Spread News & Information in S

GW00728828

Learn How!
Subscribe Now!

LotusScript Virtual Servers HTML Java ADVISOR Tips OLAP

Lotus Notes & Domino Advisor

Lotus
NOTES® & DOMINO
ADVISOR
The Independent Technical Guide to Lotus Notes and Domino

Inside
4.6

Extending Domino with Java

Sales Force Automation
Tools Reviewed

NOW MONTHLY!

☑YES! I want to subscribe to LOTUS NOTES & DOMINO ADVISOR as marked below:

❑ **MAGAZINE ONLY:** Send me 12 issues for just $75.*
❑ **MAGAZINE + COMPANION RESOURCE DISK:** Send me 12 issues + 12 disks for only $195.** I'll receive both a hard-copy magazine and sample databases, applications, add-ons, and utilities in easy-to-use electronic format each month!

Name _____

Company _____

Address _____

City _____

State/Province_____ Zip/Postal Code_____

Country _____

E-mail _____

6Q001-8

❑ Payment enclosed   ❑ Bill me

*Canada add $20.; other countries add $40.
**CA residents add $9.30 sales tax. Canada add $40.; other countries add $70. U.S. funds from U.S. banks only.

The only monthly magazine serving Lotus Notes & Lotus Domino application developers, managers and users.

Special Edition

Using

Using
Lotus® Notes
and Domino 4.6

que®

Edition Using Lotus® Notes and
4.6

opyright© **1998 by Que® Corporation.**

ll rights reserved. Printed in the United States of America. No part
this book may be used or reproduced in any form or by any
eans, or stored in a database or retrieval system, without prior
ritten permission of the publisher except in the case of brief quota-
ons embodied in critical articles and reviews. Making copies of any
art of this book for any purpose other than your own personal use
a violation of United States copyright laws. For information, ad-
ess Que Corporation, 201 W. 103rd Street, Indianapolis, IN, 46290.
ou may reach Que's direct sales line by calling 1-800-428-5331.

brary of Congress Catalog No.: 97-80538

BN: 0-7897-1535-X

98   6 5 4 3 2 1

terpretation of the printing code: The rightmost double-digit num-
r is the year of the book's printing; the rightmost single-digit
mber, the number of the book's printing. For example, a printing
de of 98-1 shows that the first printing of the book occurred
1998.

l terms mentioned in this book that are known to be trademarks
service marks have been appropriately capitalized. Que cannot
est to the accuracy of this information. Use of a term in this book
ould not be regarded as affecting the validity of any trademark or
rvice mark.

reen reproductions in this book were created using Collage Plus
m Inner Media, Inc., Hollis, NH.

Specia
Domin

Using

Lotus® Note
and Domin

Written by

Tim Bankes, David Hatter,
Marc Nadeau, R

que®

Contents at a Glance

Table of Contents

II Designing Applications

10 Creating New Databases   379

11 Designing Forms   417

IV Going Mobile

20 Setting Up to Go Remote 843

Credits

PUBLISHER
David Dwyer

EXECUTIVE EDITOR
Al Valvano

ACQUISITIONS EDITOR
Stephanie Layton

DEVELOPMENT EDITORS
Naomi Goldman
Nancy Warner

SOFTWARE SPECIALIST
Julie Maynard

DIRECTOR OF EDITORIAL SERVICES
Carla Hall

MANAGING EDITOR
Sarah Kearns

VICE PRESIDENT OF BRAND MARKETING
Greg Darling

BRAND DIRECTOR
Greg Wiegand

PROJECT EDITOR
Tom Dinse

COPY EDITOR
Gayle L. Johnson

INDEXER
Chris Wilcox

TECHNICAL EDITORS
Steve Kern
Dennis Teague

LOTUS NOTES CONVERSION SPECIALISTS
Steve Kern
MJ Kern

TEAM COORDINATORS
Stacey Beheler
Lynette Quinn

BOOK DESIGNER
Ruth Harvey

COVER DESIGNER
Dan Armstrong

PRODUCTION TEAM SUPERVISOR
Andrew Stone

PRODUCTION TEAM
Jeanne Clark
Heather Howell
Christy Lemasters
Julie Searls
Sossity Smith

Composed in *Century Old Style* and *MCPdigital* by Que Corporation.

To my parents, Ann and Bill Collins. What can I say? Without you, I couldn't do this!!
To my son, Robert. "Have I Toad You Lately That I Love You...Beary Beary Much!!"

About the Authors

Cate Richards is the Manager of Consulting and Application Solutions Services for Bay Resources, Inc., a Lotus Premium Business Partner and Key Regional Integrator in St. Petersburg, Florida. She and her team facilitate the automation and maintenance of their clients' business systems, using Lotus Notes and Domino as the platform. She also trains her clients and team in the use of Notes, reengineering business processes, and the documentation of policies, procedures, and systems. Cate has worked with Lotus Notes for over seven years and has been a beta test participant since version 2.0. This is her eighth writing endeavor on Lotus Notes for Que, and she has just recently finished her seventh book—*Teach Yourself Lotus Notes in 24 Hours* (Sams Publishing)—for the beginning Notes user. She has also contributed time to Xephon as a technical editor for their *Notes Update* magazine and has contributed material on Lotus Notes to *Windows NT* magazine. She is an L-Team member, selected by Lotus to assist users on the CompuServe Lotus Notes support forum (GO LOTUSC). She holds an M.B.A. from the Roy E. Crummer Graduate School of Business at Rollins College in Winter Park, Florida, and she also has a B.A. in Marketing from the University of South Florida in Tampa. You can reach Cate via email at `crichards@bay.com`, via CompuServe at `76702,1502`, or at `Cate Richards/STP/BAY@BAY@BAYEXT@NOTES NET`.

Tim Bankes is a partner and Principal Information Systems Consultant with Definiti, Inc., a Lotus Premium Business Partner in Cincinnati, Ohio. He has been working with Lotus Notes since version 3.0 and specializes in the design, development, and deployment of comprehensive groupware/workflow solutions. His primary responsibilities include working with clients to redesign and automate business processes and serving as the lead developer of multiple sales force/enterprise management systems. Bankes is a Certified Lotus Professional as a Principal Application Developer and System Administrator. He holds a B.B.A. in Information Systems, a B.B.A. in Management, and a certificate in International Business from the University of Cincinnati. He can be reached at `tbankes@definiti.com` or at `103163.1002@compuserve.com`.

Dave Hatter is a Groupware/Messaging Specialist with Entex Information Services, the largest PC systems integrator in the United States and the leading provider of "Total PC Management" for large organizations. He has over five years of programming experience with a variety of tools and has been working with Lotus Notes for nearly three years. He is a Lotus Certified Notes Specialist (LCNS) for Notes 3.x and a Certified Lotus Professional Developer and a Certified Lotus Professional System Administrator for Notes 4.x. In addition, Hatter teaches a wide variety of technology-related community education courses and appears monthly on a local cable TV show to discuss current technology and trends. He holds a B.S. in Information Systems from Northern Kentucky University. He can be reached via email at `dhatter@one.net`. Or visit his Web page at `w3.one.net/~dhatter`.

Stuart Hunter is a Certified Lotus Notes Engineer and a Certified Lotus Notes Instructor working for Global Dynamics Inc. in Miami, Florida. His duties include managing and maintaining the Notes network at client sites and developing tools to help with that process. Originally from Edinburgh, Scotland, Stuart came to Miami by way of Paris, France, where he looked after the European Notes network for a large detergent manufacturer. He can be reached via e-mail at `shuntera@compuserve.com`.

Ray Monahan is an Account Manager with Bay Resources in St. Petersburg, Florida. His primary responsibility is to find the right Bay Resources technical expertise to meet his customers' information and communication needs. A longtime fan of Lotus Notes, he focuses most of his skills on selling Notes-based solutions to his clients. Ray has been working in the information technology market for the past 12 years. He has held positions in senior management for the technology publishing, manufacturing, distribution, and system integration markets. He a has B.S. in Journalism from Suffolk University in Boston, Massachusetts.

Marc Nadeau is a Senior Consultant with Bay Resources, a Lotus Business Partner in St. Petersburg, Florida. His primary responsibility is to assist clients with Lotus Notes infrastructure issues, planning, and implementation. He is also responsible for working with his clients to integrate information between Lotus Notes and other database applications. In addition to client responsibilities, Marc also supports Cate Richards in managing many of the internal processes of the Lotus Notes team at Bay, and he acts as a mentor to others on his team. Prior to joining Bay Resources, he worked for Coopers & Lybrand L.L.P., where he helped support Lotus Notes and network infrastructures in the organization. Marc received a B.S. in Computer Information Systems from Thomas College in Waterville, Maine.

Roy Rumaner is a Lotus Notes Architect for Sprint Paranet in Oak Brook, Illinois, with over three years of Lotus Notes experience. He has been a beta tester for Lotus Notes since Release 4.0. He has also been a technical editor for Xephon's *Notes Update* magazine. Roy is currently a member of the L-Team, selected by Lotus to assist users in the CompuServe Lotus Notes support forum (GO LOTUSC). He is the L-Team Lotusphere party chairman, an unofficial post he has held for the past two years. He can be reached at `rrumaner@xnet.com`, `rumaner@paranet.com`, `tigger@loveable.com`, or `104125.3462` (CompuServe).

Rob Wunderlich, CLP/CLI, is an instructor and Notes consultant for ENTEX Information Systems in Bloomfield Hills, Michigan. He has written numerous articles on groupware in general and Lotus Notes in particular. In addition to doing consulting and development work with Notes, he is ENTEX/Michigan's Webmaster and has grown to love the InterNotes products by employing them on ENTEX/Michigan's Web page (`http://web1.leadgroup.com`). He is founder of the Detroit Notes Professionals Association, a user group for Notes developers, administrators, and purveyors in southeastern Michigan. He is also a board member of DANUG, the Detroit Area Network User Group. He can be reached at `rwunder@leadgroup.com`.

About the CD-ROM Content Contributors

Steve Kern is a Certified Lotus Professional and the Senior Notes Consultant for LDA Systems, headquartered in Cleveland, Ohio. He works at the Columbus, Ohio branch. Before becoming a consultant, Steve spent 15 years in Business Management, and began working with PCs in the early 1980s. Steve received a B.S. in Agriculture from The Ohio State University, and lives in Columbus, Ohio with his wife, two daughters, three fish tanks, and one Golden Retriever.

Darren Smith is a product specialist focusing on the marketing aspects of integration and development for Bay Resources, Inc., a Lotus Regional Integrator in St. Petersburg, Florida. His primary responsibility is to assist the sales and marketing process by leveraging the materials and tools provided by manufacturers and vendors for the Consulting and Applications Group. He spends most of his time working with the sales force on development and software integration opportunities, facilitating the technical sales process as well as creating the marketing programs for Bay Resources in these areas. He holds a B.A. from Purdue University in Public Relations with a minor in Marketing. He can be contacted via email at `Dsmith@bay.com` or at `Dersmith@GTE.net`.

Michael Farrugia works as a Lotus Notes Consultant for Bay Resources in St. Petersburg, Florida. He has been working with Notes for just over a year. He specializes in Lotus Domino Web administration and cc:Mail to Lotus Notes gateways and MTA. He also plans and designs infrastructures for Lotus Domino for Bay's clients. He can be reached at `mfarrugia@bay.com`, `mikefarrugia@usa.net`, or `Mike Farrugia @ Bay Resources @ Notes Net`.

Acknowledgments

When I first began using computers, I bought a few books and noted the authors' names on the cover (and then promptly forgot them). What I never took the time to do was open the book to find out who *really* was responsible for getting that book out. To put *this* book together, a team of Lotus Notes professionals and Macmillan editors collaborated to get the job done in an extremely tight time frame. My first and foremost thank yous go to this team! Not only have I been blessed with wonderful folks who really know what they're doing, but I have formed some lifetime friendships that span across the oceans! There would be no book without all of these folks, and I salute them! I encourage you to review their biographies and credits in the preceding pages.

Next in line, but first in my heart, is my family. Once again, they have stepped up to the plate to help me get this "book that would not die" out the door! The hustle and bustle of writing this book is all-consuming, because the beta releases require rewrites upon rewrites of text you just submitted the day before for the previous beta release! My parents, Ann and Bill Collins, and my son, Robert Richards, have been my cheerleaders, dietitians, exercise monitors, sounding boards, housekeepers, back massagers, and all-around sanity checkers from day one! They are also great at nagging me when I get too lazy! Mom and Dad, you are the greatest!! Without you, I would never make it through these book "things." And Robert, what can Mommy say? "I love you more than anything in the whole wide universe...infinity...infinity times!" Brother Bill and Sister Syau Li (I got it right this time), thank you for your support from afar. I promise I really will come see you at your house soon!

Heartfelt thanks go out to all the folks at Lotus who have helped throughout the course of the development of this book. Special thanks go to Landon Hunsucker and Sherry Lautenbach, our Business Partner representatives in Atlanta, who were fantastic in helping get the information we needed for this book—as well as answering all those pesky questions we always seem to come up with! Thanks also to Wizop Ildiko Nagy for her assistance and trust in the CompuServe LOTUSC forum (and for the great Lotus toys she sends every year)!

I would be remiss if I didn't thank all the folks at Bay Resources (who are too many to name individually). Cass Casucci and Bob Hamilton have been wonderful to work for since the day I started with Bay Resources. Your overwhelming encouragement in these "book things" is something I've never had before in a company, and it is greatly appreciated! In fact, the overwhelming support I receive from my own team, the Sales and Marketing team, and the rest of my coworkers is always amazing. The folks at Bay Resources are the best in the world to work with! Go Bay!!!

Thanks to all the folks at Macmillan who helped make this book happen: Al (who still picks the best time to take a vacation), Stephanie (who is still trying to figure out how we Notes folks keep writing more than anyone else), Naomi (who has finally figured out that my pager number is the best leash of all), and all the other editors who helped keep me on time! The folks at Macmillan are *the best* around—even if they do set a deadline that keeps you working all night and through the weekend!

Although I haven't been as vocal this year due to tight deadlines, I have been keeping up with the antics of the gang in the CompuServe Lotus Notes forum (GO LOTUSC). Again, I thank them for all the inspiration, fun, and answers they have provided over the past year! Deb, Roger, John, Tom, Bob, "Legs," Philip, Chet, Peter, Ron, Gerald, Zev and Zoe, Kirstin, and the rest of the forum crew have provided great examples, ideas, and laughs throughout the year! LOTUSC also provided several great authors for this book (just check the author bios)! LOTUSC is definitely the best (if not the wackiest) Lotus Notes support forum going! Congratulations, L-Team members of the forum, on your recent nomination for a Beacon award for Excellence in Customer Satisfaction!

Personal thanks to my two mentors—Linda Metcalf (and Doug, too) and Gary Strack—for jump-starting me years ago into "working at what I enjoy." You will always hold a special place in my heart! And thanks to my new Do Jang, National Tae Kwon Do Academy of Palm Harbor, for keeping me in shape, and to my miracle team at Timothy & Co.'s salon in Countryside, Florida for keeping me from looking like a sheep dog during the course of this writing! Now if only I could find a new chiropractor...

Foreword

To paraphrase a popular Mark Twain quotation, the reports of Lotus Notes' death are greatly exaggerated. Lotus' archenemy and occasional partner, Microsoft, has failed to produce a "Notes killer." Other groupware vendors have made great strides in their products. Some of them are almost equivalent to Notes Release 2. Even the World Wide Web has failed to drown Lotus in the great paradigm shift of the decade.

What is it that keeps Lotus Notes/Domino afloat amidst competitive, technology, marketing, and other pressures? I believe it's the fact that effective groupware is more than a universal inbox or email and group scheduling. Groupware that works is groupware on which you can build useful collaborative applications. Groupware that works lets you build tools for content and information sharing, workflow monitoring, control, and knowledge management. Groupware that works gives you choices—platform choices, architecture choices, and even development tool choices.

A mere glance at the size and scope of this book should convince you that Notes is either substantial groupware technology or a miserable piece of software that requires so much documentation that you'll never figure out how to use it. Since really horrible software would have collapsed under the pressure regularly applied to Notes, it must be good groupware. Let me assure you that it is.

You might find much to wish for as you become more familiar with the features of this version of Notes/Domino, but you'll find that the "wish list" is shrinking rapidly, especially where Domino tackles the Web. Developers should be especially excited about what's in Release 4.6. Many of the new features are targeted directly at making the developer's job even easier. Lotus has had a long journey with Web development. They started in Release 3 grappling with the Web by delivering publishing tools that served merely as a facade of the real groupware work going on outside of the Web. In Release 4, they integrated those tools with the server, but the first major step was when they added the Domino server and got serious with rendering HTML and integrating more Web features into Notes 4.5. Now even more of what you expect in an industrial-strength Web server is part of Domino. You'll find SSL, NNTP, POP3, and LDAP—and you can expect the list to grow as new Web technologies become mainstream.

However, the market already has plenty of Web servers, and the ordinary Web developer has no interest in Domino. After all, my teenage daughter has her own Web site. She had no trouble learning HTML and JavaScript. What's the big deal with Domino? It's time for the ordinary Web developer to step aside. The real power of Domino is in building interactive groupware applications for the Web. If you're putting up another static marketing site with some cute JavaBeans that show your byline on a marquee, you're not doing business on the

Web. Domino lets you manage documents, control workflow, build interactivity, and handle Web sites and applications where the content is constantly changing. Lotus has given you the tools to make Web-based groupware happen.

You'll find a wide array of development tools from which to choose. Lotus has stayed away from the one-size-fits-all approach. Although this means that there's more to learn, it also means that more flexibility and capability are built right into the product. It means that you can create more powerful Web applications with Notes 4.6 than with any other single tool on the market. It also means that as Web development matures and standardizes, Lotus is committed to incorporating new technology into their products.

If you're a developer, you now have the choice of the Function language, LotusScript, and Java for back-end processing. You can build user interfaces using Notes forms, views and navigators for Notes clients, or these and HTML and JavaScript for browser interfaces. You can also add OLE, ActiveX, and Java applets to both Notes and browser clients. And if that isn't enough, Lotus has made the internals available via a comprehensive application program interface (API). Sound a little daunting? It can be, but it's also exciting. Building useful and effective software is rewarding work. There's nothing like a full complement of tools to make that work easier.

So where do you go from here? Well, I'd start by reading this book. But don't just take my word for it. You'll find praise for the previous versions of this book from developers, business partners, online forums, and user groups. This is a great place to start if you're not sure if Notes is for you, if you're upgrading to Notes 4.6 from an earlier version, if you're moving from being a casual user to a developer, or if you want to know how you might better use Notes in your organization. My organization hands a copy of this book to every new Notes user and developer as the starting point for the many details that help them do their jobs better.

But after that, Notes is a tool that must be used in order to be fully understood. Use it. Take the ideas you find here and in other places and put them to work. If you aren't a developer, challenge your development staff to build the kinds of collaborative Domino applications that make your organization more competitive and more effective. And, lastly, keep your eye on what Lotus will do next.

It might seem silly to learn Notes 4.6 when another major release is just around the corner, but don't wait. Although Notes 5 promises to be the best yet, the old hands have learned that each release is additive. The fundamentals don't change. Each new release has brought new tools and has made the old tools work better. Sure, I put LotusScript in my applications where I might have tried a Function language macro before, and I'll put Java agents where I'm using LotusScript now, but I haven't stopped using either tool. The Function language is powerful and often surprisingly simple to implement. LotusScript is a fine scripting language and gives developers—especially new ones—a good look at the objects used behind the scenes. As Java becomes more popular, less LotusScript will be written, but the same was true of the Function language when LotusScript first hit the scene. What you learn now will be useful later. Don't let the promise of future features keep you from realizing the potential of the product today.

Lotus has more in store for us, but just look at what you have now. Use it. Learn it. Enjoy it. Happy reading!

Steve M. Caudill, CCP
Software Architect, Interteam Software Corporation
Editor, Lotus Notes & Domino Advisor Magazine

Introduction

In this chapter

Many people get caught up in the eternal—and often infernal—paperchase around the organizations in which they work and communicate. Coworkers send flyers reminding everyone of the company picnic. Human Resources modifies its 3-inch-thick manual and then reprints it and sends it to all employees. You must order supplies, so you fill out a purchase request and forward it to your manager for approval, who forwards it to Accounting, who forwards it to Purchasing, who forwards it to you to let you know the supplies have been ordered. Does any of this sound familiar? This paper chase that companies have struggled with has created the perfect environment for Lotus Notes to take hold and quickly become the market leader in groupware technology.

Groupware is software designed to be used by groups of people sharing information and working together. It lets a group of people use the same information, but often in different ways, depending on their particular needs. Notes lets you perform many of the common activities you currently partake of during the workday: exchanging mail, sharing ideas, accessing information, and planning for the future. Notes' aim is to replace paper documents with electronic documents, but with a twist. You can create sophisticated workflow applications that automate—and often streamline—your business processes. Notes doesn't simply create a copy of a paper form; it moves it through the business process through the use of electronic signatures, status conditions, and other indicators. Notes lets you automate your workflow, re-creating the path your document takes, often improving it as unnecessary steps are made more visible for inspection or elimination.

What Is Lotus Notes?

If you ask anyone who works with Lotus Notes to define it, you'll probably get a different answer from each person you talk to. Lotus Development Corporation representatives themselves often struggle with defining Notes, because it can mean different things to each organization that uses it. Some refer to Notes as a document database—but don't let that simple definition fool you. Notes is more than a receptacle for storing documents, like many of the more traditional types of databases.

It's perhaps better to think of Notes as a way of organizing documents and making them available to groups of people. However, the word *document* can often be misleading, because many people think only of text when they think of documents. With Notes' rich text field capability, a document can contain just about any electronic object, which is why many people refer to Notes as a storage container. You can embed or import graphics into documents, incorporate spreadsheets, insert video files that can be viewed straight from the document, insert voice messages that can be played with the click of a button, and attach any file in any format to a document for distribution to others.

Notes' open, nonproprietary format also lets it serve as the "glue" that helps your other applications talk to each other. You can use Notes to gather and distribute information around your organization as a front-end, user-friendly GUI (graphical user interface) and then schedule the information to download into your more traditional legacy mainframe applications. You can also develop sophisticated applications in languages such as Visual Basic and C and then pass the information collected in those applications to Notes to be stored or distributed throughout an organization. With Notes' new capability to work with information on the Internet through its family of products and the built-in Web browser, Notes now combines its rich text and security capabilities with the vast frontier of information on the Internet—giving you the best of both worlds.

Benefits of Notes

Notes' unique database structure lets you keep track of complex, relatively unstructured information (which is how you typically receive information) and makes that information available to groups of users on a network—whether they are connected directly to the network or are dialing in from remote locations. Notes helps eliminate much of the redundant paperwork and steps in your business processes by moving the flow of documents from paper (where typically one person at a time reviews the information) to an electronically organized workflow in which many people can review, approve, and send information with the click of a button. In a world where companies must cut costs while increasing the speed at which people must communicate to maintain a competitive presence, Notes can give companies a definite edge.

Who Should Use This Book?

This book is written for the Notes "power user" and/or "new designer"—someone who wants to use Notes for more than accessing email and using databases that have already been designed. This book is also a great resource for existing Notes users who need to get up and running on a much-enhanced version of Notes. This book also offers guidance on how to get started using Notes—sending email, composing documents, changing the way you view information, and so on—so the new Notes user will benefit too!

The CD that accompanies this book contains software applications, text, demos, screencams, white papers (research studies), adjunct product information, training information, and support numbers provided by Lotus Development and many third-party vendors. This information gives you a feel for many of the products and services available on the market, as well as ideas on how you might want to use Notes in your organization. Also available on the CD are sample Notes databases, a Database Icon Library, a Notes Architecture Guidebook, six bonus chapters, and a Formula Catalog database, among other things.

If you would like to view this book on your computer instead of reading the printed version, you can access the entire book in Notes format on the CD-ROM.

How to Use This Book

This book is divided into six parts. The earlier parts are intended for a general audience, and the later parts require an understanding of the previous parts. You will also find a wealth of information in the appendixes and on the CD-ROM to help you further understand Notes. Even if you're a Notes pro, you should check out the first chapters to review many of the changes incorporated into Notes 4.6.

Part I: Notes Basics

Part I discusses the basic nature of Notes and presents an overview of its capabilities. You will read about how and why the city of Sarasota, Florida, decided to use Notes as its communication platform.

Chapter 1, "Getting Started with Lotus Notes," introduces the concepts of working with groupware, understanding the Notes interface, and starting and exiting Notes.

In Chapter 2, "Customizing Notes," you learn how to personalize your Notes setup, create custom SmartIcons, and work with your DESKTOP.DSK and NOTES.INI files.

Chapter 3, "Using Databases," provides the foundation for working with any database. You learn about the basic components of a Notes database and how to use them.

Chapter 4, "Getting Started with Electronic Mail," walks you through Notes' email package.

To gain insight into how the Address Books act as the heart of the Notes system, read Chapter 5, "Using the Notes Address Books." It provides instructions for using the Address Books when you're addressing email creating group lists and Person documents, and performing other tasks available in the Address Books.

Chapter 6, "Advanced Mail," continues the discussion of working with email. It covers such advanced topics as working with attachments, forwarding documents via mail, and many other tips for getting the most out of mail.

Chapter 7, "Working with Text," walks you through all the commands and features available to enhance text in your documents. You learn how to change font attributes, control margin settings, use the clipboard, and work with bullets and numbering.

In Chapter 8, "Working with Documents," you explore features that add pizzazz to your documents. You learn how to create tables, hotspots, collapsible sections, links, and more. You also learn how to use the spell-checking feature.

Chapter 9, "Lotus Notes Group Calendaring and Scheduling," teaches you how to work with the new calendar feature located in your Mail database. You learn how to create appointments, invite users to a meeting, schedule resources, and more.

Part II: Designing Applications

In Part II, you learn about the basic building blocks used to create or redesign a Notes database application. This part of the book also explores design, @Function, and LotusScript terminology. If you're an experienced Notes programmer, you still might want to skim through these chapters, because quite a bit has changed in the newest release of Notes.

Chapter 10, "Creating New Databases," introduces the basic building blocks of application design, including how to create applications from templates, work with the design menus, and develop graphical navigators.

To take a deeper look into developing database forms, see Chapter 11, "Designing Forms." It shows you how to create a form from scratch. It also provides a basic overview of form design, as well as some tips on using some of the more advanced features available when you create forms.

Chapter 12, "Designing Views," delves further into application design by looking at how you design the views that report information. This chapter walks you through creating a view from the ground up. You learn the basics of view design and many advanced features as well.

Chapter 13, "Integrating Notes with Other Applications," discusses the basics of working with OLE2, FX (field exchange), and other methods that let you incorporate information from other applications into Notes databases.

Chapter 14, "Working with Formulas," and Chapter 15, "Working with Functions and Commands," give you a foundation for using Notes formula function programming. These chapters supplement the chapters on creating databases, forms, views, and other programmable objects by explaining the rules for writing formulas using Notes' functions.

Chapter 16, "Buttons and Agents," looks at designing and incorporating buttons and agents into your Notes applications to enhance their design and user-friendliness and to perform routine "housekeeping" chores.

Part III: Working with LotusScript

Chapter 17, "LotusScript Basics," provides the foundation for beginning to work with LotusScript. LotusScript is a basic compatible language (much like Visual Basic) that is used to develop applications in Notes.

Chapter 18, "Writing Scripts with LotusScript," takes you one step further into working with LotusScript. It provides detailed examples of working with this programming language and gives you a boost in becoming an expert programmer.

Chapter 19, "More LotusScript," shows that too much of a good thing sometimes isn't bad! This chapter gives you more advanced examples of working with LotusScript.

Part IV: Going Mobile

In Part IV, you learn how to work with Notes remote—that is, not connected to a network. Remote users must set up their systems to prepare for working disconnected from the server and then initiate communication with the server each time they are ready to send and receive information. This section tells you how to prepare and work off the network. Even if you aren't a remote Notes user, you might benefit from scanning these chapters, because you might communicate with remote users and would therefore benefit from seeing Notes from their point of view.

In Chapter 20, "Setting Up to Go Remote," you learn what you will need in order to work with Notes when you're away from a network. You also learn how to set up Notes to go on the road.

Chapter 21, "Working Remote," walks you through the process of working remote, which involves calling servers and replicating (exchanging) information with them. You also learn tips on keeping the size of your remote databases manageable.

Part V: Advanced Notes Topics

As you and your business become more experienced with Notes, you will undoubtedly want to take advantage of its special features. This part of the book delves further into these more advanced topics.

Chapter 22, "Security and Encryption," looks at Notes' security features. Understanding your Notes ID and certificates, managing database access control, and working with encryption are just a few of the important topics in this chapter.

Chapter 23, "Notes: Under the Hood," explains the behind-the-scenes happenings of Notes from a high level. You gain an understanding of the role that servers play, the platforms they work on, the new centralized Notes Administration interface, and other features that Notes uses to keep the people on your system communicating. This chapter is geared toward the user who needs to understand what is going on in the background so that applications are developed correctly. It can help you answer some of those "Why is this happening?" questions that frequently occur when users work with Notes.

Part VI: Working with the Web

This section is dedicated to Notes' new Internet-related features. You learn how to configure your workstation to browse the Internet using the Notes Web browser. You also learn about working with Domino and the Web Navigator. In addition, you get insight into the direction Lotus is taking with the Internet.

Chapter 24, "Lotus Notes and the Web," discusses Notes' new Internet enhancements. This chapter also discusses the reasoning behind the inclusion of Notes' Internet capabilities and the future direction of Notes with regard to Web communication.

Chapter 25, "Using the Web Navigators," teaches you how to configure your workstation and use the powerful features of the Notes Web browser. This chapter offers a soup-to-nuts explanation of working with this tool.

Chapter 26, "Using Domino Server's HTTP Service," shows you how to set up and work with the new Domino server add-on that is integrated into Notes 4.5. This powerful tool lets you publish Web databases directly to the Internet, work with mail and other databases from any Web browser, and much more.

Appendixes

You will find a wealth of information in the appendixes to further facilitate your understanding of Notes. The appendixes provide additional reference information that supports many of the chapters in this book.

Appendix A, "Database Templates," briefly describes the templates that ship with Notes 4. Use this appendix to quickly get an idea of what is available for your use.

Appendix B, "Special Characters," details the special characters that are available in Notes. Use this table as a quick reference when working with special characters (such as the registered trademark symbol).

Appendix C, "Using the CD-ROM," offers brief insight into the contents of the CD and provides you with instructions on how to access the information.

Bonus Chapters on the CD-ROM

The enclosed CD-ROM provides screencams of add-on and third-party products, application demos, sample Notes databases, and additional technical and reference information. Also included on the CD are six bonus chapters.

Bonus Chapter 1, "ODBC and Lotus Components," looks at applications of LotusScript programming, building on what you learned in Part III.

Bonus Chapter 2, "Working with Web Publisher," looks at how to use the Web Publisher to manage your Web site. Although much of this technology is also available in the new release of Domino (discussed in Chapter 26), many companies still use the Internet Web Publisher to manage their Web sites. This chapter shows you how.

Bonus Chapter 3, "Command Reference," provides a detailed list of the Notes menu commands and their corresponding hotkeys. Use this as a quick way to locate those elusive commands while finding your way around Notes.

Bonus Chapter 4, "@Functions," describes all the @Functions available when you want to work with Notes' Formula programming language. This chapter supplements Chapters 14 and 15.

Bonus Chapter 5, "Remote Troubleshooting," lists the most common problems that people experience when working remote—along with solutions. Use this chapter in conjunction with the Mobile Survival Kit and Smartform Modem Doctor databases, located on the CD-ROM, to help resolve remote troubles.

Bonus Chapter 6, "Using Domino.Action," helps you utilize one of the primary tools in Domino that can help you get a Web site up and running. Domino.Action is a Notes application that creates and maintains a whole, Domino-based Web site. It simplifies the creation of a Web site by working from preset designs into which you plug your information and graphics.

Conventions Used in This Book

Que has over a decade of experience in developing and publishing the most successful computer books available. With that experience, we've learned which special features help readers the most. Look for these special features throughout the book to enhance your learning experience.

Several type and font conventions are used in this book to help make reading it easier:

- *Italic* type is used to introduce new terms.
- Onscreen messages and code appear in monospace type.
- URLs, newsgroups, Internet addresses, and anything you are asked to type also appear in monospace type.
- Placeholders (words that stand for what you actually type) appear in *italic monospace*.

 T I P Tips present brief advice on a quick or often overlooked procedure. These include shortcuts that can save you time.

N O T E Notes provide additional information that might help you avoid problems. They also offer advice that relates to the topic at hand.

CAUTION

Cautions warn you about unexpected results, mistakes to avoid, and potential problems that a procedure might cause.

TROUBLESHOOTING

What is a troubleshooting section? Troubleshooting sections anticipate common problems in the form of a question. The response provides you with practical suggestions for solving these problems.

Sidebar

Longer discussions that aren't integral to the flow of the chapter are set aside as sidebars. Look for these sidebars to find out even more information.

▶ **See** Cross-references point you to another section so that you can get more information on a particular topic, **p. xxx**

Notes Basics

Getting Started with Lotus Notes

In this chapter, you will learn basic Notes concepts that will help you develop a good foundation for working with this software.

Welcome to Lotus Notes 4.6

The most difficult part of working with Lotus Notes is often trying to figure out just what it is. New users might think of Notes as electronic mail (email), because that is often their first introduction to Notes. Others might call it a database software package, a workflow product, a document library, groupware, or communication software. Notes is all of these things and more. Essentially, Notes is a distributed client/server database application that lets users organize, process, track, and share information. With Notes, users can access the same database at the same time and use the information to suit their individual needs. Notes consolidates the tools needed to effectively communicate and collaborate in an organization. Notes provides the following:

- Email
- Group discussion
- Workflow
- Scheduling
- Document management
- Application development
- Web publishing and browsing
- Distributed document replication
- Centralized directory services (Address Book)
- The ability to integrate with disparate email systems (Notes offers SMTP MTA, cc:Mail, and POP 3 support, for example)

Notes can be used simply as an email package that sends email to other Notes users on your network. However, with the inclusion of some special software and gateways that can be installed by your Notes administrator, your email capabilities can be extended to let you send and receive faxes, communicate with Notes users outside your network, and even send mail to and publish databases over the Internet for non-Notes users. If your network is set up to use the products and features that are available with Notes, it becomes the single, user-friendly source of access to multiple email and other communication services.

Businesses benefit greatly not only from Notes' powerful email capability but also from the ability to redefine and automate their business processes. For example, some businesses have used Notes to automate their hiring or purchase approval process to include signature authorizations at each phase. Some companies run all their business communications on Notes, often using Notes as a front-end data-gathering tool for information that eventually ends up stored on a mainframe. Many companies also build reporting applications in Notes that import data from mainframe computers to report across a wide range of users in a corporation.

There aren't many business applications that can't use Notes 4.6. Many applications are simple, easy-to-develop databases that allow better communication among a group of users, whereas other applications are sophisticated business process programs developed with a combination of Notes and other programming languages and software tools. These applications can be designed by someone in your organization or by outside consultants. As you read this book, you will learn about the tools, applications, and methods for successfully working with Notes 4.6. Throughout this book, tips and techniques used by expert Notes developers and adminis-trators will assist you. The CD-ROM accompanying this book provides you with sample data-bases, tips, demos, and other information.

N O T E Although this book focuses on what Notes is, it would be prudent to briefly discuss what it isn't. Notes isn't a relational database system, in which changes made to one record automatically update all instances of that entry throughout the system.

For example, in the banking industry, an application might exist that tracks all the information about a banking customer for each account held at the bank. If the customer changes his or her phone number, a relational system would make that change in every record in that customer's system. In Notes, if the phone number changes in a customer record, code would have to be created to update all instances of that phone number in subsequent documents related to that client—or the records would have to be edited individually to make the change. Careful database design can overcome some of these limitations, but you should keep them in mind when you're deciding which system you need to resolve your business problems.

Notes is also not meant to be a high-volume, transaction-based system in which thousands of documents are accessed and created each day. Although Notes can handle high-volume tasks with some careful planning and development, the system's responsiveness and capacity might suffer. Consider the transaction volume level when you're selecting a system for your business needs.

What's New in Notes 4.6?

If you're just upgrading from Notes 3.x or 4.x, you will notice a wealth of changes in Notes 4.6. However, if you're upgrading from Notes 4.5 to 4.6, many of the changes might seem more subtle. However, this doesn't mean that the number of changes is insignificant. This section will walk you through some of the major changes that are present in Release 4.6. The remain-der of this book will guide you through using these new features, as well as the wealth of other features already present in Notes.

- Portfolios: You can now represent a collection of databases with a single database icon, so managing related databases has become much easier. You will learn more about this feature in Chapter 3, "Using Databases."

- Integration with Lotus SmartSuite and Microsoft Office: Notes 4.6 offers better integra-tion with Lotus SmartSuite and Microsoft Office on a number of points using the Windows ActiveDoc technology. Here are a couple of the new features:

  - You can use Lotus Word Pro 97, Microsoft Word 95, or Microsoft Word 97 as an alternative email editor.

- The Document Library application is included to securely share and route documents with others by using built-in workflow. You can create proposals, budgets, and presentations within Notes by using the business productivity applications you're used to and then route them to colleagues by using the built-in workflow capabilities in Notes and Domino.

■ Enhanced Internet Web Navigation: You can use Microsoft Internet Explorer to navigate the Internet directly from inside your Notes client using the Internet Explorer ActiveX component. This allows you to render Web pages with all the power and speed of Internet Explorer but still retain the best of Notes functionality for storing and managing your Web information. Combining the two applications, you can do the following:

- Forward Web pages to colleagues via email.

- Configure the Page Minder and Web Ahead agents to do the surfing for you.

- Utilize selective local Web page storage for off-line browsing. You can selectively cache pages for off-line use, enable Page Minder or Web Ahead agents, and set database size options for performing database "housekeeping" chores. Pages not read within a certain amount of time can be reduced to links, updated pages can be forwarded to your mail file automatically, and you can cache pages manually by clicking Add Bookmark on the Action Bar.

■ Enhanced Contact Management: You can use your Notes client as a Contact Manager from your Personal Address Book. You can use the new Business Card-style addressing to store contact information, create a mail memo or meeting invitation, or go to a contact's Web site simply by highlighting a Business Card and clicking the corresponding action button.

The Person records (now called Business Cards) have been enhanced to include much more information, and fields are automatically parsed as the information is added. You can dynamically edit the form to reflect the correct contact information for each record. For example, if Robert doesn't have a pager, but instead has a phone on his dock, you can easily change his form to include "Dock Phone" as one of his contact numbers. You can also add additional contact information such as spouse and child names, as well as department and mail stops in the "More information" section of each record. User-defined categories for each contact make it easier for you to categorize and view contacts to find people faster.

■ Time savers for personal information management: You can quickly and easily convert an email to a calendar appointment for yourself, a meeting that you invite others to, or a to-do item for yourself or someone you work with. You also can create a mailing list using the members of the To: and cc: fields of a memo or meeting invitation you've received so that you can easily send mail to that same group of people in the future.

■ POP3/SMTP mail support: Notes 4.6 users can send and receive email from any POP3 account, whether on the Internet or their company's intranet—all using the same familiar Notes interface that you use for other activities such as contact management and Web browsing.

■ Printing calendar views: You can print calendar views as they are displayed or as a linear listing of the calendar entries in a date range or for all entries.

■ Java applet support in forms: Notes Designer for Domino 4.6 lets you store and execute Java applets from within forms. This allows Web developers to create a richer, more interactive experience for users by using Java applets as a part of the forms that are presented to both browser and Notes client users. Additionally, the storage of Java applets within Domino application databases lets developers take advantage of Domino's world-class replication technology for keeping their Java applets synchronized in several locations. Developers also have the ability to easily link to a Java applet that is stored in the file system.

■ Java agents: Notes Designer for Domino now includes Java agents. In addition to the previously available Simple Agents, Formula Agents, and LotusScript Agents, developers can now use Java to develop agents. These agents perform a range of tasks—from email filtering and knowledge management to automated server administration.

■ Navigator enhancements: Notes Designer for Domino gives Navigator and image map creators more control over graphical layouts, new graphical objects, and the ability to import graphic files into Domino applications. The new file formats include BMP, GIF, JPEG, PCX, and TIFF.

■ Easier addition of Domino Web elements to pages: You'll save time and energy by adding views, navigators, and folder panes more easily to your Domino pages using a new user interface option.

■ Hide design elements from browsers or Notes clients: You can use the new Hide option to show the richer, more sophisticated pieces of your application only to Notes users and not to Web browsers. Or you can show certain areas of your application only to browsers in order to exploit their particular capabilities. Application pieces can be hidden either by design or on-the-fly using the new @ClientType function.

■ Web browser preview: Notes Designer for Domino 4.6 contains a new design mode so that you can preview what an application looks like in a Web browser in addition to a Notes client.

■ LotusScript enhancements: Over 20 new LotusScript classes, events, and other enhancements have been added to Notes Designer for Domino 4.6.

■ Integrated tools added: Lotus BeanMachine for Java and Notes Global Designer are now bundled in the package in Designer. BeanMachine for Java is the only tool that lets you visually author Java applets without writing a single line of code. You can internationalize new and existing Domino/Notes databases quickly and efficiently with Notes Global Designer, which helps you translate and keep track of your design elements for each nationality you are designing for.

■ Display of Unicode characters: Release 4.6 of the Notes Client includes support for Unicode fonts. To enable this feature, add the following line to the NOTES.INI file:

```
UNICODE_DISPLAY = 1
```

If this line is missing, or if the setting is UNICODE_DISPLAY = 0, there is no support for Unicode fonts, and the Notes Client displays text by translating from LMBCS to the platform character set, exactly as in earlier releases.

If this feature is enabled, Notes interrogates the currently selected font to see if it supports the Unicode range based on the user's locale. If it does, Notes translates from LMBCS to Unicode to display text. If not, LMBCS is translated to the platform character set, just as in earlier versions.

The default setting for the North American version is UNICODE_DISPLAY = 0. Part of the localization process involves turning on this feature (UNICODE_DISPLAY = 1) for language versions in which multilingual display is important. In either case, the end user can override the system setting by editing the NOTES.INI file. There is currently no user interface in the Notes Client for enabling Unicode display.

- Keyboard switching: In conjunction with Unicode display, the Notes 4.6 Client supports keyboard codepage switching. The client pays attention to the currently selected keyboard input locale and converts keyboard input from the codepage for that locale into LMBCS.

- Groups form in Address Book: The members field in the Groups form of the Address Book is now wider. This lets you view long, hierarchical names more easily.

- Wildcard capability in Network Connection documents: Notes now allows an asterisk wildcard character in the address field in certain Connection documents. You can use this new capability with the existing capability of using asterisks as wildcards in the destination server field (which allows one connection document to apply to all the servers in a group or organization).

  When an asterisk appears as the first character of an address field in a Network Connection document or a Remote LAN Connection document, the common name of the server being sought is substituted for the asterisk in the address.

  For example, if a Network Connection document exists for destination server */BAY, specifying the protocol TCP/IP and the address *.BAY.com, you can use this connection document to connect to any BAY server (for example, Sales/BAY) as long as the BAY servers have IP addresses in the BAY.com domain (for example, sales.BAY.com).

  Using these wildcard constructions makes managing connections to servers in other domains much easier.

- Notes Connect for ISDN: A CAPI-compliant ISDN driver is now available via the Web for the Domino 4.6 Server and the Notes 4.6 Client. ISDN (Integrated Services Digital Network) is a growing public telecommunications network with a flexible infrastructure designed to integrate voice, data, video, and imaging. CAPI (Common Application Programming Interface) allows any application program to communicate with any other third-party CAPI-compliant ISDN driver and adapter cards.

This is by no means an exhaustive list of the new features available in Notes 4.6. As you work through this book, you will notice other new features that can enhance your work with Notes 4.6.

Living and Working in a Notes Culture

As mentioned earlier, some companies use Notes to run all their business communications, whereas others use it to automate specific tasks or processes in their organization. Some companies only use the email capabilities, with perhaps a few discussion databases. Regardless of the way(s) a company uses Notes, at least initially Notes is change management—it changes the way users communicate and work within an organization. Individuals at lower levels of a company now have rapid access to information never before available, as well as the ability to funnel communication directly to management when necessary.

End users have more control over the look and feel of the databases they are using. Users of Notes 4.6 can easily display information in a format that makes sense to them rather than having to use the format developed by a programmer. They can create private views of the information that is tailored to the way they want to see information, sort information in the columns (if the designer has set up the views to allow column sorting), and widen columns to display more information if needed. Applications are typically built and modified much faster than in traditional database packages. This makes it easier for organizations to match their communication structures to the ever-changing business processes caused by the pressures of the industries they are operating in. The ease and speed with which applications can be built and altered—often referred to in the industry as Rapid Application Development, or RAD—reduces development costs.

Fewer programmers are required for application development in Notes, and this often leads to radical changes in the way information systems departments are organized and staffed. Because Notes is built to run on a wide variety of platforms within a company, information systems departments are finding it easier to network various departments and locations with one communications package. This task was tedious before, if not impossible. With Notes' easy remote and Internet capabilities, many companies have moved toward creating virtual offices so that their employees can work from home.

Recent trends show that companies are building more applications that link them with their clients and vendors, thus making Notes a means of commerce and revenue generation for their businesses.

Notes changes the way a company communicates. Managing this communication and the applications that support it provides a significant challenge. In this book, you'll not only learn how to use Notes and begin developing applications, but you'll also gain insight into managing your own communications needs.

The following case study provides further insight into the benefits of Notes and the challenges faced by organizations as they begin to upgrade the ways in which they handle the increasing demand for information management. Whether you work in the public or private sector, some of the considerations that made the city of Sarasota decide to turn to Notes might be similar to the considerations that make Notes an effective choice for your needs. Some of the challenges they face might be familiar to you.

Case Study: A City on Notes

Information Services (IS) departments in the municipal and government sectors face the same challenges as their corporate counterparts. In today's ever-changing technology arena, meeting the goals of the organization and accommodating the demands of end users have become increasingly difficult. Delivering a multitude of products and services to a variety of departments presents unique challenges for even the most astute IS departments.

At one time or another, every IS department addresses concerns regarding connectivity issues involving dissimilar platforms, help desk support, software deployment, standardization of software platforms, and intranet and Internet security. At the same time, there is a need to ensure the maintenance of hardware platforms at the client, server, and midrange levels.

Sarasota's Information System Challenges   As with the business community, local government organizations must work within budget constraints. Voters, like stockholders, demand a high return on their investment. In the state of Florida, these challenges are greatly compounded, because the fluctuation in residential and tourist populations between the summer and winter months can be staggering. Tourism is one of Florida's major industries. As millions flock to the sun and sand during the winter, the population in many areas nearly doubles—and the demand on the IS departments more than doubles as city personnel seek to take care of the city's information needs in managing the winter residents' requests for information, licensing issues, and other matters involving the offices of the city. Unfortunately, budgets don't increase to reflect the demands on services.

Mary Scott, Director of IS Services for the city of Sarasota, realized her department's unique challenges. "When people think of winter in Florida, they usually think of fun and relaxation. Winter has taken on a whole new meaning for me!" Drawing from her many years of IS experience, Mary realized that she needed to utilize technology to accommodate these yearly fluctuations, stay within budget constraints, and realize the largest potential from her investment.

"I wanted to ensure that whatever solution we incorporated in the city was scalable. In other words, it can be enhanced and expanded upon when demand requires it. Secondly, the solution must be based on an open platform. We had to get away from the legacy environment. Proprietary platforms were dragging us down with hardware and software support and maintenance issues and costs."

Mary understood that whatever strategy she devised, it was paramount that her IS team be able to quickly understand the technology, learn how to use it, and then translate their expertise into support and deployment. Mary turned to Lotus Notes due to past experience with the product and its track record of success as the top groupware application on the market.

Implementing the Notes Solution   With her team on board, the next goal was to gain support from the multiple departments and their managers. Mary began to announce her plans to the various departments in the city and to solicit their feedback on information needs. "I knew that to be successful, I would have to gain support from a variety of departments and individuals— many of whom still utilized highly paper-intensive processes to accomplish some rather complex tracking requirements," she said. "By adopting Notes as an email package, we gave our end users an easy-to-use GUI interface email package at the start to gain confidence in Notes' capabilities. With the success of the NotesMail deployment, we gained support for the tool believed to be most effective in achieving our objectives and taking the city into the 21st century!"

Many managers and end users were concerned about the substantial change in which they were to communicate and had fears that too much change too quickly would do more harm than good. "Once the individual departments realized that we weren't changing their desktop tools that they had grown accustomed to [Microsoft Office], only the methodology by which we shared data, those fears quickly dissipated."

Using Notes to Upgrade Record Keeping   With NotesMail deployed, Mary's next step was to recruit some outside assistance from a high-level Notes consulting firm in the area to help her map out the remaining plan and work with her team on their new endeavor. With the assistance of the studies performed by the outside Notes consultants, it was decided that the next most critical and essential area in which to deploy Notes would be in eliminating the bottleneck that had begun to occur in publishing meeting minutes for several departments in the city for access by Sarasota employees and constituents.

Every department in every city, when conducting a public meeting, is required to store all pertinent meeting minutes or notes in a repository for access by the constituency. In the case of Sarasota, this database resided on an HP 3000 using a COBAL-based program created over a decade ago. The program was hard to use, required a tremendous amount of support, was accessible only to users who had access to the mainframe, was only 80 percent accurate in its indexing capabilities due to numerous platform changes over the years, and was poorly formatted. It was also subject to many of the date problems anticipated to occur in legacy systems with the year 2000.

Previously, members from the various departments would transcribe the meeting minutes in Microsoft Word, make a copy for the physical record book, and then upload the document to the mainframe. Once it was in the old system, it couldn't be readily accessed or easily reproduced by anyone other than the creators of the minutes. It couldn't be easily edited by anyone.

According to Mary, "If anyone wanted to research a particular topic—say, 'dog licenses'—they would have to have a clerk first search the mainframe, note the particular dates if that particular document had been indexed, and then go to the record books to copy the original. In some cases, mainframe storage did not exist for a document at all, meaning that the entire search was a manual process through printed documents. This process was extremely time-consuming and did not allow easy access to the constituency or other departments."

Using Mary's success with Notes as an email system, Bay Resources, the outside consulting firm, scheduled meetings with the various department managers to determine their needs for an online meeting minutes application in Notes. Once the criteria for performance and deployment were identified, the process of developing the application began. Using Lexstyle Publisher, a tool created by Coextant that converts documents created in most popular word processing packages to Notes documents, Bay Resources developed a routine that took existing minute meetings in Microsoft Word and published them in Notes—preserving their Word formatting, which is often lost in translation between applications. Once in Notes, end users could easily and quickly search the existing database for topics of interest or reference.

Using Notes search capabilities, everyone in the city has quick and easy access to these records. The city now has a program that can greatly reduce the time and manpower for other departments and gives the constituency greater access. It is Mary's goal to make the meeting minutes even more available to the general public by publishing the Meeting Minutes database directly to the Web using Domino.

Expanding Capabilities with Notes   Mary Scott and her department are in the process of using Notes to implement many other projects and improvements. According to Mary, "We want to leverage our Lotus Notes platform to create a 'City on Notes.' Where Notes can provide the solution to a communication need, it will be used." Projects on the burner include the following:

- A billable fee tracking system. Currently, all projects requiring city services are tracked by individual departments in old legacy systems. It is the department's responsibility to coordinate between themselves information for accurate billing. According to Mary, "We know that under the current system, the city is literally losing money in tracking billable fees. We plan on using a Notes-based solution to track all billable fees in a centralized database that is designed to notify critical personnel in the city via NotesMail when a project's billable fees are due to expire. The savings that will be realized when the new system goes online should more than pay for the development of the application in a very short time."

- Mary and her team are also ready to release their Domino-powered Web site. "Using the new Web capabilities of Notes, every department will have the ability to post information, services, and pertinent information to citizens and visitors. This element of using Notes is not only key to our infrastructure, but vital in the effort to provide large audience access to the city without costly overhead."

- Expanding on the power of Domino, the city of Sarasota will link to other very popular sites, including the Van Wizel Performing Arts Center, Ringling Museum, and other tourism-related sites so that citizens can quickly reference some of the major areas of interest in the city.

What's down the road for the progressive IS department in Sarasota? Turning the IS department into a revenue center by providing excess capacity in the city's new system to other municipalities for a fee. Mary Scott would like the city and the constituency "to reap the benefits from technology today, tomorrow, and in the future. The deployment of Lotus Notes was a monumental step onto the walkway of the year 2000!"

Starting Notes

 To start Notes, locate the Lotus Notes icon on your desktop. The location of this icon depends on how your company installed Notes on your PC.

 The person who installs Notes on your desktop can determine where the icon appears on your desktop. You might have a group, or menu option, called Lotus Notes that includes the Notes program. You might want to copy the icon to your Startup folder so that Notes starts automatically each time you start your PC. Start Notes as you would any other program. Put the mouse pointer on the Notes icon and double-click, or choose Notes from the menu. As Notes starts, it briefly presents a start-up logo. Eventually you see a screen similar to the one shown in Figure 1.1.

N O T E If you're new to Windows 95, the start procedure for Notes might appear a little different. Simply select Start, Programs. Find the menu option where your Notes program is located (usually Lotus Applications). Click this item to start Notes.

For other operating systems, follow your standard procedures for starting a program.

Understanding the Notes Workspace

As with any program, learning the various parts of the screen is the key to learning how to use Notes. In this section, you'll learn about the different parts of the Notes screen and how to control them using the mouse and keyboard. Figure 1.1 shows a typical Notes screen and some of its many features.

FIG. 1.1
Few changes were made to the workspace for Notes 4.6, but if you're just upgrading from Notes 3.x, you will find new features to surprise you!

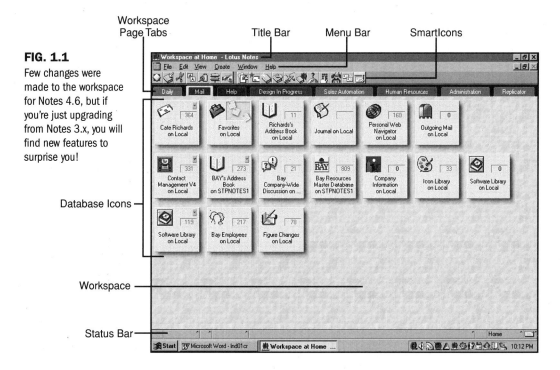

The Menu Bar

When you first start Notes, you'll see the menu bar near the very top of the Notes screen. It contains words such as File, Edit, View, Create, Actions, Window, and Help. Each word represents a menu of operations. Table 1.1 briefly summarizes the operations available through each menu on the menu bar.

 T I P Not all menu commands appear on the menus when you first start Notes. Some commands are available only when you're performing particular functions.

Table 1.1   Menu Operations

Menu	Description
File	Lets you perform database operations, print, configure your environment, work remote (not connected to a network), manipulate attachments, bring information from word processors and other programs into Notes, and save information from Notes to other programs.
Edit	Contains functions for moving, copying, and making other changes to documents; checks spelling; links; works with unread marks; searches for text; and undoes the last command you performed.
View	Lets you determine what information you see on-screen.
Create	Formerly the Compose menu in Release 3 of Notes, Create lets you create messages, documents, folders, views, agents, database designs, sections, tables, objects, hotspots, and page breaks.
Actions	Lets you perform functions on a document, text, or database. You can move documents to folders; categorize documents; enter, change, or delete field values; edit, send, and forward documents; and perform advanced features such as truncating, untruncating, and resaving documents.
Text	Lets you alter the size, color, and font style of text within your message and set tabs and margins.
Window	Provides you with a list of open Notes windows and lets you switch from one window to another. You can also elect to tile, cascade, minimize, and maximize windows.
Help	Provides you with online help to all Notes functions and helps you determine which version of Notes you're using.
Design	Provides you with menu selections available only when you're designing views, forms, subforms, navigators, fields, or agents. This menu is present only when you're in design mode.
Table	Provides you with menu selections only when the cursor is located in a table.

Menu	Description
Attachment	Available only when attachments are present in a document, this menu lets you perform actions on attachments—such as detaching selected documents.
Section	Available only when collapsible sections are present in a document. This menu gives you the ability to control attributes of a section—for example, renaming the section.

N O T E Additional menu commands not listed here appear on the menus when special functions are applied in Notes. For example, if you insert a Lotus 1-2-3 worksheet into a document, a 1-2-3 Worksheet command is offered to give you a quick way of manipulating the object's properties.

Databases and Workspace Pages

Even if you use Notes only to send and receive electronic mail, you still need to know how to manage databases, because your mailbox is a database. However, if you use Notes to its fullest, you and your coworkers will store and share many different kinds of information: status reports, customer records, sales prospects, various kinds of paperwork, budgets, and so on. You might want to access dozens of different databases at different times. Organizing this information is the key to using Notes effectively.

Each database you work with is represented by an icon located on a workspace page. When you first start up Notes 4.6, you see a set of six file folder tabs just below the SmartIcons, each representing a workspace page. Think of workspace pages as categories of data.

Just as you might use different drawers in a file cabinet to contain related files, workspace pages organize your databases into well-defined, grouped sections. You can decide what to call each workspace page and where to place the databases on each workspace page.

In Notes 4.6, you can add or delete workspace tabs as you need them. You'll learn more about how to do this in the section "Customizing Your Workspace" in Chapter 2, "Customizing Notes."

N O T E There is a seventh tab titled Replicator. This tab is predefined by Notes to replicate database information between your remote PC and a Notes server and to send and receive mail when you're working remote. You'll learn more about this tab in the section "Setting Up the Replicator" in Chapter 21, "Working Remote."

You can display any workspace page by clicking the tab associated with it. Each database appears as a box containing a name and a small icon. The icon is usually a picture that you associate with the topic of the database. A database of unsolved problems might have an icon of a question mark or a frowning face, for example. Sometimes each box displays other information about each database, depending on how you set up your preferences.

▶ **See** "Customizing Information Displayed on Database Icons," **p. 51**

If you use Notes exclusively for mail, the first workspace page might be the only one you use. Together, the six workspace pages are known as your workspace.

The organization of your workspace is completely up to you. You can arrange your workspace pages in any convenient manner and place any database on any workspace page. Notes doesn't require any particular arrangement.

The SmartStatus Strip

The SmartStatus strip, shown in Figure 1.2, appears at the bottom of the screen. It is a strip of icons and messages that displays information about network and hard disk activity, mail, database access levels, text attributes, and various status messages. The strip is divided into segments that contain indicators. Table 1.2 describes the indicators in each segment.

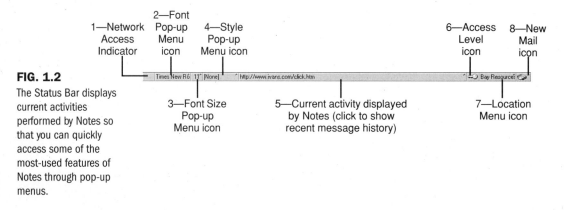

FIG. 1.2

The Status Bar displays current activities performed by Notes so that you can quickly access some of the most-used features of Notes through pop-up menus.

Table 1.2 Understanding the Status Bar Icons	
Status Bar Icon	**Description**
1	The first segment indicates disk or network activity. If a lightning bolt appears, Notes is accessing data across the network. This segment is blank when Notes isn't performing network access. If you're working remote, a modem with blinking red and green lights appears.
2	The second segment shows the current font typeface you're using. This segment is used only when you're editing a document or designing a new form and the cursor is located in a rich text field (see Chapter 7, "Working with Text"). If you click this segment, Notes displays a list of available fonts from which you can select.

Status Bar Icon	Description
3	Like the typeface segment, the third segment, font size, is available only during editing and displays the current text point size. Clicking this segment displays a list of the available point sizes. You can select a new point size by clicking one of the sizes in the list.
4	The fourth segment, style, offers predefined styles that you can select.
5	The fifth segment displays status, error messages, and Internet addresses if you're working with the Web features.
6	The sixth segment, access level, indicates your permission level for the database you're accessing. In Chapter 22, "Security and Encryption," you'll learn about the various access levels and how to interpret the icon in this segment. If you click this segment, Notes displays a message explaining the meaning of the symbol.
7	The seventh segment, location, indicates how your machine is set up for working. For example, if your computer is connected permanently to a network, you see Office (Network) in this section. Other settings, such as Travel (Remote), Island (Disconnected), and Edit Current will be discussed in Chapter 2, and in Part IV of this book, "Going Mobile."
8	The eighth segment displays an inbox icon with an envelope when new mail arrives; otherwise, it displays an envelope. Clicking this segment displays a list of actions you can perform to create, scan, receive, and send mail from your mailbox.

Context-Sensitive Menus

You can access context-sensitive menus by right-clicking anywhere in the Notes workspace. A context-sensitive menu of available commands appears, giving you easy access to the most commonly used functions performed in your current situation. The selections on this menu change as you perform different tasks in Notes. The context-sensitive menu in Figure 1.3 shows the commands available when you enter text in a mail message.

FIG. 1.3

Context-sensitive menus help speed your work with Notes by placing some of the most common features you need at the click of a mouse button.

Working with SmartIcons

Notes provides yet another way to perform common functions. Arranged along one edge of the screen (usually the top) is a row of icons, known as SmartIcons, that represent common functions (see Figure 1.4). SmartIcons represent the same operations you can access with the menus but let you invoke these functions with a single click. For example, you can display the Notes ruler (explained in Chapter 7 by clicking the SmartIcon that looks like a ruler instead of choosing View, Ruler.

FIG. 1.4

SmartIcons provide shortcuts for performing menu commands.

Notes provides a SmartIcon for almost every operation, but the entire collection of icons would fill the screen. After deciding which operations you perform most often, you can tell Notes which SmartIcons you want displayed.

▶ **See** "Customizing SmartIcon Sets," **p. 28**

Notes has the ability to display context-sensitive SmartIcons—in other words, the icons displayed in the icon bar change according to what you're doing at any given time.

Notes provides one set of SmartIcons, the universal set, for you to choose from. However, you can add more icon sets to the list of available SmartIcon sets. You can also customize the universal set by adding new SmartIcons to it. You can also select File, Tools, SmartIcons, Context Icons to have Notes automatically display different icons that are based on the tasks you're performing.

If you don't want to display SmartIcons on your workspace, choose File, Tools, SmartIcons and then deselect the Show Icon Bar option in the dialog box. Likewise, if you want to hide only SmartIcons that are context-sensitive, deselect Context Icons. If you want to hide the icon descriptions that display when you point to an icon, you can deselect Descriptions. If you later change your mind and want to display any of these features, return to this dialog box and reselect these options.

N O T E You can also change the SmartIcon set by opening the SmartIcons dialog box and selecting the set you want to use from the drop-down list box. You'll learn more about this dialog box in the next section. ▪

Changing the Position of SmartIcons You can change the position in which your SmartIcon palette is located. To do so, follow the next steps.

If you are new to Windows 95, you can also reposition the Start menu by clicking anywhere in the Taskbar and dragging it to a new position. You can also hide the Taskbar by right-clicking the Taskbar, choosing Properties, and putting a checkmark next to Auto hide. This might make your workspace appear less cluttered at the bottom of your Notes window.

1. Select File, Tools, SmartIcons. The SmartIcons dialog box appears, as shown in Figure 1.5.

FIG. 1.5
Use the SmartIcons dialog box to add new icons to your SmartIcons bar, create custom SmartIcons, and change the position of the SmartIcons box.

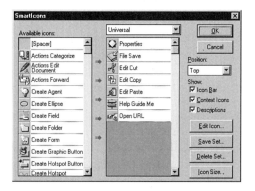

2. Click the down arrow in the Position list box.
3. Select the location in which you want the SmartIcons to be displayed: Left, Right, Top, Bottom, or Floating.
4. If you don't want to customize your SmartIcons further, click OK to save your settings and return to your workspace.

Selecting Floating from the list of positions lets you display the SmartIcons in a box that you can reposition in the window by dragging it (see Figure 1.6). You can resize this box by clicking any of its corners and dragging its borders until the box is the length or height you want. Figure 1.7 illustrates the same set of floating Mail SmartIcons after resizing.

FIG. 1.6
You can elect to have your SmartIcons float on the workspace so that you can position them near the section of the page in which you're working.

FIG. 1.7
You can resize your floating SmartIcons box so that it isn't in the way and is the shape you want.

If you want to close the floating SmartIcons set, click the close box in the upper-left corner of the window. To redisplay the window, select File, Tools, SmartIcons, Show Icon Bar.

TIP   If you select Left or Right as the position for the SmartIcons, keep in mind that the height of your screen can't display as many SmartIcons as the width. If you find that one of these settings frequently results in some of your SmartIcons being truncated, you might want to select Top, Bottom, or Floating, or customize the SmartIcon set you're using to display fewer icons.

Customizing SmartIcon Sets   Although Lotus constructed sets of icons that they thought would be useful, you aren't locked into these choices. Within each set, you can add, remove, rearrange, and even create new icons.

To customize the SmartIcons, display the SmartIcons dialog box by choosing File, Tools, SmartIcons (see Figure 1.8). The list box on the left displays all the available SmartIcons that you can put on a SmartIcon bar. Next to each icon, Notes displays the menu selections you can make to perform the equivalent operation. (All these icons are described further in Appendix A, "Database Template.")

FIG. 1.8

In addition to selecting and positioning the desired SmartIcon set, you can use this dialog box to modify any set of SmartIcons.

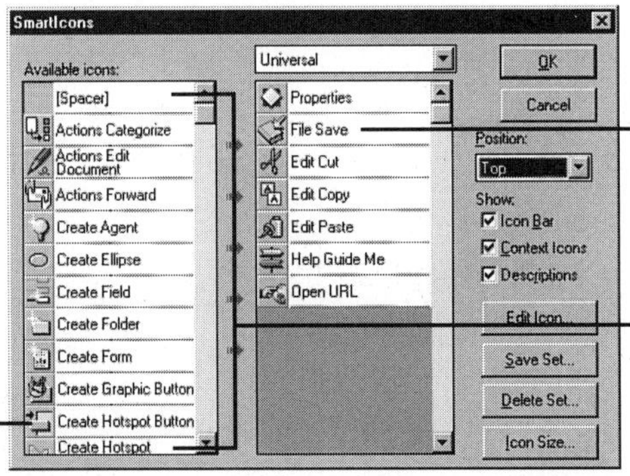

Click an icon and drag it to the desired position in the current SmartIcon set

Here's the current set of SmartIcons

This list shows all the SmartIcons

The list box in the center of the dialog box shows the icons that currently make up one of the available SmartIcons sets. (This section refers to this list box as the current set.) Select the set of icons you want to customize.

To add a new icon to an existing set, find the icon in the list of available icons and drag it to the current set. Notes inserts it into the set. You can add the same icon to as many SmartIcon sets as you want. When you have added all the SmartIcons you want to the current list, click OK to save your changes and return to the workspace.

N O T E   At the top of the list of available icons is a special item called Spacer. If you insert this item in an icon set, Notes inserts a small gap between icons.

To remove an icon from the current set, drag it from the current set off to one side, out of the current set list box. (It doesn't matter where you drag it, as long as it's out of the current set list box.) When you have removed all the SmartIcons you want from the current list, click OK to save your changes and return to the workspace.

You can also add and remove icons from the universal set of SmartIcons. Although the universal set of icons was predefined by Lotus, you might find that you want other icons to display throughout your work in Notes. Notes displays the icons in the universal set in conjunction with the context-sensitive icons wherever you are working in Notes. Context-sensitive SmartIcons don't display in the list of current SmartIcons in the dialog box but they appear to the right of them in the workspace when the situation calls for them to be active. When you're adding icons to this icon set, keep in mind that if you add too many icons, you will probably run out of display room. If you want to add many more icons to the set, you will probably need to display the set as floating to be able to view them all.

To create a new set of SmartIcons, first display an existing set and click Save Set. Notes displays the Save Set of SmartIcons dialog box, which lets you assign a name to the new set. You also must provide a filename with an SMI extension. You can then customize the new set as needed by adding and removing icons.

To delete an existing set, click Delete Set. Notes lists all the existing sets. Select one or more sets and then click OK. Notes deletes the sets you selected.

CAUTION

You can't delete the Universal set of SmartIcons from the Delete Sets dialog box, but it can be deleted using a File Manager program or your operating system's commands if you aren't careful. This SmartIcon set's filename is UNIVERSE.SMI, and it must be present in your SmartIcon subdirectory, typically C:\Notes\Data\Win, as defined in your NOTES.INI file (even if you don't use it), or you won't be able to use SmartIcons in Notes. If this file isn't present, Notes prompts you for the Icon subdirectory the next time you start Notes. You will need to click Cancel multiple times to continue the startup. You won't have access to SmartIcons if this file isn't present, even if you have other SmartIcon files defined.

Make sure that you don't accidentally delete this file when you're cleaning up the files on your hard drive. If you should accidentally delete it, you can either reinstall Notes, use your operating system or File Manager to rename another SMI file you have created UNIVERSE.SMI, or create a blank text file using any text editor and save the file with the name UNIVERSE.SMI. Notes can then start up without an error message and provide you with the ability to use SmartIcons.

There might be times when you need to change the size of the SmartIcons displayed. For example, you might want to increase the size of your SmartIcons when giving a presentation so that the audience can see which SmartIcons you're selecting. With the SmartIcons dialog box open, click the Icon Size button. The Icon Size dialog box appears, as shown in Figure 1.9.

FIG. 1.9

You can increase the size of SmartIcons so that they are easier to see by selecting Large (Super VGA) in the Icon Size dialog box.

Select Small (VGA) (the default) if you want to display the SmartIcons at their usual size. Select Large (Super VGA) if you want to display large SmartIcons. Of course, you won't be able to display as many icons when you select Large. However, large icons are ideal if you're using Notes to make a presentation.

Editing and Creating SmartIcons   You can edit and create new SmartIcons—with limitations. The existing, defined SmartIcons that perform commands such as File, Print, can't be edited. However, Notes provides several custom SmartIcons that you can use to create your own special SmartIcons to run macros easily. (Editing and creating a SmartIcon is easy, but you will need to understand formulas in order to do so. See Chapter 14, "Working with Formulas," and Chapter 15, "Working with Functions and Commands," for more information on writing formulas.)

Custom SmartIcons can be a real time-saver for frequently run commands or complicated tasks in which a macro is used. For example, if you often like to switch to the Calculator in Windows while you're working in Notes, you might want to add a custom icon to your SmartIcon set to open it automatically. To do so, follow these steps:

1. Click the Edit Icon button in the SmartIcon dialog box. The Edit SmartIcons dialog box appears.

2. Scroll through the list of Custom Icons available for you to edit. Highlight the icon you want to use.

3. Edit the icon's name in the Description text box to describe the function it will perform. In this example, type `Calculator`. This is the name that Notes displays in the bubble help that appears when you point to a SmartIcon on the workspace.

4. Click Formula to open the SmartIcons Formula dialog box, shown in Figure 1.10.

FIG. 1.10

You can enter formulas to customize the functions of SmartIcons.

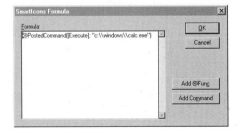

5. Type the formula you want to apply to the custom icon. In this example, you would enter the formula as it is displayed in Figure 1.10. Note that the formula contains double backslashes between the drive and subdirectory names. When you write a directory path in Notes formulas, you must use double backslashes. You'll learn more about writing formulas like this one in Chapter 14.

6. Click OK, and then click OK again to save the formula.

7. Add the newly created SmartIcon to your SmartIcon palette as described in the preceding section.

You can now use the edited SmartIcon to run the command to open Calculator whenever that SmartIcon is selected. When you exit File Manager, you return to Notes exactly where you left it.

Opening and Viewing Databases

> **N O T E** If you're opening a database for the first time during your work session, you might be prompted for your Notes password. Simply type your Notes password in the dialog box provided and click OK. Notes passwords are case-sensitive, so you need to type the password exactly as your Notes administrator set it up for you. You'll learn more about working with your Notes password in Chapter 2. ■

It's quite easy to open a database. Simply double-click a database icon corresponding to the database you want to use. A database icon appears as a square on your workspace, with the name and location of the database printed on it. Notes opens the database to display navigators, views, panes, and folders, as illustrated in Figure 1.11. This section briefly describes how you move around a database to find the information you're looking for. If you have used a previous release of Notes, you might still want to read this section, because Notes has added many new features.

> **N O T E** If this is the first time you have opened the database, you will first see the About This Database document, which usually provides you with a summary of the purpose of the database, along with any rules for using it, and a contact name in case of problems. Take a moment to read the document, and then press the Esc key to exit the document. You will see this document in subsequent uses of this database only if you select Help, About This Database, if the designer of the databases elects to have this document display upon each opening, or if it has been modified. ■

Working with Panes

When you first open a database in Notes 4.6, you'll notice that the window is usually split into two panes (unless you have the option of displaying the preview pane selected). The left pane displays the default database navigator (usually the Folder Navigator), which provides a graphical way to navigate through the documents in the database. A database designer can also build other navigators and assign one of them as the default navigator to be displayed when you open the database. Figure 1.11 displays the default Folder Navigator for the Bay Employees Company Numbers\By Location & Type view.

FIG. 1.11

Databases open to display navigators, views, panes, and folders similar to those shown in the Bay Employees database, shown here.

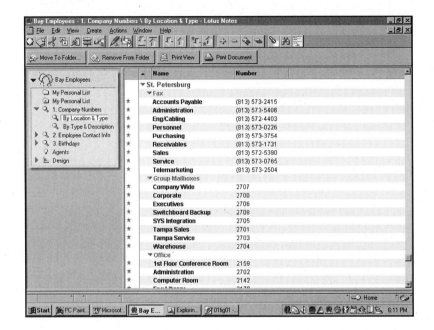

Working with Views

The person who designs the database decides how the documents are ordered and categorized and what information is displayed about each document. A view is the way in which the list is presented. When the database is open, the view pane appears on the right. Figure 1.12 shows a sample view for the Richards's Address Book database. This view shows the Location documents used for network and remote connections with the server. You'll learn more about server connections in Part IV.

The database designer might have determined that the list can be presented in several useful ways and therefore might have created several views. Consider a database that contains sales orders. A view called By Customer might present the documents (sales orders) strictly in alphabetical order by customer last name; another view, perhaps called By Sales Rep, might categorize documents by sales representative. By selecting a view, you can determine how Notes presents the list of documents.

Different views might display the documents in the same order but show different information about each document. A view called Revenue, for example, might show each document's customer name, gross sales amount, profit, and commission. Another view, called Customer, might list the same documents but show customer address and phone numbers as well.

FIG. 1.12
Views list all, or a subset, of the documents that appear in a database.

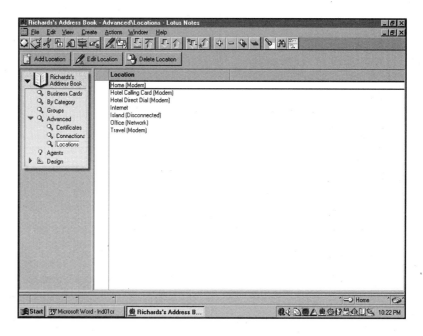

A view might not list all the documents in a database. A view called Delinquent Accounts, for example, might list only documents that represent unpaid sales orders that are at least 90 days late.

The designer of a database selects one of the views in the database as the default view that Notes uses when you open the database for the first time. You can select another view at any time, as explained in the next section.

Selecting a View

When you open a database, Notes displays a view. If you're accessing this database for the first time, you see the predefined default view. Otherwise, Notes displays the last view you selected. After you select a different view, Notes always remembers the view you last selected, even when you exit Notes. In some databases, the database designer might have created only a single view, so your choice is limited to that view unless you create a new view for yourself (as discussed in Chapter 10, "Creating New Databases"). In other databases, some views are hidden by the designers so that access is granted only to particular users of the database, or through special actions programmed into the application—for example, from a navigator. In most databases, however, you can choose from among several views.

You can select views from the navigator pane by clicking text that has a small magnifying glass next to it. You can also select a view by selecting the View menu and choosing the title of the view you want to use (see Figure 1.13). Notice that the available views are listed in the drop-down menu and in the navigator. The active view has a checkmark next to it on the View menu and has a box surrounding its title in the navigator.

FIG. 1.13

Available views in a database appear at the bottom of the View menu.

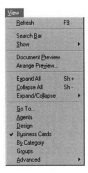

Expanding Categories in Views

Categories in views are represented by small triangles, plus signs, or other graphics chosen by the designer of a database to indicate that there are collapsible categories in the view. These *twisties* appear to the left of a category title. For example, if you select text marked by a twistie that is pointing to the right, you will expand the category to view more documents or categories. If you select text marked by a twistie that is pointing down, you will collapse the category. You can also expand and collapse views by using SmartIcons, as shown in Table 1.3. You will learn more about working with views in Chapter 3.

Table 1.3   SmartIcons that Help You Collapse and Expand View Categories

Icon	Description	Action
✚	Single plus sign	Expands one category level
▬	Single minus sign	Collapses one category level
✚	Multi-plus sign	Expands all categories
▬	Multi-minus sign	Collapses all categories

Working with Folders

Folders are similar to views but store documents as you specify by moving them in and out of the folders you use rather than using selection formulas that automatically specify which documents are displayed in views. Folders are a great tool to use when you want to sort related documents in a database according to criteria you set. You'll learn more about creating and using folders in Chapter 3.

When you select a folder icon in the navigator, documents stored in that folder display in the view to the right. If the folder is marked with a twistie, clicking the twistie displays additional folders stored within the folder. Figure 1.14 shows an example of a folder storing all Location documents, along with subfolders sorting the same Location documents by city.

Part

I

Ch

1

FIG. 1.14

You can create subfolders to further organize your documents.

Secondary folders that store a subset of documents in the primary folder

Primary folder for a group of documents

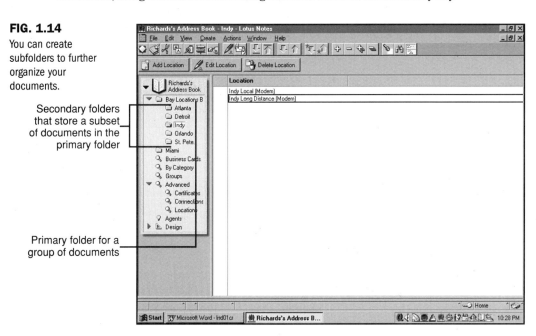

Understanding Documents

The building blocks for all databases are *documents*—which are created by putting information in a form. A *form* is a template designed and stored in the database that users select to create a document that stores information. When you create a document in a database, you select from one of the forms created by the database designer. This form serves as a template for you to enter your information. When you save the information you have entered in the form, Notes displays it as a document in the database. This section quickly walks you through understanding documents. You'll learn, in detail, how to work with documents throughout Part I, "Notes Basics."

Opening Documents

Once you have located the document you want to read in the view, Notes provides several ways to open it:

- ▪ Double-click the document's title
- ▪ Highlight the document and press the Enter key
- ▪ Highlight the document and select File, Open

When the document opens, you may scroll through its contents using the scroll bars at the right and bottom of the document window.

Creating Documents

Each database design can provide a wealth of forms to be created. Each one can be different or can contain as few as one form—as determined by the database designer. You might have forms in which you enter times into a time-tracking database, or forms that order supplies from your purchasing department. The method of creating a document is typically the same for all of them. While you are in the database, select the Create menu and then select the form name that represents the document you want to create (see Figure 1.15). The document appears in edit mode, ready for you to enter information.

FIG 1.15

To create a document in a Notes database, you may choose from the available list of documents displayed in the Create menu.

> **N O T E**   Some designers might create databases in which you are prompted to create a new document by clicking a button rather than by selecting the form name from the Create menu. You'll learn more about creating new documents in Chapter 3.

Before you enter text in a document, the document must be in edit mode. In other words, the brackets surrounding the fields must be open, as shown in Figure 1.16. If you open an existing document and don't see the open brackets, double-click anywhere in the document or select Actions, Edit Document so that it is placed in edit mode. Now you can enter or edit text as you want.

Exiting Documents

When you're ready to close a document, do one of the following:

- Double-right-click (if you have this option selected in your preferences; see Chapter 2).
- Select File, Close.
- Press the Esc key.
- Press Ctrl+W (or Ctrl+S to save).

Notes will close the document you're reading. If you entered or edited any information in the document, you will be prompted to save the document. Click Yes if you want to save the information, No if you want to discard your entries and exit anyway, and Cancel if you want to return to the document before saving.

FIG. 1.16
A document in edit mode displays open brackets around the fields, indicating that you can enter information into the fields.

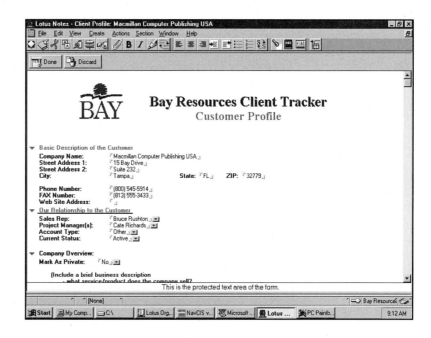

> **CAUTION**
>
> If you click No when you're prompted to save your changes, Notes closes the document without saving any information you have added, and you lose all the entries you made. Click Cancel if you want to go back and add or remove information before saving.

Getting Help

Notes includes an extensive online help system using many of the new Notes 4 features. The help system contains hundreds of documents, each discussing a Notes topic. You can access the help system at any time by pressing F1. Notes will take you to the Guide Me help panel that relates to your current tasks. You can follow the various linked documents to learn about the task you're trying to perform, or you can click the Help Topics button to exit the Guide Me panel and open the Help view. You can also access help directly by selecting Help, Help Topics, or by double-clicking the Notes Help database icon, shown in Figure 1.17.

 TIP If you will be designing databases, and you would like to see examples of the use of many of Notes' new features, the Notes Help database utilizes many of these features in its design. If the database is stored on your hard drive, you can access the design of the database to see how it is put together. Pay a visit to the design of the navigators in the database to get an idea of how Notes panels and other navigators are put together. Don't change the design, though, or your next help session might exhibit problems.

FIG. 1.17

Notes ships with two
Help databases: the full
Notes Help database
and the remote Notes
Help Lite database.

Notes provides context-sensitive help whenever you press F1. Notes looks at what you're doing and tries to select the panel from its Help database that will offer you the most useful information. For example, if you're in the middle of sending a mail message, pressing F1 displays a document that offers you information on sending mail messages. You can also click the Help Topics SmartIcon, if available, to open the Notes Help database.

Figure 1.18 shows a typical Notes help document. For long help messages, you can press the Page Up and Page Down keys to move through the text of the help document.

FIG. 1.18

Notes Help documents
provide you with
instructions on using
Notes features and
guide you through
finding additional
information on a related
topic.

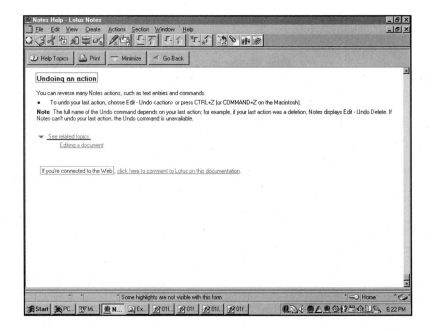

In a book, you sometimes find cross-references, in which one section of text refers to another. For example, a printed book might contain a sentence such as "See page 352 for more information." Notes includes the electronic equivalent, known as *hotspots,* which allow you to access related information in another help document.

In Figure 1.18, notice that the phrase "Editing a document" is underlined (onscreen, it's also green). This is a hotspot. The presence of this text attribute tells you that you can get more information about this phrase. If you click the text, Notes displays a different document that contains information about ways to change how paragraphs look. This document, in turn, might contain other hotspot links that can guide you to related sections. You'll learn more about hotspots in Chapter 8, "Working with Documents."

Some of the help articles also contain pop-up boxes, indicated by light green outline boxes that provide quick definitions for important terms. For example, the words "edit mode" in Figure 1.19 indicate the presence of a pop-up box. When you point at the words in the box and hold down the left mouse button, a box appears with a definition of the phrase.

FIG. 1.19

Pop-ups in Help documents indicate additional information about a word or phrase. Click anywhere in the pop-up box to view the information.

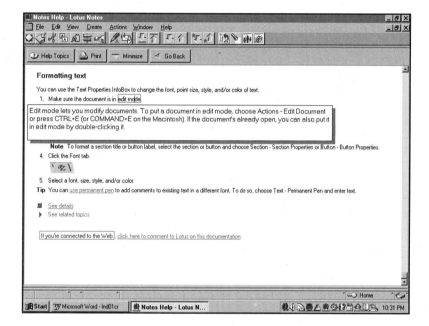

At the top of the Help window, you'll find a series of buttons that let you use Help to your best advantage. These buttons include the following:

- The Help Topics button opens the Help Index view and displays a list of all the documents in the database. The document you were viewing is still open and can be accessed by closing the current window or selecting the document from the <u>W</u>indow menu. This provides you with a fast way of looking up another document without having to close the current one.
- The Print button quickly prints the current help document.
- The Minimize button minimizes the Help window.
- The Go Back button goes back one window (this is the same as pressing the Esc key).

If you're reading an article that you accessed through a doclink or hotspot, you can either press the Esc key or click the Go Back button (if it's visible) to return to the Help document you were reading. A *doclink* is a link icon resembling a document that opens another document related to the topic when you double-click it. If you are reading a document that you invoked by pressing F1, pressing Esc closes the help system and returns you to your previous activity.

Using the Visual Index

New to the Notes 4 Help database is the Visual Index, which takes advantage of new Notes features—hotspots and graphical navigators. You can open the Visual Index by clicking the Visual Index icon in the navigator of the Notes Help database. As shown in Figure 1.20, the Visual Index has graphical representations of subjects covered in the Help database.

FIG. 1.20

The Visual Help Index displays graphical representations of the types of Visual Help documents available in the database. Just click any picture to open a Visual Help document about that subject.

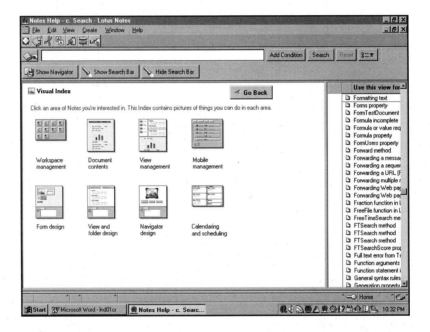

When you double-click one of these graphics, a visual representation of a subject appears (see Figure 1.21). You will notice several yellow bubbles with question marks on them. When you click one of these bubbles, you learn how to perform the action marked by the bubble. For example, clicking the bubble positioned over the bullet in Figure 1.21 displays text indicating that the feature is a bullet and then leads you to the steps for creating bullets (see Figure 1.22). You'll learn more about hotspots and graphical navigators in Chapter 8.

You can search for a particular help topic by switching to the Search view and using the Search Bar. To display it, select View, Search Bar. The Search Bar appears directly above the Help view. You can type words in the text entry box and then click the Search button. Notes searches through all the documents in the database and displays the ones that meet your search criteria. You'll learn more about using the search features of Notes in Chapter 8.

FIG. 1.21
Visual Index documents in the Help database provide quick, easy ways to learn about many of the features in Notes. Just click any of the question mark indicators to display additional information about a topic.

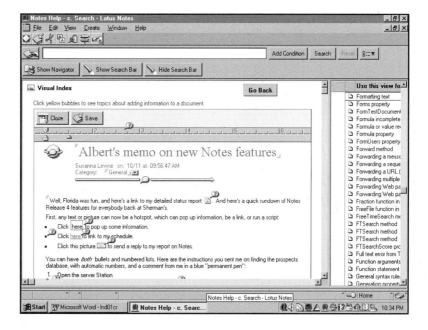

FIG. 1.22
After you click a question mark indicator, Notes opens a document describing how to use the corresponding feature.

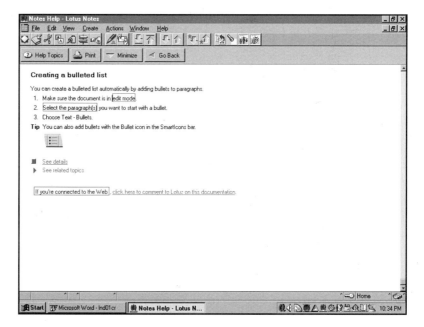

Storing Help Topics for Quick Reference

While you're viewing the Help database navigator pane, you'll notice a folder called Favorite Topics. As you read through Help documents, you might find a few that you want to reference frequently. Simply highlight the document you want to reference and drag it onto the folder. To view the topics that you stored for quick access, click the Favorite Topics folder in the View Navigator. Click the Favorite Topics folder and then choose from the list of documents in the view.

Using Notes Help Lite

Notes 4.x provides an abridged version of Notes Help called Notes Help Lite. This database installs on your hard drive when you install Notes 4.x. The purpose of this database is to provide mobile users with a Help database that minimizes the amount of hard drive space needed while continuing to supply valuable help information when you're working remote. Essentially, Help Lite provides help on the features you use when working with Notes remote. It excludes topics on design, administration, and LotusScript. The Visual Index is also excluded, because graphics take up more space.

If you look in Help Lite for topics that are not common to everyday use, Notes prompts you to access the network copy of the full Help database. If you elected to install both versions of Help during the installation of Notes 4.x, you can safely delete the Help Lite database, because the documents are duplicates of the full Help database.

Getting Lotus Internet Support Help

Notes 4.6 gives you a quick way to get assistance from Lotus if your Domino server has been set up to access the Internet. Select Help, Lotus Internet Support to choose from the following three options:

- Notes Home Page: Accesses the World Wide Web and goes to the Notes Home Page so you can begin your search for additional information on Notes.

- Lotus Home Page: Gives you a more global view of what is going on at Lotus by opening the Lotus Home page.

- Lotus Customer Support: Opens to the main Web page that guides you through locating the various support offerings on the Lotus Web site—from online Knowledgebase information to files that you can download to assist you with your Notes needs.

The shortcut provided by Notes is a quick way for you to begin your hunt for additional information that facilitates your use of Notes. Remember, though, that your Notes administrator must provide you with the means of accessing the Internet through Domino in order for you to utilize this help feature.

Help for Notes 3 Users

If you were a Notes 3 user, you have noticed by now that many of the commands and actions you memorized have now changed. Notes 4.x provides you with a quick way to discover the new command equivalents for Notes 3 commands. Just select Help, Release 3 Menu Finder. The Release 3 Menu Finder window appears, as shown in Figure 1.23.

FIG. 1.23
You can find the equivalent Notes 4 menu commands for tasks you used to perform in Notes 3 by selecting the Release 3 command you would use.

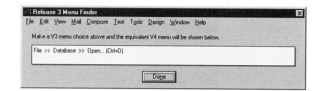

Select the menu command sequence you used to perform in Release 3 of Notes. The equivalent Release 4 command appears in the window. Perform this command to perform the same task you used to perform in Release 3.

Exiting Notes

Notes provides many ways to perform most operations, and the same is true of exiting. You can exit Notes by doing any of the following:

- Press Alt+F4.
- Choose File, Exit.
- Click the control menu box in the upper-left corner of the Notes screen. The control menu appears. Choose Close to quit Notes.
- Double-click the control menu box.

Customizing Notes

Many people who use Notes spend most of their day working with it. If your job involves a great deal of contact with other people, much of that interaction might involve exchanging messages through Notes. If you're going to work with Notes frequently, you will be pleased that you can customize most aspects of the program.

This chapter provides tips and techniques to use in customizing your Notes environment. In this chapter, you'll learn about arranging your workspace pages and icons, configuring Notes, and setting up your printer. You'll also learn a little bit about two special Notes files, DESKTOP.DSK and NOTES.INI, and the importance they have.

Customizing Your Workspace

Your workspace is the starting point for working with Notes. Even though organizing your workspace might not be as important to you as organizing the databases in which you work, it can help you quickly locate and work with the databases you need.

N O T E   As you work in Notes, you might be prompted for your Notes password. This usually happens when you first begin your session in Notes, when you try to make changes to the Access Control Lists (ACLs), or when you first try to access a database that is located on a server or one that enforces local security when you're working remote. You might also be prompted for your password even if you already entered it during the work session, if you try to access documents or a database that is encrypted on your hard drive, or if you try to change your password or call a server from a remote location.

When you are prompted for your Notes password, type it in the Password dialog box exactly; Notes passwords are case-sensitive. For more information on Notes passwords, see Chapter 22, "Security and Encryption." ▪

Arranging Workspace Pages

The Notes workspace is initially divided into six workspace pages. Each database you access appears as a box with an icon on one of the pages. When you add databases to your workspace or create your own databases, the first step is to select the page on which you want the database to appear.

When you start using Notes, you will probably work with only a few databases: your mail, the Address databases, and perhaps one or two information databases that your department uses. Because the number of databases is small, you probably will put all your databases on a single workspace page.

As your familiarity with Notes increases and your use of Notes expands, you will work with more and more databases. Eventually, you might want to use more databases than can fit on a single workspace page. You can fit a total of 99 database icons on a single workspace page. Long before that happens, however, you will probably feel that your page is cluttered and will want to organize it.

Adding New Workspace Pages

Notes 4.x lets you add additional workspace page tabs to better organize your workspace. You can have up to 32 workspace pages, in addition to the workspace page titled Replicator. Notes automatically adjusts the size of the tabs to accommodate the addition of tabs and the size of the words you're entering as tab titles. However, if you enter more text/tab combinations than Notes has room to display, the tabs on the right side of the workspace begin to disappear. If this happens, the only way you can move to those workspace pages is to highlight workspace page and press the right arrow key to view the contents of the hidden workspace pages. To add a new workspace page, follow these steps:

Part

I

Ch

2

1. Click a workspace tab to insert the workspace page to the left of the selected workspace page.

2. Choose Create, Workspace Page. If you haven't added a workspace page before, Notes asks if you want to upgrade your desktop file if you have upgraded from Notes R3.x to Notes 4.x.

3. Click Yes to add the workspace page and upgrade your desktop file, or click No to cancel.

 TIP When you want to add a new workspace page, you can also right-click and select Create Workspace Page from the menu that appears.

CAUTION

When you add additional workspace pages to your workspace, you modify your DESKTOP.DSK file, which stores your personal preferences and setup information. Once you modify this file in Notes R4.x, you can't use the file with previous releases of Notes.

Deleting Workspace Pages from Your Workspace

Just as you can add workspace pages to your workspace, you can also remove them. When you remove a workspace page, you also remove any database icons you have positioned on the page. If you don't want to remove the icons from your workspace, you need to move them to another tab before following these procedures. To remove a workspace page from your workspace, follow these steps:

1. Click the workspace page's tab.

2. Choose Edit, Clear or press Delete.

3. Click Yes to confirm the deletion or No to cancel it.

N O T E Removing the database icon and deleting the database are not the same thing. Deleting the database is accomplished by selecting File, Database, Delete and will physically remove the database (if you have access permission to do so). Removing the database icon removes only the icon from your workspace. If the file is located on your hard drive or server, you simply need to again add the database icon to another workspace page.

Naming Workspace Page Tabs

When you feel that your workspace is getting cluttered, you might want to use the other workspace pages. To name a workspace page, follow these steps:

1. Double-click the workspace tab that you want to name, or click the workspace tab and then select the Properties SmartIcon. The Workspace Properties InfoBox for the selected tab appears, as shown in Figure 2.1.

FIG. 2.1

You can name your workspace pages by opening the Workspace Properties InfoBox.

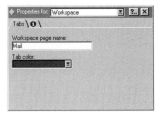

2. Type in the new name for the tab in the Workspace page name text entry box.
3. Select a color for the tab in the Tab color list box.
4. Double-click the control menu box (in this example, it's the X in the upper-right corner of the box) to close the InfoBox and accept your edits.

Moving Databases on the Workspace

You can move databases from one page to another at any time. Click the workspace page on which the database now resides and then drag the database from that page to the tab belonging to the page where you want to move the database. The Workspace page tab displays a box around the title when the cursor is positioned correctly. You can move multiple databases by holding down the Shift key, clicking each of the databases you want to move, and then dragging the icons to the new page.

As you move icons from one workspace page to another, you might find that the icons on the pages become rather disorganized. You can tell Notes to straighten up a workspace page by selecting the page and choosing View, Arrange Icons. Notes arranges all the database icons on the current page, starting from the top and moving down, with no gaps.

You can also move the icons on your Notes workspace without using the mouse. To do so, follow these steps:

1. Select the icon you want to move.
2. Hold down the Shift and Ctrl keys at the same time.
3. Use the cursor arrows to reposition your icon.
4. Release the Shift and Ctrl keys.
5. Press Enter when you have completed the move.

The icons will now appear on the newly designated workspace page.

Working with Stacked Icons

There are times when you might want to keep more than one copy of a database icon on your workspace. Perhaps you have access to the same database that is stored on more than one server on your network. Or you might be working remote and keeping a replica copy of a database that is stored on your hard drive as well as the icon pointing to the main database stored on your server. Your workspace might get cluttered with all the copies of the database icons. You can set your workspace to show all database replicas as stacked icons. Stacked icons take up less room on your workspace and make it easier to work with all the databases at once. When you stack icons, the topmost, leftmost icon appears at the top of the stack. Stacked icons appear with a stacked icon indicator in the upper-right corner of the icon, as shown in Figure 2.2.

FIG. 2.2
You can stack replica copies of icons so that they take up less space on your workspace page.

 —————— Stacked icon indicator

Stacking Database Icons   If your duplicate icons don't appear to be stacked, select View, Stack Replica Icons. A checkmark appears that indicates the selection is active. Notes remembers this setting until you turn it off.

When you stack icons, Notes checks your location and displays whichever icon you used last when you were working using that location at the top of the stack. The icons automatically display the server name or Local in the title of the icon as they are brought to the top of the stack. This lets you quickly know which copy of the database you are using: a server (a network copy) or Local (a copy stored on your hard drive). For example, in Figure 2.2, you see Cate Richards' database located on the Local hard drive.

If a database has replicas on multiple servers, and all are added to your workspace, the top-left icon on the workspace page appears at the top of the stack when you elect to stack your icons.

N O T E If you have multiple copies of database icons on your workspace, but they don't stack when you select <u>V</u>iew, Stac<u>k</u> Replica Icons, you're working with copies of the database—not replica copies. Copies of databases include all the design features of the original database but don't contain the same Replica ID, which is what Notes uses to determine if a database is a true replica or just a copy. You'll learn more about copies and replica copies of databases in Chapter 20, "Setting Up to Go Remote."

Using Stacked Icons   Typically, you store replica copies of databases on your hard drive when you're working away from a network. (See Chapter 20 for more information on creating replica copies of databases.) You may also keep replica copies of databases on your hard drive if you are making design modifications to a database and you don't want to do so directly in the production server copy.

Regardless of your reason for having multiple replicas of a database on your workspace, you might often find the need to switch between the replica copies during your work session. Because the replica that is at the top of the stack is the database that Notes works on, you simply need to select a new replica to be placed on the top of the stack. To do so, follow these steps:

1. Click the database indicator (down arrow) in the upper-right corner of the database icon. The database icon menu drops down, as shown in Figure 2.3.

FIG. 2.3

Select the database indicator to choose between replica databases when their icons are stacked.

2. Select the copy of the replica that you want to work in. For example, in Figure 2.3, the Local copy of the database is currently at the top of the stack—the checkmark displays next to that location. To bring the network copy of the icon to the top of the stack, choose the server name in which the replica is stored. In this example, you would select BRSTPNOTES01/BAY RESOURCES.

N O T E The Replicate option in the database location menu list is discussed in Chapter 20. ▦

If you decide that you don't want to stack your replica icons anymore, select <u>V</u>iew, Stac<u>k</u> Replica Icons to remove the checkmark. Your icons automatically unstack and arrange themselves on the workspace.

Customizing Information Displayed on Database Icons

In addition to arranging the workspace pages on which your databases reside, you can customize the appearance of the database information. The simplest database icon (and the default) consists of a picture relating to the content and title of the database. Figure 2.4 shows a sample workspace page with three databases.

FIG. 2.4

These three databases show the default database information.

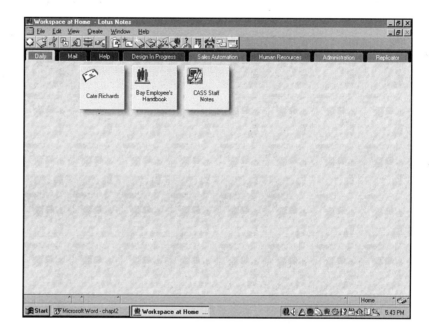

You can customize the icons to display additional information about each database. The <u>V</u>iew menu contains two options that prompt Notes to tell you more about each database on your workspace:

- Show Unread: This tells Notes to display a tiny window next to each icon, showing the number of unread documents in the database. This number tells you if you need to allocate time to read the contents of the database. Be aware, however, that Notes doesn't update this number every time someone enters a new document into the database. The Show Unread window shows only the number of documents that were in the database the last time you opened it. If you want Notes to update the number of unread documents for each database on your current workspace page, exit all your databases and then press F9 or choose <u>V</u>iew, Re<u>f</u>resh Unread Count. Notes also updates the unread document counter the next time you start up Notes. The Unread count for the database you are working in updates when you exit the database.

TIP Pressing Ctrl+Shift+F9 updates all databases on all workspace pages on your desktop.

N O T E   You can scan databases for unread documents in Notes to quickly review new information stored in your databases. Read the section "Scanning Databases for Unread Documents" in Chapter 10, "Creating New Databases," for more information on this feature. ▪

▪ Server names: This tells Notes to display the server name of each database under the database title. This information can be helpful if you need to know which server the database is located on. "Local" refers to databases that are stored on your local disk drive.

T I P   If you hold down the Shift key as you select View, Show Server Names, Notes displays the filename for each database. Notes can also display the filenames without the server names on the icons if you continue to hold down the Shift key and select View, Show Server Names again.

Figure 2.5 shows the same workspace page shown in Figure 2.4, with the addition of the unread document counter, server name, and filename.

FIG. 2.5

If the full server name, filename, or pathname is too long to display on the database icon, you can find the same information by selecting File, Database, Properties.

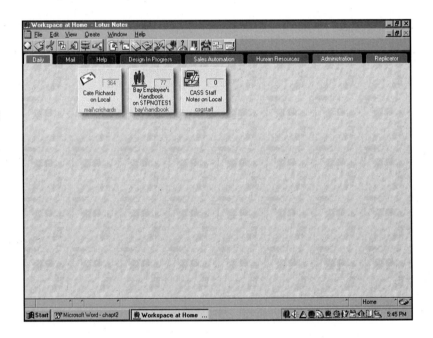

You can also elect to enlarge the size of the database icon through the Notes User Preferences settings, as described in the next section. This enlarges the entire database icon, including the text size of the titles. This is great if you have difficulty reading the database titles. Keep in mind that you will see only a few icons in the workspace at a time, and long database title names will be truncated.

N O T E For OS/2 3.1.5 Notes users, VGA fonts might appear too small when you're using IBM's S3, 32-bit, and 64-bit graphics chips. If you have this difficulty, you might want to increase the font size using File, Tools, User Preferences. You should also add this parameter to your NOTES.INI file:

`DISPLAY_FONT_INCREASE=1`

The display font options are 1, 2, and 3. 1 is the best for the video chips mentioned here. ▪

You will read more about modifying the NOTES.INI file later in this chapter.

Setting Up Your Printer

 You use your operating system software to tell your computer what kinds of printers are available. For example, in Windows 95, you use the Printer's Properties InfoBox. The only information Notes needs is the printer(s) you want to use.

Choose File, Print to open the File Print dialog box, shown in Figure 2.6. When you click the Printer button, Notes displays a list of available printers in the Print Setup dialog box, shown in Figure 2.7. If you have only a single printer available, Notes displays only that printer. Make your printer selection and click OK. After you select a printer, Notes routes all printouts to that printer until you change your selection.

FIG. 2.6

Click the Printer button to switch printers or make changes to your printer setup in the File Print dialog box.

FIG. 2.7

Select the printer you want to use, or for which you want to make setup changes, from the list of printers available to you.

N O T E The dialog box that appears when you select and set up a printer will vary, depending on the type of printer and the operating system you're working with. For example, the dialog boxes just shown are for an HP LaserJet 4P printer with a workstation running Windows 95. Your dialog boxes might vary slightly from those shown here. ■

The Print Setup dialog box also allows you to configure various options about how the printer works by clicking the Setup button. You shouldn't have to modify any of these options often unless you're printing custom work.

Perhaps the change most often made when changing printer setups is to switch between landscape and portrait printing. This change in paper orientation is made through your operating system printer setup but can be reached by selecting File, Print, Printer, Setup. The printer's properties dialog box appears, as shown in Figure 2.8.

FIG. 2.8

If your printer supports landscape printing, you can switch between landscape and portrait printing in this dialog box.

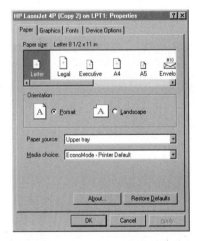

Figure 2.8 shows the dialog box that appears when you're printing to the HP LaserJet 4P printer. This setup box (and the available options) depend on the type of printer you have selected, so you might see a slightly different setup dialog box for your printer. In the Orientation combo box, select the paper orientation you want to use, click OK, and then click OK again to save your settings. Typically, the page orientation settings remain in effect until the next time you change them. However, some networks are set up and administered to always shift print settings back to their default. It all depends on how your PC is installed and what operating system you use.

If you have additional questions about the other options available for your printer, refer to your printer manual.

Changing Your Password

Notes maintains several important pieces of information about you. Some of this information, such as your user ID number, isn't of concern to you but is vital to Notes. You can display some of the information by choosing File, Tools, User ID. When Notes prompts you for your Notes password, type it and click OK. The User ID dialog box appears, as shown in Figure 2.9.

FIG. 2.9

The User ID dialog box provides you with a summary of your personal ID information. You can click the Set Password button to change your Notes password.

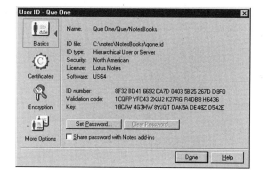

This dialog box provides the following information about your ID file:

- User name
- ID filename and location
- ID type
- Security (North American or International)
- License type
- Software number
- ID number
- Validation code
- Key

You also open this dialog box to do the following:

- Change your user name
- Work with certificates
- Configure for encryption
- Work with advanced options concerning your Notes ID

You'll learn more about managing your Notes ID in Chapter 22. For now, we will only look at changing your password.

> **CAUTION**
>
> Changing your user name removes all the certificates from your ID, so you will have to acquire new certificates before you can use any shared databases (databases not on your local drive). Contact your Notes Administrator before performing this action!

Perhaps the most important selection in the User ID dialog box lets you change your password. Security experts say that you should change your password on a regular basis, but most people change their passwords only when they have a pressing need for a new password (for example, if a trusted friend who knows the old password turns out to be a snoop!).

N O T E   Although it's beyond the scope of this chapter, I want to highlight a new feature that first appeared in Lotus Notes 4.5. Beginning with Notes 4.5, Notes Administrators can set up an administrative task on the Notes server to enforce password aging of your Notes password. Whether this option is set or not depends on the needs and policies of your company. ▪

To change your password, choose File, Tools, User ID. Enter your current Notes password when prompted, and then click the Set Password button. The Enter Password dialog box appears, prompting you for your old password (see Figure 2.10). Enter your old password and click OK.

FIG. 2.10

You must first enter your old Notes password in the Enter Password dialog box and then type your new password when prompted.

N O T E   You will notice that the hieroglyphic symbols next to your password change as you type each letter. This is just an additional Notes security feature that acts as an anti-spoofing device, making it more difficult to write programs that look like the Notes password screen but that actually steal your password. The XXXs that appear in the password entry field are provided to mask your password entry from others who might be looking over your shoulder. ▪

Notes then prompts you with the Set Password dialog box, shown in Figure 2.11. Type in your new password and click OK. As is always true when you enter a password, your new password doesn't appear on-screen as you type. To ensure your security, avoid creating passwords that can easily be guessed by people who know you, such as your child's or pet's name. Because passwords are case-sensitive, you can decrease the chance of someone guessing your password by varying the case of the letters. For example, if you want to enter pluto3 as your password, try typing plutO3, capitalizing the O (or any other letter). Adding numbers to the password also helps keep people from discovering your password.

FIG. 2.11

You can enter a new password in the Set Password dialog box, but take note of the minimum number of characters your Notes ID requires for a password.

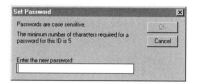

Part

I

Ch

2

N O T E The minimum number of characters you need to type to enter a new password might vary, depending on the minimum character limit that your Notes Administrator might have set when your Notes ID was issued. Typically, the minimum character limit is set at eight, as suggested by Notes, but it could be as low as zero and anywhere in between. If you try to type a new password and Notes doesn't accept it, try typing a password that has more characters.

Finally, Notes prompts you for your new password again. This is a safety feature to ensure that you typed the password correctly. Notes signals an error if you didn't type the same new password both times; otherwise, Notes accepts the new password. You must use it the next time you start Notes or clear your logon. Click Done to exit the User ID dialog box.

CAUTION

A Clear Password button in the User ID dialog box can remove your password. If you value the security of your mailbox, don't click this button. With your password cleared, anyone who has access to your laptop or PC can access your Notes mailbox and even send mail under your name.

Specifying Your Notes Preferences

Through Notes Preferences, you can customize various aspects of Notes. Choosing File, Tools, User Preferences gives you the User Preferences dialog box, which provides a single location for customizing all your global preference settings.

The User Preferences dialog box is divided into the following four sections:

- Basics: Displays a panel that allows you to control startup options, the location of your Notes data directory, trash folder setup, and your User Dictionary.

- International: Displays settings that let you customize the way Notes translates particular international symbols, casing, and collation. You can also select which international dictionary you want to use.

- Mail: Displays settings that let you specify how you want your mail treated. You can also define the location of your mail database and which mail program you're using.

■ Ports: Lets you control the serial or network port that Notes uses to connect to the Notes server. Your system administrator can assist you with any changes you might want to make in this pane if you're unsure of the settings you need to make. If you're planning to work remote, read Chapter 20 for more information on the Port settings you need to make.

Basic Settings

The User Preferences dialog box always opens to the Basics settings by default, as shown in Figure 2.12. Most of the settings you make in this section won't take effect until you restart Lotus Notes.

FIG. 2.12

The Basics settings pane lets you change many of the default startup settings in Notes.

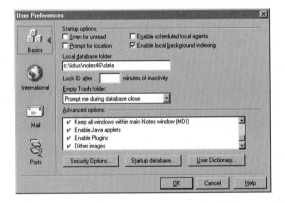

The largest portion of this dialog box is devoted to the Startup options that consist of check boxes and text entry boxes that govern the actions that Notes takes each time you start Notes. The following sections describe the options.

Scanning Unread Documents   If you choose the Scan for unread option, Notes scans some or all of your databases for unread documents each time you start Notes. You can determine which databases Notes scans in the Scan Unread dialog box (for more information, see Chapter 8, "Working with Documents").

Prompting for Location   The Prompt for location option causes Notes to display the Choose Location dialog box every time you start Notes. You might find this feature handy if you travel frequently with your laptop, because you can select from any of the locations you have defined in your Address book. The locations you define tell Notes whether it is on a network or working remote. It also lets you tell Notes which phone numbers to call if working remote and which time zone you're working in. You can also change the date and time entries when prompted for your location. You'll learn more about this setting in Part IV of this book, "Going Mobile."

Starting the Agent Manager   If you want to automatically start the Agent Manager when you start Notes, select the Enable scheduled local agents option in the User Preferences dialog box. With the Agent Manager, you can run agents (macros) in the background. This way, you can have Notes automatically perform tasks that you set up, such as filing documents, finding particular topics, or sending mail at certain times. You learn about working with agents in more detail in Chapter 16, "Buttons and Agents."

Indexing in the Background   The Enable local background indexing option lets you create full text indexes in the background, allowing you to continue working while full text indexes are created. A full text index is a collection of files that indexes the text in a database and lets you search for text anywhere in the database through queries. You'll learn more about full text indexes in Chapter 8.

Changing the Default Data Directory   The Local database folder in the User Preferences dialog box lets you specify where Notes' data files (databases, desktop settings, and so on) are kept. C:\NOTES\DATA is the default. You can use this field to specify an alternative directory in which your local databases can reside.

If you are upgrading from Notes 3 and you didn't store your databases in a subdirectory other than C:\NOTES (the default data directory for Notes 3), or you have otherwise specified C:\NOTES as your data directory, you can, and should, store your local databases in a directory other than C:\NOTES if possible. By storing the data files in a subdirectory other than C:\NOTES, you can get easier access to them and protect yourself against accidentally deleting important system files when you're housecleaning your data files.

If you leave the data directory as C:\NOTES, your data files get stored along with all the program files. Not only is this inefficient, but it can be dangerous as well. It takes longer for you to hunt through several filenames to find your database files when they aren't stored separately, and you might accidentally select a program file by mistake when copying, moving, or deleting files, which might cause problems in running Notes. Keep in mind that if you move your data files to a different directory, some Notes functions might be affected, such as the use of indexes created in R3, or any formulas you have in a database that reference a particular database by the filename and its path.

N O T E   Release 4.x of Notes uses C:\NOTES\DATA as the default data directory when the software is installed. This is different from Notes 3, which used C:\NOTES as the data directory. Unless you change your data directory, this is where Notes looks for all your data files. You will find a list of the data files that should be stored in your data directory later in this section. ▧

You can easily create a new data directory and move your data files to it. Usually this subdirectory is within the Notes subdirectory, but it doesn't have to be. In fact, there are some circumstances under which you might want to specify a different drive name as well as a subdirectory name. This is usually when you're working in a situation in which your hard drive space is limited but you have plenty of file storage space on a network drive.

N O T E   If you frequently work remote, you will want to keep your data directory on your local hard drive, because you will not always be connected to a LAN. This doesn't mean that you can't store databases on a network file server. It simply means that they will not be available to you when you're working remote. ▧

To create a data directory other than C:\NOTES, follow these steps:

1. Change the data directory setup by selecting File, Tools, User Preferences and typing the new local database directory name in the text box. For example, type `c:\NOTES\DATA` (or substitute your new directory name for C:\NOTES\DATA).

TIP Write down the new data directory exactly as it was entered in this step, or copy it to the Clipboard by highlighting it and pressing Ctrl+C. When you create the new folder, you can either type the folder name or paste it in using Ctrl+V. Using the copy/paste method will help you avoid typographical errors. You might want to reference the full path and directory name in step 5.

2. Click OK to save the entry.

3. Close Notes and open File Manager or Explorer in Windows. If you're running a different operating system, follow its procedures for making subdirectories and moving files into them. You will need to close Notes to move the DESKTOP.DSK file, because otherwise it will be in use.

    If you already have a C:\NOTES\DATA directory, and you just need to move your data files, skip to step 6.

4. Highlight the drive or directory folder where you want to locate the new data directory. For example, if you want the new data directory to be located within the Notes directory, highlight the Notes directory folder.

5. Select File, Create Directory (or select File, New, Folder in Windows 95). In the Create Directory dialog box, type the name of the new data directory. (In Windows 95, rename the folder by clicking the folder name to place it in edit mode.) In this example, create a data directory in the C:\NOTES subdirectory named DATA.

6. Select File, Search (or Start, Find, Files or Folders in Windows 95). Type `*.NSF` in the Search For (or Named in Windows 95) text box (make sure you include the asterisk). Type `c:\` in the Start From text box (in Windows 95, it's Look in) if you want to copy all the databases on your hard drive to your new data directory, and then click OK (or Find Now). Once you have located all your .NSF files, select all of them by holding down the Shift key and clicking the first filename in the list and then the last filename in the list. All the database files will be selected and ready to move into the new data directory (DATA, in this example).

NOTE If you have several subdirectories in which you store Notes databases, and you want to move only the files in C:\NOTES, you might want to type `c:\NOTES` in the Start From text box to move only the databases stored in the existing C:\NOTES subdirectory.

If your previous data directory was stored elsewhere and you want to move your files, type that subdirectory's path in the Start From text box. █

7. Select File, Move (not Copy, because that would leave a copy of the database files in the old directory and take up unnecessary hard drive space). Enter the entire path name in the To text box. For this example, type C:\NOTES\DATA as the path. In Windows 95, you need to select Edit, Cut to send the files to the Clipboard, open the new destination's folder, and select Edit, Paste.

You must also move the following files to your new data directory following the same procedures in steps 4 and 5 and then substitute the appropriate file extensions as needed:

Part

I

Ch

2

- Any Version 2 databases stored with the .NS2 extension and/or Version 3 databases stored with the .NS3 extension.
- Your DESKTOP.DSK file. You'll learn more about this file later in this chapter.
- Your CACHE.DSK file.
- Any character and language files that you have installed. These files have the .CLS extension.
- Your locally stored template files (.NTF files).
- Your personal dictionary file (where you have added words to the spell checker), USER.DIC.
- If you work with OS/2, your NOTES.INI file.

You may also want to copy your Notes ID file to this subdirectory to simplify switching to it if you use more than one ID on a workstation.

8. Click OK to move the files.
9. Exit File Manager or Explorer and restart Notes.

You now have a new data directory in which your existing Notes databases are located. You might experience a slight delay the first time you open a database that has been moved into the new data directory. This is because Notes is updating its location information.

If you receive a prompt from Notes indicating that it can't find a database in the new data directory, check to make sure that the file was moved and that you correctly updated the Local database directory name in the User Preferences dialog box.

If you experience any problems—for example, if Notes won't start after you make these changes, or you discover that your desktop is blank when Notes starts—check to make sure you correctly moved your DESKTOP.DSK file, your NOTES.INI file (if you use OS/2), and the other files just listed into your new data directory.

Setting the Automatic Log-Off Point   The Lock ID after xx minutes of inactivity option lets you specify the number of minutes you want Notes to keep your password active before logging you off when you haven't touched the keyboard or mouse. Notes will automatically log off from Notes, and you will have to reenter your Notes password the next time you begin to access your databases.

N O T E If you have a number of log-off minutes specified, Notes will log you off even when you're typing if you haven't performed any other task that actively accesses the server—such as opening another document. You'll briefly see the message `Private user information cleared` in the status bar. You can continue working, but you are prompted for your password as soon as you try to save a document, open another database, or any similar action. ▧

 T I P Don't make this setting so short that you don't have a chance to review a complex document, embedded chart, or spreadsheet. A setting between 15 and 30 minutes is usually sufficient to protect your Notes security while minimizing the number of times you spend typing your password during a Notes session.

Empty Trash Folder   Your mail database has a trash folder that contains all the mail you have marked for deletion during a session. You can tell Notes how to empty the trash folder with three options:

- ▧ Choose Prompt me during database close to have Notes ask you whether you want to clear the mail in the trash folder each time you close your mail database. This is the default selection.

- ▧ Choose Always during database close to have Notes automatically clear the mail in the trash folder each time you close your mail database.

CAUTION

Once you empty your trash folder, you can't undo this action. You won't be able to get the mail back!

- ▧ Choose Manually to cancel automatic clearing of the trash folder. If you select this option, you must select Actions, Empty Trash to clear the mail in the trash folder.

Selecting Advanced Options   You can select from many advanced options to control many of Notes' actions when it starts up. The list of options is summarized in the following sections.

Marking Previewed Documents as Read   Choose the Mark documents read when opened in the preview pane option if you want Notes to mark a document as being read when you preview it using the preview pane (even though you haven't opened it). You'll learn more about the preview pane in Chapter 3, "Using Databases."

Selecting a Font   Notes normally uses proportional fonts, in which letters require varying amounts of screen space. For example, a capital M takes up much more space than a lowercase i. The Typewriter fonts only option tells Notes to display all information (including database titles, views, and documents) in monospace fonts, in which all letters take up the same amount of space. You might find this option useful for checking the width of columns. If a column is wide enough in a monospace font to display the entire contents of the column, it will probably be wide enough when you switch back to a proportional (nonmonospace) font.

The Large Fonts Option   The Large fonts option tells Notes to display text in large letters. This increases the font size that appears in the database icons (as well as the size of the database icon). It also increases the font in the views and forms as it appears on your workstation. It doesn't change the size that the font prints or the size in which it displays to other users (unless they have also selected Large fonts). You might find this option handy if the regular characters are too small to read comfortably on-screen, if you need to view the screen from a distance, or if you give a presentation in which many people need to see the screen.

> **CAUTION**
>
> Selecting this option might cut off text in your database titles. This happens because the text becomes too large to fit in the small areas.

Make Internet URLs (http://...) into Hotspots   You can select the Make Internet URLs (http://...) into hotspots option to have Notes automatically convert Internet addresses into hotspots if you are set up to have Notes interface with the Internet through the new Web browser feature of Notes R4.x. URL stands for Uniform Resource Locator, which is the World Wide Web name for a document, file, or other resource. It describes the protocol required to access the resource, the host where it can be found, and a path to the resource on that host. If you are configured to access the Web through Notes, you can click an URL hotspot, and Notes takes you to the referenced Web site.

Changing the Texture of Your Workspace   You can choose to have Notes display the workspace with a marbled 3-D look by selecting Textured workspace. Then, when you click a database icon, it appears to flatten against the workspace to indicate that it is selected. You must have your display set to at least 256 colors to use this feature; otherwise, it doesn't appear in the list.

Keeping the Maximized Workspace in Back   The Keep Workspace in back when maximized option lets you automatically keep the Notes workspace behind other open windows when you have the Notes window maximized. This way, each time you close a window, Notes returns to the last window that was current instead of to the workspace.

Using Monochrome Settings   The Monochrome display option tells Notes to display everything in black and white (monochrome), even on a color monitor if you're using Windows-based operating systems, OS/2, or UNIX. You might find this option handy if you design databases and want to see how they would look on a monochrome monitor.

Closing Windows with Right-Double-Click   The Right double-click closes window option lets you use the right mouse button to close any open window by double-clicking it while your cursor is anywhere within the window. If you are a former Notes 3 user, you will probably want to select this option immediately if you have gotten used to exiting Notes documents by right-double-clicking.

Keeping All Notes Windows Within the Main Notes Window   You can select the Keep all windows within main Notes window (MDI) option to have Notes windows maximize only as large as the main workspace window. This option is selected by default. If you deselect this option, Notes windows that are opened within the main Notes window can be maximized to fill the entire screen—even if the main Notes window does not.

Enabling Java Applets   You can tell Notes to enable Java applets so that you can view them with the Personal and/or Server Web Navigator. By default, this option is not selected. Even if you have this feature enabled, you must also adjust the settings in the Java Applet Security section in your Location documents to use this feature.

Enabling Plug-Ins   A plug-in is a software module that extends the capabilities of the Web browser. Many available plug-ins support multimedia viewers, utilities, and applications within the context of a Web browser. Notes supports plug-ins if you download and install them on your hard drive. The first time you encounter a Web page that has the <EMBED> tag, Notes searches for plug-ins in the Netscape plug-ins folder on your system. If this folder doesn't exist, Notes prompts you for an alternative location for the plug-in folder. From that point, whenever you retrieve a page that has the <EMBED> tag, Notes displays the Execution Security Alert dialog box—unless you selected Trust Signer when you previously downloaded that plug-in—and then goes to the specified plug-in folder to invoke the plug-in module.

TIP   To make sure that Notes can find the plug-ins you have downloaded, install all of them in the same folder on your computer. If you have Netscape already installed on your computer, make sure that all plug-ins are installed in the Netscape plugins folder.

Dithering Images to Match Your Display   Selecting Dither images tells Notes to use a particular pattern of pixels to convert the graphic to something more appropriate for your particular display. This option's purpose is to attempt to fine-tune graphical images so that they appear sharper on your monitor.

Making Notes the Default Web Browser   You can tell Notes to be your default Web browser by selecting this option. You will learn more about working with your Web browser in Chapter 24, "Lotus Notes and the Web."

Security Options   Click the Security Options button to make selections in the Execution Control List (ECL) to protect your data against the threat of mail bombs, viruses, Trojan horses, or unwanted application intrusions encountered when navigating the Internet. Execution Control Lists provide a way for you to manage whether such executable files are allowed to execute—and what level of access the program should be permitted. ECLs are specific to your PC and can be controlled to a very precise level, as shown in Figure 2.13. For example, you might stipulate that when a document is signed electronically by a certain trusted colleague, programs executed by that document can access documents and databases, as well as modify environment variables, but can't access the file system or external programs. This is put in place to protect your data when you access documents from Notes and Web locations.

FIG. 2.13
Execution Control Lists (ECLs) let you indicate which types of executable files can execute—and what level of access the program should permit.

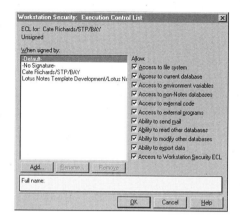

Choosing Which Database to Open Automatically When Notes Is Launched Click the Startup database button to tell Notes which database, if any, you want to open automatically when you start Notes. Databases are listed according to the workspace page they are on, as shown in Figure 2.14. You can select one database title and then click OK to save your setting.

FIG. 2.14
Notes R4.6 allows you to select a particular database to automatically open when you first start Notes.

Changing the User Dictionary Clicking the User Dictionary button causes Notes to display the User Spell Dictionary dialog box, shown in Figure 2.15. Through this dialog box, you can add, update, and delete words that you have defined in your personal data dictionary.

FIG. 2.15
You can define words, names, and phrases that you commonly use in your User Dictionary to facilitate the spell checker.

To add new words to your dictionary, type the new word in the text entry box at the bottom of the dialog box, and then click Add. To delete a word, select the word from the scrolling list box and click the Delete button. To edit an existing word, select the word from the scrolling list box, edit the text in the text entry box, and then click Update. Click OK to exit the dialog box and save your changes, or click Cancel to exit without saving your changes.

CAUTION

Do not press Esc to exit this (or any) Notes dialog box. Doing so is the same as clicking the Cancel button and causes you to lose any setting changes you have made.

International Settings

To display the options for international settings, click the International icon in the User Preferences dialog box. Notes displays the International settings panel, shown in Figure 2.16. Through this dialog box, you can control characteristics that tend to vary from one country to another. These characteristics are described in the following sections.

FIG. 2.16

You can change your dictionary, import/ export character translation sets, and other settings that typically differ according to your international location.

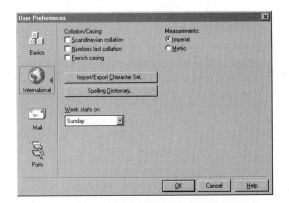

N O T E   The international settings here do not change the currency denomination indicator or the date format used in many countries outside of North America. You make these changes in your operating system.

For example, if you want to use British pounds Sterling, or the date format dd\mm\yy, you could open Control Panel in Windows and click the International icon. Change the Country setting to United Kingdom. The currency indicator and date format defaults would then be changed to reflect the common formats used in the United Kingdom.

Check your operating system information for additional information on changing the international default settings.

Controlling Collation and Casing   In Lotus Notes, database designers can specify that items listed in a view appear in a particular sort order—ascending or descending. The Collation/ Casing options let you tell Notes how to treat some of the characters when sorting. You can choose any or all of the options. If you choose Scandinavian collation, Notes puts accented characters at the end of the alphabet (which is where the Scandinavians put them). If you choose Numbers last collation, Notes considers numbers to come after letters (thus, part number 6X032 would appear after ZY512). If you choose French casing, Notes discards accent marks when you change lowercase letters to uppercase.

Notes uses Country Language Services files (.CLS files) to translate international currency symbols such as the pound (£) and the yen (¥), and accented letters, when you import or export data from Notes. Notes also uses .CLS files to determine the order in which characters are sorted.

Part

I

Ch

2

 T I P To re-sort the documents in an existing database with the selections made in this section, restart Notes and then press Shift+F9 after you open the database you want to view.

The collation and casing options are turned off by default. If you choose these options, they don't take effect until the next time you start Notes. If you can't be sure that every user will set up the collation and casing options the way you want them to appear in a particular database, be sure to incorporate the necessary sort settings into your design.

Changing the Unit of Measurement   The Measurements radio buttons allow you to specify Imperial units of measurement (inches, the default) or Metric units (centimeters). Your choice determines whether you must specify margins and tabs in inches or in centimeters. If you have the ruler displayed, this option changes the unit of measurement to inches or centimeters.

Translating Files   The Import/Export Character Set button lets you specify a file for translating foreign characters and symbols from a non-Notes file into Notes. When you click this button, you are greeted with the Choose Translation Table dialog box, shown in Figure 2.17.

FIG. 2.17
The selection you make in the Choose Translation Table dialog box determines how Notes translates characters when you import or export documents.

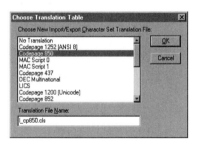

You can either select an existing translation file (.CLS) from the Choose New Import/Export Character Set Translation File list box or type the path and filename of a .CLS file that you want to use that isn't stored in your data directory. See Chapter 13, "Integrating Notes with Other Applications," for more information about importing and exporting data.

Selecting a Dictionary   The Spelling Dictionary button lets you tell Notes which dictionary (such as French or British) to use instead of the American dictionary. Here are the available dictionaries:

American English

American Medical

Australian English

Brazilian Portuguese

British (ise) English

British (ize) English

British Medical (ise)

British Medical (ize)

Canadian French

Catalan

Czech

Danish

Dutch General

Dutch Preferred

French

German

German (ss)

Italian

Norwegian

Nynorsk

Portuguese

Russian

Russian Jo

Spanish

Swedish

The dictionary files selected here are not the same as your User Dictionary, in which you add words when you select Define while using the spell checker. These files are located in your Notes program directories. The default file is English and is denoted by the filename ENGLISH.DIC.

 TIP If you write documents that must be sent from your home office to an office in a different country, change the dictionary before running the spell checker. This is particularly helpful when you're sending or receiving documents between countries that vary in their use of British (ise) English and British (ize) English spellings.

Setting the Starting Day of the Week   You can specify which day of the week your week starts on by selecting <u>W</u>eek starts on and then choosing the day of the week from the list. This setting is important if you use the Calendaring and Scheduling features, because Notes will use this setting to define the layout of the calendar pages. The default setting for this option is Sunday.

Mail Settings

You can control how Notes accesses and processes your mailbox by selecting File, Tools, User Preferences and then clicking the Mail icon on the left side of the dialog box. Notes displays the Mail setup options in the User Preferences dialog box shown in Figure 2.18.

FIG. 2.18
You can customize the way Notes treats mail in the User Preferences Mail pane.

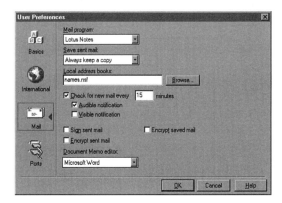

Specifying the Mail Program   The Mail program field identifies the mail system you are using. It should be set to Lotus Notes, the default, unless otherwise specified by your Notes administrator.

Saving Sent Mail   The Save sent mail option tells Notes how you want to treat mail when you click the Send button (or select Actions, Send). If you want to always keep a copy of the memos you send, select this option. If you don't want to save a copy when you send a memo, select Don't keep a copy. If you want Notes to prompt you to save every time you send a message, select Always prompt.

> **CAUTION**
>
> If you select Don't keep a copy, you won't be prompted to save a document when you click the Send button to send the message. Notes simply sends the document and closes it. If you later need to reference the document, you won't be able to do so unless the recipient forwards it back to you. It is safer to select one of the other two options if you think you'll need to review any of the messages you send.
>
> However, if you right-double-click, or press Esc to exit and send the document (rather than clicking the Send button), your default selection for saving sent mail is highlighted in the checkbox. You then can deselect the option for that instance before you click Yes to send the mail message.

Selecting Your Local Address Books   If you travel often, you might want to carry more than one Address Book with you—such as your company's Public Address Book—so that you can select users' names from the list of available recipients while you're on the road. Your Personal Address Book's filename is NAMES.NSF and is located in your Data directory.

To configure Notes to access an additional Address Book, you need to type or select the Address Book's filename in the Local address book's text box. You can use the Browse button to select the filename (recommended) or type the filename directly in the text entry box, using commas to separate each filename. You can select only one Address Book filename at a time if you use the Browse button. If you want to select more than one Address Book, simply click the Browse button again for each new selection. The Address Books entered here must be located in your data directory. The setting you make in this text box is saved to your NOTES.INI file (as discussed later in this chapter). When you click the Address button while composing an email message, you can switch from one Address Book to another.

N O T E When you send mail or use Notes' type-ahead feature to address mail, Notes looks in the first database you have listed in the Local Address Book's text box and then checks the next database, and so on. You should keep your Personal Address book, NAMES.NSF, as your first entry and then list each subsequent database in the order in which you want Notes to search them. ▪

Checking for New Mail   As you will learn in Chapter 4, "Getting Started with Electronic Mail," Mail notifies you when new mail arrives. By changing the number of minutes in the Check for new mail every *xx* minutes setting, you can control how often Notes checks the server to see whether new mail has arrived in your mailbox. If you need to quickly know when new mail has arrived, enter a small number (perhaps 3 or 4). If you rarely receive mail, or if you don't need to be notified immediately, entering a larger number (15 or 20) saves your computer the work of frequent checking. If you uncheck the associated checkbox, Notes won't automatically inform you when new mail has arrived—you've got to check for yourself periodically.

You can also tell Notes how you want to be notified of new mail. If you select Audible notification, Notes plays a short tune whenever you have new email. Selecting Visible notification results in a small dialog box appearing to notify you that new mail has arrived. You need to click OK to clear this dialog box from your window.

Signing and Encrypting Sent Mail   If you select the Sign sent mail checkbox, Notes checks the Sign box when you mail a document. Chapter 4, "Getting Started with Electronic Mail," describes in more detail the Sign checkbox that electronically signs your mail messages.

Selecting the Encrypt sent mail option automatically checks the Encrypt box when you close a mail document. See Chapter 22, "Security and Encryption," for more information about encrypting messages.

Encrypting Saved Mail   If you check the Encrypt saved mail option, Notes encrypts mail stored in your mailbox on the server, and in your hard drive if you work remote and have a copy of your mail database there. Although you can generally assume that your mailbox is private and secure, a few people (such as your system administrator(s)) can access your mailbox without your permission. You can use this option if you are particularly concerned about keeping the messages in your mailbox secure.

Document Memo Editor   You can select whether you want to use Microsoft Word, Lotus Word Pro, or None as your mail document editor. If you select Word or Lotus Word Pro, you will be able to use their respective word processing packages as the tool to type and edit text while creating documents in your mail database. If you select None, you will use the standard Lotus Notes word processing capabilities to create your mail documents.

▶ **See** Chapter 6 "Advanced Mail," **p. 207**

See Chapter 6 "Advanced Mail," p. 207

Ports Settings

The Ports panel in the User Preferences dialog box provides options and buttons that let you or your system administrator configure how your computer communicates with your server and specify what kind of network or modem your computer has. After your computer is set up, you normally don't have to adjust any of these options if you're working on the network. If you aren't experienced with the requirements of your network, consult with your system administrator if you need to change your Ports setup.

If you're working remote, you might find that you use the Ports preferences quite frequently. If you want to learn more about this preference panel, read Chapter 20, "Setting Up to Go Remote."

Configuring Options Under Windows and OS/2

Many of the most important preference choices you can make are controlled not by Notes but by Windows, Macintosh, UNIX, or OS/2. For example, through the Windows Control Panel or the OS/2 System Setup, you can specify the following parameters:

- Some screen colors (for example, the colors of borders and title bars)
- Available fonts and font sizes
- International settings (such as country name, currency symbol, and time and date formats)
- Types and configurations of printers

Consult your Windows, OS/2, or other operating system manual for more information about these parameters.

Understanding the DESKTOP.DSK File

When working with Notes, it is often helpful to understand a little something about the key files that are accessed in your daily use of the program. The DESKTOP.DSK file is one of the files you should be familiar with. It stores information about your workspace in your local data directory. This file stores the following information:

- The database icons you've added to your workspace
- The workspace page tabs and names you've added to your workspace
- Settings made in the File Page Setup dialog box, such as headers and footers

- Design information about any private views or folders you might have
- The number of documents still unread in a database

Your DESKTOP.DSK tells Notes where it should display all your database icons when you start up Notes. It also stores all your private view definitions for all databases to which you have access. Private views are ones that you have designed for yourself and that are not available to other users of a database. You'll learn how to design them in Chapter 12, "Designing Views."

CAUTION

If you delete the DESKTOP.DSK file, or if it becomes corrupted for any reason, you lose all the desktop settings (for example, database icons and tab names), and you lose all your private views. Keep this in mind when working with this file. You should back up the DESKTOP.DSK file regularly, using your operating system, perhaps once a month.

The DESKTOP.DSK file can grow as large as 50M—a big file. The larger your DESKTOP.DSK file, the slower your response time can become—not to mention the amount of space the file takes up on your hard drive. As you add private views and databases to your desktop, this file grows.

N O T E You can compact the DESKTOP.DSK file just as you would any other database. Compacting your workspace is covered later in this chapter.

When you delete database icons from your desktop, or private views from databases, the space that was taken up will become available, but the size of the file is not reduced. When you add new database icons to the workspace, or private views to databases, they first take up the freed space before the file size grows. When you compact your DESKTOP.DSK, you decrease the white space.

Changing the Location of DESKTOP.DSK

By default, Notes looks for the DESKTOP.DSK file in the data directory (defined in the User Setup dialog box). The data directory is identified in the NOTES.INI file with the following parameter:

```
Directory=[drive]:\[directory]
```

If you want to locate DESKTOP.DSK in a directory other than the data directory, add the following line to the NOTES.INI file:

```
Desktop=[drive]:\[directory]\DESKTOP.DSK
```

Whereas it is recommended that you keep your DESKTOP.DSK file in your data directory, you might find the need to locate an alternative DESKTOP.DSK file for when you perform demonstrations. For demonstrations, you don't want your normal desktop settings displayed.

For example, if you wanted to store a second copy of your DESKTOP.DSK file to be used when teaching a class, you could enter the following in the NOTES.INI file:

```
Desktop=C:\CLASS\DESKTOP.DSK
```

When you start Notes, it looks in the CLASS subdirectory for the DESKTOP.DSK file. When you no longer want to use the special DESKTOP.DSK file, you need to modify this line again to change where Notes looks for your DESKTOP.DSK file.

You also need to store your DESKTOP.DSK file in a separate directory if you are sharing your workstation with someone else. In this circumstance, consult with your Notes Administrator for assistance, because special settings need to be made to your workstation in addition to locating your DESKTOP.DSK file in a separate directory.

Part
I
Ch
2

Compacting Your DESKTOP.DSK File

As you work in Lotus Notes, you add database icons, workspace pages, private views, and other features whose definitions are stored in your DESKTOP.DSK file. As you remove some of these features, Notes leaves some white space in the database where the definition was stored. Over time, this white space builds up and takes up valuable disk drive space. However, you can remove this white space by compacting your DESKTOP.DSK file. This recovers unused disk space by removing references to databases you no longer have on your workspace. To compact your DESKTOP.DSK file, follow these steps:

1. Double-click any workspace tab, and the Workspace Properties InfoBox appears. Right-click the workspace and select Properties from the menu, or select the Properties SmartIcon while you're viewing the Notes workspace and don't have any databases highlighted.

2. Click the Information tab, shown in Figure 2.19. It is marked with a lowercase i in a circle.

FIG. 2.19

The Information tab lets you compact your DESKTOP.DSK file.

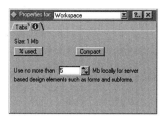

3. Click the % used button.

4. If the percentage is less than 85 percent, click the Compact button. If the percentage is greater than 85 percent, there's no need to compact yet. You are now working with a cleaner DESKTOP.DSK file that takes up less space on your hard drive. You should periodically check the size of your DESKTOP.DSK file, particularly if you are short on hard-drive space.

N O T E You might also want to limit the size of the CACHE.DSK file, which is used to cache server-based design elements to make them more readily available when you're working in Notes. To limit the size, choose the number of megabytes (normally from 1 to 16). Use no more than 1M locally for server-based design elements such as forms and subforms. When you limit the size of the CACHE.DSK file, Notes removes older, unused design elements to make room for new ones. If it appears that database design elements, such as subforms, are taking a long time to appear, you might want to increase this setting and then recompact your workspace.

Handling a Corrupted DESKTOP.DSK File

If your DESKTOP.DSK file becomes corrupted, you need to close Notes and delete the DESKTOP.DSK file through your operating system commands. When you start Notes again, a new DESKTOP.DSK file is created. Of course, you lose all your workspace customization and private view information.

T I P By having a backup copy of your DESKTOP.DSK file, you can quickly restore your workspace and private views without having to re-create them from scratch. Simply copy the backup copy of the DESKTOP.DSK file over the corrupted file in your data directory.

The NOTES.INI File

The NOTES.INI file (called the Notes Preference file on the Macintosh) is a settings file that Notes checks when you first start Notes. The NOTES.INI file resides in the Notes data directory for OS/2 Notes users and in the Windows directory for most Windows Notes users. If you upgraded from Notes Release 2 to Release 3, your NOTES.INI file might be located in the Notes directory instead.

Information in the file comes from many sources, including installation choices, server console commands, and selections made in the Setup dialog boxes discussed earlier in this chapter. Notes uses most of the variables in this file internally. You can set them through the Notes user interface (File, Tools, User Preferences) rather than having to edit the NOTES.INI file using a text editor.

N O T E When possible, make NOTES.INI settings by changing your User Preferences (File, Tools, User Preferences). It is safer to make changes using the Notes interface than by editing the file directly.

Each time Notes starts, the NOTES.INI file is used to check installation settings, Setup selections (mail, user, and location information, and your DESKTOP.DSK file), and other variables that Notes uses.

This section covers just a few of the settings that can be made in the NOTES.INI file. You'll gain an understanding of how the NOTES.INI file works, and you'll see a few of the settings that you might need to make directly in the file rather than through the User Preferences dialog box.

Part
I
Ch
2

> **CAUTION**
>
> Your NOTES.INI file must be located in the search path if you're using Windows- or OS/2-based versions of Notes. If you try to start Notes and get an error that it can't find the NOTES.INI file in the search path, edit your AUTOEXEC.BAT file to include the path to the file—usually C:\WINDOWS or C:\NOTES\DATA.

Editing NOTES.INI

Before you edit NOTES.INI, exit Notes, because the changes you make to the NOTES.INI file don't take effect until the next time you start Notes. Edit the lines of text, insert new lines, or delete lines using a text editor such as the Notepad application found in Windows applications. Make sure that your typing is exact and that no blank spaces follow any of the lines of text, or you will experience problems.

N O T E Macintosh users must edit the NOTES.INI file using a resource editor such as ResEdit. Other Notes users can do so using any simple text editor, such as Notepad in Windows. Macintosh users should consult their system's documentation before trying to edit the NOTES.INI file. ▓

When you exit the NOTES.INI document you are editing, save your changes, and then restart Notes to have your changes take place.

> **CAUTION**
>
> Make sure you create a backup copy of your existing NOTES.INI file before you edit it.
>
> Editing the NOTES.INI file can be dangerous to Notes' health if you aren't used to editing these types of files. For example, even leaving a blank space after a line of text in the NOTES.INI file can cause trouble when you try to start Notes. If you have a choice, make Notes changes through the Notes selections, or contact your Notes administrator for help.

Changing the New Mail Tune   You can change the tune that Notes uses to signal that new mail has been delivered by editing the NOTES.INI file to reference a new .WAV file—the sound file type used in Notes for the new mail tune. You may already have a few .WAV files available to you in your operating system's directory, or in a special sound file directory if you have a sound board. You can also purchase new .WAV files at most software stores or even find many of them passed along as shareware.

For most users who have .WAV files, it's a fun change to have your computer play the theme from *Leave It to Beaver* or to say "bummer" every time you get new mail.

If you have a computer that can't adjust the sound for the new mail tune, the capability to change the new mail tune, and thus edit the sound volume as well, becomes a treat. This is particularly true if you are working close to others. Changing the new mail tune is also handy if you share an office with others and you want a distinctive sound to let you know you have mail.

You must have a sound driver installed to change the new mail tune. If you don't have a sound board installed and you don't have a non-sound board speaker driver, you need to consult with your network administrator or local software dealer. Follow your operating system's instructions for installing and changing the volume on your system.

To change the New Mail Tune (for example, to have your computer say "bummer" each time you get new mail), insert the following line in your NOTES.INI file:

```
NewMailTune=drive:\directory\.WAV file name
```

For example:

```
NewMailTune=C:\WINDOWS\BUMMER.WAV
```

This tells Notes to reference the BUMMER.WAV file each time new mail is delivered to you.

You need to restart Notes to have this edit take effect.

Eliminating the Design Menu   This function generally is used by Notes administrators to keep users from being able to design new databases. However, you can also use this setting if you have no desire to design databases or manage a public workstation, if you don't want anyone to design databases from your workstation, and if you want this setting only to get mail.

Add this line to your NOTES.INI file:

```
NoDesignMenu=1
```

1 means turn on the No Design Menu function to disallow this feature and remove the menu selection from the menu bar in the Notes window.

Protecting Against Mail Bomb-Type Viruses   Although the new ECL security settings in your User Preferences dialog box go a long way toward protecting your workstation, if you want to completely protect your workstation against mail bombs—viruses sent to you via special attachments and features in your mail—enter the following line:

```
NoExternalApps=1
```

1 turns on the No External Applications command and disallows the use of any applications outside of Notes.

When you indicate this setting, you turn off all external applications that are accessed while you are working with Notes. However, this means that you can't use the following Notes features as long as this selection is made:

- DDE
- DIP
- @Command

- @DbLookup (when using non-Notes databases)
- @DbColumn (when using non-Notes databases)
- @MailSend
- @DDE*xxx*
- Object Linking and Embedding (OLE)
- Launching of file attachments
- Launch to edit (LEL)
- Subscribe (on Macintosh workstations)

Turning Off the Mail Menu   You might want to turn off the ability for people to use the Mail menu commands—for example, if you're managing a public workstation for a group of people, and all you want them to access are project databases. This function would help keep the workstation free more often.

To disable the Mail menu, enter the following line in the NOTES.INI file:

```
NoMailMenu=1
```

1 turns off the Mail menu in Notes. This selection not only eliminates the Mail menu from the workstation, but it also sets the user's mail system to None.

N O T E   If you're having trouble using Mail, and you're meant to use it, you might want to check the workstation's NOTES.INI file to make sure that this setting hasn't been enabled. This setting overrides the setting made in the Setup Mail dialog box in Notes to specify which mail package you're using. ■

Changing the Location of Your ID File   Normally, your ID file is located in your Notes directory or wherever you specified when you set up Notes. If you want to change where your Notes ID file is located, specify it by entering the following:

```
KeyFilename=<location>
```

location specifies the drive and directory in which your Notes ID is stored.

This entry is usually used when more than one person is sharing a workstation and separate NOTES.INI and DESKTOP.DSK files are created and stored in personal subdirectories for each user. This option is also useful when administering OS/2 servers—when you specify your ID file. When you open the client on the server, your ID file is used rather than the server ID.

When Something Goes Wrong with NOTES.INI

If you have problems with your NOTES.INI file that can't be resolved, you need to delete all but the first three lines in NOTES.INI, save it, and then restart Notes. Here are some examples of possible problems:

- NOTES.INI is corrupted
- You made mistakes when editing it

■ The appropriate default information doesn't seem to be present

■ You can't seem to correct the problem

Here are the three lines that you must have in your NOTES.INI file to start Notes:

```
[Notes]
KitType=1
Directory=<Notes data directory>
```

KitType indicates whether you're running the Notes workstation or server. A value of 1 indicates that you're running a workstation. A value of 2 indicates that you're running both a workstation and a server. Unless you're setting up a server, specify 1. Directory indicates the location of Notes' data directory and represents where your data files are located.

For example, the Directory line could read

```
Directory=C:\NOTES\DATA
```

You need to make your personal Setup selections again, but at least you can start up Notes with all the default information present.

N O T E   There is another file, CACHE.DSK, that also deserves mention. Your CACHE.DSK file helps speed up Notes by temporarily storing some of the server-based design elements locally for faster access during your work session. You can limit the size of this file to help conserve disk space and speed up the accessing of design elements. While working in the Notes workspace—with no database selected—choose Edit, Preferences and select the Information tab (marked by a small i). Then select "Use no more than n Mb locally for server-based design elements such as forms and subforms." You can select between 1 and 16M for this option. If you notice that your use of design features from the server becomes slower, you might want to increase your setting for this option. ■

Using Databases

Some of the thousands of companies that use Lotus Notes use it only for its email capability. Most companies, however, find that Notes can provide additional flexibility and value through the unique database and application development capabilities it offers. These capabilities allow companies to communicate, collaborate, and coordinate.

Lotus Notes databases can store, organize, and retrieve any kind of information (text, graphics, sound, and so on). Notes databases are easy to use, they allow local and remote end-users to share information in a timely fashion, and they can be developed quickly.

Understanding Databases

Once you understand the architecture of Notes databases, you can begin to harness and apply the tremendous power of Notes. Notes databases, sometimes called *object stores* because they can store any kind of electronic information, are document oriented.

Although this is not a direct correlation, it might help you to think of documents in a Notes database as records in a relational database. Each database can hold many documents, and each document can hold many fields, each with discrete information.

Because each document can store semistructured and unstructured data (meaning that the type and amount of data can vary from document to document), Notes databases are versatile and flexible, allowing Notes applications to solve many business problems.

In addition to storing and organizing data, Notes databases accept imported data from external applications such as ODBC-compliant databases (Oracle, Sybase, Access) and Excel. Notes databases can create links to external applications for dynamic data sharing (OLE and Notes/ FX) and can even have information emailed in. Notes also provides tight database security through access control lists (ACLs) and encryption to protect your data from prying eyes.

Notes databases are loosely grouped into the following categories:

- System databases
- Mail databases
- Help databases
- Discussion databases
- Document libraries
- Tracking databases
- Workflow databases

These categories show only the most common ways that Notes databases are used. The list is by no means inclusive of all the possible applications for Notes databases. In fact, many of the best Notes solutions are a mixture of different kinds of Notes applications that are linked to legacy systems.

N O T E In Notes jargon, the terms *application* and *database* are used interchangeably because Notes databases hold the design elements that make up an application. You'll learn how to begin creating databases in Chapter 10, "Creating New Databases." ▦

In Notes 4.6, the interface has been standardized, and you can use the same methods and commands to access and navigate all Notes databases. The following sections describe each type of database.

System Databases

System databases provide important information to Notes. System databases are especially important because they hold information that is needed for Notes to function correctly. Well-maintained system databases can make your Notes sessions much more productive and enjoyable. The following sections describe the system databases.

Address Books   Your Public Address Book and Personal Address Book hold information about Notes end-users in your company. They also hold server connections, locations, groups, and many other kinds of Notes control documents.

Chapter 5, "Using the Notes Address Books," describes the Address Books in detail. They are absolutely essential for Notes to work correctly. They also provide directory services, verify database access, provide system management and control information, and perform other important tasks. Figure 3.1 shows some typical Address Book icons.

FIG. 3.1
Standard databases can easily be identified on a crowded workspace page by their distinctive database icons.

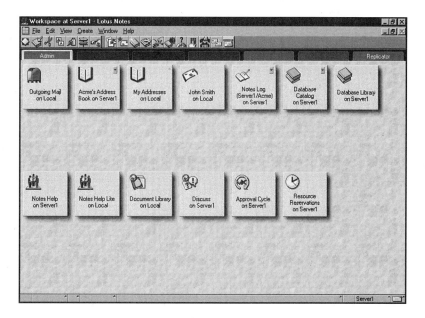

Part
I

Ch
3

Notes Log   The personal Notes log database records information about system activity that takes place while you're using Notes. Some of the many things that are tracked in the Notes Log include replication events, phone calls (if you're working remote), database usage, and other miscellaneous events.

Each Notes server also has a Notes Log database that tracks server activity. The Notes log database is an invaluable tool for troubleshooting problems.

Database Catalog   The database catalog provides information about databases that are available to you in your Notes network, including information such as the location of each database and the policy for using each database. The database catalog is automatically created when Notes is installed and is normally updated automatically each night by a server task on the Notes server.

Database Libraries   Database libraries make it easy for end-users to find databases that interest them. Database libraries can be public (when they reside on a server) or private (when they reside on a workstation).

Unlike the Database Catalog, which publishes information about all the databases available to you on a server, Database Libraries are created manually to bring together databases that might be of interest to specific user groups. For instance, all the databases regarding sales might be "published" in the Sales Library database so that other end-users can find them easily. In this regard, they are similar to Portfolios.

Mail Databases

Mail databases are used by the Notes mail system to store and route email messages. (These databases are covered in detail in Chapter 4, "Getting Started with Electronic Mail," and Chapter 6, "Advanced Mail.")

Mailbox   Your mailbox, likely to be one of your most-used databases, is where Notes stores your incoming mail, your outgoing mail, and your calendar. Chapter 4 describes the basics of using your mailbox; Chapter 6 has more advanced information.

Outgoing Mailbox   The outgoing mailbox automatically appears on your workspace when you are configured to use workstation-based mail. It is used to store all outgoing mail until you connect with the server and the router transfers the mail to the server. This database can be helpful when you're troubleshooting mail problems for a workstation configured to use workstation-based mail.

 If you are set up to use workstation-based mail (this applies primarily to remote end-users), you can open the Outgoing Mail database and select the Pending Mail view to examine mail that is waiting to be sent. If you decide, for instance, that you would rather not send that message to your boss stating that you quit, you can delete it from Outgoing Mail and she'll never know the message was written.

Help Databases

In Notes 4.6, most of the documentation is online in Notes databases. This is particularly useful, because you can install these databases on your machine and take them with you wherever you go (at the cost of considerable disk space).

Even better, you can create a Full Text Index to the Help databases so that you can find help on a given topic quickly and easily. Notes 4.6 ships with several Help databases, but the two that most end-users find most useful are the Notes Help and Notes Help Lite databases.

Notes Help　The Notes Help database (HELP4.NSF) holds the full, end-user, online documentation for Notes 4. Although this database can be useful, it is also large (approximately 5,400 documents for a total on-disk size of approximately 30M) and may be too much for end-users whose hard disk space is at a premium.

If you have the space on your local workstation, it is highly recommended that you install this database and create a Full Text Index on the database for easy searching. Using the default settings, this will consume another 8M of disk space.

Notes Help Lite　The Notes Help Lite database (HELPLT4.NSF), designed with the mobile end-user in mind, is a much smaller subset of the full Help database. (It is approximately 7M in size and contains over 1,400 documents.) If you decide to create a Full Text Index for this database, it will consume approximately 1M of disk space.

Other Help Databases　Notes also includes many other useful online help databases that you may or may not be able to access (if you can't find the following databases, see your administrator):

- Notes Administration Help (HELPADMN.NSF): This database holds detailed information geared toward Notes administrators.
- Install Guide for Workstations (WKSINST.NSF): This database holds detailed information for people responsible for Notes 4 workstation installations.
- Install Guide for Servers (SRVINST.NSF): Much like the Install Guide for Workstations, this database is geared toward Notes server installations.
- Java Programmer's Guide (JAVAPG.NSF): This contains information about the Notes classes, properties, and methods exposed to Java.
- Lotus Notes 4.6 Release Notes (READMEC.NSF for the client and READMES.NSF for the server): These databases are invaluable for people migrating from one version of Notes to another. They quickly and concisely tell you about new features and functionality.

Part
I
Ch
3

Sample Databases

Sample databases are developed by Lotus for you to use as learning tools when building your own databases.

If your workstation was set up with the default installation, these databases are in the C:\NOTES\DATA directory. The databases are called *templates,* and they have the extension NTF (Notes Template Facility).

You'll learn more about templates and how they can speed your application development in Chapter 10. For example, RESRC45.NTF is a sample database for tracking room and resource reservations. It shows you how the components of a Notes database can be assembled when building databases.

N O T E   So as not to overwrite templates that you're using from a previous version of Notes, Lotus identifies new versions of templates with a different filename and template name and usually appends the template title with the revision, such as (R4), (R4.5), or (R4.6). You will see these in the template list when you select File, Database, New. ▨

Discussion Databases

Discussion databases are one of the most common uses of Notes databases. These databases facilitate timely communication and collaboration among groups of people.

A discussion database often has very little structure, so end-users are free to use it as they want. Many companies that develop and deploy databases "cut their teeth" on discussion databases because they are usually simple and can quickly provide a high return on the investment.

An example of a discussion database is one that provides technical information and tips for end-users of Lotus Notes. Lotus includes a discussion database template, titled Discussion-Notes & Web (R4.6) for you to use as a basis for designing discussion databases (DISCSW46.NTF is the filename). The title of the template tells you that it contains enhancements for users accessing the database from a Web browser.

Document Libraries

Document libraries are an electronic repository for documents that remain relatively static but must be distributed to a large or geographically dispersed group of end-users in a timely fashion. A document library holds product information brochures, sales literature, and electronic presentations for salespeople to share and use on the road.

Lotus has included two versions of the Document Library template, Document Library (R4) (DOCLIB4.NTF) and Doc Library-Notes & Web (R4.6) (DOCLBW46.NTF), with which you can create simple document library databases. In addition, there are special versions of the Document Library for users of Microsoft Office (DOCLBM46.NTF) and Lotus SmartSuite (DOCLIBL4.NTF).

Tracking Databases

Tracking databases are usually interactive, with many end-users contributing data. One example is a complaint-tracking database used by a customer service group to track complaints and progress toward resolving them.

Another example is a help-desk database in which trouble tickets are entered. After each problem is resolved, the solution is available to other technicians so that they don't have to "reinvent the wheel" for common problems. Lotus has included the Resource Reservations (4.5) (template RESRC45.NTF), which is useful for creating a tracking application.

Workflow Databases

Workflow databases automate routine tasks to compress cycle time and increase efficiency. A common application of this concept is an expense-reports database that electronically routes expense reports to the right managers for approval, and then to payroll for the payout.

Lotus has included a workflow database template, Approval Cycle (R4) (APPROVE4.NTF), that can be useful as the basis for a workflow database.

Template Overview

Notes 4.6 ships with other useful templates; they are summarized in Table 3.1. If you want to know what a particular template does, choose a template and click the About button in the New Database dialog box.

▶ **See** "Using Templates," **p. 381**

There are also advanced system templates, primarily for use by your administrator, but these fall outside the scope of this chapter. If you are interested in these templates, click on Show advanced templates in the New Database Dialog box, select a template, and click on the About button.

Table 3.1   Useful Database Templates Included with Notes 4.6

Template Title	Template Name	Filename
Approval Cycle	StdR4Approval	APPROVE4.NTF
Discussion-Notes & Web (R4.6)	StdR46Disc	DISCSW46.NTF
Document Library (R4)	StdR4DocLib	DOCLIB4.NTF
Document Library-Notes & Web (R4.6)	StdR46WebDocLib	DOCLBW46.NTF
Lotus Smart Suite 96 Library (R4)	StdR4DocLibLS	DOCLIBL4.NTF
Microsoft Office Library (R4.6)	StdR46DocLibMS	DOCLBM46.NTF
Personal Journal (R4)	StdR4Journal	JOURNAL4.NTF
Resource Reservations (R4.5)	Std45ResourceReservation	RESRC45.NTF
Portfolio (R4.6)	StdR46Portfolio	PRTFLO46.NTF

Part
I

Ch
3

Accessing a Database

Before you can access the data in a Notes database, you must have a database icon for that database on your workspace. You can add to your workspace an icon for any database to which you have been granted access rights. (You'll learn more about access rights later in this chapter, in the section "Understanding Access Control Lists.")

 T I P You can use the database catalog and libraries to quickly find databases you might be interested in and then add their icons to your workspace.

Adding a new database icon to your workspace is quite simple. Figure 3.2 shows you the menu options to do this. Just choose File, Database, Open (or press Ctrl+O).

FIG. 3.2

The File menu options are used to add a database icon to your workspace.

You see a dialog box like the one shown in Figure 3.3, giving you a list of the Notes servers available from your machine and a list of all Notes databases on that server.

FIG. 3.3

The Open Database dialog box.

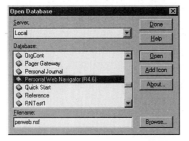

You can use the Server combo box to choose the server on which the database you want resides. When you select a server, the Database list box shows the title of each database on the server.

If the server you select is not local (for instance, you are working remote), Notes will display a dialog box that asks you whether you'd like to call the remote server.

N O T E The list of databases you see might not include every database on the server. This is because the designer or database manager might elect to hide certain databases from the Open Database dialog box, or some databases might reside in other Notes Named Networks. In addition, you don't necessarily have access rights to every database in the list.

If you don't see a database listed but you know its filename, you can type it into the Filename field and open the database. (You must have access rights to do this.) If you can't find a database that you think should be listed, or you can't access a listed database, see your administrator. Alternatively, you can look at the Database Catalog on the server (CATALOG.NSF), which lists the majority of the databases that reside on the server. Again, though, the designer or database manager might have elected to hide the database from the Catalog.

When you select a database from the list, the database's filename is displayed in the Filename box below the Database list box. At this point, if you want to add a database icon to your workspace and open the database, click the Open button. This puts the icon on your workspace and opens the database.

If you only want to add the database icon to your workspace, click the Add Icon button. This is the best way to go if you're going to add several icons, because opening each database is a waste of time.

The About button can help you identify the use of a particular database. When you click the About button, the database's About document is displayed (if one exists). This should provide information regarding the use of a database.

As in all Windows applications, clicking the Help button at this location displays context-sensitive help about using the Open Database dialog. If you can't find a database by its title, you can click the Browse button to display the standard File dialog box. This allows you to search for a database by its filename (see Figure 3.4).

Part

I

Ch

3

FIG 3.4
The Choose a Notes database or template file dialog box.

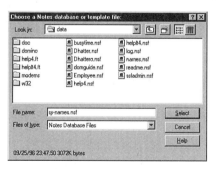

When you have added a database icon to your workspace, you are ready to begin working with the database. Before you do so, you need to understand what the different parts of a database are and how these parts interact.

Parts of a Database

Each Notes database is a distinct, on-disk structure with a filename that must meet the operating system conventions and must be unique. For example, if you're using the Notes Windows 3.11 client, you're limited to the DOS naming standard, which is eight characters for the filename and three characters for the file extension.

If you have questions about valid filenames, consult the documentation for your operating system. By default, all Notes databases have the extension NSF.

N O T E   Although Notes databases normally end with the NSF extension, a Notes database is not required to have an NSF extension. If you use an extension other than NSF, the database doesn't appear automatically in the Open Database dialog box in the list of database files. ■

Besides its filename, each database has a database title that is displayed on the database icon. Each database title can have a maximum of 32 characters, allowing much more descriptive naming of the database.

For example, you might have a Notes database that holds information about your competitors. The filename could be COMPET.NSF, and the database title might be ABC's Competitors' Information. Unless you create your own databases, the filename and database title for each database you access have already been assigned by someone else.

If multiple end-users need access to a database, it must reside on the Notes server. If you are the only end-user, you can store the database on the Notes server or keep it locally on your hard disk.

One of the nicest features of Notes is that in most instances you do not need to know where the database physically resides. Notes keeps track of database locations; all you need do is double-click the database icon to access whatever data is in the database.

When you have access to a database, it is important to understand how Notes structures and organizes information. The internal architecture of a Notes database is unique.

Like any database, a Notes database is a collection of related information. But unlike traditional relational databases, any kind of information can be stored in a Notes database. In fact, Notes is particularly well suited for storing semistructured and unstructured information.

Lotus describes a Notes database as an *object store*. It can store, organize, and retrieve any kind of data object.

It might be helpful to visualize a Notes database as an open box. Just as you can put any real-world object into an open box (if you have enough room in the box to accommodate the object), you can put any kind of data object in a Notes database.

Each Notes database is made up of several building blocks:

■ Documents

■ Forms

- Subforms
- Navigators
- Views
- Folders
- Fields
- Shared forms
- Actions
- Layout regions
- Agents
- Access control lists

Understanding Documents

The basic data storage units in a Notes database are *documents*. These correspond loosely to records in a relational database (see the following note). Each document holds one or more items that store a variety of data types: text, numbers, dates, images, sound, and so on.

All the information that applies to one specific entry in the database is stored in a document. For example, if you are using a contact-management database, one document in the database might hold information such as the company name, contact name, customer address, customer phone, and how many times you have contacted the customer. Each individual customer would have his or her own document.

Each document can hold virtually any amount of information, from a single character to several pages of text and graphics. The size is limited only by the amount of available disk space (up to 4G!). This practical lack of size limitations is in direct contrast to relational databases, in which field and record sizes are strictly defined in the database structure.

N O T E Relational databases store information by breaking it down into individual data elements and maintaining it in tabular fashion (think of a spreadsheet). Related data elements (fields) are grouped as rows in the table, and related rows (records) are stored in the same table (database).

Because of this data-centric view, relational databases are transaction oriented, meaning that they reflect only the most current state of the data. For data in a relational database to be useful, the end-user must be able to sort and query the data in various ways.

In conventional terms, a data-entry screen is called a *form* in Notes. Forms provide the structure of a document. For more information on documents, see Chapter 8, "Working with Documents."

Forms

Forms are templates that provide the format and layout when you enter data into new documents or when you display and edit data from existing documents. Each database must hold at least one form.

The designer decides which form will be used most and designates it as the default form. Each form is created by the designer and can hold static text, fields, graphics, buttons, hotspots, text links, and layout regions. You'll learn about these design elements in Chapter 11, "Designing Forms."

N O T E It might be easier for you to understand Notes forms if you consider preprinted paper forms. For example, each year the IRS has to collect certain information from you to guarantee that when April 15 rolls around, you have remitted the correct amount of income tax.

To make it as easy as possible for you to give it this information and to ensure that it gets this information, the IRS provides the 1040 form. This form has instructions to help you fill in areas (fields) that group logically related information.

If the IRS didn't provide these structured forms, it would face total chaos, because there would be no consistency between the information from one taxpayer to the next. Notes forms work exactly the same way. ▣

When you choose the Create menu to create a new document, Notes presents a list of forms that are available in the selected database (see Figure 3.5). You must choose a form from that list before you can enter data. When a form is selected, it is displayed. You can begin to enter data into the fields on the form.

FIG. 3.5

The Create menu in the Employee database.

When you save the document, Notes stores the name of the form used to create the document in a special field named Form. The next time the document is accessed, Notes examines the contents of the Form field to determine which form should be used to display the document.

If no form name is found, the document is displayed using the default form. If no default form has been created, and the form can't be located, you get an error message, and the document can't be opened. In this case, contact your administrator.

N O T E Documents can be displayed using any form in the database; however, this can cause a great deal of confusion, because fields in the form might not align with items in the document. Data that the end-user expects to see might not be displayed, and data that the end-user isn't expecting might be displayed instead. ▣

Subforms

Subforms are a feature of Notes databases that makes designing databases faster and easier. A subform is a miniform that can be inserted into a form and can hold any valid Notes design element.

Because it can be shared among multiple forms in a database, the subform allows the designer to work from one location and avoid updating several elements. In addition, subforms can be dynamically inserted into forms, based on conditions a developer specifies.

For example, if an end-user chooses certain values, you might display a subform with fields x, y, and z. Otherwise, the subform would be inserted with fields 1, 2, and 3. The use of subforms makes Notes databases more flexible, modular, and maintainable, because you can keep the design elements in the subform in one place.

Layout Regions

Layout regions are a cool feature of Notes databases that allow designers to build highly intuitive, Windows-standard databases. In a nutshell, a layout region can be put in a form or subform to provide a fixed region. This region can hold graphics, custom interface elements, and fixed fields. For more information on layout regions and their use, see Chapter 11.

Navigators

To make Notes databases more end-user–friendly and visually appealing, Lotus added a new design feature called a *navigator* in version 4. A navigator is a tool that allows end-users to manipulate Notes databases.

A good example of a navigator is the one contained in your mailbox (see Figure 3.6). Lotus has built an intuitive navigator that allows you to click icons representing the mailbox's views and folders so that you don't have to use the View menu.

FIG. 3.6
The standard navigator
for 4.6 mailboxes.

By default, all databases have a navigator that displays all the nonhidden views and folders in the database. You should familiarize yourself with this format.

Part

I

Ch

3

However, Notes designers can build custom navigators that better represent the use of a Notes database and are more visually appealing than the magnifying glasses and folders that Notes displays in the default navigator.

In Notes 4.6, the Database Navigator has been enhanced and made more graphical.

N O T E In most databases, designers use navigators for two basic reasons. The first is to supplement or replace the View menu. If views and folders are set to not display in the View menu, the user will only be able to access a view or folder for the navigator. If you can't find a view or folder that you expect to see, be sure to launch the default navigator and see whether it's shown there. Second, navigators provide a main menu or menu system that allows end-users to navigate through the entire database graphically. ■

Views

For the individual data elements in Notes documents to be useful information, they must be organized meaningfully for the end-user, and they must be easily accessible. Views and folders organize the data and allow you to navigate through it. (Folders are discussed in the following section.)

Each database must have a minimum of one view. The designer designates as the default whichever view is most likely to be used. This view is displayed the first time each new database is opened. The ability to build and use several views and folders gives the end-user tremendous flexibility when working with Notes documents.

N O T E Notes keeps track of the last view opened and displays this view each time the database is opened. This view is not displayed if you use the View menu to choose a different view before opening the database or if the designer has set the database to autolaunch a navigator that also displays a view. ■

If you have not yet opened the database, you can use the View menu to select any view created for the database you're using (see Figure 3.7). If you have opened the database, you can use the View menu or the navigator to select a view. Keep in mind that, like every element in Notes, views can be secured so that only users explicitly granted access can use them.

FIG. 3.7

The View menu for the Employee database before it has been opened.

Once you have opened a view, the documents selected by the view are displayed in the view pane. If the designer has allowed that view to be navigable from the View menu, the view title will have a checkmark beside it in the View menu to show that it is in use. In the navigator, the view in use is denoted by a blue magnifying glass rather than a yellow one.

N O T E   Be aware that as the database grows in the number and size of documents it stores, the views take more time to open.

Each view has a selection formula (created by the designer) that tells the view which documents to display. Some views have a selection formula to select and display all the documents in the database. Other views have selection formulas that select only a subset of the documents, based on some criteria.

For instance, a view in a sales-tracking database might select only orders for which the total sale price is greater than $50,000. View-selection formulas allow the designer to create customized views.

Generally, each row in a view represents a document. However, this is not always the case. In order to help organize information in a view, some rows might be categories—meaning that when you click a category, it will expand and show documents that fall into that category. Documents are categorized based on criteria that the view designer designates. In Notes 4.6, most developers use "twisties" (a small blue triangle) to indicate categories. This will be covered in more detail later in this chapter. In addition, the enhanced features of Notes 4.6 views allow documents to span multiple rows so that more information can be displayed. Each column in the view can either display data from a field in the document or use a formula to compute a value to display.

As you can see in the view pane of Figure 3.8, several columns display data from each employee document in the database. The leftmost column in the view is a special feature in Notes views and folders called the *marker column*.

Part
I
Ch
3

FIG. 3.8
The Employees by Department view.

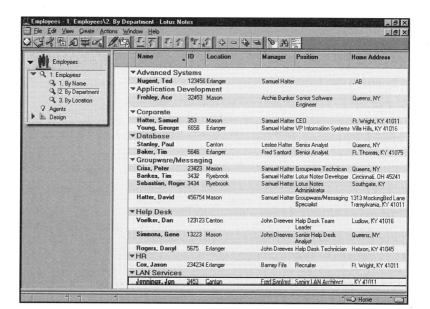

The marker column displays a variety of system information and is separated from the other columns in the view by a thin gray line that extends the length of the view. If you delete a document, for instance, you see a small blue trashcan icon in this column. If you haven't read a document, a star is displayed in this column.

N O T E   The designer chooses the icons that are displayed in columns in the views and folders. The designer also chooses the colors that indicate different aspects of a view or folder, such as unread documents. The icons that appear in the view marker column can't be changed in this version of Notes. ▣

Table 3.2 summarizes the contents of the Employees by Department view.

Table 3.2   Summary of the Employees by Department View in the Employee Database

Column	Description	Sorted	Categorized
Department	Displays the contents of the field Department	Department	Yes
Name	Has a formula that puts the last name before the first name so that this column can be sorted by last name	Last name	No
ID#	Displays the contents of the EmployeeIDfield	No	No
Location	Displays the employee's work	No	No
Location.Manager	Displays the employee's manager	No	No
Position	Displays the employee's title	No	No
Home Address	A concatenated field that displays the contents of the Address, Apt#, City, State, and Zip code fields	No	No
Home Phone/Fax	A concatenated field that displays the contents of the phone and fax fields	No	No

An outstanding feature of Notes 4.6 views and folders is the ability to dynamically resize columns (unless this feature has been explicitly disabled by the designer). To resize columns in any view or folder, simply click the line separating any two columns, drag it sideways until the column reaches the width you want, and release the mouse button.

Another great feature available when you are designing views is the option to allow end-users to dynamically change a column's sort order. If a column has this feature enabled, you see either a small up arrow, down arrow, or both in the column header.

The up arrow means that you can sort the column in ascending order. The down arrow means that you can sort the column in descending order.

If both arrows are present, you can toggle between ascending and descending order. To use this feature, simply click one of the arrows, and the view is re-sorted in the order you want.

Additionally, Notes views allow the designer to configure column headers to launch another view. If this feature is enabled, you see a long arrow pointing up. When you click this arrow, a new view is displayed.

Some other nice additions to 4.x views include Multi-line rows, Shrink rows to content, Alternate row colors, and Multi-line headings.

Multi-line rows allow columns with large amounts of data to wrap to the next line. When coupled with Shrink rows to content, Multi-line rows make the rows only as large as needed to fit the data being displayed. This is an effective way to display data.

Alternate row colors can also help differentiate rows by displaying a different color for each row, dramatically increasing readability. Multi-line headings allow the designer to use much more descriptive column headings without sacrificing horizontal space in a view.

This is all very nice, but what can a view really do for you? A view allows you to find, organize, and manipulate documents. When you open a view, a document is automatically selected.

This is either the first document in the view, the last document in the view, or the document you last selected when using the view. The selected document is highlighted by the selection bar.

N O T E The selection bar is usually black. The designer chooses the colors for various aspects of the view or folder, such as the view or folder background, the text of each column, and unread documents. To make the information displayed in the view or folder easy to read, Notes automatically chooses a contrasting color for the selection bar.

You can use several methods to select a document in a view or folder. You can use the mouse and scroll bars to navigate through the documents and then click the document you want to use. You can also use the cursor keys to move the selection bar to the document you want, or you can use the navigation SmartIcons.

 TIP If the first column of a view or folder is sorted, you can just type in the first few characters of the item you want to find. Notes displays a Quick Search dialog box that allows you to find documents in the view. When you enter the search term, Notes moves to the first document that matches whatever characters you have typed in.

continues

Part
I

Ch
3

continued

For instance, if you're using a view that displays all your customers' names sorted alphabetically by last name, and you're looking for Philip Krezewicz, typing "Krez" should be enough to move you to the right document.

When you select the document you want, you can open the document (to read or edit), print it, or delete it. The next few sections cover each of these topics in detail.

The designer, with the system end-users, decides which data elements from the underlying documents should be displayed and how they should be organized. In most databases, many views are created so that end-users can easily navigate through the database using whatever information they find most useful.

For instance, in the contact-management example, you might have the following three views:

- Contacts by Company: Displays all the customer documents in the database, sorted and categorized by company name and contact name
- Contacts by State: Displays all the customer documents in the database, sorted and categorized by state and then by company name
- Complaints by Customer: Displays all the complaint documents in the database, sorted by customer

By selecting different views, the end-user can examine different "snapshots" of the data. In fact, a view need not display all the documents in the database. A view named Calls This Week might only display a subset of customers that you spoke to this week, whereas a view named Calls Next Week might display all your calls scheduled for next week.

After using a database for some time, you might find that additional views and folders that are not currently part of the database design would help you navigate and manipulate the database. If other end-users might also benefit from the use of these new views, you can have the designer create these views for you in the server copy of the database.

If these are views that others are unlikely to use, you can build private views. Private views can sort and display the information you want to see. But these views are inaccessible by other end-users.

N O T E Shared and Shared Private on First Use views are stored as part of the database design. They can be replicated with other database design elements and data. Private views, on the other hand, are not stored as part of the database. They are stored in an individual end-user's DESKTOP.DSK file. See Chapter 2, "Customizing Notes," for more details on DESKTOP.DSK. ▪

Folders

Folders are a cool feature introduced in Notes 4.5 that are very much like views. The difference between folders and views is that folders don't need selection formulas. Instead, you move documents into and out of folders.

Folders offer an easy way to organize documents by subject matter (or any other criteria). They allow you to maintain a much smaller subset of documents than you could in a categorized view.

For example, suppose you are the manager of the Technical Services department. You often use a view that selects all 2,200 documents in an employee database and that is categorized by the Department field.

Even though you are interested only in the Technical Services employees, you still have to deal with other documents in the view. You could create a folder called Tech Services, select your employees in a view, and drag them into the Tech Services folder. This would be a smaller, faster, more manageable subset of data to work with.

In the view shown in Figure 3.9, a company's departments are organized into categories such as Application Development, Corporate, Help Desk, and Human Resources (HR). These categories aren't documents, and you can't open them as you could open documents. You can, however, perform operations on them.

FIG. 3.9

The Employees By Department view shows employees organized into categories that can be expanded or collapsed to help reduce information overload.

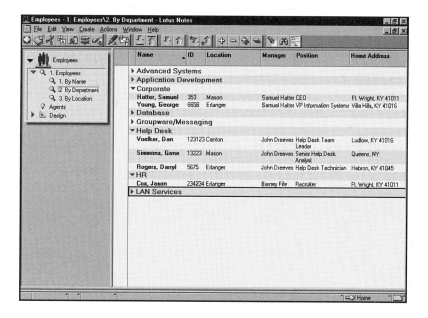

N O T E In most views, category titles stand out from document titles in boldface and are displayed with a twistie (a small blue triangle) to indicate expandability and collapsibility. However, it is up to the designer to configure these options. ▨

In Figure 3.9, you can see documents listed under categories that are expanded.

N O T E In Notes 3, most designers made the first column in a view display a plus sign (+) when the category is collapsed (when there are documents beneath the category that are not displayed) and a minus sign (–) when the category is expandable. In Notes 4.6, a twistie indicates a category.

You can click the twistie to expand and collapse the category. A twistie that points right indicates a collapsed category, and a twistie pointing down indicates an expanded category.

To help reduce information overload, you can temporarily limit the amount of information displayed in a view by collapsing a category. When you double-click the name of the category, all the documents in that category disappear.

Alternatively, you can select the category and press the minus key (–). You can select the category and choose View, Expand/Collapse, Collapse Selected Level. Or you can use the View Collapse SmartIcon. The documents themselves aren't deleted from the database, but Notes stops displaying them while the category is collapsed.

N O T E Categories are not documents; they act only as headings so that documents can be logically grouped. If you click the twistie beside any of the categories in a view (or double-click any of the categories), you expand or collapse that category. Categorization is a feature that the designer builds into views and folders to increase their usefulness.

For example, if you are interested only in employees in the Application Development department, you can collapse the HR and Advanced Systems categories so that only employees in the Application Development department are displayed. You can later expand the other categories—that is, make the employees in other departments reappear—by double-clicking the other category names.

Alternatively, you can expand the other categories by selecting them and pressing the plus key (+); by selecting them and choosing View, Expand/Collapse, Expand Selected Level; or by using the View Expand SmartIcon.

If you're working with a view or folder that has dozens of categories, and you're interested in only one, collapse all the categories. You can do this by choosing View, Collapse All; by pressing the Shift and minus (–) keys simultaneously; or by using the View Collapse All SmartIcon. Then double-click the one category you want to expand (or use any of the previously mentioned methods).

Similarly, you can expand all the categories by choosing View, Expand All; by pressing the Shift and plus (+) keys simultaneously; or by using the View Expand All SmartIcon.

The capability to quickly expand and collapse categories in views and folders makes data much easier to work with.

Viewing Database Views, Folders, and Categories

As discussed briefly in Chapter 1, "Getting Started with Lotus Notes," the way you interact with Notes databases in Release 4.6 has been significantly overhauled. In Notes 3.x, when a database was opened, it immediately displayed a view window that showed either the most recently used view or the default view for the database if that was the first time the database was opened.

The new end-user interface provides *panes*—a series of smaller windows that work together to provide easy navigation through views and folders. (Views and folders are discussed in more detail in the following sections.)

Figure 3.10 displays information from the Employee database. You can see that rather than one large view window, the screen is split into three window panes separated by gray lines. Each of these panes has a distinct and useful function:

- The leftmost pane on the top displays the navigator pane—a hierarchical structure of graphical objects that represents parts of the database.

- To the right of the navigator pane is the view pane. It displays data from documents in the database that are selected by folders and views (which are covered in detail in the following sections).

- Below the navigator pane and the view pane is the preview pane. It lets you view the contents of a document without opening it, which can save time and effort.

Part
I
Ch
3

FIG. 3.10

The various panes of the Notes 4.6 database interface.

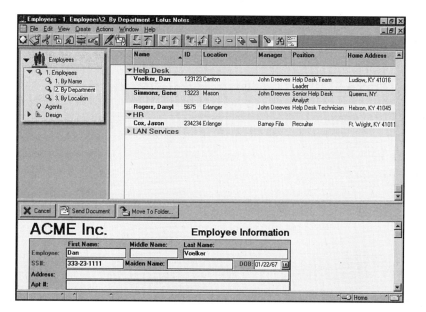

Each of these panes can be resized to suit your taste. The navigator and preview panes can be hidden if you don't find them useful or if you want to use the screen in other ways.

Using the Pane Navigator   The default pane navigator is easy to use. It has graphical icons and presents your choices in a hierarchical structure that can be expanded or collapsed. At the very top you see an icon that is the same as the database icon that appears on your workspace. To the right of the icon is the name of the database, and to the left is a twistie. Clicking on the twistie toggles between expanding and collapsing the view and folder list underneath.

Beneath the database icon is a list of the views and folders that make up the database. Some of them might have subfolders or cascaded views; these are indicated with a twistie. You can click the twistie to expand the folder or view to see the subfolders or cascaded views within. Folders are represented by a folder icon, and views are represented by a magnifying glass. The currently selected folder or magnifying glass turns blue; all other icons remain yellow.

Previewing Documents with the Preview Pane   The preview pane allows you to select a document in a view or folder. You save time by viewing the contents of the document without opening the document. You can scan through a database quickly using this tool.

The preview pane is flexible. It can be resized and placed in a variety of onscreen locations. To change the placement of the preview pane, choose View, Arrange Preview, and then click the button that corresponds to the placement you want.

Another database property can be used to set the preview pane location. Simply choose File, Database Properties (or right-click the database and choose Properties) to display the database InfoBox. Click the Launch tab, and then click the Preview Pane Default button to change the default location.

N O T E   You can disable the preview pane if you don't find it useful. The View, Document Preview menu option works like a toggle switch to enable and disable the preview pane. If a checkmark is visible next to this menu option, the preview pane is displayed midscreen. Alternatively, you can double-click the bar that separates the view pane and preview pane, or you can click and drag the separator bar to resize the preview pane to the desired size. ▓

Fields

After you select a form using the Create menu, Notes displays an empty document. Throughout the document, you see fields in which you can enter data. Most documents have several fields, which you can think of as the blanks on a paper form.

N O T E   The number, data type, and placement of fields within a form are determined by the designer. ▓

On Notes forms, editable field boundaries are delineated by small, gray, square brackets. Normally, each field has a label that explains what data should be entered into the field. Occasionally, you might see the field boundaries as red square brackets instead of gray (such as the Body field of a mail document). This means that the field is encryptable.

If the designer has included field help (a useful feature to guide end-users when they enter data), you might find additional information about the field's use and the data expected in the field by choosing View, Show, Field Help. The field help will display in a bar just above the Notes status bar at the bottom of the screen.

You can move the cursor from field to field using the directional arrows or the Tab key, or by clicking in whichever field you want the cursor located. If you're working in a rich text field, you can't use the Tab key to move to the next field. See the later section "Rich Text Fields" for details.

Like most databases, Notes has a variety of data types for fields. You might encounter a mixture of data types when working with fields inside a Notes form. Figure 3.11 shows a sample form named Employee Information. This form holds many different data types.

FIG. 3.11

Fields on the Employee form.

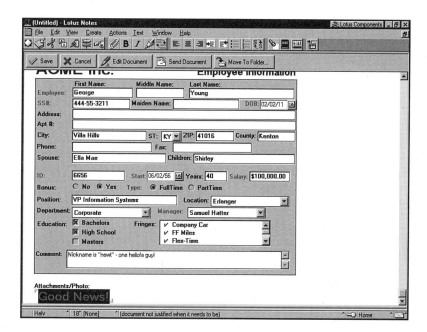

The available field types are described in the following sections.

Text Fields The text data type can be used to store alphanumeric data (essentially any character) that won't be used mathematically. Text fields, the most common type, can hold a large amount of information (up to 15K). In the document shown in Figure 3.11, Employee Name, SS#, ID#, Home Address, City, State, ZIP, and Phone are all text fields, as are most of the fields.

Numeric fields are needed only when the data values will be used in mathematical calculations. Data such as zip codes and phone numbers need not be stored in number fields, because they normally aren't used in calculations.

In addition, Notes allows designers to easily convert between data types. For more information, see the section "Function Reference by Category" in Chapter 14, "Working with Formulas," or see Chapter 17, "LotusScript Basics."

Rich Text Fields   The rich text field (RTF) data type is similar to the text data type in that it stores alphanumeric data that will not be used mathematically. However, RTF is more flexible, because it allows you to format the data.

For instance, you can change font features such as style, size, or color. You can format text, insert objects from other applications, insert file attachments, and display graphics.

In Figure 3.11, Attachments/Photo is a rich text field. Notice that the phrase "Good News" is larger than the surrounding text.

Because they can display any type of information, rich text fields can't be displayed in views. In most cases, they can't be used in formulas. Chapter 11 discusses rich text fields in more detail.

 According to the Lotus Notes Application Developer's Reference, you should use rich text fields when your data meets any of the following conditions: "includes pictures or graphs, pop-ups, buttons, or embedded objects; or if you want end-users to use text attributes such as bold, italic, underlining, or color."

Keyword Fields   The keyword data type stores text but allows you to choose a value from a list of predefined choices. Generally, designers use a keyword field when they want to ensure that the data entered into a field is from an acceptable list of values or when they want to speed data entry.

Although keyword fields store data as text, the items in the list don't have to consist of only text characters. For example, a list of possible household salary ranges could be <$10,000, $10,001–$20,000, $20,001–$40,000, $40,001–$60,000, >$60,000.

The three ways to present the list of keywords in a standard form are by using standard keywords, checkboxes, or radio buttons. If you're using a layout region, you can choose to display the list using a combo box, list box, radio buttons, or checkboxes. The following sections describe each method.

 Checkboxes are square; radio buttons are round. Checkboxes are not mutually exclusive: You can select as many checkboxes as you want. Radio buttons, on the other hand, are mutually exclusive: You can select only one button in a group of radio buttons.

Standard Keywords   When using a standard keyword field, which is not an option inside a layout region, you can choose only one of the values in the list. When the cursor is positioned on such a field, repeatedly pressing the Spacebar displays each possible value in turn.

You can also press the key for the first letter of the item you want, such as P for Programmer, and Notes fills in the rest of the word. If you want to see a list of all possible selections in a keyword field, put the cursor in the field and press Enter.

Or, if the designer has enabled it (the default setting), you can click the Entry Helper button (the small gray down arrow button next to the field). Notes displays the Select Keywords dialog box.

If you want to change the field value to one of the values listed in the dialog box, you can select an item from the list and then press Enter (or click OK).

N O T E Most keyword fields present you with a fixed set of values, and you are expected to choose one value from the list. However, the designer can allow you to enter something other than one of the predefined selections or allow you to select multiple items from the list.

If a keyword field has been designed to allow new values, the Keywords dialog box contains an input box into which you can enter new text. If the keyword field accepts multiple values, you can use the mouse to select several items from the list, and each will register with a checkmark as you select it. Each is displayed in the field when the dialog box is closed. ▪

Part

Ch

3

Checkboxes   Fortunately, checkboxes work the same way regardless of their placement in a standard form or a layout region. If the designer has enabled the Checkbox option on a keyword field, you see a list of checkboxes.

Each checkbox represents one entry in the predefined list. By default, checkboxes are not mutually exclusive, so you can select one, several, or all of the boxes if you want them to apply. Having selected a checkbox item, you can deselect it by clicking in the box again to remove the X.

For example, the Education field in Figure 3.11 lists four fringe benefits that the company provides. You can select whichever services the client uses.

An X appears in each box you select, indicating that the client uses that service. An empty checkbox indicates that the selection does not apply.

Radio Buttons   If the designer has enabled the Radio Buttons option, you see a list of radio buttons, so named because they work like the station selector buttons on early car radios. Each button represents one item in the list, and you must choose one of several mutually exclusive items. Although the radio buttons might initially be deselected, as soon as you choose one of them, you can't go back to the original state of having them all deselected. Unlike checkboxes, clicking an already selected radio button doesn't deselect it. If you have clicked a radio button in error when in fact you don't want to select any of the radio buttons, you will have to discard the document and create a new one, unless the developer has provided a reset button for this purpose.

In the Type field shown in Figure 3.11, for example, you can specify the type of employee. Clicking a button causes a black dot to appear in the button, and whichever button was previously selected is automatically deselected (the black dot disappears).

List Boxes   List boxes should be familiar to Windows end-users, because they are common in Windows applications. A list box displays a scrollable box that holds a list of valid choices.

In some instances, you can choose more than one item. This is decided by the designer. The Fringes field shown in Figure 3.11 is an example of a list box.

Combo Boxes   A combo box control should also be familiar to most Windows end-users. It is displayed as a text field and a small gray button with a black down arrow. When you click the button, a list of valid options drops down, and the end-user can select a value.

In addition, the end-user can position the cursor in the field and type the first letter of any valid entry to find the first entry in the list that begins with the typed letter. In Figure 3.11, the State, Department, Manager, and Location fields are examples of combo boxes.

N O T E   Combo boxes and List boxes are special design elements that can be displayed only in layout regions, which means that if the database designer elects not to use layout regions, you'll never see these elements. For more information about layout regions, see the section "Layout Regions" earlier in this chapter, or see Chapter 11. ▪

Time/Date Fields   The time/date data type lets you enter a time or date in a field. If the value you enter is not a valid time or date value, Notes prompts you to enter a valid one. In Figure 3.11, the Hired field holds the date that the employee was hired.

Numeric Fields   The number data type expects a numeric value (0 to 9), such as the number of employees in a company or the number of calls made to a customer. If a value entered in a number field isn't a number, Notes prompts you to enter a valid value.

The form in Figure 3.11 has two number fields: Salary and Years. (The field with a phone number can't be a number field, because it has nonnumeric characters such as parentheses, spaces, and dashes.)

Names Fields   The three names data types are Author, Reader, and Names. Each one has a special function when used on a Notes form, as explained in the following sections.

N O T E   Author and Reader fields don't override the access control list (ACL) for a database. They can only refine it. ▪

Author Fields   The Author data type has a text list of Notes names (end-user names, group names, and access roles) that determines who can edit a document.

If you have Reader access to the database via the ACL, and your end-user name appears in an Author field in a document, you can't edit that document (because an Author field can't override the ACL). To allow an author to edit his or her own documents, a developer would typically add the author's name to an Author field on the form, which refines the ACL and changes what would have been Reader access to Author access—but only for that specific document. Without that, the author wouldn't be able to edit his or her own documents. Editors can edit the document whether they are in an Author field or not, but interestingly, if they aren't specified in a Reader field, they won't be able to read the document.

If an Author field is created and no one is named in the field, only those with Editor access or higher can edit the document; it's as if the Author field weren't there. Author fields work with other Notes security features such as ACLs and Reader fields (discussed next) to provide additional database security. If all this is confusing, just remember that an Author Names field only affects those who have Author access in the ACL. Editors and above can edit the document, and readers can never edit a document (remember that the Author Names field can't override the ACL).

TIP You can click and hold an Author Names field in read or edit mode of any document to determine who has Editor access to the document.

Reader Names The reader names data type expects a text list of Notes names (end-user names, group names, server names, and access roles) that determines who can read a document. If a document has a Reader Names field and no one is named in it, anyone with Reader access or higher can read the document. Again, it's as if the Reader Names field did not exist.

As a practical example, let's say you're a member of a group that has Editor access to the database via the ACL. There is a Reader Names field in the document, but your name or group isn't in it. Can you read the document? No. In fact, you wouldn't even know it was in the database. Even managers have to be in the Reader Names list to be able to see the document.

Here's another example: You're listed as a Reader in the ACL of a database, and you're also in an Author Names field in the document. Can you edit the document? No. Remember, Author Names fields can't override the ACL, and that says you're a reader. You will be able to put the document into edit mode and make as many changes as you like, but you won't be able to save the document.

N O T E Reader and Author fields are also important to consider when replicating databases to other servers. In this situation, you can think of a server as just another user, so if a document has a Reader field and the remote server isn't listed in that field, the document won't replicate to the remote server, because the server can't *read* it. Likewise, if you have users at a remote site who are included in an Author field and are amending documents, ensure that the remote server is listed in the Author field too, or your server won't accept the changes.

Names The names data type can hold a text list of Notes names (end-user names, group names, server names, and access roles). A Names field is useful when you want to store or display a list of end-user names but not assign access rights to a document.

In a Names field, end-user names are displayed in abbreviated format—for example, Dave Hatter/Entex. But they are stored in canonical format—for example, CN=Dave Hatter/ 0=Entex.

Sections There are two types of sections in Notes. Collapsible Sections allow the developer or user to collapse or "hide" a body of text under a meaningful title. What the end-user sees is the title, underlined, with a twistie to the left of the title. Clicking the twistie expands the section, displaying the previously hidden text. Clicking the twistie again collapses the section, once more hiding the text. Note that all users can use this facility—for instance, when creating a mail message.

▶ **See** "Creating Sections in Documents," **p. 337**

Controlled Access Sections are available to the developer only when he is designing a form in a database. Typically, the section will contain other fields, and the developer can determine who will be able to edit (or read) that section. This is typically used for an approval-type application in which many people might be able to edit a document, but only a few can approve it or change its status.

▶ **See** "Editable Field Formulas," **p. 470**

Field Types   When defining a field, you not only define the type of data it can hold, but you also have the following choices for each field: editable, computed, computed for display, and computed when composed. The following sections examine the benefits and drawbacks of each of these options.

Editable Fields   An editable field can be any data type. It is stored in the document when the document is saved. The developer can provide a default value for the field or leave it blank. If there is a default value, the user can either accept it or change the value. You'll learn more about formulas in Chapter 14.

When an editable field is displayed on a form, it is delineated with small gray brackets—unless the field is an encryptable Rich Text Field, in which case the brackets are red. An example of an editable field is one named PhoneNumber in which the end-user enters a phone number.

Computed Fields   The value of a computed field is determined by a formula built into the field by the developer. This might be something as simple as displaying the user's name, or the current date and time, or it might involve complex calculations based on what the user has entered in another part of the form. In any case, the user can't edit the field directly; there are no brackets around the field that the user can click inside to begin editing. The value of the Computed field is recalculated each time the document is opened, refreshed (when the F9 function key is pressed), or saved. When the document is saved, the value of the Computed field is saved along with it.

Computed fields can be used with all data types.

Computed-for-Display Fields   The value of a computed-for-display field is determined by a formula built into the field by the developer. The end-user can't change the value of such a field, and its value is recalculated each time a document is edited or refreshed.

The difference between computed and computed-for-display fields is that the values in a compute- for-display field are not saved in the document (which means that they can't be displayed in views). You use a computed-for-display field to display to the end-user data that can easily be computed, changes frequently, and doesn't need to be displayed in a view.

Computed-When-Composed Fields   The value of a computed-when-composed field is determined by a formula built into the field that the designer develops. The end-user can't change the value of such a field, and its value is calculated only when the document is composed. This value is never recalculated. When the document is saved, all computed-when-composed fields are also saved.

An example of a use for this type of field is a field named CreatedBy that reads the end-user name from the Notes ID in use when a document is composed and stores that field when the document is saved.

Shared Fields

Shared fields are a special type of field that allow you to make your applications more modular by reusing field definitions in other parts of your database. For example, you might create a computed-when-composed field named CreatedBy that stores the name of the user who created the document. You could then share the field and use it in every form in the database rather than recording it for each form. For more information about shared fields, see Chapter 11.

Part

I

Ch

3

Agents

If you're familiar with Notes 3, you probably have worked with macros. Agents are the new and improved version of macros in Notes 4.x. Agents can work in the background to make things happen.

For example, an agent might automatically send mail, move documents into a folder, or search a database for a particular topic of interest. Custom agents created by designers or end-users can perform more powerful functions, such as manipulating field values or retrieving data from external applications.

Agents can be programmed in the traditional Notes @Function language, LotusScript, or Java.

Whether you are an end-user or a designer, agents can help you work more effectively and efficiently. For more information on agents, see Chapter 16, "Buttons and Agents."

Actions

The best way to think of actions is as small "code snippets" that can automate tasks in Notes databases. Actions can be used in forms, views, folders, navigators, and agents. They are easy to create (in fact, Lotus was kind enough to add a number of predefined Simple Actions), and they can make using a Notes database much easier. For more information on actions, see Chapter 16.

Understanding Access Control Lists

When working with a database, you might discover that you can't perform all possible operations. Each database has a manager who is responsible for that database. One of the manager's responsibilities is setting an ACL so that data security and integrity are maintained.

ACLs are a powerful feature of Notes. In Notes 4.x, database ACLs can be enforced on local databases to ensure that data remains secure for remote users.

The ACL performs three functions related to database access:

■ It defines who has access to a given database (the list can hold user names, server names, group lists, and database roles).

■ It defines what the users can do to the database.

■ It defines Roles consisting of groups for refined access to specific forms and views. (For more information on Roles, see the section "Understanding Database Security" in Chapter 22, "Security and Encryption.")

Only the database manager (or any user with Manager access) can manipulate the ACL. On the list, the manager arranges all users into one of the seven access levels listed in Table 3.3.

Users at each level can perform only certain tasks. The list can include group names so that the manager can assign the same access privileges to an entire department or workgroup with just one entry, which greatly reduces maintenance.

N O T E Throughout this book, when you read instructions for performing operations, you should keep in mind that Notes might not allow you to proceed if the database manager hasn't placed you at the access level for that operation. ■

Table 3.3 Notes Access Levels

Category	Tasks Allowed
No Access	Can't access the database
Depositor	Can create new documents but can't edit, delete, or read existing documents, even those you created
Reader	Can read documents but can't create, edit, or delete documents
Author	Can create, read, and possibly edit and delete your own documents; can read documents created by other users
Editor	Can create, edit, read, and possibly delete documents (this is a suboption that can be toggled off or on for each user), including those created by other users
Designer	Has same access rights as the Editor level and can also create, edit, or delete design elements such as forms and views
Manager	Has complete access to all facets of the database, including the ability to delete it from the hard disk and to change the ACL

Your assigned access level can (and probably will) vary from one database to another, because the manager for each database decides what level you should have. Consider the following examples:

- For a database holding sales reports, you have Author access. This allows you to create new sales reports and change them later (if you're included in an Author Names field). In addition, you can read sales reports entered by other users, but you can't edit them.

- For a database handling suggestions, comments, and complaints, you have Depositor access. You can add new suggestions to the database, but you can't read or edit them once they have been saved, much like an anonymous comments box hanging on the wall.

- For a database holding technical support material, you have Editor access. This allows you to add new documents, edit documents you have created, and also edit documents that others have created.

- For a strategic plans database, unless you're an executive, you might be assigned No Access. At this level, you can't even open the database.

Notes also allows the designer to restrict access individually to particular forms, views, sections, and fields in a database. This allows a database manager to give you access to a database but to restrict you from accessing certain information. You'll learn more about this type of access control in Chapter 10.

 TIP To find out what access level you have been granted to a specific database, open the database and look at the third block from the right on the status bar. It displays an icon representing your access level. You can click that area of the status bar to find out your access level.

Changing the Database Settings

Notes allows you to fine-tune a database by manipulating the many "database" settings that you can access through each database's database property sheet. For instance, you can make the database smaller, or you can create a full-text index so that searching the database is easier. By examining and learning about the available options, you can exert a tremendous amount of control over each database.

To access the database settings for a database, select a database by clicking its icon. You can then choose File, Database, Properties; click the Properties SmartIcon; or right-click the database icon and choose Database Properties. This displays the Database Properties InfoBox, shown in Figure 3.12.

The InfoBox allows you to use the tabs at the top of the box to select the settings you're interested in. The following sections describe the settings on each tab.

Part

I

Ch

3

FIG. 3.12

The Basics tab of the Database Properties InfoBox lets you edit particular database information.

Basics Settings

The first tab, Basics, lets you view and edit some primary database information, including the following:

- Database Title: This is the title displayed on the database icon and in the File Open dialog box. If necessary, you can change it.

- Server: This is the name of the server on which the database resides. This is basically an FYI.

- Database Filename: This is the name associated with the database file at the operating-system level.

- Database Type: Use this combo box (if you have Manager access) to change the database type from Standard, which is the default, to Library, Address Book, Personal Journal, Multi DB Search, or Portfolio. Database Types change the behavior of the database they are selected on to perform specific functionality.

  For example, the Personal Journal type doesn't allow shared agents, folders, or views to be created in the database, because the database is meant for personal use.

- Encryption: Click this button to encrypt the local copy of this database and thereby enforce local security. Encryption provides very tight security but causes a modest performance hit. Encryption is covered in more detail in Chapter 22.

- Replication Settings: Click this button to view or edit the replication settings for the database (this is covered in Chapter 23, "Notes: Under the Hood").

- Replication History: Click this button to view or clear the replication history for the database. Each time a database replicates successfully, this log is updated (see Chapter 23.

- Disable background agents for this database: This checkbox, when selected, disables any scheduled agents for this database. If you create or enable any default agents in a database, they don't run when this option is turned on. You'll learn more about agents in Chapter 16.

- Allow use of stored forms in this database: This option allows you to determine whether you want documents that have forms stored in them to be displayed with the stored form (the default action) or to be displayed with forms that reside in the database. This can be useful when documents are mailed into a database.

- Display images after loading: For databases that are to be published on the Web, this setting allows the text to be transmitted first so that the Web user doesn't have to wait while large graphics are loaded.

- Web access: Use Javascript when generating pages: Tells the Web browser to use JavaScript when accessing this database.

- Web access: Require SSL connection: For sensitive databases, the Web browser can access the database only if an SSL connection has been established.

Information Settings

The Information tab, shown in Figure 3.13, displays the following information about the database:

- The size of the database in kilobytes.

- The number of documents in the database.

- The date the database was created.

- The date the database was last changed.

- The replica ID of the database: This is a very important piece of information that you'll learn about later in this chapter and in Chapter 23.

- % Used: This button displays the amount of space in the database that is being used to store data. When this number drops below 100 percent (which it frequently does), "white space," or free space, is not being used in the database. When this number drops below 90 percent, you should compact the database to free the white space.

- Compact: This button can free unused white space by compacting the database, thus freeing valuable disk space.

- User Activity: This button lets you enable activity tracking (to log reads, writes, and updates to the database) or view each user's activity in the database if tracking has been enabled. This can be a powerful troubleshooting tool, but it does add overhead to the database.

At the bottom of the Information tab, a message might appear to indicate that this particular database can be used only by a user with a Notes Mail license (which restricts the user to certain types of databases).

Part
I
Ch
3

FIG. 3.13

The Information tab of the Database Properties InfoBox.

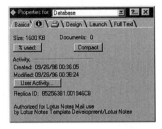

Print Settings

The Print tab (which has a printer icon) allows you to set options for printing documents and views (see Figure 3.14). These settings apply only to this copy of the database and will not replicate with other copies of the database:

- Header: The Header radio button allows you to add a header to the top of each document when it is printed. You can select the text box below it to enter a standard header. The graphic buttons below the text box allow you to insert a page number, date, time, tab, and document title (which defaults to the form name) so that you can dress up the header.

- Footer: The Footer radio button works exactly like the Header, except that a footer is added to the bottom of a document when printed.

- Font, Size, and Style: Each of these list boxes lets you apply various formatting options to the header and footer.

- Print header and footer on first page: This checkbox does exactly what it says: It prints the header and footer on the first page.

FIG. 3.14

The Print tab of the Database Properties InfoBox.

For example, you can insert a header or footer (discussed in more detail later in this chapter) or change the header and footer fonts that are sent to the printer.

Design Settings

The fourth tab, Design, displays information that concerns designers, such as the Inherit design from templates checkbox and the Database is a template checkbox (see Figure 3.15). These settings are covered in detail in Chapter 10.

CAUTION

You should not change any of these settings unless you are absolutely certain that you understand what you are doing. These settings can have deleterious effects on the selected database as well as on other databases!

- Design is/is not hidden: This is static text that tells you if the database design is locked out from changes. This is an advanced feature that allows designers to prevent changes to the underlying database code.

- Inherit design from template: When this option is enabled, you can use the Template Name text field immediately below it to choose a database template on which the current database should base its design. This feature is covered in more detail in Chapter 10.

- Database is a template: When this option is enabled, you can use the Template Name text field immediately to the right of it to enter a template name for this database so that the design of the database can be propagated to other databases. This is covered in more detail in Chapter 10.

- List as "Advanced Template" in new database dialog: This option allows you to show a database as an advanced template. It's covered in more detail in Chapter 10.

- List in database catalog: This option allows you to have the current database included in the database catalog. When this option is enabled, you can choose from the Categories field below the categories under which the database is displayed in the database catalog.

- Show in open database dialog: When this option is enabled, the current database is displayed in the File, Database, Open dialog box. If this option is deselected, the database is displayed in the list, although users can still access it if they know the path and filename.

- Include in multi-database indexing: When this option is enabled, you can index the database with other databases for cross-database, full-text searching.

FIG. 3.15

The Design tab of the Database Properties InfoBox.

Launch Settings

The fifth tab, Launch, displays checkboxes offering choices that allow you to change what happens each time a database is opened (see Figure 3.16):

■ On Database Open: Allows you to specify what happens when the user opens the database. The following table shows each option and describes what they do.

Choice	Description
Restore as last viewed by user	Opens the database exactly as it was when the user last used it
Open "About Database" document	Opens the About document each time the database is opened
Open designated Navigator	Opens a selected navigator each time the database is opened
Open designated Navigator in its own window	Opens a selected navigator in its own window
Launch 1st attachment in "About Database"	Launches the first attachment stored in the About document
Launch 1st doclink in "About Database"	Opens the first doclink stored in the About document

■ Show "About database" document if modified: Allows you to automatically redisplay the modified About database document when the database is opened only if the About database document has been modified since the last opening of the database.

■ Show "About database" document when database is opened for the first time: Allows you to decide if the About Database document is displayed upon the first opening of the database.

■ Preview Pane Default: When you click this button, the resulting dialog box can be used to set the default location of the preview pane. This can be set to one of three positions, where the Preview Pane takes up the bottom half of the screen, the right half of the screen, or the lower-right quadrant of the screen.

■ On Web Open: These options are similar to those for On Database Open. They are used to specify an action for when the database is accessed with a Web browser. The following table shows each option and describes what they do.

Choice	Description
Use Notes launch option	Uses the same option selected in the On Database Open field.
Open "About Database" document	Same as for On Database Open.
Open designated Navigator in its own window	Same as for On Database Open.
Launch 1st doclink in "About database"	Same as for On Database Open.

Choice	Description
Launch designated doclink	Having copied a doclink, choosing this option will display a button allowing you to paste the doclink that the Web user will jump to upon entering the database.
Launch first document in view	Choosing this option allows you to choose a view from which the first document will be opened to the Web user.

FIG. 3.16
The Launch tab of the Database Properties InfoBox.

Full-Text (Index) Settings

The Full Text tab, shown in Figure 3.17, provides the following buttons so that you can create and change full-text indexes. These indexes help you search for information in the database:

- Last Index Time: Shows you the date and time the database was last indexed.
- Size: Displays the size in kilobytes of the full-text index. Remember that this is additional disk space being used to store the full-text index.
- Update Index: Allows you to create a new full-text index or update an existing one. If you're creating a new index, you are prompted for a variety of settings that allow you to control the size and effectiveness of the full-text index.
- Create Index: Allows you to create a new full-text index.
- Delete Index: Deletes a full-text index.
- Update Frequency: Allows you to choose how often server-based databases are reindexed. This setting affects only server-based databases. Local databases must be indexed manually.
- Count unindexed documents: Displays the total number of documents in the database that haven't been included in the index. You can use this statistic to determine when you need to update the index.

FIG. 3.17

The Full Text tab of the Database Properties InfoBox after you create an index.

In addition, this InfoBox displays other pertinent information about how the index was created, as described in the following table:

Option	Description
Case sensitivity	Allows you to create indexes that permit case-sensitive searches. However, this increases the size of the index and decreases the speed of the search.
Index Attachments	When enabled, this option allows you to index the contents of any attachments in any document so that you can search their contents as well.
Index Encrypted Fields	When enabled, this powerful new option allows you to index the contents of any encrypted fields.
Stop word file	This option allows you to exclude from the index any words found in the Stop word file. This greatly reduces the size of the index, speeds searches, and reduces the number of irrelevant hits. The Stop word file contains common words such as "the" that could cause many hits you don't want. You can choose the default stop words file (DEFAULT.STP) or a custom stop words file that you have built.
Index breaks	By default, "word breaks only" is chosen, which helps keep the size of the index down and allows you to search based on words found in documents. "Word, sentence, and paragraph" allows the additional flexibility to search for sentences and paragraphs as well as words, but it adds significantly to the size of the database.

Working with Documents

Now that you know how the various parts of a database work, you'll learn about creating, editing, and saving documents.

To open an existing document, simply select it in a view or folder and double-click it. If you have Reader access to the database, the document is displayed onscreen in read mode.

This means that you can't edit it at this point (see Figure 3.18). It's easy to see that a document is in read mode because there are no brackets around fields.

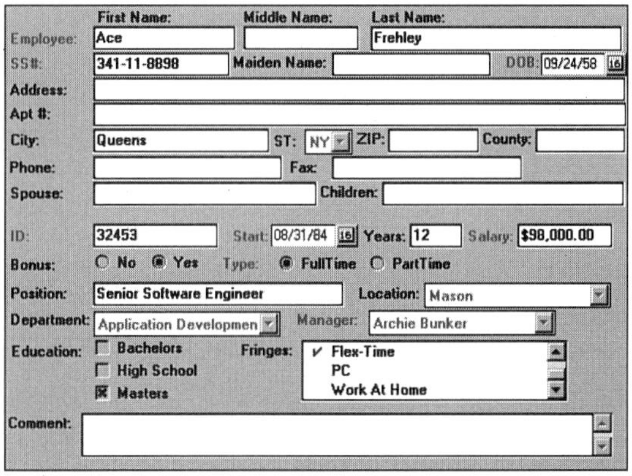

FIG. 3.18

An Employee document for Ace Frehley in read mode.

In read mode, you can see all the data in the document, and you can print the document, but you can't edit it. To edit the document, press Ctrl+E. (You can use the Actions Edit Document SmartIcon if you have the appropriate access level.) You can also double-click anywhere inside the document or select Actions, Edit Document to place it in edit mode.

When the document is in edit mode, you can change any of the data elements to which you have access, as shown in Figure 3.19. (You can see the small gray brackets around the editable fields in a standard form. In a layout region, all the controls you are authorized to use will no longer be grayed out.)

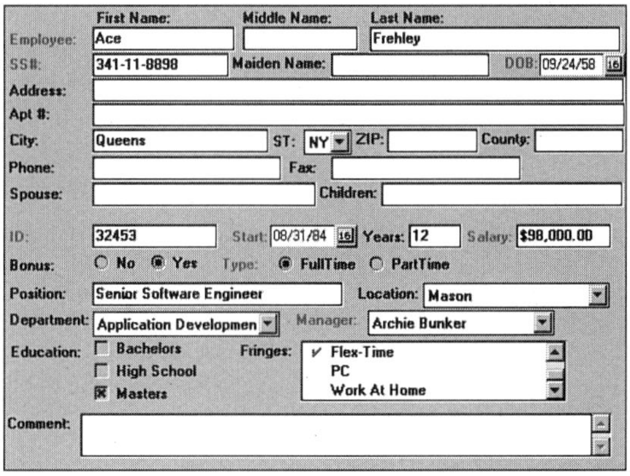

FIG. 3.19

Ace Frehley's employee document in edit mode.

To create a new document, choose Create, which displays all available forms in the database (see Figure 3.20).

Part

I

Ch

3

Create
Mail
Employee
Workspace Page
Agent...
Folder...
View...
Design

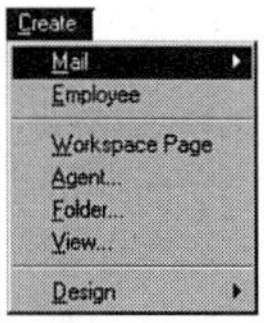

FIG. 3.20
The Create menu showing the Employee form in the Employee database.

As you can see from this figure, there is only one form in the Employee database: Employee. To create a new employee, choose Create, Employee. A new document like the one shown in Figure 3.21 is created.

First Name:
Middle Name:
Last Name:
Employee:
SS#:
Maiden Name:
DOB:
Address:
Apt #:
City:
ST: AB
ZIP:
County:
Phone:
Fax:
Spouse:
Children:
ID:
Start:
Years:
Salary:
Bonus:
No
Yes
Type:
FullTime
PartTime
Position:
Location: Canton
Department: Advanced Systems
Manager: Archie Bunker
Education:
Bachelors
High School
Masters
Fringes:
Company Car
FF Miles
Flex-Time
Comment:

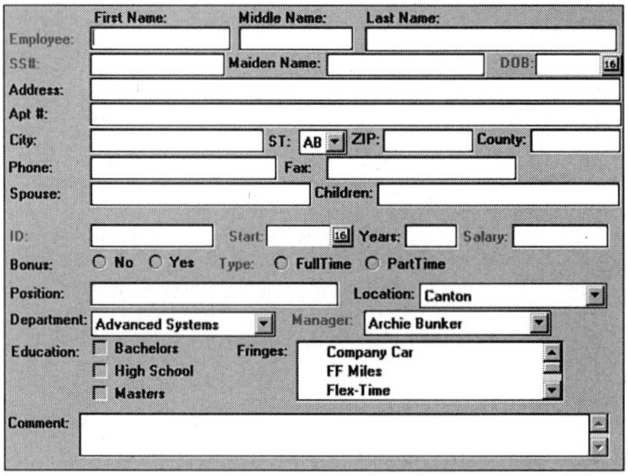

FIG. 3.21
A new Employee document.

NOTE Remember that your ability to read and access documents is controlled by the ACL for each database. The ACL is set by the database manager.

You can now enter data in the document.

Saving and Closing Documents

Now that you know how to create and edit documents, you need to know how to save or cancel your changes. When you're finished reading or editing a document, you can save the document, save and close the document, or just close the document and discard the changes.

To save any Notes document, select File, Save (shortcut Ctrl+S) or use the File Save SmartIcon. This does not close the document, but writes the data to disk.

To close a Notes document and return to the folder or view, do one of the following:

- Press Esc.
- Select File, Close (shortcut Ctrl+W).
- Click the document window's control menu box (the small application icon in the upper-left corner of the window) and then choose Close.

N O T E   You'll see two control menu boxes: one for Notes 4.6 (in the upper-left corner) and one for the window that is currently open in Notes, just below the program's control menu box. Be sure to click the view or folder's window. If you inadvertently click the Notes control menu box and then click Close, you will exit Notes. ▓

- Double-right-click anywhere in the document. This is a holdover from Notes 3.x and might not be enabled for your workstation. See Chapter 2, "Customizing Notes," to learn how to enable this feature.

Performing any of the actions just listed causes Notes to check if you have made any changes to a document. If you have made changes, you are prompted with a dialog box like the one shown in Figure 3.22.

FIG. 3.22

The Notes File Save dialog box.

To save your changes, click Yes. To close the document without saving changes, click No. To avoid closing the document (and saving the document), click Cancel.

Closing a Database

To close a Notes database, first close any open documents by using one of the methods listed in the preceding section. Then follow the same steps you would use to close a document. Don't worry if you forget to save any changes you have made to open documents—you will be prompted to save the changes.

Copying a Database

You might need to make a copy of a Notes database. For instance, if you want to make an archive database that doesn't replicate with other databases (you'll learn about this in Chapter 23), you'll need to make a new copy of the database. To do so, choose File, Database, New Copy.

Figure 3.23 shows the dialog box where you can make additional choices about the elements that you transfer to the new copy.

FIG. 3.23

The Copy Database dialog box.

You can choose a different server as the database's destination, give the copy a different title, and choose a different filename for the new copy. In addition, you can copy all the documents and design elements (forms, views, and so on) or only the design elements.

You can also choose to copy or not to copy the ACL, regardless of the other selections you have made.

The Encryption button lets you secure the database on your hard disk by encrypting it with your choice of three varying degrees of encryption—Simple, Medium, and Strong. The encrypted database won't be able to be accessed unless your user ID is used to open it. If you choose to secure your database, you should keep your user ID on a floppy disk (several for backup) and not on your local hard disk.

Finally, you can specify the maximum size of the database by clicking the Size Limit button and choosing the desired size (the default is 1 gigabyte).

When you have made your selections, clicking OK will create a nonreplicating copy of the database with a different Replica ID from the original (you can see the Replica ID in the Information tab of the Database Properties dialog box).

CAUTION

Each database has a replica ID, a unique identifier that allows it to replicate with other replica copies of the same database. (Replication is the process that synchronizes replica copies of Notes databases. You'll learn more about replication in the section "Understanding Notes Replication" in Chapter 23.

When you make a new copy of a database rather than a replica copy, the database gets a different replica ID, which means that the new copy won't replicate with other replica copies. If you want this new copy to replicate with other replicas of the same database, use the File, Replication, New Replica option rather than the New Copy option.

Working with Portfolios

One of the things to consider in Notes is how to keep logically connected databases together. One option is to create a new workspace page and move related databases there, but you might consider that wasteful if you're only trying to organize two or three databases that make up a particular application. Another option is to set up Database Libraries, but these merely point to databases. This is where a Portfolio can come in handy.

New in version 4.6, a Portfolio looks like an ordinary Notes database, but in reality it is a container where you can collect related databases.

Figure 3.24 shows the Portfolio icon that is added by default to your workspace on installation. This Portfolio, called Favorites, contains your mail file, Personal Address Book, Journal, and Personal Web Navigator. You can add to this Portfolio if you wish or create new Portfolios according to your requirements. For example, you might create a Portfolio containing your client-tracking database, product catalog, and order-entry database. Together, these databases make up your Sales application.

FIG. 3.24
The Favorites Portfolio created on installation.

Another good use for Portfolios is providing company information for employees. Many companies publish employment policies, safety regulations, organization charts, and company bulletins via Notes. Because Portfolios can be stored on the server as well as locally, new employees can add a single Portfolio to their workspace and have access to all the databases they need without having to hunt down each one individually.

N O T E   Portfolios can be deleted and replicated just like any other Notes database, but remember that these actions affect the Portfolio's NSF file and not the database collection held within. So when you delete a Portfolio, you're just deleting the Portfolio itself and not the databases referenced in that Portfolio. Replicating a Portfolio replicates the Portfolio NSF file, not all the databases referenced within. ■

Navigating Inside a Portfolio

To access a Portfolio, simply double-click its icon on the workspace. Figure 3.25 shows the Favorites Portfolio after it has been opened. The following sections are indicated in the figure:

- ■ On the top-left side you see the Portfolio Title. This displays the name of the Portfolio. Clicking it allows you to edit some of the Portfolio settings.

- ■ Below the Portfolio title, the Portfolio Navigator displays an icon representing each database that has been added to the Portfolio.

- ■ On the right is a standard view pane that reflects the contents of the database you have chosen from the Portfolio Navigator.

Each database contained in the navigator displays the icon for the database and a twistie. Clicking the twistie will expand that database, displaying the folders, views, and design elements that make up the database, as shown in Figure 3.26. Once expanded, the database behaves much as you would expect. Clicking the folders and views changes the contents of the view pane on the right, and any Action Bars associated with these views will appear in place beneath the SmartIcon Palette. Clicking the database twistie again collapses the database back to an icon.

FIG. 3.25

The contents of the
Favorites Portfolio.

Portfolio Title ──

Portfolio Navigator ──

View Pane ──

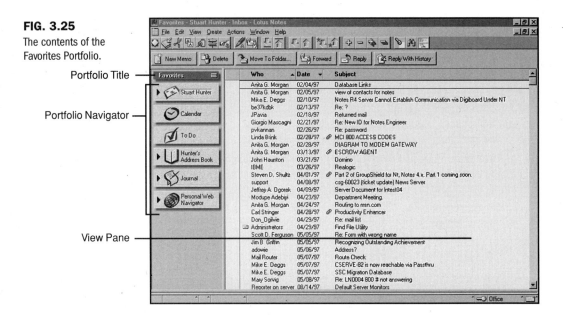

FIG. 3.26

The Portfolio Navigator
with the Mail file
expanded.

N O T E   When added to a Portfolio, your mail file is treated as a special case. The Calendar and To
Do sections are displayed individually below the main Mail icon. You can't delete these
sections, and you can't add other sections from the mail file or from any other database. ▪

Unlike databases stored on the workspace itself, you can't display the unread document count
or server name of the selected database. Right-clicking a database in a Portfolio limits you to
replicating the database or selecting another replica copy from your workspace to work with.
Therefore, instead of right-clicking, you will have to work through the menus to perform common database actions.

N O T E You might be disconcerted to find that if you add a database to a Portfolio and then delete the original icon from the workspace, the next time you start Notes, the icon will magically reappear. You can't have a database in a Portfolio that isn't also present on your workspace. The best that you can do is create a new workspace page and move the unwanted icons to it. ■

When dealing with databases, you get used to the idea that when you open a database, the view you see is the one that was active when you last closed the database. This is not how databases work within Portfolios. Regardless of the database and view you were accessing, when you exit the Portfolio and then re-enter it, the view you see in the right pane will be that of the *last* view you accessed in the *first* database in the Portfolio list. In the case of Favorites, this would normally be your mail file.

Creating a Portfolio

The Notes administrators or developers in your company might have created general-purpose Portfolios for you to use, but it's easy to create your own by following these steps:

1. Select File, Database, New to display the New Database dialog box, shown in Figure 3.27. You first choose the location for the new Portfolio, either locally (which is the default) or on a Notes server if you have the rights to do so.

FIG. 3.27

Creating a new Portfolio using the PRTFLO46.NTF template.

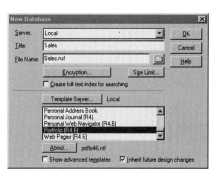

2. Give the new Portfolio a title and a filename. The most important part is to ensure that the Portfolio's design is based on the Portfolio template (PRTFLO46.NTF). Otherwise, you're creating an ordinary database, not a Portfolio.

Editing a Portfolio

Once you have created an empty Portfolio, you need to add databases to it, and you will probably want to customize the way they are displayed. The simplest way to add databases to a Portfolio is to drag and drop them from the workspace to the Portfolio icon. They will appear in the Portfolio in the order you dropped them. Unlike when you drag a database icon from one workspace page to another, the database icon won't disappear when you drag it onto the Portfolio icon; it will remain in place. Although you can continue to add databases to your Portfolio, the Portfolio Navigator is limited to displaying a maximum of 20 databases.

To further customize the way the databases appear, left- or right-click on the Portfolio Title and select Edit Portfolio, as shown in Figure 3.28.

FIG. 3.28

Selecting the Edit Portfolio command allows you to customize the way the databases appear.

Figure 3.29 shows the Edit Portfolio view of the Portfolio database. In the view pane on the right, you can see a list of all the databases that are contained in the Portfolio.

FIG. 3.29

The Edit Portfolio view.

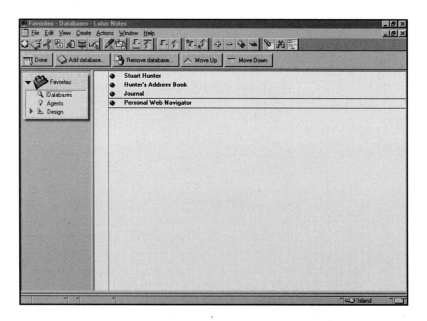

When you double-click one of the databases listed in the view, you are taken to the Database Information form for that database. Here, the only thing you can change is the displayed name of the database, as shown in Figure 3.30. Doing this doesn't change the title in the actual database, just the name as it is displayed in the Portfolio.

FIG. 3.30

Changing the displayed name for a database in a Portfolio.

Database Information

Title:	Journal
Display Title:	' Personal Journal ｣
Sequence:	3
Database Link:	
⊴	

At the top of the view, the buttons on the Action Bar let you perform various actions that affect the contents and order of the Portfolio database. Table 3.4 lists these buttons.

Table 3.4   Buttons on the Portfolio Action Bar

Button	Action
 Done	Takes you back to the Portfolio, saving any changes you have made
 Add database...	Brings up a dialog from which you can select databases from your workspace to add to the Portfolio
 Remove database...	Removes the selected database from the Portfolio
 Move Up	Changes the order of the databases by moving the selected database up the list
 Move Down	Changes the order of the databases by moving the selected database down the list

Clicking the Add database or Remove database buttons on the Portfolio action bar brings up a new dialog box. Figure 3.31 shows the dialog box for adding a database to the Portfolio.

FIG. 3.31

Adding a database to the Portfolio.

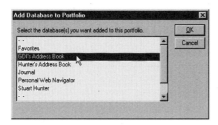

When you have finished customizing the Portfolio, click the Done button on the action bar to return to the Portfolio Navigator.

Deleting Database Icons and Databases

There are two ways to delete a database from your workspace:

■ Delete the database icon from your workspace.

■ Delete the database permanently from your hard disk or server through Notes.

Anyone can delete a database icon from a workspace, but only users with Manager access to a database can permanently delete a database from the hard disk. The following sections explain the differences between these two procedures.

Deleting Database Icons from Your Workspace

When you no longer need a database, you can delete it from your workspace without deleting the database file from the server or hard drive where it is stored. To do so, follow these steps:

1. Select the workspace on which the database resides if it is not currently showing.

2. Click the database you want to remove. (Don't double-click, or you'll open the database.)

3. To delete more than one database from the same workspace, Shift-click the other databases you want to delete (hold down the Shift key and click the other database icons you want to select).

4. Press Delete or choose Edit, Clear.

5. Notes prompts you with a dialog box that asks if you're sure you want to delete these icons from your workspace (see Figure 3.32). If you are sure, click Yes to delete the selected icon(s) from your workspace. If you have changed your mind, click No.

FIG. 3.32
The Remove Database
icon dialog box.

Deleting database icons doesn't delete the database file—it only removes the icon from your workspace. Any other users who access the database will still see the database icon on their workspaces and can still access the database. In fact, you can add the same database icon to your workspace again later.

After you delete database icons from your workspace, there are gaps where the icons used to be. You can easily fill in these gaps by dragging other database icons into the empty positions. Or, you can choose View, Arrange Icons to have Notes rearrange the icons in the workspace so that all gaps are filled in.

Deleting a Database

If you have Manager access through the ACL for a given database, you can permanently delete the database file.

> **CAUTION**
>
> The following instructions tell you how to permanently delete a database and all its information from the hard disk where the file resides. If you do this on a database, all data in that database will be lost!

To permanently delete a database, do the following:

1. Click the database icon of the database you want to delete. This selects the database.
2. Choose File, Database, Delete. Notes prompts you with a dialog box informing you that you are about to permanently delete the database and asking if you're sure that's what you want to do (see Figure 3.33).

Part

I

Ch

3

FIG. 3.33
The Delete Database Warning dialog box.

3. Click Yes to permanently delete the database from the server or hard drive, or click No to cancel the deletion.

> **CAUTION**
>
> Unless a database has been replicated to your workstation with a consistent ACL enforced in the Advanced settings of the ACL dialog, you have Manager access to all Notes databases that are stored on your workstation. This includes important system databases such as your Mail database, your Notes Log database, and your Personal Address Book database. You also have Manager access to your Mail database on the Notes server.
>
> There is no good reason to delete these databases, because you will use them (particularly your Mail database) often. You shouldn't delete any of these databases without first seeking the advice of your Notes administrator.

Using the Universal Viewer

Notes has a powerful and useful feature called the Universal Viewer that allows you to view the contents of any file attachment, even if you don't have a copy of the application that originally created the file. In fact, you don't even need to know what application created the attachment. The Universal Viewer is smart enough to determine the file type (in most cases) and display it for you.

This can be handy when you get file attachments in a format you're unfamiliar with, when you don't have a licensed copy of the application that created the file, or when you want to quickly view or print the file without launching another application, which consumes memory and wastes time.

To invoke the Universal Viewer, double-click any file attachment (or right-click the attachment and choose Attachment Properties). This displays the Attachment Properties InfoBox for the attachment, shown in Figure 3.34. If the document is in edit mode, you will see the five tabs shown in Figure 3.34. If you are merely reading the document, only the Information tab will be available.

FIG. 3.34

You can choose one of five tabs in the Attachment Properties InfoBox.

Click the View button to send the Universal Viewer into action. The file is displayed for you to look at. While the file is displayed, you can control a variety of display and print settings. To change any of the settings for the file, right-click to get a menu of options, as shown in Figure 3.35.

FIG. 3.35

You have many options with the Universal Viewer.

The Print option displays a Print dialog box. From this dialog box, you can change various print settings and then send the document to the printer. The next menu section lists display options, which vary depending on the file format of the file being viewed.

For instance, when you right-click a Microsoft Word document, you see options that apply to the document display modes in Word. The Options option displays a cascading menu like the one shown in Figure 3.36, which allows you to change many aspects of how the file can be displayed, printed, and copied to the Clipboard.

FIG. 3.36

The Options menu of the Viewer pop-up menu.

If you choose Display, you see the Display Options dialog box, shown in Figure 3.37. From there, you can change the default display font and decide how (or if) to display files that are unfamiliar to the Universal Viewer. You can click More to reach additional options, such as how to display database and spreadsheet files.

FIG. 3.37

The Display Options dialog box.

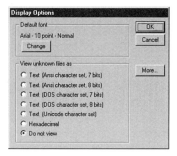

The Print menu option displays the dialog box shown in Figure 3.38. This dialog box allows you to specify a variety of printer output options, such as the printer font, the font used for the document header, whether or not a header prints, the page margins, and a name for the print job.

FIG. 3.38

The Print Options dialog box.

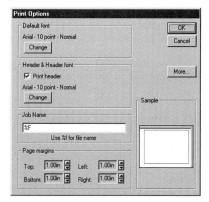

As with the display options, you can click More to reach additional options that control how certain types of files are printed. This causes the More Print Options dialog box to appear (see Figure 3.39).

For instance, you can print grid lines and cell headers for spreadsheets, grid lines and field names for databases, and borders for graphics files. In addition, when you print graphics files such as bitmaps and drawings, they can be printed in their original size or scaled to fill the entire page.

FIG. 3.39

The More Print Options dialog box.

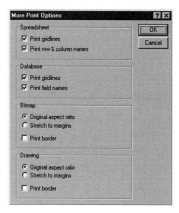

The Clipboard menu displays the Clipboard Options dialog box, shown in Figure 3.40, which lets you select a format to place on the Clipboard. As you can see from the figure, there are a variety of format types for the Clipboard.

FIG. 3.40

The Clipboard Options dialog box.

You can also change the Clipboard font. Clicking More displays another dialog box that lets you change how database and spreadsheet files are copied to the Clipboard.

The Universal Viewer is a powerful utility that can save you time and effort when you need to deal with file attachments.

Printing Documents and Views

Although Notes can bring the dream of a paperless office much closer, in reality, people still need to print hard copies of information. Notes has flexibility when it comes to printing documents and views. You have several options for what should be printed:

- Print a single document.
- Print selected documents.
- Print the entire view.

There are two ways to print a single document, each of which is slightly different:

- Print a selected document from a view or folder.
- Print an open document.

Printing a Selected Document from a View or Folder

If you're in a view or folder, you can select a document either by clicking it or by clicking in the View Marker column (to put a checkmark in it). Then choose File, Print or click the File Print SmartIcon to display the dialog box shown in Figure 3.41.

FIG. 3.41

The File Print dialog box as it appears when a single document is chosen in a view.

The File Print dialog box allows you to control many aspects of printing, such as the following:

- Click Printer to select a different printer from the one selected (this is displayed next to the printer icon) or to change the printer setup for a printer (the next section discusses specifying other printers).
- Choose Print range to set a range of pages in the document to be printed. This applies only to printing individual documents.
- Select the Draft quality checkbox to use lower-resolution printing, which speeds the printing process. This might be necessary if the selected printer doesn't have much memory.
- Use the Copies setting to indicate whether you want multiple copies of the document printed.
- Select the Graphics scaled to 100% checkbox to print graphics at their original size.

The most important options in this dialog box are in the View options section and are described in the following paragraphs.

The selections in the View options section allow you to print the entire view or print only documents that you have selected. Notice that because only a single document was selected in the view, the Print selected documents radio button is selected by default. In addition, you can choose Form Override when printing documents to select a form for printing other than the form that the document was saved with.

 TIP The Form Override feature of Notes can be useful. For instance, if you use a database in which a form is designed to speed data entry but is not very attractive when printed, a separate form can be designed for printing. When you decide to print the document, use Form Override to select the form designed for printing, which ensures that the document is printed with the more attractive format.

Document separation lets you choose from one of three options when printing multiple documents. The first option, Page Break between documents, allows you to eject a page and start printing the next document on a new page.

The second option, Extra Line, doesn't eject a new page. It inserts one blank line between each document to make the printout easier to read.

The final option, No Separation, provides no separation between documents. The next document in the queue will begin printing on the line immediately following the previous document. When you are printing only a single document, the Document separation options don't apply.

Finally, you can select the Reset page numbers checkbox, which works with the Page Break Document separation option to reset the page number to 1 for the first page of each document.

When you have made your selections, click OK to send the document to the printer.

 TIP If you want to see where the pages will break and words will wrap for a given document before you print, you can open the document and choose View, Show, Page Breaks. A heavy black line is displayed wherever a page break will occur.

Printing the Open Document

The second way to print a selected document works for a document opened in read or edit mode. Choose File, Print, or use the File Print SmartIcon, and you get a slightly altered dialog box that has fewer choices than the dialog box you would see if you began in a view or folder (see Figure 3.42).

FIG. 3.42
The File Print dialog box for a single open document.

The dialog box shown in Figure 3.42 is essentially the same as the one you saw in Figure 3.41. The difference is that you are printing a single, open document rather than a document in a view or folder. As a result, there are no view options, you can't select For_m Override, and you can't insert page breaks. Click _OK to send the document to the printer.

Printing Selected Documents

Printing selected documents is like the first option for printing a single document. Open a view or a folder, and then select multiple documents by clicking the view marker column next to each document you want to print (a small checkmark in the View Marker column indicates that you have selected a document).

Once you have chosen all the documents to print, choose _File, _Print or use the File Print SmartIcon. You see the File Print dialog box, shown in Figure 3.42. Your options are the same as when printing a single document, but the View options and Document separation selections take on new importance.

Make sure that the Print se_lected documents radio button is selected, and select Page Break as the document separator. You can also use For_m Override to print each selected document with a form other than the form with which it was last saved.

When you have made all your printing choices, click _OK to send the print job to the printer.

Printing a View

You might want to print the view instead of the documents displayed in the view. Notes makes it easy to do this. You open the view you want to print and then choose _File, _Print (or you can press Ctrl+P or use the File Print SmartIcon).

You arrive at the familiar File Print dialog box (refer to Figure 3.41). In the View options section, select the Print _View radio button, which dims the document-specific print settings such as For_m Override and Document separation. Set the other print options, such as _Copies, and then click _OK to send the view to the printer.

Printing a List of Documents in a Folder

Printing documents from folders is much like printing documents from views. To print a list of documents from a folder, just select the documents you want to print and choose _File, _Print, or click the File Print SmartIcon.

Specifying a Printer

When Windows was installed on your workstation, a default printer driver should have been installed and selected for the printer that you use most frequently. When you print from Notes, the program sends your output to the default printer unless you specify a different one.

It is often helpful to have access to a printer other than your default printer. For example, having access to a printer that uses $8\frac{1}{2}$-inch-by-14-inch paper is particularly helpful when you're printing wide views that scroll off the screen.

Part
I

Ch
3

This way, you can take advantage of some options that your default printer doesn't offer, such as an envelope feeder. Each time you print something from Notes, you see the dialog box in either Figure 3.41 or Figure 3.42, depending on what you're trying to print.

Each of these dialog boxes displays a Printer button above the selected printer (indicated by a printer icon). Click the Printer button or click the File Print Setup SmartIcon to change printer drivers.

After you click Printer, you see a dialog box that displays all the printer drivers installed on your workstation, as shown in Figure 3.43.

FIG. 3.43

The Print Setup dialog box with installed printers shown.

Click to select a printer driver from the list, and then click Setup to display a property sheet for the selected driver. Figure 3.44 shows the dialog box for the HP LaserJet 4M driver.

FIG. 3.44

The dialog box for an HP LaserJet 4M printer.

Using Headers and Footers

Another nice feature that Notes provides is the ability to set global headers and footers for all documents in a database. Headers and footers allow you to further identify documents when printing them.

A good example is the headers at the tops of the pages of this book. In the header, you see information such as the title of the chapter and the page number.

To set a header or footer, choose the Print tab of the Document Properties InfoBox, shown in Figure 3.45. From this tab, select the Header radio button to create a header.

FIG. 3.45

The Print tab of the Document Properties InfoBox.

Then, in the input box below the button, enter the text that you want your header to display. Click the button that has a green check to accept the changes or the red cancel button to reject the changes.

Clicking the Footer radio button allows you to enter text to print in the footer. It works just like the Header button.

You can see several icons immediately beneath the text box for the header and footer. These icons make it easy for you to automatically add additional information to the header or footer:

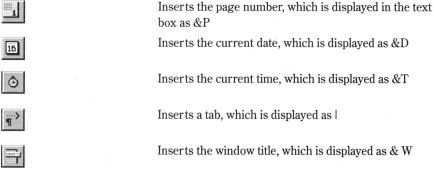

	Inserts the page number, which is displayed in the text box as &P
	Inserts the current date, which is displayed as &D
	Inserts the current time, which is displayed as &T
	Inserts a tab, which is displayed as |
	Inserts the window title, which is displayed as & W

A header formula, for example, can print the date and time, insert a tab, print the text Test Header, insert another tab, and then print the current page number. When printed, the header would look something like this:

> 10/20/97@10:10PM   Test Header   Page 1

From this Properties InfoBox, you can also adjust font settings such as typeface, size, and style for the header and/or footer. To change the typeface for the header or footer, select a new font from the Font list box.

To change the size of the font, select a font size from the Size list box. To change the font style, select the style from the Style list box.

N O T E   The font settings for the header and footer are mutually exclusive; that is, you can use different font settings for the header and footer. ▪

Getting Started with Electronic Mail

Electronic mail (email) is one of the most important and useful tools to come out of the information age, making it quick and easy to communicate with coworkers, regardless of geographical and time barriers. Although Notes provides many valuable services in addition to email, email is probably the single most used service.

The Notes email system is a friendly, durable client/server system modeled after the best-selling stand-alone email package, cc:Mail. NotesMail makes it easy to communicate with other Notes users and with other mail systems such as Microsoft Mail or Internet mail, if you have the proper hardware and software.

NotesMail is flexible. Not only can you send messages to other users, but you can also send file attachments and embed objects such as spreadsheets or graphics in the message. Understanding and using NotesMail is key to maximizing productivity when using Notes.

In this chapter, you will learn the basics of sending and receiving mail. Later chapters explain the more advanced mail features and other features of Notes that help you and your coworkers work together more effectively.

Introducing Email

Technological progress has a profound effect on the methods people use to communicate. As few as 30 years ago, the U.S. Postal Service was the way people sent messages to one another. (Paper-based mail is sometimes called "snail mail" because it's so much slower than email.) But as technology has advanced, new methods such as the fax machine and email have made it easier, faster, and often less costly to send messages to other people.

Since the mid-1980s, the popularity of email as a tool to send messages has grown exponentially. For proof of this trend, just look at the number of business cards that have an email address.

Email has revolutionized internal communications for companies that use it. Many companies now provide email links to their customers and vendors, giving them a significant advantage over competitors who rely on paper-based mail.

If you ask people who have worked with email for any length of time, most of them wonder how they ever got by without it, because it makes their jobs easier, faster, and more fun. In fact, email is rapidly becoming the preferred method of communication among technologically savvy professionals.

More and more ordinary people (not just techno-geeks, nerds, and dweebs like me) are beginning to use email because of the many advantages it provides. Before long, email will most likely supplant the postal service for all messages except those that can't be delivered by email, such as that fruitcake your Aunt Bertha sends you every Christmas.

Here are some of the advantages of email:

- ■ Paperless messaging: Because email messages are composed and delivered electronically and are generally read and stored electronically, you don't need to print the message. (All email systems provide the option of printing a hard copy of the mail message.)

- Speed: Email messages travel across the wire at the speed of light, which makes for quick delivery. Most businesses can immediately see a return on their investment. The time it takes for employees to communicate is drastically shortened, particularly in geographically dispersed companies.

- Ease of use: Most common email systems are easy to use and work, much like a word processor. Once you start the mail program, you can address your message by pulling up a directory of other email users in your network. You type your message, add any file attachments you want to send, and send the message. Some email systems even offer spell checking, so you don't have to worry about typographical errors.

   Since most people would type the letter or memo they want to send, they can save a step by using the email editor to both compose the message and send it in one step.

- Message organization: Most email systems offer power features that allow you to prioritize, sort, categorize, file, and search for your email. This makes it much easier to manage your messages than with paper mail in traditional folders or filing cabinets.

   For example, think how handy it would be to search for an important memo from your boss simply by typing in his or her name rather than digging through all the papers on your desk for the printed version.

- Flexibility: Email makes it easy to work with your messages. You can delete mail you're not interested in, forward a message to others, reply to a message, or send the same message to a large number of users just by adding their addresses.

   With electronic mail, you can do anything you can do with paper mail. Many email systems have other advanced features such as "agents," which allow you to automate mail functions. For instance, you might want a special notification each time you get mail from your boss.

- One-stop shopping: Since you probably use your computer for other jobs, having mail available on your computer helps eliminate redundancy. In addition, because the mail is an electronic file, you can export the information to other applications. For example, if I send you a picture of a new product our company makes, you can include it in a sales brochure that you are producing.

Compared to paper-based mail, email has few disadvantages. The following are examples of disadvantages:

- Expense: The initial investment in hardware, software, and configuration for an electronic mail system can be large. Many of these systems, such as Notes, are expensive in themselves. The computers to use them are expensive, and highly skilled people are needed to install and maintain the system.

   However, most modern offices have computers for their employees, and it's easy to show the advantages that email provides. The cost is outweighed by the increase in productivity.

Part

I

Ch

4

- Facelessness: Because most email messages are just text, it's hard to convey personal feelings or warmth. Many people would rather get a handwritten note from a friend than an email, even though they say the same thing.

   To learn how to make text-based mail more friendly, see the section "Email Etiquette" later in this chapter.

- As email packages improve, it's getting easier to include graphics and sound for that extra touch. But some things still need to be written by hand, like a birthday card for your son or a get-well card for a friend.

Now that you have an overview of email, let's see how NotesMail, the mail system integrated into Notes, works and how it can help you become a more productive Notes user.

Working with the Notes Mailbox

To use NotesMail, you must be familiar with your mailbox. Your mailbox is a Notes database (like what you read about in Chapter 3, "Using Databases") in which all your mail is stored. Figure 4.1 shows the database icon for a typical NotesMail user.

FIG. 4.1

A NotesMail database icon for Stuart Hunter's mailbox.

N O T E   Notes provides three core services: Document Databases, Application Development, and Messaging Services. The fact that your mailbox is actually a Notes database points to the tight integration of core services in Notes. Messaging is woven into the database structure so that any database can send and receive email messages.

In most Notes installations, your mailbox is created for you at setup, and its icon is placed on a page in your workspace, normally labeled Mail. (This is the normal configuration, but your configuration might be different. If you have trouble finding your mailbox, see your administrator.)

Because your mailbox is really just a Notes database, the procedures and techniques you use to read incoming mail and create new mail are the same as those you use when working with other Notes databases (see Chapter 3 for more information).

Two things make your mailbox special:

- The mailbox user interface resembles Lotus's cc:Mail product, which facilitates sending, storing, and organizing mail messages to and from other users.
- Notes includes native Calendaring and Scheduling capabilities. These are covered in depth in Chapter 9, "Lotus Notes Group Calendaring and Scheduling."

As you read this chapter, keep in mind that many of the techniques you will learn for working with your mailbox and mail messages (documents) apply to all Notes databases.

Another important aspect of your mail database (hereafter called a mailbox) is how you connect to the server to get your mail. If you are a mobile user with no ongoing connection to a server, you're probably set up for workstation-based mail.

If you have an ongoing connection to the server (usually via a LAN), you are probably set up for server-based mail. The type of mail you are currently using can be configured for each location.

To determine whether you're using workstation or server-based mail, open your current location document and examine the Mail File Location setting. If it's set to Local, you're using workstation-based mail; if it specifies a server name, you're using server-based mail.

Server-Based Mail   If you spend most of your time using Notes connected to a Notes server via a LAN or WAN, you're probably set up to use server-based mail. When you're set up for server-based mail, you use your mailbox on the Notes server.

Each time you create and send a new mail document, it is immediately transferred to the Notes server's mailbox. If you also save it, a copy of the document is placed in your mailbox.

The Router process on the server resolves the address of the recipient or recipients and routes the message to the intended recipient almost immediately. In addition, incoming mail is delivered to your mailbox shortly after it is delivered to your mail server.

Workstation-Based Mail   If you are a mobile user or you don't have an ongoing connection to a Notes server (for instance, you might work in a remote office or at home), and if you connect to your Notes server occasionally via modem, you're probably set up for workstation-based mail.

When your workstation is set up for workstation-based mail, you work with a replica copy of your mailbox. A special Notes database called Outgoing Mail is created on your workstation. The icon should look like Figure 4.2.

Part

I

Ch

4

FIG. 4.2
The Outgoing Mail database icon for workstation-based mail users.

N O T E   The Outgoing Mail database (whose filename is MAIL.BOX) is created by default the first time you change your location to Travel, Island, or any custom location profile where workstation-based mail is specified. You'll learn more about location profiles in Chapter 5, "Using the Notes Address Books," and Chapter 20, "Setting Up to Go Remote." ▪

Unlike server-based mail, when you compose and send a new mail message, it isn't immediately sent to the server's mailbox. Instead, the mail message is temporarily stored in the Outgoing Mail database until your next connection to the server. If you save a copy of the message, it is stored in your local mailbox, which is a replica copy of your mailbox on the server.

When you next connect to the server (if the Send outgoing mail option is enabled, which it normally is by default), your outgoing mail is automatically transferred to the server. In addition, if you replicate during this connection, your local mailbox receives all incoming mail from the server.

To enable or disable the Send outgoing mail option, choose the Replicator workspace tab. On the Replicator page, there should be an entry for Send outgoing mail that displays the Outgoing Mail database icon and a small checkbox. If the checkbox has a check in it, the option is enabled, and outgoing mail will be sent during each connection (see Figure 4.3).

FIG. 4.3

The Replicator page with Send outgoing mail enabled.

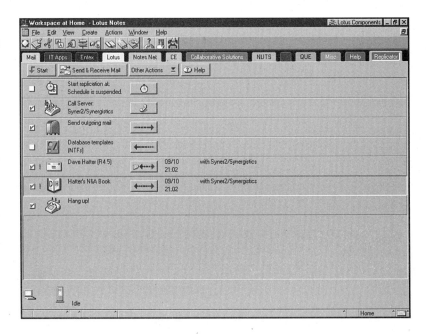

N O T E The NotesMail system is flexible, and you have considerable control over when messages get sent. For instance, you can tell Notes to make a connection immediately for High Priority mail.

You can also tell Notes to make a connection when more than a specified number of mail messages are pending in the Outgoing Mail database. You'll learn more about these options in Chapters 5 and 20. ▓

> **TIP** If you're using workstation-based mail (the current location document has the Mail File Location set to Local) and your mail isn't being delivered, make sure that the Transfer outgoing mail option is enabled during replication. You can check this by examining the Replicator page entry for Outgoing Mail.
>
> A checkmark in the small box and an arrow pointing away from the database graphic indicate that outgoing mail will be transferred. Figure 4.3 shows an Outgoing Mailbox configured to send mail on each connection.

If you didn't have a temporary storage facility for outgoing mail, you would need to connect to the server each time you sent a mail message. Not only would this be a major hassle, but it would severely limit your ability to use Notes on the road.

However, like other remote mail systems such as CompuServe, America Online, and Eudora, Notes provides this temporary storage facility, giving you tremendous freedom to create and send mail.

You can create one mail message on the plane on your way to a meeting and another while driving to a sales call. When you next connect to the server, the Router transfers the mail messages from your Outgoing Mail database to the intended recipients.

> **CAUTION**
>
> The Outgoing Mail database is a critical component of the mail system for users who don't have an ongoing connection to a Notes server. Because your outgoing mail is stored in this database until your next connection, it is very important that you not delete this database or delete it from your Replicator page.

Part
I

Ch
4

Mailbox Features

As with all Notes databases, to access your mail messages, you must first open your mailbox. In most cases, your administrator has put your mailbox icon on your workspace for you. Just double-click the mailbox icon, and the database opens. If you installed Notes 4.6 from scratch as opposed to upgrading from an existing version, Notes should have created a Favorites Portfolio for you that includes your mail file, so you can also access your mail file from there.

Remember that if you don't see the database icon you want, check the other pages in your workspace to see whether the database resides on a different page. When you open your mailbox, you should see something like Figure 4.4.

If you've used NotesMail in older versions of Notes, you can quickly see from Figure 4.4 that the mail interface has changed somewhat from version 4.5. It now includes an enhanced graphical navigator with separate sections for your Calendar and To Do views. (If you're upgrading from Notes 3.x, the changes are drastic.) If you've used cc:Mail before, you will have a leg up on users who are converting from Notes 3.x. If you haven't used cc:Mail, don't worry. Lotus has made the new mailbox much easier to use.

FIG. 4.4

The NotesMail mailbox interface.

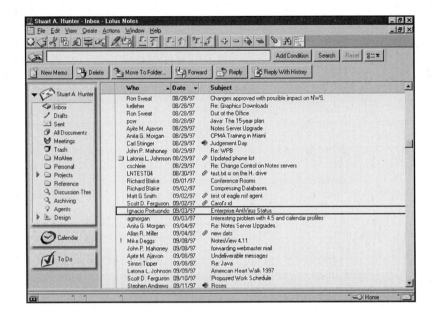

On the left side of the screen you should see the navigator pane, which has been customized for the mailbox but works the same way in every database. As you know from Chapter 3, the navigator provides a graphical representation of the elements of a database. Lotus has used this to its advantage in your new mailbox design.

To the right of the navigator is the view pane. It's like Notes 3.x views but provides more flexibility than 3.x views. The various views will be discussed shortly.

One of the most useful features is the preview pane. Although you can enable this for any database, it can be particularly useful in your mailbox, because it lets you read your mail messages without opening them. This can save you a lot of time.

To display the preview pane, choose View, Document Preview, or click the SmartIcon (the last icon on the SmartIcon bar by default). This displays the preview pane in approximately 50 percent of the screen. Alternatively, you can simply click the thick gray line at the bottom of the view pane and drag up, which displays the preview pane.

Remember, the display of your mailbox at any given time might depend on any changes that a designer made to the database and changes you might have made, such as resizing the preview pane or changing its screen location. Notes 4.6 gives you flexibility and control when working with your mail.

To make the new format of the mailbox as useful and easy as possible, Lotus has designed several default folders and views that you can access by clicking icons in the navigator:

- Inbox folder
- Drafts folder

- Sent folder
- All Documents view
- Meetings view
- Trash folder
- Folders and views

N O T E The Calendar and To Do views that were an integral part of the Mail Navigator in version 4.5 have been moved and now have their own sections underneath the Mail section. This is unique to the mail database; no other database can separate sections in this way.

The following sections examine each of these items.

Viewing Inbox Messages.   To quickly view the new mail you have received, click the Inbox icon, which opens the Inbox folder (see Figure 4.5).

FIG. 4.5
In the Inbox folder, the view pane displays the currently selected document.

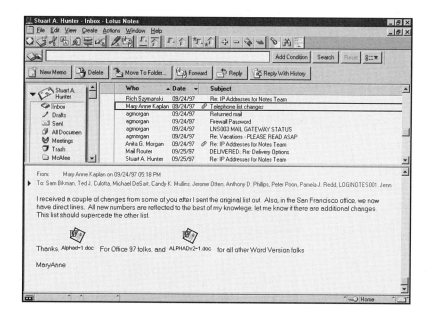

All incoming mail is stored in the Inbox folder until you move it elsewhere or delete it. (See "Moving Your Messages" later in this chapter for details on how to organize your mailbox contents.)

Viewing Draft Messages   For a view of your *drafts,* which are mail messages that you have saved but not yet sent, click the Drafts icon (see Figure 4.6).

FIG. 4.6
The Drafts view in the
mailbox database.

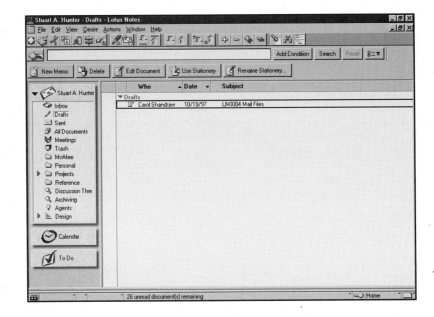

When you send a draft, it is automatically moved from the Drafts folder to the Sent folder,
unless you specify another folder.

Viewing Sent Messages   To see only the messages you have sent, click the Sent icon, which
launches the Sent view, shown in Figure 4.7.

FIG. 4.7
The Sent view in the
mailbox database.

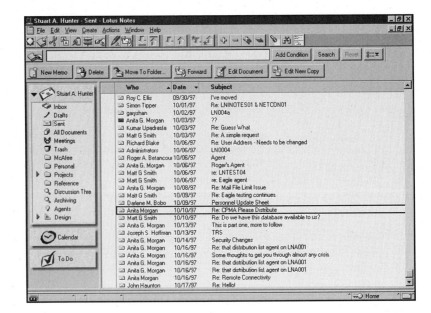

Viewing Your Calendar   Notes 4.6 has functionality that lets you do group Calendaring and Scheduling (C&S) through Notes. (Calendaring and Scheduling are covered in detail in Chapter 9.)

To view your appointments, anniversaries, and events, click the Calendar icon. This displays the Calendar view, shown in Figure 4.8, so that you can see and edit your calendar.

FIG. 4.8

The Calendar view in the mailbox database.

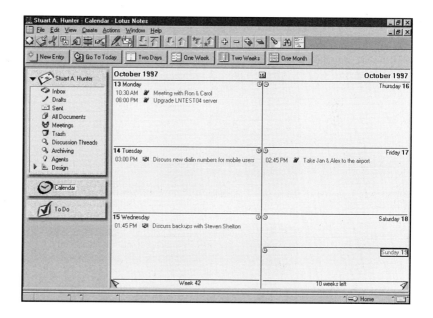

Part

I

Ch

4

Viewing To Do Documents   To Do documents let you keep track of tasks you need to perform, as well as assign tasks to other NotesMail users. To view your To Dos, click the To Do icon, which launches a folder displaying only your To Dos sorted and categorized by their status (see Figure 4.9).

Viewing Your Meetings   Another feature of the Notes 4.6 mailbox is the Meetings view, which at a glance shows you all your scheduled meetings. Figure 4.10 shows the Meetings view with several meetings scheduled.

Viewing All Documents   To see all the documents in your mailbox regardless of the folder they are in, you can click the All Documents icon. This launches a view of all the documents in the database, regardless of their status, as shown in Figure 4.11. This view is sorted on the Date column. However, you can click the arrows on the Who and Date columns to change the sort order.

FIG. 4.9

The To Do folder sorts and categorizes tasks by status.

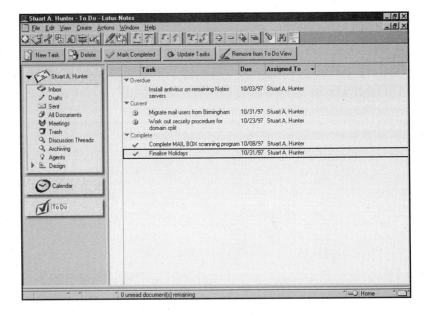

FIG. 4.10

The Meetings view in the Notes 4.6 mailbox.

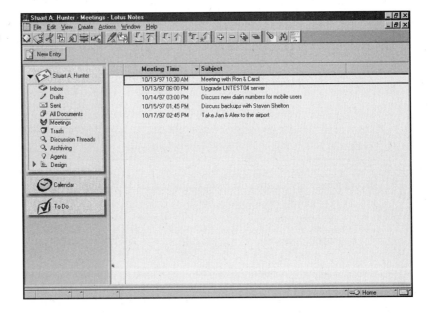

Viewing Deleted Messages (Trash)   Documents in the Trash folder are marked for deletion but are not yet deleted. To see the documents you have chosen to delete from your mailbox, click the Trash icon, which displays your trash folder (see Figure 4.12). If you see documents in the trash folder that you don't want to delete, you can move them to another folder (using drag and drop) to prevent them from being deleted, or click the Remove From Trash button.

FIG. 4.11

The All Documents view in the mailbox.

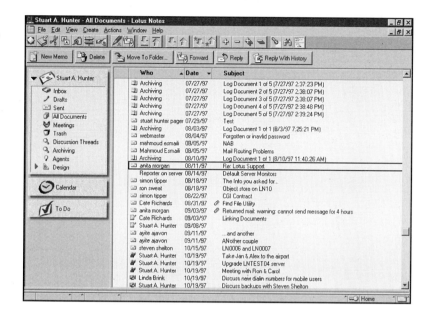

FIG. 4.12

The Trash (deleted mail) folder in the mailbox.

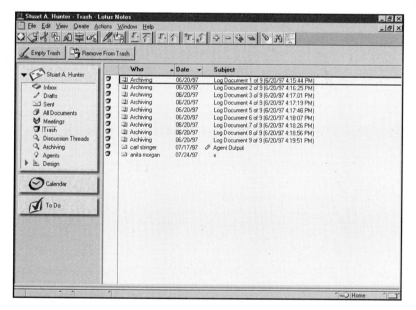

Navigating the Mailbox   In addition to the special views and folders in the mailbox, you can add private views and folders help to organize your mailbox.

For instance, you can expand the Folder and Views icon by clicking it. This displays a list of other views and folders in the database. In Figure 4.13, you can see several other views in your mailbox, each one represented by a yellow magnifying glass. Folders are represented by a file folder.

FIG. 4.13

An open folder in the mailbox.

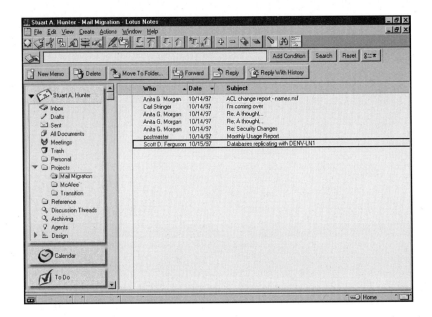

These other views and folders are covered in detail in Chapter 6, "Advanced Mail." The currently selected folder in Figure 4.13 is represented by an open blue folder, and its title is displayed in the window title.

You might also be able to access other views by pulling down the View menu and selecting the specific view you're interested in. (This option can be disabled by a designer.)

N O T E   Although the figures used here are black-and-white, this book refers to the colors used in the views so that you can identify them on your screen. ▪

Mail messages in your mailbox are displayed in the view pane. (Remember that mail messages are just specialized Notes documents. The terms *mail message* and *document* are frequently used interchangeably.)

Each column in the view pane displays either a field in a mail message or some computed value. Each row represents an individual mail message or document.

In some of the folders and views in the standard mailbox, the displayed documents are categorized. This means that documents that have the same category are grouped and displayed beneath the category (which is displayed as a separate row) in the view pane. Figure 4.14 shows the Discussion Threads view, where the indented Subject column makes it easy to follow a discussion. The following are several columns that display data from each mail message in the mailbox:

■ The leftmost column in the view pane is a special feature of Notes views and folders. It is called the Marker column, and it's separated from the other columns in the view by a thin, gray, vertical line that extends the length of the view.

This column shows a variety of system information. For instance, if you delete a mail message, you see a small blue trash can icon in this column. If you haven't read a mail message, an asterisk is displayed, and the row text is red. For example, the three messages near the bottom of the view in Figure 4.14 have a red asterisk in the Marker column.

N O T E The various icons that are displayed in these views and folders, as well as the colors that indicate different parts of the view or folder, are set by the designer. So your mailbox might look somewhat different from the figures shown here. ■

■ The first column to the right of the Marker column, the Who column, shows the name of the user who sent you the message. This column always shows a value, because Notes mail messages automatically "stamp" the sender's name into the message in the From field.

In the Who column heading, you should see an up arrow, indicating that the column can be sorted in ascending order. By default, the mail messages in this view are sorted by the date the message was sent.

■ The second column, Date, shows the date the mail message was sent. Notes automatically date/time stamps all email messages. You'll see a down arrow in the column heading, telling you that you can resort the Date column in descending order.

■ The third and final column, Subject, shows the subject of the mail message. A subject isn't necessary in an email message, so this column might be blank. (Still, email etiquette dictates that you should always enter a subject in your mail messages.) In addition, if the mail has any file attachments, this column also shows a paper clip icon to the left of the subject text.

N O T E Notes allows you to place a copy of a file inside any rich text field on any document. Once a file has been attached to a mail message, it can be transferred along with the mail message to all the intended recipients. They can then detach the file and work with its contents. (The section "Working with File Attachments" in Chapter 6 covers file attachments in more detail.) ■

Reading Incoming Mail

To access the data in a mail message, you must, at a minimum, select the document in a view or folder. Selecting mail messages is just like selecting documents in a regular Notes database. Choose the view or folder that is most useful, and navigate to the message you want.

For instance, to reply to a message your boss sent you today, the Inbox folder or the All Documents view would probably be the most helpful. When you have found and selected the message from your boss (put the selection bar on that document), you are ready to read the mail message and create a reply.

Part

I

Ch

4

FIG. 4.14
In the Discussion Threads view, note the sortable Who and Date columns.

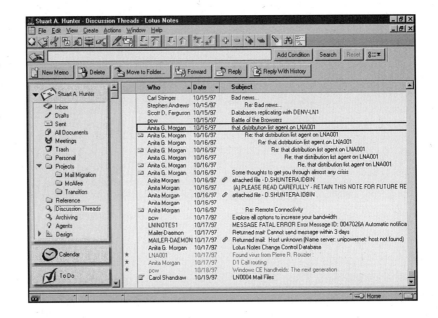

 T I P To save time, you might want to read only new mail messages. There are a couple of ways to do this. The first and easiest is to open the Inbox folder and select View, Show, Unread Only to display only the new mail messages (see Figure 4.15).

FIG. 4.15
The View menu options to show only unread mail messages.

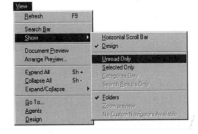

Alternatively, you can choose the All Documents view in the navigator (or select View, All Documents) and then select View, Show, Unread Only. When you select a mail message to read, you can allow the preview pane to scan the contents without opening the message. Or you can double-click the message to open it in read mode.

Figure 4.16 shows a sample mail message. Notice that the format of the standard Notes mail message, called a *memo,* is somewhat like an interoffice memo or standard business letter.

FIG. 4.16

The Memo form shown in edit mode.

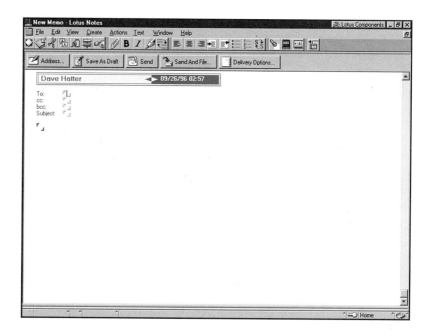

The first four lines (often called the *envelope*) provide the addressing information and the subject of the message. The parts of the envelope are as follows:

■ The To field displays the names of the primary recipients of the message. If you are reading a message you received, obviously your name appears in this field. If other names also appear in the To field, those people also got the message.

 TIP When you address a Notes mail message, you can select individual user names, group names (lists of users), or database names. In most cases, you send mail to users or groups. This is covered in more depth in Chapter 5.

■ The cc field displays the names of secondary recipients to whom the mail was sent. (cc is an abbreviation for carbon copy, a holdover from the days when carbon paper was used to make copies. Some things just never die!)

■ The bcc field displays the name or names of other recipients to whom the mail was sent. If you send a mail message with names in the bcc field, the recipients in the To and cc fields don't know that the people in the bcc field also received the mail. (bcc is an abbreviation for blind carbon copy.)

■ The From line (the colored bar at the very top of the envelope area) indicates the user name of the sender of the mail message. The name in this field is automatically generated by Notes, based on the user ID in use when a mail message is composed. In addition, the date and time the mail message was sent are normally displayed in this bar.

Part

I

Ch

4

■ The Subject line briefly tells you what the mail message is about. Although a subject isn't required, when you send a message to another user, it's common courtesy (and good Netiquette, geek slang for Internet etiquette) to include a subject so that the user has an idea of what the message is about before opening it.

The envelope is followed by the text of the message, commonly called the *body*. The body of a NotesMail message can be any length and can hold embedded objects such as pictures, sound, charts, and so on. It can also have file attachments. You'll learn about these other features in Chapter 6.

N O T E The body field in a NotesMail message is a special field called a rich text field. You learn more about the powerful features of rich text fields in Chapter 3, "Using Databases," and in Chapter 11, "Designing Forms." ■

Moving Your Messages   One of the best features of NotesMail is the ability to create folders. This allows you to organize your mail based on criteria that you set.

For example, you might create a folder named Accounting to store all correspondence from the Accounting department and a folder named HR to store all mail messages about Human Resources. Once you have created a folder, you can move mail messages into it.

To move a message into or out of a folder, you can click the message you want to move. This should make the mouse pointer display a piece of paper with one edge folded down and a plus (+) symbol above it.

You can drag it to another folder (hold down the left mouse button and move the mouse pointer over another folder) and drop it (release the mouse button). You can't drag a message to a view, only to a folder.

If you drag the message to a view, the mouse pointer changes to a circle and diagonal line (the international symbol for no), which means you can't do that.

T I P Remember that you can use the Marker column to select multiple mail messages and move them all at once.

Alternatively, you can choose Actions, Move to Folder or click the Move to Folder button on the Action Bar to display the Move To Folder dialog box, shown in Figure 4.17.

FIG. 4.17
The Move To Folder
dialog box.

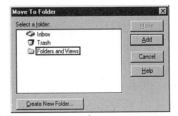

You can then select a folder to move the document into and click the Move button to move the document into the folder. You can also create a new folder from this dialog box by clicking the Add button.

Mail Notification   Most people want to know that they have new mail as soon as possible. By default, when new mail arrives in your mailbox, Notes plays a short tune to indicate that you have new mail.

You can also set a user preference that causes Notes to display a small dialog box with a visual notification of new mail. (For more information on user preferences, see Chapter 2, "Customizing Notes.")

In addition, on the status bar in the lower-right corner is an icon that gives you visual cues about new mail. A small dimmed envelope is displayed when you have no unread mail messages in your mailbox. If an inbox with a piece of paper is displayed, you have unread (possibly new) mail messages in your mailbox.

 To quickly access your new mail, click the Inbox icon in the lower-right corner of the status bar and choose Scan Unread Mail from the list.

Like most things in Notes, you can control how often Notes checks for mail and if Notes should signal you audibly and/or visually when new mail arrives. If you disable these notification features, you need to check your mailbox from time to time to see if you have new mail. In Chapter 2, you'll learn how to edit the default settings for mail notification and scanning.

To take advantage of the new mail notification features, you must leave Notes running constantly on your workstation, even if you are using other applications. You can minimize Notes if you need to run other applications.

Ending your Notes session prevents you from getting mail notifications but doesn't stop you from getting mail. If Notes is minimized and you get new mail, the Notes icon displays an envelope in addition to its usual graphic.

Understanding the Mailbox Icons

To make the NotesMail interface more intuitive, Lotus has utilized small icons displayed in the mail folders and views. At a glance, you can identify certain kinds of messages and items with an icon. Table 4.1 describes the most common icons you will see in your mailbox.

Table 4.1   Common NotesMail Graphics

Icon	Description	Location
Yellow envelope	Sent mail of Normal or Low importance	View or Folder column
Red envelope	Sent mail of High importance	View or Folder column

continues

Table 4.1 Continued

Icon	Description	Location
Paper and pencil	Draft (unsent mail message)	View or Folder column
Paper clip	Attachment	View or Folder column
Torn sheet of paper	Truncated document	View or Folder column
Trash can	Deleted message	View Marker column
Asterisk	Unread mail	View Marker column
Checkmark	Selected document	View Marker column
One piece of paper	Stationery	View or Folder column

Creating Outgoing Mail

The Notes email system is flexible and offers several different kinds of mail messages that you can send and receive. To send a mail message, choose Create. This displays a menu listing all the forms available in your mailbox.

Figure 4.18 shows the default forms available in the standard mailbox.

FIG. 4.18

The Create menu in the mailbox.

Each of the default forms in the mailbox provides a function. Let's look at the most common and useful forms.

The Memo form is the standard form. You use it to send mail messages to other users. To create a new memo, choose Create, Memo. A new memo, like the one shown in Figure 4.19, is displayed.

At the top of the Memo form is the envelope section. You can begin to address the message. Notes supplies the user ID in use at the workstation (this should be your user name if you're sending mail) and the current date and time in this section.

FIG. 4.19

A new memo in edit mode, ready to be completed and sent.

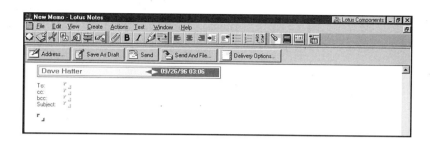

Addressing the Mail

You use the first editable field, To, to list the primary recipient of this message. If you know the recipient's exact user name, you can type it in.

N O T E Each Notes user must have an account and a Notes ID file with that Notes user name and password (among other information). Notes keeps a directory of each user name for security purposes and to identify users to the mail system.

The Public Address Book is the repository of all user information, and it plays a critical role in the Notes email system. Chapter 5 covers the Public Address Book in detail.

For example, if you want to send a mail message to Bob Dole, you could enter Bob Dole in the To field.

The Memo form has a handy feature: You can type the first few characters of a user's name in any of the address fields (To, cc, bcc), and Notes looks up the user's name in the Address Book.

If a match is found, Notes completes the name for you. If a match is not found, the status bar displays a message that the name was not found in the Address Book.

To send the message to several people, you can enter multiple names, separated by commas. Figure 4.20 shows an example of multiple recipients on a memo.

FIG. 4.20

A new memo with several (primary) recipients in the To field.

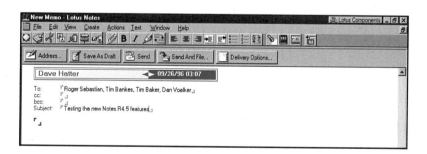

T I P You can also list each name on a new line by pressing Enter after each name but the last. Each time you press Enter, Notes provides additional room for the next name.

When you have added the names of all of the primary recipients, you can press the Tab key to move to the cc field (or click the cc field). To send a copy of this message to other users, you enter those names in this field.

For example, if you want to send mail to Roger Sebastian but want Rick Flagg and Chris Clark to get a copy, you put Roger Sebastian in the To field, and Rick and Chris in the cc field (see Figure 4.21).

FIG. 4.21

A new memo with both To and cc recipients specified.

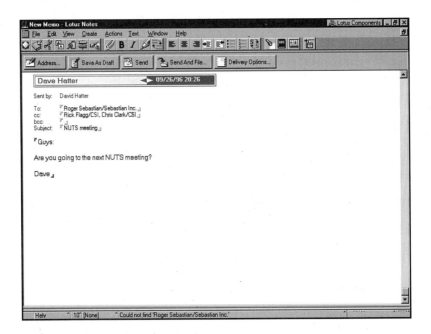

All three of these users will get the mail, just as if you had included them all in the To field. However, by putting Roger in the To field and Rick and Chris in the cc field, you are indicating to Roger that the mail is primarily for him but that you also sent the information to other users. By copying Rick and Chris, you let them know what you sent to Roger.

In some cases, you might not want the primary recipient or recipients to know that you have sent a copy of the mail to another person. If so, you can use the bcc field to send a copy of the message to other users, but the recipients named in the To and cc fields aren't notified that a copy was sent to someone else.

Figure 4.22 shows a message that is sent to Roger Sebastian, carbon-copied to Rick Flagg and Chris Clark, and blind carbon-copied to Tim Bankes.

The message sent to Roger Sebastian and the copy sent to Rick and Chris will not display the bcc field showing that Tim Bankes also received a copy. So unless Tim spills the beans, he'll be the surprise guest I'll bring to lunch on the 16th.

FIG. 4.22

A new memo with To, cc, and bcc recipients specified.

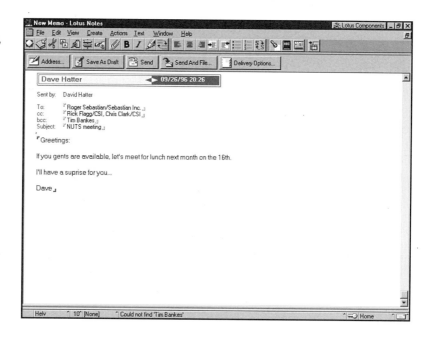

In addition to typing names into the address fields or using the dynamic lookup capability of the New Memo form, you can click the Address button on the Action Bar to display the Mail Address dialog box. This allows you to choose recipients directly from the Address Book (see Figure 4.23).

FIG. 4.23

The Mail Address dialog box.

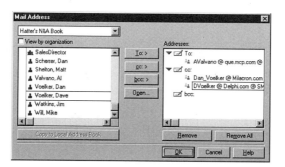

Notes is smart enough to remember the last Address Book you used in the dialog box and chooses it automatically each time you open this dialog box. To select a different Address Book, click the down arrow to display the list of Address Books you can see from your workstation.

The Address Book drop-down box selects your Personal Address Book if you are configured for workstation-based mail and the Public Address Book if you are using server-based mail. Which Address Books you can access depends on your Notes network, the configuration of your local machine, and the access levels you have been granted by your administrator.

Part

I

Ch

4

When you select an Address Book, the list box below the Address Book drop-down box displays all the users and groups in that Address Book.

A user is an individual Notes user, whereas a group is a collection of Notes users who can be addressed as one entity. Notes supplies the individual address of each person in the group and places each individual name in the field.

When you use the Mail Address dialog box, users are indicated by a small purple icon that looks like a person, and groups are indicated by a small multicolored icon that looks like a group of people. This is covered in more detail in Chapter 5.

You can use the mouse to scroll through this list to find the user or group you want to send a message to, or you can type the first character of the user or group name you are searching for. Notes searches the list to find the first entry that begins with the character(s) you entered.

For instance, to find Roger Sebastian in the list, you could type S. Notes would move the selection bar to the first item in the list that begins with S—in this case, Roger Sebastian. This feature is particularly helpful when you are dealing with a large list of users and groups.

You can also select more than one user or group from the list. This works much like selecting multiple messages from a view or folder. Just click in the small empty column (View Marker column) next to each name in the list, and a small checkmark appears, indicating that you have selected that user or group.

On the right side of this dialog box, you see another list box called Addresses. This list box displays small envelope icons representing each of the address fields. If any users or groups have been assigned to a particular field, they are displayed beneath the icon representing that field.

For example, in Figure 4.23, you can see that Al Valvano has been assigned to the To field. As with a view or folder, you can collapse or expand these lists by clicking the twisties to save space.

To add a user or group to the distribution list, select the user or group from the list of Address Book entries. Click the button that corresponds to the address field you want to place this user name in.

For example, to add Mojo Nixon to the To field, you can choose Mojo from the list and click the To button. The Addresses list box immediately reflects the new item.

If you make a wrong entry, click the entry you want to remove from the Addresses list and click the Remove button. If you want to delete every entry in the Addresses list, click the Remove All button.

TIP In large companies, there might be several users with similar names. When using the Mail Address dialog box, if you can't distinguish one user from another, or you need more information about a particular user, click the Open button to open the selected user's person document. This should give you the information you need about a specific Notes user. This also applies to group documents.

The Copy to Local Address Book button allows you to copy group and user documents from the Public Address Book and add them to your local Address Book. This is particularly useful if you are a mobile user. It allows you to address mail from your Personal Address Book, eliminating the need to know the exact address or to carry around a full replica of the Public Address Book, which can get quite large.

Just select the entry you want to transfer, and click the Copy to Local Address Book button. When you finish addressing the mail, click the OK button to update the mail message with the addresses. To discard your changes, click the Cancel button.

Specifying the Subject

When you have entered the address information, you can tab to the Subject field. This field allows you to enter a brief description of the contents of the message. It is displayed in all the default mail views and folders (see Figure 4.24).

FIG. 4.24

The new memo form with a completed subject.

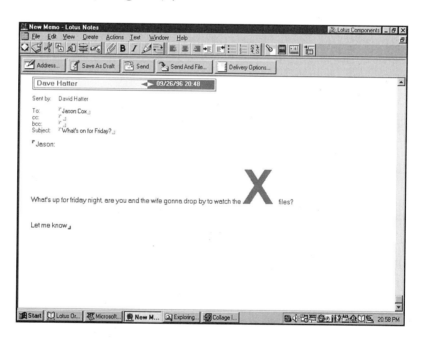

Because the subject is the first thing the user sees regarding your message contents, it should be as explicit and concise as possible.

▶ **See** "Email Etiquette," **p. 168**

Creating the Body of the Message

After you enter the address information and a brief subject, you are ready to enter your actual message, called the *body*. Although this field looks small, you can enter just about as much text as you like; this is a rich text field.

You can also embed objects from other applications, such as a 1-2-3 spreadsheet, or include file attachments. Figure 4.25 shows the completed mail memo, ready to send.

▶ **See** "Working with File Attachments," **p. 215**

 T I P Don't forget to use the integrated spell checker to make sure you don't have any spelling errors. When you are ready to spell-check your message, choose **E**dit, Check **S**pelling or use the Edit Check Spelling SmartIcon.

Delivery Options

Once you have completed your memo, you might want to control certain aspects of its delivery before finally sending it.

FIG. 4.25
A completed memo with file attachments, ready to be sent.

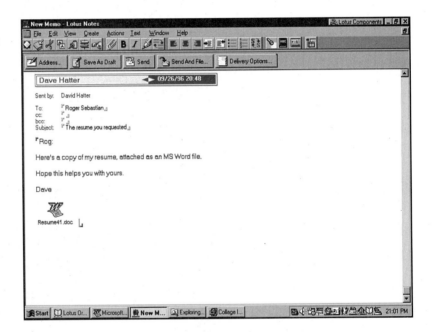

To examine or change these options, click the Delivery Options button on the Action Bar at the top of the form. The Delivery Options button launches the Delivery Options dialog box, shown in Figure 4.26.

FIG. 4.26
The Delivery Options dialog box.

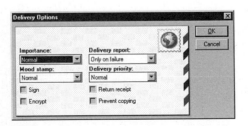

N O T E Think back, way back, to Chapter 3 and the explanation of layout regions. The Delivery Options dialog box is an example of the effective use of layout regions and dialog boxes to enhance an application both functionally and visually.

Choosing a Mood You can use the Mood stamp drop-down list to select a mood for your mail. A mood conveys a certain tone to your recipients, minimizing the facelessness problem discussed earlier in this chapter.

The default mood is Normal, which indicates a neutral tone. You can also select one of any of the following moods. Doing so inserts a graphic image between the envelope and the body to represent the tone:

 Confidential tells the recipients that they should not share this information with others.

 Flame indicates that you are angry about something.

 FYI means that this mail message is For Your Information only, and that no action is needed.

 Personal indicates that the mail is of a personal nature and should not be shared with others.

 Private is like confidential; the information in the message is for the distribution list only.

 Thank You tells the recipients that you are showing your appreciation for something.

 Good Job lets the recipients know that they are being commended for a job well done.

 Joke gives the message a light tone.

 Question tells the recipients that the message is a question that they need to answer.

 Reminder indicates to the recipients that they should not forget to do something. (NotesMail can be a great tool to jog people's memory!)

Generating a Delivery Status Report In most cases, if your mail message can't be delivered to your intended recipients, the Notes server sends you a message that it had a problem delivering the mail message, and it offers a corrective action.

Part I Ch 4

If you send a message and you don't get a Failure Report message, you can assume that your mail message was delivered. For very important messages, you might want to have the Notes server send you a Delivery Report to let you know that your mail was delivered successfully.

The Delivery Report drop-down list has four possible settings: Only on failure, Confirm delivery, Trace entire path, and None. The default setting is Only on failure. This sends a delivery report only if a routing error is encountered.

You can change the setting by typing the first letter of the setting you want (O, C, T, or N). Or you can click the down arrow and choose from the list.

If you change the Delivery Report field to Confirm delivery, in addition to notifying you of the delivery failure, the Notes server notifies you when your mail is delivered. A Delivery Report from the server appears in your mailbox like any other NotesMail message. Figure 4.27 shows a Delivery Report.

FIG. 4.27

A Delivery Report indicating that my mail was delivered to Rick's mailbox.

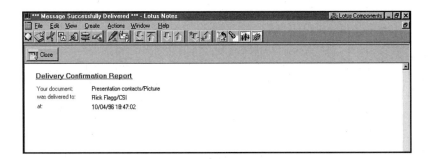

> **N O T E** A Delivery Report doesn't indicate that the mail message recipient read the message. It tells you only that the mail message was successfully delivered to the recipient's mailbox. See the later section "Requesting a Return Receipt." ▪

The Trace entire path setting returns a confirmation message from each hop along the routing path between the sender and the recipient. If you are having trouble sending and receiving mail, this can be a valuable troubleshooting tool, because you can see where the mail died on the routing path. If you communicate only with users on the same server, Trace entire path probably won't be useful.

If you change the Delivery Report field to None, you won't get a notification, even if the delivery fails. Although it isn't often used, this setting can be helpful if you're sending an unimportant message to many people (called *spamming* on the Internet) and you don't care if Notes can't deliver the message to someone. For instance, if you were going to send FYI mail to the whole organization, you might use this option.

Setting the Delivery Priority This drop-down list allows you to choose from the following settings: Low, Normal, and High.

Each of these options has an effect on the speed and cost with which the mail is routed by the server. As you would expect, high-priority mail is fastest, regardless of the cost. Low-priority mail is the slowest and most economical. Normal priority is the default and is sufficient for most mail messages.

If you communicate with other Notes users only via a LAN connection (an ongoing connection to the network) or have only one Notes server, this setting has little effect on the speed or cost of routing.

If you communicate with other Notes users across leased-line or dial-up connections, this setting is more important, because it can have a significant effect on the timeliness of delivery and the cost.

For instance, high-priority mail is routed immediately, regardless of the routing cost. Low-priority mail is sent only between 12:00 a.m. and 6:00 a.m. This is more cost-effective, because connect charges are considerably less during off-peak hours.

Normal mail is routed according to priorities set by the administrator. If you are cost-conscious and the timeliness of the mail is not important, use the Low setting. Conversely, if the mail is important and must be delivered as soon as possible, use the High setting.

▶ **See** "Advanced Connection Settings," **p. 872**

N O T E The Notes server software lets the Notes administrator set up scheduled connections to other Notes servers for routing and replication. As part of this process, the administrator can choose a routing cost to determine the most economical times and paths for mail routing and database replication.

Requesting a Return Receipt   Return receipt is used to indicate that you want to receive a message from the server when the recipient opens the mail message you have sent (see Figure 4.28). This can be useful when you need to be sure that a user has received and read (or at least opened) your mail.

FIG. 4.28

A return receipt indicating that Rick read my mail message.

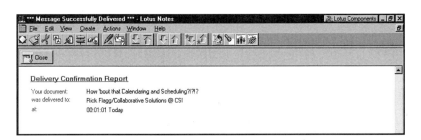

To enable this feature, select the Return receipt checkbox in the Delivery Options dialog box. An x should appear, indicating that it is enabled. To disable this feature, click the checkbox a second time to remove the x.

Many people get irritated when they frequently receive mail that generates a return receipt. It makes them feel pressured to respond to the mail immediately.

A return receipt also uses extra system resources, because a second mail message must be generated, delivered to you, and stored in your mailbox. Although this feature can be useful when necessary, you should use it sparingly.

Encrypting the Message for Security   The Encrypt checkbox lets you encrypt your mail message with the public key of the person you are sending the mail to. This provides additional security: Even if the message is intercepted en route, it can't be deciphered without the recipient's corresponding private key, and this exists solely in the recipient's ID file. If you are corresponding with a Notes user in another domain (or sending mail to an Internet user), that person's public key isn't available to you, and you won't be able to send encrypted mail. If the recipient is another Notes user in another domain, you can ask him to send you a copy of his public key. You can then enter this in a Business Card document in your Personal Address Book (see Chapter 5); you will then be able to send that person encrypted mail.

You'll learn more about encryption in Chapter 22, "Security and Encryption."

Adding an Electronic Signature   The Sign checkbox lets you attach an electronic signature to your mail. An electronic signature is derived from your unique key stored in your Notes ID.

An electronic signature is impossible to duplicate and guarantees that any mail or document signed with your Notes ID came from you (or at least your Notes ID). Electronic signatures are discussed in more detail in Chapter 22.

Electronic signatures and encryption are extremely secure methods for protecting mail messages (or any document, for that matter). But they depend on the physical security of your Notes ID.

Anyone who can access your Notes ID and knows your password can impersonate you! The moral of this story is to keep your ID secure, keep your password to yourself, and change your password frequently.

CAUTION

All Notes encryption keys are based on the Rivest Shamir Adleman (RSA) standard (named for the people who created it). This standard, which creates almost unbreakable encryption codes, needs a public key and a private key. If you encrypt a mail message or document and then lose your Notes ID file or even forget your password, chances are your information will be irretrievable! Use encryption only when security is paramount.

Disallowing the Printing or Copying of Your Mail Messages   Notes' mail interface offers another great security feature, Prevent copying. Simply put a checkmark in the Prevent copying checkbox of the Delivery Options dialog box to enable this feature.

When you enable Prevent copying, recipients of the mail message can't copy the message to the Clipboard, print the message, or forward the message to other users. This helps to ensure that confidential information isn't leaked to others through the NotesMail system.

Sending Your Message

After you select the settings you want, you are ready to save and/or send your mail message. Press Esc to close the message and display the Close Window dialog box, shown in Figure 4.29. You can send the message in the following ways:

- The Send and save a copy radio button tells Notes to send the message and put a copy of it in your mailbox. This is the default for this dialog box, and it's recommended for any mail that you might need to refer back to in the future.

- The Send only radio button tells Notes to send the message but doesn't put a copy of the message in your mailbox. If you're sending mail that you don't need to keep, such as a joke, you can use this option to save space in your mailbox.

- The Save only radio button tells Notes not to send the message but to save a draft in your mailbox. All messages that you save without sending are considered drafts until sent, and you can see them in the Drafts view. This is handy if you don't have time to finish a mail message and you want to come back and work on it later.

- The Discard changes radio button tells Notes to ignore the changes in the message. If you are composing a new message, this option causes it to be neither sent nor saved. If you are editing a message, all edits are discarded, and the saved mail stays the same.

Part

I

Ch

4

FIG. 4.29
The Close Window dialog box for mail messages.

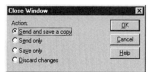

When you have chosen the option you want, click OK. Click Cancel to ignore the option and return to the mail message you are editing. Pressing Esc while this dialog box is displayed is equivalent to clicking Cancel.

 You can also use the Send or the Send And File buttons on the Action Bar to send the mail. To send the mail and store it in your sent folder without saving a copy in your mailbox, click the Send button.

To save a copy into a folder when the mail is sent, click the Send And File button. This sends the mail and launches the Move to Folder dialog box so that you can choose the folder in which to store the mail.

How Notes Validates Mail Recipients

When you try to send mail, Notes compares each of the recipients' names you have entered in the address fields against the user names in your Personal Address Book. If a match is found, the name is validated, and searching stops.

If no match is found, the Public Address Book is searched. If none of the recipient names in your memo matches any of the names in the Address Book, Notes does a soundex search (a search based on items that sound similar) to show you a list of users with similar user names.

For example, if you enter the last name Jones but the user name is Will Jones, Notes finds all the people named Jones and displays them in the Ambiguous Name dialog box, shown in Figure 4.30.

FIG. 4.30

The Ambiguous Name dialog box.

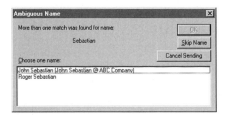

If you see the name of the person you want, double-click it or use the arrow keys to select it and click OK. Notes inserts the correct user name in place of the invalid one.

If you don't see the right name in the dialog box, click the Cancel Sending button and use the Address button on the Action Bar to pull up a list of valid names.

TIP Because the Mail Address dialog box takes its information from the Notes Address Books, using it to address your mail messages can save time and hassle by avoiding invalid user names.

Email Etiquette

Now that you know how to use NotesMail, it's important to know a little about email etiquette so as not to offend your colleagues. The following are some tips and conventions you might want to follow when sending email messages:

- Don't type your messages in ALL UPPERCASE. This is called shouting and annoys people. Always use the proper case unless you want to imply that you are SHOUTING!

- Email is private information, just like the rest of a company's business correspondence, and security is important. You should never send an email message with proprietary or confidential information outside the company without prior approval.

- Email might seem private, but in many cases, a manager can read an employee's email with impunity and without informing the employee. In addition, tape backups are often made of Notes servers, so your mail might be around for a long time. Before you send that juicy love note to your colleague, remember that others could read it.

- Email can be edited and forwarded without the originator's knowledge, unless you use the Prevent copying delivery option when you send your mail.

- Importance and Delivery priority on messages should be set to High only when essential.

- When you need to give constructive criticism or reprimand someone, it's better to do it in person. Email might not convey the tone or message you want.

- People who send frequent or unnecessary messages, or who write dissertations or diatribes, are eventually ignored, like the boy who cried "wolf."

- Subject lines should be brief and should give the recipient some idea of the message's content.

- Email should be read and edited carefully and then spell-checked before you send it. Typos make you look foolish or can convey a misleading or wrong meaning.

- Cute or cryptic use of email shorthand can cause miscommunication. The following lists many of the common email shorthand and emoticons (email shorthand is often enclosed in brackets; for example, <g> means "grin"):

BTW:	By the way
FYI:	For your information
LOL:	Laughing out loud
ROFL:	Rolling on the floor laughing
BRB:	Be right back
IMO:	In my opinion
IMHO:	In my humble opinion
CU:	See you...
PMJI:	Pardon me for jumping in
GD&R:	Grinning, ducking, and running
;-)	Wink
:-)	Smile
:-(	Frown
:-D	Big smile
:-O	Mouth open in amazement
8-)	Smile with glasses

TIP Remember that the body of a NotesMail message is rich text, which means that you can include graphics, sounds, movies, or any other object to help liven up your mail. You aren't limited to using text-based shorthand and emoticons.

Using Other Mail Forms

Your mailbox has several forms other than the Memo that can be useful. After the Memo form, the forms you'll be most likely to use are the Reply form, the Reply with History form, the Task form, and the Phone Message form, all of which are standard in the new NotesMail mailbox.

Replying to a Message

You often get a mail message that needs a reply. You can compose a new memo. But it won't necessarily reference the original message. Notes has a much easier way to create a reply.

You can reply to a mail message with two types of reply forms in your standard mailbox: Reply and Reply with History. You create a reply that references the original mail by selecting the original mail message and choosing Create, Reply or by clicking the Reply button on the Action Bar.

This is a new reply, and the To and Subject fields already have the right values. The To field is set to the user name of the person who sent you the original mail.

The Subject field reflects the subject of the original mail and adds Re: before the subject to indicate that this is a reply. Enter the text of your reply, and send the reply as you would any mail message (see Figure 4.31). When Notes sends the reply, it returns you to the original memo.

FIG. 4.31

A new reply mail message to a mail message from Roger Sebastian.

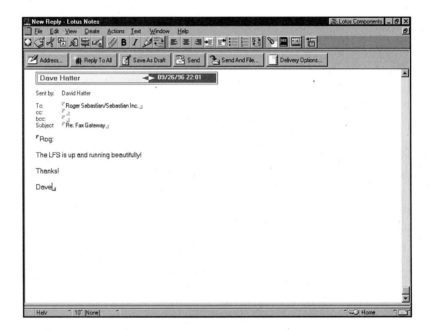

The Reply with History form is almost exactly like the Reply form, except that it copies the body of the original mail message (see Figure 4.32). This means that you can reply to specific points raised in the original mail message, saving the time it would take to retype the information.

FIG. 4.32

A new Reply with History, showing the text of the original message from Rick Flagg.

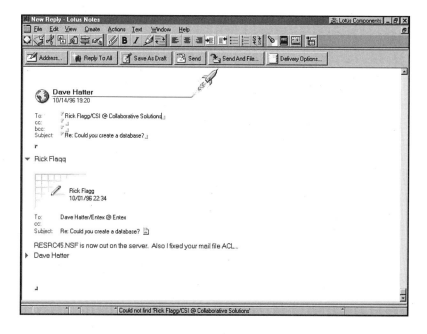

To create a Reply with History message, select the mail message you want to reply to and choose Create, Reply with History or click the Reply with History button on the Action Bar. As in the Reply form, the To and Subject fields are filled in, and the body field holds an exact copy of the original mail message body. Notes also includes a doclink, allowing you to quickly access the original message, creating a thread. You can edit this copy and insert your rebuttals.

Phone Messages

A phone message is a mail message that has a format like a written phone memo pad. If you take a phone call for someone else, you can let her know she has a phone message via Notes mail.

Not only is this faster, but it sets off the new mail indicators in Notes. To send a phone message, choose Create, Special, Phone Message.

Figure 4.33 shows a sample phone message. Your user name appears in the From field, just as it would on a real phone memo pad.

The phone message has additional fields that you can fill in, including Contact and Phone. The message also has check boxes for typical comments such as Telephoned and Please Call.

When you finish the phone message, send it as you would any other mail message.

Part
I

Ch
4

FIG. 4.33

The Phone Message form in your mailbox.

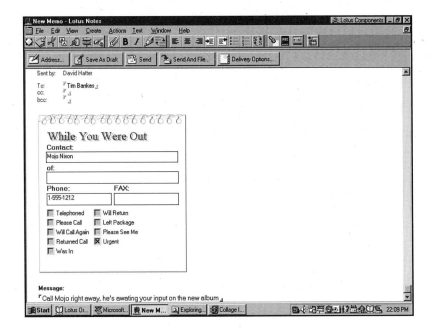

Tasks

In Notes 4.6, Tasks have been separated from the meetings, events, and anniversaries that were all together in Notes 4.5. Tasks appear in your To Do list, which you can access by clicking the To Do icon in the navigator pane. The other form types are now categorized under the Calendar icon. They are discussed in Chapter 9. To compose a new Task, choose Create, Task (see Figure 4.34).

The Task field allows you to enter a textual description of the task that needs to be done. The priority radio buttons can be used to assign a priority to the task so that you or the other assignees know the importance of the task.

None is the default setting for priority. The Start and Due fields let you enter dates to track when a task needs to be done and how many overdue tasks you have.

You can enter other comments in the Additional information field.

To assign the task to others, click the Assign to Others button on the Action Bar. This displays the Assign to and cc fields, which work just like the To and cc fields in the Memo form. Any user or group names entered into these fields cause all the named individuals to get the task via mail.

By default, tasks are not displayed in the Calendar views. If you want to see your tasks in your Calendar, click the Display Task on My Calendar button. This button will then change to Remove From Calendar View, which you can click if you subsequently change your mind.

FIG. 4.34

The Task Form to remind me to turn in my presentation.

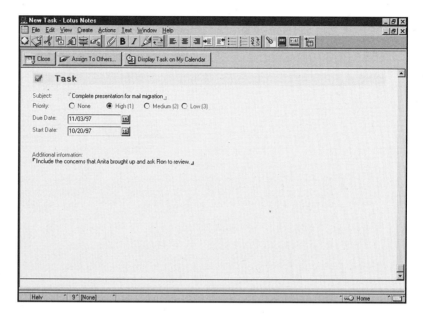

Bookmarks

Bookmarks are another incredibly useful feature of the Mailbox design. A bookmark is a customized mail message that lets you automatically create a doclink to any document.

An example of a typical use of a bookmark is if you're browsing the Technical Support database and you find a document you want to share with your team. You can copy the document into a mail message and send it to everyone on your team.

But this would be redundant, because the document already exists in the Technical Support database. Instead, you could send mail that tells the users where to find the document.

Or you could send them a bookmark. This is a dynamic link to the original document that takes the user there with a single click.

To compose a bookmark, open or select the document you want to link to, and then choose Create, Mail, Special, Bookmark.

A new form that looks like Figure 4.35 is created, with a doclink and some descriptive information that tells the recipients what the doclink points to.

When you compose the bookmark, you add the address information as you would with any other mail form and then send the bookmark. When the recipients get the bookmark, they follow the instructions beside the red arrow and click the link icon to open the linked document.

FIG. 4.35
The Bookmark form lets
you create and mail a
doclink to another
document.

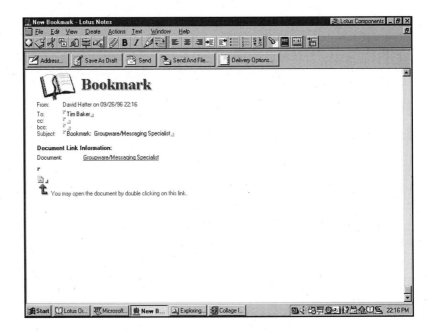

Forwarding a Mail Message

You often receive a mail message that you want to send to other users who weren't included in the original distribution list. To do so, select any mail message and choose _A_ctions, _F_orward, click the Forward button on the Action Bar, or click the Forward SmartIcon.

You see a new Memo form that looks much like a regular memo, except that the body of the memo contains the whole mail message you were reading or had selected (see Figure 4.36). (This is like the Reply with History option, but it doesn't put the sender's address into the To field and doesn't automatically fill in the subject field.)

You can address the message using the steps you saw earlier in this chapter. You can edit the body of the memo if you need to add to or change the original message, or to include additional information with the old message. Send the message as you would any other. You aren't restricted to forwarding only mail messages. You can forward any document that you can access by selecting it in a view or opening it on-screen and choosing _A_ctions, _F_orward, or by clicking the Forward SmartIcon.

You can see from Figure 4.36 that the original mail has been copied into the body of the new mail message and that other text has been added. Forwarding mail messages makes it easy to distribute information to other users.

FIG. 4.36

A message forwarded to Ron Reeves.

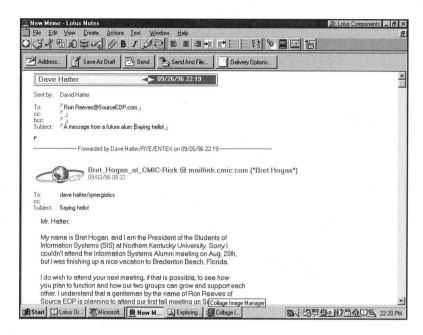

N O T E Remember that unless you enable Prevent Copying in the Delivery Options for your mail messages, any recipient can easily forward your mail messages to any number of other users without your knowledge.

This includes Internet users if the appropriate Message Transfer Agents (MTAs) are in place. A major security breach could result, so keep this in mind when mailing confidential information. ■

Printing Messages

Even though you use your mail electronically 99 percent of the time, you may occasionally want to print a copy of a mail message you have sent or received. Printing a mail message is just like printing any other Notes document.

Here is a reminder for printing documents:

1. Select the message you want to print. (Remember, if you're in a view or folder, you don't have to open the message to print it.) To print the mail message you're reading, proceed to the next step.

2. Choose File, Print, or click the File Print SmartIcon. The File Print dialog box appears. (See Chapter 3 for more information about this dialog box.)

3. Select the appropriate settings for this document in the File Print dialog box.

4. Click OK to print your document.

5. Remember that users can disable the printing capability when they send you a message.

Part

I

Ch

4

Closing Messages

When you are finished reading a mail message, you can close the message and return the folder or view you were in by doing any of the following:

- Press Esc.
- Press Ctrl+F4 or Ctrl+W.
- Click the view or folder window's control menu box and choose <u>C</u>lose. (The control menu box is the small application icon in the upper-left corner of the view or folder window.)

N O T E   You'll see two control menu boxes: one for Notes 4.6 in the upper-left corner, and one for the view or folder window just below the program's control menu box. Make sure you click the view or folder's window. If you inadvertently click the Notes control menu box, you will be prompted to exit Notes.

- Select <u>F</u>ile, <u>C</u>lose.
- Right-double-click the document. This is a holdover from Notes 3.x and might not be enabled for your workstation. See Chapter 2 for more information on how to enable this feature.

Deleting Messages

As you accumulate mail messages in your mailbox, you'll probably decide that you no longer need a number of messages. Unneeded mail messages clutter your mailbox, making it harder to find the important messages. They also occupy precious disk space and decrease your mailbox's performance.

(If you keep every mail message you get, you'll consume a large amount of disk space, and your administrator will probably call you.)

Consider the following techniques for conserving disk space:

- After you have read an incoming message, delete it unless it has information you really need to keep. Similarly, when you send a message to someone else, don't select the <u>S</u>ave checkbox in the Document Save dialog box unless you really need to keep a copy of the mail message.
- You might often need to keep messages for a long time—for example, if you work in a legal department. You might also need to keep a message or a return receipt message as proof that you responded to a problem.
- You can print the message and delete the electronic copy. You can also move the message to an archive mailbox, which is discussed in the next section.
- Regularly scan your mailbox, at least once a month, for unneeded messages. When you find messages you no longer need, delete them.

■ You might get mail messages with file attachments you don't really need, but you want to save the mail message. Deleting unneeded attachments can conserve significant space, because attachments are also stored in your mailbox.

▶ **See** "Deleting Attachments," **p. 218**

Deleting Mail Messages

Because of the way Notes allocates storage space for databases, your mailbox can eat up inordinate amounts of disk space if you don't delete mail messages frequently. This is important for remote users, because disk space on most notebooks is usually at a premium.

The moral of this story is to delete your unneeded mail frequently. This makes it easier to find mail you need to keep, saves disk space, and increases the performance of your mailbox.

As in any Notes database, to delete mail messages, open your mailbox and choose the view or folder you find most useful for reading mail. Then select the message or messages you want to delete and press the Delete key. Or click the Edit Cut SmartIcon to mark that message for deletion.

Notes doesn't delete the message immediately; it moves it to the trash folder. This is a useful feature, because if you decide you really don't want to delete any of the marked documents, you can rescue them from the trash by opening the trash folder and moving the documents back out.

If you're sure you want to delete the documents in the trash folder, click the Empty Trash button on the Action Bar, press the F9 key, or close the database. Any of these actions displays a dialog box warning you that you are going to permanently delete the documents and asking you to confirm the operation.

You can also delete a message while you're reading it by pressing Delete. Notes flags the message for deletion (using the trash can icon in the View Marker column) and takes you to the next message in your mailbox. This works only when you're reading a message, however. The Delete key has a different effect when you're composing a message.

Part

I

Ch

4

Exiting Your Mailbox

To exit your mailbox, use any of the following methods you learned earlier for closing a database:

■ Press Esc.

■ Press Ctrl+F4 or Ctrl+W.

■ Double-click the control box for your mailbox view.

■ Right-double-click (it doesn't matter what the mouse is pointing at). This method works only if the right mouse button option is enabled as a user preference on your workstation.

As with any database, if you have flagged messages for deletion, Notes asks if you want to permanently delete them. If you click Yes, the messages you have flagged are deleted permanently from your mailbox. If you click No, the messages stay in your mailbox, and the deletion flags remain.

Handling Your Mail with the Status Bar and SmartIcons

As you probably know by now, Notes provides many ways to do the same task, particularly for email. One of the most useful features is the mail section in the far-right corner of the status bar.

When a dimmed envelope icon is displayed, you have no new mail. When new mail is transferred to your mailbox, an inbox with a piece of paper in it is displayed. Clicking this icon displays the menu shown in Figure 4.37.

FIG. 4.37

You can access the Mailbox feature from the status bar.

Choose one of the following options from this menu:

- You can select the Create Memo option to open your mailbox and create a new blank mail memo, just as if you had chosen Create, Memo in your mailbox.

- Selecting the second option, Scan Unread Mail, opens your mailbox and opens the first unread mail message. You can then navigate between the unread documents until none are left. If no unread mail messages are found, the status bar says There are no unread documents in your mail file.

> **N O T E** When you use this method to read unread documents, you open the documents. This means that Notes no longer considers these messages unread. █

- You can select Receive Mail, the third option, to initiate a server connection and begin replicating your local mailbox with the server copy of your mailbox. Any new mail that is queued at the server mailbox is transferred to your local mailbox. Outgoing mail is not sent.

- The fourth option, Send Outgoing Mail, initiates a server connection and routes pending mail from your workstation to the server's mailbox. Incoming mail is not received.

- The fifth option, Send & Receive Mail, performs the actions of both Receive Mail and Send Outgoing Mail.

- The sixth and final option, Open Mail, opens your mailbox and displays the last view or folder you used.

When you open your mailbox, in addition to the status bar, Notes provides a context-sensitive set of NotesMail SmartIcons that can make your NotesMail sessions easier and more productive. Table 4.2 shows each of the default NotesMail SmartIcons and describes their functions.

Table 4.2   The Default NotesMail SmartIcons

Icon	Name	Description
	Actions Edit Document	Opens the currently selected document in edit mode.
	Actions Forward	Forwards the currently selected document.
	Navigate Next Main	Goes to the next Main document in the current view or folder.
	Navigate Previous Main	Goes to the previous Main document in the current view or folder.
	Navigate Next	Goes to the next document in the current view or folder.
	Navigate Previous	Goes to the previous document in the current view or folder.
	Navigate Next Unread	Goes to the next unread document in the current view or folder.
	Navigate Previous Unread	Goes to the previous unread document in the current view or folder.
	View Expand	Expands the current category.
	View Collapse	Collapses the current category.
	View Expand All	Expands the whole view (All Categories).
	View Collapse All	Collapses the whole view (All Categories).
	Edit Find Next	Launches the Search dialog box.
	View Show/Hide Search Bar	Toggles the full text search bar off and on.
	View Show/Hide Preview Pane	Toggles the document preview pane off and on.

Part

I

Ch

4

Using the Notes Address Books

In this chapter

Chapter 2, "Customizing Notes," briefly discussed the Public and Personal Address Book databases and how important they are to Notes' operation. In Chapter 3, "Using Databases," you learned how to address mail by choosing the names of users and groups from the Public Address Book. This chapter examines the Personal and Public Address Books in more detail.

Understanding the Personal Address Book

Figure 5.1 shows a Public Address Book icon for Acme Company and a Personal Address Book icon for Stuart Hunter. At first glance, the Personal Address Book and the Public Address Book seem very similar in form and function, but they are actually quite different in supporting the enhanced functionality of Notes 4.6. In version 3.x of Notes, the design of the Public Address Book and the Personal Address Book was the same, despite the fact that the user would never need to create server or domain documents. The design split in Notes 4, with separate design templates for the Public Address Book and the Personal Address Book. This has been taken further in Notes 4.6, where the differences are much greater.

FIG. 5.1
The Public and Personal Address Book icons.

The Personal Address Book database is created on each user's workstation when the Notes client software is installed. It is essentially a directory service that you can use to store information that pertains only to you and your workstation. For instance, if you frequently send mail to a Notes user in another company, but no one else in your organization needs that e-mail address, you should store the address in your Personal Address Book. The Personal Address Book is very useful for mobile users, because it can be used in mail addressing. If you are a mobile user, it might be impractical to carry around the Public Address Book from your domain if it is very large. Instead, you can copy the Person documents of people you intend to e-mail from the Public Address Book and paste them into your Personal Address Book, where they will be displayed with the Business Card form. Alternatively, you can add people to your Personal Address Book from mail you have received by choosing Actions, Mail Tools, Add Sender to Address Book. Having populated your Address Book, you can then edit your Location document so that the Personal Address Book is used for type-ahead mail addressing.

The Personal Address Book also contains details about how you connect to the Notes servers in your domain and rules for governing how that connection should be made, depending on your location.

The Public Address Book has a much more important role and a larger scope than the Personal Address Book. According to the Lotus documentation, the Public Address Book is the "most important database in a domain." In fact, the Public Address Book defines the Notes domain, containing information on users, groups, what servers are out there, who can access them, how they're connected, and how and when replication and mail routing take place. Your Notes administrator uses the Public Address Book as his or her primary tool for controlling the domain.

N O T E In Notes 4.6, the Public Address Book database is based on the StdR4PublicAddressBook template (PUBNAMES.NTF), which contains various forms and views for setting up and managing a domain. The Personal Address Book is based on the StdR4PersonalAddressBook template (PERNAMES.NTF) and contains only forms and views that apply to the workstation.

Figure 5.2 shows the documents you can compose using the Create menu of a standard Personal Address Book. As you can see, the Personal Address Book contains the following types of documents (described in the next sections):

- Business card
- Group
- Location
- Server connection
- Server/certifier

FIG. 5.2
The Create menu in the Personal Address Book.

N O T E The word *standard* is used to describe the design elements, such as views, folders, and forms, in your Address Book as they ship from Lotus. What you actually see might vary from the figures displayed in this chapter, because each of these design elements could be altered by Notes administrators or designers in your organization.

Business Card Documents

The most obvious change in the design of the Notes 4.6 Personal Address Book is that the Company and Person documents have been removed and replaced with Business Card documents. Lotus plans to give the Personal Address Book a more Personal Information Manager (PIM) look and feel, and these changes reinforce that goal. A completed Business Card document is shown in Figure 5.3.

Part
I

Ch
5

FIG. 5.3

A Business Card document for Stuart Hunter.

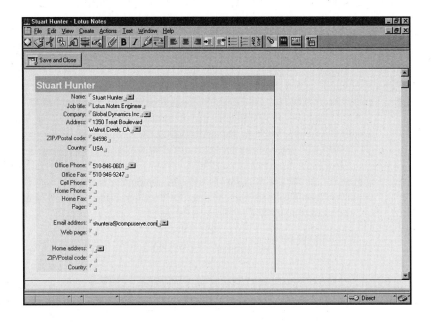

N O T E   If you have used some other application to maintain a list of contacts, you can easily import the list into your Personal Address Book without programming if the software supports exporting data as either an ASCII text file (nearly every software package supports this) or a 1-2-3 spreadsheet. Once you have exported the data, the steps you follow next will depend on the type of file format you chose when you exported the data and which fields you want to import from your old PIM into Notes. To learn more about importing data into Notes, see Chapter 13, "Integrating Notes with Other Applications." ■

You can create a new Business Card document in two ways. First, whenever you receive e-mail from someone not in your Personal Address Book, you can choose to have Notes create a Business Card document for that person. While the e-mail is open on your screen, choose Actions, Mail Tools, Add Sender to Address Book.

Second, you can add Business Card documents manually. From your Personal Address Book's Business Card view, click the action bar's Add Card button or choose Create, Business Card. A blank Business Card form opens.

The usage of this form is very straightforward; you simply fill in information on a person or company that you want to store in your Personal Address Book. In certain fields, Notes will attempt to parse the information you type into appropriate fields. As you type in a name, Notes will attempt to split it into the individual components of Title, First Name, Last Name, and Suffix. Click the entry helper button (the small down-pointing triangle) to the right of the Name field to see how Notes has assigned each component to the correct field. You can then make any necessary corrections. Figure 5.4 shows an example of this.

FIG. 5.4

Notes parses the name you enter into its component parts.

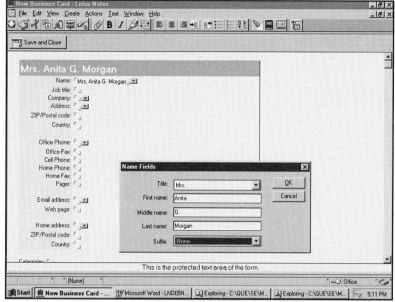

If you're filling in a Company name, Notes will attempt to match what you're typing with the name of a company you have previously entered and fill out the rest of the company name for you. Alternatively, you can click the entry helper to the right of the field and choose from a list of previously entered company names. If you select a previously entered company, Notes will copy the address information from that entry to this new Business Card.

The section of the Business Card document that contains the telephone information is actually dynamic. You can change the field labels to reflect any information you want. Click the ellipsis to the right of the Office Phone field to bring up the Phones dialog box, shown in Figure 5.5. You might not need to record this person's pager number but would instead like to record his or her birthday. Simply edit the label and then enter the birthday on the right.

If you have copied a Person document from the Public Address Book and pasted it into the Personal Address Book, it is displayed in the Business Card form. However, all the fields from the Person document are not immediately visible on the Business Card document. Fields such as Mail Domain, Short Name, and Public Key are stored under the More Info section. Click the twistie to view the information.

If the user is someone with whom you will be corresponding by e-mail, you can enter his or her e-mail address in the Email address field. You can either enter the e-mail address manually or click the ellipsis next to the field to invoke the Mail Address Assistant. The Mail Address Assistant displays a series of dialog boxes that prompt you for the information to form a correct e-mail address for several mail systems. The first dialog box prompts you for the e-mail system that your correspondent uses, as shown in Figure 5.6.

FIG. 5.5
You can change the field labels to show any information you choose.

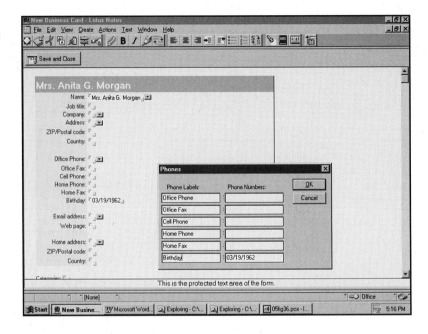

FIG. 5.6
The default value for this field is Notes, but if a user employs another mail system, it can be indicated on this list.

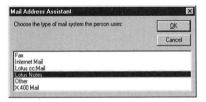

Depending on the selection made in the Mail Address Assistant, you will see one of the following dialog boxes next:

■ The Notes Mail Address Assistant: This feature provides some guidance when you enter a user's name and domain. As you can see in Figure 5.7, the names referring to the user are displayed in the User name field, and the user's domain is displayed in the Notes domain field.

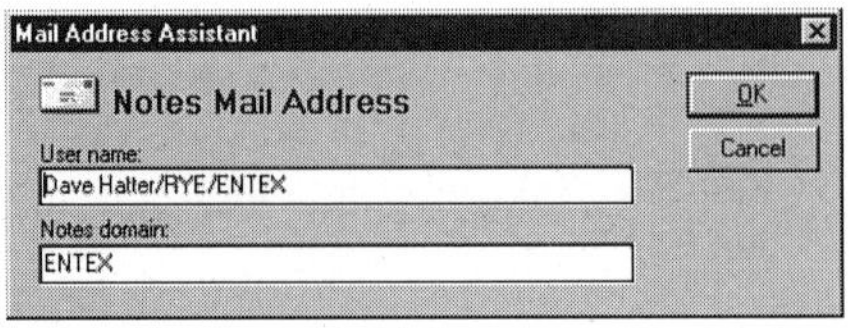

FIG. 5.7
The Notes Mail Address Assistant for Dave Hatter.

N O T E   Once you have entered the user's name, you can press the F9 key to refresh the document; Notes attempts to plug in the e-mail address for you. You will need to check the address to ensure that it is correct. ▦

■ ·The cc:Mail Address Assistant: This dialog box (see Figure 5.8) can be used to guide you when you enter cc:Mail addresses if you need to communicate with someone who uses cc:Mail.

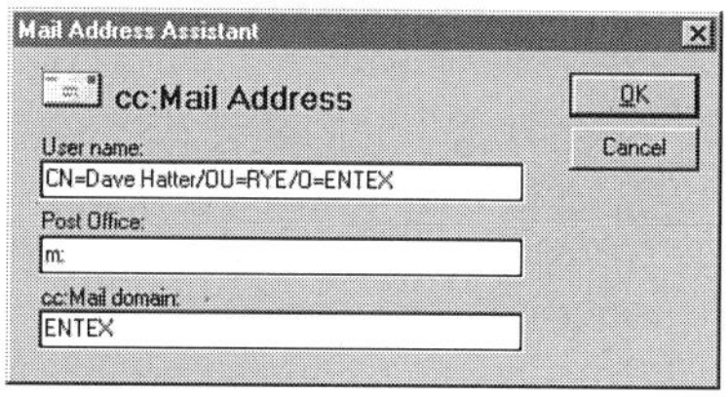

FIG. 5.8

The Notes cc:Mail Address Assistant for Dave Hatter.

■ The Internet Address Helper: As you can see from Figure 5.9, the Internet Address helper guides you when you enter an Internet Mail address. Internet mail capability is now built into the Notes 4.6 server. See Chapter 24, "Lotus Notes and the Web," for more information on connecting Notes to the Internet.)

FIG. 5.9

The Notes Internet Address Assistant for Dave Hatter.

Part

I

Ch

5

The X.400 Address Helper guides you when you enter an address for users who use X.400-compliant mail systems. As you can see from Figure 5.10, X.400 naming can be quite complicated and confusing. In most cases, you won't be able to use X.400 mail unless you have the recipient's business card with the X.400 address on it, or the address has been written out for you, because it's highly unlikely that you could correctly guess it.

The Fax Mail Address Assistant, shown in Figure 5.11, guides you when you enter a fax address. You just enter the user's name, fax number, and the Notes domain that points to your fax gateway. (In order to send a fax through Notes, you need either the Domino Fax Server (DFS) or some third-party fax gateway.)

The last choice, the Other Address Assistant, guides you when you need to enter an address for some other unlisted type of mail system that is connected to Notes through a gateway. As you can see from Figure 5.12, you just enter the user's mail address and the Notes domain that points to the other system.

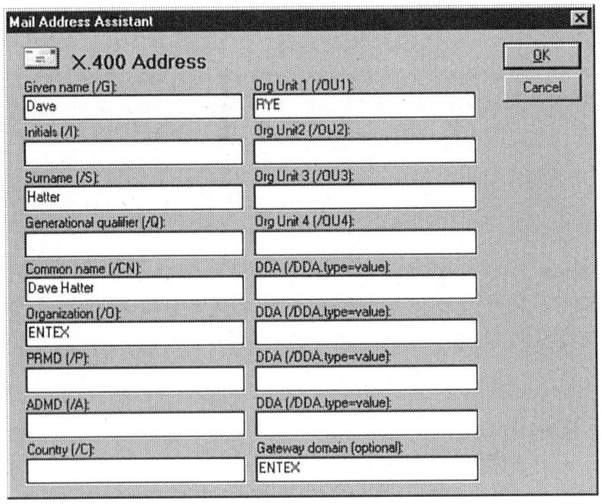

FIG. 5.10

The Notes X.400 Address Assistant for Dave Hatter.

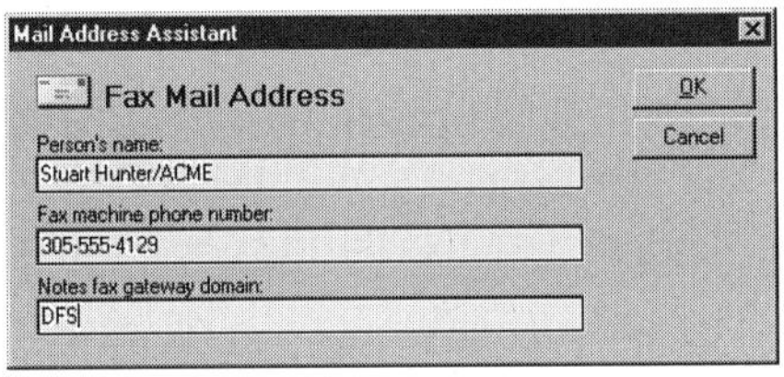

FIG. 5.11

The Fax Mail Address Assistant.

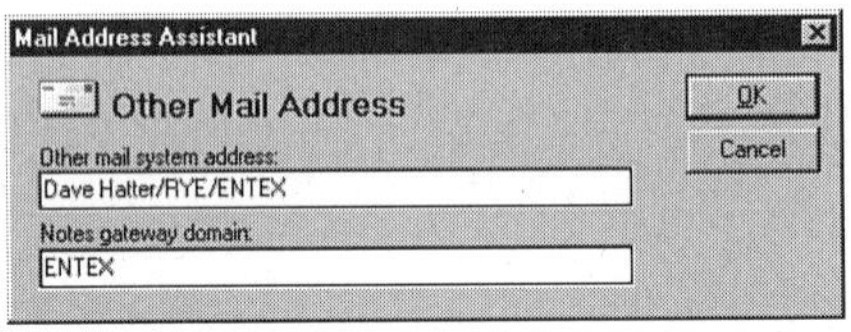

FIG. 5.12

The Notes Other Address Assistant for Dave Hatter.

The Distinguished Name

Each Notes user has a distinguished name that is based on the X.400 naming standard. The name is broken into four components: the Common Name (CN), Organizational Unit (OUN, where N is the number of the organizational unit), Organization (O), and Country (C). The following format is used:

CN/OU1/OU2/OU3/OU4/O/C

Here is an example of a fully distinguished name:

Samuel Hatter/R&D/Tech Services/Help Desk/Notes/ABC Company/US

The following list explains each component in the name:

- Common Name: Each Notes user must have a Common Name, which can be up to 80 characters long. The Common Name is derived from the user's first and last names (and middle name if entered), as displayed in the Person document and stored in the Notes user ID. Examples are Samuel Hatter or Mojo Nixon. In this example, the Common Name is Samuel Hatter.

- Organization: The Organization component of a distinguished user name is typically the name of the company, institution, or organization that is installing Notes, although it can be anything that the administrator chooses to use when the first server is installed. Each Notes user must have an Organization specified as part of his or her fully distinguished name. Some examples are ABC Company and Mojo Nixon Fan Club. In the Samuel Hatter example, ABC Company is the organization component. At this point, Hatter's distinguished name would be Samuel Hatter/ABC Company.

- Organizational Unit: Normally, the Organizational Unit is a department or group name that is added to a distinguished user name to make it unique and to provide additional levels of security within the Notes installation. If two people named Bob Smith worked at ABC Company, for instance, Notes wouldn't know which one you were sending mail to. However, if one worked in the accounting department and the other in the manufacturing department, these department names could be added to their distinguished names as Organizational Units to further qualify each person and grant or deny access at different levels. For example, Bob Smith/Accounting/ABC Company might have access to all accounting-related databases and servers but have no access to the manufacturing-related databases and servers.

  Although Notes users can have up to four Organizational Units in their fully distinguished names, Organizational Units are not required. In the Samuel Hatter example, R&D would be OU1, Tech Services would be OU2, Help Desk would be OU3, and Notes would be OU4. Hatter's fully distinguished name at this point would be Samuel Hatter/R&D/Tech Services/Help Desk/Notes/ABC Company.

- Country: This is a two-letter abbreviation that identifies your country. The country codes are defined by CCITT. (CCITT, the Consultative Committee for International Telephone and Telegraph, is a committee of the International Telecommunications Union, a United Nations treaty organization that studies, recommends, and develops standards for technical and operational telecommunications issues.) This component is optional and is used only when needed to uniquely identify a distinguished name worldwide. In the Samuel Hatter example, US is the country component that would yield the fully distinguished name. Hatter's fully distinguished name at this point would be Samuel Hatter/R&D/Tech Services/Help Desk/Notes/ABC Company/US.

Whenever you send a Notes mail message to another user, the Mailer module uses the address information you have entered to look up the distinguished name from the Address Book. The Router module of the server then uses the distinguished name to route the mail to its recipient(s). If the recipient is another Notes user, the mail will be delivered based on the mail priority and scheduled connections between servers. If the mail recipient is using another supported mail system such as cc:Mail, Internet, or X.400, you must have a connection to the other system for the mail to be routed. In other words, you must have an Internet mail connection for your Internet mail to be routed to the recipient.

Part
I

Ch
5

Group Documents

Group documents are very useful, because they can be used to refer to multiple users, servers, or even other groups, which can save you a significant amount of time when you're addressing mail messages and creating database ACLs. For example, you might need to mail the weekly sales numbers to your entire sales team. Rather than entering each name into the To field in a mail message (or choosing each name from the Address dialog box), just create a group document that references each user, and then reference the Group name in the To field of your mail message. In most cases, you will probably use Group documents that have been set up in the Public Address Book. But if there is no group covering the people you want to collectively mail in the Public Address Book, you can set this up in your Personal Address Book instead. If you think that the new group is likely to be used by more than just you, contact your administrator to ask about creating a new group in the Public Address Book. To add a group, simply choose Create, Group from the Address Book or, from the Groups view, click the Add Group button. If you know at the outset you are creating a Mailing List group, you can click the Add Mailing List button from the Groups view. Figure 5.13 shows the standard Group document in edit mode with the Administration section expanded.

FIG. 5.13
A Multi-Purpose Group in the Personal Address Book.

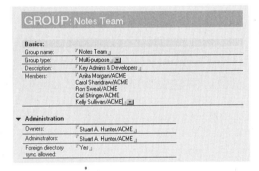

The first section, Basics, contains the fundamental fields needed to define a group—Group name, Group type, Description, and Members. The Administration section contains information that is really irrelevant in a Personal Address Book, such as who created the group (you) and who maintains the group (you again).

Basic Information   You use the Basics fields as follows:

- The Group name field: This field is required, because it is the name that Notes will use to find the group. A Group name might be Widget Sales Team or Accounting. Longer names are recommended, because they are more descriptive and generally more unique (however, if you make a name too long, it will be cumbersome to use).

- The Group type field: This field is a standard keyword list that allows you to determine how a group list will be used (this field is really geared for use in the Public Address Book). For instance, you can indicate that the group should be used only for database ACLs, which means that when you address mail, it won't be seen. You can set a group for use in mail addressing only, which means that it can't be used in ACLs, or you can use a group to deny access, which means that users in a specific group will be denied access to the server. This can also be a multipurpose group, meaning that it can be used for any of these functions. This field is not required and, in most instances, it should be left on the default setting, Multi-purpose.

- The Description field: This is an optional text field that you can use to add more detail to a Group document. For example, you might want to explain the purpose of a particular group so that other users and administrators will understand its purpose.

- The Members field: This is a multivalue list field that is used to name the members of the group. When you reference a group, it is this field that Notes uses to determine who or what is in the group. For a Group document to have any meaning, this field must be populated with the Notes usernames of the members of the group. You can click the down arrow button beside the field to launch the Names dialog box and add users or other groups to the list very quickly. Figure 5.14 displays the Names dialog box, which works exactly like the dialog box that is launched when you click the Address button in a mail Memo form. Simply choose the users or groups you want, and click OK.

FIG. 5.14

The Names dialog box.

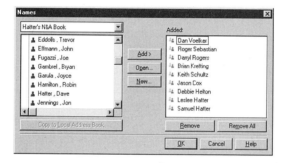

Administrative Information   The Administration section can be expanded and collapsed by clicking the twistie beside the title. Once the section is expanded, the Owners and Administrators fields can be accessed:

- The Owners field can be used to list the user or users who "own" the group. In most cases, this is the person who created the group, and it should be left alone.

- Likewise, the Administrators field can be used to identify the administrator(s) of the group. Again, this is irrelevant in the context of the Personal Address Book. The Group documents found in your Personal Address Book are identical in function and usage to those found in the Public Address Book.

- The Foreign directory sync allowed field determines whether this document can read by gateway products during directory synchronization, but this is irrelevant in the context of the Personal Address Book.

N O T E   Every Address Book, when it's created, has two groups entered by default: LocalDomainServers and OtherDomainServers. These groups are also entered into every database ACL as Manager when a database is created. If each server in your domain is entered in the LocalDomainServers group, the servers will be guaranteed access to the database. This ensures that the server can replicate with the local copies of a database.

Part
I

Ch
5

Location Documents

Location documents are probably the most important documents in the Personal Address Book (certainly the largest and most complex). They are especially important if you're constantly on the move, carrying Notes around with you on a laptop computer. For instance, you might have a Location document for your office connection that enables the LAN port and disables the modem, and a Home location configured to disable the LAN port and dial out to your Notes server by using the modem on COM2.

When the Notes 4.6 workstation software is installed on your workstation, five default Location documents will be created in your Personal Address Book automatically: Office, Internet, Home, Island, and Travel. If you travel to other sites frequently and need to communicate with Notes from those locations, you can create Location documents that match the physical configuration that your PC will need to use to connect at each site.

To create a Location document, simply choose Create, Location or, from the Locations view, click the Add Location button on the Action Bar.

▶ **See** "Setting Up Locations," **p. 858**

Location documents work hand-in-hand with Server Connection documents. Each Server Connection document contains information needed to connect to a server, such as the server's phone number if a dial-up connection is used. When you attempt to communicate with a Notes server, information from Location documents and Server Connection documents is used to make the connection.

The Location documents are used primarily when you work remote. See the section "Setting Up Locations" in Chapter 20, "Setting Up to Go Remote," for details of the settings in the Location document.

N O T E Chapter 20 assumes that you will be working with a dial-up modem. If you will be connected to the Notes server via a LAN, choose Local Area Network in the Location type field of the Location document, which will tell Notes to use the LAN card in your workstation when looking for a Notes server.

If you need to have LAN and dial-up connections available for a given location, select Both Dial-Up and Local Area Network, which will allow you to access your Notes server either way. The last choice, No Connection, can be used if you will have no connection to a Notes server but you want to work with local databases on your workstation. ▦

Understanding the Type-Ahead Feature   The Recipient name lookup field in the Location document can be used to enable and configure the type-ahead feature when you're addressing mail messages. When type-ahead is enabled, Notes will look into the specified Address Books to find a name based on the characters you have entered in the To, cc, or Bcc fields of a message. For example, if you wanted to send a mail message to a user named Ace Frehley/KISS Inc., you could position the cursor in the To field and begin typing the first few characters of the recipient's name. In this example, you could type Ace, and Notes would search the Address Book for the first user who has a name that begins with the characters Ace. It's best to enter enough characters to uniquely identify the name. For instance, it would be better to enter Ace than Ac.

Although this feature can be very handy, it can be time-consuming if your Address Book is very large. If you want to disable this feature when you're sending mail messages, select Disabled in the Recipient name type-ahead field of the Location document. If you want to attempt to fill in the field from your Personal Address Book, which can greatly reduce the lookup overhead, you can select Personal Address Book Only. If you want to have Notes search both your Personal and Public Address Books for recipients' names, select Personal and then Public Address Book. Notes will then look first in your Personal Address Book for a match; if one is not found, it will then search the Public Address Book.

The Recipient name lookup field works in conjunction with the Recipient name type-ahead field. If type-ahead is enabled, you can use the Recipient name lookup field to determine the scope of the search, as follows:

- Stop after first match: This setting tells Notes to stop searching when it finds a match for a user name.
- Exhaustively check all address books: This tells Notes to continue searching all Address Books available from your workstation even after a match has been found. If you have many Notes users in your organization, this option can take some time but might produce more accurate results.

Server Connection Documents

For each server you communicate with, you must have a Server Connection document. These documents are used to provide specific connection information about each server and, as mentioned earlier, they work hand-in-hand with Location documents. In order to create a new Server Connection document, choose Create, Server Connection. However, in most cases, your administrator should be involved in this process, because you might not necessarily know all the information you need to complete the document.

The type of connection you use to access the server determines the specific information needed in the Connection type field. These are described in the following sections.

Dialup Modem   If you dial in to the server via modem, select Dialup Modem. For details on setting up Server Connection documents for remote access, see the section "Setting Up Connections Records" in Chapter 21, "Working Remote." Figure 5.15 shows a Dial-Up Connection document.

Local Area Network   If you access the server over a LAN connection, select Local Area Network. Here you can enter the name of the server you want to connect to, the port over which you connect to the server, and optionally a Destination server address if the server isn't available via DNS or a hosts file. Figure 5.16 shows a Connection document to the Uranus server using TCP/IP where an IP address has been included.

Part
I

Ch
5

FIG. 5.15
A Dial-Up Server Connection document for the Saturn server.

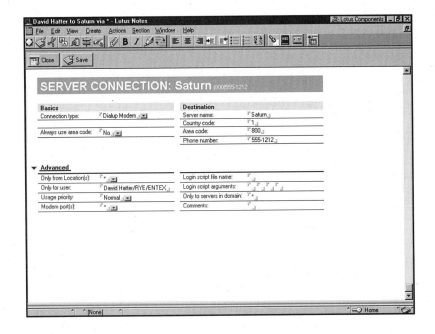

FIG. 5.16
A LAN Server Connection document for the Uranus server.

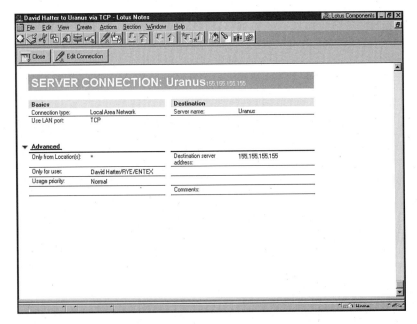

Passthru Server   If you use a Notes passthru server, select the Passthru Server option. You would enter the name of the server you ultimately want to connect to and the name of the passthru server or hunt group that you will pass through to get there. Your administrator controls which servers can be used for passthru, so you might want to call and check. Figure 5.17 shows a Passthru Connection document. You can see that to get to server Pluto, you pass through server Uranus.

FIG. 5.17
A Passthru Server
Connection document
for the Pluto server.

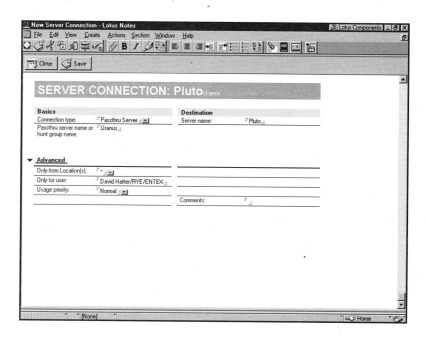

Remote LAN Service　　The Remote LAN Service option should be used only if you will be dialing in to a remote LAN service, such as AT&T Network Notes, to get connected to a server. This is similar to a passthru server. Figure 5.18 shows a Remote LAN Service Connection document to server Mars. The Remote LAN Service field allows you to select the type of remote LAN service you are using. The Remote connection name field is used to give the remote connection a name to help identify this connection when displayed in views. The Login name and Password fields work hand-in-hand to get you logged in to the remote access server via the telephone number you enter in the Phone number field.

> **CAUTION**
>
> Unless you secure your Personal Address Book, someone could access your Remote LAN Service documents and learn your user ID and password for this service. There are two good solutions to protect the confidentiality of your Personal Address Book.
>
> The first method would be to encrypt the entire database, which would allow access only to someone with your ID and Notes password. This method adds some overhead in terms of performance and disk space but is reliable and secure. To use this method, right-click your Personal Address Book and choose Database Properties. You can then use the Encryption button to secure your database.
>
> *continues*

continued

The second method will secure only specific documents. If you want to secure your Remote LAN Service document, right-click that document in a view and then choose Document Properties, which launches the Document Properties InfoBox. Then click the tab that displays a small key. On this tab, you may choose a list of people and groups that can access the document. You can also associate an encryption key with the document, which will protect the contents of your document from prying eyes.

FIG. 5.18

A remote LAN Server Connection document for the Mars server.

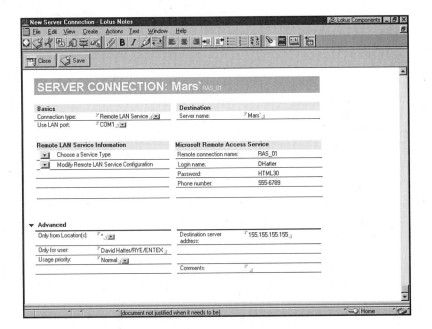

Hunt Groups Hunt Groups allows you to dial a single telephone number and be connected to one of a number of servers for passthru use. In this case, you can't specify a particular server to connect to, so the name of the Hunt group can be anything you like. You can get the telephone number of the Hunt group from your administrator.

All these documents have an Advanced section. The contents of that section vary, depending on the Connection type you have selected. These fields are discussed for mobile users in the section "Advanced Connection Settings" on page 872. For Connection types of Local Area Network or Remote LAN Service, you might want to enter the IP address or host name of the server you want to connect to in the Destination server address field.

Certificate Documents

Your Personal Address Books will also contain Certificate and/or Cross Certificate documents. When you are certified to communicate with a server, you should receive a Certificate or Cross

Certificate document. You must have one in order to be authenticated by the server. A certificate was added to your ID file when it was created. It identifies you to the servers in your organization as being part of the same family, and therefore trustworthy. Barring any other security measures, you should then be able to access those servers. A cross certificate, on the other hand, is issued by another organization. It says that even though you aren't a part of their family, they trust you enough to access their servers. For example, a supplier might issue you a cross certificate so that you can access a product catalog on their Notes server.

▶ **See** "Understanding Certificates," **p. 924**

Understanding the Public Address Book

Although few users utilize the Public Address Book for little more than mail addressing, it is much more than a simple user directory. When the first server in a domain is installed, Notes automatically creates a new Public Address Book database in the Notes\Data directory (the actual filename defaults to NAMES.NSF) from the StdR4PublicAddressBook PUBNAMES.NTF template.

N O T E In Lotus Notes, a *domain* is a group of servers and users who share the same Public Address Book, which controls mail routing. A company that has several locations can have one domain or many domains. The number of domains required is usually determined by security needs and the number of users in each domain. As a domain grows, so does its Public Address Book, which decreases overall system performance, because Address Book searches take longer and consume more disk space. Each user's domain is determined by the server that his or her mailbox resides on. Don't get confused by the preceding sentence if you use workstation-based mail; even though you access your mail messages through a local database, it is merely a replica of your mailbox on the Notes server. ▪

The Public Address Book plays dual roles in every Notes installation. First, it provides Directory Services by acting as a central repository for user, server, and group names that can be accessed for communication with others. It also acts as a server management tool for Notes administrators by providing the Notes server with information on replication schedules, mail routing, automatic tasks, mail-in databases, certificates, and other important system information. Even if you don't use Notes Mail at your company, the Public Address Book must exist in order for the Notes server(s) to operate properly.

Because the Public Address Book plays such a crucial role in every Notes installation, security of the Public Address Book is a very important issue. By default, users have Author access to the Public Address Book in such a way that they can edit their own Person documents but nothing else. You might find that your administrator has restricted that further to Reader access. If you have an occasion to add a document to the Public Address Book—say, a Person or Group document—you will probably need to send a request to your Notes administrator.

In order to make maintenance of the Public Address Book easier and more secure, Lotus automatically adds a number of roles that can be used to refine the ACL and allow users or groups

Part
I

Ch
5

to perform very specific actions on certain types of documents. For example, you can assign Author access to the administrator who needs to certify users and the UserCreator and UserModifier roles to create and edit Person documents. However, the administrator wouldn't be able to create, edit, or delete any of the other documents in the Public Address Book.

Regardless of your access level (even if you have Manager access to the Public Address Book), in order to create a document, you must be named in the appropriate Creator role. The Modifier roles apply only to users who have Author access; users who have Editor, Designer, or Manager access are automatically granted modifier rights. The following list shows the roles available in the Public Address Book:

- GroupCreator allows users or groups named in this role to create new groups, but not to modify or delete them.
- GroupModifier allows users or groups named in this role to edit or delete groups, but not to create them.
- NetCreator allows users or groups to create all documents except Person, Group, and Server documents.
- NetModifier allows users or groups to edit or delete all documents except Person, Group, and Server documents.
- ServerCreator allows users or groups to create Server documents.
- ServerModifier allows users or groups to edit or delete Server documents.
- UserCreator allows users or groups to create Person documents.
- UserModifier allows users or groups to edit or delete Person documents.

Forms within the Public Address Book create documents that fall into two basic categories of services: Directory Services and Server Management.

Directory Services

Each time you send a mail message or open a database on a Notes server, you will come into contact with the directory services aspects of the Address Book. Notes keeps track of users and servers in the Public Address Book. Whenever a mail message is sent, the Notes server looks in the Public Address Book in an attempt to find a document that corresponds to the user, server, or group names listed on the envelope of the mail message. If a match is found, the message can be routed; if no match is found, the server can't route the message.

Likewise, when the user attempts to open a database on a server, the server examines the database's ACL. (Remember, if you're working with a local database, you have Manager access by default.) If a user is listed in a group in the ACL, the server must find that group in the Public Address Book to determine if the user is in the group.

In the Public Address Book, the following four forms fall into the directory services category:

- Person documents
- Server documents (these documents serve both roles—directory services and server management)

- Group documents
- Location documents

These forms are described in the following sections.

Person Documents   Each Notes user in a domain will be identified by a Person document in the Public Address Book.

A Person document is automatically created in the Public Address Book for each user during the new user registration process (which also creates a certified user ID). Certain key fields in the Name and E-Mail sections are populated based on the registration information. If these users will be accessing Notes databases using Domino and the Web, additional fields will be added. For more information on setting up Person documents for Web users, see Chapter 26, "Using Domino Server's HTTP Service."

> **CAUTION**
>
> In most instances, with the exception of your Person document, you won't have sufficient access to the Public Address Book to make changes to any of the documents it contains. It is critically important that you not make changes to any documents in the Public Address Book without first speaking to your Notes administrator, because this can cause a wide variety of serious problems, such as mail not routing. In fact, in almost every instance, you should request that the Notes administrator make any required changes.

Server Documents.   Each server in a domain has a Server document in the Public Address Book that is created automatically when a new server is installed. The Server document identifies the server to the rest of the Notes domain. The administrator uses it to perform many security functions, such as determining who has access to the server and who can create new databases on it. Some of the key fields and sections that might affect you as a user are mentioned here. For guidance on the others, consult the online Domino Administration Help database, usually stored in the DOC directory on your Notes server.

- Server Name field: Contains the server's abbreviated name.
- Administrators field: Contains the name of the person or persons who can administer the server via the Remote Server Console. This means that you can control the server from a workstation rather than by sitting at the server console itself. If you don't know the name of your Notes administrator, it might well be the person(s) listed in this field, although the field might show a group such as Administrators rather than a list of names.
- Server's phone number(s) field: If you are a dialup user, this field might contain the telephone numbers used to connect to the server. If there is no entry, that doesn't mean that you can't dial in to the server—just that your administrator has chosen not to publish the numbers here.
- Network Configuration section: Displays the various communication protocols enabled on the server. You will need to have a protocol in common running on your workstation in order to connect to the server directly (you might be able to reach it indirectly via

passthru if you don't share a common protocol). Note that this section will note whether the X.PC protocol is enabled for dialup use, so don't take its absence as an indicator that there is no dialup for this server.

- Restrictions section: This section is one your administrator pays close attention to. It determines such things as who is allowed to access the server, create new and replica databases, and access the server via passthru.

- Agent Manager section: Determines who can run agents on the server. If you are a developer creating applications with server-based agents, ensure that the administrator has included you in the necessary fields.

Group Documents   Group documents in both the Public and Personal Address Books are identical but tend to be used for different purposes. Whereas in a Private Address Book a Group document is more than likely to be a Mailing List, in the Public Address Book it is equally likely to be an allow or deny access group for use in an ACL to restrict who can access a database.

Location Documents   Much like Group documents, Location documents in both the Public and Personal Address Books are identical and are used in the same way. The primary difference is that Location documents in the Public Address Book are shared among all users in the domain.

The rest of the documents in the Public Address Book generally fall into the Server Management category.

Server Management Documents

The Public Address Book contains the documents that are used almost exclusively by Notes administrators, so they are explained only briefly here. (For a more detailed explanation of the purpose and usage of these documents, refer to the online Domino Administration Help database, usually found in the DOC directory on your server.) Server Management documents include the following:

- Configuration documents: These documents allow the administrator to make fundamental changes to the functionality of the Notes server without having to manually edit the NOTES.INI file. The administrator can make such changes remotely, simply by completing a Notes document.

- Certifiers and Cross Certificate documents: These documents aren't created manually; they are added as the result of the process the administrator undertakes when creating certifiers and cross certificates. Certifier documents are crucial to the security of a Notes installation. For more information, see Chapter 22, "Security and Encryption."

- Domain documents: These documents can be created to allow communication and mail routing to other Notes domains or to foreign domains, such as the Internet. There are two basic types: Foreign Domain documents and Non-Adjacent Domain documents.

Foreign Domain documents are used to define a non-Notes domain, such as a cc:Mail domain, and Non-Adjacent Domain documents are used when you need to communicate with a Notes domain through an intermediary domain. For example, suppose you want to send mail to Ace Frehley in the XYZ domain, but you don't have a connection to that domain. However, you do have a connection to the ABC domain, which communicates with the XYZ domain. A Non-Adjacent Domain document would specify the route to XYZ through ABC.

- Connection documents: These are much like the Connection documents in the Personal Address Book, but rather than defining user-to-server connections, they define server-to-server communication and establish mail-routing and replication schedules.

- Program documents: These can be used to automatically start server tasks, batch programs, or API programs. For example, if you wrote an API program to transfer data from an Access database to a Notes database and you wanted it to run each night, you could create a Program document that would run the program at the specified interval.

- Setup Profile documents: These documents allow the administrator to define a common set of setup elements that can then be applied to multiple users. Profile documents can make adding new users to the system significantly less complicated and time-consuming. For example, if you wanted everyone in a certain OU, such as Accounting, to be configured exactly the same, you could create a Profile document that would let you build a common set of configuration parameters for this group.

- Mail-In Database documents: These documents let the administrator configure a database to receive mail messages. For example, you might have a sales rep on the road compose an expense report form and mail it into a centralized expense report database.

Using Views in the Address Books

Each of the Address Books contains views and folders that can be very useful. Like the documents that each Address Book contains, some of the views overlap and provide the same functionality, but on a different scale. The following sections examine some of the more useful views that exist in the Personal and Public Address Books.

Business Cards View

This view exists only in the Personal Address Book, although documents pasted in from the People view in the Public Address Book will appear here, and they contain a lot of the same information. The Business Cards view, shown in Figure 5.19, is very useful if you want to use Notes as a Personal Information Manager, with the addresses and telephone numbers available onscreen.

Part
I
Ch
5

FIG. 5.19
The Business Cards view in the Personal Address Book.

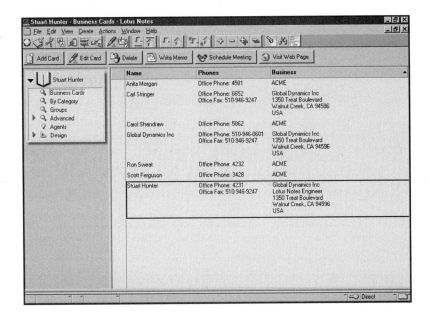

Groups View

The standard Groups view exists in both the Personal and Public Address Books. The Group column displays the name of each group, sorted in ascending order. The next column, Description, displays the group's description if one was entered.

Locations View

The Locations view in the Personal Address Book (cascaded under Advanced) displays all the Location documents that exist in your Personal Address Book, sorted by the first (and only) column, Location (see Figure 5.20). This view also exists in the Public Address Book, where you might find Location documents set up by the administrator that can be copied and pasted to save mobile users from having to create them manually.

People View

This is the view you will probably use most often when you look at the Public Address Book. The People view is very useful, because it displays every Notes user in the domain, as shown in Figure 5.21. The following is the information available in this view:

- The first column, Name, displays the name of the user, sorted in ascending order by last name.

- The next column, Telephone, displays both the office telephone number and the home telephone number if they have been entered.

FIG. 5.20

The Locations view in the Personal Address Book.

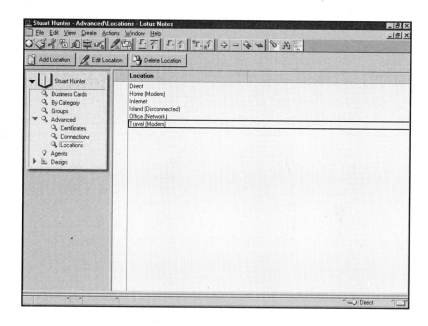

- The Company column is useful if your organization owns several companies or if you have suppliers or contractors stored in the Address Book.

- The last column, E-Mail, is pretty much self-explanatory; it displays the user's e-mail address.

FIG. 5.21

The People view in the Public Address Book.

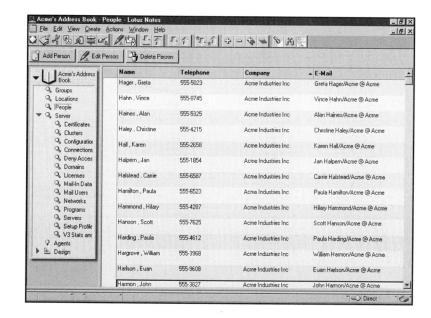

Certificates View

This view is cascaded under Server in the Public Address Book and under Advanced in the Personal Address Book. In the Public Address Book, it displays all the certificates and cross certificates held by the servers in the current domain. This might allow everyone in your domain to be able to communicate with servers in another domain that is a subsidiary of your company. In the Private Address Book, it displays all the certificates and cross certificates you hold. A certificate might have been granted to you so that you are the only one in your company who can access a supplier's Notes server to place an order.

Connections View

This view is cascaded under Server in the Public Address Book and under Advanced in the Personal Address Book. In the Public Address Book, it shows you how each server in your domain communicates with the others, and also how your servers communicate with servers outside your domain. In the Personal Address Book, this view shows you how your workstation connects to other servers in your domain and beyond (see Figure 5.22).

▶ **See** "Setting Up Connection Records," **p. 869**

FIG. 5.22

The Connections view in the Personal Address Book.

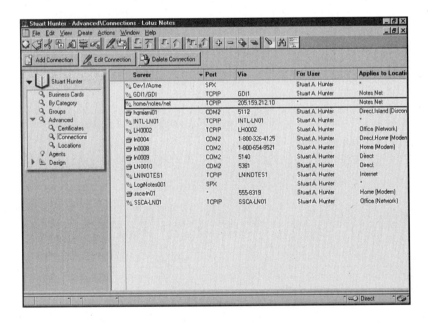

Server	Port	Via	For User	Applies to Locati
Dev1/Acme	SPX		Stuart A. Hunter	*
GDI1/GDI	TCPIP	GDI1	Stuart A. Hunter	Notes Net
home/notes/net	TCPIP	205.159.212.10	*	Notes Net
hqmiami01	COM2	5112	Stuart A. Hunter	Direct,Island (Discon
INTL-LN01	TCPIP	INTL-LN01	Stuart A. Hunter	*
LH0002	TCPIP	LH0002	Stuart A. Hunter	Office (Network)
ln0004	COM2	1-800-326-4125	Stuart A. Hunter	Direct,Home (Moden
ln0008	COM2	1-800-654-8521	Stuart A. Hunter	Home (Modem)
ln0009	COM2	5140	Stuart A. Hunter	Direct
LN0010	COM2	5361	Stuart A. Hunter	Direct
LNINOTES1	TCPIP	LNINOTES1	Stuart A. Hunter	Internet
LogiNotes001	SPX		Stuart A. Hunter	*
ssca-ln01	*	555-8319	Stuart A. Hunter	Home (Modem)
SSCA-LN01	TCPIP	SSCA-LN01	Stuart A. Hunter	Office (Network)

In the Public Address Book, this view is useful because you can see not only how the servers in your own domain are connected, but also what connections exist between your own organization and other Notes organizations.

Server/Domains View

This Public Address Book view, just like the Connections view, helps you understand how your organization's Notes communicates with other companies and mail systems. Nonadjacent domains show organizations that you can contact indirectly, and foreign domains detail how Notes mail can be transferred to users of other mail systems or things such as fax and pager gateways.

Server/Mail-In Databases View

As well as sending mail to individuals and groups, your developers might have set up databases that can accept mail. For example, you might find yourself filling in a Problem Reporting document that is mailed to a Support database, where the support staff can pick it up and deal with the problem. If your organization has set up a Resource Reservations database, the mail files representing the resources that have been created will be visible here.

Server/Programs View

Your company might have purchased or written programs that interact with the Notes server. Usually, they are required to be run at a specific time or day of the week. For example, a nightly process that imports data from a mainframe to Notes might be scheduled and visible in this view.

Replicating the Public Address Book

If you are primarily a remote user (that is, you spend most of your time using Notes not connected to a LAN), you will probably want to create a replica of the Public Address Book on your workstation so that you can take advantage of the user addresses and groups it contains. To do so, use the same steps you would use to create a replica of any database. Select the copy of the Public Address Book icon on the server and choose File, Replication, New Replica. The New Replica dialog box appears, as shown in Figure 5.23.

FIG. 5.23
Making a new replica copy of the Public Address Book.

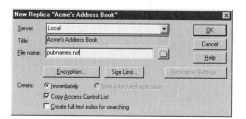

The Server box should be set to Local, and the Title box should display the title of your company's Public Address Book. Enter a new filename for the replica of your Public Address Book.

CAUTION

By default, the Public Address Book on the server has the filename NAMES.NSF. Your Personal Address Book on your workstation has the same name. If you choose to store a replica of the Public Address Book on your workstation, you must change the default filename given to the replica; otherwise, you will overwrite your Personal Address Book with your Public Address Book.

If you forget to change the filename, Notes will warn you that a file with that name already exists, and it will ask you if you want to overwrite it. Choose No and enter a new filename for the Public Address Book replica. If no standard exists in your organization for naming local replica copies of the Public Address Book, you might want to use PUBNAMES.NSF for the actual filename.

You can then use the other settings in the New Replica dialog box to set a size limit for the Public Address Book replica, limit the replica to several variations of the People and Groups views, enter encryption settings, create a full text index, copy the ACL into the replica, and choose when to create the new replica. When you are sure all the settings are correct, click OK. A New Replica Stub icon will appear.

Once the replicator has initialized and copied all the documents into your Public Address Book replica, you can begin to use the replica as you would the original database on the server.

N O T E   Remember, by default, you have Manager access to all local databases, which means that you will be able to create and modify documents that exist in the replica of the Public Address Book. However, if the administrator has done his or her job properly, your changes will be overwritten by the data in the server copy. In short, don't add or change documents in your replica of the Public Address Book, because they will be overwritten. Make them in your Personal Address Book. This brings us to another note. If you have many users in your company, your Public Address Book could grow *very* large. If space on your computer is at a premium, you might want to copy documents from your Public Address Book to your Personal Address Book instead of making a full replica copy.

Advanced Mail

In Chapter 4, "Getting Started with Electronic Mail," you learned the basics of the Lotus Notes email system. There are a number of additional features you can use to extend the capabilities of NotesMail. This chapter examines the advanced features that allow you to use NotesMail with maximum efficiency, effectiveness, and enjoyment.

NotesMail Under the Hood

NotesMail is the leading client/server store-and-forward mail system.

The following are some of the many reasons why NotesMail is so popular:

- Intuitive user interface: NotesMail sports the award-winning, industry-leading cc:Mail user interface. Because it's easy to learn and intuitive to use NotesMail, users can become productive immediately.

- Rich text support: Because the body of the mail message is a rich text field, any type of object can be put inside a mail message, including file attachments, OLE objects, graphics, and doclinks.

- Bidirectional field-level replication: Like all Notes databases, your mail database can be replicated. This allows you to keep multiple copies of your mail database in perfect synchronization, the ideal situation for remote users. Each time you connect to the Notes server, your local replica copy of your mail database will be synchronized with the copy on your server. If you delete mail in your local copy, it will be deleted on the server; if new mail is waiting on the server, it will be transferred to your local replica. For more information, see Chapter 23, "Notes: Under the Hood."

- Functionality: NotesMail has a vast array of built-in functions that power email users expect, such as Forwarding and Reply, folders, and Address Book-based addressing. Additional power features include Letterheads, Stationery, Return Receipts, Mood Stamps, Delivery Reports, automatic reply capability, and archiving utilities.

- Security: NotesMail offers two immensely powerful security features: encryption at both the message and database level, and digital signatures, which provide a level of security unmatched in other mail systems.

- Shared mail: Although shared mail is administrative (meaning that, as an end-user, you need not concern yourself with it), it is a powerful new technology. Shared mail allows the administrator to configure NotesMail so that when a message is sent to multiple recipients, the summary (envelope information) is stored in each user's mailbox, whereas the nonsummary (body) information is stored in the shared mail file on the server.

  Each user has a link to the shared information, so when the message is accessed, the user sees the full message. This allows much better disk usage, because large mail messages are not stored in each mailbox. It also helps reduce network traffic.

- Integration: Messaging is one of Notes' core services. This means that NotesMail is tightly integrated into Notes, allowing mail messages to be sent from or to users, databases, and other systems.

- Extensibility: NotesMail is easily extended to communicate with other enterprise-wide mail systems such as MS Mail or IBM's PROFS.
- Scalability: NotesMail works well for 10 users or 100,000 users. This is because Notes server software can take advantage of multiple processors and because NotesMail uses the client/server architecture.

These are just some of the reasons why NotesMail is so powerful and popular. Before we delve more deeply into the advanced features of NotesMail, here is a quick refresher course on how it works.

Each Notes workstation has a Mailer program that is used to create new mail messages and verify addresses, and each Notes server has a Router task that runs on the server and routes mail messages from senders to recipients. For the following example, assume that the user is connected to a Notes server through a LAN, only one recipient is entered, and the recipient's address is valid.

When the user creates and sends a new mail message, the Mailer on the workstation tries to verify the recipient's address against the Address Book. When the address is verified, the Mailer transfers the mail message to the Mail.box database on the user's mail server.

The router, which is constantly polling the Mail.box database, interrogates the mail message and tries to determine whether the recipient is on the same mail domain (shares the same Public Address Book). If so, the message is put into the user's mailbox almost immediately.

If the user is in another domain, the router tries to make a connection to the user's domain via connection documents and foreign/nonadjacent domain documents in the Public Address Book. When the proper route to the user's domain is determined, the router makes a connection based on the priority of the message and the connection schedules in the Public Address Book.

That, in a nutshell, is how NotesMail works. For more detailed information, see Chapter 23, or the Domino Administration Help database, usually found in the DOC directory on your server. Now that you understand the basics of how email works, let's look at the advanced features of NotesMail.

Organizing Your Mail

The ability to quickly and easily find and manipulate mail messages is paramount for effective mail use and user satisfaction. The smart folks at Lotus realized this and have added a variety of powerful tools to help you effectively organize your mail messages.

In addition, like most things in Notes, your mailbox can be tailored to your specific needs. (See Chapter 2, "Customizing Notes," to learn more about Notes customization.)

You can add a certain amount of customization to most views and folders even if you aren't a database designer—unless the database designer has disabled some of these features. In general, you have more control over folders than views.

In terms of customizing views, unless you have Designer or higher access to a database, the amount of customization you can lend to a view is somewhat limited compared to a folder. You can, however, create your own private views. (For more information on private views, see Chapter 12, "Designing Views.")

In the standard Notes mailbox, you can make some simple changes to the views that provide greater usability. You can also put your mail into folders that simplify organizing and storing the volume of mail you receive.

CAUTION

Unlike with most databases, you have Manager access to your mailbox by default, regardless of whether it resides on the server or is a replica on your workstation. This means that you have the highest level of access to the database and can change the database design. You can even permanently delete the database! This means that unless you have a backup, your mail will be lost!

In almost every case, the mailbox should provide all the functions you will ever need. It is highly recommended that you not try to make design changes to the mailbox other than those mentioned in this section.

You might also be using the NotesMail license or the Notes Desktop license, which don't allow you to make any design changes. If you feel that changes are needed, submit a request to the database design team to make the changes.

If you decide to make design changes to the database, be very careful. You might make changes that affect how your mailbox works and that can't easily be corrected.

In addition, because your mailbox is based on a template, your changes might be overwritten. You will learn more about this issue in Chapter 12.

Changing Mail Views

In Chapter 4, you learned that when you open your mailbox, Notes displays a list of incoming and outgoing messages in the view or folder that you last used. As with most databases, you can choose any of several different views and folders. Each of these presents your mail messages in a different way.

In the mail template, the views do not appear in the view menu and can be accessed only from the Navigator. At the bottom of the Navigator, you'll see two additional views, Archiving and Discussion Threads.

N O T E The design elements in your mailbox such as views and folders are standard. What you see in your mailbox, however, might vary from the figures in this chapter, because each of these documents might be changed by Notes administrators or designers in your organization. ▪

Here are the standard views:

- Discussion Threads: When someone starts an ongoing discussion that prompts responses and then responses to the responses, the collective body of related messages is called a *thread*. (This is a very common term in Internet jargon, especially in UseNet, newsgroups, and email.)

The Discussion Threads view displays in a hierarchical manner all messages that are part of the same discussion. Any message that has a reply is displayed with the reply below it, and any replies to a reply are displayed below each reply. This view makes it easy to keep track of an ongoing email discussion.

■ Archiving: This view lets you see and edit your Archive Profile and Archive Log documents for each archive session, as well as set the location of your mail archive file. (This is much like the Notes Log.) You'll learn how to archive mail messages later in this chapter, in the section called "Archiving Your Mail."

Organizing Your Mail into Folders

If you are a Notes 3.x user, this section will be particularly important to you. In the old version of the mail database, each NotesMail message had a special field named Personal Categories. This field allowed you to specify categories so that you could logically group your mail messages.

When the Personal Categories field was populated with data, NotesMail used it to categorize the mail messages in views. For instance, if you often got mail from the Finance department, you might have categorized this mail as "Finance," whereas mail from Accounting you would categorize as "Accounting." You could create as many categories as you needed to help organize your messages into groups and make the views more meaningful and less cluttered.

In the Notes 4.x mailbox, each document still has a Personal Categories field, but it is there only for backward compatibility with older email messages. Lotus has added a much more powerful feature to the new mail database: folders. (For a brush-up on folders, see Chapter 3, "Using Databases.")

When you're trying to organize your mail messages, folders are useful, because you can put messages in a folder that apply strictly to a specific issue, account, concept, and so on. For instance, you can create a folder called ABC Company and put all mail messages related to ABC Company in it.

This folder would hold only messages about the ABC Company, so the number of messages it holds would be much smaller than the number of messages that would show up in a categorized view. Searching, manipulation, and viewing are therefore quicker and easier. An additional benefit is that the folders are added to the standard Navigation pane, allowing you to find and manipulate them.

Notice that in the mailbox shown in Figure 6.1, several folders have been created, with the Projects folder itself containing three further folders. If the folders you want to store mail messages in already exist, click and drag documents to them. Or you can select Actions, Move to Folder or click the Move To Folder button on the Action Bar to display the Move To Folder dialog box, shown in Figure 6.2.

Part

I

Ch

6

FIG. 6.1

User defined folders for frequent communications in the mailbox.

FIG. 6.2

The Move To Folder dialog box displays the list of folders in the mailbox.

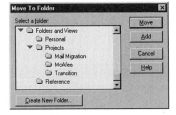

From this dialog box, you can choose a folder from the graphical list displayed in the Select a folder list box. Once you have selected a folder, you can use the Move button to move the document from the folder it's in to the selected folder.

Or you can click Add to add a document to the selected folder and leave it in its current folder as well. To create a new folder, click the Create New Folder button to launch the Create Folder dialog box.

You can create as many folders as you need to organize your mail messages in your mailbox. To create a new folder, choose Create, Folder. The Create Folder dialog box, shown in Figure 6.3, appears.

FIG. 6.3

The Create Folder dialog box displays a list of existing folders so that you can decide where to place a new folder.

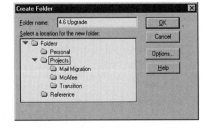

The Create Folder dialog box is easy to use. You enter a new folder name in the Folder name field and choose a location for the new folder from the hierarchy of folders shown in the Select a location for the new folder list box. (This list box displays all the folders and their hierarchy in your mailbox.)

Click the folder where you want to put the new folder, and then click <u>O</u>K. The new folder is added to your mailbox, and you can use it immediately.

To begin using your folders, select a mail message or messages the same way you would select any documents. Click and drag the messages to the proper folder. It's as simple as that!

Folders are a very powerful new feature of the new NotesMail interface. They can make your life easier when you're working in your mailbox. If you often get mail messages from another department or person, you might want to create a folder to organize them.

For instance, if you often communicate with several departments at the XYZ Company via email, you might create a folder called XYZ for general mail messages from the company and create several subfolders under XYZ, such as Purchasing, Engineering, Marketing, and Sales, to store mail messages from those departments.

Remember, customize your folders to meet your needs. You can store a mail message in one or many folders. You can move it from one folder to another at any time.

N O T E If you're upgrading from Notes 3.x to Notes 4.6, Lotus has included an agent that lets you convert the categories stored in your old mail messages to folders, which can save you a considerable amount of time. (See Chapter 16, "Buttons and Agents," for more information.) To use this agent, open your mailbox and click the Agent icon (the small light bulb) in the Navigator.

Right-click the Convert Categories to Folders agent to launch a pop-up menu. Choose <u>R</u>un to start the agent and create new folders for each category. When the agent is finished, Notes displays a brief summary of the actions carried out by the agent in the Agent Log dialog box. Your administrator may have already done this for you as part of the upgrade process if you are moving from Notes 3.x. If you open your mailbox and see folders that correspond to the categories you had in your old mailbox, you won't need to do this. ▪

Changing the Width of Columns in a View or Folder

In the view pane, the columns are separated by thin gray lines. Most columns in a view are resizable, much like the columns in an Excel or 1-2-3 spreadsheet. When you position the mouse pointer directly over any of the column separator lines, notice that the pointer changes to a solid black line with an arrow on each side.

When the mouse pointer changes, you can "grab" the column separator (hold down the right or left mouse button) and drag it to the size you want. This technique can be handy, because it allows you to dynamically determine how wide a column should be.

N O T E The first non-data column in any view or folder is called the Marker column. It is the thin, vertical gray line that extends the length of the view and separates it from the other columns. You can't resize this column. See Chapter 3 for more information on the special function of this column. ▪

Part

I

Ch

6

Changing the Sort Order

Many of the views in the mailbox, such as the All Documents view, allow you to change the sorted order of certain columns (see Figure 6.4). Any column heading that displays a small arrow pointing up, down, or both ways indicates that you can click in the column heading to change the sort order.

FIG. 6.4
You can change the sort order of columns in the All Documents view with a single click.

Sorts the column in ascending order

Sorts the column in descending order

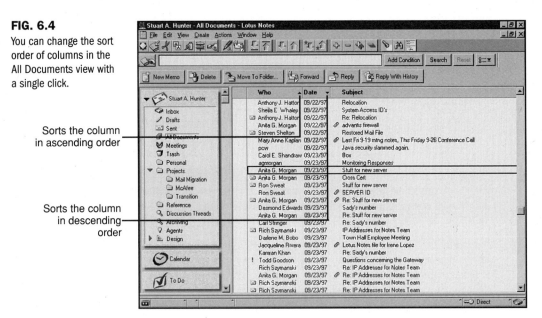

In Figure 6.4, the Who column has an arrow pointing up. This means that when you click the Who column header, that column is sorted in ascending order.

The arrow changes from black, which means that the column is in its default order, to turquoise, meaning that the column is now sorted in ascending order. You can click again to return the column to its default unsorted order, but this order is effectively by date because the documents appear in the order in which they arrived in the database.

The Date column is already sorted in ascending order (the oldest dates first). The column heading has a down arrow, indicating that you can change the sort order from the default (ascending order) to descending order (most recent dates first). A second click on this column returns the messages to ascending order.

Another useful feature allows you to view only new messages. To enable this feature, simply choose View, Show, Unread Only.

Without getting into view design, these are the only view features that an end user can customize in a mailbox. Folders, on the other hand, can not only be customized in the same ways that views can, but they can also be created from scratch. This allows you to build your own folders to organize your mail messages. The creation of views and folders is covered in Chapter 12.

Working with File Attachments

As a PC user, you probably need to share files with other users on many occasions. As you know, this is often much more easily said than done, particularly if you work for a geographically dispersed company.

However, Notes makes it easy to email a file as an attachment to your mail message to any other NotesMail user. Perhaps a coworker in Bangladesh needs a copy of the technical documentation you have prepared in Lotus Word Pro, or the plant in Düsseldorf needs your market analysis report created with Lotus 1-2-3.

Before email (and particularly NotesMail), sharing files meant copying the files to a shared disk drive on the LAN. Or it meant copying them to a floppy disk and using "sneaker net" (you got up and ran the disk down to the colleague who needed it) if the colleague was in the office, or snail mail if the person was at another location.

Notes simplifies the sharing of files by allowing you to attach a file to an email message. The following sections explain how to work with attachments.

Users new to email are often confused by the concept of a file attachment. When you attach a file to an email message (regardless of the original file format), Notes makes a copy of the whole file. It inserts the copy of the file into the body of the email message, leaving the original file unchanged.

N O T E This is like using your operating system to copy a file, except that now you can mail the file to other users, and they can use the file just as if they had created it themselves. ▓

Attaching Files

You can attach a file (or files) to any mail document. The first step is to create a new message. When the new message is onscreen, you work with it just as you would with any other mail message until you are ready to attach the file.

For instance, if you have an office in Germany that needs the latest sales figures, you can attach the 1-2-3 spreadsheet to a mail message and send it to the German office. Likewise, you can attach the Access database that has the latest inventory data and mail it to a colleague in a different office.

To attach one or more files, follow these steps:

1. Place the cursor in the body portion of the memo, and then choose File, Attach or click the File Attach SmartIcon. The Create Attachment(s) dialog box appears, as shown in Figure 6.5.

Part

I

Ch

6

FIG. 6.5

The Create Attachment(s) dialog box is simple to use. Just select the file(s) to attach.

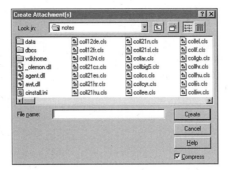

You must be in the Body field in order to attach a file. File attachments can be attached only in rich text fields, and Body is the only rich text field in the mail message.

2. You can use the Look in drop-down box to select the directory where the file(s) you want to attach reside. The list box below that displays all the files in the selected directory. By default, the Create Attachment(s) dialog box points to the last directory you accessed using this dialog box. If this is the first time you've used this dialog box, it should point to the Notes directory, C:\NOTES.

3. Select all the files you want to attach by clicking them in the list box (selected files are highlighted with a blue bar). They will be displayed in the File name text box. To select more than one file, hold the Ctrl key down as you select files. (If the files you want to select are consecutive, click the first file and then hold down the Shift key and click the last file. All the intermediate files will also be selected.)

4. Click Create. Notes inserts an icon in your document that represents each of the attached files. Notes uses the file extensions of each file you attach to scan the Windows Registry to try to identify the source application (the application that created the file) so that an icon representing the application that created the file can be displayed.

For example, if you insert a Microsoft Word document, the Word icon is displayed in the mail message to represent the file attachment. If Notes can't identify the file attachment (its ability to identify file attachments is based on your operating system), an icon that looks like a gray piece of paper with the right edge folded down is inserted.

Figure 6.6 shows a sample memo with several different file attachments.

When you have attached the files, address the mail as you normally would, enter the subject, and add any text to the message body that might help the recipient understand the attachment. Once the file is attached, you still have complete editing capability in the Body field.

You can insert text above, below, beside, or between the attachments and move the attachments as if they were text. After you finish the message and attach the files, send the message as you normally would.

▶ **See** "Sending Your Message," **p. 167**

FIG. 6.6

A mail message displays the icons of known file types when they are attached.

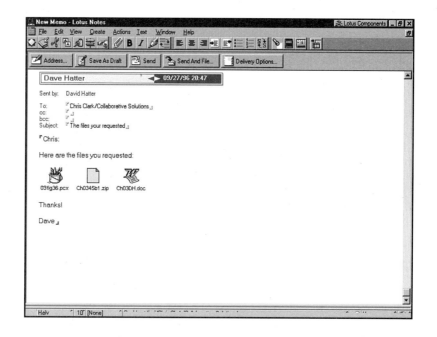

A Word About Compression

The Compress checkbox in the Create Attachment(s) dialog box is enabled by default. In most instances, you should leave this option checked so that Notes will compress the file attachment(s).

During the compression, Notes searches for repeating patterns in the file. It codes these repeating patterns and strips them out, reducing the size of the file.

In many cases, a compressed file attachment is 80 to 90 percent smaller than the original file. Because the files are smaller, they can be transferred more quickly than the original file and consume less disk space on the server. The only disadvantage of compressing attachments is that the attachment process takes slightly longer (the increased time is barely noticeable) because Notes must analyze and process each file attachment.

Certain types of files don't contain repeating patterns—for example, any file that has already been compressed by another compression utility such as PKZIP (the repeating patterns have already been stripped out) or certain graphics files that use a compression scheme by default, such as GIF and JPEG files. Having Notes compress these files won't cause any damage. But the space savings are negligible, and compression takes slightly longer.

When the recipient gets the mail message and tries to extract, launch, or view the attachments, Notes automatically decompresses the file into its original format. The recipient doesn't need to take any special actions if only the Notes compression method was used.

Part

I

Ch

6

Detaching Attachments

When you open your mailbox, you should be able to immediately identify mail messages that have attached files. This is because all the standard views and folders display a paper clip somewhere in the view pane to indicate that a file has been attached, as shown in Figure 6.7.

FIG. 6.7

The All Documents view displays messages that have attachments with a paper clip icon.

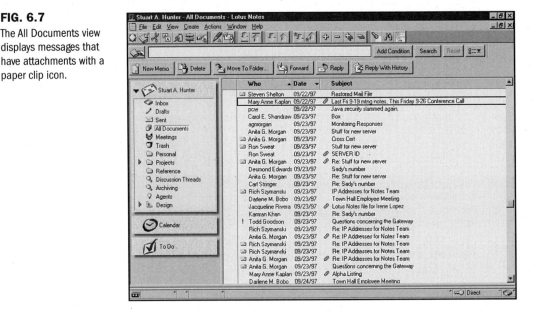

> **N O T E** The position of the paper clip might vary from view to view and folder to folder, but it is displayed in all the standard views and folders that ship with Notes 4.6. Be aware that if custom views and folders have been specified for the database, the paper clip icon might not be displayed. This is at the discretion of the designer. ■

To detach one or more of the attached files (extract the file from the mail message and store it as a file on your disk), follow these steps:

1. Open the mail message that has attachments. You see the corresponding icons in the body.

2. When you select any or all of the attachments, a new menu, Attachment, appears between the Actions and Window menus (see Figure 6.8).

FIG. 6.8

The Attachment menu on the main menu bar mimics the features that are available when you click the attachment.

3. From this menu, choose Detach (a bit of a misnomer, because this command doesn't detach the attachment from the message; it saves the file separately). Notes displays the standard File dialog box, asking where you want to copy the file and what the filename should be.

4. The original filename of the attachment is the default value for the new filename, but you can give the file a new name. Pick any directory you want. Notes detaches the file from the message onto your hard disk.

Or you can double-click any of the attachments to display the Attachment Properties InfoBox and then view, launch, or detach the attachment (see Figure 6.9).

FIG. 6.9

The Attachment Properties InfoBox allows you to set a number of options for each attachment.

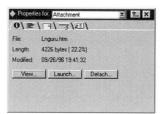

Attached files stay in a mail message even after you detach, launch, or view them (launching and viewing are described shortly). You can extract the attachment as many times as you want.

You can detach the file to your hard disk, for example, and then detach it again to a disk (specify A: or B: as the directory). If you forward the message to someone else, the attached file goes with it.

 TIP File attachments are often quite large and can quickly consume precious disk space. If you find yourself running low on space, you can open mail messages and delete their attachments while retaining the mail message itself. See "Deleting Attachments" later in this chapter for details.

Detaching Multiple Attachments

Many times, you will receive a mail message that has more than one file attached. It can be more convenient to extract several at once. To detach more than one attachment, follow this procedure:

1. Select the attachments you want to detach (hold down either mouse button and drag the pointer over the attachments; this highlights the icons with a black bar).

 TIP Notes doesn't care how much text you select in addition to the attachments, so don't worry about selecting only the attachments. In fact, if you want to detach all attachments in a message, you can right-click one of the attachments and choose Detach All from the submenu.

2. Choose Attachments, Detach All Selected.

Part

I

Ch

6

3. Notes displays the standard File dialog box that allows you to select a directory in which to store the attachments. Choose a directory (all the attachments will be stored in this directory) and click OK. Notes detaches the selected attachments.

Viewing Attachments

Sometimes you get file attachments that you want to look at before you detach them to your workstation's disk. To view only the contents of an attachment, you can select the attachment and open the Attachment property sheet by double-clicking the icon.

Click View to open the Universal Viewer and examine the file contents. Or you can select the attachment to view and choose Attachment, View.

As discussed in Chapter 3, "Using Databases," the Universal Viewer lets you examine the most popular file formats, such as Microsoft Word, Microsoft Excel, Microsoft Access, Lotus 1-2-3, Lotus Word Pro, and many others. However, you might receive files that the Universal Viewer can't understand.

For instance, many people use a compression utility such as PKZIP to compress files before they are attached because it provides superior file compression. Because the file is specially encoded, the Universal Viewer can't understand the contents of the file and can't display it correctly. If this is the case, you'll need to detach the file, unzip it, and then find the application that originally created the file in order to view it. If you don't have the original application, you could put the unzipped file into a new mail message and try the Universal Viewer on it.

Launching Attachments

Not only can you extract files to disk or view and print the contents with the Universal Viewer, you can also launch (start) the application that created the file and begin editing the file immediately. But first, a few caveats.

In order for the Launch function to work correctly, the following must be true:

- Unless the attached file is an executable file, such as a Lotus ScreenCam movie, you must have access to the application that created the file attachment, either from the hard disk on your workstation or from a drive on a network server. In other words, you can launch 1-2-3 by double-clicking a file that has a WK4 extension only if you have 1-2-3 available from your computer.

- The application that originally created the file must have been successfully installed and configured in the Windows Registry for your system. In the Registry, Windows maintains a database of applications it recognizes and the types of files that are associated with each application.

   When you launch a file, Windows examines the file's extension and searches the Registry for a match. If a match is found, Windows starts the application and opens the attached file. For example, suppose you receive mail that has the file DOSINFO.SAM (an Ami Pro 3.1 file) attached. Windows determines from the Registry that files with the extension .SAM are Ami Pro files, so it starts Ami Pro, and the attached file is opened as an Ami Pro document.

This method isn't foolproof, because end users can name a file anything they want. And although a file might look like a 1-2-3 spreadsheet (has the extension WK4), it might be an ASCII text file, which means that the file will not be launched correctly. If you can't get a file to launch, consult your operating system manuals and your Notes administrator for help.

> **CAUTION**
>
> Some malicious user could send you a virus or other harmful program as a file attachment that infects your computer when launched. If you get mail that has an executable file from a suspicious source or you are suspicious of an attached file, don't launch it! Scan the file with an antivirus program or consult your administrator to learn about Notes' Execution Control List feature. See Chapter 2 for more information on Execution Control Lists (ECLs).

To launch an attachment in its associated program, select the file and open the Properties InfoBox by double-clicking the attachment's icon. You can then click the Launch button to open the file with the application that originally created it. Alternatively, right-click the attachment and choose Launch from the submenu.

When you elect to Launch, Notes starts the application that created the file and opens the file in that application. For example, if the file was created in 1-2-3, Notes starts 1-2-3 and loads the attachment into 1-2-3 for editing. If the file is an executable program, Notes executes the program.

Deleting Attachments

Normally, attached files stay in a message until the message is deleted. This can quickly consume an inordinate amount of disk space. However, you can keep the mail message but delete the attachments to save disk space.

Here are some reasons for deleting attachments:

- The mail message has important information, but you don't need the file attachments.
- You detached or launched the files with the host application and saved the files to disk. Either of these choices creates a copy of the attached files on disk, meaning that you now have redundant copies of the files on your workstation that consume disk space. By deleting the attachment from the mail, you free up this space.
- Files were erroneously attached to the mail message. You don't want to send the files, but you do want to send the mail message. If you delete the message, it deletes the attachments, but you must retype the message.

To delete an attached file or files, the document must be opened in edit mode. If you're viewing the document in a view or you have the document open in read mode, press Ctrl+E to switch to edit mode.

With the document open in edit mode, select the files you want to delete and press the Delete key or choose Edit, Clear. You could also click the Edit Clear SmartIcon.

Part

I

Ch

6

Notes prompts you with a dialog box indicating that the delete operation can't be undone. If you are sure you want to delete the attachment, click Yes; otherwise, click No to cancel the delete operation.

Working with Mail-In Databases

Because messaging is at the core of Notes, mail messages can be sent to any database if it is enabled. This feature can be especially handy if you need to share information between two databases that don't replicate.

For example, you can create a suggestion-box-type application in which users can mail documents to a database but they don't need the database available to them. Or the Mail-In database capability can be useful if you want to design a workflow application in which documents can be routed to individuals who are part of the business process.

Before a database can get messages, you or the Notes administrator must create a Mail-In database document in the Public Address Book (see Figure 6.10). To do so, select the Public Address Book and choose Create, Server, Mail-In Database. Remember, you must have Author access or better and/or be in the NetCreator role to create a new document in the Public Address Book.

FIG. 6.10

Creating a Mail-In Database to receive Expense Reports.

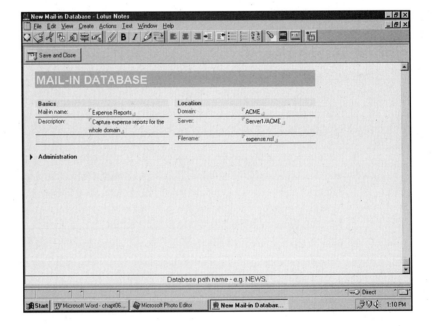

You must then enter a name for the database (this is the name users enter in the To field of a mail message), the domain of the server where the database is stored, the name of the server where the database is stored, and the filename of the database. Optionally, you may enter a description to help identify the purpose and use of the database.

Be sure to inform users that the new database is available. Explain that to send a message to the database, you must use the name in the Mail-in name field of the Mail-In Database document.

Working with Custom Forms in Your Mailbox

As they begin to understand how Notes can increase productivity through workflow automation and information sharing, many companies expand the default capabilities of the Notes mailbox by adding Custom Forms. Custom Forms usually go hand-in-hand with Mail-In Databases. They are Notes forms designed to provide added functionality to your mail system by automating manual processes.

For instance, most companies have a standardized expense report that must be routed to several people for approval before it can be processed for payment. In Notes, a Custom Form modeled from your company's standard paper expense report can be created and added to the mailbox so that the report can be filled out and mailed to the approving authority. If approved, the form is then mailed to the accounting or finance department for payment.

Another example of how Custom Forms can be useful is forms routing. You can use NotesMail to automate the process of routing a form through your company. If individuals must sign off on the form, digital signatures can be used as part of the approval process.

To access any Custom Forms that might be in your mailbox, select your mailbox and choose Create, Other. This displays the Other dialog box, shown in Figure 6.11. You can also choose Create, Mail, Other if you aren't in your mailbox to get the same dialog box.

FIG. 6.11
All the forms in your mailbox are displayed in the Other dialog box.

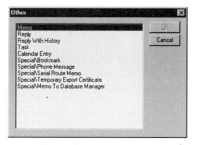
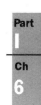

The Other dialog box displays all the forms available from your mailbox. Select the form you want, and a new one opens. At this point, you handle this form as you would any other mail message form.

In most cases, the designer who creates the Custom Forms includes a SendTo field as a minimum. He or she may include the cc, bcc, and Subject fields as well. This way, when the document is delivered to a mailbox, it is displayed like other mail messages in the folders and views.

In most organizations, all NotesMail mailboxes are based on a mailbox design template. When a database designer completes the testing of a new custom form, the form is put in the standard mailbox template. This automatically puts the new form in your mailbox on the server. If you use workstation-based mail, the form is placed in your local mailbox during your next replication.

N O T E Remember that these are "Custom" forms; they have been added by a database designer and are not included in the Mailbox templates that Lotus provides. If you upgrade your version of Notes and refresh the design of your mailbox, your custom forms will be deleted, so make provisions for this if you need the custom forms. For more information on templates, see Appendix A, "Database Templates."

Extending NotesMail with Gateways and MTAs

NotesMail is very powerful and can meet the needs of most organizations, from the smallest to the largest. Still, it might be necessary to connect NotesMail to other mail systems such as IBM's PROFS mail, Novell's MHS-based mail systems, or even the Internet.

Lotus recognizes the need to allow NotesMail to easily integrate with these other systems. It has made much progress since the Notes 3 days toward seamless connectivity for most major mail systems.

Lotus has done this in two ways: by developing internal gateways and message transfer agents (MTAs), and by encouraging Lotus Business Partners.

Before we look at two of the most popular and useful extensions, you need a better understanding of what gateways and MTAs do.

MTAs are integrated server tasks that, according to Lotus, "provide scalable, high-performance routing and relaying of messages in their native format." MTAs are completely integrated into the infrastructure of Notes. As a result, they are generally more reliable and give better performance with less cost than gateways.

In the context of NotesMail, gateways "move messages from one electronic mail system to another, acting as a protocol converter between different email formats." (For a more generic definition, see the following note.) Although they're not as tightly integrated as MTAs, gateways afford connectivity to most systems. Lotus provides a number of gateways, as do a number of third-party software vendors.

N O T E According to the LAN Times Encyclopedia of Networking, a gateway "is a computer system or other device that acts as a translator between two systems that do not use the same communications protocols, data formatting structures, languages, and/or architecture."

With this knowledge under your belt, let's examine the Domino Fax Server (a gateway) and the simple mail transfer protocol (SMTP) MTA.

Sending Faxes with Lotus Notes

The email system in Lotus Notes is very flexible and, through the use of additional software, can be used to send faxes from Notes. If your company buys the Domino Fax Server (DFS) and a machine to run the software on, you can fax any Notes document.

You can also fax documents created in other applications, such as Microsoft Word or Lotus 1-2-3. This benefits your company because it allows multiple users to share the resources of the fax server.

You can greatly reduce the need for paper, because you can send and receive faxes electronically. In fact, if you couple the fax server with a scanner, you can completely eliminate the physical fax machine!

Your Notes administrator should install this software. It means the configuring of a Foreign Domain document in the Public Address Book, a separate machine, and knowledge of your Notes installation.

When the Fax gateway is configured and running, you or your administrator needs to install the Lotus Image Viewer software on your local machine. This software installs the printer drivers that allow you to fax documents other than Notes documents and allows you to view incoming faxes.

Faxing a Message or File Attachment

After your workstation is configured, when you open your mailbox and choose Create, you see two new forms in your mailbox: Fax Request - Attachments only and Fax Request. The Fax Request form is shown in Figure 6.12.

The Fax Request - Attachments only form, shown in Figure 6.13, is almost identical to the Fax Request form, except that it has an additional field, File Attachments. File Attachments is a Rich text field that allows you to attach files, such as Microsoft Word or Lotus Word Pro, that you want to fax.

This can be useful, because you don't have to open the application that created the file and print the file to the fax gateway. The fax gateway converts the file to graphics and sends it as part of the fax.

When you fax a file attachment, the Domino Fax software converts the attached file into graphics that can be sent to the receiving fax machine. Because each file must be converted from its original format, not every type of file can be faxed (most common file types are accepted).

For instance, a file that was compressed with PKZIP won't fax correctly, because the file is specially encoded and the fax software can't convert it.

Part

I

Ch

6

FIG. 6.12

The Fax Request form for sending faxes through Notes.

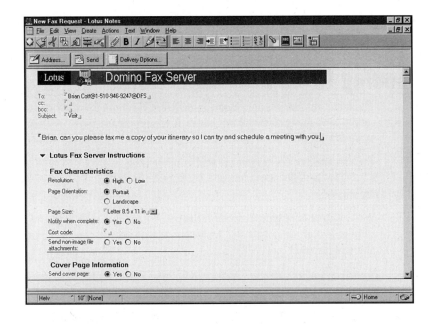

FIG. 6.13

The Fax Request - Attachments only form with a Word file attached.

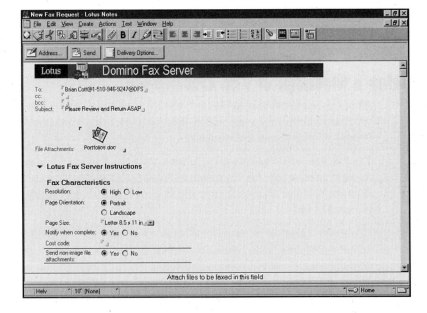

One of the advantages of using one of the Fax forms rather than sending an ordinary mail message to the Fax server is that you can choose a cover page to be sent with your fax. At the bottom of the Fax forms is the Cover Page Information section. Here, you can choose whether to send a cover page. If you do decide to send a cover page, leaving the Cover page form field blank will result in the default cover page being sent. You can request a list of custom cover pages that have been created for use in this field. If you enter a custom cover page that doesn't exist, the default cover page is used.

To tell Notes that this is a fax message and not a regular mail message, you address it in a slightly different way than you would a regular mail message. You type in a user name, which can be anything you like because it doesn't affect transmission, then the telephone number you want to send the fax to, and then the domain name that your administrator has set up. For example, if you were sending a fax to Dave Hatter at fax telephone number 1-555-555-1212 and your administrator had set up the Fax server in a domain called FAX, the address would look like this:

```
Dave Hatter@1-555-555-1212@FAX
```

N O T E To send the same message to multiple users, separate each address with a comma, as you would in a regular email message. The Fax Server software will fax the message to each listed addressee.

Once you have addressed your fax message, send it as you would any email message. The router takes over from there. When the router sees the foreign domain FAX, it transfers the mail to the fax gateway's outgoing mailbox.

The Domino Fax Server (DFS) periodically polls the DFS mailbox. When a new outbound fax is found, the DFS software renders the message as a graphic image and sends the fax.

N O T E The name of the Foreign Domain used to point to your DFS doesn't have to be FAX, and it isn't case-sensitive. This name is determined arbitrarily by your administrator. For instance, it might be called "DFS" or "Fax Gateway" or "fax server." To use this correctly, be sure to get the DFS's foreign domain name from your administrator.

Faxing Documents from Other Applications

Another way to take advantage of the Fax Server is to redirect the output of an application, such as Microsoft PowerPoint or Lotus Organizer, to the Fax Server. For instance, you might want to type up a quick letter with Lotus Word Pro and fax it to a colleague at another company.

When you finish the letter, change your printer driver to Lotus Print to Fax, and print your document. Your output is redirected to the Lotus Fax Server, which launches the Lotus Print to Fax dialog box, shown in Figure 6.14.

As you can see in Figure 6.14, the Print to Fax dialog box sports a tabbed interface that allows you to set various faxing parameters. In most cases, you only need to use the settings in the Send tab.

The first field, Name, works just like a NotesMail message: You enter the address of the recipient's fax machine in the standard Domino Fax format. The next field, Subject, is self-explanatory: You enter the subject of the fax.

Part

I

Ch

6

FIG. 6.14

Changing your printer driver to Lotus Print to Fax brings up The Lotus Print to Fax dialog box.

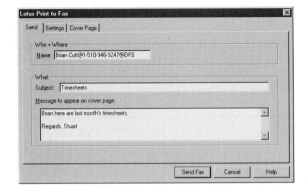

The Message to appear on cover page field allows you to enter text to print on the cover page, just like a regular fax. When you have set the appropriate options, click Send Fax. Your fax is queued at the server until a fax/modem is available to deliver the fax.

 Remember that messaging is one of the core services of Lotus Notes: You can mail any Notes document. This also applies to faxing. For example, suppose you have a lead in your Lead Tracking database who is interested in a service that your friend at another company provides, and you want to fax the information to her.

To do so, open the document you want to fax and choose Actions, Forward. A new memo is created, and the lead document is copied into the Body field. In the SendTo field, you enter the recipient's name and fax number in the UserName@PhoneNumber@Fax format mentioned earlier. The router sends the message to the Fax gateway for faxing.

The Domino Fax Server, though not cheap, is a powerful and worthy addition to any Notes installation. If your company doesn't have this capability, it's worth investigating. It can be a valuable addition to your office environment.

Sending Mail Outside Your Company

Many companies that use Notes need to send mail to other Notes users outside their company or to users who use other mail systems such as the Internet. As more companies discover the benefits of email, the need to link similar and dissimilar mail systems is growing.

In fact, there is a growing market of add-on products to allow Notes to communicate with other mail systems. Within the next decade, you should be able to communicate with almost anyone via email. The next three sections tell you how to send NotesMail to other companies that use Notes, how to send NotesMail to Internet email users through an SMTP gateway, and how to send mail to users of other mail systems, such as Microsoft Mail.

Sending NotesMail to Other Notes Users

Exchanging NotesMail between companies that use Notes requires coordination and cooperation between the companies' Notes administrators but requires no additional hardware or software.

In order for mail to be exchanged, the following must be in place:

■ Each company must have at least one server set up to communicate with a server at the other company. Each of these servers must be cross-certified so that they can communicate. Your Notes administrator should do the cross-certification to enable access for the other server.

■ At least one of the servers must call the other servers to make a connection through which mail messages can be transferred. This requires a Connection document in the Public Address Book for the server that makes the calls.

▶ **See** "Server Connection Documents," **p. 193**

■ Calling times should be scheduled in the Connection document so that mail is exchanged in a timely, cost-effective manner.

N O T E This is only a brief overview of the steps required to exchange mail between organizations. To exchange mail with another company that uses Notes, see your Notes administrator. ■

When this setup is in place, sending mail to outsiders is only slightly more complex than sending mail to your coworkers. Users in another company are outside your domain and do not appear in your Public Address Book.

This means that you must provide more routing information to Notes. When you address a message to someone outside the company, you include that person's domain (which is almost always the company name; your contact at the other company should provide this information for you), preceded by an "at" sign (@).

For example, to send a message to Dan Voelker at ABC Company, you would address the message as follows:

```
To: Dan Voelker@ABC Company
```

This notation tells Notes that Dan Voelker is not in your domain (your company's Address Book) but is outside your organization and that this message should be forwarded to the ABC Company server on the next connection. When the mail message is delivered to the mailbox on the ABC company server, it is routed to Dan Voelker's mailbox by ABC's server. Figure 6.15 shows a Person document configured to send mail to Dan Voelker, who is a Notes user at the ABC Company.

If you often communicate with people in other companies, you can make it much easier on yourself by adding their addresses to your Personal Address Book. To do so, you must add a Business Card document for each person you want to communicate with, just as you would for people in your own company who are not in your domain.

Part

I

Ch

6

FIG. 6.15
A Business Card document to help send mail to a Notes user in another domain.

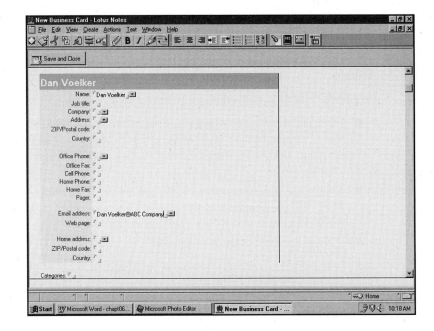

The difference for people outside your company is that you must put the person's full mail address in the Forwarding Address field. When Notes sees an address in this field, it knows that the person specified is in another domain or organization and that the mail must be transferred outside the current domain.

▶ **See** "Business Card Documents," **p. 183**

 If you have previously received mail from someone outside your company who is not in either of your Address Books, you can easily add this person to your Personal Address Book for future use. Select the mail message you received and choose Actions, Mail Tools, Add Sender to Address Book. This creates a new Business Card document and automatically copies the sender's information into it.

As the popularity of Notes continues to grow, the ability to communicate with other Notes users becomes increasingly important. In fact, many third-party service providers such as CompuServe have seen the potential for Notes. These companies have developed large Notes networks that allow you to easily transfer messages from your company to other Notes users for a small monthly charge. If your company uses Notes but can't afford the additional support to enable and maintain external connections, these services are an attractive alternative.

Sending Notes Mail Messages to Internet Users

Unless you have been living under a rock for the past five years, you must have at least heard of the Internet and might possibly use it. The Internet is a vast worldwide network of networks that allows millions of people to communicate electronically without regard to geography or time.

Lotus realized the tremendous potential of the Internet and how it can extend Notes' capabilities early on. Previously available as a separate add-in, Lotus now provides the SMTP MTA as a core component of Notes, allowing Notes users to send and receive Internet mail messages from within Notes.

To enable this capability, the Lotus SMTP MTA must be configured on a Notes server in your organization, and your company must have a connection to the Internet. If both of these conditions are met, all you need in order to send mail to someone over the Internet is an Internet address.

When the Notes administrator installs and configures this software, a foreign domain is created, much like the Domino Fax Server software, so Notes knows that this message is to be forwarded to the Internet. To send a mail message over the Internet, the SMTP domain should be appended to the user's Internet address, or it can be configured so that any mail sent to an unrecognized domain is forwarded to the SMTP MTA, which eliminates the need to append the foreign domain name.

For example, suppose you have a friend, Rose Wezel, who works at XYZPDQ Manufacturing, which has an Internet account. You want to send a message to her, so you create a new mail message and address it as follows:

```
Rose Wezel@XYZPDQ.com
```

When the NotesMail router sees this message, it reads but does not recognize the domain XYZPDQ.com and transfers it to the SMTP agent for conversion to the Internet format.

Sending Notes Mail to Users of Other Email Systems

Many large companies have a mixture of email systems, such as Microsoft Mail on one LAN and cc:Mail on another. In most cases, this lack of standardization is because when LANs and email were first introduced, each department chose the system it found most suitable.

If your company uses other email systems in addition to NotesMail, you can buy software products that allow Notes to send and receive messages from most popular mail systems.

Here are some of the other mail gateways and MTAs that are available for Notes:

- cc:Mail MTA: Allows seamless message transfer and directory synchronization with Lotus cc:Mail, the leading file-based messaging system.
- X.400 MTA: Provides native connectivity to X.400 environments.
- MHS gateway: Provides seamless connectivity between Notes and Novell's Message Handling System.
- Pager gateway: Provides the capability to send NotesMail messages to alphanumeric pagers.
- Soft-Switch: Provides connectivity to Microsoft Exchange and many others.

For an inclusive listing of third-party gateways and MTAs, visit the Lotus Web site at www.lotus.com, or pick up a copy of the Lotus Notes & cc:Mail guide from your Lotus representative.

Part

I

Ch

6

Working with cc:Mail

With cc:Mail being the best-selling email system, it is only natural that Lotus would make it easy to use cc:Mail as an alternative messaging system to NotesMail or to integrate Notes with cc:Mail.

If your organization already has a large number of cc:Mail users, it's easy to use cc:Mail in place of NotesMail. You tell Notes that you want to use cc:Mail instead of NotesMail through the configuration of your user preferences.

However, there are limitations to using cc:Mail instead of NotesMail. To enable cc:Mail, select File, Tools, User Preferences, and then click the Mail icon.

From the Mail Program combo box, choose cc:Mail. This displays a path to the cc:Mail executable. If this is right, leave it. Otherwise, type the correct path or use the Browse button to search for the cc:Mail executable.

You are also prompted to enter or browse for the local copy of your cc:Mail address book. Now you see the limitations of NotesMail mentioned earlier: Many of the NotesMail options are disabled.

Also, you'll notice that the NotesMail menu system is replaced by one that has the more limited functionality of cc:Mail. The new commands are as follows:

- Open: Runs cc:Mail's client program.
- Forward: Renders the contents of the open or selected document(s) to text and sends the text as a cc:Mail message.
- Forward as attachment: Converts the open or selected document(s) to an encapsulated Notes database and attaches the database to the message you're sending. The recipients of the message must have Lotus Notes in order to read the attached file.
- Send: Converts the open or selected document into the format in the document's MailFormat field. If none exists, the document is converted to an encapsulated Notes database. The names of the recipients are taken from the SendTo, CopyTo, and BlindCopyTo fields in the document.

As you can see, it's easy enough to use cc:Mail as an alternative mail system. But with NotesMail's new, friendlier interface and powerful client/server technology, NotesMail is a much better choice.

Accessing Your Mailbox from Another PC on the Network

If you use Notes for any length of time, sooner or later (probably sooner) you'll need to use Notes from someone else's PC. For instance, your PC might be down and you need to check your mail to see whether you got that big promotion. Or you might be in a different location for the day and you need to check your mail.

Accessing Notes from another PC in your company is easy, but you must be prepared in advance. The following sections explain what you need to do in order to use Notes from any PC.

TIP You should create an ID disk, as described in the next section, sometime in the very near future. You never know when your PC might crash, leaving you unable to get your mail or access your databases.

Creating an ID Disk

When Notes is first installed on your computer, a Notes ID file is created for you. This file holds the information that Notes needs before you can access the Notes server, such as your user name and password. You can think of your ID file as a key that allows you to unlock the door of the Notes server.

Your ID file, which is normally stored in your Notes data directory (C:\NOTES\DATA\), has an extension of ID. Normally, the first part of the filename is part of your real name. For instance, Darryl Rogers might find a file called DROGERS.ID in his Notes directory.

If you can't locate your ID file, choose File, Tools, User ID. You'll see the User ID dialog box, shown in Figure 6.16.

FIG. 6.16

The User ID dialog box.

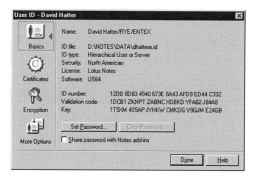

As you can see in Figure 6.16, the second line, ID file, displays the full path to the file, as well as the filename.

Because you must have this file in order to use Notes, the best plan for using Notes from other PCs is to copy this file to a disk. You can use the same method that you would to copy any file to a disk.

After you copy the file to the disk, put a label on the disk as soon as possible. On the label, identify the disk as your Notes ID, and be sure to write down the filename of the ID file. In addition, write down the name of the mail server on the disk (how to find this will be explained shortly). You use this information to access Notes from the other PC.

Part

I

Ch

6

T I P Your Notes ID file is critically important to your success in using Notes. Without an ID file, you can't use Notes. If you lose or corrupt your ID file or forget your password, you won't be able to access Notes. Although a new ID can be created, this can cause problems if you have encrypted any documents.

Make several backup copies of this file, and keep them in a secure place. (Remember, if someone else can get your ID file and knows your password, that person can pose as you!) In addition, make backup copies of this file regularly, since information stored in the file can change.

You can save yourself a lot of pain by making regular backups of this file. If you change your password in your current ID and then have to use a backup copy of your ID file, it might have an old password. The moral of this story is to back up your ID file often!

You need one more piece of information to access your mailbox from another PC. You must know the name of your mail server (the server where your mailbox database is stored). To find out the name of your mail server, choose File, Mobile, Locations. You'll see the Locations view in your Address Book.

Open any of the location documents, and you'll see the Home/mail server field in the Servers section in the right section of the form (see Figure 6.17). Or click the second box in the status bar (which displays the name of your current location setup) and select Edit Current. This also opens the current location document in your Personal Address Book.

FIG. 6.17

A location document for the Home location.

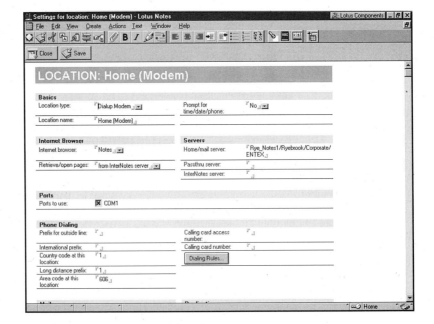

When you have your ID file on a diskette and you know the name of your mail server, you can use Notes from another PC. To access your mailbox from someone else's PC, do the following:

- Log into Notes.
- Add the icon for your mailbox to the workspace of the workstation you're using.

The next two sections cover the steps to do this.

> **N O T E** Because Notes is truly a cross-platform application, you can easily move between workstations that have different operating systems. Notes has the same look and feel on all platforms.
>
> However, you might have trouble if you try to use a UNIX or Macintosh workstation. These machines might not be able to read a disk that was formatted by DOS, Windows, or OS/2. If you need to use one of these workstations, consult your Notes administrator or Help Desk for advice on creating a cross-platform Notes ID disk that can be read by these machines.

Logging On to Notes with Your ID Disk

To log on to a Notes server with your ID disk, follow these steps:

1. If Notes is running on the workstation, go to step 2. If Notes isn't running, start it. You might be asked for a password. If so, click Cancel and go to step 2.
2. Insert your ID disk in the machine.
3. Choose File, Tools, Switch ID. Notes displays the Choose User ID to Switch To dialog box (see Figure 6.18), which shows the filename of the ID file in use on the workstation. This is the ID of the last person to log on to Notes from this workstation.

FIG. 6.18

Use the Choose User ID to Switch To dialog box to use a different ID.

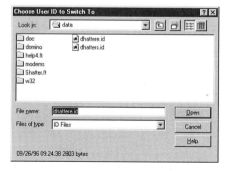

4. Click the down arrow of the Look in box and select the drive you inserted your disk into.
5. In the File name list, choose your ID file and click OK. Or you can click the File name box and type the drive letter you put the disk into, followed by a colon and the name of your ID file. For example, if you are switching to Samuel Hatter's ID, you would type `A:SHATTER.ID`.

6. You are prompted for your Notes password. Type your password and click Enter. Notes displays the User ID dialog box with key information about your Notes user ID. This includes your user name, type of license, and your internal Notes ID number (refer to Figure 6.16).

7. Choose <u>O</u>K.

At this point, you are logged in to Notes. You can do anything you can do on your workstation, unless you have databases on your machine that are not on this machine. You could, however, open them on this workstation.

Remember, though, that because the workspace on this computer is arranged by the user, you might not find things the way you have them on your workstation. For instance, you won't find your mailbox on any of these workspace pages (unless you added the icon earlier); you must add it. The next section explains how to access your mailbox when you are logged on.

 T I P It's a bad idea to rearrange the workspace on another person's workstation without explicit permission. If you do, you should try to put it back the way it was.

Adding Your Mailbox Icon to the Workspace

After you have logged in and are using someone else's workstation, you can access your mailbox. But first you must add an icon for the mailbox. Adding your mailbox is exactly like adding any other database icon.

▶ **See** "Accessing a Database," **p. 86**

To add a mailbox icon to your workspace, follow these steps:

1. Select a workspace page on which to add your mailbox. (Courtesy dictates that you ask the owner of the workspace before you arbitrarily add the icon.)

2. Choose <u>F</u>ile, <u>D</u>atabase, <u>O</u>pen or press Ctrl+O.

3. Select the name of the server that houses your mailbox. (You wrote the name of your mail server on the disk label, didn't you? If not, you need to know the name of your mail server before you continue.)

4. When you select a server, the database displays a list of the databases on the specified Notes server. You probably won't see your mailbox in the list. But if you scroll through the list, near the end you should see a list of directories, one of which should be MAIL.

   This is the MAIL subdirectory on the server, where mailboxes are stored by default. Like most things in Notes, the mail databases can be stored elsewhere. It's up to the administrator where the mail databases are stored.

   If you can't find the mail subdirectory, contact your administrator for the location of your mail file. When you have the appropriate directory, select it and click <u>O</u>pen, or double-click the MAIL entry.

TIP You can type M to index down to the first entry that begins with M (this is slightly faster than using the scroll bars). This method works in all list boxes.

5. The Database list displays the mailboxes in the MAIL directory. Each mailbox is identified by the name of the user to whom the mailbox belongs. Scroll through the list of names until you find your own name, and select it. (Remember, you can type the first letter of your name to index to the first mailbox that begins with that letter.)

   To add the icon and open the database in one fell swoop, click the <u>O</u>pen button. This puts the icon on the current workspace page and opens the mailbox. Or double-click the entry in the Database list. To add the icon without opening the mailbox, click the <u>A</u>dd button.

You now can access your mailbox from this workstation as you would from your own workstation. Your mailbox is available until you or the owner of the workstation removes the icon from the workspace.

If you plan to use this workstation to access your mailbox often, leave your mailbox icon on the workspace page to save time. But if you don't plan to use this machine again or if you use it infrequently, remove the icon from the workspace when you have finished reading your mail. To do so, select the icon and press the Delete key.

▶ **See** "Deleting Database Icons from Your Workspace," **p. 126**

When you open your mailbox on this new workstation, you should be able to see your mail the same way as on your own PC. This means that only new documents will appear as unread. If you read new documents at this workstation, they will appear as read when you return to your own workstation.

Logging Off the Other Workstation

When you finish using another workstation, be sure to clear your user information. If you don't clear your user information or switch back to the owner's ID, you stay logged in to Notes as long as that session remains active.

This means that anyone can access your mailbox and read your mail or—worse—send mail as you. Just imagine your boss getting a message from you detailing what a jerk she is. In addition, anyone may have access to any of the databases you have access to.

To maintain security (and your job), always do one of the following to make sure that you are logged off the system:

▪ Exit Notes: If you didn't copy your ID file to the workstation's hard disk but just used it from the floppy disk, there is absolutely no way anyone can access your information. If you did copy your ID to the workstation's hard disk, the user would have to know your password to log in as you (and you'd never tell anyone your password, would you?).

Part

I

Ch

6

- Press F5 (or click the Lock ID SmartIcon): This key tells Notes to clear all private user information, logging you off the system. Anyone trying to access a mailbox must enter your password.

- Ask the workstation's owner to log on while you watch: When the owner of the workstation selects File, Tools, Switch ID to select his ID file and log on to his account, you are automatically logged out.

Logging On After Someone Uses Your Workstation

As soon as someone else logs on at your workstation, your Notes session ends. When you're ready to use Notes again on your workstation, you log on to Notes again. The following procedure is almost identical to the one you used to log on to someone else's workstation:

1. If Notes is still running, go to step 2. If Notes isn't running, restart it. If Notes prompts you for the last user's password, click Cancel and go to step 2.

2. Choose File, Tools, Switch ID. Notes asks for the location of your ID file. The File name box displays the filename of the ID last used on your workstation.

   Your ID file should be in the C:\NOTES\DATA directory on your local hard disk. If the path doesn't point to this directory, change the Drive and Directory boxes to point to this directory. The File name box should display your ID file. (As a shortcut, if you know the path and name of your ID file, you can type this into the File name box and click the OK button.)

   For example, if your user name is Roger Sebastian, your ID path and file name probably is C:\NOTES\DATA\RSEBASTI.ID. If you can't find your ID file, contact your Notes administrator or your help desk. You can't reestablish a Notes session without your ID file.

   When you identify your ID file, you are prompted to enter your password. After you have done this successfully, Notes acknowledges that you are logged on, and you can begin to use Notes as usual.

N O T E   You can also use Notes via a dial-up connection from outside your company. See Chapter 20, "Setting Up to Go Remote," for more information on how to work with Notes remote. ▪

Working with the Mail Trace Feature

Mail Tracing is a new Notes 4.x feature that allows the route of a mail message to be traced from sender to recipient. This can be a useful tool when mail is routing incorrectly, because it tells you how far along the route a message went before failing.

Mail Tracing can be configured so that the router at each "hop" along the path sends a verification or so that the router just sends a verification at the final destination. This allows the user or administrator to see the exact route a mail message took on the way to its destination.

To enable Mail Tracing for a mail message, choose the Trace Entire Path for the Delivery Report option.

The Mail Tools Menu Option

Notes 4.6 has a flexible email interface that end users can customize to make NotesMail more productive and enjoyable. A good example of this is the folders feature, which allows you to specify folders in which to sort and organize your email messages based on your own criteria.

This section explores several additional features that let you add your own distinctive flair to your mail messages and make your NotesMail sessions easier and more productive. Figure 6.19 shows the options available when you select Actions, Mail Tools. This menu option is context-sensitive: It is available only when you are in your NotesMail mailbox.

FIG. 6.19

The Actions, Mail Tools menu option in the NotesMail mailbox.

As you can see from Figure 6.19, the options in this menu are

- Add Sender to Address Book
- Archive Selected Documents
- Choose Letterhead
- Create Stationery
- Delegation Profile
- Out of Office

The rest of this section covers each of these six options.

Adding a Sender to Your Address Book

As mentioned earlier, when you receive a mail message, you can easily add the sender's address to your Personal Address Book for future use. Just choose Action, Mail Tools, Add Sender to Address Book, and a new Person document will be created in your address book for this person.

Archiving Your Mail

Although it's a good idea to delete mail messages that are no longer needed, many jobs require that you keep some mail messages for long periods of time. For instance, if you work in a purchasing department and do electronic commerce with your suppliers via email, you might need to keep copies of these email messages for legal reasons.

If this is the case, you can improve your mailbox's response time and make it more manageable from an organizational perspective by creating an Archive mailbox and storing old mail messages there.

N O T E An Archive mailbox can be useful to store email messages for long periods of time and you don't want to incur the overhead of doing so in your mailbox. But you consume more disk space because you are storing more mail messages. ▪

To create an Archive mailbox, first decide where it will be stored—on your local machine or on the Notes server.

If you decide to store the Archive mailbox on the Notes server, common courtesy (and the possible wrath of the Notes administrator) dictates that you speak to your administrator before you put the database on the server. In fact, in most Notes installations, only administrators can put new databases on the server. So you might have to consult the Notes administrator for help.

After you've decided where the Mail Archive database should be stored, it's easy to create. You can select the Archiving view and click the Setup Archive button, or select your mailbox (if you aren't using it) and choose Actions, Mail Tools, Archive Selected Documents. If this is your first time making an archive, you will be asked to confirm that you want to create a new Archive Profile. Then a new Archive Profile document is created, as shown in Figure 6.20.

FIG. 6.20

An Archive Profile document.

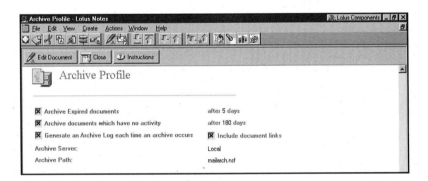

As you can see from Figure 6.20, the Archive Profile form is straightforward. If you need help with these fields when you're filling in your Archive Profile, click the Instructions button on the Action Bar. When you check Archive Expired documents, the after *xx* days field allows you to enter a value for the number of days you want to elapse before inactive documents are archived.

N O T E Any document can have an expiration date—a date after which the author of the document thinks it will no longer be valuable. To set an expiration date for a mail message, ensure that the document is in Edit mode (Ctrl+E) and then choose Actions, Special Options and enter an expiration date in the Special Options dialog box. ▪

When you check Archive documents which have no activity, the after *xx* days field allows you to enter the number of days to wait before an inactive document (a document that hasn't been edited and saved) is archived.

To generate an Archive Log each time you archive messages (an Archive Log is a summary of what the archive action did), check the option Generate an Archive Log each time an archive occurs. This option creates a log entry that you can look at in the Archiving view.

If you check this option, you see the checkbox Include document links. The Archive Log will include a doclink to each archived document. If you want to be able to open the Archive Log and quickly jump to any archived document, enable this feature.

Next, you must click the Specify Archive Location button on the Action Bar in order to specify whether the archive is stored locally or on the server. You also choose a path and filename for the archive database. When you have finished, save and close the document.

The Archive Profile editors field (not visible in the figure) lets you define a list of users who can edit this Archive profile; it defaults to your distinguished username.

When you have configured your Archive Profile, you are ready to begin archiving your mailbox.

Storing Mail in the Archive

You can archive mail messages in one of two ways. The first is through the use of an agent. Lotus provides an archiving agent, Periodic Archive, that by default runs on a weekly schedule and archives your mail messages based on the criteria you set in the Archive Profile.

This schedule can be changed. For more information on agents, see Chapter 16, "Buttons and Agents." To enable the Periodic Archive agent in your mailbox, click the Agents icon in the Navigator. This displays all the agents in your mailbox, as shown in Figure 6.21.

The Periodic Archive agent has a small empty checkbox on the left. This checkbox isn't checked because this agent isn't set to run by default. To enable the agent, click the checkbox. This launches the Choose Server To Run On dialog box, shown in Figure 6.22.

Click the drop-down list and choose the server on which this agent should run. If the archive file is stored on your workstation, choose Local. Otherwise, choose the name of the server where the archive file is stored. When you enter this information, the Periodic Archive checkbox becomes checked, and periodic archiving begins.

The second way to archive mail messages needs some user interaction. You can at any time select mail messages in your mailbox and choose Actions, Mail Tools, Archive Selected Documents to move the selected messages into the archive file. This is useful if you get many messages and you don't want to wait for the agent to run.

N O T E Remember that your new Mail Archive database is only a copy of your mailbox, not a replica. This means that the archive gets new messages only when the Periodic Archive agent runs or when you select Actions, Mail Tools, Archive Selected Documents.

Part

I

Ch

6

FIG. 6.21
Preparing to enable the
Periodic Archive agent.

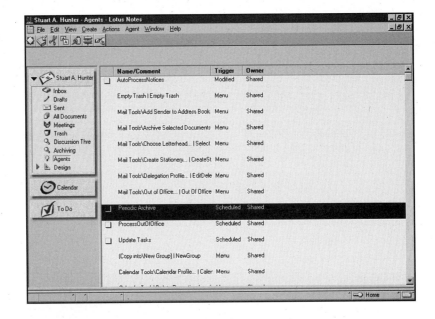

FIG. 6.22
The Choose Server To
Run On dialog box lets
you tell the agent where
to run.

As you use your Mail Archive database, it grows quickly. You should periodically check for mail messages you no longer need and delete them.

Using the Archive

Occasionally, you'll need to use the mail archive file to refer to old mail or delete messages. To access mail messages stored in your archive, you can either follow a doclink from the Archive Log or open the archive database by double-clicking it.

Delegation Profile

The Delegation Profile is a key component of Group Calendaring and Scheduling. This form allows you to define who can access your mailbox to see your calendar and schedule appointments for you. In addition, it lets you determine whether other users can read and manage your mail and even send mail on your behalf. This could be a very handy option if you're a busy executive. Because this form is used primarily for Calendaring and Scheduling, it will be covered in detail in Chapter 9, "Lotus Notes Group Calendaring and Scheduling." Figure 6.23 shows the Delegation Profile form.

FIG. 6.23
The Delegation Profile form.

FIG. 6.23
The Delegation Profile form.

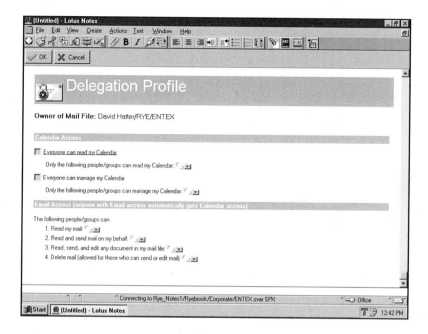

Out Of Office Profile

If you use email, particularly if you work for a large organization, you probably know what happens when you go on vacation or you have to be out of the office for an extended period of time. People keep sending you email, because they don't know you're gone. When you return, your mailbox is full, and people are angry because you haven't answered their messages.

NotesMail provides a simple way to solve this problem. If you're going to be out of the office for a while, you can create an Out Of Office Profile so that users will be notified of your absence (see Figure 6.24).

You can enter a Leaving date and a Returning date. Notes fills in a default subject and message, which you can edit to say whatever you want.

Any mail messages that are sent to you within the time specified in this document cause a return message to be generated. This return mail tells the senders that you are out for the specified time period, as well as any other information you put in the section My Out of The Office message for most people/groups.

In addition, you can put a special message for certain people in the special people/groups field. These are people who should receive a special message. You can also make a list of people and groups who get no message.

Part

I

Ch

6

FIG. 6.24

The Out Of Office Profile helps you notify co-workers of your absence automatically.

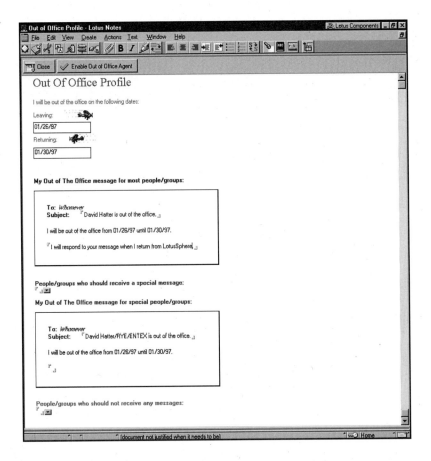

When you have entered the appropriate information, click the Enable Out of Office Agent button; you are asked which server to run this agent on. Be sure to put it in your Home/Mail server. (See the earlier section "Creating an ID Disk" for information on how to determine your Home/Mail server.)

Upon your scheduled return, you get a Welcome Back! message, and the Out Of Office Profile is disabled.

N O T E   In order for the Out Of Office Profile to run correctly, you must be granted the ability to run agents on your server. Be sure that the administrator has enabled this for you. ■

Creating Letterhead

In your mail file, you can select from several letterhead styles to display at the top of your mail messages. In the standard mail Memo form, the letterhead is the multicolored bar that displays your user name and the time and date the mail was composed.

This capability allows you to add personal flair to your mail messages. To change your letter-head, open your mailbox and choose Actions, Mail Tools, Choose Letterhead. This displays the Choose Letterhead window, shown in Figure 6.25.

FIG. 6.25
The Choose Letterhead window.

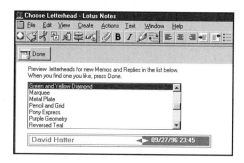

This window displays a list of all the available letterheads in your mailbox. Select one of them from the list, and the new letterhead is applied to all your mail messages. The From the Desk Of letterhead is the default letterhead used in all NotesMail forms.

Creating Stationery

Notes also lets you create stationery, a mail message whose format and recipients list you can use again. This is very useful if you often send messages to the same people.

For instance, if you send a weekly sales report to your sales team, you could create stationery for this purpose that specifies the recipient list.

To create stationery, open your mailbox and choose Actions, Mail Tools, Create Stationery. This launches the Create Stationery dialog box, shown in Figure 6.26.

FIG. 6.26
The Create Stationery dialog box displays the existing stationery forms.

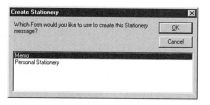

Part

I

Ch

6

You see a list of the stationery you can use. Choose one and click OK. This displays the se-lected Stationery so that you can edit it. When you finish editing, complete the recipient list, add whatever text you need, and send the message.

When the message is sent, you are asked whether you want to save the message as stationery (see Figure 6.27). If you click Yes, you are prompted for a name for the new stationery. Enter a name and click OK.

FIG. 6.27
The Save Stationery
dialog box.

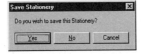

Notes tells you that the new stationery has been saved in the Drafts folder. To compose a new mail message with this stationery, open the Drafts view and open the stationery you want to use.

Other Useful Mail Tools

A variety of other extremely useful Mail tools are available. They are discussed in the following sections.

The Calendar Tools

Notes includes a very powerful Group Calendaring and Scheduling capability that is accessed through your mailbox and that comes with several tools that make it easy to use. Because Group Calendaring and Scheduling is such a powerful feature, it is covered in detail in Chapter 9, "Lotus Notes Group Calendaring and Scheduling."

Resend

If you get a delivery failure, you can use Resend to correct the address and resubmit the mail for delivery. This way, you don't have to re-create the mail message with a corrected address. To use the Resend action, either from a view or from the open document, choose Actions, Resend.

Delivery Information

This action is visible only on the Actions menu when the document is open. It is not available from a view. When you select Actions, Delivery Information, you see the dialog box shown in Figure 6.28.

FIG. 6.28
The Delivery Information
dialog box shows you
mail routing information.

The Delivery Information dialog box shows you who sent the message, the delivery options, and the mail-routing information in one convenient, visually appealing place.

Save As Stationery

Save As Stationery appears on the Action menu when a new mail message is being composed or existing mail is in edit mode. It allows you to convert the open mail message to stationery.

Special Options

The last action, Special Options, is available on the Actions menu and is context-sensitive. It works only for open messages not yet sent. When you select Special Options, the dialog box shown in Figure 6.29 appears.

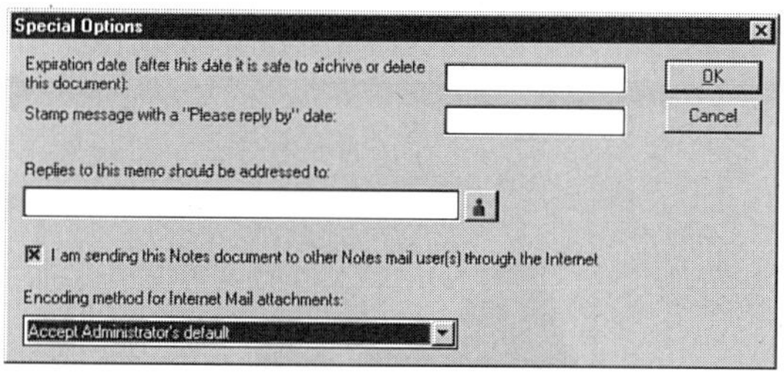

FIG. 6.29

The Special Options dialog box helps you manage advanced mail options.

The first field, Expiration date, allows you to enter the date used by the Archive macro to determine that a document is safe to archive.

The second field, Stamp message with a "Please reply by" date, allows you to enter a date from which Notes generates a `Please reply by` message in the mail message.

The Replies to this memo should be addressed to field allows you to have replies to your mail message routed to another user. You can even use the address helper to choose the user, so you don't need to know the user's address.

The I am sending this Notes document to other Notes mail user(s) through the Internet checkbox is used to tell Notes to encapsulate the message so that rich text items will be retained when they are received at the other end.

Finally, the Encoding method for Internet Mail attachments combo box allows you to choose a number of standard mail attachment transfer protocols such, as UUENCODE and MIME. For more information on Internet mail transfers, consult your Notes administrator.

The Copy Into Menu Option

The Copy Into menu option appears on the Actions menu. It provides you with a variety of tools that allow you to use information from your email to create groups, calendar entries, tasks, and memos.

The following options are available:

- New Memo: With a document highlighted in the view pane, this option creates a new memo addressed to all addressees in the original mail message, including the sender. The original mail message is included in the body of the new mail message.

■ New Calendar Entry: A new Calendar entry is created, the Subject field of the selected memo is copied to the Brief Description field, and the body of the original message is included in the Detailed Description field.

■ New Task: A new Task is created, the Subject field of the selected or open memo is copied to the Subject field of the new Task, and the body of the original message is included in the Additional Information field.

■ New Group: The addressee information from selected documents in the view is used to create the member list of a new Group document in your Personal Address Book. Figure 6.30 shows the addressees from selected documents about to be included in a new group document.

FIG. 6.30

Creating a new Group document using information from selected mail memos.

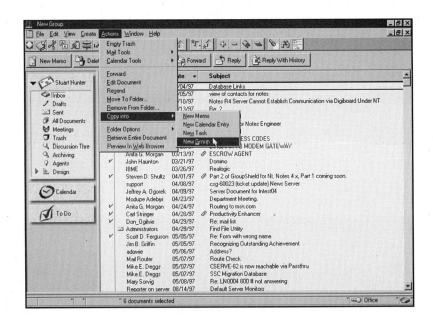

Using Microsoft Word or Lotus Word Pro as Your Mail Editor

For some users, the basic word processing features available in Notes aren't powerful enough to generate complex documents. Other users might prefer to utilize the skills they have acquired in a particular word processing application rather than learn how to use yet another editor. Because of this, users would often create a document in Word or Word Pro and then attach the document as a file attachment to a NotesMail memo. Now Notes gives you the opportunity to compose your NotesMail with Word or Word Pro directly without having to attach a file. This allows much more sophisticated content than what is available with the standard NotesMail editor.

N O T E You can only use Word or WordPro as your *mail* editor. You can't use it as the editor in any other Notes database. In addition, you must be using Microsoft Word 95, 97, or later, and Lotus Word Pro 97 or later. █

To change from the standard Notes editor to Word or Word Pro, select File, Tools, User Preferences, and then select the Mail icon. Figure 6.31 shows the Document Memo editor field, where you can change the default of Notes to Microsoft Word or Lotus Word Pro.

FIG. 6.31

Selecting Microsoft Word as your NotesMail editor.

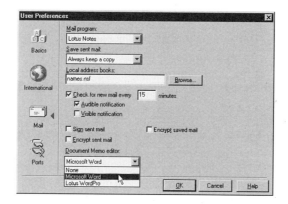

Once you have selected your NotesMail editor, you will have a new option on the Create menu. In addition to creating a memo that uses the standard NotesMail editor, you can choose either a Word memo or a Word Pro memo, depending on which editor you selected (see Figure 6.32).

FIG. 6.32

Creating a new memo using Word Pro.

It may take a few seconds longer than usual to open the mail editing window as your chosen editor is loaded, but you will then be presented with your word processor displaying a blank screen and an addressing window open on top of it. You can choose to address the mail memo now or cancel it and address it later. You can now compose your mail message using all the tools of your chosen editor, utilizing the same menus and toolbars you're used to.

A new button also appears on the Action Bar—the Envelope button (see Figure 6.33). In a standard NotesMail memo, you can address the mail memo directly in the memo itself. You don't have this facility with either of the two other editors. This button brings up an addressing dialog box where you can enter the names of the memo's recipients. This is the same addressing dialog that opened when you composed the memo.

FIG. 6.33

The Envelope button allows you to address mail to the recipients.

Figure 6.34 shows a mail message being edited in Lotus Word Pro with the addressing dialog open. Figure 6.35 shows the same mail message being edited in Microsoft Word. Notice the specific differences in the menus and toolbars. Although the File menu still displays standard Notes options, the other menus reflect those of the editor you have chosen.

FIG. 6.34

Addressing a mail message with Word Pro as your NotesMail editor.

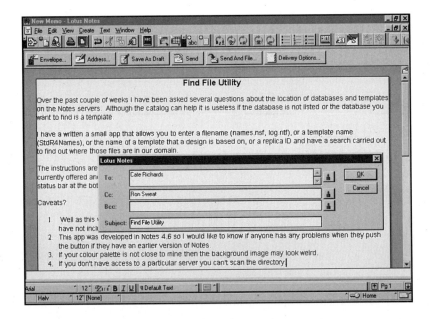

If you pull down the Help menu (see Figure 6.36), you will see that it allows you to choose between help for Notes and help for your chosen editor.

When you have completed entering and formatting your email message using the tools available to your selected editor, you can send the memo in the normal way.

When the recipient opens the memo to read it, if he has the editor used to create the memo in the first place, Word or Word Pro, that editor will automatically be opened and the memo displayed. If the recipient doesn't have the editor used to create the memo, it will be displayed in the standard NotesMail editor, and some formatting might be lost.

FIG. 6.35

Editing a memo with Microsoft Word.

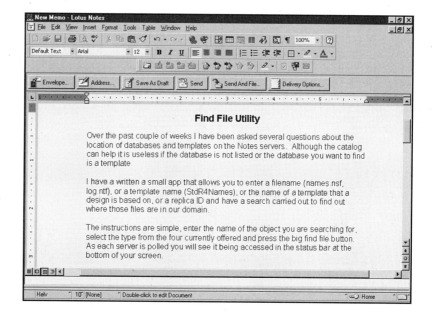

FIG. 6.36

Choosing Help allows you to select between Help for Notes or for your chosen editor.

Using POP3/SMTP Mail from Notes

With more and more people accessing the Internet, it was only a matter of time before Lotus built support for Internet email directly into the client. In Notes 4.6, Lotus has opened the Notes client to the POP3 and SMTP protocols—the prevalent mail messaging protocols used on the Internet.

If you have an Internet email account, you probably receive your email from a POP3 server, perhaps using a mail client such as Eudora. If you are already familiar with NotesMail, it might be more convenient for you to use the same client for Internet mail as you do for NotesMail. The next section describes how to set up your Notes workstation to send and receive POP3/SMTP mail. First, here are some definitions:

POP3: Post Office Protocol 3. This determines how you *receive* mail. It is the protocol that allows a mail server to receive mail and hold onto it until you connect to the mail server to retrieve mail.

Part

I

Ch

6

SMTP: Simple Mail Transfer Protocol. This protocol is responsible for formatting and sending messages from your client to the mail server. In its pure form, it can't handle the sending of file attachments, but MIME has extended the capabilities of SMTP to include attachments. However, they can't be viewed in-line with the rest of the text as with Notes.

Before you begin, make sure that you have TCP/IP installed on your workstation and that you have some way of accessing the Internet, either via LAN or modem connection. You don't specifically need to have TCP/IP configured within Notes. Like other applications designed to work with the Internet, Notes will look for a TCP/IP stack when attempting a connection with the mail server, despite the fact that you haven't added it as a protocol within Notes.

Your first decision is where to store your Internet email. The standard Notes 4.6 mail template supports Internet mail, so you might consider just using your standard NotesMail database. However, perhaps your Internet mail is personal, not work-related. Also, you need to consider what would happen if you tried to reply to one of your Internet email messages when you were connected to the company network. If the company has no Internet access, the message will bounce back. For these reasons, it's probably better to set up a separate mail database for POP3 mail.

Creating a New Database for POP3 Mail

If you decide to create a new database to host your POP3 mail instead of using an existing mail file, carry out the following steps to create it:

1. Move to the workspace page where you want your new mail file to appear. You might want to make sure that this is separate from your standard NotesMail database to avoid confusion.

2. Select File, Database, New.

3. Choose a server to store the mail file on. If you're going to use this new database purely for Internet mail, you should choose Local, because that will be the only choice when you create the Location document later. If you're using this database for Notes *and* Internet mail, you can choose to store it on a Notes server.

4. Enter a name for the mail file, making it different enough from your standard NotesMail database so that you won't confuse the two. "POP3 Mail" is a good choice.

5. Enter a filename for the mail file. Again, try and make it different enough so that you won't confuse it with your standard NotesMail database. "POP3Mail.NSF" would be a good choice.

6. Scroll down the template list and choose the Mail (R4.6) template, whose filename is MAIL46.NTF.

7. Click OK.

You have now created your new mail file that will hold your POP3 mail. You may also want to change the icon of this new file to avoid confusion with your standard NotesMail database. To do this, open the database and click the twistie next to Design in the database navigator on the left. Click Other, which is the last item in the submenu. Double-click Icon from the list of objects in the view pane. You can now use the icon designer tools to modify the default mail icon. Figure 6.37 compares the standard NotesMail database icon to the one designed for POP3.

FIG. 6.37
Change the design of the POP3 mail icon to avoid confusion with your standard NotesMail database.

The most important part of setting up for POP3 mail is creating the Location document, which allows you to connect to the Internet mail servers.

Creating the Location Document for POP3 Mail

You need a way to tell Notes, via a Location document, that you want to go to the Internet to send and receive Internet Mail.

To create a Location document for POP3 Mail, open your Personal Address Book and choose Create, Location. Then do the following:

1. Ensure that the Location type field is set to Local Area Network. Even if you're dialing in to your Internet Service Provider (ISP), the connection appears to be a direct network connection to all the applications that use it, including Notes.

2. Enter a Location name. This is how you will identify the Location document, so make it relevant. "POP3" would be a good choice.

3. In the Mail section, click the entry helper for the Mail system field and choose Internet (or Notes and Internet if you're using the same mail database for both Notes and Internet mail).

4. The mail file location will be set to Local, and you won't be able to change this unless you have selected Notes and Internet as the Mail system, in which case, you can enter the name of a Notes server in the Home/mail server field in the Servers section.

5. The mail filename should reflect the database created earlier—POP3Mail.NSF, for example.

6. In the Internet Mail section, Send outgoing mail will be set to Directly to Internet. If you have chosen Notes and Internet as your mail system, you have the additional choice of sending through a Domino server (your Home/mail server).

7. The Internet mail address field will hold the return address for messages you send, so it should be your standard Internet email address.

8. The Outgoing (SMTP)Internet mail server field will hold the name of the server that you send Internet email to. You should get this name from your ISP.

Part

I

Ch

6

9. The Incoming Internet mail server field holds the name of the POP3 server that you connect to to pick up your email. Often, this will be the same as the server in the Outgoing (SMTP) Internet mail server field. Check with your ISP to be sure.

10. The Internet username field will contain the username supplied to you by your ISP.

11. Enter the password given to you by your ISP by clicking the icon and entering your password. Note the warning about encrypting the document with your Public Key (see Figure 6.38).

FIG. 6.38

Configuring a Location document for Internet mail.

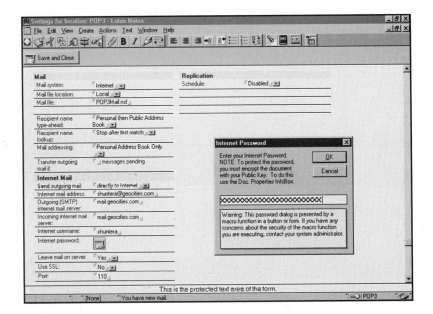

12. If you want to leave mail on the POP3 server after you have received it in your mail file, choose Yes in the Leave mail on server field. This will mean that if you delete some messages, they will be pulled from the POP3 server again when you next connect.

13. Save and close the Location document. This will result in the creation of a new mailbox file called SMTP.BOX. When you create new messages destined for the Internet, they will reside here until you transmit them when you're connected to your SMTP mail server.

14. Switch to your new Location document, and you are ready to test the connection.

Replicating Mail

You send and receive Internet email the same way you replicate mail when you're a mobile user. To test your setup, start by creating a few mail messages to friends and colleagues using their Internet email addresses. These will be stored in your SMTP.BOX file until they are ready to transmit.

If your Internet connection is via dialup, establish your connection to the Internet now. When the connection comes up, you can attempt to replicate your Internet mail in one of many ways:

■ Click the mail tray at the bottom right of your Notes screen and choose from among Receive Mail, Send Outgoing Mail, and Send & Receive Mail.

■ Open the SMTP.BOX file and click the Deliver Mail button on the Action Bar.

■ From the Replicator page, click the Send & Receive Mail button on the Action Bar.

■ From the Replicator page, click the Other Actions button and choose Send Outgoing Mail.

■ From the Inbox of your POP3 mail database, click the Retrieve Mail button on the Action Bar.

When a connection is established, mail will start to flow. Figure 6.39 shows the connection in progress, retrieving mail from the Internet Mail server.

FIG. 6.39

Retrieving mail from the Internet mail server.

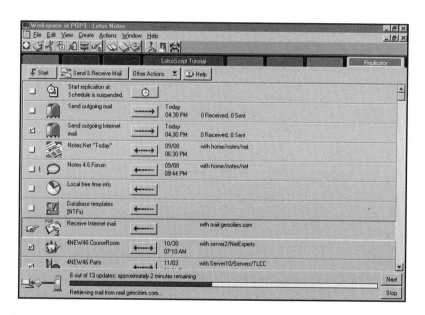

When the connection has closed, you can hang up the modem to your ISP and view your mail. Because this mail is now held in a Notes mail database, you can perform the usual tasks on it, such as replying to messages, creating Tasks from messages, and forwarding mail messages to others. ●

Part

I

Ch

6

Working with Text

In earlier chapters, you learned how to compose simple documents. Although the techniques you learned are adequate for getting information across to your coworkers, you can communicate much more effectively by using the wealth of enhanced features that Notes offers. These features add emphasis to your writing and facilitate communication as you work with Notes.

Editing Text Fields

If you have used a word processor before—anything from Word Pro to WordPerfect—you're used to rearranging, highlighting, and manipulating text. Notes includes a sophisticated text processor that provides many of the same features you have come to appreciate in word processors. If you're familiar with Windows-based word processors such as Microsoft Word for Windows, Word Pro, or WordPerfect for Windows, you will find that many of the keystrokes are the same.

Even if you haven't used a word processor before, by now you probably have done some experimenting in Notes and have discovered that you can make some simple corrections by performing the following basic actions:

- Pressing the arrow keys lets you move up, down, left, and right within your document. The arrow keys also let you move from field to field.
- Pressing the Home key positions the insertion point at the beginning of the line.
- Pressing the End key positions the insertion point at the end of the line.
- Pressing the Page Up and Page Down keys scrolls one screen up or one screen down, respectively.
- Pressing Ctrl+Home positions the insertion point at the beginning of the document; pressing Ctrl+End moves it to the end.
- Pressing Ctrl+left arrow moves the insertion point back a word; pressing Ctrl+right arrow moves it forward a word.
- Pressing the Delete key deletes the character to the right of the insertion point.
- Pressing the Backspace key deletes the character to the left of the insertion point.
- You can reposition the insertion point by clicking anywhere in the text.

As you read through this chapter, keep in mind that Notes offers a quick mouse trick to bring up a list of some of the most popular formatting selections, as well as the Text Properties InfoBox, which gives you a wealth of text and paragraph settings to enhance your documents. To use this shortcut, right-click anywhere in the Notes document. Notes displays the context-sensitive menu shown in Figure 7.1.

In the following sections, you will learn about powerful editing commands.

FIG. 7.1

You can make quick formatting selections by right-clicking anywhere in the document.

Selecting Text

Some of the most powerful editing and formatting operations involve a two-step process. You first must identify the text that you want to do something to and then tell Notes what to do with that text. As you read through the next few sections and learn how to perform editing tasks such as copying and changing text styles, you first must select the text as a way of telling Notes that this is the text you want to work with.

> **N O T E** If you haven't typed any text yet, you can set font attributes for the new text first. After you set the font attributes (such as style, size, and color), all the text you type appears with those attributes until you change them or exit the document.

To select a section of text, place the mouse pointer at the beginning of the text you want to work with, hold down the left mouse button, move the pointer to the end of the text, and release the mouse button. If you prefer to use the keyboard, position the insertion point at the beginning of the text you want to select, hold down the Shift key, and move the insertion point to the end of the text using the arrow keys. Using either method, you can select any amount of text.

After you select the text, it appears in reverse video—that is, the text appears as a light color with a dark box surrounding it (see Figure 7.2).

 You can select just one word quickly by double-clicking while the pointer is on the word. This is a great time-saver if you want to check the spelling or change the font attributes of just that one word.

After you select the text, you can tell Notes what you want to do to it.

One of the simplest and most common operations is deleting the selected text, which you can do by pressing the Delete key. Other ways to delete selected text include selecting Edit, Clear, clicking the Edit Clear SmartIcon, and pressing the spacebar.

Another common operation is typing over a selected section of text with new text. After you select the text, start typing new text to replace the old. The instant you start typing, Notes deletes all the selected text and begins inserting the new text you type.

Part

I

Ch

7

FIG. 7.2

You can select text in documents by clicking and dragging the mouse cursor over it.

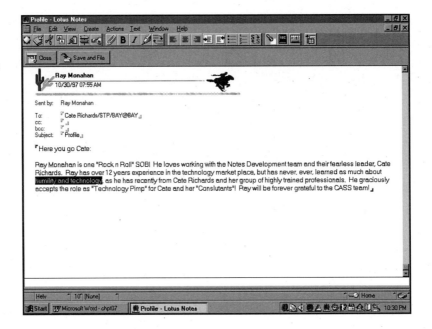

CAUTION

Be careful that you don't accidentally type text while you have text selected. If you type new text while old text is selected, Notes thinks that you want to replace the old text with the new. Many users have experienced momentary panic at seeing a large block of selected text disappear because they accidentally pressed a key. If you make such a mistake, select Edit, Undo Typing before you type anything else or perform any other function.

Using the Clipboard

The clipboard is a storage area shared among Notes and other Windows, Macintosh, and OS/2 applications. It serves as a temporary holding location for data that you are moving or copying between Notes and other word processors, spreadsheets, and many other programs. You can use the clipboard to cut text, bitmaps, or other inserted objects (such as spreadsheets and other graphic files) from a Notes document—for example, switch to a Windows word processor such as Word for Windows or Word Pro—and paste them into a Word or Word Pro document. You can also use the clipboard to cut and paste a document from one database to another. (You'll learn more about cutting and pasting documents in Chapter 8, "Working with Documents.")

N O T E   You can use the clipboard to copy data between any applications that are designed to work with the clipboard. ■

The clipboard is a temporary storage location. You can store data there only during a single Windows or OS/2 session. If you turn off your PC or exit Windows or OS/2, the clipboard is cleared, and the data is lost.

> **CAUTION**
>
> Copying something else to the clipboard will erase whatever you currently have stored there, unless you're appending text to the clipboard (this is discussed in a moment). You will lose the old data when you copy the new data to the clipboard.

The following sections explain how to use the clipboard as a way to copy and move data with Notes and between Notes and other applications.

Although this section discusses the copying, cutting, and pasting of text, these procedures apply to all objects found in Notes documents. For example, you can follow these same procedures to copy attachments, graphics, and other objects stored in the database.

Moving Text   As you type your text, you might decide that your thoughts make better sense in a different order, so you want to move text from one place to another. This process—known as cutting and pasting—comes from the days when editors cut snippets of text from a paper document and pasted them elsewhere in the document. As the technique's name implies, cutting and pasting is really a two-step process: You remove the text from its old location (cut it) and insert it into its new location (paste it).

You must be in edit mode to cut and paste data. To enter edit mode, double-click anywhere in a document that is in read mode to open it for editing. Field brackets will appear to indicate that you are in edit mode.

To cut and paste text, follow these steps:

1. Select the text you want to move.
2. Press Ctrl+X, choose Edit, Cut, or click the Edit Cut SmartIcon. Notes removes the text from your document.
3. Position the insertion point where you want to paste the text.
4. Press Ctrl+V, choose Edit, Paste, or click the Edit Paste SmartIcon. Notes copies whatever text is in the clipboard into your document wherever the insertion point is.

Copying Text   Copying text is very similar to moving it. As with moving, you want to put the text somewhere else in your current document or another document, but with copying, you also want the text to remain at its current location. You can be in read or edit mode to copy text, but you must be in edit mode to paste it.

Part

I

Ch

7

Like the procedure to move text, copying text is a two-step process using the clipboard as an intermediate holding place. Only the second step is different, as you can see from the following steps:

1. Select the text you want to copy.
2. Press Ctrl+C, choose Edit, Copy, or click the Edit Copy SmartIcon. The text remains where it is, and nothing seems to have happened. However, Notes has copied the selected text to the clipboard.
3. You can now move the insertion point to a new position and paste as described in the preceding set of steps or by using any of the other methods described earlier. Notes copies the text from the clipboard to the document in the new location.

 If you prefer to use the keyboard whenever possible, you can press Shift+End to highlight all the text on a line that is to the right of the insertion point. Or, you can press Shift+Page Down to copy everything from the insertion point to the bottom of the page. Holding the Shift key down while pressing the arrow keys will highlight everything in the direction of the arrow key you press until you release the arrow key. However, be careful! If you accidentally press Shift+Insert instead, Notes will copy whatever is on the clipboard into your document. If this happens, immediately select Edit, Undo Typing to correct the mistake.

Many applications provide cut, copy, and paste operations but use a different set of shortcut keys. Notes supports two sets of shortcut keys, as shown in Table 7.1. If you choose to use the keyboard for editing operations, you can use either set of keys. Keep in mind that the Macintosh uses the Command key rather than the Ctrl key for keyboard commands.

Table 7.1   Shortcut Editing Keys

Operation	Standard Keys	Alternative Keys
Cut	Ctrl+X	Shift+Delete
Copy	Ctrl+C	Ctrl+Insert
Paste	Ctrl+V	Shift+Insert
Undo	Ctrl+Z	Alt+Backspace

Copying Multiple Pieces of Text   You might find yourself in a situation where you want to copy several different pieces of text from several different documents and paste them all into a new document. If you use the copy-and-paste technique described a moment ago, you must copy a piece of text to the clipboard and then paste it into the new document before you copy the next piece of text. Each new copy operation replaces what is already on the clipboard. However, Notes provides a better operation for this situation:

1. Use the usual key combination—Ctrl+C—to copy the first piece of text to the clipboard.

2. For a subsequent piece of text, press Ctrl+Shift+Insert. Notes copies the selected text to the clipboard, but rather than replacing the clipboard's existing contents, Notes appends the new text so that the clipboard contains both pieces of text.

   You can also hold down the Shift key and choose Edit, Copy or Edit, Cut for each piece of text you want to add to the clipboard.

N O T E When you copy more than one noncontiguous section to the clipboard, Notes doesn't put a space between the last character of the first section copied and the first character of the next unless you copy a space or blank line at the same time you copy the text. It simply adds the text to the end of the section you copied previously.

This might create a messy copy on the clipboard, so that you have to spend time cleaning up when you paste the information into a new document. If keeping paragraphs, sentences, or words separate is important to you, make sure you highlight the spaces you want copied as well.

By repeating step 2 for additional text, you can accumulate as much text as you need on the clipboard. Place the cursor in the location in which you want the copied text to appear, and then press Ctrl+V (or Edit, Paste). Notes pastes the entire contents of the clipboard into the new location.

More About Moving and Copying Text

After you cut or copy text to the clipboard, you don't have to paste it into its new location immediately. The text remains on the clipboard until you cut or copy something else (or until you exit Windows or OS/2). If you need to perform other operations at the location where you cut or copied the text, feel free to as long as you don't cut or copy other text. However, to avoid accidentally losing your data, it's best if you paste the data that's on the clipboard into its new location as soon as possible—particularly if you're busy or often distracted and run the risk of forgetting where you left off in your work.

Pasting copies text from the clipboard into your document, but the text remains on the clipboard. If you want to place another copy of the same text elsewhere, you need only move the insertion point to the new location and paste again. Thus, from a single cut or copy, you can perform as many paste operations as you like.

You can do more than just cut (or copy) and paste within the same document. After you cut or copy text to the clipboard, you can close the current document, open another document, and then paste the text into the second document.

In fact, you need not even paste within the same application or database. You can cut or copy a section of text in Notes, switch to another application that is designed to use the clipboard, and then paste into a word processing document, spreadsheet, or other file in that application. Similarly, you can perform a cut or copy in other applications, switch to Notes, and then paste. This capability to move and copy from one application to another is one of the most important advantages of using applications that support the clipboard.

Pasting Text into Dialog Boxes   Often, you might want to copy (or cut) and paste information into a dialog box, but the Cut, Copy, and Paste commands aren't available when you choose Edit. Don't worry. You can use Ctrl+C to copy (or Ctrl+X to cut) the information to the

Part

I

Ch

7

clipboard and then use Ctrl+V to paste the information. This is particularly helpful when you're trying to enter information into a dialog box, where the Edit, Copy and Edit, Paste commands aren't available.

For example, you can use this tip when you're trying to fill the contents of a formula box when designing a field in a document. In Figure 7.3, the formula in the formula definition box is quite long and would take the designer a good bit of time to type. However, if the designer already has this formula defined elsewhere, he can copy the formula from there and paste it into the field. The designer is now free to customize the formula as needed.

FIG. 7.3

You can easily paste text into a formula dialog box by copying from one location using Ctrl+C and then pasting into the new formula entry field using Ctrl+V.

 Designers often use Notes databases to store copies of formulas—particularly complicated ones—in simple text fields. Then, when the formula is needed, the designer simply opens the database document that references the type of formula needed, copies the formula text, and pastes it into the field formula definition box currently being defined. The designer might need to customize the formula—editing references to other fields, forms, or views, for example—but the formula, with its particular syntax, provides a great template to work from.

This database is often stored on a server, and all database designers can contribute and use the formulas. This lets companies maximize the use of database design using the trusted CASE method of Notes development—Copy And Steal Everything! You can use the CASE method with the Notes Formula Catalog database, which is included on the CD-ROM that accompanies this book. In this database, you will find numerous formulas that you can copy directly into the design of your application!

Undoing Changes

Everybody presses the wrong key or chooses the wrong menu option occasionally, so you might wind up cutting when you meant to paste, or deleting when you meant to copy. Fortunately, with Notes, all isn't lost.

Whenever you perform an operation that modifies a section of text—such as delete, cut, copy, or paste—Notes offers you a chance to change your mind. You can reverse the effects, or undo, the last operation by choosing Edit, Undo, pressing Ctrl+Z, or clicking the Edit Undo SmartIcon.

The exact wording of the first option on the Edit menu varies, depending on the last operation you performed. If you last did a cut, the command is Undo Cut; if you last did a paste, the command is Undo Paste. If you choose the command, Notes undoes the last operation by restoring the deleted text, removing the pasted text, or reversing whatever action you performed.

Notes also lets you change your mind about Undo. If you undo an operation, such as boldfacing text, and then you decide you want to perform that function after all, choose Edit, Redo. The bold text will reappear. Like the Undo command, the Redo command will change, depending on what action you're performing.

Undo is useful only if you realize immediately that you have made a mistake, because you can undo only the most recent operation. Suppose that you delete a piece of text and then perform another operation (for example, typing another character or copying another piece of text to the clipboard). If you realize then that the deletion was a mistake, you're out of luck—it's gone for good.

CAUTION

The Undo command can't be used to bring back entire documents that have been deleted from a database.

Understanding Rich Text Fields

The most common type of field you encounter in Notes documents is a text field. You can enter any kind of text into such a field—words, sentences, names, and so on. Notes has two types of text fields: plain text fields and rich text fields.

N O T E The body of your Notes email memo is an example of a rich text field, and the Subject field in the memo is a text field.

A rich text field is so called because you can enter text, objects, and formatting information. Associated with any portion of rich text is a particular color, type style, justification, line spacing, and many other characteristics. By changing the characteristics for any portion of rich text, you can tell Notes to display (and print) that portion in any one of various colors, sizes, and type styles. You also can enter tables, graphics, document links, buttons, and other objects in rich text fields.

Part

I

Ch

7

In the following sections, you'll learn how to make the most of text attributes. In Chapter 8, you will learn how to insert objects such as tables, document links, and buttons.

N O T E   Rich text fields are the only fields in which you can change the font attributes; format paragraphs; and insert graphics, embedded objects, attachments, tables, document links, pop-up boxes, and other special items. They are also the only fields in which you can import data from other applications. If you're trying to use one of these features and the menu command isn't available, your cursor isn't located in a rich text field.

Information entered in rich text fields won't be displayed in views. Text (and other field types) is used when the information needs to be displayed in a view. ■

Spotting Rich Text Fields

How can you tell whether a field is plain text or rich text? You can't tell by looking at an empty field, but you can try to use some of the features described in this section. If you try to change the style of the field—by adding color or changing the type style—and Notes won't let you, the field isn't a rich text field. Also, with the cursor located in the field, you can look at the text section of the status bar at the bottom of the Notes window. If the type and size of the font appear, you're in a rich text field; otherwise, you aren't.

Finally, you can distinguish between the two types of text fields by placing the insertion point anywhere within the field and pulling down the Text menu. If the insertion point is on a plain text field, most of the menu choices, such as Bold, Italic, and Underline, are grayed out, indicating that they aren't available.

Generally, rich text fields are fields in which you might have good reason to use different fonts and type styles, such as a description of a customer problem or notes about a meeting with a client. Other fields that contain simple pieces of data, such as an author's name or the subject of a meeting, are plain text fields.

As you become acquainted with various databases, you might notice that plain text fields tend to contain small amounts of data—the name of an addressee, a zip code, or a Social Security number, for example—whereas rich text fields tend to include much longer amounts of text, such as a description of a meeting or the body of a memo.

Many documents consist of a few short plain text fields and a single potentially long rich text field. A memo, for example, has several short plain text fields (To, Cc, Bcc, Subject) and a single rich text field (the body of the memo) that can contain thousands of lines of text and other objects.

Some database designers exclude rich text fields from documents to keep users from attaching files in the document. This is the designer's way of trying to minimize database size or maximize the speed at which documents are replicated from one copy of the database to another. If you're using a database in which attaching documents is necessary, you must contact the database manager to see whether the field type can be changed.

Changing the Appearance of Text with the Text Menu

The Notes Text menu gives you control over text characteristics, such as text attributes (bold-face, italic, underline), fonts, justification, spacing, and so on (see Figure 7.4). You can use a single set of procedures to manipulate any of these characteristics. Many of the selections on the Text menu, such as Italic, Bold, and Underline, are quick selections for options that are also available in the Text Properties InfoBox. You will learn about these features when you work through the attribute settings found in the Text Properties InfoBox.

FIG. 7.4

You can change text attributes from the Text menu one at a time or access the Text Properties InfoBox to change them all at once.

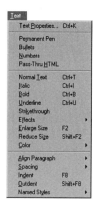

You must be in edit mode to type text and change the font attributes. If you don't see open brackets positioned around each field in the document to signify that the document is in edit mode, right-double-click anywhere in the document. You can use the Actions Edit Document SmartIcon if you have it available in your set of SmartIcons. If you're composing a new document, it's already in edit mode.

Selecting Text to Modify

To control the characteristics of new text you are about to type, follow these steps:

1. Position the insertion point where you want to type the new text if it isn't already in the proper location.

2. Choose Text, Text Properties, or press Ctrl+K.

3. Choose the characteristic you want to change (such as Font or Size).

The new text you type at that location will take on the characteristics you selected.

Suppose that you are about to type the phrase "This task is critical to our success," and you want the word "critical" to appear in bold and in red. Type the first part of the sentence (This task is). Next, change the text color to red and then change the style to bold by following these steps:

1. Choose Text, Text Properties (or click the Text Properties SmartIcon).

2. Choose Red in the Text Color drop-down list, and choose Bold from the Style list box.

3. Whatever you type now will appear in bold red. Type critical.

Before you finish the sentence, you need to switch back to nonbold black, which you can do by following the preceding steps but choosing Black rather than Red and Normal rather than Bold in step 2. Then, finish the sentence by typing to our success.

You also can change characteristics for existing text. Suppose that you have already typed the sentence "This task is critical to our success," and then you decide that you want "critical" to appear in bold red. Follow these steps:

1. Select the text you want to change—in this example, the word critical.

2. Choose Text, Text Properties.

3. The Text Properties InfoBox appears. Choose Red and Bold.

The word "critical" changes from black to red. The surrounding text remains normal black. The text you have highlighted remains in reverse video when you click OK to change the font attributes. Simply click anywhere in the document to view your font changes.

Even if you know as you type the sentence that you want the word "critical" to be in bold red, you might find that typing the complete sentence and then changing the color and style for the word "critical" is easier.

When you change fonts and font sizes, keep in mind that some fonts naturally appear smaller to the reader. For example, the Helvetica 10 font is the default and is relatively easy to read onscreen. If you change the font type to Script and leave the font size at 10, you will notice that it is quite difficult to read the text. You will need to increase the font size in order for the Script font to be readable onscreen.

Also, although Helvetica 10 is easy to read onscreen, it is often difficult for some people to read text with this font size when it is printed. You might want to increase the font size to 12 or greater if you are printing the document or if you're fairly sure that the reader will want to print the document.

Working with the Text Properties InfoBox

The first selection on the Text menu, Text Properties, lets you control the appearance of the characters that make up a section of text. The Text Properties InfoBox lets you control the characters' size, color, type style, and other attributes (see Figure 7.5). This InfoBox contains the following five tabs:

- Font: Controls font sizes, styles, and colors. The font attributes used by the Permanent Pen (discussed near the end of this chapter) are also adjusted through this tab.

- Alignment: Controls how the text in a paragraph aligns in relation to the left margin. The options on this tab also include automatic bulleting and numbering for text and line spacing for text in a paragraph.

- Pages/Tabs: Controls the pagination and tab settings for the paragraph. This tab also contains the right margin setting for printing purposes.

- Hide: Controls when Notes displays a paragraph. Notes lets you hide text based on numerous conditions.

■ Style: Gives users the ability to define frequently used paragraph styles. The styles defined on this tab are available for selection in the style section of the status bar at the bottom of the Notes window.

Each of the settings on these tabs is discussed in detail in the following sections.

N O T E If you don't have a mouse and you need to select a tab in the Text Properties InfoBox other than the one that is currently displayed, use the right and left arrow keys to cycle through the five tabs until the tab you want to work with is visible. If you press the right or left arrow key and nothing happens, try pressing the Tab key until you notice a dotted-line box surrounding the current tab's icon. Then press the right or left arrow key until the tab you want appears. ■

FIG. 7.5

The font tab of the Text Properties InfoBox is used to change font style, height, color, and other attributes.

Setting Fonts In the Font tab of the Text Properties InfoBox, you can select the font type (Figure 7.5 shows Helv selected), the size of the font, the color, and the type style.

For many common characteristics, Notes provides Text menu commands and shortcut keys that you can use instead of the Text Properties InfoBox (see Table 7.2). When you choose the Text menu, Notes displays the shortcut keys next to their corresponding commands (refer to Figure 7.4). Rather than choosing Text, Bold, for example, you can press Ctrl+B and skip the Text menu altogether.

N O T E New to Notes 4.6 is the ability to format text as passthru HTML, which is a formatting option typically used by developers creating applications that will be published to the Web. Use passthru HTML formatting to flag text in a form or document as HTML-only. To edit the text later from a Notes workstation, choose View, Show, Pass-Thru HTML. If you hid the text from Notes users, choose View, Show, Hidden from Notes. ■

You can now preview documents in a Web browser from the Actions menu, which can greatly speed up the development of your Web-enabled applications. To do so, select Actions, Preview in Web Browser. You can also get to the HTML code by selecting Actions, Edit HTML Body Attributes. Again, this is a simpler and faster method of working with HTML than what was available in previous versions of Notes.

Part

I

Ch

7

Table 7.2   Text Menu Quick Command Reference

SmartIcon	Command	Shortcut
	Text, Text Properties	Ctrl+K
	Text, Permanent Pen	
	Text, Bullets	
	Text, Numbers	
	Text, Pass-Thru HTML	
N	Text, Normal Text	Ctrl+T
I	Text, Italic	Ctrl+I
B	Text, Bold	Ctrl+B
U	Text, Underline	Ctrl+U
	Text, Shadow	
	Text, Emboss	
	Text, Extrude	
AA	Text, Enlarge Size	F2
A'A	Text, Reduce Size	Shift+F2
	Text, Color (select a color from the list)	
	Text, Align Paragraph, Center	
	Text, Align Paragraph, Full	

SmartIcon	Command	Shortcut
≡	Text, Align Paragraph, Left	
≡	Text, Align Paragraph, Right	
	Text, Align Paragraph, No Wrap	
	Text, Spacing, Single	
	Text, Spacing, One and a half	
	Text, Spacing, Double	
	Text, Spacing, Other (opens the Properties InfoBox)	
	Text, Indent	F8
	Text, Outdent	Shift+F8
	Text, Named Styles	F11 (to use Cycle list)

You can change the text style to highlight portions of your text in various ways. The style includes characteristics such as text color and font, and attributes such as boldface, emboss, shadow, extrude, and italic. Different text styles can add emphasis to important phrases, add interest to your document, and draw your reader's attention to crucial passages.

The following sections discuss the different text attributes available in the Text Properties InfoBox and offer some suggested uses.

Changing Fonts You can choose one of many fonts. Helv 10pt is the default font used by Notes (except in Macintosh, where Geneva is the default font). The following are three examples of fonts:

Helv

`Courier`

Times Roman

You can also view fonts as Typewriter fonts. The Typewriter fonts option under File, Tools, User Preferences tells Notes to display all information (including database titles, views, and documents) in monospace fonts, in which all letters take up the same amount of space. You might find this option useful for checking the width of columns. If a column is wide enough in a

Part
I

Ch
7

monospace font to display the entire contents of the column, it will probably be wide enough when you switch back to a proportional (nonmonospace) font. This is a particularly useful feature when you're designing export views.

Changing the Point Size   You can choose from any of the font sizes in the Size list box or type an entry in the box below the list. Clicking the up and down arrows next to the Size box causes the text size to increase or decrease one step for each click.

Changing the Color   When you click the down arrow next to the Text color selection box, Notes presents a list of 16 colors. Colors are especially helpful in headings and important passages.

Changing the Text Style   You can choose from any of the following text styles:

- **Bold** causes text to stand out from the surrounding text. Typing important points or names in boldface helps your reader spot the topic of a paragraph instantly.

- *Italic* puts extra emphasis on text. Use italic to highlight especially important words or phrases or for foreign phrases.

- Underline also adds emphasis.

- ~~Strikethrough~~ puts a line through the text you have selected. Using strikethrough helps your reader immediately identify areas of the text that you want removed from a document or that you don't agree with.

- Superscript is used to slightly raise text and make it smaller. This attribute is used in mathematical expressions such as 2^2 and with some symbols such as copyright or registered trademarks. You can also use it to show degrees.

- Subscript lowers one or more characters, as in chemical symbols such as H_2O.

- Shadow creates a gray shadow effect behind each letter. This feature typically is used in form or section titles to jazz up a document's appearance. Be careful with this feature, however. If the font size is small, using the shadow attribute can cause the letters to look blurry onscreen. This attribute isn't applied to printed text, just onscreen text.

- Emboss creates a three-dimensional raised effect that highlights the text you're working with. Be careful with this feature, however. If the font size is small, embossing it will cause it to look blurry. This attribute isn't applied to printed text, just onscreen text. This attribute is especially appealing with text that is shown in three-dimensional layout regions.

- Extrude creates a three-dimensional sunken look. As with embossing and shadowing, applying this attribute to text that has a small font size might cause it to look blurry. This attribute isn't applied to printed text, just onscreen text. This attribute is especially appealing with text that is shown in three-dimensional layout regions.

You can also enlarge and reduce the size of text one point size at a time using the Text menu or by using the following function keys:

- Enlarge size: Press F2 or choose Text, Enlarge to enlarge text by one point size. Pressing F2 repeatedly makes the text increasingly larger.

- Reduce size: Press Shift+F2 or choose Text, Reduce Size to reduce text by one point size. Pressing Shift+F2 repeatedly makes the text smaller.

You can also change fonts and font sizes quickly by clicking the font name or font size portions of the status bar at the bottom of the Notes window. The available font types and sizes will appear as a pop-up list when you choose the status bar option. Which fonts are available depends on which fonts are installed on your PC.

Working with Strikethrough The Text Properties InfoBox offers a selection called strikethrough, which is very useful (but often overlooked) if you're responsible for editing someone else's documents. For example, if you're reviewing a memo that lists the anticipated price on a contract, and you determine that the dollar amount is incorrect, you can simply change it and then save the document. However, this doesn't leave a "flag" to let the author easily know what has been changed in the document. You can, however, strike through the original number (and even make it red) and then enter the new number to the right of the old number (see Figure 7.6). The author can then review the changes and delete the strikethrough number if he agrees.

Another use of the strikethrough feature is in "To Do" lists in documents. You can use strikethrough to indicate to others who read the document that an item in the list has been completed. Strikethrough can also indicate edits made to a document (such as all the changes the editors of this book requested during author review). An example of this application of the strikethrough feature appears in Figure 7.6.

FIG. 7.6
Using the strikethrough command helps you highlight changes you have made to a document.

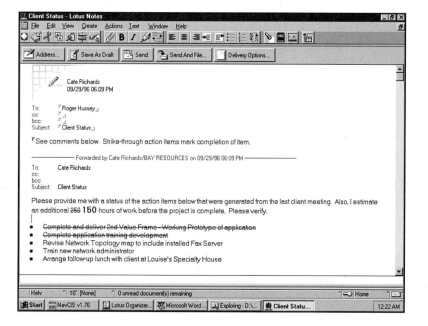

Part

I

Ch

7

Working with Font Attributes Avoid using characteristics that you can't print if you're unsure of the audience that is reading the document. You can choose different colors for your text, for example, but most people don't own color printers, and thus can't print in color. However, using color in documents that will be published to the Web is important to attract the reader's interest. Although using color to add pizzazz and emphasis to your document isn't wrong, don't depend solely on color to convey crucial information. You shouldn't include an instruction that says all steps in red are mandatory, for example, because some people might print your document and won't be able to tell from the printed copy which text was originally red. Similarly, laptop users often have a monochrome display and can't easily differentiate colors— particularly lighter shades. In cases such as these, you might want to use font size or bold text to convey your message. These will print and display on monochrome screens.

Figure 7.7 shows a sample document that uses several different text styles.

FIG. 7.7

You can highlight your text by using different types of styles.

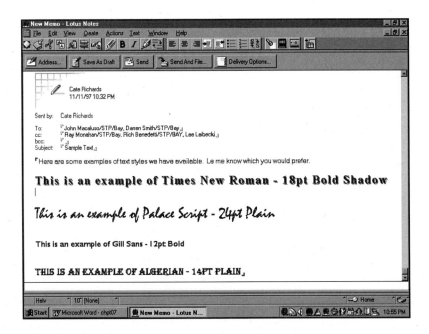

Don't get carried away with using typefaces, color, sizes, and other attention-grabbing characteristics. Bright colors, large type, and attributes such as boldface and italic are meant to emphasize and draw attention. If every paragraph in your document is a different color, size, and style, you might have created a work of abstract art, but you will give your reader a headache trying to find the important parts of the document.

You might find that responding to another user's message by using the Text options is helpful. For example, in Figure 7.8, Larry Cook received a memo from Kelly Sloan requesting some information on an upcoming meeting. Larry chose <u>A</u>ctions, <u>F</u>orward (or clicked the Forward button in the mail database, as discussed in Chapter 3, "Using Databases") to return the message to Kelly, indicating his responses in indented bold red text. Kelly then responded by forwarding the memo to Larry, typing her response using a different font attribute. This technique lets people respond to each other's questions while leaving the question in the memo for easy reference. At the end of the discussion, Larry and Kelly only have to reference the last memo if they want to review all the material at a later date.

FIG. 7.8

You can use text-formatting options to help you communicate with others in a forwarded message.

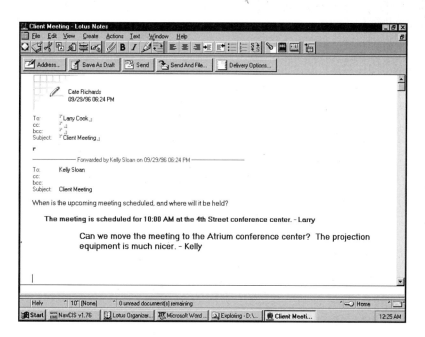

TIP Other ways to respond to a message and keep the original text with it include using collapsible sections to display the original message (see Chapter 8). Your email database will do this if you use the Reply with History button when responding to a message. You can also use paragraph indenting to emphasize your answer to a message.

A common method in many Internet discussion groups is to use the symbols >> and << before and after the message you're responding to. Any of these methods will help the reader see the original message along with any corresponding feedback to make the communication more effective.

Setting Paragraph Justification As with any good word processor, you can set margins if you want part or all of your document to have margins different than the one-inch default. You can also use tabs to indent text to predefined positions you select. The following sections explain how to set margins.

Although some characteristics, such as type style and size, can apply to any portion of text, other characteristics, such as justification, apply only to whole paragraphs—that is, a section of text that ends with a carriage return. You can't have part of a paragraph with one kind of justification while another part of the same paragraph has a different type. If you change the justification of any portion of a paragraph, the whole paragraph changes.

Part
I

Ch
7

For these paragraph-only characteristics, Notes provides a shortcut. If you want to adjust a characteristic for a single existing paragraph, you don't have to select the paragraph; just place the insertion point anywhere in that paragraph. Then, from the Alignment tab in the Text Properties InfoBox, choose the characteristic you want to adjust. If you want to adjust more than one paragraph, however, you must select all the paragraphs.

To change the attributes of paragraphs, you can open the Text Properties InfoBox by choosing Text, Text Properties, or the menu commands and bullets as described in Table 7.2. To set paragraph alignment, bulleted lists, numbered lists, margin settings, and line spacing, choose the Alignment tab, shown in Figure 7.9. The following selections are available:

- Alignment
- First line
- List
- Left margin
- Spacing

FIG. 7.9

You can change paragraph settings in the Text Properties Alignment InfoBox.

Setting the Alignment Alignment controls how each line of text is aligned along the left and right margins. To set the alignment, select the text alignment icon in the InfoBox that represents the type of alignment you want to use. Here are the types of alignment:

- Left: Notes aligns each line of text at the left margin. This style—the same as you see in typewritten text—is especially appropriate for memos. Because the text isn't aligned along the right margin, the right side of the text has an uneven appearance. As a result, this style of alignment sometimes is known as ragged right.
- Center: Notes centers each line of text between the left and right margins. You might want to use this kind of alignment for headings.
- Right: Right alignment causes Notes to align each line against the right margin, but not the left, resulting in a ragged left paragraph. This is beneficial if you're trying to align numbers, particularly in column design. Otherwise, this alignment option tends to have little use for the average user.
- Full: Notes aligns each full line of text along the left and right margins. By adding tiny amounts of space almost imperceptibly between words, Notes manages to make each line exactly the same length. For partial lines, such as those at the end of a paragraph, Notes aligns only the left margin.

Newspapers and many books use this type of alignment, which tends to give your document a more professional, pleasing appearance. Many people dislike editing a document that has full alignment, however, because Notes' constant changing of spacing between words during editing distracts them.

- None: Notes displays each paragraph as a single long line. If a paragraph is longer than Notes can display onscreen, you must use the scroll bars or left and right arrow keys to view the rest of the line.

 TIP If you need to edit text that has been fully aligned, you can change the alignment to left alignment, edit the text, and then change the alignment back to full. This will make it easier for you to edit the paragraph, because you won't have to work around Notes' continuous adjustment of the font alignment as you're editing.

You can also set alignment by using the SmartIcons.

Setting the First Line (Indent/Outdent)   The First line group of icons tells Notes how to treat the first line of text in a paragraph. You use these settings to indent or outdent the paragraph:

- Standard: Notes doesn't indent or outdent the paragraph. Instead, it aligns the first line of text with the rest of the paragraph.
- Indent: To indent the first line of the paragraph, click the Indent button and then type in the amount you want to indent the text in the text box that appears. The default setting is .25".
- Outdent: To outdent the first line of the paragraph, click the Outdent button and then type in the amount you want to outdent the text in the text box that appears. The default setting is .25".

You can see an example of these settings in Figure 7.10.

Working with Bullets and Numbers   Notes will automatically indent and insert bullets and numbers in documents when you click the Bullets and Numbers buttons in the List section of this tab.

You can also insert bullets and numbers (see Figure 7.11) by selecting Text, Bullets or Text, Numbers.

 TIP Select the bullet or number styles before typing your text. This will make entering text easier, because Notes will automatically add the next bullet or number while you're typing so that you can keep your thoughts organized as you work.

Setting the Left Margin   Enter the left margin setting for the paragraph. You can use whole numbers and/or decimals to indicate your setting. The standard left margin setting is 1". The maximum limit for this setting is 22.75". You should ensure that the margins are displayed onscreen so that readers of the document will be able to see the paragraph.

Part

Ch

7

FIG. 7.10

You can add pizzazz to your documents by indenting or outdenting paragraphs.

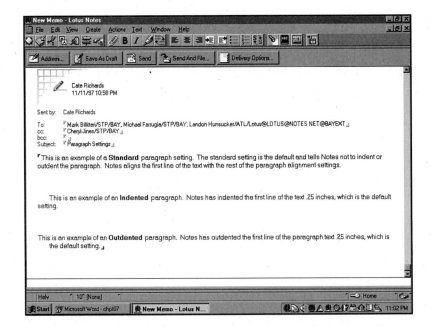

FIG. 7.11

You can add impact (and sometimes fun) to your documents by using the bullet and numbering features.

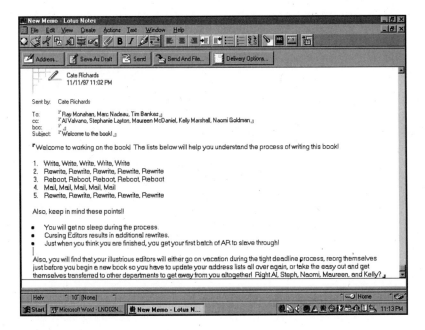

 TIP You can set margins for a hotspot, button, attachment, or object by highlighting the item and selecting Edit, Properties. (Notes will set the margins for the paragraph that contains the item.) You will learn more about these features in Chapter 8.

You can select the Top, Bottom, Left, and Right margin settings for the entire document by choosing File, Page Setup. The Page Setup dialog box appears. Here is where you can alter global document settings. You'll learn about these settings in Chapter 8.

Setting the Line Spacing The spacing options in Notes control the amount of spacing between paragraphs and between the lines of text in a paragraph. The following selections are available:

- Interline: How many blank lines Notes inserts between the lines of a paragraph
- Above: How many blank lines Notes inserts before each paragraph
- Below: How many blank lines Notes inserts after each paragraph

When you click the down arrow next to each of these options, Notes displays a selection list from which you choose the number of blank lines. Notes uses the same type of notation you might have encountered when adjusting the spacing setting on a typewriter:

- Single (no extra blank space)
- 1 $\frac{1}{2}$ (half a line's worth of blank space)
- Double (a full line's worth of blank space)

If you choose Below and then Double, for example, an extra line of blank space follows each paragraph.

CAUTION

If you select options for both Above and Below for a paragraph, you might be left with up to four lines between paragraphs. If this isn't your intention, choose one option or the other.

Setting Page Breaks and Tabs As you work with Notes, sometimes you will want to set the pagination so that Notes inserts a page break where you want it rather than when a page is filled up with text. You might also want to adjust tab settings and set the right margin for printing purposes. To perform any of these functions, highlight the paragraph you want to "control" and then open the Text Properties InfoBox. Choose the Pages/Tabs tab, shown in Figure 7.12.

FIG. 7.12

The Pages/Tabs tab of the Text Properties InfoBox lets you specify settings that affect your document when it is printed.

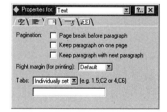

Setting Pagination The first section of the tab controls pagination. You can specify the following:

- Page break before paragraph: Notes inserts a page break before the selected paragraph. This setting is ideal if you want to insert a page break to ensure that a particular paragraph is printed at the top of the following page. For example, if you're writing sections within a proposal document, you might want the heading of each section to begin at the top of a page.

  This setting can also be used with your email if you want to print the body of the memo but don't want to include the To, From, Date, and Subject fields. Place the cursor on the first line in the body of the memo, and then select this option. Notes prints the address information on one page, and the remainder of the memo starts at the top of the second page.

- Keep paragraph on one page: Notes keeps the lines of text highlighted together when printing. Notes breaks the page either before or after the selected paragraph but not within the text. This is ideal if you want to make sure that an entire paragraph prints on the same page to make reading easier.

- Keep paragraph with next paragraph: Notes keeps the selected paragraph on the same page as the following paragraph. Notes breaks the page before the selected paragraph if it doesn't fit on the same page as the following paragraph. This is ideal if you're providing an example and you want the descriptive paragraph below the example to print on the same page.

TIP You can also set a page break by choosing <u>C</u>reate, Page Brea<u>k</u>. This option acts as a toggle for setting page breaks. Selecting <u>C</u>reate, Page Break once will enter a page break, and selecting it again will remove the page break.

A line appears across the page to indicate any page breaks you specify.

Removing a Page Break If you decide that you want to remove a page break, place the cursor in the first line of the paragraph immediately following the page break and choose <u>C</u>reate, Page Brea<u>k</u>. Notes will remove the page break.

Setting the Right Margin for Printing Use the Right margin (for printing) field to specify the right margin. This option applies only to the printed document. The right side of the screen is always the right margin when you display a document, so make sure that you specify this setting based on the paper size. Keep in mind that many printers (such as lasers) won't print any closer than $1/4$ of an inch from the edge of the paper—regardless of the margin you specify.

The default is traditionally 1" to 1.25", but this depends on your specific printer's capabilities. If you select Other for this setting, you must enter a value in the text entry box that appears. When you specify settings for Other, make sure you do so in relation to the paper size. For example, to have a one-inch right margin on the standard 8.5×11-inch paper, type `7.5` in the text entry box. This tells Notes that you want the margin to be 7.5" from the left side of the paper.

Setting Tabs   You can set tab spacing for your text by using the Pages/Tabs settings in the Text Properties InfoBox. You can set tab stops for one or more paragraphs by entering specific tab stops in the text entry box provided. Setting tab stops is a two-step process. You must first indicate how you want the tab stops to be set and then specify the factor that Notes will use in setting the tab. Follow these steps to set tabs:

1. Click the down arrow next to the Tabs text box. You have two options:

    Individually set: This lets you enter the places you want tab stops to occur. You can enter numbers in inches or centimeters (for example, .5" or .5 cm). If you enter more than one tab stop, separate them with semicolons (for example, .5"; 1.35"; 4").

    Evenly spaced: Notes evenly spaces tab stops based on the interval you provide. For example, you can tell Notes to set a tab stop every .45".

    You can set four types of Tab stops in Notes by typing their corresponding letter before the tab stop or by using the mouse to set the tab stop with the ruler. (See "Setting Margins and Tabs with the Ruler" later in this chapter for more information.) The following list describes each type of tab stop, its corresponding letter, and the corresponding tab indicator that is displayed in the ruler:

    Right: This is represented by the letter R before the tab stop in the Tabs entry box. Right tabs cause text to be aligned flush-right at the tab stop. You often use this setting when you're trying to align currency values.

    Left: This is represented by the letter L before the tab stop in the Tabs entry box. Left tabs cause text to be aligned flush-left at the tab stop. You often use this as the standard tab entry.

    Decimal: This is represented by the letter D before the tab stop in the Tabs entry box. Decimal tabs cause text to be aligned according to the decimal point location in the text. This setting is ideal when you're trying to align numbers in a list.

    Center: This is represented by the letter C before the tab stop in the Tabs entry box. Center tabs cause the text to be centered on both sides of the tab stop. This option is ideal when you're trying to display a list of items to a reader.

2. Once you have made your Tabs type selection, specify the interval for the tab settings. If you are individually specifying the tab stops, type in the exact location for each tab, using semicolons to separate multiple entries. If you are telling Notes to evenly space the tab stops, type in the interval space between each tab setting.

N O T E   You don't have to enter semicolons to separate multiple entries (as shown in the following example). If there is a space between the number settings, Notes will insert the semicolon when you save your selections. However, inserting the semicolon helps delineate the individual tab stops when you review your settings—decreasing the chance of your running your numbers together and ending up with an incorrect setting. ■

You have flexibility when setting tab stops. To set tabs at 1.5, 2, and 4 inches, for example, type the following:

```
1.5 2 4
```

You don't need to type " after the number; Notes adds it to all numbers that represent inches.

N O T E   Notes always displays the current tabs in this box using semicolons, even if you entered the tabs using spaces. ▪

If you prefer to measure a specific tab stop in centimeters, you can type cm after a number. For example:

```
1 2.3 10cm 15cm 6
```

In this example, Notes will set five tabs. The 1, 2.3, and 6 represent inches, but the 10 and 15 represent centimeters.

If you have chosen metric measurements as your default measurement (see Chapter 2, "Customizing Notes"), Notes assumes that all measurements you enter are in centimeters unless you enter a " to indicate that a measurement is in inches. For example, if the default is set to metric, and you set tabs at the following positions:

```
10 20 6"
```

Notes sets a tab at 10 and 20 centimeters and at 6 inches. After you set tabs, you can press the Tab key to move to the next tab stop in your document.

Hiding Text   Notes lets you hide text within a document during particular functions. Although this feature is typically used by database designers when designing the forms that will be used, it is discussed here briefly. You will find more information on hiding fields in the database design sections in Chapter 11, "Designing Forms."

With the Text Properties InfoBox open, click the Hide tab, shown in Figure 7.13.

FIG. 7.13

You can hide text in documents depending on how you're working with the document. You make the hide-when selections in the Hide, tab of the Text Properties InfoBox.

Notes provides the following options:

■ Notes R4.6 or later and Web Browsers: You can hide forms, views, navigators, folders, subforms, and agents that aren't supported or that are irrelevant in a particular environment. For example, if you have two versions of design elements (a Web version and a

Notes version), give them the same name or alias and then hide one from Notes users (by selecting Notes R4.6 or later) and hide the other from Web users (by selecting Web Browsers). Domino displays the correct version based on the user's system.

■ Previewed for reading: Hidden information isn't visible when users read documents in the preview pane. However, users can read the text if they open the document for reading or if they have Editor-level access and place the document in edit mode from the preview pane—unless additional restrictions are selected, as described later.

■ Opened for reading: This option hides any text selected when users open a document to read it. However, users can read the text if they have Editor-level access and place the document in edit mode—unless additional restrictions are selected, as described later. This option is ideal in designing documents if the designer wants to provide instructions on completing a field when the user is composing a document but the designer doesn't want the user to be bothered with the instructions when reading the document.

■ Printed: This tells Notes to print everything but the highlighted text. You can use this option when you want to omit portions of sensitive text when printing a document for someone else to read or otherwise limit the text that prints.

■ Previewed for editing: This option lets readers of the document see the text when reading (unless additional restrictions are selected) but not when composing or editing a document when they are viewing the document in the preview pane.

■ Opened for editing: This option lets readers of the document see the text when reading a document (unless additional restrictions are selected) but not when composing or editing a document. This option is usually used by designers who have fields displaying information in a format that is different than when the document is composed. For example, the user selects a keyword series that identifies the product name, price, and catalog number while composing a document (which is easier than having to make three separate selections in three separate fields). The database designer, however, elects to hide that keyword field when someone is reading the document and sets up separate fields to display this information for ease of reading and editing at a later date.

■ Copied to the clipboard: This tells Notes to ignore this text when copying text to and from the clipboard. This is a handy command when you want to copy all but a part of a document or when the database designer has set security in the fields that shouldn't be overridden if text is copied to the clipboard. This setting also affects text when a document is forwarded from a database. The text marked for hiding won't appear in a message forwarded from the database. This setting doesn't affect entire documents that are copied and pasted at the view level.

■ Hide paragraph if formula is true: By entering a qualifying formula in the Formula window, the database designer can set conditions for when the text is hidden. For example, if the designer wants only the author of the document to be able to see the text in the field, he can write an author formula to provide this criteria for viewing the text. You will learn more about writing formulas in Chapter 14, "Working with Formulas," and Chapter 15, "Working with Functions and Commands."

Part
I

Ch
7

Setting Styles   You can define and save combinations of paragraph and text properties that you use regularly as named paragraph styles. This is a handy way to define particular styles that you use frequently so that you don't have to continuously set the attributes individually through the Text Properties InfoBox. To set up a named paragraph style, follow these steps:

1. Place the document you're working on in edit mode by double-clicking anywhere in the document.

2. Select a paragraph and make all the attribute settings you want. This is the paragraph style you will save in the following steps. For example, if you want to create a style to use as a response to other memos in which the text is numbered, bold, and red, create these settings for the existing paragraph.

3. Select Text, Text Properties, and then choose the Style tab, shown in Figure 7.14.

FIG. 7.14

You can create styles that can be reused by highlighting a paragraph whose style you want to copy and then accessing the Style tab of the Text Properties InfoBox.

4. Click Create Style. The Create Named Style dialog box appears, as shown in Figure 7.15.

FIG. 7.15

Provide descriptive names in the Create Named Style dialog box to make it easier to remember what the style is used for.

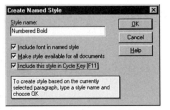

5. Enter a name for the paragraph style in the Style name text box. For example, you could name the style Numbered Bold.

6. Check Include font in named style, which is the default, if you want to include all font settings as well as paragraph settings.

7. Check Make style available for all documents if you want to have this style setting available regardless of the document you're working in. Selecting this option adds the style name to the status bar pop-up selection list at the bottom of the Notes window.

8. Check Include this style in Cycle Key (F11) if you want this style to appear when you cycle through the available styles using the F11 key.

9. Click OK.

Once you have defined the style name, you may highlight a paragraph and select the setting by returning to the Style tab or by selecting Text, Named Styles and then clicking the name of the style you want to apply. If you elected to display the style when pressing F11 to view the cycle key, you will be able to select the style through those options as well. You can also select styles by clicking the Styles option on the status bar to display the list of currently defined styles, as shown in Figure 7.16.

FIG. 7.16
You can quickly change the style of a paragraph by clicking the Style option on the status bar and then selecting one of the defined styles in the pop-up menu.

Available styles

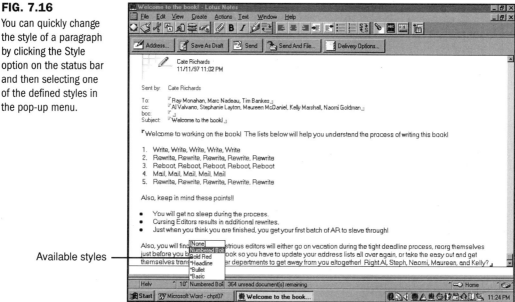

The following three predefined styles appear under Text, Named Styles:

- Headline: This displays the selected text in bold, purple, 12-point Helvetica.
- Bullet: This displays the selected font in bullet style.
- Basic: This changes the selected font size to 10-point Helvetica but maintains any other text formatting options defined previously.

You can use the Redefine Style button on the Style tab to redefine a named style based on the current paragraph selection. Or you might want to "clean house" periodically (get rid of old styles) by clicking the Delete Styles button and then selecting the style to delete.

Setting Margins and Tabs with the Ruler

Notes provides two methods for setting the margins and tabs: You can access the Text Properties InfoBox, as discussed earlier in this chapter, or you can use the ruler. Whether you use the ruler or the Text Properties InfoBox to set margins and tabs, you might want to have the ruler present to guide you in making your settings.

Part

I

Ch

7

Displaying the Ruler   When controlling margins and tabs, you might find displaying the Notes ruler helpful. The ruler is a bar near the top of the screen marked off in inches like a ruler but with special marks indicating your margins and tab settings (see Figure 7.17). The ruler helps you visualize distances in your document and provides a simple means of setting margins and tabs.

FIG. 7.17

Use the ruler to help guide you in setting margins and tabs.

Ruler ⌐

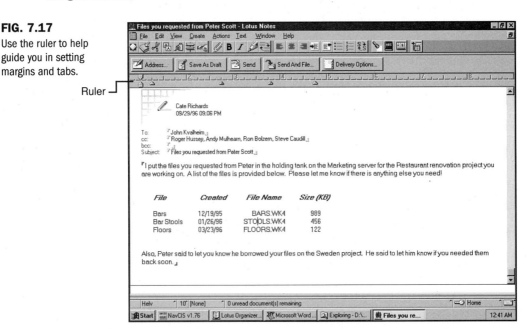

To display the ruler, choose <u>V</u>iew, <u>R</u>uler (or click the View Ruler SmartIcon if it is present in your current SmartIcon group). Along with measuring the document in inches, the ruler shows margins and tabs. Notes displays tabs as triangles pointing up and the left margin as two pentagonal arrows. Choosing <u>V</u>iew, <u>R</u>uler again causes the ruler to disappear.

N O T E   Table column settings are represented in the ruler by a mark that looks like a T. You will learn more about creating tables in Chapter 8. ▪

In addition to changing margins, you can use the ruler to set tabs, as explained in the next section.

Changing Margins and Tabs with the Ruler   To change the left margin of the first line using the ruler, click the top pentagonal arrow and drag it to its new location. If you want to adjust the left margin of the paragraph to indicate a setting other than the one set for the first line, click the bottom pentagonal arrow and drag it to a new location.

By specifying one left margin for the first line and another for all other lines, you can create the paragraph styles shown in Figure 7.18.

FIG. 7.18
You can use the ruler to define margin settings in your documents.

Top pentagonal arrow

Bottom pentagonal arrow

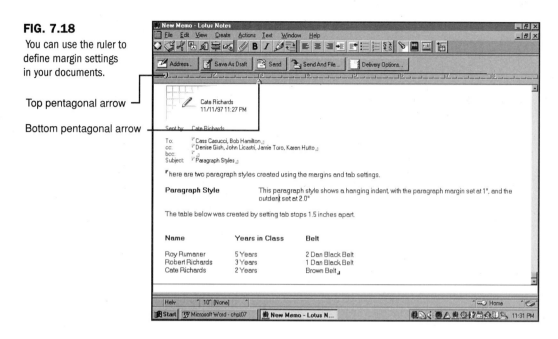

You can also set tabs using the ruler. Display the ruler if it isn't showing, and then select the paragraphs you want to change. You can then change the position of a margin by dragging the corresponding triangle to a new position. Recall that the upward-pointing triangles are tabs. Figure 7.19 shows all four types of tabs you can define.

To set a new tab, place the mouse pointer on the ruler at an empty position and click. A tab arrow appears to mark the tab stop. To clear an existing tab, click the corresponding tab arrow a second time. To change the tab setting, click and drag the corresponding tab arrow to a new position and release the mouse button.

FIG. 7.19
You can define tab stops by clicking the ruler. If you want to use the special tab attributes such as right-align, left-align, and decimal point-align, you can use the Text Properties InfoBox or right-click the tab stop to display a pop-up menu box with the four tab stop styles available for selection.

Part

I

Ch

7

As discussed earlier, you can place four types of tabs in your documents. To place these tabs using the ruler, do one of the following:

- Left tab: Left-click on the ruler.
- Right tab: Right-click on the ruler.
- Center tab: Shift+right-click on the ruler.
- Decimal tab: Shift+left-click on the ruler.

Figure 7.19 shows examples of each of these tab settings.

N O T E   Setting margins and tabs using the ruler is one of the few Notes operations that requires the mouse; there are no corresponding hot keys. If you don't have a mouse, you must choose Text, Properties and use the Pages/Tabs pane to set margins and tabs.

Setting Margins Quickly with the Keyboard

Notes provides several keystrokes for quickly changing margins. After selecting the paragraphs you want to affect, you can do the following:

- Press F7 to indent the first line by a quarter of an inch. By pressing this key several times, you can indent the first line by any multiple of a quarter of an inch. Press Shift+F7 to outdent the first line by a quarter of an inch.
- Press F8 to indent every line by a quarter of an inch. Pressing Shift+F8 outdents every line by a quarter of an inch.

You can create a hanging indent (that is, paragraphs in which the first line is farther to the left than the other lines) by indenting all lines one or more times by pressing F8 and then unindenting the first line by pressing F7.

Working with the Permanent Pen

The Permanent Pen option lets you use revision marks to quickly add comments that stand out in a document. When you use the Permanent Pen, you don't have to reset the font every time you move somewhere else in the document. For example, if you're answering questions in a document and you want to write all your answers in bold red, you can set up your Permanent Pen to use these font attributes. Then, you can type text in multiple places in the document without having to redefine the font attributes each time you move to a new location.

Before you use your Permanent Pen, you might want to change the font attributes. To do so, select Text, Properties, and select the font, size, style, and color you want to assign to the Permanent Pen in the Text Properties InfoBox. Once you have made your settings, click the Set Permanent Pen font button to save your selections.

To use the Permanent Pen, follow these steps:

1. Select Text, Permanent Pen.
2. Click at the beginning of the section where you want to add a comment.

3. Type your text. The text you type will be in the style, size, and color you specified for the Permanent Pen.

4. Reposition the cursor where you next want to use the Permanent Pen, and type your comments.

5. Continue using the Permanent Pen until you have completed all your comments.

6. Deselect the Permanent Pen by selecting Text, Permanent Pen to disable this option.

N O T E If you want to change the font characteristics of the Permanent Pen, choose Text, Text Properties. In the Text Properties InfoBox, make all the necessary font, size, style, and color selections, and then click the Set Permanent Pen font button. Notes will use the new Permanent Pen font characteristics until you use this process again.

Using Special Characters

Occasionally, you might have to use special characters that don't appear on your keyboard, such as currency, copyright, and trademark symbols. Notes lets you enter hundreds of special characters into a document by pressing special key combinations.

To type a special character, press Alt+F1 followed by the code that represents the special character. Each code, consisting of one or two keys, is supposed to remind you of the special character. For example, to type the symbol for the Japanese yen (¥), you press Alt+F1, Y, =. Appendix B, "Special Characters," lists more characters that are available.

Using this feature, you can enter letters from non-English alphabets, fractions, international currency designations, and so on.

N O T E Not all printers can print all special characters, so Notes might have to drop some special characters when printing documents. In particular, most daisywheel printers are limited in their selection of characters. Keep this limitation in mind when composing documents if you're sharing information with people who use older printers or daisywheel printers.

In the next chapter, you'll learn even more Notes features that will add pizzazz to documents and increase functionality. ●

Part

I

Ch

7

Working with Documents

Notes 4.6 has a wide variety of features that help make it a robust environment for communicating with others. These features can be added or applied directly to a rich text field within a document that has already been designed. You can also build some of these features into the design of the database forms, as you will learn in this chapter.

Checking Your Spelling

No matter how professional your document or how insightful your message, you won't impress readers if misspellings litter your document. And if you are like many who have used word processing software for quite some time, your ability to spell even the simplest words has somehow disappeared! Notes includes a spell checker that looks for misspelled words and other common mistakes.

 TIP As discussed in the section "International Settings" in Chapter 2, "Customizing Notes," you can select from one of 28 dictionaries by selecting File, Tools, User Preferences, clicking the International icon, and then clicking the Spelling Dictionary button.

Switching from one dictionary to another is a big plus in organizations that work internationally. A proposal can be written in the U.S., for example, forwarded to the U.K., and spell checked there using the British (ise) dictionary to pick up on differences in spelling between the two countries. For example, in the U.K., "organization" is spelled "organisation," with an s instead of a z.

To check the spelling of a document, position the insertion point at the top of the document then choose Edit, Check Spelling. If Notes finds a misspelled word or detects some other irregularity that it regards as a mistake, it displays the dialog box shown in Figure 8.1. In this example, the word "developed" was misspelled.

FIG. 8.1

Use Spell Check to find misspelled words and other common errors in documents.

 TIP You can check the spelling of just one word or a group of words without having to check the spelling of the entire document. To do so, highlight the word(s) and then select Edit, Check Spelling.

At the bottom of the dialog box, you will see the status field, which will tell you the problem Notes found with the highlighted word or phrase. For example, in Figure 8.1, the status field displays Unknown Word, meaning that the word isn't one that Notes recognizes as being spelled correctly. The offending word is highlighted in your document and displayed in the Replace text box. At this point, you must decide what to do:

■ If the word is misspelled, as in the example here, you can fix it in the Replace box and then click Replace. Notes replaces the misspelled word in the document with the fixed word. If you misspelled the same word in the same way elsewhere in the document, Notes fixes the word in only one location at a time and asks you what to do each time it encounters the misspelled word.

■ If you agree that the word is misspelled but you don't know how to spell it correctly, you can view the guesses that Notes makes. Notes searches its dictionary for words that are similar to the misspelled word and displays them in the Guess list box. Figure 8.1 shows the guesses that Notes produced for "developped."

■ Often, the first word in the Guess list box is the correct spelling. In this example, Notes guessed the correct spelling as "developed." Select the correctly spelled guess and then click Replace. Alternatively, you can double-click the correctly spelled word. Notes replaces the misspelled word in the document with the correctly spelled word.

N O T E Notes can't always guess the correct spelling. If too many letters are wrong, or if you transpose letters, Notes might not be able to produce the correct word. ■

■ You might want to prompt Notes to accept an incorrectly spelled word or phrase. For example, if you intentionally misspell a word or phrase, such as Ye Ol' Shoppe, but you want Notes to point out similar misspellings later that might be unintentional, you can click Skip to skip just this one instance of the spelling or click Skip All to always skip this misspelling during this spell checking session.

This feature is most useful for acronyms, names, and technical words that occur several times throughout the document that you know are correct but that you don't want to add to your dictionary.

■ If you know the word is spelled correctly and it's a word you use often, click Define. Notes adds the word to your personal dictionary so that it will consider the word valid whenever you check spelling in the future, whether in this document or another. This feature is most useful for technical terms or proper names that you use often.

■ If you want to exit Spell Check before Notes tells you that it is completed, click Done. Notes will halt the spell checking process at that point and return you to your document.

N O T E Words that you define during spell-checking sessions are entered into your personal dictionary (USER.DIC). For more information on adding words to or removing words from your personal dictionary, refer to the section "Changing the User Dictionary" in Chapter 2. ■

Along with catching misspelled words, Notes watches for other common errors, such as unusual capitalization and repeated words (such as "I saw the the dog"). As with misspelled words, you can tell Notes to ignore the problem or specify how to fix it.

After Notes displays all the questionable words, it displays a final dialog box telling you that spelling is complete. Click OK to close this dialog box.

CAUTION

Although the spell check is a wonderful aid for producing error-free documents, it can't replace proofreading. The spell check can't catch grammatical errors or incorrectly used words. Worst of all, it doesn't catch words that you misspell if they happen to be different words that are spelled correctly. For example, if you meant to write "I hear that we have hired ten new people" but you mistakenly omit the "a" in "hear," Notes won't catch "her" as a misspelled word. Likewise, if you spelled the word "here," Notes won't see it as an error, even though it's not the correct usage.

Searching for Text

No good word processor is complete without the capability to locate text wherever it occurs within a document. Notes includes features that let you search for text strings and replace one phrase with another. Notes also lets you search entire databases for text strings so that you can quickly locate documents that relate to the same topic. Notes contains several ways to search for information in databases. If the database has a full-text index, you can do more advanced searches. All Notes databases provide the following capabilities:

- You can search for text in a document that you are reading. If your document is in edit mode, you can also elect to replace the text you find with new text.

- You can search for text in document titles that appear in a particular view. Notes will find and highlight the first document in a view whose title matches your word or phrase.

- You can find all documents that contain a word or phrase anywhere in the document. Using this search method shows the documents in the view, with a checkmark next to them. The words within the document that match the search criteria won't be highlighted, however, as they will be if the database is indexed for full-text search (as described in the following list).

If a database has a full-text index, you can enhance the capabilities of your search as follows:

- You can find all documents that contain a certain word or phrase and have Notes outline the search words with red boxes to highlight them.

- You can use the Search Builder feature to help you quickly create search formulas to find documents.

- You can save search formulas to reuse at a later date.

- You can define your search in the following ways:

    Make your search case-sensitive.

    Include synonyms of search words.

    Search for words that are located near one another in a document.

    Include variations of the same word in your search.

Customize the way your search results are displayed.

Search for documents in multiple databases at the same time.

In the following sections, you will learn about all these features.

Performing General Searches for Text

The following sections will walk you through searches you can perform whether or not your database is indexed. As you will see, the general search capabilities on any database are pretty powerful!

Searching for Text in a Document You Are Reading   Notes makes it simple to find (and replace if you're in edit mode) a word or phrase in a document whether you are reading or editing the document. You can search for a word or phrase anywhere within a field by choosing Edit, Find/Replace. Notes displays the Find and Replace dialog box, shown in Figure 8.2. In the Find and Replace text boxes, enter the word or phrase you want to find.

FIG. 8.2

Finding and replacing text is easy when you use the Find and Replace feature in Notes.

 T I P   If the phrase you want to find or replace is now on-screen, you can select the phrase so that it appears as the phrase to find when you perform a find or replace operation. Suppose that onscreen you now see a paragraph discussing money market funds, and you want to find other places in the document that also discuss them. Select the phrase "money market fund." When you choose Edit, Find/Replace (or Edit, Find Next), the phrase "money market fund" already appears in the phrase to find.

After you enter the search phrase (if it's different from the one Notes displays), you can choose any of the following checkbox options in the Match section to change the way Notes performs its search:

- Whole word: Normally, Notes looks for the search phrase without regard to word boundaries. If you ask Notes to find "cat," for example, it stops not only on the word "cat," but also on "scat" and "catalog" because they both contain "cat." If you're searching for especially short phrases, you can choose Whole word to tell Notes that you are interested only in the word "cat," not these three letters within any word.

- Accent: Normally, when Notes searches text, it ignores diacritical marks when finding phrases. If you choose this option, Notes considers diacritical marks when searching for text. Suppose that you are writing a document that includes the name Björn. If you want to search for this word and you don't check Accent, Notes finds the word if you enter only Bjorn. If you do check Accent, however, Notes will find only Björn if you enter it with its umlaut. (See "Using Special Characters" in Chapter 7, "Working with Text," for information about entering special characters.)

■ Ca<u>s</u>e: When you choose this option, Notes looks only for phrases capitalized exactly the way you typed the search phrase. During a search for "cat," for example, Notes won't stop on "Cat" or "CAT."

Click Find Ne<u>x</u>t to begin the search. Notes searches for the phrase from the current insertion point position and repositions the insertion point on the next occurrence of the phrase. If Notes reaches the end of the document without finding the phrase, it displays a dialog box telling you that it couldn't find the phrase.

Often, the first occurrence of the phrase isn't the one you want. Choose <u>E</u>dit, Find Ne<u>x</u>t or press Ctrl+G to repeat the last search. Notes searches for the same phrase using the same combination of selected options. By pressing Ctrl+G enough times, you can find each occurrence of the phrase throughout the document.

 TIP You can also search for phrases that include tabs and that are separated by a hard return by typing \t and \n, respectively. (\n stands for new line.) If you want to find the words "cat" and "mouse" separated by a tab, for example, you would enter cat\tmouse as the search phrase.

Replacing Text On occasion, you might need to change a phrase that occurs several times throughout a document. For example, a particular function formerly performed by your Denver office might have been transferred to Atlanta, and you need to find all instances of "Denver" in a document and change them to "Atlanta." You can use the Find feature to find and change each occurrence individually, but Notes provides a related feature, replace, that makes this kind of wholesale replacement easier.

To perform a replace, you must be in edit mode. Press Ctrl+E to switch to edit mode if you're now in read mode (brackets appear around each field when you're in edit mode). Position the insertion point at the top of your document and choose <u>E</u>dit, <u>F</u>ind and Replace. Notes displays the Find and Replace dialog box, shown in Figure 8.3.

FIG. 8.3

To quickly find and replace text, use the Find and Replace dialog box, but make sure you're in edit mode first.

The Find and Replace dialog box offers exactly the same checkbox options as the Edit Find dialog box, and you use them in the same way. After you enter the phrase to find and the replacement phrase, choose any options that apply and then click Find <u>N</u>ext. Notes locates the first occurrence of the search phrase from the point at which the cursor was located when you began the search. Notes then highlights the phrase and waits for you to click one of the following buttons:

■ If you click Find <u>N</u>ext, Notes leaves the current occurrence of the phrase unchanged and finds the next one.

■ If you click Find Previous, Notes searches for the occurrence just before the current one (or the cursor location if you're just beginning your search).

■ If you click Replace, Notes replaces the current occurrence with the replacement phrase.

■ If you click Replace All, Notes replaces every occurrence of the search phrase with the replacement phrase.

CAUTION

Think carefully before using Replace All. If you make a mistake, you can't undo the operation using Edit, Undo. It is much too easy to make incorrect changes to your document that will take you hours to fix. If, for example, a woman replaces your male personnel manager, you might want to revise a certain memo by changing "he" to "she." If you forget to check Whole word, however, and then you click Replace All, Notes changes "other" to "otsher," "there" to "tshere," and similarly messes up all other words that have the letters "he" in them.

■ If you click Done, Notes stops the search, leaving the current occurrence of the search phrase as is.

 Save your document (choose File, Save) before using Replace All. If you make an error in your replacing, you can always exit the current document without saving and then reopen the document from its saved version.

Searching for Documents in a View   Not only can you search for a phrase within a single document, but you can also search in other useful ways when you're looking at a view. You can search for documents within a view to have Notes highlight documents that contain your search word or phrase anywhere within view columns (any of the text showing in the views).

To perform a search within a view, follow these steps:

1. While in a view, select Edit, Find, or Edit, Find Next. The Find dialog box appears, as shown in Figure 8.4.

FIG. 8.4
To search for a word or phrase within a view, type the text you want to search for in the Find dialog box.

2. In the Find text box, type the text you want to find. As an option, you can select Whole word, Accent, and/or Case. (See the earlier section "Searching for Text in a Document You Are Reading" for information on these features.)

3. Click Find <u>N</u>ext or Find <u>P</u>revious. If you click Find <u>N</u>ext, Notes highlights the first title that contains the text after the location of the cursor. If you click Find <u>P</u>revious, Notes highlights the first title that contains the text before the location of the cursor.

4. Repeat step 3 until you are through with your search for documents.

5. Click <u>D</u>one when you are through with your search.

Full-Text Searching in Databases

Notes provides a more powerful search mechanism known as a full-text search. Using this search feature, you can search for documents that contain several phrases rather than a specific single phrase. Perhaps you want to find documents that discuss stock prices and quarterly earnings, for example. This type of search also lets you search an entire database or even more than one database at a time, displaying all the documents that meet your search criteria in a view.

To use a full-text search, the database must have been indexed for full-text searches. The indexing process creates a special file that allows Notes to quickly determine which words or phrases a document contains. If a database isn't indexed, you can perform only limited searches by choosing <u>E</u>dit, <u>F</u>ind or by using the Search Bar without an index, as discussed earlier.

Indexing a Database   You can index any databases that you create on your local hard disk, unless the database is enforcing a consistent access control list and you aren't the manager or designer. Only someone with Designer or higher access can index a database that is shared with other people on a server. You can index a database in one of the following two ways:

■ Choose <u>F</u>ile, Database, <u>P</u>roperties to bring up the Properties InfoBox. Select the Full Text tab and then click <u>C</u>reate Index to bring up the Full Text Create Index dialog box, shown in Figure 8.5. This dialog box controls how the database will be indexed.

FIG. 8.5

To index a database, access the Full Text Create Index dialog box from the Database Properties InfoBox.

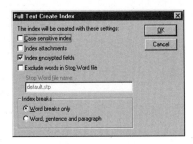

■ You can also tell Notes you want to index a database by selecting <u>V</u>iew, Search <u>B</u>ar while in a database that isn't indexed. Notes will display the Search Bar and provide you with a Create Index button. If you click this button, the dialog box shown in Figure 8.5 will appear to begin the process.

N O T E Because you are the manager of your email database located on the server, you can index that database if you want to. If your server capacity is low, however, indexing your mail database might overburden your server as it produces the index and keeps it updated. If your Notes administrator indicates that you shouldn't index your mail database located on the server, this is usually a sign that the server doesn't have enough memory or space.

You can create an archive email database using the archiving capabilities within mail, which allow you to periodically move documents to the archive file. The archive is typically stored on your hard drive. Notes users often prefer this process because there is less need to index the active mail databases where so many changes are taking place every day and that require continuous updates of your index. Most often, you are trying to search through older memos to find the information, and you can search for this kind of information easily in the archive copy of the email database. ▪

In the Full Text Create Index dialog box, you should normally accept the default selections, as shown in Figure 8.5. The following sections describe the indexing options.

Case Sensitivity   The Case sensitive index option lets you indicate whether you want Notes to distinguish between uppercase and lowercase letters. For example, it will treat "cat," "Cat," and "CAT" as different entries. If this is unnecessary (which is usually the case), don't select this option—it can greatly increase the size of the index and might exclude documents that you really want to find. Use this option only if case-sensitive searches are required—for example, if you index a database full of C programming concepts and structures.

Indexing Attachments   With the Index attachments option, you can indicate whether you want Notes to index any attachments containing text that you inserted in a document. If you select this option, you will be able to search the database for words or phrases stored in Notes documents and any files attached to the documents. For example, if you attached a WordPro document to a document stored in a database that maintains this selection in its indexing setup, you will be able to search the Notes text and the WordPro text when you query the database. Choosing this option might significantly increase the length of time it takes to index the database, however, as well as the amount of space the index takes up on the hard drive. Also, Notes can't highlight the words in the search phrase in the attached document. Instead, it highlights the attachment icon in the document.

Indexing Encrypted Fields   If you want to include text in encrypted fields in a full-text index, choose Index encrypted fields. You can index encrypted fields only if you have the appropriate encryption key, and only people who have the encryption key can search the fields. Using this option increases the size of an index by the number of encrypted fields in a database and the amount of text they contain. See Chapter 22, "Security and Encryption," for more information on working with encryption.

Using Stop Word Files   The Exclude words in Stop Word file option tells Notes not to search for words that are extremely common (the, and, if, it, and so forth). These common words are called stop words and are defined in the file listed in the field following this selection. You will probably want to select this option, because it reduces the number of documents selected to only those that match the remainder of your search criteria.

If your database is local, however, and you find that you need to keep a word in the search, such as "off," so that a search for articles on "Off Broadway," for example, can be run successfully, you will need to edit the Stop Word file to remove the word "off"—or not use the Stop Word file to index the database. The default Stop Word file, DEFAULT.STP, is located in your Notes directory. Although it can be edited using any ASCII text editor, you can make a copy of the file and then edit the copy. That way, you can revert to the original file when needed.

TIP The line ' [0-9]+ in DEFAULT.STP tells Notes not to index numbers. You might want to create a Stop Word file with only this line in it and give it a name that reminds you of its purpose, such as NUMBERS.STP. You can then select this file when users don't need to search for numbers.

You can also create additional Stop Word files and customize them for specific local databases. For example, if you have a local database for computer topics, you can create a Stop Word file for the database to include words such as "computer," "keyboard," "mouse," and so on that appear so frequently in documents that they're not useful in searches.

If you create an additional Stop Word file, you must do so before you create the index that uses it. Once you create the Stop Word file, you can select it when you create the index. The filename must be eight characters or less and use the extension STP—for example, COMPUTER.STP. The Stop Word file must be located in the program directory, typically in C:\NOTES.

TIP In large databases, a Stop Word file can reduce the index size by about 20 percent (on average), according to indexing dynamics. Of course, don't bother searching for "To be or not to be" in a Shakespeare database!

NOTE Indexes created with customized Stop Word files don't replicate along with the database, either from server to server or from server to workstation. In fact, indexes don't replicate at all.

Working with Index Breaks The Index breaks section has two options: Word breaks only and Word, sentence and paragraph. You will normally use Word breaks only unless you're trying to perform fancier searches. If you select Word, sentence and paragraph, Notes lets you perform more complex searches that specify that all the search words have to be in the same sentence or paragraph. This can lengthen the time of your search and can also take up a large amount of space. Because most documents you search are fairly short, particularly in your email database, selecting Word, sentence and paragraph isn't necessary.

Completing the Indexing Process When you have finished making your selections, Notes tells you that the indexing of the database has been queued if the database is located on the server. If you index a database on your hard drive, Notes will inform you that it is performing a local index. If the database is located on the server, you can continue working in other databases while the database is being indexed, but you won't be able to work in the database the server is indexing until it is finished. You won't get a message that the indexing is finished—you will know it is done when you can open the database. If the database is local, you won't be able to continue working in Notes until the indexing is complete, unless you have chosen Enable local background indexing in the User Preferences dialog box (select File, Tools, User Preferences). This is selected by default. In local indexing, you will know the indexing is complete when the Indexing Database status box disappears or the status bar indicates that the process is complete.

When you create a full-text index, Notes creates a subdirectory and stores the index files there. Notes names this subdirectory according to the name of the indexed database and gives it the file extension FT. For example, if you index a database named MARKET.NSF, Notes creates the subdirectory MARKET.FT and places it in the same directory as the database—usually the Notes data directory.

> **CAUTION**
>
> If you're running short on hard disk space, don't index your database. If you begin indexing a database and you run out of disk space before the indexing is complete, you won't be able to use the index. You will need to delete the index, clean up space on your hard drive, and then create a new index on the database.

Updating the Index   If you add, delete, or change any documents in a database that has been indexed, the index will no longer accurately reflect the database; new words will have been omitted, and words no longer in any document will continue to remain in the index. This causes your searches to behave unexpectedly if you're searching for words that have changed. You will have to periodically update a database index.

If the database is on a server, updating the index occurs automatically, although you can "force" the update as well. Select File, Database, Properties, choose the Full Text tab, and click Update Index (see Figure 8.6). You control how often an index update occurs automatically by editing the information. Click the arrow next to Update frequency (servers only) and choose between Immediate (the default), Daily, Scheduled, and Hourly, depending on how often you want the database to be indexed. Because setting indexing options affects server resources, you should contact your Notes administrator before performing this function.

FIG. 8.6

You update database indexes in the Full Text tab of the Database Properties InfoBox. You also can specify how frequently a server copy of a database index should be updated.

T I P If you are unsure which setting to select for scheduling indexing, select Immediate. If you discover (or if users report) that the database's response time is very slow, reduce the frequency of the updates.

If users access a database on the server infrequently or if the database isn't modified often, select Daily, which will update the index at night based on the server task Updall runs. (Updall settings are made by the Notes administrator.) This will help conserve server resources, making everyone happy.

You can also schedule the updates for an off-peak time to reduce the drain on server resources when many people are trying to use the server. Selecting Scheduled updates the index according to a schedule in the Public Address Book Program document for the Updall server task (a task set by your Notes administrator). If you select this option and no Program document for Updall exists, scheduled updates don't occur. Check with your Notes administrator if you are unsure of this option.

If you're working with a database index on your hard drive, you must "force" the indexing by clicking the Update Index button. Notes immediately updates the index, presenting you with a status box to show how many documents it's indexing. When the Database Properties InfoBox disappears, you can resume working in Notes with a newly indexed database.

N O T E The larger the database and the more complicated the index selections, the larger the file space and memory it will take to maintain. Make sure that you will really use the indexing feature in a database before you index it. ■

Indexing in the Background   As mentioned earlier, you can enable background indexing at startup, creating full-text indexes in the background. With this feature set, you can keep working in Notes without having to wait until Notes completes the indexes. To do this, follow these steps:

1. Select File, Tools, User Preferences.
2. Select Enable local background indexing and click OK.
3. Click OK when Notes tells you that some preferences won't take effect until you restart Notes.

If background indexing is enabled when you replicate databases, Notes automatically updates each database's full-text index and views in the background after replication is completed.

Deleting an Index   You can delete a full-text index if you no longer want a database indexed. You should also delete the index and then re-create it if you are experiencing full-text index problems or if you want to change index options. In the latter two cases, create a new index after deleting the original. Do not delete the index from the index subdirectory directly; instead, use the following procedure:

1. Select the database and choose File, Database, Properties. The Database Properties InfoBox appears.
2. Select the Full Text tab.
3. Click the Delete Index button. Notes displays the dialog box shown in Figure 8.7.

FIG. 8.7
You can delete
database indexes that
you no longer use to
conserve disk space.

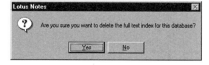

4. Click Yes when prompted to delete the index.

Notes deletes the index for the database and removes the subdirectory created for this index from your hard drive. If you want to reindex the database after selecting new indexing options, or if the index was experiencing problems, follow the procedures to create a full-text index described in the earlier section "Indexing a Database."

Performing a Full-Text Search   If a database has been indexed for full-text searches, choosing View, Search Bar causes Notes to display the Search Bar dialog box across the top of the document window, as shown in Figure 8.8. This is quite different from the Find dialog box you saw earlier. The Search Bar consists of two areas into which you can enter one or more phrases.

Opens Search Builder   Clears the search results

FIG. 8.8
Use the Search Builder
to perform queries
against indexed
databases.

Lets you enter
search text directly

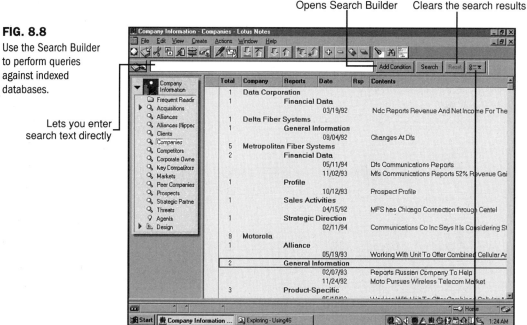

Lets you further refine
your search results

If you're performing a simple search for just a word or phrase, you can type it in the text entry box to the left of the Search Builder and click Search. Notes will perform a search on a database's documents and display the results in the view according to how you choose to see them. You can work with the documents displayed in the view, but if you exit the database, you will clear the results of your search. You can also choose to clear the results of the search by clicking the Reset button. (You will read more about how Notes displays query results in the next few sections.)

If you want to perform a more detailed query, you can click the Add Condition button to be more specific about the query you want to build in the Search Builder. When you're finished building a query, you can click Search, and Notes will display the results of your query in the view according to how you chose to see them. The next sections will walk you through building a query, selecting viewing options, and interpreting your view results.

 T I P   You can create complicated, extensive search queries by using any of the search techniques described in the following sections. You can also use a combination of any of these search methods to further refine your search query. For example, you can define a search for a particular author's documents by selecting the By Author search (see the later section "Searching by Author"), making your selections, and then clicking OK to save your entry. You can then select another condition and input words or phrases that you want the document to contain to further enhance your query.

Searching for Specified Text   In the previous examples, you learned how to search for a single word or phrase in a database. If your database is full-text indexed, however, you can use Search Builder to find documents that contain the words and phrases in a list.

Before you conduct the search, be sure that the database is open to the view you want to search, and then follow these steps:

1. If the Search Bar isn't visible, choose View, Search Bar.
2. Click the Add Condition button. The dialog box shown in Figure 8.9 appears.

FIG. 8.9

By typing words or phrases into each of the entry boxes, you can narrow your search results by selecting only those documents that meet all the criteria.

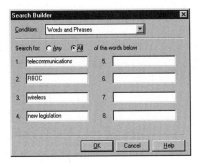

3. In the Condition drop-down list, leave the default value Words and Phrases.
4. Select All to have Notes display only documents that contain all the words or phrases you enter into the Search Builder. Selecting Any, as described later in this chapter, will display documents that contain any of the words or phrases you type.
5. Type a word or phrase in as many of the numbered text boxes as you want. Search Builder searches for documents that contain all these words and phrases.

6. Click <u>O</u>K. Notes displays the query you have built in the text box of the Search Builder. Entries you created in the fields are separated by AND to signify that these words and phrases must all be in the document in order for it to be displayed in the results.

7. Click the Search button on the Search Bar.

TIP If you need to include more than eight words and phrases in your search, repeat steps 2 through 6 until all your criteria have been entered.

For example, Figure 8.9 shows a query that has been built to search a company information database for all documents that contain the words "telecommunications," "RBOC," "wireless," and "new legislation."

The results of this query would be any documents in the database that contained all the words and phrases listed in Figure 8.9. In this example, only one document contained all the words and phrases, as shown in Figure 8.10.

FIG. 8.10
The view will display the results of a full-text query against a database.

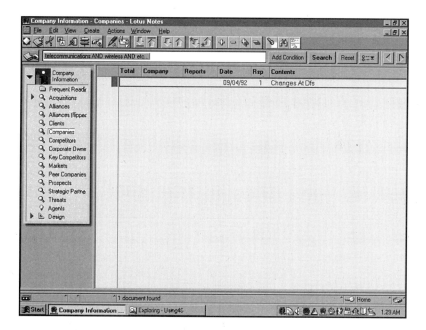

Opening the document displayed in the view displays all the words and phrases defined in the query highlighted with red boxes, as shown in Figure 8.11.

If you want to find documents containing any of the words or phrases you have specified, choose <u>A</u>ny in step 4. Entries you created in the fields are separated by OR to signify that at least one of these words or phrases will be displayed in the results for the document.

FIG. 8.11

Words and phrases appear with red boxes highlighting them when you open a document displayed after a query when the database is indexed.

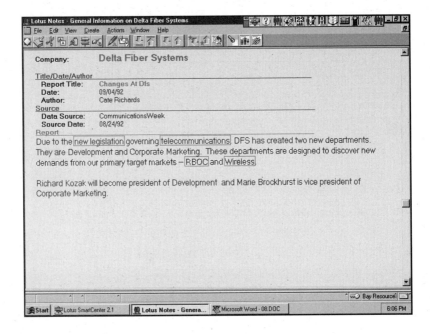

Notes will display the results of this query in the current view, as shown in Figure 8.12. In this example, several documents meet the criteria defined in the query.

FIG. 8.12

If two or more documents meet the search query, they will be listed in the view according to the criteria you defined.

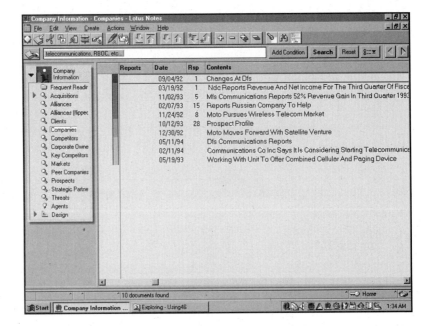

Searching Multiple Databases You can search more than one database at a time, if necessary. To do so, follow these steps:

1. Select the database icon for each of the databases you want to search (they must all be on the same workspace page) by holding down the Shift key and clicking each database icon.

2. While holding down the Shift key, double-click any of the database icons you selected.

3. A view will open in which the titles of the selected databases appear in the navigator (almost like category titles in a database view), as shown in Figure 8.13.

FIG. 8.13
When you're searching multiple databases for text, the database titles appear in a temporary navigator when they are selected for query.

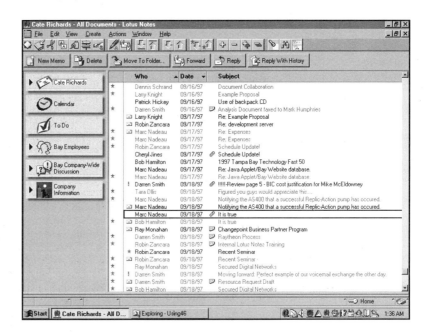

4. Perform a full-text search as usual.

5. To see the results of the search in each database, click the small triangle to the left of each database title in the view. That database title will open to display all the documents found to contain your search criteria. Switch between views and folders as usual in the database to see all documents.

Searching by Author If your database is indexed, you can define a query to search a database to display all documents composed by a specific author or group of authors.

Before you conduct the search, be sure that the database is open to the view you want to search. Then follow these steps:

1. If the Search Bar isn't visible, choose View, Search Bar.

2. Click the Add Condition button. The Search Builder appears, as shown in Figure 8.14.

FIG. 8.14

When you query a database for documents By Author, Notes changes the appearance of the dialog box.

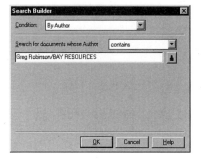

3. In the Condition drop-down list, select By Author.

4. In the Search for documents whose Author drop-down list, select contains if you want documents created by the authors you select or does not contain if you want to exclude documents created by a specific author.

> **N O T E**   In any query you build, if you choose to exclude an entry based on a selection or term that you enter, Notes will insert NOT before the phrase to indicate that Notes should exclude any documents that contain that entry. You can also type NOT before any word or phrase to get the same effect. For example, if you want to exclude documents written by anyone named Larry, enter NOT Larry in the search formula by author. This principle works for all searches you build, not just searches by author. ■

5. Do one of the following:

Type the name of an author in the text box. To include more than one name, separate the names with commas.

Click the Author icon (the icon of a person) and select the names of the authors you want from the Address Book (see Figure 8.15). If you're working on the network, Notes will display the Public Address Book. If you're working remote (off the network), Notes will display your Private Address Book. If you have more than one Address Book available, you can switch between them as usual.

FIG. 8.15

You can select the author(s) you want to search for from your Address Book to make sure you have the correct spelling for your query.

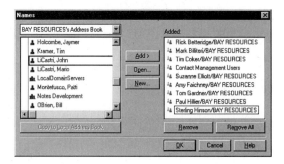

To select a person's name in the address list (group names have no effect in this search), highlight the name and click Add. Notes will add the name you have selected to the list on the right. Continue to select names until all the authors you want to include in your query are selected.

6. Click OK in the Names dialog box and again in the Search Builder dialog box.

7. Click the Search button on the Search Bar.

N O T E You can search by author in all databases created using Notes 4.x as long as there is an author field in the database's design. You might have difficulty searching databases created in versions earlier than Release 4, however. You won't be able to search by author in anonymous databases (databases meant to hide the identity of the author of a document). ▨

Searching by Date If your database is indexed, you can search for documents based on the date they were created or modified. Before you conduct the search, be sure that the database is open to the view you want to search. Then follow these steps:

1. If the Search Bar isn't visible, choose View, Search Bar.

2. Click the Add Condition button. The dialog box shown in Figure 8.16 appears.

FIG. 8.16

This query searches for documents created after 11/19/96.

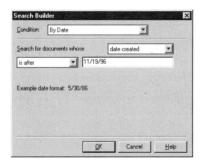

3. In the Condition drop-down list, select By Date.

4. In the Search for documents whose drop-down list, select date created or date modified.

5. In the next drop-down list, specify how the date for which you are searching is related to the documents for which you are searching.

6. Type a date in the date text box. If there are two text boxes, type dates in both of them. Make sure you use the format displayed below the list box when typing your dates. The date format depends on the format used by your operating system.

7. Click OK. Repeat steps 2 through 7 if you need to include more dates in your search.

8. Click the Search button on the Search Bar.

Notes will search the database for all documents that meet your date criteria and display them in the view.

Searching by Field Contents   If a database is indexed, you can search for documents that have a specific entry in a particular field. For example, in a Marketing database, you might want to find documents that contain the word Competitor in the `ClassificationR` field.

Before you conduct the search, be sure that the database is open to the view you want to search. Then do the following:

1. If the Search Bar isn't visible, choose <u>V</u>iew, Search <u>B</u>ar.

2. Click the Add Condition button. The dialog box shown in Figure 8.17 appears.

FIG. 8.17

This query looks for the word "Competitor" in the `ClassificationR` field of the database.

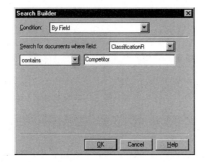

3. In the <u>C</u>ondition drop-down list, select By Field.

4. In the <u>S</u>earch for documents where field drop-down list, select the field you want to include in the search. This drop-down list box has a list of all the fields contained in the design of the database.

5. In the other drop-down list, make a relationship choice: The field either does or doesn't contain the entry.

6. In the text box (or text boxes), type the text, dates, or number for which you want to search. For example, type `Competitor`.

7. Click <u>O</u>K. Repeat steps 2 through 7 if you need to include more fields in your search.

8. Click the Search button on the Search Bar.

If you aren't familiar with the design of the database and you don't know the name of the field you want to use in your query, you can review the field design information by highlighting a document in the database view you're searching and selecting <u>E</u>dit, <u>P</u>roperties. Notes will display the Document Properties InfoBox for the document, as shown in Figure 8.18. Select the Fields tab. A list of all the fields will appear in the left list box. As you select a field name, Notes displays in the right list box the design and contents of the field for the document you selected. Reviewing this information should help you find the appropriate field to use in this query.

FIG. 8.18
You can view the form's field content in the Fields tab of the Document Properties InfoBox for the document.

Searching by Criteria in a Form   If your database is indexed, you can search for documents by entering criteria into any database form, as long as the database designer indicated that the form could be displayed in Search Builder.

Before you conduct the search, be sure that the database is open to the view you want to search, and then follow these steps:

1. If the Search Bar isn't visible, choose View, Search Bar.
2. Click the Add Condition button.
3. In the dialog box that appears, click the Condition drop-down list and select By Form.
4. In the Form drop-down list, select the form you want to use in the search. All forms in the database will appear in the drop-down list unless the database developer designed the forms to not appear. See Chapter 11, "Designing Forms," for more information on form design.
5. In the form you selected, type entries (text, numbers, and so on) in as many fields as you want to include in the search in the fields defined in the database form. What you type in each field is what you search for. Type your entries into the fields that appear in the form just as if you were typing in a regular Notes document.
6. Click OK.
7. Click the Search button on the Search Bar.

Notes will search for documents that include all the entries you make.

Searching for Documents Created with a Certain Form   If a database has been indexed, you can use the Search Builder to find documents that were created using a specific form. For example, you can create a query in a Marketing database to show only documents created using the Company form. Typically, you use this type of search when you know that a particular word or phrase appears in many different documents in a database and when you're interested in information that would be contained in only one particular type of form. For example, the word "hotel" might appear many times in a company travel database, but if you're preparing a report on all problems with hotels reported by employees, you're interested only in the instances of the word that appear in a Trouble Report form in the database.

Before you conduct the search, be sure that the database is open to the view you want to search. Then follow these steps:

1. If the Search Bar isn't visible, choose View, Search Bar.

2. Click the Add Condition button. The dialog box shown in Figure 8.19 appears.

FIG. 8.19

This selection indicates that you want to search in the Activity Report and Company Profile forms.

3. In the Condition drop-down list, select By Form Used.

4. In the Form list box, select one or more forms. A checkmark will appear next to each form selected.

5. Click OK.

6. Click the Search button on the Search Bar.

Refining Your Search Results   Notes provides you with many ways to view and alter the results you receive when you run a search query. You can alter the order in which documents are displayed, use synonyms in your search, change the maximum number of entries displayed, and save a search formula. You make these settings using the Options button on the Search Bar. When you refine your searches by clicking the Options button before running the query, the menu in Figure 8.20 is displayed.

Here are the options from which you can select in this drop-down menu:

■ Include Word Variants: This option tells Notes to include any words in which the base part of the word you're looking for is present. For example, if you enter "training" as the search criteria, documents containing "train" would also be selected. If you enter "train," Notes would also display "training," "trained," and so on.

■ Use Thesaurus: With this option, you can include synonyms of search words in your search. For example, if you search for documents that contain the word "doctor," Notes also finds documents that contain the word "physician." This selection will remain active until you reset the Search Builder or exit the database.

■ Sort by Relevance: By default, the search results in databases queried with the Full Text Search feature are displayed in the order of significance, which means that the more times the word or phrase is found in a document, the higher up in the list the document will be displayed. You can ascertain the significance of the document in the search by looking to the left of the documents in the view. A vertical bar indicates the relevance of each document to the search criteria, as shown in Figure 8.21. The darker the portion of the bar, the more relevant the document.

FIG. 8.20
By clicking the Options button, you can change the way Notes displays your results.

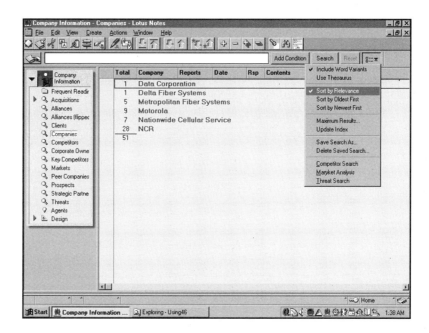

FIG. 8.21
By default, search results are displayed in the view according to relevance.

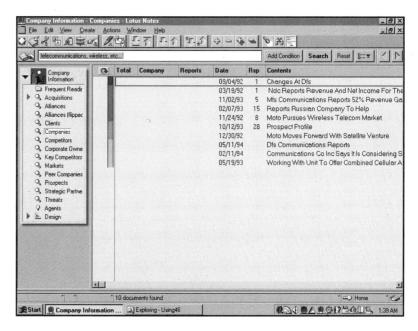

■ Sort by Oldest First: This option displays the documents found in the search according to their compose date, with the oldest documents displayed first. This sort order is ideal if you're trying to follow a discussion on a topic and you want to read the discussion from beginning to end.

■ Sort by Newest First: This option displays the documents found in the search according to their compose date, with the newest documents displayed first. This sort order is ideal if you're looking for the latest information regarding a particular topic—for example, if you're reviewing a database of customer contact reports and you want to see what is current for a particular topic.

■ Maximum Results: This option lets you determine the maximum number of documents you will accept in the results of a search. The default setting is 250 documents, which is usually adequate for your needs. If you're interested only in receiving documents that best suit your query, and you want to speed up the search process, reduce this setting.

■ Save Search As: This option lets you save a search formula so that you can use it whenever you use the database in which you created it. If you have Designer or Manager access to the database on a server, you can also make the search formula available to anyone who uses the database by selecting Shared search in the Save Search As dialog box, shown in Figure 8.22. Saved search formulas appear at the bottom of the Options menu in the Search Bar, as shown in Figure 8.23.

FIG. 8.22

You can save search formulas in the database in which you used them.

FIG. 8.23

Saved searches are displayed at the bottom of the Options menu in the database in which you saved them.

■ Delete Saved Search: With this option, you can remove saved search formulas. When you select this option, Notes displays the Delete Saved Search dialog box, shown in Figure 8.24. Select the saved search name you want to remove, and then click Delete.

FIG. 8.24
You should delete old, saved queries that you will no longer use to keep your menu list from becoming cluttered.

Notes will display a checkmark next to selected items to tell you what options you have selected. Once you have made your selections, you can click the Search button on the Search Bar to begin searching the database.

In addition to the methods of refining your queries that you have learned about in the preceding sections, you can also use the following terms in your query field entries to further enhance your query capabilities.

If you selected Word, sentence and paragraph as the index break when you created the full-text index, you can use the proximity operators to increase the relevance ranking of words that are close to each other. The following proximity operators are available:

- Near: The closer the words or phrases are to each other, the higher Notes will rank their relevance in the sort view. For example, if you entered `Competitor near Threat` in a query field, Notes would sort the documents in which these terms are closer to each other at the top of the view.

- Sentence: This option works much the same as Near, but all the words or phrases must be in the same sentence. For example, if you entered `Competitor sentence Threat` in a query field, Notes would sort the documents with both of these terms in the same sentence at the top of the view.

- Paragraph: This option works much the same as Near, but the words or phrases must all be in the same paragraph. For example, if you entered `Competitor paragraph Threat` in a query field, Notes would sort the documents with both of these terms in the same paragraph at the top of the view.

You can also use wildcard characters in place of other characters when you search for text:

- Use a question mark (?) for a single character. For example, typing `owe?` will return documents containing words such as "owed" and "owes."

- Use an asterisk (*) for multiple characters. For example, typing `fl*` will return documents containing words such as "Florida," "Floridians," "flow," and "flop."

Wildcard characters work only in text fields; they don't work in fields that contain dates or numbers.

To further refine your query, you can perform a second search based on the results of the first search. For example, suppose you searched a company information database for the names of companies that are considered threats to your organization. If this search came up with so many documents that it was ineffective, you might want to refine the search to include only companies that are threats *and* whose product line focuses on the same target market as yours.

You can do this by performing the first query on the database to find companies that are considered threats. Then, with that query's results still displayed, perform another query on documents containing target market names that are the same as yours. Notes will search only the documents listed in the first query to find matches with the second.

Working with Document Read Marks

You have seen that Notes displays an asterisk next to documents that you haven't read. In databases such as your mailbox, these markers can serve as important reminders that you need to read certain documents. Sometimes, however, you might decide that you don't want to read certain documents in a database or in your mailbox at a particular time.

Suppose that your company maintains a database of important scheduled events that you want to keep abreast of. Someone in your company routinely adds notices about the company softball team, which doesn't interest you. After a long vacation, you return to your desk and find 14 softball announcements in the database. You really don't want to read them, but they all have asterisks next to them.

You can use the Unread Marks option to tell Notes to remove the asterisks and make the documents appear as though you have read them. To mark documents as read, open the database and choose Edit, Unread Marks. The Unread Marks submenu appears (see Figure 8.25), allowing you to select one of the following four options:

- Mark Selected Read: This option marks all selected documents as read.
- Mark All Read: This option marks all documents in the database as read.
- Mark Selected Unread: This option marks all selected documents as unread.
- Mark All Unread: This option marks all documents in the database as unread.

Note that the last two choices let you mark read documents as unread; that is, you can read a document and then tell Notes to mark it as though you hadn't read it. At first glance, this capability might seem like a feature in search of a use, but you actually might find it useful, especially if you keep old memos in your mailbox that you think might be important later.

When you open your mailbox, you probably look for asterisks, which call your attention to newly arrived mail. Suppose you read a message just before quitting time one afternoon, and then you realize that the memo will require significant attention tomorrow. If you close the message, Notes now considers it one of the many previously read messages and removes its attention-getting asterisk. You can put it back by marking the document as unread so that it will again attract your attention the next time you read your mail.

FIG. 8.25
You can mark documents as read to indicate that you have already read them or as unread to draw your attention to those documents at a later date.

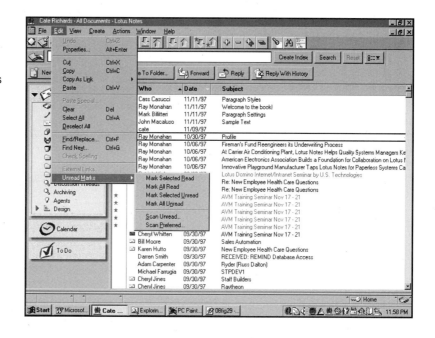

 You can now open documents directly from the preview pane rather than just through the view. If you want to make sure that documents you read in the preview pane are also marked as being read, select File, Tools, User Preferences. In the Basic settings, select Mark documents read when opened in preview pane in the Advanced options section. Notes will mark any documents you open through the preview pane as well as those you open directly through the view as being read.

Scanning for Unread Documents

Many people work with several different databases and must constantly be on the lookout for new documents showing up in those databases. Suppose that your company has several databases that contain status reports from different departments, and one of your jobs is to monitor these status reports for customer problems. You might find it cumbersome to check each database several times a day to see whether new documents have appeared. Instead, you can select Edit, Unread Marks, Scan Unread to learn about new documents.

Scanning Preferred Databases   You can use the Scan Unread feature in several ways, but the most common—and most useful—method involves a two-step process. In the first step, you tell Notes which databases you want to watch for unread documents; these databases are known as your preferred databases. Then, at any time, you can ask Notes if there are any unread documents in any of your preferred databases.

To supply Notes with your list of preferred databases, select Edit, Unread Marks, Scan Preferred. The Scan Unread dialog box appears, as shown in Figure 8.26. When you select Choose Preferred, the Scan Unread Preferred Setup dialog box appears, as shown in Figure 8.27.

FIG. 8.26

You can use the Scan Unread dialog box to begin setting up preferred databases to scan.

FIG. 8.27

You must select each database you want to mark as preferred individually from the list. Workspace page names are indicated with a hyphen before and after the name; you can't select them.

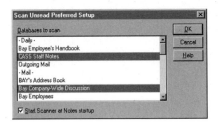

Notes lists all the databases on all your workspace pages. Workspace pages themselves have a hyphen on either side of the name:

`- Misc -`

Select the databases that you want scanned for unread documents. You must click each database title individually. Click OK to save your selections.

N O T E The Scan Unread Preferred Setup dialog box includes a checkbox labeled Start Scanner at Notes startup. If you check this box, Notes will automatically scan your preferred databases for unread documents each time you start Notes. ■

When you have selected your preferred databases, you can scan them for unread documents by making sure no databases are selected on the workspace (click anywhere in the blank gray portion of the workspace) and choosing Edit, Unread Marks, Scan Preferred. Notes displays the Scan Unread dialog box (refer to Figure 8.26). It displays the name of the first of your preferred databases and shows the number of unread documents in the database. You can choose any of the following actions:

- View First Unread: Notes opens the first document in the first database. You can then read the unread document. Press Tab to move to the next unread document in the database, and press Esc to exit the current document and open the database view.

- Mark All Read: Notes assumes that you don't want to read the documents and marks them as read from this database only. All other databases you're scanning won't be affected by this selection.

- Skip This Database: Notes displays the name of the next preferred database and the number of unread documents in that database.

After Notes scans all databases, it loops back to the first and begins scanning again. When you see the same databases appearing again, click <u>D</u>one to exit scanning.

Scanning a Single Database   To scan a single database for unread documents, highlight the database you want to scan by clicking the database icon. Select <u>E</u>dit, Unread <u>M</u>arks, <u>S</u>can Unread. Notes will open the first unread document in the database. Press Tab to open the next unread document. Press Esc to end the scan and exit the document. You will be returned to the database view.

Scanning Multiple Databases   You can select multiple databases and then scan them. To do so, press the Shift key and then select each of the databases you want to scan. Select <u>E</u>dit, Unread <u>M</u>arks, <u>S</u>can Unread. Notes opens the Scan Unread dialog box. Follow the procedures in the section "Scanning Preferred Databases" to scan the databases you have selected.

Copying and Pasting Documents

Not only can you use the clipboard to copy pieces of text from one document to another as described in the section "Copying and Pasting Text" in Chapter 7, but you can also use almost the exact same technique to move or copy documents from one database to another. Do the following:

1. Open the database in which the documents now exist.

2. Select one or more documents by clicking in the left margin next to each. A checkmark will appear next to selected documents, as shown in Figure 8.28.

FIG. 8.28

Selecting documents in a view allows you to perform a function— such as copying—on all the documents at one time.

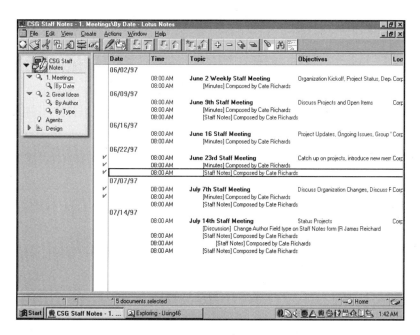

3. If you want to copy the documents, choose Edit, Copy, press Ctrl+C, or click the Copy SmartIcon. If you want to move the documents, choose Edit, Cut, press Ctrl+X, or click the Cut SmartIcon.

4. Close the current database and open the database in which you want to place the documents.

5. Choose Edit, Paste, press Ctrl+V, or click the Paste SmartIcon.

Notes inserts the documents into the new database. This procedure works best if both databases contain the form that you used to compose the documents. If, for example, the documents were composed with a form called Client Information, and both databases contain forms by that name, Notes can perform the move or copy easily. Otherwise, Notes will display the document using the database's default form, which might not contain the same field names. In that case, you might see a blank document when you open it using the default form or see only some of the fields in the document, or you might not see the document in the view at all if the view is using a selection formula based on the form or other field contents.

> **CAUTION**
>
> Trying to copy documents into a database that doesn't contain a copy of the form in which they are created can result in Notes being unable to display any of the information in the form or displaying only a small portion of the information. Read Chapter 11 for information on working with form design.

Applications of Copying and Pasting Documents

The ability to copy text, fields, or even entire documents is a Notes feature that is often overlooked but that contains a great deal of power. Here are some excellent applications of the capability to copy (or cut) documents to the clipboard:

- Although Notes provides you with an automatic archival agent for your email, which is date-driven if activated, sometimes you might simply want to archive specific documents out of your email database on demand. You can cut documents from your active mail database and store them in an email "archive" database for safekeeping. With this archive, you can keep your active mail database relatively small as well as have the capability to keep important documents in case you need to get to them quickly at another time. As mentioned earlier, make sure that the document's form design is also present in the archive database to ensure that you can read the documents clearly. It's best if your archive mail database is a copy of your active database design. Read Chapter 10, "Creating New Databases," for more information on database design.

- You can temporarily protect against losing documents while you perform other functions in the database. For example, suppose you're getting ready to run an agent against several documents in a database to replace some text but you want to make sure the documents are protected against errors, such as being deleted. Before you do so, you can copy them to the clipboard, run your macro, and then verify that your results appear as you expected in your original documents.

If something went wrong when you ran the macro, you can always delete the modified documents and paste the documents from the clipboard back into the database so that the information is restored to its original condition (before you began the agent).

- Copying and pasting documents within the same database is a time-saver if you want to edit small portions of a document but want to keep the old, unedited document intact, such as a large proposal that someone else in your organization wrote. Copy the document to the clipboard and then repaste it into the database by selecting Edit, Paste. Open the copy of the document and edit it. Your document will contain the edits without disturbing the original document.

  Often, depending on the design of the database, your copy of the document will appear slightly indented below the original document as a response document if you highlighted the original document before pasting. (Your database designer might have bypassed your need to do this by selecting one of the following options in the Form Property InfoBox during the creation of the form design: New versions become responses, Prior versions become responses, or New versions become siblings. See Chapter 11 for more information on the Form Property InfoBox.)

Linking Documents

Often, you will want to guide readers to other areas where there is information related to the topic they are currently reading about. For example, perhaps a document that you are composing discusses a topic that is mentioned in another document.

For example, if you're discussing the health benefits of broccoli, you might want to create a link to another document that contains a recipe for actually making the stuff edible! The link need not even be in the same database as the document you're reading.

You can create links to the following:

- Documents
- Views
- Databases

A link appears as a piece of paper with its corner folded down, as shown in Figure 8.29. Associated with each link is a location, called the link pointer, within the link document. When the user double-clicks the link, Notes displays the link document showing the section of text containing the link pointer. When the user closes the link document, Notes returns to the original document that contained the link.

To create a link, follow these steps:

1. Start with one of the following:

   Open the link document (the document you want to link to—it doesn't have to be in the same database) and select a link point by clicking the position within the document that you want Notes to display when the doclink is activated. Note that if you open the document in read mode, the insertion point flashes only momentarily, but Notes still knows where it is.

Open the view in which you want to link (the view doesn't need to be in the current database). Press F6 and select the view or folder you want to link to in the navigator pane.

Highlight the database you want to link to by clicking its icon.

2. Choose Edit, Copy as Link.

Select whether the link you are creating is a Document Link, View Link, or Database Link. Notes puts a link on the clipboard that corresponds to the link point you selected. Notes will indicate that the link has been copied to the clipboard in the Status Bar at the bottom of the Notes window.

3. Open the document in which you want to insert the link. You must open the document in edit mode.

4. Paste the link into any rich text field in the document just as you would a section of text (select Edit, Paste or press Ctrl+V).

FIG. 8.29

Notes can link a document to other documents, views, or databases.

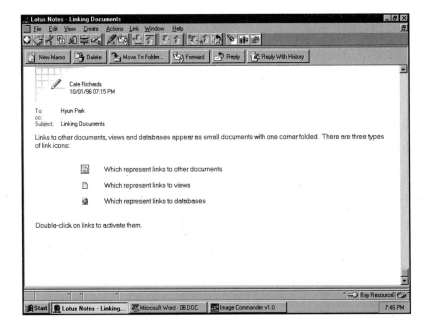

CAUTION

The following circumstances might keep links from working:

- If the database ID or document ID referenced in the doclink is changed, you will have to make the link again. This often happens when the database is copied to another server (as opposed to making a replica copy) and the original database is deleted. It can also happen if the document is cut out of the linked database and stored in another database.

- The user doesn't have access to the database, server, or directory on the server in which the referenced database is located. The user must have at least Reader access.

- The user doesn't have form access to read the document referenced in the link. Form access is assigned when the form is created by the database designer. The default is All Users (who have access to the database).

- The user doesn't have view access, necessary to read the view that is linked. The access level for reading a view is created by the database designer. The default is All Users (who have access to the database).

- Remote users won't be able to use the link unless the referenced database is located on their hard drive or they are dialed out to a server hosting a copy of the database.

If you're working on the network and you double-click a link and the referenced database isn't located on your workspace, Notes will search the servers to which you have access and add the database icon to your workspace, opened to the link point.

Because links are simply a set of numbers referencing the database ID and document ID, you can use them in messages to users to have them add a new database to their desktop and open the database to the referenced link point. When you close the database to which you have been linked, you will notice that the database icon has been added to your desktop. The database icon will remain on the workspace page until the reader removes it.

This is an ideal way for database managers to help users access a new database. There is another way: using buttons that specify exactly which server you should access, as well as the name of the database (and possibly the document). You will learn more about buttons in Chapter 16, "Buttons and Agents."

You can use links in designing databases to guide users to referenced information. For example, if you have a discussion database, you can create a link in the form design of the response documents to always link back to the parent document if the reader wants to review the original topic. You will learn more about designing forms and views in Chapter 11, "Designing Forms," and Chapter 12, "Designing Views."

Adding Hotspots to Your Documents

Hotspots let you communicate additional information. Depending on its type, a hotspot might display pop-up text, switch to a linked destination, or perform a Notes action. For example, a pop-up hotspot displays pop-up text, as shown in Figure 8.30.

Notes can also use hotspots to link to another document. For example, Figure 8.31 shows a document with underlined text. The author of the document created a hotspot for this text so that when users double-click the text, they will open a related document. You will see many examples of this use of text hotspots in the online Lotus Notes Help database. (Text hotspots appear as underlined green text in the help documents. They link you to information related to that help topic.)

FIG. 8.30

Pop-up hotspots are handy when you want to display information in a document that only some readers will be interested in seeing, such as directions to your house.

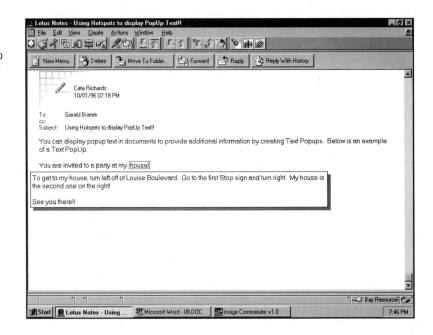

FIG. 8.31

You can use text hotspots to link readers to related text.

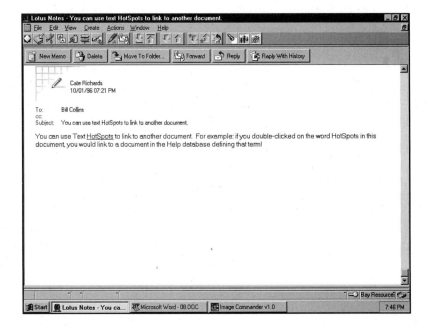

Finally, Notes can use hotspots to perform actions. For example, you could define an action to compose a document titled "Registration" whenever someone clicks a hotspot called Register (see Figure 8.32).

FIG. 8.32

You can use action hotspots to perform functions—such as composing a new form—whenever someone clicks them.

N O T E Before you create a hotspot, the cursor must be located in a rich text field, and your document must be in edit mode. You must be in read mode to display or activate a hotspot.

N O T E There is one final type of hotspot—buttons that you can create in documents as well as in the design of a form. Button hotspots are covered in detail in Chapter 16.

Pop-Up Hotspots

To define a text pop-up hotspot, in which text pops up whenever the user clicks and holds the left mouse button on a particular hotspot, follow these steps:

1. Make sure the document is in edit mode.

2. Select the area to which you want to add the hotspot. This area can be text that you have typed or a graphic that you have copied from the clipboard.

3. Do one of the following:

   Choose Create, Hotspot, Text Popup and enter the text you want the pop-up to display. For example, you can type help information about a particular form in the text box to provide help information, particularly when the instructions are too long to fit in the field help line displayed at the bottom of the window.

Choose Create, Hotspot, Formula Popup and enter a formula in the programmer pane that will set the text you want the pop-up to display. For example, you can set a formula that looks up a list of current products in a product database whenever someone clicks the hotspot. You will learn more about writing formulas in Chapter 14, "Working with Formulas," and Chapter 15, "Working with Functions and Commands."

 TIP If the text you want to enter has already been typed in another Windows or OS/2 document, you can highlight the text and select Edit, Copy to copy the text to the clipboard. Then, with the cursor in the pop-up text field, press Ctrl+V to paste the text from the clipboard. (The Edit, Paste function isn't available because you are in a dialog box.) This is a quick way to put a large amount of text in a pop-up. The formatting and font attributes won't be present in the pop-up, however.

As mentioned earlier, database designers most often use pop-ups to include additional help or reference information in the design of a form. You too can use the pop-up feature in the body of documents to limit the amount of information a reader has to filter through to get to the information needed in the document you are creating.

For example, if you're working with a team on a proposal and you've been exchanging information about it (close dates, dollar amounts, and so forth) but you also want to define for the readers some of the terms within the contract, you can create a pop-up around the terms. If a reader needs a definition, he can access it; otherwise, he doesn't need to waste time reading the definition, and he can continue through the rest of the document.

You can also copy information from a previous memo and paste it into a pop-up box when links aren't applicable. The reader then has the option of reading previous information, if needed, by clicking the pop-up you created or just reading the current information. To paste text from the clipboard into a pop-up box, create the pop-up box as usual, and then press Ctrl+V to paste the text from the clipboard into the dialog box.

One last example of using Formula pop-ups is to display editing information about the particular document you're reading. The developer of the application can provide a pop-up hotspot (perhaps in a graphical format) with a Notes formula that tracks the history of the original author and any editors of the document. People interested in seeing that information can click the graphic to display it. Otherwise, the information is tucked out of sight from the main body of the document.

 TIP The Online Help database provides some great examples of the use of pop-up hotspots in documents and navigators.

Link Hotspots

You can add a hotspot that allows users to switch to another document, view, folder, or database. This is an example of a link hotspot that leads to another document (much as you learned in the section "Linking Documents" earlier in this chapter). The difference between creating a link and creating a link hotspot is in the appearance of the "trigger" that initiates the link.

When creating links, you paste an object that looks like a document into a document. In creating link hotspots, any area that you highlight will serve as the "trigger" for making the link. For example, you could highlight a graphic of an airplane to have Notes link you to a policy on airline travel in another database.

To create a link hotspot, follow these steps:

1. Begin by choosing any of these options:

   In the view pane, click the document to which you want to link.

   In the navigation pane, click the view or folder to which you want to link.

   In the workspace, click the database to which you want to link.

   In a document, click the area of the document to which you want to link.

2. Choose Edit, Copy as Link.

3. Open the document to which you want to add the hotspot in edit mode.

4. Highlight the area to which you want to add the hotspot. (This area can be text or a graphic.)

5. Choose Create, Hotspot, Link Hotspot.

Action Hotspots

You can add a hotspot to an area of a document (such as text or a graphic) that lets users perform a Notes action. For example, you can add a hotspot that creates a document that you can type and send, such as a registration form in a training database. A good example of action hotspots can be found in many of the new V4 navigators, in which clicking a graphic opens a navigator, view, or document for you to read. Other examples in the Help database include action hotspots that are programmed around each of the book icons in the navigator pane. Clicking a book opens another navigator and view for quick access to the information you need the most.

To create an action hotspot, do the following:

1. Make sure the document is in edit mode.

2. Highlight the area to which you want to add the hotspot. The area can be text or a graphic.

3. Choose Create, Hotspot, Action Hotspot. The programmer pane appears, as shown in Figure 8.33.

4. In the programmer pane, do one of the following:

   Specify a preprogrammed action that Notes includes by selecting Simple action(s) and clicking Add Actions. Then select an action, specify any settings Notes needs to perform the action, and click OK.

   To enter a formula that performs an action, select Formula and enter the formula. The formula you use can be a simple formula, such as telling Notes to close the database, or it can be quite complex.

FIG. 8.33

To create action hotspots, you need to be in the Programmer pane.

To enter a script that performs an action, select Script and enter the script. The script you use can be a simple script, such as composing a document, or it can be quite complex.

N O T E You will learn about programming simple actions, formulas, and scripts in Part II, "Designing Applications." ■

   5. Click anywhere within the document to close the programmer pane and continue working.

You can remove the green border that surrounds a hotspot by highlighting the hotspot while you're in edit mode or the design pane and selecting Edit, Properties. The HotSpot Button Properties InfoBox appears, as shown in Figure 8.34.

Deselect Show border around hotspot. You can also hide the hotspot; change fonts, colors, and other text attributes; and perform any paragraph formatting options by making the appropriate selections in the hotspot's Properties InfoBox.

To use a hotspot, click anywhere within the border of the hotspot—with the exception of pop-up hotspots. To use a pop-up hotspot, click and hold the left mouse button anywhere within the hotspot's borders. The text will be displayed as long as you press the mouse button.

FIG. 8.34
Use the HotSpot Button Properties InfoBox to control how the hotspot is displayed in the document or form.

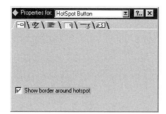

Using Tables in Your Documents

As you use Notes to compose documents, you might find tables handy for representing data. Tables consist of data arranged in rows and columns in any manner you choose. The intersection of each column and row is a cell. Most often, lines surround each cell so that the table forms a grid. Like most other advanced formatting features, tables can appear only in rich text fields.

You can include tables in the design of your database forms by following the instructions for creating tables provided in the next section. Rather than entering text into all the cells, however, you will define fields. Figure 8.35 shows an example of a form using a table as part of its design (in design mode). See Chapter 11 for additional information.

FIG. 8.35
You can create tables as part of the form design. Each cell can contain static text or a separate field design.

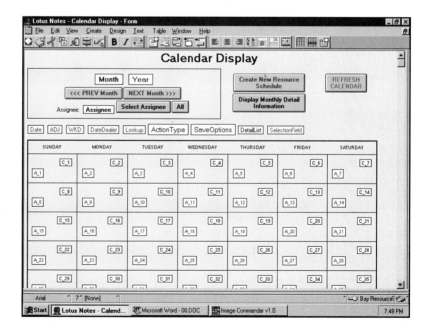

In the following sections, you will learn how to create tables in documents, add data to tables, and change tables' characteristics.

Creating Tables

To create a new table, position the insertion point where you want the table to appear, and then choose Create, Table. Notes opens the dialog box shown in Figure 8.36.

FIG. 8.36

Enter the number of rows and columns for your table.

Enter the number of rows and columns you want for this table. Notes immediately creates a table in your document with the numbers of rows and columns you specified. Notes also adds a new menu to the menu bar at the top of the Notes window: Table. You can use this menu to control the attributes of the table you're working with.

You can add and delete columns and rows from a table and change cell widths, borders, and other table attributes at any time. The following sections provide details.

Adding and Deleting Columns

To add a new column to your table, click where you want to add the column. Select Table, Insert Column. Notes adds another column to your table to the left of the cursor location.

If you want to add multiple columns to your table, click where you want to add the columns and select Table, Insert Special. Notes displays the Insert Row/Column dialog box, shown in Figure 8.37.

FIG. 8.37

By selecting Table, Insert Special, you can add multiple columns or rows to your table.

Type the number of columns you want to add in the text box provided, and then select Column(s). Next, select from the following options:

- Insert: Inserts the number of columns specified to the left of the current cursor location.
- Append: Adds the number of columns specified to the far-right side of the table.
- Cancel: Lets you exit without adding any columns.
- Help: Accesses the online help in Notes.

Notes adds the columns to your table.

You can also delete columns from your table by placing the cursor in the columns you want to remove and selecting Table, Delete Selected Column(s). Notes will ask whether you want to delete the columns; click Yes. You can also delete multiple columns by placing the cursor in the first column you want to delete and then selecting Table, Delete Special. Select Column(s) and specify how many columns you want to remove. When you have made your selection, click Delete. Notes removes the current column and any additional columns to the right of the current one, according to the number of columns you specified.

Adding and Deleting Rows

To add a new row to your table, click where you want to add the row. Select Table, Insert Rows. Notes adds another row above the current cursor location.

If you want to add multiple rows to your table, click where you want to add the rows, and then select Table, Insert Special. Type the number of rows you want to add in the text box provided, and then select Row(s). Next, choose from the following options:

- Insert: Inserts the number of rows specified above the current cursor location.
- Append: Adds the number of rows specified to the bottom of the table.
- Cancel: Lets you exit without adding any columns.
- Help: Accesses the online help in Notes.

Notes adds the rows to your table.

You can delete rows from your table by placing the cursor in the rows you want to remove and selecting Table, Delete Selected Row(s). Notes will ask whether you want to delete the row; click Yes. You can also delete multiple rows by placing the cursor in the first row you want to delete and then selecting Table, Delete Special. Choose Row(s) and specify how many rows you want to remove. When you have made your selection, click Delete. Notes removes the current rows and any additional rows below the current one, according to the number of rows you specified.

Changing Table Attributes

You can change the way your table looks by changing border attributes, column widths, space between columns and rows, and cell colors; splitting cells; joining cells; and selecting margin settings. To change these attributes, place the cursor in the first column or row that you want to modify. If you want to modify multiple cells, select the first cell, click and hold the left mouse button, drag the cursor over all the cells you want to modify, release the mouse button, and select Table, Table Properties. The Table Properties InfoBox appears with the Borders tab selected, as shown in Figure 8.38.

You can specify border widths ranging from 0 (no border) to 10 (the thickest border) for each side of the cell's border. You can also specify whether you want the table border to be

- Standard (a plain black line)
- Extruded (a "pushed in" 3-D effect)
- Embossed (a raised 3-D effect)

FIG. 8.38

You can change the borders for your table in the Table Properties InfoBox to add pizzazz to your table and highlight important information.

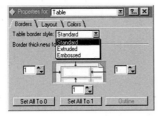

To change border settings (the thickness of the lines and appearance surrounding your table's cells), follow these steps:

1. With the Table Properties InfoBox opened to the Borders tab, do one of the following:

    To change the table's border style, click the down arrow and choose Standard, Extruded, or Embossed. This selection affects all the table's cells, not just the ones you have highlighted.

    To set the border on one or more sides, click the up/down arrow next to each border thickness to increase or decrease the width of each border.

    To set the border on all sides to single, click Set All To 1.

    To remove the border from all sides, click Set All To 0.

    To set the outline of the cells you have highlighted to a particular thickness or style, click Outline and then select any of the other options available to you.

2. If necessary, select another cell in the table and repeat step 1 until all the cell's borders are set as you would like them.

3. Close the dialog box.

To change borders only for the outer sides of the table, select the entire table and click Outline. Then select the border styles and settings for each side of the table. This feature makes it easy to frame your table with a special border setting.

You can also highlight the entire table and remove the border or select border styles that affect the entire table, including each individual cell's borders.

To make adjustments to the margins, column widths, and spacing between rows and columns, select the Layout tab of the Table Properties InfoBox, shown in Figure 8.39.

FIG. 8.39

Adjusting margins, spacing, and column widths helps add impact to your tables.

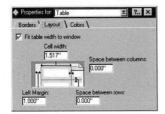

You can control the following settings:

- Fit table width to window: This setting tells Notes to always adjust the column widths to fit within the current window. That way, people who view the table can easily see all the columns, regardless of the size of their monitor or window.

N O T E Large tables can sometimes be difficult to read if Fit table width to window isn't selected, because the user will have to scroll back and forth in the window to see all the information.

Also, tables can sometimes be difficult to read on different platforms, screen sizes, and/or resolutions. Keep your user in mind when you create tables in documents. ▨

- Left Margin: To indent the table, enter a number larger than the default (1.25"). Notes will move the left margin of the table accordingly.

- Space between rows and Space between columns: With these options, you can specify how much blank space Notes displays between the text and the cell's borders. The default is 0.000".

- Cell width: This setting lets you specify in inches the width of the cells in each column. You can set the current cell's column and then click in another cell to adjust its width. Notes records which cell you're adjusting next to the Cell width text entry box.

Notes provides the capability to highlight certain cells with color. To add color to any cell in your table, highlight the cell(s) and select the Colors tab in the Table Properties InfoBox (see Figure 8.40). Select the color from the Background Color drop-down list. Notes will fill the cell(s) with the color you have selected. Click Apply to Entire Table if you want the selected color to fill all the cells in the table. You can also click Make Transparent to remove the color from any cell(s) you have selected.

FIG. 8.40

The top row of cells in the table will be filled with black to empha-size the table's column headings. This is just one use of color in your tables.

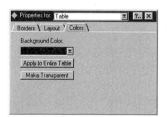

When you have made all your adjustments, close the Table Properties InfoBox to continue working with your table.

N O T E Large tables in documents tend to slow down the PC's response time when it reads and prints documents. Keep this in mind when you decide to insert a table. ▨

Merging and Splitting Cells

Notes gives you the ability to merge and split cells. Merging and splitting cells provides you with an enhanced way to draw attention to your form and communicate information to your readers. It also lets you duplicate the design of many simple paper forms more accurately in Notes.

To merge cells, follow these steps:

1. Highlight the cells you want to merge, as shown in Figure 8.41.

FIG. 8.41

You can merge cells in Notes 4.6 to change the size and shape of areas of a table.

N O T E   You must highlight more than one cell before the Merge Cells menu command becomes available. However, at the time this chapter was written, merging cells could throw off the width of the columns dramatically. ▨

2. Select Table, Merge Cells.

Notes merges the cells into one. If you have text in any of the cells, Notes will display the combined text from the single cells in the newly created cell.

To split cells, follow these steps:

1. Place the cursor in the cell you want to split.

N O T E   The cell you want to split must be a previously merged cell before the Split Cell command becomes available. ▨

2. Select Table, Split Cell.

Notes splits the highlighted cell into the original number of cells and copies any text in the merged cell into one of the new cells.

Entering Data in the Table

Suppose that you need to represent revenue figures for the fourth quarter in each of your company's three business units, along with totals. At first, you might think you want a table with four columns and four rows, but an extra row and column would let you label each month and business unit. So enter 5 as the number of rows and 5 as the number of columns. When you click OK, Notes creates the table.

You can enter data in the new table just as you can anywhere in the document. Figure 8.42 shows what the table might look like after data is typed into the cells (but before its characteristics are adjusted to enhance its attractiveness). In this example, the data was typed individually into each cell, including the totals. If the table were part of the design of the form, you could design a formula to automatically put the numbers in the Total row. You will learn more about creating formulas in Chapter 14.

FIG. 8.42

Tables such as the one shown here communicate information correctly but are bland and don't highlight important information.

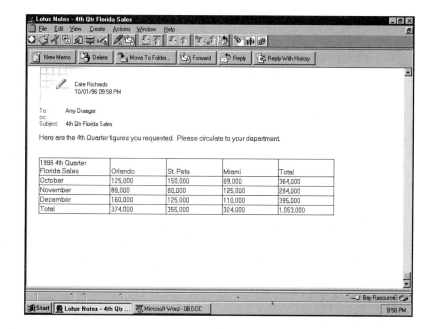

Once you have set the table's design, you can adjust the borders, cell widths, and other text formatting characteristics to add impact and highlight information to attract the reader's attention. Figure 8.44 (shown in a moment) displays the same table shown in Figure 8.42 but is formatted to enhance the presentation of information. As you enter data into a table, keep the following points in mind:

- You can use the arrow keys to move around within a table just as you can use them to move anywhere in a document. Within a table, however, you can also press Tab to move from one cell to another and Shift+Tab to move to the preceding cell (that is, the cell to the left, or the last cell in the preceding row if you're at the beginning of a row).

- If you enter text that is too wide for the cell, the cell extends to as many lines as necessary to hold the text.

- If you enter a single word that is too long to fit in a cell, Notes extends the height of the cell and splits the word. Notes never increases the width of a cell to accommodate long words. If a word is too long to fit, type a hyphen and press Enter to divide the word. When you press Enter, Notes adjusts the height of the cell to accommodate the additional line.

Creating a One-Cell Table

You can highlight text in a document to emphasize a point by creating a table that has one cell and one column, as shown in Figure 8.43. In this example, the author created a one-cell table with the right and bottom borders defined as double, while the top and left borders were left as single. This creates a shadow effect that adds some pizzazz to your documents.

FIG. 8.43

You can use table settings to accentuate the contents of the table.

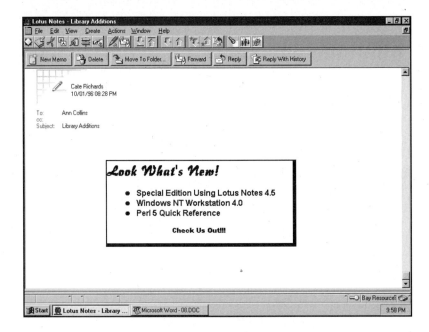

Once you have created the one-cell table, you can enter text into it. Notes won't let you put a box around text that has already been typed, so if you want to try this feature with previously entered text, you will need to create a box and then cut and paste the text into it.

Changing Table Text Characteristics

You can change many characteristics of the table text at any time, just as you would with any text. You can use the Text menu and Text Properties InfoBox to change the color, size, and other font attributes for the text in the table.

You can also change the justification of an entire column or row. Highlight the columns or rows for which you want to set justification and then select Text, Align paragraphs. You can specify whether the entire column or row should be left, right, centered, or full (you can't specify none in tables). In Figure 8.44, the columns of numbers have been right-justified so that the numerals align properly.

FIG. 8.44
You can align text and modify table settings to enhance a table's readability. This is the same table shown in Figure 8.42, but it's now formatted to enhance its presentation.

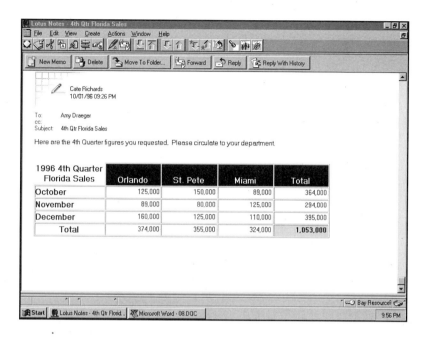

Part
I

Ch
8

Creating Sections in Documents

You can use sections to collapse one or more paragraphs in a document into a single line, referred to as the Section Title. The reader can see more detail than that displayed on the Section Title by clicking the twistie (down arrow) next to the Section Title to expand the section to reveal more information. Sections make navigating large documents easier.

Readers can expand a section when they want to read its contents or ignore the section if it doesn't apply to them. When designing forms, database designers can create hide-when formulas to provide logic to determine when a particular section can be seen. In this section, you will learn how to create sections in documents. You will learn more about designing forms in Part II.

N O T E You must be in a rich text field in order to create a collapsed section.

Figure 8.45 shows a document concerning an upcoming meeting in which sections have been created. One section, "Directions to Roy Rogers," has been expanded to display further information. The twistie to the left of the section title tells you that there is a collapsible section.

To create a section, follow these steps:

1. Highlight the paragraphs, graphics, and other information you want to collapse into a section.

2. Choose Create, Sections. Notes will immediately collapse the section and display the title of the section as the first line of text in the paragraphs you selected. If the first line you had highlighted was blank, your section heading will be blank.

FIG. 8.45

Collapsible sections can make navigating through documents easier for the reader.

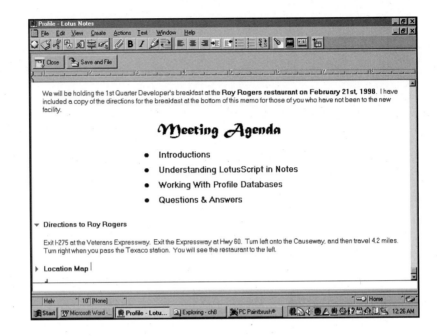

Changing the Title of a Section

If you want to edit the title of a collapsed section after it is created or change any of its other attributes, click anywhere within the collapsed section and select Edit, Properties. Notes displays the Section Properties InfoBox, as shown in Figure 8.46.

FIG. 8.46

You can change collapsible section titles in the Section Properties InfoBox.

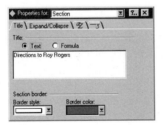

In the Title tab of this InfoBox, you can change the section title by typing a new one. You can also select the Formula option and have Notes compute the title of the section based on a formula you enter. After you have entered the title of the section, you can select the border style and color from the drop-down selection boxes.

Controlling How Notes Displays Sections

In Notes, you can control how collapsible sections are treated when you first open the document. With the Section Properties InfoBox open, select the Expand/Collapse tab, shown in Figure 8.47

FIG. 8.47

You can control how Notes displays the collapsible sections when you open and print the document.

The following options are available for each mode the document is in—Previewed, Opened for reading, Opened for editing, and Printed:

- Don't auto expand or collapse indicates that the section will appear in the state that it was left in the last time you opened the document.
- Auto expand section tells Notes to always expand this section when you open the document.
- Auto collapse section tells Notes to always collapse this section when you open Notes.

You may also select Hide title when expanded if you don't want to display the section title when the section is expanded, which can help conserve space in the document. Select Preview only if you want the section feature active only when you're previewing a document. In any other mode, the expand/collapse capability won't be available, and the section title won't be displayed.

 It is often useful, regardless of how you want documents to be viewed online, to tell Notes to Auto expand section when printing to make sure that you see all the data on the form in the print-out.

Also, it's a good idea not to include required fields (fields into which you require users to enter data before they can save the form) in sections that are automatically collapsed. Hiding the field from display in that manner might frustrate users when they try to save the form and discover required fields that they couldn't see.

Changing Section Fonts and Hiding Sections

In Chapter 7, you learned how to change fonts and hide text you were working with. Likewise, Notes lets you change the font color, size, and style of the section title through the Font tab of the Section Properties InfoBox. Make the necessary settings just as you would for regular text. Likewise, you can hide the section based on the documents' status or condition by accessing the Hide when tab of the Section Properties InfoBox. You learned about this feature in Chapter 7, and you'll learn more about it in Chapter 11.

You can create nested collapsible sections by highlighting more than one and selecting Create, Sections. Figure 8.48 shows multiple layers of collapsible sections for an account profile document.

FIG. 8.48

You can create multiple layers of collapsible sections.

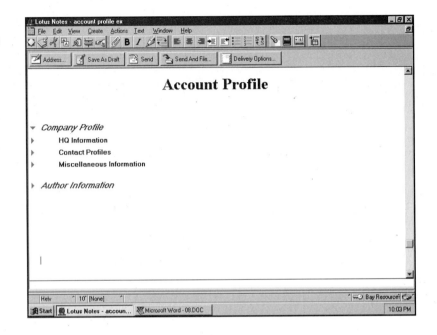

N O T E   You can incorporate sections into the design of your form and control access to those sections so that only certain readers can see them. You will learn more about controlling access to sections of a form in Chapter 11.

Deleting Sections

Sometimes you might not want to keep the section setting in your document. For example, some people don't want to keep the collapsible section created when you elect to reply with history in your email database; they would rather see just the contents of the section. If you decide that you don't want a collapsible section in your document, you can easily remove it, as long as it isn't part of the form's design. To remove a section, highlight the section title and select Sections, Remove Section. Notes will remove the section but leave all the text, graphics, and other objects in the document.

Using Folders to Organize Your Documents

You can use existing folders in a database—or design your own—to organize your documents in a manner that makes sense to you. For example, in your email database, you might want to create a folder called Hot Topics to store memos on issues of great importance to you. (This is similar to selecting a category for the mail memo in Notes 3.x.) When you find a document in a view that you want to store in your folder, simply click the document title and drag it to the folder. When the mouse pointer is located over the appropriate folder (the folder will be highlighted with a box when it is selected), you can release the mouse button. The document will move into the folder. When you click the folder, you will see your document located in it.

Creating Folders

Folders can take on the characteristics of views in that you can copy the column design of the views so that they appear the same in the folder. For example, you can create a folder called Executive Correspondence and base the folder design on the People view in the database, which sorts documents according to people's names.

To create a new folder, do the following:

1. Select or open the database where you want to create the folder.

2. Choose Create, Folder to access the Create Folder dialog box, shown in Figure 8.49.

FIG. 8.49

You can enter or edit the name of a folder in the Create Folder dialog box.

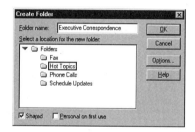

3. Enter a name for the folder in the Folder name box. The name should be descriptive and can contain any characters. The name's length is limited by the number of characters you can type in the Folder name box (between 14 and 26 characters, depending on capitalization). If you want to place the folder inside an existing folder, click the existing folder title in the Select a location for the new folder list. This list will vary depending on whether you create a Private folder (the default) or select Shared (see the next step).

4. If you have at least Designer-level access to a database and the database manager has granted you permission, you can click Shared to tell Notes that this is a folder that you want everyone who uses the database to have access to.

5. Click OK.

Notes creates the folder, and it appears in the navigator according to the options you selected.

If you want to select a view or folder on which to base the folder's design, follow these steps:

1. In the Create Folder dialog box, click Options to display the Options dialog box, shown in Figure 8.50.

FIG. 8.50

Select the view design that you want the design of your folder to inherit.

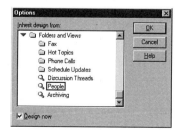

2. Choose a view or folder from the Inherit design from list. If you want to change the design of the folder as soon as the folder is created, select the Design now option. When you click OK to create the folder, Notes will automatically open its programmer pane.

3. Click OK.

Deleting Folders

Occasionally, you might find that you no longer need a particular folder in your database and you don't want it to clutter up your navigators. You can easily delete a folder by doing the following:

N O T E You must have Designer- or Manager-level access in order to delete, rename, or move shared folders (those used by everyone) in a database. ■

1. Select the folder you want to delete from the navigator pane.

2. Select Actions, Folder Options, Delete Folder.

3. Click Yes when you're prompted to delete the folder. Notes removes the folder from your navigator.

The documents displayed within the deleted folder don't get deleted, however. You can switch to any view designed to display the documents to see them.

 T I P You can also delete a folder by highlighting the folder's name in the navigator and pressing F6 and then pressing the Delete key. Click Yes when prompted to delete the folder.

Renaming Folders

Sometimes you might want to rename a folder to further define its contents. You can do so by selecting the folder you want to rename and then selecting Actions, Folder Options, Rename. The Rename dialog box appears, as shown in Figure 8.51. Type the new folder name in the Name box and click OK.

FIG. 8.51

You can open the Rename dialog box by selecting the folder you want to rename, pressing F6, and selecting Actions, Folder Options, Rename.

Moving Folders

Just as you might want to rename a folder, you might also want to move a folder to display within another folder or move a folder out of another folder. To move a folder, highlight the folder you want to move and select Actions, Folder Options, Move. The Move dialog box appears, as shown in Figure 8.52. Highlight the location where you want to relocate the folder, and then click OK. Notes will move the folder to the new location.

Part

I

Ch

8

FIG. 8.52
You can also open the Move dialog box by highlighting the folder you want to move, pressing F6, and selecting Actions, Folder Options, Move.

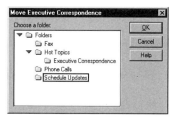

Moving Documents Into and Out of Folders

You can move documents to folders by clicking the document titles in the view and dragging them to the folder in which you want to store them. Alternatively, you can select all the documents you want to move to the folder by placing a checkmark next to each document title and selecting Actions, Move to Folder. Notes will prompt you to select the folder into which you want to move the documents. Moving a document to a folder doesn't move the document out of a view. Instead, it works somewhat like creating a category sort for the document. If you return to the view that originally displayed the document, you will still see it displayed there.

You can remove documents from a folder by clicking the document titles (or select multiple documents by placing a checkmark next to each name) in the folder and selecting Actions, Remove from Folder. Notes will remove the selected documents from the folder. This doesn't delete the documents from the database, however; you can still see the documents if you switch back to a view designed to display those documents.

> **CAUTION**
>
> Don't select the documents and press the Delete key, send the documents to the Trash, or select Edit, Clear unless you want to permanently delete the document from Notes. Unlike selecting Remove from Folder, these actions permanently delete the documents from the database.

In Part I, you have learned to work with many of the advanced options available when you're working with documents. You have learned to search text, insert options that enhance your communication, work with tables, create folders, and create sections. You will learn more about many of these features and their use in Part II. ●

Lotus Notes Group Calendaring and Scheduling

In this chapter

For years, stand-alone Personal Information Managers (PIMs) such as Lotus Organizer have helped people better organize and schedule their time and priorities. However, the fundamental problem with these tools was their inability to share information in a workgroup. In order to be truly effective, group scheduling must be able to deal with people who are geographically disparate and not necessarily connected via the same LAN. If you've ever tried to schedule a meeting with a group of people—particularly in a large company or one for which people are on the road frequently—you understand the frustration of not being able to get in touch with key people.

Lotus Notes Group Calendaring and Scheduling (C & S) effectively addresses these problems. This chapter introduces you to the concepts of Group C & S and shows you how to use Notes for C & S in your workgroup.

An Overview of Group Calendaring and Scheduling

As more and more companies of all shapes and sizes begin to understand the synergy and tremendous return on investment that can be realized by implementing collaborative technologies such as Lotus Notes, they demand more functionality from the underlying architecture. In its usual fashion, Lotus has risen to the occasion by delivering a very powerful, user-friendly Group Calendaring and Scheduling solution based on its award-winning Organizer PIM.

This section briefly explains what C & S is and does, in case you haven't had the opportunity to work with one of the user-friendly C & S tools, such as Organizer, Goldmine, or MS Schedule.

In a nutshell, Notes Calendaring and Scheduling lets you schedule and track appointments, events, tasks, and anniversaries for yourself as well as members of your workgroup, team, or organization. In addition, you can send invitations to meetings, view your colleagues' free time, and even schedule company resources, such as conference rooms, auditoriums, training rooms, and A/V equipment. The best part is that—because it's Notes-based—it replicates! This gives you the capability to schedule meetings, send invitations, and reserve resources even as a remote user.

N O T E In a group Calendaring & Scheduling system, free time refers to any user's availability. It is absolutely critical to be able to determine when other users are available so that you can schedule meetings with and for them. If you don't know when other users are available (that is, when they have free time), you will not be able to harness the power of C & S in scheduling activities for them!

If you've used Organizer, you'll love the powerful group C & S capabilities of Notes. (This even includes remote dialup users!) If you haven't used Organizer, be prepared for a real treat: The easy-to-use interface makes organizing your time a piece of cake.

Lotus set out to make Notes the client for enterprise-wide cross-platform C & S by building Notes C & S around its proven technologies and allowing seamless integration into existing groupware and messaging infrastructure. The following are some of the primary benefits of group C & S capabilities:

- Tight integration with NotesMail
- Legacy system migration or coexistence
- Remote/mobile access to schedules, free time, and resources
- Extensibility through programming
- Tight security through Notes native security
- Real-time access to scheduling information
- Delegation of authority for reading mail and scheduling appointments
- Ease of use and accessibility based on the award-winning Organizer interface
- Access to C & S data through Web client with Domino
- Ability to be woven into existing applications, increasing their effectiveness

Notes' group C & S capabilities can be a tremendous asset to your organization and will make your users much more effective.

Part

I

Ch

9

Getting Started with Notes C & S

Calendaring & Scheduling was introduced in Notes 4.5, so if you're upgrading from a version prior to that, your administrator needs to do a few things before you can start to use the C & S features:

- Because you access your calendar through your mail file, the design of your mail file must be upgraded with the C & S elements.
- Your Notes server needs to be running at least Notes 4.5. The free time system requires the Schedule and Calendar Connector tasks to be running on the server, and these weren't introduced until 4.5.
- The Public Address Book needs to be upgraded to at least the 4.5 design because a number of views and forms are required for C & S that didn't exist in the older designs.

Figure 9.1 shows one of these updated documents in the Public Address Book; note the Calendar section. This Domain document would allow you to schedule meetings with employees of another company you are connected to via Notes—a very powerful feature.

Recognizing C & S Tiles and Views

Once you have taken care of the preliminary considerations, you can begin using Notes C & S by opening your Notes 4.6 mailbox. You'll see a number of items relating to C & S that you'll need to become familiar with (see Figure 9.2).

FIG. 9.1

Note the Calendar section in this Domain document from the Public Address Book.

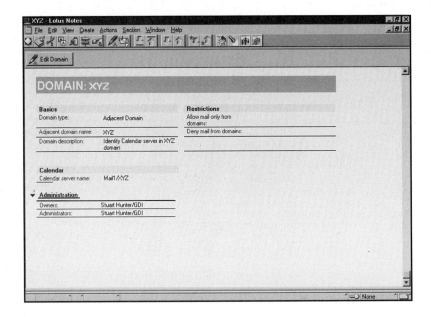

FIG. 9.2

The 4.6 NotesMail Navigator has special views to support Calendaring & Scheduling.

- Meetings view: Displays details of any meetings you have created. Meetings are also displayed in your Calendar view.
- Calendar tile: Displays your calendar in the familiar Lotus Organizer style.
- To Do tile: Displays any tasks you have set up. You can choose to display these tasks in your calendar or keep them separate.

In addition, the Create menu has Task and Calendar Entry forms and several actions that are used to configure your C & S options. The Calendar Entry form is used to create Standard Appointments (Meetings), Anniversaries, and Events, such as the monthly alumni club meeting that you always forget to go to. (These items will be covered in detail throughout the rest of this chapter.) But before you start creating and managing your appointments, you'll need to configure your Calendar Profile and, if necessary, your Delegation Profile.

Creating a Calendar Profile

In order to maximize the usefulness and functionality of Notes C & S, you must create a Calendar Profile for yourself that defines how you want to use C & S. In order to create a Calendar Profile, open your NotesMail mailbox and choose Actions, Calendar Tools, Calendar Profile. Figure 9.3 displays a Calendar Profile document.

FIG. 9.3

The Calendar Profile allows you to configure your Calendaring defaults.

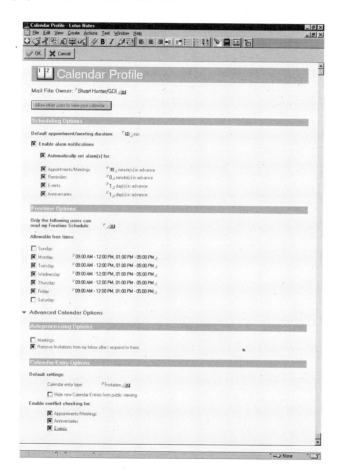

The first field on the form, Mail File Owner, is used to tell Notes to whom this profile belongs. It defaults to the username on the ID that is in use when the form is composed. It allows you to choose a different user from the Public Address Book.

Below that is a button called Allow other users to view your calendar. This button takes you to the Delegation Profile, which allows you to decide who can access your calendar and what actions they can perform there. The Delegation Profile is described in the next section.

N O T E   Allowing others to see your calendar is very different from allowing others to see your free time. Be careful with this selection. If you allow others to see your calendar, they will see appointments you've entered into your calendar, except for those you specifically mark as "not for public viewing." You can also give people access to your mail, but you should carefully consider who can have this kind of access.

The Scheduling options section contains a number of fields that let you configure your scheduling defaults. The first field, Default appointment/meeting duration, is used to set a default value for meeting length in minutes, meaning that for each new appointment you create, its length will be set to the default value you enter here. It defaults to 60 minutes. The next field, Enable alarm notifications, is a checkbox that acts as a toggle switch for setting alarms. When this feature is checked, it tells Notes to scan your calendar for appointments that have alarms so you can be notified. If you have checked the Enable alarm notifications option, the Automatically set alarm(s) for option becomes enabled so that you can set alarms and default values for each type of appointment. The usage of these fields is self-explanatory.

The Freetime Options section lets you define who can access your free time information and what days and time ranges should be considered when calculating your free time.

The first field in this section, Only the following users can read my Freetime Schedule, is a keyword field that pulls up a dialog box displaying users from your Address Book. Just select the users you want to be able to access your free time information. The rest of this section is pretty simple. To enable a day, simply check its box and then enter the times that should be considered available. For example, if you don't want to be scheduled for Saturday meetings, don't check the Saturday checkbox.

The section Advanced Calendar Options contains two additional sections, Autoprocessing Options and Calendar Entry Options. They let you enable settings that can make Group C & S more productive for you.

The Autoprocessing Options section contains options that allow you to automatically process items in your calendar. Currently, you can autoprocess only meetings. If you want to do so, simply check the Meetings checkbox and then choose the people you want to autoprocess from the keyword list that the option Autoprocess meetings only from the following people presents. You can click the Remove invitations from my inbox after I respond to them checkbox to tell Notes to automatically delete meeting invitations from your mailbox once you have accepted them, saving you the time of having to look for invitations and delete them manually.

The Calendar Entry Options section is divided into two categories: Default settings and Enable conflict checking for. In the Default settings options, the Calendar entry type field allows you to choose from the different kinds of Calendar Entries so that each time you create a new appointment, it will be set to the type chosen here. For example, if you tend to have more appointments than meetings, you might want to change the default from Meeting to Appointment. The Hide new Calendar Entries from public viewing checkbox tells Notes to allow only users explicitly named in your Delegation Profile to view your Calendar Entries.

The Enable conflict checking for section contains a series of checkboxes that allow you to tell Notes to check for conflicts on certain types of appointments. Your choices are Appointments/Meetings, Anniversaries, and Events. To enable any of these options, simply place a checkmark in the respective box. Notes will then check for scheduling conflicts when you create any of these types of Calendar Entries. If a conflict is detected, a dialog box will appear, warning you of the conflict. You have the option of scheduling the entry anyway, in which case the conflicting entry will appear in the calendar with a red bar to the left of the entry. You might be tempted to enable conflict checking for all Calendar Entry types, but you should consider this carefully for types such as anniversaries and events. For example, if you schedule an event because you're attending a two-day seminar, you will receive conflict warnings when you attempt to schedule the times for the lectures you will be attending during the seminar. Likewise, a conflict warning would be inappropriate when scheduling a business meeting that happens to fall on your daughter's birthday.

Once you have set your desired options, save the document. Your Notes client will begin using your new configuration.

Creating a Delegation Profile

If you travel a lot or work as part of a very close-knit team, it might often be necessary to have someone else read and respond to your mail and schedule. Notes adds this capability through delegation—the ability to give access to your mailbox to a user or group that you specify.

To enable delegation, you must create a Delegation Profile. Open your NotesMail database and choose Actions, Mail Tools, Delegation Profile. Figure 9.4 shows a Delegation Profile.

FIG. 9.4

The Delegation Profile allows you to delegate access to your mailbox and calendar.

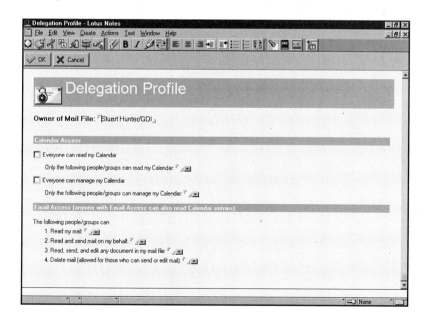

As you can see, the Delegation Profile is relatively simple to complete. The first field, Owner of Mail File, tells Notes to whom this Delegation Profile belongs. When a new Delegation Profile is created, this field defaults to the username of the Notes ID in use.

The first section, Calendar Access, contains calendar delegation options. If you'd like everyone to be able to read your calendar, click the Everyone can read my Calendar checkbox, which will hide the Only the following people/groups can read my Calendar field. If you want only certain users to access your calendar, you can use the Only the following people/groups can read my Calendar field to select people or groups that should have access. As you might expect, the Everyone can read my Calendar and the Only the following people/groups can read my Calendar fields are mutually exclusive.

You can also allow other Notes users to manage your calendar. If you'd like everyone to be able to manage your calendar (this is not recommended), click the Everyone can manage my Calendar checkbox, which will hide the Only the following people/groups can manage my Calendar field. If you want only certain users to access your calendar (this is the better choice), such as an assistant, you can use the Only the following people/groups can manage my Calendar field to select people or groups that should have access. As you might expect, the Everyone can manage my Calendar and the Only the following people/groups can manage my Calendar fields are mutually exclusive.

> **N O T E** There is a *big* difference between read and manage access to your calendar. If you grant manage access to everyone, anyone can add, edit, or delete your appointments. You should use that level of access judiciously.

The second section, E-mail Access, enables you to define people or groups that can access your mailbox. The first thing you should note is that anyone you grant e-mail access to will automatically have Calendar access. You can use the four fields in this section to control a number of e-mail access options:

- Read my mail: This field can be used to select a list of users who can read mail in your mailbox.

- Read and send mail on my behalf: When users or groups are named in this field, they will be allowed to not only read your mail but also send mail on your behalf. It will be denoted on the mail that someone else sent it for you.

- Read, send, and edit any document in my mail file: This field allows any users named in this field to not only read and send mail but also edit any type of message in your mailbox. This is a very powerful delegation and should be given judiciously.

- Delete mail: This field allows you to name users who can delete mail from your mailbox. Note that if you have given people or groups send or edit access, they get this access by default.

> **N O T E** As long as your mailbox's Access Control List is set correctly, you will have no worries: Only the people you name in the E-mail Access section will have access. If you don't specify any users, only you will be able to read your mail.

Once you have created a Calendar Profile and a Delegation Profile (if necessary), you're ready to begin using Notes Calendaring and Scheduling to manage your time and that of your colleagues.

Using Your Calendar

Everyone—no matter what the size of their organization—occasionally must attend a meeting. Notes' native C & S capabilities make it easy to manage your schedule, because you can create meetings, reserve resources, and even invite others to your meetings electronically whether you are a local or remote user.

Part

I

Ch

9

Creating a Calendar Entry

When you're ready to schedule a meeting, you simply open your mailbox and choose Create, Calendar Entry or, from the Calendar view, click the New Entry button on the Action Bar. This launches a new Calendar Entry form, as shown in Figure 9.5. The default type is Invitation unless you changed this in your Calendar Profile.

FIG. 9.5

The Invitation type Calendar Entry with invitees selected.

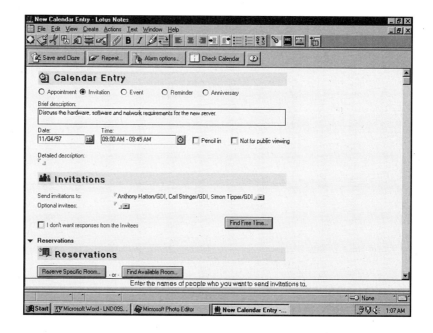

NOTE You can also create a Calendar Entry from any mail message that you have in your mail file. To do so, select a document in any view in your mail file, or open the document. Select Actions, Copy Into, New Calendar Entry. ■

▶ For an explanation of the other options in the Copy Into menu option, see the section in Chapter 6 titled "The Copy Into Menu Option," **p. 247**

The first thing you'll notice about this form is a series of five radio buttons that you can use to choose the type of entry you'd like to create. As you work with the Calendar Entries, you notice that each of the five form types has many overlapping fields, but each has fields specific to the purpose of the form. Since there are differences between the forms, we'll examine each one individually. Here are your choices:

- Appointment: As you'd expect, appointments are used to add meetings to your schedule.

- Invitation: Invitations let you create an appointment and invite other people or groups. These people will receive an invitation by e-mail.

- Event: Events are used to denote special meetings—a trade show or a presentation—on your schedule.

- Reminder: Reminders are just that—they are added to your calendar to help you remember to do something. For example, they can work hand-in-hand with anniversaries to help you remember to purchase an anniversary present for your spouse.

- Anniversary: Anniversaries are used to enter recurring things such as birthdays, wedding anniversaries, and holidays to your schedule.

Appointments

Creating an appointment is simple. Just click the Appointment radio button. The Calendar Entry form, shown in Figure 9.6, appears.

FIG. 9.6

The Appointment form.

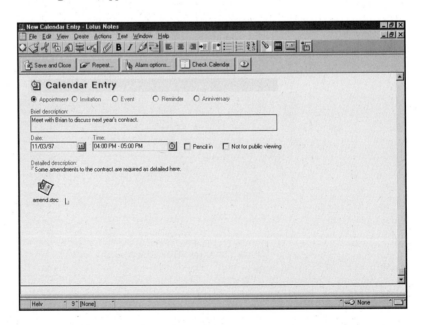

The first field, Brief description, is used to enter text that describes the appointment. It will be displayed like a mail message subject in the views and folders in your mailbox, so it's important to enter a description that makes sense.

The Date and Time fields are pretty much self-explanatory: They are used to store the date and time of the appointment. The Date field will default to the current date, and the Time field will default to the current time. However, you should pay special attention to these fields, because they implement two of the controls that Lotus has "borrowed" from Lotus Organizer—the Date control and the Time control.

Notice that beside the Date field is a small button with a calendar graphic. When this button is clicked, it launches a graphical calendar control (see Figure 9.7). You can move forward and backward a month at a time by clicking the small black arrows in the upper corners of the control. When you find the date you want, simply click it, and it will be inserted into the Date field.

FIG. 9.7

The calendar control lets you easily select date values.

You'll also notice that beside the Time field is a button with a clock graphic. Much like the calendar control, when clicked, this button displays a graphical time bar so that you can select the time range for your appointment (see Figure 9.8). To select a time range, you can click and drag the clocks at each end of the time bar to the appropriate start and end times. If you need to see more of the time control, just click the up and down arrows to scroll through the times.

FIG. 9.8

The time control lets you point and click your way toward setting the time of your appointment.

N O T E   Both the Date and Time controls are standard design elements that are available to Notes application developers for use in their applications. Kudos to Lotus, because this functionality has been needed for a long time.

The Pencil in checkbox, when checked, is just like "penciling in" something in your day planner. It just indicates that the appointment is tentative.

The Not for public viewing field is a checkbox that acts as a toggle to let you indicate that this appointment is confidential and should not be displayed to other users.

The final field, Detailed description (indicated by gray angle brackets), is a rich text field that can be used to enter a detailed description, add file attachments, or insert objects that help further describe the appointment.

You'll also notice the Save and Close, Repeat, Alarm Options, Check Calendar, and Help buttons on the Action Bar. These action buttons extend the functionality of C & S. The Save and Close button saves the appointment and closes the current window.

If you'd like to make the appointment repeat without rekeying the information, you can click the Repeat button, which will launch the Repeat Rules dialog box, shown in Figure 9.9.

FIG. 9.9

The Repeat option allows you to quickly and easily schedule recurring appointments.

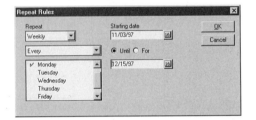

The Repeat Rules dialog box allows you to easily choose repeat options. You can use the Repeat drop-down field to tell Notes how often this appointment will repeat:

- Weekly: This tells Notes to create an entry in your calendar each week on the day and time you specify. An example would be your weekly staff meeting every Friday at 9:00 a.m.

- Monthly by Date: This tells Notes to create an entry in your calendar each month on the date and time you specify. For example, you attend the monthly Notes users' meeting on the 10th of each month.

- Monthly by Day: This tells Notes to create an entry in your calendar each month on a specific day rather than on a date. For example, you might get paid on the last Friday of each month.

- Yearly: This tells Notes to create an entry in your calendar each year on the date and time you specify. For example, you attend an annual marketing convention every year.

- Custom: This is the most powerful option. You tell Notes to create entries based on the criteria you specify.

Once you have made a choice for repeating your entry, use the other fields to define the specifics of the repeating appointments. For example, if you choose monthly on the 2nd and that falls on a weekend, you have the option of moving the meeting forward or backward for that one specific instance. This is a very powerful tool that can make scheduling recurring appointments easy.

The Alarm options button launches the dialog box shown in Figure 9.10. Here you can set the alarm parameters for this entry. The first field, When, is static text that displays the time and date of the entry.

FIG. 9.10

The Set Alarm dialog box is very handy when you need to remember important appointments.

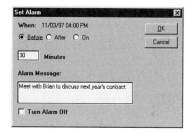

N O T E If you haven't enabled alarms in your Calendar Profile, you will be prompted to do so before the Set Alarm dialog box is displayed. ▪

The next two fields work together to determine when the alarm will notify you. The Minutes field lets you enter a time in minutes that, when the Before, After, or On button is set, will cause you to be notified before, after, or on the appointment time and date.

The Alarm Message field lets you enter a message that will be displayed when the alarm occurs. This value defaults to the value of the Brief description field, but you can enter any value you like.

The Turn Alarm Off checkbox toggles the individual alarms off or on.

N O T E If you enabled alarms in your Calendar Profile, the Minutes and Before/After/On fields will default to the values you entered for the Automatically set alarm(s) for Appointments/ Meetings field. You can override this on an individual basis by entering a new time for the alarms. To change this value permanently, just edit your Calendar Profile. ▪

Once you have enabled an alarm for an entry, a dialog box will appear on-screen at the designated time to remind you that you are scheduled to attend the appointment.

The Check Calendar button on the Action Bar will open your Calendar view so that you can quickly check your schedule for available times. When you're finished, you simply press Esc to return to your appointment.

The final button on the Action Bar is the Help button. When clicked, it displays a context-sensitive dialog box that explains how to complete the Calendar Entry you are creating.

N O T E In order to make the C & S process as easy as possible, Lotus made the usage of the Brief description, Not for public viewing, Pencil in, and Detailed description fields, as well as the Date and Time controls, consistent throughout the five types of Calendar Entries, helping to decrease the learning curve and make Notes C & S more user-friendly. In addition, the Alarm and Repeat, Check Calendar, and Help action buttons are consistent across all the Calendar Entries. ▪

Now that you know how to create an appointment, using the other Calendar Entry forms is easy because of the overlapping fields. Rather than reiterate the same information for each of the forms, we'll examine the divergence from the Appointment form in the remaining four forms.

Invitations

Sometimes you'll want to schedule other people to attend a meeting. That's where the invitation comes into play. To create an invitation, just create a new Calendar Entry and click the Invitation radio button. Notice that an invitation contains all the same information as an appointment but adds a subsection that allows you to specify the invitees (see Figure 9.11).

FIG. 9.11

The Invitations section allows you to schedule meetings with colleagues.

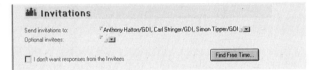

Because the Invitation form is identical to the Appointment form except for the Invitations section, only the Invitations section will be examined here. The first field, Send invitations to, is a keyword list that allows you to select from the Address Book a list of users or groups that you'd like to send an invitation to. The next field, Optional invitees, is identical to the Send invitations to field, except that people and groups selected here aren't required to be in attendance but could benefit from attending.

The Find Free Time button lets you search the Free Time database for each of the named recipients to ensure that they are available at the designated time (see Figure 9.12). The I don't want responses from the Invitees checkbox lets you tell Notes not to have the recipients send you mail responses in regard to the invitation.

FIG. 9.12

The Free Time dialog box showing a conflict for the desired meeting time.

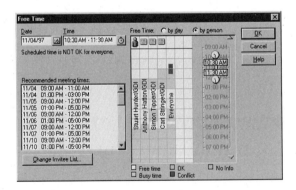

N O T E The free time information is held in a Notes database on the server called BUSYTIME.NSF. Notes lets you check free time even when you're working remote by replicating a subset of this database containing the free time of the colleagues you specify.

▶ **See** "Setting Up to Check Free Time," **p. 882**

If you want to reserve rooms or resources for your meeting, you can click the Reservations twistie. Reservations is an expandable section that contains three buttons: Reserve Specific Room, Find Available Room, and Reserve Resources (see Figure 9.13).

FIG. 9.13
The Reservations section lets you reserve rooms and other assets for your meeting.

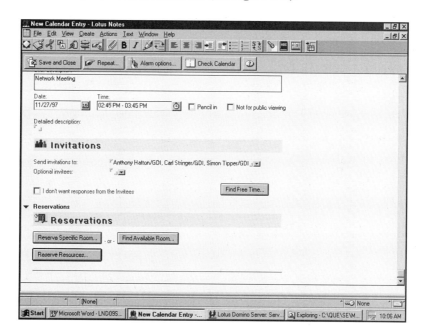

The Reserve Specific Room button launches a dialog box that displays a list of available resources. When you select a room, Notes will check to see if it is available at the specified time and date; if so, it will be reserved for your meeting. The Find Available Room button allows you to search the Resource Reservation database for any room that is available during the time and date you have specified for the Calendar Entry. The Reserve Resources button works in a way that is very similar to the Reserve Specific Room button; you can choose a resource from the list, and Notes will check to see if it is available. If it is, it will be reserved for your meeting.

The final field, Chairperson, is a display-only field that, when the document is saved, will display the common name of the Notes ID in use.

Events

If you'd like to schedule an event, such as a trade show or conference, simply create a new Calendar Entry and click the Event radio button. This will change the appearance of the form slightly, as shown in Figure 9.14.

FIG. 9.14

Events allow you to schedule multiday entries easily.

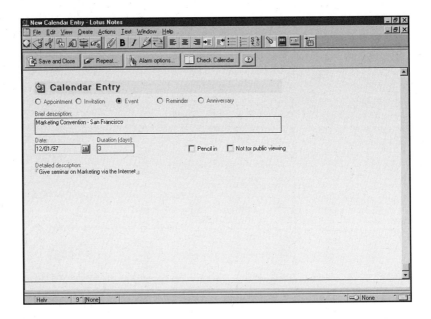

The primary difference between an event and an appointment or invitation is the fact that events are entered on a daily basis rather than an hourly basis. This is why you have a Duration field in which you can indicate the number of days the event lasts. Notes will create an event in your schedule for each of the days you indicate in the Duration field.

Reminders

Reminders are almost identical to appointments, except that the Time field expects a discrete time rather than a time range (see Figure 9.15).

Anniversaries

The last type of Calendar Entry, Anniversary, lets you keep track of important anniversaries such as birthdays, wedding anniversaries, Mother's Day, and so on. Figure 9.16 shows an anniversary.

Tasks

Although you don't create Tasks from the Calendar Entry form, it is useful to include them here, because you have the option of presenting them in your Calendar view. (How to do so is discussed later in this section.)

Chances are that as well as attending the meetings you have been creating entries for, you will also have to prepare some work for them. If you're working on specific projects, you might be assigned tasks that must be completed within a certain time frame. Task documents allow you to track these items and their status in a variety of views.

FIG. 9.15
Create a reminder when you have to be somewhere important at a particular time.

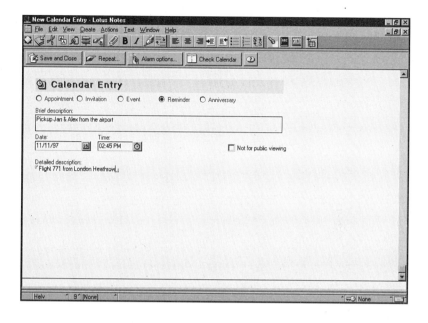

FIG. 9.16
Stay on your spouse's good side: Use Anniversary to keep track of important dates.

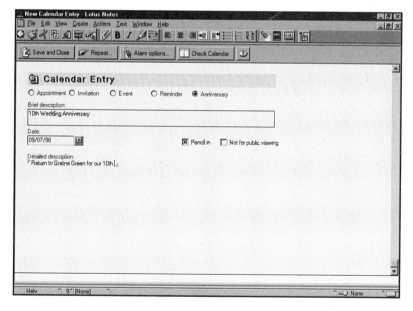

Tasks have their own view, which you can access by clicking the To Do "tile" at the bottom of your mail navigator. Figure 9.17 shows your mail file with the To Do view open.

FIG. 9.17

The To Do view shows your Tasks sorted by urgency.

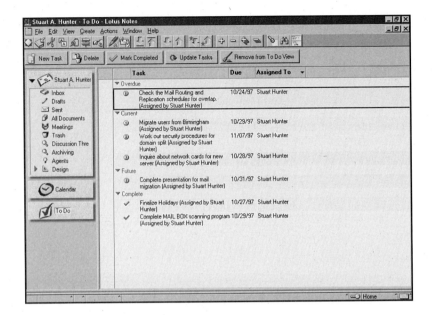

The To Do view sorts your Tasks by urgency and priority. Tasks that are overdue come first, followed by tasks that are current but haven't passed their due date yet. Next come future tasks, and the least priority goes to tasks that have been marked as Completed. Within each of these categories, the priority a task has been given (High (1), Medium (2), or Low (3)) determines its position in that category.

You can create a new Task in several ways:

- If you aren't in your mail file, you can select Create, Mail, Task.

- If you are presently in your mail file, you can select Create, Task.

- If you are currently in your To Do view, you can click the New Task button on the Action Bar.

- From any view in your mail file, or while looking at a specific mail document, you can select Actions, Copy Into, New Task. This will create a new Task with the Subject field of the selected or open memo copied to the Subject field of the new Task, and the body of the original message included in the Task's Additional information field.

The Task form, shown in Figure 9.18, has many fields in common with other Calendar Entry documents, but it contains two date fields for setting a Start Date and a Due Date. These fields affect how the Task is sorted in the To Do view. You can also decide to display the Task in your Calendar view by clicking the Display Task on My Calendar button. In the Calendar view, the Task will be displayed under its Start Date; there will be no indicator on the Due Date. If you subsequently decide you don't want the Task in your calendar, you can click the Remove From Calendar View button.

FIG. 9.18

The Task form has two date fields between which the Task is "current."

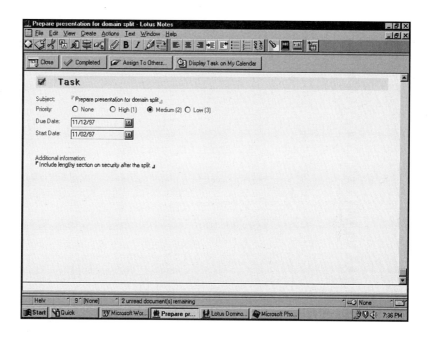

If you are managing a project, you can assign tasks to others working on the project. After filling in the details of the Task, click the Assign To Others button. The Assign To and CC fields are where you can type in the names of the people you want to assign the Task to. You can use the Address button on the Action Bar to select the names from the Public Address Book. When you save the Task, you are prompted to mail the Task to the Assignee.

You can mark a Task as complete from the To Do view by selecting the Task and clicking the Mark Completed button, or by accessing the Task document and clicking the Completed button on the Action Bar.

The To Do view contains a button called Remove from To Do view. This button is useful for getting rid of Tasks that you have marked as Complete but that you don't want cluttering up the To Do view. These Tasks will still appear in the All Documents view of your mail file.

Viewing Your Calendar Entries

Once you have created Calendar Entries, or have been invited to appointments, you obviously need to be able to view, edit, and delete them. Lotus has made it easy to do so. To find your standard appointments, you can use the Calendar view, Meetings view, or All Documents view.

The Meetings View The Meetings view, shown in Figure 9.19, displays all your appointments. It's a quick and easy way to manage your schedule.

FIG. 9.19

The Meetings view displays all your Calendar Entries in a basic format for ease of use.

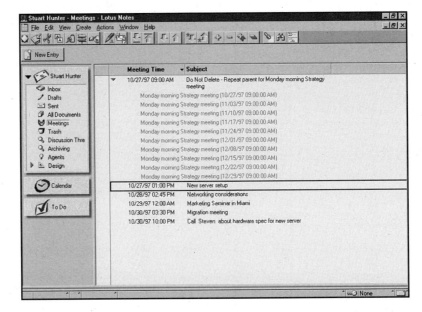

The first column, Meeting Time, is sorted in ascending order based on the meeting's time and date. Notice the down arrow on the column header, which indicates that the column can be resorted in descending order.

The second column, Subject, displays what the user entered for the brief description of the meeting.

The Calendar View   The Calendar view, shown in Figure 9.20, is a very powerful feature that brings the award-winning look and feel of Organizer to Lotus Notes. It allows you to view your appointments through a calendar metaphor so that it's easy to manage your schedule. Because this is such a powerful feature that can be used by application developers in their own applications, it warrants its own section. See "Navigating Through the Calendar View" later in this chapter.

Notice the Calendar-related action buttons on the Action Bar. Each of these buttons allows you to change the views of your calendar so that you can display as much data as needed to suit your personal preferences—from two days at a time to as much as a month's worth of data.

The All Documents View   By now, the All Documents view is probably old hat to you, but it can be used for C & S because it displays your appointments (see Figure 9.21). However, because it doesn't discriminate between the documents it displays, it can be somewhat overwhelming. In addition, in the All Documents view, Calendar Entries display the date they were created, not the date for which the entry was set. In Figure 9.21, you can see that all the Calendar Entries were created on the same day, but you get no idea as to when the events actually take place.

FIG. 9.20
The Calendar view displaying a week of Calendar Entries.

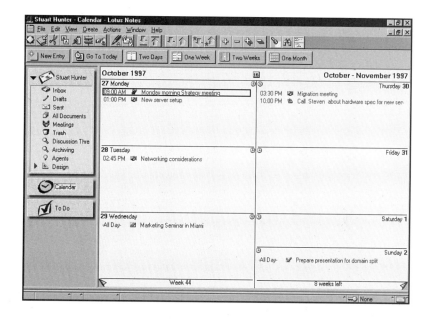

FIG. 9.21
The All Documents view displays special icons for Calendar Entries.

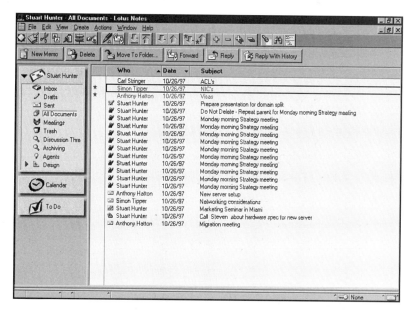

As you can see, many different types of documents are displayed in this view. However, Lotus did add several icons to this view to indicate that a document is a Calendar Entry.

Once you have learned how to use the views, you can quickly find your appointments and begin to edit and delete them.

Editing a Calendar Entry

To edit an existing entry, you use the same techniques that you would use to edit any Notes document. Using one of the C & S views or the All Documents view, find the document and then open it by double-clicking it and pressing Ctrl+E, or by choosing File, Edit Document. Once you have opened the document, make the appropriate changes and save it. Notes will then examine the document and recompute the scheduling information to see if a conflict exists for any of the invitees. If not, the invitees will be notified of the new date, time, and location. If a conflict exists, you'll be notified so that you can take the appropriate action.

Deleting a Calendar Entry

Again, you can find an appointment that you want to delete by using the C & S views. Then you can select the document and press the Delete key. When the document is deleted, Notes will remove it from all the invitees' schedules.

Responding to a Meeting Invitation   If you receive an e-mail invitation to a meeting, there are several ways you can respond to it. Figure 9.22 shows a meeting invitation similar to one you might receive.

You have the following choices:

- Accept: If you choose to accept the invitation, click the Accept button, or choose Actions, Accept. An entry will be added to your calendar, and an acceptance will be sent back to the person who invited you.

- Decline: If you choose to decline the invitation, click the Decline button or choose Actions, Decline. The invitation will be marked as such in your mail file, and no entry will be made in your calendar. The person who invited you will automatically be informed that you have declined.

- Other/Delegate: If you click the Other button or choose Actions, Other, you can select from a variety of actions, such as Delegate, which allows you to select another person to attend the meeting on your behalf.

- Other/Propose Alternative Time/Location: This option brings up an additional section where you can choose an alternative date, time, or location for the meeting if the original isn't convenient. This counterproposal will be mailed back to the chairperson.

FIG. 9.22
A meeting invitation.

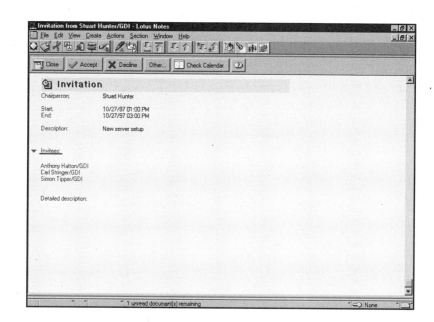

- Other/Pencil In: You can tentatively accept the invitation. An entry will be made in your calendar with the Pencil in field checked. The chairperson will be told that you have penciled in the invitation.

- Check Calendar: If you want to, you can have a quick look at your calendar before deciding on your actions. Clicking this button will display your standard Calendar view. Press Esc to return to the invitation.

Making Resource Reservations

Although you can reserve resources when you create an Invitation type Calendar Entry, there will be times when you want to reserve a resource without having first created a Calendar Entry. This is where the Reservation form in the Resource Reservation database comes in handy. This form does just what it says: It allows you to reserve a resource. It works somewhat differently, depending on whether you elect to reserve a room or a resource.

Reserving a Room

The first thing you will have to do is identify the Resource Reservation database that your administrator has created and add it to your desktop. The Resource Reservation database, unlike other key system databases, doesn't need to have a particular title or filename, so you will need to check with your administrator as to its location and name. In a crunch, you could try looking in the Database Catalog.

To create a room reservation, open the Resource Reservation database and choose <u>C</u>reate, <u>R</u>eservation.

When you create a new reservation, the Reserved by field defaults to your username, but you can choose another user from the Address Book by clicking the down arrow next to the Reserved by field. You can use the Phone number/Extension field to enter the phone number of the person who reserved the resource, making it easy to get in touch with him or her quickly. You then answer a series of questions that will define the actions Notes will take.

The reservation form will take you through a series of steps to help you achieve your goal. First, you are asked whether you want to reserve a room or a resource. In this case, leave the default selection, which is Room, and click the Continue button. You can then choose between the options described in the following two sections.

Finding an Available Room at a Specific Time   Choose this option and then click the Continue button. You can then enter details for the date and time of the reservation, number of people attending, and at which site. After completing that, click the Find an Available Room button to allow Notes to find a room that fits your criteria using the Free Time dialog box. If there is a match, the room will be displayed in the Room field. The completed form appears in Figure 9.23. When you save the reservation, the free time for that room will be updated to take into account the new reservation you have just created.

FIG. 9.23
A completed Room
Reservation form.

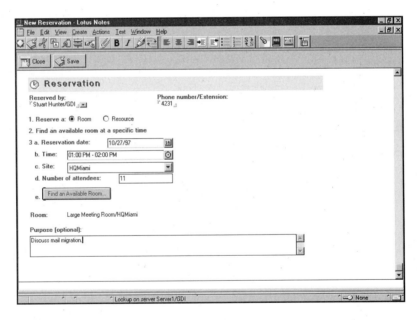

Finding an Available Time for a Specific Room   There might be times when you know you need a particular room, so you try to find a time when the room is free. In these cases, you would choose this option and then click the Continue button. Click the Choose a Specific Room button. You will see the Rooms dialog box, shown in Figure 9.24, where you can choose the desired room. Having made that selection, you can choose the date and the number of hours for the reservation. Click the Find an Available Time button, and Notes will present you with the Free Time dialog box, where you can choose a time for the reservation. Optionally, fill in a Purpose for the reservation and save the document. The free time for this room will be updated to block out the time you have selected.

FIG. 9.24
Selecting a specific room from a list of available resources.

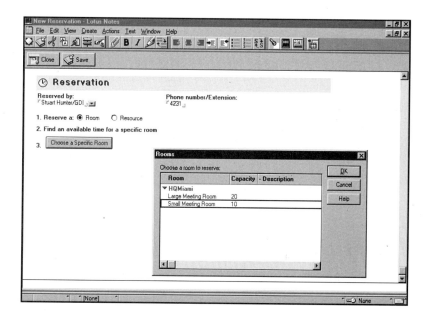

Reserving a Resource

The process of creating resource reservations is very similar to creating room reservations. Just choose the Resource Reservation database and choose Create, Reservation (or click the Create Reservation button that appears on the Action Bar of all the views). You'll see a new Reservation form. The next step is to click the Resource radio button, followed by the Continue button. As with reserving a room, you now have a choice between finding an available resource at a specific time and finding an available time for a specific resource.

Finding an Available Resource at a Specific Time   Choose this option and then click the Continue button. You can then enter details for the date and time of the reservation, which site you want to reserve, and the category of the resource. When you then click Find an Available Resource, the first resource that matches your requirements and that is available at that date and time is placed in the Resource field. If this choice isn't suitable, click the Find an Available Resource button again to pull up the next resource that matches your criteria (see Figure 9.25). Save the document to reserve the resource.

FIG. 9.25

An asset about to be reserved with the Resource Reservation form.

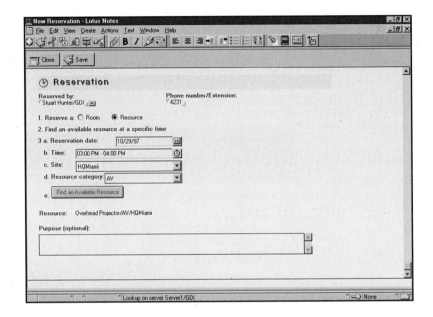

Finding an Available Time for a Specific Resource   Choose this option and then click the Continue button. This causes the Choose a Specific Resource button to appear. When you click it, you see a dialog box listing all the resources in all sites in your domain (see Figure 9.26). Choose the desired resource and click OK. You can then choose a date for the reservation and how many hours you need it for, and then click the Find an Available Time button. The Free Time dialog box will appear (see Figure 9.27), showing any conflicts with an existing reservation. If there is a conflict, you can change the date and time of the reservation to fit, or abandon it and choose another resource. Save the document when you have finished to reserve that resource.

FIG. 9.26

The Resources dialog box displays resources sorted by site and category.

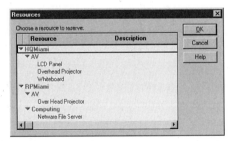

FIG. 9.27

The Free Time dialog box showing availability for a particular resource.

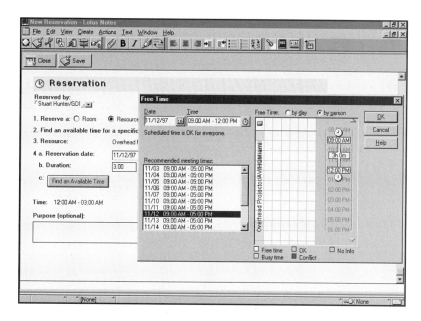

Navigating Through the Calendar View

The Calendar view lets you graphically display your schedule in a day-planner metaphor. In fact, each view looks similar to an actual piece of paper. You navigate through the calendar by clicking the "dog-eared" edges of the page. You can also print the view to have a nice copy of your schedule (printing your Calendar views is covered in the next section).

NOTE The best thing about this view style is that it isn't limited to your schedule; your developers can use this style of view in any Notes database.

The Calendar view can be configured to display data in several ways: two days at a time, one week at a time, two weeks at a time, or one month at a time. The two-day view, shown in Figure 9.28, displays the most detailed information and looks similar to a page from a day planner. It includes the appointment's time of day and a description of the appointment.

This view is very easy to use. When opened, it defaults to today and tomorrow. To view the preceding or the following day, simply click the page's upturned edge to move through your schedule one day at a time. You'll also notice a small white calendar icon. You can click this to display a calendar control in order to move through your schedule in much bigger chunks. In addition, the bottom of each page displays the day number (out of 365 days) and how many days are left in the current year. Notice the small clock icon that appears on each day. If you click it, it displays the time slots for the day, with arrows to help you scroll through them. If you right-click any day, you see a menu that lets you jump to today's date, change the Calendar view to display one of the other time periods, and show the time slots for the day.

FIG. 9.28

The two-day Calendar view displays detailed information about your schedule.

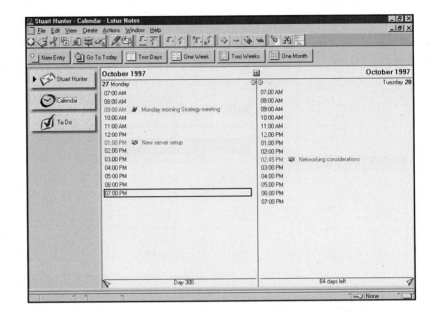

To access any scheduling information, simply double-click it to open the appointment. If you want to add a new appointment, find an open time and double-click anywhere on the line the time is on. This will launch a new Appointment form.

The one-week version of the view works exactly like the two-day view, except that it displays slightly less detail (see Figure 9.29). It shows you only the descriptions for any appointments you have scheduled within a given week. By default, it displays the current week. At the bottom, it displays the week number (out of 52) and the number of weeks left in the year.

The two-week view, shown in Figure 9.30, also works exactly like the other views, but it displays even more of your schedule with less detail. Each of the two pages displays a week's worth of data. The default is the current week and the following week. At the bottom, you see the weeks' numbers (out of 52) and the number of weeks left in the year for each of the two weeks displayed.

The one-month version of the view is probably the most useful for a quick "one-stop shopping" view of your schedule (see Figure 9.31). It displays an entire month of your schedule at one time with minimal detail. For each day that you have something scheduled, you'll see an icon (the same one used in the standard views) that indicates you have appointments on a particular day. The bottom of the view displays the number of the month (out of 12) and the number of months left in the year.

FIG. 9.29
Get a handle on your week with the one-week view of your calendar.

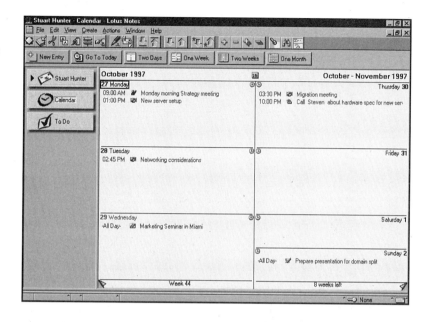

FIG. 9.30
The two-week version of the Calendar view can be useful to see the current week's schedule and to plan for the next week.

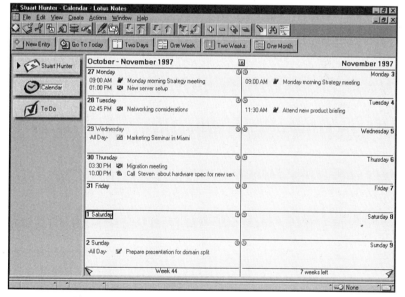

FIG. 9.31

The one-month view
displays your schedule
on the "macro" level,
displaying very little
detailed information.

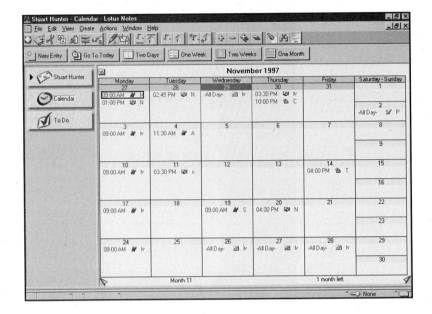

FIG. 9.31

The one-month view
displays your schedule
on the "macro" level,
displaying very little
detailed information.

Printing Calendars

If you need a printed version of your calendar to carry around with you, Notes will print it
using whatever Calendar view you have chosen. This didn't work in Notes 4.5 but has been
fixed in Notes 4.6.

First, choose the Calendar Style you want to print (Two Days, One Week, Two Weeks, or One
Month). Then choose File, Print. If you simply want to print the Calendar Style you selected
earlier, press Enter or click OK.

If you want to print your calendar only for a specific number of days, you can use the date controls in the Print selected days section of the Print dialog to control the start and end days (see
Figure 9.32). If you do override this setting, regardless of the Calendar Style you selected
previously, you will receive a line-by-line listing of your Calendar Entries.

The C & S Process in Action

Examining a real-life example is a good way to integrate all the information in this chapter and
get a feel for the capabilities of Calendaring and Scheduling. Let's follow the scheduling of a
standard appointment for three invitees from start to finish. The process begins when a user,
Leslee Hatter, composes an invitation. She chooses to invite Dan Voelker. She also chooses to
reserve the Management Conference Room, which is pulled from the list of available resources
in the Resource Reservation database, and she sets the date for 10/31/97 from 1:00 to 3:00
p.m.

FIG. 9.32

Choosing the calendar print range.

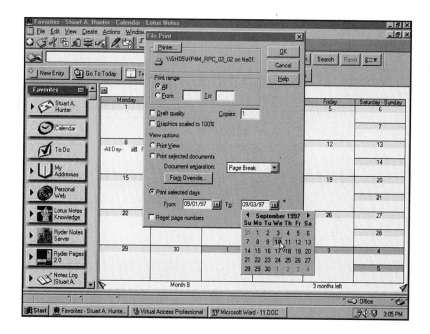

In order to save time and ensure that the date and time she selected are open for the invitee, Leslee elects to determine the invitee's free time by clicking the Find Free Time button, which displays the Find Time dialog box. Notes then sends a query to Leslee's mail server, "Ace." Ace looks for Dan Voelker's Person document in the Public Address Book and, depending on whether or not Dan's Person document is found, will do two very different things.

If Dan's Person document is found, Server Ace examines Dan's Mail Server field. If Dan's MailServer is also Ace, Notes examines his free time in the Free Time database and displays this information to Leslee. If Dan's MailServer is another server in the same domain, Notes forwards the query to Dan's MailServer and looks up his free time for Leslee. If Dan's MailServer is outside the Domain, Notes uses the Calendar Domain field to determine where Dan's free time information resides.

If the Free Time system can't find Dan's Person document in the Public Address Book, it has no choice but to assume that Dan's mailbox is in a different domain. If Leslee appends the domain name to Dan's address, or if Dan's hierarchical name has enough information to tell the Free Time system where Dan's domain is, the Free Time system attempts to search the Public Address Book for a domain document for Dan's domain and take one of the following actions based on what it finds.

If the Free Time system finds an adjacent domain document, it looks at the CalendarServer field for the name of a server that accepts free time requests for Dan's mail domain. If the data in this field has been entered correctly, the Free Time system opens the Free Time database on Dan's MailServer and then returns Dan's information to Leslee. If the CalendarServer field is incorrect or empty, the free time request fails, and the Find Time dialog box indicates that Dan's information is unavailable.

If the Free Time system finds a Foreign Domain document, it knows that Dan is using a different scheduling application, such as Organizer. The CalendarServer field in the Foreign Domain document identifies the name of a server that processes free time requests for Dan's domain. The CalendarSystem field identifies the name of the plug-in program that will perform the free time lookup on Dan's server. The Free Time system forwards the query to Dan's server for processing and, if successful, will return the results to Leslee.

If no Domain documents are found by the Free Time system, Leslee's request fails, and the Find Time dialog box indicates that Dan's information is unavailable by displaying all Dan's time as a solid gray bar.

N O T E   A free time query will fail if the invitee's home server is down or any of the links that are used to get from your server to the invitee's server are down. If this happens, you'll receive an error message indicating that the server is down, and the Find Time dialog box will indicate that the user's time is unavailable.

If no conflicts exist, Leslee can use the Find Time dialog box to select a different time; otherwise, when she saves the form, an invitation is generated and mailed to each of the invitees, and the appointment is added to Leslee's schedule—which updates her Free Time database and puts a reservation in the Resource Reservation database to inform other users that the Management Conference Room is booked on October 31.

When the invitees receive their invitations, they can check their schedules. (They should be free, because Leslee elected to check for conflicts.) When Dan Voelker receives the invitation, he accepts, and his schedule is updated to reflect the meeting with Leslee.

Barring natural disasters or a higher-priority event popping up, Dan should show up at 1:00 p.m. on October 31 for Leslee's meeting because they have their schedule to remind them every day. (They could even set an alarm!) In addition, when other users try to schedule Dan, they will see that he is booked on that date. ●

Designing Applications

Creating New Databases

Throughout this book, you have learned about the databases created by Lotus—the Mail database, the Address Book, and so on. In this chapter, you will learn how to create your own customized databases, which you can use to store and share almost any kind of data you can imagine.

Getting Started

Users of many skill levels can design and build Notes databases. Even beginners with limited Notes experience can learn to build simple but useful databases for many purposes, because Notes comes with many helpful templates. Databases can be created to manage small amounts of data used by only a few people, or even one person, or they can manage enterprise-wide applications involving tens of thousands of documents. Enterprise applications are typically made up of several databases and are more complex to design and maintain.

Throughout this chapter, you will learn about the various tools for designing and building databases. As you build databases, you might not perform these actions in exactly this order, although creating the database obviously comes first! Utilizing Notes' rapid application development environment, after creating the database it is typically most efficient to create the forms first (which actually capture the data) and create the views and navigators later since their design, and the information they display, are based on the data captured on the forms.

N O T E Lotus Notes comes in three different workstation license types designed for varying levels of users:

- Lotus Notes
- Lotus Notes Desktop
- Lotus Notes Mail

Lotus Notes Mail licenses and Lotus Notes Desktop licenses can create and use some design templates but can't use all the design features made available by Notes. You can determine what type of license you are currently using by simply reading the window title while viewing the Notes workspace. If you're going to create databases, design forms and views, and so on, you will probably want to use the full Lotus Notes license. Contact your system administrator and ask how you can upgrade your version of Notes to the full Lotus Notes license.

When creating new databases, you have three options to get started. You can

- Create a new database based on an existing template
- Copy an existing database and modify its design
- Create a new database from scratch

Since Notes ships with many fully functional database templates that might already perform the functions you hope to design in your database, it makes sense to begin there. Later sections discuss your other two options.

Using Templates

Notes comes with a collection of templates—ready-made databases—that you can use as a starting point for creating your own databases. A *template* is a special type of Notes database (with an .NTF extension) from which other databases are modeled. Templates contain no data, only design elements that you can use to serve as a guideline when you start creating new databases. This will minimize your development time since these databases already have various forms, views, agents, navigators, script libraries, and other design elements. However, keep in mind that when you create a new database, it can also be just as efficient to copy an existing database and modify the design where appropriate.

If you use a template, the first step in creating a database is deciding which template should serve as the starting point for your new database. In some cases, you might find that one of the supplied templates meets your functional requirements. If none of the templates matches your needs exactly, an existing template still might contain many of the design elements you require and therefore can serve as a starting point for creating your new database.

Before you begin to create a new database, think about how you or others are likely to use it. Are you creating it to serve as a central storage location for some type of document? Will the database serve as a discussion group for sharing ideas? Consider the information you want to store in the database, and also give some thought to the various ways you want the data displayed and printed. In addition, most of the databases that ship with Notes (the Mail database, the Address Book, and so on) are also available as design templates. In the following sections, you will learn how to create a database by using a template.

Reviewing the Notes Templates

Notes comes with 44 templates (including advanced ones). A few in particular are extremely useful and can be used to create your own databases, including powerful Web pages, with little or no customization on your part. If you design new databases often, you might come back to these as starting points or create your own templates with standard views, forms, subforms, agents, script libraries, and so on, thus minimizing development time. Notes templates are fully functional databases that can be used "off-the-shelf." However, because no two businesses operate in the same manner using the exact same processes, you might need to customize your applications to meet the needs of your organization. Nevertheless, in these cases, templates can still be utilized as starting points for your database design.

Other templates (those that become visible when you select the Show Advanced Templates checkbox) are useful only to system administrators or when you use system databases such as mailboxes. Table 10.1 lists several of the Notes templates.

▶ **See** "Database Templates," **p. 1091**

Part

II

Ch

10

Table 10.1 Standard Templates Available with Notes

Template Name	Description
Approval Cycle (R4)	Used to create databases that manage and track the submission and approval of electronic forms. Application profiles can be created for the various approval forms, which determine how a particular approval should be processed. The approval cycle logic can be reused for other electronic forms and easily modified when the approval policy changes.
Discussion - Notes and Web (R4.6)	Discussion databases are databases in which workgroups can share thoughts, ideas, or knowledge. Team members can read and contribute to discussion threads in which the history of each topic is preserved. This template is designed to be accessed from both Notes clients and Web browsers and is fully functional for both types of clients.
Document Library (R4)	Used for storing and describing documents, much like an electronic filing cabinet. Typically, this serves as an object store and allows for the set-up document approval cycles and archiving.
Doc Library - Notes and Web (R4.6)	This has the same features as the Document Library (R4), except that it can be accessed from both a Notes client and a Web browser.
Microsoft Office Library (R4.6)	Similar to the Document Library template, except that it focuses on documents created with Microsoft Office Suite applications using OLE 2. Microsoft Word, PowerPoint, Excel, and PaintBrush documents can be easily created, launched, and modified from within Notes using the Microsoft application as an OLE server and Notes as an OLE client. This database also supports creating review cycles for the documents. For more information on this database and OLE 2, see Chapter 13, "Integrating Notes with Other Applications."
Lotus SmartSuite 96 Library (R4)	Similar to the Document Library template, except that it focuses on documents created with Lotus SmartSuite 96 applications. Lotus 1-2-3, Freelance, and Word Pro documents can be easily created, launched, and modified from within Notes using the specific Lotus application as an OLE server and Notes as an OLE client. This database also supports creating review cycles for the documents. For more information on this database and OLE 2, see Chapter 13, "Integrating Notes with Other Applications."

Template Name	Description
Personal Address Books	Used to create additional Address Books. The template is the same one used for your Personal Address Book.
Personal Journal (R4)	Lets you keep a diary or journal and categorize entries into folders. This also contains "clean sheets" and serves as a scaled-down word processor with versioning control.
Personal Web Navigator (R4.6)	Gives you access to the Internet directly from the Notes workspace using Notes as the browser (with an embedded Browser applet) or Internet Explorer within Notes (assuming that the user has a connection to the Internet).
Web Pages (R4.6)	Allows WebMaster and WebSite designers to easily create and store Web pages for corporate intranets or Web sites that can be published via Domino.
Frameset (R4.6)	Similar to the Web Pages (R4.6) template, except that this template is designed to take advantage of frames, supporting 18 predefined layouts ranging from 2 to 4 frames.
Portfolio (R4.6)	A collection of Notes databases that share a common view pane among various databases. The Favorites database is based on the Portfolio template. (The Favorites database is created automatically when Notes 4.6 is installed on your system.) This database allows the user to view documents from multiple ("favorite") databases without changing the user interface. The various "favorite" databases can be added, removed, or repositioned within the portfolio database, as shown in Figure 10.1.
Search Site	Allows users to search multiple databases using only one search.
Resource Reservations (R4.5)	Formerly called Room Reservations, this template is used to manage and track room and resource reservations. It can be easily modified to track reservations for almost anything and has been designed to work with the calendar views available in Notes 4.5.

Part
II

Ch
10

FIG. 10.1

The new portfolio database allows the user to view multiple databases from a single screen.

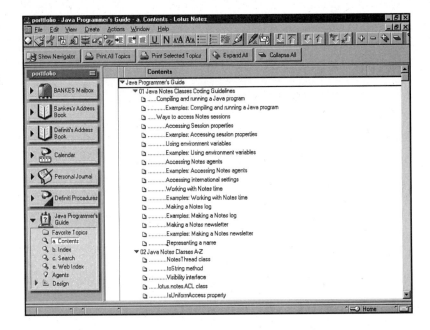

Creating a Database from a Template

Once you decide on a template, follow these steps to create your database:

1. Select the workspace page on which you want to create the database.

2. Select File, Database, New or press Ctrl+N. Notes displays the New Database dialog box, shown in Figure 10.2.

FIG. 10.2

The New Database dialog box.

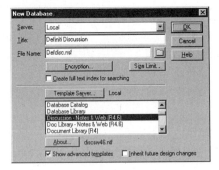

The top half lets you set the database's server location, title, filename, and other options. The bottom half contains a list of available templates.

3. In the Server list, select the server on which you want your database to reside.

N O T E When you choose to create a database on Local, by default Notes places the database in the Notes data directory located on your computer unless you specify an alternative drive and/or directory with the filename. You can specify a network or local drive and a particular folder by clicking the button that has a folder on it (it's to the right of the File Name field). It's a good idea to design your databases locally and replicate them to a development server or development directory so that there will be multiple copies in case your local copy becomes corrupt or the design is accidentally deleted. However, until the database is ready for production, the database design properties List in database catalog and Show in "Open Database" dialog should be disabled.

In addition, you might not be permitted to create new databases or replicas on the server. If this is the case, you must contact your Notes administrator. ▨

4. In the Title box, enter a descriptive title for the database that is up to 32 characters long, such as `Legal Contract Library` or `Equipment Requests`.

T I P The title is an easy way to quickly identify this particular Notes database from your workspace. The title appears in the title bar at the top of the screen when the database is opened. This is also the title that appears in the database list when the user selects File, Database, Open. Your database will be much easier for users to find if the title is descriptive and complete.

Notes doesn't require unique database titles, but you should avoid duplicate titles to reduce confusion among users. Also, consider implementing naming conventions for database titles and filenames. Giving related databases titles that begin with the same words helps delineate them in the Open Database dialog box.

5. In the File Name box, enter the name of the database file. The name should have an NSF extension (unless you're creating a database template), such as CONTRACT.NSF or REQUESTS.NSF. (Notes automatically adds the extension if you leave it out.) Notes does support extended filenames (for Windows 95 and NT), and, by default, the database filename is the same as the title you just typed. However, because Notes supports multiple platforms, it is generally good practice to limit filenames to eight characters. Also, consider the implications of using mixed case, since platforms such as UNIX are case-sensitive. It is generally good practice to establish a standard naming convention for filenames and establish how uppercase and lowercase letters should be used (such as all uppercase, all lowercase, proper case, or mixed case). Also, set a standard for creating directories and grouping databases according to function, department, and so on.

6. If you are creating a local database, you have the option of encrypting it. To do this, click the Encryption button, select Locally encrypt this database using, and then choose an encryption type (see Figure 10.3).

FIG. 10.3
You can locally encrypt
a database using the
Encryption for dialog
box.

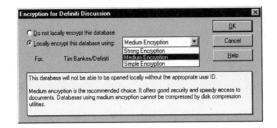

N O T E   If you encrypt a local database, anyone who uses your computer must use your ID file and
enter your password to access the encrypted database. This is especially useful if you have
a laptop computer and are worried about someone taking your computer and possibly accessing
sensitive information in your Notes database.

Desktop security is also useful in an office environment, because it helps ensure the confidentiality of
the data stored on your personal machine.

You don't have to encrypt the database when it's created. Therefore, you can decide to encrypt the
database later if you're unsure whether this will be necessary.

▶ **See** "Security and Encryption," **p. 919**

7. To set a size limit for your database, click the Size Limit button. The default size limit of
   1G is probably enough for most Notes databases, unless your database will contain a
   great deal of rich text objects. The maximum database size can be 4G, but this is highly
   inefficient! Designers should consider the performance implications of a database of this
   size, as well as physical limitations of hard drive space (especially when replicated to
   laptop computers). If a database of this size is anticipated, designers should consider
   breaking the database into multiple databases, implementing reader names, choosing
   selective replication, storing only on the server, or exploring alternative solutions. This
   parameter can't be changed after the database has been created.

8. To create a full text index for the database, put a checkmark next to Create full text index
   for searching.

▶ **See** "Full Text Searching in Databases," **p. 298**

9. From the template list, select the template you want to use to create your database.
   When specifying a template, keep the following notes in mind:

   - If you select Blank from the template list, Notes creates an empty database with no
     forms or views. Use this to create a database from scratch.
   - The template list contains a list of templates available locally on your computer. To
     select a template located on a server, click the Template Server button and choose
     the server on which the template is located. The template list will update to list the
     templates available on the server you selected.
   - Templates might or might not be installed on your personal machine, depending
     on how the Notes installation was performed. If you don't have templates available
     on your machine, make sure you look for them on a template server.

- If you check Show advanced templates, the template list will include system templates such as the Notes Log and Mail Router Mailbox, as well as any other templates marked as advanced templates. In most cases, you won't need to create databases with these templates. If you have upgraded your machine from Notes 3.x to 4.x, other, older templates might also appear in this list. Templates that have (R4) in their titles are specifically geared to take advantage of Notes 4.0 features such as new GUI features and LotusScript. R4.5 templates take advantage of Notes 4.5 features such as Calendaring and Scheduling, and R4.6 templates take advantage of new features discussed in this book, such as extensive Web integration, new GUI features such as view navigators and portfolios, and better Internet mail, Calendar, and OLE support.

 T I P   For more information on a particular Notes template, click the <u>A</u>bout button in the New Database dialog box.

Part

II

Ch

10

10. By default, Notes checks the <u>I</u>nherit future design changes check box. Deselect this option if you don't want design changes to be inherited, which is typically the case. When design changes aren't inherited, databases can be tweaked to display corporate logos, conform to design standards, add and remove functionality, and so on. Keep these issues in mind:

- When this box is checked, the design of your database is automatically synchronized with the design of the template when the Design task runs on the server or the database design is manually refreshed. This is useful if your database will be based exactly on the design template. If you have several databases based on a single template—for example, you have several document library databases—you can change the single underlying template, and those changes will propagate to all databases based on that template. If you are using the template only as a starting point for your database, you should deselect this checkbox. You can always reselect it later.

- Design inheritance isn't limited to the database level. It is possible to have only individual design elements inherit changes or to disable inheritance.

N O T E   A centralized development team might create design templates with standardized design features to be used when creating new databases; this can shorten development time and reuse previous design work. These databases might or might not have the .NTF extension, even though the database property Database is a template might be selected. The .NTF extension doesn't ensure that the database's design will propagate to the respective databases (although it does ensure that the database won't appear in the File, Database, Open dialog and will appear in the File, Database, Replace Design dialog). Whether a database is a design template or inherits its design is determined in the Design tab of the Database Properties InfoBox, shown in Figure 10.4. In order for a database to function as a template, the parameter Database is a template must be selected on the Design tab and an appropriate template name supplied. ▓

FIG. 10.4
Setting the database
template in the
Database Properties
dialog box.

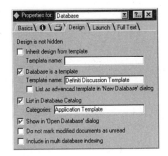

- It is generally a good idea to have all production databases whose design won't be modified by the end users to be set up to inherit their design from a design template. Therefore, when changes in design are made, they can be made and tested on the template with bogus data (since only the design is inherited). Once testing is verified, the newly created and modified design elements won't take effect until the Server Design task runs or the design is refreshed manually. This also helps protect against unauthorized users' accidentally (or intentionally) modifying the design of the production databases.

▶ **See** "Designing Forms," **p. 417** and "Designing Views," **p. 485**

- If you click Inherit future design changes and you later make design changes to your database, you might be surprised to find that your changes were overwritten by the design in the template.

- When a database inherits design changes from a template, it inherits the design from the template on the workstation or server on which the database resides. This means that if you create a database using a template on your workstation and later move the database to a server, you should make sure that the template on the server matches the one on your workstation. Otherwise, the design of your database could be changed without your knowledge—with potentially disastrous results.

CAUTION

Be careful when copying a database. The Inherit Future Design Changes checkbox isn't available in the Copy Database dialog; however, this database setting is automatically copied. Therefore, the new copy will automatically be set up to inherit its design if the original database had that property selected, which is typically not what you want!

TIP The About Database document, the Using Database document, and private agents aren't refreshed when the database design is refreshed. These design elements must be copied and pasted into their respective elements.

11. Click the <u>O</u>K button to create your database. After a few moments, Notes will create a new file in your data directory, add a database icon to your workspace, and open the new database automatically.

12. Notes displays an About document, which briefly describes the database. Close the About document by pressing Esc, by pressing Ctrl+W, by selecting <u>F</u>ile, Close, or by double-right-clicking anywhere within the document (if this user preference has been enabled).

After you complete these steps, you see your newly created database, which doesn't contain any documents yet. If the template exactly matches your needs, you are ready to begin entering documents and using your database.

More often than not, however, you must customize the database to make it meet all your organization's needs. No two businesses use the same processes, and the functional requirements for a database might grow throughout its existence. Templates can serve as good starting points in database design, but often, customization is required. Throughout the rest of this book, you will learn all you need to know in order to customize your database designs.

Selecting a Location for Your Database

As you create a database, you must select a server from the New Database dialog box's <u>S</u>erver list and then enter a filename for the database. Together, these two pieces of information determine where the database resides. The location you select for your database will depend on who accesses your database and what directories are on your server.

Note that you shouldn't use network drives to share databases with other people. If multiple people access a database without going through a Notes server, the database could become corrupted.

In the <u>S</u>erver list box, you have the following options:

- Local: When you select this entry, the database will be created on the workstation's hard drive. Because it is local to your workstation, users can't access the database unless they are using your computer.

- Server: When you select this entry, the database will be created on the selected Notes server. Since it is on the server, it will be available to everyone on your Notes network, assuming that they are given access in the database's Access Control List and have been granted access to this file directory via server directories and links settings.

After you have selected a server, enter a filename in the <u>F</u>ile Name box. You have three options here:

- You can enter a filename such as PROBLEMS.NSF. The database will be put into the default data directory for the selected server. For example, if the data directory is C:\NOTES\DATA, the full path and filename would be C:\NOTES\DATA\PROBLEMS.NSF.

- You can enter a directory and filename such as DATABASE\PROBLEMS.NSF. The database would then be put into C:\NOTES\DATA\DATABASE\PROBLEMS.NSF if C:\NOTES\DATA is the data directory.

- If you selected Local as your server, you can enter a full path and filename for your database, such as D:\DATABASE\PROBLEMS.NSF. This is useful if you want to put your database on another disk drive or a network drive.

Adding and Changing Design Elements in the Database

Now that you have created your database, you are ready to customize its design to fit your needs. You do this by adding, deleting, or changing its design elements. Notes databases have six main design elements:

- Forms define the data that will be entered into a document. They consist of static text, fields, graphics, buttons, subforms, sections, and actions. Forms are the heart of an application. They are the primary user interface for entering data into your database and contain many of the actions that users invoke while using the application. However, user data is stored in documents (a collection of data items). Forms simply provide a way to display and capture the data; they typically aren't a part of the document itself.

- Views are a list of the documents contained in the database that display specific information about each document using rows and columns to delineate the information. Views are indexes to the information in your databases. A single database usually has many views that list different subsets of documents or different information or sort the documents in different orders or categories. A well-designed set of views makes information in your databases easy to find and more useful.

- Subforms are reusable groups of fields, graphics, and other form design elements. They are somewhat of a form within a form. Subforms can include many of the same elements that are placed on forms. You should use them if you have part of a form that is common to several forms. By using them, you don't have to add design elements to each form individually; you can just insert the subform. Also, if you need to make changes to the subform, you can make the changes once—in the subform—and they will propagate to all forms using the subforms.

- Navigators are graphical interfaces to your databases. They can contain icons, buttons, bitmaps, hotspots, and static text. Clicking an element on a navigator can execute Simple Actions (such as opening a view or another navigator), @Function formulas, or LotusScript programs. Navigators make your applications more intuitive and easier for your users.

- Script Libraries allow Notes developers to build reusable LotusScript modules that can be invoked from multiple places within a Notes database.

- Agents are programs written in either LotusScript or the formula language using @Functions and @Commands. You can run them at predetermined intervals from a menu or event. Agents can be either private (created by a user and used only by that user) or shared (created by the database designer and used by all users). Some good uses for agents include archiving a set of documents, categorizing documents into folders, updating groups of documents, or storing common tasks that might be performed from multiple locations within a database.

Accessing Existing Elements with the Folders Navigator

The navigation pane, shown in Figure 10.5, lets you access all existing design elements of your database with just a few clicks. When you are designing a database, the first thing you should do is display the folders navigator if it isn't already showing. If another navigator is currently selected, select <u>V</u>iew, Show, <u>F</u>olders.

FIG. 10.5
You access existing design elements of a database in the navigation pane.

The following headings are under the Design category in the navigation pane:

- Forms
- Views
- Folders
- Shared Fields
- Subforms
- Navigators
- Script Libraries
- Other

Clicking any of these items displays a list of the corresponding existing elements in your database where the current view is normally displayed. For example, selecting Forms lists all the forms in your database, as shown in Figure 10.6.

If you click a form name, you are put into design mode for the selected form (see Figure 10.7). Likewise, if you choose Views, Folders, or any other heading, you will get a list of views, folders, and so on.

Part
II

Ch
10

FIG. 10.6
Selecting Forms
displays all existing
forms.

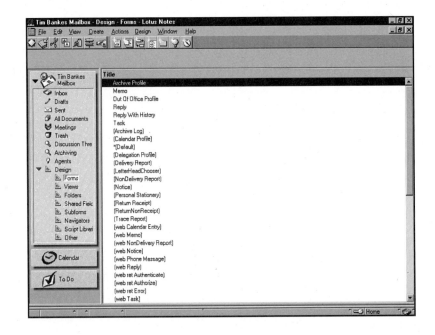

FIG. 10.7
The form design screen.

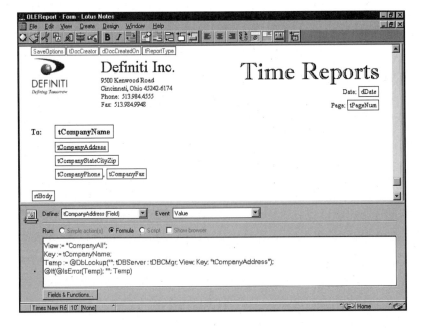

Creating New Elements with the Create Menu

The folders navigator allows you to edit existing elements, but suppose you want to create a new form, view, and so on. You use the Create menu, shown in Figure 10.8.

FIG. 10.8

You create new elements using the Create menu.

Table 10.2 lists each design element and its corresponding item(s) on the Create menu.

Table 10.2   Creating Elements with the Create Menu

Element	Create Menu Selection
Agent	Create, Agent or Create, Design, Agent
Folder	Create, Folder or Create, Design, Folder
View	Create, View or Create, Design, View
Form	Create, Design, Form
Navigator	Create, Design, Navigator
Script library	Create, Design, Script Library
Shared field	Create, Design, Shared Field
Subform	Create, Design, Subform

You will learn more about each of these options and how to use them in the following sections.

Manipulating Design Elements

You can also easily delete, copy, and paste design elements from your Notes database. First, choose the type of element you want to remove or copy from the navigation pane.

For example, you can select Forms to get a list of forms saved within the database. Then choose the actual element (in this case, form) you want to delete from the list on the right. Next, to delete the element, press the Delete key, choose Edit, Clear, or use the Edit Clear SmartIcon. In addition, you can also copy or cut these elements to the clipboard and paste them into other databases. Select the design element and choose Edit, Cut (or press Ctrl+X or choose the SmartIcon) to cut the element to the clipboard, or choose Edit, Copy (or press Ctrl+C or choose the SmartIcon) to copy the element to the clipboard. Then open the destination database and select the design element type in the Design category in the navigation pane. Then simply paste the element by choosing Edit, Paste (or pressing Ctrl+V or choosing the SmartIcon).

 TIP Except for agents, you can select multiple design elements to delete, cut, or copy at one time by pressing and holding the Ctrl key while selecting various design elements, or pressing and holding the Shift key to select all elements between the first and last selection (see Figure 10.9).

FIG. 10.9
Use the Ctrl or Shift keys to select multiple design elements.

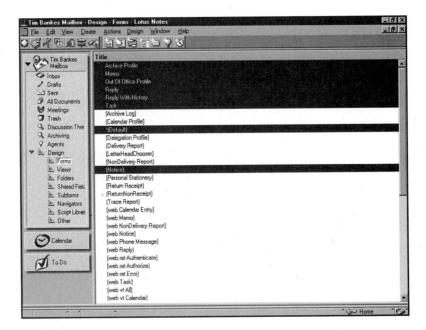

Understanding Database Access

Now that you have created a database, you need to decide who should access it. Once you put your database on a server, it's out there for everyone on your Notes network to see unless the database design properties List in database catalog and Show in "Open Database" dialog are disabled. However, you probably want only certain people to access your database and might want to vary their respective access levels. Even if you want everyone to see the data in your database, you will want to restrict certain functions. For example, you probably want only one person, or a group of people, to be able to change the design of your database (you probably will be part of this group). You will probably want only certain people to edit existing documents, while others will only enter new documents, and still others will only be able to read documents. If you didn't restrict these functions to specific people or groups, your data and database design would be in jeopardy, because anyone could make changes to your database. This is why controlling access to your database is vitally important. Notes is equipped with a powerful and robust security framework, which is important for native Notes applications or databases that will be published on the Web by Domino.

The key to controlling access is your database's Access Control List (ACL). Within your ACL, you define which people or groups of people have access to your database and what functions they can perform. Additionally, the ACL defines which servers can access your database and what they can replicate.

▶ **See** "Security and Encryption," **p. 919**

Part
II
Ch
10

N O T E By default, the database ACL affects only databases stored on a server. To enforce the ACL locally and across all other servers where replica copies are created, choose File, Database, Access Control. Click Advanced tab and select the option Enforce a consistent Access Control List across all replicas of this database (see Figure 10.10). ▨

FIG. 10.10

Enforcing consistent ACL across all database replicas.

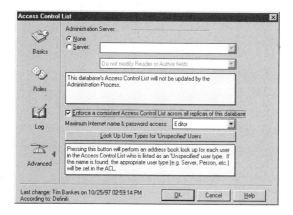

To gain a better understanding of how the ACL affects security, we should step back and take a quick look at the entire Notes security framework.

Notes has four layers of security:

- ▨ Server-level security: Before users can access a database on a server, they must have access to the server. Server access is controlled by the server administrator through the use of certificates attached to users' ID files and server access lists. This is the first and most general layer of security.

- ▨ Database-level security: Database security for any database on a server is handled by the database ACL. The ACL lists users and servers and assigns them rights to the database. Access levels range from Manager, who has total access to the database, to No Access.

The database manager creates and controls the ACL. An additional database-level security feature is Local Encryption, which causes local databases to be encrypted, so that only the user who set Local Encryption can access them.

■ Document-level security: Document security consists of the document's Read Access list. This list is defined by the form's Read Access list, any Reader Names fields in the document, and the Read Access list in the Document Properties dialog box. The Read Access list refines the ACL for that document, meaning that if someone has Reader access or above in the ACL but isn't listed in any Read Access list, he can't read the document. If a person isn't a reader in the ACL, he can't read the document even if he is listed in the document's Read Access list.

■ Field-level security: Certain fields on a form can be encrypted using encryption keys, so that only users with the correct key can read those fields. The database designer specifies which fields are encryptable. When a key is associated with the document, all encryptable fields are encrypted with that key.

One good way to think of the various levels of Notes security is as a funnel. At the top level, the administrator controls who has access to a particular server. The next level is access to a particular database. Database ACLs can work only within the constraints of what security the administrator has set. All the security options work like a funnel, where you can control access to a particular level of security based only on what the previous level allows you to do. Within this framework, the ACL is the highest level of security that a database designer can use to control access to a database. Therefore, it is very important that you give serious thought to who will access your database and set up the ACL correctly.

Assigning Access Levels

When planning your Access Control List, you will decide who gets what level of access. You can assign seven levels:

■ Manager

■ Designer

■ Editor

■ Author

■ Reader

■ Depositor

■ No Access

In the Access Control List, you list users and servers who need access to your database. In the ACL, users and servers are listed together and are given one of the access levels just listed. The access levels have a slightly different, but similar, connotation, depending on if they are given to a person or a server. For a person, the access levels define what actions the user can perform on the database. For servers, access levels define what information the servers can replicate.

▶ **See** "Understanding Database Security," **p. 926**

TIP It is useful to create a group in your Public Address Book containing the names of all administrators and provide that group's Manager with access to all databases.

Likewise, you can create a group containing all developers and give that group's Designer access to all databases. Using a group, it is easy to control and add people to a database ACL, because they are stored in the shared Address Book.

Names, Servers, and Groups in the ACL

Now that we have listed the access levels you can assign in the Access Control List, we should look at how people and servers are listed in the ACL. Each entry in the ACL is one of the following:

- User Name
- Server Name
- Group Name
- Database Replica ID
- Anonymous User

User names in the ACL should be entered exactly as they appear in the user's ID file. If your organization uses hierarchical names, you should enter the fully distinguished hierarchical name—for example, Jane Doe/Marketing/Standard. If the server your database is on and the person you are adding are in the same organization, you can enter just the common name in the ACL, but the fully distinguished name is more secure, since two people can't have the same fully distinguished name.

Server names are entered in much the same way as user names. You should use the server's fully distinguished name—for example, Server1/Marketing/Standard. But you can use the common name if the servers are in the same organization.

N O T E Notes lets you use the asterisk (*) wildcard to replace any component of a hierarchical name below the organization. Using wildcards, one ACL entry can grant access to everyone within a single organization or organizational unit. For example, the entry */Definiti gives access to anyone in the Definiti organization (including Tim Bankes/Definiti or Dave Hatter/Development/ Definiti). The entry */Development/Definiti applies to anyone who has an organizational unit of Development and an organization of Definiti (Dave Hatter/Development/Definiti but not Tim Bankes/ Definiti). ▪

CAUTION

It is possible that a user will be listed in multiple groups that have conflicting access rights within a database. The general rule is that the user will be granted the highest access rights available. However, if a user is listed with his or her fully distinguished hierarchical name, this will take precedence over another ACL

continues

continued

entry that is listed in the Common Name format, even if the Common Name entry has higher access. Therefore, it is best to maintain a minimal, though thorough and logical, number of groups in the Address Book and to use the fully distinguished hierarchical name.

Group names in the ACL can be any group of people or servers that is defined in the Public Address Book. Using group names in your ACLs has several advantages over using individual names:

- One group representing many users keeps the number of entries in the ACL low. This makes managing the ACL much easier.

- If a group of people needs its access changed, you only need to change the access for a single group rather than for several individual users.

- A single group can be in the ACL in several databases. Simplify administration by centralizing changes within the Public Address Book.

- Using groups, you can list a descriptive name that makes up a set of people, so you don't have to worry about typing in each individual entry, just the group name.

Standard ACL Entries

Four standard entries are, by default, automatically created for every new database: Default, LocalDomainServers, OtherDomainServers, and the database creator (the user name of the person who creates the database). When you plan the ACL for your database, you should first assign access levels to these four entries. You don't have to include all four standard ACL entries, but using them is one way of making your ACLs uniform across databases, which make the ACL easier to administer and more secure. The following list describes each entry:

- The Default entry defines the access level for anyone who isn't listed anywhere else in the ACL. It is recommended that Default be either No Access, Reader, or Author. Your selection depends on the purpose and content of the database and whether it is to be published to the Web. A database with confidential information, such as a human resources database, has a Default of No Access. One with general enterprise-wide information, such as a company policy database, has a Default of Reader. One in which everyone composes documents, such as a discussion database, has a Default of Author.

CAUTION

By default, when you create a new database, the Default access is set to Designer (unless the database is created from a template with the default ACL specified). This exposes the design elements to any user who has access to the database. It is good practice to immediately set the ACL levels appropriately after creating the database.

■ LocalDomainServers is a group in every domain's Address Book that contains the names of all the servers in your domain. You might want to create your own server group in the Address Book, give it a meaningful name based on your organization or domain, and enter the names of the servers that require access to these respective databases. This makes managing the access of servers more scalable and anticipates the addition of new servers, domains, and multiple server groups (that have varying functions). It also anticipates the possibility of certifying with other servers (outside your domain). Therefore, you have unique access groups, even for your servers. You will want to give the LocalDomainServers group (or whatever internal server group name your organization uses) Manager access so that replicas of the database on all servers can replicate the entire database, including changes to the ACL. There are two cases in which you don't give this group Manager access:

- When you want to control ACL or design changes from a central server, you should give the group a lower access level (probably Editor) and the central server Manager access.

- When you don't want your database replicated to all servers in your domain, you should give the group No Access.

■ OtherDomainServers is also a group in every domain's Address Book. It contains the names of servers in other domains within your organization with which you regularly replicate. This group typically has Designer access if the database is replicated to other domains (to keep the designs in sync among replicas). If the database isn't replicated to other domains, the group has No Access. As with the LocalDomainServers, you will probably want to create your own unique group name to perform this function.

■ The creator of each database is put in the ACL with Manager access. You don't have to keep this person in the ACL, but Notes does require that at least one person be given Manager access to the database. If there were no Manager, it is possible that everyone could be locked out of a database with nobody able to add people to the ACL.

N O T E By default, when creating a new database, Notes assigns the creator Manager access, assigns LocalDomainServer and OtherDomainServers Manager access, and gives the Default group Designer access. You will want to modify the access granted in each case to conform to your organizational standards and protect the database design and information. ■

CAUTION

Notes will let you give the Default group any access level, all the way up to Manager. However, you should never set it higher than Author for a database in production. Doing so would pose a serious security threat. Even Author access should be used sparingly. In fact, many organizations impose a standard that Default is given No Access. Then people, groups, and servers are specifically added with their respective access.

If you need to give a large group a high access level, you are better off leaving Default no higher than Reader. Then create a group in the Public Address Book to which you can grant a higher access level.

N O T E If you replicate with servers in other domains outside your organization, those servers are usually listed in the ExternalServers group in the Address Book. OtherDomainServers should refer only to servers in other domains within your organization. ■

Beyond these standard entries in the ACL, you will add additional entries for users, servers, and groups of users or servers. These additional entries will affect the bulk of database users.

Creating the ACL

The first step you take in creating the ACL is to plan who needs access to your database. As part of this process, you collect all the names of your users and organize them into any necessary groups. If you use any groups, now is the time to either create the groups yourself or ask the administrator to create them for you.

The groups you create should have descriptive names. You can describe either the group's tasks (for example, PO Approvers) or members (for example, Account Managers). A descriptive name tells you who belongs in a certain group when ACL changes are made, possibly months or years down the road.

If you have an administrator create the groups for you, make sure he includes you as a group owner. As an owner, you can add or remove people from the groups you use. Therefore, if an administrator isn't available, you can make access changes immediately.

Table 10.3 lists a sample ACL. It contains the standard server groups (LocalDomainServers and OtherDomainServers), two individual names, two groups of users, one name using wildcards, and the Default entry.

Table 10.3   Sample ACL Entries

Entry	Access Level
LocalDomainServers	Manager
OtherDomainServers	No Access
Roy Rumaner/NotesAdmin/Bay	Manager
Bill Harris/Development/Bay	Manager
Document Editors	Editor
Account Managers	Author
*/Executives/Bay	Reader
Default	No Access

Once you have defined who needs access to the database, you are ready to create the ACL using the Access Control List dialog box. Follow these steps:

1. Click the database icon for which you want to set up an ACL, and select File, Database, Access Control. Or right-click the database and select Access Control (see Figure 10.11).

FIG. 10.11

Right-click a database to view its pull-down menu.

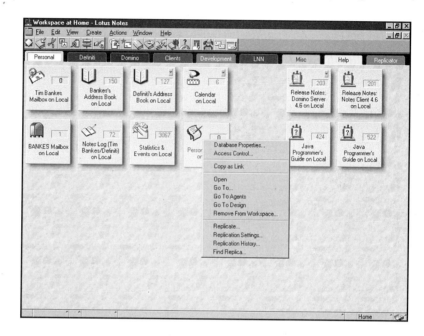

2. Notes prompts you for your password if you haven't already entered it and then displays the Access Control List dialog box, shown in Figure 10.12.

FIG. 10.12

The Access Control List dialog box.

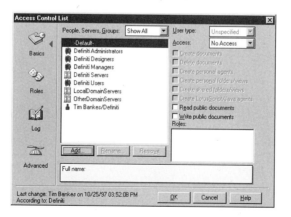

The People, Servers, Groups list shows all the entries in the ACL. You can add, delete, or update entries in this list. Use the following procedure to add names to the list:

1. Click the Add button (located below the list of people, servers, and groups). Notes displays the Add User dialog box, shown in Figure 10.13.

FIG. 10.13

Enter names into the Add User dialog box.

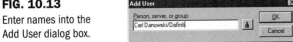

2. Enter a single name in the Person, server, or group box. Or click the Person button in the Names dialog box, which is used for looking up names in an Address Book (see Figure 10.14). This dialog box is very similar to the one you use to address NotesMail. You can select names from the list on the left and click Add to add them to the list on the right. In addition, you can select groups of individuals from the Address Book.

FIG. 10.14

You add names from an Address Book using the Names dialog box.

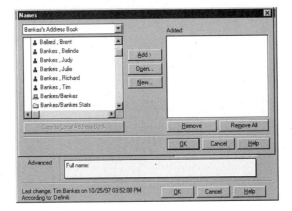

3. When you have added all the names, click OK. The names will now show up in the People, Servers, Groups list.

CAUTION

When you add new entries in the database ACL, the default access level of new people, groups, or servers will be the same as the access level of the currently highlighted person, group, or server. Therefore, be careful not to grant too much or too little access when creating new entries.

To rename an item in the list, follow these steps:

1. Select the name you want to rename, and click the Rename button. The Rename User dialog box, shown in Figure 10.15, appears.

FIG. 10.15

The Rename User dialog box.

2. From this point on, the procedure is the same as for adding new names, except that the name you enter will replace the one you selected. Notes tries to reconcile a name in the ACL with one in your Address Book by looking for spelling matches.

To delete a name from the list, select the name you want to delete and click Remove.

Once you have entered the correct names, you can assign access levels to them using the following procedure:

1. Select a name from the list of People, Servers, Groups.

2. If you want, select a user type from the User type pull-down list (see Figure 10.16).

FIG. 10.16

Selecting a user type.

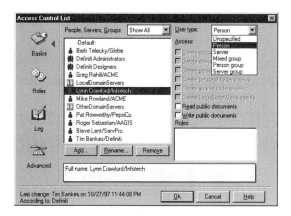

3. Select the appropriate access level from the Access pull-down list (see Figure 10.17).

FIG. 10.17

Selecting an access level.

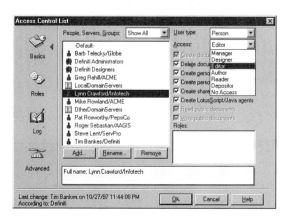

4. Below the Access list are eight checkboxes that you should check to further refine a user's actions. The actions available for selection depend on the access level you assigned the user. For example, the Create documents box is unavailable for a user who

has Reader access because a reader, by definition, can't create documents. Any unavailable items are grayed out. Actions that are selected *and* grayed out are automatically available to that level of access, and those actions are inherent to the particular access level. Conversely, actions that are grayed out and *not* selected can never be performed by users with the assigned access rights (see Figure 10.18).

FIG. 10.18

Grayed out options cannot be performed.

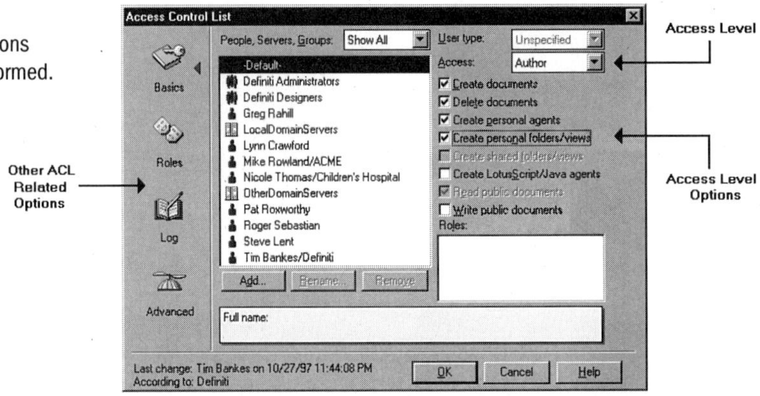

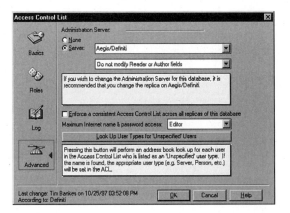

5. Finally, you can select any roles assigned to this user, if any are defined, in the Roles list box.

You can also set other ACL-related options by clicking the icons on the left side of the Access Control List dialog box. Figure 10.19 shows the advanced options you can set.

FIG. 10.19

Setting other ACL-related options.

With these advanced options, you can control whether this database's ACL can be automatically updated by an agent and enforce the ACL for databases on local workstations:

■ Basics: This option is used to set up names and access levels.

- Roles: This option allows you to set up roles for the database. Roles let you define more specific security entries for a database. Using roles, you can give a subset of users or servers access to specific database components.

- Log: This option displays a history of changes to the ACL.

- Advanced: This option allows you to select advanced options, such as selecting the Administration Server or the option Enforce a consistent Access Control List across all replicas of this database.

Customizing Database Icons

For each database, Notes displays an associated icon. Most database templates have a default icon associated with them that the Lotus designers considered appropriate for that type of database. It can be challenging to create an appealing icon, because Notes limits your ability as a designer. The dimensions of each icon are limited to 32 by 32 pixels and the standard 16 colors typical of earlier versions of Notes (Release 3, for example). However, some good examples are contained in some of the newer templates, and since the icon is the first element your users are exposed to, it is important to make sure that it's meaningful and appealing. Figure 10.20 shows the icon that Notes assigns to a database created from the Document Library template (as described earlier in this chapter).

FIG. 10.20

The Document Library icon.

frameset
on Local

TIP You should create at least a simple icon for every database to help users distinguish databases on the desktop.

Having common icons for similar databases can cue the user to the type or purpose of the database.

Using the Icon Editor

You can modify an icon as you want or even create new icons. To edit an existing icon or create a new icon for your database, double-click it in your Notes workspace. Once it's open, click Design in the navigation pane on the left side of the screen and then select Other. Notes displays several unique aspects of the database that you can change in the view pane on the right side of the screen. Double-clicking Icon opens the Design Icon dialog box, the built-in icon editor (see Figure 10.21).

You can experiment with the various tools on the left side of the Design Icon dialog box. They allow you to draw freehand, draw lines, erase, fill large areas of the icon with certain colors, and perform other special editing.

Part

II

Ch

10

FIG. 10.21

Double-clicking Icon opens the Design Icon dialog box.

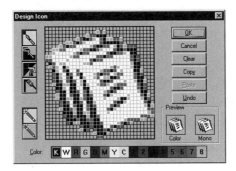

Copying and Pasting Icons from Another Source

Even if you aren't artistic, you can still add more interesting icons to your databases. If you know of another database that has an interesting icon, for example, you can "borrow" that icon for your database. To copy another database's icon, follow these steps:

1. Open the database that has the icon you want to use.

2. Click Other under Design on the folders navigator and select Icon. The Design Icon dialog box appears.

3. Click the Copy button. Notes copies the icon to the clipboard.

4. Click Cancel to close the dialog box, ensuring that you haven't made any changes to this icon, and then press Esc to close the database.

5. Open the database in which you want to use the icon.

6. Again, click Other under Design on the folders navigator and select Icon to access the Design Icon dialog box.

7. Click the Paste button. The icon you copied from the other database appears in the icon editor area of the dialog box.

8. Click OK to close the dialog box. Your new icon is in place.

You can also use icons from other sources. If you have access to Windows and OS/2 icons and can copy them to the clipboard, you can paste them into the icon editor of the Design Icon dialog box. You might also have access to an icon library database that contains all kinds of icons that others have created, and you can use them for your databases. If the icon you paste is larger than 32 pixels by 32 pixels, the edges of the graphic will be truncated.

Remember that when an icon is changed for a database on a server, people won't see the new icon until the next time they access that database on their PC or refresh the database on their workspace page.

Creating Standard Help Documents

Every database has two standard help documents, an About document and a Using document. These standard help documents will help your users by telling them the purpose of your database and how to use it. Also, they eliminate some of the questions asked of you. You should therefore take some care in creating these documents before deploying your database.

The user can access these documents from the Help menu. For example, if the user is reading the Company Procedures database, the Help menu will show two items, About Company Procedures and Using Company Procedures.

Creating an About Document

A database's About document tells people about the database—that is, what kind of information the database contains, who should use it, and how to get the most benefit from that particular database. If you create a database for your private use, you probably won't create an About document. However, if your database will be used by others who might not be familiar with it, you should always create an About document that includes a brief description of the database, who should use it, and the names of the database managers.

The About Document can also display default information or your company logo, or perform automated events when a database is opened, propagating information to all database users in a simple way.

To create or modify an About document, open the database. Click Design in the navigation pane, and then select Other. Now select About Database Document from the view pane on the right side of the screen.

Notes displays the current About document, or a blank screen if no About document exists, and enters an edit mode very similar to the one used to edit forms (see Figure 10.22). You can type new text, delete existing text, or perform almost any editing function on your About document.

After you complete your About document, close the window. When Notes asks if you want to save your changes, click Yes.

 TIP You should list any important database contacts, such as the database owner or manager, in the About document. That way, the users will know who to contact if they have any problems. Better yet, add a button that will automate a process allowing the user to send e-mail to the owner or manager.

Creating a Using Document

A Using document is very similar to an About document, except that it describes how to use the database. It usually describes the forms and views in the database and how they function.

Part

II

Ch

10

FIG. 10.22

A sample About document for the Web Pages database.

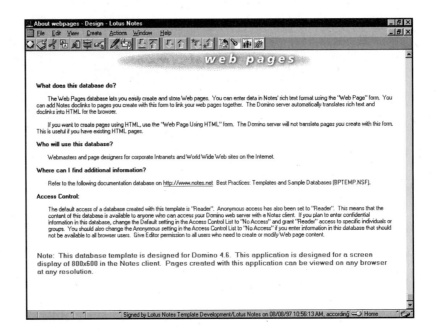

The Using document is also useful if you use doclinks. Many designers create a form with a name such as Help Document, which they use to compose many documents, each describing some facet of working with the database. These designers then insert doclinks into the Using document that reference these other documents. This technique creates a very powerful help system but complicates the database views because each view must include a specific selection formula so that the Using documents don't appear in any of the views. That selection formula might look like this:

```
SELECT Form != "Help Document"
```

Figure 10.23 shows how a portion of the database Using document might appear.

N O T E The Using document and About document don't have any properties exposed, but they can contain objects, buttons, links, Java applets, Web elements, OLE objects, plug-ins, and so on. However, the Launch tab of the Database Properties InfoBox does allow you to automatically open the About database, launch the first attachment, or launch the first doclink in the About document. ■

Creating Graphical Navigators

The following chapters will show you how to create and modify forms and views in your database. These are essential design elements included within the database. Forms are the framework, a skeleton, for entering, modifying, and viewing information within the database. Forms contain the fields, text, graphics, objects, actions, and buttons that facilitate data entry for the user. Views list the documents stored in a database in rows and columns and provide an entry point for the user to view and open the document.

▶ For more information on designing forms and views, see Chapter 11, "Designing Forms," and Chapter 12, "Designing Views."

FIG. 10.23

A sample Using document that describes how to use the database.

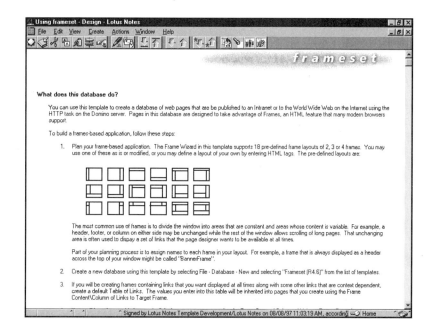

Once you have created forms and views for your database, you will want to build a user interface that helps users maneuver through it. Graphical navigators are that interface, similar to views. Navigators provide a graphical way for users to do such things as switch views, open documents, file documents into folders, and just about any other action you can program in Notes.

Navigators are made up of objects (text, pictures, or shapes) that cause actions to occur when they are clicked. One common use of navigators is a graphical table of contents. The Notes Help database uses this style of navigator, as shown in Figure 10.24.

You have already worked with at least one navigator, the default navigator. Each database automatically has a navigator that splits your screen into two different panes, which allows easier access to your Notes information.

Even though the navigator provides a good interface to a database, you undoubtedly will want to create your own specialized navigators.

Part
II

Ch
10

FIG. 10.24

A table of contents navigator from the Notes Help database.

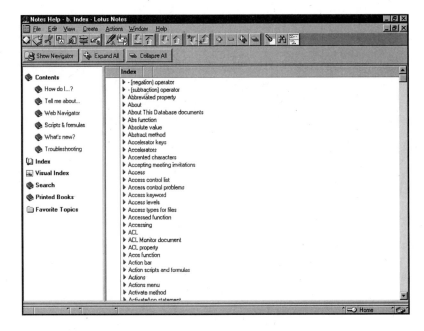

Working with Navigator Objects

To begin working with navigators, choose Create, Design, Navigator or use the Create Navigator SmartIcon. All these objects can be added to a navigator using the Create menu.

There are six types of navigator objects:

- Graphic backgrounds: A graphic background is a bitmap that is pasted into the navigator. Each navigator has only one background, and you can't attach actions to it. In fact, a graphic background is the only element that can't perform an action. You can think of a graphics background as wallpaper behind the information that appears on-screen.

N O T E Graphical backgrounds can't be resized once they are pasted into a navigator.

Use a graphics design program such as PC Paintbrush Pro, Photoshop, or Paint32 to size your graphic. This will allow you to size the graphic and paste it into the navigator. ▦

- Graphic buttons: These are small images that can be pasted into a navigator. They can appear like icons on-screen and perform specific actions when clicked. Graphic buttons can't be transparent, and any caption must already be part of the graphic.
- Graphical shapes: Similar to buttons, graphical shapes can be rectangles, polygons, polylines, or ellipses. They are drawn using Notes drawing tools and can be any shape you choose. Like graphic buttons, you can assign Notes tasks to be performed when they are clicked. Graphical shapes can be transparent and can have captions.

- Hotspots: Hotspots are very similar to graphical shapes, except that they are displayed on-screen in a more discreet manner. For example, a hotspot might be a green pop-up box that appears around text. When it's clicked, additional information might appear. They are transparent so that they don't take up a lot of room on-screen. Hotspots are always transparent and don't have captions.

- Text boxes: Text boxes are simply blocks of text that can be placed on the navigator and that can have actions associated with them. Text boxes can be transparent. Of course, they have captions, since they are text boxes!

- Command buttons: Command buttons are normal buttons with a text caption on their face. Command buttons are useful for initiating any actions that don't have graphical depictions. Command buttons can't be transparent and can have captions.

 TIP When you're designing applications for Notes, the quality and color palette you use depends on where this database will be used. The following types of graphic images can be pasted or imported into a navigator for Windows and OS/2:

- Bitmap
- GIF
- JPEG
- PCX
- TIFF 5.0

When you're importing or pasting graphic images, the color scheme is sometimes distorted after it's brought into Notes. To minimize the distortion of graphic images, limit the quality of the images to 256 colors. If you're designing graphics that will only be seen via Notes clients, use the Lotus color palette (Lotus.act or Lotus.pal). This file is available for downloading from Lotus at `http://www.lotus.com/devtools/2106.htm`.

If you're creating graphics that will be displayed on the Web, Domino supports the formats just mentioned (graphics are stored in a 256-color platform-independent format). However, because Web browsers support GIF and JPEG formats, you might make the images turn out better by creating the graphics in these formats. Domino converts all graphic images to either GIF or JPEG formats when they are published, depending on which option is set in the HTTP section of the server document.

Polyline objects, Highlight when attributes, and the auto-adjust option for navigators aren't currently supported by Domino.

In order to use a navigator within a Web application, you must select the navigator property Web browser compatible. This instructs Domino to convert the graphic to an HTML image map. If you don't select this, Domino will only display the graphic background, hotspot polygons, hotspot rectangles, and circles.

Navigator objects can be created or drawn within the navigator design space using the Create menu. Table 10.4 lists the procedures used to create each type of object.

Table 10.4   Creating Navigator Objects

Object	Procedure
Graphic background	Create a picture in any drawing program, copy the picture to the clipboard, and select Create, Graphic Background. The graphic will be pasted into the navigator. You can also set the navigator's background color by editing its properties (choose Design, Navigator Properties).
Graphic button	Create a picture in any drawing program, copy the picture to the clipboard, and select Create, Graphic Button.
Graphic shapes	From the Create menu, select the type of shape you want to draw. Then use the mouse to draw the shape.
Hotspots	Select either Create, Hotspot Rectangle or Create, Hotspot Polygon. After drawing the hotspot, double-click it to display its Properties InfoBox. Select the HiLite tab. In this box, you can specify if the hotspot should become highlighted when touched or clicked.
Text box	Select Create, Text and draw a box using the mouse. After you draw the box, the Text Box Properties InfoBox appears. Enter the text you want to display in the Caption box, and then close the Properties InfoBox.
Command button	Select Create, Button and draw the button with the mouse. The Button Properties InfoBox will appear. Enter the text for the face of the button in the Caption box, and then close the Properties InfoBox.

Navigator Actions

 To make sure that your navigator is fully displayed, use the Auto Adjust option and place a small (one-space) hidden object just to the right edge of the completed navigator.

Creating a navigator whose vertical dimensions are larger than the available screen real estate will force the vertical scroll bar to appear.

You might find it helpful to use a transparent rectangle that is one character wide.

Up to this point, we have referred to objects having actions associated with them. But what can these actions do? An action can be one of three types:

- A simple action
- A formula
- A script

You define actions in the bottom portion of the navigator design screen, as shown in Figure 10.25.

FIG. 10.25

The navigator design screen.

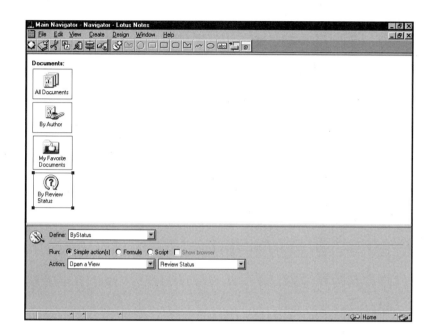

To define an action for an object, you should first click the object. This activates the bottom portion of the design screen. Then click the radio button that corresponds to the type of action you will define—either Simple action(s), Formula, or Script.

If you select Simple action(s), you must select an action from the Action pull-down list. Table 10.5 lists the type of simple actions you can select.

Table 10.5 Types of Simple Actions

Simple Action	Description
Open another Navigator	This action causes the current navigator to close and another to open in its place. When you select this option, another list box opens from which you select the navigator you want to switch to.
Open a View	This action switches the user to the specified view. When you select this option, another list box opens from which you select the view you want to switch to.

continues

Part

II

Ch

10

Table 10.5   Continued

Simple Action	Description
Alias a Folder	This action causes any documents dragged from the view pane onto the object to be placed in a specified folder (such as your mail database). When you select this option, a list box opens from which you select the folder you want to alias.
Open a Link	This action opens a specified document. Before selecting this option, go to a document and select Edit, Copy as Link. The object will link to the specified document.
Open an URL	This action switches the user to a specified URL. The user must be connected to a Domino server that has access to the WWW in order for this option to work.

If you select either a formula or a script, a box opens in which you can write any @Function formula or LotusScript program, respectively. Formulas are described in more detail in Chapter 14, "Working with Formulas," and LotusScript is discussed in Part III, "Working with LotusScript."

Displaying a Default Navigator When Your Database Opens

Once you have created several navigators, you might want to select one and have it open every time the database opens. Setting a default navigator this way ensures that the same screen will always display upon startup. By creating a default navigator, you can link to different views, documents, and other navigators, creating a graphical user interface to your Notes database.

To select a default navigator, open the Database Properties InfoBox (from the workspace, right-click the Database icon and select Database Properties) and select the Launch tab, as shown in Figure 10.26.

FIG. 10.26

You select a default navigator from the Launch tab of the Database Properties InfoBox.

You have three options regarding navigators in the On Database Open pull-down list:

■ Open designated Navigator: This option opens the designated navigator within the normal three-paned window (the navigator is on the left, the view is on the right, and the preview is on the bottom).

- Open designated Navigator in its own window: This option displays only the navigator when the database is opened; the three-paned window won't appear until the navigator is closed.

- When you're designing for Web usage, the option Open designated Navigator in its own window is available in the On Web Open list box, or you can set it up to use the Notes launch option (see Figure 10.27).

FIG. 10.27
You select a default Web navigator from the Launch tab of the Database Properties InfoBox.

The Preview Pane Default button allows the developer to force the database to open in one of the three preview pane modes (see Figure 10.28). However, forcing a preview of the currently selected document and/or selecting Maximize document preview on database open can affect performance.

FIG. 10.28
Choosing a location for the preview pane.

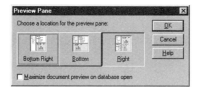

Part
II

Ch
10

TIP Opening a navigator in its own window is a convenient way of displaying a welcome screen or graphical "front door" to your application each time the database is opened. This is helpful when your application is made up of multiple databases but you want to give your users an intuitive entry point.

In the Navigators Properties dialog box, on the grid you can set the navigator to have all objects snap to grid (you can also set the grid size in pixels). This is helpful when you're aligning your objects on-screen.

You can easily preview how your navigator will look and function (partially) by selecting Design, Preview. If you are designing a navigator for the Web, you can preview it by selecting Design, Preview in Web Browser.

Designing Forms

Now that you have learned how to create a database, you're ready to create a form. Forms contain the fields you will use in your application, as well as text and graphics to help make your application more intuitive and easier to use. Lotus Notes uses forms for entering data, displaying data, and controlling the field structure in documents. When users open documents, they see the data "through" the form. A database might have a variety of forms used for displaying different data, or even for displaying the same data in different formats.

What's Contained in a Form?

A form contains several design elements that help define the structure of your database. When you design a form, you place these objects where you want them displayed.

Here are the most widely used components for designing forms:

■ Fields: Fields hold various types of data, including text, numbers, time/date values, keywords, names, and rich text. You can place fields anywhere you want on a form. A field can be unique to that form or shared among forms within a database. Fields are the basis for how data is stored and displayed from within Notes. Besides storing data, you can use fields to calculate data and even add LotusScript programs that run when the user enters and exits fields. Field attributes such as font type, style, size, and color affect the way data is displayed in the finished document. Fields can also be dynamically hidden or exposed, depending on the document mode, a formula, or even whether the current user is using version 4.6 of Notes or a Web browser! This allows designers to create a single form that will display properly, regardless of whether the user is using a Notes client or a Web browser. However, not all field attributes are supported via Web browsers.

▶ **See** Part III, "Working with LotusScript," **p. 679**

■ Text: You can place static or dynamic text anywhere on a form, and you can apply any text attribute to it—color, size, font, style, and so on. You generally want to label fields with text that helps users understand the purpose of each field.

In previous versions of Notes, designers couldn't add dynamic text to a form without creating a Notes field that displayed text dependent on an evaluation. With Notes 4.6, you can create computed text fields based on formula results, allowing for the dynamic rendering of text on both Web and Notes documents. However, there might still be instances when using a computed field better suits the application (for example, when using a rich text field, which isn't limited to 64K of data and which allows for variable text properties and other objects). Also, consider using layout regions to gain control over the exact placement of text. However, layout regions don't support rich text or computed text and aren't supported on the Web.

▶ **See** "Layout Regions," **p. 472**

■ Graphics: You can place a decorative graphic anywhere on a form, and it will appear on every document created with the form, unless it is dynamically hidden. For example, if you're designing a form for correspondence, you can place your company logo at the top of the form to create a letterhead.

N O T E   Consider the limitations imposed when pasting and importing graphics into your application. Using the Lotus color palette, limiting your graphic to 256 colors, or using TIFF or JPEG images when working with Web forms will help minimize distortion when the form is rendered to the user. You can paste bitmap images or import bitmap, GIF, JPEG, PCX Image, and TIFF 5.0 bitmap files into Notes forms.

▶ **See** "Creating Graphical Navigators," **p. 408**

- Hotspots: Hotspots allow users to perform simple tasks that mimic the Notes menus or complex tasks that are defined by formulas or LotusScript. Hotspots are placed directly on the form in the form of buttons, graphic hotspots, pop-up text, actions, links, and formulas. They are a useful way to automate static text and decorative graphics.

- Action Bars: Action Bars are a nonscrolling set of buttons displayed at the top of the form automatically. They can't be stacked, and the graphics assigned to each action are limited by the predetermined icons that ship with Notes. However, they can contain @Functions, @Commands, or scripts and can be published to OLE2 objects. Actions are also available via the A̲ctions menu during runtime.

- Tables: Tables are useful for summarizing information or lining up fields, text, or graphics in rows and columns. You can disable the cell borders (lines that surround each table cell) if you want to create an "invisible" table, make the border extruded or embossed, alter the border width, make the table transparent (when displaying a graphic background behind it), and make different cells display different background colors. In addition, tables can contain rich text, graphics, links, and so on. However, they can't contain layout regions.

- Layout regions: Layout regions allow for graphical interfaces similar to those other visual design application tools. Within layout regions, you can create and drag fields, graphics, text, and hotspot buttons. You can set layout regions to show a border or display fields in a 3D style. In addition, they automatically show useful calendar and time buttons when time/date fields or keyword fields are placed onto layout regions.

▶ **See** "Layout Regions," **p. 472**

- Attachments: Any file can be attached to a document and later viewed (with the File Viewer that ships with Notes), launched, or detached to the local hard drive. Attachments can also be full-text searched.

- Links: Links to databases, views, folders, documents, and URLs can be inserted into documents to allow for easy switching between data with a single mouse click.

- Java applets: Java programs (applets) can now be included in your Notes applications! This is accomplished by either directly including the applet design in the form design so that all documents created with this form will contain the applet, or by including it in a document's rich text field. An applet is typically a collection of files and can't be created directly by Notes. It must be created from a Java applet authoring tool.

▶ **See** Chapter 13, "Integrating Notes with Other Applications," **p. 539** for details on using Java applets.

Part
II

Ch
11

■ OLE objects: A form that has an OLE (Object Linking and Embedding) object lets you use Notes with other OLE server applications. OLE automation can also be accomplished using LotusScript and Notes/FX 2.0 when supported. See Chapter 13, "Integrating Notes with Other Applications," for details on using OLE with Notes.

■ Other form design features: Other design options you can apply to the form design include the following:

- Automatically create bulleted lists by selecting Text, Bullets.

- Automatically create numbered lists by selecting Text, Numbers.

- Enter blank lines (horizontal rules) in the form to visually separate the document by selecting Create, Horizontal Rule.

- Modify the background color of the form and choose from the 256-color palette, by using the Form Properties dialog box, described in the later section "Background Settings."

- Create a graphic background on the form (either BMP when copying and pasting into the form or a BMP, GIF, JPEG, PCX Image, or TIFF 5.0 bitmap file when importing into the form). If the graphic is as large as the document, only a single image is displayed. Otherwise, the graphic is tiled. This process is described in the section "Background Settings."

- Enter LMBCS characters by using compose sequences from the LMBCS table.

N O T E Notes stores characters with the LMBCS (Lotus Multibyte Character Set) but displays and prints characters with the ANSI (American National Standards Institute) character set. You can use the LMBCS to print and display characters that aren't on your keyboard, such as the lowercase Icelandic thorn. Refer to the Notes help document to view the LMBCS table for corresponding codes and sequences. ■

Design Features in Notes 4.6

When designing or modifying forms, if you don't see Design Folders in the view and folder navigator, select View, Show, Design. Figure 11.1 shows a sample database in design mode, which was created using the document library template.

Notice that in the Navigation pane you see the various components of the database, such as the folders and views, agents, and design. Click Design to expand the design components. This displays the forms, views, folders, shared fields, subforms, navigators, and other components that exist in the database.

When you click Forms in the Navigation pane, the Title pane on the right displays all the forms that exist in the database. You can double-click one of these forms to go into edit mode. Figure 11.2 shows the Document form in edit mode. Once in form design mode, you can show up to three different window panes. This user interface is referred to as the Integrated Development Environment (IDE). The three-pane IDE is consistent throughout the designs of the various forms, views, and folders. It also has a similar interface when you're designing navigators, agents, and script libraries.

Available forms   Title Pane

FIG. 11.1
In design mode, the Navigation pane displays the design objects that currently exist in the database, whereas the Title pane displays the type of design elements currently being viewed.

Click Design to expand

Navigation Pane

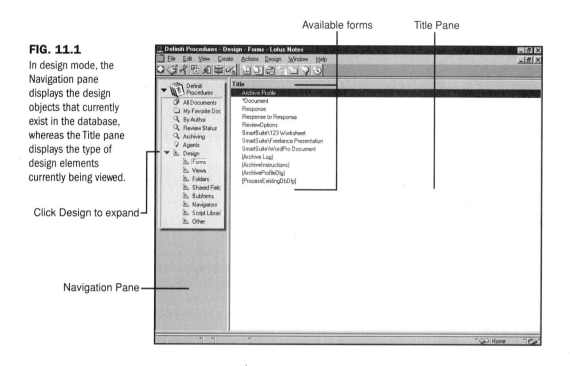

Action Pane

FIG. 11.2
While editing a form, you can easily maneuver between panes to design the form and its attributes.

Form Pane

Event Box
Define Box

Programmer Pane

Errors Box

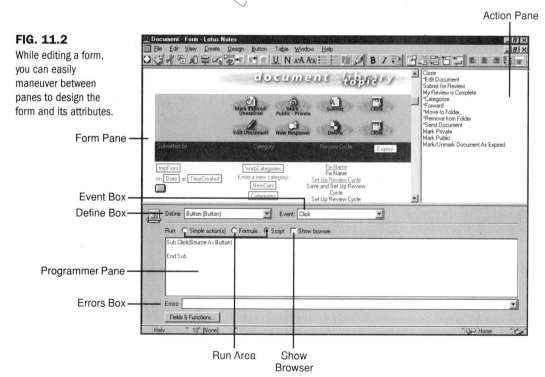

Run Area   Show Browser

N O T E The default form is designated by an asterisk (*). There should be one default form with every database. The default form is the one used to open documents that don't have a form associated with them. In other words, they don't have a value stored in the Form field. Avoid designing applications that will create a situation in which you need to open a document with the default form, because this might create unexpected results. There is also always one default view in each database, also designated by an asterisk. For more information on views, see Chapter 12, "Designing Views." ■

 T I P Select View, Action Pane to toggle the Action pane. Select View, Design Pane to toggle the Design or programmer pane, right-click to pull up display options, or position the cursor on the frame separating each pane from the rest of the form until the crosshairs are visible and then double-click.

On the top left, the form itself is displayed in the main design window, or the Design pane. This is where you can enter static text, fields, tables, layout regions, objects, and so on. On the top right is the Action pane, which allows you to define various actions that can be performed on the database. This pane is hidden by default. To open it, choose View, Action Pane. On the bottom center is the Programmer pane, which allows you to define the formulas, scripts, and actions for all the design elements associated with the form. This is where the programming work is accomplished. The Programmer pane consists of the following:

- The Define box: A combo box that shows all the objects and actions that have been exposed to the designer and that are programmable.

- The Event box: A combo box that shows all the events that have been exposed for each object selected in the Define box. Every object has its own set of events, and some, such as default actions, have none at all. Fortunately, each new release of Notes has more exposed objects and events.

- The Run area: The three radio buttons dictate the type of programming available for the currently selected object and event.

- The Errors box: This box is only used when you're programming with LotusScript. It displays all syntax errors that are detected. If multiple errors are detected, they can be seen in the drop-down box. Selecting the error from the box positions the cursor on the offending line of code.

- The Show browser checkbox: This control exposes the object browser, which lists information on LotusScript, the Notes classes, constants, subs and functions, variables, and registered OLE objects.

The text displayed in the Programmer pane can be customized to use different colors, fonts, and font sizes. In addition, scripts written within the Programmer pane can be searched (and replaced), imported, and exported. For more information on using the Design pane with the formula language, see Chapter 14, "Working with Formulas." For more information on using LotusScript, see Chapter 17, "LotusScript Basics."

T I P A powerful, yet often underutilized, design feature when you're creating forms is the ability to right-click and bring up a properties/design menu (see Figure 11.3). When you're creating forms, a single right-click shows the properties of the currently selected text or object and gives you options to create new fields and shared fields and the ability to toggle the Action pane and the Design pane.

FIG. 11.3
Displaying the object
properties menu.

Now that you're aware of the new features that you'll encounter when designing a form, you can begin creating a form. The next few sections detail how to define a form and its attributes.

Understanding Form Hierarchy and Types

Before jumping in and selecting Create, Design, Form to create a new form, you need to understand the structure or hierarchy of a Notes database. Each form created for any application has a form type associated with it. The following three types of forms can exist in a Notes database (they follow a hierarchical order):

- Document
- Response
- Response-to-response

Document is the default form type and is the highest-ranking form in the hierarchy. If you create only one form in the database, it should be of type document.

Response and response-to-response type forms are used to create responses to documents and other responses. It is important to remember that you create the relationship between the document and the response by highlighting the appropriate document before composing the response. When building views, Notes will display these three types of documents by indenting the response beneath the parent by three spaces (assuming that the developer has created the appropriate column formulas and attributes to allow Notes to thread discussions correctly).

N O T E The threading functionality is controlled by $Ref fields in the response documents. Each response document contains this $Ref field, which stores the value of the parent document's unique ID. ■

Figure 11.4 shows an example of response documents in a hierarchical view.

FIG. 11.4
Response documents create a hierarchy in a view. The responses and response-to-responses appear below the main documents and are indented by three spaces.

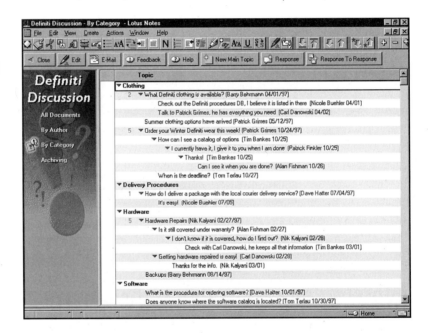

N O T E Response-to-response type forms give the user more flexibility when composing documents, because they can be associated with either a document or any response-type document. ■

Table 11.1 summarizes the three different form types.

Table 11.1   The Three Form Types

Form Type	Description
Document	Used to create any main document. Independent of all other documents.
Response	Used to create responses to a main document. Dependent on the main document. In a view that uses a response hierarchy, a response document appears underneath the main document that is highlighted when the user chooses Compose and is indented by three spaces under a main document. You can display 32 levels of responses. However, since the maximum width of a view is 22.75 inches, be sure that the display of indented responses and their labels doesn't exceed this limit.
Response-to-response	Used to respond to either a main document or another response document. Indented under another response document. Multiple levels are allowed.

Planning and Formatting a New Form

In order to create a form, you need to have at least Designer access to the database (unless it's local). Similar to the method used to create a new database, there are several ways to create a new form:

- Copy an existing form from the current database.
- Copy an existing form from another database.
- Create a form from scratch (possibly using existing design elements such as subforms and shared fields).

Effective Form Layout and Design

When laying out a form, you should always attempt to think the way a user would when inputting data. Your goal is to make the form appealing and the data entry logical and free-flowing. Developers in a company should focus on using their company's defined formatting standards to increase their organization's corporate identity—for example, logo in the left corner, a specific font size and color, and so on).

Keep in mind the following tips when designing your forms:

- You should always try to keep a standard or consistent look and feel in your forms, especially if you're developing applications for a company that wants to maintain a corporate image.

■ You can sketch the form on paper before designing it on-screen to indicate the layout of the various design elements. However, because Notes is a rapid application development environment, this step might be unnecessary. Since the design elements can easily be maneuvered during the design, focus on the functionality first (which is typically more challenging)—such as what data needs to be captured, how the fields are defined, and what design elements need to be created to support the functions. Then perfect the actual layout as the design progresses.

 TIP Use common sense when designing applications. Limit the number of colors used on each screen to three if possible. Although Notes lets designers use almost any color as a background on the form, stick with conservative, user-friendly colors and avoid gaudy colors such as magenta. If possible, use the same font type throughout the form, and limit font sizes to three. Take the time to line up the fields and be consistent.

■ Look at other databases' forms to discover new form design techniques. Open them up and learn. If appropriate, copy and paste desired parts of other forms.

■ You should consider how your forms will appear when used in various screen size resolutions. Try to use light-colored or white backgrounds for easy viewing.

■ Utilize tab settings, tables, or layout regions for consistent alignment. Don't use too many fields in each form or section, because users become frustrated when forced to enter large amounts of data. Create default values and keywords for fields when possible to assist the user with data entry.

Creating a New Form

When first designing a new form, you can define the fields, graphics, text, margins, and tabs in any order, because Notes doesn't create any predefined structure on the form. To create a form, you need to perform the following steps:

1. Select the database you want to add to the form.

2. Choose Create, Design, Form or click the Create Form SmartIcon to create a blank, untitled form (see Figure 11.5).

FIG. 11.5

Selecting Create, Design, Form lets you begin designing a new form. The form's InfoBox lets you define the form's properties.

3. To define the properties for a form, you need to select <u>D</u>esign, Form <u>P</u>roperties to display the Form Properties InfoBox. In the box's title, notice that "Form" is automatically selected. The Form Properties InfoBox lets you modify the settings for your form, such as its name, what to do when the document is opened or closed, and other default options.

 TIP Right-click the Form pane and select Form Properties to gain quick access to the Form Properties InfoBox.

4. Lay out the form by placing fields, text, graphics, and other objects on the form as needed.

5. Save the form by choosing <u>F</u>ile, <u>S</u>ave (Ctrl+S). If you didn't name the form in the Form Properties InfoBox, you will be prompted to name it before saving. The form name is significant, because Notes can reference it from within field formulas, form formulas, selection formulas, and view column formulas.

 TIP You can preview your design of the Notes form or Web page during the design process by selecting <u>D</u>esign, Preview in <u>N</u>otes or <u>D</u>esign, Preview in <u>W</u>eb Browser.

If you preview the form in a Web browser, Notes loads the Notes HTTP task and serves the form to the Domino server using the browser that has been selected for that particular location document in your Personal Address Book.

The ability to preview Notes forms with a browser is available only to Windows 95 and Windows NT workstations. You can shut down the HTTP process that runs the Web browser by choosing <u>F</u>ile, <u>T</u>ools, Stop Local Web <u>P</u>review Process.

In order for you to preview databases, they must reside in the Notes data directory on the local machine or server running the HTTP task.

You can also preview navigators in design mode. In addition, you can preview existing documents and shared views (however, views can't be previewed in design mode).

Adding Static Text to a Form

You can add static text to a form in design mode the same way you type characters into any Notes document: Type directly on the form, exactly where you want the text to appear. Figure 11.6 shows a form in design mode with static text. Often, static text is used as field labels, placed directly above or to the left of the appropriate field.

FIG. 11.6

Static text identifies and labels your fields.

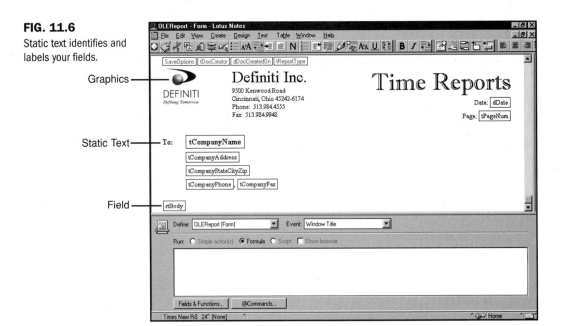

Graphics

Static Text

Field

TIP Information entered into a field is usually of variable length. For example, a customer name field would be variable, while a Social Security number field would be of constant length. Therefore, place fields of variable lengths where the user could enter more than one line of data on a line by itself or within tables, since Notes will move any fields to the right of the data as data is entered. In addition, using layout regions lets you control where fields, buttons, and graphics are displayed on the form, the dimensions of the fields, overlapping graphics and fields, and special keyword and calendar entry buttons.

The default font and color for static text on new forms is 10-point black Helvetica. Usually, static text should have a different color or size or appear in boldface to set it off from the field contents.

Choose Text, Text Properties; press Ctrl+K; click the Text Properties SmartIcon; or right-click and select Text Properties to change the size, color, and other attributes of static text. By default, Notes automatically displays SmartIcons used to modify some of the most common text attributes.

▶ **See** "Changing the Appearance of Text with the Text Menu," **p. 267**

TIP You can create your own SmartIcon set that has the SmartIcons that you use most often during design. Most of the commands that modify text attributes have already been created and can easily be added to your personalized SmartIcon set. Furthermore, you can create your own SmartIcons that quickly perform the commands you use most often. For more information on creating SmartIcons, see Chapter 1, "Getting Started with Lotus Notes."

You can add tabs by using the ruler to align fields. To toggle the ruler display, choose <u>V</u>iew, <u>R</u>uler or click the View Ruler SmartIcon. To set margins and tabs using the ruler, you must use the mouse.

▶ **See** "Setting Margins and Tabs with the Ruler," **p. 286**

 Notes designers and Web page designers can use any color in the Lotus 256-color palette for text. Earlier versions of Notes only allowed 16 colors for text. However, any colors selected with a 4.6 client will display with full fidelity in all 4.x versions of Notes.

Copying a Form from Another Database

Occasionally, you might want to copy a form from one database and use it in another, possibly modifying it to meet the new application's needs. This procedure can save you a lot of development time, especially if you begin using consistent formatting standards in your databases.

▶ **See** "Database Templates," **p. 1091**

To copy and paste a form, follow these steps:

1. Select the database containing the source form.
2. Verify that you are in design mode (select <u>V</u>iew, <u>S</u>how, <u>D</u>esign).
3. In the Navigation pane, click Design to expand the design components.
4. Click Forms to display the available forms in the database in the Title pane.
5. Select the form (or forms) you want to copy from the Forms list.

 You can select a range of forms by holding down the Shift key while clicking. To select individual forms, hold down the Ctrl key while clicking.

6. Select <u>E</u>dit, <u>C</u>opy, or click the Edit Copy SmartIcon.
7. Switch to the database where you want to paste the form, click Design in the Navigation pane, and then click Forms to display the list of forms.
8. Select <u>E</u>dit, <u>P</u>aste, or click the Edit Paste SmartIcon. The new form's name will appear in the Forms list.

Part
II

Ch
11

> **CAUTION**
>
> If you're copying and pasting from the same database a form (or another database) that has the same name as an existing form, the form is pasted into the list of forms but is renamed "Copy of" followed by the original form name. All subsequent copies are named "Another Copy of" followed by the original form name.

You can make a quick backup of a form by simply copying and pasting it in the same database. However, be sure to open the backup form and deselect the Include in Menu option in the form properties. In addition, put parentheses around the form name to hide the form from the users. It's good practice to rename the form, including the date of the backup in the name.

▶ **See** "Naming a Form," **p. 431**

 If you're copying and pasting a form from a different database whose "Database is a template" design property has been enabled, you will be asked whether you want this new design element to inherit future design changes when the database is refreshed, as shown in Figure 11.7. This feature allows your new form to inherit design changes from the original form (even though the original database isn't set up as the template to this database). In other words, design inheritance is available not only at the database level but at the design element level as well. Therefore, when you're using the same form (subform, script library, and so on) among multiple databases, you can allow them to inherit their design from the original form. When you do this, future design changes will only have to be made to the original form; the changes will propagate to all respective forms. Keep in mind that design inheritance works in only one direction. All design changes must be made to the original form. Any design changes made directly to the forms set up to inherit their design will be lost.

FIG. 11.7

Setting up form-level design inheritance from a form in another database.

Form Properties

Adding static text is just the initial step in creating a form. You also need to define the form's overall attributes, such as its name, type, read access, compose access, whether to hide it, and whether to make it the default form in the database. Then you will be ready to add the fields. Form attributes are defined in the Form Properties InfoBox (see Figure 11.8), which you access by selecting Design, Form Properties. The following sections describe how to use the settings on the various tabs in this InfoBox.

FIG. 11.8

The Form Properties InfoBox lets you define the properties of a form. Each tabbed section lets you define different attributes.

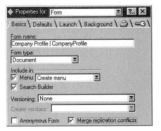

NOTE You must be designing or editing a form to select Form Properties.

The six tabs in this dialog box correspond to the form's properties:

- Basics
- Defaults
- Launch
- Background
- Printer Settings
- Security

Basic Settings

The Basics tab in the Form Properties InfoBox for a form is the default tab (the one you will always encounter first). In this section, you can name the form, select the form type (for example, document, response, or response-to-response), decide whether to include it in the Create menu or the Search Builder, specify versioning, and so on.

The following sections explain in more detail the options you can use to define a form's properties or attributes in the Basics tab.

Naming a Form In the Form name box, enter a name for this form. The name can be any combination of characters, including spaces, and it's case-sensitive. A name can't exceed 256 bytes (or characters, unless you're using multibyte characters, in which case 256 bytes isn't the same as 256 characters). This 256-byte limit includes synonyms and any cascading names. Only the first 64 characters will appear on menus and in dialog boxes.

Keep the following points in mind when naming a form:

- Use descriptive names: The form names appear on the Create menu. Essentially, the form name is the Create command to create a specific document, so its name should indicate its purpose. For example, if it's a response form, try to use the word "Response" in its name.

- Use accelerator keys: By default, the first unique letter in the form name is used as the form's accelerator; the accelerator is underlined on the Create menu. To force Notes to use a different letter as the accelerator, insert an underscore (_) before that letter. For example, to force the letter A to be the accelerator key for a form named Loan Analysis, enter the name as Loan _Analysis. Even though you can designate the same letter as an accelerator key several times, it's good practice to use a different letter for each form that will appear on the Create menu.

- Use cascading form names for forms that can be grouped by function: Enter the top-level form name, followed by a backslash (\) and the additional form name. For example, entering Action Item\Invitation causes the name Action Item to appear on the Create menu and the Invitation form to cascade from it, as shown in Figure 11.9. Notes allows one level of cascades.

Part
II

Ch
11

FIG. 11.9
Cascading form names
are useful for organizing
your forms on the
Create menu.

- Use synonyms: Synonyms let you change the form's name on the Create menu without tracking down and rewriting formulas that reference the original form name, which is a great time-saver. For example, if you changed Action Item\Meeting form to Action Item\Group Meeting, you would attain errors in various formulas that reference that form.

Create form synonyms (aliases) when you first create the form (even if the synonym is the same as the form), and use this when referring to the form in all formulas. This way, you can change the displayed form name at any time without affecting the existing code. You can create multiple aliases, but the rightmost alias is the value stored in the Form field of all documents created with this form.

Notes will automatically sort the forms alphabetically from the Create menu. However, this isn't always what you want. Typically, forms are sorted in order of occurrence or frequency of use. To ensure that the forms are sorted in the proper order, simply number the forms when you name them—for example, 1. Create Project, 2. Create Task, and so on.

To use synonyms, enter the form name followed by a vertical bar (|) and the synonym's name. The first name in the Form name box is the name that appears on the Create menu. If you're using both a cascade and a synonym, put the cascade name before the synonym. For example, in 1. Action Item\Appointment | Appointment, 1. Action Item\Appoinment will appear on the Create menu, but the document will be saved with Appointment as the value stored in the Form field.

CAUTION
Web users won't have access to Notes menus, because they are accessing the databases with a browser. Therefore, in order to allow those users to create and edit Notes documents, you must add @Command formulas in the Action Bar or add buttons to the form's design to allow users to perform menu equivalent functions, such as creating documents and opening views.

Specifying the Form Type   As mentioned earlier, a Notes database has three types of forms: documents, responses, and responses-to-responses. In the Form type drop-down list box, you can select the desired form type, as shown in Figure 11.10. The default form is document.

▶ To fully understand the hierarchy of forms, see the earlier section "Understanding Form Hierarchy and Types," **p. 423**

FIG. 11.10

Select the desired form type in the Form type drop-down list box.

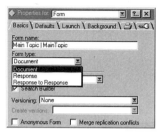

Including the Form in the Create Menu   Select the Include in Menu option if you want to display the form on the Create menu. If you deselect this option, the form is effectively hidden from the database's users. For example, your NotesMail database has several hidden forms that are used only to display information. Developers use this feature to prevent users from composing a certain form, but they can still use the form to read documents. This is also useful when you want to control what forms are used through navigators. Keep in mind that the Create menu can display only nine forms unless cascading is used.

CAUTION

Deselecting Include in Menu doesn't guarantee that the form is truly hidden. This is because users could use it in form formulas (to select which form will be used in a particular view) or use Form Override. To permanently hide a form, you can place parentheses around the form's name in the Form name box. Using parentheses not only hides the form on all menus but also prevents users from using Form Override to print the document. However, the form can still appear in form formulas and be referenced by your code. Developers like to use this technique to hide forms used in dialog boxes, forms reserved for specific purposes, old forms that they want to store for future use or backup, and so on—basically, any form they want to permanently hide from the end user.

You could select the Include in Menu option and then choose the Create other option in the list box. This removes the form from the Create menu and moves it to the Other dialog box (see Figure 11.11), which you access by selecting Create, Other. This is useful if you don't expect a form to be used frequently or you want to shorten the list of forms shown on the Create menu because many forms are listed.

FIG. 11.11

You access the Other dialog box by selecting Create, Other.

Including the Form in the Search Builder   If the database has been full-text indexed, the Search Builder option lets you use the form in a Search Builder for a full-text search. In a full-text search, users can select a form to use in a search and enter search criteria in the fields on the form (see Figure 11.12). This option even lets users search for text in attachments and embedded objects.

▶ **See** "Full-Text Searching in Databases," **p. 298**

FIG. 11.12
The Search Builder lets you select the condition By Form; then the desired form can be used in conducting a query.

If the form is used to display documents, it generally should be made available for queries so that users can attempt a full-text search using a familiar layout versus having to enter more-complex query commands when a form isn't made available.

Tracking the Version   Normally, every time you save an updated document, it replaces the original document, whose original field values are lost forever. With the versioning option, you can allow this to happen, force a saved update to become a new response document, or let the user decide. Figure 11.13 shows the available options that let you begin version control by utilizing the functionality of the Notes document response hierarchy.

FIG. 11.13
Versioning lets you incorporate whether documents become responses or siblings upon being updated. This is a great way to track who is editing and saving the documents while maintaining previous versions.

The following options are available for incorporating versioning into your database:

■ None: This is the default option that designates no versioning will occur.

- New versions become responses: This lets you incorporate document version control in your application. If a document created with this form is modified, the original remains intact, and all updated copies are stored as responses to that original, providing a history of changes. This method of version control is immune to replication and save conflicts. For example, if users on different servers modify and save the same main document, their versions are treated and displayed as two separate response documents when the databases replicate.

   A replication conflict occurs when two or more users edit the same document in different replicas between replications. A save conflict occurs when two or more users edit the same document in a database on a server at the same time. At the next replication, after two users edit and save the same document, Notes designates as the main document the document that has been edited and saved most frequently. It displays the other(s) as responses to the main document labeled [Replication or Save Conflict] with a diamond symbol in the left margin.

- Prior versions become responses: This is another method of version control, except in this case, if a document created with this form is modified, the updated copy replaces the original main document, which is then stored as a response to the new version. Again, this gives an application the ability to maintain a history of changes.

- New versions become siblings: In this situation, the original document is listed first, and all successive versions or siblings follow as additional main documents. You should choose this option if you want to leave the original document as a main document without introducing the risk of replication or save conflicts, which can occur if the database resides on multiple servers.

- When you're using versioning, a second drop-down list is available to control how the new versions are created. They can be Manual - File, New Version, which won't automatically save edited documents as new versions but will create an option to save the document as a new version if you select File, Save As New Version. If the option Automatic - File, Save is selected, the edited document will create a new version every time the document is saved. If neither option is selected but versioning has been enabled, Automatic - File, Save will be selected by default.

▶ **See** "Understanding Form Hierarchy and Types," **p. 423**

Anonymous Form Setting   Selecting the Anonymous Form checkbox allows for true anonymous creation and editing of documents. Notes typically tracks who has created and edited a document with the reserved $UpdatedBy field. However, when Anonymous Form is enabled, this field isn't created. Instead, the $Anonymous field is created with a value of 1 (true).

T I P When using the anonymous form feature, be sure *not* to include any fields on the form that track who has created or edited the document.

Merge Replication Conflicts   This feature helps reduce (although not eliminate) the possibility of replication conflicts. When this feature is enabled, if two users edit different fields in the same document, rather than automatically creating a [Replication or Save Conflict] document,

Notes will merge the two documents, modifying only the fields that have changed in each respective document. However, if both users edit the same field, a [Replication or Save Conflict] document is still created, as described in the section "Tracking the Version," to ensure no loss of data.

Default Settings

In the Defaults tab of the Form Properties InfoBox, you can select options that specify how that form will be used. Figure 11.14 displays the Defaults tab options for the Form Properties InfoBox.

FIG. 11.14

The Defaults tab in the Form Properties InfoBox lets you specify the default settings for how the form will function.

The following sections describe the options that are available in the Defaults tab.

Specifying the Form as the Default Form   Selecting the Default database form option makes the current form the default form for the database. A database can have only one default form. Figure 11.15 shows the list of available forms in the database. The default form is designated by an asterisk.

> **CAUTION**
>
> When you designate a form as the default form, another form in the database that might already have that designation loses default form status. The new default form setting takes precedence.

Using a default form ensures that if a another form is renamed without a synonym or is deleted from the database, users can still view documents created with that form through the default form. Whenever Notes can't find the form used to create a document, it always reverts to the default form for the database. This method might not always display the information contained in the document, because the document must contain the fields that are in the form design. The form that is used to display a document is based on the following criteria, listed in order of precedence:

- The form has been stored in the document. This isn't recommended, because it creates additional overhead by storing design elements with the document in multiple $ fields. This method is occasionally used if the document will be sent to another user who doesn't have access to the document.

FIG. 11.15

The default form, Main Topic, is indicated by an asterisk (*) beside the name in the design folder.

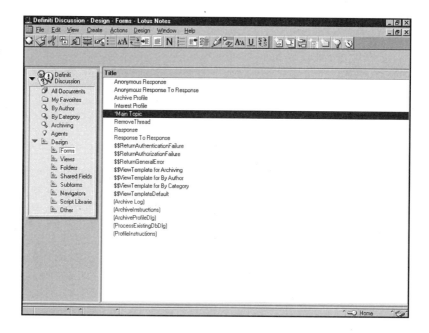

- The Form formula is used in views to override the form used to open a document. This is helpful when you want the form that is used to display the data to be dynamic, depending on the current view or a formula evaluation. For example, suppose a document is being routed through an organization, but not every person who views the document needs to see the document in the same format, or the document is displayed differently depending on its status.

- The value stored in the Form field in the Notes document is used to open the document. This field is automatically created by Notes when a document is saved by assigning the value of the current form or its alias to the reserved field name, Form. This is the most common scenario. However, a form design element must exist with the same name as defined in the Form field, or the default form will be used.

- The database default form is used to open the document (none of the preceding criteria have been met). Typically, it's not a good idea to allow this scenario to occur, because each form has specialized actions and display features. If a document is forced to revert to the default form, you can't be guaranteed that the associated form design will properly display the document.

Automatically Refreshing Fields The Automatically refresh fields option recalculates all the form's computed fields (fields are described later in this chapter) every time the user moves the mouse pointer to the next field during data entry. This allows you to automatically update calculated fields for users as they move through the document during data entry. By default, this option isn't enabled, which means that the calculated fields in the form will be updated only when the document is saved or refreshed.

CAUTION

If the form contains many computed fields, constant recalculation will significantly slow data entry and irritate the user. Use this option sparingly or only when it's necessary to see the result of a calculation when proceeding to the next field. Also, it might be possible to perform such calculations using LotusScript within the exiting and entering events of each field.

 TIP   The user can always update fields manually by pressing F9.

Storing Forms in Documents   Normally, only the data entered in the fields of a form are stored within a document. The Store form in document option automatically stores the form design with each document, allowing you to retain the layout of that form with that document. This is a relatively significant setting, because documents that are created with a form using this setting aren't updated if the form is changed, the form stored with the document is stored only when the document is created, and the design is never updated. It also causes the database to become very large, because the entire form design is stored with each document, possibly using as much as 20 times more disk space.

You should use this option if you intend to mail documents from the database to users' mail files because the mail file wouldn't contain the original form design; if the form contains an OLE object or subscription, and changes between the Notes document and the object must be in synch; or if the documents have been stored as encapsulated documents to be mailed to cc:Mail users. Otherwise, you should avoid using this setting.

N O T E   You can determine the size of a form by viewing the forms in the design folder. Select a form and then choose <u>D</u>esign, Design <u>P</u>roperties. Select the Design tab to view the size of the form in bytes. ■

Enabling Field Exchange   With the Disable Field Exchange option, you can disable or enable field exchange to occur between a Notes document and fields from another application that supports Notes/FX technology, such as a Lotus 1-2-3 spreadsheet. Notes/FX uses OLE technology to allow Notes and any OLE server application to share data fields. The contents of fields in an OLE server application file can automatically appear in a corresponding field in a Notes document, and vice versa. Furthermore, depending on the type of field, the contents of the field can be updated from either direction (bidirectional). For more information, see Chapter 13, "Integrating Notes with Other Applications."

Inheriting Values from the Selected Document   In the On Create section of the Defaults tab, select the Formulas inherit values from selected document option if you want documents created with this form to inherit or copy values from the highlighted document in a view or open document in a form. An example of inheriting field values would be if a document were created where the field CustomerName contained "Definiti, Inc.," a response to that document were then created, and the Customer Name appeared in the response document's `CustomerName` field upon creation. The subsequent document doesn't have to be a response document; data inheritance works when you create new main documents as well.

This option is very useful in discussion databases where you utilize the three different types of forms (document, response, and response-to-response) and you want to have similar information filter down to the child documents. For example, you might want to copy relevant information, such as the subject from a main discussion document to a response document in the discussion database. The discussion template (discsw46.NTF) has two forms, response and response-to-response, that utilize this option and is an excellent starting point in learning this Notes development technique.

From a developer's standpoint, inheriting fields from parent documents is useful for making a Notes database more closely associated with a "relational" database rather than the general "flat-file" Notes database. Inheritance happens only when a document is first created. If the parent's information changes, the child won't reinherit the data. Therefore, designers will have to program methods to ensure the data integrity of the documents. Also, inheritance isn't limited within a single database. New documents created in another database can still inherit values from the currently selected, or open, document. When incorporating these techniques, be sure to consider data synchronization issues among the databases, possibly creating agents to ensure data integrity.

Part

II

Ch

11

CAUTION

When creating applications for the Web, the Domino server can't translate commands based on the currently selected document in a view, because the Web doesn't support a "selected document."

Inheriting a Document into a Rich Text Field   Another feature for developers is the Inherit entire selected document into rich text field option. This option lets you choose how you want the inherited document to appear: as a link, collapsible rich text, or rich text. If you select rich text, you can also choose which rich text field the document should appear in. For instance, a new response document can automatically inherit the contents of its main document. Just make sure that you have created a rich text field to store the inherited document. After selecting Inherit entire selected document into rich text field, you can select the rich text field you created. Then select one of the following full document display options:

- Link: This creates a doclink to the original parent document.
- Collapsed rich text: This option displays the parent document as a collapsed section and gives users the opportunity to review the parent document, but it doesn't clutter the form.
- Rich text: This inherits the fully expanded contents of the parent document.

Figure 11.16 shows an example of a document (a Reply With History form from the Mail database) if "Inherit entire selected document into rich text field: Body as Collapsible rich text" was selected.

FIG. 11.16

Inheriting a selected document as collapsible rich text into the Body field.

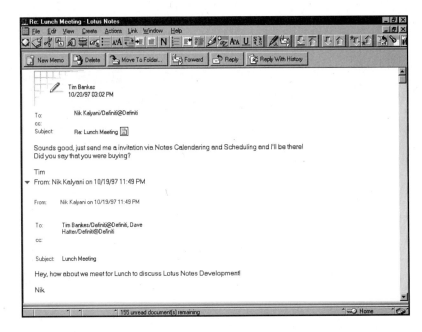

Automatically Opening a Document in Edit Mode   If the Automatically enable Edit Mode option is selected, you can place an accessed document in edit mode when it has been opened from a view by either double-clicking the appropriate document or highlighting the document and pressing the Enter key. Not selecting this checkbox opens the document in read mode and doesn't allow for immediate data entry. Typically, you want to automatically enable edit mode to facilitate easier data entry for the users. If edit mode isn't enabled, users must double-click, press Ctrl+E, choose Actions, Edit Document, or use an Action Bar created by the designer. However, disabling automatic edit mode might be a good option for documents that don't need user input, such as help documents, policies, procedures and other corporate documents, or documents with security considerations in which not all users have rights to edit documents but it might be necessary to open documents in read mode.

Show Context Pane   You can also govern how a document appears when it is open by selecting the Show context pane option and its associated appearance option, either Doclink or Parent.

Present Mail Send Dialog   To facilitate document mailing, you could include a text field called SendTo on the form. Then, if the Present mail send dialog option is selected, and a SendTo field exists on the form with a person's name, Notes will prompt the author of the document to send, save, or discard the document, as shown in Figure 11.17.

This is a great feature if you want to mail-enable forms in your databases. It's especially useful for creating workflow-type applications, such as sending approvals.

FIG. 11.17
The Close Window
dialog box appears
when you save a
document if a SendTo
field exists on the form.

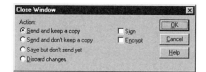

> Did you know that you can mail any document to a fellow user by choosing Actions, Forward?
> Occasionally, in applications that require workflow procedures, you might want to automate this
> procedure.

Treat Document Contents as HTML   Select this checkbox when you're designing applications
that are only to be published as Web pages via Domino. This tells Domino to convert the contents of the form to HTML on-the-fly when serving the document to a Web browser.

> You can tell Domino to pass HTML directly to the Web browser and ignore all other fields by adding a
> field named HTML to the form. Then you can add HTML code as the field value or default value. In
> essence, this allows for the same functionality as "Treat document contents as HTML," except that only
> the field value of the HTML field is converted and published. Therefore, you can have other fields on the
> form for native Notes users. The HTML field can be computed or editable. (However, if it's editable, you
> can change the HTML on a per-document basis, as opposed to creating it once for the whole form.)
> Also, if the HTML code placed within the HTML field is greater than 15K, you must use a rich text field.
> Otherwise, you can use a text field.

Settings for Launching Objects

The Launch tab in the Properties InfoBox for a form initially displays only an Auto Launch
drop-down list box with a default of None. Here you can select the object type or application
that you want to launch from within your form and any associated actions. These actions are
covered in more detail in Chapter 13, "Integrating Notes with Other Applications."

Background Settings

The Background Color option lets you select the form's background color from a 256-color
palette (see Figure 11.18). Keep in mind that monitor resolution and size affect color, and that
background color affects the visibility of text. Select light colors such as white, light blue, and
yellow for easier viewing.

Use the graphic background buttons to create a graphic background on the form (either BMP
when copying and pasting into the form or a BMP, GIF, JPEG, PCX Image, or TIFF 5.0 bitmap
file when importing into the form). If the graphic is as large as the document, only a single
image is displayed. Otherwise, the graphic is tiled. You might want to hide the graphic when
designing, because the layout in design mode won't match how the form is displayed (because

of additional design elements, such as hidden fields, that aren't displayed at runtime). If the graphic contains more than 16 colors, you can select the checkbox Hide graphic on 16 color displays.

You can also allow users to override background properties in order to improve performance if this form is designed to be rendered as a Web page.

FIG. 11.18
The Background tab for Form properties.

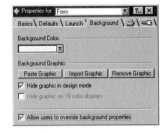

T I P   Because graphic backgrounds are automatically tiled, it's easy to create a textured background for a form when you're designing applications that will be published on the Web.

Printing Options

The Print tab, which has a printer icon, lets you define a header and/or footer in your form and set its corresponding font, size, and style attributes (see Figure 11.19).

▶ **See** "Using Headers and Footers," **p. 134**

FIG. 11.19
It's easy to set the Header and Footer options for your form when printing. Unfortunately, these options aren't WYSIWYG, so you must print the header and footer to see how they will appear.

T I P   To specify a multiline header or footer, press Enter at the end of each line of the header or footer.

Security Settings

Sometimes you will want to restrict who can create or read specific documents. The Security tab, which has a key icon, lets you establish whether a user can read or author a certain document with this form (see Figure 11.20). The following sections describe these options.

FIG. 11.20

The Security tab in the Form Properties InfoBox allows you to define who can and can't see specific documents using this particular form.

Restricting Read Access   By default, anyone with at least Reader access to the database can read all documents. You can define a read access list that restricts the form so that documents created with the form are available only to a limited list of people. Then, every document created with the form receives this list.

▶ **See** "Working with the Access Control List," **p. 784**

Follow these steps to define the list of users allowed to read documents composed with this form:

1. Deselect All readers and above in the section called Default read access for documents created with this form.

2. Select each user, group, server, or access role you want to include.

N O T E   The database ACL and any access roles should have already been defined by the manager using File, Database, Access Control. This setting doesn't override the database ACL; it can only refine it at the form level.

3. If a person doesn't exist in the ACL, you can click the Person icon to select a name from a Public or Private Address Book.

   Repeat steps 2 and 3 for each name you want to add to the list. To remove a name, click the name again to remove the checkmark.

4. Save the form.

N O T E   The read access list refines the ACL; it doesn't override it. If a user doesn't already have Reader access to the database, he won't be able to read the documents created with this form, even if you list him in the read access list.

Create Access   You can restrict the form to a limited list of people for creating documents. The create access list is designed just like the read access list. By default, anyone with at least Author access to the database can create documents with any of the database's forms. To define the subset of users who will need a specific form, follow these steps:

1. Deselect All authors and above in the Who can create documents with this form section.

2. Select each user, group, server, or access role you want to include.

3. If a person doesn't exist in the ACL, you can click the Person icon to select a name from a Public or Private Address Book.

   Repeat steps 2 and 3 for each name you want added to the list. To remove a name, click the name again to remove the checkmark.

4. Save the form.

Other Methods of Securing Forms   The Security tab in the Form Properties InfoBox also lets you select the following options:

- Default encryption keys: This option lets you select and associate any defined encryption keys for the form. To use this feature, you must define one or more fields on the form as encryptable. Every document created with the form will automatically have its encryptable fields encrypted, using the keys you specify here. Be sure to distribute the keys to people who will be using the form.

- Disable printing/forwarding/copying to clipboard: This option prevents users from printing, forwarding, or copying restricted information. This feature greatly helps prevent accidental or intentional distribution of confidential information. It doesn't prevent users from using screen-capture programs, however.

- Available to Public Access users: Selecting this checkbox allows documents created with this form to be available in the associated views and folders to users who have been defined in the access control list of the database with public access read or write privileges.

Creating a Window Title

It is important that you assign a meaningful window title to each form, because this title will appear in the Notes title bar when the form has focus. It also appears on the Window menu when the user tasks between multiple Notes windows. However, the form title doesn't have to be static; you can use limited @Functions to create dynamic titles. For example:

```
@If(@IsNewDoc; "New Company Document"; "Company Profile for " + tCompanyName)
```

To create a form window title, click empty space in the Form Design pane or select the form object from the Define combo box in the lower pane of the IDE. Then type a character string or formula into the formula box.

Adding Fields to a Form

Once you have defined a form, you can add fields to it. Fields are the individual elements by which you enter data into Notes and display the data stored in Notes. A form can accept and display only data for which there are fields. For example, if you want users to enter their employee ID numbers on the form, you must add the EmployeeID field to the form layout. Fields store various types of data, such as text, numbers, dates, names, rich text, and so on.

You create a field by giving it a name and selecting some attributes for it, such as the data type, field type, and format. Notes then places the field on your form. Each field definition is composed of five basic elements:

- A field name
- A data type
- A computed or editable attribute
- Display options
- Field formulas and script

The following sections explore the various types of fields you can use in your forms.

Single-Use and Shared Fields

Notes supports single-use and shared fields. A single-use field is a normal field. You define it, select attributes for it such as its data type, and then place it on a form. If you want to use it again in a different form, you can define a new field using the same name and define the attributes or copy the field from the existing form and paste it into the new form, but in both cases, the new field has no relation to the original. Single-use fields are stored within the form itself and are available only on that level.

Shared fields are used in multiple forms in the same database and require the same attributes and formulas in each form. These fields are stored as separate entities in the database design and can be accessed from any form design. You access a shared field by selecting Create, Insert Shared Field, which lets you place the shared field at the insertion point for any form in the database. Every time you update one instance of the shared field, all other instances are automatically updated too, because they use the same field definition. If you make a shared field a text field instead of a number field, for example, all instances of that shared field are updated automatically to reflect your changes.

Shared fields are useful when you want to use the same field in multiple forms and you want to make sure that the exact same definition is used everywhere. For example, your database might use the InterestRate field in three different forms. To make sure that all the forms use the same field definition, you define a single shared field called InterestRate and then use it in each form. To create a new field, follow these steps:

1. Place the mouse pointer on the form where you want the field to appear.
2. Select Create, Field or click the Create Field SmartIcon to insert a single-use field. Notes inserts a new field called Untitled on your form and displays the Field Properties InfoBox, shown in Figure 11.21. You can now rename the field and change other properties of the field.

FIG. 11.21

Inserting a new field onto a form. A single-use field is identified by its light rectangular outline.

Inserting a single-use field

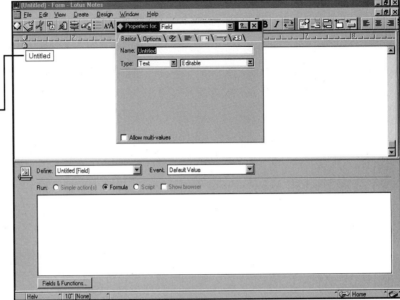

3. Select Create, Insert Shared field or click the Create Insert Shared Field SmartIcon to display the Insert Shared Field dialog box, shown in Figure 11.22. Select the shared field and then click OK to insert it onto the form (see Figure 11.23).

FIG. 11.22

Inserting a shared field called tCompanyName onto a form.

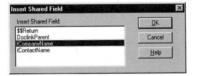

If you haven't defined a shared field, this dialog box will be blank. To define a shared field, you must return to the Navigation pane, select Create, Design, Shared Field, and then name and define the shared field. Or you can select an existing field and then select Design, Share this field. Once saved, this newly named shared field will appear in the Insert Shared Field dialog box for reuse.

 TIP You can copy and paste fields between forms by using the clipboard. However, a shared field will revert to a single-use field when copied and pasted, because its definition isn't stored with the field.

If you define a shared field and then place it in a form that has the Store Form in Documents option selected, that instance of the field is automatically converted to a single-use field whenever a document is created and saved using that form. This ensures that if the document is mailed or pasted into another database, the field will be accessible even if the new database doesn't contain a copy of the shared field's definition (this is true of any field, not just shared fields).

FIG. 11.23
Shared fields are designated by a heavy rectangular outline.

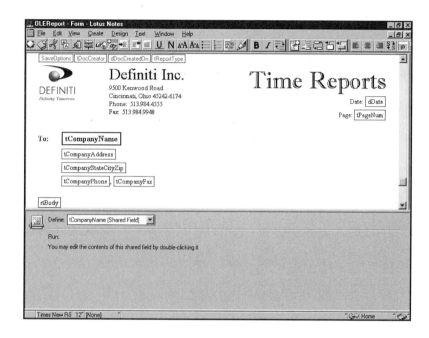

If you delete a field from a form, the data entered through that field can't be displayed in that form. There is no message, and the data itself can't be altered with that form, although it can be altered with agents and/or LotusScript. You can still display it by adding the field to another form. The contents of the field are still considered part of the document, but because there is no field to display them in, they are not displayed on the form.

NOTE You can use another form or create a new field with a formula that displays the contents of the previously deleted field or view the document properties of the document from a view (see Chapter 12, "Designing Views"). ▓

 Be careful when creating many shared fields. Overloading your form with shared fields can affect performance, because shared fields take slightly longer to load.

Only the design elements of shared fields are "shared" across different forms, not the values that are stored within them.

Fields can't be shared across databases.

Defining Fields

Once you've chosen whether the field on the form is single-use or shared, you must define the field's characteristics—for example, its data type, field type, format, paragraph attributes, and so on. This is accomplished in the Field Properties InfoBox.

 TIP Double-click an existing field, select Design, Field Properties, or press the spacebar while a field is selected to display its Field Properties dialog box.

Basic Settings   Use the Basics tab, shown in Figure 11.24, to name the field, select the data type, and select the field type.

FIG. 11.24

The Properties InfoBox for a field allows you to define the attributes for the fields in your form.

The following options appear in the Basics tab:

- Name: Name the field first. The field name must begin with a letter, but it can include numbers and the symbols __ and $. Fields beginning with $ are internal type fields used by Notes that you usually won't have to worry about unless you do more-complex Notes database programming or are designing Web pages. (Table 11.2, shown later in the chapter, lists internal fields used by Notes and Domino.) When naming a field, remember that it might be used in a formula, so you should try to choose a short name that is easy to remember. There are about a dozen reserved field names, such as Categories, SendTo, Save Options, and Sign, that have special meaning in Notes. Fields that have these reserved field names behave in a predefined way. (Table 11.3, lists reserved fields used by Notes.) Field names might contain up to 32 bytes (if you're using multibyte characters, 32 bytes is different from 32 characters).

- Type: Notes supports nine data types for fields. You select a data type to indicate how this data will be stored and used. These data types are discussed in the next section.

- The Editable and Computed attributes: Every field is either editable or computed. Editable fields are typically text, numeric, rich text, or keywords. Computed fields must contain a formula to calculate their values and are usually number, time/date, authors, readers, and names field types. They can't be edited by the user.

Editable fields can contain three formulas:

The default field value: The initial value of the field when the field is first created in the document. An example would be prepopulating the value of a status field to New on a new document.

The input translation formula: Modifies the contents of the field when the document is recalculated or saved. An example would be using the @Trim function to eliminate redundant spaces.

The input validation formula: Verifies the contents of the field against predefined criteria when the document is recalculated or saved. Failing to meet the specified criteria can result in a condition that doesn't let the user save the document until the condition is satisfied. For example, this is often used to verify that a value has been entered for a field, such as checking to see if the field is null (using double quotes) and returning a failure condition. When formulas in input validation formulas return a failure condition, a prompt box is automatically displayed that refers to the offending field, and the cursor is automatically placed in the respective field.

For more information on using field formulas and @Functions, see Chapter 14, "Working with Formulas," and Chapter 15, "Working with Functions and Commands."

Computed fields are used to automatically enter or compute data based on other fields' values, document status, and many other conditions (see Chapter 14). There are three types of computed fields:

- Computed: Computed fields contain formulas that recalculate every time the user creates, recalculates, or saves the document.

- Computed When Composed: Computed when composed fields contain formulas that calculate only when the document is first created. The values of these fields can still be changed using buttons, agents, and LotusScript, but they will never recalculate on their own. They are typically fields that store information that becomes static after the document has been created, such as the author or the created date.

- Computed For Display: Computed for display fields contain formulas that recompute every time the document is opened or recalculated, but their contents are never saved with the document. They are temporary fields whose values are relevant only to the currently open document. Because they aren't saved with the document, they can't be displayed in a view.

■ Allow multi-values: If multiple values will be accepted in a field, select the Allow multi-values checkbox. Multivalue fields are useful if you have a field that can contain more than one value. For example, you might want to have a field where someone can enter names of people who can edit a document, or where someone can assign multiple dates or numbers.

■ Compute After Validation: Computed fields are typically recalculated every time the document is created, recalculated (refreshed), or saved. Selecting the Compute After Validation option ensures that the formula for this field won't be calculated until after all the other fields have been validated. This is useful when the formula of one field is dependent on the values stored in other fields.

For more information on field types and formula types, see the section "Field Types" later in this chapter.

Table 11.2 Internal Fields

Field Name	Description
Form	The name of the form used to create the document or the name of the form most recently used to save the document. Use the form in views to select documents created with the form.
PostedDate	Indicates that a document has been mailed and shows the time and date it was mailed.
$Title	Used with a form that is stored in the document.
$Info	Used with a form that is stored in the document.
$WindowTitle	Used with a form that is stored in the document.
$Body	Used with a form that is stored in the document.
$Actions	Used with a form that is stored in the document.
$UpdatedBy	Lists the document's authors and editors. Anonymous forms don't have this field.
$Anonymous	If Anonymous Form was enabled for this form, there is no $UpdatedBy field. Instead, there is an $Anonymous field with a value of 1.
$Readers	Lists authorized readers if the document contains a read access list.
$Revisions	Lists the date and time of each editing session since the first time the document was saved.
$File	Shows an entry for each attachment in the document.
$Links	Shows an entry for each link in the document.
$PublicAccess	Assigning a value of 1 gives users with No Access or Depositor access the ability to view specific documents or forms without giving them reader access to the entire database.
$VersionOpt	Contains a value from 1 to 6 that allows users to create new versions of edited documents on a document-by-document basis.
$$HTMLHead	Lets you pass HTML information (for example, meta tags and JavaScript) to the head tag for a document. This is valid only when the form property is "For Web access: Treat document contents as HTML."
$$Return	Lets you override the default confirmation message when Web pages are submitted to Domino.

Table 11.3 Reserved Field Names

Field Name	Value	Description
BlindCopyTo	Names	Blind-mails recipients.
Categories	User-defined	Used to categorize documents in views.
CopyTo	Names	Copied mail recipients.
DeliveryReport, DeliveryPriority	L, N, H	Values dictate low-, medium-, or high-priority options.
Encrypt FolderOptions	1, 0	Use 1 to encrypt mailed documents.
MailFormat	T, E, B, M	Lets cc:Mail users view Notes documents in a variety of predefined formats.
MailOptions	1, 0	Use 1 for automatic mailing.
ReturnReceipt	1, 0	Use 1 to send a receipt when the document is opened by the recipient.
SaveOptions	1, 0	Use 1 to save mailed documents.
SecretEncryptionKeys	User-defined	A function of using secret encryption keys.
SendTo	Names	Mail recipients. Required for all forms that mail documents.
Sign	1, 0	Use 1 to an add an electronic signature to fields. Applicable only if a form also contains sign-enabled fields.

Choosing Options   In the Options tab, shown in Figure 11.25, you can define help descriptions, address security issues, and define multiple-value separators. The following list details these options:

- Help description: If provided, the optional Help description appears as a one-line prompt at the bottom of the form window when the mouse pointer is placed in that field. For example, "Enter the date that the loan closed" is a poor example of field help description, because it fails to inform the user how to enter the date. A better example would be "Enter the date that the loan closed using the format MM\DD\YY."

 TIP   Try to make the Help description useful and indicate the field's general purpose. Use a pop-up on the form if you can't fit all the information into this field's text box. To toggle the display of field help, select View, Show, Field Help. The document must be in edit mode in order to display the field help.

FIG. 11.25

The Options tab in the Field Properties InfoBox is where you supply help instructions and apply multivalue features.

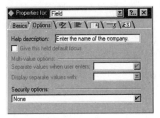

- Give this field default focus: This feature automatically moves the mouse pointer to a particular field location when the document is created or opened in edit mode. If this option isn't selected, the cursor moves to the first editable field on the form.

- Multi-value options: This section lets you handle multivalues in a field. This section is available only if Allow multi-values was selected on the Basics tab. You have two options when working with multivalue options. The Separate values when user enters option determines the multivalue separator when the field is being edited. The Display separate values with option determines how multivalue fields are displayed in read mode. You need to define either of these options and then the corresponding separator value (Space, Comma, Semicolon, New Line, or Blank Line).

  The Separate values when user enters option lets you give users choices for entering text. If the field is editable, it's best to allow several kinds of separators so that users can separate entries as they want.

  If you allow only one separator, such as a comma, users must use that separator to prevent Notes from reading multiple entries as a single entry.

  The Display separate values with option lets you define how the multivalue entries appear. To align and separate multiple values on the form, use the ruler (Ctrl+R) to create a hanging indent where the field begins. Select New Line for both the input and display separator.

- Security options: Here you can select Sign if mailed or saved in section, Enable encryption for this field, or Must have at least Editor access to use to enable security features for particular situations.

  Select Sign if mailed or saved in section to determine whether mailed documents are signed or encrypted automatically during mailing. These override the users' settings in the Document Save dialog box. Select Enable encryption for this field to activate the encryption of a field when it is saved. Select Must have at least Editor access to use to define whether a user must have at least Editor access to modify the field.

The following options aren't supported by Domino on the Web:

Help description

Give this field default focus

Sign if mailed or saved in section

Enable encryption for this field

Note that Web users can read data in encrypted fields.

Setting the Font The Font tab, shown in Figure 11.26, has the letters A and Z in custom fonts. The options on this tab let you easily set or modify the field's font, size, style, and text color. You can also set the permanent pen font for adding comments to a document in a different font.

FIG. 11.26

The Font tab in the Field Properties InfoBox.

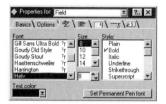

Alignment Settings The Alignment tab, shown in Figure 11.27, lets you define how a field appears. This tab has left-aligned rows of text on it. You can specify the field's alignment, where the first line begins, whether the field is displayed within a list using bullets or numbers, where the left margin begins, and the desired spacing of lines.

FIG. 11.27

The Alignment tab in the Field Properties InfoBox.

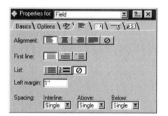

NOTE Make sure these alignment settings work with the settings of the static text in the form. Typically, you set and modify these settings from the form display while you're viewing all the design elements.

Pagination Settings In the Pagination tab, shown in Figure 11.28, you can specify how a form is paginated. This tab looks like a page with the number 1. The Page break before paragraph option lets you keep all the lines in one paragraph on the same page. The Keep paragraph on one page and the Keep paragraph with next paragraph options let you keep consecutive paragraphs on the same page. You can also specify the right margin when printing and the spacing of tabs.

Options for Hiding Fields The options on the Hide tab, shown in Figure 11.29, are often used by Notes developers. (This tab has a window shade.) These options are used to hide data when users are a particular type of client (Web versus Notes 4.6 or later) or when the client is reading, editing, printing, or being evaluated. Developers usually have fields on a form that they use for calculations or to store information that the user doesn't need to see. This information is generally stored at the top or bottom of a form and is hidden from the users.

FIG. 11.28

The Pagination tab has features that are very useful when you're printing documents.

FIG. 11.29

You can hide lines of your form, depending on whether a user is reading, editing, previewing, or printing a form.

> **CAUTION**
>
> Hiding fields is more useful as a formatting option than as a security measure. A user could see hidden data, such as salaries, by selecting File, Document Properties and then going to the Fields tab in the InfoBox when a document is selected. If you want to ensure that data is hidden from users, you should encrypt those fields.

The following sections describe the Hide tab's options for hiding fields.

Hide Paragraph From

- Notes R4.6 or later: When you're designing applications that will be accessible via both native Notes and Web browsers, it might be necessary to hide certain design elements (for example, Web-specific design features) from the Notes clients.

- Web Browsers: This is essentially the opposite of the option Notes R4.6 or later. This hides design features from browsers because either it is not supported by the browser or by Domino, or the functionality has been separately designed for Web browsers.

These two properties are used together when you're designing forms that will be used by both Notes clients as well as Web browsers.

N O T E If you select Hide paragraph from Notes R4.6 or later, Notes automatically sets the Hide paragraph settings when the document is Previewed for reading, Previewed for editing, Printed, and Copied to the clipboard.

It is no longer necessary to use the @UserRoles function to determine whether the client is a Notes or Web client. Now developers can use the @ClientType function. If the client is a Notes client, @ClientType returns "notes." If the client is a Web client, @ClientType returns "web." Therefore, developers can use this function in the Hide formula of a paragraph to hide text, images, and fields, depending on the client type. ▨

Hide Paragraph When Document Is

- Previewed for reading: This option hides the text or field when the document is being read in a preview pane. It can still be seen when it's read or edited.

- Opened for reading: This option hides the text or field when the document is being read. Whenever you hide information in read mode, it is automatically hidden during printing, too.

- Printed: This option hides the text or field when the document is printed. The data isn't hidden when the document is being read unless you also select Opened for reading.

- Previewed for editing: This option hides the text or field when the document is being edited in a preview pane.

- Opened for editing: This option hides the text or field when the document is being edited.

- Copied to the clipboard: This option hides the text or field when the document is copied so that the hidden information isn't copied to the clipboard.

- Hide paragraph if formula is true: You must provide the formula. These formulas can be based on field values, user name, and so on and can be made into complex evaluations. However, using a lot of hide-when attributes decreases the form's performance. Therefore, optimize the evaluations used within these formulas.

N O T E If you select Opened for reading, Notes automatically selects Previewed for reading and Printed. If you select Opened for editing, Notes automatically selects Previewed for editing. ▨

To hide a field or paragraph using any of these options, follow these steps:

1. Select the paragraph(s) or field(s) you want to hide. You can hide only entire lines or paragraphs (delimited by a hard return). Therefore, if you set the properties for one element on a line, all elements on that line (text, graphics, fields, and so on) take on the same hide when properties.

T I P You can use tables (without visible borders) to hide or show multiple design elements in the same row. Each cell in a table has its own paragraph attributes, including its hide-when attributes. Tables also help you with consistent spacing when you're laying out design elements on the form.

2. Select the Hide tab. In the Hide paragraph when document is section, you can select any of the options detailed a moment ago.

Some developers like to place all their hidden fields that are only to be displayed when edited at the very top or bottom of the form with a Hidden Fields label. This makes hidden fields easy to locate if the form has to be modified. With that in mind, read the following Caution.

CAUTION

Notes calculates fields from top to bottom and from left to right in a document. Therefore, the placement of hidden fields is important. Place hidden fields that "reference" fields used throughout the rest of the form at the top of the form, and place hidden fields that are summary or calculated fields at the bottom of the form.

Often, when creating a hidden field, you want the field to be hidden in all cases. Rather than checking all six checkboxes to hide the paragraph or object, simply select Hide paragraph if formula is true and put a 1 in the formula box. This will always evaluate to `true`, thus hiding the object. This also makes it easier to unhide and hide when you're designing, testing, and debugging your applications.

Saving Paragraph Properties as Styles   You can use the Style tab to save combinations of paragraph properties that you use regularly, such as alignment, indentation, and margins, as a named paragraph style. These named styles can then be used to quickly format existing paragraphs.

Suppose that you often write financial reports in italic text with a 2.25-inch left margin. You could save the italic and left margin paragraph properties as a named style called Reports. Then, when you write financial reports, you could format them with the Reports style without having to specify the italic and left margin properties each time. You could select Text, Named Styles, Reports, or you could assign Reports to the cycle key F11, which would allow you to cycle through each of the named styles you have created and assigned to the key.

To create a named style, follow these steps:

1. Create and customize a paragraph to your liking. With the paragraph selected, choose Text, Text Properties to display the Text Properties InfoBox.

2. Select the Style tab. Choose Create Style to display the Create Named Style dialog box, shown in Figure 11.30.

3. Enter a name for the paragraph style.

4. (Optional) Deselect Include font in named style if you don't want to save the selected paragraph's font in the named style.

5. (Optional) Select Make style available for all documents to make the style available when you format paragraphs in other documents in the database.

FIG. 11.30

Creating a named paragraph style is a great time-saving tool for quickly formatting lines in a form.

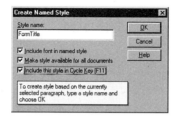

6. (Optional) Select Include this style in Cycle Key (F11) to make the style available when you press F11 to cycle through named styles.

7. Click OK to save your style.

After you create named styles, you can format paragraphs with those styles. To format a paragraph with a named style, follow these steps:

1. Make sure the document is in edit mode.

2. Select the paragraph(s).

3. Do one of the following:

   • Choose Text Named Styles and select a style from the menu that appears.

   • Click the Named Styles indicator on the status bar and select a style from the list that appears.

4. Press F11 or click the Text Style Cycle Key SmartIcon to cycle through the named styles when you format paragraphs.

Understanding the Data Types

Nine data types are available when you create a field. The data type definition lets you define what type of data can be entered into the field. In most cases, you will be dealing with text fields that can accept alphanumeric data such as phone numbers or regional office names. However, you will encounter situations in which your form will require the use of other data types, such as Time, Number, Rich Text, Reader, Author, and Keyword type fields.

It's easy to select and format these field types, but once you begin developing more complex formulas that manipulate the entered data, you will want to know how each data type is stored. The following sections explain in further detail each of the available data types.

▶ **See** Chapter 14, "Working with Formulas," **p. 583**

Text   Text consists of letters, punctuation, spaces, and numbers that are not used mathematically. Company names, addresses, and phone numbers with hyphens are all good examples of the Text data type. Individual text within a Text data type field can't be styled by the user (bold, color, and so on); it can only be plain. The developer of the form, however, can globally change the format for all the data contained in the field.

N O T E To allow a user to format individual pieces of text within a field, you should use rich text as the data type. Here a user can designate bold, underline, and color for various text, lines, and paragraphs. ■

CAUTION

Unlike text fields, whose size is limited to 64K, rich text fields can contain large amounts of data. You should use rich text fields when you need to display text with various formatting styles, graphics, attachments, and OLE objects. However, although you can access the attributes of a rich text field, the contents of the field can't be evaluated. For example, you can't display the contents of a rich text field in views or formulas by using the @Prompt or @Text functions. (For more information, see Chapter 14, "Working with Formulas.")

Time   The Time data type is comprised of both the time and the date; it is made up of letters, numbers, and punctuation. You must use the Time data type if you want Notes to recognize a value as a time-date value; otherwise, it is treated as text.

When the Time data type is selected, the Field Properties InfoBox changes to display the available time and date options, as shown in Figure 11.31.

FIG. 11.31

Notes can format time data in several different time, date, and overall time formats. It's as simple as selecting the displayed option.

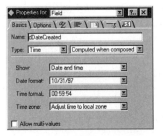

Dates can range from 1/1/1000 through 12/31/9999, whereas times can range from 00:00:00 to 23:59:59 in the 24-hour format and from 12:00:00 a.m. to 11:59:59 p.m. in the 12-hour format. When you're creating time fields, four drop-down boxes determine the formatting of the field:

- Show: Determines whether the field shows the Date and time ("11/22/97 10:35:06 AM"), which is the default, Date only ("11/22/97"), Time only ("10:35:06 AM"), or 'Today' and time ("10:35:06 AM Today"). Using the 'Today' and time setting will display "Today," "Yesterday," or "Tomorrow" rather than the actual date when appropriate.

- Date format: Determines the format of the month, day, and year. The options for the format are mm/dd, mm/yy, and mm/dd/yy (the default).

- Time format: Determines how the time values are stored. The options are hh:mm:ss (the default) and hh:mm.

- Time zone: Determines how the time/date value is handled when you're working with multiple time zones. The options are Adjust time to local zone, which is the default, Always show time zone, and Show only if zone not local.

N O T E You can use formulas to convert text fields to date fields, or vice versa. For example, @TextToTime("07/31/64") converts the text string "07/31/64" to the date 07/31/64. On the other hand, @Text(@Today) converts the value of today's date to text. In addition, when using the @Text function, you can pass parameters that will modify the format to a preferred format. ■

▶ **See** Chapter 14, "Working with Formulas," **p. 583**, for details on writing formulas to convert data types.

As you read in Chapter 1, "Getting Started with Lotus Notes," Notes 4.6 provides some new ways to display date and time fields. If you want your users to be able to select a date or time, you can add the following date and time controls to the design of your form (provided that they are contained within a layout region) by making some special field formatting selections in the Field Properties dialog box:

- Calendar Control: Design a field, set its type to Time, and specify Show Date.
- Time Control: Design a field, set its type to Time, and specify Show Time.
- Time Duration Control: Design a field, set its type to Time, select Allow multiple values, and indicate to separate values with a blank line in the Options panel.

Numbers   The Number data type is used to represent all numbers that need to be displayed or calculated mathematically. It can include any of the 10 numerals (0 to 9), the minus and plus signs (– and +), the decimal point (.), scientific notation (E), and the constant e.

When the data type Number is selected, the Field Properties InfoBox displays the available number options, as shown in Figure 11.32.

Part II

Ch 11

FIG. 11.32
The Number type in the Basics tab lets you define the format for your number field, which is how it will be displayed in Notes.

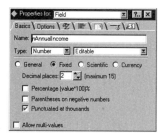

Here are the available Number formats:

- General: Displays numbers as they are entered, with zeroes being suppressed.
- Fixed: Displays numbers with a fixed number of decimal places, as specified in the Decimal places list box.
- Scientific: Displays numbers using exponential notation.
- Currency: Displays values with a currency symbol and two digits after the decimal point.

You can also choose whether to display percentages, parentheses, and punctuation at thousands. Table 11.4 summarizes the available number formats.

Table 11.4 Number Formats

Format	Examples
Integers	123, –123
Decimal fractions	1.23, 0.12, –.123
Scientific notation	1.23E4, 1.23E–4, –1.23E4
Currency	$1.23, ($1.23)

Keywords Keywords are a list of predefined values for a field that a user can select from. For example, you might want the user to select from a list of keywords for a field named BranchOffice. Notes stores keywords as text, but the keywords don't have to be made up of text characters. Using keywords lends consistency to the values that appear in the database documents, because each user has the same set of values to choose from when entering information into a keyword field.

To create a keyword list, follow these steps:

1. After creating the field, select Keywords as the data type in the Type list box, as shown in Figure 11.33.

FIG. 11.33
Creating a simple keyword field will allow the user to select from predefined lists of data when entering data.

2. Select whether the field is to be editable or computed. Keyword fields are editable because you want the user to choose the desired keyword from the list you provide. If you want the value calculated, make the field a text field instead.

3. In the Choices list box, select one of the following:

    Enter choices (one per line): This is the quickest option when you're building keyword lists. It can work well if the keywords will always be simple options such as Yes, No, and Maybe. However, read the following Tip.

    Use formula for choices: Developers like to use this technique to query other databases (mainly Notes) and bring in a view column of keywords. Using @DbLookup or @DbColumn makes your code more modular and easier to maintain. See the following Tip.

It's common practice for new Notes developers (and some experienced developers) to hardcode the keyword lists when designing applications using the Enter choices option. However, this limits the option of customization, because only Notes developers can go back in and change the options within a keyword (and with some schedules, corporate policies, and bureaucracies, this can take time). It is more efficient to have these keyword lists based on a formula using the @DbLookup function (or @DbColumn) against documents in a special hidden keyword view. Then, you can allow only designated administrators (or developers) access to modify the documents in a restricted access view. Using this method, all keyword lists can be easily administered in a single location, by non-Notes developers, in a timely fashion. For more information on using @DbLookups and @DbColumns, see Chapter 14, "Working with Formulas."

Use Address dialog for choices: This lets you use the Address Book as the keyword list, which is convenient if you're building a keyword list of names contained in your Address Book. When you select this option, another checkbox appears, allowing you to set Look up names as each character is entered. Selecting this option causes Notes to automatically look up names that match the text currently typed in the field, similar to the type-ahead functionality used when addressing mail using NotesMail.

Use Access Control List for choices: This lets you pull in the predefined Access Control List for the current database to build the keyword list. This handy feature lets Notes developers build more flexible security features into a database, such as possibly allowing users to choose who can access a document that they create. This might not be as useful if you have defined groups in the ACL instead of actual user names.

Use View dialog for choices: This lets you select a view to display choices from. The dialog box actually displays the Notes view within the dialog window, similar to using the @Picklist function. The column number value determines the value returned based on the user selection, which doesn't have to be displayed in the dialog box. In fact, the value returned by the dialog can actually be a hidden column in the view. This feature is useful when the selections in a keyword list aren't based on static lists but on a dynamic list of values determined by existing Notes documents—for example, all the current categories saved with existing documents.

4. If the Choices are based on Enter choice (one per line), in the keyword text section, enter each keyword followed by a hard return. Figure 11.33 has a "one per line" keyword list using Yes, No, and Maybe. You can sort the list after entering it by clicking the Sort button.

If the Choices are based on Use formula for choices, enter the formula in the formula window. This is typically a @DbColumn or @DbLookup formula that returns a text list for options. You can click the Formula Window button to open the Edit Formula window. This displays a larger window to edit the formula, as well as the Fields & Functions button, which helps you with the formula design. Here is an example of a formula that returns a text list based on values in the first column of a view with an alias of Category that is in the same database as the current form:

Part II
Ch 11

```
View := "Category";
Temp := @Unique(@DbColumn(""; ""; View; 1));
@If(@IsError(Temp) ¦ Temp = ""; "There currently are no categories
created."; Temp)
```

For more information on writing formulas, see Chapter 14, "Working with Formulas."

5. Select Allow values not in list if you want users to be able to enter additional keywords in your list. This checkbox is available for all the keyword types except when the view dialog is used for choices and when keywords are used within layout regions. You can also select Allow multi-values to allow the user to select multiple entries from the keyword list.

TIP Select Allow multi-values when you want to associate a document with multiple keywords. This is very useful when you're building views that require a document to be shown in multiple categories.

CAUTION

Any keywords entered by users will be accepted in the field but won't be added to the list permanently. The newly added keyword will appear in the keyword list only for that document.

To determine how you want the keyword list to be displayed, select the Display tab (the second tab) in the field's Properties InfoBox to choose an interface style for displaying the keywords (see Figure 11.34). You can choose from three methods for displaying the list of keywords to users, plus designate the frame type and number of columns.

FIG. 11.34

Selecting the interface style for your keyword list lets you creatively display your available options when a user inputs the data.

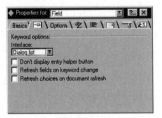

- Dialog list: Presents a standard field interface. Users can press the spacebar to cycle through the list and type the first letter of the appropriate item to display it. If several items have the same first letter, users can begin to type the first few letters of the word to display the appropriate choice or press Enter to display the keyword dialog box that lists all the items. This interface gives you the option of allowing users to enter items not included on the list (select Allow values not in this list); however, the additional items are not added to the list for future use.

- Checkboxes: Presents a list of checkboxes, each representing one list item, as shown in Figure 11.35. Users can select more than one of the available keywords.

FIG. 11.35
Keywords can be formatted with checkboxes using a 3D frame, standard frame, or no frame with one or more columns. Checkboxes let users select multiple keywords.

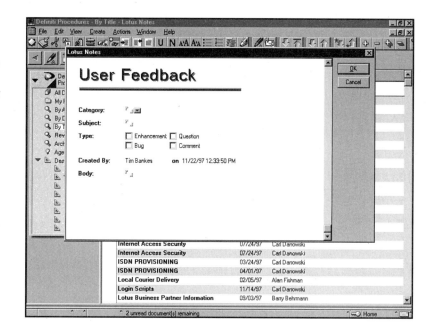

■ Radio buttons: Presents a horizontal list of radio buttons, each representing one list item. Users can select only one item. Figure 11.36 shows how radio button keywords will appear.

FIG. 11.36
Keywords can be formatted with radio buttons using a 3D frame with two columns. Radio buttons let users select only one keyword.

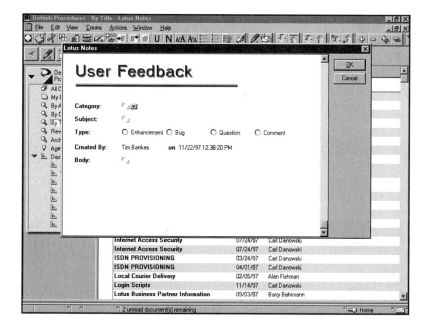

Part
II

Ch
11

N O T E You can also change the way the Checkbox and Radio Button keywords display on the form by selecting the Keyword Options tab (it has a rectangle on it) in the Field Properties dialog box. You can elect to have the keywords displayed horizontally rather than vertically. You can also choose to display them in 3D, with the standard frame or no frame around the selections. You can also choose to refresh fields on keyword change and refresh choices on document refresh.

Keep the user in mind when you're deciding how the keywords will be displayed. Users can get confused if each instance of keywords looks different than the last. Stay consistent throughout your design. Also, although using checkboxes and radio buttons can help facilitate data entry, they can take up quite a bit of room when you're reading your documents. You might want to create a second field on the form that inherits the values from the keyword selections but is displayed only when you're reading and printing. Then set the keyword selection fields to display only when you're editing. ■

Select Don't display Entry Helper button if you don't want to display the Entry Helper button (see Figure 11.37). This is available only for dialog box list keywords. This button helps the users easily identify keyword lists when inputting data. It also lets them enter data using the mouse instead of pressing a key in the field.

FIG. 11.37
The display Entry Helper button displays the dialog box list of keywords when clicked.

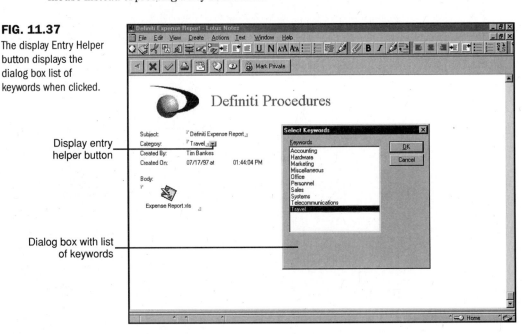

Display entry helper button

Dialog box with list of keywords

You can also select Refresh fields on keyword change to automatically change other fields within the document that might be using that keyword selection in a formula. This is important if other fields are based on the current keyword selection, because you want them to be updated to display the correct information.

After you finish setting up the keyword field, apply any formatting options you want, close the Field Properties InfoBox, and save the form (or press Ctrl+S or click the File Save SmartIcon).

TIP Always test your keyword list by selecting <u>D</u>esign, Preview in No<u>t</u>es when editing the form's design. This is a quick and accurate way of testing the functionality and layout of all the design elements.

You can also create synonyms for your keywords, which allows you to display one set of keywords to the user while storing another in the document. This is helpful if the keyword is actually a phrase, but it is only necessary to store a single value or to store a value of 1 or 0 instead of a Yes or No value. Keyword synonyms are designated by using | followed by the synonym. Here is a keywords list for a Type of Loan field with synonyms:

- Commercial | C
- Private | P
- Real Estate | R

The leftmost name is displayed within the document, while both the name and the synonym (the rightmost name after |) are stored internally. If you categorize a view based on a keywords field, the keyword synonyms will be used as the category names.

NOTE Keyword fields aren't rendered on the Web client the same as they appear with a Notes client. Here are some points to consider when designing keyword fields for Web browsers:

- The option Allow values not in list isn't supported. The user will be forced to select from the keyword list.
- When you use Allow multi-values, multiple values can't be selected. In addition, all the choices will be visible at once.
- The Entry Helper button isn't supported on the Web and won't be visible.
- When you use Refresh fields on keyword change, fields are refreshed after the document is submitted.
- The option Refresh choices on document refresh isn't supported by Domino. The document must be submitted and then reopened for editing in order to recalculate the fields.

Rich Text   Rich text information may contain text, tables, embedded or linked objects, file attachments, URL links, Java applets, or graphics. The text in a rich text field can be individually styled (bold, color, and so on) with the Text Font command. A text field can't be individually styled, and all its contents are the same font and size.

Rich text fields are more versatile than text fields, but they have two limitations: They can't be combined with other data types in a @Function, and they can't be displayed in a view. However, they aren't constrained by the physical 64K limit imposed on other field types, including text fields. Because Notes is a rich object store, if there is an object that you can store in a computer, you can probably put it into a rich text field!

Authors   Authors is a data type that contains a list of user names (group names and access roles may also be used) that indicates who can edit a given document (see Figure 11.38). The user name should always be entered as a Notes user name. For instance, if a user's name in

Notes is Jim Brown/ABC Corp, his name should be entered the same way in an Authors field. The name entered is stored in the document as a fully distinguished name in hierarchical format. Authors fields are an interesting and integral part of security in Notes applications and documents, because they provide another level of security beyond the ACL.

FIG. 11.38

An Authors field lets you indicate who can edit a given document.

Most often, few applications will allow anyone to edit all the documents in a database (Editor-level access), so an Authors field should be included in all your forms. If an Authors field has been created but its value is null, it enforces no restrictions, as if it weren't even there. However, once it is populated with even one name, all people (given Author access in the database ACL) not listed will no longer have rights to edit this document.

In most situations, you will want the user who originally composed a document to be able to edit the document later. To enable this option, include at least one field that is an Authors data type. This field should be a Computed When Composed field that has @UserName as the default field formula.

A document can contain multiple Authors fields. This is useful when you want to display the name of the document's original author in one field and then designate Editor access to additional users with another field. Any user listed in any of a document's Authors fields can edit the document.

N O T E The Authors field can't override the database access control settings; it can only refine them. Any names listed in the Authors field are, by default, given Reader access even if they aren't listed in the Readers field (if one exists). ■

▶ **See** Chapter 14, "Working with Formulas," **p. 583**

CAUTION

If the Authors field on a document is blank, it acts as if the field isn't there. Unless the original author has Editor access or above in the ACL, he won't be able to edit the document. This can occur quite often (if you don't include a formula, it still calculates the username) if you allow the field to be editable and the user accidentally removes his name as the author.

T I P Click and hold the Authors field in read or edit mode to display the contents of the $UpdatedBy field.

N O T E If a user says he can't edit his own documents, verify that an Authors field exists and that it contains the user's name.

If you choose to make the Authors field editable, you can generate the list of choices in the Authors field by choosing one of the following options from the Choices list box on the Basics tab:

- None: In this situation, you must rely on a formula or on the authors to create the list of names.
- Use Address dialog for choices: This option displays the Names dialog box so that users can select names from a Personal or Public Address Book. Select Look up names as each character is entered to help users fill in a name quickly. Notes looks for a match for the character in the open Address Book.
- Use access control list for choices: This option brings up a list of people, servers, groups, and roles in the access control list, which is a smaller subset than the Address book.
- Use View dialog for choices: This option brings up a dialog box containing entries from a column in a Notes database view. Select the database to look up, select a view, and select a column number. This is similar to using a @DbColumn formula to obtain a list of users.

N O T E You must select Allow multi-values for an Authors field to store a text list with multiple names. Concatenate the names in the formula with colons.

N O T E The ability to use the Address dialog, the access control list, and the View dialog isn't supported by Domino when you're publishing to the Web because the access of Web users is based on the authenticated name.

Readers Similar to the Authors data type is Readers, which contains a text list of usernames (group names and access roles may also be used) that determines who can read documents.

If the list is provided, users can control read access to a particular document. If the document also contains a read access list, the two lists are combined. If a Readers field doesn't exist, the ACL defines who can read the documents. Users not included in a Readers field (regardless of ACL rights) can't see the document in any view and therefore can't read the document. In fact, if a user who isn't listed in the Readers field makes a local replica of the database, the document won't be replicated. This includes database managers. A Readers field has the same choices to generate a list of readers as an Authors field. See the preceding section for an explanation of these choices.

Part

II

Ch

11

N O T E   Readers is similar to Authors, except that it limits read access to a document instead of granting edit access. It is important to remember that Readers and Authors fields can further restrict, but can't extend, a user's capabilities.

If a Readers field exists on a document but is null, Notes will act as though the field doesn't exist, thereby granting reader rights to all users (assuming that they have sufficient database access rights).

Names provides a means of displaying distinguished names in various formats. Distinguished names are always stored internally in their canonicalized format, listing all components of the name along with their labels. The Names field displays only the Common Name component of a distinguished name—that is, the person's first and last name.

A Names field converts hierarchical names to a cleaner, abbreviated form, such as

```
Richard Bankes/Management/US
```

instead of

```
Richard Bankes=CN/Management=O/US=G
```

Use this type of field when you want to show usernames as they appear on Notes IDs.

Use the Names field to display a list of usernames or server names where an Author Names or Reader Names field is inappropriate because you aren't trying to assign read or write access, such as when you're using a SendTo field in a workflow application.

Field Types

The field type determines whether the data is user-entered or calculated. Not all field types are available for all data types, so be sure your selection makes sense. The four field types are Editable, Computed, Computed for Display, and Computed When Composed.

All three of the Computed field types are noneditable, meaning that the developer supplies the data or value automatically via a formula; the user can't modify it. The purpose of Computed fields is to automatically generate data, such as time and author names, and then protect that information from being updated by the user.

Editable

Every form will contain some Editable fields, because you usually want the user to enter some data. After the user enters data, it is stored with the document. As part of an Editable field, you can do the following:

- Optionally define a default value formula that forces an initial value to appear when the user composes the document
- Utilize an input translation formula that converts the date the user enters or an input validation formula that checks the validity of the user's input

■ Begin utilizing the LotusScript programming language to create an event to run when the user enters or exits a field

Computed

Computed fields are automatically calculated upon composing and can be used with any data. Computed fields allow only one formula. You enter this formula in the Programmer pane by selecting the event Value. As a developer, you supply the value using either a constant or a formula that calculates the value.

Computed fields are used to provide field values based on calculations and manipulation of entered data. It is important to remember that this value is recalculated every time the document is refreshed and saved. An cxample of the use of Computed fields is to capture the name of the document's author in an Authors field and the date the document was created in a date.

▶ **See** Chapter 14, "Working with Formulas," **p. 583**

Computed When Composed

This field is very similar to a Computed field, except as the type states, the field value is computed only when the document is first created. This field type can be used with any data type except rich text. Fields that inherit information from another document are often Computed When Composed fields, since inheritance also happens only when a document is first created (see Figure 11.39). See the earlier section "Understanding Form Hierarchy and Types," which explains response documents. These values aren't permanently locked, because these and other fields can still be changed through other field formulas or agents that are contained in the document.

Part

II

Ch

11

FIG. 11.39
This field in a response document would inherit the Subject field from its parent document. The field name OriginalSubject dictates that the form will inherit the Subject data in the parent document.

Computed for Display

The value of a Computed for Display field is determined when the document is opened. The value isn't stored in the document. Instead, it's calculated for display every time the document is opened for reading or editing and is recalculated every time the document is refreshed. You can use this with any data type except rich text.

A good example of its use is to display the current time or the date the document was created, because these values are automatically stored internally with each document. Developers also use Computed for Display fields to present information contained in another field in a different format.

> **CAUTION**
>
> You can't display the contents of a Computed for Display field in a view because it isn't a value stored in the document. Also, it's not a good idea to use a lot of these field types on a form, because they can slow down performance when you open a document.

N O T E With Computed or Computed for Display fields, you can delay computing until after input validation formulas have been run by selecting Compute After Validation. Input validation formulas are used to verify that the information entered in a field meets certain criteria or to verify that a required field has been filled in. This can help you speed up data entry.

The ability to compute after validation isn't supported by Domino or Web clients. For more information, see the section "Basic Settings" earlier in this chapter. ■

Editable Field Formulas

Every field type accepts at least one formula. Editable fields can accept up to three formulas, and Computed (noneditable) fields can contain one formula. The three field formulas for editable fields are Default Value Formula, Input Translation Formula, and Input Validation Formula.

The formulas are optional, meaning that you don't have to supply a formula for any of the three. But if you want to manipulate or automate data entry, you will have to provide formulas. For example, after the user enters his data, you could convert the entry to proper case letters, trim the value, and then validate the entry to make sure it meets certain requirements.

Formulas are written in the Programmer pane, which is located at the bottom of the screen when you're editing a form. You can display it by selecting View, Design Pane. You can easily switch between the various fields by selecting the desired field in the Define list box to display the field's corresponding events, such as Default, Input Translation, and Input Validation formulas, in the Event list box.

When building formulas, you can also easily click the Fields & Functions button in the Programmer pane to display a list of available Fields and Notes programming functions.

Default Value Formula

Default Value formulas provide an initial value for the field, which the user can either accept or edit. Providing a default value ensures that the field gets filled in and often removes the need for users to enter data such as their names or the date.

You can supply a constant such as "U.S.A." for a text field or 0.05 for a number field, or a formula that resolves to an appropriate value, such as Subtotal * 1.05. To construct the default formula, just write the expression; no assignment statement is needed (see Figure 11.40). However, if the Subtotal field used in the formula Subtotal * 1.05 is blank, an error will occur.

FIG. 11.40

Supplying the constant "OH" for the text field tCompanyState.

N O T E At first you might assume that the default field value is calculated only once when the document is first created. However, technically this isn't true. When a document is opened with a particular form, the default value will calculate *whenever the field doesn't already exist in the document*. Of course, when a document is first created, it has no fields, so all the respective fields are populated with the default values. But if a field was removed from the document and opened again with the form, it would be populated with the default field value again, since it doesn't exist. Similarly, if an existing document was opened with a different form than the form it was created with, any fields with default values in the new form that don't already exist in the document would be populated with their respective default values. In most cases, documents are opened with the same form they were created with, but it's important to note that just because it is an old document doesn't mean it will ignore default field values. ▓

 T I P If you want a text string in the formula to be entered as text (literally), you must enclose it in quotation marks (" "). For number fields, you need to enter the number. For example, 100 enters the number 100. You might want to have the default formula use another field and its value. For example, entering Price in the formula enters the value of the field named Price. Field names don't need quotation marks.

Input Translation Formula

An Input Translation formula converts information entered by the user to adjust the field value or make the field conform to a specific format. Developers generally use Input Translation formulas to convert text to proper capitalization or to delete blank spaces. It's important to remember that this formula executes when the document containing the field is saved or refreshed, and it must evaluate to a value suitable for storage in the current field.

When constructing the formula, be sure to reference the field name. For example, an input translation formula for the Company Name field might trim the user input (for example, @Trim(tCompanyName)), and for the phone field, apply a certain format.

Input Validation Formula

The Input Validation formula compares the data entered by the user to criteria specified by you in the formula. If the data satisfies the criteria, it is accepted; otherwise, a message is displayed. For example, an Input Validation formula for the tCompanyName field might ensure that a value exists:

```
@If(tCompanyName = ""; @Failure("You must enter a Company Name prior to sav-
ing!"); @Success)
```

The important point to remember is that this formula executes after the Input Translation formula and when the document is saved or refreshed.

If a particular field fails when the validation formula runs, the cursor is automatically placed in the offending field.

An Input Validation formula usually uses the following three @Functions:

- @If: Lets you test a condition and perform actions based on the result.
- @Success: Instructs Notes to accept the value if the condition is true.
- @Failure: Instructs Notes not to accept the value if the condition is false and to prevent the user from saving the document. This displays the message that you supply as an argument in this @Function. Be sure to display a message that clearly indicates what is wrong and how the user can correct it.

TIP If a field is required, you should indicate this in the field's Help description.

Validation evaluations can be moved to the Query Save event of the form so that more complex operations can be performed, depending on their current values. See Part III, "Working with LotusScript."

Layout Regions

Notes 4 and later releases have a great new design feature called layout regions, which let you more easily design visually enticing forms. Layout regions allow for the design of combo boxes (drop-down boxes, really), checkboxes, list boxes, radio buttons, and useful calendar and time buttons when Time/Date fields or keyword fields are placed on layout regions (see Figures 11.41 and 11.42). They also allow you to predetermine the vertical and horizontal dimensions of a field and enable scroll boxes, multiline fields, and so on. However, they don't support rich text, shared fields, subforms, computed text, and other robust features. Layout regions aren't supported on the Web. (However, text and fields contained within a layout region will display when viewed from a Web browser, although the formatting is lost because they are automatically left-justified, don't display 3D effects, and so on.) Therefore, don't use layout regions when designing applications for the Web. However, when you're designing applications for native Notes, layout regions facilitate the design of powerful and friendly user interfaces.

FIG. 11.41

The 3D calendar button helper when used within a layout region.

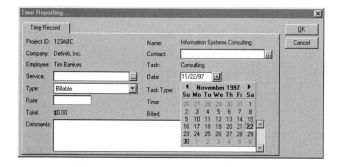

FIG. 11.42

The Time calendar button when used within a layout region. Here it is used as a mulivalue field.

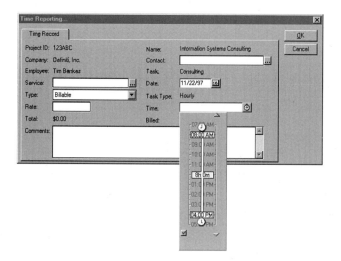

N O T E In order to use the Calendar and Time helper buttons within layout regions, the Time/Date fields must be set up in the following manner:

Calendar helper: The Show setting on the Basics tab of the Field Properties InfoBox must be set to Date only, and it must be a single-value field.

Time helper: The Show setting on the Basics tab of the Field Properties InfoBox must be set to Time only. This can be either a single-value field or a multivalue field. If it is a single-value field, there is only one sliding time bar in the drop-down helper. If it is a multivalue field, there are two slide bars and they returns a date range. ▪

The Personal Journal template (JOURNAL4.NTF) has an excellent example of a layout region in the Docinfo form. Figure 11.43 shows a Time Record form being used in a Time Record database, and Figure 11.44 shows the layout region for that form in design mode.

Part
II

Ch

11

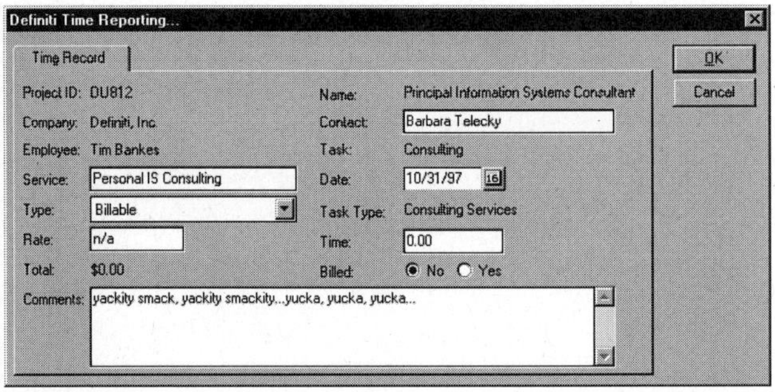

FIG. 11.43
The Time Record
dialog box.

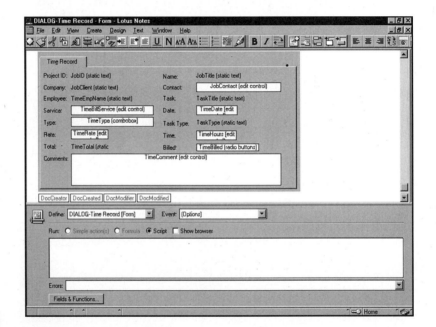

FIG. 11.44
A look at the layout
region in design mode.

Follow these steps to create a layout region:

1. Select the database and choose View, Design.

2. In the Navigation pane, select Design, Forms.

3. Double-click the form you're designing.

4. Move the mouse pointer to the line where you want to place the layout region, and choose Create, Layout Region, New Layout Region. This inserts a frame representing the layout region.

5. Add the desired text, fields, and objects in the region. You can add the following to a layout region, just as you can with forms and subforms: static text, graphics (either in the

background or as graphic buttons), hotspot buttons, and all fields (with greater numbers of display options) except rich text.

6. Save the form.

N O T E Layout regions can't contain rich text, so you can't add the following to a layout region: links, tables, objects, attachments, popups, sections, Java applets, and rich text fields. In addition, layout regions can't contain subforms, computed text, or shared fields. See Table 11.5 for a quick summary. Layout regions aren't supported on the Web. ▪

Table 11.5   Design Elements Within Layout Regions

Allowable Design Elements	Design Elements Not Allowed
Static text	Computed text
Graphic buttons	Popups and hotspots
Graphic background	Links
Field types other than rich text	Rich text
Buttons	Objects
Calendar entry buttons	Attachments
Combo boxes	Sections
List boxes	Tables

T I P When creating layout regions, you will need to define the properties for the region in the Layout Properties InfoBox, shown in Figure 11.45. You can access it by selecting the layout region and then selecting Design, Layout Properties. Here you can define margins, widths, 3D effects, borders, snapping to grid, and hiding options.

N O T E As you will discover quickly if you use layout regions, printing layout regions can often be a problem. One of the most commonly reported problems with printing layout regions is that many of the field values don't print with the layout region, or they aren't properly positioned on the page. If you experience these problems, try making a second field on the layout that is computed and that inherits its value from the field used for data entry. Have this second field display only when printing, and have the original field used for data entry hidden when printing. You can stack these fields on top of each other in the layout's design to stay consistent with your design. You should now be able to see your data when it is printed. Of course, this creates additional fields and overhead on the layout region and form. You might also consider creating separate sections or forms that are used when printing the document. ▪

Part
II

Ch
11

FIG. 11.45
The Layout Properties InfoBox allows you to choose various options for your layout region.

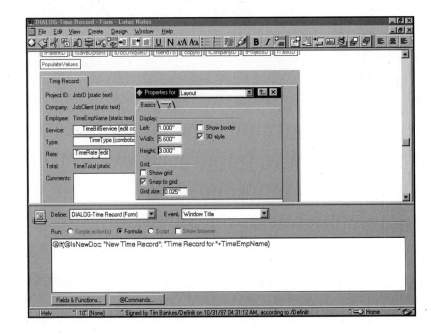

> **CAUTION**
>
> Do not use layout regions in Web-enabled applications. They will render the fields to the screen, but they will become automatically left-justified and won't perform in an expected manner.

Subforms

A subform is an excellent form-building shortcut that allows you to store often-used fields and other form elements together. Subforms are objects placed within forms that can be reused across multiple forms and applications. Subforms are similar to shared fields, because they allow you to use the same fields in multiple forms within the database. However, subforms act more like forms, sharing much of the same functionality. Subforms can contain static text, images (such as a corporate logo), a set of fields, buttons, Action Bar buttons, tables, layout regions, and LotusScript that can be applied across various portions of the application. Changes made to an existing subform are immediately reflected to all the forms using that subform.

N O T E The formula for computed subforms is evaluated only once, when the form is first loaded. Therefore, the variables used in the computed subform formula must be valid when the document is loading and won't recalculate when the document is recalculated. Subforms can't contain other subforms. ▪

The Document Library R4.6 (DOCLIBM.NTF) provides an excellent example of using a subform in the database. Figure 11.46 shows the subform Shared Response Header and its elements. Figure 11.47 shows this subform inserted in another form within that same database. This development technique will save you a lot of time.

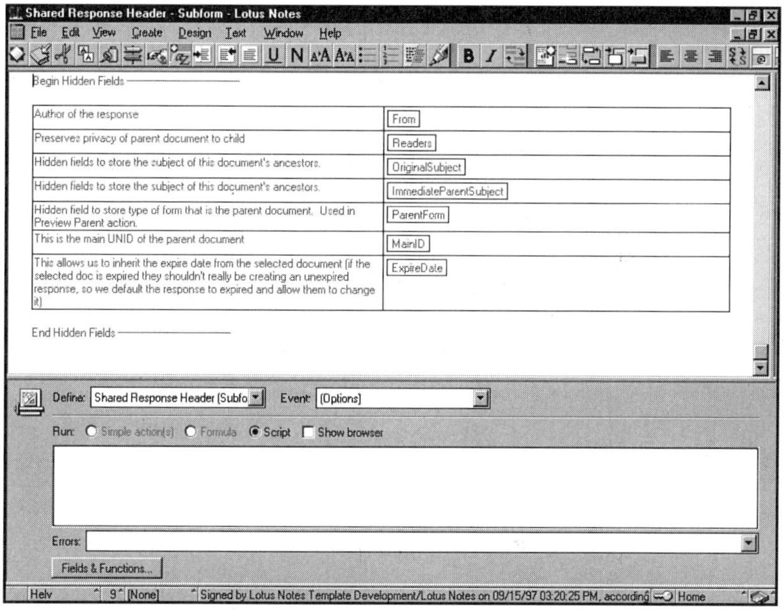

FIG. 11.46
The subform Shared Response is used multiple times in other forms in the Document Library R4.6 database.

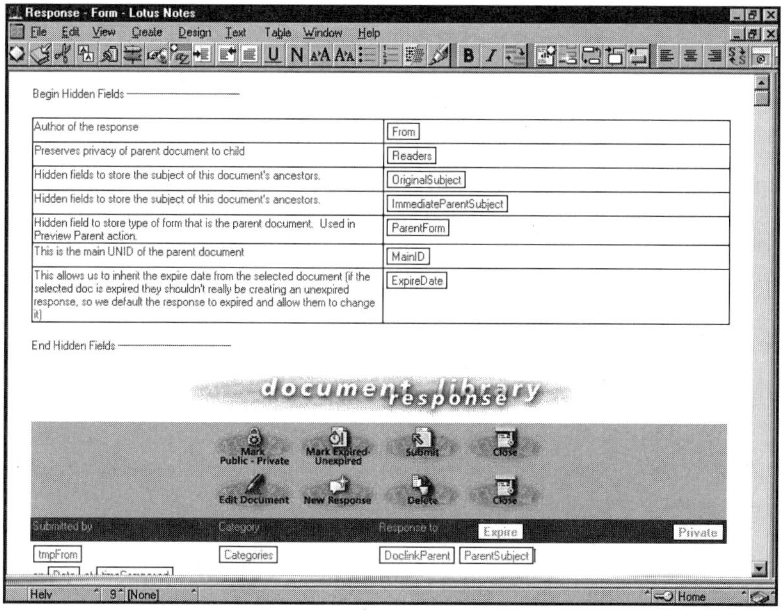

FIG. 11.47
Here's the subform being utilized in the Response form of the Document Library R4.6.

N O T E You can edit previously created subforms by clicking them directly in a form or by selecting Design Subforms in the navigation pane. ■

CAUTION

You can't add other fields to the form that have the same name as those on the subform, because this would be an attempt to have two fields with the same name on one form.

The subform, which stores a group of form elements as a single design element, must have been created in advance. Subforms can contain the same components as regular forms. To create a new subform, follow these steps:

1. Select the database that will have the new subform, and choose Create, Design, Subform.

2. Choose Design, Subform Properties.

3. Name the new subform using the same rules as for forms.

4. In the Basics tab, choose the desired options for the subform: Include in Insert Subform dialog, Include in New Form dialog, or Hide Subform for Notes 3 users.

5. Save the subform.

To insert a previously created subform, follow these steps:

1. Open the desired form in edit mode, place the insertion point where you want to paste the subform, and choose Create, Insert Subform. The Insert Subform dialog box appears, as shown in Figure 11.48.

FIG. 11.48
The Insert Subform dialog box lets you place previously created subforms into your forms. Think of subforms as libraries of grouped fields that can be reused.

2. Select the subform you want to use, and click OK to insert the subform into your form.

3. Save the form.

N O T E Subforms can be loaded into the host form based on a subform formula. Therefore, entire blocks of content can change, depending on a formula evaluation. This allows for reusable code and objects stored within the subforms and is more efficient than overusing hide-when formulas. However, subform formulas evaluate only once—when the form loads—and can't be recalculated. ■

▶ **See** Chapter 14, "Working with Formulas," **p. 583**

Tables

Tables are useful for summarizing information or lining up fields in rows and columns. A table placed on a form appears in every document created with the form. You can use tables to organize information or line up fields in rows and columns. Tables within forms can contain text, buttons, objects, or graphics. You can even omit the cell borders if you want to create an "invisible" table.

To create a table on a form, follow these steps:

1. In the selected form, move the mouse pointer to the location where you want to place the table.

2. Choose Create, Table.

3. Specify the starting number of rows and columns for the table, and click OK. Figure 11.49 shows a three-row, two-column table.

Table Menu

FIG. 11.49

Tables in forms are great for organizing and aligning fields. Use the Table menu or the Table Properties InfoBox to modify your tables.

Inserted Table

Table Properties InfoBox

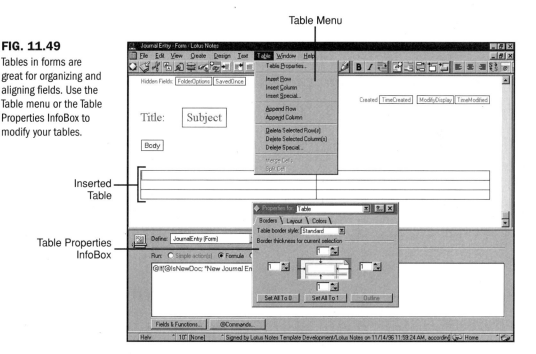

Part II

Ch 11

Use the Table Properties InfoBox to change border styles (standard, extruded, or embossed) and spacing for the currently highlighted area within the table. You can also highlight the table or individual rows or columns and choose Text, Text Properties to change the style of text or to hide text for the highlighted area.

Each individual cell has its paragraph attributes. Therefore, you can apply different hide-when formulas, text attributes, and so on to each cell.

Tables can contain rich text, graphics, objects, links, horizontal rules, hotspot buttons, attachments, computed text, and so on. However, they can't contain layout regions, subforms, or tables within tables.

Notes 4.6 lets you merge cells either horizontally or vertically to allow you to use one table with various sizes of rows and columns.

You can also set the background color of any, or all, cells in a table as well as make the table transparent so that a graphic background will be visible behind the table.

4. Click the form and save it.

N O T E Tables are especially useful when you're designing Web pages since HTML ignores spaces, tabs, and carriage returns. Keep the following points in mind when designing tables that will be rendered with a browser:

- Domino will use the column widths defined in the table.
- Table lines are either on for the entire table or off for the entire table. Therefore, if any cell border is turned on, all the cell borders will be visible.
- Tables are useful when you're formatting multicolumn keyword fields, such as radio buttons and checkboxes.
- You can add HTML code to a table cell to further enhance elements within the cell. ■

Sections

Sections are useful for organizing documents that contain a lot of information. You can use sections to collapse one or more paragraphs in a document into a single line or to limit access to specific areas of a form. Sections make navigating large documents easier. Readers can expand a section when they want to read its contents. Developers like to group related information in a large document into different sections.

▶ **See** "Creating Sections in Documents," **p. 337**

To create a collapsible or controlled-access section, follow these steps:

1. Open the desired form in edit mode.
2. Select and highlight the paragraph(s) you want to collapse into a section.
3. Select Create, Section, Standard or Create, Section, Controlled Access.

 Notes uses the first paragraph as the section title by default. To change a section's title, you must use the Section Properties InfoBox.

N O T E When designing applications for the Web, Domino supports collapsible sections and access-controlled sections. In addition, the following section properties are supported on the Web:

- The ability to display and hide section titles
- The ability to control when a section is expanded or collapsed
- The ability to control when a section is hidden
- The ability to control the lines that surround a section ▨

Hotspots

Hotspots are very useful for displaying pop-up text, using buttons to invoke a formula process, switching to linked destinations, or activating a Notes action.

▶ **See** "Adding Hotspots to Your Documents," **p. 323**

You can add a hotspot to an area of a document, such as text or a graphic. To create a hotspot, follow these steps:

1. Open the desired form in edit mode.
2. Select the area you want to add the hotspot to.
3. Choose Create, Hotspot. You can now select any of the following:
    - Link Hotspot: This lets you link to a specific document, such as a Help document designed for your database, view, or anchor link. You must select Edit, Copy as Link a portion of text on a target document before selecting this hotspot option.
    - URL Link: This lets you link the selected text or graphic to a specific URL, such as http://www.lotus.com.

N O T E In earlier versions of Notes, any valid URL found in a document was rendered as a hotspot link that wasn't carried over to the Web. Now Domino automatically converts any valid URL found in any part of a document (not only rich text) to a highlighted link on the Web page. ▨

Button: Use this option to create a button and corresponding formula to perform some type of task.

Text Pop-up: This lets you enter the text you want the popup to display.

Formula Pop-up: This lets you enter a formula in the Programmer pane that will set the text you want the popup to display.

Action Hotspot: Use this option to create an action hotspot that performs a specific action defined in the database.

Figure 11.50 displays the Create menu options for the available hotspots.

Part
II

Ch
11

FIG. 11.50

Hotspots are useful for displaying help information, switching to linked destinations, and performing Notes actions.

 In previous versions, Domino recognized only the first button in a document and treated it as a Submit button that closed and saved the document. Now, multiple buttons (or none at all) can be used on forms for Web display. Buttons on forms are no longer evaluated by Domino when they are displayed. Instead, they are evaluated when the user clicks the button. (However, formulas on hotspots and actions are evaluated when the button is displayed.) In order to use multiple buttons on a form (or no buttons at all), the database property "Web Access: use JavaScript when generating pages" must be selected. When creating buttons for Web pages, keep the following tips in mind:

- Domino will hide buttons if the @Commands and @Functions they contain aren't supported on the Web.

- Create only one Submit button per form.

- Images can't be buttons.

- Action Bars and hotspots support only a limited set of actions.

- Navigator image regions can't be used as submit buttons.

- @Command([FileSave]), @Command([FileCloseWindow]), and @Command([ViewRefreshFields]) are now supported.

Improving Form Performance

Because of the many powerful features that you can incorporate into the design of these forms, their performance can sometimes suffer as a result. Here are some general guidelines to follow that will help improve the performance of your Notes forms:

- Avoid overusing graphics and bitmaps, especially if they are large. Notes will compress these images and delay interface load time.

- Don't set the form property to automatically refresh fields. If it's necessary to perform calculations with certain fields, use LotusScript within the entering and exiting events of the respective fields.

- Avoid using long tables or many tables that contain significant number of fields. Also, keep in mind that it takes additional time to load layout regions, subforms (especially computed subforms), and shared fields.

- Try to replace field calculations, form events, and conditional formulas with LotusScript events. This also makes maintenance easier and allows for savvier error-handling routines.

- Optimize the use of @DbLookups and @DbColumns. Design these fields to perform these lookups only once and only when necessary. Combine multiple lookups into a single lookup, parse the data, and then populate the respective fields. Also, minimize script methods that perform similar functions in the same manner.

Designing Views

The secret to developing and building views in Notes is knowing the database's structure and having a vivid understanding of what you want to accomplish with the view. You need to understand what fields, data types, and forms exist in your database. When you know that information, creating views can be very easy. If you have not already created the database forms, stop and go back to Chapter 11, "Designing Forms." The design of the views is directly dependent on the data captured within those forms.

In each Notes database, views list documents and provide a means to access them. Views essentially are tables of contents listing the documents (or subset of documents) in a Notes database. Unlike most printed books, a database can have many tables of contents, each of which selects, sorts, or groups the documents in the database in a specialized way.

In addition to listing the documents stored within a database, views facilitate the following functions:

- Selecting documents to open or to perform an action against.
- Copying and pasting documents, which creates a new unique ID for each document.
- Marking documents for deletion. The user is prompted to delete the selected documents, which are deleted when the view is refreshed or closed.
- Printing selected documents using their respective forms or printing the display of the view.
- Forwarding selected documents via email.
- Searching the documents for specific text.
- Refreshing the view to see changed documents, new documents, or the absence of deleted documents.

Every database must have at least one view; most have multiple views. A view might display all the documents in the database, or it might show only a subset of documents. Which documents are displayed is determined by values stored within them, the access rights of the current user, or various selection formulas defined by the developer. At times, you will want to view the same information in different ways. You might, for example, want to see the information from a Contact or Address database organized and listed by last name, by state, by the date it was created, or by who created it, just to name some possibilities.

Notes allows you to create multiple views for each database. You can design views to display only the documents you specify and to sort them so it's easy to interpret the information. In addition, users can create private views for their own purposes. A private view is accessible only by its creator, though the documents displayed are still accessible by all users with sufficient access control rights.

Understanding the Logistics of Views

As previously mentioned, views are lists of documents in a Notes database. Each row represents a document within the database (or a category of multiple documents). Depending on how they're designed, views can select, sort, or categorize documents in a variety of ways. Views can also show information about the documents listed, such as the author's name or the date of creation. It is important to remember that views might show all documents in a database or only a selection of documents. You can split a view into the following three panes:

- Navigation pane
- View pane
- Preview pane

FIG. 12.1

The three panes that can be displayed within a view. The menu choices and SmartIcons will change depending on which pane has focus.

Navigation pane

View pane

Preview pane

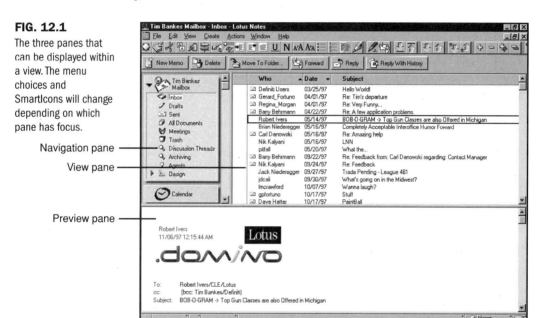

 TIP Select View, Document Preview to toggle the Preview pane. Select View, Arrange Preview to change the location of the View pane and the Preview pane.

NOTE If the design of the database allows for it, you can resize columns by dragging, change the sorting in a column, or change to another view by clicking its title. ■

Views are created by the designer of a database. Users can customize panes and columns to some extent, but they cannot affect a view's design. Each view consists of one or more columns, each of which displays a field or the results of a formula. Think of a view as a report with each column in the report displaying the field information for the individual documents (rows).

Each line (row) in a view usually represents a single document. Notes allows multiple rows or word wrapping for a single document. Columns represent one (or more) type of information (fields) available in the document. The developer writes a selection formula for each view; this formula selects which documents are displayed in that view. The formula can select all documents in the database, or it can select only those that meet certain criteria.

As a user, you can perform several tasks in a view. The following is a list of tasks that can be performed by users. Some of these tasks, however, are dependent on the access control rights assigned to the user (see Chapter 22, "Security and Encryption"):

- Open a document.
- Navigate between documents.
- Find unread documents.
- Forward documents (email) to other Notes users.
- Select documents to act upon (print, export, refresh fields, and so on).
- Delete documents.
- Copy documents.
- Move and copy documents to folders.
- Run agents against selected documents.
- Refresh the view.

Views can be either shared or private. Shared views are available to all database users, unless restricted by a Read access list assigned to the view. A private view can be seen only by the person who created it. Private views are useful when a user wants to see documents organized in a particular way. Think of private views as predetermined queries created by the user. A user's private view, however, can display only documents to which the user already has access; encrypted data and documents that the user does not have Read access for cannot be displayed.

Like forms, views can contain Action Bars at the top of the window. Action Bar buttons can contain simple actions, @Functions, @Commands, a combination of these, or LotusScript. The buttons act the same as within forms; they are nonscrollable and can act on (though are not limited to) the currently selected document(s).

N O T E When designing applications to be published by Domino for Web clients, users do not have access to Notes menu choices. Therefore, you need to create Action Bars, buttons, and hotspots that perform the necessary actions. Select the database property "Web access: Use JavaScript when generating pages" in order to enable all the buttons and to allow specific @Commands. If this property is not set, Domino only recognizes the first button as the submit button, which closes and saves the document. ■

CAUTION

The Domino server displays all buttons, actions, and hotspots regardless of whether the @Commands and @Functions are supported for Web applications.

Be sure to test all views from a Web browser on the Domino server running the HTTP task to make sure the views perform in an expected manner.

Planning a View

Before creating a view in Notes, you should have an idea of what information is important in each document and how it can best be presented to the users. You could sketch the idea on paper, but Notes is a rapid application-development environment and views are not difficult to design or modify. Therefore, it might be quickest to put some basic views together, then simply modify their design per user specifications. Your views should answer questions that might arise when creating views and should include the following information:

- Identify and state the purpose of each view. If the database is made up of main and response documents, it is a good idea for at least one view of the database to show each main document associated with its response documents. It also is a good idea to have a flat, nonhierarchical view that sorts documents by date.

- Do you want to see all the documents or just a subset? Which subset of documents will be displayed? What are the different subsets of the information needed to display.

- Decide how to sort documents in the view. To reduce the number of views, use columns that users can sort themselves using column titles.

- Try to visualize the columns of information (fields). Do you want to include all the fields in columns or just specific fields? Try to avoid using so many columns that the user has to scroll horizontally to see all the data. This is inefficient and annoying for the user. Use multiline rows or multiple views with different categories to display the data. Remember, views represent a summary of the data contained in the documents. They are not meant to display all the fields of each respective document.

- Will unread markers be displayed? Do you want unread documents to appear in a different color or be marked with a star?

- Will the column display field data or be manipulated in a column formula? Sometimes developers combine two fields, such as City and State, into one column using a column formula like City + ", " + State.

- Should responses be indented beneath the parent documents to display the hierarchical relationship? Indenting allows you to organize your related parent/child documents for easier viewing.

■ Do you want to include any view statistics? You might, for example, want to indicate whether a contact entry has had five call reports (responses).

■ Do you want to categorize any columns? Categorization allows you to sort and organize your data to locate information.

■ Decide whether access to read the documents in each view should be restricted. For tighter security, you can add access lists to forms rather than views.

■ Decide whether any shared or private-on-first-use folders are needed.

■ Identify any hidden views and respective columns that are necessary for special sorting or for other applications' lookups.

■ Decide on the view's style, such as colors for view elements, the view background, and the number of lines per row. Are there standards that currently exist within your organization? Is there a need to create view design standards? Although each view should show different information (or related information sorted in a different way), try to maintain consistency among the views.

■ Decide on column colors, type styles, and widths (either resizable or set).

CAUTION

Creating an excessive number of views can significantly add to the database size, can affect performance, can make maintenance more difficult, and can confuse the user.

Creating Views

After designing and planning a view, you can create it in Notes by performing the actions outlined in this section.

Select Create, View or Create, Design, View, or press the Create View SmartIcon to display the Create View dialog box, as shown in Figure 12.2. The Select a location for the new view list box defaults to creating a private view.

FIG. 12.2

The Create View dialog box allows you to select and name the type of view you want.

In the View name box, enter a name for the view. This can be left as Untitled and changed from within the View Properties Info box, or you can enter the entire view name, with cascading levels.

▶ **See** "Naming the View," **p. 500**

Click Shared if you want to create a shared view. When designing database applications, you typically are creating shared views. Shared views are visible to everyone with at least Read access to the database. Otherwise, the views will not be visible to all members of your team or organization. This view type cannot be changed after the view has been created. This can be further defined by selecting Personal on first use. Notice that the Select a location for the new view list box changes to display the current view folders (see Figure 12.3).

FIG. 12.3
The Create View dialog box changes to reflect a shared view.

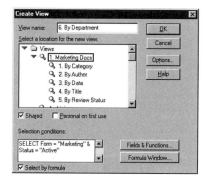

N O T E When creating shared views, Notes automatically creates the new view as a cascading view under the currently selected view location. The Views folder is selected by default, which places the newly created view directly under the Views category, without cascading. ▪

A personal-on-first-use view combines the attributes of shared and private views. It is created as a shared view; after it is used by an individual for the first time, however, it becomes a private view. Developers use this option when they want to create specialized private views for each user, but they don't want to have each user's name on the View menu. This also allows users to modify views and to personalize the way they display the data without affecting how other members view the data. In addition, because they become personal (private) views, they do not inherit future design changes made to the original view.

Shared views always are stored as design elements in the database; personal views are stored either in the database or in the user's workspace file (DESKTOP.DSK). This is determined by the ACL setting "Create personal folders/views" in the database ACL. If the user has rights to create personal views or folders, the views are stored as design elements within the database. Otherwise, the views are stored in the user's DESKTOP.DSK file. You can force a personal-on-first-use view to be stored in the user's DESKTOP.DSK by selecting the Store in desktop checkbox that appears when creating personal-on-first-use views (see Figure 12.4).

Part
II

Ch
12

FIG 12.4

When creating personal-on-first-use views, the Store in desktop option and the database access control determine where the personal view will be stored.

You can enter the Selection conditions within this dialog, or you can wait and enter them later. If left blank, it will assume the default condition, SELECT @All, which selects all the documents in the database.

Clicking Add Condition brings up the Search Builder dialog box (see Figure 12.5). This works like a wizard, setting certain criteria for the documents to display within the view. Selecting the Select by formula option reveals the default view formula, the Fields and Functions button, and the Formula Window button. These can easily be modified after the view has been initially created.

FIG. 12.5

The Search Builder wizard makes it easy even for non-Notes developers to create personal views based on specific criteria.

Clicking the Options button allows you to create the view from an existing view design. Selecting Design Now from the Options dialog causes the view to be immediately opened in design mode for editing. When creating views, you usually modify the design immediately after creating. Otherwise, the view is added to the list of existing database views.

Click OK to create and save the view. The newly created view appears in the Design pane when Design Views is selected in the Navigation pane, as shown in Figure 12.6.

FIG 12.6

The view, titled 1. Marketing Docs\6. By Department, appears in the Design pane after being created and saved. If you did not name the view, the name appears as Untitled.

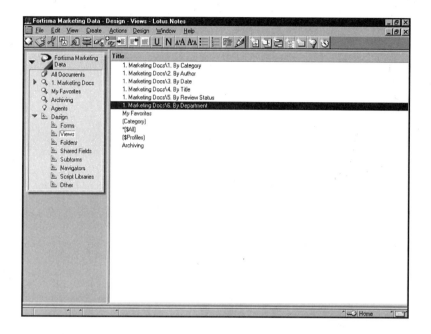

Double-click the new view to open the view in design mode, as shown in Figure 12.7.

The new view is identical to the view designated as the default design view (unless an alternate view was chosen using the Options button when creating the view). Figure 12.7 shows a view based on a default design view. Notice the preexisting columns. If no view has been designated as the default design view, the new view contains only one column that displays the document number (@DocNumber). An example is shown in Figure 12.8.

At this point, you can modify the view by adding and modifying columns and their corresponding attributes.

Each view can display a maximum of 32 levels of responses or categories. If there are more levels to be displayed (which is highly unlikely), change the view design to a flat, nonhierarchical view that displays all the documents on a single level.

N O T E   A view can contain as many columns as you want but can not exceed 22.75 inches wide. ▪

Part

II

Ch

12

FIG 12.7

The newly created view is opened in design mode. This is where you begin defining the structure of the view.

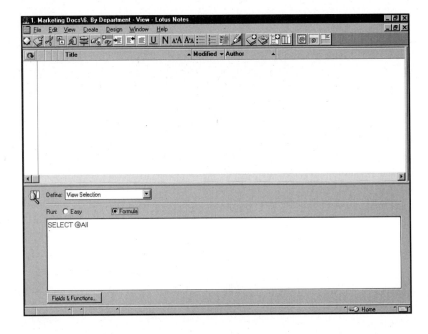

FIG 12.8

This is an untitled view opened in edit mode that has not been based upon a default design view.

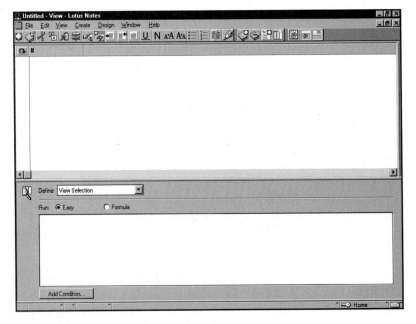

The total number of sublevel forms, views, and agents that cascade from the top level should not exceed 200; otherwise, the top-level views will not display properly. When designing Web pages, Domino allows no more than 200 cascading view and folder names.

Copying a View

Occasionally, you might want to copy a view from one database to another, possibly modifying it to meet the new application's needs.

▶ **See** "Database Templates," **p. 1091**

To copy and paste a view, perform the following steps:

1. Select the database containing the source view.
2. In the Navigation pane, select Design Views to display the available list of views in the Title pane.
3. Select the view you want to copy from the Views list.

 TIP You can select more than one view by using Ctrl+Shift as you click your selections.

4. Select Edit, Copy, or Cntl+C, or click the Edit Copy SmartIcon.
5. Switch to the database where you want to paste the form.
6. Select Edit, Paste, or press Ctrl+V, and the new view's name appears in the Views list.

> **CAUTION**
>
> If you are copying and pasting a view within the same database, the view is pasted into the list of views but is renamed by changing the view name to Copy of *viewname*. This can then be renamed using the View Properties InfoBox.

▶ **See** "Naming the View," **p. 500**

Be careful when copying and pasting views. newly created views inherit some design properties from the original view. For example, its inheritance is based on the design template that the original view inherits its design from, and whether it is visible or hidden from Web clients versus Notes clients, and so on.

These settings are available by selecting the view from the View list in design mode, then selecting Design, Design Properties from the pull-down menu, then selecting the Design tab from the dialog (see Figure 12.9). For more information, see the view design properties in the "Using View Design Properties" section of this chapter.

Using Views and Folders on the Web

When views are displayed on the Internet, they are published by Domino as a collection of dynamic Web pages. As documents are added to the database/Domino site, all views containing those documents are automatically updated to display the new contents. Any design changes made to the view are displayed the next time the user accesses the view. The view contains the following elements:

Part
II

Ch
12

FIG 12.9

Be careful when copying and pasting views because the design properties for views are copied as well.

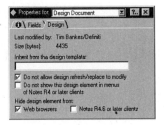

- Action Bar (which can be customized)
- Navigational bar
- Title of the view
- Column headings
- Body of the view containing the documents
- Ending navigational bar

Every time a Web client opens, scrolls, expands, or collapses in a view, the view is regenerated as a new HTML page on-the-fly by Domino. Views rendered with Domino have the same column and row format as standard Notes views (unless HTML is used to modify the format), except for the following:

- A Web navigation bar is generated at the top and bottom of the screen with buttons to expand, collapse, scroll, and search documents within the view (if the database is full-text indexed).
- Documents are opened by clicking a document link rather than by double-licking anywhere in the document row.
- When working the views on the Web, there are no currently selected documents.

▶ **See** "Setting the Style for the View," **p. 507**

Embedding Views and Folders on the Web

When designing applications that will be published on the Web by a Domino server, you can embed a view, the folder pane, or a navigator in a form or document. This gives designers the capability to customize the appearance of the view with specific elements instead of using the default described in the previous section. This allows you to create forms that display multiple windows within the same screen. This can be further enhanced through the use of frames.

Prior to Release 4.6, these Web elements were exposed to Web clients through the use of $$ViewBody, $$ViewList, and $$NavigatorBody fields. These fields are no longer necessary because view, folder, and navigator elements can be directly added to the form design or document. These fields, however, are still supported. They must be editable text fields or any computed type field. One $$ViewBody, one $$ViewList, and several $$NavigatorBody fields can be used on a single form.

Embedding a view displays the view within a document and replaces the `$$ViewBody` field used in Release 4.5. The value of the embedded view element is the view name in qoutes or a formula that computes the view name. Using embedded views allows the Notes developer to customize the appearance of the view, as opposed to using the default view attributes created by Domino.

Embedding the folder pane displays a list of views and folders (using the standard folders navigator with links to the views and folders) and replaces the `$$ViewList` field used in Release 4.5. There is no value associated with the folder pane element, it is dynamically updated as views are added or removed. The font style applied to the field is the font style used to display the folders. The capability to drag and drop documents is not supported by Domino.

Embedding a navigator displays the navigator within a document and replaces or supplements the `$$NavigatorBody` field used in Release 4.5. You can still create multiple `$$NavigatorBody` fields on a form by appending an underscore and character to each additional field name. To use a navigator in a Web application, you must select the Web browser compatible option in the Basics tab of the Navigator Properties dialog box. This setting informs the Domino server to convert the navigator to an HTML image map. If this is not selected, only the graphics background, hotspot polygons, rectangles, and circles will display; all other objects will not display. For more information about navigators, see Chapter 11.

CAUTION

All objects used in navigators behave the same on the Web as they do in Notes. The exception is polylines, which display on the Web but have no effect.

You can only add one embedded view and one embedded folder pane in each form. However, you can embed these Web elements anywhere within a document, form, table, or collapsed section, and they can be left, right, or center justified. You can add multiple navigators to a form.

N O T E   Domino disregards view titles and background colors of embedded views. A field containing the `@ViewTitle` function, however, can return the title of the view for display. Domino uses the Server document setting to determine the number of lines to display. In addition, if there are Create or Read access lists on the form, the embedded views will not display. ▪

In embedded views, the default view navigation bar does not display. To give users the capability to perform navigation functions, use the functions outlined in Table 12.1 to replace their respective action.

Part

II

Ch

12

Table 12.1   Navigation Commands for Embedded Views

Action	Command	Description
Next	@DbCommand("Domino"; "ViewPageUp")	This allows the user to see the next set of results in a view when the number of documents exceeds the default lines per view.
Prev	@DbCommand("Domino"; "ViewPageDown")	This allows the user to see the previous set of results in a view when the number of documents exceeds the default lines per view.
Expand	@Command([ViewExpandAll])	Expands the contents of the view to see more results.
Collapse	@Command([ViewCollapseAll])	Collapses the contents of the view to see fewer results.
Search	@Command([ViewShowSearchBar])	Allows you to search the database if it is full-text indexed.

To embed a view, folder, or navigator within a form, perform the following steps:

1. Open the form in design mode or the document in edit mode.
2. Position the cursor in the area of the form or document where the embedded object is going to be displayed.
3. From the Create menu, insert a Web element into the form, as shown in Figure 12.10.

FIG 12.10

From the Create, Web Element pull-down menu, you can embed a navigator, view, folder pane, or file upload control.

4. When embedding views and navigators, you can either specify a view or navigator to display every time, or you can write a formula by selecting the checkbox for Choose a view based on formula or Choose a navigator based on formula. After clicking OK, you can create a formula in the Programmer pane. The result of the formula has to be a text string for the name of the respective view or navigator.

5. Select Pane, View Pane Properties to modify object properties such as alignment, spacing, margins, "hide when" attributes, and so on.

6. When finished, save and close the form.

N O T E To delete an embedded element, select the element then select Edit, Clear from the pull-down menu. You also can simply press the Delete key. ▪

To find examples of using embedded views, folders, navigators, and frames, look at the Discussion Notes and Web (Release 4.6) template, the Doc Library Notes and Web (Release 4.6) template, and the Frameset (Release 4.6) template.

Using a Form as a View Template

When designing applications that will be used on the Web, you can create an association between a form and a view (or navigator), thus allowing views to be customized when published by the Domino server. This association is accomplished by assigning a reserved fieldname to the form. Domino then uses this form when the Web user opens the view or navigator. The reserved form names used to create these associations are as follows:

- ▪ $$ViewTemplate for *viewname*: This creates an association between the form and the view specified by *viewname*. The form must have an embedded view or $$Viewbody field contained within it. The *viewname* is the actual name of the view or its alias name. A form that is named $$ViewTemplate for Categories, for example, associates the form to the Categories view.

- ▪ $$ViewTemplateDefault: This creates an association between this form and all Web views that have not been associated with another form. The form must have an embedded view or $$Viewbody field contained within it. This form essentially becomes the template for all Web views not associated with a specific form using the $$ViewTemplate for viewname. In order to use this form, the database must contain a form with $$ViewTemplateDefault as an alias. Any additional fields, text, and graphics must be included in the form.

N O T E When the Web view is referenced by a Web client, the Domino server searches for a form that contains an alias to the view in the form $$viewTemplate for *viewname*. If the alias doesn't exist, Domino then searches for the form with the alias of $$ViewTemplateDefault to display the view using this default form. If this form is not found, then Domino displays the view with the standard appearance to the user's browser. ▪

Part
II

Ch
12

■ `$$NavigatorTemplate for` *`navigatorname`*: This creates an association between the form and a navigator specified by *navigatorname*. The form must have an embedded navigator or `$$NavigatorBody` field.

■ `$$NavigatorTemplateDefault`: This creates an association between this form and all Web navigators that have not been associated with another form. The form must have an embedded navigator or `$$NavigatorBody` field. For more information about creating navigators, see Chapter 10, "Creating New Databases."

Defining View Attributes

Before you begin laying out columns in the view, you need to define some basic attributes—such as the view's name, styles, and default options—in the view's Properties InfoBox.

To open this InfoBox, perform the following steps:

1. Open the desired view in design mode.

2. You can either select <u>D</u>esign, View <u>P</u>roperties, click the Properties SmartIcon, or right-click and choose View Properties.

The Basics tab in the View Properties InfoBox, as shown in Figure 12.11, essentially allows you to supply a name, alias, and comment for the view.

▶ **See** "Using Aliases (Synonyms)," **p. 502**

FIG 12.11

The Basics tab in a view's Properties InfoBox is used to define the name, alias, comments, and style for a view.

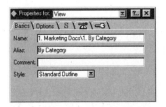

Naming the View   The name you type in the Name text box can be any combination of characters (including spaces), and it is case sensitive. A name can have up to 130 characters, but only the first 64 characters will appear on each cascading level in the view menus and in dialog boxes.

View names appear on the <u>V</u>iew menu; thus, when you name a view, you are giving it the title used to access it. The name should be logical and should indicate the criteria or sort order (for example, View By Contact). The following sections describe in more detail the specifics of naming a view.

Specifying Accelerator Keys   When naming a view, you should also use accelerator keys (or shortcut views). By default, the accelerator key is the first unique letter in the view name that has not already been used by a preceding view. To force Notes to use a different letter as the accelerator, insert an underscore before the desired letter. In By _Contact, for example, the underscore forces the letter C to be used as the accelerator.

Ordering View Names   Consider the order of views on the <u>V</u>iew menu. The View menu automatically sorts names in alphabetical order. If you want more frequently used views to appear first, you can use numbers as the first character. For example:

```
1. Current Week
2. by Task
3. by Client
```

 TIP Using view names with numbers provides easy accelerators for users because the numbers are unique and become the accelerator keys. They are still treated as text when sorting, however, so if there are more than nine views, the number 11 is listed before 2. Therefore, if you are numbering views and there are more than nine in the database, use two-character numbers such as 01, 02, 03, and so on.

Grouping Views with Cascading Menus   You can use cascading views to group a series of views in a cascading submenu under a single name. This shows the user that the views are related and can save space on the menu. Define a cascading view by entering the top-level view name, followed by a backslash (\) and the additional view names. Notes allows one level of cascade. These view names, for example, would appear under <u>V</u>iew, By <u>C</u>ontact:

```
1. Marketing Docs\1. By Name
1. Marketing Docs\2. By Author
1. Marketing Docs\3. By Date
1. Marketing Docs\4. By Title
1. Marketing Docs\5. By Review Status
1. Marketing Docs\6. By Department
```

When the user chooses <u>V</u>iew and highlights 1. Marketing Docs, a cascading menu appears, as displayed in Figure 12.12.

FIG 12.12
Cascading view names enable you to organize your views for quick, easy access.

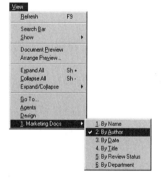

Hiding a View   Occasionally, you might want to "hide" a view from users by not displaying it on the <u>V</u>iew menu. Developers like to hide views for keyword lookups or to save views for future use. To hide a view, enclose the view name in parentheses. For example:

```
(Client List)
```

> **CAUTION**
>
> Hidden views usually exist for use with formulas or LotusScript and Agents. Hiding a view is not a security measure. Though the user cannot see the actual view, users can still make a private view and see its documents if they have Reader access to the database and have been given permission to create private views.

Using Aliases (Synonyms)   Aliases (also called synonyms) in views work exactly like synonyms in forms. Aliases allow you to change the view's name on the <u>V</u>iew menu without tracking down and rewriting formulas that reference the original name. If you don't use aliases, these formulas and even doclinks from other databases generate errors. (Figure 12.11 displayed an example of naming a view with an alias.)

> **CAUTION**
>
> If you want to rename a view, be sure to keep the original name as a synonym so any doclinks pointing to that view can still be opened.

When creating views that will be referenced with `@Dblookups`, `@DbColumns`, `@Picklists`,and so on, always create a view alias and reference this alias in all formulas. Therefore, if the displayed view name ever changes, all formulas and LotusScripts that reference that view can still function properly.

Defining the View Style   Currently two view styles are available when creating new views, Standard Outline and Calendar. Unless you are creating a view to display a calendar, choose Standard Outline.

The Calendar view, new in Notes 4.5, is a neat design feature used in the Calendaring & Scheduling portion of your NotesMail database. It also can be used, however, in the design of any database you are using. Calendar view style is similar to the standard outline view except that the Calendar view is limited to sorting only on a Time/Date field, which must be the first column in the view.

You might have a Training Schedule database, for example, in which you want to display all the upcoming classes in a calendar format. Prior to Notes 4.5, programming this task was quite tedious.

Other advantages to using Calendar views include:

- Options for viewing the calendar by two days, one week, two weeks, or by the month
- Point, click, and drag functionality among various dates
- The capability to print calendar entries and set date ranges when printing (a new feature with Release 4.6)
- Integrated task, event, and anniversary display functionality

To display a view as a calendar, the first column must be a Time/Date field. Follow these steps to accomplish this:

1. Select the database and choose View, Design.
2. In the Navigation pane, click Design, Views.
3. Double-click the view.
4. Create the first column based on a field with a Time/Date value. Specify that the view should sort according to this column. It is important that the Time/Date value include both Date and Time, even if the time value is 00:00. You will want to hide this column.
5. Create the second column based on a field with a number value that specifies the duration (in minutes) of a calendar entry. You will want to hide this column and create a separate column to display the time.
6. Create a view-selection formula that selects all documents containing the Time/Date field.
7. Choose Design, View Properties.
8. Select Calendar as the style.
9. Close and save the view.

TIP If date values defined in the first column have multiple date values, select the column sorting value "Show multiple values as separate entries" to display events across multiple days. Otherwise, only the first date is displayed.

Domino supports Calendar views by converting them to tables so Web clients can view calendar entries. Certain calendar features, however, are not supported because of their dynamic, graphical attributes. Conflict bars and the clock, scrolling through entries for a single day, and creating new appointments are not supported.

Setting the View Options   The Options tab in the view's Properties InfoBox (shown in Figure 12.13) enables you to further define the properties of your view. You can designate whether the view is the default view, how the view opens (expanded or collapsed), whether response documents appear in a hierarchy, and even whether the view appears in the View menu.

FIG 12.13

The Options tab displays various default options for your view.

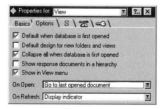

Part
II

Ch
12

The following list describes the available selections in the Options tab:

- Default when database is first opened: Designates the view as the default view; when the database is first added and opened by a user, this view appears. Only one default view is allowed per database. The default view is marked with a asterisk in the list of views in the Title pane. Your default view should not place restrictions on who can access the view because it is the first view shown to users when they open the database.

N O T E   When you select the Default when database is first opened option in one view, it automatically deselects this option in the previously selected default view because there can be only one default view. ▦

- Default design for new folders and views: Enables the developer to use the view as the default when designing other views and folders in the database. If this option is enabled, the design of newly created views will initially be identical to the design of this view. The view used for this should display all documents in the database so that users who create folders with this view are not excluding documents that they move to a folder.

- Collapse all when database is first opened: When enabled, the view collapses existing documents into their categories when the view is opened.

T I P   This option helps users to easily locate categorized documents in a very large view.

N O T E   The option Collapse all when database is first opened is not supported on the Web. This is because Web views do not expand and collapse all at once; they expand and collapse only one category at a time (at which point the entire Web page is regenerated). ▦

- Show response documents in a hierarchy: Indents response documents and response-to-response documents under their parent documents. This option allows you to indent response documents an additional three spaces under main documents. A response hierarchy is useful when readers want to see the progression of a discussion thread or want to see related topics grouped together. Discussion databases often use this format in a Main view. Figure 12.14 shows a view in which the option Show response documents in a hierarchy has been selected.

A flat, nonhierarchical view doesn't distinguish between main and response documents. This is useful when the listing doesn't focus on topics, as in a By Author view, or when there are no response documents, as shown in Figure 12.15.

To indent response-to-response documents, create a column immediately to the left of the column containing your main documents (see Figure 12.16). This new column needs to have Show Response Only selected and a formula written to display the response documents.

FIG 12.14

A hierarchical view indents and associates response documents under corresponding main documents.

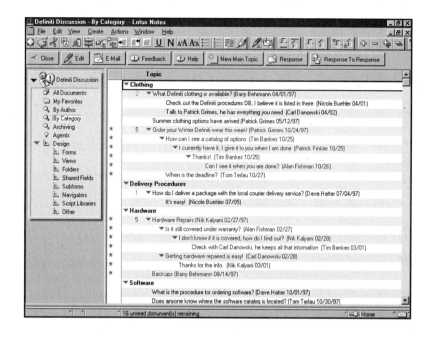

FIG 12.15

A nonhierarchical view does not indent response-level documents under their corresponding main parent documents.

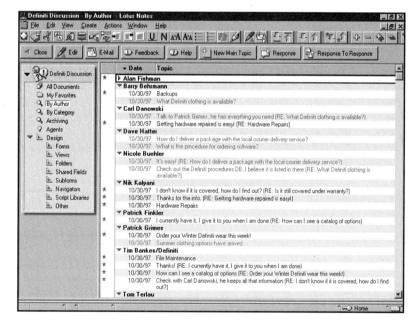

FIG 12.16

To show the response-document hierarchy in a view, create a column to the left the column containing the main documents.

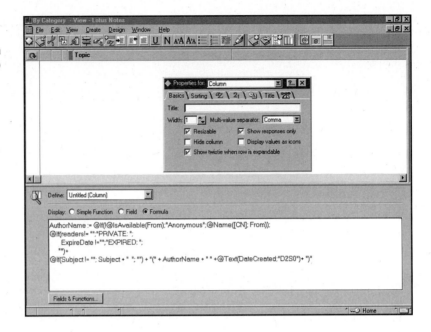

Creating a hierarchical view requires two important columns: one to display the main-level documents and one to the left of that for displaying response-level documents. The view options are as follows:

▶ **See** "Showing Responses Only," **p. 518**

    ■ Show in View menu: This option displays the view in the <u>V</u>iew menu. Deselecting this is similar to adding ( ) around a view name and hiding the view; in this case, however, the name does not contain ( ). Be aware that this does not truly hide the view. Unless you put parentheses around the view name, it is still visible in the <u>V</u>iew, <u>G</u>o to... dialog box. Therefore, when designing views not intended to be visible to the users (such as views used programmatically for @DbLookups, @DbColumns, @Picklists, LotusScript, and so on), make sure to parenthesize the view name and deselect the Show in View menu option.

N O T E   Deselecting the Show in View menu option applies only to Notes clients, not Web users, because Web users do not have access to Notes menus. The view still appears in the folders pane when <u>V</u>iew, <u>S</u>how, <u>F</u>olders is selected. To hide the view from Web users, you must set the design properties of the view to hide it from Web users (**see** "Using View Design Properties" on **p. 514**) or enclose it in parentheses. ■

    ■ On Open: You can control where the user is in a view each time it is opened. You can select Go to the last opened document, Go to the top row, or Go to the bottom row.

    ■ On Refresh: A view that's ready to be refreshed has the Refresh icon in the top-left corner of the View pane. This allows you to display the Refresh indicator button when the view needs to be refreshed, as shown in Figure 12.17.

FIG 12.17

The Refresh indicator is displayed when the view needs to be refreshed to show any newly created documents.

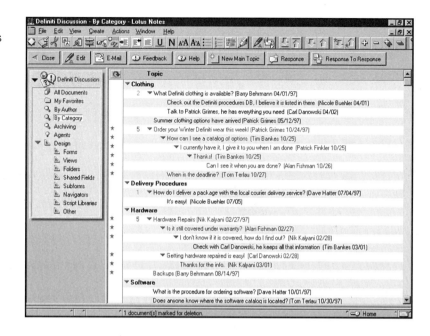

N O T E   The On Open, Goto... options and the On Refresh options are not supported by Domino for Web applications. ▨

Setting the Style for the View   Notes Release 4.5 dramatically improved how a view can appear. These features can be found in the Styles tab of the View Properties InfoBox, as shown in Figure 12.18.

FIG 12.18

The Styles tab enables you to set properties, such as color, and to use multiple rows for headings and rows.

Developers can find a variety of options in the Styles tab that affect how a view appears. In the Styles tab of the View Properties InfoBox, you can define the color of the following:

- ▨ Background: Generally, a light-colored background is best for viewing data. White is the default. The 256-color palette is available when choosing the background color.

- ▨ Column totals: This can help column totals stand out from other data. Gray is the default. The 16-color palette is available when choosing a color for the column totals.

- ▨ Unread rows: Color can be used to indicate whether a document in a view has been read. Black is the default. The 16 color palette is available when choosing a color for unread rows.

■ Alternate rows: This new feature allows developers to alternate row colors and high-lights for easier reading.One row might be highlighted in yellow, for example, the next row white, the next yellow, and so on. Use a light color that contrasts the background but is still visually appealing. The 256-color palette is available when choosing colors for alternate rows.

■ Show selection margin: The selection margin is used for selecting documents and displaying certain icons. If you need to show only documents without other identifier information, you can remove the document selection margin at the left. Only in rare development situations would you deselect this option to prevent users from marking or selecting documents. Readers can still select documents by holding Shift as they click document names, but they won't be able to see which documents are selected. The selection margin shows the following icons:

- Checkmark: Signifies which documents are currently selected.

- Star: Signifies unread documents or documents that have been marked unread.

- Trashcan: Signifies a document that has been marked for deletion, but not yet deleted.

- Diamond: Represents a replication conflict that needs to be resolved.

 TIP Hide the selection margin when using special views in @Picklists functions in which the user should only select a single document. For more information about functions see Chapter 15, "Working with Functions and Commands."

N O T E   The Unread Rows, Alternate Rows, and Show Selection Margin options are not supported on Domino Web pages. ■

■ Show column headings: If deselected, the view's column headings are hidden.

■ Beveled or Simple headings: In the Show column headings list box, you can indicate how you want column headings to appear. Beveled headings is the default option. It bevels the appearance of view columns, giving the headings a three-dimensional appeal and making the distinction between multiple column headings more clear. In Figure 12.19, you can see that the Beveled headings option displays the view columns with column separators.

N O T E   Beveled column headings are not supported on Domino Web Pages. ■

■ Lines per heading: You can select the number of rows (1–5) the column heading can have. This is a great feature for using long column-heading names, also shown in Figure 12.19. Avoid using more than two to three lines per heading, however, unless the view is used only for printing. Using more lines occupies valuable screen real estate and is more difficult to read and understand. If the column title cannot be represented in one or two lines, it might not be a good column description.

FIG 12.19

Use the Beveled headings option to display the column headings.

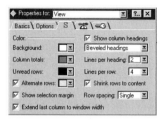

N O T E   When designing views for the Web, setting the Lines per heading option to 1 causes Domino to convert this setting to a NOWRAP HTML attribute. This also is true for the Lines per row setting.

- Lines per row: This feature allows you to have multiple rows in the view (up to nine). This gives you the opportunity to use word wrapping and to improve the reporting capabilities of Notes (also shown in Figure 12.19). Avoid using more than three to five rows per document if possible. Using more (especially nine) uses a lot of screen real estate and minimizes the number of documents visible on-screen. The view should display a summary of the document data. If the user needs to view more information, it is more efficient to view the document using the Preview pane or by opening the document.

N O T E   If it is necessary to display information from a rich-text field, keep in mind that rich-text fields cannot appear in a view as rich text. In addition, they normally contain long strings of text that you would want to word wrap. You might want to convert the rich-text field to a text field before attempting to use the word wrapping feature for a field in a view column.

- Shrink rows to content: If the Lines per row option is set to more than one, this eliminates extra rows not used by a document, thus saving view and reporting space.
- Row spacing: Spacing—the vertical space between documents—can be single, 1¹/₄, 1¹/₂, 1³/₄, or double. Typically, spacing should be set to single. This allows the greatest amount of information to be displayed at one time.

When designing views for a Web page, you can override the default row and column settings by using HTML formatting attributes defined within the column formula. The HTML in the column formula must define all formatting and document linking for the view. The setting For Web access: Treat view contents as HTML must be selected on the Advanced tab (described in the "Using Advanced Features" section of this chapter).

Using Advanced Features   The Advanced tab (with the beanie hat icon) allows you to select more advanced view features, as shown in Figure 12.20. This section allows you to specify when Notes should refresh or discard the view index, how to display unread marks, and which forms to use when a document is opened in this view. The attributes you can designate are described in the following sections.

FIG 12.20

The Advanced tab allows you to establish when to refresh or discard the view index, set up unread marks, designate a Form formula, and set up ODBC and Web access.

Refreshing the View   In the Refresh index list box, you can select Auto, after first use; Automatic; Manual; and Auto, at most every use. A view index, unrelated to a full-text search index, is an internal filing system that lets Notes create the most current list for a view. When documents are changed, added, or deleted, the view index must be refreshed to display the changes. The view index can be refreshed by the user pressing F9, as a result of the Updall server process, or as a result of the specified view design. To improve performance time, you can change how frequently the view index is refreshed by selecting one of the following options:

■ Auto, after first use: This default option updates the view every time it is opened, after the first time. It adds changes incrementally to the view index. Users never need to be concerned about whether the view displays the latest changes. It does, however, take a little longer for a view to display the first time it is opened. After being opened, it is cached for the user during each session, but it might have to be refreshed depending on the user's actions.

CAUTION

Take time to consider performance issues when deciding on a refresh strategy. Users have little patience when it comes to waiting for a view to refresh. Refreshing views (a result of the nonrelational document structure of Notes databases) can take considerable time with larger databases and on under-powered desktops and laptops.

■ Automatic: This option keeps the view updated by adding changes incrementally to the view index, whether or not users ever open the database. Users never need to be concerned about whether a view displays the latest changes, and views open more quickly. This option works well on databases that reside only on servers.

■ Manual: This option relies on the user to refresh the view. This option is useful with large databases—if it isn't critical for the view to be kept up-to-date—because it allows large databases to open faster. If users want to look for a new document, they can refresh the view by clicking the refresh indicator.

■ Auto, at most every: This option allows you to specify how frequently the view index should be updated. This is a good compromise between Automatic and Manual indexing for large databases that change fairly often. The view's index is updated automatically only at the specified interval, entered in hours. If a user opens a database in which changes have been made since the last indexing, a blue arrow appears at the top left of the view to indicate changes have been made that are not visible in the view. Users have the option of manually refreshing the view to see the updates.

Discarding the Index   If slower view displays are acceptable, you can change the Discard index option from Never to one of the other choices to save disk space. If the view index is deleted, users have to wait for the view index to be re-created. You have the following options:

- Never: This option preserves the view index permanently; updates are added to the existing index. The view index never has to be re-created, but this option takes up more disk space than the other options. Use this for views that users frequently need, so they don't have to wait for a new view index to be created when they open the database. For large databases, this can take several minutes.

- After each use: This option deletes the view index as soon as the database is closed. This option saves the most disk space, but the index must be rebuilt the next time the view is opened. Select this option when the view is used infrequently but on a predictable basis; for example, use this option only on Friday afternoons when an agent is run.

- If inactive for n days: This option deletes a view index only if the view hasn't been used in the specified number of days. If the view is deleted, the it is rebuilt the next time the database is opened. (This option doesn't affect local databases.) Select this option when a database is used infrequently and on an unpredictable basis as a compromise between the Never and After each use options.

N O T E   The Updall server task runs on the server that updates all views that have been accessed at least once. It updates all full-text indexes for all the databases on the server. Arguments can be included to modify how it runs. Updall deletes and updates the view index when it runs, which is at 2 a.m. by default.

N O T E   Refresh index options and Discard i ndex options are not supported by Domino on the Web. Views can only be re-indexed at the Notes server.

Displaying Marks for Unread Documents   The Unread marks combo box provides three options for displaying marks for unread documents. They are the following:

- Standard (compute in hierarchy): This option displays asterisks by unread main documents and response documents as well as by any collapsed categories containing unread documents. Because this choice displays unread marks at every level, it displays the view the slowest. It does, however, give the readers the most information about documents they need to read.

- Unread documents only: This option displays asterisks only for unread main documents. Unread marks do not appear next to response documents or collapsed categories. This choice displays the view faster than the Standard display and is a good compromise between showing unread marks at every level and not showing them at all.

■ None: This option does not display unread marks. It displays the view fastest, but it doesn't help users see which documents they haven't read. Use this only if users don't need to see asterisks next to new or modified documents they haven't read, or if this is a reference-type database in which the users never read all the documents. Users can still navigate to the next unread document using SmartIcons.

Using the Form Formula

What would you do if you wanted to have users compose a document using one form, but then have them view the data entered in an entirely different form? You could use form formulas.

A form formula decides which of a database's forms is used for composing and displaying documents, based on a formula evaluation. This allows you to display the same information in different ways, to arrange fields differently, or to omit some fields in the alternate form. The Address Label view of a Contact Information database, for example, could use the form formula `frmAddressLabel` to display documents using the Address Label form. The `frmAddressLabel` form could be a shortened version of the Contact Information form that includes only the Name and various Address fields.

The form formula is optional. If you do not create one, Notes displays the documents in the view using the following rules, which are listed in order of precedence:

■ The form stored in the document if the Store form in document option was selected when the document was created.

■ The form name returned from the form formula.

■ The form name defined in the Form field of the document. By default, this is the form with which the document was created.

■ The default form designated in the database (Design, Form Properties).

N O T E If a document is created with a form that has the Store form in Document option selected, the form formula is ignored and the document is displayed using the stored form. Storing the form in documents allows documents to display correctly, even in databases where the form has not been defined, has been renamed or deleted, or was mailed to a user who does not have access to the original database. One note of caution, however: Storing the form with the document increases the size of the database and prevents any modifications to the design of the form. For more information about stored forms see Chapter 11. ■

To create a form formula, perform the following steps:

1. Open the desired form in edit mode and select Design, View Properties to display the view's Properties InfoBox.

2. Click the Advanced tab.

3. Click Formula Window, which displays the Design Form Formula dialog box, as shown in Figure 12.21.

FIG 12.21

This formula creates new documents using the New Discussion form and accesses existing documents using the Main Topic form.

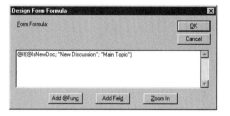

4. Write the form formula and then click OK. A form formula must evaluate as the name of a form.

Using the Form Formula for ODBC Access

You can use the Open Database Connectivity Standard (ODBC) to access data from external databases (using formulas and LotusScript) and to bring that data into Notes documents. After being brought into Notes, it can be summarized in Notes views for reporting and searching.

If a view is to be used with an external ODBC data source, you can set it to generate unique keys in the index. For more information about using Notes with ODBC, see Bonus Chapter 1, "ODBC and Lotus Components," on the CD-ROM.

Using the Form Formula for Web Access

When designing for Web clients, it is possible to allow the Domino server to publish the contents of the view as HTML. To do this, select the Treat view contents as HTML option. This allows Web pages more flexibility with certain design features (such as overriding the default row and column settings) by using HTML formatting attributes defined within column formulas.

You can add HTML to forms, documents, fields, views, columns, and agents to create Web-specific instructions and formatting for databases designed for Web usage. Domino automatically combines HTML code with data and displays it to the browser. Domino supports most tags in HTML 3.2, as well as some additional tags.

N O T E   For more information about writing HTML code, visit the HTML Web site at `http://www.w3.org/pub/WWW/markup`. For more information about HTML 3.2, visit the site `http://www.w3.org/pub/WWW/markup/wilbur`.

Using Security Options

You can select the Security tab (with the key icon) to define a limited list of users who can access a view or folder. Figure 12.22 shows the Security options for a view. The default option is All readers and above, which utilizes what has been defined in the ACL for the current database. This is not a true security measure, however, as users can create private views to mimic any view you have created.

Part

II

Ch

12

FIG 12.22

The Security tab enables you to decide who (users and groups) can access the view.

To refine this list further, follow these steps:

1. Deselect All readers and above.

2. Click the Person icon to select a name or group from a Personal or Public Address Book.

3. Select the Available to Public Access Users option. This allows users with Read or Write public documents privileges (in the database access control) to access the view.

N O T E In order to add a user to the Read access list for a view, the reader must already have at least Reader access in the database access control list. Entries in the Read access list for views can not expand user access, they can only refine it. Be sure to add any servers that need to replicate this view (perhaps to replicate design changes to the view). Do not put Read access controls on the default view of a database.

Using View Design Properties

View and folders—like forms, navigators, and the like—are design documents with their own design properties. The design properties track when a view was created, modified, added to the database, modified within this database, and last accessed. They also display the unique ID of the view document, the fields it contains, and some specific design settings. To access the design properties of a view, follow these steps:

1. Select the database and choose View, Design.

2. In the Navigation pane, expand the design and select Views.

3. Highlight a view in the Main view pane and select Design, Design Properties. This displays the Design Document properties dialog box, as shown in Figure 12.23.

The Fields tab displays all the internal $ fields that make up the design document (see Figure 12.24).

The Design tab (see Figure 12.25) displays who last modified the design document, the size of the document, and the following design settings:

■ Inherit from design template: Design inheritance is available not only on the database level but for individual design elements as well. Therefore, views can inherit their design from views in other databases when their design is refreshed, without refreshing other design elements within the database. The value of this field should be the design template name of the database that contains the original view.

FIG 12.23

The design document properties allow you to view when the document was last modified and what fields it contains, and to set design-specific parameters.

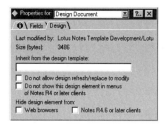

FIG 12.24

The Fields tab reveals internal fields used by Notes to define the view.

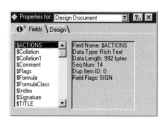

- Do not allow design refresh/replace to modify: If the database is set up to inherit its design from another database, you can protect individual design documents (such as views) by selecting this option. Therefore, when the database design is refreshed or replaced, the view design is not altered. For more information about database design inheritance see Chapter 10.

- Do not show this design element in menus of Notes Release 4 or later clients: This allows you to hide the view from displaying in the View pull-down menu and the Folders pane. Select this setting if this view is only going to be used by Web clients, and you want to remove this view from both the View menu and the Folders pane.

- Hide design element from Web browsers: When designing databases that will be accessed by both Web clients and native Notes clients, you can hide or display certain views depending on the client type. Therefore, if you have designed views that do not render properly to Web browsers, select this option so only Notes clients will access the view.

- Hide design element from Notes Release 4.6 or later clients: If your Notes database will be accessed by a mix of clients running Release 4.6 as well as prior releases, you have to create views specially designed for older clients. Because of their archaic design, however, you will want to hide these views from upgraded clients using Release 4.6 or higher.

Part

II

Ch

12

FIG 12.25

The Design tab displays who last modified the view design, its size, and other view-specific design settings.

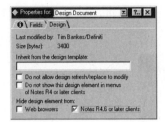

Creating Columns in a View

To fully create a view, you need to create columns. A column displays the contents of a field or the result of a formula, which can involve one or more fields. A new view always includes a column labeled "#" (using the formula @DocNumber to number the documents in the display) or columns included in the default design view that you might not want to keep. Keep the following tips in mind when creating columns:

- Delete any columns you do not want to use. Either select them and press the Delete key, choose Edit, Cut, or press Ctrl+X if you want to reuse and paste the column in another location.

- You can have as many columns as you can fit within 22.75 inches.

- It is best to fit the columns on-screen so the user is not forced to horizontally scroll the display to see them.

- Always place the categorized columns in the leftmost position of the view, followed by sorted columns then unsorted columns.

To create a column, perform the following steps:

1. Select the column to the right or left of where you want the column to appear.

2. Choose Create, Insert New Column to insert a column to the left of the currently highlighted column. If you want to add another column to the right of the last column in the view, choose Create, Append New Column instead. If you are pasting columns into a view, they will appear to the left of the currently selected column.

3. Double-click the new column header to display the column's Properties InfoBox, as shown in Figure 12.26.

 Right-click the column header and select Column Properties to display the Properties InfoBox.

CAUTION

If you edit a view that contains documents by adding a column or modifying an existing column, you should click the Refresh indicator button to update the view so you can immediately view your design changes.

FIG 12.26

The column's Properties InfoBox allows you to establish how the column appears.

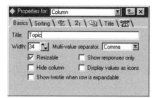

Using Basic Settings

In the Basics tab of the column's Properties InfoBox, you can set many options, including the following:

- Enter the name of the column
- Set the width of the column
- Decide whether to hide the column

Figure 12.26 in the preceding section displayed the basic options available for a column. The following sections describe these options.

Adding a Column Title   In the Title text box, enter a title to be displayed at the top of the column; using a title is optional. If the title is longer than the defined column width, it will be truncated to fit the width unless you have designated multiple rows for the column header. Regardless of the number of lines per heading, the total length of the column title can not exceed 80 characters. For more information about the Lines per heading option, see the section "Setting the Style for the View" earlier in this chapter.

> **N O T E**   Columns that are only one or two characters wide should not contain titles. Generally, these types of columns are categorized, and the categories themselves are self-evident for naming purposes.

Determining the Column Width   Enter the desired width of the column, in characters, in the Width text box. Notes assigns a default width of 10 characters to new columns, but you can make a column as narrow or as wide as you want. Depending on the font and point size, a variable amount of characters can fit in the length, not just 10 characters.

> **T I P**   Drag the column header lines with the mouse to size the column.

Choosing a Separator for Multiple Values   If the column shows several values (usually generated by a multivalue field), you can specify how you want to separate the values with the Multi-value separator field. If None is selected, the Multiple-value field is displayed as a single text string.

▶ **See** "Keyword Fields," **p. 102**

▶ **See** "Basics Settings," **p. 110**

Controlling Column Resizing   Select the Resizable option if users are allowed to adjust column width themselves as they use the database. The width reverts to the design setting when the database is closed.

Hiding Columns   The Hide column option is useful for columns that are needed by the view's design but not by the users, such as a column used only for sorting purposes. Figure 12.27 shows an example of a hidden sort column using the DateCreated field. The column is sorted in ascending Date order.

N O T E   Hidden columns are not hidden when designing a view in design mode. They are hidden only when viewed in the View pane. The width of a hidden column does not affect the view size on the screen.

Showing Responses Only   Select the Show responses only option to display the column only if it displays documents of the response or response-to-response document types. All response documents are displayed under their corresponding main documents; each level of response is indented an additional three spaces. This option is widely used in discussion databases or databases in which you want to show the parent (main document) to child (response) relationship. For more information about the Show response documents in a hierarchy option, see the section "Setting the View Options" earlier in this chapter. You can define only one column as a responses-only column in a view.

FIG 12.27

A hidden sort column is used to force a sort on preexisting fields.

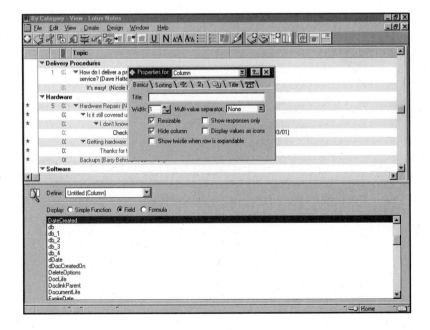

CAUTION

Always place a Show responses only column to the left of columns that display only main document information. This is because all columns defined after the responses-only column will display data for main documents only. Normally, Notes allows for information to be displayed only within the limitations of a column's width. But when Show responses only is selected, that restriction is bypassed. To see the difference, use Ctrl+X to cut the column containing Show responses only, then refresh the view. Notice how the view changes? Now, paste (Ctrl+V) the column back into the view.

Displaying Values as Icons   Select the Display values as icons option to use one of over 170 predefined icons to graphically represent special values (such as attachments) in the column. Write a formula for the column; the result of the formula determines which icon is displayed. The following formula determines whether a document has an attachment and, if so, displays the appropriate attachment icon:

```
@If(@TextToNumber(@Version) > 122;
@If(@IsDocTruncated;
30;
@IsAvailable($ContentIcon);
$ContentIcon;
(@Contains(@LowerCase(From); " pager ") ¦ @Contains(@LowerCase(SendTo); "
pager "));
46;
@Attachments;
@If(@Contains(@LowerCase(@AttachmentNames); "message.wav" :
 "vmsg_hdr.wav");
44;
@Contains(@LowerCase(@AttachmentNames); ".wav");
15;
@Contains(@LowerCase(@AttachmentNames); ".tif");
47;
5);
0);
@IsAvailable($ContentIcon); $ContentIcon; @Attachments; 5; 0)
```

Use 0 as the false case when you want to leave the column blank. The preceding formula returns 0 when the document has no attachments, so nothing is displayed. Figure 12.28 displays a table of the column icons' values.

Indicating Expandable Rows   The Show twistie when row is expandable option displays a green triangle that users can click to see categorized documents within a collapsed view or folder, as shown in Figure 12.29.

N O T E   The Show twistie when row is expandable option is not fully supported by Domino for Web pages. Triangles are always shown when the row is expandable. ▪

Part

II

Ch

12

FIG 12.28

The available icons that can be displayed in view columns.

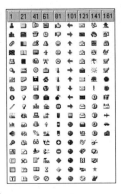

FIG 12.29

Twisties allow users to quickly navigate views by expanding and collapsing categorized columns.

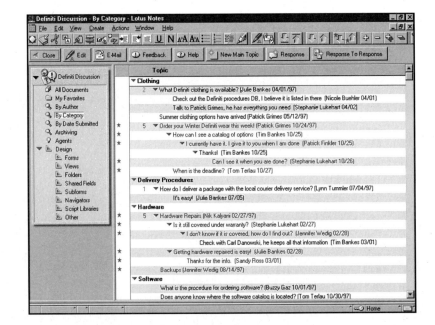

Sorting Options

Sorting and categorizing is an important part of building views. It allows you to be creative in how you display documents to users. You should organize documents in a way that makes it easier and quicker for users to find what they are looking for. You should always sort the view on at least one column; otherwise, documents and responses appear in the order they were composed.

The Sorting tab in the column's Properties InfoBox, displayed in Figure 12.30, allows you to define how the column will be sorted and categorized. The options available are described in the following sections.

FIG 12.30

The Sorting tab allows you to specify sorting and categorization attributes for your view.

Using Sort Order In the Sort section, select None, Ascending, or Descending. For alphabetical listings, ascending order is usually preferred. For Date columns, however, descending is preferred to display the most recent documents first. Figure 12.31 shows a view that sorts the Creation Date in descending order and the Author's first name in ascending order. You can sort views in multiple ways and combinations. Remember, however, that columns are sorted from left to right.

FIG 12.31

This view is sorted first by the document's creation date and then by the author's first name.

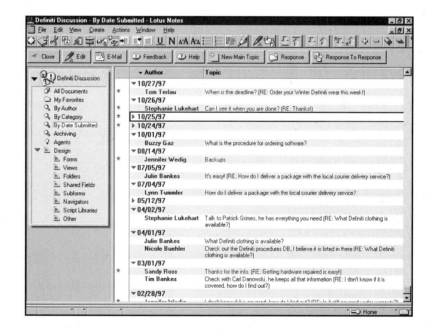

Using Sort Type In the Type section, choose Standard or Categorized. Standard is the default option, but you should select Categorized if the view contains categories. The value of the categorized field is not displayed on every row. In fact, it cannot be opened by double-clicking on it in the view window. Double-clicking on the category (or single-clicking on the twistie, if it is displayed) will only collapse or expand the category, thus revealing or hiding the documents that belong to it. Refer to Figure 12.29 to see a view with categories.

Part

II

Ch

12

When selecting multiple documents in a view using the selection margin, the status bar counts checkmarks made on categories as if they are valid documents. This can be misleading. Because they are categories, however, and do not represent actual documents, actions cannot be performed against them (see Figure 12.32).

FIG 12.32

Twelve rows (represented by the checkmarks) have been selected within the selection margin; however, only nine are actually selected documents.

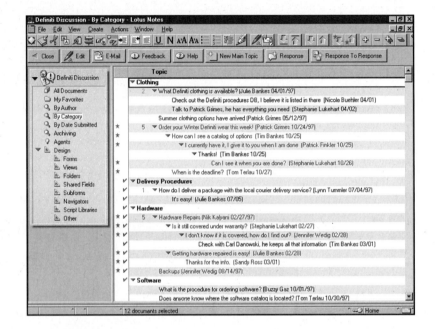

N O T E   If you are sorting a view by chronological order, you must sort using a formula with either @Created or another field that tracks the date the document was composed. The formula function @Created returns the date that the document was created. Using this time value, you can sort the column in ascending or descending order. ◼

When sorting and categorizing by date, you might notice that documents with the same date are not always categorized together. This happens if @Created was used in a sorted and categorized column. This is because even though the date (9/28/71, for example) is displayed in the view, the actual date value used in the sort also contains a time value, therefore creating multiple categories. One work-around for this is to modify the column formula in the categorized column so it converts the Time/Date value to text with the @Text formula. When doing this, pass the parameters that format the Time/Date value to display a date only, @Text(@Created; "D0S0") for example. For more information about using @Text, @Date, and other @Functions, see Chapter 15.

CAUTION

A similar situation might arise when working with international dates. Depending on how the Time/Date value was saved with the document, it could be displayed using the United States format (12/25/97), a European format (25.12.97), and so on. You might want to format how the date is displayed so all documents are displayed in a consistent manner.

In addition, the default separator used in date values is dependent on the operating system Notes is running on. When using Windows, UNIX, or a Macintosh, the default separator is a slash (/); when using OS/2, the default separator is a hyphen (-).

Using Case-Sensitive and Accent-Sensitive Sorting   Deselect the Case sensitive sorting option if you do not want the sort to be case sensitive. If this option is selected, uppercase letters are displayed before lowercase letters.

Deselect Accent sensitive sorting if you do not want the sorting for this column to be accent-sensitive. If this option is selected, accented letters are sorted with respect to the language being used at the workstation.

Using Show Multiple Values as Separate Entries   If the field value displayed in the sorted column contains multiple values (it is defined as a multivalues list), select the checkbox for Show multiple values as separate entries so that each value is displayed as a separate row. Otherwise, only the first value is used in the sort, and all values are displayed in a single row.

Clicking on a Column Header to Sort   You can designate one or more columns in a view as sortable on demand, or you can link them to automatically open another view when clicked. Users click these special columns and see the documents in the order defined by the column or easily change views.

To establish this feature, select the Click on column header to sort option. You can choose between Ascending, Descending, Both, or Change to view. The Change to view option lets you select a view for Notes to switch to when the user clicks the special curved arrow that appears in the column title.

In the column header, the Ascending option is represented by an upward pointing arrow, the Descending option displays a downward pointing arrow, the Both option displays both arrows, and the Change to view option displays a curved arrow. Figure 12.33 shows a column heading with the Click on column header to sort option selected, using an ascending sort in the who column, a descending sort in the date column, and the change to view option in the subject column.

If Ascending, Descending, or Both is selected, you can select the Secondary sort column to display list boxes that enable you to designate a second column and its sort order to automatically sort upon. Figure 12.34 shows the dialog for a secondary sort set up for the Who column displayed in Figure 12.31.

Part

II

Ch

12

FIG 12.33

Users click these special columns and choose a sorting method to see the documents in the order they want.

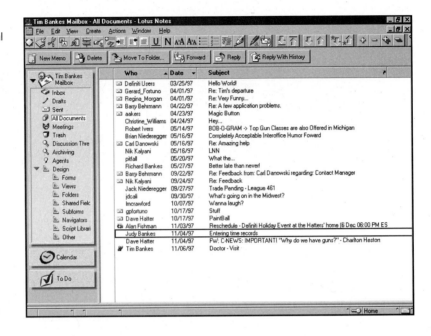

FIG 12.34

Selecting a secondary sort column gives the user more flexibility in re-sorting documents on-the-fly.

You can use the column heading title text to warn users what will happen if they use the Change to view option. For example, you might title the column Click here to switch to the By Author view. Because this design feature is relatively intuitive, it shouldn't take long for users to become familiar with sorting and switching between views. To prevent users from getting lost, however, the view they switch to should probably specify an option for returning to the original view.

N O T E Sorting view columns is now supported by Domino on the Web. Therefore, column images can now be clicked on to sort from a Web browser. ■

Displaying Totals The Totals option enables you to specify how you want totals to appear. The following are the options available for displaying totals:

- None
- Total
- Average per document
- Average per subcategory
- Percent of parent category
- Percent of all documents

N O T E You can click the Hide details option to hide the details row but still show the totals for the categories.

Defining the Style for the Column

The Styles tab in the Column Properties InfoBox (its icon shows A and Z) allows you to define the style attributes for the selected column. Figure 12.35 displays the Styles tab options available in the column's Properties InfoBox. By now, this dialog box should look very familiar because it is used throughout Lotus Notes to define text properties. Here, you can define the following attributes to improve the appearance of your view:

- Font
- Size
- Style (select any predefined styles.)
- Text Color (you are limited to the predefined 16-color palette.)
- Justification (Align the data in your column to be Left, Right, or Center.)

FIG 12.35

The options in the Styles tab are very logical.

Part
II

Ch
12

 TIP Select Left when working with text and Time/Date values, Right when displaying numbers (especially numbers with decimal places), and Center when working with small values you want to stand out (such as Yes, No, icons, and so on).

One helpful feature developers will appreciate is that style changes are automatically reflected in the view. If the database already contains documents, and the view selection formula allows some of those documents to be displayed in the view, simply click on the Refresh icon or press F9 to view how the documents will appear in the view. This saves an immense amount of time because you don't have to close a dialog box to preview any changes. Also, you can click Apply to All to apply any changes made to all the existing columns in the view, so you don't have to individually change each column.

N O T E When viewing documents in a view while designing the view, all categories are automatically expanded. ■

Displaying Numbers

The Numbers tab in the Column Properties InfoBox (its icon is a large 2 and a small 1, as shown in Figure 12.36) allows you to define how columns with numbers appear. You can choose from the following four number formats:

FIG 12.36

The Numbers tab enables you to define the numbering format for the column.

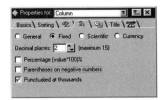

- General: This option displays numbers as they are entered. Zeroes to the right of the decimal point are suppressed; for example, 8.00 displays as 8.

- Fixed: This option displays numbers with a fixed number of decimal places; for example, 8 displays as 8.00. You can select the desired number of places from the Decimal places list.

- Scientific: This option displays numbers using exponential notation; for example, 80,000 displays as 8.00E+04. You can select the desired number of decimal places from the Decimal places list.

- Currency: This option displays values with a currency symbol and two digits after the decimal point; for example, 8 displays as $8.00.

After selecting the numbering format, you also can set the following options:

- Percentage (value × 100)%: This displays values as percentages; for example, it displays .80 as 80%.

- Parentheses on negative numbers: This displays negative numbers enclosed in parentheses; for example, it displays (8) instead of –8.

- Punctuated at thousands: This displays large numbers with the thousands separator; for example, it displays 8,000 instead of 8000.

Displaying Times and Dates

The Time and Date tab in the column's Properties InfoBox (displaying a clock and calendar icon, as shown in Figure 12.37) allows you to define the following time and date attributes:

■ Show: You have four choices for controlling combinations of time and date: Date and time, Date only, Time only, and 'Today' and Time. If you select the last choice, values indicating the current date display the word "Today" instead of the date. Values indicating the previous day display the word "Yesterday" instead of the date. Values indicating the next day display the word "Tomorrow" instead of the date. All other values display the date.

■ Date format: You can select from MM/DD, MM/YY, and MM/DD/YY.

■ Time format: You can select HH:MM or HH:MM:SS to display the time using a 12-hour or 24-hour clock format.

■ Time zone: You can select Adjust time to local zone, Always show time zone, or Show only if zone not local. The Adjust time to local zone option displays the time relative to the time zone of the reader. For example, a document created at 3:00 P.M. in New York that is read by a user in Los Angeles adjusts to Pacific Standard Time; the creation time is displayed as 12:00 P.M.

The Always show time zone option displays the time zone where the document was created. With this option, the creator's time zone is always shown. The Show only if zone not local option displays the time zone where the document was created only when the document is read by someone in a different time zone.

FIG 12.37
In the Time and Date tab, you can select the date, time, and time zone formatting attributes.

Changing the Style of the Column Title

Using the Title tab in the column's Properties InfoBox, you can modify how the column heading appears.

The available options are identical to the Styles tab, except that any changes made are reflected in the column title. You also can use multiple rows in the header by switching to the view's Properties InfoBox and selecting the Style tab. For more information about the Lines per heading option, see "Setting the Style for the View" earlier in this chapter.

Using Advanced Features

The Advanced tab (with the beanie hat icon) allows you to select more advanced view features. The programmatic names assigned to columns are the internal field names assigned and used by Notes (recognizable by the $Fieldname). Avoid manipulating or changing this value.

When designing Web pages that will be published by Domino, select the For Web Access checkbox to instruct the Domino server to convert the values displayed in the columns as links. Web clients can use this feature to open a document instead of double-clicking a document as they would in native Notes (see Figure 12.38).

In previous releases of Notes, when viewed from a Web browser, Domino automatically rendered the first visible column as a link. This limited the functionality of the programmer and could be misleading for the Web client because the first visible column might not have been the document title. A view that sorted by date, for example, forced the date column to display the document link rather than the title. Now, however, the designer can choose which column or columns should be displayed as links (or no column links at all). Databases designed with previous releases of Notes will still automatically use the first visible column as a link.

FIG 12.38

Using the Advanced tab, you can determine which columns are rendered as document links by the Domino server.

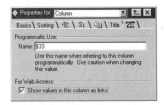

Defining Column Formulas

Column formulas specify what information should be displayed in this column of the view. The formula can be a field name (if you want to display the data for a particular field), a formula, or one of 13 simple functions. Typically, developers do require more complex formulas than just the field name or a simple function.

TIP   When writing a formula for the column definition, first select the Field display radio button. This lists all available fields in the database. Highlight the field you will be working with when applying @Functions, then select the Formula display radio button. The field name will automatically be carried over into the Programmer pane for editing. This prevents you from misspelling the field name and from having to debug your code.

To start writing a column formula, open the desired view in edit mode. Display the Programmer pane if necessary. Then select the column heading you want to write the formulas for. You also can click the Define list box in the Programmer pane to select the desired column. Figure 12.39 displays the first column in the selected view and its corresponding formula.

Entering the formula into the Formula box is easy. You must select one of these Display options to enter your formula: Simple Function, Field, or Formula. These options are described in the following sections.

N O T E   A column formula must evaluate to a text string.

FIG 12.39
This column formula specifies the column contents to be Categories.

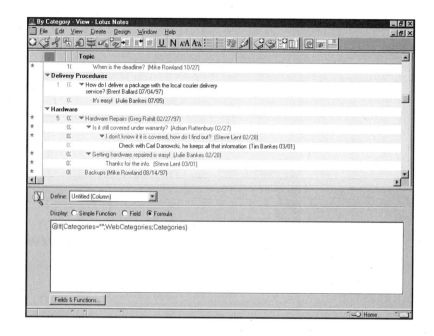

Using Simple Functions

Selecting the Simple Function option displays a list of multiple, simple, often-used functions that saves you from writing formulas from scratch. These functions let the columns you design display information about authors, attachments, documents, time and date, responses, the view, or the folder. Figure 12.40 displays a column using the simple function Creation Date and displays all 13 simple functions. This quick shortcut is identical to selecting Formula as the display option and writing the formula @Created in the formula window.

The following is a list of available simple functions:

- Attachment Lengths: Uses @AttachmentLengths to return the size(s) in bytes of the document's attachment(s). The data type is a number list. The values returned are the size of the attachment based on its uncompressed file size, so the returned value might differ slightly from the actual hard drive space taken up by the attachment.

- Attachment Names: Uses @AttachmentNames to return the filenames of the document's attachments, as they are stored on the operating system. The data type is a text list.

- Attachments: Uses @Attachments to return the number of files attached to the document. The data type returned is a number.

- Author(s) (Distinguished Name): Uses @Author to return the names of the document's author(s) in hierarchical format, as in Tim Bankes/Definiti.

Part
II

Ch
12

FIG 12.40

Simple functions are a great development time-saver when creating formulas for columns.

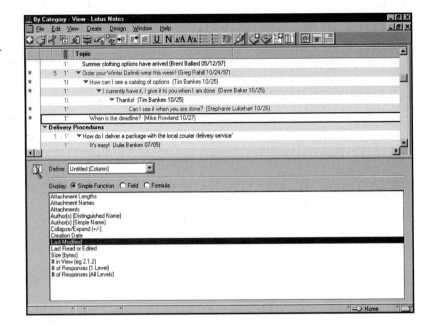

■ Author(s) (Simple Name): Uses `@Name([CN];@AUTHOR)` to return the author's name without its fully distinguished format, as in Tim Bankes.

■ Collapse/Expand (+/-): Uses `@IsExpandable` to return a plus symbol (+) if the view entry has descendants that are not visible because the main document or category is collapsed, or a minus symbol (-) if there are no subordinate documents or if subordinate documents are currently visible. This is a feature left over from Notes Release 3 and should be replaced by selecting the Show twistie when row is expandable option defined within the column's Properties InfoBox.

■ Creation Date: Uses `@Created` to display the time and date a document was created. The data type is a Time/Date.

■ Last Modified: Uses `@Modified` to determine when a document was last saved. The data type is a Time/Date.

■ Last Read or Edited: Uses `@Accessed` to determine the last time and date a document was read or edited. The data type is a Time/Date.

■ Size (bytes): Uses `@DocLength` to return the size of the active document in bytes. The data type returned is a number.

■ # in View (for example, 2.1.2): Uses `@DocNumber` to display a number for each document, indicating its order in the view. Responses are numbered in outline style under Main documents; for example, the first response to the first main document would be 1.1.

■ # of Responses (1 Level): Uses `@DocChildren` to return the number of direct descendant (response) documents for a document or the number of next-level subcategories for a category. The data type returned is Special text.

■ # of Responses (All Levels): Uses @DocDescendants to return the total number of descendant (response and response-to-response) documents for a document or subcategories for a category.

▶ **See** Chapter 14, "Working with Formulas," **p. 583**

Using Fields

Selecting the Field option in the Programmer pane displays a list of the fields currently available in the database. This is a great time-saver if you are not sure of the field names or their correct spellings. Figure 12.41 displays the DateCreated field being selected from the list of available fields for the second column of this view.

FIG 12.41

This quick shortcut is the same as selecting Formula in the display and typing the field name.

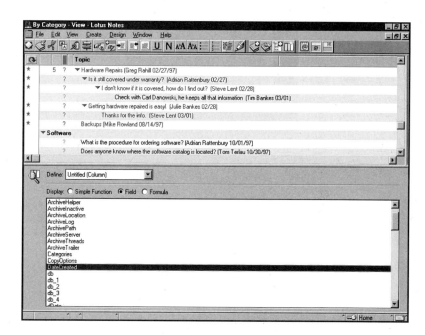

Using Formulas

Choosing the Formula option is the traditional way to enter a column formula. You will encounter situations in which the Simple Function and Field displays are not enough to perform detailed column formulas, as shown in Figure 12.42.

When in the formula window, you can enter the formula. You can even click the Fields & Functions button to display a list of available fields and functions that can be pasted into the formula.

The following formula reformats the contents of From to put the last name first followed by a comma, a space, and the first name (for example, Bankes, Tim):

```
@If(@Contains(From; " ");
@Right(From; " ") + ", " +
@Left(From; " "); From)
```

FIG 12.42

The Formula option allows you to create broader and more detailed formulas to capture the column contents that you want.

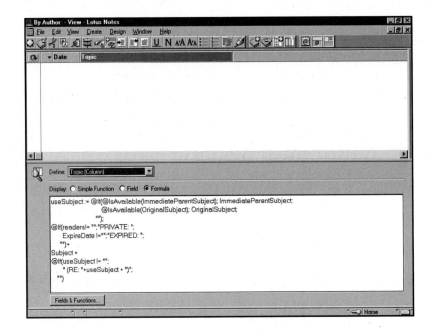

The following formula is useful for a categorizing column that displays each month as a category name. Dates need to be converted to a text value to be displayed in a view:

```
m :=@Text(@Month(Date));
@If(
m = 1; "January";
m = 2; "February";
m = 3; "March";
m = 4; "April";
m = 5; "May";
m = 6; "June";
m = 7; "July";
m = 8; "August";
m = 9; "September";
m = 10; "October";
m = 11; "November";
m = 12; "December";
"")
```

To show people's names and phone numbers together in one column, create a column that is sorted in ascending order. The following formula separates the two field values with a blank space:

```
Name + @If(Phone = ""; ""; " (" + Phone + ")")
```

For more information about using @Functions and programming using the formula language, see Chapter 14, "Working with Formulas," and Chapter 15, "Working with Functions and Commands."

Defining Selection Formulas

Usually, in each database you design a Main view that displays all the documents. It is often useful, however, to have one or more selective views that include only documents relevant to a particular topic or that meet certain criteria. The view's selection formula selects which documents are displayed in a view.

> **N O T E** Every view has a selection formula. If you do not define one, Notes defaults to SELECT @All, which selects every document in the database.

To create a selection formula, perform the following steps:

1. Open the desired view in edit mode.

2. In the Programmer pane, select View Selection from the Define list box or click anywhere in the upper view pane.

3. Write the selection formula in the formula box and refresh the view to see whether your formula evaluates correctly. Figure 12.43 shows a sample selection formula that selects only those documents in which the From author field equals Cate Richards.

FIG 12.43
Selection formulas allow you to eliminate extra forms and documents you do not want to display.

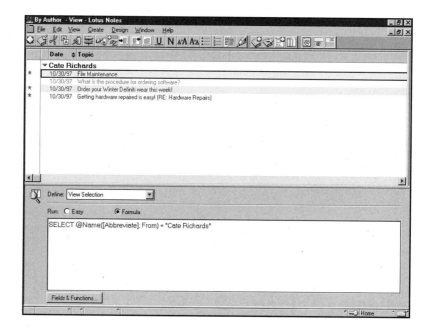

Part
II

Ch
12

Using Folders

Folders are very similar to views. In fact, you design a folder nearly the same way you design any Notes view. Why create folders? Designing a folder is useful when none of the existing views of a database shows information the way you want to see it. Folders let you store and manage related documents without putting them into a category. This would require a categories or keyword field in the form used to create the documents. In fact, you can easily add and remove documents from folders by dragging selected documents.

The best way to describe folders and their advantages is to compare them to the folders used for email, favorite URLs and bookmarks, and within file directories. They allow you to move documents into logical subsets of data. They are user friendly because they allow dragging and dropping of documents into them (as well as actions performed by menus, buttons, and so on). Figure 12.44 displays the Discussion template database with the folder My Favorites, which displays documents that have been selected and moved into this folder.

FIG 12.44

Folders allow you to organize selected documents.

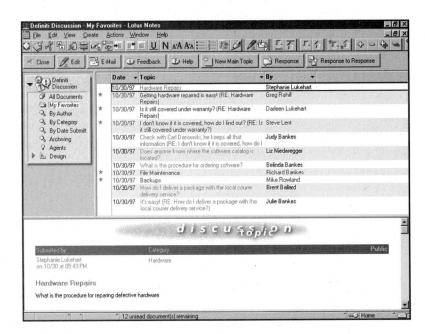

When you create a folder, its design is automatically based on the design of the default view of the current database. You can choose to base the folder's design on a different existing view or to design the folder from scratch. After you create a folder, it appears in the Navigation pane until you delete the folder.

Designing Folders

You can keep a folder private or share it with other users of a database. No one else can read or delete your private folders. To create private folders in a database, you must have at least Reader access to the database. To create shared folders in a database, you must have at least Designer access.

▶ **See** "Understanding Database Security," **p. 926**

When you create a private folder, Notes stores it in one of two places:

- If the manager of the database has allowed it, your folder is stored in the database, letting you use the folder at different workstations. To see whether a database allows storage of folders, select the database, choose File, Database, Access Control, and see whether the Create personal folders/views option is turned on, as shown in Figure 12.45.

FIG 12.45
The Access Control List dialog box allows you to see whether you can create personal folders and views.

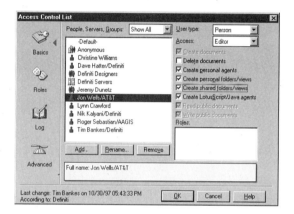

- If the manager has not allowed storage of folders in the database, Notes stores your folder in your desktop file (DESKTOP.DSK).

Creating a Shared Folder

If you cannot find a folder that is similar to the one you need, create a new folder. Creating and editing a folder works exactly like creating and editing a view. Its initial design is copied from the default design or from the default view if you haven't set up a default design. Follow these steps to create a shared folder:

1. Select or open the database where you want to create the folder. Choose Create, Folder or choose Create, Design, Folder. The Create Folder dialog box appears.

2. Enter a name for the folder in the Folder name box.

3. Select Shared (folders are private by default). To learn more about creating private folders, see Chapter 10. Private folders are displayed in a gray color; shared folders are displayed in yellow.

4. Click Folders to store this folder at the top folder level, or click the name of another folder to place this new folder inside an existing folder.

5. Select the Personal on first use option if this is a private folder that you're distributing to multiple users. Select the Store in desktop option if you want the folder always stored in the user's DESKTOP.DSK file.

6. (Optional) To select a view to base the folder's Inherit design on, select Options. This allows you to choose the desired folder or view and to set the Design now checkbox to immediately modify the folder design.

7. Click OK to create the folder.

If a view or folder already in the database is similar to the one you need, you might be able to use it with only minor modifications. To copy a folder, perform the following steps:

1. In the selected database, choose View, Design.

2. In the Navigation pane, click Design, Folders.

3. Click the folder you want to copy and choose Edit, Copy (or use press Ctrl+C or the SmartIcons).

4. Choose Edit, Paste (or use Ctrl+V or the SmartIcons). This automatically creates a copy of that folder; the name starts with Copy of. If no existing view or folder suits your purpose, create a new one. Its initial design is based on the default design you have set for new views and folders, or on the default view if you haven't set a default design. You also could copy a folder from another database.

Setting Folder Properties

After creating the folder, you might want to further define its properties. Using the Properties InfoBox, you are able to define both basic properties (such as the folder name and alias) and more advanced properties (such as its style and security levels). To do so, perform the following steps:

1. In the selected database, choose View, Design.

2. In the Navigation pane, click Design, Folders, and then double-click the desired folder. This opens the folder in design mode.

3. Right-click the mouse and choose Folder Properties or select Design, Folder Properties. This displays the Folder Properties InfoBox, as shown in Figure 12.46.

While designing a folder, you also can create more advanced options using actions and navigators. These allow the user to automate moving documents between folders. Folder actions allow users to perform specific tasks on documents without having to open them, and navigators allow the user to switch and move easily between folders.

Renaming and Deleting Folders

You can rename, move, or delete any private folder and any public folder to which you have Designer or Manager access. To rename a folder, follow these steps:

1. In the Navigation pane, select the desired folder.

2. Choose Actions, Folder Options, Rename to display the Rename dialog box.

3. In the Name box, enter a name of up to 64 characters, unless cascading one level.

4. Click OK.

FIG 12.46

The Folder Properties InfoBox enables you to select and define the attributes for your folder.

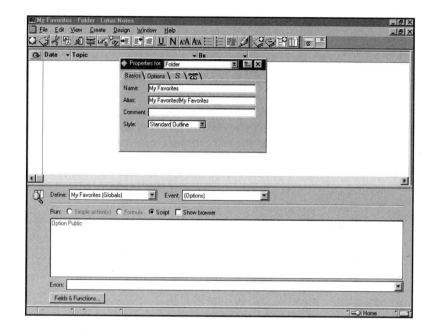

To delete a folder, perform the following:

1. In the selected database, choose View, Design.
2. In the Navigation pane, click Design, Folders.
3. Highlight the folder you want to remove.
4. Choose Edit, Clear or press the Delete key.
5. Click Yes to confirm the deletion.

Another way to delete a folder is the following:

1. In the Navigation pane, select the desired folder.
2. Choose Actions, Folder Options, Delete Folder.
3. Click Yes.

Moving Folders

You can move the folders under Folders and Views in the Navigation pane into other unrelated folders. You cannot, however, move a folder into its parent folder, any of its children, or itself. To do so, perform the following steps:

1. Display the Navigation pane.
2. If Folders and Views is collapsed (its triangle is pointing to the right), click the triangle.
3. Drag the folder you want to move into the folder you want to move it to.
4. Using the menu, select the folder you want to move.

Part
II

Ch
12

5. Select Actions, Folder Options, Move.

6. In the Choose a folder list, click the folder into which you want to move the selected folder.

7. Click OK to move the folder.

Integrating Notes with Other Applications

With Lotus Notes, workgroup members can share documents and data created in other applications and use those documents to collaborate on ideas, issue reports, track clients, monitor projects, and customize workgroup processes. Notes enables you to integrate data from other programs by importing, exporting, linking, embedding, and accessing back-end data through the power of LotusScript.

Lotus Notes includes a suite of tools, called NotesFlow, designed to extend the power of Notes by providing methods to build applications that share information and integrate with other desktop products. Notes flow tools allow designers to build cross-product, workflow applications that automate business processes, simplify tasks, reduce risk, and drive the flow of work. After you integrate your data with Notes, you can use the power of Notes—and its great security and replication features—to manage your documents. This approach is more powerful, secure, and manageable than saving files to a shared group network drive.

By incorporating Notes Field Exchange (Notes/FX) and Object Linking and Embedding (OLE), you can create dynamic applications that use the best programs with Notes. This functionality is not new to Notes, but has been more tightly integrated and enhanced with Release 4.6. An excellent example of Notes OLE integration is the new user preference to use Microsoft Word or Lotus Word Pro as your document memo editor with e-mail (see Chapter 4, "Getting Started with Electronic Mail").

Importing and Exporting Data with Other Applications

Lotus Notes provides several ways to import information from other programs into Notes documents or views. Conversely, Notes data can be exported to other software programs and file formats.

In Notes the File, Import and File, Export commands allow you to transfer information through various standard file formats. Whether you want to exchange data with a Windows, OS/2, or DOS application or with your company's mainframe, you'll discover an easy way to do it with Notes.

Transferring data to and from Notes is performed from a view or from within a specific document. Views are used to exchange tabular information between the Notes database and another application. You use documents only when you want to transfer data from a specific document. In most cases you probably will import or export large numbers of records and, therefore, will need to work from a view.

To import or export tabular data from the view level, switch to the desired view; select File, Import or File, Export; choose the desired file format; and name or select the file to be imported or exported. Notes supports the following file formats when exporting or importing tabular data at the view level:

- Lotus 1-2-3 worksheet (.WKS, .WK1, .WRK, .WR1, .WK3, and .WK4 extensions)
- Structured text
- Tabular text

When exporting or importing rich text data at the document level, Notes supports the following file formats:

- Lotus Ami Pro (1.x or later)
- ASCII text
- Binary with text
- BMP image
- CGM image
- Excel 4.0/5.0
- GIF image
- JPEG image
- Lotus 1-2-3 worksheet
- Lotus PIC
- Microsoft Word RTF
- Microsoft Word for Windows 6.0
- PCX image
- TIFF image 5.0
- WordPerfect 5.x, 6.0/6.1

Importing a File into a Document

You can easily convert data from another application so that a Notes document can use the data. To import a file from another document, perform the following steps:

1. Open the document in edit mode.
2. Select the field where you want the imported data to appear. You must be in a rich text field to import.
3. Choose File, Import or click the File Import SmartIcon to display the Import dialog box (see Figure 13.1).
4. Select a file type in the Files of type list box.
5. Locate the desired file using the Look in list box and then select the file; alternatively, just enter the path and filename in the File name box.
6. Click Import to import the file. Figure 13.2 displays a file imported into a rich text field.

N O T E You may need to adjust the margins and tab settings to align some portions of an imported file. ▮

FIG. 13.1

Use the Import dialog box to specify the file to import into your Notes document.

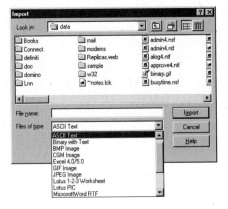

FIG. 13.2

The file is imported into the Notes document.

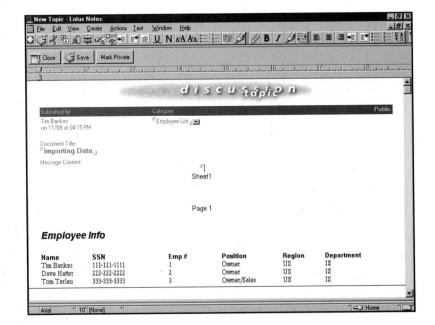

7. If the type of imported file is either a Lotus 1-2-3 or Symphony Worksheet, specify whether the entire worksheet file should be imported or a specific named range and its respective name (see Figure 13.3). If the file is an ASCII text file, specify whether line breaks should be preserved

Importing Pictures

You can use the clipboard to copy pictures into a document. You can also import picture files into a document using File, Import. To copy a picture or graphic object into a document, perform the following steps:

FIG. 13.3

When importing a Lotus
1-2-3/Symphony file,
specify the range of
data to import into the
rich text field.

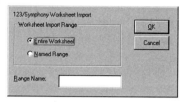

1. Copy the picture in the source application (press Ctrl+C or choose Edit, Copy).

2. Switch to Notes and open in edit mode the document you want to add the picture to (press Ctrl+E or choose File, Open).

3. Do one of the following:

    - If you are creating/editing a document, select the rich text field where you want to place the picture.

    - If you are designing a form, place the cursor where the graphic should be displayed.

4. Choose Edit, Paste; press Ctrl+P; or click the Edit Paste SmartIcon.

It is important to note that you can only paste and import pictures into a rich text field of a Notes document. To import a picture file into a document, perform the following steps:

1. Open the Notes document in edit mode (press Ctrl+E or choose File, Open).

2. Do one of the following:

    - If you are creating/editing a document, select the rich text field where you want to place the picture.

    - If you are designing a form, place the cursor where the graphic should be displayed.

CAUTION

The Import menu is unavailable if you don't import an image into a rich text field.

3. Choose File, Import or click the File Import SmartIcon to display the Import dialog box (refer to Figure 13.1).

4. Specify the file type and name of the picture file; then click Import. The image is inserted into Notes (see Figure 13.4).

N O T E If the file type for your image file does not appear, open the image in its source application and use a copy/paste procedure to copy the image into Notes. You can import BMP, JPEG, PCX IMAGE, GIF, and TIFF 5.0 bitmap files into documents.

Part
II

Ch
13

FIG. 13.4

The image is imported into your Notes document where you specified.

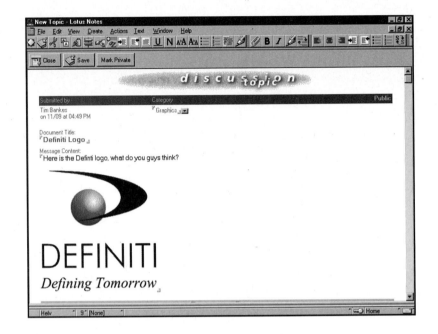

Sizing Graphics for Rich Text Fields and Navigators

Two questions typically come up when working with importing pictures:

Q. The pictures that I import come in very large. How can I change their appearance in Notes?

A. After a picture file has been imported into Notes, you can easily adjust or resize the graphic. To do so, click the picture once and then drag the box in the picture's lower-right corner in the desired direction to resize. Notes treats the picture as one unit, so you must resize the entire picture. To help you gauge the picture's dimensions, Notes displays the picture's current width and height as a percentage of its original width and height above the status bar.

Q. After resizing a picture, I discovered that the original dimensions of the imported picture were more appropriate. How do I return a picture to its original size?

A. Open the document containing the picture in edit mode and click the picture. Next, choose Picture, Picture Properties to display the Properties InfoBox. Click the Basics tab and then click the Reset width and height to 100% button.

Notes treats the graphic images and backgrounds you paste into navigators differently than it treats pictures imported into rich text fields. You must size all graphics you plan to paste into navigators before you paste them into Notes. You cannot size them after they are pasted into the navigator.

When pasting or importing images into Notes, colors may be slightly adjusted to match the Lotus color palette. This modification can produce undesirable results. To minimize distortion of graphic images, limit the quality of the graphic images to 256 colors and use the Lotus color palette (Lotus.act or Lotus.pal). This file is available to download from Lotus at http:// www.lotus.com/devtools/2106.htm.

The User Preferences setting called Dither Images instructs Notes to adjust the bitmap rendering to more closely match that of the original graphic. This setting is available only on systems with 256 colors and doesn't help users running at a higher-quality resolution. However, because this option is a user-defined setting, you can not be sure if it is enabled on your user's systems. Therefore, you should create graphics that work independently of this setting. Dithering also significantly slows document loading and often produces undesirable results.

Importing Structured Text Files

Importing data from ASCII files is relatively painless, and with a little preparation and setup, Notes can offer quite a bit of flexibility. For example, if your company's MIS reporting department provides your group with customer mailing lists in ASCII file format (generally mainframe downloads are in ASCII or tabular-text format), you can set up Notes to make importing the data a simple matter. The important step to remember when importing data into Notes is that you will be importing from the view level. Choose File, Import and then in the Import dialog box you can select from three basic types of data files:

- Structured Text
- Tabular Text
- 1-2-3 Worksheet

If you are working with ASCII text files, you must select either the Structured Text or Tabular Text type. A structured text file is an ASCII text file that contains labels that identify each field. It retains its structure in fields and values when imported into Notes. Generally, records and fields in structured text files are separated by a form-feed ASCII character or delimiter. The following example displays a comma-delimited text file:

```
"Joe Lotus","123 Main Street","Bartlett","IL","60103"
"Mary Smith","456 Oak Street","Streamwood","IL","60107"
```

When you import a structured text file into a view, the field names in the text file must correspond to the field names in the Notes document. To do so, you create a form that contains the names of the fields you're importing. Figure 13.5 shows an example of a structured text file that imports data into a contact list database.

N O T E When importing or exporting structured text files, they must have an .LTR, .CGN, or .STR extension.

To import structured text files into Notes, follow these steps:

1. Choose File, Import or click the File Import SmartIcon. The Import dialog box appears (see Figure 13.6).
2. In the Files of type list box, select Structured Text as the file type. Then select the path and name of the structured text file.
3. Choose Import. Notes displays the Structured Text Import dialog box (see Figure 13.7).

Part
II

Ch
13

FIG. 13.5

You can import a structured text file into a Notes view.

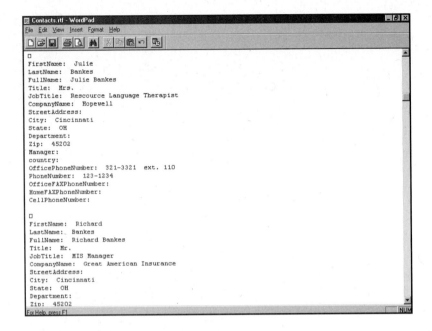

FIG. 13.6

This example displays the structured text file, CONTACTS.TXT, being imported.

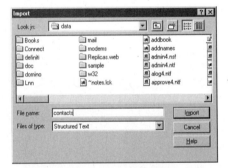

FIG. 13.7

The Structured Text Import dialog box specifies how to import the CONTACTS.TXT file into your Notes database.

4. In the Use Form list box, select the desired form into which you want the data imported. This list displays all the available forms in the database.

5. Select an Inter-document delimiter to indicate how to separate the records—either Form-feed or Character-Code.

NOTE The order of the labeled fields does not have to match the order of the fields in your Notes form. Each record could have fields of various sizes. You must separate records with a specific delimiter, however, such as ASCII Code 12 (the form-feed character). Each structured text field is limited to 256 bytes per field. ▪

6. Leave Main Document(s) selected in the Import As list unless you are creating Response documents. For example, if your Notes database has contact information contained in main documents and call report information contained in response documents, you would select this option to import call report data into a corresponding call report response document.

7. Leave Justify selected in the For body text list to wrap text to fit the Notes window, or you can choose to maintain the existing line breaks in the source file by adding a return character at the end of each line of text.

8. (Optional) If you want the imported documents to contain every field of the form you selected, select Calculate Fields on Form During Document Import. This setting creates in the document any of the calculated fields that exist on the form, even if you are not importing them.

9. Click OK. Notes imports the data into the fields in your Notes database using the selected form (see Figure 13.8).

FIG. 13.8
Using the selected form, import the records into the view.

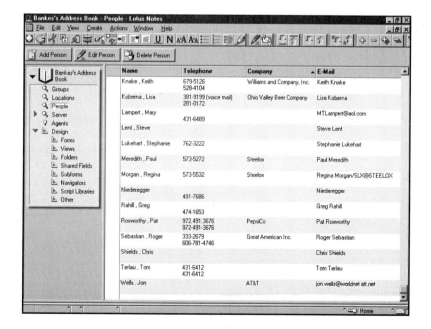

N O T E If the worksheet file being imported contains multiple sheets, Notes imports the sheet (or range from the sheet) that was last selected when the file was closed. ▪

You can now use existing views or design new views to display the imported data in any desired way. For example, you could design a view that includes contact name and address information sorted alphabetically on the contact name. This view could then be exported to an external application for printing mailing labels.

▶ **See** "Adding Fields to a Form," **p. 444**

▶ **See** Chapter 12, "Designing Views," **p. 485–538**

Importing Tabular-Text Files

Reports from mainframes or client/server databases are downloaded in the format of tabular-text files. Tabular-text files contain ASCII text in distinct rows and columns because records and fields are separated with equal amounts of tabs, spaces, or other delimiters. When importing or exporting tabular text files, they must have a .TAB, .TXT, .PRN, or .RPT extension.

If you have a Notes database with a view in which field names and widths exactly match the contents of the tabular view, you might be able to import the database directly into the view with little trouble. The tabular-text file doesn't always provide data for all the target fields, however, and also might not properly identify to Notes the contents of each field. Situations like this arise if you are attempting to import a file that has not been parsed. A nonparsed file is an ASCII file in which delimiters or tabs have not been defined.

N O T E When importing tabular text into a view, each record is limited to a maximum of 999 characters. ▪

Suppose that a file contains a listing of customer information from your company's customer contact system that must be downloaded in comma-delimited format (see Figure 13.9). Each field in a comma-delimited file is surrounded by quotes, and each field is separated by a comma. Each record must contain the same number of fields or items.

Next, suppose that you want to import this file into a Notes database you have designed. The Customer Profile form you are importing into the database should contain the fields listed in the CONTACTS.COL file shown in Figure 13.10. You can create a COL file with any ASCII text editor and give it the extension .COL. The target form can contain more fields than the tabular-text or comma-delimited file and the fields can be in a different order.

Column descriptor files (COL files) are used with tabular text files and worksheet files to map a notes view, more specifically, the Notes fields, to the imported source file. When the source file and the Notes view do not have the same format, COL files tell Notes how to interpret the text file and map the information to Notes field names. Because COL files are saved and can be reused, they are helpful for importing multiple source files that have the same structure.

FIG. 13.9

The comma-delimited file CONTACTS.TXT shows records as rows; the field data is separated by commas.

```
contact.txt - Notepad
File  Edit  Search  Help
Ballard,Brent,561-0886  ext. 119,,Cincinnati,OH
Bankes,Belinda,732-7595,,Cincinnati,OH
Bankes,Judy,369-5901,,Cincinnati,OH
Bankes,Julie,231-8771,Hopewell,Cincinnati,OH
Bankes,Richard,369-5901,Great American Insurance,Cincinnati,OH
Behrmann,Barry,513.984.4555 x104,Definiti,Cincinnati,OH
Buehler,Nicole,513.984.4555 x112,Definiti,Cincinnati,OH
Crawford,Lynn,583-0004,Infotech,Cincinnati,OH
Danowski,Carl,513.984.4555 x109,Definiti Inc.,Cincinnati,OH
Fishman,Alan,513.792.7983,Definiti Inc.,Cincinnati,OH
Fortuno,Gerard,583-0004,Kendle,Cincinnati,OH
Gibbs,David,606-781-9840,Hamilton County Justice Center,Cincinnati,OH
Hassebrock,Rick,232-2096,,Cincinnati,OH
Hatter,Dave,513-984-4555 x105,Definiti Inc.,Cincinnati,OH
Kalyani,Nik,513.792.7981,Definiti Inc.,Cincinnati,OH
Koberna,Lisa,381-9199 (voice mail),Ohio Valley Beer Company,Cincinnati,OH
Lent,Steve,343-6409,,Cincinnati,OH
Lukehart,Stephanie,762-3222,,Cincinnati,OH
Meredith,Paul,573-5272,Steelox,Cincinnati,OH
Morgan,Regina,573-5532,Steelox,Cincinnati,OH
Niederegger,Brian,491-7686,,Cincinnati,OH
Niederegger,Liz,491-7686,,Cincinnati,OH
Niederegger,Jake,491-7686,,Cincinnati,OH
Niederegger,Leah,491-7686,,Cincinnati,OH
Niederegger,Jack,491-7686,,Cincinnati,OH
Rahill,Greg,474-1653,The Chop House,Cincinnati,OH
Roxworthy,Pat,972.491.3676,PepsiCo,Cincinnati,OH
Sebastian,Roger,333-2679,Great American Ins.,Cincinnati,OH
Shields,Chris,,,Cincinnati,OH
Terlau,Tom,431-6412,,Cincinnati,OH
Wells,Jon,,AT&T,Kansas,KS
```

Column descriptor files are ASCII text files that contain column definition statements and formulas that control how data in the source file is mapped to fields located in the view. One statement is written for each column in the source file that describes how to modify values in the source file to the columns in a view. The formulas can use @If formulas to test values or they can use text manipulation functions to trim or concatenate values or to assign default values.

To create a COL file, follow these steps:

1. Open any ASCII text editor and create a file using the .COL extension.

2. Enter the name of the column in the source file followed by a colon. This name must be identical to the name of the field on the form.

3. (Optional) Specify the data type after the column name using the TYPE expression, followed by the data type. The data type must be Text, Number, or DateTime. If no data type is defined for each field, Notes automatically determines the data type based on the appearance of the data. In addition, if the imported data doesn't match the data type specified, Notes automatically converts the data type to the type it most resembles. The following COL file example shows all three data types:

```
tCustomerAddress: TYPE TEXT
nCustomerAge: TYPE NUMBER
dDate: TYPE DATETIME
```

4. Specify the format of the data source (for example, the delimiter of fixed position of the column). If the tabular text file uses a delimiter character to separate columns of data,

use the UNTIL keyword to specify the delimiter for each field. The syntax for the UNTIL statement is

```
tCompanyName: UNTIL ","
```

If no delimiter character occurs at the end of the row, specify the last field delimiter as null (""), as shown in Figure 13.10.

5. If it is necessary to write formulas within the COL file, create a section with the keyword FORMULASTART and FORMULAEND. This section must appear after all column definition statements, and only one such section can fall within each COL file. The formula start must appear alone on a line before any formulas. Subsequently, the FORMULAEND must appear alone after the last formula. Every line within this section (appearing between the keywords) must end with a semicolon (similar to programming with @Functions elsewhere within Notes).

Here are some other keywords that can be used in COL files:

■ START and END define fixed-width columns of data, rather than defining a delimiter character. The first column position always starts with 1. The following example of a column definition uses the START and END keywords to define the tCustomerName field as 20 characters wide:

```
tCustomerName: TYPE TEXT START 1 END 20
```

■ WIDTH is used with the START keyword. It also defines fixed-width columns of data, rather than using a delimiter character, by defining the length of the keyword. For example:

```
tCustomerName: TYPE TEXT START 1 END 20
tCustomerAddress: TYPE TEXT START 21 WIDTH 40
```

■ HEADER tells Notes to ignore header information for the number of lines specified after the HEADER keyword.

■ FOOTER tells Notes to ignore footer information for the number of lines specified after the FOOTER keyword.

■ LINESPERPAGE sets the maximum number of lines per page. The LINESPERPAGE count includes header lines and footer lines even if they have been suppressed with the HEADER and FOOTER keywords:

```
HEADER 3 FOOTER 1 LINESPERPAGE66
```

■ WKSCOL allows you to associate a field with a specific worksheet column. The syntax for the WKSCOL statement is

```
fieldname: WKSCOL columnletter
```

fieldname is the name of the field in the view, and columnletter is the column in the worksheet source file.

■ RANGE allows you to specify the range to be imported from the worksheet. Setting values in the COL file will override settings entered in the Worksheet Import Settings dialog box. The syntax for the range statement is

```
RANGE rangename
```

rangename is a the name of a valid range in the imported file. When using the RANGE keyword, the first WKSCOL statement in the COL file must refer to the first column in the range.

Keywords can be put together on the same line or each on their own line. The settings created in the COL file override values in the Tabular Text Import dialog box.

> **N O T E** Field names that are defined in the COL file but are not displayed in the Notes view are still imported into the Notes document. Field names must be created within Notes that match the field names as defined in the COL file. ■

FIG. 13.10

The CONTACTS.COL file tells Notes how to interpret the contents of the comma-delimited text file (shown in Figure 13.9) into documents, using a specified form in the database.

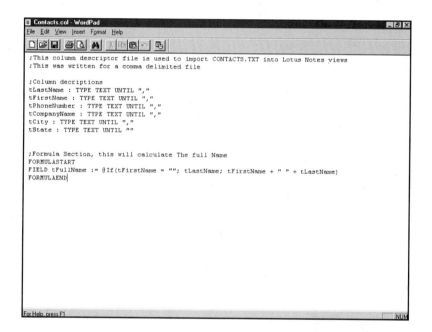

After creating the COL file, switch to Notes and the database that should receive the imported data. Then perform the following steps:

1. Choose File, Import or click the File Import SmartIcon to display the Import dialog box.

2. Select the Files of type list box and select the text file that will be imported in the File name list box, using the Look in list boxes if necessary.

3. Click Import to display the Tabular Text Import dialog box (see Figure 13.11).

4. Select the desired form in the Use Form list box.

5. Select Use format file. Click Choose format file to display the Choose an Import Format File dialog box to select the COL file that you created.

6. Click OK to import the data based on the COL file.

Figure 13.12 displays the sample CONTACTS.TXT file that was imported into a Notes database.

FIG. 13.11
With the Tabular Text Import dialog box, you can choose various options for importing the comma-delimited file.

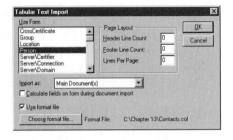

FIG. 13.12
The CONTACTS.TXT file has been imported into the database.

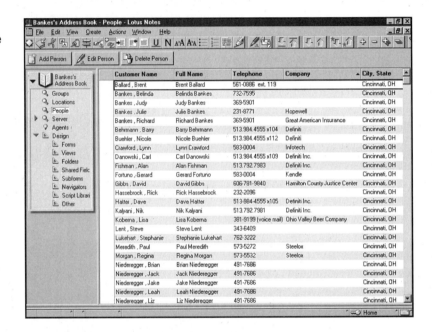

 TIP To quickly see whether the data was imported in the correct fields, open a document or choose File, Document Properties, and select the Fields tab.

Using Notes with Spreadsheet Programs

Occasionally, you might need to extract Notes data into a format that allows you to perform what-if analysis or to build graphs for financial analysis. One option is to embed an object (such as a spreadsheet or chart component) and use LotusScript to pass variables to the object and display the results (see the first Bonus Chapter, "ODBC and Lotus Components"). Another option is to export the Notes data to a spreadsheet program. Because Notes can export and import data to and from Lotus 1-2-3 worksheet file format, any program that can read or write a WK* file can effectively share data with Notes.

N O T E To export Notes data into Microsoft Excel, you can export the view data into Lotus 1-2-3 format and then open the file in Excel as a Lotus 1-2-3 file type (at which point Excel will convert the file to an Excel format) or use 1-2-3 to save the data as an Excel spreadsheet. ▪

Exporting Notes Data to a 1-2-3 Worksheet   To export data from Notes to a 1-2-3 worksheet file, you must start from a view because you can't export to a worksheet file from within an open document. When you export a view to a worksheet, each document becomes a worksheet row and each field becomes a worksheet column, with field contents becoming cell contents. The view does not need to display all the fields available in the Notes database, but it must contain all the fields you want to export.

▶ **See** "Creating Views," **p. 490**

▶ **See** Chapter 14, "Working with Formulas," **p. 583**

Using the same sample documents from the previous exercise, suppose that you want to export the contact information from the view shown in Figure 13.12. With the desired view selected, perform the following steps:

1. Choose File, Export or click the File Export SmartIcon to open the Export dialog box (see Figure 13.13).

FIG. 13.13
With the Export dialog box, enter the filename, extension, filetype, and location for the new file

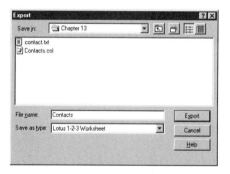

2. Enter a filename in the File name box; then choose Lotus 1-2-3 Worksheet in the Save File as Type list box.

3. Specify the drive and directories in which you want to save the file in the Save in list boxes and then click the Export button. The 1-2-3 Worksheet Export dialog box appears (see Figure 13.14).

4. Select All Documents if you want to export all the documents appearing in the view, or select Selected Documents if you have preselected a subset of the available documents.

5. Select the Include View Titles checkbox if you want to export the column titles along with the data. The column titles will populate the first row in the spreadsheet.

6. Click OK. The view information is imported into 1-2-3 worksheet format.

If you open the exported file in 1-2-3, you will see something like Figure 13.15.

FIG. 13.14

In the 1-2-3 Worksheet Export dialog box, you can specify how you want to export the data.

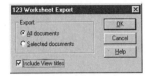

FIG. 13.15

The fields in the original view have become columns and every document has become a row.

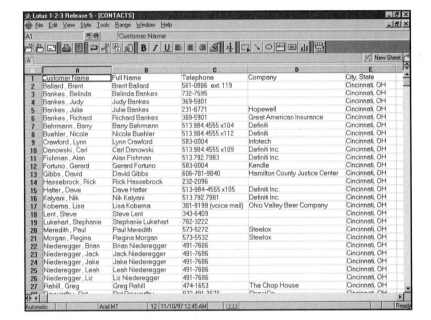

> **CAUTION**
>
> When you export a view to a new spreadsheet file, Notes exports the file as plain worksheet data without any formatting or styles unless you specify a file extension. If the filename does not include a file extension (for example, `Contacts`), when you open the exported file in 1-2-3, you may see the message `File or extension converted`, indicating that the worksheet has been converted to the appropriate format for the 1-2-3 version that you're using. You may also need to reformat some data, (for example, time values) into the desired format and resize the column widths. Reformatting will be necessary when working with other programs such as Excel, Word, and Quattro Pro.

Importing Spreadsheet Data   Importing data into Notes from a spreadsheet file requires more preparation than exporting from Notes. You should assign a range name to the data range in the file that you want to import, and you might need to build a view to receive the spreadsheet data. When you import a spreadsheet into a view, each spreadsheet row becomes an individual document and each spreadsheet column becomes a field, with the cell contents becoming field contents. You must create both a form and a view before you import a spreadsheet file into a view.

T I P Don't include any column headings in this range name because Notes imports the column headings as a document.

 T I P Before importing large amounts of data, always import small test files. Before importing an entire spreadsheet, for example, you might want to import a named range of several rows and columns.

To understand how to import a spreadsheet, you can import the data CONTACTS.WK4 that you just exported (refer to Figure 13.15). This worksheet data will be imported into a view designed to receive the worksheet data. Follow these steps:

1. Create and save the view that will import the spreadsheet data. In the Import view, columns are ordered and fields are designated to accept the data. The columns in the receiving view should not be categorized and must exactly match the columns in the worksheet. For example, if the first column in the worksheet's range contains a name, you should set the first column of the view to contain those names.

▶ **See** "Creating Views," **p. 490**

▶ **See** "Sorting Options," **p. 520**

2. Switch to the view into which you'll be importing the data.

3. Choose File, Import to display the Import dialog box (see Figure 13.16).

FIG. 13.16

The Import dialog box is similar to the Export dialog box.

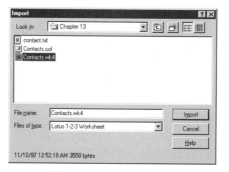

N O T E Notes will not wrap lines of the imported worksheet. Display the horizontal scroll bar with the View, Show, Horizontal Scroll Bar and scroll across the view, adding the necessary columns. You can add as many columns as you can fit within the maximum view width of 22.75 inches. ▪

4. Specify 1-2-3 Worksheet in the Files of type list box. If you select a 1-2-3 Worksheet file, the file type will change to the appropriate type automatically.

5. Select the file in the File name box; use the Look in list box if necessary.

6. Click Import to open the Worksheet Import Settings dialog box (see Figure 13.17).

FIG. 13.17

In the Worksheet Import Settings dialog box, choose the appropriate Notes form and other options to use for importing the data.

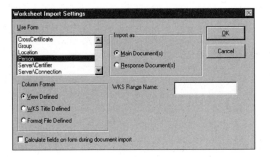

7. Choose the form that will receive the data from the Use Form list. This form should be the one that contains the fields that exactly match the data you are importing.

▶ **See** "Creating a New Form," **p. 426**

8. Select the desired column format. This example uses View Defined because you're mapping the columns in the spreadsheet to the Notes view. The following list describes when to use the various column format options:

   - View Defined: Select this option if the format of the worksheet columns (the column names and widths) exactly matches the format of the columns in the view. The columns in the view must contain the field name; otherwise, the data will appear in the view after the import but will not be contained in the corresponding field.

   - WKS Title Defined: Select this option if the cell contents in the first row of the worksheet file are to become column headers in the database. These cell contents must be labels. Field names will be created from the column titles and can be used in the database forms.

   - Format File Defined: Select this option (the most reliable import method) if you created a separate column format descriptor file (COL file) as described earlier in the section "Importing Tabular Text File."

9. Select the desired option in the Import As section. Generally, you want to import each worksheet row as a main document, so leave the Main Document(s) option selected. If you need to, however, you can import the spreadsheet data into Response Document(s).

10. If you're importing the whole worksheet, leave the WKS Range Name box blank. Otherwise, enter the name of the named range you want to import. A named range is a name assigned to a range of cells or a single cell in a worksheet.

11. If you are importing data that needs to be calculated, select Calculate Fields on Form during Document Import. This option allows Notes to calculate any computed fields on the form during the import procedure. For example, suppose you have a computed field called Region that contains the following formula:

```
@If(State = "IL";"Midwest";State = "CA";"West";State = "OH";
"Mideast"; State = "NY";"East";"")
```

This code would calculate the Region field based on your formula.

CAUTION

Notes imports information more quickly when you do not select Calculate Fields on Form because it is not required to calculate each field on the form when importing. Also, some calculated fields may not be meant to be used in this manner and may create unexpected results.

12. Choose OK or press Enter to import the data into the Notes database.

N O T E Notes uses a character translation file to translate foreign symbols and characters. This file (CLS) must be located in the Notes program directory. To change the character translation set, select File, Tools, User Preferences; click International; click Import/Export Character Set; and select the appropriate CLS file. ▨

Understanding Object Linking and Embedding (OLE)

NotesFlow is an assortment of tools that help to expose the open development platform and information-sharing capabilities of Notes. The tools can be used singly or together to facilitate OLE, publishing actions, Notes/FX, autolaunching objects, and using ODBC. You can use the NotesForm tools to perform the following:

- Design forms that contain embedded objects. Each document created with the form can contain the same object or can contain linked objects that refer to a shared source file.

- Design forms that launch objects automatically based on certain form settings.

- Set up Notes forms to exchange data with OLE-compliant applications. The data can be unidirectional or bidirectional, using default field names or user-defined field names.

- Design actions that use formulas or LotusScript and publish those actions so that they appear in the action menu of the OLE server application.

- Use the ODBC standard to access external databases and bring the information into Notes for routing, searching, reporting, and sharing (see the first Bonus Chapter, "ODBC and Lotus Components").

OLE technology allows data to be shared between OLE-compliant applications for Windows and Macintosh systems. OLE 2.0, which is supported by Notes4, is the second generation of OLE. OLE 2.0 is an expansion on the Microsoft Windows OLE that lets you share data in additional ways. For example, you can use OLE 2 features such as drag-and-drop and "in-place" editing to create and manipulate object data more easily. OLE information generally can be linked, embedded, or both. Some of key benefits from OLE 2 are

- Drag-and-Drop: OLE 2 objects can be created in Notes by simply dragging data from an OLE 2 server application and dropping it into Notes.

- "In-Place" Editing: OLE 2 objects can be edited using the server application's commands and menu bar from within the Notes window.

Part
II
Ch
13

- Link Server: Document links, view links, and database links can be created in OLE 2 client applications.
- Storage Server: OLE 2 objects can be embedded into Notes documents with links to the embedded data and other OLE 2 client applications.

To use OLE 2.0, customers must have two OLE 2.0–compliant applications: a server and a client. The server application contains the source data, and the client application is the recipient of the source data. For example, if you embed a 1-2-3 worksheet object into a Notes database, 1-2-3 is considered the server application and Notes the client application. Linking an OLE object means getting a copy of the object or data from the server, placing it in the client, and maintaining a link to the server application so that the client is kept up-to-date.

N O T E OLE linking is similar to Dynamic Data Exchange (DDE) linking in that the link is dynamic; that is, the data updates when the original file changes. Unlike DDE, however, users can double-click an OLE link and load the server application to modify or update information. With a DDE link, you would need to first load the source application and locate and open the file to modify the data. Check your source application to determine whether it is DDE or OLE 2.0 capable. ■

Embedding an object means placing the entire object into the client application. Unlike linking, the connection is not dynamic; embedding does not maintain a continuing link to the server application. As a result, if data in the source file changes, it will not change in the embedded object within Notes; an embedded object immediately becomes a physical, static part of the client application. Compared to linked objects, embedded objects take up more physical space, but because the embedded object is contained within Notes, users do not need access to the source file. Therefore, using the source file and sharing it among team members (some of which may be mobile, disconnected clients) is easier since users are not required to open the source file (which might be stored on a server).

Linking an Object

A linked object is a pointer to data in another file. If you make any changes to the original source file, those changes are automatically reflected in the Notes document containing the linked object because of the link that was created. Because there is a link to a source file (typically stored on a shared server), users must have access to the server, directory, and source file. In addition, they will have to have a drive mapped to the location of the source file. Therefore, if they are not currently connected to the server (disconnected users), they will not be able to access the linked object. To link a file created with another application to a Notes document, perform the following steps:

1. Select the desired data in the file and copy it to the clipboard using Edit, Copy (or Ctrl+C).

CAUTION

If the application is a DDE server, but not an OLE server, make sure that you keep the server application and linked file open when updating a link between the DDE server and the Notes document containing the linked object.

2. Switch to Notes and open in edit mode the document to which you want to add the linked object (press Ctrl+E to place the document in edit mode).

3. Do one of the following:

   - If creating/editing a document, position the cursor into the rich text field where you want the object to appear.

   - If modifying the design of a form, place the cursor where the object should appear on the form.

4. Choose Edit, Paste Special or click the Edit Paste Special SmartIcon to display the Paste Special dialog box (see Figure 13.18).

FIG. 13.18

In the Paste Special dialog box, you can link an object in a Notes document to the object's source file.

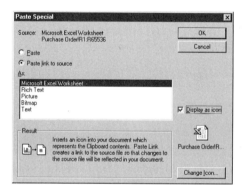

5. Select Paste link to Source to create a linked object. You also could select the Paste option to paste the object without any linking features (see Figure 13.19).

FIG. 13.19

The linked Excel 97 object (in this case, a worksheet) is inserted into the Notes document.

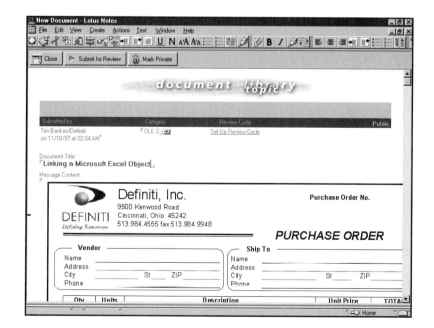

Part

II

Ch

13

6. Select a display format for the object from the <u>A</u>s list box. The options available in the <u>A</u>s list box will change, depending on the type of source data.

7. If available and desired, select <u>D</u>isplay as Icon to display an icon, instead of the linked data. (To display a different icon, click Change <u>I</u>con and make your selection.) Choose this option if you do not want to display everything that is copied or you don't want the object to take up a lot of space in your Notes document.

8. Click <u>O</u>K.

This process inserts a picture of your clipboard contents into your document. Paste <u>l</u>ink to Source creates a link to the source file so that any changes to the source file are reflected in your Notes document. If you make any changes to the source file, Notes prompts you to update the linked object when you open the document (see Figure 13.20).

FIG. 13.20
Notes detects whether the object is linked and prompts you to update the object in the Notes document if desired.

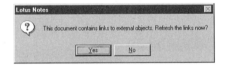

You can update linked objects automatically on activation or update them manually. To change a linked object's update type, start in edit mode and perform the following:

1. Click the object.

2. Select <u>E</u>dit, External L<u>i</u>nks to display the External Links dialog box. This dialog box lists the links that are currently available in your document and allows you to edit the link, update the link, open the source, or break the link.

3. Select <u>A</u>utomatic to update the object each time you activate it; select <u>M</u>anual to update the object as needed (see Figure 13.21).

4. Click <u>O</u>K to save your changes.

FIG. 13.21
The External Links dialog box allows you to set automatic versus manual updates, update the object now, open the source file, edit the link, or break the link.

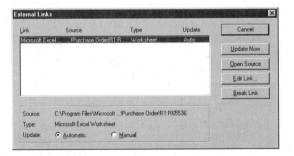

T I P   To display or edit an object's data when the object is displayed as an icon, double-click the icon.

When you link a file to a Notes document, keep the following in mind:

- You must be in a rich text field to add an object.

- You must save the source file. Without a filename, Notes does not know what file to link to.

- If the server application is an OLE server, Notes creates an OLE object. If the server application is a DDE server, but not an OLE server, Notes creates a DDE object. When you create or activate a DDE object in Notes, you must have both the server application and Notes open.

- In Notes you can display objects in four display formats (rich text, bitmap, picture, and text), as well as in a format corresponding to the server application. The server application determines which display formats are available, however. If you select a display format the server application does not provide, Notes displays the object in picture format instead.

- If you select the Display as Icon option in the Paste Special dialog box (refer to Figure 13.18), Notes displays the server application's icon by default. To display a different icon, click the Change Icon button, which appears when you select Display as Icon. From the Change Icon dialog box, you can choose between the current and various default icons available for that application or even choose a different file to select another icon.

Embedding Part or All of a File

Recall that an embedded object is basically a copy of data from another file. Changes made to the original source file are not reflected in the Notes document. To embed a portion of a file, start in the source application and perform the following steps:

1. Select the data you want to embed and then copy it to the clipboard by choosing Edit, Copy (or pressing Ctrl+C).

2. Switch to Notes and open in edit mode the document to which you want to add the embedded object. (Do so by choosing File, Open or pressing Ctrl+E.)

3. Do one of the following:

   - If creating/editing a document, position the cursor in the rich text field where you want the object to appear.

   - If modifying the design of a form, place the cursor where the object should appear on the form.

4. Choose Edit, Paste Special, or click the Edit Paste Special SmartIcon to display the Paste Special dialog box (refer to Figure 13.18).

5. Select Paste.

6. Select the way you want the pasted data to appear from the As list box.

7. If available and desired, select Display as Icon for Notes to display an icon, instead of the embedded data.

▶ **See** "Linking an Object," **p. 558**

8. Click OK.

Part
II

Ch
13

This procedure inserts an embedded picture of your clipboard contents into your document. It looks the same as a linked object, but it acts differently in that any changes you make to the source file will not be reflected in your Notes document. In fact, double-clicking the object activates a new file based on the original object that you can modify and save back to Notes. Embedding files is ideal for document-versioning applications.

When you embed an object in a Notes document, keep the following in mind:

- You must be in a rich text field to add an object.
- If you select the Display as Icon option, Notes displays the server application's icon by default. If Display as Icon is selected, you can click Change Icon to choose a different icon to be displayed.
- If Notes cannot determine the format of the data in the original file, it will display the server application's icon instead of the data.
- If you embed a blank object using a server application that can also serve as a client application, then you can embed other objects into the object you're creating. For example, you could embed a Word 6.0 document into a Notes document, and then within that same Word 6.0 document, you could embed an Excel 5.0 object. In this way you can build compound documents using different source applications.

To embed an entire file in a document, perform the following steps:

1. In Notes, open in edit mode the document to which you want to add the embedded object (press Ctrl+E).

2. Do one of the following:

    - If creating/editing a document, position the cursor in the rich text field where you want the object to appear.

    - If modifying the design of a form, place the cursor where the object should appear on the form.

3. Choose Create, Object or click the Create Object SmartIcon to display the Create Object dialog box (see Figure 13.22).

FIG. 13.22
With the Create Object dialog box, you can select the object type and file to insert.

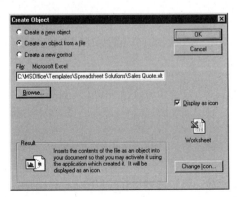

4. Select Create a <u>n</u>ew Object to display the available options. Notes displays the object types that have been registered to your operating system.

5. (Optional) Select Create an Object from a <u>fi</u>le; then in the Fil<u>e</u> text box, enter the path and filename. Alternatively, you can click the <u>B</u>rowse button and select the desired file.

N O T E You can also select Create a New <u>c</u>ontrol from the dialog box to select a new control that you have created to insert into a Notes document. For example, you may have created a DLL or OCX control that you want to insert into a document in Notes. You will also see these controls appear in the Create a <u>n</u>ew Object list—possibly flagged by a symbol. Selecting the control from either location is an acceptable way to work with these controls.

6. (Optional) Select <u>D</u>isplay as Icon to have Notes display an icon, instead of the embedded data.

7. Click <u>O</u>K to insert the object file. Double-click the embedded file to activate it for editing. If the application that created the embedded file is not currently running, Notes starts the application.

This new and separate object is not related or linked to the existing object. Any changes or updates made in the original file will not be incorporated into this object.

Embedding a Blank Object in a Document

You can embed a blank object in a Notes document. Embedding blank objects is useful when you want to insert a new object that is not based on any preexisting data. If you embed a blank object using a server application that can also serve as a client application, then you can embed other objects into the object you're creating.

N O T E Notes will display only the object types that have been installed on your system. For instance, Lotus Approach would not be shown as an object-type option if it was not installed or registered. Check your `WIN.INI` and `REG.DAT` files for more details.

When you add a blank object, Notes opens a blank work file in the application you select so you can enter data. After selecting File, Save within the server or source application, the data and embedded object will be saved in Notes. Starting in Notes, follow these steps to add a blank object:

1. Open in edit mode the document to which you want to add the embedded object (press Ctrl+E).

2. Click to position the cursor where you want the object to appear.

3. Choose <u>C</u>reate, <u>O</u>bject or click the Create Object SmartIcon to display the Create Object dialog box.

4. Select Create a <u>n</u>ew object to display its available options (see Figure 13.23).

Part

II

Ch

13

FIG. 13.23

You can select a 1-2-3 worksheet object to insert into the current document.

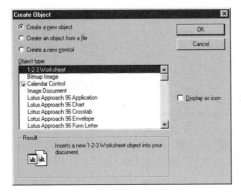

5. Select the desired object type from the Object Type list box.

6. Select an object type that corresponds to the application you want to use (for example, Freelance Presentation or 1-2-3 Worksheet).

7. (Optional) Select Display as Icon to have Notes display an icon instead of the embedded data.

8. Click OK to insert the selected object into your Notes document.

You now can create new data in the blank work file.

After working with the file and if the embedded object is OLE 2.0–compliant, you can click anywhere on the Notes document to save the object data and return to Notes. You can easily double-click the object to activate the object to edit and modify.

Using the OLE Launch Features in a Form

You can design document management databases that automatically open blank embedded objects when you create a new document. Compared to using a network drive, this type of Notes database is better for organizing and managing databases because users may not have access to your network drive or may not know the correct path to the files. Using Notes, any user with the appropriate access (designated in the Access Control List) can locate documents using the views in the database. The Microsoft Office Library template, doclbm46.NTF, and the Lotus SmartSuite 96 Library (Release 4), doclibl4.NTF, use this workflow.

To create a form that automatically launches another application, start in the database in which you want the launch to happen and perform the following steps:

1. Create a new form or edit an existing one and add fields to store the desired information (for example, AuthorName, Category, Title, DateCreated, and Body).

2. Choose Design, Form Properties to display the form's Properties InfoBox or click the Design Form Properties SmartIcon.

3. Click the Launch tab to designate the launching properties for this form (see Figure 13.24).

FIG. 13.24

The Launch tab allows you to set Auto Launch options for OLE objects and specific launch options.

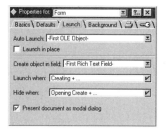

4. In the Auto Launch drop-down list box, Notes displays the available applications installed on your PC that your operating system recognizes. You can select the application that you want to launch automatically. Also, Notes will display the following three options if an object or attachment already exists on your form:

- First Attachment: Automatically launches the first file attachment contained in the form.

- First Document Link: Automatically launches the first linked document contained in the form.

- First OLE Object: Automatically launches the first OLE object contained in the form. Selecting this option will display more options to further define how this object will launch.

5. You can select from the following options if you previously selected First OLE Object in the Auto Launch drop-down list box:

▶ **See** "Settings for Launching Objects," **p. 441**

- Launch In-Place launches the object in place, enabling the user to edit the object directly within Notes. This feature is called *in-place editing* because the menu in Notes changes to adapt to the corresponding application. In other words, you don't have to launch the embedded object's application and then have Notes switch to that application. The menus, toolbars, palettes, and other controls necessary to interact with the object temporarily supplement the existing menus and controls of the active window. If an object is not launched "in-place," then it is launched "out-of-place," causing focus to shift to the application and sending Notes to the background.

N O T E Only objects that support OLE2 can launch in place. Objects that support only OLE1 will launch out-of-place regardless of the Launch In-Place setting. Embedded objects that are stored as icons always launch out-of-place.

- Advanced Options displays additional options such as hiding and creating when the object is selected.

- Create Object in Field allows you to select None, select First Rich Text Field, or specify which rich text field to create the object in. All the rich text fields that currently exist on the form will appear as options in the drop-down list box. If

Part

II

Ch

13

another rich text field is available in the form, you could select it here. This will save the object in the indicated field.

- Launch When instructs Notes when to launch the indicated object. You can activate the object when creating, editing, and/or reading. The Creating option launches the embedded object when the document is created. The Editing option launches the object when the user edits a document that was created with this form. The Reading option launches the object when the user opens a document created with this form and uses it in read mode. If the form autolaunches a new object, the Launch When setting must include Creating because Creating is the only event that launches a new object. Also, if the form has been set to Automatically enable edit mode, any "Launch When" attributes for Reading will be ignored.

- Hide When instructs Notes when to hide the object. You can hide the object when you select the following options: Opening Create, Opening Edit, Opening Read, Closing Create, Closing Edit, and Closing Read. Some of these options will be grayed out depending on the settings for Launch When and the Present Document as Modal Dialog. The Hide When options are not available when Launch In-Place is selected. You can design a form that hides the Notes document during any of these activities, and you can select more than one available option.

- Present Document as Modal Dialog displays a dialog box with the form when returning from the object; otherwise, the form is presented in a full pane. Figure 13.27 shows an example of this option. The user can also select actions not shown in the modal dialog box by clicking the Action button. These actions are the Action Bar buttons designed for the form. To modify the design of these buttons, select View, Action Pane in the design mode of the form.

6. Save the form.

Depending on which options you selected, you can now create a new form by selecting it from the Create menu. Figure 13.25 displays a Microsoft Word document object that is launched automatically when the user selects the form from the Create menu. Because the object has been set to launch in place, Microsoft Word menu options are available even though the object is contained within Notes. Action Bar buttons designed with the form are also available. The user can enter data into the document and then save the data and switch back to Notes.

In this example the Document Info dialog box appears when the user returns to Notes, prompting the user for the document title and category (see Figure 13.26).

Other Features of OLE 2.0 Available in Notes

OLE 2.0 offers several enhancements to OLE 1.0 and provides additional versatility in Notes 4. For example, if a user double-clicks an object that was created by an OLE 1.0–compliant application and that object is contained within an OLE 2.0–compliant application that supports in-place editing, a new editing window is activated in the OLE 1.0 style.

FIG. 13.25
Automatic launching of a Word 97 object with Launch In-Place enabled.

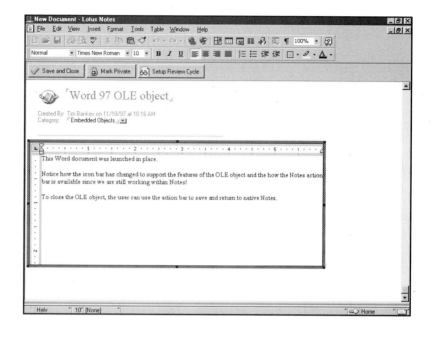

FIG. 13.26
The Present Document as Modal dialog option was selected in this example, so the user is prompted to enter a title and category.

N O T E   OLE 2.0 is backward compatible with OLE 1.0, which means that programs written to the OLE 1.0 specification can interact with OLE 2.0-compliant applications (and operating systems) as if both used OLE 1.0. ■

The following list describes some features of OLE 2.0 available in Notes:

- ■ Nested object support allows users to directly manipulate objects nested within other objects and to establish links to nested objects. Essentially, therefore, you can embed objects within other embedded objects.

- ■ Drag-and-drop allows users to drag objects from one application window to another or drop objects within other objects.

For example, you can drag an illustration from a Word 97 application window and drop it into a Notes document (see Figure 13.27).

FIG. 13.27

You can drag and drop a Word 97 object into a Notes document and the object will then be embedded.

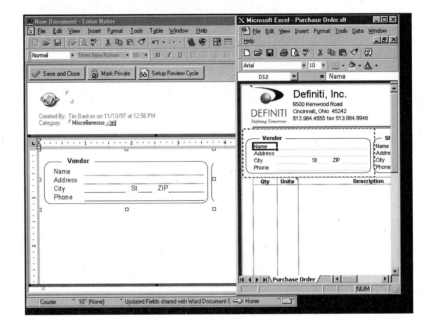

■ Storage-independent links support links between embedded objects that are not stored as files on disk but within Notes documents. In other words, embedded objects within the same or different documents can update one another's data, whether or not the file system recognizes embedded objects.

■ Adaptable links maintain links between objects in certain move or copy operations, which means that if you move a linked object to a new file path, the link will be maintained and recognized in its new location.

■ Programmability allows the creation of command sets that operate both within and across applications. For example, a user could use LotusScript to invoke a command from Notes 4 that sorts a range of cells in a spreadsheet created by Excel.

■ Logical object pagination allows objects to overlap page boundaries and break at logical points.

■ Version management allows objects to contain information about the application in which they were created, including what version of the application was used. This feature gives programmers the ability to handle objects created by different versions of the same application.

■ Full-text searching allows embedded objects and attachments to be included in full-text searches. However, when a word match is found, the object or attachment is launched but the word/phrase is not highlighted.

■ Object conversion allows an object type to be converted so that different applications can be used with the same object. For example, an object created with one brand of spreadsheet can be converted so that it is interpretable for editing by a different spreadsheet application.

The following sections describe in more detail some of the new OLE 2.0 features in Notes 4 that allow you to create remarkable compound documents using the power of Notes/FX.

> **CAUTION**
>
> Keep in mind that UNIX does not support autolaunching.

Using Application Field Exchange

The latest releases of most productivity applications—1-2-3, Word Pro, Freelance, Word, PowerPoint, Excel, and so on—support a powerful feature of application integration called Notes Field Exchange (Notes/FX).

Notes/FX uses OLE technology to enable Notes and any OLE server application to share data fields or to swap information. The contents of fields in an OLE server application file can appear automatically in a corresponding field in a Notes document, and vice versa. Furthermore, depending on the type of field, you can update the contents of the field from either application.

> **N O T E** Lotus SmartSuite products use Notes/FX 1.1, the latest version, which includes enhancements to the handling of OLE objects. Microsoft Office products still use Notes/FX 1.0, an older version, however.
>
> If you install the 32-bit version of Notes on your client workstations, you may experience problems using FX between Notes and other applications. The 32-bit version of Notes supports OLE 2 technology—the technology used by FX. Some Microsoft applications do not support all the additional functionality added in Notes OLE 2 technology. Therefore, if you want to use FX, you may need to install the 16-bit Notes client or upgrade to Microsoft Office 97. ■

This Notes-driven technology greatly extends the application potential of Notes. For example, you can use 1-2-3 to create sophisticated worksheets or use Word Pro to create robust documents and then users can save, categorize, and view these worksheets or documents in a Notes database. By working within Notes, you leverage the information stored in Notes and exploit the workgroup collaboration services of Notes. Why is Notes/FX more useful than just using object linking and embedding documents? Notes/FX expands the capabilities of OLE by enabling you to build fields of information that can be shared between a Notes document and the object. These fields can then be shown easily in either application. Notes/FX fields fall into three category types:

■ One Way: These fields support the exchange of data in only one direction. They usually supply basic file information such as author, creation date, and file size.

■ Two Way: These fields support bidirectional exchange of data between the OLE server application and the OLE client application. These fields allow updates in either direction for the default fields that are defined in the OLE application such as description or subject.

■ User Defined: These fields support bidirectional exchange of data between the OLE server and client application and can be defined by the developer. Both sets of fields must be created in both the server application and the Notes form. This type of field is the most robust type to exchange.

From the desktop perspective, you now have a powerful way to store, browse, organize, share, and collaborate on desktop documents throughout an organization. No one will ever again have to say, "Here's a disk with marketing files" or "The financial spreadsheets are somewhere on drive G."

Benefits of Notes/FX Applications

Notes/FX can seamlessly integrate workgroup applications with Notes by extending Notes to use the powerful editors and features provided by other applications. Designing a Notes/FX application yields the following benefits:

■ You can replicate documents and templates throughout the company.

■ You can use security and access control features from Notes to regulate data access.

■ You can use version control to implement and maintain documents.

■ You can automated approval management.

■ You can build groupware applications quickly by using existing desktop applications, thereby facilitating rapid application development.

■ You can categorize and sort desktop documents.

■ You can search and retrieve quickly.

Table 13.1 lists some of the many business applications that could be used in developing a Notes/FX application.

Table 13.1   Business Applications of Notes/FX

Application	Examples
Managing workflow	Travel planning, expense authorization, customer support, call tracking
Collaboration and review	Budget planning, sales projections, contract management, document versioning
Sharing documents	Presentation libraries, form letters, marketing materials, corporate policies

How Does Notes/FX Exchange Data

Notes/FX uses OLE-embedded objects to exchange information with fields in a Notes form. For example, if you embed a 1-2-3 worksheet document in a Notes database using OLE, then 1-2-3 makes data in cells and ranges available to Notes, along with some document information. Notes can use these fields in views or calculations and can return new values to the 1-2-3 worksheet.

For Notes/FX to exchange data with an OLE-enabled server application, the field names in the embedded file (server) must correspond exactly to the field names in the Notes form being used. For more information about fields in any other application that exchanges data with Notes, see the Help documentation for that application.

Using Application Field Exchange

Three major steps are involved in setting up a Notes/FX application:

1. Create the application document that will be used with Notes; then use Edit, Copy to copy a portion or all of the document to the clipboard.

2. Embed the application in a Notes document or form. By embedding the object, you are initializing a live OLE link that enables the field exchange.

3. Define the user-defined fields that will be used to exchange information (as described by your application's Help instructions).

The following example creates a Notes/FX application using 1-2-3 and Notes that tracks expense reports. The expense reports are created in a 1-2-3 worksheet and then stored in Notes for easy document management and categorization.

All you must do is to identify and match Notes field names with 1-2-3 range names or cell addresses. To exchange data between 1-2-3 and Notes, a 1-2-3 worksheet object must be embedded in a Notes form. In the worksheet object, you need to create a two-column table of data you want to exchange.

Preparing the Notes Form   The Notes form must be designed to store the fields that will exchange data with the object (in this case, a 1-2-3 worksheet) and to store the 1-2-3 worksheet object itself. To create such a form, start in Notes and follow these steps:

1. Select or create a new database. Choose Create, Design, Forms; alternatively, you can edit an existing form.

▶ **See** "Creating a New Form," **p. 426**

2. Create and name fields to contain text and numbers from the 1-2-3 worksheet object (see Figure 13.28). Use descriptions and instructions to tell database designers how the form works.

Part

II

Ch

13

FIG. 13.28

The Notes form contains fields that will exchange data with the embedded Lotus 1-2-3 object.

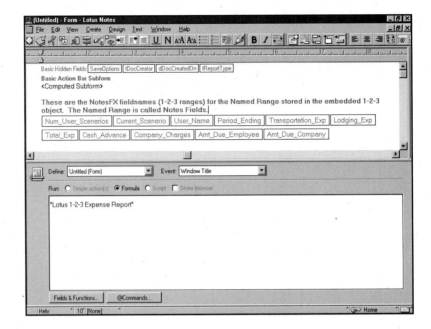

3. Choose Design, Form Properties to display the form's Properties InfoBox; then click the Launch tab to reach the options shown in Figure 13.29.

FIG. 13.29

You can select an Auto Launch option from the form's Properties InfoBox.

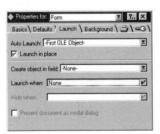

4. Select First OLE Object in the Auto Launch drop-down list box. Doing so indicates that you want Notes to launch the first OLE object encountered on the form. (You will embed this object in the next section.)

5. Save the Notes form.

Preparing the Embedded Object To create a Notes/FX application using 1-2-3 and Notes, perform the following steps:

1. Open the desired 1-2-3 worksheet or create a new file. Figure 13.30 displays the 1-2-3 worksheet object that will be embedded in a Notes form.

FIG. 13.30

The Lotus 1-2-3 Expense Report worksheet template is already NotesFX enabled.

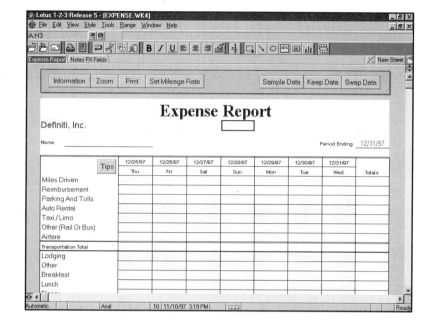

2. Create the fields to exchange data with Notes. Figure 13.31 shows the two-column table in the worksheet. The first two columns are essential for Notes/FX to work. The first column lists the field names in the Notes form that will receive and send 1-2-3 data. The second column defines the range names or values of the corresponding information in the 1-2-3 worksheet. This range of field names is then named with the range name Notes Field, which enables FX to find and exchange the field information.

N O T E The headings in the first row are not part of the Notes Field range—these are for reference only. They are not necessary for Notes/FX to occur and should not be included in the Notes Field range. █

 T I P Use Range, Name, Add in 1-2-3 Release 5 to name the two-column table Notes Field.

3. Arrange and position your worksheet area. Highlight a portion or all of the document and then choose Edit, Copy to copy the part of the worksheet that you want to display in the Notes form (see Figure 13.32). The selected range does not have to display the information that you want to exchange, but it is easier to recognize in Notes if the copied range is displayed.

4. Switch to your Notes form and then click to position the cursor where you want the object to appear.

5. Choose Edit, Paste, Special to display the Paste Special dialog box.

FIG. 13.31

The Notes Field range is required for Notes to exchange data with a 1-2-3 object.

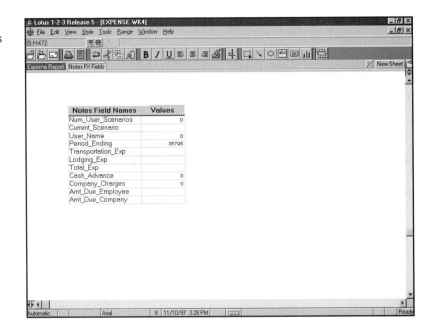

FIG. 13.32

Copy a range of data to display in Notes.

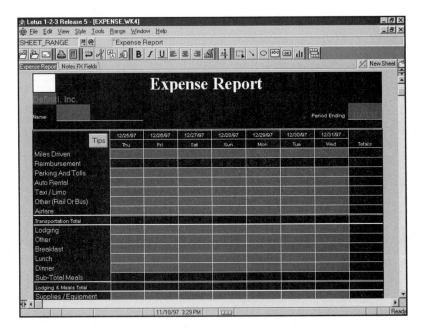

6. Select <u>P</u>aste and then 1-2-3 Worksheet in the <u>A</u>s list box to embed the 1-2-3 worksheet object in the form (see Figure 13.33).

7. Save the Notes form.

FIG. 13.33

The Embedded Lotus
1-2-3 object pasted
into the Notes form.

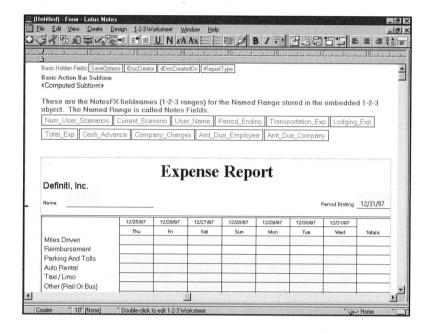

Using the Notes/FX Application You now can begin using the Notes/FX application you designed in the preceding section. To create a new Notes document using the embedded 1-2-3 worksheet object, perform the following steps:

1. Choose Create and then select the name of the form that you just created. If you selected First OLE Object in the Properties InfoBox, Notes creates a new 1-2-3 worksheet document based on the embedded object.

2. Edit the data in the 1-2-3 expense worksheet.

3. Choose File, Exit & Return to have Notes close 1-2-3 and return to Notes. Or choose File, Close to close the worksheet object without exiting 1-2-3. The fields in the Notes document that match the 1-2-3 data are updated (see Figure 13.34).

Your new document, including the new data entered in the 1-2-3 expense report template, appears in the view.

N O T E You can update the existing templates by opening the document that launches the 1-2-3 object. In 1-2-3, make any necessary changes; then update the document and return to Notes. Notes now reflects the modifications you made in 1-2-3. ▪

Publishing Actions to OLE Server Applications

By publishing an action, it becomes available within the Action Bar inside the OLE server application. Notes designers can then write formulas and LotusScript that run within the OLE

Part
II

Ch
13

application. You can use this powerful feature of NotesFlow to automate the routing and workflow of Excel and 1-2-3 spreadsheets, Word and WordPro documents, or any OLE 2–compliant application.

FIG. 13.34

The updated embedded Lotus 1-2-3 object after receiving NotesFX field values.

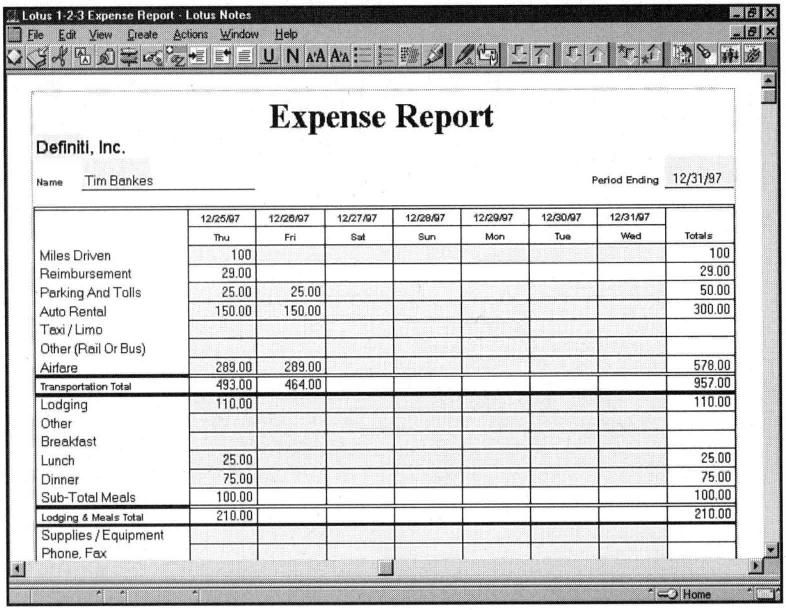

Using published tasks, you can coordinate and integrate tasks among various desktop applications and help the user to focus on the workflow process. For example, the Notes application could route a product order that was created in Microsoft Excel but stored as an OLE object within a Notes document for routing. The Action Bar could contain sequential routing steps for sending the document to next user, changing the document status, automating the sending of e-mail, providing the user with help, and so on. This feature speeds up cycle time, reduces risk of error, and provides an audit trail for management all within the security model and sharing capabilities provided by Notes.

OLE actions are Action Bar buttons that are modified to work with OLE applications. To create and publish actions, perform the following steps:

1. Open the form in design mode

2. Open the Action pane by selecting View, Action Pane.

3. Double-click on an action or create a new action by selecting Create, Action. Assign the action a Title, assign an icon (optional), and complete the basic action information. For more information on creating actions, see Chapter 11, "Designing Forms."

4. Click the NotesFlow Publishing tab. This tab displays the properties of the action when published to the OLE application (see Figure 13.35).

FIG. 13.35

From the NotesFlow Publishing tab, you can enable the action to appear in OLE objects and determine what the action should do when selected.

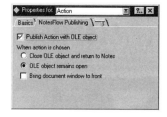

5. Select Publish Action with OLE Object.

6. Select a property that determines what should happen after an action runs. You have two choices:

   - Close OLE object and Return to Notes: This option causes the OLE object to save any changes that were made to the OLE document, close the OLE object, and return focus back to Notes.

   - OLE Object Remains Open: This option allows the focus to remain with the OLE object. Use this option when the user still needs to perform other tasks after the action has run.

7. Depending on the outcome of the action, you can select Bring Document Window to Front. This optional setting allows the focus to be returned to Notes without closing the OLE object. The OLE object will not be saved unless it is done programmatically or the user returns focus back to the OLE object to save. This feature will not work if the Notes document window has been hidden.

8. Enter code in the Programmer's pane of the IDE. Here you can use simple actions, @Functions, @Commands, or LotusScript. For more information, see Chapter 14, "Working with Formulas," Chapter 15, "Working with Function and Commands," and Chapter 17, "LotusScript Basics."

9. Save the form.

N O T E Make sure that the form property Disable Notes/FX is not selected in the form properties default tab. ■

Two excellent examples of publishing actions are the Microsoft Office Library (4.6), `doclbm46.ntf`, and the Lotus SmartSuite 96 Library (4), `doclib14.ntf`. They both use published Action Bars but the Microsoft template launches the OLE applications in-place, whereas the Lotus template launches the OLE application as a modal dialog (see Figure 13.36).

FIG. 13.36

The Microsoft Office Library autolaunches OLE objects in-place and publishes four actions to the OLE application.

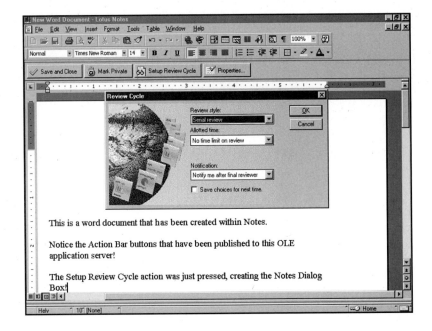

Using OCX Support

An OCX is an OLE custom control that allows designers to create and embed small, self-contained software modules within Notes documents. These modules are commonly referred to as ActiveX controls. They are similar to the Visual Basic controls (VBX controls) used with 16-bit versions of Visual Basic before Release 4.0. OCX controls can be both 16-bit and 32-bit controls; however, 16-bit OCX controls must be used with 16-bit applications, and 32-bit OCX controls must be used with 32-bit applications. In general, most new custom controls will be OCX controls. These controls are sometimes called plug-ins (not to be confused with Netscape Plug-ins). OCX controls are currently supported only on Windows 95 and Windows NT. Each OCX module contains the data and software it needs to run. To add an OLE custom control to a form, perform the following:

1. Open the form in design mode if you are adding the OCX to the form design,

   or

   open a document in edit mode and select the appropriate rich text field if you are adding the OCX to a rich text field.

2. Select Create, Object from the pull-down menu (see Figure 13.37).

3. Select the origin of the object:

   - Create a new Object: Select a custom control from the registered list of controls installed on your computer.

- Create an Object from a file: This option allows you to enter the path of the control file to insert a nonregistered control.

- Create a New control: This option shows only OLE custom controls, such as Lotus Components.

FIG. 13.37

The Create Object dialog box allows you to create a blank new object based on registered types, create an object based on a file, or create a new control.

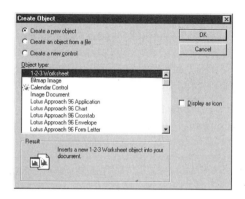

NOTE If a custom control does not display in the Create Object dialog box, you must use LotusScript to access and insert the control. ▪

Figure 13.38 shows a Calendar Control that was created by selecting the Create New Control option and then selecting the Calendar Control in the Create Object dialog box. (The options on your system will vary depending on what controls are installed and registered in your system.)

FIG. 13.38

The Calendar Control is one of many controls that you can embed within a Notes form or document.

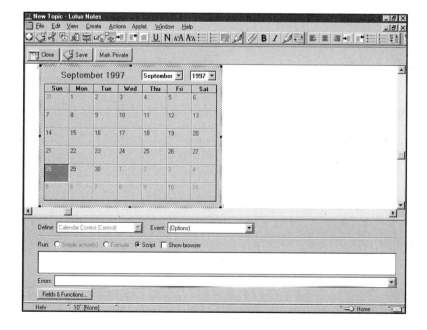

Part

II

Ch

13

4. Select the control and then select Applet from the pull-down menu to reveal several options and settings that apply to the control. From the Applet pull-down menu, you can view the control properties, edit its design, and freeze the control.

The following options are available via the Applet pull-down menu:

- Object Properties: Displays the formatting properties dialog box of the object, similar to the standard text properties dialog box (see Figure 13.39). To view the Object Properties of the control, select the control, choose Applet, and then choose Object Properties from the pull-down menu. The Info tab (the first tab) displays the following settings:

  - Object Name: This setting allows you to rename the object

  - Size Object to Window: This setting causes the custom control to expand and automatically fill the entire window when the document is opened in edit mode. Other data that is currently displayed in the form becomes invisible while the custom control is expanded.

  - Size Object Below Fields: This setting causes the custom control to fill the area of the Notes window below the layout region when the document is opened in edit mode. If no layout region exists on the form, the control automatically fills the entire screen. Any other information below the layout region will not be visible while the custom control is expanded. If the form contains multiple layout regions, the control automatically appears under the first layout region, and all other layout regions will be hidden while the control is expanded.

N O T E These settings will not take effect until the document is saved, closed, and reopened.

- Run Object When Reading Document: This setting allows you to make changes to the custom control while the document is in read mode. These changes cannot be saved until the document is in edit mode. However, these changes can be printed. While in read mode, the settings to Size Object to Window and Size Object Below Fields still take effect.

FIG. 13.39
The Applet Property dialog box allows you to rename the control, modify its size, set it to run in read mode, and set formatting options.

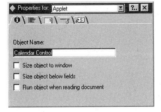

- Copy and Cut: This setting allows you to copy and cut the entire control using the Notes internal clipboard. Using the internal clipboard, a Paste operation pastes the control object while a Paste, Special pastes a representation of the object.

- Copy External: This setting copies the entire object using the OLE clipboard. When you use the OLE clipboard, a Paste, Special operation within Notes or another application pastes the actual object; in contrast, a Paste operation pastes a representation of the object.

- Edit Events: This setting opens the Design pane (displaying the calendar events) and the Programmers pane.

- Show Property Pages: This setting edits the control's own properties.

- Design Mode: This setting sets the control's mode to design or run.

- Freeze Events: This setting toggles freezing or unfreezing the control's events.

N O T E All properties and methods of an OLE custom control can be accessed in the same manner as other Lotus Notes objects. To examine the properties and methods for registered OLE controls, open the LotusScript browser and select OLE Classes. For more information on using LotusScript and using controls see Chapter 18, "Writing Scripts with LotusScript," and the Bonus Chapter "ODBC and Lotus Components." ▪

Using Java Support

Notes 4.5 gave Notes clients the capability to run Java applets. However, you could not directly insert the applet into a Notes document or form. First you had to convert a Web page that contained an applet to a Notes document using a Web Navigator. Then you could copy and paste the applet into the document. Now with Notes 4.6, Java applets can be directly inserted into a Notes form or document. The applets will run automatically after they are inserted into the form or document. The forms or forms containing the applets are served by Domino to any Java 1.0x- or Java 1.1-compliant browser.

Because applets can be made up of one or more classes and reference resources, the process of adding applets to forms and documents varies. Shipping with Notes Designer, Lotus BeanMachine allows nonprogrammers to enhance their Web site and easily create Java applets. BeanMachine is a visual, point-and-click authoring tool that combines Java Beans and Java applets. For more information on using Java and creating Web sites, see Chapter 25, "Using the Web Navigators," and Bonus Chapter 2, "Working with Web Publisher." ●

Part
II

Ch
13

Working with Formulas

The Lotus Notes formula language is a *nonprocedural language* (also called a *declarative language*) that has been around since the inception of Notes and that continues to grow in both features and capabilities. Although it has been supplemented (and in many ways supplanted) by LotusScript and now Java, it still provides a powerful way to accomplish fairly complex tasks with relatively little coding. It's a very useful tool in your developer's toolbox. In fact, there are several situations in Notes where you must use the formula language if you want to automate a process.

The following are objects that can only be programmed using the Notes formula language and/or Simple Actions (which are nothing more than predefined formulas you can use to "codelessly" automate your applications):

- Default Field formulas
- Form formulas (in a view)
- Input Translation formulas
- Keyword formulas
- Replication formulas
- View Column formulas
- View Selection formulas
- Window Title formulas

Each of these objects (and many more) will be covered in this chapter.

What Is a Formula?

Simply put, a *formula* is an expression that Notes evaluates to find a value. This value is then used in whatever context is appropriate at the time of evaluation. Many formulas are simply evaluated and have no side effects. For example, the following is a simple formula:

```
100 + 100
```

It adds 100 to 100, which, of course, equals 200.

However, some formulas do have side effects. For example, a formula might use the @Prompt function, which would cause a message box to appear:

```
@Prompt([Ok];"Reminder";"Don't forget to run backup tonight.")
```

When this formula is evaluated, the result is a dialog box that displays the message Don't forget to run backup tonight.

Taking side effects even further, a formula can also be a sequence of expressions that come close to being a program—in essence, all side effect and little evaluation. If fact, some people would argue that formulas are little programs in their own right.

So, writing a formula is a type of programming. Through formulas, you instruct Notes to accomplish some task. If you happen to be a programmer, you will find similarities between formulas and the programming languages with which you are familiar. In fact, you might be more comfortable using LotusScript. If you're not a programmer, don't panic; you don't need a degree in computer science to use formulas.

▶ **See** "What Is LotusScript?," **p. 682**

Formulas let you create variables and use control logic. Most of the complicated tasks that formulas perform require the use of @Functions. These functions, such as @Today, @If, @SetField, and @Prompt, seen earlier, are discussed more extensively in Chapter 15, "Working with Functions." Even though this chapter uses @Functions in examples, it is more concerned with the basics.

Notes formulas perform calculations according to strict instructions you provide. In almost any situation where Notes needs to use or display a value, you can provide a formula that tells Notes what steps to take to calculate the value. Formulas also let you express relationships between fields, cause Notes to choose between courses of action based on the values of fields, calculate values, and perform other complex actions.

One of the most common uses of formulas—and probably the easiest to understand—is using formulas in the columns of a view. Each column is usually set to a field name, so the value of that field is displayed. Simply by specifying the field name, you have created an extremely small formula. A more complicated formula would be conditionally displaying an icon in a column based on the value in a field. Figure 14.1 shows a view with a column that displays icons that visually represent the status of an item. For example, completed items have a green checkmark beside them, while items on hold are represented by an hourglass.

FIG. 14.1
A formula has been created to place an icon indicating the status of each name.

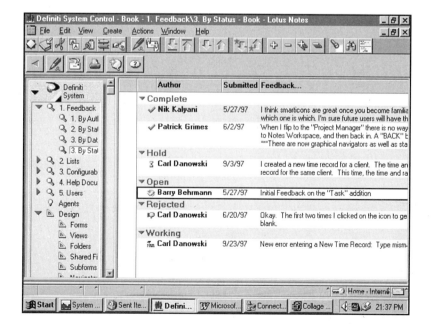

Part
II

Ch
14

When you edit a column formula in Notes in the programmer's pane, you can see what the view will look like in the designer's pane window in the top section of the screen. This makes checking your formulas very easy, because you can press F9 to have Notes recalculate the formulas and display the view.

▶ **See** "Creating Columns in a View," **p. 516**

Here are some other situations in which formulas can be useful:

- When you define a view, you can define a formula that selects which documents Notes displays in the view. This is called a *selection formula* and is instrumental in making views select only the documents you need.

- When you design a view, you create columns that display information for each of the documents in the view. A column can either display the contents of a field stored in a document, or it can have an elaborate formula that will be evaluated and its result displayed.

- A view can have a Form formula that is used to determine which form in a database will be used when the user elects to open a document displayed in a view.

- Forms can have a Window Title formula that is used to specify the title bar text that Notes displays when someone reads or composes a document.

- The fields on a form can use formulas to set their default value, to validate the data that has been entered in the field, and to manipulate the data in a field. For example, you might have the name entered in the CompanyName field converted to proper case when the document is saved.

- You can create buttons, hotspots, and actions and use formulas to accomplish a task. For example, you might create a button which, when clicked, calculates the amount of commission that should be paid on a particular sale based on the formula you have written.

This short list doesn't even begin to describe the plethora of ways you can use formulas in Notes. Later in this chapter, the section "Where Are Formulas Used?" details every formula type in Notes and gives examples of each.

Evaluating Formulas

When you use a formula, you are asking Notes to either compute a value or perform an action. But before we delve deeper into how and where you can use formulas, some brief coverage of the terms used when discussing and writing formulas is in order. Table 14.1 lists some common programming terms and their meanings.

Table 14.1 Common Programming Terminology

Term	Definition
Constant	Similar to a variable in that it temporarily stores data and is referred to by a name. However, by definition the value of a constant, unlike a variable, can't be changed by the program.
Expression	A statement that is used to describe some data and/or perform some action.
Equation	A mathematical expression that equates one set of conditions to another.
Keyword	A reserved word that has special meaning in a programming language.
Literal	Similar to a constant, a literal is a hard-coded value that won't be changed by the program. However, a literal isn't referred to by a name. For example, X might be a constant, but 8 is a literal.
Operator	A symbol used as a function, usually for arithmetic and logic.
Variable	A temporary storage area for data used in a program, referred to by a name chosen by the programmer. Variables by definition can be used to store changing data.

The most basic formula is a simple expression. For example, the formula

```
"This is an expression"
```

consists of a single string literal (which is just an unchanging value). Expressions can also consist of a field name or variables interspersed with operators. (Operators are just symbols used as functions. They are discussed in the section "Using Operators" later in this chapter.) For example, the formula

```
storeCost * 1.2
```

demonstrates calculating a 20 percent markup on the original price of the value contained in the storeCost field. The operator, in this case *, or multiplication, serves to connect the variable and a numeric constant.

Notes formulas can also consist of multiple expressions. When this happens, the last expression evaluated becomes the value of the entire formula. This is where some programming comes into play, because variables are usually involved. For example, a two-step process might be involved in determining a total cost column:

```
customerCost := customerPrice * 1.2;
taxToAdd := customerCost * .06;
customerCost + taxToAdd;
```

The first line uses `customerCost` as a temporary variable to simplify the calculation. It also helps isolate the different parts of a formula. If the `customerCost` expression needs to change in the future, only one line needs to be changed. Temporary variables have local scope, meaning that the contents of the variable are stored only for the life of the formula. When the formula is finished, the temporary variables vanish.

Notice that the `:=` operator is used to assign a value to a temporary variable (unlike most programming languages, which use `=`). You should also note that a semicolon ends each line. The semicolon tells Notes that the expression is complete and that it should be evaluated before continuing. Every line in a Notes formula must end with a semicolon (except the very last line, but it's good practice to get into the habit of ending every line with a semicolon).

When the last line of a formula is evaluated, the resulting value is returned as the result of the formula. For example, if the preceding code sample were placed in a view column formula, the column would display the total cost of the item plus tax.

Every formula must evaluate to some value, and every value must be one of the following five data types:

- Numeric values: These are numbers and include fields that you define as numbers. The example of `storeCost * 1.2` used a moment ago would evaluate to a number.

- Time/date values: These values represent a time or date and include fields that you define as a time or date. Formulas that evaluate to time/date values are useful as view column formulas. For example, you can use the `@Adjust` function to calculate when an invoice should be paid. The `@Adjust` function can add 14 days to the invoice date to arrive at the due date.

- Logical values: These values don't correspond to fields you define in a document. They always represent the answer to questions that can be answered "true" or "false." For example, Hide When formulas must return either a `true` or `false` value. In the Notes formula language, `true` is represented by `1` and `false` by `0`.

- Text values: These values include most other types of fields, including those you defined as text, rich text, or keyword. Because Notes is document-oriented, you will probably find yourself using text values quite often. For example, you might want to change a person's name to all uppercase characters to make searching easier. You could use the `@Uppercase` function to do this.

- List values: These values contain more than one element. These elements can be either number, text, or time/date values. However, usually each list contains only one type—for example, a list of cities or a list of birth dates. Notes provides special functions that let you perform different types of list processing. You could also think of lists as a one-dimensional array.

N O T E You can't mix data types within an expression. For example, if you multiply `10` by `"12"`, you will get an error, because `10` is numeric and `"12"` is text. You could, however, convert `"12"` to a number and successfully multiply these two numbers. ▪

Now, let's discuss constants and how they can be used in formulas.

Using Constants

Constants let you specify values that never change. For example, a formula that computes average monthly sales might sum the sales of each month and divide by 12 (the number of months in a year). Because the number of months in a year won't change, a constant can be used.

In the next few sections, you will read about number, text, date, and list constants.

Number Constants Perhaps the most familiar constants are numeric. If you see the number 3.1415, you might recognize it as pi—one of the most famous numeric constants. When constants are used in formulas, nothing special is done; you just type in the number—for example, 36.23 or 4. Notes also recognizes a style of writing numeric constants called *scientific notation;* see the sidebar titled "Understanding Scientific Notation" for more information.

One of the simplest formulas is one that simply consists of a constant. For example, the default value of a state tax field might be 0.06, which represents six percent. As you design the field, you might create a default value formula of 0.06.

From then on, Notes will set that field to 0.06 each time a new document is composed. The user can change it as needed.

Text Constants You can also specify constant text. This is done by surrounding a group of characters with quotation marks (" "). Suppose you're defining a city field in a form, and you expect that in most cases the user will want to enter Park Hills. You would specify the default value for the field as the following:

```
"Park Hills"
```

The quotation marks are crucial to a proper text constant; without them, Park Hills looks like a field name. If you omit the quotes, Notes thinks that you want to initialize the city field with the value in the Park Hills field. Since this field doesn't exist, an empty string (" ") will be returned, and your formula won't do what you expected.

TIP If you're having trouble with a formula, check to make sure that the quotes are correct. You might be referencing a field name when you meant to use a text constant, or vice versa. For example, the following two functions demonstrate @Functions in which field names are referenced with quotes and without quotes.

As you can see in this function:

```
@SetField("CompanyName";"Definiti");
```

the @SetField function expects the field name (CompanyName in this case) to be enclosed in quotes. In the following function, on the other hand, the field name isn't enclosed in quotes:

```
@IsAvailable(CompanyName);
```

Time/Date Constants   The Time/Date constant is probably the least used. It is specified by enclosing a time or date in square brackets ([ ]). Times can be a.m. or p.m. and can include a time zone. For example, suppose you have a database in which you track company meetings. Most meetings begin at 8:30 a.m., so you might initialize the field that contains the meeting start time with the following time constant:

```
[8:30 AM EDT]
```

You can write dates as numbers separated by slashes or dashes, depending on whether your computer is running Windows or OS/2. If you're using Windows, use slashes for dates:

```
[11/9/96]
```

If you're using OS/2, use dashes:

```
[11-9-96]
```

> **N O T E**   When using Date/Time constants in formulas, you need to be aware of where the formula
> is being evaluated—the server or the workstation. For instance, Date/Time constants in
> views are calculated by the server. If these fields are editable, computed, and computed for display,
> @Created, @Modified, and @Accessed are calculated by the server; @Now, @Today, @Yesterday,
> and @Tomorrow are calculated at the workstation; and @Modified is computed at the workstation
> the first time it is executed. For fields that are computed when composed, the server computes
> @Created, and the workstation computes @Now, @Today, @Yesterday, @Tomorrow, and @Modi-
> fied. @Accessed doesn't display.
>
> Use the Date/Time format (slashes or dashes) associated with the operating system of the machine
> that evaluates the formula.

List Constants   List constants are the most powerful and complicated type of constant. A list constant consists of one or more elements of the same data type. If the list constant has more than one element, the elements are separated by a list concatenation operator (:). For example, the following is a list containing the names of four cities:

```
"Boston" : "New York City" : "Orlando" : "Cincinnati"
```

Notice that each element is a text value. You could also use number or date values to form a list. For example, the following might be a list of quarterly billing dates:

```
[03/15/97] : [06/15/97] : [09/15/97] : [12/15/97]
```

To summarize, you write text constants surrounded by quotes, date and time constants surrounded by brackets, and number constants surrounded by nothing, and list constants are combinations of other constants connected by the list concatenation operator.

Understanding Scientific Notation

To express very large and very small numbers, Notes supports scientific notation, which most often is used by scientists and engineers. A number expressed in scientific notation consists of a number (called the *mantissa*), the letter E, and one or two digits (called the *exponent)* representing a power of 10:

```
1.73E14
```

You can read this number as "1.73 times 10 to the 14th power," which in turn is 173,000,000,000,000. (In general, don't type commas in numbers; Notes won't recognize them.)

You can also use negative exponents to represent numbers that are smaller than 1. For example:

`1.73E-4`

is equal to 0.0173.

People who must deal with very large or very small numbers appreciate this notation, because you can tell at a glance how large the number is. Unless you are involved in some type of scientific endeavor, you probably won't run into this notation.

Performing Calculations

Most formulas perform simple actions—adding, subtracting, multiplying, and dividing numbers to compute values, manipulate text strings, and calculate dates. The following sections explain how to use operators, which are symbols, that represent actions that Notes can perform on data.

Using Operators   Four of the most common operators represent the basic arithmetic operations. They are listed in Table 14.2.

Table 14.2   The Four Most Common Arithmetic Operators

Operator	Description
+	Addition
-	Subtraction
*	Multiplication
/	Division

Notice the symbols for multiplication (*) and division (/). You must use these symbols for these operations. You can't, for example, use x for multiplication as you would if you were writing a formula on paper.

Suppose that your database contains documents that have information about a sale your company made last month. In each document is a field called `customerPrice`. Normally this field is displayed without a shipping charge. However, in one view's column, you need to display the price including a $6.00 shipping charge.

When you define the Total Price column, you can enter

`customerPrice + 6`

as the default value formula. Yes, this default value formula is a bit overworked as an example, but you will use it a lot in real life.

The first operand of the expression, `customerPrice`, represents the value of the `customerPrice` field in a document. The 6 is a numeric constant. The plus sign (+) tells Notes to add two values together—the value in the `Price` field and the number 6—for each document and display the resulting value in the column.

You can also perform calculations that involve several fields. Suppose you have the following fields:

Field	Description
productCost	The amount you paid for the product
laborCost	Your cost for getting the product set up and ready for delivery
customerPrice	The price the customer paid for the product

In one column of the view, you might want to display the profit for each sale. When you define the column, however, you can't enter a simple field name as the formula, because no field in the document contains the profit on the sale. Instead, you can enter a formula that calculates the amount of the profit by subtracting the cost of the product and the labor from the price, as follows:

```
customerPrice - productCost - laborCost;
```

As Notes reads this formula from left to right, it takes the value of `customerPrice`, subtracts `productCost`, and then subtracts `laborCost`. The result of this expression is the value Notes displays in the Profit column, using the appropriate values for each document.

To take this example one step further, suppose you want to display the preferred customer's price, which reflects a discount off the customer price. The discount percentage isn't contained in any of the fields in the document, but it's always 85 percent of the regular customer price. So the formula for the Discount Price column would be as follows:

```
customerPrice * 0.85
```

Notes evaluates this formula and then displays the resulting value in the column.

Suppose you had a Discount Price column that also showed a Profit After Discount column. This column would use the following formula:

```
(customerPrice * .85) - (productCost - laborCost)
```

Notice that the discount price formula is simply embedded into the profit formula by enclosing it in parentheses. The next section has more information about how to use parentheses and what they mean.

Operator Precedence   As Notes computes the value of a formula, it usually reads the formula from left to right. For example, if you write the following:

```
fudgeFactor + increaseAmt - decreaseAmt + otherAmt;
```

Notes takes the value of the `fudgeFactor` field, adds the value of the `increaseAmt` field, subtracts the value of the `decreaseAmt` field, and adds the value of the `otherAmt` field.

The *operator precedence,* or the order in which the operators are evaluated, is the same for addition and subtraction.

However, there are factors that override the usual left-to-right rule. Some operators have a higher precedence than others, which means that they will be evaluated first. For example, if a formula uses addition or subtraction mixed with multiplication or division, Notes does the multiplication and division first because they have higher precedence.

Let's look at the evaluation order more closely. Suppose that a document contains information about an employee's pay, and one of the formulas looks like this:

```
empBonus + hoursWorked * hourlyRate;
```

If you read this formula from left to right, you might think that Notes adds `empBonus` and `hoursWorked` and then multiplies the result by `hourlyRate`. But because multiplication has a higher precedence, Notes does the multiplication first, computing the value of `hoursWorked` times `hourlyRate`, and then adding the result to `empBonus`.

Understanding the precedence of operators is vital to ensuring that you derive the correct values from your formulas. Table 14.3 displays the order of precedence. Keep in mind that a precedence of 1 is the highest, meaning that operators with this precedence will be evaluated before lower-precedence operators.

Table 14.3   Notes Operators and Their Precedence Levels

Operator	Operation	Precedence
:=	Assignment	N/A
:	List concatenation	1
+, -	Positive, Negative	2
*	Multiplication	3
**	Permuted multiplication	5
*/	Permuted division	5
+	Addition, concatenation	4
*+	Permuted addition	5
-	Subtraction	5
*-	Permuted subtraction	5
*=	Permuted equal to	5
<>	Not equal to	5
!=	Not equal to	5

Part

II

Ch

14

continued

Table 14.3 Continued

Operator	Operation	Precedence
=!	Not equal to	5
><	Not equal to	5
<	Less than	5
*<	Permuted less than	5
>	Greater than	5
>*	Permuted greater than	5
<=	Less than or equal to	5
>=	Greater than or equal	5
*>=	Permuted greater than or equal	5
!	Logical NOT	6
&	Logical AND	6
¦	Logical OR	6

▶ **See** "Using the @If Function," and "Logical Operators," **p. 626 and 629**

The assignment operator doesn't have a precedence level because it is used only in assignment statements. The permuted operators are used for list operations. Both of these topics will be covered in a moment.

The Assignment Operator   The assignment operator, :=, is one that you will use frequently. It allows you to assign a value to a variable or field. For example, the following simple formula assigns the product of hoursWorked and hourlyRate to a variable named empWage, which is then used in the next expression to derive the employee's total wage:

```
empWage := hoursWorked * hourlyRate;
empWage + empBonus;
```

The following formula sets the value of the field CompanyName to Definiti:

```
FIELD CompanyName:="Definiti";
```

Now that you've seen the assignment operator in action, compare the following example to the formula shown a moment ago:

```
(hoursWorked * hourlyRate) + empBonus;
```

Although the same result is achieved here, using the variable empWage makes the formula easier to understand, because it reduces the complexity of the formula's statements, and this value could be used elsewhere in the formula without the need to recalculate it. Remember, though, that once the first formula completes, the value stored in empWage will be lost. The only way to permanently store a value is to save it as a field in a Notes document or write it to the Notes INI file.

The next section shows you how to use parentheses to explicitly change the order of operation. Parentheses are also useful in documentation to show future users of your formulas that you intended the formula to be evaluated in a certain way.

Using Parentheses to Prioritize Operations

Usually Notes performs arithmetic from left to right, except when the order of precedence dictates otherwise. However, you can force Notes to perform specific operations first by surrounding portions of a formula with parentheses. In essence, the parentheses tell Notes that the operators inside have a higher priority and need to be evaluated first.

Suppose you want to display a discount price in a column, and you compute the discount price by adding the item cost and the item profit and multiplying by 90 percent. You might try to create a formula like this:

```
itemCost + itemProfit * .9
```

If you have an `itemCost` of $10 and an `itemProfit` of $2, this formula would be $10 + $2 * .9, or $11.80.

However, this isn't the result you want. Notes performs multiplication first, so it multiplies `itemProfit` by .9 and then adds the `itemCost`. To get the result you want, you need to explicitly tell Notes what to evaluate first, like this:

```
(itemCost + itemProfit) * .9
```

When the same values as before are used (an `itemCost` of $10 and an `itemProfit` of $2), this version of the formula becomes ($10 + $2) * .9, or $10.80.

Surrounding the addition portion of the formula with parentheses forces Notes to add first and then multiply.

You can also nest parentheses if needed. The following simple example shows the technique. If you consistently get a two-percent reduction in the `itemCost` because you pay your bills in cash, you might represent this fact in the formula as follows:

```
((itemCost * .98) + itemProfit) * .9
```

In this formula, the `itemCost` is multiplied by .98 to reflect the two-percent reduction for cash payments. This is enclosed in parentheses so that it will be the first operation performed. Then Notes will add the result to `itemProfit` and multiply that result by .9.

Using the previous values (an `itemCost` of $10 and an `itemProfit` of $2), the formula becomes (($10 * .98) + $2) * .9, or $10.62.

Concatenating Text

Concatenate means to connect end to end, an operation you often want to perform on text. When the plus sign (+) appears between two text values, it tells Notes to concatenate two pieces of text. By using plus signs between text or fields, you can concatenate as many pieces of text information as you need.

Suppose that a form has two fields that contain a person's first name and last name, respectively. In a view, you want to display the last name, a comma, and the first name. You can use the following formula to define the column:

```
lastName + ", " + firstName
```

This formula evaluates to a single text value that contains the last name, followed by a comma and a space, and then the first name.

N O T E   Remember that using quotes in a formula causes Notes to use the text inside the quotes exactly as is. In the case of `lastName`, however, you don't actually want Notes to use the word "lastName" in constructing the person's full name; instead, you want it to access the value of the `lastName` field and use the field value. If you used quotes, Notes would print the literal word "lastName."

List Operations

Earlier in this chapter, you saw that list constants look like the following:

```
"Boston" : "New York City" : "Orlando" : "Cincinnati"
```

Each city is an item in this four-element list. In Notes, the colon (:) acts as a list concatenator in the same fashion that the plus sign (+) acts as a text concatenator.

You can use the assignment operator to store this list in a variable:

```
destinationCities := "Boston" : "New York City" : "Orlando" : "Cincinnati"
```

Now the variable `destinationCities` has a list with four elements. If you needed to expand this list, you could do the following:

```
expandedList := destinationCities : "Park Hills"
```

The `expandedList` variable holds a five-element list. This formula shows that the list concatenation operator works on list variables as well as on list constants.

This section looks at the different operations you can perform on lists. List operations fall into the following types:

- Pair-wise: These operators act on two lists in parallel fashion. The first element in list A pairs with the first element in list B. If one list is shorter, the last element in the shorter list is repeated for each remaining element in the longer list.

- Permuted: These operators act on two lists by pairing each element in list A with every element in list B. Thus, every possible combination of values (all permutations) is used.

Of the four basic arithmetic operators, only the addition operator will be discussed since the addition, subtraction, multiplication, and division operators all work on lists in a similar fashion.

List Addition   The addition operator works differently depending on whether the lists being added are numeric or text. The numeric lists act as you probably would expect them to. The following formula:

```
listOne := 5 : 10;
listTwo := 1 : 2;
listOne + listTwo
```

results in a list consisting of the following:

```
6 : 12
```

which is 5 + 1 and 10 + 2.

If one of the lists is longer than the other, the last element of the shorter list is repeated as many times as needed to make up the difference. For example, the following:

```
listOne := 5 : 10 : 20 : 30;
listTwo := 1 : 2;
listOne + listTwo
```

will result in a list consisting of the following:

```
6 : 12 : 22 : 32
```

which is 5 + 1, 10 + 2, 20 + 2, and 30 + 2. Notice that the 2 in the listTwo variable is repeated twice.

Text lists, when added, result in the concatenation of an element in list A to an element in list B. For example, the following:

```
listOne := "A" : "B";
listTwo := "1" : "2";
listOne + listTwo
```

will result in a list consisting of the following:

```
A1 : B2
```

which is A + 1 and B + 2.

Again, if one of the lists is longer than the other, the last element of the shorter list is repeated as many times as needed to make up the difference.

Permuted List Addition   Let's use the previous examples to show permuted addition. The following example:

```
listOne := 5 : 10;
listTwo := 1 : 2;
listOne *+ listTwo
```

results in a list consisting of the following:

```
6 : 7 : 11 : 12
```

which is 5 + 1, 5 + 2, 10 + 1, and 10 + 2. All possible combinations of values are used.

Lists with mismatched lengths don't need any special consideration when doing permuted operations. For example, the following:

```
listOne := 5 : 10 : 20 : 30;
listTwo := 1 : 2;
listOne *+ listTwo
```

will result in a list consisting of the following:

```
5 : 6 : 11 : 12 : 21 : 22 : 31 : 32
```

which is 5 + 1, 5 + 2, 10 + 1, 10 + 2, 20 + 1, 20 + 2, 30 + 1, and 30 + 2. Again, all possible combinations of values are used.

Permuted text list addition works exactly as you might expect. For example, the following:

```
listOne := "A" : "B";
listTwo := "1" : "2";
listOne *+ listTwo
```

results in a list consisting of the following:

```
A1 : A2 : B1 : B2
```

which is A + 1, A + 2, B + 1, and B + 2.

N O T E The elements from the first list control the ordering of the resulting list. The first element of the first list is matched against the first element of the second list, and then the second element of the second list, and so on.

This might be important if you need to know the order of the list. I don't know of any situation where this is critical, but you never know when a fact like this might save you a couple of hours of frustration looking for a bug in your formula. ▨

Formula Keywords

You have read about the basics so far; let's move on to some more complicated concepts. Several things make formulas into little programs; temporary variables and multiple expressions are among the most important.

However, Notes also has keywords that can be used in formulas. These statements are more executed than evaluated and therefore might also fuel the "formulas are small programs" argument. No values are associated with keywords, just actions.

Five keywords are used with formulas:

- DEFAULT
- ENVIRONMENT
- FIELD
- REM
- SELECT

The next five sections discuss each of them in detail.

The _DEFAULT_ Keyword   This keyword lets you assign a default value to a field. It also lets you create a temporary field (which lasts while the formula is being evaluated) with a default value. And, since you can use a statement more than once in the same formula, you can have dynamic defaults.

The syntax of the DEFAULT keyword is as follows:

```
DEFAULT variableName := value ;
```

The Notes online help has a great example of how this statement might be used. You can use the following column formula:

```
@If(@IsAvailable(keyThought); keyThought; topic);
```

to display the topic field if the keyThought field isn't available.

▶ **See** "Using the @If Function," **p. 626**

You can also perform this same task by using the DEFAULT statement:

```
DEFAULT NewTopic := topic;
NewTopic
```

You might consider the second method easier to understand and less error-prone. When using the DEFAULT method, the field NewTopic is used for the computed value. In cases where the field NewTopic doesn't exist, the value of Topic is substituted.

The _ENVIRONMENT_ Keyword   This keyword is used to create and/or set environment variables in the NOTES.INI file under the Windows, OS/2, and UNIX operating systems and in the Notes Preferences file under the Macintosh operating system. This means that each machine (and each user) can have different values for the same environment variable.

The syntax of the ENVIRONMENT keyword is as follows:

```
ENVIRONMENT variable := textValue ;
```

Notice that environment variables must be text values. If you need to use numbers with environment variables, check out the @Text and @TextToNumber functions in Chapter 15, "Working with Functions and Commands." They can be used to convert between text and number data types.

N O T E   The @Environment function can retrieve the value of an environment variable. It can also be used, along with the @SetEnvironment function, to set the value. Both of these functions are discussed in Chapter 15, "Working with Functions and Commands." ▓

Environment variables are frequently used to create sequential numbers for Notes applications in which all the users access the same database on a server (this won't work for users who have replica copies). The idea is that the first time you access the variable, it doesn't exist. So you create it with a value of 1. The next time you need a sequential number, read the value, increment it, set the environment with the new value, and use the new value in your document as needed.

Environment variables are also used to personalize databases since each user can have a different value. For example, if your company uses regional sales offices, the address of the local sales office can be stored in an environment variable and used in default value formulas in fields. For example:

```
@Environment("salesOfficeAddress");
```

You also need to be aware of where the formula is being evaluated. Some formulas are evaluated at the server, so the NOTES.INI or Notes Preferences file will be different than the one on the client workstation.

The Notes online help topic "Examples: @Environment, @SetEnvironment, and ENVIRONMENT" does a good job of explaining the details and intricacies of this keyword.

The inclusion of profile documents in Notes has rendered the ability to write to the NOTES.INI file less useful, because profile documents are generally faster, and each user can have one stored in a database.

▶ **See** Chapter 19, "More LotusScript," **p. 749**

The *FIELD* Keyword The FIELD keyword is used to assign a value to a field. It is also used to tell Notes which fields will be assigned values later in the formula.

Before you use @SetField in a formula, if the field receiving the assignment doesn't exist in the document, you must declare it within the same formula. One way to do this is to declare it at the beginning of your formula with the FIELD keyword. The syntax of the FIELD keyword is as follows:

```
FIELD FieldName:=FieldName;
FIELD Fieldname:=Fieldname;
```

> **CAUTION**
>
> If FieldName doesn't already exist in the document, it will be created. Make sure that you want a permanent field and not a temporary field when using the FIELD keyword. Also, when you use FIELD intending to create a new field, make sure that you aren't overwriting an existing field by accident.

When using the FIELD keyword to tell Notes that you might set its value later, you can use this form of statement:

```
FIELD myField := myField;
```

This formula sets myField to the value stored in myField. In other words, the value doesn't change. You can blank out a field by using the following:

```
FIELD myField := "";
```

If you aren't certain that the value of the field will be changing in your formula, set the field equal to itself. Set the field equal to blank text only if you intend to never use its value again.

The FIELD statement can also be used to delete fields in combination with the @DeleteField function:

```
FIELD myField := @DeleteField;
```

This keyword doesn't work in Column, Selection, Hide When, Window Title, or Form formulas.

The *REM* Keyword *Remarks,* also known as *comments,* are notes that you make, as part of your formula, to explain to yourself or others how your formula works. Lotus Notes completely ignores remarks but keeps them as part of your formula so that you can see them when you examine your formula.

If you become very proficient with formulas, someday you might work on a very complex formula for hours before getting it to work just right. If you—or worse, someone else—need to make a change six months later, the nuances of the formula might have been forgotten. Perhaps you had the foresight to jot down a few notes about what your formula does in some internal documentation. But, of course, those notes are gone also. Adding comments to your formulas will help avoid this problem.

The syntax of the REM keyword is as follows:

```
REM " [remark text] ";
```

For example:

```
REM "This formula selects only dogs without rabies vaccine";
REM "Written 10-17-97 by Mojo Nixon, Chief Programmer";
```

Good programmers know that no matter how fresh your thoughts are in your mind today, six months from now they might be stale. You might not have the slightest idea why you wrote a formula the way you did.

In complicated formulas, you can use remarks to separate different sections of the formula. For example:

```
REM "********************";
REM "Set up the first list";
listOne := 5 : 10;
REM "Set up second list   ";
listTwo := 1 : 2;
REM "Add the two lists.   ";
listOne + listTwo
REM "********************";
```

You can use any character to create a line. Some people use underscores, and others use asterisks. It all depends on what you find readable, but you should try to be consistent and always use the same character.

It's generally considered good form and common courtesy to include ample REM statements to explain your code.

The *SELECT* Keyword   The SELECT keyword defines criteria for the selection of documents in an agent that runs a formula, in a view selection formula, or during replication. You use a SE-LECT statement before an expression to define the set of documents that you want to change, see in a view, or replicate.

The syntax of the SELECT keyword is as follows:

```
SELECT expression ;
```

You can use this formula:

```
SELECT @All;
```

to have your formula see all the documents in the database. Or you can have a complex expression, as in the following:

```
SELECT Form = "myForm";
```

This SELECT statement ensures that only documents created using the form named myForm will be seen by the formula.

> **N O T E**   The Form field is a field that Notes automatically adds to each document when it is saved. Its value is the name of the form used to create the document. ▪

This keyword doesn't work in Column, Hide When, Section Editor, Window Title, Hotspot, Field, Form, or Form Action formulas.

Where Are Formulas Used?

One of the things that makes Notes so powerful and flexible is that there are so many different ways to customize your databases using formulas. Notes has almost 30 different types of formulas that can be used.

This section describes each formula type. The brief descriptions let you know the context in which a particular type of formula is found. For example, Column formulas can only be found in the View design mode.

You'll also see an example of each formula type. This small example gives you an idea of how each formula type can be used and what data type it needs to return. Some formula types, like a Replication formula or a Hide When formula, must return only a true or false value. SmartIcon, Agent, Action, Button, and Hotspot formulas don't require any return value. Instead, they are designed to perform a task.

Any @Functions that are designed to work well with that particular formula type are also pointed out. For example, the @All function can be used only in Replication, Agent, and View selection formulas.

Another important consideration is where the formula will be evaluated. If the formula is evaluated on the server, you won't be able to access information stored in INI files as environment variables at the client.

Formulas can generally be assigned to categories such as workspace formulas, form formulas, and so forth. However, some formulas fit in multiple places. We'll look at these first.

Action Buttons

Action buttons let the user perform tasks with a click of the mouse. Each action button is associated with either a view or a form and is displayed in the area just below the SmartIcons palette, known as the Action Bar. The Action Bar is a nonscrolling region that stays fixed when the user scrolls a document. Figure 14.2 shows you what action buttons in a view look like.

FIG. 14.2

The Inbox folder has six action buttons on the View Action Bar.

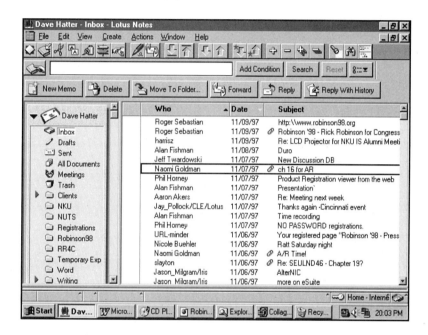

There are six predefined actions to which you can attach buttons:

- Categorize
- Edit document
- Send document
- Forward
- Move to folder
- Remove from folder

Each of these actions is automatic. You can't change their functionality, but you can change their appearance. If the action doesn't do what you want, you'll need to define your own custom action instead.

Part

II

Ch

14

N O T E   Notes' predefined actions aren't available for publishing to the Web with Domino. ▪

The next section shows you how to create custom action button formulas.

Action Button Formulas   Figure 14.2 showed the action buttons from the Inbox view of the Mail file. Now let's take a look at one of the definitions. Open your mail database. In the navigator pane, select _Design, Folders and then double-click ($Inbox). This puts you into design mode. Now choose _View, _Action Pane and double-click the New Memo action in the action pane that appears. This screen should look similar to Figure 14.3.

FIG. 14.3

The ($Inbox) view in design mode with the InfoBox and action and programmer panes displayed.

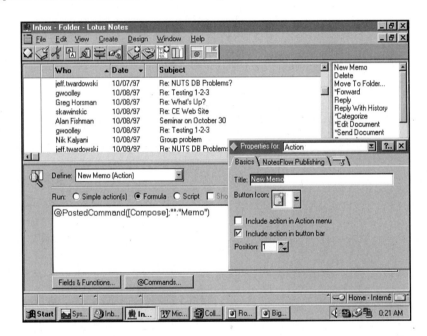

This is a busy figure. At the top left, the columns for the view are displayed. The top right holds the action pane. The bottom half of the screen holds the programmer pane with the action button formula. The InfoBox at the bottom right is where you can choose the various options that affect the action buttons. You'll notice that the Include action in button bar option has been checked.

The New Memo action (the selected one in the action pane) has the following formula:

```
@PostedCommand([Compose];"":"Memo")
```

When the action button is clicked, Notes evaluates the formula, which results in the creation of a new document based on the form Memo.

Form action formulas are a good place to automate some tasks for the user or to control field values. A simplistic example of this might be to use a form action formula to control a status field. For example, consider the following lines of code:

```
FIELD docStatus := docStatus;
question := "Has this account been verified?"
response := @Prompt([YESNO]; "Verfied?"; question);
fld := "docStatus";
@if(response; @SetField(fld ; "Yes"); @SetField(fld; "No"));
```

This formula asks the user whether an account has been verified. If it has, the Status field is changed to Yes. When controlling field content like this, you might want to change the field type to Computed.

▶ **See** Chapter 12 "Using Fields," **p. 531**

Notice that the FIELD statement is needed in this formula. Before passing a document field to the @SetField function, you need to declare it with the FIELD statement. You could assign any value you'd like to the field in the FIELD statement. This example leaves the value unchanged.

> **N O T E** The @IsDocBeingEdited, @IsDocBeingLoaded, @IsDocBeingMailed, @IsDocBeingRecalculated, and @IsDocBeingSaved functions can't be used in an action button formula. ▪

Hide Action Button Formulas   The hide action button formulas are used to control when actions are shown to the user, either in the Action menu or the Action Bar. When the Hide Action formula evaluates to true, the actions will be hidden.

> **T I P** If you want to hide a button from users who have read access but display the button to users who can edit a document, enable the Hide action if formula is true option in the Action Properties InfoBox, and use the following formula:
>
> !@Contains(@UserRoles; "Revisions")
>
> In order for this formula to work, in the ACL create a role called Revisions, highlight the person(s) or group(s) defined in the ACL, and click the role. Under Advanced, enable the option Enforce a consistent Access Control List across all replicas of this database.

This ability might come in handy if your weekend staff has a different set of tasks to perform than your weekday staff. The following formula:

```
day := @Weekday(@Now);
@If(day = 1 ¦ day = 7; 0; 1)
```

displays a given action only on Sunday (day equals 1) and Saturday (day equals 7).

Figure 14.4 shows the Hide tab of the Action Properties InfoBox for the Task action. When the formula shown in the InfoBox is true, the action will be hidden if the checkbox is checked.

Part

II

Ch

14

FIG. 14.4

An InfoBox showing a
Hide When formula that
will hide the action
button based on a
user's common name.

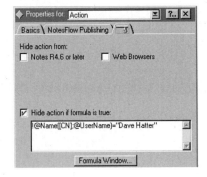

Each view or form action button also has an associated hide action button formula that you can
set.

Hotspots

A *hotspot* is a highlighted object that performs a task when clicked. A hotspot can display text
in a pop-up window, execute a hypertext link, or perform an action. Hotspot formulas can be
added to words in rich text fields, rectangles, and polygons in navigators, and buttons in layout
regions.

The next section discusses how hotspots can perform actions and display pop-up windows.

Hotspot Formulas   A hotspot formula is evaluated when the hotspot is clicked.

You might want to use a hotspot to offer your user some commentary, or you might link the
hotspot to a field on the document. Figure 14.5 shows how to use a corporate logo as an action
hotspot to connect to a WWW site.

You can also use a hotspot formula to display a dialog box to request additional details. For
example, your main form might be an inventory control form. If you need to display additional
information about a supplier or detailed information about stock on hand in a particular ware-
house, you can use a layout region and a dialog box to display the additional information. More
information can be found in the topic "Showing users a dialog box instead of a document" in
the HELP4.NSF database that comes with Notes.

You can create hotspot formulas for rectangles and polygons in navigators. Their use in a navigator is unrestricted. Whatever you can dream up, you can do. For example, you might create a
navigator to act as a graphic-based menu. In this case, each menu item might have a hotspot
rectangle formula to execute whatever menu option is selected.

FIG. 14.5

A hotspot action formula to connect to a WWW site.

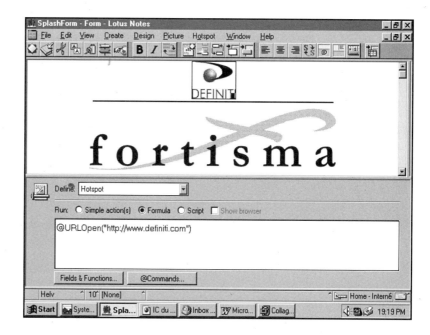

Hotspot formulas also come in handy when you're editing a document. You can create a hotspot formula simply by selecting words in a rich text field and then choosing Create, Hotspot, Formula Popup. The most common usage of this capability is to add a formula that acts as additional online help. For example, the following formula:

```
"World Wide Web"
```

could be linked to the abbreviation "WWW." Later, readers of the document could click the hotspot to see an explanation of the abbreviation.

If the hotspot is already defined, you can change its properties by right-clicking the hotspot and choosing Hotspot properties from the menu, or by choosing Hotspot, Hotspot Properties. If the hotspot supports coding, such as the Button, Formula Pop-up, and Action hotspots, you can open the programmer's pane by selecting the hotspot and choosing Hotspot, Edit Hotspot.

The @Command, @DbColumn, @DbLookup, @DialogBox, @Platform, @Prompt, @Return, and @SetField functions are designed to work well in hotspot formulas. The SELECT statement can't be used in hotspot formulas. Table 14.4 contains a concise listing of the six types of hotspots.

Part
II

Ch
14

Table 14.4   Hotspots

Type	Description
Link hotspot	A link hotspot is a graphical button that can link to a document, view, or database, providing a quick and easy way for users to navigate.
URL link	You can mimic the functionality of hypertext links on the Web with a URL link hotspot. You enter a URL, and when the user clicks the highlighted text, if an Internet connection exists, the URL will open in the user's default browser.
Text pop-up	When clicked, a text pop-up hotspot displays a text literal entered by the application developer. This can be useful for providing small help "snippets" for data entry.
Button	When clicked, a button runs a simple action, formula, or LotusScript program.
Formula pop-up	When clicked, a formula pop-up hotspot displays the result of a formula entered by an application developer.
Action	When clicked, an action hotspot can perform some action, such as opening a view, deleting a document, or sending an e-mail message.

Buttons

A *button* is a clickable object that you can add to a form to automate tasks. A Notes user can also add buttons inside a rich text field. When the button is clicked, Notes executes the code associated with it. Button formulas are covered in the next section.

Button Formulas   A common use of a button is to use the @Prompt function to display a list that the user can choose from. The following formula sets the value of the State field based on the values the user chooses from the list presented in the prompt. The following code sets the default choice to "KY":

```
FIELD State:=State;
List:="KY":"OH":"IN";
@SetField("State";@Prompt([OKCANCELLIST];"Choose State";
➥"Choose a state from the list below";"KY";List))
=
```

N O T E   Notes lets you perform a task many different ways. The preceding example could also be used in an action button formula or as an agent. You could have also elected to make the State field a keyword field using a list box or combo box interface. Keep in mind that there is no absolute right way to program in Notes (but there are ways to optimize performance). It all depends on acceptable performance and the style that you are comfortable using. ■

If you want to use the @Command function in a button formula, you must make sure that the formula switches to the right context. For example, view-level menu options such as @Command([NavigateNext]) that attempt to move to the next document in a view won't work unless Notes is in view mode.

Workspace Formulas

Formulas that act at the workspace level are global to all databases. They can perform any menu command and manipulate databases. For example, you might use a SmartIcon to add a database to the user's workspace.

SmartIcons   A SmartIcon is a customizable button that performs actions. It acts just like the buttons on toolbars that you see in many Windows applications. Each SmartIcon has a formula associated with it. There are over 100 predefined SmartIcons, with formulas that map to one of the menu commands. Many people find that clicking a SmartIcon is faster than selecting menu options and easier than recalling keyboard shortcuts. You can create your own SmartIcon by choosing File, Tools, SmartIcons and clicking the Edit Icon button. Then select one of the customizable icons from the list, enter a description, click Formula, and enter a formula.

For instance, the following formula, when used in a SmartIcon, will format text in the current rich text field to be left-aligned 9-point Arial:

```
@Command([EditSelectAll]);
@Command([TextAlignLeft]);
@Command([TextSetFontFace];"Arial");
@Command([TextSetFontSize]; "9")
```

SmartIcons come in sets that are oriented around related tasks. For example, there is a set for editing a document and a set for designing a form. When you create a SmartIcon, you need to either assign it to an existing set or create a new one.

Figure 14.6 shows the SmartIcons Formula dialog box, which you can access by choosing File, Tools, SmartIcons. Choose an icon and click the Edit Icon button, which opens the Edit SmartIcons dialog box. You can then click the Formula button. The formula shown will open a dialog box that allows the user to enter a URL.

FIG. 14.6
A SmartIcon formula to open a Web site that the user specifies.

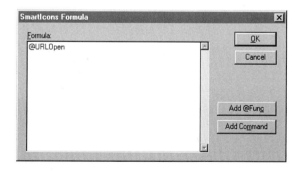

The @Command, @DbColumn, @DbLookup, @IsNewDoc, @MailSend, @Platform, @Prompt, @Return, @SetField, and @ViewTitle functions are designed to work well in SmartIcon formulas.

Database Formulas

Three types of formulas act at the database level. One type, the Replication formula, controls replication. The second type, Agents, replaces the macros used in Notes 3. The third type, Database Events, is new as of Notes 4.5.

Replication Formulas   A *replication formula* controls which documents will be replicated. It is applied to each document in the database; only documents that meet the criteria will be replicated. The formula is evaluated wherever the database is located—usually at the server.

You might use a replication formula to replicate all client documents that came from IBM or Compaq, as in the following:

```
SELECT Form="Client" & (Source="IBM" ¦ Source="Compaq")
```

If the formula evaluates to true, the document is replicated.

 T I P   Although replication formulas can be used to limit which documents can be replicated, this isn't a truly secure way to control document access, because a savvy user can change the replication formula. If security is a factor, using Reader Names fields provides a much more secure way to do this. You can learn more about Reader Names fields in Chapter 3, "Using Databases."

By using @IsResponseDoc in a replication formula, you cause all response documents in a database to replicate, not just those that meet the selection criteria. To avoid this, use @AllChildren or @AllDescendants instead.

The @All, @AllChildren, and @AllDescendants functions and the SELECT keyword are designed to work well in replication formulas. In fact, all replication formulas must contain a SELECT statement.

The @DbLookup, @Environment, @Now, and @UserName functions can't be used in a replication formula.

Agent Formulas   An *agent* is a procedure that can be made up of simple actions, a formula, a LotusScript, or even a Java program. You can have the agent triggered manually, from another agent, when new mail arrives, when documents are created or changed, when documents are pasted, or on a preset schedule.

Formula-based agents can be run on all documents in a database, all new or modified documents since the last run, all unread documents, all documents in a view, all selected documents, or the current document. In addition, you can use a SELECT statement to build a subset of documents on which to run.

The agent is run at the client if the agent is triggered manually, when documents are created or changed, or when documents are pasted. The agent is run at the server when the trigger is new mail or a preset schedule.

You might use an agent to set the status of a field. For example, suppose your organization needs to highlight valued customers for a beginning-of-the-month sales promotion. You could create an agent triggered monthly that looks at new or changed documents since the last run. The formula might look like this:

```
SELECT monthlySales > 200000;
FIELD promoStatus := "Valued";
```

This formula sets the promoStatus field to Valued for any customer with monthly sales over $200,000. Once the agent is run, you might have a view that selects only documents in which the promoStatus field contains "Valued".

Database Scripts

Starting in Notes 4.5, Lotus added a very handy and powerful new feature called Database Scripts to your developer's toolbox. You can use either LotusScript or the Notes Formula language to react to various database-level events such as the closing of a database or the deletion of a document. Currently, there are five database-level events for which you can write formulas: Postopen, Postdocumentdelete, Queryclose, Querydocumentdelete, and Querydocumentundelete. Table 14.5 lists these events and tells you when they will be run.

Table 14.5 When Database Event Formulas Are Executed

Event	When the Formula Is Run
Postopen	After a database is opened
Postdocumentdelete	After a document is deleted from a database
Queryclose	Just before a database is closed
Querydocumentdelete	Just before a document is deleted from a database
Querydocumentundelete	Just before a document is undeleted

 TIP Although it might not seem intuitive, the QueryOpen and PostOpen events of a view are fired before the PostOpen event of a database.

View Formulas

Formulas that operate at the view level are used to control what information is seen in each view column, which documents are seen, and which forms are used to display information.

View Column Formulas   A *view column formula* controls what information is shown in a view column. It must evaluate to a value that can be converted into text. It is evaluated either at the client or the server, depending on the database's location.

View column formulas are one of the most common types of formulas in Notes, because views are the primary way in which information is communicated in Notes and Domino.

▶ **See** "Creating Columns in a View," **p. 516**

Notes columns are very versatile. Here is a simple column formula that tells you whether a document was created on a weekend or a weekday:

```
day := @Weekday(@Created);
@If (day = 1 ¦ day = 7; "Week End"; "Week Day")
```

The @Created function returns the time and date on which the document was created.

The @Weekday function looks at a time/date value and indicates which day of the week the time/date value falls on. A value of 1 represents Sunday, 2 represents Monday, and so on. This value is then assigned to the day variable.

The second line, with the @If function, looks at the value of the day variable and chooses between two text constants—Week End and Week Day. If the day variable is equal to Sunday (1) or Saturday (7), the value of Week End is selected; otherwise, the value of Week Day is used.

N O T E   The @Command, @DeleteDocument, @DeleteField, @DialogBox, @Do, @DoesDbExist, @GetDocField, @IsAgentEnabled, @IsDocBeingEdited, @IsDocBeingLoaded, @IsDocBeingMailed, @IsDocBeingRecalculated, @IsDocBeingSaved, @MailDbName, @MailSend, @NewLine, @PickList, @PostedCommand, @Prompt, @SetDocField, @SetField, @Unavailable, @UserPrivileges, @UserRoles, @Version, @ViewTitle, and @WhatIsUserAccess functions and the FIELD statement can't be used in a Column formula. In addition, none of the DDE functions can be used.

The @IsNewDoc function always has a value of false or 0 in a Column formula, which makes sense if you think about it: How can a document be new if it's displayed in a view? ▪

Event Formulas   Event formulas are evaluated whenever a specific event occurs. There are 11 different view-level events for which you can create formulas: Queryopen, Postopen, Regiondoubleclick, Queryopendocument, Queryrecalc, Queryaddtofolder, Querypaste, Postpaste, Querydragdrop, Postdragdrop, and Queryclose. Table 14.6 lists these events and tells you when they will be run.

Table 14.6   When Event Formulas Are Run

Event	When the Formula Is Run
Postdragdrop	After a drag-drop operation in a Calendar view
Postopen	After a view is opened
Postpaste	After a document is pasted into a view
Queryaddtofolder	Just before an add to folder operation
Queryclose	Just before a view is closed

Event	When the Formula Is Run
Querydragdrop	Occurs just before a drag-drop event in a calendar view
Queryopen	Just before a view is opened
Queryopendocument	Just before a document is opened
Querypaste	Just before a document is pasted into a view
Queryrecalc	Just before the view is recalculated
Regiondoubleclick	After the current region is double-clicked in the current view

N O T E The Regiondoubleclick and Postdragdrop events currently are available only when the view is a Calendar-type view.

Form Formulas Normally, when a document is saved in Notes, a special field named Form is created, and the name of the form that was used to create the document is stored in this field. When the document is opened, the contents of the Form field are used to determine which form should be used to display the document. A Form formula can be used to override the Form field and select a different form with which to display the document. The formula is evaluated on the client and must evaluate to the name of an existing form. A form that is stored in the document will take precedence over the Form formula.

N O T E You can store the form used to create each document inside the document. This will eat up disk space quickly, because each document will contain the form information as well as the document information. This practice is useful primarily when you are mailing a document to some other database and you can't be sure that the proper form exists.

You enable this feature by selecting Design, Form Properties while editing a form and then choosing the Defaults tab in the InfoBox. Check the Store form in document checkbox.

T I P If you'd like to see how large a form is, open a database in design mode and choose the Forms view. Then select the form in question and choose Design, Design Properties. This will launch an InfoBox for the form. When you choose the Design tab, you'll see the size of the form, as well as a plethora of other useful information.

Form formulas are generally used to allow a document to be created with one form but viewed with another. This works especially well with Domino applications, because many of the advanced features of Notes forms (layout regions in particular) don't work in a Web browser. You can create two forms: one optimized for a Notes client, and one optimized for a Web browser. When Web users open a document from a view using the form formula, they see one form, and Notes users see a different form.

For example, you might have one form that makes heavy usage of layout regions to make your application look and feel more like a Windows application and a different form for the Web, because layout regions don't work right on the Web. The following formula demonstrates how you can display one form when a document is open from a view in a Notes client and a different form when a Web client opens the document:

```
@If(@Contains(@UserRoles;"$$WebClient");"WebContactForm";"NotesContactForm")
```

TIP If you're using Notes 4.6, you can use the new @ClientType function instead of @UserRoles. @ClientType will return Notes for Notes clients and Web for Web clients.

To enter a Form formula, open the view in design mode and choose <u>D</u>esign, View <u>P</u>roperties; this will launch an InfoBox. When you choose the Advanced tab (it has a cute little propeller beanie on it), you'll see the Form formula Formula Window button. Click this button to open the Design Form Formula dialog box, and enter the appropriate formula.

N O T E The @Command, @IsDocBeingEdited, @IsDocBeingMailed, @IsDocBeingRecalculated, @IsDocBeingSaved, @Modified, @NewLine, @Now, @PickList, @PostedCommand, @SetField, and @Unavailable functions and the FIELD statement can't be used in Form formulas. ▮

Selection Formulas A Selection formula controls which documents appear in a view. The formula should begin with the keyword SELECT and be followed by a conditional expression. The conditional expression must evaluate to either true or false and is applied to each document in the database. Any document in which the expression evaluates to true is included in the view. Selection formulas are evaluated at the database's location, either at the client or the server.

You might use a selection formula that lists all customers who have a negative account balance. For example, consider the following statement:

```
SELECT accountBalance < 0
```

If you have a database that includes several different forms, you might decide to show only documents created with a single form in a view. For example, in a database of veterinary patients, you can select only cats—composed with the Feline Profile form—using this formula:

```
SELECT Form = "Feline Profile"
```

If you don't specify a selection formula, Notes will use a default formula of

```
SELECT @All
```

This means that the view will display every document in the database.

Form-Level Formulas

Form-level formulas are used when a document is being rendered through a form. They help you control actions, buttons, events, hotspots, paragraphs, subforms, and titles.

Form-Level Event Formulas   Just like event formulas in a view, form-level event formulas are evaluated whenever a specific event occurs in the form. There are seven different events for which you can create formulas: Queryopen, Postopen, Postrecalc, Querysave, Querymodechange, Postmodechange, and Queryclose. Table 14.7 lists these events and tells you when they will be run.

Table 14.7   When Event Formulas Are Run

Event	When the Formula Is Run
Postmodechange	After changing into or out of edit mode
Postopen	After a document is displayed
Postrecalc	After a document has been refreshed
Queryclose	Just before a document is closed
Queryopen	Just before a document is displayed
Querymodechange	Just before changing into or out of edit mode
Querysave	Just before a document is saved

Form-level event formulas provide tremendous functionality (especially when they are coded with LotusScript) and can be used to do things such as validate field values or display information automatically. For example, the Postmodechange event formula can be used to reset some field information when going into edit mode, and Querysaveevent can be used to automatically send mail when a new document is saved. The following formula shows you how to send mail when a new document is saved:

```
@IF(!@IsNewDoc;@Return("");"");
@MailSend( "Dave Hatter" ;"";"";
➡"A new chapter has been submitted";"";"";[IncludeDocLink])
```

This formula uses the @IsNewDoc function to determine if this is a new document. If it isn't new, @Return is called to stop the formula and return an empty string. If the document is new, the formula continues to execute, and the @MailSend formula sends a mail message with a brief subject and a doclink.

Hide Paragraph Formulas   Hide Paragraph formulas can be used to hide individual paragraphs depending on a given set of conditions. For example, you could hide paragraphs depending on which value of a field named State is entered. This can be very useful for an employee handbook in which the rules in California are different from those in New York. One source document could serve both states. Paragraphs that are unique to New York might have the following Hide Paragraph formula:

```
! State = "New York"
```

and paragraphs that are unique to California would use this:

```
State != "California"
```

As you can see, these formulas can be written in different ways. The first essentially says, "Not State equals New York," and the second says "State not equals California."

Another use of Hide Paragraph formulas might be to show a certain set of fields only when the document is new. In this case, you would select the fields and enter the following Hide When formula:

```
! @IsNewDoc
```

N O T E   Remember that the paragraph is hidden only if the formula evaluates to true.

The ability to conditionally hide objects is a powerful tool in your developer's toolbox. You'll probably find yourself using it frequently.

T I P   Users can also hide paragraphs inside rich text fields if needed.

Insert Subform Formulas   Subforms are a good way to group a bunch of related fields together so that several forms can access them. This helps keep form designs consistent. At times, you might want to dynamically determine which subform(s) to use with a given form. This is where the Insert Subform formula comes in handy.

The Insert Subform formula lets you dynamically determine the name of a subform to display in your form. It must evaluate to the name of an existing subform, or a runtime error will result. This formula is run on the client.

An example of using an Insert Subform Formula in an inventory control system might be to display different information depending on the inventory type. Your formula might look like this:

```
@If(invType = "Medical"; "Medical Detail"; "Standard Detail")
```

Insert Subform formulas are evaluated only when the document is opened. If the basis of the condition (such as the inventory type) changes, you must close and reopen the document to reevaluate the Insert Subform formula.

Section Access Formulas   Sections let you group portions of a document. When a section is collapsed, only a title shows. When it's expanded, the section contents are readable. Sections provide a way to organize information, because you can group logically related information into one section that can be expanded when needed, allowing you to maximize screen real estate in your form.

In addition to a standard section, you can create an access-controlled section to limit who can edit the information in the section. This type of section uses a Section Access formula to control access.

N O T E The Session Access formula specifies who can edit the section, not who can read it. In addition, the formula won't override the database's access control list.

Section Access formulas must evaluate to a name or list of names. This formula will run on the client.

You can specify names explicitly in the formula, like this:

```
"Roger Sebastian" : "Sean Gaiser"
```

which restricts edit access to just these two users. Or you might want to use a view and the @DbColumn, like this:

```
@DbColumn(""; ""; "(View of Section Readers)"; 1)
```

which looks at the list of names in the first column of a view in the current database named View of Section Readers. Additionally, you can make the list of names editable.

N O T E The @Command, @IsDocBeingLoaded, @Modified, @PostedCommand, and @ViewTitle functions and the SELECT statement can't be used in Section Access formulas.

Section Title Formulas   A Section Title formula is used to determine what is displayed as the section title. The formula must either be a single field or evaluate to a text or numeric value.

If you use sections to collapse a series of fields, perhaps the education information in a personnel form, you could use a Section Title formula to display some key information in the title. For example, examine this formula:

```
"Education: (" + yrGraduated + ") " + @Left(collegeName; 25)
```

This formula might display Education: (1964) Rutgers University when evaluated. Pulling out the most important information in this way can make your forms easier to understand and also make them appear less cluttered.

T I P Users can also create sections inside rich text fields and create their own section title formulas if needed.

Window Title Formulas   Window Title formulas determine what text is displayed in the Window Title bar when a document is opened. If a form has no Window Title, when a document is opened, the Window Title will display "Untitled," which is rather uninformative.

You might use a Window Title formula to display one title for new documents and another for existing documents. For example, if your database describes an animal patient at a veterinary clinic, you might want to use the title New Patient when the document is first composed, and then use a title with the pet's and owner's names when the document is read later. The following formula accomplishes this task:

```
@If (@IsNewDoc; "New Patient"; patientName + " (" + ownerName + ")")
```

Part
II

Ch
14

You can also make very complicated window title formulas. The next example displays New Patient for new documents, patient (Owner) for existing documents, and patient (Unknown Owner) for existing documents whose owner is unknown. It's a contrived example, but the technique is useful nonetheless:

```
isFldThere := (@IsAvailable(ownerName) & ownerName != "");
ifFldYes := @Trim(patientName) + " (" + ownerName + ")";
ifFldNo := @Trim(patientName) + " (Unknown Owner)";
@If(@IsNewDoc; "New Patient"; @If(isFldThere; ifFldYes; ifFldNo));
```

The key element in this example is the first line:

```
isFldThere = (@IsAvailable(ownerName) & ownerName != "");
```

which sets the variable isFldThere to true or false. The last line actually determines which text is displayed in the title.

Like the Section Title formula, the Window Title formula must either be a single field (except for rich text fields) or evaluate to a text or numeric value.

Field Formulas

Field-level formulas can be used to manipulate the values of fields in a document as well as validate the data entered in a field. There are five basic types of field-level formulas: Default Value, Input Translation, Input Validation, Computed Field, and Keyword Field.

Default Value Formulas   Default value formulas allow you to specify the value that appears automatically in a field when a user composes a document. The default value is calculated only when a new document is created; it won't fire when a document is saved or refreshed or when an existing document is opened.

A good example of a default value is a field that stores the name of the user who created the document. You could create a field called DocAuthor with a default value formula of

```
@Name([CN];@UserName)
```

The @UserName function equates to the name of the user who created the document, and the @Name function uses the [CN] parameter to return only the common name component of the user name.

Another example of a default value that is often used is a field that holds the current date. This can be done by using the following function:

```
@Today
```

The @Today function returns the current date. When used in field-level formulas, it is evaluated at the client.

Input Translation Formulas   Input Translation formulas let you tell Notes to perform some type of automatic conversion on the information in a field. Notes executes the formula when the document is refreshed and/or saved.

For example, you might want to make sure that all supervisors' names start with a capital letter and that the rest of the letters are lowercase. Notes has a function called @ProperCase that does this for you. Using it in an input translation formula would look like this:

```
@ProperCase(supervisor)
```

When the user enters a value into this field in lowercase letters, @ProperCase provides the correct capitalization as the document is saved. For example, if the user enters samuel hatter, this formula would convert it to Samuel Hatter.

If you required the user to consecutively enter all nine digits of his Social Security number, an Input Translation formula, used in a text field, would add the hyphens in the appropriate place:

```
@If(SSN = ""; ""; (@IsDocBeingRecalculated ¦
@IsDocBeingSaved) & @Length(SSN) = 11; SSN; @Left(SSN; 3) +
"-" + @Middle(SSN; 2; 2) + "-" + @Right(SSN; 4))
```

Input Validation Formulas   Input validation formulas let you tell Notes how to determine whether or not data entered by the user is valid. These formulas differ from other kinds of formulas because they answer only a yes-or-no question: Is the data valid?

Almost all input validation formulas contain an @If function, which determines whether the field contains valid data. Two special functions tell Notes whether the data is valid: @Success returns 1, meaning that the value in the field is acceptable, and @Failure returns 0, indicating that the value isn't acceptable.

Suppose that you have a field called ClientName, which must contain a name. You can use the @Length function to determine the length of the field. The entire validation formula for the field might look like this:

```
@If( @Length( @Trim(ClientName)) = 0;
@Failure( "You must enter a Client Name" );
@Success )
```

The @If function determines whether the ClientName field is blank. If it isn't, @If signals to Notes (through the @Success function) that the data is valid. Otherwise, it uses the @Failure function to signal that the data is invalid. @Failure requires you to provide a description of the problem, which Notes displays as an error message (see Figure 14.7). Furthermore, Notes doesn't let the user save the document until he fixes the problem (in this example, the user needs to fill in the Client Name).

FIG. 14.7
This sample error message is produced through a validation formula.

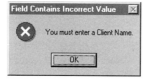

Field Contains Incorrect Value

You must enter a Client Name.

OK

The "Examples: @Environment, @SetEnvironment, and ENVIRONMENT" and the "Examples: @SetDocField" topics in the Notes online help system have more good examples of input validation formulas.

Computed Field Formulas   Document fields can be editable, computed, computed for display, and computed when composed. All the computed field types must have a formula associated with them. When evaluated, the result data type must agree with the field's data type. A text value needs a formula that evaluates to the text string, a date field needs a formula that evaluates to a date, and so on.

For example, you might want a computed numeric field that calculates the sum of other document numeric fields. You could do this with either of the following formulas:

```
monRevenue + tueRevenue + wedRevenue + thuRevenue + friRevenue;
```

or

```
@Sum(monRevenue : tueRevenue : wedRevenue : thuRevenue : friRevenue);
```

Keyword Field Formulas   Keyword fields are used to display a list from which the user can select the information that will be used in a field. The list can be explicitly created by the form designer, or a formula can be used to create dynamic lists.

One of the most common @Functions used in Keyword Field formulas is @DbColumn, which is used to get a list of keywords from a column in a view. For example, to get a list of all clients in your database, you might use this formula:

```
@DbColumn( "":"NoCache"; ""; "Client List";  Name; 2)
```

Figure 14.8 shows this formula in use in an InfoBox. To get there, select a field and then select Design, Field Properties.

FIG. 14.8
The Field Properties InfoBox shows the keyword field formula and its options.

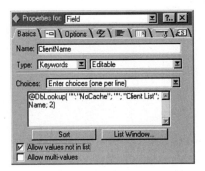

If you check the Allow values not in list checkbox, the user can add information to the list as needed. Otherwise, you'll need to create another way to update the view to add selections.

TIP These dynamic lookups are very powerful and make creating lookup tables very easy to do. At least, they'll be easy once you get the hang of it. However, dynamic lookups decrease an application's performance, so using too many of them will make your users unhappy. However, you can optimize lookups by using the "cache" option (which is the default) to cache the results of the lookup after its first execution if the contents don't change frequently. You can concatenate several fields into one view column so that all the information you need can be retrieved with one lookup and parsed into individual components. This is an excellent way to increase the performance of a slow application, but it requires some planning and practice.

When the user clicks the down arrow button beside a keyword field, a dialog box similar to the one shown in Figure 14.9 appears.

FIG. 14.9

An example of a Keyword Field formula.

From the Select Keywords dialog box, the user can select from the list or type a new keyword in the New Keywords box.

This chapter discussed where formulas can be used and gave examples of how to use them. However, it just skimmed the surface of what you can do with formulas. When used creatively, formulas have few limits. ●

Working with Functions and Commands

As you learned in Chapter 14, "Working with Formulas," the Notes formula language is extensive and powerful. This chapter examines the Notes formula language in detail and gets "under the hood" of many of the most powerful and useful functions and commands.

 The companion CD-ROM includes a complete reference to all @Functions and @Commands. Many programmers enjoy being able to browse the function reference without being tied to a computer. This chapter gives you that chance. You can look through the lists and get a feel for the vast amount of control that the @Functions and @Commands give you.

Understanding Function Basics

When you ask Notes to find the value of a field, Notes looks for that value in the database. When you ask Notes to find the value of a function, Notes needs to perform some task associated with that function. For instance, the @Today function requests Notes to find the current date. To determine the current date, Notes does not need to reference the database.

 All functions in the Notes formula language begin with an at sign (@), as in @Success or @Year. Users of Lotus 1-2-3 will recognize the @ notation.

Here's another example. Suppose that you defined a column with the formula

```
effectiveDate
```

which consists of a single field name. For each document, Notes fetches and displays the value of the effectiveDate field in that column.

Compare the preceding example with the formula

```
@Created
```

which consists of a single function name. @Created returns the date a document was created; using this function in a column formula displays the appropriate date for each document. If you use this function in a default value formula, the creation date becomes the value of the field.

 While coding a formula, you can at any time click the Fields & Functions button to display a list of all Notes functions. You can then select a function and press F1, or click the Help button to get online help for that function. When you are in the help document, you can select the function, copy it to the clipboard (Ctrl+C), and then paste it into your formula (Ctrl+V). The @Commands button works in the same fashion for all @Commands.

Function Arguments

Most functions require you to provide information with which they can work to produce a result. For example, if you want a function to determine which day of the week a certain date falls on, you must tell Notes exactly which date you are interested in.

The @Weekday function calculates the day of the week on which a date occurred; in order for this function to do its work, you must give it a date. Pieces of information that are required by functions are called arguments or parameters. Some functions perform a simple action that requires no arguments—for example, the @Created function examined earlier. Most functions, however, expect a certain number of arguments of a specific data type, which are "passed" to the function inside the parentheses. In the case of @Weekday, you need to provide a single-date argument. Consider the following formula, which might appear in the definition for a column:

```
@Weekday(effectiveDate)
```

The @Weekday function operates on the value contained in the effectiveDate field and returns an integer value between 1 and 7 representing the seven days of the week (Sunday through Saturday, respectively).

> **N O T E** This chapter follows the convention adopted by many developers of using the terms *argument* and *parameter* interchangeably.

If a function requires more than one argument, you must list all the arguments inside the parentheses, separated by semicolons. Suppose that your documents contain a homePhone field, which you use to store home phone numbers with area codes. Suppose next that you want a column to display just the area code for each person. The @Left function allows you to extract characters from the left end of a text value. You must provide @Left with a text value and the number of characters you want to extract. The following formula displays the leftmost three characters:

```
@Left(HomePhone; 3)
```

Nesting Functions

You can use the result provided by one function as the data for another function to process, a technique called *nesting*. You have already seen that @Created gives you the date that a document was created and that @Weekday tells you on which day of the week a date occurred. Thus, to display a number that represents the day of the week on which the document was created in a prompt (a message box), you can use the following:

```
@Prompt([OK];;"Weekday"; "The Weekday is: " & @Trim(@Text(@Weekday(@Created))))
```

Notes starts inside the parentheses and works its way out. @Created tells Notes to compute the date that the document was created; then @Weekday uses that date to compute the day of the week on which the creation occurred. @Text then converts that numeric value to text (a prompt can only display text), and @Trim lops off any leading or trailing spaces. Figure 15.1 displays the result of this formula.

FIG. 15.1

The result of an
@Prompt function.

Using the *@If* Function

One of the most widely used functions is @If, which allows you to write a formula that chooses between several possible values based on the outcome of a conditional test.

In its simplest form, the @If function returns one of two values. You supply a conditional expression, a true expression, and a false expression. The first step that Notes takes is to evaluate the conditional expression; it must evaluate to true or false. Next, depending on the result of the conditional test, either the true expression or the false expression is calculated and returned.

For example, suppose that each document in a customer database contains a field named CreditRating, which contains an A or B value. The A customers have credit limits of $10,000; the B customers have $3,000 limits. The following formula defines a column that displays the customer's credit rating:

```
@If(CreditRating = "A"; 10000; 3000);
```

Notice the three required parts:

- The first part is a condition that can be true or false; in this case, the condition asks whether the CreditRating field is equal to A.
- The second part is the expression used if the condition is true; in this case, the value is 10000.
- The third part is the expression used if the condition is false; in this case, the value is 3000.

In effect, this function says that if the value of the creditRating field is A, display the value 10000; otherwise, display 3000.

Now suppose that each document in a database describes one of your customers and has a field named areaCode that contains a customer's area code. Your courier considers every destination with an area code that starts with 328 to be local; all other destinations are long-distance calls and thus are more expensive. In a column you want to display either Local or Long Distance. Consider this function:

```
@If(@Left(areaCode; 3) = "328"; "Local"; "Long Distance")
```

The nesting function makes this example much trickier than the preceding example. The condition asks whether the first three digits of the area code are 328. If so, Notes displays Local; otherwise, it displays Long Distance.

The text constants in this example could be replaced with any Notes expression. Therefore, you can use field names, operators, and @Functions to accomplish different tasks. For example:

```
localCost := .10
longCost := .30
@If(@Left(areaCode; 3) = "328";
callTime * localCost;
callTime * longCost)
```

This example covers most of the concepts that have been discussed so far. It uses variables, constants, functions, and fields. If the phone call is local, then the first expression that is evaluated will multiply the contents of the callTime field by .10 (the contents of the localCost variable). Otherwise, the callTime field is multiplied by .30.

The Conditional Operators

Notes provides operators that you can use in the @If condition expression for comparing values. These are summarized in Table 15.1.

Table 15.1   The Conditional Operators

Operator	Description
=	is equal to
!=	is not equal to
=!	is not equal to (same as !=)
<>	is not equal to (same as !=)
><	is not equal to (same as !=)
<	is less than
<=	is less than or equal to
>	is greater than
>=	is greater than or equal to

You can also use predicate functions and logical operators in conditional expressions. See the "Predicate Functions" and "Logical Operators" sections that follow for more information.

For example, you can use the following formula in a column formula to alert you to customers who have spent too much:

```
@If (currentBalance > creditLimit; "Over Limit"; "")
```

This formula decides which of two values to display in the column. The formula asks whether the value of the currentBalance field is greater than the value of the creditLimit field. If so,

Notes displays the value Over Limit; otherwise, Notes displays nothing, specified as two adjacent quotes with nothing in between.

> **N O T E** The true expression and false expression can include any functions or combination of functions that you need. You are not limited to using constants. ■

The @If function has a related format that allows you to select from any number of values. In this format, the @If function includes any number of pairs of conditions and values. Notes begins checking conditions. As soon as Notes finds a condition that is true, the @If function selects the value that follows that condition.

Suppose that your company manufactures cameras. Throughout its existence, the company has manufactured cameras with three kinds of focusing mechanisms. All the cameras made before March 1981 were manual focus. After that date, manual cameras were discontinued, and all your factories produced cameras with fixed focus, except the Cleveland factory, which produced auto-focus cameras.

If each document in the database describes a camera and includes fields for the date and place of manufacture, you can define a column formula that displays the type of focus mechanism the camera uses:

```
@If (mfgDate < [3/1/81]; "Manual"; mfgSite != "Cleveland"; "Fixed"; "Auto")
```

This formula gives Notes the following orders: If the manufacture date is prior to 3/1/81, display Manual; otherwise, check the manufacture site. If it's not Cleveland, display Fixed; otherwise, display Auto.

Predicate Functions

Many Notes functions don't manipulate data, but instead examine data, testing for the existence of some condition. These functions—called *predicate functions*—are meant to be used with the @If function so that you can take some action if a specific condition exists.

For example, suppose that you want to change the title of a document to read

```
Customer Complaint Meeting (James Owens)
```

when a user reads or edits a document. The first part of the title will be pulled from the document's subject field, and the name in parentheses will be the document author's name.

When a user first creates a document, however, the document doesn't have a subject, so a better title might include the words New Document with the author's name, as follows:

```
New Document (James Owens)
```

You can use the predicate function @IsNewDoc to distinguish between an existing document and one that is in the process of being created. By using the @IsNewDoc function as the condition of an @If function, you can construct one Notes formula to display either of the needed titles. The window title formula might look like this:

```
@If (@IsNewDoc; "New Document"; Subject) + " (" + @Author + ")"
```

This formula tells Notes to determine whether this document is new, and to display the phrase New Document if it's new or the value of the Subject field if it isn't new. Onto that value, Notes should concatenate an opening parenthesis, the author's name, and a closing parenthesis. The resulting text becomes the title of the document window.

TIP Predicate functions can help you create a unique key for a document. You can create a computed text field named Key (the name selected here is arbitrary) that is hidden and set its value formula to

```
@If(@IsNewDoc and IsDocBeingSaved;@Unique;Key);
```

This formula tells Notes to generate a unique value using the @Unique function if the document is new and is being saved when this formula executes. (This condition can happen only when a new document is being saved for the first time.). Otherwise, just return the current value of the field. Because the value is computed at the moment the document is saved and only happens once, you can be assured of getting a unique value.

Logical Operators

In some situations, you may need to test for combinations of conditions. You can test for these combinations using the logical operators AND (&) and OR (¦) to combine individual conditions.

N O T E Logical operators are often called *Boolean operators.*

The AND operator (&) allows you to determine whether all of two or more conditions are true. For example, one way to determine which magazine subscribers are eligible for renewal is to create a column formula that displays "Renew" if the subscription expires this month and the customer has a good credit rating. The column formula might look like this:

```
@If (@Month(@Today) = renewalMonth & creditRating = "Good";
 "Renew";
 "")
```

In this @If function, the AND operator separates two conditions. When evaluated, Notes selects one of two values to display: Renew or " " (nothing). The @Today function returns today's date; the @Month function determines which month that date occurs in. Notes determines whether that month is equal to the value in the renewalMonth field and checks whether the creditRating field contains the value Good. For Notes to display Renew, both conditions must evaluate to true; otherwise, Notes displays nothing.

The OR operator (¦)allows you to determine whether any of two or more conditions are true. Suppose that your rental car fleet database contains documents describing vehicles in your corporate fleet and you want to display an asterisk (*) in a column if the vehicle is due for maintenance. Vehicles are scheduled for maintenance every 3,000 miles or if the driver complained of a problem during the last run. The column formula might look like this:

```
@If (currentMiles > lastServiceMiles + 3000 ¦ complaint = "Y";
 "*";
 "")
```

This @If function selects between displaying an asterisk or displaying nothing. If the value in currentMiles is greater than lastServiceMiles plus 3000 or if the complaint field is equal to Y, Notes uses the asterisk; only one of the conditions has to be true.

The NOT operator (!) changes true values to false and false values to true. Continuing with the rental car fleet example, let's say that you have a very rich, peculiar customer who insists that her rented car be red in February and December and blue in all other months. The following formula will evaluate to either Blue or Red:

```
@If (customerName = "Morganna" &
!(rentalMonth = "February" ¦ rentalMonth = "December");
 "Blue" :
 "Red")
```

When trying to understand a complex statement like this one, always start with the innermost parentheses. In this case, you need to look at the part about the rental months:

```
(rentalMonth = "February" ¦ rentalMonth = "December")
```

This formula clause or fragment evaluates to true if the rental month is either February or December. However, the original formula has a NOT (!) operator directly in front of this clause:

```
!(rentalMonth = "February" ¦ rentalMonth = "December")
```

This operator reverses the value of the clause so that it will be true only if rental month is not February or December.

Now you can look at the next larger clause that checks the customer name. If the customer name is Morganna and the month is not February or December, then the whole formula will evaluate to Blue; otherwise, it will evaluate to Red.

Conditional expressions can get pretty complicated. But if you start in the middle and work your way out, you can read them one bit at a time.

Function Reference by Category

Notes includes more than 100 functions. To help you organize them, this section groups the functions into different types. For example, some functions deal with text manipulation and others are mathematical.

To save space, only the function names are listed here. The syntax and a brief description of each function appear in the "Alphabetical Function Reference" section on the CD-ROM.

The User Environment

The user environment is the client computer unless the formula is being evaluated in the following situations: replication formula, agent whose trigger is If New Mail Has Arrived or On Schedule, selection formula, or column formula.

The following functions are useful when dealing with the user environment:

@MailDbName	@Name	@OptimizeMailAddress
@Password	@UserName	@UserRoles
@Version	@V3UserName	@ClientType

Retrieving Notes Data

As with any database-oriented application, the need to retrieve data from multiple data sources often arises. Lotus has several functions that allow you to retrieve data from Notes databases, as well as from any other ODBC-compliant database. Because ODBC adds both a new level of power and complexity, it's covered in its own Bonus Chapter, "ODBC and Lotus Components," on the companion CD-ROM.

In particular, you should become familiar with three important data-retrieval functions:

@DbColumn

@DbLookup

@PickList

As you become a more proficient Notes/Domino developer, you'll find yourself using these functions often.

▶ **See** "Using Functions to Retrieve Data," **p. 635**

Defining View Columns

Because view column formulas and views can make up a large part of a Notes application, many functions are useful in defining columns:

@Begins	@DocChildren	@DocDescendants
@DocLength	@DocLevel	@DocNumber
@DocParentNumber	@DocSiblings	@DocumentUniqueID
@Elements	@Ends	@If
@InheritedDocumentUniqueID	@IsAvailable	@IsCategory
@IsExpandable	@IsNotMember	@Keywords
@Length	@Matches	@NoteID
@Subset	@Unique	@UserRoles
@Word		

For example, to display the size of a document in bytes in a view column, you could use the following formula:

```
@DocLength;
```

You can use @If to conditionally display values or fields in a view column. For example, the following formula tells Notes to display the CompleteDate field if the Status field contains "Complete"; otherwise, Notes displays the DueDate field.

```
@If(Status="Complete";CompleteDate;DueDate);
```

 T I P   If you try to use @DocumentUniqueID or @InheritedDocumentUniqueID in a view column, it will not display properly unless you use the @Text function to convert it. For example, @Text(@DocumentUniqueID).

Manipulating Dates and Times

Notes has several functions that let you manipulate date and time values. Functions such as @Month and @Day allow you to determine the parts of a date or time. @Adjust allows you to compute a time or date in the future or past; for example, you can compute the date 30 days from today. Most useful of all is @Today, which gives you today's date. This function is especially helpful as the default value formula of a date field because it allows you to specify the current date as the initial value for a field when the user creates a document.

The following functions also are useful in dealing with dates and times:

@Accessed	@Adjust	@Created	@Date
@Day	@Hour	@Minute	@Modified
@Month	@Now	@Second	@Text
@Time	@Today	@Tomorrow	@Weekday
@Year	@Yesterday	@Zone	

Working with the Current Document

When writing formulas that act on the current document (the document that is currently open, or selected in a view), the following functions are useful:

@All	@AllChildren	@AllDescendants
@AttachmentNames	@AttachmentLengths	@Author
@Attachments	@DeleteDocument	@DeleteField
@DocLength	@DocMark	@DocumentUniqueID
@InheritedDocumentUniqueID	@IsAvailable	@IsDocBeingEdited
@IsDocBeingLoaded	@IsDocBeingMailed	@IsDocBeingRecalculated
@IsDocBeingSaved	@IsNewDoc	@IsResponseDoc

@IsUnavailable	@MailSend	@NoteID
@Responses	@SetField	@Unavailable
@SetDocField	@Set	@IsDocTruncated

The DEFAULT, FIELD, and SELECT statements also are important when working with a selected document.

Manipulating Lists

Lists can be a powerful way to manipulate data in Notes. In fact, the many functions that Notes provides for manipulating lists can help you in ways you might not have expected. For example, you can use the list processing features of Notes to easily manipulate strings. The following functions are useful when dealing with lists:

@Elements	@Explode	@Implode
@IsMember	@IsNotMember	@Keywords
@Member	@Replace	
@Subset	@Unique	

Manipulating Numbers

You can use mathematical functions to manipulate numbers. For example, the @Max function returns the largest number from a list of parameters that you pass it; the @Sum function, as you might expect, returns the sum of a number list.

Here is a list of the functions that are useful in dealing with numbers:

@Abs	@Acos	@Asin
@Atan	@Atan2	@Cos
@Exp	@Integer	@Log
@Ln	@Min	@Modulo
@Max	@Pi	@Power
@Random	@Round	@Sign
@Sin	@Sqrt	@Sum
@Tan	@Text	

Manipulating Text

Text functions allow you to manipulate text in various ways and to convert data from text to another type, or vice versa. For example, the @Left function, which allows you to extract the beginning portion of a text value, is a function that can manipulate text. Other text functions allow you to check for the length of a field, manipulate text in various ways, and extract any portion of the field.

Suppose that a document requires the user to enter a part number in a field named partNumber. Letters in this field always are supposed to be in uppercase, but you want the user to be able to enter them in uppercase or lowercase. You can specify the following input translation formula:

```
@UpperCase (partNumber)
```

Another real-world example is storing a user's name as First Name, Last Name (the native format in Notes) but displaying it as Last Name, First Name in views so the user can easily find people by their last names. For example, Samuel Hatter is the value stored in the Contact field, but Hatter, Samuel is displayed in a view. The following code is a simple demonstration of how you could use this technique in a view column:

```
@Trim(@ProperCase(@Right(Contact;" ")))+ ", "+@Trim(@ProperCase(@Left(Contact;"
")));
```

The following functions allow various types of text manipulation:

@Abstract	@Begins	@Char
@Contains	@Date	@Ends
@Explode	@Implode	@Left
@LeftBack	@LowerCase	@Middle
@MiddleBack	@NewLine	@ProperCase
@Replace	@Right	@RightBack
@Trim	@UpperCase	

Converting Data Types

When working with different data types, you frequently need to convert from one data type to another. For example, suppose that you have a time/date field that holds the order date of an invoice and you want to create a window title formula that shows the customer name and the year of the invoice. The window title, when finished, should look like this:

```
John Doe - 1996
```

Here is the formula that will create this title:

```
@ProperCase(customerName) + " - " + @Text(@Year(orderDate))
```

You've seen the @ProperCase function before—it makes sure that each word is capitalized. Let's concentrate on the right side of the formula. The @Year function looks at the orderDate field and extracts the year as a number date type. In order to concatenate the year to the customerName field and the text constant, the year needs to be changed into a text data type. The @Text function performs this conversion for you.

The following functions allow various types of data-type manipulations:

@Explode	@Implode	@Text
@TextToNumber	@TextToTime	@Time

The following functions allow various types of list-type manipulations:

@Contains	@Elements	@Explode
@GetPortsList	@Implode	@IsMember
@IsNotMember	@Keywords	@Member
@PickList	@Replace	@Subset
@Unique		

WWW Access

The following functions allow applications to access the World Wide Web:

@URLGetHeader

@URLHistory

@URLOpen

Using Functions to Retrieve Data

The main functions for data retrieval were listed in the preceding reference section. This section provides more details on using the @DbColumn, @DbLookup, and @PickList functions to retrieve data.

@DbColumn Function

You can use the @DbColumn function to retrieve a list of values from a view column. This function can be very useful for building lists of choices for a keyword field or an @prompt that dispalys a list. The syntax of the @DbColumn function when used with Notes databases is as follows:

@DbColumn(class : **"NoCache"** ; server : database ; view ; columnNumber **)**

The first argument, class, tells Notes what type of database you are accessing. To indicate a Notes database, you can either enter an empty string ("") or enter "Notes". The next parameter (which is optional) tells Notes whether the result set should be cached or not. Caching the result improves performance, but if the list has frequently changing values, you may not see a complete list. The default value is to cache the results; if you want the results to be recalculated each time, include the "NoCache" keyword.

The next argument is a text list that should contain the name of the server and database that you want to access. For example, if the server name is Gonzo/Trusted/definiti and the database name is employee.nsf, you would enter "gonzo/trusted/definiti:employee.nsf". You can also use the Replica ID of a database in place of a server name and database name. The server parameter should be an empty string ("") for local databases or the server name for server databases.

N O T E Using a Replica ID, rather than a database name, makes your code much more difficult to maintain. Another developer may have no idea what database this ID points to, causing him or her to have to try and find it! Also, if you ever make a nonreplica copy of the database (for example, to eliminate whitespace), this code will abruptly break. ▪

 T I P If you elect to use Replica ID for this function, open the database properties box and copy it to avoid possible typographic errors.

The next parameter, `viewname`, is the name of the view that should be searched. You use either the view name, or, if it has one, the view alias.

T I P Use a view alias whenever possible to avoid the possibility of the view name changing, which will bungle your formulas.

The final parameter, `columnNumber`, tells Notes which column of the view to return. Although this step might sound simple, for developers new to Notes, this process can often be a source of frustration because not every column is necessarily counted in a view.

The following method ensures you get the right column every time: Open the view in design mode and count all the columns from left to right, ignoring any columns that contain a constant value such as `"Created On:"` or that contain only the following @Functions: @DocChildren, @DocDescendants, @DocLevel, @DocNumber, @DocParentNumber, @DocSiblings, @IsCategory, @IsExpandable. Notes does not count these columns.

You can use the `@Dbcolumn` function to build two types of lists. The following examples demonstrate using both dynamic and static lists. A *dynamic list* changes as users create, update, and delete documents; one example would be a list of contact titles from the contact records in a database. A *static list* is not based on user input and rarely if ever changes —for example, a list of states in the United States.

The following code builds a list of unique choices for an editable keyword field using the first sorted column of a view.

```
List:=@dbcolumn("";@Subset(@dbname;1):"contacts.nsf";"Titles";1);

@if(@Iserror(List);@Return("Lookup error");@Unique(List));
```

In this code, the first line executes a `@Dbcolumn` that returns the a list of values based on the Titles view in the Contacts database. You'll notice that the `@Subset` and `@Dbname` functions determine the server name; this handy technique eliminates the need to hard code a server name, which diminishes portability of the code. If you're confused, refer to the Tip that follows.

 T I P A handy function that will make your code more portable and maintainable when using `@Dbcolumn` or `@Dblookup` is the `@DbName` function. `@Dbname` returns a list containing the name of current server and database. This information is especially useful because if a database is local (not on a server), `@Dbname` returns an empty string (`" "`) as the first element of the list. If the database is on a server,

@Dbname returns the name of the server. For example, if a database named `contacts.nsf` is on `Gonzo/Trusted/Definiti`, @Dbname returns `"Gonzo/Trusted/Definiti"`:`"Contacts.nsf"`. You can the use the ever-handy @Subset function to extract only the server name from the list.

The second line uses an @If to ensure that the @Dbcolumn did not return an error. If no error was returned, you can use @Unique to strip duplicate values out of the list and to return the unique list. Otherwise, a programmer-defined error message is returned.

@*DbLookup* Function

The @DbLookup command is similar to the @DbColumn command, but rather than returning all the values in a view column, it returns only values that match a key that you provide as one of its arguments.

The syntax of the @DbLookup is

```
@DbLookup( class : "NoCache" ; server : database ; view ; key ; columnNumber );
```

or

```
@DbLookup( class : "NoCache" ; server : database ; view ; key ; fieldname );
```

As you can see, the syntax of this function is very similar to the @dbColumn function so this section examines the differences. The first difference is the inclusion of another parameter, key. The key value tells Notes which documents in the view should be read, based on the values in the first sorted column in a view.

T I P The view against which you perform an @DbLookup must contain a sorted column; otherwise, a null value is returned. Additionally, although the search is not case sensitive, spacing and punctuation must be precise because an exact match must be made.

N O T E Using @DbLookup against a view column that contains a multivalue field that is sorted but not categorized can lead to inaccurate results.

The other difference in syntax is that you can use either a column number or a field name as a parameter for the data you want returned. If you use a column number, the same rules apply as for @DbColumn. The field name parameter is actually a better alternative than the column number because the field simply has to exist in the document found during the search; the field does not have to be displayed in a view. Therefore, you can keep view indexes small by including only the minimum number of columns. Often when a column is added or removed, @DbColumn and @DbLookup formulas that rely on a column number fail to produce the desired result because the column number that was originally referenced has changed. Keep in mind, however, that using the field name can cause a lookup to be marginally slower because the document must be searched until the field is found.

The following example should help you understand how you can put @DbLookup to work.

In this example, suppose users compose documents in an orders database (orders.nsf), and as part of the process, they need to get a list of products and product information from your products database (products.nsf). One way to accomplish this task with minimal user input is to create a keyword field that generates a unique list of all product numbers in the products database by using an @DbColumn formula. Figure 15.2 illustrates the InfoBox and the Edit Formula dialog box for this field.

FIG. 15.2

Using @DbColumn to return a unique list of values in a keyword field.

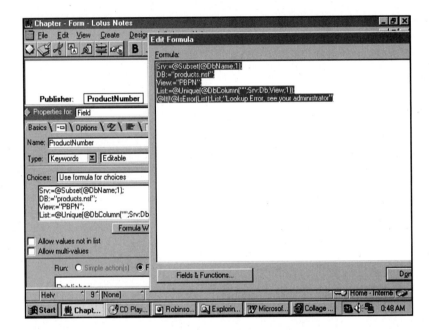

When the user chooses a product number from the list presented in the Product Number field, the other product information such as the unit price, cost, description, and quantity on hand are automatically filled in via an @DbLookup in a hidden computed field (which is refreshed by the Product Number change). This processing is done through the magic of view in which all the required information is concatenated into one column. The view in Figure 15.3 is optimized for looking up multiple values.

N O T E The field delimiter in the view column, "@#@", was chosen because it is a series of characters that are very unlikely to appear in real data. You can choose whatever character(s) you like as a delimiter; just be sure that it has a slim chance of appearing in the data you intend to delimit. ■

FIG. 15.3

A view optimized for looking up multiple values in one shot.

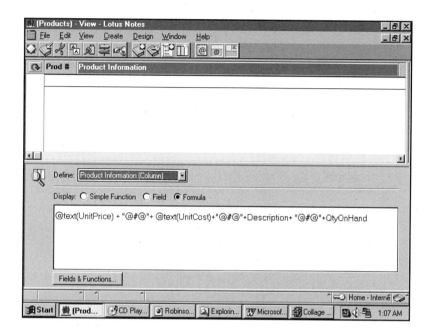

One way to structure the code is to add a hidden, computed-for-display field that performs the lookup into the view that was just created based on the value of the `ProductNumber` field. The following code would be in the hidden field called `Prodinfo`:

```
@Explode(@DbLookup("";@Subset(@DbName;1):"products.nsf";"View";ProductNumber;2);"@#@");
```

This code performs a lookup against the hidden view in the products database. When a match is found, `@DbLookup` returns a column containing the rest of the product information, delimited by "@#@". For example, product number 11118 might retrieve "15.00@#@6.00@#@Widget@#@10" where 15.00 is the unit price, 6.00 is the unit cost, Widget is the description, and 10 is the quantity on hand. The `@Explode` function is called to create a list of individual values from the text string, which would result in the following list:

```
"15,00":6.00:Widget:10"
```

Then all product-related fields on the form (they should be either computed or computed-for-display) would have a formula that reads a specific element from the list contained in the hidden `ProdInfo` field. The code required to set the `Unit Price`, `Unit Cost`, `Description` and `QtyOnHand` fields would look something like the following:

```
@TexttoNumber(@Subset(ProdInfo;1));
@TexttoNumber(@Subset(@Subset(ProdInfo;2);-1));
@Subset(@Subset(ProdInfo-2)-1);
@TextoNumber(@Subset(ProdInfo;-1));
```

N O T E @DbColumn and @DbLookup can return only 64K of data (which doesn't sound like much, but is actually a fair amount of data). If you need to retrieve more data than that, you'll need to consider the @PickList function, which is covered next. ▓

@*PickList* Function

The @PickList function is a very powerful way to retrieve data from Notes databases. When called, it can do one of two things: display a view named by the programmer and return a view column for the selected document(s). Or it can display the Notes Address dialog box (the same one used when addressing mail).

Although @PickList is new to Notes 4.6, according to Lotus, @PickList is faster than the older @DbColumn and @DbLookup, and is not constrained by the 64K limit.

The following code illustrates the syntax of the @PickList function:

```
@PickList( [Custom] : [Single] ; server : file ; view ; title ; prompt ; column )
```

or

```
@PickList( [Name] : [Single] )
```

When used with the [Name] parameter, @PickList displays the Address dialog box, as shown in Figure 15.4.

FIG. 15.4

The Address dialog box displayed by @PickList.

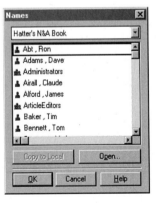

When used with the [Custom] parameter, you specify the server and database that contains the view you want to display as well as the name of the view to display. The *title* parameter allows you to specify a message to display in the Window Title of the dialog box, and the *prompt* parameter specifies a message in the dialog box to help the user understand what to do. The [Single] parameter allows you to determine whether more than one document can be selected, which affects what is returned by the last parameter, *column*.

The *column* parameter determines which column is returned from the view. If the [Single] parameter is specified, only a single discrete value will be returned; if a user can select more than one document ([Single] is not specified), a list will be returned.

The following code uses @PickList to display a dialog box like the one shown in Figure 15.5 and return column 3 from the view:

```
@PickList([custom]:[single];
@Subset(@dbname;1):"contacts.nsf";"Customers";"Lookup Contact";"Select a Con-
tact"; 3)
```

FIG. 15.5

An @PickList dialog box.

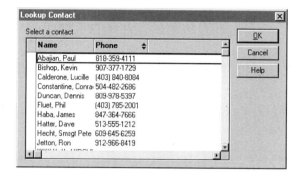

N O T E @PickList cannot be used on the Web because it uses a modal dialog box. In fact, none of the Notes functions that manipulate the user interface such as @Prompt and @DialogBox can be used with Domino.

@*Command* Reference by Category

Notes includes more than 350 commands for use in formulas and functions. They are used in buttons, agents, and action items. In this section the commands are grouped by type. For example, some commands deal with administration issues, whereas others deal with form and view design and manipulation, text editing, and replication.

Only the names are listed here. The syntax and a brief description of each command appear on the companion CD-ROM.

All commands use the following syntax:

```
@Command([commandname]; parameters )
```

For example, you could create action buttons in a form or a view using the following @Commands to print the current document, close the current window, create a new document in the specified database using a specified form, initiate replication, and run an agent.

```
@Command([FilePrint]);
```

```
@Command([FileCloseWindow]);
```

```
@Command([Compose]; server : database ; form ; width : height);
```

```
@Command( [ToolsReplicate] ; repMethod  )
```

```
@Command([ToolsRunMacro];"AgentName");
```

Because all @Commands use the same syntax, the @Command portion in the listings isn't repeated.

Administration

AdminCertify	AdminCreateGroup	AdminCrossCertifyIDFile
AdminCrossCertifyKey	AdminDatabaseAnalysis	AdminDatabaseQuotas
AdminIDFileClearPassword	AdminIDFileExamine	AdminIDFileSetPassword
Administration	AdminNewCertifier	AdminNewOrganization
AdminNewOrgUnit	AdminOpenAddressBook	AdminOpenCatalog
AdminOpenCertLog	AdminOpenGroupsView	AdminOpenServerLog
AdminOpenServersView	AdminOpenStatisticsView	AdminOpenUsersView
AdminOutgoingMail	AdminRegisterFromFile	AdminRegisterServer
AdminRegisterUser	AdminRemoteConsole	AdminSendMailTrace
AdminStatisticsConfig	AdminTraceConnection	RenameDatabase
PublishDatabase	SetCurrentLocation	

Agents

AgentEdit	AgentEnableDisable	AgentLog
AgentRun	AgentSetServerName	AgentTestRun

Attachments

AttachmentDetachAll	AttachmentLaunch	AttachmentProperties
AttachmentView		

Calendar

CalendarFormat	CalendarGoTo	FindFreeTimeDisplay

Create

CreateAction	CreateAgent	CreateControlledAccessSection
CreateEllipse	CreateFolder	CreateForm
CreateLayoutRegion	CreateNavigator	CreatePolygon
CreatePolyline	CreateRectangle	CreateRectangularHotspot
CreateSection	CreateSubForm	CreateTextform
CreateView		

Design

DesignDocumentInfo	ChooseFolders	RemoveFromFolder

Forms-Related Commands

DesignFormAttributes	DesignFormFieldDef	DesignFormNewField
DesignForms	DesignFormSharedField	DesignFormUseField
DesignFormWindowTitle	DesignHelpAboutDocument	DesignHelpUsingDocument
DesignIcon	DesignMacros	DesignRefresh
DesignReplace	DesignSharedFields	DesignSynopsis

Views-Related Commands

DesignViewAppendColumn	DesignViewAttributes	DesignViewColumnDef
DesignViewEditActions	DesignViewFormFormula	DesignViewNewColumn
DesignViews	DesignViewSelectFormula	
PasteBitmapAsBackground	PasteBitmapAsObject	
DatabaseReplSettings	DebugLotusScript	
DesignDocumentInfo	InsertSubFormPictureProperties	

Edit

Compose	EditBottom	EditButton
EditClear	EditCopy	EditCut
EditDeselectAll	EditDetach	EditDocument
EditDown	EditEncryptionKeys	EditFind
EditFindInPreview	EditFindNext	EditGotoField
EditHeaderFooter	EditHorizScrollbar	EditIndent
EditIndentFirstLine	EditInsertButton	EditInsertFileAttachment
EditInsertObject	EditInsertPageBreak	EditInsertPopup
EditInsertTable	EditInsertText	EditLeft
EditLinks	EditLocations	EditMakeDocLink
EditNextField	EditOpenLink	EditPaste
EditPasteSpecial	EditPhoneNumbers	EditPrevField
EditProfile	EditResizePicture	EditRight
EditSelectAll	EditSelectByDate	EditShowHideHiddenChars
EditTableFormat	EditTableDeleteRowColumn	EditTableInsertRowColumn
EditTop	EditUndo	EditUntruncate
EditUp		

File

FileCloseWindow	FileDatabaseACL	FileDatabaseCompact
FileDatabaseCopy	FileDatabaseDelete	FileDatabaseInfo
FileDatabaseRemove	FileDatabaseuseServer	FileExit
FileExport	FileFullTextCreate	FileFullTextDelete
FileFullTextInfo	FileFullTextUpdate	FileImport
FileNewDatabase	FileNewReplica	FileOpenDatabase
FileOpenDBRepID	FilePageSetup	FilePrint
FilePrintSetup	FileSave	FileSaveNewVersion

Folder

Folder	FolderCollapse	FolderCustomize
FolderExpand	FolderExpandAll	FolderExpandWithChildren
FolderMove	FolderProperties	FolderRename

Form

FormActions	FormTestDocument

Help

Help	HelpAboutDatabase	HelpAboutNotes
HelpFunctions	HelpIndex	HelpKeyboard
HelpMessages	HelpTableOfContents	HelpUsingDatabase

HotSpot

HotSpotClear	HotSpotProperties

Layout

LayoutAddGraphic	LayoutAddText	LayoutElementBringToFront
LayoutElementProperties	LayoutElementSendToBack	LayoutProperties

Mail

MailAddress	MailComposeMemo	MailForward
MailForwardAsAttachment	MailOpen	MailRequestCrossCert
MailRequestNewName	MailRequestNewPublicKey	MailScanUnread
MailSend	MailSendCertificateRequest	MailSendEncryptionKey
MailSendPublicKey		

Navigate

NavigateNext	NavigateNextHighlight	NavigateNextMain
NavigateNextSelected	NavigateNextUnread	NavigatePrev
NavigatePrevHighlight	NavigatePrevMain	NavigatePrevSelected
NavigatePrevUnread	NavigateToBackLink	

Navigator

NavigatorProperties	NavigatorTest

Object

ObjectDisplayAs	ObjectOpen	ObjectProperties

Open

OpenDocument	OpenNavigator	OpenView

Replicator

ReplicatorSendReceiveMail	Replicator
ReplicatorReplicateHigh	ReplicatorReplicateNext
ReplicatorReplicateSelected	ReplicatorReplicateWithServer
ReplicatorSendMail	ReplicatorStart
ReplicatorStop	

Section

SectionCollapse	SectionCollapseAll	
	SectionDefineEditors	
SectionExpand	SectionExpandAll	SectionProperties
SectionRemoveHeader		

ShowHide

ShowHideLinkPreview	ShowHideParentPreview	ShowHidePreviewPane

Show

ShowProperties

Text

TextAlignCenter	TextAlignFull	TextAlignLeft
TextAlignNone	TextAlignRight	TextBold
TextBullet	TextCycleSpacing	TextEnlargeFont
TextFont	TextItalic	TextNormal
TextNumbers	TextOutdent	TextParagraph
TextParagraphStyles	TextPermanentPen	TextReduceFont
TextSetFontColor	TextSetFontFace	TextSpacingDouble
TextSpacingOneAndAHalf	TextSpacingSingle	TextUnderline

Tools

ToolsCall	ToolsCategorize	ToolsHangUp
ToolsMarkAllRead	ToolsMarkAllUnread	ToolsMarkSelectedRead
ToolsMarkSelectedUnread	ToolsRefreshAllDocs	ToolsRefreshSelectedDocs
ToolsReplicate	ToolsRunBackgroundMacros	ToolsRunMacro
ToolsScanUnreadChoose	ToolsScanUnreadPreferred	ToolsScanUnreadSelected
ToolsSetupLocation	ToolsSetupMail	ToolsSetupPorts
ToolsSetupUserSetup	ToolsSmartIcons	ToolsSpellCheck
ToolsUserLogoff		

User

UserIDCertificates	UserIDClearPassword	UserIDCreateSafeCopy
UserIDEncryptionKeys	UserIDInfo	UserIDMergeCopy
UserIDSetPassword	UserIDSwitch	

View

ViewArrangeIcons	ViewBelowFolders	ViewBesidesFolders
ViewCertify	ViewChange	ViewCollapse
ViewCollapseAll	ViewExpand	ViewExpandAll
ViewExpandWithChildren	ViewHorizScrollBar	ViewMoveName
ViewNavigatorsFolders	ViewNavigatorsNone	ViewRefreshFields
ViewRefreshUnread	ViewRenamePerson	ViewShowFieldHelp
ViewShowObject	ViewShowOnlyCategories	ViewShowOnlySearchResults
ViewShowOnlySelected	ViewShowOnlyUnread	ViewShowPageBreaks
ViewShowRuler	ViewShowSearchBar	ViewShowServerNames
ViewShowUnread	ViewSwitchForm	

Window

WindowCascade	WindowMaximize	WindowMaximizeAll
WindowMinimize	WindowMinimizeAll	WindowNext
WindowRestore	WindowTile	WindowWorkspace

Workspace

WorkspaceProperties	WorkspaceStackReplicaIcons

Other

RefreshHideFormulas	ZoomPreview

Compatibility Commands

HelpRelease3MenuFinder	V3EditNextField	V3EditPrevField

N O T E　A complete alphabetical @Function and @Command reference can be found in the Notes Help database (`help4.nsf`). ▇

@Command and *@PostedCommand* Action List

In addition to the functions already discussed, you have a couple of other functions at your disposal. You can access most of Notes menu options through the @Command and @PostedCommand functions.

Both @Command and @PostedCommand can handle the same actions—the key difference is when the actions are performed. @Command performs an immediate action in the Notes environment, whereas @PostedCommand defers actions until the end of the formula. ●

Buttons and Agents

Although buttons aren't new to Notes, the way they're programmed and the things you can do with them have been enhanced with a new interface and LotusScript functionality.

In Notes Release 4.6, there's more flexibility than ever before in defining tasks or executing script programs. Behind a button might be some quite complex code, yet the user is presented with a simple, non-intimidating interface. Be aware, however, that programmability can have a downside as well, which will be discussed later in this chapter.

Don't be intimidated by the idea of automating your database applications. After working with buttons and agents for a while on local databases, you'll be ready to begin adding them to some production databases. In this chapter, you'll learn basic concepts and some advanced tips you can begin using today.

Understanding Agents

Agents allow you to automate daily tasks or build powerful tools you can use to execute complex programs. Users of previous versions of Notes will recognize the similarity of the Agent Builder window with that of the Macro Design window from Notes 3.x. Basically, agents are macros, but more powerful and updated to include the new LotusScript and Java capabilities.

TIP If you've recently migrated to Release 4.x of Notes, you might want some assistance in converting your knowledge of Release 3.x menus to the current version. You can choose <u>H</u>elp, Release 3 Menu Finder to activate a stay-on-top window showing the conversions in a display window as you click the familiar Release 3 menu interface.

Agents can automate daily tasks, help you organize yourself, and keep you better informed. Agents carry out your instructions, pull information from other sources, and file it away until you need it—and these are just a few of the many tasks agents can perform.

Agents can be run manually from the Notes menu, can be scheduled to execute on their own, can run in response to a database event (such as new mail being received), or can run at the touch of a button.

The type of agent a user creates depends on the user's access level (determined by the database's ACL) and the intended audience.

Public Agents

Public, or shared, agents are meant to be run by other users and are typically created by administrators and application designers. An example might be an agent that automatically searches a sales contract database, sending to the appropriate salesperson a reminder of clients with an approaching contract renewal date.

To create a public agent, you must have at least Designer access to the database. To run an agent, you must have at least Reader access. Agents are sensitive to the access level of the user and do not allow them to perform tasks they wouldn't be able to perform manually.

Agents are stored within the database in which they are created. For Notes to activate an agent, the database must be stored in the Notes data directory (usually C:\NOTES\DATA) or one of its subdirectories on the computer where the database is kept. Directory links, which are text files pointing to data-storage locations other than the Notes data directory, can be utilized; however, that link file must be stored in the Notes data directory.

N O T E Once an agent is designated as public or private, that designation cannot be changed. If you create a private agent and want to make it public (or shared) later, you'll need to create a new agent and designate it as shared. You designate a public agent by selecting the Shared Agent checkbox in the Agent Builder window.

Private Agents

Users with ACL access below Designer access but who have the Create personal agents access (this is a checkbox in the ACL settings) can create agents for their own use. These private agents are stored in the database and can act on their own computer or on public databases.

N O T E To create a LotusScript or Java agent, you must also have the Create LotusScript/Java agents checkbox checked in the Database ACL for each user or group that needs this permission.

You might want to create a private agent, for example, to organize your mail database or copy documents from a public database to a newsletter database.

A user must have at least Reader access to a database to create a personal agent. Personal agents can't carry out a task that the user wouldn't be able to perform manually in a given database. For example, a personal agent cannot update a document if the user doesn't have at least Editor access to the database.

Creating Agents

With Designer or better access to a database, you can create both public and private agents. If you have Editor, Author, or Reader access, you are limited to creating private agents. Agents can be created in one of three ways:

- You can copy an agent that performs a function similar to the one you require from the same database you're designing.
- You can copy an agent from another database.
- You can create an agent from scratch using the Agent Builder window reached through the Create, Agent menu choices. Again, you need Designer or better access to create public (or shared) agents and at least Reader access to create agents for your own use.

The following sections cover each method.

Copying an Agent in the Current Database

To copy an agent from the current database, follow these steps:

1. Choose View, Agents and highlight the agent you want to copy.
2. Choose Edit, Copy from the menu; press Ctrl+C; or use the Edit Copy SmartIcon.
3. Choose Edit, Paste from the menu; press Ctrl+V; or use the Edit Paste SmartIcon. Notice that the copied agent will have the name "Copy Of *agentname*."
4. Double-click the newly pasted agent to open the Agent Builder window. Edit the agent to fit your needs. If you have Designer-level access and want to create a shared agent, select the Shared Agent checkbox in the Agent Builder window.
5. Press Esc and choose Yes to save your changes.

Copying an Agent from Another Database

To copy an agent from another database, follow these steps:

1. Highlight the icon of the database containing the agent you want to copy, and choose View, Agents.
2. Highlight the agent you want to copy. Choose Edit, Copy from the menu; press Ctrl+C; or use the Edit Copy SmartIcon.
3. Press Esc to close the database.
4. Open the database you want to paste the agent into.
5. Choose View, Agents.
6. Choose Edit, Paste from the menu; press Ctrl+V; or use the Edit Paste SmartIcon.
7. Double-click the newly pasted agent to open the Agent Builder window. Edit the agent to fit your needs. If you have Designer-level access and want to create a shared agent, select the Shared Agent checkbox in the Agent Builder window.
8. Press Esc to close the database, and choose Yes to save it.

If you copy an agent from a database that is a design template, you'll be asked whether you want to accept future design updates. Choose Yes if you want to receive design updates from the original template. Choose No if you want to update it yourself. See Chapter 10, "Creating New Databases," for more information on working with database template files.

It is possible to change this option later. To accept or deny changes to an agent after it has been created, follow these steps:

1. Click the agent name.
2. Choose Agent, Agent Properties, or right-click the agent name and choose Agent Properties. The Agent Properties InfoBox appears.
3. Click the Design tab in the InfoBox (see Figure 16.1).

FIG. 16.1

Choose the Design tab in the Agent Properties InfoBox to change template update choices.

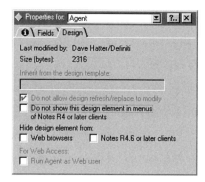

4. Choose the Do not allow design refresh/replace to modify option.

5. Close the Agent Properties InfoBox.

In Chapter 10, you learned that Notes ships with sample databases that can be used as templates for new databases. These databases are also an excellent place to find agents you can use in other databases you create. Be sure to check out the templates that ship with Notes for Agents you can put to immediate use with few or no modifications.

Creating an Agent from Scratch

You can build an agent from scratch if you cannot find one suitable to copy and edit. Keep these tips in mind when building agents from scratch:

- Write down the steps you'd follow if you were going to perform a task, or series of tasks manually. This will help you get the basic steps in the right order. Next, consider making a flowchart of the agent. This can help you to identify any holes or gaps in the process.

- Consider creating a "library" database to store copies of agents that you find useful. Agents can be copied here for later reference by you or other developers. This can be a big time-saver, especially when using complex formulas and LotusScript programs!

Before building an agent, consider the following:

- What do I want the agent to do? The things that agents can do have greatly increased with this version of Notes. Simple Actions allow users to create agents even without knowledge of Lotus's @Functions. The addition of LotusScript and now Java allows you to answer this question in ways users of previous versions only dreamed about! Have a clear idea of the tasks the agent should accomplish and how to have Notes do it.

- What should I name the agent? What you name a Notes agent matters. See the section on "Choosing a Name" for more information.

    Users who create private agents have only themselves to consider here. The workday can be frustrating enough without adding complications yourself. Do yourself a favor and use descriptive names so you don't have to remember exactly what "Delete" is going to do when you run it.

■ When do I want the agent to run? For planning purposes, consider the time(s) that your agent will run. Are there periods during the day that you use your computer more than others? Are there times when the server you're using is busier than others, or perhaps unavailable? Consider scheduling agents that are resource-intensive (those requiring more time or processing power to complete) at times when resources are least strained.

The details of scheduling your agent will be covered in the "Choosing When to Run the Agent" section later in this chapter. Right now, be aware that agents can be scheduled to run manually, in response to a database event (such as received mail), at a particular time, or repeatedly. For example, agents that archive public databases should be run when those databases aren't in use. Mail agents should run at least daily. You may want some agents only to be run manually.

■ Which database elements should it act on? The scope of the actions for your agent should be considered. Agents can be run against an entire database, selected documents, or a single document. It is important to understand and plan your agent so that it affects only those database elements you desire. Otherwise, you could lose important information or negatively affect other people's jobs or your own!

By thinking about these questions before you begin, you'll find that you have the necessary elements in your grasp to easily create a useful agent.

Using the Agent Builder Window

To build an agent, follow these steps:

1. Highlight the icon of the database you want to design the agent in.

2. Choose Create, Agent. The Agent Builder window opens (see Figure 16.2).

3. Choose the desired options in the Agent Builder window. If you have Designer level access and want to create a shared agent, select the Shared Agent checkbox in the Agent Builder window.

4. Specify the action, formula, script or Java program for the agent. Check the format of your formulas by clicking the green checkmark to the left of the Programmer pane. If there is an error in the format, a pop-up window will appear with text summarizing the problem. Make the necessary changes to the formula and click the checkmark again to verify that at least the formula is valid.

5. Press Esc.

6. Make sure you test the formula before allowing it to be used on live data. Use the simulated run option to verify that the agent will select the intended documents and act the way it's intended. You may place important data at risk, otherwise. Refer to the section "Testing Your Creations" later in this chapter for more details on testing agents.

Some options in the Agent Builder window are not available for all agents. Agents that are run manually from the Actions menu present the greatest number of options to the creator. Agents that run in response to defined actions like new mail or pasted documents are more limited because they run only on the documents that have changed.

FIG. 16.2

Open the Agent Builder by choosing <u>C</u>reate, <u>A</u>gent from the menu or double-clicking the name of an existing agent to edit choices for that agent.

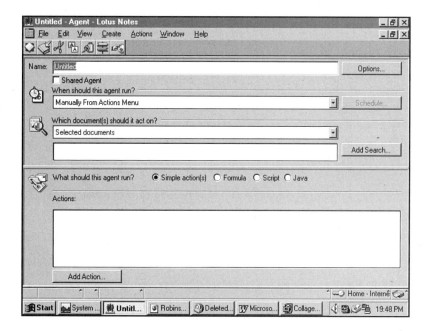

Part

II

Ch

16

As you may suspect, there are four elements required of an agent:

- Name
- Schedule
- Document selection
- Actions

The following sections describe the options for these required elements.

See Chapter 13, "Integrating Notes with Other Applications," and Chapter 14, "Working with Formulas," for more information on @Functions, and Chapter 17, "LotusScript Basics," for information on LotusScript programming.

Choosing a Name

First, give your agent a name so that users can refer to it. Naming it first lets you refer to the agent by name as you work. If you save an agent without a name, it will appear as Untitled in the menu. Naming conventions aren't as innocuous as you might suspect.

 TIP Use the Options button to the right of the Name field on the Agent Builder window to add a comment about the agent. You can use the Show search in search bar and Store highlights in documents options to control how Notes handles the results of searches done by agents. The Available to public access users checkbox determines whether users who are accessing the database as "public access" (users with No Access or Depositor access) can run the agent.

An agent's name should be descriptive of its actions—for example, Save to Newsletter folder. A descriptive name will help users decide which agent to run from the <u>A</u>ctions menu. Because your agent names can contain up to 32 alphanumeric characters (including spaces and punctuation), you should be able to create names that describe the function of an agent. Being specific can reduce mistakes and user anxiety. The function of an agent named Send article to Sales team is easy to understand.

Naming Conventions   Standardized naming conventions help users to work efficiently because agents with similar functions will have similar names in all the databases they use. It also provides a more cohesive look and feel to your company's Notes/Domino environment. This is especially important if you're considering publishing databases on the Internet.

Specifying Name Order   Notes will sort agent names, on the <u>A</u>ctions menu, in alphabetical order (see Figure 16.3). If you want your agents to appear in a particular order on the menu, you'll have to name them appropriately or prepend them with a number. For example, if tasks are carried out in a particular order, you'll want to set the order of agent names accordingly.

FIG. 16.3

Agent names sorted alphabetically.

 You can number your agents so that they are not necessarily sorted in alphabetical order. However, Notes will convert the numbers to text, and they will be sorted based on their text value rather than their numerical value, meaning that 10 will be listed before 1, not after 9 as you might expect. Circumvent this problem by using 01, 02, 03, and so on when naming rather than 1, 2, 3. Notes will then list the agents in "numeric" order.

Specifying Accelerator Keys   Windows, OS/2, and UNIX users can select an agent by typing the first letter of its name or the underlined letter in the agent's name. These underlined letters, referred to as accelerator keys, can be programmed by the agent's creator. To do so, place an underline character (_) in front of the letter you want to use as the accelerator key when naming the agent.

If you do not specify a default accelerator key, Notes will create one for you. Because the first unique letter in the agent's name will be used, the program's choice might not be intuitive to the user. For example, if you have two agents whose names begin with Copy, the first will use C as its accelerator key, and the second will use O.

Naming agents alphabetically will allow users to select an agent by simply typing that letter. If two agent names begin with the same letter, the default accelerator key will be the first unique letter in the name of the second agent.

Grouping Agents with Cascading Menus   If a database contains several agents that perform similar functions, consider creating a cascading menu. This alternative presents a more cohesive and efficient menu to the user by grouping agents by function. When you click the first level, a submenu appears with additional choices. This option is helpful in reducing clutter on the Action menu.

To set up a cascading menu, first decide on a descriptive name for the top-level menu that the user will see. For example, if there are several agents that copy selected documents to different folders, place them under one menu item with a name such as Copy To Folder.

When naming the agent, begin with the descriptive name (from the preceding paragraph), followed by a backslash (\). Next, type the agent name that the user will see in the submenu. For example, to create the menu shown in Figure 16.4, name the agents as shown here:

```
Copy \ Documents to Finance folder

Copy \ Documents to Marketing folder

Copy \ Documents to Sales folder
```

FIG. 16.4
Agents grouped by function.

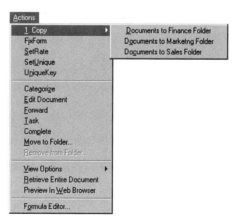

Notes supports one level of cascaded names. These appear on a submenu. Each agent name cannot contain more than 64 bytes. Multibyte characters (such as the \ character in the cascading name) limit the number of characters, as opposed to bytes, that the name can contain. The name of the top menu can be up to 32 bytes in length, and the cascaded names can be up to 30 bytes.

Part
II

Ch
16

Choosing When to Run the Agent

Some agents require user intervention to run. These manual agents are useful for tasks that are run at the user's discretion. Agents can also be set to run on a schedule or in response to certain database events. Let's look at how to create these agents and consider some examples of situations in which they might be useful in your day-to-day work. The following choices are available in the field When Should This Agent Run?:

- Manually From Actions Menu
- Manually From Agent List
- If New Mail Has Arrived
- If Documents Have Been Created or Modified
- If Documents Have Been Pasted
- On Schedule Hourly
- On Schedule Daily
- On Schedule Weekly
- On Schedule Monthly
- On Schedule Never

 TIP   If you're a laptop user and you choose to receive truncated documents during replication (see the Receive summary and 40K of rich text only option under Replication), agents will not run against these documents. If you want to run agents against these documents, you must have Notes send the full document(s).

You can also choose not to receive agents when replicating a database. If you don't want agents to replicate to a local copy of a database, follow these steps:

1. Click the icon of the replica database.
2. Choose File, Replication, Settings, Advanced.
3. Under the Replicate incoming field, clear the checkmark from the Agents option.

Running Manually from the Actions Menu   Database designers who create public agents for use by others will find the Manually From Menu option the most useful. This allows users to run an agent by clicking the Actions menu in a database and choosing an agent by name.

This option can be useful when you're testing the component pieces of a complex agent before changing its run option to Manually From Agent List. Checking the function of component agents can save you from repairing the damage caused by unexpected results.

Hiding Agents and Running Agents from Other Agents   You can choose to hide an agent so that it doesn't show up in the Actions menu. Hidden agents can be run from another agent, or you can run a hidden agent by highlighting it in the Agents view and selecting Actions, Run. To hide an agent, choose Manually From Agent List in the When Should This Agent Run? field in the Agent Builder window. Keep the following points in mind:

- Use the <u>A</u>ctions, <u>R</u>un option to test hidden component agents when creating large or complex agents. The Agent Log will appear after the hidden agent is run via the <u>A</u>ctions, <u>R</u>un menu options in the Agents view.

- Use the Run Agent action in the Programmer pane to combine existing agents. (If you want to run an agent from another database, you'll have to copy it into your database.) Use this technique to combine component agents using Simple Actions, @Function formulas, or LotusScript into a single agent.

- Actions will be carried out sequentially, in the order in which they occur in the agents. Document selection is performed by the primary agent. The main agent (perhaps one chosen from the <u>A</u>ctions, <u>R</u>un menu) runs and passes the resulting information to a secondary agent for its processing. For example, the first component agent searches for all documents within a folder for a particular author name and marks them as unread. The next component agent performs the programmed action on all the documents selected by the first agent.

Scheduling Agents   Scheduled agents require no user intervention to run. They do exactly what their name implies. This also makes them one of the most useful tools in the never-ending battle to stay informed in a constantly changing market.

In the When Should This Agent Run? section of the Agent Builder window, choose the desired schedule:

- On Schedule Hourly
- On Schedule Daily
- On Schedule Weekly
- On Schedule Monthly
- On Schedule Never

A Daily agent can be used, for example, to run periodic checks of published databases you subscribe to. This option might be useful if you need to keep informed of your competitor's movement within a given market. Several companies now publish news and information databases for users of Notes. Lotus's Newsstand and WorldCom provide a source for published databases.

Perhaps you are responsible for the department newsletter or a weekly meeting. You might use a weekly agent to remind others to submit an article or complete an action item (or just to show up for a meeting).

TIP If you are responsible for the company newsletter and you're one of the millions of people surfing the Web nowadays, check out Lotus's Newsstand. It offers a neat list of published databases you can subscribe to for industry and special-interest information. For an up-to-date list, point your Web browser at **http://www.newsstand.lotus.com/**.

Part

II

Ch

16

An agent that runs monthly might be useful for copying documents more than six months old to an archive database for storage and reference. This could also serve to keep the size of a production database smaller, thus reducing the need for disk space on remote servers in branch offices, reducing indexing time for views, and reducing replication times.

The On Schedule Never option is reserved for background macros from Notes 3.x that were scheduled to run Never. If you want one of these to run, change the schedule to one of the Release 4 options.

Keep in mind that an agent runs on the computer where the database is stored. If you're running an agent from a database on your local machine, you can do more because you have Manager access, unless Local Security is enabled. Running an agent from the server requires you to pay closer attention to the user's Access Control rights.

To run scheduled agents when you start Notes, follow these steps:

1. Choose File, Tools, User Preferences.
2. Select Enable scheduled local agents.
3. Click OK when you get the message that some changes won't take place until Notes is restarted.
4. Click OK.

Using the Schedule button on the Agent Builder window, you can take the following actions (see Figure 16.5):

- Decide which server or workstation an agent runs on.
- Set the starting and ending dates.
- Set the frequency and starting and ending times of hourly agents.
- Set the starting time for a daily agent.
- Set the day of the week and time of day a weekly agent runs.
- Set the day of the month and starting time of monthly agents.

These options will be handy for agents that run time- or system resource-intensive tasks, such as archiving large databases or compiling a report. You can choose when you can afford to dedicate those resources. Some tasks lend themselves to being run during off-hours.

A salesperson who's on the road visiting a customer might want his computer to dial into his home server at night, while the phone rates are less expensive, and pull all the orders he wrote for a client between the 1st and 20th of the month from the company's Projected Sales database, for example. Perhaps he also wants those orders that mention a certain part or product. Agents can also be set to query other databases for documents by certain authors or dates, or even those including or excluding certain keywords. Look at the "Building Search Queries" section later in this chapter.

FIG. 16.5

Click the Schedule button in the Agent Builder window to choose the times this agent will run. Note that the agent in the example can be found in the Room Reservation template file.

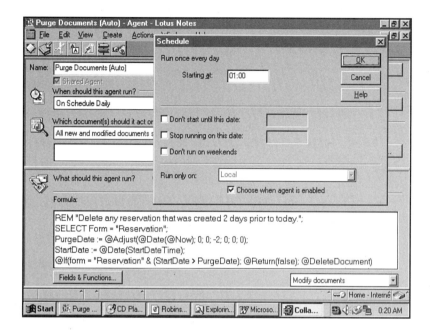

Triggering Agents with Events An agent that is set to activate whenever new mail arrives in the database might, for example, check the username and Delivery Priority fields and forward any High Priority item from the District Vice President to your assistant for action while you're on vacation. To activate the agent with email, choose If New Mail Has Arrived in the When Should This Agent Run? section of the Agent Builder window.

> **CAUTION**
>
> Using If New Mail Has Arrived as a trigger for LotusScript agents will not work in Notes 4.5. This is a well-known bug, and as of this writing, it is not known whether this bug has been fixed in Notes 4.6. Use this feature with caution.

Agents can also be set to activate when a document is modified or if a document has been pasted into a database. Any important document from an employee work schedule to a customer contract might need to be sent to a Person or Group defined in the Name and Address Book if it was modified. To choose one of these options, select If Document Has Been Modified or If New Documents Have Been Pasted in the When Should This Agent Run? section of the Agent Builder window.

Specifying Documents Affected by the Agent

Deciding which documents within a database an agent will act on is required for the successful creation and execution of any agent:

■ Manual agents present the greatest number of selection options. They allow the agent to select a single document, a set of documents in a folder or view, an entire folder or view, or the entire database.

■ Scheduled agents can be run against all documents in the database or on documents that were added or modified since the agent last ran.

■ Change-activated agents present the user with the fewest selection options because they run only against those documents specified by the type of change that occurred—for example, new mail items, pasted documents, or documents modified since the agent was last run.

To specify which documents will be affected by the agent, select one of the following options in the Which Document(s) Should It Act On? section of the Agent Builder window:

■ All documents in the database—The agent will attempt to modify all the documents within the database.

■ New and Modified documents—Only documents that have been created or modified since the agent last ran will be processed.

■ All unread documents—The agent will run against documents marked as unread. You can use another agent to select documents by author, for example, and mark those as unread before triggering a secondary agent.

■ Selected documents in the open view—This option can be most useful to process documents selected by another agent, or you can select documents manually and then run the agent from the Actions menu.

■ All documents in the open view—This choice instructs the agent to run against all documents within the view that is currently open.

■ Current document—The agent will make changes only to the document currently open.

■ Pasted documents—Documents that are pasted into the database will be acted on when the agent runs.

Building Search Queries The use of search queries allows you to fine-tune document selection by agents. This section will introduce you to the options available for search queries.

The Add Search button in the Agent Builder window allows you to define search parameters for an agent. This feature lets you, more specifically, define criteria to select which documents should or shouldn't be acted on by your agent.

Clicking the Add Search button displays the Search Builder dialog box, in which you can choose search options for documents, including author names, dates, field values, or forms used. You can build compound searches by adding parameters to more than one of the option fields in the Search Builder window.

For example, you might want to search a folder for documents by a particular author, created in a given date range. To do this, just complete the necessary fields in the By Author, By Date, and In Folder options in the Condition field. The resulting query will be shown in the field to the left of the Add Search button in the Agent Builder window.

Notes allows searches of encrypted fields and file attachments as long as the database is full-text indexed and the index was created to include these items. If Notes does not allow a search, contact the Manager of the database and ask for a new index to be created that includes attachments and encrypted fields.

N O T E If the database is full-text indexed, make sure that it is current. Open the database properties InfoBox and click the Fulltext tab. You can then click the Count Unindexed Documents button to see whether all the documents are indexed. If the database is not full-text indexed, click Update index; otherwise, your search results might not be accurate. Databases that are full-text indexed will produce better results than those that aren't. If the database resides on a server, set the full-text index's refresh frequency so that the index stays current. ∎

To check the criteria used for the database's full-text index, follow these steps:

1. Highlight the database icon on the workspace.
2. Right-click your mouse on the icon.
3. Choose Database Properties.
4. Select the Full Text tab.

Databases that are stored on a server can use scheduled updates of full-text indexes. You'll need Designer access or above to create, update, or delete a full-text index. Contact your Notes administrator for assistance in setting up a schedule that meets your needs. Remember that full-text indexes require both disk space and processor resources. The administrator can help balance the need for indexing with the resources available on the server.

Table 16.1 describes each type of search.

Table 16.1   Types of Full-Text Searches

Type	Description
By Author	Allows you to search for documents created by a specific author.
By Date	Allows you to search for documents based on the date they were created or modified.
By Field	Allows you to search for documents that contain the field you specify (you select a field from the list of all the fields in the database) and that contain a value that matches your query.
By Form	Allows you to choose a form from the database and fill out fields in the form to build a query that will select documents.

continues

Table 16.1   Continued

Type	Description
By Form Used	Allows you to search for documents that were created with the form(s) you specify.
In Folder	Allows you to search for documents stored in a particular folder.
Words and Phrases	Allows you to search for documents that contain any or all of the words/phrases you specify. You can enter up to eight separate words and phrases.

Figure 16.6 displays the Search Builder dialog box being used to build a search for documents that were created on December 21, 1995.

FIG. 16.6
The Search Builder dialog box is an easy, yet powerful, way to further refine your queries.

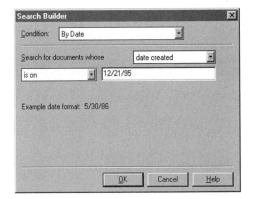

Programming the Agent's Function

Up to this point, you've learned the details to consider when naming an agent. You've considered, in general terms, when it should run and on which elements of the database it should act. Now you'll look at how agents work. Using the Programmer pane, you'll define the specific functions an agent actually carries out (see Figure 16.7).

An agent doesn't have to be complex to be useful. There are four ways to program an agent's function:

■ Using Simple Actions (predefined Notes functions), a user can create an agent with no programming experience. Simple Actions are discussed in the following section.

■ Using the formula language, you can select and process documents. Agents that use @Functions and @Commands require an understanding of programming with the Notes formula language, but they allow significantly more flexibility than Simple Actions.

■ Using LotusScript, Lotus's BASIC-compatible scripting language, you can write very powerful and complex agents that perform almost any action you can think of.

■ Using Java, you can also create very complex agents that can do almost anything.

FIG. 16.7
The Programmer pane is the portion of the screen that asks the question What should this agent run?

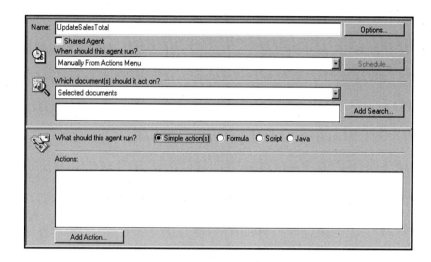

Part
II

Ch

16

Using Simple Actions   Simple Actions are predefined Notes functions that can be strung together to carry out a desired task. These allow manipulation of documents, fields, mail, and folders. You can use Simple Actions to trigger other agents, allowing you to combine component parts into a larger, complex agent.

To program the agent with Simple Actions, follow these steps:

1. With the Agent Builder window open, click the Simple action(s) radio button in the Programmer pane.

2. Click the Add Action button on the bottom of the Programmer pane. The Add Action dialog box appears onscreen (see Figure 16.8).

FIG. 16.8
Clicking the Add Action button in the Programmer pane allows you to program one of Notes's predefined functions.

3. Click the arrow on the right side of the Action field to see a drop-down list of the actions available. You can choose from these 15 Simple Actions available in Notes 4:

Copy to Database	Move to Folder
Remove from Folder	Copy to Folder
Reply to Sender	Delete from Database
Run Agent	Mark Document Read
Send Document	Mark Document Unread
Send Mail Message	Modify Field
Send Newsletter Summary	Modify Fields by Form
@Function Formula	

N O T E You can combine Simple Actions and @Functions by choosing the @Function Formula action and writing an @Function formula. ▪

4. Note that the fields in the lower part of the Add Action dialog box change, depending on the Action you choose. Complete the fields in the lower part of the dialog box.

5. Click OK to save, or click Cancel to close the box without saving your choices. The resulting command will be shown in the Programmer pane.

Notes will carry out multiple Simple Actions in the order listed in the Programmer pane. To program an agent to carry out multiple Simple Actions, repeat steps 2 through 5. Each command you add will be shown in the Programmer pane next to the preceding command (see Figure 16.9).

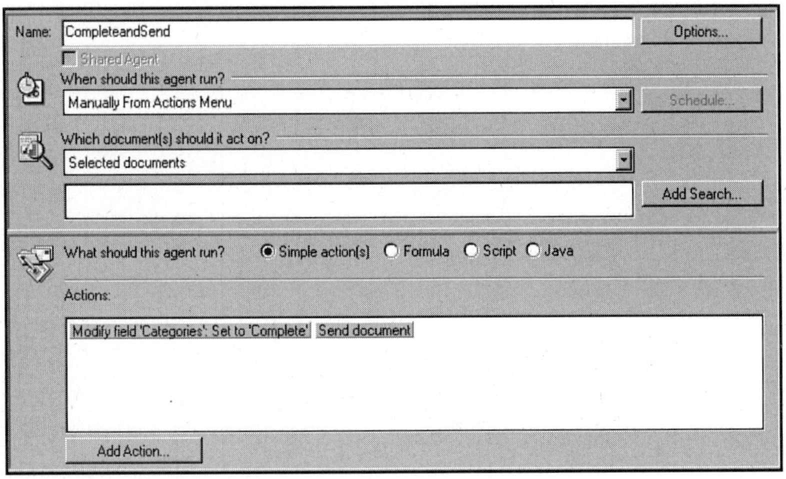

FIG. 16.9

The Programmer pane shows the multiple Simple Actions selected.

Using @Function Formulas   Using @Functions, you can perform the following actions:

- Modify and save existing documents.
- Create new documents by making a copy of an existing document and modifying the copy, preserving the original.
- Select documents in a view but not process them. Use this option to test your selection formula before actually processing documents.

> **N O T E**   Use of the @Command functions is limited within agents. @Command and
> @PostedCommand can be used only with agents that act on the currently selected
> document. Scheduled agents cannot use @DbColumn or @DbLookup to access information in
> databases on another server. They can, however, be used to access other databases on the same
> computer that the agent resides on. ■

Agents that use the formula language cannot be combined with Simple Actions or LotusScript programs in a single agent. Refer to Chapter 13, "Integrating Notes with Other Applications," and Chapter 14, "Working with Formulas," for detailed information on working with @Functions.

Use @Function formulas to select and process documents within a database. To program an agent using @Functions, follow these steps:

1. Choose Formula in the Run field on the Programmer pane.
2. Click the Field & Functions button. The Fields and Functions dialog box appears on-screen (see Figure 16.10).

FIG. 16.10

Click the Fields & Functions button to display a list of @Functions and field names to add to your formula.

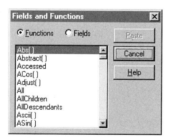

3. Click either the Functions or the Fields button:

   Clicking Functions will show a list of @Function commands that can be pasted into the Programmer pane. The keywords Environment, Field, Rem, and Select are also available. One of these must be the first word used in a formula statement. Highlight the desired selection and click Paste to add it to your formula.

 If you are unsure what a function does, or have forgotten which parameters it requires, simply select it from the list and click the Help button, or press F1 to see online help regarding the function you selected. You can then select it and copy it to the clipboard (Ctrl+C) and paste it into your formula (Ctrl+P), saving you time and effort.

Part

II

Ch

16

Clicking Fields will show a list of the fields defined in the database. Highlight the desired selection and click Paste to add it to your formula.

4. Write an @Function formula in the Programmer pane. As you enter parameters in the Programmer pane, you'll note the appearance of a green checkmark and a red X to the left. Clicking the green checkmark allows you to check the format of the @Function formula you've written. If the formula's format is incorrect, clicking the checkmark will produce a dialog box with a summary of the problem. Clicking the red X will clear the Programmer pane.

5. On the bottom right side of the Programmer pane is a pull-down menu; open the menu and select one of the following options:

   - Modify Documents will modify the original and save the new document.

   - Create New Documents will make a copy of an existing document and modify the copy, preserving the original.

   - Select Documents In View will mark documents with a checkmark but not process them. Use this option to select documents to be processed by an agent or to test your selection formula before actually processing documents.

Using LotusScript Programs   Agents defined as Script in the Run field on the Programmer pane cannot be combined with Simple Actions or formulas in a single agent. However, you can use the Evaluate function in LotusScript to execute most @Functions.

▶ **See** Chapter 17, "LotusScript Basics," **p. 681**

Use LotusScript to create sophisticated programs that can process database documents, act on the database ACLs, write to the file system, or interact with other programming languages.

To program an agent using LotusScript, follow these steps:

1. Choose Script in the Run field on the Programmer pane.

2. Write or copy-and-paste a LotusScript program that selects the documents you want to process and performs the actions you desire. You can check the Show browser checkbox to show a list of LotusScript commands that can be pasted into the Programmer pane (see Figure 16.11).

Using Java Programs   If you have Java expertise on your team, you can easily write Java agents for Notes/Domino 4.6. Click the Java radio button in the Programmer's pane, and you'll see several new options such as the Base Class field and the Import Class Files button, which are illustrated in Figure 16.12. Writing Java agents is beyond the scope of this chapter; for more information on this topic, the following two sources will be very helpful:

   ■ `Java Programmer's Guide` (javapg.nsf), a new Notes database that is installed with Notes 4.6 in the DOC subdirectory.

   ■ `Special Edition Using Javascript` from Que Publishing, which, conveniently enough, is included on the CD-ROM.

FIG. 16.11

Enable the Show Browser to display a list of LotusScript programming parameters.

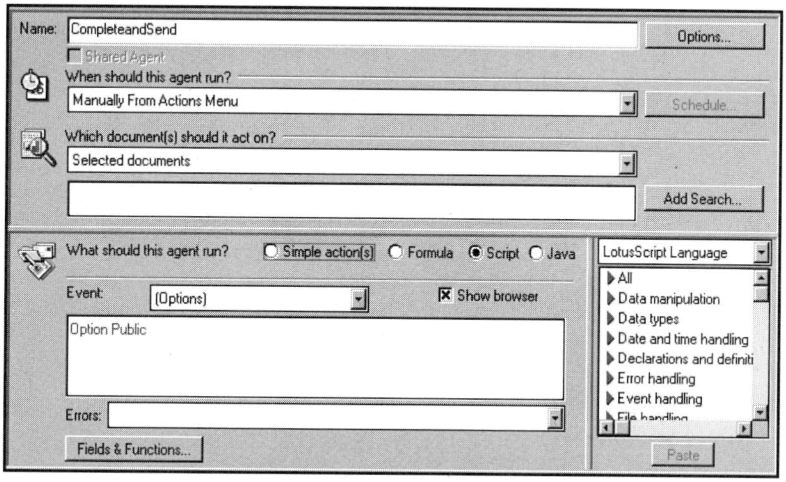

FIG. 16.12

The Programmer's pane for Java programs.

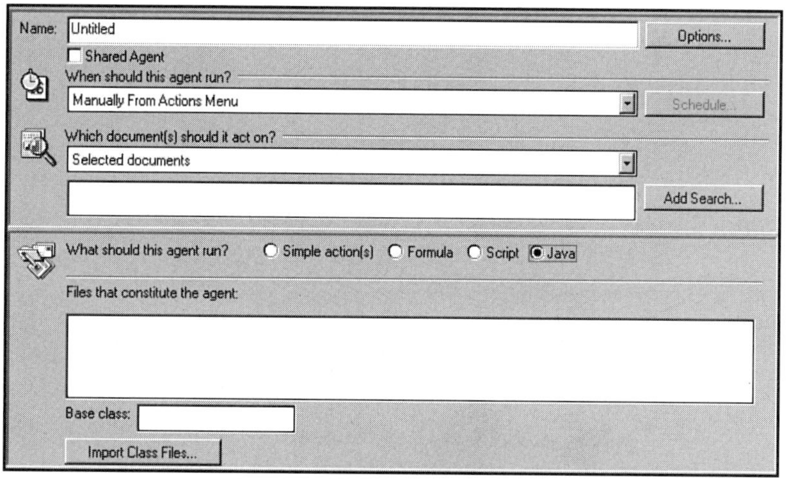

Completing the Agent

After you finish specifying what you want the agent to do, save the agent. Then test it to be sure it works as expected. Begin writing agents in local database copies so that you won't corrupt important data. Begin testing your agent with the Simulated Run option, which identifies the changes that would occur if you were to actually run the agent.

Refer to the "Testing Your Creations" section of this chapter for information on how to test your agent before running it on live data. The more complex an agent is, the more places things can go wrong. If you are writing formula agents, consider using the @Prompt statement to help you troubleshoot and debug. Placing @Prompt statements in your formula code can help you determine where the code is failing. For example:

```
Ret:=@DbLookup("";"Aegis/Definiti":"employee.nsf";"EMPBID";EMPID,2);

@Prompt([OK};"Debug 1"; "Passed lookup, return value is: " + Ret);
```

If you are writing LotusScript agents, you have the added advantage of using the Debugger, as well as using the Print statement or the Messagebox statement to help you debug your code. For example:

```
Print "Current Employee ID =" & Cdoc.EmpID(0)

Ldoc=Lview.GetDocumentByKey(Cdoc.EmpID(0))

Msgbox "You got document " & Ldoc.NoteID & "Emp ID = " Ldoc.EmpID(0), 64, "Debug"
```

The preceding example prints the value of the EmpID field of the current document on the status bar, does the LotusScript equivalent of an @DbLookup, and then pops up a dialog box that displays the Note ID of the document that was retrieved, as well as the value of the EmpID field.

Using Buttons and Hotspots

A button is a graphical representation of a push button you can place on a form (or subform) or in a rich text field to carry out Notes commands or run a script. Buttons allow users to run agents, formulas, or scripts from the form or document level by double-clicking. Again, users can complete only actions allowed by their access level defined in the ACL.

The button interface has been updated in Notes 4. You have more options than with previous versions for creating and displaying the button itself, as well as the underlying code. From the Button Properties InfoBox, you can determine whether a button appears on a form and format the text, alignment, and style.

Notes 4 adds a new design element called a hotspot. Whereas a button is an independent graphic, a hotspot usually appears as text or a graphic, with a green border around it.

As with a button, users can click a hotspot to perform Notes actions or run scripts. You can use hotspots, like hypertext, to link documents together. For example, if a memo mentions a corporate policy, consider using a link hotspot to allow the user to read the policy document for clarification. Hotspots can be used to annotate phrases and graphics, test formulas, or carry out a script. Figure 16.13 illustrates Notes buttons and hotspots.

Creating and Removing Hotspots

Hotspots can execute Simple Actions, @Functions, and LotusScript just like buttons. The presentation is the major difference between a hotspot and a button. A button appears as a graphical object, but a hotspot can appear as a bordered area of text—and even the border can be removed! In essence, a hotspot can do what a button can without taking up additional space in the document.

FIG. 16.13

Buttons and hotspots can be linked to text or graphics. They carry out Notes's commands and actions much like buttons.

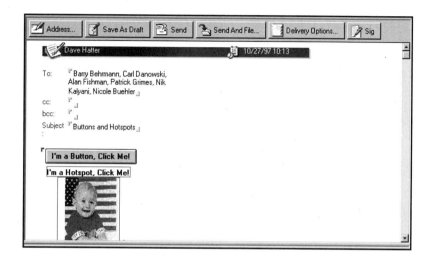

Part

II

Ch

16

To add a hotspot, follow these steps:

1. Open the document or form you want to add the hotspot to.

2. When adding a hotspot to an existing document, choose Actions, Edit Document. While in edit mode, select the area in the rich text field where you want the hotspot. When creating a hotspot in a new form, highlight the rich text field where you want the hotspot to appear.

3. Choose Create, Hotspot.

4. Choose the type of hotspot to be created:

    Link Hotspot   Formula Popup

    Text Popup   Action Hotspot

    Button

5. If you choose a Formula Popup or Action Hotspot, you need to write a formula in the Programmer pane that appears onscreen. Format the hotspot as desired, and close the Properties InfoBox for the hotspot. Test your formulas to ensure that the actions taken are what you want before using them on live data.

6. Save the form or document.

To remove a hotspot, right-click the hotspot while in edit mode and choose Remove Hotspot from the menu.

Link Hotspots   Link hotspots can be used to create a link to another document, view, or database—these are similar to doclinks. To create the link, follow these steps:

1. Go to the document, view, or database you want linked by this hotspot.

2. Choose Edit, Copy As Link to copy a doclink to the clipboard.

3. Close the object.

4. Open the document or form you want the hotspot in.

5. Highlight the area of the rich text field you want to link. This can be text or even a graphic.

6. Choose Create, Hotspot, Link Hotspot.

N O T E When you create a link hotspot, Notes doesn't copy the object into the field but uses a pointer to the destination. If the object you link to is not reachable due to ACL levels or if the server the object resides on is unavailable, Notes presents a menu asking where it should search for the object. For this link to function properly, ensure that the object will be available to the intended user. ▪

You can find the object linked to a hotspot by double-clicking the hotspot. Clicking once and holding the left mouse button down shows the destination of the linked object.

Text Pop-Up Hotspots   Text pop-ups display a simple text message when the left mouse button is clicked once and held down while on the hotspot. This message can be used to provide commentary or additional explanation for a field or a caption. To create a text pop-up hotspot, follow these steps:

1. Highlight the area of the rich text field you want the text to appear by when the hotspot is activated.

2. Choose Create, Hotspot, Text Pop-up. The HotSpot Pop-up Properties InfoBox appears (see Figure 16.14).

FIG. 16.14

The text entered into the HotSpot Pop-up Properties InfoBox appears when the hotspot is clicked.

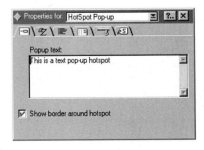

3. In the Properties InfoBox, enter the text you want to appear when the hotspot is clicked.

4. Click the green checkbox in the left border to accept the text as entered. Click the red X in the left border to clear the text box.

Formula Pop-Up Hotspots   Formula pop-up hotspots are very similar to text pop-up hotspots, except that instead of entering a simple, static text string, you can use @Functions to generate a more dynamic message. A user will see the result of this formula by clicking and holding down the left mouse button on the hotspot. The result of the hotspot formula must be a text string, such as "Click the Reschedule button to send a new invitation to invitees".

To create a formula pop-up hotspot, follow these steps:

1. Highlight the area of the rich text field you want the result of the @Function formula to appear by when the hotspot is activated.

2. Choose Create, Hotspot, Formula Hotspot. The HotSpot Pop-up Properties InfoBox appears along with the Programmer pane.

3. Enter an @Function formula in the Programmer pane.

Figure 16.15 shows the result of a user named Roger Sebastian clicking a Formula pop-up hotspot that contains the following formula:

```
@if(@Name([CN];@UserName)="Roger Sebastian";"Don't you have anything better to do
than click this hotspot? Go write some code!";"Thanks for clicking this hotspot,
have a nice day!");
```

Part
II

Ch
16

FIG. 16.15

The result of the formula is displayed when a formula hotspot is clicked.

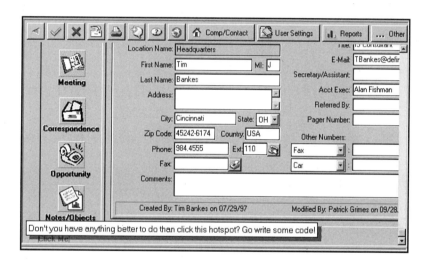

Action Pop-Up Hotspots   Action pop-up hotspots allow a user to execute an @Function or @Command when the hotspot is double-clicked, provided that the user has adequate ACL access to carry out the specified operations.

The following steps show how you create these hotspots:

1. Highlight the area of the rich text field where you want the hotspot to appear.

2. Choose Create, Hotspot, Action Hotspot. The HotSpot Properties InfoBox appears on-screen along with a Programmer pane.

3. In the Programmer pane, enter Simple Actions, an @Function formula, or a LotusScript program to control the hotspot.

Be aware that a hotspot could be a Trojan horse that executes another program by using the @Execute command. If you are unsure what a hotspot will do, make sure that the Execution Control List Default options are all unchecked.

▶ **See** Chapter 22, "Security and Encryption" **p. 919**

Making a Hotspot Invisible

You can remove the green border from around the hotspot, making it "invisible" to the user. To do so, follow these steps:

1. Click the inside of the hotspot.

2. Choose Hotspot, Hotspot Properties. The HotSpot Properties InfoBox appears.

3. Deselect Show Border around Hotspot. You'll see that the border disappears.

4. Close the HotSpot Properties InfoBox and save the form or document.

Editing a Hotspot's Function

You can edit the function of a formula or action hotspot, replacing or editing the underlying actions or formula. Button formulas are edited in a similar fashion:

1. Open the document or form in edit mode.

2. Click the hotspot (or button).

3. Choose Hotspot, Edit Hotspot from the main menu, or right-click the hotspot and choose Hotspot properties from the pop-up menu. (If editing a button, use the Button, Edit Button menu choice or button pop-up menu properties.) The HotSpot Properties InfoBox appears along with the Programmer pane.

4. Make your changes to the code.

5. Save the changes and close the document.

Creating Buttons

Buttons manually execute Simple Actions, @Functions, or LotusScript programs with the double-click of a mouse. They add automation to the database. Users don't have to use the menus to choose commands or the name of the agent necessary to carry out the actions programmed into a button.

To create a button, follow these steps:

1. Open the document or form you want to add the button to.

2. While in edit mode, place the cursor in the rich text field where you want the button to appear.

3. Choose Create, Hotspot, Button. A small button will appear on the form at the point you selected with your cursor. The Button Properties InfoBox and Programmer pane will appear on the screen (see Figure 16.16).

FIG. 16.16

The Button Properties
InfoBox.

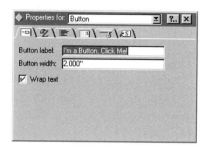

4. Click the first tab of the Button Properties InfoBox (it looks like a button on a document).

5. In the Button label text box, type the label you want the user to see on the button.

6. The formatting options for buttons are the same as those for normal text. (These were discussed in greater detail in Chapter 7, "Working with Text.") With the formatting options in the Button Properties InfoBox, format the button as desired:

   Click the Fonts tab to format the attributes of the font used for the button's label.

   Click the Alignment tab to format the alignment and spacing used for the text in the button's label.

   Click the Pagination tab to format pagination, printing margins, and tab spacing for the text in the button's label.

   Click the Style tab to choose or manage the style of the button's text.

7. When you have finished selecting options for the button, close the Button Properties InfoBox.

8. In the Programmer pane, program the actions the button will carry out. As with agents, program the buttons using Simple Actions, @Function formulas, or LotusScript. Again, the code doesn't need to be complex to be useful. Buttons that transport users to a related document or add a database icon are relatively easy to create, and save time over completing the same action manually.

The default button settings create a functional button. To edit the properties of an existing button, follow these steps:

1. Open the document in edit mode by pressing Ctrl+E or selecting Actions, Edit Document from the menu.

2. Right-click the button and select the Button Properties option to bring up the Button Properties InfoBox. (Alternatively, you can choose Button, Edit Button from the menu.)

3. Select the tab of the property you want to edit (button title, text, and the rest).

4. Make the desired changes. As you make changes, they are reflected in the button on-screen. If you edit the button label, a green checkmark appears next to the Button Label field. Click the checkmark for the changes to the label to take effect.

5. Close the InfoBox.

Hiding Buttons and Hotspots

The Properties window has an additional choice that allows control over the display of a paragraph, including buttons, hotspots, sections, or attachments.

You might want to hide a paragraph due to either formatting or security concerns. For example, when a form is printed, buttons and other graphic objects might detract from its aesthetic appeal. Humans are visual creatures. The way a form looks often affects whether it even gets read! You might also want to hide sections with confidential or non-essential information. Refer to Chapter 14 and Chapter 15 for more ideas on using this option.

 Although hiding objects using Hide When formulas is often seen as a security feature, it is easily circumvented in various ways and should not be used to secure highly sensitive information. Consider using reader name fields or encryption, or both, if information absolutely must remain secure.

You can choose to hide a paragraph under conditions defined here. The options in the Button Properties InfoBox are relatively self-explanatory. You can hide a paragraph while the form is being read, printed, edited, or copied.

In the InfoBox, you'll notice the option Hide paragraph if formula is true. Below this is a formula window that allows you to enter an @Function formula. By clicking the Formula Window button at the bottom of the InfoBox, you can get a larger window to be displayed.

The Field and Functions button on the bottom allows selection of @Functions and field names. You might want to utilize this capability, for example, to hide the button or hotspot from certain users or groups. The following code snippet demonstrates a simple hide-when formula for hiding a button that sets the Status field to complete.

```
Status="Complete"
```

Testing Your Creations

In this chapter, we've learned that agents, buttons, and hotspots can automate Notes databases. What you might have realized by now is that, improperly programmed, they could potentially cause a good deal of grief as well!

Think about what would happen if you created an agent on a Sales Commission Reports database that erased documents—or worse, deleted the file. How many other files or records can you think of whose loss or erroneous alteration would cause disastrous results?

To save yourself and others a lot of grief, think about ways to test your agents, buttons, and hotspots before they're used on live data. Following are some ways to accomplish safe testing without pain.

Use Local Databases

When you're starting a new development project, consider using nonreplica copies or templates on a local workstation rather than a server. This tactic will limit your exposure if an error should occur. This is especially true with vital databases such as the server's Address Book.

Considering the functionality of LotusScript or the inexperience of a new developer, it's a good safeguard.

 T I P Unlike with the formula language code, with LotusScript code, documents are not automatically saved when modified. You must explicitly call the Save method to save your changes. Knowing this, when you get LotusScript code nearly complete, you can test it against real data without calling the Save method, thus ensuring that data is not changed until you are certain the agent works correctly.

Protect Server Data

If your agents are acting on mailed documents, the test database needs to be on a server. Any time you test on a server, take precautions to protect your investment. The first precaution should be to involve your Notes administrator. He or she can advise you on server resources, data availability, index issues, and the best time to conduct testing.

Using these steps on your workstation or server will protect your data:

- Perform a clean backup of the server before testing agents that will interact with the Public Address Book or other databases that are likely to be open when the server is running.

- Create a nonreplica copy of the database you're manipulating and rename it. Have the agent interact with the renamed database rather than the one containing your live data.

- If possible, choose an execution time that will affect the fewest users if the unthinkable happens.

 T I P You can turn off all scheduled mail- or change-activated agents within a database by following these steps:

1. Choose File, Database, Properties.
2. Select the Disable agents for this database option.

This might prove to be useful while you're troubleshooting problems with agents on workstations or servers.

Simulation—Test Option

Notes provides a feature that will let you simulate the execution of an agent. To simulate an agent, follow these steps:

1. Highlight the database to be tested.
2. Highlight the agent to be tested.
3. Choose Actions, Test.
4. Look at the Test Report, which shows the number of documents that would be processed and describes the actions that would be taken if the agent were actually run.
5. Fix any problems encountered in the agent's code and test again.
6. Repeat until everything checks out. Close and save the agent.

Testing Complex Agents

When testing complex agents or scripts, break them into component parts and execute the parts in the order in which they will execute when run as a single agent or action. You can use the simulated run option to test individual components. Check the test log to identify problems with each component. This action allows you to easily and quickly isolate the problems that occur.

T I P Remember, if you are writing LotusScript, the Debugger is a very valuable troubleshooting and debugging tool. To enable the Debugger, choose File, Tools, Debug LotusScript. You'll learn more about the Debugger in Chapter 17.

This chapter has shown you how to create your own agents, buttons, and hotspots. Automating databases with these techniques can either save users time or cripple their ability to perform their jobs. Making life easier is the whole idea of database automation! Keep it simple and protect your company's investment in its people and data. ●

Working with LotusScript

LotusScript Basics

In previous chapters, you learned how to use Lotus Notes @Functions and @Commands. In this chapter, you'll start learning about LotusScript, the cross-platform programming language used in Lotus products. This chapter investigates the syntax and structure of the LotusScript language from a practical point of view, looking at everything from comments to data types, functions, and error-handling. You can apply what you learn in this chapter to any product that uses LotusScript (virtually all the SmartSuite products). Chapter 18, "Writing Scripts with LotusScript," looks more specifically at the way LotusScript is used in Lotus Notes.

This chapter assumes that you are not new to programming and have some experience with event-driven scripting languages, such as Visual Basic, JavaScript, or REXX.

What Is LotusScript?

LotusScript is an event-driven, BASIC-compatible, embedded scripting language with object-oriented extensions. LotusScript first appeared in Lotus Improv, the innovative dynamic spreadsheet product released for Windows in 1992. Gradually, more Lotus products were shipped with LotusScript, including Lotus Forms, Lotus Notes ViP (which subsequently was sold to Revelation), Notes Pump, and the products in SmartSuite (WordPro, 1-2-3, Freelance, Approach, and Organizer). LotusScript Release 3 is available in Lotus Notes Release 4.x.

Event-Driven Programming

For those of you who have programmed in older languages and remember those days of punching in line after line of code, you are in for a treat! LotusScript uses an event-driven paradigm that causes code to run (or not run) in response to events that take place in the Notes/Domino environment. For example, opening a database, opening a view, opening a document, or clicking a button are all events that occur as users proceed through a database. You can write code that automates a process, prompts a user for input, checks for data entry errors, or prevents certain actions.

Although this might sound complicated, if you've programmed with the Notes Formula language, you're already familiar with this concept. When you create a button and code it with Notes formulas or LotusScript, for example, the code does not execute until the user clicks the button. Likewise, validation formulas in fields don't fire until certain events take place (in this case, saving or refreshing a document).

Every user-programmable object in Notes has events that are exposed so that you can write code that will be executed when that event takes place. For example, a button has, among other items, a Click event that executes the code it contains after the button is clicked.

N O T E   Not all objects can be scripted. You'll learn more about which objects can and can't be scripted in Chapter 19, "More LotusScript." ■

Every object that supports LotusScript has the following four events (most objects have many others as well):

- **Options:** Use the `Options` event to code special statements, such as `Option`, `Use`, `UseLSX`, and `Const`. (You'll learn more about each of these statements later in this chapter and in Chapter 18, "Writing Scripts with LotusScript.")

- **Declarations:** The `Declarations` area allows you to write non-executable statements that apply to all events in the object. You can declare global variables that can be used throughout the other events and subroutines in your script, for example.

- **Initialize:** `Initialize` is always the first event to fire and can be used to write executable code that prepares objects and variables for other events; or, it can contain the entire script.

- **Terminate:** The `Terminate` event is often used as a clean-up area. `Terminate` is always the last event to execute and is useful for closing files and explicitly releasing variables.

Although the Notes event hierarchy won't be covered here (it will be discussed in detail in Chapters 18 and 19), it's very important for you to begin to understand this concept early so you'll know where (and why) to put your code. For the examples in this chapter, the executable code will be written in the `Initialize` event or the `Click` event of a button.

Part

III

Ch

17

Adding Comments to Your Code

The first and most important set of statements to learn in any new programming language is the one that lets you put comments (non-executable code that allows you to make notes in your code) into your scripts. You'll surely agree to the importance of these statements if you have ever had to modify someone else's uncommented code (or even the code that you wrote three months ago and never quite got around to commenting!).

In LotusScript, a comment line begins with the apostrophe character. In fact, anything after an apostrophe is considered a comment, so you can easily add comments to the ends of lines. You can also use %REM and %END REM to comment blocks of code, as in the following example:

```
' A single line comment . . .
'  . . . and another
%REM
The first line in a multi-line comment
.
.
The last line in a multi-line comment
%END REM
```

N O T E Be kind to maintenance programmers (and yourself) by commenting your code as you go. This avoids the chore of adding comments to code after it has been written.

TIP If you can get a block of code to save, you can use the `%REM %END REM` construct to "rem out" the entire block so that you can save your script and debug it later.

Understanding LotusScript Variables

In LotusScript, as with all programming languages, variables are used to store and manipulate data. Although you may use variables in the same way in other programming languages, you should be aware of a few things when naming variables in LotusScript:

- The first character must be a letter.
- The other characters must be letters, numbers, underscore characters, or type declaration characters (more on this in a moment).
- Variable names can contain a maximum of 40 characters.
- Variable names are not case-sensitive. For example, COUNT and count are the same variable name.

In fact, these rules apply to all names within LotusScript, such as the names for the following:

- Constants
- Types
- Classes
- Procedures such as functions, subroutines, and properties.

Understanding LotusScript Constants

In the most basic terms, a *constant* is nothing more than a value that won't change during the course of a script's execution. Notes provides you with the capability to create user-defined constants by using the Const statement. Notes also provides a bevy of built-in constants to make your programming life easier. Table 17.1 lists the built-in constants.

Table 17.1 LotusScript Built-In Constants

Constant	Description
FALSE	The Boolean value False. Represented by 0.
TRUE	The Boolean value True. Represented by –1.
NULL	For variables of type Variant, NULL indicates that the variable does not have a value.
NOTHING	For variables that can refer to objects, NOTHING indicates that the variable does not currently refer to an object.
PI	The ratio of the circumference of a circle to its diameter.

N O T E If you are familiar with Notes Formula programming, you know that Boolean True is represented by 1 in the Formula language. But in LotusScript, True is represented by -1. This distinction can be very frustrating until you get it burned into your brain.

Additional programming constants are defined in special files you can include in your scripts. The files are known as *Include files* and have a file extension of .LSS that indicates a LotusScript Source file. Use the %INCLUDE directive in the Declarations section of a script to include an .LSS file. For example, you might want to use the following:

```
%INCLUDE "LSCONST.LSS"
```

These constants make your scripts more readable. You can use MB_OK and MB_OKCANCEL, for example, with the LotusScript MsgBox function to represent the values 0 and 1, respectively.

 TIP In a standard Notes installation, all the .LSS files are stored in the Notes program directory. A good way to learn more about these files and the constants they define is to view them using a text editor, such as Notepad or WordPad.

You can define your own constants by using the Const statement. This is a useful way of making your code more readable. To define constants to represent product sizes, for example, you could use the following code fragment:

```
Const SIZE_SMALL  = 1
Const SIZE_MEDIUM = 2
Const SIZE_LARGE  = 3
```

As a general convention, constants are always given names in uppercase. Table 17.2 lists the Include files.

Table 17.2 LotusScript Include Files

Filename	Description
lsconst.lss	General LotusScript constants
lserr.lss	General LotusScript error constants
lsxbeerr.lss	Error constants for the Notes back-end classes
lsxuierr.lss	Error constants for the Notes front-end classes

Understanding Data Types

All variables in a LotusScript program have a data type associated with them. The type essentially defines two things:

■ How much memory LotusScript should reserve for the data to be stored by the variable

■ The types of statements in which you can use the variable

After you declare a variable of type Integer, for example, LotusScript reserves two bytes of memory for the value to be stored by the variable and checks that the variable is used only in statements applicable to integer values. A variable of type Double reserves 8 bytes for a floating-point value.

Table 17.3 lists the data types that LotusScript supports.

Table 17.3   LotusScript Data Types

Data Type	Bytes Stored	Range	Suffix
Integer	1	-32,768 to 32,767	%
Long	4	-2,147,483,648 to 2,147,483,647	&
Single	4	-3.402823E+38 to 3.402823E+38	!
Double	8	-1.7976931348623158E+308 to 1.7976931348623158E+308	#
Currency	8	-922,337,203,685,477.5808 to 922,337,203,685,477.5807	@
String	2 per character		$
Variant	16	None	

Declaring LotusScript Variables

Strictly speaking, you don't have to explicitly declare variables in LotusScript, because the first time you use a new variable, LotusScript automatically (implicitly) declares it for you. If you don't declare a variable or don't include a type-declaration character, LotusScript automatically assigns it a type of Variant, which consumes the most memory.

TIP   Always use the LotusScript Option Declare statement in the general declarations section of your code. This statement forces you to explicitly declare all the variables you use. You will save a lot of debugging time and effort by using Option Declare. If you don't use this statement, you could waste time tracking down an error, only to find that you have misspelled a variable name, which LotusScript then treats as a new variable.

You declare LotusScript variables by using the Dim statement. For example, the following code fragment declares three variables—iCount as an integer, strName as a string, and curPrice as a currency value:

```
Dim iCount As Integer
Dim strName As String
Dim curPrice As Currency
```

You can add any of the prefixes shown in Table 17.4 to a variable declaration to declare a variable of the corresponding type. For example, the following lines of code declare a `Single` and a `Double` value:

```
Dim sRatio!
Dim dLimit#
```

N O T E Using suffixes for your variables makes it much easier to debug your program, because you can tell at a glance exactly what type of value can or should be stored in a particular variable. Additionally, in a very large program, you can save a lot of keystrokes by using suffixes instead of keying in the full type name for each declaration.

If you don't explicitly give a variable a type, LotusScript treats it as a variant. The following two lines of code both declare variables of type `Variant`:

```
Dim varFontType As Variant
```

```
Dim varFontName
```

 T I P It is good programming practice to always declare variable types, even when optional. This method removes any doubt about the type you intend to use, makes your program easier to maintain, and consumes less memory.

Notice the prefixes used as part of the variable names. Although they are not strictly necessary, it's a good idea to prefix your variable names so that you can work out their types from the names. This practice helps you check that you're working with the correct type of variable in an expression. Just by looking at the variable names in your code, for example, you should be able to see whether you are using values of different types in the same statement.

People use many different naming conventions. I tend to use the prefixes shown in Table 17.4.

Table 17.4 Suggested Prefixes for Variable Names

Data Type	Prefix	Example
Integer	i	iDocsDeleted
Long	l	lFileLength
Single	s	sWeightCoefficient
Double	d	dAcceleration
Currency	c	cSalaryIncrease
String	t	tDocTitle
Variant	v	varName

You can easily extend this naming convention to include additional types and procedure names. If I use an integer as a Boolean value, for example, I prefix its name with f (for flag). Or, if a function returns an integer, I prefix its name with i. This can be useful, because it clearly shows what type of value the function returns.

Converting Data Types

In many cases, when you assign data of one type to a variable of a different type, LotusScript converts the data for you. In general, LotusScript converts data of different types using the following sequence:

- Integer
- Long
- Single
- Double
- Currency

LotusScript has a range of functions that lets you convert between variables of different types. The functions are listed in Table 17.5 and allow you to do the following:

- Convert data from one type to another
- Convert a number to a string
- Convert a string to a number
- Convert a string or a number to a date
- Check the data type of a variable

Table 17.5 LotusScript Data-Conversion Functions

Statement or Function	Description
Bin$	Converts the supplied number to a string representing its binary value.
CCur	Converts the supplied value to Currency data type.
CDat	Converts the supplied value to Variant of type Date.
CDbl	Converts the supplied value to Double data type.
CInt	Converts the supplied value to Integer data type.
CLng	Converts the supplied value to Long data type.
CSng	Converts the supplied value to Single data type.

Statement or Function	Description
CStr	Converts the supplied value to its string representation.
DataType	Returns an integer representing the data type of the supplied value.
Hex$	Converts the supplied number to a string representing its hexadecimal value.
Oct$	Converts the supplied number to a string representing its octal value.
Str$	Converts the supplied number to a string.
TypeName	Returns a string representing the data type of the supplied value.
Val	Converts the supplied string to a number of type `Double`.

Converting Data from One Type to Another

Use CCur, CDat, CDbl, CInt, CLng, CSng, and CStr to convert data from one type to another. You typically do type conversions to make sure that the result of a calculation is a certain type. The following code fragment, for example, shows how to make sure that the price calculation is returned as a Currency value:

```
Dim iQuantity As Integer
Dim curPrice As Currency
Dim curTotal As Currency

curTotal = CCur(iQuantity * curPrice)
```

Converting a Number to a String

At times, you'll need to convert a number to its string representation. LotusScript has a number of functions that let you do this. Str$ converts the numeric value you supply to its string representation, prefixing the resulting string with a space if the number is positive. For example, the following code prints 143:

```
Print Str$(143)
```

> **NOTE** When you use LotusScript inside Notes, the Print statement will direct its output to the status bar if the script is running on a Notes client or to the Notes Log if the agent is running on a server.

If you don't want the leading space, use CStr instead. Bin$ takes the number you supply and converts it to a string containing its binary representation. For example, the following code prints 101:

```
Print Bin$(5)
```

Similarly, Hex$ and Oct$ convert numbers to their hexadecimal and octal representations.

Converting a String into a Number

Use the Val function to convert a string to a number. You supply Val with a string, and if the string can be converted to a number, Val returns a Double value containing the numeric representation of the string. If a string value cannot be converted to a number (if, for example, you pass Val "xyz"), a 0 will be returned.

Checking the Data Type of a Variable

If you need to check the data type of a variable or an expression, you can use the DataType or TypeName function. DataType returns an integer representing the data type of the variable or expression being checked. LSCONST.LSS contains a set of predeclared constants you can use to interpret the value returned by DataType. TypeName is similar to DataType, except that instead of returning an integer, it returns a string describing the data type. For example, the following code prints STRING:

```
Dim strName As String
Print TypeName(strName)
```

Understanding LotusScript Data Structures

LotusScript supports the common programming data structures of arrays, lists, and user-defined types. It also supports object-oriented constructs; for example, you can create your own classes, methods, and properties. You can also use LotusScript to work with OLE and ActiveX objects. Let's start simple and look at arrays first.

Working with Arrays

Arrays are common to almost every programming language and can be very useful. In the most basic terms, you can think of an array as a kind of *virtual table* (it's *virtual* in the sense that it exists only in RAM). Like a table or spreadsheet, a virtual table has rows and columns that can be used to store data. The intersection of a row and column (a *cell* in a spreadsheet or a *field* in a table) is called an *element*. An array's dimensions tell you how many columns it has. A one-dimensional array has only one column, whereas a three-dimensional array has three columns.

In LotusScript, you can declare two types of arrays: static and dynamic. A *static* array is an array of fixed size and contains a fixed number of elements. You can't add or delete elements. A *dynamic* array can be resized at any time; you make it larger or smaller by adding or removing elements. Table 17.6 shows the LotusScript functions you can use to work with arrays.

Table 17.6   LotusScript Array-Handling Functions

Statement or Function	Description
Dim	Declares a static array and initializes its elements.
Erase	Reinitializes each array element (for fixed arrays). Removes all elements from the array (for dynamic arrays).
IsArray	Returns True (given a variable name or expression) if the supplied expression is an array.
LBound	Returns the lower bound of the dimension of the array (given an array name and an optional dimension of the array).
Preserve	Allows you to resize a dynamic array while maintaining its current values.
ReDim	Declares a dynamic array and allocates storage for its elements or changes the size of an existing dynamic array.
UBound	Returns the upper bound of the dimension of the array (given an array name and an optional dimension of the array).

Part

III

Ch

17

You declare a static array by using the Dim statement. You specify the following:

- The number of dimensions for the array
- The subscript bounds for each dimension
- The type of data to be stored

Dim allocates storage for the array and initializes each element of the array to a default value. Unless you specify otherwise, the first element of an array has an index of 0. If necessary, you can change this default to 1 by using the Option Base 1 statement. The following declarations specify static arrays:

```
Dim strPrinterNames(9) As String        'Declares a one dimensional string
array with 10 elements, bounds are 0 to 9
Dim strQueueNames(19) As String * 32     'Declares a one dimensional string
array with 32 characters allotted to 20 elements, bounds are 0 to 19
Dim iRoutingMatrix(9, 9) As Integer      'Declare a nine dimensional integer
array of 100 elements
Dim iPrintJobIDs(1 To 50) As Integer     'Declares a one dimensional string
array of 50 elements, bounds are 1 to 50
```

You can also use Dim to declare dynamic arrays. When you declare a dynamic array using Dim, however, you specify only the type. You don't specify the number of elements in the array, and no storage is allocated for the array. Before you can use a dynamic array, you have to use the ReDim statement to allocate some storage for its elements. For example, the following code shows how to declare a dynamic array and then allocate some storage for it:

```
Dim iDatabases As Integer                'Declare the number of elements to use
Dim strDatabaseNames() As String         ' Declare a dynamic array
```

```
iDatabases = 25                     ' Initialize the number of elements
ReDim strDatabaseNames(iDatabases)  ' Allocate storage for this 25 integer
element in this one dimensional array
```

You can also declare and initialize an array using ReDim. To declare an array containing six elements of type Integer and initialize each element to 0, for example, use the following:

```
Option Base 1                       ' Specify that the first element of any array
has an index of 1
ReDim varWidgets(6) As Integer      ' Declare a dynamic one dimensional integer
array with 6 elements
```

You can use ReDim to change the size of a dynamic array with the option of preserving the existing contents of the array or reinitializing all elements. Suppose that you have a dynamic array, iCustomerIDs, containing 50 elements. You need to increase its size to 100 elements while preserving its current contents. You can use the following code:

```
ReDim Preserve iCustomerIDs(99)
```

If you need to find the size of a dynamic array at runtime, you can use the LBound and UBound functions. You supply these functions with the name of an array, and (optionally) with the dimension for which you are seeking the bounds. LBound returns the lower bound of the specified array dimension, and UBound returns the upper bound. After resizing the iCustomerIDs array, for example, LBound(iCustomerIDs) is 0 and UBound(iCustomerIDs) is 99.

You can use the Erase statement to delete all the elements in a dynamic array and free up the storage the array uses. With a static array, you can use Erase to reinitialize each element.

You can assign an entire array to a variable of type Variant. Consequently, you might need to check whether a variable contains an array by using the IsArray function. If the variable or expression you supply to IsArray is an array, the function returns True, as shown in this example:

```
Dim varIcons As Variant
Dim lIconIDs(255) As Long
Print IsArray(varIcons)       'False
varIcons = lIconIDs
Print IsArray(varIcons)       'True
```

Accessing the Contents of an Array   To access the contents of a specific element, you simply refer to its subscript—also known as the *index*. The following example shows how to get the contents of the twenty-fourth element of the array:

```
Dim sOverDue(25) as Single
Dim sOverDueValue as Single
SOverDueValue =SOverDue(24)
```

Array Processing with Loops   Most array processing is done using loops to navigate through the elements in an array and conditional tests to determine whether an element contains the value you are seeking. The following code snippet demonstrates a simple For/Next loop that allows the user to enter an employee's name (courtesy of the Inputbox$ function) to find in a one-dimensional dynamic array of employee names:

```
Dim tEmpNames(250) As String
'Load array via some code
```

```
Dim tTestName$
tTestName$=InputBox$("Enter an employee's name", "Find Employee","")
For I%=0 to Ubound(tEmpNames)
If tEmpNames(I%) = tTestName$ Then
Print tEmpNames(I%)
Exit For
End If
Next
```

Let's examine this example. The first line declares a string array to store the employee names. The second line is a REM statement, and the third line declares a string variable to store the name entered by the user. The next line uses Inputbox$ to pop up a dialog box with a text field that allows the user to enter a value that will be returned by the function—in this case, to the tTestName$ variable. The third line initializes a For/Next loop that will loop a discrete number of times; in this case, it uses the Ubound function to determine the number of times the loop is needed.

The fourth line uses an If statement to test the value the user entered against the current array element. If the value matches, the Print statement is used to print the current element to the status bar and the loop terminates, compliments of the Exit For statement. If a match is not found, the loop continues until all the elements in the array have been tested and the loop terminates normally.

Working with Lists

A list is similar to an array because it contains a set of elements. It differs from an array in the way you identify and work with its elements. With arrays, you identify the element you are working with by using an index. With lists, you identify elements by using a list tag. A *list tag* is simply a string used to uniquely identify a particular element in the list. Table 17.7 describes the LotusScript functions used with lists.

Table 17.7   LotusScript List-Handling Functions

Statement or Function	Description
Dim	Declares a list.
Erase	Removes all elements from a list (for lists). Or, removes the element from a list (for list elements).
ForAll	Loops through the elements of a list.
IsElement	Returns True if the string is a list tag for any element in the list (given the name of a list and a string).
IsList	Returns True if the supplied expression is a list (given a variable name or expression).
ListTag	Returns the name of the element in the list that is being processed. Can be used only inside a ForAll block.

You use `Dim` to declare an empty list, as in the following example:

```
Dim curAmountOutstanding List As Currency
```

When you declare a list, it has no elements and no storage is allocated for it. You add elements to the list by assigning new list tags. You can create two new elements in the list, for example, with list tags ABC and XYZ by using this code:

```
curAmountOutstanding("ABC") = 12.99
curAmountOutstanding("XYZ") = 52.00
```

You use the tag to refer to a list element in much the same way you use an index to refer to an array element. To add the two list elements you just created, for example, use the following:

```
Dim curTotal As Currency
curTotal = curAmountOutstanding("ABC") + curAmountOutstanding("XYZ")
```

Use `Erase` to delete specific elements from the list or to delete all elements. For example,

```
Erase curAmountOutstanding("ABC")
```

removes the ABC element from the list, whereas

```
Erase curAmountOutstanding
```

erases all elements from the list.

If you need to check whether you have already added an element to a list, you can use the `IsElement` function. You supply the list tag for the element you are looking for, and the function returns `True` if the tag belongs to an element in the list. Continuing this example, the following code returns `True`:

```
IsElement(curAmountOutstanding("XYZ"))
```

In a similar way, you can use `IsList` to check whether a variable is a list. For example, the following returns `True`:

```
IsList(curAmountOutstanding)
```

To process elements in an array, you typically use a loop to step through each index in the array. When using lists, the only way to identify an element is by its list tag. So how do you loop through all elements in a list? The answer is to use a `ForAll` loop with the `ListTag` function. For example, the following code prints all the elements in your example list:

```
ForAll varElement In curAmountOutstanding
    Print ListTag(varElement); " owes ";  varElement
End ForAll
```

You should note a few points when using `ForAll`. In the example, the variable `varElement` is known as a *reference variable*. A reference variable is a special kind of variable used by LotusScript when processing `ForAll` loops. In the body of the loop, each element in the list is assigned to the reference variable. You never have to declare a reference variable; LotusScript takes care of that for you and declares all reference variables to be of type `Variant`. In fact, if you do declare a reference variable, you'll get an error when you try to compile your script.

Inside a ForAll loop, you can use the ListTag function to find the list tag that corresponds to the current element. ListTag works only inside a ForAll loop.

> **CAUTION**
>
> LotusScript supports only arrays and lists of up to 64K. Be aware of this limitation when allocating large arrays and lists.

User-Defined Types

You can define your own data types in LotusScript by using the Type statement. You give your new type a name and then define one or more member variables for the type.

> **N O T E** The term *member variable* is used to refer to any variable included in a user-defined type. ▪

To declare a new type with four member variables suitable for holding a customer ID, first and last name, and current balance, you could use the following type declaration:

```
Type Customer
    lCustID As Long
    tCustFirstName As String
    tCustLastname As String
    cBalance As Currency
End Type
```

You can then use Dim to declare new variables of this type:

```
Dim custNew As Customer
Dim custMailingList As List Customer
Dim custMostFrequentBuyers(99) As Customer
```

You refer to member variables by using *dot notation* (you'll get very familiar with this concept as you learn more about LotusScript), which has the form *VarName* .*MemberName*, where *VarName* is the name of the variable of the user-defined type and *MemberName* is the name of the member variable. To set the values of a variable of type Customer, you would do the following:

```
custNew.lCustID = 14829
custNew.tCustFirstName = "Jon"
custNew.tCustLastname = "Jennings"
custNew.cBalance = 100.00
```

Working with User-Defined Classes and Objects

You can define your own classes and objects within LotusScript. The Class statement is similar to the Type statement, except that in addition to defining member variables (*properties*, in object-oriented lingo), you can also define member procedures (*methods*, in object-oriented lingo). You can define two special procedures within a class: New and Delete. You define New to initialize the member variables for an object of the class. You define Delete if you need to do any special processing when an object of the class is deleted. The following example shows a simple class with four member variables and four member procedures:

```
Class custObject

' Declare member variable
lCustID As Long
tCustFirstName As String
tCustLastname As String
cBalance As Currency

' Define constructor
Sub New(lID As Long, tFirstName As String, tLastname As String,
cBal As Currency)
lCustID = lID
tCustFirstName = tFirstName
tCustLastname = tLastname
cBalance = cBal
End Sub

' Define destructor
Sub Delete
Print "Customer ";tCustFirstName;" ";tCustLastname; " deleted."
End Sub

Sub SetBalance(cBal As Currency)
cBalance = cBal
End Sub

Function cQueryBalance As Currency
cQueryBalance = cBalance
End Function

End Class
```

As with other variables, you use `Dim` to declare object variables. When you use `Dim` with a class name, you are actually declaring a reference to an object. You then use `New` to create a new object and `Set` to assign the object to the reference variable:

```
Dim custNew As custObject
Set custNew = New custObject(15565, "Sean", "Gaiser", 100.00)
```

By default, the member variables you declare are private to the class, whereas the member functions are public. That is, you cannot refer directly to member variables using dot notation, but you can use dot notation to refer to member functions. For example, to update a balance, you use

```
custNew.SetBalance(50.00)
```

instead of

```
custNew.curBalance = 50.00
```

which would give you an error, because `curBalance` is private to the class. Similarly, to query a balance, you would use

```
cCurrentBalance = custNew.curQueryBalance
```

instead of

```
cCurrentBalance = custNew.cBalance
```

The With statement gives you a shorthand way of accessing public procedures and member variables within an object. You use With to point to a particular object, and then you use dot notation to refer to the object. The following example shows how to use With to set and query a customer balance:

```
With custNew
Call .SetBalance(50.00)
cCurrentBalance = .cQueryBalance
End With
```

When you are finished with an object, you can delete it by using the Delete statement:

```
Delete custNew
```

If you have defined a Delete subroutine within your class, it is executed before the object is deleted. When you delete the customer object in your example, the Delete subroutine prints Customer Sean Gaiser deleted. Table 17.8 lists the statements and functions related to working with classes and objects.

Table 17.8   LotusScript User-Defined Object-Handling Functions

Statement or Function	Description
Class	Declares a user-defined object class.
Delete	Executes the Delete subroutine for a user-defined object.
IsObject	Returns True if the supplied expression is an object.
New	Creates a new user-defined object.
Set	Associates an object with a variable.
With	Accesses public procedures and variables within an object using a dot notation.

OLE and ActiveX Objects

You can access the classes, methods, and properties of OLE and ActiveX objects by using LotusScript and Notes. This means that you can use Notes to transfer data to applications such as Microsoft Excel and Lotus WordPro and then work with the data using the object classes within the application. You can also program ActiveX objects, such as Lotus Components, directly from LotusScript. Table 17.9 describes the LotusScript functions that deal with working with objects.

Table 17.9 LotusScript OLE and ActiveX Object-Handling Functions

Statement or Function	Description
CreateObject	Creates an OLE object given an OLE object class.
GetObject	Opens the OLE object contained in a file (given a path to a file and the name of an OLE class).
IsObject	Returns True if the supplied expression is an object.
Set	Associates an object with a variable.

You can create a new OLE or ActiveX object by using the CreateObject function. You supply the name of the class of object you want to create, and LotusScript creates the object. If necessary, LotusScript will start the application required to create the object. The following example shows how to create a new WordPro document from a SmartMaster and save it:

```
Dim objDoc As Variant
Set objDoc = CreateObject("WordPro.Application")
objDoc.NewDocument "", "", "C:\DOCS\EBS.MWP", "", "", ""
 ' Update the document here . . .
objDoc.SaveAs "C:\DOCS\REPORT.LWP", "", "", False, True, False
Call objDoc.Close(False)
```

To open an existing object, use GetObject. You supply the path to the file containing the object and, optionally, the name of the class. LotusScript finds and opens the object. The following example shows how to open a Word object—in this case, the file C:MYDOCUMENTS\RESUME.doc:

```
Dim objDoc As Variant
 ' Open a WordPro Document
Set objDoc = GetObject("C:\MYDOCUMENTS\RESUME.DOC")
```

Understanding LotusScript Operators

In LotusScript, operators are used to perform the following types of functions:

- Mathematical
- Logical
- Comparison
- String concatenation

Table 17.10 lists the mathematical operators.

Table 17.10   LotusScript Arithmetic Operators

Operator	Description	Example	Result
–	Negates a number	-34	-34
–	Subtracts two numbers	7-5	2
+	Adds two numbers	5+9	14
*	Multiplies two numbers	7*6	42
/	Divides two numbers	16 / 5	3.2
\	Performs integer division on two numbers	16 \ 5	3
Mod	Performs modulo division on two numbers	16 Mod 5	1
^	Raises a number to a power	5 ^ 2	25

Table 17.11 shows the LotusScript comparison operators.

Table 17.11   LotusScript Comparison Operators

Operator	Description	Example	Result
=	Returns True if two values are equal	5 = 6	False
<> ><	Returns True if two values are not equal	5 <> 6	True
<	Returns True if one value is less than another	7 < 9	True
>	Returns True if one value is greater than another	7 > 9	False
>= =>	Returns True if one value is greater than or equal to another	8 >= 8	True
<= =<	Returns True if one value is less than or equal to another	8 <= 8	True
Is	Returns True if two object references refer to the same object	objA Is objB	True if objA and objB refer to the same object

Table 17.12 shows the logical operators you can use in LotusScript.

Table 17.12   LotusScript Logical Operators

Operator	Description	Example	Result
Not	Logical negation	Not B	True if B is False; False if B is True
And	Logical And	A And B	True if both A and B are True; False otherwise
Or	Logical Or	A Or B	True if A or B is True; False otherwise
Xor	Exclusive Or	A Xor B	True if A or B is True, but not both; False if A and B are both False or both True
Eqv	Logical equivalence	A Eqv B	True if A and B are both False or both True; False if either A or B (but not both) is True
Imp	Logical implication	A Imp B	True if A is False or both A and B are True; False if A is True and B is False

Table 17.13 shows the available string operators.

Table 17.13   LotusScript String Operators

Operator	Description	Example	Result
&	Concatenates two strings	"AB" & "CD"	"ABCD"
+	Concatenates two strings	"AB" + "CD"	"ABCD"
Like	Returns True if a string matches a supplied pattern	"ABC" Like "A*"	True

N O T E   Although + and & both concatenate string values, & is the preferred operator to help avoid confusion, because + is an overloaded operator that also can be used to add numeric values. ■

Using Functions and Subroutines

In LotusScript, you can define functions and subroutines (subs) that you can call from within a script to perform specific functions. You could define a function to convert a date with a two-digit year into a date with a four-digit year, for example, and keep your boss happy well into the next century! The main difference between a function and a sub is that a *function* returns a value and a *sub* does not.

Declaring Functions and Subs

You declare a function by using the `Function` keyword:

```
Function fIsWeekend(iDay As Integer) As Integer
```

You give it a name and then define the list of arguments you are going to pass to it; finally, you define the type of value it is going to return. To set the return value, assign a value to the function name, as shown in the following example:

```
Function fIsWeekend(varDate As Variant) As Integer
If Weekday(varDate) = 1 Or Weekday(varDate) = 7 Then
    fIsWeekend = True
Else
    fIsWeekend = False
End If
End Function
```

Part
III

Ch
17

You define subs in much the same way by using the `Sub` keyword. The only thing to remember is that you can't return a value from a sub, so you don't have to declare a return type. A typical sub declaration follows:

```
Sub GoToBeach(tResort As String, iMilesToResort As Integer)
```

To create a new sub, open any event that can be coded with LotusScript and begin typing in the new sub header. After you press Enter upon completion of the header, a new sub will be added (as will an `End Sub` statement), and you'll be ready to code your sub. Functions work exactly the same way.

Calling Functions and Subs

To access the code you have written in a sub or function, you must *call* it. After a sub or function is called, program execution is transferred to the called routine. When the routine finishes, control is transferred back to the calling program, and execution continues at that point. To call a function, you simply assign it to a variable, as in this example:

```
Dim fGoToWork As Integer
Dim varToday As Variant
 ' Use the built in function Today to get today's date
varToday = Today
 ' Use the fIsWeekend function
fGoToWork = fIsWeekend(varToday)
```

To call a sub, you can use any of the following methods:

```
Call SubName(Arg1, Arg2 ...)
```

or

```
Call SubName arg1, arg2
```

or

```
SubName(Arg1, Arg2 ...)
```

The following example uses one of these methods:

```
If fIsWeekend(varToday) Then
    Call GoToBeach("Maui", 4000)
End If
```

When you pass values to subs and functions, you need to be aware of two ways LotusScript can pass arguments:

- By reference: LotusScript passes a reference to the argument. The function works with the argument. Any changes the function makes to the argument are reflected in the original.

- By value: LotusScript passes a copy of the argument to the function. The function works with the copy. Any changes to the copy do not affect the original.

Some arguments—such as arrays, lists, and objects—are always passed by reference. With other arguments, you have a choice. If you always want an argument to be passed by value, use the ByVal keyword when you declare that argument in the function or sub declaration. In the following example, the second argument is always passed by value:

```
Sub DeleteDocument(iDocNumber As Integer, ByVal tDocTitle As String)
```

 TIP Technically, functions return one value through their name, and subs return no value. However, by passing values by reference (the default), you can change the values of a parameter inside the function/sub, and it will be reflected in the calling program.

Understanding Flow Control: Sequential Processing, Selection, and Iteration

Like most programming languages, LotusScript provides three basic ways to control the flow of execution in a script: *sequential processing*, *selection* (branching), and *iteration* (looping).

By default, all code for a given event will execute in sequence until it hits the last line. However, you can alter the serial flow of a script by using looping and branching. Loops allow you to repeatedly execute a set of statements based on certain conditions being met. Branches can conditionally execute different parts of a script, based on the results of comparisons or the value of variables. Let's look at loops first.

For...Next Loops

You use the For...Next loop to execute a set of statements a specified number of times. You specify the following:

- A control variable for the loop.
- A start value for the variable.
- An end value for the variable.
- (optional) A step value to add to the control variable after each execution of the loop. If you don't specify a value, the default is 1.

The first time the loop is executed, the control variable has the start value. After each execution of the loop, the control variable is incremented by the step value. If you use a positive step value, the loop finishes when the control variable is greater than or equal to the end value. You can use a negative step to make the loop operate in reverse or step backward. This also dictates that you make the start value greater than the end value for the control variable. The following example shows a typical For...Next loop:

```
Dim iCount As Integer
For iCount% = 1 To 10 Step 2
' Do something . . .
Next
```

In this example, the loop is executed five times, with iCount% having the values 1, 3, 5, 7, and 9.

ForAll Loops

You already had a sneak preview of the ForAll loop when you looked at using lists in LotusScript. However, you aren't restricted to using ForAll loops with lists. You can also use them with arrays and object collections. You can use a ForAll loop, for example, to loop through all elements in an array named tCompanies:

```
ForAll vElem In tCompanies
                ' Do something here
End Forall
```

Do...While Loops

Do...While loops repeatedly execute a block of statements while a specified condition is True. This type of loop is very handy when you need to process a nondiscrete number of items. Before the loop is executed, the condition you specify is tested; if it evaluates to True, the block of statements within the loop is executed. If the condition evaluates to False, the loop is not executed and control passes to the next statement after the loop. The following loop, for example, executes three times and prints 17, 18, and 19:

```
Dim iCount As Integer
Dim iMax As Integer
iMax% = 20
iCount% = 17
Do While iCount% < iMax%
    Print iCount%
    iCount% = iCount% + 1
Loop
```

An alternative form of the Do...While loop tests the condition after the loop is executed, as shown here:

```
Dim iCount As Integer
Dim iMax As Integer
iMax% = 20
iCount% = 17
Do
    Print iCount%
    iCount% = iCount% + 1
Loop While iCount% < iMax%
```

The main difference between the two loops is that you can guarantee that the second loop is always executed at least once.

Do...Until Loops

A closely related type of loop is the Do...Until loop. With this kind of loop, the set of statements in the loop is executed until the loop condition evaluates to True. For example, if you change the first of the Do...While loops to a Do...Until loop, the statements inside this loop are never executed, because the condition iCount% < iMax% is True before the loop is entered. Consider this example:

```
Dim iCount As Integer
Dim iMax As Integer
iMax% = 20
iCount% = 17
Do Until iCount% < iMax%
    Print iCount%
    iCount% = iCount% + 1
Loop
```

The Do...Until loop also has an alternative form that checks the condition at the end of the loop:

```
Dim iCount As Integer
Dim iMax As Integer
iMax% = 20
iCount% = 17
Do
    Print iCount%
    iCount% = iCount% + 1
Loop Until iCount% < iMax%
```

This loop is executed only once and prints 17.

If...Then...Else Branches

You can use If...Then...Else statements to select which statements are executed based on a condition you specify. If the condition is True, one set of statements is executed; if the condition is False, a different set is executed, as demonstrated by this example:

```
If iCount% > iMax% Then
    Print "Too many items!"
```

```
Else
    Print "Processing "; iCount%; " item(s) . . ."
End If
```

You can omit the `Else` part of the statement if you only want to execute a set of statements when a condition is `True`, as shown in this example:

```
If iDaysOverdue% > 14 Then
    Print "Time to send a nastygram!"
End If
```

You can use the `ElseIf` statement with `If` to test multiple conditions, as shown in this example:

```
If iDaysOverdue% <= 7 Then
    Print "Time to send a reminder note!"
ElseIF iDaysOverDue% <=14 Then
    Print "Time to send a nastygram!"
ElseIF iDaysOverDue%<=21 Then
    Print "Time to put a lien on their property"
Else
    Print "Time to send Vito to break some kneecaps!"
End If
```

Select...Case Branches

Using the `Select...Case` statement is similar to using the `ElseIf` statement with `If`. It lets you select a block of statements to execute based on the value of an expression. The primary difference between `Select Case` and `If/ElseIf` is that `Select Case` is faster and easier to code (and requires less typing!), because after a `True` condition is found, execution continues at the next line of code after the `End Select` statement. Consider this example:

```
Select Case iBoxesOrdered%
    Case Is <= 0
        Call ProcessInvalidOrder(iBoxesOrdered%)
    Case 1
        Call ProcessSmallOrder(iBoxesOrdered%)
    Case 2 To 15
        Call ProcessMediumOrder(iBoxesOrdered%)
    Case 16 To 31
        Call ProcessLargeOrder(iBoxesOrdered%)
    Case Else
        Call ProcessHugeOrder(iBoxesOrdered%)
End Select
```

GoSub and On...GoSub

Within a sub or function, you can use `GoSub` and `On...GoSub` to branch to a specific label within the procedure. A *label* is simply a way of identifying a place in your code. The code at the label can execute a `Return` statement to branch back to the statement following the `GoSub`. The following code, for example, branches to the label `lblLogError` if the order quantity is negative:

```
Sub ProcessInvalidOrder(iOrderQuantity As Integer)
If iOrderQuantity% < 0 Then
    GoSub lblLogError
End If
```

```
Exit Sub

lblLogError:
Call LogError
Return
End Sub
```

You can use `On...GoSub` to branch to one of a number of labels based on a supplied value—for example, when the following statement is executed:

```
On iErrorNumber% GoSub lblA, lblB, lblC
```

If `iErrorNumber%` is 1, the program branches to `lblA`; if `iErrorNumber%` is 2, the program branches to `lblB`; and if `iErrorNumber%` is 3, the program branches to `lblC`. If `iErrorNumber%` is 0 or greater than 3, the `On...GoSub` statement is ignored.

GoTo and On...GoTo

`GoTo` and `On...GoTo` are similar to `GoSub` and `On...GoSub`, because they let you branch to specific labels. However, `GoTo` statements are one-way branches. You cannot use a `Return` statement to return control back to the statement after the `GoTo`.

> **N O T E** It's generally frowned upon and considered bad form to use `GoTo`, because it leads to fairly unstructured code that can be very difficult to follow and debug. The only exception is in error-trapping routines, because using `On Error Goto` is the only way to programmatically handle runtime errors. Error checking is handled later in this chapter in the "Handling Errors at Runtime" section. ■

Working with Strings

LotusScript has a rich set of functions you can use to manipulate strings. In this section, you'll look at the following:

- Creating strings
- Creating substrings
- Formatting strings
- Finding and comparing strings

Table 17.14 lists the statements and functions you can use to manipulate strings.

Table 17.14 LotusScript String-Handling Functions

Statement or Function	Description
Asc	Returns the ASCII character code for the first character in a string.
Chr	Returns the character that corresponds to a given ASCII character code.

Statement or Function	Description
Format	Evaluates an expression and formats the result according to the format string given. This is a very powerful and useful function.
InStr, InStrB	Returns the position of the character (InStr) or byte (InStrB), where one string first occurs within the other.
LCase	Converts a supplied string to lowercase.
Left, LeftB	Returns the number of characters (Left) or bytes (LeftB) from the left of a string (given a string and number).
Len, LenB	Returns the number of characters (Len) or bytes (LenB) used to store a string or number (given a string or number).
LSet	Assigns one string to another and left-aligns the result, using spaces for padding if necessary.
LTrim	Removes the leading spaces from the supplied string.
Mid	Returns the substring of the specified length that starts at the specified position (given a string, a start position, and a length).
Right, RightB	Returns the number of characters (Right) or bytes (RightB) from the right of the string (given a string and number).
RSet	Assigns one string to another and right-aligns the result, prefixing it with spaces if necessary.
RTrim	Removes the trailing spaces from a supplied string.
Space	Returns a string containing the number of spaces (given a number).
StrCompare	Compares two strings according to the supplied comparison method.
Trim	Removes the leading and trailing spaces from the supplied string.
UCase	Converts a supplied string to uppercase.
UChr	Returns a character that corresponds to the Unicode character code given.
Uni	Returns the Unicode character code for the first character in a given string.
UString	Returns a string of the specified characters of the supplied length (given a length, and either a Unicode code or a character).

Part III

Ch 17

Creating Strings

You use Dim to declare string variables. You can declare strings as variable or fixed-length:

```
Dim tVariableLength As String
Dim tFixedLength As String * 20
```

As declared, tFixedLength contains 20 characters. If you want to set a string to a particular length after it has been declared, you can use the Space$ function to set the string to a specified number of spaces. The following code, for example, sets tName to 32 spaces:

```
Dim tName As String
tName$ = Space$(32)
```

Alternatively, you can use the String$ function to set a string to any number of a specified character. You supply the number of characters and either the character or ASCII character code of the character to use. For example,

```
tName$ = String$(32, "x")
```

and

```
tName$ = String$(32, Asc("x"))
```

both set tName to contain 32 x characters.

If you are working with Unicode character codes, you can use UString$ to do the same thing, as long as you supply the Unicode character code:

```
strName = UString$(32, Uni("x"))
```

N O T E   The Asc function returns the ASCII character code that corresponds to the character you specify. Similarly, the Uni function returns the Unicode character code for a character. If you already know the appropriate code, you can find the corresponding character by using Chr for ASCII codes and UChr for Unicode codes. ▪

Creating Substrings

After you have a string, you can use any of the following functions to create substrings from it. With Left or Left$, you can create a substring consisting of a specified number of characters from the left of the string. The following example shows how:

```
Dim tName As String
Dim tFirstName As String
tName$ = "Daniel A Voelker"
tFirstName$ = Left$(tName, 6)    'tFirstName$ is set to 'Daniel'
```

Similarly, you can use Right or Right$ to extract characters from the right of the string, as in this example:

```
tLastname$ = Right$(tName, 7)     'tLastname$ is set to 'Voelker'
```

Use Mid or Mid$ to extract characters from anywhere in a string. You supply the start position and the number of characters, as shown here:

```
tMiddleInitial$ = Mid$(tName, 8, 1)    'tMiddleInitial$ is set to 'G'
```

To find the length of a string, you can use Len, as in this example:

```
Dim iLength As Integer
iLength% = Len(tName)    'iLength is set to 16
```

N O T E Many LotusScript functions have two versions—one that ends in a $ and one that doesn't. If you use the version that ends in $, the return data type is `String`. If you use the version without a $, the return data type is `Variant`. ■

You can remove leading and trailing spaces from strings using `Trim`, `LTrim`, and `RTrim`. `Trim` removes both leading and trailing spaces, `LTrim` removes leading spaces, and `RTrim` removes trailing spaces.

CAUTION

Several of the string-handling functions have one version that works with characters, such as `Left`, and another version that works with bytes, such as `LeftB`. This is fine when one character is stored in one byte. However, because the Unicode encoding scheme used by LotusScript represents each character with a two-byte character code, you should be wary of using the byte-oriented string functions `LeftB`, `LenB`, `MidB`, and `RightB`. They may give unexpected results with Unicode strings. Use `Left`, `Len`, `Mid`, and `Right` instead.

Formatting Strings

You can change the case of a string to lowercase by using `LCase` or to uppercase by using `UCase`. For more advanced formatting, use the `Format` function. You can use this function to format a string, date/time, or number according to a format string. The three following examples barely scratch the surface of the power and functionality of the `Format` function. In the first example, a message box uses `Format` to convert a Boolean value to the text string `"Yes"` or `"No"`. In the second example, `Format` is used to convert a `Double` value to a text string formatted as currency. The third example converts a date from one format to another.

```
' Format Example #1 converts a boolean value to a "Yes/No" string - Format
returns "No" in this case
Choice%=0
Msgbox "The user chooses: " & Format$(Choice%,"Yes/No"), 64, "Choice"

'Format example #2 converts a number to a currency value - Format returns
"$1,000,000,000"
NationalDebt#=1000000000
Msgbox "The amount is: " & Format$(NationalDebt#,"Currency"), 64, "Amount"

'Format example #3 converts a date in the format month/day/year (mm/dd/yy) to
day-month-year (dd-mmm-yyy) - Format returns 21-Dec-1995.
BirthDate="12/21/95"
Msgbox "The Birthdate is: " & Format$(Birthdate,"dd-mmm-yy"), 64, "Birthdate"
```

If you need to make sure that strings are aligned correctly, you can use the `LSet` and `RSet` statements. Use `LSet` to assign and left-align a string. `RSet` is similar, except that the string is right-aligned, as in this example:

```
Dim tLabel As String
tLabel$ = Space$(8)
LSet tLabel$ = "ABC"    'Sets tLabel$ to "ABC      " because the current
length of tLabel$ is 8'
```

```
RSet tLabel$ = "XYZ"     'Sets tLabel$ to "     XYZ"
tLabel$ = "ABC"          'Sets tLabel$ to "ABC"
```

TIP If you need to convert a string to the proper case, you could do it the hard way—by parsing out each piece and using Lcase on the first character. Or, you could use the Evaluate function in Lotus with the @Propercase formula, as shown in the next example.

```
Dim PCaseName As Variant
tUserName$="jason d cox"
PCaseName=Evaluate("@ProperCase(tUserName)")' In this example, tUserName
represents a field in Notes document, you'll learn about that as well as the
Evaluate function in Chapters 18 and 19.
Print PCaseName(0) ' prints "Jason D Cox" to the status bar.
```

The Evaluate function allows you to take the most advantage of the Formula language @Functions inside LotusScript. You simply pass the @Function and its arguments as a string argument to the Evaluate function, and Evaluate will return a variant value containing the result (this is why a subscript is used to refer to the value).

Finding and Comparing Strings

If you need to find a string contained within a string, you can use InStr to find the position of the first character of the embedded string. You supply the following:

- (optional) The position in the string to be searched at which to start searching. The default is the start of the string.
- The string to look for.
- The string to be searched.
- (optional) A number to indicate whether the search is case-sensitive—0 for case-sensitive and 1 for case-insensitive.

The following code shows how to find the position of the first occurrence of one string within another, regardless of case:

```
Dim tMain As String
Dim tSearch As String
Dim iPos As Integer

tMain$ = "Hello world!"
tSearch$ = "wor"
iPos% = InStr(1, tMain$, tSearch$, 1)  ' Look for 'wor' within 'Hello world!'
```

You can compare two strings by using StrCompare. With StrCompare, you supply the following:

- The two strings to compare.
- (optional) A number to indicate how to compare the strings. For example, you can specify that the comparison is case-sensitive.

StrCompare returns the following:

- -1 if the first string is less than the second
- 0 if the strings are equal
- 1 if the first string is greater than the second

TIP In most instances, you won't know the position of a character or substring within another string, but you can use the functions that were just covered to write code that will handle almost any instance. The following example demonstrates how you can extract any number of characters as a string:

```
Dim Pos as Integer, tCustName as String
tCustname$="Darryl Rogers"
Pos%=Instr(tCustName$, " ")
If Pos% Then
    Print "First Name = " & Left$(tCustName$, (Pos%-1))
    Print "Last Name = " & Right$(tCustName$, (Len(tCustName$)-Pos%))
End If
```

Date and Time Handling

Table 17.15 describes the LotusScript functions you can use to manipulate dates and times.

Table 17.15   LotusScript Date and Time-Handling Functions

Statement or Function	Description
Date	Returns the current system date as a date/time value or sets the current system date to a specified value.
DateNumber	Returns the corresponding date/time value, given a year, month number, and day of the month.
DateValue	Returns the corresponding date/time value, given a string representing a date.
Day	Returns the day of the month, given a date/time value.
Hour	Returns the hour, given a date/time value.
IsDate	Returns True if the supplied expression represents a date (given an expression).
Minute	Returns the minute, given a date/time value.
Month	Returns the month, given a date/time value.
Now	Returns the current system date and time as a date/time value.
Second	Returns the second, given a date/time value.

continues

Table 17.15   Continued

Statement or Function	Description
Time	Returns the current system time as a date/time value.
TimeNumber	Returns the corresponding date/time value, given an hour, minute, and second.
Timer	Returns the number of seconds that have elapsed since midnight.
TimeValue	Returns the corresponding date/time value, given a string representing a time.
Today	The same as the Date function.
Weekday	Returns an integer representing the day of the week, given a date/time value. Day 1 is Sunday.
Year	Returns the year, given a date/time value.

To find the current date, use the Date or Today function. Both return a date/time value containing the current system date. You can find the current time by using the Time function to return a date/time containing the current time. If you want both the date and time, use Now. To set a date to a specific value, you can use DateNumber or DateValue. DateNumber returns a date value when supplied with a year, month, and day. DateValue returns a date value when supplied with a string representing a date. Consider this example:

```
Print DateNumber(1995, 12, 21)    ' Prints 12/21/95
Print DateValue("Dec 21, 1995")   ' Prints 12/21/95
```

DateNumber is also useful in date calculations. For example, to find the date two years, three months, and twelve days before Dec 21, 1995, you could use the following:

```
Print DateNumber(1995 - 2, 12 - 3, 21 - 12)   ' Prints 10/09/93
```

You can use two similar functions to set a time to a specific value. TimeNumber returns a time value when supplied with an hour, minute, and second; TimeValue returns a time value from a string representing a time:

```
Print TimeNumber(20, 40, 3)   ' Prints 8:40:03 PM
Print TimeValue("20:40")      ' Prints 8:40:00 PM
```

You can find the number of seconds since midnight by calling the Timer function.

TIP   You can use the Timer function to time parts of your program. To see how long it will take to read a large file from a network file server, for example, call Timer before and after reading the file and subtract the two values. Timer is accurate to the nearest hundredth of a second.

After you have a date/time value, you can use Year, Month, Day, Hour, Minute, and Second to extract its constituent parts. You can use Weekday to return an integer representing the day of the week.

Working with Files

You can work with files by using LotusScript in many ways. Table 17.16 lists the functions available to you.

Table 17.16   LotusScript File-Handling Functions

Statement or Function	Description
Close	Closes one or more open files.
EOF	Indicates whether the end of a file has been reached. The exact condition used to determine the end of the file depends on the type of file being read.
FileAttr	Returns the access type or the operating system file handle for the file (given a file number and a flag).
FileCopy	Copies a file.
FileDateTime	Returns a string containing the date and time the file was created or modified (given a filename).
FileLen	Returns a filename's length in bytes.
FreeFile	Returns a file number you can use to open a file.
Get	Reads data from a binary or random file.
GetFileAttr	Returns a file or directory name's file system attributes.
Input #	Reads data from a sequential file into a list of variables (given a file number).
Input	Reads a specified number of characters from a sequential or binary file into a String variable (given a file number).
InputB	Reads a specified number of bytes from a sequential or binary file into a String variable (given a file number).
Kill	Deletes a file.
Line Input #	Reads a line from a sequential file into a String or Variant variable (given a file number).
LOC	Returns the current position of the file pointer in a file (given a file number).
Lock	Locks the file (given a file number)—or, optionally, a record or range of bytes within the file—so that other processes cannot update it.
LOF	Returns the length of a file (given a file number).
Name	Renames a file or directory.

Part

III

Ch

17

continues

Table 17.16   Continued

Statement or Function	Description
Open	Opens a file.
Print #	Prints a list of variables to a file.
Put	Writes data to a binary or random file.
Reset	Closes all open files.
Seek	Returns the current file pointer position, given a file number. Or, given a file number and a position, sets the current file pointer position.
SetFileAttr	Sets the file system attributes for a file.
Spc	Inserts a specified number of spaces into a Print or Print # statement.
Tab	Moves the print position to a specified column.
Width #	Specifies the line length of a sequential file.
Write #	Writes a list of variables to a file. Similar to Print #, except that delimiter characters are written automatically when necessary.
Unlock	Unlocks a file previously locked using Lock.

Types of Files

LotusScript can work with the three types of files listed in Table 17.17.

Table 17.17   LotusScript File Types

File Type	Description
Sequential	A text file
Random	A file consisting of a series of formatted records
Binary	A file with a program-defined structure

Getting File Information

If you know the name of a file, you can use GetFileAttr, FileDateTime, and FileLen to access file information. Use GetFileAttr to check the attributes for a file. The FileDateTime function returns the date when the file was last modified, and FileLen returns the length of the file in bytes. The following code, for example, checks whether a file is hidden; if it is, the code sets its Hidden attribute.

```
%Include "LSCONST.LSS" ' this would be placed in the options section
Dim iAttributes As Integer
iAttributes% = GetFileAttr("C:\TEMP.TXT")
If (iAttributes% And ATTR_HIDDEN) Then
    Call SetFileAttr "C:\TEMP.TXT", ATTR_READONLY
End If
```

N O T E LotusScript agents that attempt to manipulate system time, perform file I/O, or execute operating system commands are considered *unrestricted* agents. For users to be able to run these agents, they must have been granted Run Unrestricted Agents access in the Server document of your Public Address Book. You can learn about this topic in the Notes Help database (help4.nsf). ▓

Creating and Opening Files

Part

III

Ch

17

To open a sequential file, use the FreeFile and Open statements. Use FreeFile to allocate a new file number for the file. You then use this file number in the Open statement. For example, to open a new sequential file for output, use this code:

```
Dim iFileNumber As Integer
iFileNumber% = FreeFile
Open "C:\RESULTS.TXT" For Output As iFileNumber%
```

You can open a sequential file for Input, Output, or Append. After you open a file, you use the file number to refer to it thereafter.

To open a random file, you also use FreeFile and Open, but this time, you specify the Random option on the Open statement:

```
Dim iFileNumber As Integer
iFileNumber% = FreeFile
Open "C:\RECORDS.DAT" For Random As iFileNumber% Len = 80
```

The Len option is used to indicate the number of bytes per record in the file.

Use the Binary option in the Open statement to open a binary file, as shown in this example:

```
Dim iFileNumber As Integer
iFileNumber% = FreeFile
Open "C:\RECORDS.DAT" For Binary As iFileNumber%
```

After you open a file, you can use LOF to check the number of bytes in the file.

Reading Files

You can use the Line Input # and Input # statements, or the Input function, to read data from an open sequential file. Line Input # reads one line of data from the file:

```
Do Until EOF(iFileNumber%)
    Line Input #iFileNumber%, tInputLine
Loop
```

The EOF function returns True when the end of the file has been reached.

Use `Input` # to read data from a line in a file into a set of variables. For example, if your input file contains lines of the format

```
11111, "Samuel", "Hatter", 100.00
22222, "Leslee", "Hatter", 850.00
```

you could use the following code to read a line from the file:

```
Dim lID As Long
Dim tFirstName As String
Dim tLastName As String
Dim cBalance As Currency
    ' . . . Open the file as in previous examples
Input #iFileNumber%, lID&, tFirstName$, tLastName$, cBalance@
```

The `Input` function is another option for reading data from a sequential file. With `Input`, you supply the number of characters to read. You could read the ID number from the beginning of a line in the file by using the following code:

```
strID = Input$(5, iFileNumber%)
```

When you are working with random or binary files, use `Seek` and `Get` to find and read records from the file. Working with binary files can be tricky and is beyond the scope of this chapter. For more information, see the Lotus Notes Help database (`help4.nsf`).

Writing Files

You can use `Write` # to write the contents of a set of variables to a sequential file. For example, to write a line to an open file, use this code:

```
Dim lID As Long
Dim tFirstName As String
Dim tLastName As String
Dim cBalance As Currency
    ' . . . Open the file for output or append as in previous examples
    ' . . . Assign values to variables
Write #iFileNumber%, lID&, tFirstName$, tLastName$, cBalance@
```

`Write` # automatically adds delimiting characters to the output line, such as quotation marks around strings and commas between values. Notice the similarity between `Write` # and `Input` #; they are designed to work with each other to write and read lines in the same format. You can also use the `Print` # statement to write data to a sequential file. However, when you use `Print` #, you have to add your own delimiting characters. You can use a couple of functions with `Print` # to help format the line. Use `Spc` to add a specified number of spaces to the line and `Tab` to move the print position to a specified position within the line. For example, take a look at the following code:

```
tFirstName$ = "George"
tLastName$ = "Young"
Print #iFileNumber%, "*"; Tab(4); tFirstName$; Spc(2); tLastName$; "*"
```

This code prints the following:

```
*   George   Young*
```

Use `Put` to write data to random and binary files.

In some cases, you might want to block access to the file until your program finishes with it. LotusScript provides the Lock and Unlock statements to allow you to do so.

Closing Files

After you finish with a file, you should close it using the Close statement; this will flush the buffers to disk as well as close the file. If you want to close all the files that are open, you can use Reset. Here is an example of how to use the Close statement:

```
Close #iFileNumber%
```

Deleting Files

To delete a file, use the Kill statement. You supply Kill with the name of the file to be deleted:

```
Kill "C:\TEMP.TXT"
```

Input/Output

When you are using LotusScript within Notes, you often use Notes forms to get information from users and to display results. But sometimes you need to use different methods to communicate with a user. The LotusScript functions in Table 17.18 offer you some alternatives.

Table 17.18 LotusScript Input/Output Functions

Statement or Function	Description
Beep	Causes the PC speaker to emit a beep.
InputBox	Displays a dialog box in which a user can enter a value.
MessageBox	Displays a message box to a user.
Print	Writes some text to the Notes status bar.

Use InputBox to display a dialog box with an entry field. A user can enter a string into the entry field and click an OK button. You can then access the string the user typed from your script, as shown here:

```
tName$ = InputBox$("Please enter your name")
```

If you want, you can specify a window title for the dialog box and a default value:

```
iOrderQuantity% = CInt(InputBox$("Enter the order quantity",
 "Order Quantity", "10")
```

You can display values from your script by using MessageBox or Print. Use MessageBox to display a dialog box containing a message of your choice. If you want to display a message to confirm this order, for example, you could use this code:

```
If MessageBox("You are about to order " & CStr(iOrderQuantity%) &
 " widgets.  Is this correct?", MB_YESNO, "Confirm Order")= IDYES Then
```

```
    'Do something
End IF
```

MB_YESNO and IDYES are two of several constants relating to the MessageBox function that are defined in the LSCONST.LSS file. Additional constants are available that you can use to add icons and buttons to the message box. See the "MsgBox Parameters" section in the LSCONST.LSS file for more details.

In Notes, the LotusScript Print function displays a line of text in the Notes status bar. This feature can be very useful if you are writing a LotusScript agent that may take some time to execute, because it gives you an easy way to keep the user informed about its progress. In an agent that processes documents in a database, for example, you could use the code

```
Print "Processing document " & CStr(iCurDoc%) & " of " &
CStr(iTotalDocs%) & " . . ."
```

inside the main processing loop to display a constantly updated status message to your users. To top it off, why not let your users know when you're done by using Beep to wake them up!

The LotusScript Mathematical Functions

Table 17.19 describes the LotusScript mathematical functions.

Table 17.19   LotusScript Mathematical Functions

Statement or Function	Description
Abs	Returns any number's absolute value.
ACos	Returns a number's arccosine in radians (given a number between -1 and 1).
ASin	Returns a number's arcsine in radians (given a number between -1 and 1).
ATn	Returns a number's arctangent in radians.
ATn2	Returns the polar coordinate angle in radians, given the coordinates of a point in the Cartesian plane.
Cos	Returns the cosine of an angle in radians.
Exp	Returns the exponent of a number.
Fix	Returns the integer part of a number.
Fraction	Returns the fractional part of a number.
Int	Returns the nearest integer that is less than or equal to the supplied number.
Log	Returns the natural logarithm of a number.
Round	Rounds a number to a specified number of decimal places.

Statement or Function	Description
Sgn	Identifies the sign of the supplied number. Returns -1 for negative numbers, 0 for zero, and 1 for positive numbers.
Sin	Returns the sine of an angle in radians.
Sqr	Returns the square root of the supplied number.
Tan	Returns the tangent of an angle in radians.

Handling Errors at Runtime

LotusScript detects two types of errors:

- Compiler errors
- Runtime errors

Compiler errors are due to mistakes in your LotusScript code. You cannot run your code until you have fixed any compiler errors LotusScript has detected. You'll look at the Notes *Integrated Development Environment* (IDE) in the next chapter and explore some of the features that help reduce the number of compiler errors you'll have to fix.

Runtime errors are errors that occur when LotusScript attempts to run a script. A runtime error occurs when a script attempts to open a file that has been deleted, for example. LotusScript identifies many runtime errors and assigns each one an error number and an error message describing the error. You can add code to your programs to provide special handling for any or all of these errors. You can even define your own errors and assign them error numbers and messages. Table 17.20 describes the LotusScript functions that relate to error-handling.

Part III

Ch 17

Table 17.20   LotusScript Error-Handling Functions

Statement or Function	Description
Erl	Returns the LotusScript line number of the most recent error.
Err	Returns or sets the current error number, depending on how it is used.
Error	Returns an error message or signals an error, depending on how it is used.
On Error	Sets up error-handling for a procedure.
Resume	Determines where a LotusScript program resumes execution after an error.

Whenever LotusScript detects an error at runtime, it stores the following information:

- The line number in the LotusScript source file where the error occurred
- The error number
- The error message

You can use the Erl function to get the line number for the most recent error. The Err function returns the most recent error number, and Error$ returns the associated error message.

After LotusScript stores this information, it looks for an On Error statement in the current procedure that can handle the error. If it can't find one, it checks in the procedure that called the current one, and so on, until it has checked all the calling procedures. If a suitable On Error statement isn't found, LotusScript displays the error message associated with the error and stops execution of the script. If an On Error statement is found, LotusScript transfers control to the On Error statement.

The On Error statement can do either of the following:

- Ignore the error. If you specify On Error Resume Next, LotusScript ignores the line that caused the error and executes the line immediately after it.
- Specify a label to go to. If you specify On Error GoTo followed by the name of a label, LotusScript transfers control to the code at that label. The code should handle the error. Use a Resume statement to restart the script.

The following example shows how to define your own error and set up an error handler to process it. The example Sub defines an error with error number 600 and then initializes an error-handling routine to process errors with this number. It then forces the error to occur. Control is passed to the error-handling routine, which prints the error number and line number of the statement where the error occurred. Control is then returned to the statement following the one that forced the error.

```
Sub ErrorTest
' Define an error
Const ERR_MY_ERROR = 600

' Set up error handling to detect this type of error
On Error ERR_MY_ERROR GoTo lblHandleError

' Force an error to occur
Error ERR_MY_ERROR

' After the error is handled, control returns here . . .
Print "Finished."

Exit Sub

lblHandleError:
Print "Error number "; Err; " occurred on line "; Erl
Resume Next
End Sub
```

This chapter covered the syntax, structure, and main features of LotusScript. In the next chapter, you'll learn how LotusScript fits into Notes and how to use LotusScript and Notes to develop great Notes applications. ●

Writing Scripts with LotusScript

Chapter 17, "LotusScript Basics," introduced you to LotusScript and explained some of its basic features and syntax. In this chapter, you build on these basics and learn how to use LotusScript within Notes.

Extending Notes Capabilities with LotusScript

LotusScript extends the Notes programming interface beyond @Functions and @Commands. You use LotusScript to write scripts to perform various functions and tasks in Notes. You attach scripts to various objects in Notes, depending on what you need to accomplish. For example, you might use LotusScript to create an agent to update documents at a scheduled time. LotusScript provides many capabilities that Notes formulas do not, such as the following:

- Manipulate the ACL of a Notes database
- Print a list of all databases that reside on a server or local hard disk
- Read and write files of any type
- Most importantly, process iteratively (loop)

You enter LotusScript code into Notes using the Notes Integrated Development Environment (IDE). Notes contains an integral LotusScript compiler that translates your code into executable LotusScript.

Working with the Notes Integrated Development Environment

The Integrated Development Environment (IDE) in Notes lets you design forms, views, navigators, script libraries, and agents in a consistent, user-friendly way. However, for each form, view, or agent that you design, the IDE interface will vary slightly to reflect the features of each design element. This section focuses on the IDE interface as it relates to form design, but the Script Editor and debugger work similarly when working with other design elements. The Forms IDE is displayed, as shown in Figure 18.1.

The screen is divided into three areas or panes.

The Form Layout Pane

The large pane in the upper-left part of the screen is the Form Layout pane. You use this pane to design and lay out your form. You can add fields, static text, graphics, subforms, buttons, hotspots, actions, sections, and layout regions to the form.

FIG. 18.1
The Notes IDE for form design.

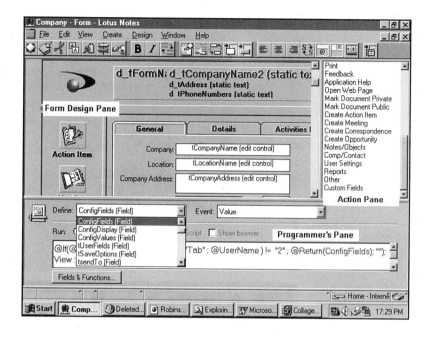

The Action Pane

The small pane in the upper-right part of the screen is the Action pane. You use this pane to define the actions that are associated with the form. By default, the Action pane is not visible when you first open the IDE. To display the Action pane, choose View, Action Pane or drag the vertical bar at the right edge of the screen to the left until the Action pane is the size you want. Finally, if you're a SmartIcon fan, you can click the View Show/Hide Action Pane SmartIcon.

To hide the Action pane, either choose View, Action Pane again to uncheck the menu option; drag the vertical bar to the right edge of the screen; or click the View Show/Hide Action Pane SmartIcon.

The Design Pane

The Design pane (often referred to as the programmer pane) is the pane displayed at the bottom of the screen. This is where you write your LotusScript code. By default, the Design pane is visible. If you want to hide it, choose View, Design Pane, or drag the horizontal bar (the one that separates the Design pane from the rest of the window) down to the bottom of the screen.

The Design pane consists of a number of components that you use to write the LotusScript code. The following sections look at each in turn.

Define Box   The Define box, which is visible in Figure 18.1, is a drop-down combo box that you use to select the object or action that you want to script.

For example, in Figure 18.1, the tCompanyName field is being scripted. You can use the Define box to quickly switch to another object or action. To select a different object to script, click the arrow on the Define box. A list of the scriptable elements in the current design object will appear. After you select the object or action that you want to script, it will be opened in the Design pane.

Event Box   The Design pane contains a second drop-down box, the Event box, which is also visible in Figure 18.1.

The Event box lists all of the scriptable events that are associated with the currently selected object or action. The Event box shows the event currently being programmed. For example, in Figure 18.1, the event being programmed is the tCompanyName field's Entering event. To program a different event, simply select it from the list in the Event box.

If the selected object or action has no events associated with it, such as one of the standard form actions, the Event box is not displayed. Figure 18.2 shows how the Design pane looks when the standard Edit Document action is selected.

FIG. 18.2
The Design pane appears without the Event box when a standard form action is selected.

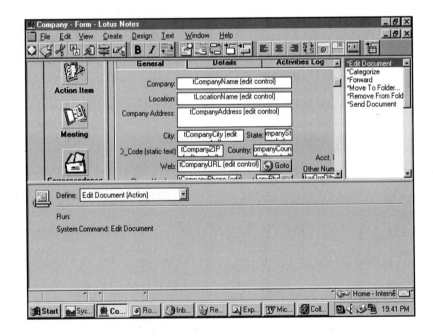

N O T E   If you add your own LotusScript functions and subs to a form, they are shown in the Event box when you select the Globals object for the form. ▧

The Run Radio Buttons   Depending on the type of object you have selected in the Define box, you can use the Run radio buttons to select the type of programming for the object (see Figure 18.3).

FIG. 18.3
The Run radio buttons
are used to select
LotusScript as a
programming option.

The radio buttons present you with three choices:

- Simple Action(s)
- Formula
- Script

N O T E When scripting agents in Notes 4.6, you also have the option to use Java.

Select the Script radio button to program using LotusScript.

The Script Browser After you have selected the Script radio button, you can display the Script Browser by checking the Show Browser check box. Figure 18.4 shows the Script Browser.

Part
III

Ch
18

FIG. 18.4
The Script Browser is a
very handy tool.

The browser lets you display the following:

- A list of the functions and features available in LotusScript.
- All of the Notes classes and their associated methods, properties, and events. (You will learn about these in detail in the next chapter.)
- All of the OLE2 and ActiveX classes that are available to you.

You select what you want to display using the browser combo box. You can select the following:

- LotusScript language
- Notes classes
- Notes constants
- Notes subs and functions

■ Notes variables

■ OLE2 classes

For example, if you want to see what functions LotusScript has available for Error Handling, follow these steps:

1. If it is not already selected, select LotusScript Language in the browser combo box. A list of categories of functions is displayed.

2. Click the twistie next to Error Handling. The names and syntax of the LotusScript Error-Handling functions are shown (see Figure 18.5).

FIG. 18.5

The LotusScript error-handling functions shown in the Script Browser.

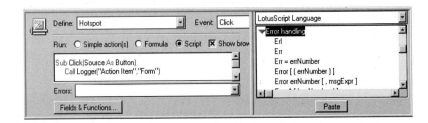

If you want to add an item from the browser to the code (such as a function name), follow these steps:

1. Position the cursor in the LotusScript code where you want to insert the item.

2. In the Script Browser, double-click the item you want to insert. The item is inserted into the code where you placed the cursor.

The browser can be very useful when you want to do the following:

■ Check for availability of a specific function.

■ Check the parameters for a function.

■ Check the properties, methods, and events of a Notes, OLE2, or ActiveX class.

The Script Editor   You will type your LotusScript code in the area of the Design pane called the Script Editor. The Script Editor understands LotusScript syntax and helps you by reviewing the script as you enter it. The Script Editor does the following:

■ Checks for syntax errors as you enter the script.

■ Automatically capitalizes LotusScript key words.

■ Formats the script by automatically indenting blocks of code.

■ Completes certain types of LotusScript block statements, such as If...Then statements and For...Next loops.

■ Provides colors to display different types of statements in your script.

You'll look at how to use the Script Editor in more detail later in the chapter.

The Errors Box   The Errors combo box is used to display syntax and compilation errors. For example, Figure 18.6 shows how a simple syntax error is detected and reported.

FIG. 18.6

The Errors box reports a syntax error.

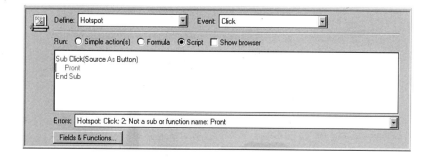

Using the Script Editor

If you can use a text editor, you can use the Script Editor! It works just like most text editors and supports the familiar key combinations for moving the cursor and for cutting, copying, and pasting text. For example:

- Home moves the cursor to the start of the current line.
- End moves the cursor to the end of the current line.
- PageUp moves the cursor up one "page" at a time.
- PageDn moves the cursor down one "page" at a time.
- Ctrl+C copies the selected text to the clipboard.
- Ctrl+X deletes the selected text from the Script Editor and copies it to the clipboard.
- Ctrl+V pastes text into the Script Editor from the clipboard.

Part

III

Ch

18

> **CAUTION**
>
> The Script Editor does not have an Undo feature. So, if you accidentally make a mistake, just press the Esc key and choose not to save the changes.

Configuring the Script Editor

New to the Script Editor as of Release 4.5 of Notes is the capability to choose the font used by the Script Editor, and to display different types of statements in different colors. You can choose color for:

- Identifiers
- Keywords
- Comments
- Directives
- Errors

To define the font and colors, follow these steps:

1. Right-click the Script Editor. A pop-up menu is displayed.
2. Select Design Pane Properties. The Design pane properties are displayed in the Properties InfoBox, as shown in Figure 18.7.

FIG. 18.7

Use the Design Pane Properties InfoBox to configure the Script Editor.

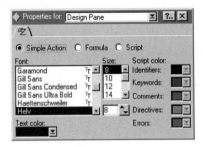

3. Select the Script radio button.
4. Select the font type and size you want to use.
5. Choose a color for each type of statement.

Entering Code

Follow these steps to enter code:

1. Select the object or action that you want to script.
2. Select the event that must be triggered to run the code.
3. Type the code into the Script Editor.

You can select the object or action to be programmed in different ways. For example, to select an object, you can do one of the following:

- Select its name from the drop-down list in the Define box.
- Click the object in the Form Layout pane.

To select an action to program, you can do one of the following:

- Select its name from the drop-down list in the Define box.
- Click the action in the action pane.

The Script Editor automatically checks the syntax of your code as you enter it. For example, as soon as you make a typographical error on a LotusScript statement or Notes object, the Script Editor lets you know by displaying an error in the Errors Box. If you have configured the colors for the Script Editor, the error is highlighted in the color you chose for errors (by default, red). Keywords, identifiers, comments, and directives are also highlighted when the Script Editor identifies them.

The code you enter using the Script Editor is stored in a LotusScript module. Notes stores a separate module for each form, view, and agent that you design. Some of the names listed in the Define box refer to parts of the LotusScript module rather than to objects or actions. The parts of the module that you use are:

- The (Options) area of the (Globals) section.
- The (Declarations) area of the (Globals) section.

You use the (Options) area to define options that affect the entire LotusScript module that you are writing. For example, if you want to use the `Option Declare` statement to make sure all variable names are explicitly declared, you add it to the (Options) part of the (Globals) section. The (Declarations) section can be used to define objects and variables that can be accessed anywhere in your module.

The Script Editor attempts to complete blocks of code and moves them to the correct location. For example, if you begin a `Type` statement on a new line in your script by entering `Type MyTypeName` and pressing Enter, the Script Editor automatically moves it to the (Declarations) part and adds the matching `End Type` statement. The Script Editor automatically moves the following blocks of code to the correct location:

- `Type`: Enter `Type` followed by the name of the type and press Enter. The Script Editor creates an empty `Type...End Type` block and adds it to the end of the (Declarations) section.
- `Dim`: If you type a `Dim` statement anywhere outside of a sub or function, the Script Editor moves the `Dim` statement to the end of the (Declarations) section.
- `Function`: Type `Function` followed by the name of the function and press Enter. The Script Editor creates an empty `Function...End Function` block and adds the name of the `Function` to the Event box.
- `Sub`: Type `Sub` followed by the name of the `Sub` and press Enter. The Script Editor creates an empty `Sub...End Sub` block and adds the name of the `Sub` to the Event box.
- `Option`: Type any of the LotusScript `Option` statements, such as `Option Declare` or `Option Base`, and the Script Editor moves the statement to the end of the (Options) section.
- `Class`: If you begin a class definition by typing `Class` followed by a class name and pressing Enter, the Script Editor moves the definition to the (Declarations) section and adds an `End Class` statement for you.
- `Property`: For either `Property Set` or `Property Get`, the Script Editor automatically creates a new block for the property and adds its name to the Event box.

The Script Editor also completes the following blocks of code for you:

- `For` loops: Type in the first line of the loop and press Enter. The terminating `Next` is automatically added for you.
- `Forall` loops: The terminating `End Forall` is added when you press Enter after typing the first line.

Part
III

Ch
18

- **If** statements: The End If is added for you.
- **Select** statements: The End Select is automatically added.
- **Do While** loops: The terminating Loop statement is added.
- **While** statements: The terminating Wend is added.

Compiling a Script

The Script Editor automatically compiles your LotusScript code for you. It does so at the following times:

- As you enter the script, the Script Editor partially compiles the script. This is how it detects syntax errors and knows when to complete blocks of code.
- When you save the script or when you click outside of the Script Editor, the Script Editor compiles the entire LotusScript module. It finds those errors that it cannot detect during the partial compilations. For example, this is the time that it can detect a call to a nonexistent sub or function.

You cannot save a script that contains compile errors; you must correct them all before you save the script.

 TIP If you want to save a script containing errors, you can put %REM and %END REM directives around the part of the script that contains the errors. This comments out the entire section and hides the error so you can save the script.

Using LotusScript Within Notes

Notes uses an object-oriented, event-driven programming model. The interface between LotusScript and Notes is a set of object classes—the Notes object classes. Objects of each class generate and respond to different events. For example, a button object can respond to being clicked, or a field object can respond to the cursor being placed in the field. When you program using LotusScript in Notes, you write LotusScript code that responds to these events.

You can attach LotusScript to events in the following types of objects:

- Buttons
- Actions
- Hotspots
- Fields
- Forms
- Views and folders
- Databases
- Agents

For each object, you need to know the events to which it responds.

Buttons, Actions, and Hotspots

Buttons, actions, and hotspots generate the events shown in Table 18.1. You will use the `Click` event most often. It is generated whenever the button, action, or hotspot is clicked. The `ObjectExecute` event is designed so that an OLE2 server application can use NotesFlow to execute Notes actions.

Table 18.1   Button, Action, and Hotspot Object Events

Event	Trigger
Click	When the button, action, or hotspot is selected.
Initialize	When the button, action, or hotspot is being loaded, before any other events.
ObjectExecute	When the action is activated by an OLE2 server that is FX/NotesFlow enabled.
Terminate	When the button, action, or hotspot is being unloaded as a document is closed. This is the last event.

The following steps show how to add a button and write some LotusScript to handle the `Click` event:

1. Create a new blank database.
2. Create a new form in the database. The Forms IDE is displayed.
3. Choose <u>C</u>reate, Hotspot, Button. A button is added to the form, and its Properties InfoBox is displayed.
4. Give the button a label by typing `"Hello World!"` in the Button label field in the InfoBox.
5. Click the Script Editor pane.
6. Select the Script radio button. By default, the Formula setting is selected for a new button.
7. Add the following code to the `Click` event:
   ```
   Messagebox "Hello World!", 64, "Button Test"
   ```
8. Choose <u>D</u>esign, Preview in Notes. You are asked to enter a name for the new form.
9. Enter `Test` as the form name and click OK. The new form is saved and displayed.
10. Click the "Hello World!" button. Your Hello World message box is displayed with the information icon.

Fields

You can attach LotusScript to the Field object events shown in Table 18.2.

Part
III

Ch
18

Table 18.2 Field Object Events

Event	Trigger
Entering	Fired when a user places the cursor in the field.
<Exiting	Fired when the cursor is moved out of the field.
Initialize	Fired when the field is loaded.
Terminate	Fired when the field is unloaded as the document closes. This is the last event.

The Entering event is useful for responding to the user placing the cursor in the field. For example, as soon as a user tabs into a field, you can enter some data into the field or clear its contents. You can use the Exiting event to see if a field has been correctly filled as soon as the user moves the cursor out of the field, rather than waiting until the document is saved. You also can use the Exiting event to calculate values for other fields in the document based on data the user entered in the current field. The following steps show how to use the Exiting event to help validate a field:

1. Create a new blank database.
2. Create a new form in the database. The Forms IDE is displayed.
3. Choose Create, Field. A field is added to the form and its Properties InfoBox is displayed.
4. Use the InfoBox to give the field the name ProductID.
5. Click the Programmer's Pane pane.
6. In the Event box, select the Exiting event.
7. Enter the following script:

```
Sub Exiting(Source As Field)
    Dim uiWorkspace As New NotesUIWorkspace
    Dim uiDoc As NotesUIDocument
    Dim tProductID As String

    Set uiDoc = uiWorkspace.CurrentDocument

    tProductID = uiDoc.FieldGetText("ProductID")
    If Len(tProductID) <> 5 Then
        Messagebox "Please enter a five character product ID", 16,
            "Re-enter
    Product ID"
        Call uiDoc.GotoField("ProductID")
    End If
End Sub
```

8. Create another field and name it ProductName.
9. Save and test the form. Place the cursor in the ProductID field and press Tab to move to the ProductName field. A message box displays to tell you to enter a five-character ID. Click OK and the cursor goes back to the ProductID field.

TIP Using field exiting events to calculate values for other fields in a document instead of using automatic refresh will vastly improve the performance of any form that has many computed fields. For example, the user selects a product ID from a keyword field that is set to Refresh fields on keyword change so that other field values can be retrieved using lookups based on the product ID. When a value is selected, all of the computed fields (except for those computed when composed), as well as any input translation, and input validation formulas will be executed, exacting a heavy performance toll. Instead, you could use the Exiting event of the field to run a script that retrieves the values and sets the fields without firing all of the other formulas.

Forms

Notes forms expose the events listed in Table 18.3. The QueryOpen event occurs when a request has been made to open a document. You can use it to set default values in the document—for example, looking up a set of keyword values from an external database. You can also use QueryOpen to see whether you should allow a document to be opened. For example, you can see who is trying to open the document or its current status before allowing it to be opened. Just after the document has been opened, the PostOpen event occurs. PostOpen keeps a history of who has read a document by adding his or her name to a list each time a PostOpen event occurs.

Table 18.3 Form Level Events

Event	The Event Is Triggered...
Initialize	When the form is loaded, before any other events.
Queryopen	Before the form is opened.
Postopen	After the form is opened.
Postrecalc	After the form has been refreshed.
Querysave	Before the form is saved.
Querymodechange	Before the form is changed to or from edit mode.
Postmodechange	After the form is changed to or from edit mode.
Queryclose	Before the form is closed.
Terminate	When the form is unloaded as the document is closed. This is the last event.

NOTE Lotus added two new form level events in Notes 4.6: WebQueryOpen and WebQuerySave. These events were not included in the previous table because they cannot be scripted and because they only work with Domino. To use these events, enter the name of an agent that you want to run when you open a document from the Web (WebQueryOpen) or save a document (WebQuerySave) from the Web. ▪

Part
III

Ch
18

When a document is open, the `QueryModeChange` and `PostModeChange` events let you respond to the document being switched to and from edit mode. `QueryModeChange` occurs just before the document changes mode (either from edit to read mode, or read to edit mode) and `PostModeChange` occurs just after. You can use `QueryModeChange` to decide if a user should edit a document. For example, if a document in a workflow system has been marked as an approved document, `QueryModeChange` can stop it from being edited.

The `PostRecalc` event occurs after all of the formulas on a document's form have been recalculated. `QueryClose` and `QuerySave` let you respond to a user's request to close or save a document. For example, you can use `QuerySave` to check that all of the fields in a document have been filled in correctly.

The following example shows you how to use the `PostOpen` event to keep a list of the people who have edited a document:

1. Create a new blank database.
2. Create a new form in the database. The Forms IDE is displayed.
3. Choose Create, Field. A field is added to the form and its Properties InfoBox is displayed.
4. Use the InfoBox to name the field DocEditors and make the field computed.
5. Click the Programmer's Pane pane.
6. In the Define box, select `Untitled` (Form), then select `Postopen` in the Event box.
7. Enter the following code:

```
Sub PostOpen(Source As Notesuidocument)
    Dim s As New NotesSession
    If Source.EditMode Then
        Call Source.FieldAppendText("DocEditors", s.CommonUserName & Chr(10))
    End If
End Sub
```

8. Save the form.
9. Create a document using the form and save it.
10. Edit the document. Your name is automatically added to the DocEditors field each time you edit the document.

Views and Folders

The view and folder object (see the `NotesUIView` class in Chapter 19) is new as of Release 4.5 of Notes. It responds to the events listed in Table 18.4. `QueryOpen` occurs just before a view is opened. `PostOpen` occurs just after a view has opened. When a user attempts to open a document displayed in the view, the `QueryOpenDocument` event occurs. You can use this event to see whether a document should be opened, or to ask the user to enter some information before he or she can look at the document.

Table 18.4 View and Folder Object Events

Event	The Event Is Triggered...
Initialize	When a view is being loaded, before any other events.
Queryopen	Before the view has opened.
Postopen	After the view has opened.
Queryopendocument	Before a document is opened from the view.
Queryrecalc	Before the view is recalculated.
Queryaddtofolder	Before a document is added to a folder.
Querypaste	Before a document is pasted into the view.
Postpaste	After a document has been pasted into the view.
Queryclose	Before the view is closed.
Terminate	When the view or folder is being unloaded. This is the last event.
RegionDoubleClick	After a region has been double-clicked (Calendar views only).
Querydragdrop	Before a drag-and-drop operation (Calendar views only).
Postdragdrop	After a drag-and-drop operation (Calendar views only).

Part
III

Ch
18

There are two events you can use to process documents that are pasted into the view. QueryPaste occurs just before a document or set of documents is pasted into a view; PostPaste occurs just after. You can use PostPaste to trigger specific processing of the documents that have just been pasted into the view. For example, you can store the date and time that the documents were pasted into the view. The QueryAddToFolder event occurs just before a document is copied to a folder. You can use it to check whether to allow the document to be added to the folder, or to ask the user to enter some filing information about the document. QueryRecalc occurs just before a view is recalculated and gives you the opportunity to stop the recalculation. The QueryClose event occurs just before the view is closed.

There are three events that are designed for use with the new calendar type of view. QueryDragDrop and PostDragDrop occur just before and just after a drag-and-drop operation. You can use them to decide whether to allow the drag-and-drop operation to continue or to perform some processing after the operation has completed. RegionDoubleClick occurs when a user double-clicks a date region in a calendar view.

The following steps show how to use the PostPaste event to store the date and time that a document is pasted into a folder:

1. Create a new discussion database from the Discussion Notes & Web (R4.6) template.
2. Choose Design, Folders and open the My Favorites folder in design mode. The Views IDE is displayed.

3. Choose the Folders object in the define box and select the `PostPaste` event in the Event box.

4. Enter the following code:

```
Sub Postpaste(Source As Notesuiview)
    Dim iDoc As Integer
    Dim doc As NotesDocument

    For iDoc% = 1 To Source.Documents.Count
        Set doc = Source.Documents.GetNthDocument(iDoc%)
        doc.PasteTime = Now
        Call doc.Save(True, True)
    Next
End Sub
```

5. Save the folder and close it.

6. Create a new Main Topic document and save it.

7. Switch to the All Documents view, select the document you just created, and copy it to the clipboard (press Ctrl+C or choose Edit, Copy).

8. Switch to the My Favorites folder and paste the document.

9. Check the Properties InfoBox for the document. The date and time you pasted the document are stored in a new field called `PasteTime`.

Databases

Databases (see the `NotesUIDatabase` class in Chapter 19) can now be scripted and will generate the seven events shown in Table 18.5.

Table 18.5   Database Object Events

Event	The Event Is Triggered...
`Initialize`	When the database is being loaded, before any other events.
`PostDocumentDelete`	After a document has been deleted from the database using Cut or Clear.
`PostOpen`	After the database has been opened.
`QueryClose`	Before the database is closed.
`QueryDocumentDelete`	Before a document or group of documents is deleted from the database.
`QueryDocumentUndelete`	Before a document or group of documents is undeleted.
`Terminate`	When the database is being unloaded, after all other events.

The `QueryDocumentDelete` event occurs just before a document or documents are deleted from the database. `PostDocumentDelete` occurs just after the documents have been deleted. The

QueryDocumentUndelete event occurs when a document or set of documents (that have been marked for deletion) are unmarked. QueryClose occurs just before the database is closed.

N O T E The PostOpen event for the database occurs after the QueryOpen and PostOpen events for view open.

The following steps show how you can use the PostDocumentDelete message to automatically alert someone when documents are deleted from a database:

1. Create a new discussion database from the Discussion – Notes & Web (R4.6) template.
2. Choose Design, Others and open the Database Script.
3. Select the PostDocumentDelete event in the Event box.
4. Enter the following code:

```
Sub Postdocumentdelete(Source As Notesuidatabase)

    Dim db As NotesDatabase
    Dim doc As NotesDocument
    Set db = Source.Database
    Set doc = New NotesDocument( db )
    doc.Form = "Memo"
    doc.Subject = CStr(Source.Documents.Count) & " documents deleted at "
    & CStr(Now) & "."
    Call doc.Send( False, "Leslee Hatter" )

End Sub
```

5. Save the script.
6. Exit from the database and reopen it.
7. Create a new Main Topic document and save it.
8. Switch to the All Documents view, select the document you just created, and mark it for deletion.
9. Exit from the database and delete the newly created document.
10. A mail message is automatically created and sent.

Agents

An *agent* is a user procedure you can use to automate many tasks within Notes, such as the archiving of old documents or the automatic generation of replies to mail messages. An agent can be triggered in a number of ways, including a menu command, a predefined schedule, the arrival of mail, or the pasting of documents. You can write LotusScript programs to create agents, and you can use Notes-supplied agents.

Agents run at either of the following locations:

■ The user workstation, if the agent's trigger has been set to any of the following: Manually from Actions Menu, Manually from Agent List, If Documents have been Created or Modified, or If Documents have been Pasted.

Part
III

Ch
18

■ The server or workstation containing the agent, if the agent's trigger has been set to either If New Mail Has Arrived or On Schedule.

Whenever an agent is executed, it runs the code attached to the Initialize event, so this is where you should put your agent code (see Table 18.6).

Table 18.6 Agent Object Events

Event	Trigger
Initialize	When the agent is loaded.
Terminate	When the agent is unloaded.

The following code example demonstrates how you can send e-mail to all users selected in a view. You'll learn about the Notes objects and classes that are being used in this example in Chapter 19.

```
Sub Initialize
    Dim S As New NotesSession
    Dim CDoc As NotesDocument
    Dim Count%
    Dim Subject As String, Msg As String
    Subject$="This is an automatic mail notification"
    Msg$=Inputbox$("Enter a brief message to send", "Mail Message","")
    Set CDoc=S.CurrentDatabase.UnprocessedDocuments.GetFirstDocument
    Do While Not CDoc Is Nothing
        Count%=Count%+1
        Call MailNotification(Subject$, Msg$, Cdoc.MailAddress(0),
S.CurrentDatabase)
        ' User defined sub that actually sends the mail message.
        Set CDoc=S.CurrentDatabase.UnprocessedDocuments.GetNextDocument(Cdoc)
    Loop
    Print Trim$(Str$(Count%)) & " mail notifications were sent"

End Sub

Public Sub MailNotification(Sbj As String, Message As String, MailAddress As
String, cDB As NotesDatabase)
    Dim MDoc As New NotesDocument(cDB)
    MDoc.Form="Memo"
    MDoc.Subject=Sbj$
    MDoc.Body=Message$
    Call MDoc.Send(False, MailAddress$)
End Sub
```

Using Script Libraries

Script libraries are a powerful and useful way to share LotusScript code across a database. Prior to Notes 4.5, if you wanted to use a function or subroutine in several forms or views, you had to include the code in each of those objects, or you had to save it as a text file and use the

%Include directive to include the code across the entire database. The first method requires significantly more maintenance; the second method means that your code will not replicate and you have to ensure that it makes it to each desktop.

However, you can write a sub or function and place it in a script library, which is a design element of a Notes database. You can then use the Use statement to make the code available to any module in a database, greatly enhancing usability and modularity! Table 18.7 shows the script library events.

Table 18.7 Script Library Object Events

Event	Trigger
Initialize	When the script library is loaded.
Terminate	When the script library is unloaded.

N O T E If your Domino applications are designed to run without authentication (that is, anonymous access), any agent run as an OpenAgent is treated as a Restricted LotusScript Agent, disallowing the use of the Use directive. To overcome this obstacle, you have two rather unpalatable choices: You can copy and paste all of the needed subs and functions into the OpenAgent and delete the Use directive, or you can set the Run Unrestricted LotusScript Agents field in the Server document to *. However, this second option is dangerous and discouraged by Lotus. ▩

Using the Debugger

The debugger lets you check how a script is executing, line by line if you like. You can start and stop the script at any time and check the values that have been assigned to specific variables or properties. This can help you quickly find errors in those scripts that are behaving improperly. The debugger displays its own window showing the script being executed. An arrow indicates which line of script is about to be executed and, as lines are executed, the arrow moves to the next line. You can use the debugger to do the following:

- ▩ Step through a script one line at a time.
- ▩ Set breakpoints in the script so it temporarily stops executing at each breakpoint.
- ▩ Examine and modify the value of variables and properties.

Enabling the Debugger

When you want to start debugging, you enable the debugger by choosing File, Tools, Debug LotusScript from the Notes menu bar.

To disable the debugger just choose File, Tools, Debug LotusScript again.

Once the debugger is enabled, it starts automatically when you run any LotusScript. When the debugger starts, it will do the following:

■ Display the debugger window (see Figure 18.8).

FIG. 18.8
Use the debugger
window to find errors
in your scripts.

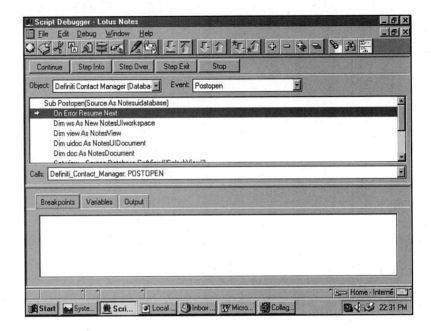

■ Highlight the first line in the script.

■ Pause execution of the script at the first line.

The following sections look at the areas of the debugger window.

The Button Area

You can control how the debugger steps through a script using the five buttons at the top of the
screen. The buttons work as follows:

■ Continue: Continue execution of the script until you reach a breakpoint or the end of the
script.

N O T E   Clicking the Continue button will cause all future invocations of the script to run either until
it hits a breakpoint, hits an error, or ends without launching the debug window. In fact, it
will not be displayed again until you close the parent object and reopen it. Consider the following
example: You have a script in the click event of an action in a view. You click the button (the debugger
launches) and then you click Continue. Until you close the view and reopen it, the debugger will not be
displayed unless you have a breakpoint set. This can be very frustrating until you figure out what Notes
is doing. ■

■ Step Into: Execute the current statement and stop at the next one. If the current statement is a sub or function call, stop at the first executable statement in the sub or
function. In addition to clicking the button, you can use Step Into by choosing Debug,
Step Into, or pressing F8.

- Step Over: Execute the current statement. If the current statement is a call to a sub or function, execute the sub or function and stop at the first statement immediately after the call. If the statement is not a sub or function call, execute the statement and stop at the next statement. To use Step Over, you can click the Step Over button; choose Debug, Step Over; or press Shift+F8.

- Step Exit: Continue execution of the current sub or function until the end of the sub or function is reached, then stop at the statement immediately following the one that called the sub or function. Use Step Exit by clicking the Step Exit button; choosing Debug, Step Exit; or pressing Ctrl+F8.

- Stop: Stop executing the script.

The Object Box

The Object drop-down displays the name of the object containing the script now running. For example, Figure 18.8 shows that the current script is being executed because the PostOpen event of the Database Script has been fired. To see the code attached to any other objects, select the specific object(s) by using the Object box drop-down list.

The Event Box

The Event drop-down shows the name of the event to which the script is attached. Similar to the Object box, the Event box drop-down list can be used to examine the code attached to any events within the current object. Figure 18.8 shows that the code displayed is attached to the Postopen event.

The Debug Pane

The Debug pane displays the LotusScript that you are debugging. An arrow points to the line about to be executed.

The Calls Dialog Box

The Calls dialog box lets you trace the route your script has taken to reach the current line. Every time a sub or function calls another sub or function, its name is added to the Calls dialog box and a history of calls is built up. The subprogram that is being executed is displayed at the top of the list. You navigate through the hierarchy of calling and called programs by selecting them from the list.

The Breakpoints Tab

The breakpoints tab displays any breakpoints that you have set. You can double-click a breakpoint to have the line displayed in the Debug pane. You'll look at breakpoints in more detail shortly.

The Variables Tab

Figure 18.9 shows the Variables tab, one of the most useful features of the debugger. It shows all the defined variables and lets you examine and change their current value. The Variables tab shows the variable name, its current value, and its type. Twisties are shown next to variables that represent objects or complex data structures. You can use the twisties to expand a variable, showing its properties or component values. You can change the value of a variable by typing a new value into the New Value field.

FIG. 18.9

Click the Variables tab to display LotusScript variables.

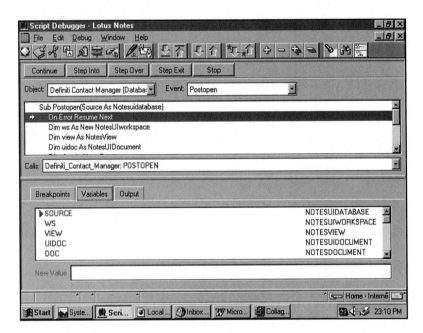

N O T E Working with items in a document in the Debugger can be frustrating because the items are displayed using a subscript-like notation (for example, [13] indicates the thirteenth item in the document). Once you find the item you are looking for, be sure to note its number. ▪

The Output Tab

The Output tab is used to display the output from Print statements in your script.

Using Breakpoints

Breakpoints are a way of interrupting the execution of the script at a specific line. When the script has been interrupted, you can examine the current value of variables and properties. You can use the debugger to do the following:

■ Set or clear a single breakpoint: To set a breakpoint, double-click in the Debug pane the line that you want to be a breakpoint. A red stop sign appears to the left of the line to show that it is a breakpoint, and the new breakpoint is added to the list of breakpoints shown on the Breakpoint tab.

N O T E Breakpoints can only be set on executable code, so non-executable statements such as Dim and REM cannot be used to set breakpoints. ■

- Clear a breakpoint: To clear a breakpoint, double-click the line containing the breakpoint you want to clear. It will then change to a stop sign with a yellow slash through it. Then double-click it again and the stop sign will vanish, indicating that it is now disabled.
- Clear all breakpoints: To clear all of the breakpoints you've set, choose Debug, Clear All Breakpoints.
- Temporarily enable or disable a single breakpoint: To temporarily disable a breakpoint, select the breakpoint in the Debug pane and choose Debug, Disable Breakpoint. The stop sign changes to a yellow slash, indicating that the breakpoint is disabled. To re-enable the breakpoint, choose Debug, Enable Breakpoint.
- Temporarily enable or disable all breakpoints: To temporarily disable all breakpoints, choose Debug, Disable All Breakpoints. You can re-enable all breakpoints by choosing Debug, Enable All Breakpoints.

N O T E You can also set and clear breakpoints by choosing Debug, Set/Clear Breakpoint or by pressing the F9 key. ■

Part
III
Ch
18

Additional Debugging Techniques

You can use a variety of techniques to test your scripts besides stepping through the code using the debugger.

Using Messagebox

You can test your scripts by using the Messagebox statement to display debugging messages. Simply define a debug sub that uses Messagebox to show text that you supply to indicate the progress and status of your script. Then call the debug sub when you need to show debugging information. A debugging sub example is shown below:

```
Sub ShowDebugMsg(strMsg As String)
    Messagebox strMsg, 64, "Debug Message"
End Sub
```

Using Print

You can also use the LotusScript Print function. If you are testing a script that runs on a client, Print writes its messages to the Notes status bar. If the script is running on a server, the messages are written to the Notes server log database. When you are debugging your script, the output from Print statements is shown on the debugger output tab.

N O T E Using the `Dialogbox` method of the `NotesUIworkspace` object to display a `Dialogbox` that uses LotusScript can be very frustrating as any LotusScript code in a dialogbox cannot be debugged in the debugger! If you need to debug code in a dialog box, use the `Print` or `MessageBox` techniques mentioned above. ■

Using an Error Handler

You may want to define an error-handling routine to catch an error, display some details about it, and continue executing the script. Otherwise, the debugger stops executing the script when it detects an error. Include the handler in all event routines you use so that every error is detected. LotusScript specifies a standard set of errors, and corresponding error numbers (as constants) in the file lserr.lss, so remember to use `%Include` to include this file in your script if you want to use the constants.

The following sample handler pops up a message box to show the error details. If an error occurs anywhere in the script, the code after the `lblShowError` label is executed, then control is returned to the statement following the one that generated the error. You can easily modify the code to write the error details to a log file for a permanent record of each error.

```
Sub Click(Source As Button)
  ' Set up the error handler
    On Error Goto lblShowError

  ' Put your button code here . . .

    Exit Sub

    lblShowError:
    Messagebox "Line: " & CStr(Erl) & " - " & Error(Err), MB_OK,
    "Error: " & CStr(Err)
    Resume Next
End Sub
```

Using Dynamic Link Libraries

With LotusScript, you can call functions and subroutines in external function libraries, such as dynamic link libraries. You can use the features and functions of the underlying operating system via its programming interface, or you can call functions in your own libraries. For example, when running on Windows 95, you can use LotusScript to call external C language functions in the Windows 95 dynamic link libraries (DLLs). You can call external functions on all of the following platforms:

- Windows 3.1
- Windows 95
- Windows NT
- OS/2
- UNIX
- Macintosh

N O T E   The functions available and the calling conventions you use differ from platform to platform. If you need to write LotusScript to run on different operating systems, use the %IF directive to check the platform type on which your script is running; then call the appropriate function for that platform. See the LotusScript documentation on %IF for details. ■

To call a function in an external DLL, follow these steps:

1. Use the LotusScript Declare statement in the Declarations section of your script to declare a reference to the routine as either a sub or function.

2. When the routine has been declared, call it as if it were a LotusScript sub or function.

For example, the following script shows you how to declare and use the external function GetFreeSystemResources. This function is available only in Windows 3.1 and returns system information about how Windows is managing its memory. When you run the script on a Windows 3.1 Workstation, it displays the available system resources in the Notes status bar:

```
Sub Click(Source As Button)
    Declare Function GetFreeSystemResources
Lib "User" (ByVal iFlag As Integer)

    Dim iSystemResources As Integer
    Dim iGDIResources As Integer
    Dim iUserResources As Integer

    Const GFSR_SYSTEMRESOURCES = 0
    Const GFSR_GDIRESOURCES   = 1
    Const GFSR_USERRESOURCES  = 2

    ' Get the available Memory, GDI and User resources
    iSystemResources% = GetFreeSystemResources(GFSR_SYSTEMRESOURCES)
    iGDIResources% = GetFreeSystemResources(GFSR_GDIRESOURCES)
    iUserResources% = GetFreeSystemResources(GFSR_USERRESOURCES)

    ' Display them on the Notes status bar
    Print "System Resources =" & Str$(iSystemResources%)
    Print "GDI Resources =" & Str$(iGDIResources%)
    Print "User Resources =" & Str$(iUserResources%)
End Sub
```

T I P   LotusScript automatically converts the function name in a Declare statement to uppercase. This is fine in Windows 3.1; however, the function names used by Windows 95 and Windows NT are case-sensitive. So, if you call external functions in Windows 95 and Windows NT, you should always use the Alias part of the Declare statement to specify the function name with the correct case.

By default, arguments are passed to external functions by reference. You can override this for certain types of data and have the argument passed by value using the ByVal keyword. For example, the following declarations pass both arguments by value:

```
Declare Function iMax Lib "MYFUNCS" Alias "iMax"
 (ByVal iX As Integer, ByVal iY As Integer) As Integer
```

Part

III

Ch

18

Using Evaluate and Execute

The LotusScript Evaluate and Execute functions let you compile and execute Notes @Functions and LotusScript programs on-the-fly. Use Evaluate to calculate an @Function formula. You supply two arguments, both the @Function formula and the object used to execute that formula. For example, you can run the @Function shown in the next example against a particular Notes document to display the total size of all attached files:

```
Sub Click(Source As Button)
    Const STR_FORMULA = "@if(@Attachments > 0; @Sum(@AttachmentLengths); 0)"
    Dim varTotalSize As Variant
    Dim uiWorkspace As New NotesUIWorkspace
    Dim uiDoc As NotesUIDocument
    Dim doc As NotesDocument

    Set uiDoc = uiWorkSpace.CurrentDocument
    Set doc = uiDoc.Document

    varTotalSize = Evaluate(STR_FORMULA, doc)
    Messagebox "Total size of all attached files is
    " & CStr(varTotalSize(0)) & " bytes."
End Sub
```

N O T E You must define a formula to evaluate when the LotusScript is compiled, so you can't use a variable to define the formula. However, after you've looked at the Execute function, you'll look at a way of fooling LotusScript so you can define a formula at runtime to use with Evaluate. ■

Using the Execute function, you can compile and execute a text string as a LotusScript program. LotusScript takes the contents of the string, compiles it, and runs it as a separate program. If you want to pass data between your main program and the program created by the Execute function, you can declare variables as Public. In this way, both programs have access to the variable and can use it to pass data back and forth between them. The following example uses a separate script to add the number one to another number.

First, in the (Declarations) section of the script, declare a Public variable to pass the number to and from the script being run by the Execute function:

```
Public piTempNumber As Integer ' for a button of form, place this code in the
Global Declaration area
```

T I P As a convention, consider starting the names of Public variables with the letter p to make it easy to tell that they are public.

Then, declare a sub to build a mini-program and call Execute to run the mini-program and display the results:

```
Sub Increment(iNumber As Integer)
    Dim tScript As String
    piTempNumber% = iNumber%
    tScript$ = ¦piTempNumber% = piTempNumber% + 1¦
```

```
        Execute(tScript$)
        Messagebox CStr(piTempNumber%)
End Sub
```

Finally, create a button on the form in order to call the new sub:

```
Sub Click(Source As Button)
    Dim i As Integer
    I% = 3
    Increment I%
End Sub
```

When you click the button, the Increment sub is called and the mini-program (which will add one to the supplied number) is compiled and executed.

Although this is a simple example, it demonstrates how powerful this feature is. You can use Execute to compile and run any text as a LotusScript program. For example, you can combine Evaluate and Execute to avoid the problem of supplying the formula to Evaluate as a constant. You will first need to declare a Public variable to get the resulting formula:

```
Public pvarResult As Variant
```

Then, create a sub that creates and executes a mini-program using the supplied string as a formula:

```
Sub ExecuteFormula(tFormula As String, varResult As Variant)
    Dim tScript As String

    ' Create a mini-program with the supplied formula and
    ' assign the result to a Public variable so that the
    ' main program can get at it.
    tScript$ = ¦Const STR_FORMULA = "¦ & tFormula$ & ¦"
    Dim uiWorkspace As New NotesUIWorkspace
    Dim uiDoc As NotesUIDocument
    Dim doc As NotesDocument
    Set uiDoc = uiWorkSpace.CurrentDocument
    Set doc = uiDoc.Document
    pvarResult = Evaluate(STR_FORMULA, doc) ¦

    ' Run the mini-program
    Execute(tScript$)

    ' Save the result returned by the formula
    varResult = pvarResult
End Sub
```

To call the new sub, add a button to a form and use the following script to pass a formula to the new sub:

```
Sub Click(Source As Button)
    Dim tFormula As String
    Dim varResult As Variant
    tFormula$ = Inputbox$("Enter a Notes formula to
    calculate for the current document:")
    On Error Goto lblExecutionError
    Call ExecuteFormula(tFormula$, varResult)
```

Part

III

Ch

18

```
Messagebox "The result of calculating " &
tFormula$ & " is " & CStr(varResult(0))

lblExit:
Exit Sub

lblExecutionError:

Messagebox "Unable to calculate the formula for this document."
Resume lblExit
End Sub
```

To test the new sub, follow these steps:

1. Click the button.

2. Type a formula, such as @attachments, into the input box and click OK.

3. A message box is displayed, as shown in Figure 18.10.

FIG. 18.10
A message box showing
the results of executing
a Notes formula.

Using LotusScript Extensions

LotusScript extensions, or LSXs, are just that—extensions to LotusScript. A software developer or tools vendor can use them to add extra classes to Notes. For example, IBM has produced a set of LotusScript extensions for MQ Series Link for Lotus Notes that lets you access transactions and data on other systems. Lotus has used LSXs to add three classes to Notes that you can use to access ODBC data sources.

N O T E   For more information on MQ Series Link for Lotus Notes, point your Web client to http://
www.lotus.com. ■

To use a LotusScript extension, include the UseLSX statement in the (Options) part of the (Global) section of a script. For example, to use the ODBC LotusScript Extensions in a script, add the following line to the (Options) part:

```
UseLSX "*LSXODBC"
```

The command loads the DLL that contains the three classes that form the ODBC extensions to LotusScript.

This is covered in more detail in Bonus Chapter 1, "ODBC and Lotus Components," on the CD-ROM. ●

More LotusScript

In previous chapters, you learned about the basics of the LotusScript language—the nuts and bolts you need to start building simple LotusScript programs. In this chapter, you learn the Lotus Notes object classes, and how you can use them to build more sophisticated Notes applications that exploit the full power of both LotusScript and Notes. The key to building these applications is a good understanding of the Lotus Notes object classes.

Understanding the Lotus Notes Object Classes

The Lotus Notes object classes let you use LotusScript to access databases, views, documents, and items, to name a few Notes objects. For example, from your LotusScript programs, you can use the Notes object classes to create, open, or delete databases and add, modify, or delete documents in those databases. In this chapter, you take a detailed look at each of the Notes object classes and see how each one can best be used from LotusScript. Before that, you need to understand the differences between the different class types.

Currently, two types of classes let you work with Notes objects: front-end, or user interface (UI) classes, and back-end classes.

> **N O T E** The two types of classes discussed in this chapter are not the only classes available to you from LotusScript. Other types of classes can be added as LotusScript extensions, such as the Open Database Connectivity (ODBC) classes, which are explained in more detail in Bonus Chapter 1, "ODBC and Lotus Components," on the CD. ■

The UI classes let you work with databases, views, and documents that are displayed in the active Notes window. For example, you can work with the document that is currently on-screen using the NotesUIDocument class. The methods and properties of the UI classes let you work with views and documents in the same way a user works with them. You can type text into fields, move the cursor, use the clipboard, and refresh views.

Four UI classes are represented:

- The Notes workspace
- The current document
- The current view
- The current database

The second type of class, the back-end classes, represents the constituent parts of Notes. They include some obvious elements, such as databases, views, documents, fields, and some more abstract concepts, such as sessions and collections of documents.

You need to understand the differences between the two types of classes because they are interlinked. For example, a document displayed on-screen has two different representations: the UI document and the back-end document. When you type data into the UI document, the corresponding back-end document is not updated until you save your changes. Conversely, if an agent updates the back-end part of a document, the UI document does not display the changes until it is refreshed. In this chapter, you will look at some of the methods you can use to keep both parts of the document in step.

The rest of the chapter looks at each class in detail. The following section starts at the Notes workspace by looking at the `NotesUIWorkspace` class.

Working with the *NotesUIWorkspace* Class

The `NotesUIWorkspace` class represents the current Notes workspace window. The class lets you use LotusScript to perform some of the actions that you normally perform from the Notes workspace, such as opening databases or creating and editing documents. If a document is already displayed in the active window or highlighted in a view, you can use this class to work with the document.

The class has only two properties, `CurrentDocument`, which returns the document that is currently open in the user interface, and `CurrentCalendarDateTime`, which returns the date and time of the currently selected region in a calendar view. Normally, you use `CurrentDocument` to get a handle on the open document, and then you use the methods and properties of the `NotesUIDocument` class to work with the document. For example, the following script finds the current document and displays in a message box the value of a field called `Title`:

```
Dim uiWorkspace as New NotesUIWorkspace
Dim uiDoc as NotesUIDocument
Set uiDoc = uiWorkspace.CurrentDocument
MessageBoxuiDoc.FieldGetText("Title"), 64, "Testing"
```

The `NotesUIWorkspace` class has twelve methods that let you open databases and URLs, create and edit documents, check for alarms, find free time, use LotusScript Extensions (LSX), and refresh views. You add a database to your workspace using the `AddDatabase` method. You supply the server and filename for the database, and it is added to the current workspace tab. You open a database by using the `OpenDatabase` method, the LotusScript equivalent of the @Command `FileOpenDatabase`. If you compare the `OpenDatabase` method with the `FileOpenDatabase` @Command, you see that their parameters are very similar. The `FileOpenDatabase` method accepts up to six parameters. The first two parameters specify the server and filename of the database to open. You use the remaining parameters to specify how to open the database. You can open the database to a specific view or navigator.

For example, you can supply the name or alias of a view as the third parameter so that the database opens to that view. If the first column in the view is sorted, you can supply a key as a fourth parameter. In this case, the database is opened at the view you specify, and the first document matching the key is highlighted. Alternatively, you can use the third and fourth parameters to open a navigator. You supply the name of a navigator as the third parameter and `True` or `False` as the fourth parameter to indicate whether the navigator should open in its own window. The fifth parameter specifies whether the view or navigator opens in a new window, even if an open window already contains the view or navigator. Specify `True` to open a new window or `False` to use an existing window. You use the last parameter to indicate whether the database should open without adding it to your workspace. Specify `True` to open the database temporarily or `False` to add the database to your workspace.

Part
III

Ch
19

To open a database from a button, use the following LotusScript:

```
Sub Click(Source As Button)
    Dim uiWorkspace As New NotesUIWorkspace
    Call uiWorkspace.OpenDatabase("Gonzo/Definiti", "fortisma\cmgr.nsf"_
, "Customers ", "Active", True, False)
End Sub
```

> **N O T E** The "_" character shown in the preceding code is called the *line continuation* character. It allows you to break a long line of code into several lines, which makes it much easier to read and manage. ▪

This opens the database CMGR.NSF in the FORTISMA directory on server Gonzo to the Customers By Region view and selects the first document whose status is `"Active"`. The last two parameters ensure that a new window opens for the view and that the database is always added to the user's workspace.

You can also use the `FileOpenDatabase` method to open a navigator. Instead of a view name, you supply the name of a navigator, and instead of a key, you supply `True` or `False` to specify whether the navigator opens in its own window. The other parameters are the same as for opening a view. For example, the following script opens a navigator called `Main Navigator` in its own window:

```
Sub Click(Source As Button)
    Dim uiWorkspace As New NotesUIWorkspace
    Call uiWorkspace.OpenDatabase("Gonzo/Definiti", "Fortisma\cmgr.nsf"_
, "Main Navigator", True, True, False)
End Sub
```

After you choose a document in a view, you can open it by using the `EditDocument` method. To have the button open the document for Digital Processing Systems in edit mode, use the following updated script:

```
Sub Click(Source As Button)
    Dim uiWorkspace As New NotesUIWorkspace
    Dim uiDoc as NotesUIDocument
    Dim Customer$
    Customer$="DigitalProcessingSystems"
    Call uiWorkspace.OpenDatabase("Gonzo/Definiti"_
, "fortisma\cmgr.nsf", "Active
Totals", Customer$, True, True)
    Set uiDoc = uiWorkspace.EditDocument(True)
End Sub
```

To open the document in read mode, specify `False` as the parameter to `EditDocument`. To open a document other than the current document, you can pass this method a Notes document object. The following code is an example:

```
Sub Click(Source As Button)
    Dim uiWorkspace As New NotesUIWorkspace
    Dim uiDoc as NotesUIDocument
    Dim LDB as New NotesDatabase("Gonzo/Definiti","fortisma\cmgr.nsf")
```

```
    Dim Lview as NotesView
    Dim LDoc as NotesDocument
    Set Lview=LDB.GetView("Active")
    Set Ldoc=Lview.GetfirstDocumentbyKey("DigitalProcessingSystems")
    Set uiDoc = uiWorkspace.EditDocument(True,Ldoc)
End Sub
```

N O T E You probably noticed that the previous examples reference some classes that you haven't learned about. They are covered later in this chapter. ▨

You can create new documents in a database by using the ComposeDocument method. For example, the following script creates a sales totals document for the Eastern region whenever you click the button:

```
Sub Click(Source As Button)
    Dim uiWorkspace As New NotesUIWorkspace
    Dim uiDoc as NotesUIDocument
    Set uiDoc = uiWorkspace.ComposeDocument("", "", "SPerson")
    Call uiDoc.FieldSetText("Region", "Eastern")
End Sub
```

Notes 4.5 introduced *profile documents* and along with them, the EditProfile method. You can use EditProfile to create or edit a hidden profile document in the current database. A profile document lets you store and update database-specific information, and it is more dynamic and less archaic than using environment variables in the NOTES.INI file. You open a World Wide Web page by using the URLOpen method. You can specify the URL and some parameters that determine whether to find the latest copy of the Web page. Alternatively, if you don't supply any parameters, URLOpen displays the Open URL dialog box for you to enter the URL you want to open.

EnableAlarms and CheckAlarms let you use the alarm features of Notes Calendaring and Scheduling. EnableAlarms starts the process that monitors alarms. Then, after this process is running, CheckAlarms lets you check whether any alarms are scheduled.

The FindFreeTimeDialog also works with the Calendaring and Scheduling capabilities of Notes to allow you to perform free time searches by using the Notes Free Time dialog box.

You can use the DialogBox method to really spice up your user interfaces. Use the method either to display the current document or to build a special form that should be displayed in a dialog box. This is really useful when the form contains a single layout region because, in this case, the form behaves just like a standard dialog box. You fill in the fields and click OK or Cancel when you finish. The neat part is that if the form you specify has any field names in common with the current document, the contents of those fields appears in the dialog box. If the user changes the contents of any of the fields and clicks OK, the corresponding fields in the current document are updated.

To see a good example of how a form is displayed in a dialog box, create a new memo in your Mail database and click the Delivery Options button. The Delivery Options form is displayed in a dialog box, and the values you enter are updated in the memo when you click OK.

Part

III

Ch

19

The UseLSX method allows you to load LotusScript Extension (LSX) extension files. You can also accomplish this in the Options area of a module by using the UseLSX directive. You will learn more about using LSXs in Bonus Chapter 1, "ODBC and Lotus Components," on the CD-ROM.

The last method in the NotesUIWorkspace class is ViewRefresh. You use ViewRefresh to refresh either the view that is currently displayed or, if a document is currently displayed, the view from which the document was selected. Refreshing a displayed view is straightforward; just call ViewRefresh and you're finished. The steps get a little more complicated when you want to refresh a view from within a newly created document because you first need to refresh the back-end view, using the Refresh method of the NotesView class, so that the new document is included in the view. Then you need to refresh the front-end view by using the NotesUIWorkspace ViewRefresh method so the updated view is displayed.

Table 19.1 lists the properties of NotesUIWorkspace, whereas Table 19.2 lists the methods.

Table 19.1 *NotesUIWorkspace* **Properties**

Property	Description	Data Type	Usage
CurrentDocument	The document that is currently being displayed.	NotesUIDocument	Read Only
CurrentCalendar DateTime	Date and time of the current region in a calendar view.	Variant of type Date	Read Only

Table 19.2 *NotesUIWorkspace* **Methods**

Method	Description	Return Data Type	Return Value
AddDatabase	Add a database to the workspace.	None	None
CheckAlarms	Check for new alarms in the mail database.	None	None
Compose Document	Create a new UI document in a specified database by using a specified form, and display it in edit mode.	NotesUIDocument	The new UI document
DialogBox	Display a dialog box with OK and Cancel buttons that contains current document displayed by using a form you specify.	Boolean	True if the user clicks OK on the dialog box

Method	Description	Return Data Type	Return Value
EditDocument	Use True to open the current document in edit mode. Use False to open it in read mode.	NotesUIDocument	The UI document just opened
EditProfile	Create a new profile document or open an existing profile document in edit mode.	None	None
EnableAlarms	Set to True to start the background process that checks for alarms.	Boolean	True if the process is enabled
FindFreeTime Dialog	Launch the Free Time Search dialog box, which allows you to perform free time searches in the Notes Calendaring and Scheduling system.	None	None
OpenDatabase	Open a database at a specified view and optionally highlight a specific document.	None	None
URLOpen	Open a Uniform Resource Locator (URL).	None	None
UseLSX	Open an LSX.	None	None
ViewRefresh	Refresh the current view.	None	None

Working with the *NotesUIDocument* Class

The NotesUIDocument class lets you work with the active document—that is, the document that is currently open on your workspace or highlighted in a view. You use this class to do the following:

- Update the contents of the fields in a document
- Position the cursor within a document
- Create and manipulate objects
- Change how a document is displayed
- Mail, forward, or delete a document

N O T E In the world of Notes databases, discrete data elements stored in a document are normally referred to as *items,* while the term *fields* refers to the data entry fields on a form. Understanding this distinction will help you as you work through this chapter. ∎

Part
III

Ch
19

Take a look at these options in more detail. Table 19.3 lists all properties of the
NotesUIDocument class, and Table 19.4 lists its methods.

Table 19.3   *NotesUIDocument* Properties

Property	Description	Data Type	Usage
AutoReload	Set to True to automatically update the currently displayed document to reflect any changes that have been made to its associated back-end document. Read to check the current setting.	Boolean	Read/Write
CurrentField	Designate the name of the field in which the cursor is.	String	Read Only
DialogBox Canceled	Indicates how a user exited a dialog box. Set to True if user pressed ESC or clicked cancel, and set to False if user clicked OK.	Boolean	Read Only
Document	The back-end document associated with the current UI document.	NotesDocument	Read Only
EditMode	Set to True to put the current UI document into edit mode or read to check whether the current UI document is in edit mode.	Boolean	Read/Write
FieldHelp	Set to True (when the UI document is in edit mode) to display field help. Read to check whether field help is currently displayed.	Boolean	Read/Write
HiddenChars	Set to True (when the UI document is in edit mode) to display hidden formatting characters. Read to check the current setting.	Boolean	Read/Write
HorzScrollBar	Set to True to display the horizontal scroll bar. Read to check whether the horizontal scroll bar is shown.	Boolean	Read/Write

Property	Description	Data Type	Usage
InPreviewPane	True if the document is currently displayed in the preview pane.	Boolean	Read Only
IsNewDoc	Set to True if the document has never been saved.	Boolean	Read Only
PreviewDocLink	Set to True to display the preview pane for a link. Read to check whether the preview pane is shown.	Boolean	Read/Write
PreviewParent Doc	Set to True to display the parent of the current UI document in the preview pane. Read to check whether the preview pane is shown.	Boolean	Read/Write
Ruler	Set to True to display the ruler. Read to check whether the ruler is shown.	Boolean	Read/Write
WindowTitle	Use for the window title for the current displayed document.	String	Read Only

Table 19.4 *NotesUIDocument* **Methods**

Method	Description	Return Data Type	Return Value
Categorize	Put the document into a category.	None	None
Clear	In edit mode only, delete the currently selected text, graphics, or object.	None	None
Close	Close the current UI document.	None	None
CollapseAll Sections	Collapse all the sections in the currently open UI document.	None	None
Copy	Copy the currently selected text, graphics, or object to the clipboard.	None	None
CreateObject	For a UI document in edit mode with the cursor in a rich text field, create an OLE or ActiveX object.	Variant	A handle to the newly created object

Part
III

Ch
19

continues

Table 19.4   Continued

Method	Description	Return Data Type	Return Value
Cut	In edit mode only, cut the currently selected text, graphics, or object from the document and place it on the clipboard.	None	None
DeleteDocument	In read mode only, mark the document for deletion and then close the document.	None	None
DeselectAll	Deselect any currently selected text, graphics, or objects.	None	None
ExpandAll Sections	Expand all the sections in the currently open UI document.	None	None
FieldAppend Text	In edit mode only, append the supplied text to the contents of a named field (or the current field if no name is supplied).	None	None
FieldClear	In edit mode only, clear the contents of a named field (or the current field if no name is supplied).	None	None
FieldContains	Set to True if a named field (or the current field if no name is supplied) contains the specified text.	Boolean	True if the field contains the text you specified
FieldGetText	Get the contents of a named field (or the current field if no name is supplied). Convert the contents into a text string.	String	The contents of the field converted into a text string
FieldSetText	In edit mode only, set the contents of a named field (or the current field if no name is supplied) to the supplied value. Automatically convert the supplied value to the correct type for the field.	None	None
FindFreeTime Dialog	Display the Free Time dialog box.	None	None

Method	Description	Return Data Type	Return Value
Forward	Create a mail memo containing the currently open UI document.	None	None
GetObject	Given the name of an OLE or ActiveX object, return a handle to the object found.	Variant	A handle to the object
GotoBottom	In edit mode only, put the cursor in the last editable field.	None	None
GotoField	In edit mode only, put the cursor in the named field.	None	None
GotoNextField	In edit mode only, put the cursor in the next editable field below and to the right of the current cursor position.	None	None
GotoPrevField	In edit mode only, put the cursor in the next editable field above and to the left of the current cursor position.	None	None
GotoTop	In edit mode only, put the cursor in the first editable field.	None	None
InsertText	In edit mode only, insert the supplied text at the current cursor position.	None	None
NavBarSetText	Use to set the text of the URL navigation bar of the Internet Explorer browser.	None	None
NavBarSpinnerStart	Starts the URL navigation bar spinner for an Internet Explorer browser.	None	None
NavBarSpinnerStop	Stops the URL navigation bar spinner for an Internet Explorer browser.	None	None
Paste	In edit mode only, paste the contents of the clipboard at the current cursor position.	None	None
Print	Print the current document. Optionally, display the File Print dialog box.	None	None

Part

III

Ch

19

continues

Table 19.4   Continued

Method	Description	Return Data Type	Return Value
Refresh	In edit mode only, compute all the formulas for the computed fields in the document.	None	None
RefreshHide Formulas	Compute all the hide-when formulas in the document.	None	None
Reload	In edit mode, update the UI document with any changes that have been made to the associated back-end document.	None	None
Save	In edit mode only, save the document.	None	None
SaveNewVersion	In edit mode only, save the document as a new version (provided the document's form has the appropriate version options enabled).	None	None
SelectAll	In edit mode, select the contents of the current field. In read mode, select the contents of the entire document.	None	None
Send	Mail the document.	None	None

Updating Fields

The NotesUIDocument class lets you access the data stored in the fields within a document. Depending on what you want to do, you can use two groups of methods: those starting with Field and those starting with Goto. The Field methods are most useful when you need to refer to a field by name. If you know the position of the field within the document or you want to move the cursor within the document, use the Goto methods.

Look at the Field methods first. There are five of them, and each expects you to supply a field name as its first parameter. A nice twist is that if you supply a blank field name, the method assumes you're referring to the current field. You can find the name of the current field by querying the CurrentField property. After you identify a field, you can get its contents with the FieldGetText method. This returns the contents of the field you specify, converted to a text string. If you want to change the contents of a field, use FieldSetText, FieldAppendText, or FieldClear. FieldSetText replaces the current contents of the field with the text you supply. FieldAppendText is similar, but it appends the text to the current value of the field rather than replacing the value. FieldClear deletes the contents of the field. If you need to check whether a field contains a specific text value, use `FieldContains`. You supply the field name and a value for which to look, and the method returns `True` if the value occurs anywhere within the field. For example, when added to the `QuerySave` event of a form containing two editable text fields, Title and Priority, the following script checks whether the Title field contains the word Urgent and, if it does, the script sets the field Priority to High:

```
Sub QuerySave(Source As Notesuidocument, Continue As Variant)
    If source.FieldContains("Title", "Urgent") Then
        Call source.FieldSetText("Priority", "High")
    End If
End Sub
```

The other way of working with fields is to move the cursor into a field and then work with its contents. Five methods let you do this. If you know the name of the field where you want to put the cursor, use the `GotoField` method. You supply the name of the field, and the method places the cursor in that field. `GotoTop` moves the cursor to the first editable field in the document, whereas its companion, `GotoBottom`, places the cursor in the last editable field. If you want to navigate through the fields in a document, use `GotoNextField`; use `GotoPrevField` to move the cursor from field to field.

 T I P   The document must be in edit mode for the previous methods to work.

After the cursor is in a field, you can use any of the `Field` methods with a blank field name to work with the field contents. Alternatively, you can use `InsertText`, or you can use a combination of the `SelectAll` method and the clipboard methods `Cut`, `Copy`, `Paste`, and `Clear`.

Use `InsertText` to add text into a field at the current cursor position. To copy the contents of the current field to the clipboard, use `SelectAll` to highlight the field contents, and then use `Cut` or `Copy` to copy the contents to the clipboard. After you have some data on the clipboard, you can use `Paste` to paste the clipboard data into a field. If you want to delete the contents of the field, use the `Clear` method.

The following button script, when executed in a form containing two fields, Title and History, selects and then copies the contents of the first editable field, Title, to the History field and then appends the current date to the History field. Make sure that you enter some text into the Title field; otherwise, there is nothing to select, and you get an error.

```
Sub Click(Source as Button)
    Dim uiWorkspace As New NotesUIWorkspace
    Dim uiDoc As NotesUIDocument
    Set uiDoc = uiWorkspace.CurrentDocument
    Call uiDoc.GotoTop
    Call uiDoc.SelectAll
    Call uiDoc.Copy
    Call uiDoc.GotoField("History")
    Call uiDoc.Paste
    Call uiDoc.InsertText(" " & Date$)
End Sub
```

Part
III

Ch
19

NOTE You can also use the back-end classes to update the fields on the current form. The following example briefly demonstrates how you can work with both types of classes.

```
Sub Click(Source As Button)
    Dim uiWorkspace As New NotesUIWorkspace
    Dim uiDoc As NotesUIDocument
    Set uiDoc = uiWorkspace.CurrentDocument
    uiDoc.Autoreload=False
    Dim Doc as NotesDocument
    Set Doc= uiDoc.Document
    If Doc.Status(0)="Hold" Then
        Doc.Priority="High"
        Call uiDoc.reload
    End IF

End Sub
```

In the preceding example, you obtain a handle to the back-end document by accessing the document property of the UIDocument. Then if the Status item is set to "Hold", the Priority field is set to "High". The Reload method of UIDocument is called to update the field in the form with the data from the underlying items. You will learn more about this later in this chapter. ■

Working with OLE Objects

A powerful feature of the NotesUIDocument class is its capability to work with OLE objects. When a document is in edit mode with the cursor in a rich text field, you can use the CreateObject method to create and insert a new OLE object. If you don't supply any parameters to the method, Notes displays the Create Object dialog box so you can choose from the list the type of object to create. Alternatively, you can supply parameters to define the type of object to create. The first parameter is the name of the new object. You can use this name later to refer to the object from within a script. Then, depending on the type of object you want to create, you specify either the type of object or the path to the file containing the object.

For example, to automatically create a new Lotus Project Scheduler Component whenever a new document is created, use the following:

```
Sub PostOpen(source As NotesUIDocument)
 Dim objNewSchedule As Variant
     If source.IsNewDoc Then 'the isNewdoc property tells you if a document has
been saved
         Source.GotoField("Body")
         Set objNewSchedule = source.CreateObject("Project Schedule",
"Lotus.Project.1","")
     End If

End Sub
```

The previous code automatically creates the new scheduler component in the first rich text field in the document.

To create an Excel Spreadsheet object from an existing file, in a rich text field called Sheet in an open document, use the following button script:

```
Sub Click(Source As Button)
    Dim uiWorkspace As New NotesUIWorkspace
    Dim uiDoc As NotesUIDocument
    Set uiDoc = uiWorkspace.CurrentDocument
    Call uiDoc.GotoField("Sheet")
    Call uiDoc.CreateObject("Expenses", "", "C:\EXPENSES.XLS")
End Sub
```

N O T E With CreateObject, you supply either the object type or the filename, not both. ▪

If a document contains an object, you can get the OLE handle to the OLE object by using the GetObject method. You supply the name of the object; either the method returns the handle to it, or the method returns Nothing if it cannot find the object.

For example, to manipulate the Excel spreadsheet you created in the last example, use the following:

```
Dim uiWorkspace As New NotesUIWorkspace
Dim uiDoc As NotesUIDocument
Dim objSheet As Variant
Set uiDoc = uiWorkspace.CurrentDocument
Set objSheet = uiDoc.GetObject("Expenses")
```

Changing How the Document Is Displayed

You can set a number of properties to change how the current document is displayed. You can turn field help on or off by using the FieldHelp property. Set the Ruler property to show or hide the ruler, and HorzScrollBar to add or remove the scroll bar at the bottom of the document. When you need to show or hide the preview pane, you can use either PreviewDocLink or PreviewParentDoc, as appropriate. You can check whether the document is displayed in the preview pane by checking its InPreviewPane property.

Part
III

Ch
19

N O T E The PreviewParent property has a corresponding @Command, ShowHideParentPreview, that lets you show and hide the preview pane. ▪

If you need to switch the document from read to edit mode, or vice versa, set the EditMode property. After the document is in edit mode, you can use the HiddenChars property to have fields display their formatting characters, such as carriage returns and tabs.

You can also set the title that Notes displays for the document by using the WindowTitle property.

Several of the NotesUIDocument properties and methods deal with how and when the document is updated. The AutoReload property is used to make sure that the displayed document is always refreshed whenever its corresponding back-end document changes. The default for AutoReload is True, so unless you change it, your document is always kept in step with its back-end document (while the document is in edit mode). If you set AutoReload to False, you need to use the Reload method to update the displayed document so that it includes any changes that have been made to its back-end document.

> **N O T E** Reload does not update the look of any rich text items that were changed in the back-end document until you close and reopen the document. ▪

The Refresh method recalculates all the computed fields in the document, just as if you had pressed F9. The RefreshHideFormulas method recalculates all the hide-when formulas for the current document. You typically use RefreshHideFormulas when a value has changed in the document that may affect how you want to display the document. For example, you may want to show or hide a section within a document, depending on the value of a field. When that field value changes, call RefreshHideFormulas to make sure that the section is shown or hidden, as appropriate.

You can also change the way all sections within the current document are displayed by using the CollapseAllSections and ExpandAllSections methods. You will not get any prizes for guessing what these methods do!

If you use Microsoft's Internet Explorer, you can use the NavBarSetText method to populate the Address box with a URL, and you can use the NavBarSpinnerStart and NavBarSpinnerStop methods to start and stop the navigation bar spinner. These three methods are new to Notes 4.6.

Working with the Document

After you open a document, what can you do with it? To start you can check whether it's a new document by using the IsNewDoc property. The property returns True if the document has never been saved to disk. You can print the document by using the Print method. You can have Notes display the File Print dialog box by calling the method with no parameters. Alternatively, you can supply parameters for the number of copies to print, for the start and end pages, and whether to print in draft mode. If you use these parameters, Notes prints your document without displaying the File Print dialog box.

You can categorize the document by using Categorize. You supply the name of a category, and the method places the document in that category. If the document is mail-enabled—that is, the document contains a SendTo field—you can use Send to mail it to the list of recipients in the SendTo field. If the document contains a CopyTo or BlindCopyTo field, the recipients named in these fields are also mailed a copy of the document. You can forward a copy of the document by using the Forward method. Forward creates a new mail memo containing the document, and you complete and mail the memo as you would any other mail memo.

After you finish with the document, you can close it by calling the Close method. If you made any changes to the document, Notes asks whether you would like to save your changes. If you no longer want the document, you can delete it, provided that the document is in read mode, by using the DeleteDocument method. This method closes the document and marks it for deletion, the same way you mark documents for deletion in a view. The document is deleted only when you refresh the view or when you exit from the database and choose to delete marked documents.

Saving Your Changes

After you have finished making changes to a document, two methods let you save your changes. The Save method saves the document to disk in exactly the same way as choosing File, Save from the menu. The SaveNewVersion method saves a new version of the document. For SaveNewVersion to work, the document's form must have the following settings:

■ Versioning must be switched on—that is, the Versioning setting for the form must be one of the following:

New versions become responses

Prior versions become responses

New versions become siblings

■ Versions must be created manually—that is, the Create Versions setting must be Manual—with File, New Version.

If both these conditions are met, SaveNewVersion creates a new version of the appropriate type.

Working with the *NotesUIView* Class

The NotesUIView class was introduced in Notes 4.5, and the class represents the currently displayed view. NotesUIView has only one method (which is new to Notes 4.6), SelectDocument, which when passed a valid NotesDocument object, will select that document in the view. Its three properties are shown in Table 19.5.

Table 19.5 *NotesUIView* Properties

Property	Description	Data Type	Usage
CalendarDateTime	Only applicable in calendar views; the date and time of the selected area.	Variant of type Date	Read Only
Documents	A collection of all the documents in the current view.	Notes Document Collection	Read Only
View	The back-end view that corresponds to the current view.	NotesView	Read Only

CalendarDateTime is designed to be used with the calendar view. It returns a string containing the date and time associated with the area that is currently selected in the calendar view. The Documents property returns a NotesDocumentCollection object that contains all the documents in the view. You use the View property to access the back-end NotesView object that corresponds to the view with which you are working.

Working with the *NotesUIDatabase* Class

The NotesUIDatabase class represents the Notes database that is currently open. It has only one method, OpenView. When passed a valid view name, this method opens that view. OpenView does not return a value. Its two properties are displayed in Table 19.6.

Table 19.6 *NotesUIDatabase* **Properties**

Property	Description	Data Type	Usage
Database	The back-end database that corresponds to the current database.	NotesDatabase	Read Only
Documents	A collection of all the documents in the current database.	NotesDocument-Collection	Read Only

The Database and Documents properties let you access some of the back-end objects that correspond to the current database.

Working with the *NotesSession* Class

This section looks at the first back-end class, NotesSession. The NotesSession class is the parent of all the back-end classes and represents the environment of the current script.

You can use NotesSession classes to answer the following questions about the current script:

- In which database is the script running?
- Is the script running on a Notes server or workstation?
- If running on a server, what is the server name?
- If running on a workstation, who is the current user?
- On what version of Notes is the script running?
- On what platform is it running?
- For agents, when was the agent last run, what happened, and was any data saved?

Table 19.7 lists all properties of the NotesSession class, and Table 19.8 shows its methods. You can use NotesSession methods to do the following:

- Read and write to environment variables in the NOTES.INI file
- Open databases
- Create other Notes objects, such as NotesDateTime, NotesLog, NotesNewsletter, and NotesDBDirectory
- Mark documents as having been processed by an agent

The next section explains how to find the current database.

Table 19.7 *NotesSession* **Properties**

Property	Description	Data Type	Usage
AddressBooks	The address books that are available to the current script.	Array of Notes Databases	Read Only
CommonUserName	The common name part of the person or server running the script.	String	Read Only
CurrentAgent	The agent, if any, that is currently running.	NotesAgent	Read Only
CurrentDatabase	The database in which the script is located.	Notes Database	Read Only
DocumentContext	For agents that have been started via the Notes API and have created a document, this property returns the newly created back-end document. This is very useful in Domino (Web) applications.	Notes Document	Read Only
Effective UserName	If on a workstation, the property returns the fully distinguished name of the person running the script. If on a server, the property returns the fully distinguished name of the person who last edited the script.	String	Read Only
International	The international settings for the machine on which the script is running.	NotesInternational	Read Only
IsOnServer	Returns True if the script is running on a server. Returns False if the script is running on a workstation.	Boolean	Read Only
LastExitStatus	For agent scripts only. The status code with which the agent ended the last time it ran.	Integer	Read Only
LastRun	For agent scripts only. The date when the agent last ran.	Variant of type DATE	Read Only
NotesVersion	The release of Notes on which the script is running.	String	Read Only

continues

Table 19.7 Continued

Property	Description	Data Type	Usage
Platform	The type of operating system on which the script is running.	String	Read Only
SavedData	For agent scripts only. A Notes document stored within the database that can be used to store data between executions of the agent.	Notes Document	Read Only
UserName	If on a workstation, returns the common name of the person running the script. If on a server, returns the common name of the person who last edited the script.	String	Read Only

Table 19.8 *NotesSession* Methods

Method	Description	Return Data Type	Return Value
CreateDateRange	Create a new NotesDateRange object.	NotesDateRange	The newly created NotesDateRange object
CreateDateTime	Given a string representing a valid date and NotesDateTime time, create a new NotesDate Time object.	NotesDate Time	The newly created NotesDateTime object
CreateLog	Given a string used to give the log a name, create a new NotesLog object.	NotesLog	The newly created NotesLog object
CreateName	Given a string representing a valid Notes user or server name, creates a new NotesName object. If an abbreviated or hierarchical canonical name is not used, a flat name is assumed. NotesName is the newly created NotesName object.		
CreateNewsletter	Given a NotesDocument Collection object, create a new NotesNewsletter object.	NotesNewsletter	The newly created NotesNewsletter object

Method	Description	Return Data Type	Return Value
CreateRich TextStyle	Creates a new NotesRich TextStyle object.	NotesRich TextStyle	The newly created NotesRich TextStyle object
CreateTimer	Create a new NotesTimer object.	NotesTimer	The newly created NotesTimer object
FreeTimeSearch	Search for free time slots for Calendaring and Scheduling.	NotesDateRange	An array of NotesDateRange objects that represent the available free slots
GetDatabase	Given the server and file-name for a database, create a new NotesDatabase object that can be used to access the database and, if possible, open the database.	NotesDatabase	The newly created NotesDatabase object
GetDbDirectory	Given the name of a server, create a new NotesDbDirectory object that can be used to list the databases on the server.	NotesDbDirectory	The newly created NotesDbDirectory object
GetEnvironment String	Given the name of a string environment variable, get its value. When running on a server, get the value from the server's NOTES.INI. When running on a workstation, use the current user's NOTES.INI.	Variant	The value of the environment variable
GetEnvironment Value	As in GetEnvironmentString but for a numeric environment variable.	Variant	The value of the environment variable
SetEnvironment Var	Given the name of an environment variable and a new value, store the new value in the appropriate NOTES.INI file. When running on a server, use the server's NOTES.INI. When running on a workstation, use the current user's NOTES.INI.	None	None
UpdateProcessed Doc	For agent scripts only, mark a document as having been processed by an agent.	None	None

Part

III

Ch

19

Finding the Current Database

One of the most common uses of the NotesSession class is to get the name of the current database—that is, the one in which the script is running. The CurrentDatabase property returns a NotesDatabase object representing the database in which the script is running.

The following example displays the name of the database in which the script is run:

```
Dim s As New NotesSession
Dim db as NotesDatabase
Set db = s.CurrentDatabase
MessageBox"This script is running in the database " & db.Title, 64, "Testing"
```

Using CurrentDatabase is a useful technique because you don't have to hard-code the name of the database into your script.

Finding Where a Script Is Running

Use the NotesSession class IsOnServer property when you need to know whether your script is running on a server or a workstation. If your script is running on a server, IsOnServer returns True.

For example, if an agent must be run on a server, the following code displays an appropriate message if you attempt to run it on a workstation:

```
Dim s As New NotesSession
Dim db as NotesDatabase
If Not s.IsOnServer Then
MessageBox"This script must be run on a server.", 16, "Error"
End If
```

Checking Who Is Running the Script

The NotesSession class gives you three slightly different ways to find out the name of the person or server running a script.

The UserName property returns the fully distinguished name of the current user. For scripts running on a workstation, the current user is the person currently logged on to Notes at the workstation. For scripts running on a server, the current user is always the server. Use this property when it is important that you have the fully distinguished name of the current user.

For example, when I manually run an agent script from the agent menu on my workstation, UserName returns Dave Hatter/Definiti. If I change the script so that it is triggered on an hourly schedule and, therefore, runs on the server, UserName returns Aegis/Definiti.

When you need only the common name part of a user's name, use the CommonUserName property. As its name suggests, this property returns just the common name part of the current user's name. When I manually run an agent from the agent menu on my workstation, CommonUserName returns Dave Hatter; when I run the same agent on a server, it returns Aegis.

The third property that allows you to find out a username is the EffectiveUserName property. For scripts running on workstations, this returns exactly the same value as the UserName property. The difference occurs for scripts running on servers where EffectiveUserName returns the fully distinguished name of the last user to edit the script.

Checking How Notes Is Set Up

You can find out both the type of operating system and the release of Notes on which your script is running. The Platform property lets you find the type of operating system. As with many of the other NotesSession properties, Platform gives you a different answer depending on where the script is running. For scripts running on a workstation, Platform returns the type of workstation operating system. For scripts running on a server, Platform returns the type of server operating system.

> **N O T E** Platform does not return the full details of the operating system. For example, Platform returns UNIX for all flavors of UNIX, including AIX, Sun, HP-UX, and SCO. ▪

Use the NotesVersion property of NotesSession to find out on which release of Notes the script is running. For example, the following script displays Notes Release 4.6 ¦September 19, 1997 in a simple message box.

```
Sub Click(Source As Button)
    Dim s As New NotesSession
    Messagebox "Your version of Notes is: " & s.NotesVersion, 64, "Testing"
End Sub
```

You can use the International property to check the current international settings, such as the currency symbol and date/time format.

Reading and Writing to Environment Variables

The NotesSession class contains three methods to give you access to Notes environment variables stored in the NOTES.INI or Preferences file. If your script is running on a server, the server's NOTES.INI is used; otherwise, the current user's NOTES.INI is used.

You return an environment variable by using either GetEnvironmentString or GetEnvironmentValue. Use GetEnvironmentString to return a string environment variable and GetEnvironmentValue to get a numeric environment variable. With each method, you supply the name and type of the environment variable, and the method returns the value. There are two types of environment variables: user variables and system variables. User variable names start with a dollar sign; system variable names don't. The following code demonstrates reading the Notes data directory (a system variable) and user variable named LastUser.

```
Dim S as new NotesSession
Dim vDataDir as Variant, vLastUser As Variant
vDataDir=S.GetEnvironmentString("Directory",True)
vLastUser= S.GetEnvironmentString("LastUser", False)
MsgBox "Notes Data Directory is: " & VdataDir & " Last User was: " & vLastUser,
64, "Testing"
```

Use SetEnvironmentVar to create a new system or user environment variable or to change the value of an existing one. You supply the name of the variable and its new value, which must be a string, an integer, or a date. Additionally, you can supply a boolean value that indicates if this should be a system or user variable. If `false`, the variable starts with a "`$`" to indicate a user environment variable. The method converts the supplied value into a text string and writes the text string to the NOTES.INI file with the name you supplied.

Opening Databases

Use the `GetDatabase` method with a server and filename to open an existing database. Provided the database exists on the specified server with the correct filename, a new `NotesDatabase` object is created and opened. If, for any reason, the database cannot be found, the method returns a closed `NotesDatabase` object. The `GetDbDirectory` method is useful when you need to process a set of databases in the data directory. When supplied with the name of a server, the method returns a `NotesDbDirectory` object, which points to the Notes data directory on that server. You can then use methods in the `NotesDbDirectory` and `NotesDatabase` classes to process the databases in the directory.

If you are writing LotusScript code that can run on either a client or a server, you can use the following to make your code more portable:

```
Dim S as New NotesSession
Dim LDB as NotesDatabase
Set LDB=S.GetDatabase(S.CurrentDatabase.Server,"cmgr.nsf")
```

This code uses the `Server` property of the `CurrentDatabase` object as the server parameter of the `GetDatabase` method. If the current database resides on a client, the `Server` property returns " " (empty string); otherwise, the property returns the name of the server. This makes your code more portable and more maintainable because you are not hard-coding the server name. You will learn more about the properties and methods of the `NotesDatabase` object later in this chapter.

Working with Agents

One of the useful features of the `NotesSession` class is its capability to store information from the last time an agent ran. In this way, you can build a history of what an agent has done.

You can use three properties from a LotusScript agent to get information about the last time the agent ran.

The `LastRun` property returns the date the agent was last executed, or `12/30/1899` if the agent has never run before. The following script checks whether an agent has been run before:

```
Sub Initialize
    Dim s As New NotesSession
    Dim datLastRun as Variant, Msg AS String
    datLastRun = s.LastRun
    If datLastRun = CDat("12/30/1899") Then
        Msg$="This agent has not been run before."
    Else
        Msg$="This script was last run on " & CStr(datLastRun)
    End If
    MessageBox Msg$, 64, "Agent Information"
End Sub
```

The LastExitStatus property is the exit code that the Agent Manager returned the last time the current agent ran. If the agent ran without any errors, LastExitStatus is 0.

The SavedData property returns a NotesDocument object that the current agent can use to store data. This is how you save information between runs. For example, suppose that an agent runs every night to check whether anyone has been added to or removed from the ACL for a database. The names of the people in the ACL can be stored in the SavedData document each time the agent runs so that the agent can then check the saved names against the current names.

NotesSession also has one agent-related method—the UpdateProcessedDoc method. This is used with some of the methods and properties of the NotesDatabase class to ensure that documents get processed by the agent only once. We will look at an example of how to use UpdateProcessedDoc later in the "NotesDatabase" section.

Working with Other Notes Objects

You can create several other Notes objects by using methods in the NotesSession class. Use CreateDateRange, CreateDateTime, CreateLog, CreateName, CreateRichTextStyle and CreateNewsletter to create NotesDateRange, NotesDateTime, NotesLog, and NotesNewsletter objects. We will cover these objects in more detail later in the "NotesDateRange," "NotesDateTime," "NotesLog," "NotesName," NotesRichTextStyle," and "NotesNewsletter" sections.

Working with the *NotesDbDirectory* Class

This is one of the easiest classes to understand because it has just one property and three methods. The NotesDbDirectory class represents the Notes data directory on a specific server or workstation, and its main use is for looping through a set of databases of a specific type or that meet certain criteria. For example, you can loop through all the databases on a server that are available for replication.

You create a new NotesDbDirectory object in one of two ways. You can use the GetDbDirectory method of NotesSession, as we saw in the last section, or you can use the New method. You specify the type of database for which you are looking. See Table 19.9 for details.

Table 19.9   Base Types for *NotesDbDirectory*

To Find This Type of Database...	Use This Constant...
Any Notes database	DATABASE
Any Notes database template	TEMPLATE
All Notes databases available for replication	REPLICA_CANDIDATE
All Notes databases that can be a template	TEMPLATE_CANDIDATE

Part
III

Ch
19

After you have a NotesDbDirectory object, you can access the databases in the directory by using GetFirstDatabase and GetNextDatabase. You can use the Name property to find out the name of the server whose directory you are accessing. For example:

```
Sub Click(Source As Button)
    Dim S as New NotesSession
    Dim uiWorkspace As New NotesUIWorkspace
        Dim DbDir As NotesDbDirectory
    Dim db As NotesDatabase
    Dim tDbsAvailToReplicate
    UIWorkspace.Currentdocument.Autoreload=False
    Set DbDir = New NotesDbDirectory(S.CurrentDatabase.Server)
    Set db = DbDir.GetFirstDatabase(REPLICA_CANDIDATE)
    Do While Not (db Is Nothing)
        tDbsAvailToReplicate = tDbsAvailToReplicate + db.Title + Chr(10)
        Set db = DbDir.GetNextDatabase
    Loop
      UIWorkspace.CurrentDocument.Document.ServerName=DbDir.Name
    UIWorkspace.CurrentDocument.Document. DbsAvailToReplicate=
tDbsAvailToReplicate
    Call UIWorkspace.CurrentDocument.reload
End Sub
```

The preceding script uses New to create a new NotesDbDirectory object for the current server. Rather than create a bunch of unnecessary variables, the script uses Notes dotted notation (also called the Extended Class Syntax) to access the back-end NotesDocument object through the Document property of the NotesUIDocument class which is being accessed through the CurrentDocument of the NotesUIWorksapce object. It then opens each database on the server that is available for replication and stores its name in the DbsAvailToReplicate field in the current document using the back-end NotesDocument object. It also uses the Name property to store the name of the server in the ServerName field. The Name property is the only property of the NotesDBDirectory class, and it returns a string value containing the name of the current server. Table 19.10 shows the methods of the NotesDbDirectory class.

Table 19.10 *NotesDbDirectory* **Methods**

Method	Description	Return Data Type	Return Value
GetFirstDatabase	Given a type of database to search for, return the first database of that type. You can search for any database, any template, any database that is allowed to replicate, or any database that can be a template.	NotesDatabase	The first database of the type you specified
GetNextDatabase	Provided you have already used the GetFirstDatabase method, return the next database of the type you specified.	NotesDatabase	The next database of the type you specified

Method	Description	Return Data Type	Return Value
New	Create a new NotesDbDirectory object.	NotesDbDirectory	The newly created object

NotesDatabase

The NotesDatabase class represents a Notes database. You use the class to do the following:

- Create, modify, and delete databases
- Create copies and replicas of databases
- Modify access control lists
- Create documents
- Find documents

The class also gives you access to other classes, such as NotesDocumentCollection, NotesView, and NotesDocument. See Table 19.11 for a list of the properties of the NotesDatabase class. Its methods are listed in Table 19.12.

Table 19.11 *NotesDatabase* **Properties**

Property	Description	Data Type	Usage
ACL	The ACL for the database.	NotesACL	Read Only
Agents	All the agents defined in the database.	Array of NotesAgents	Read Only
AllDocuments	A collection containing all the documents in the database.	NotesDocument Collection	Read Only
Categories	All the categories to which a database belongs.	String	Read Only
Created	The date the database was created.	Variant of type DATE	Read Only
CurrentAccess Level	The ACL access level for the current user.	Integer constant	Read Only
DelayUpdates	True if multiple updates to documents on a server are processed together for better performance.	Boolean	Read/Write
DesignTemplate Name	The name of the design template for the database.	String	Read Only
FileName	The file name and extension of the database.	String	Read Only

Part III

Ch 19

continues

Table 19.11 Continued

Property	Description	Data Type	Usage
FilePath	The full path and file name of the database, including drive letter, directory, filename, and extension.	String	Read Only
Forms	The forms in the database.	Array of NotesForm objects	Read Only
IsFTIndexed	True if the database has a full-text index.	Boolean	Read Only
IsMultiDBSearch	True if the database can search multiple databases.	Boolean	Read Only
IsOpen	True if the database is currently open.	Boolean	Read Only
IsPrivateAddress Book	True if the database is a Personal Address Book.	Boolean	Read Only
IsPublicAddress Book	True if the database is a Public Address Book.	Boolean	Read Only
LastFTIndexed	For databases with a full-text index, the date that the index was last updated; 12/30/1899 for databases with no full-text index.	Variant of type DATE	Read Only
LastModified	The date the database was last modified.	Variant of type DATE	Read Only
Managers	All the people, groups, and servers who are managers of the database.	Array of strings	Read Only
Parent	The NotesSession that contains the database.	NotesSession	Read Only
PercentUsed	The percentage of the database that is currently in use.	Double	Read Only
ReplicaID	The 16-character replica ID for the database.	String	Read Only
Server	The name of the server on which the database is stored.	String	Read Only
Size	The size, in bytes, of the database.	Double	Read Only

Property	Description	Data Type	Usage
SizeQuota	The maximum size, in bytes, to which the database is allowed to grow.	Long	Read/Write
TemplateName	For databases that are templates, the name of the template. If the database is not a template, returns an empty string.	String	Read Only
Title	The title of the database.	String	Read/Write
Unprocessed Documents	All the documents that are considered to be unprocessed by the script.	Notes Document Collection	Read Only
Views	All the public views and folders within the database. If the database is stored locally, personal folders are included.	Array of NotesViews	Read Only

Table 19.12 *NotesDatabase* Methods

Method	Description	Return Data Type	Return Value
Compact	Compact a local database. Note that you cannot use this method to compact the database in which the script is running.	Long	The number of bytes recovered by compacting the database
Create	Given a server and filename, create a new database on disk.	None	None
CreateCopy	Given a server and filename, create a copy of the database. Give the copy the same title and ACL as the original.	NotesDatabase	A NotesDatabase object representing the newly created copy
CreateDocument	Create a new, empty document in the database. Note that you must save the document before you close the database; otherwise, the document will be lost.	NotesDocument	The newly created document

Part
III

Ch
19

continues

Table 19.12   Continued

Method	Description	Return Data Type	Return Value
CreateFrom Template	Given a server, filename, and the name of a template, create a new database based on the template.	NotesDatabase	A NotesDatabase object representing the newly created database
CreateReplica	Given a server and filename, create a replica copy of the of the database. Give the replica the same title and ACL as the original.	NotesDatabase	A NotesDatabase object representing the newly created database
FTSearch	Given a string representing a valid full-text query, full-text search the database.	Notes Document Collection	A collection of documents matching the query sorted so that the most relevant documents are first in the collection
GetAgent	Get an agent by its name.	NotesAgent	The agent
GetDocumentByID	Given a document's Note ID, find the document.	NotesDocument	The document
GetDocument ByUNID	Similar to GetDocumentByID, but the method uses the UNID.	NotesDocument	The document
GetDocumentByURL	If the database is a Notes Web Navigator database, return the Notes document that corresponds to the Web page with the URL you specify. If required, you can force the Web Navigator database to reload the Web page.	NotesDocument	The document corresponding to the URL
GetForm	Get a form by its name or alias.	NotesForm	The form
GetProfile Document	Get a profile document from the database.	NotesDocument	The profile document
GetURLHeader Info	Given an URL and header string for Web Navigator databases, return the requested URL header information.	String	The header information
GetView	Given either the name or the alias of a view or folder, return the view or folder.	NotesView	The requested view or folder

Method	Description	Return Data Type	Return Value
GrantAccess	Change the ACL for the database to give a person, group, or server a specified access level.	None	None
New	Create a new Notes Database object. Note that this method does not create a new database on disk.	NotesDatabase	The newly created object
Open	Given a server and filename, open an existing database.	Boolean	True if the database was found and successfully opened
OpenByReplicaID	Similar to Open, but use the supplied server name and replica ID to find the database	Open	True if the database was found and successfully opened
OpenIfModified	Given a server, filename, and date, open an existing database, only if it has been modified since the date you specified.	Boolean	True if the database was found and successfully opened
OpenMail	Open the current user's mail database.	None	None
OpenURLDb	Open the default Web Navigator database.	Boolean	True if the database was found and successfully opened
OpenWithFailover	Given a server and filename, attempt to open the database. If the database cannot be opened and the server is in a server cluster, attempt to open a replica of the database on another server in the cluster.	Boolean	True if the database was found and successfully opened
QueryAccess	Given the name of a person, group, or server, return their access level to the database.	Integer constant	The access level
Remove	Delete the database.	None	None
Replicate	Given a server name, replicate the database with its replica copy on that server.	Boolean	True if the database replicated successfully

continues

Part

III

Ch

19

Table 19.12   Continued

Method	Description	Return Data Type	Return Value
RevokeAccess	Remove a person, group, or server from the ACL for the database.	None	None
Search	Given a Notes selection formula and a cut-off date, search the database for all documents that match the formula.	Notes Document Collection	All the documents that match the formula and have been modified since the cut-off date
Unprocessed FTSearch	For agent scripts only, the same as FTSearch, except that only those documents that the agent considers unprocessed are searched.	Notes Document Collection	The documents
Unprocessed Search	For agent scripts only, the same as Search, except that only those documents that the agent considers unprocessed are searched.	Notes Document Collection	The documents
UpdateFTIndex	For any database with a full-text index, update the index. For local database, create the index, if necessary.	None	None

Creating a Database

The NotesDatabase class gives you several methods with which you can create a new database on disk. The most straightforward is Create, which creates a new blank database. You specify the server and filename to use and whether to open the database after it has been created.

N O T E A database has to be open before you can use the majority of its properties or methods. You can test the IsOpen property in your script to determine whether a database is open. ■

After you create a new database or open an existing one, you can use any of the following methods to create new databases based on the original: CreateCopy, CreateReplica, or CreateFromTemplate.

Use CreateCopy to create a copy of the current database. The copy contains all the forms, views, and agents of the original, and the copy has the same ACL and same title. You can create a replica of the current database by using the CreateReplica method. You supply a server and filename, and the method creates a replica copy of the database at the new location. If the current database is a template, you can create a new database based on the template by using `CreateFromTemplate`. As with the other methods, you supply a server and filename for the new database. You can also specify that the new database inherits future design changes from the template. The following example uses these methods to create new databases:

```
Dim s As New NotesSession
Dim db As NotesDatabase
Dim dbTemplate As New NotesDatabase("", "report.ntf")
Dim dbReplica As NotesDatabase
Dim dbCopy As NotesDatabase
Dim dbNew as NotesDatabase
Set db = s.CurrentDatabase
 'Create a replica of the current database Set dbReplica = db.CreateReplica("",
"stock.nsf")
 'Create a backup copy of the current database
Set dbCopy = db.CreateCopy("", "backup\stock.nsf")
dbCopy.Title = "Backup of New Stock Control Levels"
 'Create a new database based on a template
Set dbNew = dbTemplate.CreateFromTemplate("", "report.nsf", True)
```

 TIP Scripts running on a server can create or access databases only on that server—all the more reason to use the `Server` property of the `CurrentDatabase` object for the server parameter of any method.

Opening, Closing, and Deleting a Database

Before you can access any of the properties or methods of a database, the database must be open. After you open the database, all its properties and methods are available to you.

You can use the `IsOpen` property to check whether a database is open. If the database is not open, the simplest way to open it is to use the `Open` method. You supply a server and filename, and the database opens—provided it exists—and the script has at least reader access to it. If you know the replica ID of the database, you can use the `OpenByReplicaID` method. This works the same way as the `Open` method, but you supply the replica ID rather than the server and filename. `OpenIfModified` is useful for agents that must periodically check for updates to databases. You supply a server and filename as for `Open`, but, in addition, you supply a `NotesDateTime` object. The database opens only if it has been modified since the date represented by the `NotesDateTime` object. If your Notes servers are configured as part of a server cluster, you can use the new `OpenWithFailover` method to attempt to open a database on one server and, if unsuccessful, automatically try to open a replica of the database on another server in the cluster.

You can also use a couple specialized `Open` methods. `OpenMail` finds and opens the mail database for the current user. As with some other methods, `OpenMail` behaves differently when run on a workstation than when run on a server. On a workstation, the method finds the mail database for the current user. On a server, the method finds the mail database for the last person who modified the script.

If a Notes Web Navigator database has been set up at your location, you can use OpenURLDb to find and open it.

All the open methods return True if the specified database was successfully opened, and the methods return False if the database could not be opened for any reason.

TIP To open a database, your script must have at least reader access to the database. If the script is running on your workstation, you must have reader access to the database you want to open. If the script is running on a server, the server must have reader access to the database.

When your script finishes running, Notes automatically closes all the databases that the script has opened. After a database is closed, you cannot access its properties and methods. Use the Remove method if you want to delete a database.

Working with a Database

After you open a database, a wealth of information is available to you about it. Some properties tell you when it was Created or LastModified. You can get the database's server, filename, and replica ID by using the Server, FilePath, FileName, and ReplicaID properties. You can find its title by using the Title property, and you can check what categories the database belongs to by using the Categories property. The Parent property of a database returns the NotesSession that contains the database.

If you are working with full-text indices, you can check that the database is indexed by using the IsFTIndexed property, or use LastFTIndexed to find the date and time when the index was last updated. You can use the new IsMultiDbSearch method to check whether the database contains a multi-database full-text index. If you need to update the index, you can call the UpdateFTIndex method. You can also use UpdateFTIndex to create a full-text index for a database if the database is stored locally on a workstation. If you try to use UpdateFTIndex on a server-based database that has no full-text index, you get an error. The following script example checks whether a database has a full-text index and creates one if necessary. If the database already has a full-text index, the script updates it only if the database has been modified since the last time the full index was updated:

```
Sub Click(Source As Button)
    Dim s As New NotesSession
    Dim db As NotesDatabase

Set db = s.CurrentDatabase

    If (Not db.IsFTIndexed) Then
        Print "Creating Full Text Index ..."
        Call db.UpdateFTIndex(True)
    End If

    If (db.LastModified > db.LastFTIndexed) Then
        Print "Updating Full Text Index ..."
        Call db.UpdateFTIndex(False)
    End If
```

```
        Print " FT Indexing Complete."
End Sub
```

You can track the size of the database by using the `Size`, `SizeQuota`, and `PercentUsed` properties. `Size` gives you the size of the database in bytes, and `PercentUsed` gives you the percentage of this size that contains data (versus empty space). `SizeQuota` returns the maximum bytes that your Notes administrator has allowed for this database. For example, you can use `Size` and `SizeQuota` to monitor a database and issue a warning if its size approaches the quota limit. Or, if the `PercentUsed` is higher than a certain percentage, you can use the `Compact` method to reclaim the empty space.

 You can compact local databases only by using the `Compact` method. If you run a script on your workstation, you can compact databases only on your workstation. If you need to compact server databases, make sure that you run the script on the server.

If the database is a template, you can find the name of the template by using the `TemplateName` property. Similarly, if the database inherits its design from a template, you can find the name of the template from which it inherits its design by using the `DesignTemplateName` property.

If you are interested in Notes Address Books (well, who isn't!) and have used the `AddressBooks` property of `NotesSession` to get the currently available Address Books, you can check whether each is a Public or Private address book. `IsPublicAddressBook` and `IsPrivateAddressBook` return `True` if the database is of the appropriate type. For example, the following script counts the number of public and private address books currently available.

CAUTION

As of this writing, on a Notes 4.6 client, the `IsPublicAddressBook` property does not work properly. The following example illustrates code that should work after the bug is fixed.

```
Sub Click(Source As Button)
    Dim s As New NotesSession
    Dim iPublicAddressBooks As Integer
    Dim iPrivateAddressBooks As Integer

    Forall NAB In s.AddressBooks
        If BookNAB.IsPublicAddressBook Then
            iPublicAddressBooks% = iPublicAddressBooks% + 1
        End If
        If NAB.IsPrivateAddressBook Then
            iPrivateAddressBooks% = iPrivateAddressBooks% + 1
        End If
    End Forall

Messagebox "This session has" & Str$(iPublicAddressBooks%) & " public address
book(s) and"_ _
& Str$(iPrivateAddressBooks%) & " private address book(s).", 64, "Address Books"
End Sub
```

You can get a list of all the agents in a database by using the Agents property. Actually, what you get is an array of NotesAgent objects. You can then use the properties of the NotesAgent class to display information about each agent. If you know the name of an agent, you can get its corresponding NotesAgent object by using the GetAgent method. In a similar way, you can use the Forms property and the GetForm method to work with forms in the database.

You can force a database to replicate with a specified server by using the Replicate method. You supply the server name, and the method initiates replication and returns True if the replication was successful.

Working with the Access Control List

The NotesDatabase class gives you several methods and properties that let you examine and modify ACL settings for the database. You can get the ACL for the database by using the ACL property. This returns a NotesACL object, which represents the current ACL. You can then use the properties and methods of the NotesACL and NotesACLEntry classes to read and modify the ACL.

Even if you don't use a NotesACL object, you can still work with the ACL for the database. You can use the QueryAccess method to check the access level for a person, group, or server. Give the method a person, group, or server name, and it returns an integer constant that represents the current access level to the database for the name you specified. See Table 19.13 for details.

Table 19.13 Access Level Constants for *NotesACL*

Access Level	Constant
No access	ACLLEVEL_NOACCESS
Depositor	ACLLEVEL_DEPOSITOR
Reader	ACLLEVEL_READER
Author	ACLLEVEL_AUTHOR
Editor	ACLLEVEL_EDITOR
Designer	ACLLEVEL_DESIGNER
Manager	ACLLEVEL_MANAGER

You can use QueryAccess to check whether a user is allowed to perform certain tasks on the database. For example, the following script checks that the current user has at least Editor access to the database:

```
Sub Click(Source As Button)
    Dim s As New NotesSession
    Dim db As NotesDatabase
    Dim iAccessLevel As Integer

    Set db = s.CurrentDatabase
```

```
    IAccessLevel% = db.QueryAccess(s.UserName)

    Select Case iAccessLevel%
        Case ACLLEVEL_MANAGER
            Print "You have Manager access to this database."
        Case ACLLEVEL_DESIGNER
            Print "You have Designer access to this database."
        Case ACLLEVEL_EDITOR
            Print "You have Editor access to this database."
        Case Else
            Print "You  have less than Editor access to this database."
    End Select

End Sub
```

You can find the access level for the current user by using the NotesDatabase CurrentAccessLevel property. This returns the same set of integer constants as QueryAccess. You can also get a list of the names of the people, groups, or servers who have Manager access to the database by using the Managers property. This property returns a list of the names of the managers of the database.

If you need to alter someone's access level, you can either use the ACL property to get the NotesACL object and then use its methods, or you can use the GrantAccess and RevokeAccess methods of NotesDatabase. Use GrantAccess to give a person, group, or server a specified access level. Use RevokeAccess to remove a name from the ACL.

Creating a Notes Document Using the *NotesDatabase* Class

Use CreateDocument to create a new document in the database. This method returns a NotesDocument object, which you can then use to add data to and save the new document. NotesDocument will be covered in detail later in the "*NotesDocument*" section.

Part

III

Ch

19

Finding a Document Using the *NotesDatabase* Class

All documents in Notes databases have two unique numbers that can be used to identify them. The Note ID is an 8-character ID that uniquely identifies a document within a particular database. The Note ID is specific to the database—that is, a copy of the document in a replica database may have a different Note ID. The Universal ID for a document is a 32-character ID that uniquely identifies the document in all replica copies of the database. The NotesDatabase class has methods that let you find a document by either its Note ID or its Universal ID.

Use GetDocumentByID when you know the Note ID and use GetDocumentByUNID if you know the Universal ID.

If the current database is a Web Navigator database, you can use GetDocumentByURL to find a document by its uniform resource locator (URL). For example, to get the latest update of the Lotus home page from the Web Navigator database, you can use the following:

```
Dim s As New NotesSession

Dim LotusHomePage As NotesDocument
 'Assume that the current database is the Web Navigator
```

```
Set LotusHomePage = s.CurrentDatabase.GetDocumentByURL("http://www.lotus.com",
True)
```

If you need to do fancy things with the HyperText Transport Protocol (HTTP) header informa-tion for a Web page, you can use GetURLHeaderInfo to return a specified header value. Supply the URL and the name of the header value you want, and the method returns that header value. If the Web page doesn't contain the requested header, the method returns a null string.

Finding a Group of Documents

You can find every document within a database by using the AllDocuments property. AllDocuments returns a NotesDocumentCollection containing all the documents in the data-base. If you want to find a subset of the documents in the database, you can use two different methods: Search and FTSearch.

If you want to select the documents by using a Notes selection formula, you can use the Search method. You supply Search with the following three parameters:

- A Notes selection formula, such as Form = "Main Topic".
- A NotesDateTime object. Only documents that have been modified since the date specified by the date-time object are included in the search results.
- The number of documents to return (or 0 for all documents).

The method returns a NotesDocumentCollection containing all the documents that match the selection and date criteria.

If it is easier to find the documents you want by using a full-text query, use the FTSearch method. With FTSearch, you supply two parameters: a Notes full-text query and the number of documents to return. The method searches the database and returns a NotesDocumentCollection that contains the matching documents, sorted in order of relevance. Don't worry if the database you want to search isn't full-text indexed; the method still works, albeit much more slowly than if the database is full-text indexed.

N O T E If you use the FTSearch method on a database that is not full-text indexed, you may get mixed results. If possible, create a full-text index for best results.

When you're working with agents and want to further restrict the set of returned documents to include only those documents the agent hasn't already processed, you can use the UnprocessedDocuments property and the UnprocessedSearch and UnprocessedFTSearch meth-ods. Exactly which documents an agent defines as unprocessed varies, depending on how the agent is set up. See the Notes Help database for details on how an agent defines an unproc-essed document.

You can also use the GetView method to find a specific view with the database. After you have the view, you can use the search methods in the NotesView class to find documents within the view—which leads nicely to the next class.

Working with the *NotesView* Class

The NotesView class lets you work with Notes views and folders and the documents they contain.

By using NotesView properties and methods, you can do the following:

- Examine view attributes
- Navigate up and down a view hierarchy
- Search for documents within a view
- Delete a view

See Table 19.14 for all the properties of the NotesView class. Its methods are listed in Table 19.15. Note that you can't create new views within a Notes database from LotusScript; you can access only existing views. You can get a specific view by using the GetView method of NotesDatabase, or you can get all the views in a database via its Views property.

Table 19.14 *NotesView* Properties

Property	Description	Data Type	Usage
Aliases	The aliases for the view.	Array of strings	Read Only
AutoUpdate	Set to True to have the front-end view automatically updated if the back-end view changes.	Boolean	Read/Write
Columns	All the columns in the view or folder.	Array of NotesView Columns	Read Only
Created	The date and time when the view or folder was created.	Variant of type DATE	Read Only
IsCalendar	True if the view is a calendar view.	Boolean	Read Only
IsDefaultView	True if the view is the default view for the database.	Boolean	Read Only
IsFolder	True if the view object represents a folder.	Boolean	Read Only
LastModified	The date and time when the view or folder was last modified.	Variant of type DATE	Read Only

continues

Part
III

Ch
19

Table 19.14 Continued

Property	Description	Data Type	Usage
Name	Result depends on how you accessed the view object—either its name, its alias, or its name and alias.	String	Read Only
Parent	The database that contains the view or folder.	NotesDatabase	Read Only
ProtectReaders	Set to True to protect the $Readers item during replication.	Boolean	Read/Write
Readers	The names of the people, groups, and servers that can read the view.	Array of strings	Read/Write
UniversalID	A 32-character ID that uniquely identifies the view or folder in all replicas of a particular database.	String	Read Only

Table 19.15 *NotesView* Methods

Method	Description	Return Data Type	Return Value
Clear	If a view has been filtered by using a full-text search, reset the view so that all documents are displayed.	None	None
FTSearch	Given a string representing a valid full-text query, full-text search the database and display in the view only those documents that match the query.	Integer	The number of documents that match the query
GetAllDocuments-ByKey	Given a key, find all documents in the view that match the key.	Notes Document Collection	A collection of documents that match the key
GetChild	Given a document within the view, find the first response to the document.	NotesDocument	The first response to the document

Method	Description	Return Data Type	Return Value
GetDocumentByKey	Given a key, find the first document in the view that has the supplied key.	NotesDocument	The first document with the key
GetFirstDocument	Get the first document in the view.	NotesDocument	The first document in the view
GetLastDocument	Get the last document in the view.	NotesDocument	The last document in the view
GetNextDocument	Given any document in the view, find the next document.	NotesDocument	The document
GetNextSibling	Given any document in the view, find the next document at the same level as the supplied document.	NotesDocument	The document
GetNthDocument	Given an index into the view, find the document at that position.	NotesDocument	The document
GetParentDocument	Given any response document in the view, find its parent document.	NotesDocument	The parent document
GetPrevDocument	Given any document in the view, find the previous document.	NotesDocument	The document
GetPrevSibling	Given any document in the view, find the previous document at the same level as the supplied document.	NotesDocument	The document
Refresh	Update the view to show any changes.	None	None
Remove	Delete the view from the database.	None	None

Part
III

Ch
19

Working with View Properties

You can find the name of a view by using the Name property. If you need to find the aliases for the view, you can get them by using the Aliases property. The IsFolder property can be used to determine whether you are working with a folder or a view.

Use Created and LastModified to find out when a view was created and the last time its design was modified. You can check whether a view is the default view in a database by using the IsDefaultView property.

The Columns property gives you access to all the columns within a view or folder. When you read the property, you get an array containing a NotesViewColumn object for each column in the view. You can use Columns in a loop to get all columns, or you can specify an index into the array to get a specific column.

Navigating a View Hierarchy

After you have a view, you can navigate through the documents in the view by using a variety of methods. Use GetFirstDocument and GetNextDocument or GetLastDocument and GetPrevDocument to step through all the documents in the view in the order in which they are displayed. If you want to skip to a document based on its position within the view, use GetNthDocument. The following code fragment demonstrates looping through all the documents in a view:

```
Dim S as New NotesSession
Dim Doc As NotesDocument
Dim View As NotesView
Set View=S.CurrentDatabase.GetView("SalesbyRegion")
Set Doc =View.GetFirstDocument
Do While Not Doc is Nothing
    If Doc.Status(0)="Open"
        Doc.Priority="High"
        Call Doc.Save(True,False)
    End If
Set Doc=View.GetNextDocument(Doc)
Loop
```

If you're working with documents in a response hierarchy, you can use methods to find documents at different levels in the hierarchy. After you find a document, you can use GetChild to get the first response to the document or GetParentDocument to get its parent. To get documents at the same level, use either GetNextSibling or GetPrevSibling.

Finding a Document in a View

Use GetDocumentByKey to find a single document based on the column values that are displayed in a view. You supply a key in the form of an array of strings—one string for each column value you want to compare. The first string in the array is compared with the contents of the first sorted or categorized column, the second string with the next sorted or categorized column, and so on for each string you supply. If all the strings match the column values, the document with those column values is returned.

N O T E   If your key consists of more than one string, each column you compare must be sorted. ■

You can use GetAllDocumentsByKey to retrieve a collection of NotesDocuments from a view. For example, the following code builds a collection of NotesDocuments where the Priority field is set to "High".

```
Dim S as New NotesSession
Dim Doc As NotesDocument
Dim Docs As NotesDocumentCollection
```

```
Dim View As NotesView
Set View=S.CurrentDatabase.GetView("SalesbyRegion")
Set Docs=View.GetAllDocumentsByKey("Northern")
If Docs.Count>0 Then ' ensure that you retrieved at least one document
    Set Doc=Docs.GetFirstDocument
    Do While Not Doc is Nothing
        Doc.Priority="High"
        Call Doc.Save(True,False)
        Set Doc=Docs.GetNextDocument(Doc)
    Loop
End if
```

Searching for Documents in a View

You can use the power of Notes' full-text queries to find a set of documents within a view. The FTSearch method lets you execute a full-text search query on the view. The view is filtered to include only those documents that match the query. You can then use any of the NotesView navigation methods to process documents in the view. To reset the view so that all documents are included, use the Clear method.

Updating a View

Changes to a view—for example, new documents or deletions—are not automatically reflected in the NotesView object. To get the most up-to-date view contents, use the Refresh method.

Deleting a View

You can use Remove to delete a view permanently from a database.

Working with *NotesViewColumn*

The NotesViewColumn object represents a column in a view or folder. Its properties are listed in Table 19.16.

Part

III

Ch

19

Table 19.16 *NotesViewColumn* **Properties**

Property	Description	Data Type	Usage
Formula	If the column uses an @Function or a simple function to calculate the value to display, returns the textual representation of the formula.	String	Read Only
IsCategory	True if the column is categorized.	Boolean	Read Only
IsHidden	True if the column is hidden.	Boolean	Read Only

continues

Table 19.16 Continued

Property	Description	Data Type	Usage
IsResponse	True if the column is a responses-only column.	Boolean	Read Only
IsSorted	True if the column is sorted.	Boolean	Read Only
ItemName	If a column displays a field value, returns the name of the field; otherwise, returns an internally generated name.	String	Read Only
Position	The position of the column in its view. Column numbers start at 1.	Integer	Read Only
Title	The title of the column, if it has one.	String	Read Only

You can't directly update any of the columns, but you can query their properties. You can check the position of a column within a view by using the Position property.

N O T E All column positions start at 1, whereas by default LotusScript array indices start at 0. Remember to add 1 to the array index to get the column position.

The Title property returns the column title, and you can check whether the column is visible by using the IsHidden property. You can check whether the column is sorted or categorized by using IsSorted and IsCategory.

You can check how the column calculates the values it displays by using either Formula or ItemName. Only one of these properties is valid for any particular column. If the column uses a Notes formula to calculate its value, Formula returns the formula as a string. If the column displays the contents of a field, ItemName returns the name of the field.

N O T E NotesViewColumn represents the design of a column. To get the contents of the column for a document, use the ColumnValues property of NotesDocument.

Working with the *NotesDocument* Class

Notes is all about working with documents, and the NotesDocument class is all about working with documents by using LotusScript. The class is rich in function and large in terms of the number of properties and methods it contains, but after you gain a good understanding of how the class works, you're on your way to understanding how to work with Notes documents. Table 19.17 lists the properties for the NotesDocument class, and Table 19.18 lists its methods.

Table 19.17 *NotesDocument* **Properties**

Property	Description	Data Type	Usage
Authors	The names of the people who have saved the document.	Array of strings	Read Only
ColumnValues	For documents retrieved from a view, the values that appear in each view column for the document.	Array of variants	Read Only
Created	The date the document was created.	Variant of type DATE	Read Only
EmbeddedObjects	All the OLE or ActiveX objects within a document.	Array of NotesEmbedded objects	Read Only
EncryptionKeys	The keys used to encrypt the document.	String or array of strings	Read/Write
EncryptOnSend	True if the document is to be encrypted when it is mailed.	Boolean	Read/Write
FTSearchScore	If the document was retrieved by a full-text search, the relevance score.	Integer	Read Only
HasEmbedded	True if the document contains at least one embedded or linked object or file attachment.	Boolean	Read Only
IsNewNote	True if the document has never been saved.	Boolean	Read Only
IsProfile	True if the document is a profile document.	Boolean	Read Only
IsResponse	True if the document is a response to any other document.	Boolean	Read Only
IsSigned	True if the document contains at least one signature.	Boolean	Read Only
IsUIDocOpen	True if this document was accessed from a NotesUIDocument.	Boolean	Read Only
Items	All the items stored within a document.	Array of NotesItems	Read Only
Key	For a profile document, the key for the document.	String	Read Only

Part
III

Ch
19

continues

Table 19.17 Continued

Property	Description	Data Type	Usage
LastAccessed	The date the document was last read or modified.	Variant of type DATE	Read Only
LastModified	The date the document was last modified.	Variant of type DATE	Read Only
NameOfProfile	For a profile document, the name of the profile document.	String	Read Only
NoteID	An 8-character ID that uniquely identifies the document within a particular database.	String	Read Only
ParentDatabase	The database that contains the document.	NotesDatabase	Read Only
ParentDocument UNID	For response documents, a 32-character ID that uniquely identifies the document's parent.	String	Read Only
ParentView	For documents retrieved from a view, the view from which the document was retrieved.	NotesView	Read Only
Responses	The immediate responses to the document.	Notes Document Collection	Read Only
SaveMessageOn Send	True if the document is to be saved when it is mailed.	Boolean	Read/Write
SentByAgent	True if the document was mailed by a script; False if the document was mailed by a person.	Boolean	Read Only
Signer	If a document has been signed, the name of the person who signed the document.	String	Read Only
SignOnSend	True if the document is to be signed when it is mailed.	Boolean	Read/Write
Size	The size of the document in bytes (including any file attachments).	Long	Read Only

Property	Description	Data Type	Usage
UniversalID	A 32-character ID that uniquely identifies the document in all replicas of a particular database.	String	Read Only
Verifier	If a document has been signed, returns the name of the certificate that verified the signature.	String	Read Only

Table 19.18 *NotesDocument* **Methods**

Method	Description	Return Data Type	Return Value
AppendItemValue	Either create a new item in the document and set its value, or append a value to an existing item.	NotesItem	The new item
ComputeWithForm	Execute all the default value, input translation, and validation formulas for the document by using its form.	Boolean	True if all formulas executed successfully
CopyAllItems	Copy all items from the document to another document.	None	None
CopyItem	Copy an item into the current document.	NotesItem	The new item
CopyToDatabase	Copy the document into a database.	NotesDocument	The new document
CreateReply Message	Create a new document, formatted as a reply to the current document.	NotesDocument	The new reply document
CreateRich TextItem	Create a new rich text item in the document.	NotesRichTextItem	The new rich text item
Encrypt	Encrypt the document.	None	None
GetAttachment	Get a named file attachment from the document.	Notes Embedded Object	The file attachment
GetFirstItem	Get the first item with the supplied name from the document.	NotesItem	The item

Part

III

Ch

19

continues

Table 19.18   Continued

Method	Description	Return Data Type	Return Value
GetItemValue	Get the value of the item with the supplied name from the document.	String for rich text items; Array of strings for text or text list items; Array of doubles for numbers, number lists, or datetime items	The value
HasItem	True if the document has an item with the supplied name.	Boolean	True if the item exists
MakeResponse	Make the current document a response to the supplied document.	None	None
PutInFolder	Put the document into the specified folder. Create the folder, if necessary.	None	None
Remove	Delete the document.	Boolean	True if the document was deleted
RemoveFromFolder	Remove the document from the specified folder.	None	None
RemoveItem	Delete all items with the specified name from the document.	None	None
RenderToRTItem	Create a picture of the document and store it in a rich text field.	Boolean	True if the picture was created
ReplaceItemValue	Replace all items that have the specified name with a new item, then assign the new item a value.	NotesItem	The new item
Save	Save any changes to the document. Any of the changes you make to a document take effect only after the document has been saved.	Boolean	True if the document was saved
Send	Mail the document to the specified recipients.	None	None
Sign	Add the current user's signature to the document.	None	None

Creating a Notes Document

You create a new document by using either the CreateDocument method in NotesDatabase or the New method.

Finding a Notes Document

There are many ways to find an existing document. You can use methods in the NotesView and NotesDatabase classes to find documents. Use methods in NotesView to do the following:

- Find a document based on its position within a view or that match a key value

Use methods in NotesDatabase to do the following:

- Find all documents in a database
- Find documents based on their Note ID or Universal ID
- Find documents that match a Notes full-text query
- Find documents selected by a Notes selection formula

If the current document was found by using a Notes full-text search, the FTSearchScore property is set to the relevance score calculated by the search. If the document was retrieved from a view, you can use the ParentView property to find the view that contains the document. The ColumnValues property is another property that gets set only if the document was found in a view. This returns an array representing the values that appear in each column of the parent view for this document.

▶ **See** *"Working with NotesView Class"* and *"NotesDatabase,"* **p. 787 and 775**

The NotesDocument class also has properties that let you find the responses to a document or the parent of a document. You will learn about these later in the section, "Working with Response Documents."

Part III

Ch

19

Working with Document Properties

After you have a document, you can use some of the properties of the NotesDocument class to examine the document. You can tell whether the document has just been created by using the IsNewNote property. If the document has never been saved, the property returns True. Created tells you when the document was created, and if the document has been saved, you can use LastAccessed and LastModified to see when the document was last updated. If you need to know how big a document is, the Size property gives you the document's current size in bytes.

The NoteID and UniversalID for the document are also available to you as properties.

You can check whether a document contains an electronic signature by using the IsSigned property. If IsSigned is True, the Signer property contains the name of the person who signed the document, and Verifier stores the name of the certificate used to verify the signature. If the document isn't signed, you can use the Sign method to sign it. The following example shows how to sign a document:

```
Sub Click(Source As Button)
    Dim Ws As New NotesUIWorkspace
    Dim doc As NotesDocument

    Set doc = Ws.CurrentDocument.Document

    If Not doc.IsSigned Then
        Call doc.Sign
        Call doc.Save( False, True )
        Messagebox "Document signed by " & doc.Signer &_
        " and verified by " & doc.Verifier & ".", 64, "Signatory Information"
    Else
        Messagebox "Document is already signed.", 16, "Signature Error"
    End If
End Sub
```

If security is important, you can also encrypt the document by using the Encrypt method. Be sure to set the EncryptionKeys property to the names of the encryption keys you want to use before encrypting the document. You can also check who has edited the document by reading the Authors property.

> **CAUTION**
>
> Mail encryption works differently from document encryption, so if you want to mail an encrypted document, set the EncryptOnSend property to True, and then mail the document by using the Send method.

If you are searching for embedded objects or file attachments within the document, you can use the HasEmbedded property to check whether any embedded objects exist. You can get some, but not all, embedded objects by using the EmbeddedObjects property. Use GetAttachment to get a file attachment, given its filename.

> **CAUTION**
>
> The EmbeddedObjects property does not return any file attachments or OLE/1 objects created in Notes Release 3. If you need to get at these objects, use the NotesRichTextItem version of EmbeddedObjects.

Working with Profile Documents

Profile documents are new to Notes as of Release 4.5. They are documents that you can create to store database specific items. For example, you may want to store some parameters that define how and when documents should be archived from a database. Profile documents are also useful to store information between databases instead of using environment variables. You can use either the EditProfile method of the NotesUIWorkspace class or the GetProfileDocument method of the NotesDatabase class to create new profile documents. You can check whether a document is a profile document by using the NotesDocument IsProfile property. After you have a profile document, you can manipulate it in the same ways that you

manipulate a normal Notes document. To accesses a profile document's name, use the
NameOfProfile property. The key value is available from the Key property.

Creating and Modifying Document Items

Although you already looked at quite a few document properties, you still haven't looked at one
of the most important properties—the Items property. You can use Items to get a list of all the
items stored in a document. The property returns an array of NotesItem objects, which you
can then examine by using the properties and methods of the NotesItem class. You can use
GetFirstItem to get the first item in the document by the name you specify.

If you're looking for a particular item, you can see whether it exists by using HasItem. You
supply the name of an item, and HasItem returns True if the document contains that item. You
can get the contents of an item in several different ways. Either use GetItemValue and supply
the name of the item as a parameter, or use what's known as *Extended Class Syntax*, which lets
you access the item as though it is a property of the document. For example, the following two
scripts both get the contents of the Quantity item. The following script uses GetItemValue:

```
Sub Click(Source as Button)
    Dim uiWorkspace As New NotesUIWorkspace
    Dim uiDoc As NotesUIDocument
    Dim doc As NotesDocument
    Dim iQuantity As variant

    Set uiDoc = uiWorkspace.CurrentDocument
    Set doc = uiDoc.Document

    iQuantity = doc.GetItemValue("Quantity")
End Sub
```

The following script does the same as the preceding one, but this script uses Extended Class
Syntax:

```
Sub Click(Source as Button)
    Dim uiWorkspace As New NotesUIWorkspace
    Dim uiDoc As NotesUIDocument
    Dim doc As NotesDocument
    Dim iQuantity As Integer

    Set uiDoc = uiWorkspace.CurrentDocument
    Set doc = uiDoc.Document

    IQuantity% = doc.Quantity(0)' Use the subscript notation to indicate the
first value in the item
    NsgBox "The quantity is: " & Trim$(Str$(iQuantity%)), 64, "Quantity"
End Sub
```

Part

III

Ch

19

N O T E Extended Class Syntax lets you treat an item within a document as though it is a property.
The items within a document, in effect, become extra properties of the document. You can
read and set them the same way as any other property. For example, if a document contains an item

continues

continued

called DocAuthor, you can access its value by using the same syntax as for a property. The following example should help reinforce this concept:

```
Dim Ws as NotesUIWorkspace
Dim Cdoc as NotesDocument ' This is the current document
Dim tDocAuthor As String
Set Cdoc=Ws.CurrentDocument.Document
tDocAuthor$=Cdoc.DocAuthor(0)
```

 T I P GetItemValue always returns an array even if the item contains only one value. If the item contains a single value, it is stored as the first element of the array. Likewise when you use the Extended Class Syntax, you must use subscript notation unless you want to access all the values in the array.

You can use `AppendItemValue` and `ReplaceItemValue` to create a new item or update the contents of an existing one. If an item of the name you supply doesn't exist, a new one is created. The following script uses the two methods to create new items in a document:

```
Sub Click(Source as Button)
    Dim uiWorkspace As New NotesUIWorkspace
    Dim uiDoc As NotesUIDocument
    Dim doc As NotesDocument
    Dim itmTitle As NotesItem
    Dim itmPrice As NotesItem

    Set uiDoc = uiWorkspace.CurrentDocument
    Set doc = uiDoc.Document

    Set itmTitle = doc.AppendItemValue("Title", "The Quest for Knowledge")
    Set itmPrice = doc.ReplaceItemValue("Price", 50)
    Call doc.Save(True, True)

End Sub
```

You can also create new items using Extended Class Syntax. For example, to create a new item called Title, you can do the following (the example shows how to use Extended Class Syntax to its fullest potential):

```
Sub Click(Source as Button)
    Dim uiWorkspace As New NotesUIWorkspace
    uiWorkspace.CurrentDocument.Document.Title="Monte Taylor: Southern Region"
    Call uiWorkspace.CurrentDocument.Document.Save(True, True)
End Sub
```

You can also create rich text items by using the `CreateRichTextItem` method. The following example demonstrates manipulating a rich text field with Lotus Script:

```
Sub Click(Source as Button)
    Dim S As New NotesSession
    Dim Ws As New NotesUIWorkspace
    Dim Mdoc As NotesDocument
    Set MDoc=S.CurrentDatabase.CreateDocument
```

```
     Set RTF = MDoc.CreateRichTextItem( "Body" )
     Mdoc.Form="Memo"
     Mdoc.Subject="Please review the new sales report from the Western Region"
     Call RTF.Appendtext("As new sales summary report has been created on:" &
Date$)
     Call RTF.AddNewLine(2)
     Call RTF.AppendText("Click this DocLink to view the report")
     Call RTF.AppendDocLink(WS.CurrentDocument.Document, "Click me!")
     Call Mdoc.Send(False, "Sales_Managerment")
End Sub
```

Using the *ComputeWithForm* Method

The methods you just learned let you bypass the Notes user interface and create documents directly from a LotusScript program. Usually, you create documents by completing a form in the Notes user interface. When you save the document, the field validation formulas on the form are computed, and, if any of the field values are incorrect, the field validation formulas tell you, and you can't save the document. By bypassing these validation formulas and creating documents in the background, we can create documents that would not pass the field valida- tion tests. If it is important to check that the document you have created meets the field validation criteria for a form, you can use the ComputeWithForm method to force the validation formulas to be executed.

This can be useful if you have changed the design of a form to include new validation code, and you need to test whether the existing documents are still valid. You can check each document by using ComputeWithForm, and you can update those that no longer meet the new validation criteria.

```
Sub Click(Source as Button)
     Dim S As New NotesSession
     Dim Ws As New NotesUIWorkspace
     Dim TargetDb As NotesDatabase
     Set TargetDB=S.getDatabase(S.CurrentDatabase.Server,"leads.nsf")
     Dim Ndoc As NotesDocument
     Dim Errors As Integer
     Set NDoc=TargetDB.CreateDocument
     NDoc.Form="Lead"
     Call Ws.CurrentDocument.Document.CopyAllItems(NDoc, True)
     Errors%= NDoc.ComputewithForm( True, True)
     If Not Errors% Then
          Call Mdoc.Send(False, "Sales_Management")
     Else
          Msgbox "A error occurred during validation!", 16, "Error"
     End If
End Sub
```

Copying and Deleting Document Items

Two methods let you copy items between documents. CopyItem copies a single item from one document to another, whereas CopyAllItems copies every item in the document. For example, the following code demonstrates how you can create a new document in another database, and copy all items in the current document to it:

```
Sub Click(Source as Button)
    Dim uiWorkspace As New NotesUIWorkspace
    Dim OtherBD as New NotesDatabase("Aegis/Definiti","testing.nsf")
    Dim NewDoc as NotesDocument
    Set NewDoc=OtherDB.CreateDocument
    Call uiWorkspace.CurrentDocument.Document.CopyAllItems(NewDoc, True)
    Call NewDoc.Save(True, True)
End Sub
```

To delete an item from the document, call RemoveItem. The following example demonstrates how you can use the RemoveItem method to delete an item from the currently selected Notes document in a view:

```
Sub Click(Source as Button)
    Dim S As New NotesSession
    Set Cdoc=S.CurrentDatabase.UnprocessedDocuments.GetFirstDocument
    If Cdoc.HasItem("Status") Then
        Call Cdoc.RemoveItem("Status")
        Call Cdoc.Save(True, False)
        Print ¦ "Status" Item was deleted from document¦, 64, "Testing"
    End If
End Sub
```

Working with Response Documents

It's really easy to find all the immediate responses to a document. Just look at the Responses property. This returns a NotesDocumentCollection containing all responses to the current document. If you need to check whether the current document is a response document, that's easy, too. Check the IsResponse property. If it's True, you're working with a response document. You can then use the ParentDocumentUNID property to find the Universal ID of the document's parent.

Sometimes you need to change a document's position in a view hierarchy—for example, to make one document a response to another. Use the MakeResponse method to make this change. You call the MakeResponse method in one document to make that document a response to another.

Moving and Copying Documents

Not only can you alter a document's position in a hierarchy, you can also copy the document between databases. The CopyToDatabase method creates a new copy of the document in the database you specify. For example:

```
Sub Click(Source as Button)
    Dim uiWorkspace As New NotesUIWorkspace
    Dim TargetDB as New NotesDatabase("Aegis/Definiti","testing.nsf")
    Dim NewDoc as NotesDocument
    Set NewDoc=uiWorkspace.CurrentDocument.Document.CopyToDatabase( TargetDB )
    Call NewDoc.Save(True, True)
End Sub
```

You can also move documents between folders within the database. Use PutInFolder to add a document to a folder, and use RemoveFromFolder to remove it from a folder.

Mailing a Document

One of the great features of Notes is its tight integration with the mail system. All documents are potentially mail messages. The NotesDocument class lets you exploit this by making it very easy to mail-enable your documents. You can mail any document by using the Send method. Simply supply a list of recipients, call the Send method, and the document is sent to those recipients. If the document contains a SendTo field, your list of recipients is ignored, and the document is sent to the recipients listed in the SendTo field. If you set the SaveMessageOnSend property, the document is automatically saved after it is sent. You can also specify some mail options, such as SignOnSend and EncryptOnSend. The following example demonstrates just how easy it is to send mail using LotusScript.

```
Sub Click(Source as Button)
    Dim uiWorkspace As New NotesUIWorkspace
    Dim Mdoc as NotesDocument
    Dim RTF as new NotesRichTextItem(Mdoc, "Body")
    Set Mdoc=uiWorkspace.CurrentDocument.Document.ParentDatabase.CreateDocument'
Create a new document in the current database
    Mdoc.Form="Memo"
    Mdoc.Subject="A new sales summary report has been created"
    Call RTF.Appendtext("As new sales summary report has been created on:" &
Date$)
    Call RTF.AddNewLine(2)
    Call RTF.AppendText("Click this DocLink to view the report")
    Call RTF.AppendDocLink(uiWorkspace.CurrentDocument.Document, "Click me!:")
    Call Mdoc.Send(False, "Sales Group")

End Sub
```

N O T E Notice that the preceding code specifically creates an item named "Form". This is because a form is not used to create the document. If a form field with the name of the form the document should use is not set, the document opens with the default form; if there is no default form, the user gets a big ugly error message and can't open the document. Be sure that you create a form field when creating documents with script, and if you are mailing a document to a user's mailbox, be sure that you set the form field to "Memo". If you are mailing a document to a mail-in database, either store the form in the document or ensure that you set the value of the form field to the name of a form in that database. ■

RenderToRTItem is a useful method to use when you are mailing documents. The method creates a picture of a document and places it into a rich text field, just the same way as when you use Mail, Forward to forward a document.

You can also create a reply to the current document by using CreateReplyMessage. This method creates a new document that is formatted as a reply to the original. This can be useful for automatically generating and sending acknowledgments when you're designing a workflow application. For example, you can automatically acknowledge the receipt of an expenses claim form.

Saving and Deleting a Document

None of the changes you make to a document have any effect until you save the document. If you don't save your document, all your changes are lost when you close the document. Use the Save method to save your changes. You supply Save with two or three parameters. Set the first parameter to True to save the document, even if someone else has edited a copy of it while you've been working with it. If you use this parameter, your copy of the document overwrites the original. If you set the first parameter to False, the second parameter determines what happens when you save the document.

If you set the second parameter to True, your document becomes a response to the original. If you set this parameter to False, the document is not saved and your changes are discarded.

The optional third parameter is new as of Release 4.5, and you use it to indicate whether the saved document should be marked as read. Set this parameter to True to mark the document as read or False to mark it as unread.

You can delete a document from the database by using the Remove method.

Working with the *NotesForm* Class

The NotesForm class is new as of Release 4.5. It allows you to examine and work with form properties (which you will notice are similar to the view properties). You can also use the class to delete a form from a database. The Notesform class has only one method, Remove, which allows you to delete a form from a database. The properties for this class are shown in Table 19.19.

Table 19.19 *NotesForm* **Properties**

Property	Description	Data Type	Usage
Aliases	The aliases for the form.	Array of strings	Read Only
Fields	The names of the fields on the form.	Array of strings	Read Only
FormUsers	The names of the users that can use the form (the contents of the $FormUsers field).	Array of strings	Read/Write
IsSubForm	True if the form is a subform.	Boolean	Read Only
Name	The form name.	String	Read Only
ProtectReaders	Set to True to protect the $Readers item during replication.	Boolean	Read/Write

Property	Description	Data Type	Usage
ProtectUsers	Set to True to protect the $FormUsers item during replication.	Boolean	Read/Write
Readers	The names of the users that can read the form (the contents of the $Readers field).	Array of strings	Read/Write

Working with the *NotesItem* Class

The NotesItem class lets you work with the contents of a Notes document. When you enter a value into a field on a form and save the document, Notes stores the value you enter as an item within the document. NotesItem lets you examine and modify these items. You can use the properties and method within NotesItem to do the following:

■ Examine item properties
■ Create items within a document
■ Modify items within a document
■ Delete items

See Table 19.20 for the NotesItem class properties and Table 19.21 for the methods.

Table 19.20 *NotesItem* Properties

Property	Description	Data Type	Usage
DateTimeValue	For date-time items only, a NotesDateTime object representing the item.	NotesDateTime	Read/Write
IsAuthors	True if the item is an Authors item.	Boolean	Read Only
IsEncrypted	True if the item is encrypted.	Boolean	Read Only
IsNames	True if the item is a Names item.	Boolean	Read Only
IsProtected	True if the item can be modified only by users with at least Editor access.	Boolean	Read Only
IsReaders	True if the item is a Readers item.	Boolean	Read Only
IsSigned	True if the item contains an electronic signature.	Boolean	Read Only

Part
III

Ch
19

continues

Table 19.20   Continued

Property	Description	Data Type	Usage
IsSummary	True if the item is a Summary item. Only Summary items can be displayed in views and folders.	Boolean	Read Only
LastModified	The date that the item was last modified.	Variant of type DATE	Read Only
Name	The name of the item.	String	Read Only
Parent	The document containing the item.	NotesDocument	Read Only
SaveToDisk	True if the item should be written to disk when the document containing it is saved.	Boolean	Read/Write
Text	A textual representation of the item. List items are separated by semicolons.	String	Read Only
Type	The type of item.	Integer constant	Read Only
ValueLength	The size, in bytes, of the item.	Integer	Read Only
Values	The values stored within the item.	String for rich text items; Array of strings for text or text list items; Array of doubles for numbers, number lists, or datetime items	Read/Write

Table 19.21   *NotesItem* Methods

Method	Description	Return Data Type	Return Value
Abstract	Abbreviate the text of the item.	String	The abbreviated text
AppendToTextList	For a text list item, add another value to the end of the list.	None	None
Contains	For items containing lists, check whether the value you supply is one of the values in the list. You can search text lists, number lists, or date lists.	Boolean	True if the value is in the list

Method	Description	Return Data Type	Return Value
CopyItemTo Document	Copy the item to a document.	NotesItem	The new item
New	Create a new item.	NotesItem	The new item
Remove	Delete the item from the document.	None	None

Examining Item Properties

Use the Name property to find the name of an item. You can find out what type of item you are working with by examining its Type property. For example, Type lets you know whether an item is a text item. You can find out more about the item by using IsNames, IsAuthors, and IsReaders—that is, to see whether it is one of these special types. The LastModified property returns the date when the item was last updated.

You can check the item's security settings by using IsEncrypted, IsProtected, and IsSigned.

Creating and Modifying Items

Use the New method to create new items within a document. You supply the document, the name of the new item, and its initial value. If you're creating a text item, you can optionally set it to be a Names, Readers, or Authors item. You can also create a new item by copying an existing item from one document to another by using CopyItemToDocument.

N O T E To create a new "names" type item (reader names, for example), you can create a new NotesItem object and set the "SpecialType" flag to one three constants (found in lsconst.lss): NAMES, READERS, or AUTHORS. Otherwise, you can use the Isreaders, IsAuthors, or Isnames properties of a NotesItem.

You can read or modify the contents of an item by using its Values property. When it is read, Values returns the item contents in the appropriate format—for example, as an array of strings for a text or text list item. Similarly, when you use Values to modify the contents of an item, you must supply the values in the correct format—for example, an array of doubles for a number or number list item. Alternatively, you can use the Text property to convert an item value into its textual representation—for example, the Text property of a number field containing 42 is the string "42".

If you're working with a text list item, you can use the AppendToTextList method to add new values to the end of the list.

Finally, you can use the Abstract method to abbreviate the contents of a text item. You specify the maximum number of characters to return and information on how to abbreviate the text. The method returns the abbreviated contents of the item.

Deleting Items

To delete an item from a document, use the Remove method. Remember to save the document so that your changes take effect.

Working with the *NotesRichTextItem* Class

The NotesRichTextItem class lets you create and modify rich text fields within documents. You can do the following:

- Add text, formatting characters, and doclinks to a rich text field
- Combine rich text fields
- Find the embedded or linked objects or file attachments that are contained in a rich text field

The NotesRichtextItem class has only one property, EmbeddedObjects, which returns an array of NotesEmbeddedObjects containing all the OLE or ActiveX embedded and linked objects and file attachments in the rich text item. It is a read-only property. The methods of this class are shown in Table 19.22.

Table 19.22 *NotesRichTextItem* **Methods**

Method	Description	Return Data Type	Return Value
AddNewLine	Append one or more new lines to the rich text item.	None	None
AddTab	Append one or more tab characters to the rich text item.	None	None
AppendDocLink	Given a database, view, or document, create a link to the supplied object and append the link to the rich text item.	None	None
AppendRTItem	Append one rich text item to another.	None	None
AppendStyle	Append a NotesRichTextStyle to the end of a NotesRichText Item. Any text following the style is rendered using that style's attributes until another style is appended.	None	None
AppendText	Append the supplied text to the rich text item.	None	None
EmbedObject	Given the name of a file or application, create an embedded object, link, or file attachment and store it in the rich text field.	NotesEmbedded-Object	The newly created object

Method	Description	Return Data Type	Return Value
GetEmbedded Object	Given the name of an embedded object, link, or file attachment within the rich text item, return the corresponding NotesEmbeddedObject.	NotesEmbedded- Object	The object
GetFormattedText	Return the contents of the rich text item as a text string.	String	The text of the text item
New	Create a new rich text item.	NotesRich- TextItem	The newly created rich text item

Creating and Modifying a Rich Text Item

As with many of the other classes, you can create objects in the NotesRichTextItem class in different ways. If you have a NotesDocument object, you can use its CreateRichTextItem method to create a new NotesRichTextItem object. Alternatively, you can use New in the NotesRichTextItem class.

To find and use rich text fields that already exist in a document, use the GetFirstItem and GetNextItem methods of NotesDocument. The following script shows how to find a rich text item called Body:

```
Dim doc As NotesDocument
Dim vItem As Variant
 '... Set value of doc ...
Set vItem = doc.GetFirstItem("Body")
    If (vItem.Type = RICHTEXT) Then
    'The item is a rich text item, so you can use the NotesRichText item  methods
    End If
```

After you have created or found a rich text item, you can add text to it by using the AppendText method. You can also add any number of tabs and new lines by using AddTab and AddNewLine, or you can append the contents of one rich text field to another by using AppendRTItem. In Notes 4.6, you can use AppendStyle to manipulate the formatting of the contents of a rich text field. The following code sample demonstrates many of these concepts:

```
Sub Click(Source as Button)
    Dim Ws As New NotesUIWorkspace
    If Not Ws.CurrentDocument.IsnewDoc Then
        Dim vRTF As Variant
        Set vRTF=Ws.CurrentDocument.Document.GetFirstItem("Body")
        vRTF.Appendtext("Testing 1-2-3")
        vRTF.AddNewLine(2)
        vRTF.AppendText("More Testing")
        Call Ws.CurrentDocument.Document.Save(True, False)
    End If
End Sub
```

You can create embedded objects or file attachments in a rich text field by using `EmbedObject`. The following is an example:

```
Sub Click(Source as Button)
    Dim WS As New NotesUIWorkspace
    Dim vRTF as Variant
    Dim Object as NotesEmbeddedObject
    Set vRTF=Ws.CurrentDocument.Document.GetFirstItem("Body")
    vRTF.Appendtext("New Sales Report Attached")
    vRTF.AddNewLine(2)
    Set Object = VRTF.EmbedObject(EMBED_ATTACHMENT, "",
"c:\notes\data\sales.xls", "SalesReport")
    Call uiWorkspace.CurrentDocument.Document.Save(True, False)
End Sub
```

> **CAUTION**
>
> You can attach files on any supported Notes platform, but you can create embedded or linked objects only on platforms that support OLE.

One of the most useful methods supported by the class is `AppendDocLink`. This method lets you create any of the three types of Notes links—a database link, a view link, or a document link—and append it to a rich text field. This is great for creating summary documents. For example, you can create a script that searches all your organization's newswire databases for new documents, and the script mails you a summary document containing database links to the databases you should check.

Reading a Rich Text Item

You can get the text of a rich text item in a couple ways. If you want to reformat the text, you can use the `GetFormattedText` method. This gives you the option of removing any embedded tab characters and wrapping the text after a specified number of characters. If you want just the text and don't care about the formatting, just access the rich text item in the same way you access a plain text item.

You can get a named embedded object from a rich text field by using `GetEmbeddedObject`. You supply the name of the object, and the method returns a `NotesEmbeddedObject` that represents the object. You can then use the properties and methods of `NotesEmbeddedObject` to work with the object.

Working with the *NotesRichTextStyle* Class

The `NotesRichTextStyle` class, new to Notes 4.6, allows you to manipulate the visual attributes of a `NotesRichTextItem`. Interestingly enough, this class has no methods. Table 19.25 summarizes the `NotesRichTextStyle` properties.

Table 19.25 *NotesRichTextStyle* **Properties**

Property	Description	Data Type	Usage
Bold	Use this property to make text bold.	Integer	Read/Write
Effects	Use this property with one of several constants to apply text effects.	Integer	Read/Write
Font Size	Use this property with the appropriate font size.	Integer	Read/Write
Italic	Use this property to make text italicized.	Boolean	Read/Write
NotesColor	Use this property with one of the defined constants to change the color of rich text.	Integer	Read/Write
NotesFont	Use this property to change the font of the text.	Integer	Read/Write
StrikeThrough	Use this property to make text appear with a line through it.	Boolean	Read/Write
Underline	Use this property to underline text.	Boolean	Read/Write

The NotesRichTextStyle class is relatively straightforward; you simply set the properties listed in the preceding table to change the attributes of text in a rich text field. Many of these properties use constants. See the following example:

```
Dim S As New NotesSession
    Dim ws As New NotesUIWorkSpace
    Dim rtStyle As NotesRichTextStyle

    Set rtStyle = S.CreateRichTextStyle

    Dim richText As New NotesRichTextItem(Ws.CurrentDocument.Document, "Body")

    ' You can stack the style attributes

    rtStyle.NotesColor = COLOR_BLACK
    rtStyle.FontSize = 24
    rtStyle.Effects = EFFECTS_SHADOW

    ' and then apply them all to the text that follows...
    Call richText.AppendStyle(rtStyle)
    Call richText.AppendText("LotusScript is ")
```

Part

III

Ch

19

```
' now change the color and set the Bold and Italic attributes
rtStyle.NotesColor = COLOR_BLUE
rtStyle.Bold = True
rtStyle.Italic = True
Call richText.AppendStyle(rtStyle)

' and add some more text
Call richText.AppendText("GREAT!!!")


' modifications to rich text fields do not show up until the doc is closed
and reopened
' so force the user to close the document. Save it first to make sure the
change gets there!
Call Ws.Currentdocument.Document.Save(True,True)
Call Ws.CurrentDocument.Close
```

The preceding example adds the text "LotusScript is GREAT!!!" to the Body field. The first two words are in black, 24-point, shadowed text. "GREAT!!!" is then set to blue, bold, and italic. Note that for this change to become visible, because it is a rich text item, the document must be closed and then reopened.

Working with the *NotesEmbeddedObject* Class

The NotesEmbeddedObject class can represent either a file attachment, an embedded object, or a linked object. You use this class to do the following:

- Find the OLE class and properties of an embedded object
- Find the OLE verbs that the object supports
- Activate any of these OLE verbs

The properties for the class are shown in Table 19.23, and the methods are shown in Table 19.24.

Table 19.23 *NotesEmbeddedObject* Properties

Property	Description	Data Type	Usage
Class	The name of the application that created the object.	String	Read Only
FileSize	The size, in bytes, of the object.	Long	Read Only
Name	The name used to refer to the object.	String	Read Only
Object	The OLE handle to the object.	Variant	Read Only
Parent	The rich text item that contains the object.	NotesRichTextItem	Read Only

Property	Description	Data Type	Usage
Source	For file attachments, the name of the file; for other object types, an internal name used by Notes.	String	Read Only
Type	Whether the object is an embedded object, linked object, or file attachment.	Integer constant	Read Only
Verbs	For OLE2 objects, the verbs that the object supports.	Array of strings	Read Only

Table 19.24 *NotesEmbeddedObject* Methods

Method	Description	Return Data Type	Return Value
Activate	For embedded or linked objects only, load the object and activate its OLE server application.	Variant	A handle to the object
DoVerb	For embedded objects only, execute the supplied verb.	None	None
ExtractFile	For file attachments only, copy the file attachment to the supplied filename.	None	None
Remove	Delete the supplied embedded or linked object or file attachment.	None	None

Part
III

Ch
19

Creating an Embedded Object

You create embedded objects in a rich text field within a document by using the EmbedObject method of the NotesRichTextItem class.

Finding an Embedded Object

You can find all the embedded and linked objects within a document by using the EmbeddedObjects property of NotesDocument. If you need to look only in a particular field, you can use the NotesRichTextItem property, EmbeddedObjects, to get all the embedded objects in the field. Both properties return an array of NotesEmbeddedObjects. When you know the name of the rich text field and the name of the object, use GetEmbeddedObject in NotesRichTextItem to get the object.

Getting the Properties of an Embedded Object

After you have an object, you can use the properties in this class to get the details of the object. Use Type to check whether the object is an embedded object, linked object, or file attachment.

Then for embedded objects, you can use Class to get the OLE name of the application that created the object. Use Name to get the name of the object. If the object was created by using the Notes Create Object dialog box, the name created appears in the Object Type list in the dialog box. Object gets the object's OLE handle, and Verbs gets a list of all the OLE verbs the object supports. For file attachments, use Source to get the filename of the attachment. For all object types, the FileSize property gives you the size in bytes of the object or attachment.

Activating an Embedded Object

You can load an OLE embedded or linked object by using the Activate method. You can show or hide the user interface of the OLE server application. The method returns the OLE handle for the object, which you can then use to access the object's methods.

You can also execute any of the verbs supported by the object by using the DoVerb method.

Extracting a File Attachment

If you are dealing with a file attachment object, you can copy the file attachment to disk by using ExtractFile. You supply a path for the file, and the method copies the file to disk. The following example demonstrates extracting a file:

```
Sub Click(Source as Button)
    Dim WS As New NotesUIWorkspace
    Dim vRTF as Variant
    Set vRTF=Ws.CurrentDocument.Document.GetFirstItem("Body")
    Dim Object as NotesEmbeddedObject
    Set Object = vRTF.GetEmbeddedObject("Sales.xls")
    Call Object.ExtractFile(InputBox$("Where would you like to store this file?",
"Save File", "c:\notes\data"))
End Sub
```

Deleting an Embedded Object

You delete an embedded object by calling its Remove method. As with the other methods that delete items from documents, you must save the document to have your change take effect.

Working with the *NotesDocumentCollection* Class

The NotesDocumentCollection class lets you work with a subset of the documents in a database. You have a lot of flexibility in how you select the documents in the collection. For example, you can get the following:

- All the documents in a database
- Those documents found by a full-text query of a database

- Those documents selected by a Notes selection formula
- Those documents selected by using a key
- All documents that have not been processed by an agent
- All the responses to a document

See Table 19.26 for the class properties and Table 19.27 for the methods.

Table 19.26 *NotesDocumentCollection* **Properties**

Property	Description	Data Type	Usage
Count	The number of documents in a collection.	Long	Read Only
IsSorted	Whether the collection is sorted. Only collections produced by full-text searches of a database are sorted.	Boolean	Read Only
Parent	The database that contains the collection.	NotesDatabase	Read Only
Query	If the collection was produced by a search, the query that was used.	String	Read Only

Table 19.27 *NotesDocumentCollection* **Methods**

Method	Description	Return Data Type	Return Value
FtSearch	Performs a full-text search on the documents in a collection and further limits the documents in the collection to those selected by the search.	None	The filtered document
GetFirstDocument	Get the first document in the collection.	NotesDocument	The first document
GetLastDocument	Get the last document in the collection.	NotesDocument	The last document
GetNextDocument	Given any document in the collection, get the next one.	NotesDocument	The document
GetNthDocument	Given an index into the collection, find the document at that position.	NotesDocument	The document

Part
III

Ch
19

continues

Table 19.27 Continued

Method	Description	Return Data Type	Return Value
GetPrevDocument	Given any document in the collection, get the previous one.	NotesDocument	The document
PutAllinFolder	Given the name of a folder, this methods adds all the documents in collection to the folder. If the folder doesn't exist, this method creates the folder.	None	None
RemoveAll	When called, this method deletes all the documents in the collection.	None	None
RemoveAllfromFolder	Given the name of a folder, removes all the documents in the collection from the folder. Does nothing for documents not in the folder.	None	None
StampAll	Given the name of an item and value to set, replaces the item value for all documents in the collection. If the item does not exist, the item is created.	None	None
UpdateAll	Marks all documents in the collection as processed by an agent.	None	None

N O T E Collections are not as efficient as views for accessing documents because collections have to be created for you, whereas views are built into the database. If you can get the documents you want by using a view, use the view instead of a collection. ▪

Creating a Collection

You use properties and methods in the NotesDatabase, NotesDocument and NotesView classes to get a collection of documents. The simplest collection is all the documents in a database, and the collection is available by using the AllDocuments property of NotesDatabase. You can restrict the documents that are included in the collection by using either the FTSearch or Search methods in the NotesDatabase class. You supply the FTSearch method with a Notes full-text query and a maximum number of documents to find, and the method returns a collection of all documents that match the query. For example, to find the first 10 documents containing the words Holly and Bracken, use the following:

```
Sub Click(Source As Button)
    Dim s As New NotesSession
    Dim db As NotesDatabase
    Dim coll As NotesDocumentCollection
    Set db = s.CurrentDatabase
    Set coll = db.FTSearch(¦"Holly" & "Bracken"¦, 10)
End Sub
```

To find all documents that match the query, specify 0 as the number of documents to return.

 TIP Use the vertical bar to delimit the search string. If you use quotation marks as string delimiters, you have to double up any quotation marks in the search string, which soon makes it very difficult to read.

Use the Search method when you want to select documents by using a Notes selection formula. For example, to select all the Server documents in the current database that have been modified in the last week, use the following:

```
Sub Click(Source As Button)
    Dim s As New NotesSession
    Dim coll As NotesDocumentCollection
    Dim dtLastWeek As New NotesDateTime("Today")
    Call dtLastWeek.AdjustDay(-7)
    Set coll = S.CurrentDatabase.Search(¦Form = "Server"¦, dtLastWeek, 0)
End Sub
```

If you are using an agent to access the collection, you can use the UnprocessedDocuments property or the UnprocessedFTSearch and UnprocessedSearch methods to further limit the collection by including only those documents the agent considers to be unprocessed.

If you use one of the full-text search methods to create a collection, the documents are sorted with the most relevant documents first. All the other methods return unordered collections. If you need to check whether a collection is ordered, use the IsSorted property.

The GetAllDocumentsByKey method of the NotesView class can be used to get all the documents from a view that match the key that you supply, as follows:

```
Sub Click(Source As Button)
    Dim s As New NotesSession
    Dim View As NotesView
    Dim coll As NotesDocumentCollection
    Set View=S.CurrentDatabase.GetView("by Title")
    Set coll=View.GetAllDocumentsbyKey("Special Edition: Using Lotus Notes 4.6")
    If Coll.Count>0 Then
        Call coll.StampAll("Status","Closed")
        Call coll.UpdateAll
    End If
End Sub
```

Part

III

Ch

19

Finding Documents in a Collection

After you have a collection, you can use the Count property to check how many documents were returned. You can refine the documents in the collection by performing a full-text query on the returned documents. Use FTSearch to specify the query, and the method modifies the collection to contain only those documents that match the search criteria.

You then have several methods of finding documents in the collection. You can use GetFirstDocument and GetNextDocument to step through all the documents. If you want to step through the collection in reverse order, use GetLastDocument and GetPrevDocument. You can get a specific document in the collection by using GetNthDocument. The following example demonstrates one way to traverse a collection.

```
Sub Click(Source As Button)
    Dim s As New NotesSession
    Dim View As NotesView
    Dim Coll As NotesDocumentCollection
    Dim Cdoc As NotesDocument
    Set View=S.CurrentDatabase.GetView("by Title")
    Set coll=View.GetAllDocumentsbyKey("Special Edition: Using Lotus Notes 4")
    If Coll.Count>0 Then
        For I%=1 To Coll.Count
            Set Cdoc=Coll.GetNthDocument(I%)
            Print "Cdoc.NoteID=" & Cdoc.NoteID
        Next
    End If
End Sub
```

Working with Documents in a Collection

Notes 4.5 introduced several new methods that you can use to work with document collections. You can add all the documents in a collection to a specified folder by using the PutAllInFolder method, or remove them with RemoveAllFromFolder. You can delete all the documents in a collection, using RemoveAll. If you want to add or update a specific item in all the documents in a collection, you can use StampAll. You supply the name of the item and its new value, and StampAll updates the item in every document in the collection. If the item doesn't exist, StampAll adds it. When you're working with agents, you can use UpdateAll to mark all the documents in the collection as having been processed by the agent.

Working with the *NotesAgent* Class

The NotesAgent class represents any public or private Notes agent or Notes 3.x macro. Agents let you automate tasks within Notes, such as archiving documents, sending mail messages, or routing documents through a workflow system. As a database designer, you can create shared agents and make them available to users of your database. You can also create personal agents to help automate routine tasks.

N O T E You must have at least designer access to a database to be able to create shared agents. To create personal agents in a database, the Create Personal Agents option in the ACL must be selected for your name or for a group to which you belong. For server-based databases, you must also be included in the group of people allowed to create personal agents on the server. See the Agent Manager Restrictions section of the server documentation for details about who can create personal agents. ▦

You can use NotesAgent to examine the properties of an agent or delete it from the database.

The NotesAgent class properties are listed in Table 19.28, and the methods are shown in Table 19.29.

Table 19.28 *NotesAgent* **Properties**

Property	Description	Data Type	Usage
Comment	The comment associated with the agent.	String	Read Only
CommonOwner	The common name of the person who last edited the agent.	String	Read Only
IsEnabled	True if the agent is enabled.	Boolean	Read/Write
IsPublic	True if the agent is available to all database users.	Boolean	Read Only
LastRun	The date that the agent last ran.	Variant of type DATE	Read Only
Name	The name of the agent.	String	Read Only
Owner	The fully distinguished name of the person who last edited the agent.	String	Read Only
Parent	The database in which the agent is stored.	Notes Database	Read Only
Query	The text of the query used to select the documents on which the agent runs.	String	Read Only
ServerName	For server-based agents, returns the fully distinguished the name of the server on which the agent runs. For workstation-based agents, returns the fully distinguished name of the current user.	String	Read/Write

Part
III

Ch
19

Table 19.29 *NotesAgent* **Methods**

Method	Description	Return Data Type	Return Value
Save	If you change the IsEnabled property or the ServerName property, you must call this method to save your changes.	None	None
Remove	Delete the agent from the database.	None	None
Run	Run an agent.	None	None

Working with the *NotesACL* Class

The NotesACL class represents the Access Control List for a database. You can use the NotesACL class to do the following:

- Create new entries in the ACL
- Examine existing entries in the ACL
- Modify ACL settings
- Add, rename, or delete roles in the ACL

See Table 19.30 for the class properties. The class methods are shown in Table 19.31.

Table 19.30 *NotesACL* **Properties**

Property	Description	Data Type	Usage
Parent	The database that contains the ACL.	NotesDatabase	Read Only
Roles	All the roles defined within the ACL.	Array of Strings	Read Only
UniformAccess	Indicates whether uniform access is set for this database.	Boolean	Read/Write

Table 19.31 *NotesACL* **Methods**

Method	Description	Return Data Type	Return Value
AddRole	Given the name of a role, add that role to the ACL.	None	None
CreateACLEntry	Given a person, group, or server name and an access level, create a new ACL entry.	NotesACLEntry	The newly created ACL entry

Method	Description	Return Data Type	Return Value
DeleteRole	Given the name of a role, delete that role from the ACL.	None	None
GetEntry	Given a person, group, or server name, find the corresponding ACL entry.	NotesACLEntry	The ACL entry for the person, group, or server
GetFirstEntry	Find the first entry in the ACL.	NotesACLEntry	The first entry in the ACL
GetNextEntry	Given any ACL entry, find the next one.	NotesACLEntry	The next early in the ACL
RenameRole	Given the name of a role, find that role and rename it.	None	None
Save	Save any changes that have been made to the ACL.	None	None

Creating ACL Entries

The CreateACLEntry method lets you create a new ACL entry for a person, group, or server. You specify the name and the level you want to assign, and the method creates a new entry in the ACL.

Finding ACL Entries

You can get a specified ACL entry from the ACL by using the GetEntry method. You supply the name of the person, group, or server, and the method returns you a NotesACLEntry object containing the ACL details for that name. You then use the NotesACLEntry properties to examine or modify the entry. You can also loop through all the ACL entries by using GetFirstEntry and GetNextEntry. The following script is an example:

```
Sub Click(Source As Button)
    Dim s As New NotesSession
    Dim ACL As NotesACL
    Dim Entry as NotesACLEntry
    Set ACL=S.CurrentDatabase.ACL
    Set entry = acl.GetFirstEntry
    Do While Not Entry is Nothing
        ' Some processing here
        Print "The Current ACL Entry is: " entry.Name
        Set entry = acl.GetNextEntry(entry).
    Loop
End Sub
```

Modifying ACL Settings

New in Notes 4.5 is the ability to modify the ACL setting so that you enforce a consistent Access Control List across all replicas of this database. Set the UniformAccess property to True to make the Access Control List consistent.

Part III

Ch 19

Modifying Roles

You can find all the roles that have been defined in the ACL by using the Roles property. You can also add, rename, or delete roles from the ACL by using AddRole, RenameRole, and DeleteRole.

Saving Your Changes

Any changes that you make to an ACL take effect only after you have saved the NotesACL object by using the Save method. If you close the database before calling Save, any changes you have made are lost.

Working with the *NotesACLEntry* Class

The NotesACLEntry class represents an individual entry in the ACL for a database. You can use the NotesACLEntry class to do the following:

- Add or delete names in the ACL
- Change some of the actions that a user can perform in the database
- Change the roles assigned to a name in the ACL

See Tables 19.32 and 19.33 for the properties and methods for the class.

Table 19.32 *NotesACLEntry* Properties

Property	Description	Data Type	Usage
CanCreate Documents	True if the ACL entry can create documents in a database.	Boolean	Read/Write
CanCreate PersonalAgent	True if the ACL entry can create personal agents in the database.	Boolean	Read/Write
CanCreate PersonalFolder	True if the ACL entry can create personal folders in the database.	Boolean	Read/Write
CanDelete Documents	True if the ACL entry can delete documents from the database.	Boolean	Read/Write
Level	The access level for this ACL entry.	Integer constant	Read/Write
IsPublicReader	True if the current entry is a public reader in the database.	Boolean	Read/Write
IsPublicWriter	True if the current entry is a public reader in the database.	Boolean	Read/Write

Property	Description	Data Type	Usage
Name	The name associated with the ACL entry.	String	Read/Write
Parent	The ACL that contains the entry.	NotesACL	Read Only
Roles	The roles that are defined for this ACL entry.	Array of strings	Read Only

Table 19.33 *NotesACLEntry* **Methods**

Method	Description	Return Data Type	Return Value
DisableRole	Given the name of a role, remove that role from the ACL entry.	None	None
EnableRole	Given the name of a role, add that role to the ACL entry.	None	None
IsRoleEnabled	Given the name of a role, check whether the ACL entry has that role enabled.	Boolean	True if the role is enabled
New	Create a new ACL entry.	NotesACLEntry	The newly created entry
Remove	Delete the supplied ACL entry from the ACL.	None	None

Creating and Deleting ACL Entries

In addition to using the CreateACLEntry method of the NotesACL class, you can use New to create new entries in an ACL. For example, the following button script creates a new entry in the ACL for the group SupportTeam and gives the group Reader access to the database:

```
Sub Click(Source As Button)
    Dim s As New NotesSession
    Dim db As NotesDatabase
    Dim acl As NotesACL

    Set db = s.CurrentDatabase
    Set acl = db.ACL
    Dim aclGroup As New NotesACLEntry(acl, "SupportTeam", ACLLEVEL_READER)
    Call acl.Save
End Sub
```

If you need to delete an entry from an ACL, use the Remove method.

Part
III

Ch
19

Modifying ACL Entries

You can find the name associated with an ACL entry by using the Name property, and you can find the current level of access by using the Level property.

You can examine or modify the actions that are available to the ACL entry by using the following four properties: CanCreateDocuments, CanCreatePersonalAgent, CanCreatePersonalFolder, and CanDeleteDocuments. The properties correspond to the Create Documents, Create Personal Agents, Create Personal Folders, and Delete Documents settings in the ACL.

Modifying Roles

The NotesACLEntry class contains a similar set of methods and functions to the NotesACL class for working with roles. As you might expect, the methods in NotesACLEntry refer only to the roles for the entry with which you are currently working. For example, the Roles property lists the roles that are enabled for the current ACL entry. You can add the current entry to a role by using EnableRole or remove the entry by using DisableRole. Use IsRoleEnabled to test whether a specific role is enabled for the current entry.

Working with the *NotesLog* Class

The NotesLog class lets you keep track of your scripts. You have several options for how you record your script's progress. You can log messages to a Notes database, which is useful when you want to keep a rolling history of what your scripts have done. Alternatively, you can store messages in a mail memo and automatically send the memo when your script has finished running. This is useful to alert people when a script has something useful to tell them, such as, "I know I was supposed to copy all those documents last night, but it was late, the server was running slowly, and...." You get the idea. A third option, if your script is running locally, is to write your log messages to a file. For scripts that are agents, you have an additional choice. Each agent has a log associated with it, and you can write messages to that log. You can display the log for an agent by selecting the agent and then choosing Agent, Log from the Notes main menu.

You can use the NotesLog class to do the following:

- Open a database, mail, or file log
- Log actions or errors to the log

See Table 19.34 for a list of the NotesLog class properties and Table 19.35 for its methods.

Table 19.34 *NotesLog* Properties

Property	Description	Data Type	Usage
LogActions	True if actions should be logged.	Boolean	Read/Write

Property	Description	Data Type	Usage
LogErrors	True if errors should be logged.	Boolean	Read/Write
NumActions	The number of actions that have been logged so far by the script.	Integer	Read Only
NumErrors	The number of errors that have been logged so far by the script.	Integer	Read Only
OverwriteFile	If the log is being written to a file, returns whether an existing log file should be overwritten or appended.	Boolean	Read/Write
ProgramName	A name that identifies the script and is used to identify the log entries.	String	Read/Write

Table 19.35   *NotesLog* Methods

Method	Description	Return Data Type	Return Value
Close	Close a log.	None	None
LogAction	Write an action message to a log.	None	None
LogError	Write an error message to a log.	None	None
LogEvent	Generate a Notes event.	None	None
New	Create a new log.	NotesLog	The newly created log
OpenAgentLog	Open a log for an agent.	None	None
OpenFileLog	Given a filename, open the file and write any subsequent action or error messages to the file.	None	None
OpenMailLog	Create a new mail memo addressed to the recipients you specify. Write any subsequent action or error message to the memo and mail the memo when the log is closed.	None	None

Part

III

Ch

19

continues

Table 19.35 Continued

Method	Description	Return Data Type	Return Value
OpenNotesLog	Given a server and filename, open the specified log database. Write any subsequent action or error messages to the database.	None	None

Creating a Log

You create a new log by using either the CreateLog method in NotesSession or the New method of NotesLog. With either method, you supply a name to identify the new log. You can access this name later by using the ProgramName property.

Opening a Log

You have four options for the type of log you want to create, and each type of log has a method to open it. OpenNotesLog opens a specified Notes database as the logging database. The database must be based on the StdR4AgentLog template, which comes with Notes. If you look at the design of the template, you see that it is designed to store and display log entries. You can create one log database for all your agents or individual log databases for heavily used agents. When you log messages to the database, a new Log Entry document is created for each message.

 TIP If you're going to open a log database from a server-based script, make sure that the log database is on the same server. Scripts that run on servers can't open databases on other servers.

To open a mail log, use OpenMailLog. You supply the method with the names of the people or groups to receive the mail memo and optionally supply the subject line for the memo. Any log entries you write are stored in the mail memo until you close the log. The mail memo is then mailed to the list of recipients. The third open method is OpenFileLog. With this method, you supply the fully qualified path and filename where you want to store your log messages. The last open method is OpenAgentLog, and you use this method to log messages to the log associated with an agent.

Specifying What to Log

By default, actions and errors are written to the log. If you don't want to log either of these, set the LogActions or LogErrors property to False. You can check how many actions and errors have been logged so far by reading the NumActions and NumErrors properties. These properties are useful if you want to limit the size of a log to a specified number of log entries. If you're using a log file, you can set OverwriteFile to True to overwrite any existing file with the same name as your log file. If OverwriteFile is False, your log messages are appended to the log file.

Writing to a Log

When you want to write a log message to your log, call one of the `LogAction`, `LogError`, or `LogEvent` methods.

`LogAction` does one of the following, depending on the type of log you open:

- If you're logging to a Notes Database, `LogAction` creates a new Log Entry document in the database that contains the text you supply to the method.
- If you're using a Mail log, the method writes the current date and time, which is followed by your log message, to the Body of the mail memo.
- For file logs, `LogAction` writes the current date and time, which is followed by your log message, as the next line in the file.

`LogError` is similar, except that you supply the method with an error code and a description, which then is written to the log the same way as in `LogAction`.

`LogEvent` is different in that the method sends a Notes event message over the network. You can use `LogEvent` to send alerts to systems management software such as NotesView.

Closing a Log

After you are finished logging messages, you close the log by using the `Close` method. If you are using a mail log, `Close` sends the mail memo to its intended recipients. The following example demonstrates using the `NotesLog` class.

```
Sub Initialize
    Dim S As New NotesSession
    Dim CLog As New NotesLog( "Check Status Agent" )
    Call CLog.OpenMailLog( "Definiti_SalesManagers",  "Log for Check Status
Agent" )
    Dim Coll As NotesDocumentCollection
    Dim Cdoc As NotesDocument
    Dim Count%
    Set Coll = S.CurrentDatabase.AllDocuments
    Set CDoc = Coll.GetFirstDocument
    Do While Not  CDoc Is Nothing
        count% = count% + 1
        Call CLog.LogAction( "Processed document " +  Cstr( count% ) )
        Set CDoc = Coll.GetNextDocument( CDoc )
    Loop
End Sub
```

Working with *NotesDateTime*

One of the potentially confusing things about working with dates and times in LotusScript is that you have to deal with two different date-time formats: the Notes date-time format and the LotusScript date-time format. The `NotesDateTime` object represents a date and time in Notes format. As such, the `NotesDateTime` object has a date component, a time component, a time zone component, and a daylight savings time adjustment. The object stores times to an accuracy of hundredths of a second. Contrast this with the LotusScript date-time variant, which has only a date component and a time component that stores times to the nearest second.

When you get a date-time value from a Notes document, you get it as a NotesDateTime object. You can use the NotesDateTime object to do the following:

- Convert between the Notes date-time format and the LotusScript date-time format
- Convert between the Notes date-time format and text strings
- Modify the date and time components of a Notes date-time

See Table 19.36 for the class properties and Table 19.37 for its methods.

Table 19.36   *NotesDateTime* Properties

Property	Description	Data Type	Usage
DateOnly	A string containing only the date part of a date-time value.	String	Read/Write
GMTTime	The date-time converted to Greenwich mean time.	String	Read Only
IsDST	True if the computer running the script is set to observe daylight savings time, and daylight savings time is currently in effect.	Boolean	Read Only
LocalTime	The date-time in the local time zone.	String	Read/Write
LSGMTTime	The date-time converted to Greenwich Mean Time.	Variant of type DATE	Read Only
LSLocalTime	The date-time in the local time zone.	Variant of type DATE	Read Only
TimeOnly	A string containing only the time part of a date-time value.	String	Read/Write
TimeZone	The current time zone.	Integer	Read Only
ZoneTime	The date-time adjusted for the TimeZone and IsDST properties and returned as a string.	String	Read Only

Table 19.37 *NotesDateTime* **Methods**

Method	Description	Return Data Type	Return Value
AdjustDay	Add or subtract the number of days you specify from the date-time.	None	None
AdjustHour	Add or subtract the number of hours you specify from the date-time.	None	None
AdjustMinute	Add or subtract the number of minutes you specify from the date-time.	None	None
AdjustMonth	Add or subtract the number of months you specify from the date-time.	None	None
AdjustSecond	Add or subtract the number of seconds you specify from the date-time.	None	None
AdjustYear	Add or subtract the number of years you specify from the date-time.	None	None
ConvertToZone	Convert a date-time to a specified time zone.	None	None
New	Create a new date-time object.	NotesDateTime	The newly created date-time object
SetAnyDate	Set the date part of the date-time so that it matches any date. The time part of the date-time is not changed.	None	None
SetAnyTime	Set the time part of the date-time so that it matches any time. The date part of the date-time is not changed.	None	None
SetNow	Set the date-time value to today's date and the current time.	None	None
TimeDifference	Given two date-time values, return the date-time difference in seconds between them.	Long	The number of seconds between the two times

Creating a *NotesDateTime* Object

To create a new `NotesDateTime` object, you can use either the `CreateDateTime` method of `NotesSession` or the `New` method. You supply a string representing a date and time, and the methods return a new `NotesDateTime` object representing that date. You can specify the date and time in many different formats. Following are some of the formats:

- MM/DD/YYYY HH:MM:SS PM—for example, `'05/29/1992 14:30:00 PM'`
- MM/YYYY—for example, `'12/2001'`
- MM/DD HH:MM:SS—for example, `'07/27 17:04:00'`

 TIP You are using four-figure dates in all your LotusScript programs, aren't you? It's not that long to the year 2000!

After you have a `NotesDateTime` object, you can set it to the current date and time by using the `SetNow` method. You can also use `SetAnyDate` and `SetAnyTime` (which work like wildcards) to set the date and time parts of the object to match any date or time.

Converting a Date to and from LotusScript Format

Two properties let you convert between the different date-time formats. `LSLocalTime` lets you convert a Notes date-time format to its equivalent LotusScript date-time format. You can also set the `LSLocalTime` property to convert a LotusScript date-time into a Notes date-time. The following example shows how to convert a Notes date-time format date and time into a LotusScript date-time format:

```
Dim dtNotes As New NotesDateTime("12/21/1995 2:47:03 AM")
Dim datLotusScript As Variant
datLotusScript = dtNotes.LSLocalTime
```

In this example, the LotusScript date-time is set to represent 12/12/1995 2:47:03 AM, irrespective of the time zone for the computer.

You can also set the `LSLocalTime` property to convert a LotusScript date-time into its Notes date-time equivalent.

The second property, `LSGMTTime`, not only converts the Notes date-time into LotusScript format, but also converts the time component into Greenwich mean time.

If you need to find the time zone for a Notes date-time, use the `TimeZone` property. The property returns an integer representing the time zone. When you need to know whether daylight savings time is in effect for a Notes date-time, you can use the `IsDST` property to check. If the computer on which you run the script is set to observe daylight savings time and daylight savings time is currently in effect, `IsDST` returns `True`.

Converting a Date to and from a Text String

If you need to convert a date-time between a Notes date-time value and a text string, you have two properties to help you. `LocalTime` and `GMTTime` work in a similar way to their LotusScript equivalents, except that they translate Notes date-time values to and from text strings. You can also use the new `ZoneTime` property to get a date-time value displayed in its original time zone.

Modifying a Date and Time

You can modify parts of a date-time by using the `AdjustYear`, `AdjustMonth`, `AdjustDay`, `AdjustHour`, `AdjustMinute`, and `AdjustSecond` methods. For example, to calculate the date two weeks ago, use the following script:

```
Dim dtNotes As New NotesDateTime("Today")
Call dtNotes.AdjustDay(-14)
```

The methods are smart enough to adjust any parts of the date-time that need to be updated. For example, if the script runs on July 2, the month part of the date-time is automatically changed to June. You can convert a date-time from one time zone to another by using `ConvertToZone`.

Performing Date and Time Calculations

Use the `TimeDifference` method to calculate the number of seconds between two Notes date-time values.

Working with the *NotesDateRange* Class

The `NotesDateRange` class represents a time span. See Table 19.38 for the class properties.

Table 19.38 *NotesDateRange* Properties

Property	Description	Data Type	Usage
EndDateTime	The end of the date range.	NotesDateTime	Read/Write
StartDateTime	The start of the date range.	NotesDateTime	Read/Write
Text	The date range as a string.	String	Read/Write

Set the `StartDateTime` property to a `NotesDateTime` object representing the beginning of the time span, and set the `EndDateTime` property to another `NotesDateTime` object representing the end of the span. You can then read the start and end dates by using the `Text` property. For example, the `Text` property of a `NotesDateRange` object could be `10/01/96 11:15:00 AM—10/03/96 11:15:00 AM`.

Working with the *NotesName* Class

`NotesName` is another class that was introduced in Notes 4.5. It represents a user or server name within Notes and lets you access the various components of hierarchical names. For example, you can use a `NotesName` object to extract the organization component of a user's name.

N O T E All the properties of the NotesName class are Read Only, so you can't use this class to update user or server names. ▪

The NotesName class has only one method, New, which you use to create a new NotesName object. The properties of this class are listed in Table 19.39.

Table 19.39   *NotesName* Properties

Property	Description	Data Type	Usage
Abbreviated	The abbreviated form of a hierarchical name.	String	Read Only
ADMD	The administration domain name part of a hierarchical name.	String	Read Only
Canonical	The name in canonical format.	String	Read Only
Common	The common name (CN) part of a hierarchical name.	String	Read Only
Country	The country (C) part of a hierarchical name.	String	Read Only
Generation	The generation part of a name.	String	Read Only
Given	The given part of a name.	String	Read Only
Initials	The initials of a name.	String	Read Only
IsHierarchical	True if the name is hierarchical.	Boolean	Read Only
Keyword	The name in keyword format.	String	Read Only
Organization	The organization (O) part of a hierarchical name.	String	Read Only
OrgUnit1	The first organizational unit (OU1) part of a hierarchical name.	String	Read Only
OrgUnit2	The second organizational unit (OU2) part of a hierarchical name.	String	Read Only
OrgUnit3	The third organizational unit (OU3) part of a hierarchical name.	String	Read Only
OrgUnit4	The fourth organizational unit (OU4) part of a hierarchical name.	String	Read Only

Property	Description	Data Type	Usage
PRMD	The private management domain name part of a name.	String	Read Only
Surname	The surname part of a name.	String	Read Only

Working with the *NotesInternational* Class

The NotesInternational class is also new to Notes as of Release 4.5, and the class gives you access to the international settings on the machine running a script. For example, on a machine running Windows, you can access the international settings that have been configured by using the Control Panel.

N O T E If any of the international settings are changed, Notes immediately recognizes the change. ▨

The class properties for NotesInternational are shown in Table 19.40; it has no methods.

Table 19.40 *NotesInternational* **Properties**

Property	Description	Data Type	Usage
AMString	The string that indicates a time before noon in the local language.	String	Read Only
CurrencyDigits	The number of digits after a decimal point.	Integer	Read Only
CurrencySymbol	The currency symbol.	String	Read Only
DateSep	The character used to separate the year, month, and day in a date.	String	Read Only
DecimalSep	The character used to separate the parts of a decimal number.	String	Read Only
IsCurrencySpace	True if there is a space between the currency symbol and the amount.	Boolean	Read Only
IsCurrencySuffix	True if the currency symbol is displayed after the amount.	Boolean	Read Only
IsCurrencyZero	True if a fraction has a leading zero when displayed as a decimal.	Boolean	Read Only

Part
III

Ch
19

continues

Table 19.40 Continued

Property	Description	Data Type	Usage
IsDateDMY	True if the date format is day-month-year.	Boolean	Read Only
IsDateMDY	True if the date format is month-day-year.	Boolean	Read Only
IsDateYMD	True if the date format is year-month-day.	Boolean	Read Only
IsDST	True if daylight savings time is in effect.	Boolean	Read Only
IsTime24Hour	True if the time format is 24-hour.	Boolean	Read Only
PMString	The string indicating a time after noon in the local language.	String	Read Only
ThousandsSep	The thousands separator character for numbers.	String	Read Only
TimeSep	The character used to separate the hours, minutes, and seconds in a time.	String	Read Only
TimeZone	The time zone setting.	Integer	Read Only
Today	The string that means today in the local language.	String	Read Only
Tomorrow	The string that means tomorrow in the local language.	String	Read Only
Yesterday	The string that means yesterday in the local language.	String	Read Only

Working with the *NotesNewsletter* Class

Suppose that you have a collection of Notes documents, which are the results of a full-text search of a database or a set of documents that haven't been processed by an agent. Wouldn't it be great if you could create a summary document containing doclinks to all the documents in the collection? By using the NotesNewsletter class, you can.

The class lets you create two types of summary documents. The first type is based on all documents in the collection; the second type includes information from just one of the documents in the collection.

See Table 19.41 for the NotesNewsletter class properties and Table 19.42 for the class methods.

Table 19.41 *NotesNewsletter* Properties

Property	Description	Data Type	Usage
DoScore	For newsletters created by using the FormatMsgWith Doclinks method; True if the relevance score for each document should be included.	Boolean	Read/Write
DoSubject	For newsletters created by using the FormatMsgWith Doclinks method; True if the subject of each document should be included. (Use SubjectItemName to define which field to use as the subject.)	Boolean	Read/Write
SubjectItemName	For newsletters created by using the FormatMsgWith Doclinks method; the name of the field to treat as the subject or title of the document.	String	Read/Write

Table 19.42 *NotesNewsletter* Methods

Method	Description	Return Data Type	Return Value
FormatDocument	Given the position of a document within the newsletter, create a picture of that document. Then create a new document in the supplied database and store the picture as the body of the new document.	NotesDocument	The newly created document
FormatMsgWith Doclinks	Given a database, create a newsletter document in the database.	NotesDocument	The newsletter document
New	Create a new newsletter.	NotesNewsletter	The new newsletter

Creating a Newsletter

You have two ways to create a new NotesNewsletter. You can use the CreateNewsletter method of NotesSession or the NotesNewsletter New method. With both methods, you supply a document collection that contains the set of documents you want to include in the newsletter.

Formatting a Newsletter

After you have created a Newsletter object, you can choose between two options to create a summary document from the Newsletter object. You can use the FormatMsgWithDoclinks method to create a document containing links to all the documents within the collection. You supply the method with the database in which to create the new document.

The new document has a summary line for each document in the collection. By default, each line contains the relevance score for the document, which is followed by a doclink to the document. If you don't want to include the relevance score, set the DoScore property to False. You can also include a title for each document by using the DoSubject and SubjectItemName properties. You set SubjectItemName to the name of the field that contains the text you want to use as the title. You then set DoSubject to True to include the title in each line of the newsletter. For example, suppose that the documents in the collection all contain a field called DocTitle, which stores the subject of the document. If you set SubjectItemName to DocTitle and DoSubject to True, each line in the newsletter consists of the relevance score for the document, a doclink to the document, followed by the text from the DocTitle field.

You can use the second option, FormatDocument method, to create a new document containing a picture of a particular document from the collection. This is similar to forwarding a document, where the new mail memo displays a picture of the forwarded document. You supply the method with the database in which to create the new document and a number to indicate which of the documents to include from the collection. The method creates the new document, which contains a picture of the document from the collection.

Saving or Mailing a Newsletter

The document you create by using the NotesNewsletter methods is, in Notes terms, the same as any other document. You can call the document's Save method to save the document, or you can use the Send method to mail the document.

Working with *NotesTimer*

The NotesTimer object lets you set a timer that you can use to trigger an event. You specify a time interval, and when the time interval has passed, an Alarm event is triggered. The NotesTimer class has only one method, New, which you use to instantiate a new NotesTimer object. Its properties are listed in Table 19.43.

Table 19.43   *NotesTimer* Properties

Property	Description	Data Type	Usage
Comment	A comment to identify the timer.	String	Read/Write
Enabled	Set to True to enable the timer. By default, a timer is enabled.	Boolean	Read/Write

Property	Description	Data Type	Usage
Interval	The number of seconds to wait before triggering an Alarm event.	Integer	Read/Write

To use a timer, do one of the following:

- Declare a NotesTimer object in the (Declarations) or (Options) part of a script.
- Create a NotesTimer object by using New or CreateTimer method of NotesSession. You supply a time interval and an optional comment.
- Use the On Event Alarm statement to define a sub to call at each passing of the time interval.

You use the Interval property to set the time interval for the timer and the Comment property to add an identifying comment to the timer. You can enable and disable the timer by using its Enabled property.

For example, to set up and use a timer to call a sub every minute, you first declare the timer in the (Options) or (Declarations) section, as follows:

```
Dim tmrMinute As NotesTimer
```

Then, in part of your script, you create the timer and define the sub to call when the timer time period has expired:

```
Set tmrMinute = New NotesTimer(60, "One minute timer")
On Event Alarm From tmrMinute Call DoOneMinuteProcessing
```

Because, by default, the timer is enabled, the DoOneMinuteProcessing sub will be called approximately every minute.

> **CAUTION**
>
> Don't rely on the accuracy of the timing too much, because other events can delay the time at which the Alarm event is triggered.

Part III

Ch 19

Working with the *NotesRegistration* Class

The NotesRegistration class is new to Notes 4.6, and the class allows you to use LotusScript to create and administrate Notes user IDs. The class properties and methods are listed in Tables 19.44 and 19.45.

Table 19.44 *NotesRegistration* **Properties**

Property	Description	Data Type	Usage
CertifierIDFile	The complete file path to the certifier ID to use when creating Notes IDs.	String	Read/Write
CreateMailDb	If True, tells Notes to create a new mail database with an ID file when calling RegisterNewUser.	Boolean	Read/Write
Expiration	The expiration date to use when creating Notes ID files.	NotesDateTime	Read/Write
IDType	The type of ID file you want to create when calling Register NewUser, RegisterNewServer, and RegisterNewCertifier.	Integer	Read/Write
IsNorthAmerican	If True, ID file will be created as a North American ID file.	Boolean	Read/Write
MinPassword Length	Given an Integer value, determines the minimum number of characters required for an ID's password.	Integer	Read/Write
OrgUnit	Indicates which Organizational Unit should be used when creating an ID file.	String	Read/Write
RegistrationLog	Indicates which log file should be used when creating ID files.	String	Read/Write
Registration Server	Specifies which server to use when creating IDs. This property is used only when the new ID is stored in the server's Address Book, or when a mail database is created for the new user.	String	Read/Write
StoreDInAddress Book	If True, the ID file will be stored in the Public Address Book.	Boolean	Read/Write
UpdateAddress book	If True, the server entry in the address book is updated when the ID file is created.	Boolean	Read/Write

CAUTION

The `StoreIdInAddressBook` is listed in the Notes Help for this class as `StoreIdtoAddressBook`, but it is listed in the LotusScript browser as `StoreIdInAddressBook`, which is the proper syntax.

Table 19.45 *NotesRegistration* **Methods**

Method	Description	Return Data Type	Return Value
`AddCertifier ToAddressbook`	When called, adds the Certifier ID to the Public Address Book.	None	None
`AddServerTo Addressbook`	Creates a new Server document in the Public Address Book.	None	None
`AddUserProfile`	When called, adds a user profile document to the ID file.	None	None
`AddUserTo AddressBook`	Used to add a new user to the Public Address Book.	None	None
`CrossCertify`	Call this method to cross-certify an ID file.	Boolean	True if cross-certification was successful
`DeleteIDOnServer`	Call this method to delete an ID file from the server.	None	None
`GetIDFromServer`	This methods allows you to get an ID file from a Notes server.	None	None
`GetUserInfo FromServer`	Use this method to retrieve information from the server about a user.	String	Various information about a user
`Recertify`	Call to recertify an ID file.	Boolean	True if recertification completed successfully
`RegisterNew Certifier`	This method allows you to create a new certifier ID.	Boolean	True if the certifier was successfully registered
`RegisterNew Server`	Use this method to create a new server ID.	Boolean	True if server was successfully registered

continues

Part

III

Ch

19

Table 19.45   Continued

Method	Description	Return Data Type	Return Value
RegisterNewUser	Call this method to register a new Notes user.	Boolean	True if user was registered successfully
SwitchToID	This method allows you to switch the current ID to an ID file that you specify.	String	The username of the new ID file

Automating Notes Registration

The NotesRegistration makes it easy to use LotusScript to automate the Notes registration process. The following example shows you how you can use a custom dialog box to get the new user registration information from a user and then create a new Notes user ID.

```
Sub Click(Source As Button)
    Dim Session As New NotesSession
    Dim Ws As New NotesUIWorkspace
    Dim RegIDoc As NotesUIDocument
    Set RegDoc=Ws.CurrentDocument.Document
    Dim NR As New NotesRegistration
    ' You have to set the registration Server and use the full path and id
    ' for the CertifierIDFile
    NR.registrationServer="Aegis/Definiti"
    NR.CERTIFIERIDFILE = "f:\idfiles\Cert.ID"
    NR.StoreIDInAddressBook=True
    ' In this example, the dialogbox contains a fields whose contents will be
used as the RegisterNewUser method's parameters
    If Ws.DialogBox("(UserRegistration)", True, True, False, False, False,
"Register a new  Notes user") Then
        NR.StoreIDinAddressBook = True
        NR.CreateMailDB = True
        NR.UpdateAddressBook = True
        If NR.RegisterNewUser(RegDoc.Lname(0), RegDoc.UserIDFile(0),
RegDoc.MailServer(0), RegDoc.Fname(0)_
        , RegDoc.FwdDomain(0), Reg.Doc.MiddleInitital(0),
RegDoc.CertPassword(0), RegDoc.Mlocation(0)_
        , RegDoc.Comment(0), RegDoc.UserMailPath(0), RegDoc.UserPassword(0))
Then
            Msgbox "The new user: " & RegDoc.FName & " " & RegDoc.LName(0) & "
was registered Successfully", 64,_ "Success"
        Else
            Msgbox "Sorry, " & RegDoc.FName & " " & RegDoc.LName(0) & " was
NOT registered, please try again", 64,_ "Registration Error"
        End If
    End If
End Sub
```

Going Mobile

Setting Up to Go Remote

This chapter is for Notes users who need to set up their PCs to work on Notes away from the office—that is, users who aren't connected to a Notes server through a local area network. You can work remote all the time (referred to as *remote only*) or part of the time (referred to as *network/remote*). With Lotus Notes' remote capability, you can easily send and receive mail, use public databases, and participate in Notes discussions as though you're working on-site.

N O T E   As you will learn in Part VI, "Working with the Web," you can also work with databases and get your email using an Internet Browser if Lotus' Domino server is set up in your company to allow access in this manner. However, this chapter and the next focus on remotely connecting directly from your Notes client to your Notes server through a dial-up connection. To learn how to access Notes' database via the Internet, check out Part VI of this book. ■

What Does It Mean to Work Remote?

When you connect to a Notes server through a local area network, your PC, whether a desktop or a laptop, is connected by cables directly through a LAN to one or more servers. You have direct access to databases on the servers in your network. Usually, you also have access to printing resources and other file servers (servers used to store files and applications for you). This access often lets you work with a large amount of information without having to have a large hard disk to store it all. You can also work with the current database information and send and receive email instantly.

However, Notes functions quite differently when you work remote. When you set up Notes on your remote PC, you must use a modem to connect to a Notes server through a telephone line connection. You create copies of all the databases you want to use and store them on your PC's hard disk (unless you're working strictly through Interactive Connection, discussed in Chapter 21, "Working Remote"). If you're using a printer, you typically have the printer cables attached directly to your PC. In other words, you have to be in physical possession of just about every-thing you need to work with when you're off the network. You control the times when informa-tion is passed between you and others on the network, because you must initiate the call to the server in order to begin the communication process.

Most often, a remote PC is a laptop that you use when you travel. You can also work remote with Notes on a desktop PC at home or in another office. Regardless of the type of equipment you use, keep in mind that you will require more disk space when working remote because you will have to store replica copies of databases on your hard drive. You will learn more about replica copies in the rest of this chapter and in Chapter 21.

The size of these copies depends on the amount of information the databases store and how much of it you elect to carry with you remotely. In Notes 4.x, the maximum size a database can grow to is 4G. Although most databases won't grow to their maximum allowable size, they can be quite large and can require a significant amount of space. The minimum recommended amount of free hard disk space for running Notes and working with the databases you need on your remote PC is 100M—and that might be cutting things close if you're accessing multiple databases! You will find tips on minimizing your hard disk space usage in Chapter 21, which explains how to make and use databases while working remote.

Consider Disk Space When Going Remote

If you're getting ready to work remote but you haven't yet purchased the PC you will use, talk with your Notes administrator to find out how much disk space you will need to successfully work remote and access all the applications you will require within your company. If you install the full version of Notes on your PC (all the operating files, Help files, documentation files, sample databases, and so on), you're looking at using at least 55M of disk space before you make the first copy of a database you will use from the server! Keep in mind that most operating systems don't perform efficiently if you don't allow for at least 5M of free disk space to be used as swap file space while you're working.

You can elect to install Notes without all the documentation to minimize the disk space used. This type of installation is recommended if you're working away from the office only part of the time and you have access to these files when you're on the network in case you need them.

If you're not planning to design databases, you can safely elect not to install these databases on your hard drive. Documentation databases, which are stored in a directory called DOC, are online copies of Notes documentation. You might want to install the documentation databases and then delete the databases you don't find useful for your needs.

The Notes Help database (HELP4.NSF) is very large, but it provides online help for most Notes questions. When you were installing Notes 4.x, you or your Notes administrator also installed a database called Notes Help Lite, unless you deselected this option during the installation. The filename for Notes Help Lite is HELPLT4.NSF, and it's stored in your C:\NOTES\DATA subdirectory (unless you specified a different directory during setup).

Help Lite contains a subset of the Notes Help documents. It provides help while you travel, but it uses less disk space than the full Help database. Help Lite contains information you are more likely to need when you use Notes away from the office, such as information on working remote. It doesn't contain much information on nonremote topics, such as database design.

If you work remote all the time, you might want to delete the Help Lite database (by highlighting its icon and selecting File, Database, Delete, Yes) and keep the full Notes Help database, because you will most likely need to access help information on topics not covered in Help Lite. You can conserve some disk space by not carrying two copies of the same information on your hard drive.

However, if you typically work remote only part of the time, you might want to delete the full Notes Help database from your PC's hard drive and carry only the Help Lite database on your hard drive to conserve disk space. You can always access the full version of the Notes Help database from the network when you're working in the office.

Your Notes administrator can help you decide which of these databases you need while working remote. It is always recommended that you consult with your Notes administrator to ensure that you are working within the standards set for your company.

Part

IV

Ch

20

What You Need to Work Remote

To work remote, you need the following:

- A PC with Notes 4.x installed
- A modem connected to your PC with an asynchronous (serial) port enabled and a modem (MDM) file that's compatible with your modem
- The exact name of the Notes server(s) you will access
- The phone number(s) for the modem connection to the Notes server(s)
- A direct-dial analog phone line
- A certified Notes User ID

Your Notes administrator also must do the following:

- Grant you appropriate access to the Notes server(s)
- Set up the Notes server(s) to receive incoming calls through a modem

In the following sections, you will learn about modems and phone lines. The remainder of this chapter walks you through configuring your PC to work remote.

Using Modems

Modems, which are the most common type of communications processor, convert the digital signals from your computer at one end of a communications link into analog frequencies, which can travel over ordinary telephone lines. At the other end of the communications line, a modem converts the transmitted data back into digital form that the receiving computer can process.

You can buy several types and speeds of modems. An internal modem (located inside your PC) is more convenient when you travel with a laptop, but it isn't always the recommended type of modem for your needs and isn't supported in some older laptops. An external modem connects through a port outside your PC. External modems are now available in desktop models (meant for stationary use) and pocket models, known for their compact, lightweight, portable features.

N O T E　Most new laptops support *PCMCIA cards*—often referred to as *PC cards*—which are about the size of a credit card and fit into small slots on the side of your laptop. One of the most popular PCMCIA cards is the modem card. These credit card-size modems are very popular due to their high-speed data transmission capabilities—typically 14,400 baud to 28,800 baud—and their lightweight, compact features (which helps keep the laptop weight down when you are lugging around a PC all day!). They are also popular because they are easy to take in and out of a laptop. ▪

When you choose a modem, one of the most important factors is the modem's speed, which is measured in bits per second, also known as the *baud*. A higher baud means your PC and the server can exchange information more quickly, which results in a shorter (and cheaper) phone call. In business settings today, most users use 9,600 to 28,800 baud modems. The least expensive modems in use today are 2,400 baud modems, which have longer exchange times and higher phone costs. Several popular modem models on the market today offer speeds from 9,600 baud to 36,000 baud. Recent modems have speed capabilities even greater than 36,000 baud.

Paying attention to what type of baud the modem speed is manufactured for is also important. *Fax modem speed* refers only to the speed that a *fax* can be transmitted through the modem; *data modem speed* refers to how fast *data* can be transmitted through the modem. A 9,600/ 2,400 fax data modem, for example, transmits faxes at 9,600 baud and data at 2,400 baud. Lotus Notes transfers data (the information you are exchanging when you work in databases). Therefore, you must pay attention to the data baud that your modem supports. You should try to get a modem that supports at least 28,800 baud to help keep your phone bill down, as well as to keep the server from being tied up for long periods of time. Table 20.1 illustrates three average times for data transmission based on the baud of the modem you and the server are using.

Table 20.1   Comparison Transmission Times for Three Baud Values

Time	Baud Value
25 minutes	9,600
15 minutes	14,400
7 minutes	28,800

N O T E   When working remote with Lotus Notes, you will be prompted in the status bar at the bottom of the Notes window when you have connected to the remote server, and you will be told at which speed you have connected. The prompt information tells you the port connection speed, which is the speed at which your port is transmitting data to the port on the server.

However, in many cases, this speed isn't the actual speed at which data is being transmitted. The speed at which the carrier can successfully transmit data is also a factor. For the purposes of using Notes remote, think of a carrier as everything in between your modem and the server's modem, including phone lines, hotel switchboards, and so on.

When connecting internationally, through old phone systems, or even through hotel switchboards, the carrier speed might be greatly reduced. You might receive a prompt that you have connected to the server at a port rate of 9,600 baud, for example, but everything will seem to be happening in slow motion. This problem is most likely due to the slow carrier speed of the transmission. ■

Notes can work with all the many different makes and models of modems, as long as you can locate or create a modem command file for your modem (see the next paragraph). Many manufacturers sell modems that are known as *Hayes-compatible,* indicating that software can control them using commands that were standardized by a company called Hayes. Notes works well with these types of modems.

Part

IV

Ch

20

Notes comes with files called *modem command files,* which have an MDM extension. These files provide the commands that PCs need in order to use your modem. If you use a non-Hayes-compatible modem, you need to search for a modem command file configured for your modem or spend time editing a modem command file to meet your needs. Editing a modem command file can be a considerable chore, and it's best done by an expert or with assistance from one.

CAUTION

Before you buy a modem, check with your Notes administrator to make sure that your modem is compatible with the server's modem. Otherwise, you might experience problems with your modem connections, have to connect only at very low speeds, or sacrifice some of your modem's special functionality in order to talk to the Notes server. Typically, Hayes-compatible modems are your best bet, because Notes runs very well with them.

Getting Help with Your Modem Setup If you have trouble with your modem, you have resources to turn to for additional help. Your Notes administrator is the first resource available to you for assistance with modem installation and troubleshooting.

The modem's manufacturer and documentation might also provide the key to getting your modem set up properly. Look for a section in your modem documentation that indicates the appropriate modem files that might be compatible with your modem, as well as any special settings that might be required.

Available from Lotus is the Mobile Survival Kit database, which provides debugging information regarding problems with modems, as well as additional modem files that might work better with your particular modem. You can find this database in CompuServe by entering GO LOTUSC and checking out the Library in this forum, or by accessing the database from Lotus' Web site: www.lotus.com. You will find the Mobile Survival Kit in the Notes support section. A copy of this database is also on the CD that accompanies this book. You will find it as an attachment in the Using Lotus Notes 4.6 database.

This database, if it's available to your company, will most likely be installed on a Notes server(s) on your network. Check your network's Database Catalog to see whether this database is available to you. If you don't see it listed, ask your Notes administrator if this database was acquired for use by your company through partnership agreements. As just mentioned, you can also find this database on the Lotus Web site. It is updated weekly, so you will find the most up-to-date files there. Finally, several other outside resources, bulletin boards, and help services might be available to you if you have substantial trouble with your modem.

Phone Line Requirements

When you communicate with a server remotely, your modem converts the data signals sent from your PC into analog signals that can be sent over a telephone line. The modem on the server then converts the analog signals back into a digital form that your PC can understand. Having the proper type of phone line to transmit the signals being sent from your modem is therefore important.

To work with a modem, you need a direct-dial analog phone line, also referred to as a voice line. Most residential locations have an analog line into the home. Digital lines transmit digital signals that your modem can't interpret. You typically find digital lines in office buildings.

You also must make sure that special telephone services such as call waiting and call park (similar to putting a call on hold), which can interrupt communications on your line, are discontinued or disabled when you work with your modem. Even a split-second interruption in the phone signal can cause your modem connection to be terminated. Contact your local phone company for details on the specific services it offers that might interfere with your modem.

 If you can temporarily disable a special telephone service by pressing a particular number/character sequence (*70 on a touchtone phone or 1170 on a rotary phone in most of North America), you might also be able to disable this service through Notes each time you dial the server. Enter this number sequence as part of the prefix number when you call a server. You might need to experiment or contact your phone company for additional information. More information on how to enter phone numbers is provided in the section "Setting Up Connections Records" later in this chapter.

Ideally, you would have a dedicated phone line to use if you were planning to work a great deal with Notes from your home. If you need to install a phone line, specify to the phone company that you want a POTS (plain old telephone service) line. This request will ensure that you will receive the type of line you need to work remote. You might also consider getting Integrated Services Digital Network (ISDN) service—particularly if you're planning to send a lot of data back and forth with a server or servers. ISDN sends digital signals, which are more compatible with computer systems than analog systems, and the speed in which the data is transmitted is much greater. However, this type of service is more expensive, and you will need to get a special modem in order to use it.

Getting Started

Although Lotus Notes provides you with all the software capability you need to work remote, you first need to set up your system before you can work away from the network. Each step is discussed in detail later, but the following list gives you an overview of the steps you must perform on your PC:

1. Enable a port.
2. Enable your modem.
3. Create a location or locations.
4. Create a server connection or connections.

The remainder of this chapter discusses these steps in more detail. An additional step, setting up Notes for remote mail, is covered in Chapter 21, because the settings you make will depend on how you elect to work with the Notes server.

Part
IV

Ch
20

Enabling a Port

Before you can work with Notes remote, you must make sure that the proper communications ports are set up correctly on your system. Communications ports serve as a gateway through which your PC can communicate with other hardware through special connections. To use Notes on a network, you enable a LAN port, which is often denoted by the letters LAN and a number (such as LAN0). When you're working remote, you use a communications port, which is denoted by the letters COM and a number (such as COM1). Notes makes it easy to set up the type of communications ports you need to work with.

TIP If you use your computer to work on a LAN at one site and to work remote at another, you can enable the LAN port and the COM port at the same time. Notes switches to the appropriate port as necessary based on the location you select for your work session. You will learn more about setting up locations shortly.

Follow these steps to verify, change, or set up your network port(s):

1. Choose File, Tools, User Preferences to open the User Preferences dialog box.
2. Select the Ports icon to display the Ports Setup panel, shown in Figure 20.1.

FIG. 20.1

To set up your communication ports, you use the Ports Setup panel of the User Preferences dialog box.

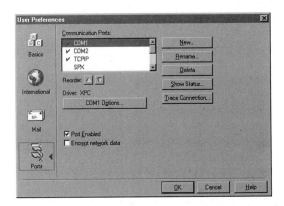

N O T E You might not see as many ports listed in your Ports Setup panel as shown in Figure 20.1. The number of ports displayed depends on the setup of your computer. ■

3. In the Communication Ports scroll box, select the COM port attached to your modem. (COM2 is often used with modems for portable PCs, particularly internal modems. COM1 is often used for external modems. Check your PC's user manual to determine which COM port you need to choose.)
4. To see the status of the COM port you have selected, select the COM port in Communication Ports scroll box, and then click Show Status (see Figure 20.2). If you see a message indicating that the COM port is performing a function, select another COM port for your modem. The Port Status dialog box in Figure 20.2 indicates that no activity is taking place. Click Cancel to close this dialog box and return to the Ports Setup panel.

FIG. 20.2

Opening the Port Status dialog box is a fast way of determining whether another device is utilizing the port you have selected.

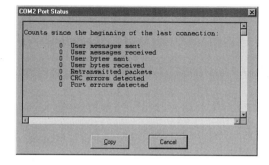

5. Select Port Enabled so that a checkmark appears in the checkbox and next to the selected COM port in the Communication Ports scroll box.

6. If you need to encrypt the data as it's sent over the modem, choose Encrypt network data. This selection slows down the transmission of data by turning off the ability to use data compression. It really isn't recommended unless you're transmitting highly sensitive data or you suspect that someone is tapping into your transmissions.

   Encryption causes Notes to encode data in such a way that anyone wiretapping a phone line can't read the data. Notes encodes the data before transmitting it over the phone line and decodes it at the other end. Eavesdroppers see meaningless data if they try to analyze the line.

Leave the Ports Setup panel open. You'll need it to set up your modem in the next section.

 You can reorder the way the ports are sorted in the Communication Ports scroll list by highlighting the COM or LAN port name you want to reorder and clicking the up or down arrow next to the Reorder option. Clicking a Reorder arrow causes the highlighted port to move up or down in the list of ports. Use this technique to move the port names you work with frequently to the top of the list for easier reference.

Defining a New COM Port

If you don't see any COM ports listed in the Communication Ports scroll box, you must define one before you can move forward. This procedure is very simple. When you add a port, you are telling Notes what communications port on your PC to use and specifying what driver and buffer size to use. With the Port Setup panel open, follow these instructions to define a port:

1. Click New to display the New Port dialog box.

2. Enter the following information in the appropriate text fields:

   Name: Enter the COM port that you want to set up. For example, enter COM1. If you are unsure of which port you need to activate, consult your PC and modem documentation.

   Driver: Select XPC to specify the driver for dialup use.

continues

Part
IV

Ch

20

continued

> Select which location(s) will use this port name in the Use Port at the following locations list box. (You'll learn more about locations later in this chapter, in the section "Setting Up Locations.")
>
> Your new port setup should look similar to the example in Figure 20.2 if you are setting up a COM1 port.

    3. Click <u>O</u>K to return to the Port Setup panel.

Setting Up Your Modem

Before you can use your modem, you need to specify the particular modem command file to work with your modem, the modem speed (baud) for your modem, and whether your dial setup is pulse or tone. You also might want to customize some additional settings. To set up your modem, follow these steps:

    1. If you are not already in the Port Setup panel of the User Preferences dialog box, select <u>F</u>ile, <u>T</u>ools, <u>U</u>ser Preferences, and then click the Ports icon. Otherwise, skip to step 2.

    2. Click the port's <u>O</u>ptions button (it's below the Driver information label in the center of the dialog box). The title of this button changes according to the port you have highlighted in the <u>C</u>ommunication Ports list box. The Additional Setup dialog box appears, as shown in Figure 20.3.

FIG. 20.3

You can adjust modem settings in the Additional Setup dialog box.

    3. In the Modem <u>t</u>ype list box, choose the type of modem you're using. If your exact modem type isn't available, choose the closest compatible type. Refer to your modem's user's guide to determine modem compatibility. If your modem type isn't listed, see the next section.

    4. Adjust the remaining modem settings if necessary. (These settings are described in later sections.)

N O T E   Ignore the <u>A</u>cquire Script button and the Log script <u>I</u>/O checkbox. Script files are written and managed by Notes administrators on the Notes servers and are not covered in this book. Script files are similar to modem command files in that you use both to set up communications equipment to work in your environment. For example, if you try to connect to CompuServe's Lotus

Notes server to send email to non-Notes users, you will need a script file provided by CompuServe to log on and navigate through its complex services to reach the Lotus Notes servers. Your Notes administrator will contact you if you need to make adjustments to these features. ▇

5. Click <u>O</u>K, and then click <u>O</u>K again to save your modem and network ports selections.

What to Do if Your Modem Isn't Listed

If your modem type isn't listed in the Additional Setup dialog box, choose Auto Configure (for unlisted modems only) from the Modem <u>t</u>ype list. Notes will usually be able to adapt to the modem connected to your PC. If you later change your modem type, Notes automatically tries to adapt to the new modem if this file is selected.

If your modem type isn't listed, and the Auto Configure MDM file (for unlisted modems) doesn't let your modem connect with the server, try selecting modem files that might be similar to your modem. If you still can't get your modem to work with an existing MDM file, you will need to create or edit an existing modem command file. You can do this by choosing one of the generic or null modem files to use as a template and then clicking the Modem <u>F</u>ile button. Editing or creating a modem command file isn't an easy task for most users; consult your modem's user guide or your Notes administrator for the technical assistance you need.

When possible, choose a modem file specifically designed for your modem. Often, when you use a modem file that is similar to the type you need but not quite the same, you experience some problems or lose some of your modem's features. Refer to the "Remote Troubleshooting" chapter on the CD-ROM if you have problems making connections with your modem.

N O T E If you don't see any modem files listed when you open the Additional Setup dialog box, you
might have a line missing from your NOTES.INI file. Exit to your command prompt and edit
the NOTES.INI file to include the following line:

```
ModemFileDirectory=C:\Notes\Data\Modems
```

If you specified a different data directory when you installed Notes, you will need to modify this entry to show the path to your MODEMS subdirectory (or wherever you have your MDM files stored). Save your new NOTES.INI file and exit. You must restart Windows and Notes before the edits will take effect. For more information on editing your NOTES.INI file, read Chapter 2, "Customizing Notes." ▇

Part
IV

Ch
20

Port Speed

In the Additional Setup dialog box, the Maximum port <u>s</u>peed option specifies the fastest speed at which transmission can take place, depending on the type of modem you use. If you chose Auto Configure as the modem type, choose 19,200; Notes automatically adjusts to the appropriate speed during each session for your particular modem.

Lotus Notes uses data compression when passing information across phone lines, unless the data you're sending is encrypted. For the most part, data compression effectively doubles the speed at which the data is passed across the connection. For example, a modem with a maximum baud of 9,600 can transfer data at the relative speed of 19,200 baud with data compression, because twice the amount of data is being passed within the same amount of time.

The speed actually used will be the lesser of the maximum speed you select in this setting and the maximum speed specified in the MDM file you have selected. For example, if you selected 19,200 bps in the Maximum Port Speed option, and the MDM file limits your modem to 9,600 bps as the maximum, you will see a warning like the one shown in Figure 20.4.

FIG. 20.4
This sample error message signals an incompatible modem speed.

If you dial from a hotel or on noisy phone lines, you might need to choose a slower speed than the maximum allowed by your modem to improve your connection. The large amount of electronic noise being processed by your modem as it is trying to process the data can cause connection problems, and the hotel's PBX switch might not be able to handle high-speed transmissions. Lowering the baud helps your modem distinguish between what is data and what is noise.

Speaker Volume

The Speaker volume option in the Additional Setup dialog box determines what you can hear when you dial the server. To hear the modem as it dials, choose any option except Off. If you listen to the modem, you can determine whether it is dialing, whether the carrier connection is established, and whether the server's modem and your modem are "shaking hands" (sort of a "Darth Vader with a cold" sound). Hearing the modem is also useful if you dial into the server manually. You should choose to hear the modem tones unless you are scheduling your PC to call the server during times when you need quiet, such as during the night in your hotel room!

Dial Mode

Use the Dial mode option in the Additional Setup dialog box to specify what mode of dialing you should use: Tone (as used on a touchtone phone) or Pulse (as used on a rotary phone). The mode of dialing refers to how you dial to make a phone connection, not how the data is transferred (see the earlier discussion of analog signals). If you use a rotary phone or you have a modem style that doesn't support touchtone dialing, select Pulse.

Tone is the most common selection in most of North America. You might need to experiment if you're working internationally or on old phone systems. To verify a tone line, lift the receiver of the telephone connected to the analog phone line, and enter a phone number. If the tones on the line vary depending on the numbers you press, you are working in tone mode. If the tones for all the numbers sound the same, you are working in pulse mode.

N O T E Keep in mind that if you travel, you might need to make changes to the dial mode based on where you're trying to dial from. If you try to dial a server and you receive an error message indicating that a dial tone can't be found (or another strange error message), try changing the dial mode. Typically, locations with relatively modern phone systems support a tone mode for dialing. ▪

Dial Timeout

The Dial timeout option in the Additional Setup dialog box sets the number of seconds to wait for a connection to a server before canceling the call. The default setting is 60 seconds. If you have problems connecting to a busy server, you're dialing overseas, you include a calling card number in your dialing, or you find that your modem is particularly slow, increase the Dial timeout setting. You can also increase the Dial timeout setting for a particular session in the Call Server dialog box. You will learn more about this setting in Chapter 21.

Notes uses this setting to determine how much time it will spend trying to dial and connect (log on) to the server. Don't increase this setting to too high of a number, or you will find yourself waiting for long periods of time if there is an error in trying to dial a server. Also, don't set it too short, or you will rarely connect to the server in the time allotted. You might need to adjust this setting a few times if you experience problems connecting to the server within the default 60 seconds. Typically, a setting of 60 will work. A maximum setting of 90 seconds is usually the upper limit you will need.

Hang Up/Idle Time Setting

Use the Hang up if idle for option in the Additional Setup dialog box to set the number of minutes your system stays connected to the server without any activity taking place against the server. The default time is 15 minutes. Increase this setting if you need more time. Decrease the amount of time if you don't need a long waiting period. You save in telephone costs and tie up the server for less time if you keep this setting low.

The Hang up if idle for setting is based on activity with the server, not activity being performed solely on your hard drive. For example, if you are reading a document in a server copy of a database while connected from a remote location, Notes doesn't count the time spent reading the document as performing a function against the server, because the document is local to your workstation once you open it. Notes begins the idle countdown from the time you open the document until you perform another activity that accesses the server, such as indexing the database, opening another document, saving the document, and so on. You will know that the server is being accessed when you see the green and red lights flashing in the modem icon in the lower-left corner of the Notes window. Two nonblinking green lights on the modem icon indicate that you are connected but not actively performing a function with the server.

Part
IV

Ch
20

> **CAUTION**
>
> While you're connected, if you set up your PC to perform any selection that "talks" to the server at least once during the time that is specified in the Hang up if idle for section, you won't be disconnected after the Hang up if idle for time is met, even if you leave the room or otherwise stop working on the server.
>
> Three direct examples come to mind: If you have set up your Mail Preferences to check for mail by selecting File, Tools, User Preferences, Mail more often than the time set in the Hang up if idle for setting; if you have set up a macro that accesses a server database to perform its task while you're working on the server as well; or if you set up your locations to replicate with the server more often than the time set in the Hang up if idle for setting.

The server also has a Hang up if idle for setting, and the shorter of the two times is used. If increasing the Hang up if idle for time on your system doesn't keep you from disconnecting from the server before your work is finished, contact your Notes administrator.

Logging Modem Input/Output

The Log modem I/O setting in the Additional Setup dialog box enters modem responses in your system's log entries. Under normal circumstances, you don't need this option, but it can help if you need to troubleshoot modem problems.

If you select Log modem I/O, each time you try to make a call (or perform just about any function in which your modem is involved), a document is written in your Notes Log database, which is stored on your hard drive. After a while, this database becomes quite large, depending on how often you call your server.

▶ **See** "Working Smart Remote," **p. 909**

Using Log Entries

Notes provides a special template that creates a Notes log on your PC that records all modem activity if you choose Log modem I/O. (Your server also has a Log database that logs all activity—calls, replications, database access, and so on.) When Notes logs a modem activity, it creates a document that lists the details of the call. The log reports successes and failures in dialing remote and provides you with a record of what occurred during communication with the server.

To view this information, add the Notes log from your C:\NOTES\DATA directory to your desktop (the log filename is always LOG.NSF), and then open the modem log as you would any other database. The Notes log is very beneficial in helping you troubleshoot problems while working remote.

Hardware Flow Control

The Hardware flow control option in the Additional Setup dialog box specifies what Notes should do if more data exists than can fit in your system buffer when receiving and transmitting. (In Notes 3.0, this option was called RTS/CTS Flow Control.) Choose this option unless your modem or serial card can't support flow control. (Consult your modem/serial card documentation.) Activating this setting is especially recommended for transmission speeds of 9,600 baud or greater in order to protect against impaired performance.

Editing the Modem File

You can edit your modem command file if necessary. For example, if you're receiving a large number of errors indicating that the modem can't detect a dial tone (perhaps Notes doesn't recognize an international dial tone, or you're trying to dial through or out of a PBX system, which can be found in many offices and hotels) and Notes doesn't recognize its dial tone, you might want to edit the modem command file you're using.

To edit your modem file, highlight it in the Additional Setup dialog box, and click the Modem File button to open the Edit Modem Command File dialog box, shown in Figure 20.5. Scroll through the settings you want to change, and edit them as you would any other text in Notes.

FIG. 20.5

Use this dialog box to edit your modem file to deal with special circumstances.

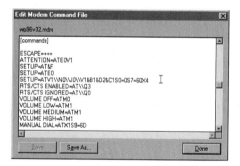

For this example, you would scroll down to the section headed [commands] and look for a line that starts with SETUP and contains the characters X4. You might need to look closely, because these characters are often hidden in a cluster of command strings. In Figure 20.5, the I-beam pointer is next to the appropriate character string for this modem file.

Change X4 to X1. This command tells Notes to ignore listening for dial tones, ringing, and so forth and to continue trying to connect to the server. You won't need to change the command file back to its original state once you can make connections successfully. Notes will continue to function well with the change in any situation.

A great application of this edit is when someone is overseas and wants to use the company's 800 number or other corporate phone access to connect to a Notes server through its internal phone mail system (provided that the company's PBX system will allow this). This person can then take advantage of cheaper rates and possibly have a direct connection to the server. Keep in mind that in some countries, such as Mexico, special arrangements might need to be made with the local phone company to set up connections to 800 numbers.

Click Save to save the new settings, click Save As to save the new settings under a different name that you specify, or click Done to exit the dialog box. If you try to exit the dialog box

Part

IV

Ch

20

without having saved any changes you have made, Notes prompts you to do so. Click No if you don't want to save your settings, Yes to save your changes, or Cancel to return to the dialog box.

CAUTION

If you're editing a command file, make a backup copy of the file, or save the edited file under a different name. This copy will allow you to easily return to the original modem command file if you have made errors in the edited one or you switch to a new modem that requires the original configuration. If you have never edited a modem command file, you might want to get assistance from someone experienced in doing so before attempting this yourself.

Setting Up Locations

A *location* is a place where you work with Notes using specified communication settings. For example, you might use a network port when you work in the office and are connected to a network, and you might use a remote port (COM) when you're disconnected from the network and working remote.

Notes lets you create Location documents in your Personal Address Book to store specific communications settings for each location in which you work. You can create as many Location documents as you want and then switch to those locations when you want. The Location document tells Notes how you're working in Lotus Notes (remote or network-based), how to call the server, how to treat mail during your work session, and many other communication details (as discussed later in this chapter). The Location document you select when you begin your work session also defines the databases you elect to replicate. In the Location document, you specify the following items:

- The location type (local area network, dial-up modem, both dial-up and local area network, or no connection)
- Phone information (such as dialing prefixes)
- Ports to use
- Replication information
- Servers
- Mail information

When you first installed Notes, you automatically created the following five Location documents in your Personal Address Book:

- Island (disconnected)
- Office (network)
- Travel (modem)
- Home (modem)
- Internet

You can edit these documents and customize them or create your own. You can then choose between the different locations you have defined to tell Notes how it will work with the server and mail the work session.

N O T E An occasional problem when editing existing documents might occur, particularly if you aren't the original "owner" of that document. Notes might not see the edited location as being available to you when you try to select it. If this happens and you review your entries and don't discover any errors, simply create a new Location document with the correct information to identify your location. Notes should be able to "see" that location when you want to switch to it.

With locations, a remote user can easily define multiple types of location connections to use while working away from the network and then quickly switch back to the network when in the office by selecting a network-defined location. Here are some tips for location settings:

- If your home and office are typically in different area codes, create a location called Home, and specify 1 and your office's area code as a dialing prefix. When you use the Home location to call a server, Notes automatically dials 1 and the area code before it dials the server's phone number.

- If you work in an office that is disconnected from a network and is located in a different area code, create a location called My Office, and specify 1 and your office's area code as a dialing prefix. When you use the My Office location to call a server, Notes automatically dials 1 and the area code before it dials the server's phone number.

- If you're working from a hotel room and you typically use a calling card when you make long distance calls from a hotel room, create a location called Hotel, and specify your calling card number. Then, when you use the Hotel location to call a server, Notes automatically uses your calling card number. You might also want to specify a prefix for gaining an outside line when calling from a hotel room.

Entering a New Location

Location documents are stored in your Personal Address Book, which is usually defined as your last name followed by the words Address Book. You can view your current Location documents by opening your Personal Address Book and selecting the Locations view from the navigator, as shown in Figure 20.6, or by selecting the File Mobile Edit Current Location SmartIcon.

Figure 20.6 shows the five default locations created when you first install Notes 4.x, along with several locations created by the user of this workstation. You can customize the default locations or create new ones. To create a new location, follow these steps:

1. While in the Locations view, select Create, Location or press the Add Location action button. The new Location document will appear, as shown in Figure 20.7.

FIG. 20.6

Check out your defined Location documents in your Personal Address Book.

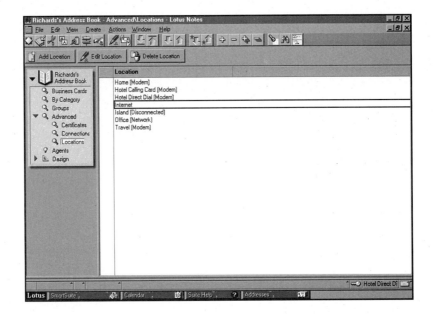

2. Specify that you are setting up for remote use by entering the information as described in the following sections. The Location form shows nine sections for this type of setup: Basics, Internet Browser, Servers, Ports, Phone Dialing, Mail, Replication, Advanced, and Administration. Make the appropriate entries. (Entries for each section are discussed in a moment.)

3. When you have completed your entries, press Esc to exit the document, and then click Yes to save it. You will see your new Location document appear in the view.

To edit an existing Location document, open the Location document you want to edit, and then double-click anywhere in the body of the document. Notes will place the Location document in edit mode for you to make the necessary changes. Exit and save the document as described in step 3.

N O T E The new Location document uses a new Notes 4 technique called Hide-When. The sections and field entries for this form change as you enter information into the preceding fields. The following section of this chapter discusses the options available to you when you specify that you are working as a dial-up modem location. For additional information on the Personal Address Book, see Chapter 5, "Using the Notes Address Books." ■

Basic Location Settings   The first section of the Location document, Basics, controls the basic information that Notes uses to determine how you are working. The following are your options:

T I P   Most of the field labels in this document are hotspots. You can click and hold the left mouse button to show help for each field.

FIG. 20.7

Use this document to define a new location.

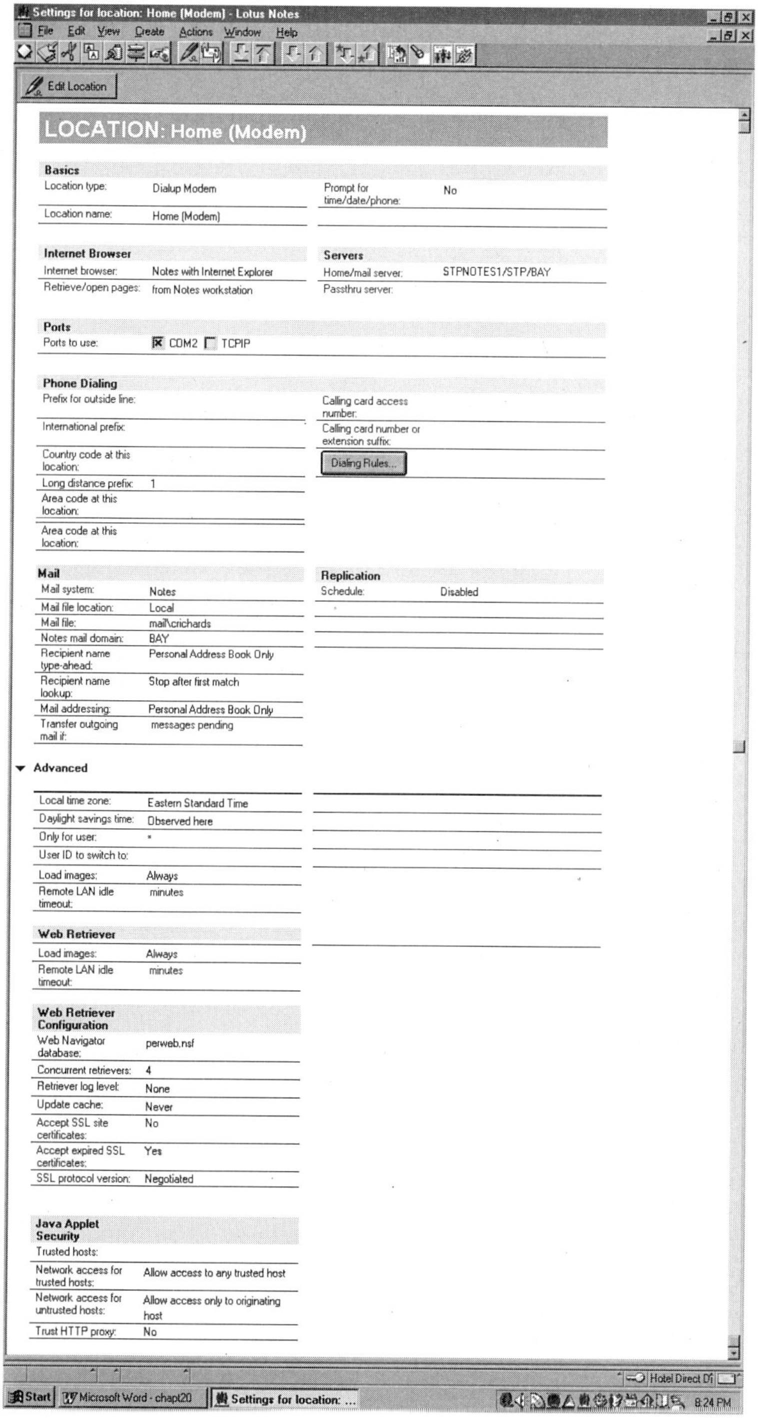

Settings for location: Home (Modem) - Lotus Notes

File   Edit   View   Create   Actions   Window   Help

Edit Location

LOCATION: Home (Modem)

Basics

Location type:	Dialup Modem	Prompt for time/date/phone:	No
Location name:	Home (Modem)		

Internet Browser

		Servers	
Internet browser:	Notes with Internet Explorer	Home/mail server:	STPNOTES1/STP/BAY
Retrieve/open pages:	from Notes workstation	Passthru server:	

Ports

Ports to use: ☒ COM2 ☐ TCPIP

Phone Dialing

Prefix for outside line:		Calling card access number:	
International prefix:		Calling card number or extension suffix:	
Country code at this location:		Dialing Rules...	
Long distance prefix:	1		
Area code at this location:			
Area code at this location:			

Mail

		Replication	
Mail system:	Notes	Schedule:	Disabled
Mail file location:	Local		
Mail file:	mail\crichards		
Notes mail domain:	BAY		
Recipient name type-ahead:	Personal Address Book Only		
Recipient name lookup:	Stop after first match		
Mail addressing:	Personal Address Book Only		
Transfer outgoing mail if:	messages pending		

▼ **Advanced**

Local time zone:	Eastern Standard Time
Daylight savings time:	Observed here
Only for user:	*
User ID to switch to:	
Load images:	Always
Remote LAN idle timeout:	minutes

Web Retriever

Load images:	Always
Remote LAN idle timeout:	minutes

Web Retriever Configuration

Web Navigator database:	perweb.nsf
Concurrent retrievers:	4
Retriever log level:	None
Update cache:	Never
Accept SSL site certificates:	No
Accept expired SSL certificates:	Yes
SSL protocol version:	Negotiated

Java Applet Security

Trusted hosts:	
Network access for trusted hosts:	Allow access to any trusted host
Network access for untrusted hosts:	Allow access only to originating host
Trust HTTP proxy:	No

Hotel Direct Di

Start   Microsoft Word - chap(20   Settings for location: ...   8:24 PM

- Location type: Select Dialup Modem to tell Notes that this location is used when you are disconnected from the network.

- Location name: Type in the name of the location. This name can be anything you want to use that is descriptive of the location in which you would want to use this profile. For example, you could use Hotel (Calling Card) to define a Location document that you plan to use when staying at hotels where you want to have the call billed to your calling card. You could enter another Location document called Hotel (Direct Dial) to use when you stay at hotels that don't accept calling cards for dialing long distance.

- Prompt for time/date/phone: Select Yes if you want Notes to prompt you for these settings each time you start up Notes. If you select Yes, the dialog box shown in Figure 20.8 appears whenever you switch to this location or start Notes with this location defined. This option is recommended if you frequently work from different locations, particularly if you often work on and off the network or often cross time zones.

FIG. 20.8

This dialog box appears if you tell Notes to prompt for time, date, time zone, and phone prefix information in the new Location document.

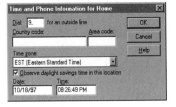

Internet Browser   These settings indicate which Internet browser you want to use and where you want to retrieve and open Web pages. You'll learn more about these settings in Chapter 25, "Using the Web Navigators."

Server Settings   The Servers section of the Location document specifies your home/mail server, as well as passthru and InterNotes servers if applicable. Make the following entries in the Servers section:

- Home/mail server: Specify the exact name of your Mail server (often referred to as your Home server). This is the server in which your mail file is located. If you are unsure of your Mail server name, highlight the network copy of your Mail database and select View, Show Server Names (a checkmark appears when this option is highlighted). The server name displayed in your network mail icon is the entry you must make in this field.

- Passthru server: A passthru server configuration allows you to dial into one server location and access any other servers defined in the network through that dialup connection. If your company uses this configuration, enter the server's name exactly as it is defined by your Notes administrator in the Public Address Book. If you don't know your passthru server name, contact your Notes administrator for assistance before you make an entry in this field.

- InterNotes server: If your company uses the Lotus InterNotes product, you can define the InterNotes server in this field. Contact your Notes administrator for particulars about this entry. You will learn more about working with the Internet features of Notes in Chapter 25, "Using the Web Navigators."

Ports   Here you select the ports to use for this location. The available selections are determined by the ports you defined when you set up your modem. To select a port, click in the box located to the left of the port's name. For example, Figure 20.7 indicates that the port COM2 will be used to connect to the server from this location. If you don't see the port you want to use in the available options, that port hasn't been enabled in Notes. Refer to the earlier section "Enabling a Port" for information on setting up a port for remote use.

Phone Dialing Information   The Phone Dialing section of the location is used to enter the phone dialing information you will use in conjunction with the phone number defined in the connections record. (You will learn about the connections record in the next section.) Notes adds the information you specify to a server's phone number as a prefix (outside line prefix, country code, area code, and calling card access number) or as a suffix (calling card number). In the Phone Dialing section, you set up the dialing instructions to connect to the server, as well as modify any server numbers that you might call when working from your particular location:

- Prefix for outside line: Enter any dialing prefix you must use to get an outside line when dialing the server from this location. For example, if you're in a hotel and you must dial 9 to get an outside line before you can call the server, enter 9 in this field. (See the later sidebar "Entering Prefixes and Suffixes" for more details.)

- International prefix: Enter any international prefix you need to use when dialing to another country from your location. For example, from the United States, it's 011.

- Country code at this location: Enter a country code if you always call the same country from the same location.

- Long distance prefix: Enter the prefix you must dial to make a long distance call. For example, to direct dial in the U.S., it is 1.

- Area code at this location: Enter the area code for this location if you didn't enter this information directly with the phone number in the connections record. Typically, if you define a connections record for access to a server that is always outside your area code, you will enter 1, the area code, and the remainder of the number in the Connections document.

- Calling card access number: If you plan to use a calling card when using this location, and your phone long distance calling card plan requires you to enter an access number before dialing the phone number, enter that number in this field. You might want to include a comma or two after this number to have Notes pause to allow time for the long distance access number to register. You might need to experiment with the number of commas you use to reach your long distance service.

- Calling card number: If you plan to use a calling card when using this location, enter the calling card number you would normally dial after you have dialed the phone number. You might want to add a comma or two before this entry to have Notes pause between dialing the server number and entering your calling card number. You might need to experiment with the number of commas you use to successfully enter your calling card number.

■ Dialing Rules: Click the Dialing Rules button to open the Dialing Rules dialog box, shown in Figure 20.9. This dialog box displays all your connections records and the phone numbers defined for each of these records. Select the server names to view the phone numbers that will be dialed when working from this location. You might want to edit these phone numbers for dialing from this location only to meet your needs. You will learn more about defining server phone numbers in the section "Setting Up Connections Records." Click OK to save your changes and return to your Location document.

FIG. 20.9

Check out your connections records in the Dialing Rules dialog box. Clicking the More Options button allows you to change modem settings.

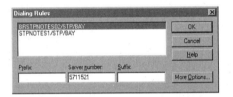

N O T E   An occasional problem might occur when you're trying to select a server to call by clicking the Dialing Rules button (or by selecting File, Mobile, Call Server), particularly if you edited an existing Connections document when setting up your Notes workstation. Notes might not see the connection as being available to you when you try to select it. If this happens and you review your server connection entries and don't discover any errors, simply create a new Connections document with the correct server information. Notes should be able to "see" that server connection when you want to select it. You will learn how to create a Connections document in the section "Setting Up Connections Records." ■

Entering Prefixes and Suffixes

When you're entering dialing instructions, keep in mind that the phone number can include any numbers you normally dial before or after a phone number, including calling card numbers. Insert one comma after the prefix and before calling card numbers for every two seconds you normally would pause between dialing the phone number and entering your card number:

        ,,calling card number

Two commas (four seconds) are usually adequate before the calling card number, but you might need to experiment. It is best that you be able to hear your modem dialing when trying to work with calling card numbers to help you determine whether the entry is correct.

If you dial out of a hotel, and an operator comes on the line to ask for the calling card number you are dialing, you probably need to increase or decrease the number of commas between the server phone number and the credit card number. If the pause between these numbers is too long, an operator will come on to ask you what number you want to dial before Notes dials the credit card

continues

continued

number. You will need to hang up, remove a comma, and try again. If the pause is too short, your modem will try to enter the card number before the phone system is ready for it, and then an operator will come on the line to try to assist you. You will need to hang up, add a comma or two, and try again.

If your modem is an older model, check its documentation to determine the maximum number of digits it can dial. To fit as many numbers as possible into the sequence, don't use any hyphens in the phone number defined in the Connections document or prefix and suffix entries in this document, and use as few commas as possible.

Some hotel phone systems might not let you use your calling card number for remote dialing. If not, you might need to dial direct and charge the call to your hotel room bill. Also, pay attention to the calling information in your hotel. Some hotels are set up to have you enter a 9 when making some outside calls and an 8 when making others. If you are unsure of which prefix to use, contact your hotel operator.

Finally, some hotels use an older PBX system that doesn't let you use your modem, or lets you use it only at very slow speeds. Although this situation is rare in North America, it can be quite common elsewhere. Refer to the "Remote Troubleshooting" chapter on the CD for additional help before you give up completely.

Mail Settings   The Mail section of the Location document specifies how Notes treats your mail when you're working remote. Make the following entries when setting up your location records:

- ■ Mail file location: Select Local if you want Notes to use the copy of your mail file that is stored on your hard drive. Choose On Server if you plan to work interactively with your Mail database file that is located directly on the server.

N O T E   When you select Local, Notes stores all the mail you send in your Outgoing Mail database, which acts as a holding tank for your outgoing mail until you call the server and replicate your mail to pass it on to the recipients. When you select On Server, Notes immediately transfers the mail to the recipients when you send it, so you must be directly connected to the server to use this selection. It is recommended that you select Local for this option when working remote. You will read more about how mail is used in Chapter 21, "Working Remote." ▒

- ■ Mail file: Specify the exact path and filename of your mail file. If you selected Local for your mail file location, you need to specify the path and filename of the mail file on your hard drive. Typically, your mail file is located either in the mail subdirectory of your data directory or in the data directory itself and is named using the first initial of your first name followed by the first seven letters of your last name. For example, the mail filename for Cate Richards would typically appear as mail\crichards. Keep in mind that the path is relevant to the Notes data directory! If your Notes administrator performed a standard installation of Notes on your workstation, the appropriate directories and filenames should already be present for you.

If you selected On Server for your mail file location, you need to specify the path and filename of your mail file on your mail server. Typically, this mail file is also located in the mail subdirectory on your server and appears similar to the preceding example.

 T I P   When possible, it is best to always name and store your mail file on your hard drive exactly as it is stored on your mail server. This setup makes it easy to change the mail file location without having to edit the mail filename.

- Notes mail domain: Enter the mail domain to be used for this location. This entry is not required. If you are unsure of your mail domain, contact your Notes administrator.

- Recipient name type-ahead: Select where you want Notes to look for address names when using the type-ahead feature of Notes 4 (see Chapter 5, "Using the Notes Address Books"). You can specify one of the following:

  Selecting the Personal Address Book Only option means that Notes looks only in your Personal Address Book for entries. If a match isn't found in the Personal Address Book, Notes quits trying to use the type-ahead feature and accepts whatever you type in the recipient fields of a memo.

  Selecting the Personal then Public Address Book option means that Notes looks first in your Personal Address Book for entries. If a match isn't found, Notes searches the Public Address Book. To use this entry, you must be connected to the server when addressing a memo or have a replica copy of the Public Address Book stored in your local data directory and identified in your File, Tools, User Preferences, Mail, Local Address Books setup, as discussed in Chapter 2, "Customizing Notes."

  Selecting the Disabled option causes Notes to disable the type-ahead feature completely. If you don't have any names listed in your Personal Address Book, and you don't have a copy of the Public Address Book stored on your hard drive, you might want to select this option so that Notes doesn't bother to look for the spelling when you mail a document.

- Recipient name lookup: Select Stop after first match to have Notes find only the first name that matches the recipient name when you send mail from the location. Select Exhaustively check all Address Books to have Notes find all the names that match the recipient name when you send mail.

- Transfer outgoing mail if: Enter the number of outgoing mail messages that you want to automatically initiate a call to the server. In order for this feature to work, your modem must be connected to a phone line, and you must have background replication running for this location. (You will learn more about setting up background replication in the section "Meeting the Requirements for Background Replication.")

Replication   You can create entries that tell Notes how often you want to replicate with your server(s) when you are set up for a particular location. Replication is the process of calling the server and exchanging information. You'll learn more about it in Chapter 21.

To use these settings, you must be set up for background replication. You will learn how to do this in the section "Meeting the Requirements for Background Replication." To set up a replication schedule, make your entries in the following fields:

- Schedule: Select Enabled if you want Notes to perform background replications with the server at set times during the day. Select Disabled if you want to prompt Notes each time you want to perform a replication with a server.

- Replicate daily between: Specify the time frame in which you want Notes to try to call the server. Notes will try to dial the server during this time frame, based on the settings you make below this entry.

  You can enter a range of numbers by placing a hyphen between the start and end times, as follows:

  `08:00AM - 10:00 PM`

  You can also enter specific times by separating the entries with commas, as follows:

  `08:00 AM, 01:00 PM, 05:00 PM`

- Repeat every: Specify how often you want Notes to repeat its replication with the server. For example, if you specify 60 minutes, Notes will try to replicate every 60 minutes during the time frame specified for this location.

- Days of week: Specify which days of the week you want Notes to replicate with the server. You might elect to have Notes replicate every day of the week, in which case you would select all seven days. However, if you work at this location only on weekends, you might want to specify Fri, Sat, and Sun, because these are probably the only days on which you want Notes to try to call.

N O T E Notes uses the replication information to replicate databases located on the Replicator tab of your workspace. You'll learn more about this tab in Chapter 21. ■

Advanced Settings   You have two settings available to you if you select the twistie next to the Advanced section in the Location document:

- Local time zone: Select the time zone that is typically used for your location. For example, if you typically use this location profile when you are working in Georgia, you would choose Eastern Standard Time. This selection changes the time and date information that Notes uses during the work session to agree with that of the local time zone.

- Daylight savings time: Select Observed here if you want daylight savings time observed for this location. Notes will automatically change the time stamp it uses to match daylight savings time. Otherwise, select Not observed here.

- Only for user: If you are using a shared workstation, and this location profile is to be used only by a particular person or group, specify the names of the users in this field exactly as they are named in the Public Address Book. Otherwise, leave the asterisk (*) in this entry to indicate that anyone can use this location setting.

- User ID to switch to: Click the flashlight icon to select a new user ID to switch to whenever you're working at this location. For example, if you're a Notes developer and you maintain a separate Notes ID for testing, you can create a location called Testing and specify a Notes test ID in this field. Whenever you switch to this location, Notes will switch your user ID and prompt you for that ID's password.

- Load images: To facilitate your working with the Web, you have the capability to tell Notes when you want it to load an image in the document when you first open the document. You can have Notes always load the images when the document is loaded, or load the images only on request.

- Remote LAN idle timeout: If you're using a remote LAN service, such as Microsoft Remote Access Service or AppleTalk Remote Access, you can use a remote LAN server to connect to other servers on the network. The setting in this field identifies how long Notes will maintain this connection with no activity passing between your workstation and the network before disconnecting.

- Web Retriever Configuration: This section of the Advanced settings tells Notes how you want to retrieve Web pages in Notes. You will learn more about these features in Chapter 24, "Lotus Notes and the Web."

- Java Applet Security: This section of the Advanced settings tells Notes how you want to work with Java applets that appear in Notes. You will learn more about these features in Chapter 25, "Using the Web Navigators."

Administration Settings   The Administration section of the Location document is used to identify people who are allowed to make changes to this document. Make the following entries in this section if applicable:

- Owner: Type the full name of the person who is allowed to modify this Location document exactly as it is spelled in the Public Address Book. If you leave this field blank, any user can modify this document. If you are the only person using this workstation, you don't need to use this field.

- Administrators: Enter the full name of any groups or individuals allowed to edit this document. If you leave this field blank, any user can modify this document. If you are the only person using this workstation, you don't need to use this field.

Switching and Editing Locations

You can easily switch between locations at any time by selecting the Location box in the status bar at the bottom of the Notes window, as shown in Figure 20.10. Click the Location box to open the list of defined locations, and then select the location you want to use.

You can edit a current location by selecting Edit Current from the list of options. The current Location document will open in edit mode for you to modify. The changes occur when you exit and save the entries. (You can also edit a location by opening its document in your Personal Address Book in the Locations view.)

FIG. 20.10
You can switch
locations from the
status bar.

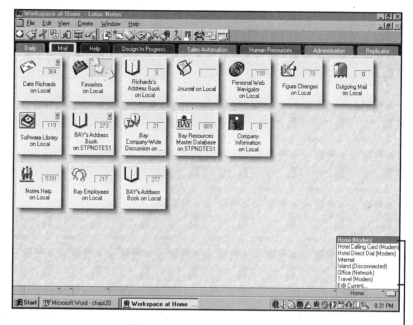

List of defined locations

Setting Up Connections Records

To specify the server(s) you want to use, add their entries to your Personal Address Book as
Server Connections.

N O T E When your PC was initially set up for remote use, an entry for your Mail server (where your
Mail database is located) was created automatically in your Personal Address Book. ■

To add server entries to your Address Book, follow these steps:

1. Open your Personal Address Book. (For information on using Notes Address Books, see
   Chapter 5, "Using the Notes Address Books.")

2. Click the twistie next to Advanced in the navigator, and then select Connections.

   If you have had a connection previously set up for you, you will see the Connections
   document appear in this view. The view looks similar to the one shown in Figure 20.11.
   This view indicates that three servers and an Internet location have been set up with
   connections records:BRSTPNOTES02/STP/BAY, and home/notes/net, STPNOTES1/
   STP/BAY.

Part

IV

Ch

20

FIG. 20.11

The Server Connections Records view lists your defined connections.

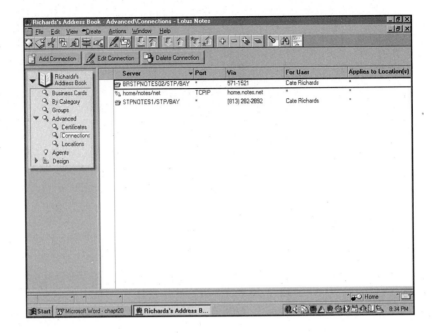

To view the connections record and make edits as necessary, highlight the connections record and press Ctrl+E, or open the document and double-click anywhere in the document to place it in edit mode, and then make the necessary changes as described next. If you don't have the Server Connections document you need, you must create a new one as described in step 3.

3. Choose Create, Server Connection. The Server Connection form opens, as shown in Figure 20.12.

4. Enter the necessary information. (The list following these steps describes the information needed.)

5. Close the window and click Yes to save the connections record.

Repeat this process for each remote connection you want to make.

In the Server Connection form, you need to provide the following basic information:

■ Connection type: Select Dialup Modem to indicate that you will be accessing this server via a modem.

■ Always use area code: Select Yes if you will always use an area code to reach a server and you want Notes to dial the area code—even if it is the same as the area code entered in the Location document. Otherwise, enter No. If you enter No, you will reference your Location document for an area code to use.

FIG. 20.12

Use this form to create a new connections record.

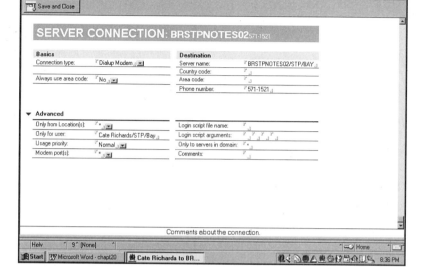

You must also make some Destination settings, as follows:

- Server name: Type the exact name of the server you are connecting to. You need to include all hierarchical naming in this entry. You can determine the exact server entry you need to enter by opening the Public Address Book and viewing the server connections.

- Country code: Select the country (or type in the country code) in which this server is located. Notes will automatically list the country code for the server if its country location is defined in the list of countries.

- Area code: If necessary, enter an area code for this server's phone number. You might want to leave this field blank in this document and enter the area code via the Location document, as discussed in the earlier section "Setting Up Locations." Leaving this field blank allows you to use this server connection's definition in all your locations, without having to individually edit the phone number each time you set up a location.

- Phone number: Type the unique part of the phone number that must be dialed to connect to the Notes server. The unique part of the phone number is the portion you have to dial no matter where you're calling from. When you dial the server, an entry box allows you to enter a prefix for the server you dial so that you can include any numbers that you need in order to get an outside line. You can also specify the nonunique part of the server phone number when you set up locations, as discussed in the earlier section "Setting Up Locations."

You can use hyphens between numbers; they don't affect the dialing. However, if your modem doesn't support entering a long string of numbers, you might want to exclude entering hyphens.

To include pauses in the dialing, type a comma between numbers for every two seconds you want the modem to pause. Each comma equals two seconds. For example, typing 9,,, (with three commas) causes a six-second pause after you dial the 9. You might need to experiment with the number of commas you need to dial successfully.

If your server has multiple modems with their own phone numbers and they are not set up in a hunt group (in which you call one number and a hunt group automatically switches you to each of several server numbers until it finds one that is open), separate the phone numbers with a semicolon (;). If the first number is busy, the next one is tried, and so on.

Advanced Connection Settings

To enter advanced settings for a connection record, select the twistie next to the Advanced section heading in the Remote Connections form. A group of advanced settings will appear. Make entries for any of the following settings as needed:

- Only from Location(s): Select the locations in which you want this Connections document to be used. Typing an asterisk (*) in this field allows this Connections document to be used for all locations.

- Only for user: By default, the document author's name is entered in this field. If you want to enter additional users for this connections record if you are sharing a workstation, enter their full Notes names here.

- Usage priority: Select Low if you plan to use the database's priority settings to create a replication schedule for accessing a server based on the importance of a database's sending and receiving information and if you don't place importance on this database's replicating on a frequent basis. Select Normal for routine scheduling of database replications with the server. You can also elect to replicate high-priority databases through the Replicator tab, as you will learn in Chapter 21.

  Typically, this setting is made for connections between servers rather than between remote workstations and servers. However, you can use this option to control the number of times your database replicates with the server during a scheduled replication by using these settings.

- Modem port(s): Select which modem ports can use this connections record. Typing an asterisk (*) in this field allows all modem ports to use this record.

- Login script file name: If applicable, enter the filename for the login script that you need to use to connect to your server. Contact your Notes administrator for information on any script files that might be required.

- Login script arguments: If you use a login script, and you must pass unique arguments to the script as you connect to the server (for example, passwords, name, and so on), type those arguments in the four fields provided in the order in which they are requested by the login script. Contact your Notes administrator for additional information on these entries.

■ Only to servers in domain: If you want to connect only to particular remote domain servers, specify their names in this field. This entry is optional for remote users. Typing an asterisk (*) in this field allows this connections record to connect to servers in all domains.

■ Comments: Specify any additional comments in this field to document the connections record.

Setting Up for Background Replication

Notes lets you schedule calls to a server to perform background exchanges of information by making setup selections in the Location document, as discussed in the earlier section "Setting Up Locations." A background exchange lets you continue working in Notes remotely as your modem (if it's on) dials and performs an exchange with the server. It also allows you to schedule calls while you aren't working so that you can have up-to-date information when you next begin working.

Meeting the Requirements for Background Replication

You might want to take advantage of the background replication feature if you're traveling and you want to have Notes update the information in your databases while you're out of your hotel room. You can set up Notes to call the server at 5:00 p.m. to exchange information so that you will be working with the latest updates when you return to your room at 6:00 p.m.

You can take advantage of the scheduled calling while you are asleep, at meetings, or possibly at times when calling costs are lower. You might also want to check with your Notes administrator, or check the Phone Calls view in the server's Notes Log database, to determine times when server modems are usually not as busy. Schedule your calls during their slack time, particularly if you are continuously getting busy signals when you call the server during regular work hours.

Keep in mind that you can always force a call to the server outside of the times set in this section when you want to make contact at an unscheduled time.

Notes performs the background replication if the following conditions are met:

■ Notes is running.

■ Your modem is plugged into a phone line.

■ You have switched to a location that has enabled background replication.

When you start Notes, it checks the replication schedule defined in the location setup and performs the next background replication according to that location's settings. You can follow the progress of the background replication by switching to the Replicator tab. You will learn more about the Replicator in Chapter 21.

Part

IV

Ch

20

Setting Up Windows for SHARE.EXE

If you work on a DOS/Windows workstation and you want to take advantage of the background replication option, you must first load the DOS SHARE.EXE program before you try to run a background replication. (SHARE is often already loaded on your system, but if it isn't, you will need to load it.) To load the program, exit Windows and Notes, and then type SHARE at the DOS prompt. Restart Notes and Windows, and proceed to run a background replication.

To automatically load the SHARE program every time you start your PC, follow these steps at the DOS prompt:

1. Type EDIT C:\AUTOEXEC.BAT.
2. Insert the following line in the AUTOEXEC.BAT file—typically about three to four lines down:

   LOADHIGH C:\DOS\SHARE.EXE

3. Exit and save the modified AUTOEXEC.BAT file.

When you restart your computer, the SHARE program will load automatically.

> **CAUTION**
>
> When you use the background replication method, Notes will keep trying to call the server within the time parameters you set, which ties up your phone line for any incoming calls you might receive.
>
> Also, if you begin a database exchange using background exchange with the server, and something happens to terminate the connection, Notes will keep trying to call the server to continue completing the task until the replication is complete.
>
> If you have a large document, perhaps one that contains several attachments and is over 1 or 2M in size, you might be disconnected continuously before the replication successfully completes, because large documents often have difficulty making it over phone lines in one piece, particularly if you connect at a low baud. Notes will keep trying and will tie up your phone line, as well as the server's, for as long as it takes to be successful, unless you terminate the process manually.
>
> Be careful using this feature unsupervised unless you take precautions to not replicate large documents or attachments.

If you have followed the instructions in this chapter, your PC and modem should now be configured to successfully use Notes remotely, and you should have at least one location and connection record set up to use when working remote. Often, your Notes administrator has already configured your system for you. It is still wise to scan through this chapter so that you are familiar with the configuration of your equipment. This information will help you if you ever have trouble while working remote. Don't forget to review the CD-ROM for any troubleshooting you might need to do!

Working Remote

If you followed the procedures in Chapter 20, "Setting Up to Go Remote," your PC and connections should be all set up to begin working with Notes remote. As described at the beginning of Chapter 20, working remote involves some different equipment and procedures than when you're working on the network and are directly connected to the server. This chapter briefly describes the process involved in working remote.

Understanding Remote Access

When you connect to a Notes server through a local area network, you work with the most current database information and have continuous access to databases stored on a server. As you edit, create, or delete documents, Notes instantly updates the database on the server. Notes transfers mail instantly, too, so that mail you send is routed immediately through the server to the destination you specify.

Notes functions quite differently, however, when you work remote. When you set up Notes on your remote PC, you must create replica copies (you will learn more about this term shortly) of all the databases you want to use on your PC's hard disk (unless you're working strictly via Interactive Connection; this is discussed in the section "Using the Interactive Connection Method"). When you first begin to work with Notes remote, the database copies on your PC match the databases on the server. They don't match for long, however. As you travel, you edit, delete, and create new documents in the databases stored on your hard disk. Back at the office, other users are doing the same things to the original databases. Soon you have documents on your PC that aren't on the server, and vice versa.

Every so often you connect your PC to a phone line and tell Notes to perform a replication. Notes calls one or more of your servers, and your PC and the server determine what changes have taken place since the last time you exchanged information. If you have created new documents, Notes transfers them to the server; if you have deleted documents, Notes deletes them from the server. Similarly, any changes that other people have made to the server databases are transferred to your PC. If you're working with NotesMail, you might also be transferring email when you call the server.

After the exchange is complete, Notes disconnects the phone line, and again the database copies on your PC match the databases on the server. As a result, the information in these local copies is only as current as the last time you performed an exchange with Notes.

You can work remote in two ways:

- *Replication* means that you work disconnected from the server in replica copies of databases, dial the server, exchange information, hang up, and then continue working disconnected from the server.

- *Interactive* means that you dial the server and then work connected on the server in network copies of the databases, as though you were on a network. With this method, the information you have added to or read into the server copies isn't copied to your hard drive and therefore isn't available to you when you hang up.

Each method is discussed in detail in the following sections.

Understanding How Mail Works Remote

How you set up your NotesMail while working remote depends on how you plan to work with the server. You can use replication, work interactively, or use a combination of the two methods. To understand why it is important to prepare your NotesMail, it is necessary to understand how Notes works with Mail both on and off the network.

A mail message is a Notes document that is composed using a special form. This form contains a field called SendTo (CopyTo and BlindCopyTo also work this way) that tells Notes to send the document to the recipients. Your standard email memo form, reply forms, and so forth all contain this field to alert Notes that the document is to be treated as mail. You can put this field in any form design to create a mail document. An application developer must take a few additional steps to turn the form into mail; if you're interested in learning about form design, check out Chapter 11, "Designing Forms."

When you're working connected to a network and you mail a document that has a SendTo field, you send it to a Notes mail router for delivery to the recipients listed in the field. The mail router runs on a Notes server and carries messages from your workstation to the destination (much like the post office handles paper mail) by looking up the names and groups listed in the To, cc, and bcc fields of your message and comparing them to the names and groups listed in the company's Address Book, which is located on every server. The router verifies that each individual name is valid. If a name is invalid, the router will try to find someone with a similar name in the Address Book and will then prompt you to make a selection. A name can be considered invalid if you have misspelled it, if the person listed has been denied access to Notes by the Notes administrator, or if you have otherwise gotten the name wrong.

Once the router has reconciled the names in your memo with the names in the Address Book, it delivers the message to the recipient's mail database anywhere in the network. If the recipient's mail database is located on the same server as yours, the message is delivered immediately. If the recipient is located on another server, the router finds the path to that server based on the information stored along with your recipient's name in the Address Book.

When you're working disconnected from the server, however, you turn on a switch (select a Location document that indicates you're working remote) that tells Notes to store any documents to be mailed in a holding database called Outgoing Mail. This database's filename is MAIL.BOX, and it performs the same service as the mailbox outside your home. When you send messages, Notes looks up the names and groups in your Personal Address Book stored on your hard drive (and your Public Address Book if you have created a replica copy of it). If the message is addressed to any groups, Notes substitutes the names in the group listing for the group name in your memo.

> **N O T E** For more information on setting up your remote Location documents, read Chapter 20. ■

Notes also checks to see whether individuals listed in your memo have forwarding addresses associated with their names in the Address Books stored on your hard drive and then substitutes the forwarding names for the names listed in the memo. Notes then uses the Outgoing

Mail database to store the messages, because you have no mail router available to you until you call the server.

Notes will prompt you if you have misspelled a name or otherwise have it incorrect when you're working remote but will send the message anyway because you aren't required to carry the Public Address Book, which is the official listing, on your hard drive. It is the Public Address Book listing that tells Notes where to deliver mail. If the name you type doesn't match the names listed in this book, Notes won't know where to route the mail.

When you call the server and send your mail (you'll learn more about this process later), your workstation transfers all the messages you have stored in your Outgoing Mail database to the router on the server in one batch. Because all the memos are dumped on the server at one time, the server receiving the memos doesn't check to see whether the addressees are valid at that time. As a result, remote users aren't prompted if any names are wrong. If the names are wrong, remote users receive a Delivery Failure report the next time they call the server to exchange database information.

After your outgoing mail is transferred to the server, Notes begins updating your mail database with any incoming mail that has been sent to you. Notes will also update the server copy of your mail database with any mail you saved in your local copy of your mail database. If you selected any other databases to update that have replicas on the server, Notes will update them during the session as well.

Settings for Mail

When you're working remote and plan to use Mail, you must first decide how you're going to communicate with the server. If you're working using the replication method, choose the Local Mail option in the Location document you're using in order to tell Notes to hold all the mail you're sending in the Outgoing Mail database until you call the server. If you plan to use the interactive method, select the On Server Mail option to tell Notes to immediately transfer the mail to the recipients in the memos you send. When you use the replication method, you work in a replica of your Mail database that is stored on your hard drive. When you work interactively, you typically use the network copy of your Mail database stored on the server. (The section "Preparing a Replica of a Database" discusses how to create a replica of your Mail database.)

Interactive Mail Setup   To set up your workstation to work remote using the interactive method, verify that the On Server option is selected in the Location document you are using for this session. To check whether this option is set, select the Locations box in the status bar at the bottom of the Notes window, as shown in Figure 21.1.

CAUTION

Using the Interactive connection feature of Notes more often than not will result in slower response times for your work with the server. It also tends to tie up the server's modem lines for long periods of time, which can get you in deep trouble with your Lotus Notes administrator and fellow users! Use this option sparingly!

FIG. 21.1

Select a location to edit or review settings.

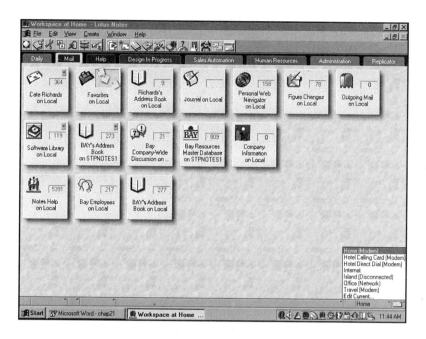

Select Edit Current from the pop-up list to view the current location document. Verify that the Mail File Location field is set to On Server. If it isn't, place the cursor in that field and press the spacebar to change the setting. You'll learn more about working with the interactive method in the section "Using the Interactive Connection Method" toward the end of this chapter.

N O T E On Server is the Mail File Location selection that is used when you're working on the network. When On Server mail is selected, your Outgoing Mail database is turned off, and the Public Address Book is referenced first when you send mail. When you send a mail message, the server immediately routes it to the recipient's mailbox.

If you select Local as the Mail File Location, your Outgoing Mail database is turned on, and your Personal Address Book is used for addressing messages. If the recipients you enter aren't listed in your Personal Address Book, Notes lets you mail your message, but it doesn't verify the name until the message is sent to the server for routing. ■

Replication Mail Setup   If you choose to work using the replication method (which is typically the preferred method of connection), you must have a replica of your Mail database stored on your hard drive. If you installed Lotus Notes as remote (or as network/remote), a replica of your Mail database was created for you at that time. To check whether you have a replica of your Mail database on your workstation, select View, Show Server Names and then look through the database icons on your workspace for a database called *Your Name* on Local (see Figure 21.2).

Part

IV

Ch

21

FIG. 21.2

Locating your local Mail database is easy when the icons aren't stacked, but your workspace might otherwise begin to get quite cluttered.

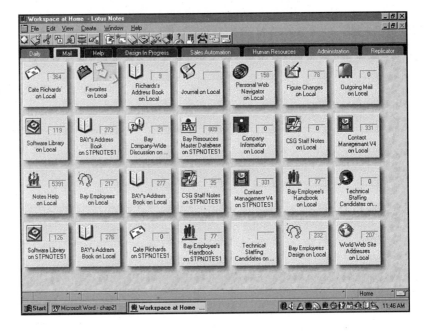

If your icons are stacked, click the down arrow in the upper-right corner of the database icon to see whether the Local selection is present, as shown in Figure 21.3. If you see the Local selection, you already have a remote Mail database installed on your workspace. Otherwise, follow the procedures in the section "Preparing a Replica of a Database" later in this chapter to create a replica of your Mail database on your workspace.

Switching Between Local and On Server Mail

If you frequently switch between Local and On Server mail, you should define separate Location documents for these options, as described in Chapter 20. If you selected Network and Remote installations when you first installed Notes, these documents were created for you. When you first begin a work session, switch to the appropriate location so that the correct mail settings are activated. You can switch locations at the beginning of a work session or at any time during a work session by clicking the Locations box in the status bar in the bottom-right corner of the Notes window or by selecting File, Mobile, Choose Current Location, as shown in Figure 21.4. The Choose Location dialog box, shown in Figure 21.5, appears. Select the location you want to use and then click OK.

TIP As described in Chapter 20, make sure you name your Location documents so that they are descriptive of the location you're working in. It is highly recommended that you include the type of connection, network or remote, in the name of the location to make choosing locations for work easy. Otherwise, you might have to open and review the Location documents frequently to see what type of location setup you're working from.

FIG. 21.3

Usually your local Mail database icon is positioned on top when you're working at a remote location. However, if you need to switch to the local database, click the small down arrow in the upper-right corner of your Mail database icon and then select Local.

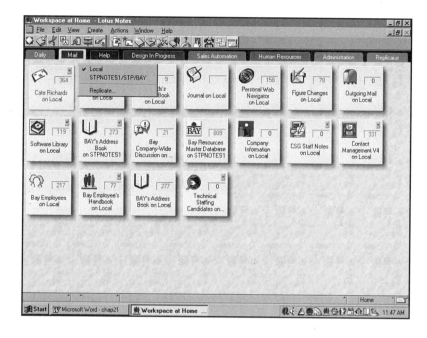

FIG. 21.4

You can use menu commands to switch locations.

FIG. 21.5

Choose the location you want from the Choose Location dialog box.

When You Work Both On and Off the Network

If you frequently work on and off the network, choose File, Tools, User Preferences, Prompt for Location to have Notes ask you what location you are working from each time you start Notes. Your location must have the Local option selected in order for you to work remote, or you will be prompted to call the server each time you send mail.

Specifying the Local option turns on the Outgoing Mail database and tells Notes to look only in your Personal Address Book. If your location specifies Local mail while you are working on the server, however, all mail that you send is still held in the Outgoing Mail database until you perform the next replication with the server instead of being routed immediately to the addressees specified in the memo.

Part

IV

Ch

21

continues

continued

If you frequently travel across time zones, check your Date and Time each time you start Notes by selecting the Prompt for time/date/phone option in the Location document, as described in Chapter 20. Selecting this option ensures that any scheduled replications that you might have set up in your server locations (see Chapter 20 for further information on scheduled replications) and any timed agents are running at their proper times (see Chapter 16, "Buttons and Agents," for more information on agents).

Setting Up to Check Free Time

You can set up Notes to check the free time available for selected individuals in your company while you are working remote. In Chapter 9, "Lotus Notes Group Calendaring and Scheduling," you learned how to schedule appointments and check on the free time for each person you were inviting to a meeting. However, when you're working remote, you typically don't have access to each user's free time unless you tell Notes to replicate this information to your remote workstation.

When Notes 4.6 was installed on your workspace, a database entry for checking free time was automatically entered on your Replicator tab (you will learn more about this feature shortly), as shown in Figure 21.6. When you click the replicator arrow (the blue arrow next to the database icon), you might be prompted to call the server to check free time. To set up free time, however, you don't need to call the server, so click No if prompted. The Local free time settings dialog box will appear, as shown in Figure 21.7.

FIG. 21.6

Notes 4.6 automatically adds the Local free time info replication entry to your workspace. Place a checkmark next to its icon if you want to poll the server for free time information when you replicate.

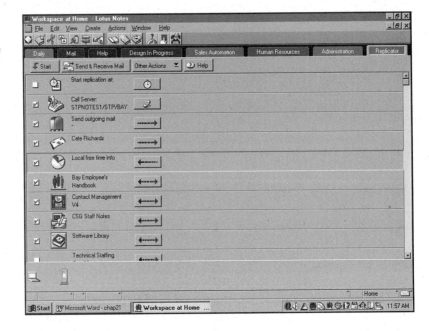

FIG. 21.7

You can tell Notes whose free time schedules you want to maintain while working on the road.

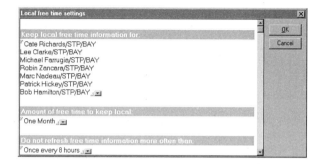

Make the following settings in the Local free time settings dialog box:

- Type or select the users' names for which you want to replicate free time schedules. Make sure your name is in this list. Click the down arrow next to the Keep local free time information for field to open the Address Books you have access to if you want to select the users' names (recommended).

- Select the Amount of free time information to keep local from the keyword list. For example, if you want to keep up to a month's worth of free time information for scheduling purposes, select One Month from the list.

- Select the length of time you want Notes to wait before checking with the server for free time in the Do not refresh free time information more often than list box. For example, select Once every 8 hours if you want Notes to check for free time only once during the workday.

Click OK to save your settings. Notes is now configured to keep track of the free time for the people you have selected.

N O T E Keep in mind that keeping track of users' free time will take up space on your hard drive and increase the amount of time it will take to replicate with the server. Set up only those users for which it is important to keep track of free time—or you might find yourself short on disk space pretty quickly! Also, limit the amount of time you want to keep the free time information to further reduce the amount of disk space used. Finally, limit the number of times you poll the server to check free time to eliminate several calls to the server while you're working remote.

Replicating a Database

Replication is the process of updating replica copies (or replicas) of a database. After you create a replica of a server database on your hard drive, you work in that copy and then dial the server to exchange new, modified, and deleted documents in the databases.

N O T E You can learn even more about replication in Chapter 23, "Notes: Under the Hood."

To work with a replica of a database (one stored on your hard drive), it is helpful to understand how to tell a local copy of a Notes database from a server copy. The icon for a local copy of a database includes the word Local with the database title, whereas a server icon displays the server name. To verify which databases are local and which are on the server, select View and make sure that the Show Server Names option is selected. If a server name is present below the title of the database, it is a server copy of the database; otherwise, it is a local database.

Double-clicking a server copy's icon when you're working disconnected from the server results in a prompt for you to call a server in order to open the database. Double-clicking a local database icon opens the database from your hard drive when you're working remote. Figure 21.8 shows examples of network and local database icons for the same database.

FIG. 21.8

Examples of local and network database icons.

If your database icons are stacked (if you selected View, Stack Replica Icons), click the down arrow in the right corner of the database icon to view a list of where each copy of the database is referencing. If Local is one of the options in that list, you have a local copy of the database stored on your hard drive. You might see multiple server names in the drop-down box if you have added the same network copy of the database icon from multiple servers, as shown in Figure 21.9.

Having multiple database icons for the same database that is stored on multiple servers is common for many remote users and is often convenient for updating purposes (see Figure 21.9). Databases that users access frequently (such as the Database Catalog) might be located on all servers in an organization to facilitate users' accessing them—from the network or when calling in from a remote location. Having a popular database stored on many servers often reduces the number of phone calls a remote user needs to make in order to update all his databases.

To replicate a database, you follow these general steps:

1. Prepare a first-time replica of a database.
2. Choose appropriate replica options.
3. Verify access levels.
4. Replicate the database.

The following sections discuss these steps in detail.

FIG. 21.9

An example of stacked icons referencing multiple servers.

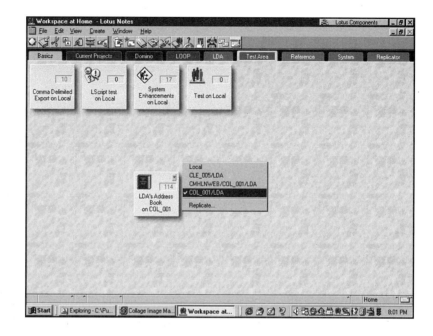

Preparing a Replica of a Database

Before you use the replication method, you must prepare a replica icon of each database you plan to use. Replicas of server databases are duplicates of the server databases, including the identification numbers, called Replica IDs, that distinguish each database from all others. When you access a Notes database, Notes looks at the Replica ID, not the name of the database, to determine which database you are trying to access. If the numbers don't match, Notes won't access the server's copy of the database during replication.

> **CAUTION**
>
> If you don't create replicas of databases when you work remote, your databases won't be able to exchange information with the server! Don't confuse creating replicas of a database (File, Replication, New Replica) with creating copies (File, Database, New Copy). Copies of databases contain all the database's designs and documents, but not the same Replica ID—which is what the Notes server looks for when exchanging information with a database. If the Replica ID between your database and the server doesn't match, you won't be able to replicate the database.

To create a replica of a database, follow these steps:

1. Select the database icon you want to use to create a replica. You might need to connect to the server and add the database icons you want to use to create replicas.

2. Choose File, Replication, New Replica to display the New Replica dialog box, shown in Figure 21.10.

Part

IV

Ch

21

FIG. 21.10

Use this dialog box to create replicas.

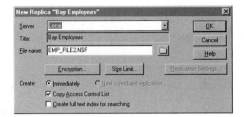

3. In the Server list box, select the server where you want to store the replica database—Local in this case, because that is the name given for databases stored on your local hard drive.

4. By default, Notes enters the network title of the database you selected. You can't change it later unless you have Designer level access or greater for the database.

5. Type the File name of the database to include its path as you want it stored on your hard drive or floppy disk. By default, Notes enters the filename as it is stored on the network.

N O T E   Be sure to name replicas of any database the same as they're named on the server. Although this practice isn't mandatory, naming databases this way helps eliminate confusion—unless you're creating a replica copy of the Public Address Book (see the following Caution). If you highlight a copy of a database that you want to make a replica of, Notes automatically fills in the appropriate server and filenames for you when you select File, Replication, New Replica. ■

If you're making a replica of your Mail database, always give the replica the same name as the original database on the server, including any subdirectory names (for example, MAIL\CRICHARD). Otherwise, Notes might not be able to find your Mail database when you switch from On Server mail (on-site) to Local mail (off-site) operations.

CAUTION

If you're making a replica copy of the Public Address Book, you *must* rename the file, because your Personal Address Book maintains the same name—NAMES.NSF. If you don't rename the Public Address Book, you will overwrite your Personal Address Book!

6. Select either or both of the following options:

The Copy Access Control List option (recommended) copies the original database's Access Control List to the new replica. If you don't select this option, you will be listed as the Manager of the database, but servers might not be listed, which will create problems when you try to replicate later.

The Create full text index for searching option automatically creates a full-text index at the time you make the replica of the database so that the Full Text Search option is immediately available. If you don't select this option now, you can always create an index later. Depending on the size of your database, creating an index might take some time; keep this in mind when you select this option.

7. Choose Immediately to immediately create a replica of the database that is initialized and filled with the contents (or a subset) of the original database or choose Next scheduled replication to create a shell (often called a Replica Stub) of the database that will be filled with the contents the first time you perform an exchange.

 TIP Select the Next scheduled replication option if you plan to make several replica copies of databases or you expect that the initial replication of the database will be lengthy. You can then replicate with the server once to fill all the database shells at the same time.

8. Make any Encryption, Size Limit, or Replication Settings you want for this replica database. Each of these options is discussed in the following sections.

9. Click OK to create the replica database.

N O T E If you don't have a copy of the network database icon available on your workstation when you want to make a replica copy to take on the road, choose File, Database, Open to add the database icon to your workstation before following the preceding steps to make a replica copy. If you're working remote and you don't have a copy of the icon, you can select File, Mobile, Call Server and call, or select File, Replication, New Replica and select the server name where the database is located. Notes will prompt you to call the server.

After you connect to the server, the Choose database dialog box appears. Choose the database you want to create a replica of and then click Select. Notes will display the New Replica dialog box with the relevant information entered for you. Complete the settings as described in the preceding list to create your replica. ▪

Setting Database Encryption Options

You can set the security of your local database so that only someone who has your Notes ID and password can open it. Follow these steps:

1. Click the Encryption button in the New Replica dialog box. The Encryption dialog box appears, as shown in Figure 21.11.

FIG. 21.11
Use this dialog box to encrypt a local database.

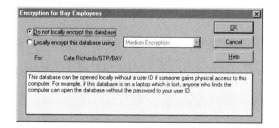

2. Select Locally encrypt this database using:.

3. Select Simple, Medium, or Strong Encryption from the drop-down list box. Simple Encryption lets you open the database much quicker than you can with Medium or

Strong Encryption, so unless you must carry a higher level of security on this database, choose Simple.

4. Click OK to return to the New Replica dialog box.

Notes uses the public portion of your Notes ID encryption key to secure this database from other people accessing it without your Notes ID and password. Keep in mind, however, that if you're sharing a public workstation and you locally encrypt a database that others also need to use, they won't be able to access the database with their IDs. For more information on encryption, see Chapter 22, "Security and Encryption."

Identifying a Size Limit

You can specify the maximum size for this database by clicking the Size Limit button in the New Replica dialog box. The Size Limit dialog box, shown in Figure 21.12, appears.

FIG. 21.12
Use this dialog box to set the size limit of a local database.

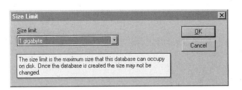

Size limits are set in gigabytes, so you will probably be able to leave the default (1 gigabyte) as your entry. Click OK to exit and save your selection. Chances are your remote PC won't be able to host databases larger than this amount anyway.

N O T E You can also set limits on the size of the database (to make limits less than 1G) through the administration pane. ▨

▶ **See** "Accessing System Database Information," **p. 982**

Choosing Replication Settings

To conserve space, speed up replication time, control what is sent to the server, or make any other settings that affect the way a replica database replicates with a server or servers, you can click the Replication Settings button in the New Replica dialog box. You can also modify replication settings at a later date by highlighting a replica of a database and selecting File, Replication, Settings to display the Replication Settings dialog box, shown in Figure 21.13.

To set or change replication settings for a database, follow these steps:

1. Select the database whose replication settings you want to change.

2. Select File, Replication, Settings while highlighting an existing replica database icon to display the Replication Settings dialog box, shown in Figure 21.13.

3. Choose all the options that meet your needs, and then click OK.

The Replication Settings dialog box offers four panels to facilitate making all the replication settings for the database. The following sections describe the options available in each panel.

FIG. 21.13

Use the Replication Settings dialog box to control different aspects of the replication process.

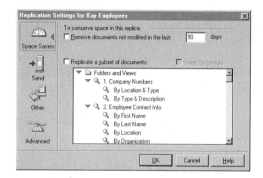

Saving Space The first panel to appear when you open the Replication Settings dialog box is the Space Savers panel. You may select from any of the following options:

- Remove documents not modified in the last *xx* days: This option purges documents that haven't been edited within the specified time period. If your database has documents meeting the criteria specified in this option, you will be prompted each time you open the database until you click Yes to remove the documents, change the number of days, or disable this option. The purging process removes from this replica all references to the deletion stub that can be copied to other replicas of the database. This option, which is a great way to save space, is discussed in more detail in the section "Working Smart Remote." Selecting this option in your remote copy of the database doesn't remove documents from the server copy of the database.

- Replicate a subset of documents: This option lets you specify the criteria that will define the specific documents you receive from the server during replication. You can select particular views of documents to replicate or specify a formula to use to limit the documents you replicate with the server. You will learn more about this feature in the later section "Selective Replication."

Limiting What Is Sent to the Server Just as you can limit what information is received from the server, you can also limit what information is sent to the server by clicking the Send icon in the Replication Settings dialog box. The Send panel of the Replication Settings dialog box appears, as shown in Figure 21.14.

FIG. 21.14

Use the Send panel to limit the information that is sent to the server.

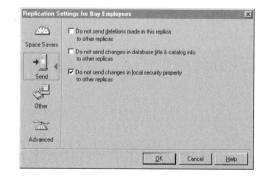

Part
IV

Ch
21

You can make any of the following selections:

- Do not send deletions made in this replica to other replicas: When this option is selected, you can delete documents from your local copy of the database without worrying about passing those deletions on to other replicas on the server. This selection is handy if you can't define a particular selective replication setting (date created, author name, subject matter, and so on) to limit the documents in your local database and you need to reduce the size of the database you are storing locally. Your deletions won't be passed on to the server.

  This option is also handy in case you accidentally delete documents from a local copy and you don't want to risk passing those deletions to the server. If you have the correct access to delete documents from the server copy of the database, you could delete all instances of a particular document if this option isn't selected.

- Do not send changes in database title & catalog info to other replicas: Select this option if you want to make changes to the title of your local replica of the database and update the catalog information without having the change replicate to the server copy of the database. This setting is used primarily by managers or designers of applications who want to work with them locally. You must have at least Designer level access on the server copy of the database to change database titles on the server copy and catalog information.

- Do not send changes in local security property to other replicas: Select this option if you want to change Access Control information for this replica of the database without changing the Access Control information in other replicas. This setting is used primarily by managers of applications who want to work with them locally. You must have Manager level access to change Access Control settings on the server copy of the database.

Other Replication Settings   You can temporarily disable replication, assign replication priority, limit documents received during replication according to a specified date, or identify a CD-ROM publishing date. Click the Other icon in the Replication Settings dialog box to display the Other panel, shown in Figure 21.15.

FIG. 21.15

Use this panel to further control replication.

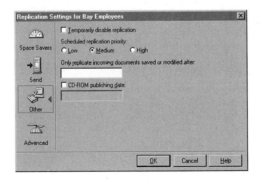

Select from any of these options:

- Temporarily disable replication: When this option is selected, the database won't be included in any replications with other replicas, even if it is selected when you schedule a replication. This option is ideal if you think your application might be corrupted and you don't want to risk passing on corrupt data to another copy of the database. You can also use this option to disable a database that changes infrequently so that the server won't spend time trying to read it during a scheduled replication. You can later deselect this option when you want to begin replication again.

- Scheduled replication priority: With this option, select Low, Medium, or High to indicate the level at which this database will replicate during scheduled replications. Notes provides options that let you opt to replicate only databases that have a particular priority setting during a session. The Replicator will let you elect to replicate only high-priority databases as a way to limit the number of databases replicated during a scheduled replication. This is particularly useful if you are in a hurry and only want to receive information from databases you have indicated as being very important.

- Only replicate incoming documents saved or modified after: In this box, enter the cut-off date you want to use to limit the documents you want replicated. This option lets you minimize the number of documents you're replicating to only those created or edited on or before the date specified so that you can reduce the amount of hard disk space that's used and the length of replication time. This setting is ideal if you want to get only the latest information from a database while working remote, particularly if you typically access this database on a frequent basis when you're connected to the network.

 TIP The Only replicate incoming documents saved or modified after option is a great feature to use if, for some reason, there is a very high volume of documents being added to a database and you go on vacation. This will allow you to replicate only a small subset of the documents rather than everything (which could take a long time).

- CD-ROM publishing date: If you're creating a CD-ROM in which you're publishing a replica of this database, you can tell Notes to specify the publishing date for the replica with this option. The recipient of the CD-ROM copy of the database can then copy the CD-ROM file to his or her local drive (or server) and then replicate with the original database without having to perform a full replication—only the documents created after the publishing date will have to be replicated.

Advanced Replication Options   If you want to get really sophisticated with your replication strategies, click the Advanced icon in the Replication Settings dialog box to open the Advanced panel, shown in Figure 21.16.

FIG. 21.16

The Advanced panel contains more replication options.

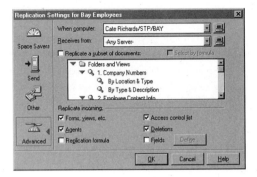

If more than one server contains a replica of a database, you can select the server your replica receives. If you receive from more than one server, you can select different documents or different parts of a database's design to receive from each. To select only particular servers to replicate with, do the following:

1. Leave the When computer option at the default, which is your Notes name.

2. Click the server indicator (the computer icon) next to the Receives from box and then select the server you want to replicate with in the Servers dialog box that appears (see Figure 21.17). Click OK.

FIG. 21.17

You can specify which servers you want to receive from in the Servers dialog box.

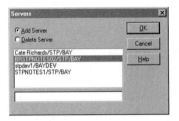

 You can also use this dialog box to remove servers that you want to exclude replication with by highlighting their names and selecting the Delete Server option before clicking OK.

3. To receive only selected documents from the server, select the Replicate a subset of documents option and do one of the following:

   Select the folders and views you want.

   Choose the Select by formula option and specify a formula.

4. To receive only selected parts of a database's design, do one or more of the following:

   Select Forms, views, etc., to receive a database's basic design.

   Select Agents to receive a database's agents.

   Select Replication formula to receive the formula a database uses to select the documents it receives.

Select Access control list to receive a database's Access Control List (ACL).

To prevent receiving document deletions from the server copy, deselect Deletions.

Select Fields and then click the Define button if you want to replicate only certain fields in the database with the server. When you click the Define button, you will be able to select All Fields or Custom from the drop-down list box. If you select Custom, you will see a list of all fields that are present in the database, as shown in Figure 21.18.

FIG. 21.18

You can tell Notes to replicate only information in specific fields when you exchange information with the server.

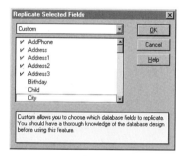

5. Select the fields that you want to replicate (a checkmark is put next to the names of selected fields) and then click OK.

6. Click OK to exit the Replication Settings dialog box.

CAUTION

Be careful using this option in Notes. If you aren't familiar with the design of the database, you could end up replicating the wrong information and have views that don't sort because the correct fields of information weren't brought down, and so on. Although this option can substantially reduce the amount of information that you replicate over the phone lines, it can also cause problems.

NOTE You'll learn more about using the selective replication sections of the Space Savers and Advanced panels in the section "Selective Replication" later in this chapter.

Verifying Access Levels

When you first make a replica of a server database, you must verify, and possibly modify, the access level for yourself and for the server(s) you will dial into to perform an exchange. To do so, follow these steps:

1. Select the replica of the database you want to verify.

2. Choose File, Database, Access Control (or click the File Database Access Control SmartIcon). The Access Control List dialog box appears, as shown in Figure 21.19.

Part
IV

Ch

21

FIG. 21.19

Use this dialog box to verify the Access Control List settings.

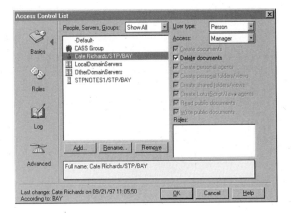

3. Select your name in the People, Servers, Groups list box. If your name isn't listed, click the Add button to enter your name—exactly as it is defined in Notes. You may either type your name (including any hierarchical naming conventions) or select the Person icon to open the Address Book, where you can select your name from the list of users.

4. Choose Person from the User type list box if it isn't already selected.

5. Choose Manager from the Access list box if it isn't already selected.

6. Go through the list box to find the Notes server name(s) where the database is located. Select the server name(s) with which you will replicate this database.

7. Choose Server from the User type list box if it isn't already selected.

8. Choose Manager in the Access list box for each server to ensure that it can read, write, and modify the databases you replicate.

 You should also have two server entries in your database access list titled LocalDomainServers and OtherDomainServers. If you access the same database on multiple servers in your domain (the more likely case) or across multiple domains (not quite as common), grant one or both of these entries Manager-level access as well.

If your company maintains only one domain, you can update the access for LocalDomainServers only and feel safe in removing access for the OtherDomainServers setting. Making these updates helps eliminate the possibility of replication problems if the database is moved to another server and that server's name isn't entered in this access list.

In order for these server group names to work in your remote environment, you must have their entries in the group list of your Public Address Book or have made a replica copy of the Public Address Book on your hard drive.

9. Repeat steps 6 through 8 for each server you dial to update this database.

10. Choose OK to exit the dialog box and save your changes.

Repeat this process for each replica database on your desktop.

CAUTION

If the server name isn't present, you must enter it in the text box directly below the People, Servers, Groups list box. The server name must be spelled exactly as the Notes administrator designated; Notes is case-sensitive about this spelling. (To avoid misspellings, select the name of the server by clicking the Add button and then selecting the Person icon next to the Person, Server, or Group text entry box to choose the server name from the Address Book.)

Identify the server as Server in the User type list box, assign the server Manager access, and choose Add User. If the server isn't listed in the ACL, it can't update your replica of the database after you create it the first time.

Setting Up the Replicator

Notes 4.x provides a feature called the Replicator. With the Replicator, you can replicate multiple databases with different servers with a single click of the Start button. You can also do other work while Notes replicates in the background.

To display the Replicator, click the Replicator tab in your workspace. When you switch to the Replicator, the workspace appears as shown in Figure 21.20.

FIG. 21.20

The Replicator lets you manage the replication of your local databases in one place.

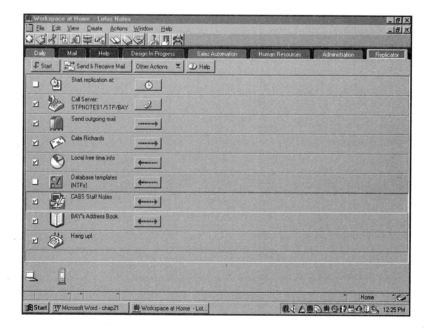

When you use Notes away from the office, you can have the Replicator call each server you want to replicate with automatically. If you're using a passthru server or a remote LAN server, you can have the Replicator make a single call and replicate all your local databases at one time, even if they're on different servers. The Replicator also lets you customize replication based on the location you're working from. It also provides additional ways to replicate. For example, you can assign High priority to selected databases and replicate only those databases. The following sections describe the Replicator.

Understanding the Replicator Page   The Replicator is always the last page on your workspace; you can't delete it. The Replicator automatically contains the following types of entries:

- Database: The Replicator contains a database entry for each local replica you have unless you deleted the entry from the Replicator page. When you add replicas of databases to your workstation, they are automatically added to the Replicator. To remove replicas of databases that you don't want on your Replicator, highlight the database entry and press the Delete key. Click Yes to indicate that you want to remove the entry.

- Start replication at: Use this entry to specify a replication schedule and enable scheduled replication. Which replication schedule is used depends on the location you're using and the settings you made in its Location document. If you want to modify the time at which you start replication, click the clock icon displayed on the Start replication at entry, and Notes will open your current Location document (refer to Figure 21.20). After you have made any necessary changes, press the Esc key and click Yes to save your changes. If you aren't using scheduled replication, this option will be blank. To replicate, you will need to click the Start button manually, as described in the later section "Performing a Replication."

  The Start replication at entry is always first and can't be deleted.

- Database templates: You can use this entry to refresh the designs of template-based databases. You can't delete the Database templates entry.

- Send outgoing mail: You can use this entry to send all pending messages from your Outgoing Mail database (MAIL.BOX). You can't delete the Send outgoing mail entry.

You can also create the following types of entries for mobile locations (such as Home and Travel):

- Call: When you create a Call entry, you specify the server you want to call, and the Replicator uses the information from the Server Connection record, along with any special location prefix and suffix numbers that might have been defined, when it dials. You can use a Call entry to connect to a server.

- Hang up!: You can use a Hang up! entry to end a connection to a server. The Hang up! entry tells Notes to end a call to the current server.

To set up the Replicator, perform any of the tasks described in the following sections.

Moving a Replicator Entry   Except for the Start replication at entry, which always comes first, you can arrange Replicator entries in any order you want. For example, you might want to group Replicator entries according to the server on which you want to replicate so that the Replicator has to call that server only one time to exchange all databases in common. To move a Replicator entry, follow these steps:

1. Click and hold the left mouse button over the entry you want to move. Be careful not to drag over the actual button, or you might start the procedure for that button!

2. Drag the entry to its new position.

3. Release the left mouse button.

Creating a Replicator Entry   You can create entries that automatically connect and disconnect from servers when you replicate over a modem. You can create a Call entry or Hang up! entry, as explained in the following steps.

N O T E   The Replicator automatically adds Database entries when you create replicas of databases. However, if you have deleted a database replication entry and you want to add it to the Replicator again, follow these steps:

1. Switch to the workspace page that has the replica of the database and click the replica's icon.

2. Hold down the left mouse button and drag the icon to the Replicator tab.

3. When the mouse cursor is positioned over the tab, release the mouse button.

Notes adds the Database entry to the Replicator again. ▧

To make a Call entry, follow these steps:

1. If necessary, switch to the location where you use your modem to connect to the Notes servers.

2. On the Replicator tab, click where you want the Call entry to be located. Notes will place the Call entry directly above the entry you choose.

3. Select <u>C</u>reate, Call Entry. Notes automatically creates the entry for your Home server by default.

4. If you want to create a Call entry to a server other than your Home server, double-click the new Call entry's action button (it has a small yellow phone handset as its icon). Select the server you want to call and then click <u>O</u>K.

When creating Call entries, keep the following tips in mind:

■ If you have set up a server connection for a passthru server or a remote LAN server, create a single Call entry for this server on the Replicator tab. When you do this, the Replicator can make just one phone call to replicate with all the servers. You will need to ask your Notes administrator about passthru and remote LAN server connections specific to your company.

Part
IV

Ch
21

- When the Replicator calls a server, it stays connected to the server until it reaches another Call or Hang up! entry. You don't need to create a Hang up! entry for each Call entry, just the last one.

- If you create two or more Call entries next to each other, the Replicator tries each call in turn. When the Replicator makes a connection to a server, it then skips to the first entry that is not a Call entry.

- You can replicate over a modem without Call entries. If you don't have Call entries created, the Replicator tries to call the last server that the first Database entry replicated with.

You can create a Hang up! entry so that the Replicator automatically disconnects from a server when you replicate over a modem. To create a Hang up! entry, follow these steps:

1. On the Replicator tab, click where you want the Hang up! entry. Notes will add the Hang up! entry immediately above the entry you choose.

2. Select Create, Hangup Entry. Notes adds a new Hang up! entry to the Replicator.

If you want to make the Hang up! entry the last entry in the list, click and hold the left mouse button over the Hang up! entry and drag it to the last position. Remember, you need only one Hang up! entry, even if you have more than one Call entry. When the Replicator reaches a new Call entry, it automatically hangs up the current call.

Specifying Replicator Options   Replicator entries contain action buttons, which you can use to specify Replicator options. The following options are available (see Figure 21.20):

- You can click the clock action button on a Start replication at entry to specify a replication schedule for the current location. The current Location document opens in edit mode for you to make any changes you like. Press the Esc key and then click Yes to save your new settings.

- You can click the arrow action button on a Database entry to specify whether you want to send and/or receive documents from a server. If you select the Receive Documents from Server option, you can reduce the length of time it takes for replication by selecting to receive full documents, document summaries and the first 40K of rich text only, or document summaries only.

N O T E   The Receive summary and 40K of rich text only option lets you shorten a document by removing bitmaps, other large objects, and all attachments from the document copies received from the server. When you select this option, Notes retrieves only the document summary (basic document information, such as the author and subject) and the first 40K of information. Notes doesn't remove large objects and attachments from the documents stored on the server, however—just from the copies you receive. This option helps reduce long exchange times and saves valuable disk space by keeping file sizes low. If you later decide that you want to get the information you excluded during replication, you can deselect this option or work interactively in the server copy of the database to review the entire document.

The following are a few things that you need to keep in mind when selecting this option:

- When you open a shortened document, Notes displays (TRUNCATED) as part of the document's title in the title bar.

- You can't categorize or edit shortened documents.

- Agents don't work on shortened documents.

- Notes doesn't send shortened documents to another replica unless the replica has the Receive summary and 40K of rich text only option selected.

- If you elect to shorten documents, you can retrieve the entire document by selecting Actions, Retrieve Entire Document while reading the document. Notes will dial the server and retrieve the rest of the document for you to review. ▪

 TIP If you find errors in your replication with a server and you are either not receiving or not sending documents during a session, check to see if the arrow action button is set to send (arrow pointing to the right), receive (arrow pointing to the left), or send and receive (arrow pointing both ways). Make changes as necessary.

If you still have difficulty, check the access control to make sure that both you and the server you're replicating with have the appropriate access level for the database. Finally, check to make sure that your database is a replica of the one located on the server, not just a plain copy.

- ▪ You can click any Call entry action button to specify a different server to call. Select the server from the pop-up list that appears when you click this action button. In this list, Notes displays the servers for which you have already defined phone numbers.

▶ **See** "Setting Up Connections Records," **p. 869**

Deleting a Replicator Entry   You can easily delete Replicator entries by clicking the entry you want to remove and pressing the Delete key. Click Yes to confirm the deletion.

Replicating with the Server

When you're ready to replicate with the server, either to fill the database shells you might have created in the preceding section or to exchange information with the server on an ongoing basis, you will need to plug your modem into your PC and connect the modem to the telephone jack. You can either carry your own telephone cable with you when working on the road or unplug the cable from the connection in back of the phone (if possible) and plug it into your modem jack. Make sure that the other end of the cable is plugged into the telephone jack in the wall!

It is recommended that you carry a telephone cable with you. In the United States, the telephone jack connector is commonly referred to as an RJ-11; you might need to verify the appropriate cable connector you will need if you're working internationally, because this varies by country. If you need to dial manually (you must dial through an operator to get an outside line), if the closest phone cable is permanently attached to the phone, or if the phone cable you're trying to use is damaged, you will be thankful you have a spare.

Part
IV

Ch

21

N O T E Some phones have data ports located in the back of the phone. In this case, you run a telephone cable from your modem to the back of the phone rather than directly to the jack. You will need a second cable in this case. When possible, running the telephone cable directly from your modem into the wall jack is preferable. This setup makes your replications much smoother. ■

Performing a Replication   You can replicate information between the server and one (or many) of the replica databases located on your workspace. When you perform an exchange (replication), you dial the server, send and receive database information, and hang up. There are two ways to replicate with a server:

■ Replicate selected databases in the foreground.

■ Replicate selected databases with the Replicator.

The following sections describe both options.

Replicating in the Foreground   To replicate with a server in the foreground, follow these steps:

1. Select the database you want to replicate.

2. Select File, Replication, Replicate, or click the File Replication Replicate SmartIcon. The Replicate dialog box appears, as shown in Figure 21.21.

FIG. 21.21

You can elect to replicate in the background using the Replicator tab, or in the foreground with options when you select File, Replication, Replicate.

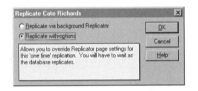

3. Select Replicate with options and click OK. The Replicate dialog box displays additional settings, as shown in Figure 21.22.

FIG. 21.22

You can choose additional settings in this Replicate dialog box.

4. Select a different server to replicate with by clicking the down arrow next to the with drop-down list box, if necessary.

5. Select one or both of the following:

<u>S</u>end documents to server.

<u>R</u>eceive documents from server. If you select this option, you may also specify whether you want to receive full documents, document summaries and the first 40K of rich text only, or document summaries only.

6. Click <u>O</u>K. Notes prompts you for permission to dial the server you selected. Click <u>Y</u>es to begin the replication.

When you use the Replicate with <u>o</u>ptions setting to replicate databases, Notes calls the server and performs the replication in the foreground. You will have to wait until the replication is complete before you can continue working, but you will receive a more detailed report of your replication activity than what is displayed on the Replicator page. If you want to continue working while Notes is replicating, you must use the Replicator (background replication) as described in the following section.

 If you work both onsite and offsite, you can decrease the amount of time required to perform remote database exchanges. While you're still connected onsite to the server, perform a database exchange for all your local replicas, as described earlier. You leave the office with the most recent database information and decrease the amount of time needed to perform a remote replication, because you don't need to send and receive as many documents. Database replication with the server is also a great deal faster to perform when you do it on the network.

Replicating Databases with the Replicator   You can replicate databases in the background with the Replicator by switching to the Replicator tab and clicking Start (recommended) or by selecting <u>F</u>ile, <u>R</u>eplication, <u>R</u>eplicate, <u>R</u>eplicate via background Replicator. When you replicate in the background, you can continue to do other work while Notes replicates. If your modem is connected to a phone line, Notes begins calling the first server identified on the Replicator tab and replicates information until it handles the last replication entry.

 You can easily add a replica database icon to your Replicator by clicking its replica icon and dragging it to the Replicator tab. When you click the Replicator tab, you should see the newly added replica database icon. Make sure that there is a checkmark in the selection box next to the icon if you plan to replicate the database.

N O T E   If your current location is set up for scheduled replication, you don't need to do anything to have the Replicator begin background replication when the replication settings criteria are met. When the criteria for replication are met, Notes will automatically begin the replication sequence set up on the Replicator tab.

Watch the bottom of the Replicator tab to see the progress of each database as it replicates (see Figure 21.23). Notes communicates each step in the replication process to you, as well as the estimated time it will take for the replication of each database to be complete. Notice that a hand icon points to each entry on the Replicator tab as it becomes active.

Part
IV

Ch
21

FIG. 21.23

A replication in progress.

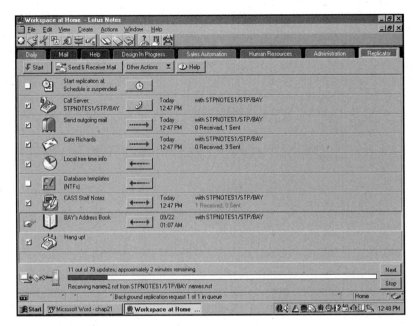

N O T E Notes indicates how many "Updates" you are sending and receiving when it replicates. However, the term "Updates" can often be misleading to the new remote Notes user. Notes considers any element that must replicate to be an update—including deletions, design elements, documents, edits, and so forth. For example, you might get a notice indicating that you are receiving 50 updates in your mail database, but when you open your database, you see only three new documents. The other updates could have been design changes, deletion stubs, or edits to existing documents that occurred in the network copy of the database. ■

If you click Next, Notes stops replicating the current database and moves to the next entry. Click Stop if you want to end the current replication. Notes stops replicating the current database, ignores the remaining entries on the Replicator tab, and hangs up the connection. If you want to hang up manually, select File, Mobile, Hang Up.

N O T E If you work offsite and on a network, keep in mind that any information you have entered into your local replicas doesn't appear on the server copy of the database when you return to the office unless you performed a database exchange after your last entry. To update the server copy of the database, perform a background replication as soon as you connect to the network again. ■

Using Some Special Actions with the Replicator Often, when working remote, you might want to replicate mail, replicate only one database, replicate only selected databases, replicate with a selected server, or replicate high-priority databases only. The Send & Receive Mail and the Other Actions buttons let you perform the following actions during a replication:

- Click the Send & Receive Mail button if you only want to replicate mail during a particular replication. Notes immediately calls your Home/Mail server and exchanges Mail databases. It also transfers all the mail you might have created and stored in your Outgoing Mail database.

- Click Other Actions, Replicate High Priority Databases to begin replicating only those databases whose replication settings indicate High Priority. (See the earlier section "Other Replication Settings" for information on setting database priorities.) High Priority databases are distinguished by a red exclamation point beside the database icon on the Replicator page. You can also set a database to High Priority by right-clicking the entry and choosing High Priority from the menu.

- Select the databases you want to replicate by clicking in the boxes next to their entries. Select Other Actions, Replicate with Server, and then select the server you want to replicate with. Click OK to begin the replication. Notes calls only that server to replicate with. Keep in mind that if the databases you select don't have replicas on that particular server, and you aren't calling a passthru server, your databases won't be updated.

- Select the databases you want to replicate by clicking their entries in the Replicator. Select Other Actions, Replicate Selected Database Only. Notes calls the server and replicates only those databases.

- Select the databases you want to replicate by clicking the box next to their entries (make sure that you also deselect those that you don't want to replicate). Select Other Actions, Replicate Selected Databases Only. Notes calls and replicates only the selected databases.

- To send only your outgoing mail, select Other Actions, Send Outgoing Mail. Notes will call your server and transfer only your outgoing mail to the server. You will not receive any updates or send any updates to other server databases.

Monitoring Replication History   After you replicate using the Replicator, you see how many documents you sent and received logged directly on each database entry that was selected for replication. However, you might want to view the history of past replications to see who replicated with a particular database and when. You can do so by highlighting the database you are interested in on the regular workspace page and then selecting File, Replication, History or by right-clicking the database entry on the Replicator page and selecting History from the menu. The Replication History dialog box appears, as shown in Figure 21.24.

FIG. 21.24
You can view the replication history of a database in this dialog box.

You can Copy the information to the clipboard to paste into a report, Clear the history, or change the way you view the information (by Date or by Server name). Click Done when you're ready to exit the Replication History dialog box. This technique is ideal for database managers who need to review database activity!

TIP If you don't think you're replicating correctly with the server—for instance, you aren't receiving all the documents you should be getting—you can elect to Clear the history of the replication. The next time Notes calls the server, it will begin to replicate as though this were the first time instead of performing an incremental replication of only the items in the database that have changed since the last time you replicated. Keep in mind, though, that if the database is large, it might take a long time to perform your next replication.

More About Using Mail Remote

Notes makes sending and receiving mail documents easy while operating remote. A few points about using mail remote warrant further discussion, however. In the following sections, you will learn more about using the Outgoing Mail database (MAIL.BOX) and working remote with the Notes Address Books.

Understanding the Outgoing Mail Database

When you use mail remote, Notes stores all mail that you send (including any return receipt reports for documents you received and opened) in a special Outgoing Mail database named MAIL.BOX. The Outgoing Mail database appears on your workspace automatically if you set up Notes for remote use when you first installed Lotus Notes. If you installed Notes as a network-only user and later created a replica of your Mail database, Notes automatically created the Outgoing Mail database at that time.

If you think the Outgoing Mail database is present, but you don't see its icon on your workspace, select File, Database, Open. With Local highlighted in the servers list, type MAIL.BOX in the Filename text box. Click Add Icon and then click Done. If an error message appears indicating that the file doesn't exist, there is a strong chance that the file might be corrupted or was somehow deleted after you started your session with Notes. Shut down Notes, delete the MAIL.BOX file from your Notes data directory if it's present, and then start Notes again. Notes will automatically create a new Outgoing Mail database for you.

If you want to verify whether you sent a Mail document from your Mail database (you might not remember whether you chose to mail a document you were working on, or you might suspect that your remote mail capabilities aren't working correctly), open the Outgoing Mail database. If the Mail document title is displayed, the message will transfer to the server the next time you perform a database exchange when you replicate your Mail database. If you decide that you don't want to mail the document, you can delete the document from this database before you perform an exchange.

Likewise, to make sure that all the mail you send is transferred to the server during the last exchange, open the Outgoing Mail database. No documents will be displayed in the Mail view if your exchange was successful.

Using Address Books Remote

In order for mail to be routed properly, the recipient names listed in the To, cc, and bcc fields must be spelled exactly as they are in the server's Address Book. Usually, only users listed in the server's Address Book can receive Notes mail, because the server's Address Book displays all Notes users set up to receive mail on your network. The exception is if special gateways are installed to work with Notes on your network to route mail to other foreign Notes domains or other types of email systems. (Refer to Chapter 6, "Advanced Mail," for additional information on this exception.)

As discussed earlier, Notes looks in your Personal Address Book first to find recipients. If the recipient isn't listed there, Notes transfers the document to the server anyway during a database exchange. The server then looks for the recipient in the Public Address Book. If the server can't find the name, it sends a nondelivery report to your mail file on the server. You aren't aware of the delivery failure until the next time you perform a database replication.

If you are a remote-only user, you can use the interactive connection method to connect to your Notes server to update your Personal Address Book with other Notes users' names so that you have their names available when you address mail. There is an alternative (and recommended) method: replicating the Public Address Book to your hard drive (also discussed in this section). This first method is used mainly for users who, for some reason, can't replicate a copy of the Public Address Book to their hard drives.

To update your Personal Address Book with users' names, follow these steps:

1. Open your Public Address Book on the server.
2. Select View, People, or choose the People view in the navigator.
3. Highlight the name of the person you want to add to your Personal Address Book.
4. Click the Copy to Personal Address Book action button.
5. Click OK when prompted by Notes that the documents were copied.

 TIP You can copy more than one Person document at a time by selecting all the people you want to copy to your Address Book and then clicking the Copy to Personal Address Book action button. To do so, click in the left margin next to each name you want to copy. A checkmark will appear next to each selected name. When all the names you want to copy are selected, click the Copy to Personal Address Book action button to begin the copying process. Notes will tell you how many documents you copied at the completion of the task.

TIP As noted in Chapter 5, "Using the Notes Address Books," you can also add a person's name to your Personal Address Book while reading a mail message from him by selecting Actions, Mail Tools, Add Sender to Address Book. Using this method, you can add users to your Address Book as you receive mail from them. By adding only users you regularly correspond with to your Personal Address Book, you can substantially cut down on the size of the Personal Address Book database.

Rather than adding individual Person documents from the server's Address Book to your Personal Address Book or not having Notes users' names available to you, follow the next steps for a simpler, recommended, alternative method.

CAUTION

Although the following information works for most Notes users, check with your Notes administrator to make sure that carrying a replica of the Public Address Book for your company doesn't interfere with any special setup or policy that the administrator might have made.

Also, depending on the number of users you have on your network, this database can be quite large, and therefore might be impractical to carry on your hard drive.

Finally, users can make changes to the network copy of this database several times a day, and you might find it too time-consuming to replicate this database frequently. Turn off replication or limit it to a few times a month.

1. Make a replica stub of the Public Address Book in your local directory (refer to the earlier section "Preparing a Replica of a Database"). Enter any filename other than NAMES.NSF, because that is being used by your Personal Address Book. For this example, enter the filename NAMES2.NSF.

2. In the Space Savers settings of the Replication Settings dialog box, locate the Include drop-down dialog box and select Minimal Address Book, as shown in Figure 21.25.

FIG. 21.25

You can minimize the amount of information you replicate from the Public Address Book by selecting Minimal Address Book from the Include list box in the Replication Settings InfoBox.

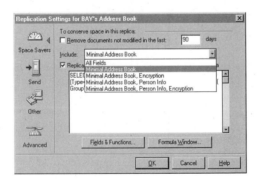

N O T E   You can also expand the amount of information you replicate to your Personal Address Book by selecting one of the following options from the Include drop-down list box:

- Minimal Address Book, Encryption: This includes the encryption key information for that person as well as the address information.

- Minimal Address Book, Person Info: This includes personal information such as phone number, address, and so on, as well as address information.

- Minimal Address Book, Person Info, Encryption: This includes both encryption and personal information in the Person document as well as address information.

Keep in mind, however, that the more you elect to replicate, the more hard disk space you will require. ■

   3. Click OK.

When Notes replicates with the Public Address Book, it replicates only the minimal information you need for group lists and Person documents to address your mail—unless you choose an expanded option to include additional information.

You also need to add a line to your NOTES.INI file to tell Notes that you have another Address Book to use when addressing mail remote. You can do this by choosing File, Tools, User Preferences, Mail and selecting the name of the new Address Book (for example, NAMES2.NSF) from the list. Click OK to exit the User Preferences dialog box. Notes will update the NOTES.INI setting for you. For details on updating NOTES.INI for multiple Address Books and to set user preferences, see Chapter 2, "Customizing Notes."

After modifying your NOTES.INI file, you should be able to switch between your Personal and Public Address Books while working remote. You can update your replica of the Address Book by replicating it just as you would any other database. For more information on using the Address Books, see Chapter 5.

You now have a replica of the Public Address Book to use with the mail address feature when you're working remote. To access the names in the list remote, follow the instructions in Chapter 5. All the addressees appear in your Public Address Book.

Using the Interactive Connection Method

An interactive connection establishes a direct link between your remote station and the server, requiring a constant telephone connection. Although your PC is connected to the server by telephone lines rather than LAN cables, you can use the databases stored on the server and receive the most up-to-date information in the databases just as though you were working on-site. You receive mail directly from the mail router, and the mail you send is transferred through the mail router directly to the recipient you specify as soon as you send it.

However, interactive connections tie up the server for a longer period of time, resulting in higher phone costs. Plan to use an interactive connection only when you work with a very large database and you don't have the resources to install the database on your remote PC, or when you're adding a database so that you can create a replica of it. An interactive connection can also be useful if you don't use the database frequently.

> **CAUTION**
>
> If you use an interactive connection, save documents often. Otherwise, if your connection to the server is discontinued before you complete and save an entry, you might lose the information. If you lose the connection, keep the document you're trying to work with open on your desktop until the connection can be re-established. Save the file when you're connected back to the server.

To work interactively, you must first call the server. After you're connected, you can work in the databases on that server as though you were connected on a LAN.

> **N O T E**   If the databases you want to work in are on different servers, you must repeat this process for each server after you complete the work on one unless you're connecting to a passthru server. ▓

To call the server, follow these steps:

1. Choose File, Mobile, Call Server or click the File Mobile Call Server SmartIcon. The Call Server dialog box, shown in Figure 21.26, appears.

FIG. 21.26

Use this dialog box to call the server directly.

2. Select a server from the server list. The servers listed are the ones for which you have Connection documents in your Personal Address Book.
3. Specify any prefix or suffix options you want to use.
4. Click Auto Dial to have the computer dial the server immediately or click Manual Dial if you want Notes to prompt you to pick up the phone to dial manually.
5. Select File, Mobile, Hang up when you're through working with the server.

If you are unsuccessful in connecting to the server, Notes prompts you with an appropriate message. Try to dial the server again. If you're still unsuccessful, refer to the "Remote Trouble-shooting" chapter on the CD-ROM.

CAUTION

If you plan to use NotesMail and you want the memos routed immediately upon sending, make sure you have selected a location that is set up for On Server mail. Use your network copy of your Mail database while working interactively.

▶ **See** "Setting Up Locations," **p. 858**

You are now connected to the server and can open any database on it for which you have been granted access. (It's just like a network connection at this point, only slower and less reliable.) If you don't have the server's database icon already on your desktop (the icon will have the server's name on it if you have View, Show Server Names selected), you can add it. If you have stacked your replica icons, click the icon indicator on the database you want to use and high-light the server name you have just connected to in the drop-down list.

N O T E When you use the interactive connection method, you might lose your connection to the server on several occasions. An interruption in the phone line causes this problem most often; the problem also might be caused when you don't perform an activity for a long time (for example, if you're reading a long document) and the Hangup if Idle for time expires. If this problem occurs too frequently, increase the Hangup if Idle for setting. ▨

▶ **See** "Setting Up Your Modem," **p. 852**

Working Smart Remote

This section has a wide variety of tips and techniques you can use while working remote to take advantage of Notes capabilities, reduce the amount of hard disk space you're using, mini-mize the amount of time you spend on the network, and otherwise work smart!

Transporting Databases on a Floppy Disk

If you work away from the office and you use a different remote computer than on the network, you can reduce the cost and time involved in performing an offsite database exchange for the first time by copying a database to a floppy disk while you're onsite and then copying it to your remote computer offsite. This process takes much less time to perform than setting up a re-mote replica offsite and then dialing in to perform the first exchange to fill the database with documents.

To copy a database to a floppy disk and then install it on your remote PC, follow these steps:

1. While onsite, make a full replica of the database you want to install on your remote system to your C:\NOTES\DATA directory. (You will want to delete this copy after the procedure, so take note of the file's location.)

Part
IV

Ch
21

2. Check the database file size by choosing File, Database, Properties and switching to the Information tab (marked by a small i). Check the size of the file to make sure it will fit on a single floppy. If the file is too large to fit on a single disk, refer to some of the suggestions in the remainder of this section for solutions.

3. Using your operating system's commands, copy the database to a floppy disk. After the database is copied to the floppy disk, delete the copy on your hard drive—unless you have other reasons for keeping it there.

   At the remote site, copy the replica of the database on your floppy disk to your remote C:\NOTES\DATA directory (or whichever directory you have specified as your Notes data directory) by using your operating system's commands.

4. Launch Lotus Notes.

5. Add the newly copied database to your workspace.

CAUTION

Keep in mind that you must maintain replica copies of databases on your local hard drive if you want to replicate with the server. Using the operating-system commands to copy a database to and from a disk will maintain the replica copy status of the database. If you copy the database to or from the floppy disk using Notes commands, make sure you select File, Replication, New Replica to make the copies. This method is actually slower than using the operating-system commands.

If the replica is too large to fit on a single floppy disk (check the file size you found in step 2), use one of the following methods:

- Make only a partial replica of a database (as discussed in "Preparing a Replica of a Database" earlier in this chapter). Restrict the number of documents in the database replica by selecting the Only replicate incoming documents saved or modified after option in the Replication Settings dialog box when you create the new replica. Make sure you change the settings back after you copy the database to your remote workstation so that a full replica can be obtained.

- Use compression programs (such as PKZIP) to reduce a database's size. Your local software dealer can recommend several programs that can help you. PKZIP can often have tremendous returns on compression due to the database structure of Notes. However, if the size of the database when zipped still exceeds the space available on the disk, you can tell PKZIP to compress onto multiple disks by including the -& command when zipping the file.

- Use your operating system's Backup command to create a backup copy of the replica database in your C:\NOTES\DATA directory onto multiple floppy disks. Then use the operating system's Restore command to load the database onto your remote PC. (Refer to your operating system's manual for details on backup and restore procedures.)

- Use any of the other space-saving replication settings, such as selective replication (discussed later in this chapter), to reduce the size of the database being copied as a new replica.

Maintaining Replica Databases

You can use the options in the Replication Settings dialog box (see the section "Choosing Replication Settings") and a few other techniques to clean out your offsite replica databases from time to time. These options allow you to automatically purge (delete) documents from a database replica, delete documents from a database replica manually without copying the deletions back to the network, reduce the size of a database replica through selective replication, compact a database, and delete a database replica from your system. The following sections discuss these techniques in more detail.

Deleting Documents from Replicas   You can remove older documents by deleting them from your database without deleting them from other replicas. This option is usually used when you can't automatically remove documents based on the date they were last saved and/or modified (as described in the next section). Follow these steps:

1. Select the database from which you want to remove documents. Display the Replication Settings dialog box by choosing File, Replication, Settings or clicking the File Replication Settings SmartIcon. Select Send to display the Send panel.

2. Choose the Do not send deletions made in this replica to other replicas option if you don't want to copy any deletions made in this database to the server.

3. Click OK and then delete any documents from the database without worrying that they will also be removed from other replicas. See Chapter 3, "Using Databases," if you need instructions on deleting documents manually.

> **CAUTION**
>
> If you don't select the Do not send deletions made in this replica to other replicas option and you have permission on the server copy of the database to delete documents, you will delete all the documents from the server copy that you delete in your local copy. The server, in turn, will delete all these same documents from other users' replica copies the next time they replicate with the server. Be sure that you have the selection checked.

Automatically Reducing the Number of Documents   You can have Notes automatically reduce the number of documents in a database by filling out the Remove documents not modified in the last *xx* days option. Notes automatically removes from your replica documents that were saved and/or modified prior to the cutoff date without deleting the documents from the server or leaving deletion identifiers (which take up space!) in your database.

For most databases, this method is preferable to deleting documents, because you don't have to constantly manage the deletions; however, it isn't always feasible. Some databases (such as library databases and the Address Book documents) might contain information that is important because of its topic (or other classification) rather than the date it was created or modified. For these types of databases, you might want to either delete the unwanted documents or set up a selective replication formula (as described later in this section) to limit the database to only those documents you want.

Part
IV

Ch
21

Compacting the Database   Although deleting documents might reduce the number of documents in the database, the document deletion identifiers take up space within the database. Also, after you use a database for a while, it begins to contain an increasing amount of "whitespace," just as your hard drive begins to get fragmented over a period of time.

You can remove this whitespace by highlighting the database icon and selecting File, Database, Properties and then selecting the Information tab (marked by a small i). Click the Compact button to begin compacting your database (squeezing out the whitespace).

It is usually necessary to compact a database about once a month or when there is about 10 to 15 percent unused space in the database. You can find out how much space is used by selecting File, Database, Properties and then selecting the Information tab (marked by a small i). Click the % Used button to show how much space is being used. Subtract the amount of space used from 100 percent.

N O T E   Compacting might take a while if the database is large. When Notes compacts a database, it makes a temporary copy of the active or selected database and copies it over the original file, preserving the original Read/Unread markers while removing unused space. If you try to open the database during the copying process, you see the message `Database is in use by you or another user`. ▓

CAUTION

If you wait until you have very little free disk space available before you try to compact your databases, you might not have enough free space to perform this function! Be diligent in performing your housekeeping tasks.

If you do find that you don't have enough disk space free to compact a large database, try compacting smaller ones first to see whether you can free up enough space for the larger ones. You might also need to consider deleting from your hard disk databases (or other files) that you no longer use.

Maintaining Special Databases   When working remote, pay special attention to your Mail, Notes Log, and Outgoing Mail databases. The following tips give you guidance for maintaining these databases in particular, but they can apply to other databases as well:

■   Your Mail database will most likely be the most active database while you're working remote and will therefore require compacting quite frequently. Consider carrying only the last week or two of mail in your database by following the instructions in the section "Automatically Reducing the Number of Documents." (You can always access older mail documents by working interactively with the server in the network copy of your Mail database, as long as you haven't deleted them.) You might also consider making an Archive Mail database to store documents that you want to carry with you that are older than the specified replication cutoff date. (Refer to Chapter 10, "Creating New Databases," for further information on creating databases.)

■ If you have received and detached attachments in email documents, delete the memo containing the attachments. (If you need to retain the memo, place it in edit mode and remove the attachments.) You might also be able to use the attachments you receive without detaching them from the memo (if you only need to read the attachment) by selecting Launch, which lets you read the attachment information without having to save it on your hard drive. For more information on using attachments, refer to Chapter 6.

■ If you selected Log Modem I/O when you set up your modem, Notes creates a document every time you call the server. Even if this selection wasn't made, your Notes Log database will grow over time and must be cleaned out. You can either set a purge interval, as discussed a moment ago, or simply delete the entire database (if you don't need any of the Log history anymore) through your operating system's file manager or the DOS prompt. (You can't delete it straight from Notes, because it is always considered in use when Notes is running.) If you delete the database, you must then re-create it using the Notes Log template available to you. Make sure you name the new database LOG.NSF and store it in your local data directory. (Refer to Chapter 10 for additional information on creating databases from templates.)

■ If you don't have enough disk space available to compact any databases, deleting the Notes Log database and then re-creating it after you have compacted all the other databases might be the best way to go. Also, you might get an error message if you try to compact your Log database, because Notes might be accessing it for a background process. If you want to reduce your Log file size under this circumstance, you have to either set a purge interval or delete and re-create the database.

■ Over time, your Outgoing Mail database will grow just like other databases, even though documents are being stored there only temporarily. Make it a habit to compact this database whenever you compact your Mail database. You might occasionally receive an error message indicating that your Outgoing Mail file is in use and can't be compacted. This message occurs primarily when background replication is underway. It is typically easier to find a time to compact this database when you first start Notes.

If you don't have enough space to compact the Outgoing Mail database (or others), you can permanently delete the database. Notes will re-create it the next time you start Notes.

Deleting a Database Replica   You might want to permanently delete a database replica from your hard disk. (Removing a replica file from your hard disk doesn't affect other replicas of the database on the server.) The steps to delete a replica are the same as deleting any other database:

1. Click the database icon.
2. Choose File, Database, Delete.
3. Click Yes to acknowledge the deletion of this database.

Part
IV

Ch
21

CAUTION

You will lose all the information stored in any database replica you elect to delete that you haven't replicated to the server. Make sure that any information you want to keep is replicated with the server or copied and stored in another database before you delete the database.

Selective Replication   Selective replication lets you control what type of information will transfer from the source database on the server to a replica of a database. You can identify particular folders or views of documents to replicate or use replication formulas to limit the number of documents replicating from the server. Replication settings are a part of the database in which they're created, but they only apply to replication with a particular server. The default is Any Server.

Replication formulas are very similar to the View Selection formulas you might write when designing a view in a database. For example, if you had a Sales Tracking database for all the regions in which your company does business, and your Western Sales Manager, Bill Moore, only wanted to receive the documents in his replica of the database that are for the Western region, you could create a replication selection formula in Bill's replica of the database that tells Notes to receive only the documents that contain the criteria specified in the formula. The selection formula would look like this:

```
Select SalesRegion = "Western"
```

SalesRegion is the field name used in the database form design to specify the sales regions for this company, and Western is the name of Bill's region. This selection formula limits the data Bill receives to only those forms in which there is a field titled SalesRegion and the entry in the documents with this field is Western. For more information on writing formulas, refer to Chapter 14, "Working with Formulas."

You automatically have Manager-level access for all local replicas of databases unless Enforce a consistent ACL across all replicas is checked in the File, Database, Access Control, Advanced settings for the database, so you have the correct access level to set up selective replication on those databases. However, you must have Designer- or Manager-level access to create replication formulas on the server copies of the database, because those formulas might affect all database users.

The following information provides you with the steps to follow to set up selective replication for a database. Refer to Part II, "Designing Applications," for further information on formulas and database design.

NOTE   Keep in mind that selective replication formulas can work only if the design of the database allows you to select the information in the manner in which you want. For example, if there were no fields distinguishing the sales region in Bill's database, he wouldn't be able to select on that criteria. If you are designing databases that will be replicated to users or other servers, keep this fact in mind as you proceed.

To take advantage of selective replication, follow these steps:

1. Highlight the database you want to set up and then select File, Replication, Settings. The Replication Settings dialog box appears, as was shown in Figure 21.25.

2. In the Space Savers panel, you must first decide whether you want to create a selective replication by highlighting folders and/or views available in the database design or whether you need to write a formula to provide yourself with the selective replication you need.

3. If you want to replicate based on the folders and/or views available to you in the database design, enable Replicate a subset of documents. Then select the folders or views you want to replicate to your hard drive. This method is by far the simplest, particularly for novice users, so if the view or folder definitions will provide you with the subset of information you want, choose this method.

4. If you can't get the subset of information you require by selecting folders or views to replicate, click the Select by formula option. Enter the selective replication formula in the text entry box below this setting. The default formula is SELECT @All, which tells Notes to copy all the documents from the server. Notes adds the word SELECT to all selection formulas when they are saved, so you don't have to type it. Enter the selection formula just as you would any other Notes formula (refer to Chapter 14 for assistance with formulas).

5. Click OK to save your settings and exit the dialog box.

Notes will now limit the number of documents you replicate from the server based on the criteria you have chosen.

NOTE You can also create selective replication formulas in the Advanced panel of the Replication Settings dialog box to have Notes selectively replicate information based on specific servers you replicate with. You could set up replication formulas to replicate all documents with one server but only documents meeting specific criteria from another server, for example.

Follow the earlier instructions for creating the subset replication settings. Refer to the section "Choosing Replication Settings" for additional information on the Advanced panel settings.

Replication formulas that the source database Manager writes and applies to a database take precedence over all formulas written and applied to local copies of a database. For example, if the source database Manager creates a selective replication formula telling Notes to replicate only documents created by the user, the user of a replica can't use a selective replication formula to replicate all documents, because Notes will ignore it. The user can, however, create formulas to further restrict the documents received, as Bill did in the previous example.

The capability to effectively work remote can be a distinct advantage to businesses today as the need to communicate between the home office and the field becomes critical. As you have seen, Notes makes this capability quite easy, whether you always work as a remote user or work onsite part of the time. ●

Advanced Notes Topics

Security and Encryption

Whenever people store and distribute data, there is always the danger that prying eyes will want to intercept or even alter that data. Some data might be subject to simple nosy snooping— perhaps an employee who wants to examine other employees' personal records. Other data might be critical to a project's success, making it attractive to corporate spies.

Whatever the reason, much of the information passed around inside companies and across the Internet needs to be protected to ensure security.

Understanding the Benefits of Notes Security

The Notes designers understood that, in order to be effective, a security system should meet certain basic requirements. The security that Notes offers has the following benefits:

- The system includes security features that can protect information from even knowledge-able snoops. Simple, unsophisticated measures might stop nosy employees or hackers who are just casually curious. However, more-sophisticated features are necessary to thwart corporate spies who are well-versed in computer security systems and how to defeat them.

- The system protects data from being altered or forged. For example, when you receive a mail message, you should be confident that the message was sent to you by the person listed in the From field and that the contents of the message were not altered after it was sent.

- Security features are easy to use. This should reduce the urge to forgo security in order to get the job done faster.

Understanding the Five Levels of Security

Notes offers significant control when it comes to securing your data. By implementing several varying levels of security, Lotus clearly had the integrity of your databases in mind when developing Notes. Several security options are available to you, ranging from protecting a Domino server from unwanted eyes to verifying the author of a single field of information to prevent forgery. The following list introduces you to the five levels of Notes security:

- Server-level security: Before users can access a database on a server, they must have access to the server. Server access is controlled by the server administrator through the use of certificates attached to users' ID files and server access lists. This is the first and most general layer of security.

- Secure Sockets Layer (SSL): Since non-Notes clients such as Web browsers don't have Notes IDs, server-level security can't be enforced. SSL provides privacy and even authentication for server tasks over TCP. SSL offers client authentication using SSL certificates and basic password authentication using SSL encryption. This is the strongest security available for non-Notes clients.

- Database-level security: Database security for any database on a server is handled by the database access control list (ACL). The ACL lists users and servers and assigns them rights to the database. Access levels range from Manager—who has total access to the database—to No Access. The database manager creates and controls the ACL. An additional database-level security feature is local encryption, which encrypts local databases so that only specified users can access them.

- Document-level security: Document security consists of the document's read access list. The read access list is defined by the form's read access list, any reader name fields in the document, and the read access list in the Document Properties InfoBox. The read access list refines the ACL for that document—meaning that if someone has Reader access or better in the ACL but isn't listed in any read access list, that person can't read the document. If that person isn't a reader in the ACL, he can't read the document even if he is listed in the document's read access list.

- Field-level security: Certain fields on a form can be encrypted using encryption keys so that only users with the correct key can read those fields. The database designer specifies that fields are encryptable. When a key is associated with the document, all encryptable fields are encrypted with that key.

Using Your Notes ID

The key to protecting your information in Notes is your Notes ID file. All security features in Notes work through the information contained in your ID file. Through your ID file, Notes grants you access to the information you're supposed to see and keeps you out of documents and databases that are off-limits to you.

Your Notes ID file contains the following information:

- Your name
- Your Notes license, which gives you permission to use Notes
- Your private and public encryption keys, which Notes uses to encrypt and decrypt messages
- Your password
- Encryption keys and certificates

The name of your Notes ID file usually consists of your first initial, last name, and the letters ID. For example, Marc Nadeau's ID file would be MNADEAUID. You can usually find your ID file in the Notes Data directory, but some users keep their ID file on a floppy disk as extra security because it can be locked up at night, they can take the file with them when they travel, or they can place it in their home directory on their LAN so that it can be accessed from any workstation on the LAN.

N O T E On your computer, Notes might have named your personal ID file USER.ID instead of using your first initial and last name.

Safeguarding Your Password

If your ID file is your gateway to Notes, your password is your key to your ID file. Notes won't let you use the information stored in your ID file until you have entered your correct password. By requiring you to enter your password, Notes can ensure that only you can use your ID file and the information it contains.

It is crucial that no one but you knows your password. Every security feature in Notes works under the assumption that no one else knows your password. With your password and access to your ID file, someone else can access your mailbox, read and compose documents in databases you have access to, send messages with your name, and decrypt messages you receive.

Before your system administrator installs Notes on your PC, he creates an ID file that contains your initial password. You should immediately select a new password and store it in your ID file. The following sections explain how.

Selecting a New Password   Your choice of passwords plays an important role in determining the security of the information you store in Notes. However, too many Notes users put more effort into choosing this morning's parking space. The privacy of your mailbox and all the databases you have access to depends on the fact that only you know your password, and therefore only you can use your Notes ID file. You must select a password that no one else can discover but that is easy for you to type and remember. Choose your new password carefully and consider these points when making your decision:

- Anyone attempting to guess your password will probably try the names of your pets, spouse, parents, children, and other relatives, as well as number combinations that represent your birthday, Social Security number, and anniversary. Similarly, don't choose words that reflect your interests, such as the name of your favorite sports team. People who know you can guess such passwords.

- A password such as starshine491 is much harder to guess than simply starshine.

- StarsHinE491 is an even more secure password than starshine491 because it expands the realm of characters used.

- Choose a password that is at least eight characters long. Notes will let you use passwords that have as many as 31 characters.

- You might recall the line "Three rings for the eleven kings under the sky" from *The Lord of the Rings* by J.R.R. Tolkien. From it you could construct the password 3r4tekuts. It is very unlikely that anyone could guess such a password, and yet you can remember it easily by recalling that famous phrase.

After you have selected your password, follow these rules to protect it:

- Never write down your password. Someone might find it.

- Never tell anyone your password. (A possible exception would be a secretary who processes the boss's mail.)

Changing Your Password After you have selected a new password, you can use the following procedure to change your existing password:

1. Choose File, Tools, User ID. Notes asks you to type in your current password before you can access any of your user options.

2. After you've typed your password, click OK to display the User ID dialog box, shown in Figure 22.1. You'll be working with this dialog box a lot, because this is where many security options can be selected.

FIG. 22.1

Notes lets you change your password from here.

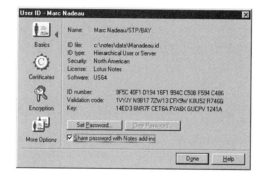

3. Click the Set Password button to change your Notes password.

4. Notes prompts you for your current password to make sure that it is really you trying to change your password.

5. Notes displays the Set Password dialog box, shown in Figure 22.2. It reminds you that Notes passwords are case sensitive, which means that if you capitalize any letters in your new password, you must capitalize those same letters each time you use your password in the future. Enter your new password and click OK.

FIG. 22.2

All the Xs hide your password so that people can't read it while you type.

6. Notes displays another Set Password dialog box. Enter your new password again and click OK. By making you repeat your password, Notes ensures that you didn't mistype it the first time. If the two attempts don't match, Notes will make you repeat steps 3 and 4.

TROUBLESHOOTING

Why do I get more Xs than what I typed? As you type your password, you might notice that a random number of Xs appears for every letter or number you type. This is so that anyone looking over your shoulder can't tell how many characters are in your password simply by counting the Xs.

If You Forget Your Password   If you can possibly avoid it, try not to forget your password. If you do, ask your system administrator to create a new ID file for you with a new password.

Forgetting your password can cause some difficulty, because unique encryption information is stored within each ID file, and it can't be re-created. You will permanently lose access to information encrypted by your user ID. If Domino and Windows NT user synchronization is used, forgetting your Notes password will also affect your access to the NT network. Check with your system administrator for recommended ID backup procedures.

 T I P   It's a good idea to put a copy of your Notes ID on a floppy and keep it in a secure off-site place. When you forget your password after a password change, you can replace your existing ID with the backup copy containing the known password.

Understanding Certificates

One of the crucial components of your ID file is your certificate. You can think of your certificate as your company's seal of approval on your Notes ID. The certificate is the electronic equivalent of a notary's seal, telling the Notes servers throughout your company that your ID was properly created by an authorized administrator within your company. Certificates play a key role in preventing hackers and spies from creating bogus ID files and infiltrating your company's Notes system.

N O T E   Most users have a single certificate in their ID file, but some people have several. If you regularly access databases that belong to other companies (perhaps you provide technical support for your clients, for example), you might have a certificate in your ID file from each of those companies. Each server wants to see a certificate it trusts before you can access that server. ▪

Much like your driver's license, certificates have an expiration date—usually two years from the date they were issued. As the expiration date on your certificate approaches (within 60 days), Notes displays a dialog box warning you that your certificate is about to expire.

When you receive this message, you must have your certificate recertified, just as you must get your driver's license renewed from time to time. To request recertification, you must first mail a "safe copy" of your ID to your system administrator using the following procedure. (A safe copy of your ID is simply a shell of a normal ID file that lets you send, request, and obtain certificates. Just think of it as a secure courier system that is protected by your personal password.)

1. Before you begin, make sure you know the name of the person in your company who certifies IDs.

2. Choose File, Tools, User ID to bring up the User ID dialog box. Select the Certificates pane and then click Request Certificate. Notes displays the Mail Certificate Request dialog box, shown in Figure 22.3.

FIG. 22.3

You request a certificate via email through the Mail Certificate Request dialog box.

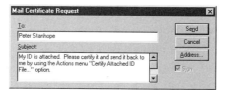

3. In the To text box, enter the name of the person in your company who certifies IDs. If you're unsure of the spelling, you can click Address to access the company's Public Address Book.

4. Click Send. Notes sends a mail message to your system administrator with the safe copy of your Notes ID attached and a message requesting that he recertify your ID.

Your system administrator will recertify your ID and send it back to you by mail. (You hope he accomplishes this task before your certificate expires. Otherwise, you might need to make a few phone calls.)

To accept the new certificate, follow this procedure:

1. Choose File, Tools, User ID to access the User ID dialog box.

2. Notes prompts you for your Notes password. Enter it and click OK.

3. Choose the More Options pane, shown in Figure 22.4.

FIG. 22.4

You control your advanced Notes ID options from this pane.

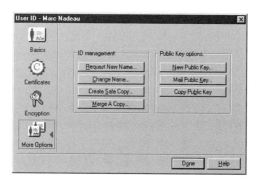

4. Click the Merge A Copy button and select the ID file to merge. Notes copies your new certificate into your Notes ID file, and you're good for another two years.

Although this process describes how to update a Notes certificate, you follow the same steps to request a new certificate. You've just got to ensure that you mail the safe copy of your ID file to the correct person for certification.

Understanding Database Security

Each time you access a database, Notes applies various security features to determine which operations you are allowed to perform. In this section, you will learn how Notes decides who can perform various database operations and how you can change the way people access databases.

Access Levels

Whenever you attempt to access a Notes database, Notes classifies you into one of several access levels that determines what you are allowed to do while working with that database. Your access level is different for each database you access and is determined by the manager of the database.

Here are the seven possible access levels:

- No Access: You can't access the database in any way.
- Depositor: You can create new documents in the database, but you can't read any documents stored in the database, even if you created them.
- Reader: You can read documents, but you can't create new documents or modify documents already stored in the database.
- Author: You can create new documents and read existing documents. You can modify documents if you created them.
- Editor: This has the same privileges as Author, except that you can also modify documents created by other people.
- Designer: This has all the privileges of Editor. In addition, you can modify the database design (such as forms and views).
- Manager: You can perform any operation in the database. Only the Manager can delete the database and control what others can do to it. Every database must have at least one Manager.

If you have any permissions other than Manager, your only exposure to database security involves learning what you and your coworkers are allowed to do. However, if you are the manager of a database, you're responsible for deciding what others can do. In the following section, you'll learn how to control access to the database.

The Access Control List

Associated with every database is an ACL that specifies who can access a database and what they're allowed to do with it. Anyone who has access to the database can view the ACL, but only someone with Manager access can modify it.

To display the ACL for a database, select or open the database and choose File, Database, Access Control. Notes displays the Access Control List dialog box, shown in Figure 22.5.

FIG. 22.5
You check the
database's ACL
settings here.

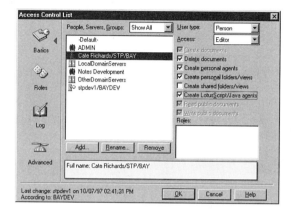

The People, Servers, Groups combo box lists the names of all the people, servers, and groups for which the Manager wants to specify access. Whenever the Access Control List dialog box is displayed and one of the names is selected, the remainder of the dialog box shows the access permissions for the name. You can change the selected name just like you change the selected item in any combo box.

In Figure 22.5, Cate Richards's name is selected. The Access combo box shows that she has Editor privileges for this database, and the User type combo box shows that this is a Person entry in the list. Notice the eight checkboxes to the right of the list box. They let you further refine the person's creation and deletion rights.

If you select a different name from the People, Servers, Groups combo box, the Access combo box, the User type combo box, and the checkboxes change to reflect the permissions for the newly selected name.

Which checkboxes appear depends on the person's privileges. For example, if the selected name has Editor access, Notes grays out Create documents, Read public documents, and Write public documents so that they are always marked, because all Editors can always perform these functions.

In addition to the names of people, the ACL can contain the names of groups. Every member of that group has the same privileges.

The ACL can contain both the name of a group and the name of one or more people in that group. When deciding what permissions should apply to a specific user, Notes first looks for the person's name. If the name isn't found, Notes then looks for a group to which that person belongs. If a person is listed in an ACL and is also a member of a group listed in the same ACL of different access, the individual access takes precedence. This feature lets you override group permissions for a specific person by making an entry for that person. If an individual is listed in multiple groups contained in the same ACL, the group with the highest access takes precedence. Remember that using groups to define your ACL requires that your company's Public Address Book be secure; otherwise, individuals could be added to groups and have access to databases they shouldn't.

Every ACL also has an entry for Default. Notes applies these permissions for anyone not listed by name and who is not a member of any group.

Two predefined names always appear in the ACL:

- LocalDomainServers: The access level for this entry determines the access for other servers within your domain, which probably represents your company. For databases that are replicated on other servers within your company, LocalDomainServers must be Reader access or better.

- OtherDomainServers: The access level for this entry determines the access for servers outside your domain (probably your company). You will probably want to set this entry to No Access unless you're building databases that can be accessed by other companies.

If you have Manager privileges for the database, you can change the permissions for a name in the ACL. Simply select the name you want to change and choose the option that represents the access you want that person to have.

Roles

Notes security includes the concept of roles, which can help you organize the people who need to access the forms and views in a database. A role is any group of people you define who need to have similar access to the forms and views within a database.

A role is most useful when you can identify a group of people who all need to perform the same operations on a database and will therefore need the same privileges. By creating a role for this group, you are simply adding and removing privileges for the entire group.

You can add to the list of roles for a database by selecting the Roles pane from the Access Control List dialog box (see Figure 22.6). Notes displays the list of roles. In this example, three roles—Trainers, Managers, and Developers—have been defined.

FIG. 22.6

You set your Notes roles from the Access Control List dialog box.

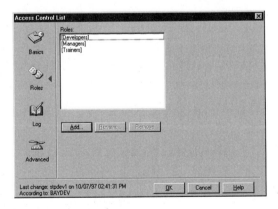

To create a new role, click Add. Notes prompts you for the name of the new role and adds it to the list. To delete a role, select the role from the list and click Remove. To rename a role, click Rename.

To control which users are included in a role, click the Basics icon to return to the Basics pane and select a name. Any roles that the person belongs to are listed in the Roles box. To add another role for the person, click the role in the Roles box. The role will appear with a checkmark next to it. To remove someone from a role, uncheck the role in the Roles box. Figure 22.7 shows Cate Richards assigned to the Trainers role.

FIG. 22.7
Cate Richards is assigned to the Trainers role.

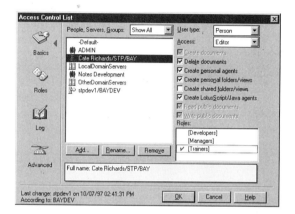

After you have created a role, you can specify the role in place of a user name in the Read Access Control List dialog box and the Compose Access Control List dialog box for forms and views. If you specify that the Supervisor role can access a particular form, all the users you placed in the Supervisor role can access that form. Later, if you decide that they no longer need to access the form, you simply remove the role, and none of those users has access.

Understanding Encryption

You might think that because your company isn't building nuclear warheads or involved in national security (then again, maybe it is), you really don't have much need for privacy. However, in even the most mundane of businesses, you might encounter sensitive information that you must protect at all costs. Encryption lets you keep your secrets secret.

If you have no concerns about who sees your data—if you deal exclusively with information that isn't particularly private—Notes's database security is probably all the security you'll ever need, and you can skip the rest of this chapter. But even so, if you want to know how the cloak-and-dagger folks hide their information, read on. This is fascinating stuff!

A Quick History of Encryption

Throughout history, people have constantly sought methods to store and convey information in ways that kept it secret from enemies who might try to intercept the information. The oldest technique for sending secret information was concealment, in which the sender might simply try to hide the secret information. The sender might send a package that contains a secret compartment or bury a secret message in a letter among otherwise innocent-looking text.

More commonly in recent times, people have relied upon encryption to conceal information, a process in which the sender scrambles the message in some way to make it unreadable. The receiver then performs a related operation, known as decryption, that converts the scrambled message back to its original form. An enemy who intercepts the message along the way sees only the scrambled message.

The earliest forms of encryption relied on keeping the decryption technique secret. The sender encrypted information by using a complex method that he hoped an enemy couldn't figure out. In Roman times, simply substituting one letter for another (A=B, B=C, C=D, and so on) was good enough, but today many newspapers routinely publish such encrypted messages on their puzzles page, and amateur cryptographers crack them in minutes.

Before the twentieth century, there was a practical limit to how complex an encryption technique could be. The more complex an encryption system was, the greater the chance that the person encrypting or decrypting the message would make a mistake. Also, quite often encrypted messages are needed in a hurry, such as on a battlefield. If an encryption technique is too complex, people can't use it quickly.

Computers changed everything. They could handle complex encryption and decryption techniques flawlessly and quickly. However, they also helped code-breakers crack complex encrypted messages. The techniques that let you securely encrypt your messages today are very sophisticated, and in the following sections, you'll come to understand the basics of how they work.

Understanding Encryption Keys

Of all the things to learn about Notes, possibly few topics are less understood by users than encryption. Perhaps that's because most users don't feel that their information is sensitive enough to require such secrecy. But as with a lot of features, once you know encryption is available, you'll probably find opportunities to use it.

Most encryption schemes today involve some type of scrambling that is controlled by a key. The sender selects a secret phrase, word, or number—the key—and uses the key along with some process to encrypt the information. The receiver, who must know the key, applies a reverse process using the same key to decrypt the message and retrieve the original information. If an enemy intercepts the message (and the encryption technique is sophisticated enough), he can't recover the information without the key, even if he knows how the encryption/decryption technique works.

This technique is known as single-key encryption. Notes has the capability to encrypt a message using a single key and later decrypt the message back into its original form. In fact, single-key encryption plays an important part in Notes (see "Creating Encryption Keys" later in this chapter).

However, single-key encryption isn't well-suited for exchanging email because of an important drawback: Both the sender and the receiver must have the same key, but they must manage to keep it secret from the rest of the world. You must figure out some way to exchange the key ahead of time, and if an enemy should intercept it, he can read your secret messages as easily as the intended receiver.

One of the greatest advances in modern cryptography is the development of a technique that doesn't require you to exchange keys in secret. This technique is the focus of Notes encryption and of most modern encryption systems.

Understanding Public-Key Encryption   The most recent innovation and the central technique in Notes is called public-key encryption. In this technique, everyone has two keys. Public-key encryption is based on the fact that the keys are related in such a way that a message encrypted with either of the keys can be decrypted only with the other key.

In any public-key encryption system (including Notes), you create two keys. (In the case of Notes, Notes performs this operation for you.) You keep one of the keys—known as your private key—secret, but the other key—known as your public key—can be widely distributed and given to anyone.

If someone wants to send you a secret message, he uses your public key, which you have distributed to all your friends and coworkers, to encrypt the message. When you receive the message, you use your private key to decrypt the message. Remember that messages encrypted with one key can be decrypted only with the other key. The crucial feature of public-key encryption is that messages can't be decrypted with the same key that was used to encrypt them. Thus, an enemy can't decrypt your message even if he knows your public key. Because your public key only lets others encrypt messages for you, you can distribute your public key through normal means without worrying about enemies intercepting it.

How Safe Is Encryption?

Your public and private keys are always related in such a way that messages encrypted with one key can be decrypted only with the other. However, the relationship between the two keys is so complex that the chances of anyone figuring out your private key, even if they know your public key, are virtually nil.

How safe is public-key encryption? Cryptographers widely believed that a good public-key system was virtually uncrackable. In 1977, three leading cryptographers encrypted a short message using a public-key technique, and jokingly offered a $100 prize to anyone who could crack the message. The public-key technique they used was very similar to the technique used by Notes. They believed that the calculations needed to determine the private key and thus uncover the message would require more time than the lifetime of the universe.

Imagine their surprise when the code was cracked in eight months!

Arjen Lenstra at Bellcore (the research and development outfit jointly owned by the regional Bell telephone companies) couldn't resist the challenge and organized a team of code breakers at Iowa State, MIT, and Oxford, along with 600 code-breaker wanna-bes on the Internet. After a massive effort that required eight months and a lot of mainframe and supercomputer time, Lenstra and his team cracked the code.

continues

continued

For us mere mortals, this exercise probably doesn't mean much. The effort that Lenstra and his team devoted to cracking the message was enormous, and probably no one is willing to devote such an enormous amount of effort and equipment to cracking anything that regular people are likely to send through email. And cracking this one message wouldn't lessen the effort that Lenstra would have had to expend to crack a different message encrypted with a different key.

However, it does illustrate that given enough time and money, nothing is ever 100 percent secure.

Oh, and the message? It turned out to be, "The magic words are squeamish ossifrage."

Notes creates your private and public keys for you. Both are extremely huge numbers (hundreds of digits each) that Notes selects at random. You don't need to know the specific numbers that Notes selects for your keys. What's important is that they are available for Notes to use when encrypting and decrypting messages and that they have that crucial relationship: Messages encrypted with one key can be decrypted only with the other key. Your private key is stored in your ID file, and your public key is stored in the Notes Address Book along with your other public information. In this way, everyone can access your public key, because everyone has access to the Address Book. But only you have access to your private key, because only you can access your ID file.

Encrypting Outgoing Mail   If a determined spy really wants to intercept email, he can find lots of opportunities. As your electronic message travels from your machine to your recipients, it might pass through numerous machines, miles of network cable, and possibly thousands of miles of public telephone lines. With the proper equipment, your message can be intercepted anywhere along the way.

You can ensure the privacy of an outgoing mail message by encrypting it. Sending encrypted mail is easy with Notes; most of the work happens automatically without any action on your part. You can encrypt a message simply by clicking the Delivery Options button at the top of the screen when composing a mail memo. This brings up the Delivery Options dialog box, shown in Figure 22.8. To encrypt, select the Encrypt option before clicking QK.

FIG. 22.8

You change your delivery options in the Delivery Options dialog box.

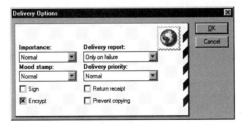

N O T E   If you usually want to encrypt your mail, you can choose File, Tools, User Preferences to bring up the User Preferences dialog box. Choose the Mail pane and select Encrypt sent mail. From then on, Notes marks the Encrypt option for you each time you send mail. If you don't want to encrypt a particular message, you can turn off the Encrypt option for that message when you send it.

When you tell Notes to encrypt a message, it locates your recipient in the Notes Address Book and retrieves his public key. It uses the public key to encrypt the body of the message and then sends the message as it does any other message. When the recipient retrieves the message, Notes recognizes that the message is encrypted and automatically decrypts it using the recipient's private key, which is stored in his ID file.

If you send an encrypted message to several recipients, Notes encrypts the message in such a way that it can be decrypted using the private key of each of the recipients.

CAUTION

When you encrypt a message, Notes encrypts only the body of the message—not the other fields, such as the subject, date, sender, or recipient's name. Therefore, you defeat the purpose of encryption if you convey too much information in these fields, especially the subject. For example, if the subject of your message, which isn't encrypted, is "Hostile corporate takeover is on for tomorrow," and if your message is intercepted, it won't matter that the body of the message is encrypted; the subject gives it all away!

Obtaining Missing Public Keys   In order for outgoing mail encryption to work correctly, Notes must know the recipient's public key. As you sit at your desk at work, sending mail to your coworkers, you shouldn't have a problem. Notes will retrieve recipients' public keys from your company's Public Address Book, and you can happily encrypt any mail you want.

However, in the following two situations, you might find that Notes doesn't have your recipient's public key:

- If you send a message to someone outside your company, he won't have an entry in your company's Public Address Book.

- If you're using Notes remote and composing mail for later replication (see Chapter 21, "Working Remote"), Notes doesn't have access to your company's Public Address Book.

If Notes doesn't have access to the public keys it needs, and therefore can't encrypt your message, Notes warns you by displaying the Mail Encryption Failure dialog box. You can click OK to Send to tell Notes to send the message even though it can't be encrypted. Otherwise, click Cancel Sending if you aren't willing to send the note without encryption.

Because Notes can't find the entry it needs in the company Address Book in these situations, you can encrypt messages by placing an entry for the recipient in your Personal Address Book along with the public key. The following two sections describe procedures you can use to accomplish this task.

Finding the Public Key for Someone Inside Your Company   You can get the public key for someone inside your company from your company's Public Address Book. Every person's public key is contained in his Person document. If you're a remote user, you can copy the entry from your company's Public Address Book into your Personal Address Book by following the next steps. (Remember, you won't need to perform this procedure if you aren't a remote user, because Notes can access the Public Address Book automatically when you send encrypted mail.)

1. Dial into your home server by selecting File, Mobile, Call Server.

2. If your company's Public Address Book isn't already on your workspace, choose File, Database, Open, Add Icon.

3. Open your company's Public Address Book database.

4. If the People view isn't already showing, choose View, People to display it.

5. Locate the document describing your recipient and select it by clicking it or moving the selection bar to it. (Do not open it by double-clicking it.)

6. Click the action button Copy to Personal Address Book.

7. Click OK when the copy confirmation pop-up box appears.

Now that you have the individual's Person document containing his public key, your Notes client can access that public key for encryption when you aren't connected to the server.

Getting the Public Key for Someone Outside Your Company If you want to be able to send encrypted mail to another Notes mail user outside your company, you must have the recipient send you her public key. Suppose you want to exchange encrypted mail with your friend at another company. She will need to send you her public key, which she can do using this procedure:

1. Choose File, Tools, User ID. Notes asks for a password and then displays the User ID dialog box.

N O T E Many of the techniques you will learn in this chapter involve the User ID dialog box. You will undoubtedly notice that every time you access this dialog box, Notes prompts you for your Notes password. Because working with encryption is such a sensitive activity, Notes needs to ensure whenever you access this dialog box that it really is you typing commands at the keyboard and not someone who happened to sit down at your desk while you were away. You might find it annoying to have to type your password each time you work with this dialog box, but be thankful that Notes is looking out for your security. ■

2. Choose the More Options icon.

3. Click Mail Public Key. Note displays the Mail Public Key dialog box, shown in Figure 22.9. Your friend should enter your name in the To field. (If she wants to use the Address Book to help with the addressing, she can click Address.) Notes supplies an appropriate subject for the memo.

FIG. 22.9
You choose the recipient of your public key from this dialog box.

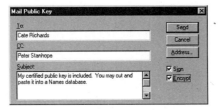

4. Click Se<u>n</u>d. Notes will send you a mail message containing your friend's public key.

5. Click D<u>o</u>ne to close the User ID dialog box.

Recall that you don't need to worry about someone intercepting this message. If an enemy intercepts your friend's message containing her public key, he has only intercepted something that your friend wanted to make public anyway. Remember: Having your friend's public key will only allow someone to send encrypted mail to her, not read her encrypted mail.

When you receive the message containing your friend's public key, the subject of the message will explain what the message contains. The body of the message appears as a huge, seemingly meaningless number.

When you receive your friend's Notes mail message, follow this procedure to extract the key:

1. Open the message.

2. The body of the message will contain your friend's public key and nothing else. Select the body of the message—all 500 or so digits.

3. Choose <u>E</u>di<u>t</u>, <u>C</u>opy to copy the key to the clipboard.

4. Close the message and your mailbox and then open your Personal Address Book.

5. Choose <u>C</u>reate, Person to create a document describing your recipient.

6. Complete the first two sections that contain the information about your recipient's name and location.

7. Later in the document, in the Advanced section, there is a field called Public Key. Place the insertion point there.

8. Choose <u>E</u>dit, <u>P</u>aste to paste your recipient's public key into the field.

9. Close and save the document by pressing Esc.

After you complete this procedure, Notes can access your friend's public encryption key, and you can send encrypted mail to her. If she wants to send encrypted Notes mail to you, you must perform the first procedure described in this section to send her your public key, and she must perform the second procedure in this section when she receives your message to insert the key into her Address database.

Sending Encrypted Mail Internationally

The U.S. State Department considers encryption technology to be a matter of national security and won't permit the export of the most sophisticated encryption software outside North America. Lotus created three versions of Notes to accommodate this restriction: one for sale in North America, an international version for sale elsewhere, and a third version that combines security features for the whole world. The three versions work identically, except that the North American version can use either of two encryption methods: a very secure method that is restricted by the State Department, and a different, slightly less-secure method that isn't restricted. The international version includes only the less-secure method. The third version (North American Worldwide Security) uses a combination of the other two versions to maintain its security

Similarly, each Notes user purchases one or both types of licenses: a North American license or an international license. The North American version grants you permission to use the more-secure North American encryption scheme, and the international version doesn't. Your license is included in your ID file. You can tell which type of license you have by checking the User ID dialog box (choose File, Tools, User ID).

Regardless of which type of license you have, you can use any version of Notes either within North America or internationally. However, if you send encrypted mail, Notes will use the more-secure North American encryption method only if you're using the North American version of Notes and you have a North American license.

Note that if you're using the North American version of Notes and you have a North American license, you can't send encrypted mail to an international user. Your version of Notes will use the robust North American encryption method to encrypt your message, but your international recipient won't be able to decrypt the message with his international version. In this case, you'll want to use the North American Worldwide Security version of Notes, which is ideal for companies that are international Notes users or that require employees to travel out of the country.

However, an international user can send encrypted mail to a North American user. The North American version of Notes will be able to decrypt the message, because it includes the capability to use either decryption method.

Encrypting Incoming and Saved Mail

This chapter has shown you how to encrypt mail that you send to others so that it is unreadable as it makes its way to your recipient's mailbox. Another option, encrypting saved mail, lets you tell Notes that all mail, whether sent in encrypted form or not, should be encrypted when stored in your mailbox. This feature is particularly useful if you store sensitive messages—both sent and received—in your mailbox for long periods of time, because it ensures that no one can look through your mailbox.

NOTE Your system administrator can configure Notes so that all mail messages arriving in mailboxes on a particular server are encrypted, regardless of the users' settings. This option might be appropriate in a high-security environment, such as a defense contractor or for a server in a company's Human Resources department, which naturally deals with sensitive issues. ▪

You can encrypt your saved copy of mail that you send to others. Choose File, Tools, User Preferences. Notes displays the Preferences dialog box. Click the Mail icon and check the Encrypt Saved Mail checkbox. Even when you send mail that isn't encrypted, the copy you store in your own mailbox will be encrypted. This feature will also encrypt incoming mail, but only after you have read the mail.

The Confidentiality of Personal Mail

If you get along well with the people you work with, it's natural that some of the communication that goes on at work isn't strictly business-related. Officially, most companies frown on using the company's email system for personal messages, but realistically, everybody knows that some small fraction of any company's email traffic isn't about department budgets and sales proposals. As long as everybody keeps his or her personal messages to a minimum, most companies look the other way.

However, you should understand that your right to privacy on your company's email system is virtually nonexistent. Consider this excerpt from a large company's corporate policy document:

"Electronic mail systems such as Lotus Notes are not public electronic communications services as defined by 28 USC 2510. They are the property of the company that you work for, are restricted to use solely by authorized users for business purposes, and the contents of any such systems are subject to random or periodic monitoring and disclosure by management without notification to users."

People in most Western countries have come to expect complete privacy of mail sent through the postal service, but don't be fooled into thinking that this privacy extends to your company's email system. In the U.S., at least, the courts have upheld the right of your company to peruse your mailbox and to insist that you decrypt encrypted mail for their examination. If one of your Notes messages contains evidence of inappropriate or illegal behavior, and a company administrator should happen to see the message in your mailbox, you won't be able to claim that the company illegally searched your personal mail, as some employees have tried to do. Unless you work in a country where the rules are different, your mail belongs to your company.

So give a little thought to what you send through Notes. If you work in a particularly sensitive environment (such as the defense industry), you can bet your company does occasional spot checks in employees' mailboxes. Your plans for a palace coup are best reserved for the U.S. mail.

Encryption and Performance

Should you encrypt all your mail? Are there any disadvantages to encryption? Just one.

Encryption takes time. Every time you encrypt a message, there is a delay of a few seconds while Notes encrypts your message. The larger the message, the longer it takes to encrypt it. Similarly, when the recipient reads your message, it takes a few seconds for Notes to decrypt the message. When you're deciding whether to use encryption, you must weigh the extra privacy that encryption provides against the slight increase in time it takes Notes to process the encrypted message.

Encrypting Documents

The previous sections showed you how to encrypt mail. However, Notes includes a second type of encryption that is unrelated to the public-key encryption technique you saw earlier. This second type of encryption lets you encrypt data not only in mail messages but in other types of documents as well. You can encrypt fields within almost any kind of document if the database designer has enabled this feature. Using encrypted fields, you can ensure that sensitive data stored in databases is as secure as the data you exchange through mail messages.

N O T E Many beginning Notes users, struggling to learn about Notes encryption, never realize that Notes contains two separate schemes for encrypting things: public-key encryption and single-key encryption. Although they share some characteristics and can often be used together in some combination, keep in mind as you read the next section that you are learning about a completely new technique. ▪

Understanding Single-Key Encryption

Public-key encryption is used almost exclusively to encrypt mail. With email, one person encrypts the message and sends it to a recipient, who decrypts it. But what if you want to encrypt a document that is stored in a database, and you want to make sure that only certain people can decrypt it? Single-key encryption is a better choice.

Unlike public-key encryption, which involves a public and a private key, the scheme Notes uses for encrypting fields involves only a single key, known simply as an encryption key. As with public-key encryption, you use a key to encrypt data, but unlike public-key encryption, you use the same key to decrypt the data.

As a Notes user, you can create any number of encryption keys, which Notes stores in your ID file. You can use these keys to encrypt data so that only you can read it, or you can distribute any of these keys to other users so that they too can decrypt the data.

You can think of your ID file as an electronic version of a key ring. Your key ring can contain keys that you create, as well as copies of keys that other people create and give to you. You can lock (encrypt) data with one of the keys, and other Notes users can unlock (decrypt) the data if they have a copy of the same key. Similarly, they can encrypt data with their keys, and you can decrypt it if you have a copy of the same key.

You can have any number of keys on your key ring, and you will probably share different keys with different groups of people. For example, you might have one key that you use to encrypt data that you expect to share with people in the sales department. Each member of the sales department has a copy of that key and thus can read any data encrypted with that key. Others outside the sales group can't read the information, because they don't possess the key.

You might create another key and use it to encrypt data that you want to share with people in your Seattle office. Of course, you will need to give a copy of that key to everyone in the Seattle office. The sales group and the Seattle group won't be able to read one another's data, because members of one group don't possess the key that members of the other group use to encrypt data. You will be able to read both sets of data, because you possess both keys. (Obviously, a salesperson in the Seattle office will also possess both keys and will be able to read data from both groups.)

Finally, you might have a key that you use to encrypt data that you don't want to share with anyone. You wouldn't give a copy of this key to anyone.

By knowing who has a copy of a particular key, you can control exactly who can read any data you encrypt.

You have learned that one of the characteristics of public-key encryption is that you can freely distribute your public key to anyone, because this key can be used only for encrypting data—not decrypting. In contrast, you must carefully control who possesses a particular key in single-key encryption. If the wrong person obtains a key, he will be able to read anything that was encrypted with that key.

Table 22.1 summarizes the differences between public-key encryption and single-key encryption.

Table 22.1 Public-Key Encryption Versus Single-Key Encryption

Public-Key Encryption	Single-Key Encryption
Each user has only two keys: one public and one private.	Each user can create as many encryption keys as he likes.
Your public and private keys are created by Notes when your Notes ID file is created.	You create encryption keys whenever you want by using the procedure described in this chapter.
Notes uses the public key to encrypt messages and the private key to decrypt messages.	Notes uses the same key to encrypt and decrypt messages.
Each user keeps his private key secret but can distribute his public key to anyone.	The key's creator must carefully consider who receives a key.
Only the person with the private key can decrypt data.	Anyone with the key can decrypt data that was encrypted with the same key.

Using encryption keys depends on various people performing these procedures:

- Creating encryptable fields
- Creating encryption keys
- Distributing the keys to other users with whom you want to share encrypted data
- Encrypting and decrypting data

In the following sections, you'll learn how to perform these procedures.

Creating Encryptable Fields

When someone designs a database form (see Chapter 3, "Using Databases," for more information about designing forms), he can specify that specific fields are encryptable, which means that they can contain encrypted data. (The data in an encryptable field doesn't *have* to be encrypted; giving a field this attribute simply gives users the option of storing encrypted information in the field.)

You can spot an encryptable field when you compose a document by the corners that surround the field. For most fields, the corners are white, but for encryptable fields they are red.

If you are a database designer, you can make a field encryptable by following these steps:

1. Enter edit mode for the form if you haven't already done so. In the database's navigator pane, choose Design and then Forms. In the document selection window (on the right side of the screen), select the form that the field resides on.

2. Double-click the field you want to make encryptable. Notes displays the field's Properties InfoBox, as shown in Figure 22.10.

FIG. 22.10
You can make a field encryptable from this InfoBox.

3. Select the Options tab.

4. Access the Security options combo box and choose Enable encryption for this field.

5. Close the Field Properties InfoBox.

Creating Encryption Keys

To encrypt fields within a document, you must use an encryption key, which you or someone else must create. Typically, you create a new key when you identify a group of people who want to be able to share encrypted data. After you create a key, you distribute that key among the members of that group. For example, when a member of the word processing department realizes that it would be nice for the members of her department to share encrypted data, she creates a key and distributes it to everyone in the word processing department.

To create an encryption key, follow this procedure:

1. Choose File, Tools, User ID.

2. Notes prompts you for your Notes password. Enter it and click OK. Notes displays the User ID dialog box.

3. Click the Encryption icon. Notes displays a list showing all the keys currently stored in your ID file, as shown in Figure 22.11. The first key is selected. The Comment box shows a comment for the selected key if there is one. This dialog box also shows the date the selected key was created and restrictions on the key (explained later in this chapter).

4. Click New to create a new encryption key. Notes displays the Add Encryption Key dialog box, shown in Figure 22.12.

FIG. 22.11

The User ID dialog box shows the available encryption keys.

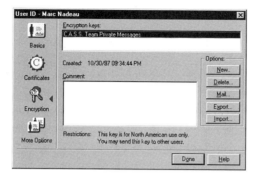

FIG. 22.12

You type your new encryption key's name here.

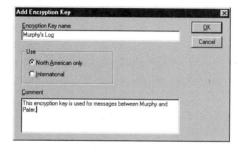

5. Enter a name for your key in the Encryption Key name field. You should select a name that describes who will use the key or what kind of data will be encrypted using the key.

6. Choose either North American only or International use. As with public-key encryption, Notes has two schemes for single-key encryption. If you select North American only, Notes uses its more-secure encryption method, but you can't share the key with coworkers outside North America. If you select International, you may share the key with anyone, but Notes uses a less-secure encryption method.

7. In the Comment text box, enter any additional information that you might want to keep with the key for future reference. Your comments can help you remember what a particular encryption key should be used for.

8. Click OK. Notes returns to the User ID dialog box.

9. If you want to create more keys, repeat steps 3 through 8. Otherwise, click Done to close the User ID dialog box. Notes adds the keys that you created to your ID file.

CAUTION

Notice that the User ID dialog box contains a Delete button that you can use to delete keys from your ID file; simply select the key you want to delete and click Delete. However, after you delete a key, you won't be able to read any data encrypted with that key without getting another copy from someone. Worse, if everyone who has a copy of that key has deleted his or her copies, all data encrypted with that key is forever unreadable. Even though someone can create another key with the same name, it isn't the same key and can't be used to decrypt data that was encrypted by the old key. So think twice—or three times—before deleting a key.

Part

V

Ch

22

Creating an encryption key is only the first step in making it useful. Unless you intend to use the key to encrypt data that you don't want to share, you next must distribute the key to other people. The next two sections tell you how to distribute encryption keys.

Distributing Encryption Keys by Email

Most often, you will distribute encryption keys to other users through Notes mail. To mail one of your encryption keys to another user, follow these steps:

1. Display the User ID dialog box by choosing File, Tools, User ID. Notes prompts you for your password.

2. Click the Encryption icon. Notes displays the list of encryption keys in the Encryption pane.

3. Select the encryption key you wish to send and click Mail. Notes displays the Mail Address Encryption Key dialog box, shown in Figure 22.13.

FIG. 22.13

You send your encryption keys to the users indicated in the Mail Address Encryption Key dialog box.

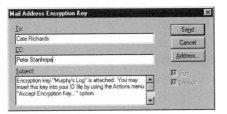

4. Enter the names of the people to whom you want to mail the key. You can access the Address Book to help with the addressing, just as you can with any mail message, by clicking Address. Note that this dialog box doesn't let you deselect the Sign and Encrypt checkboxes. All mail messages containing encryption keys must be signed and encrypted.

5. When you have entered all the names, click Send.

6. Notes displays a dialog box asking if you want your recipient to be able to send the encryption key to other people. If you want to be sure that no one has the key other than the people you send it to, click No. If you click Yes, people who receive the key from you might pass it on to other users. After you click Yes or No, Notes sends a message containing the encryption key to the people you specified.

Now, consider the recipient of a mail message that contains an encryption key. Fortunately, when someone sends you an encryption key, the subject of the mail message explains what the message contains and tells you what to do.

The encryption key itself appears as an attachment with a strange-looking filename. However, don't use the usual technique to extract this attachment (as described in Chapter 5, "Using the Notes Address Books"). Instead, follow these steps:

1. Choose Action, Accept Encryption Key. This item is new to the Action menu.

2. Notes prompts you for your Notes password. Enter it and click OK.

3. Notes displays the Accept Encryption Key dialog box, shown in Figure 22.14, which shows the name of the key, the date it was created, and what restrictions it carries (where it can be used and whether you can pass the key on to others). The dialog box also displays the comment that was entered (if any) when the key was created. You can modify or add to this comment if you want.

FIG. 22.14

You accept encryption keys while reading email.

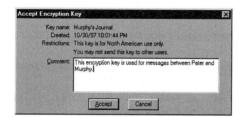

4. To insert the key into your ID file, click Accept.

Distributing Encryption Keys by File

You will usually distribute encryption keys to other users by mail, but occasionally you might need an alternative method. For example, consider these situations:

■ Perhaps one of your client companies uses Notes, but people in that company can't send or receive mail outside their company. You have made a copy of a database that you want to send them on a floppy disk (using the database-copying procedure you learned in Chapter 3). Some of the data in the database is encrypted, so you want to send them the encryption key as well.

■ As secure as NotesMail is, a floppy disk in your shirt pocket is even more secure. You know your encryption key hasn't been intercepted if you put it on a floppy disk, take it to a coworker, and put it on his machine.

Notes lets you create a file that contains an encryption key. You can write this file to a floppy disk or a network drive, and from there distribute it to other people. You can also make a copy of such a file for safekeeping to ensure that you don't lose an important encryption key.

To create a copy of an encryption key on a floppy disk, follow these steps:

1. Display the User ID dialog box by choosing File, Tools, User ID. Notes prompts you for your password.

2. Click the Encryption icon. Notes displays the list of encryption keys.

3. Select the key you want to write to floppy disk and then click Export. As shown in Figure 22.15, Notes lets you type in a password to protect this encryption key should it fall into the wrong hands.

4. Notes lets you place restrictions on the encryption key you write to the floppy disk. If you click Restrict Use, Notes displays the Encryption Key Restrictions dialog box, shown in Figure 22.16. It provides you with a text box in which you can specify the name of a

single user. Notes won't let anyone except that user extract the encryption key stored on the floppy disk. In addition, a checkbox (marked by default) lets that user pass the encryption key on to other users. If you uncheck the checkbox, the user can't pass the key on to other users.

FIG. 22.15

You enter a password to protect your encryption key.

FIG. 22.16

You can specify who can use this encryption key.

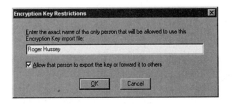

5. After you have entered a user's name and optionally unchecked the checkbox, click OK. Notes returns to the User ID Encryption Key Export dialog box.

6. The Password and Confirmation text boxes let you enter a password to protect your encryption key. No one will be able to read the encryption key from the floppy disk into his ID file without this password. This feature prevents the floppy disk from falling into the wrong hands. Choose a password and enter it in both the Password and Confirmation boxes (the password doesn't appear onscreen), and click OK. If you're willing to forego the safety of password-protecting the key (say, if your coworker is just down the hall), you can bypass entering the password by clicking No Password instead of OK.

7. Notes displays a dialog box so that you can enter the name of the file you want to create. To write the file to a floppy disk, enter a filename that begins with A: or B: (depending on which drive you want to access) followed by an extension of KEY. For example, if the key is used by the sales department, you might name the file A:SALES.KEY.

8. Click OK. Notes writes the key to the floppy disk.

Instruct your recipient to use the following procedure for importing the key from the floppy disk into his ID file or perform this procedure yourself if you receive a floppy disk containing an encryption key:

1. Display the User ID dialog box by choosing File, Tools, User ID. Notes prompts you for your password.

2. Click the Encryption icon. Notes displays the list of encryption keys.

3. Click Import. Notes displays a dialog box asking you for the name of the file that contains the key you want to import. Type the name of the file. Alternatively, type A: or B: to produce a list of all the files on the floppy disk and then select the proper file from the list. Click OK.

4. If a password was assigned to the encryption key, Notes asks you to type it in. Notes displays the Accept Encryption Key dialog box (refer to Figure 22.14). As before, it displays the name of the key, the date it was created, and what restrictions the key carries (where it can be used and whether you can pass it on to others). To add this key to your ID file, click Accept.

 When you import an encryption key, the original isn't removed from the disk you used. Use Windows Explorer to remove the encryption key from your disk. You might even want to format the disk to ensure that file recovery tools can't recover the encryption key should the disk fall into the wrong hands.

Encrypting Data with Encryption Keys

You can use any of your encryption keys, whether you created them yourself or someone else sent them to you, to encrypt data in any document:

1. Choose File, Document Properties. Notes displays the Properties InfoBox for the document.

2. Click the tab that has the key icon to display the document's security information.

3. Choose the Encryption keys combo box. Notes shows all the encryption keys stored in your ID file, any of which you can use to encrypt the document. If the document is currently encrypted, a checkmark appears next to the keys currently in use.

4. Select any of the keys from the Encryption keys list and then close the list.

5. Close the Document Properties InfoBox.

When you encrypt a document, only the encryptable fields (the ones with the red corners) are encrypted. All other fields can still be viewed by anyone. As you're entering sensitive information into a document, be sure that you don't enter anything private into a field that isn't encryptable (that has white corners).

You can remove encryption keys from an encrypted document by using the same dialog box. You might want to remove a key if a document is encrypted with several keys, and you later realize that the group that shares a particular key shouldn't be allowed to access the document. Follow the same procedure you used earlier to select encryption keys. If you click a key that is currently in use (and has a checkmark next to it), the checkmark disappears, and Notes no longer uses the key to encrypt the document. If you deselect all the encryption keys used to encrypt a document, the document is no longer encrypted.

N O T E   If you design databases, sometimes you might want all documents within a database to be
encrypted. You can specify one or more keys to use by default for encryption. While editing
a form in a database's design, choose File, Document Properties. Notes displays a Properties InfoBox
similar to the Properties InfoBox you see for individual documents. As before, select the tab that has a
key icon and select one or more encryption keys from the Encryption keys combo box. When users
create new documents, Notes automatically uses those keys to encrypt the documents. If the users
want to specify other keys to use, or if they want to specify that some of the default keys are not to be
used, they can display the Document Properties InfoBox to add or remove any keys they want.

Accessing Encrypted Documents

To access a document that contains encrypted fields, you don't need to do anything out of the
ordinary. When you attempt to open an encrypted document, Notes looks in your ID file to see
if you have a copy of any of the encryption keys that were used to encrypt the document. As
long as you have at least one of the keys, you can read or edit the document as you normally
would.

If you don't have a copy of any of the keys, your access to the document is restricted. If you
open the document for viewing, you see only the unencrypted fields. If you attempt to edit the
document, Notes displays a dialog box explaining that the document is encrypted and that you
can't edit it unless you have a copy of one of the keys.

Understanding Electronic Signatures

In Chapter 4, "Getting Started with Electronic Mail," you learned that you can sign email by
marking the Sign checkbox when you send the mail. Now that you have learned how encryption works, you can understand how an electronic signature works.

Encryption lets you prevent an enemy from intercepting and reading or altering the body of
your message. An electronic signature prevents an enemy from forging the other fields in a
message. Without electronic signatures, an enemy who is knowledgeable about Notes could
write a message and, by forging the From field, make the message appear to be from you.
Electronic signatures prevent such tampering.

When you sign a message, Notes attaches a hidden electronic code that proves to the receiver
that you are the sender of the message and that the message hasn't been altered along the way.
The electronic signature is possible through a curious twist involving public-key encryption.

In the section "Understanding Public-Key Encryption," you learned that each Notes user has a
private encryption key (known only to that user and stored in his ID file) and a public encryption key (known to everyone and stored in the Address Book). You also learned that the main
characteristic of public-key encryption is that data encrypted with one key can be decrypted
only with the other.

As you've seen, when someone sends you encrypted mail, Notes uses your public key to encrypt the data. When you receive the mail, Notes uses your private key to decrypt the data. At first, you would think that in order for public-key encryption to be useful, the public key would always be used to encrypt data, and the private key would always be used to decrypt data. But recall the definition of public-key encryption: The keys are related in such a way that a message encrypted with either one of the keys can be decrypted only with the other key.

This definition doesn't say that you must use the public key for encryption and the private key for decryption. It says that either key can be used to encrypt data, and the other key is used to decrypt the data. In other words, it's possible to encrypt data with your private key and to decrypt it with your public key. At first, that doesn't appear to be a very useful thing to do, because the whole world knows your public key, so anyone can read the data that's encrypted with your private key. But in the case of electronic signatures, that's exactly what we want.

In constructing an electronic signature, Notes uses your public and private keys in a technique that's the opposite of the usual encryption scheme. When you send signed mail, Notes builds a 16-byte block of data, called a fingerprint, from the message's recipient name, your name, cc field, domain name, and subject. Notes then encrypts the fingerprint with your private key and attaches it to the message.

When your recipient receives your mail, Notes spots the encrypted fingerprint and uses your public key to decrypt the data. Notes then checks the fingerprint against the message's recipient name, sender name, and other fields. If everything still matches, Notes can be sure that the message hasn't been altered along the way, because only you (with your private key) could have encrypted the fingerprint in such a way that it could be decrypted correctly with your public key. As your recipient opens your message, Notes displays a message on the status line that reassures your recipient that all is well:

```
Signed by Marc Nadeau on 9/30/97 10:32:34, according to BAY
```

Cases can arise in which Notes can't verify the validity of a signature, even though the message was properly signed. Most often, problems in verifying a signature occur when you receive mail from outside your company. Depending on how your system administrator has set up the connection with the other company, Notes might not be able to ensure the validity of the sender's public key. In such a case, Notes displays a message telling you that it can't verify the signature. This message doesn't mean that Notes has detected anything wrong with the message. It just means that Notes doesn't have the information it needs to ensure a proper signature.

Encryption Hazards

Using encryption to secure your data seems like a good idea, and something you would always want to do. But there are hazards to using encryption:

- The risk of losing a key: If you lose an encryption key, your data is lost. This seems like an unlikely occurrence, but all it takes is a disk going bad, and you could lose the key.

■ The risk of losing your ID: If you lose your ID, you lose your private key, meaning that you can't read your encrypted mail. Also, forgetting your password is as good as losing your ID.

■ Difficulty in administering keys: If you're using encryption keys, you have to make sure that you distribute them to all users who need the data. This can become difficult when you have more than a few users.

For these reasons, use encryption with care. If an application absolutely requires encryption, use it. Otherwise, use encryption sparingly.

Execution Control Lists

The Execution Control List (ECL) lets you protect your data from mail bombs, viruses, Trojan horses, and unwanted application intrusions encountered when you navigate the Internet. Execution Control Lists provide a mechanism for managing whether such executable files should be allowed to execute, and what level of access the program should be allowed.

ECLs are managed on a per-user basis via the User Preferences panel, and they can be controlled with more precision in the Execution Control List (see Figure 22.17). For example, a user might stipulate that when a document is digitally signed by a certain trusted colleague, programs executed by that document can access documents and databases, as well as modify environment variables, but can't access the file system or external programs.

FIG. 22.17

The Execution Control List dialog box.

 TIP It's a good idea to leave the Default options blank. This helps reduce the chances of someone causing damage to your system.

Password Expiration and Reuse

Passwords protect and ensure the security of the Notes system by preventing other users from using someone's ID file. Lotus recommends that all users password-protect their ID files and keep their passwords private. The Password Expiration feature was designed to protect the Notes system from situations in which a malicious user obtains a user's ID file and password and impersonates that user. The feature lets Notes administrators specify and enforce an expiration period/date on passwords for user ID files. When the authentication dialog box appears, the user is notified that his password has expired and that he must supply a new one. A list of previous passwords prevents users from reusing any of their old passwords. ●

Notes: Under the Hood

Millions of Notes users now know that its many powerful and unique services allow it to deliver in ways no competing product can. Understanding what these services do and how they work is crucial to having a happy and healthy Notes installation. This chapter is written with the Administrator in mind and takes an in-depth look at how Notes works its magic.

Understanding Notes Replication

In today's business environment, as teams become the prevalent work force model, the need to share information across time and geographic boundaries is increasing. Thus the ability to synchronize databases so users in disparate locations can share information on a timely basis is becoming more and more critical to maintaining a competitive advantage. One of the most powerful and complicated features of Notes is its capability to synchronize multiple copies of Notes databases stored on different servers or client workstations. This process, known as *replication*, allows users on different networks—even in different time zones or in different countries—to share the same information in a timely and effective manner.

N O T E Lotus Notes was the first product on the market to support true client/server replication, and many companies now claim that their product supports replication. This claim must be scrutinized very carefully, because most of these products are file-system based, meaning they must transfer an entire file, or are messaging-based, meaning they must send messages that contain data between "replicas." As of this writing, Lotus Notes is the only product that supports client/server replication at the field level. Currently, no other product can support this claim. ■

The primary reason to use replication is so users who do not have direct access to the server where a database resides can work collaboratively with the information it contains. For instance, people who don't have a persistent connection to the LAN, such as salespeople, people who work from home, or people who use a server in a different location, can work with a replica of the database and have their replica synchronized with the original database through the replication process.

A good example of the need for replication is demonstrated by users configured for workstation-based mail. When mail messages are delivered to you, they are placed in your mailbox on the server. With workstation-based mail, you have a replica of your mailbox on your workstation. Each time you replicate with your Notes server, the Replicator synchronizes the local copy of your mailbox with the copy on the server.

Replication is not merely a file-system based process, where an entire file is copied from one machine to another, but a true client/server-based process that bidirectionally synchronizes each replica of the database with changes from the other copy. In Notes 3.x, this was a document-level process; if any changes were made to a document, the entire document was replicated. In Notes 4.6, replication is a field-level process. If only one field in a document changes, only the information contained in that field is sent to the other database.

To illustrate the importance of field-based replication, consider this example. Company XYZ has a Marketing Encyclopedia database used to store PowerPoint and Freelance graphics presentations, video, and sound files as file attachments in a rich text field. In Notes 3.x, when a user edited a document and changed the Presentation Format field from PowerPoint to Freelance, the entire document—including the large presentation stored as an attachment—was replicated to all replica databases. This can consume a vast amount of time and system resources.

If the same scenario takes place in a Notes 4.6 database, only the fields that actually change—in this case, the Presentation Format field—are replicated, thus saving a tremendous amount of time and system resources, particularly for dialup users.

Part

V

Ch

23

N O T E In some cases, field-based replication is desirable. It adds overhead on the front end of the process because each database must be searched more thoroughly to determine which fields have changed. If a particular database has frequent changes to large documents, field-based replication can be very useful; otherwise, it might actually take slightly more time. ■

For the replication process to be efficient and effective, Notes must track several pieces of information at the database level, such as the Replica ID and Replication History, and at the document level, such as the Document ID, Created date, Modified date, and Added to file date. Each of these will be examined in detail.

As you will see in the following sections, replication is a very powerful but very complicated feature of Notes, and this chapter can only scratch the surface. In most instances, the Notes Administrator will configure your workstation and you need not worry about these issues. If you need more information, refer to your Notes manuals and online Help database.

N O T E Much of the replication process is controlled by database-specific settings accessible through the Replication Settings dialog box. To access this dialog box, right-click the database icon and choose Database Properties to display the Database Property InfoBox. Click the Replication Settings button to display the Replication Settings dialog box. For details on how to use and change these settings, see the section "Choosing Replication Settings" in Chapter 21, "Working Remote." ■

Replica ID

Each Notes database, when it is first created (when the File, Database, New operation is performed), gets assigned a unique Replica ID. When two or more databases share the same Replica ID, this is a signal to the Notes server that these databases are linked and should be synchronized. Only databases with identical Replica IDs will be synchronized.

To see the Replica ID of any database, choose File, Database, Properties, right-click the database icon and choose Properties, or select the database and click the Properties SmartIcon.

Any of these actions displays the Database Properties InfoBox. You can then click the i tab to see the Replica ID of the database. Figure 23.1 displays the i tab of the properties for the mail database.

FIG. 23.1

You can use the Database Property InfoBox to quickly and easily view the Replica ID.

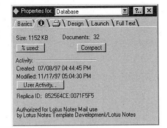

When you create a new replica of a database by choosing File, Replication, New Replica, the new database is assigned the same Replica ID, and replication between the two databases can begin.

> **CAUTION**
>
> If you have the capability to create replica databases on your server (which can be limited by the Notes Administrator), it is very important that you understand the distinction between a *replica database* and a *database copy*. A copy of a database made by choosing File, Database, New Copy assigns a new Replica ID to the copy, although the database looks the same and contains the same data.
>
> This means that the new database will *not* replicate with the original database. If you want to make a copy of a database that will *not* replicate with the original, such as a Mail Archive database, this is the method you should use.

Replication History

The first time a database is replicated successfully, a *Replication History* is created that tracks the time, date, username or servername, and actions of that last replication. To access the Replication History of a database, select it and choose File, Replication, History, or right-click the database icon and choose Replication History. The Replication History dialog box shown in Figure 23.2 is displayed.

FIG 23.2

The Replication History dialog box.

When a database replicates successfully, it is recorded in the Replication History. The Domino server uses the replication history to help determine which documents to replicate. Only successful replications are logged in the Replication History for a database. For instance, if you are a dialup user and initiate a replication session while the server's lines are busy, the Replication History will not be updated until the database actually replicates.

When the Notes server knows the date and time of the last successful replication, it uses special time and date information stored in each document to determine which documents have been added, modified, or deleted since the last successful replication. This is known as *incremental replication* and can drastically reduce the time needed to replicate. If the last successful replication time and date cannot be determined, which could happen if the Replication History was cleared or if the database in question is a brand new replica, a full replication is performed. This takes much longer and consumes more resources, because each document in each database must be examined for changes.

Part

V

Ch

23

 TIP The Replication History can be a valuable troubleshooting tool for experienced Notes Administrators, because you can quickly determine when a database last replicated, with whom it replicated, and whether information was sent, received, or both. In addition, some replication problems can be solved by clearing the Replication History of a database. For example, if a user's time or date gets out of synch with the time and date of the server, replication may not work properly. After the time and date are properly set, clearing the replication history gets the process back on track. If you have Manager access to a server database or are working with a local copy of a database, you can use the Clear button on the Replication History dialog box shown in Figure 23.2 to delete the Replication History of the database and ensure a full replication when the next replication takes place.

Document ID

Much like the Replica ID of a database, each Notes document has a unique Document ID. Each document actually has three different IDs used by Notes to provide varying levels of identification and uniqueness. The value displayed in the Document Property InfoBox for the ID is all three of the following values concatenated:

- The primary identifier is the *Document ID*, which can be used to distinguish a document within a database.
- The *Universal ID* is unique between replica databases, but is the same for all replicas of the same document.
- The highest level identifier is the *Originator ID*, which is unique among all documents in all replica copies of a database.

In addition, Notes keeps track of several time/date values that it uses for replication and auditing purposes. The five time/date values it tracks are Created, Modified, Added to this file, Modified in this file, and Accessed in this file. You can view these dates with the information tab of the Document Properties InfoBox. To do so, select any document and choose File, Document Properties; right-click a document in a view or folder and choose Document Properties;

or select a document and click the Properties SmartIcon. Figure 23.3 displays the Document Properties InfoBox that appears and shows these dates and the document's unique ID.

N O T E   An important part of the Replication process is the Sequence Number, which you can see in the second row of the ID starting with "SN." Notes uses this number to compare with other replicas of the document to determine if replication needs to take place. ■

FIG. 23.3

The Document Properties InfoBox displays pertinent document-level replication information.

The following sections describe the individual date values.

Created   Every Notes document has a Created time/date associated with it. This is the date when the document was originally created (regardless of the replica it was created in) and is database-independent. The Created time/date value is the same in each replica copy of a document in each database and will never change.

The dates associated with a document, such as the Created, Modified, and Added to file dates, as well as dates associated with a database, are dependent on the system date of the workstation or server in use when the document is added, updated, or replicated. If the system date is inaccurate, it can cause replication problems. You should occasionally check your system time and date to ensure that they are correct, and edit as needed.

Modified   Each time a document is modified after its creation, the Modified date is updated. The Modified date is crucial for replication because Notes uses this date in conjunction with the Replication History to perform incremental replication. The Modified date can vary for replicas of the same document if a user updates a copy of the document in a replica of the original, or vice versa. During replication, Notes views the differences in the dates as a signal that the document has changed and at least one of the fields needs to be replicated. After the databases have replicated, the Modified date should be the same in each copy of the document until the next edit takes place.

Added to This File Date   The Added to this file date is database-dependent in that it reflects the date when a particular document was placed into the copy of the database you are using. For example, if a document originates in the server copy of a database, the Added to this file date reflects the date the document was saved in that database. When the database next replicates and that document is transferred to the replica, the Added to this file date of the document in the replica displays the date it was placed into the replica.

Modified in This File   The Modified in this file date is also database-dependent and displays the date on which a particular document was last modified in the current database. In any given document, this date changes when a user updates a document or the replicator updates a document that was changed in a replica copy.

Accessed in This file   The Accessed in this file date is database-dependent. As its name implies, it displays the date the selected document was last accessed.

The Replication Process

The ABC Company, for example, maintains a database named Marketing Discussion on Server_A in the Atlanta office. When a new office opens in Chicago, a new replica of the database is made on the Server_B in Chicago, which copies all the documents in the database from Server_A to Server_B. When the initial replication is completed, the Replication History in the Marketing Discussion database on Server_A should look something like this:

```
10/19/97 08:25:16 PM Server_B/ABC Company DATA\MDISCUSS.NSF (Send)
```

From this Replication History, you can see that Server_A sent data from this database to its replica on Server_B on 10/19/97 at 8:25 p.m. No data was received from the new database, because it was a Replica Stub and contained no data.

N O T E   A *Replica Stub* is a new replica database that has not been initialized, meaning that it shares a Replica ID with another database but has yet to actually replicate. ▪

The Replication History of the replica database on Server_B should look something like this:

```
Server_A/ABC Company DATA\MDISCUSS.NSF 10/19/97 08:26:38 PM (Receive)
```

This Replication History tells you that the replica database received data from the Marketing Discussion database on Server_A and took just over a minute to transmit the data. As you have probably guessed, the amount of time required for replication depends on the size of the data being transmitted and the volume of changes transmitted.

In most instances, if replication is functioning correctly, you will see two distinct entries in the Replication History of any database that replicates with another database. One entry indicates that data was sent to the other database (Send), and the other entry indicates that data was received from the other database (Receive).

As users begin to use the new database on Server_B, new documents are added and existing documents are updated or deleted. As an example, follow six documents through the process. Table 23.1 shows the two databases as they exist after the replication on 10/19/97 at 8:25:55 p.m.

Table 23.1   Replication Example 1

Doc #	Doc ID*	Created	Modified	Added to File	Server	Delete
1	ABC234:364VBC	10/20/97 7:22:40 a.m.	10/20/97 9:31:56 a.m.	10/21/97 6:22:11 a.m.	Server_A	
2	AB1X42:BN456X	10/20/97 12:45:32 p.m.	10/21/97 3:44:11 p.m.	10/20/97 12:45:32 p.m.	Server_B	
3	AXV567:CBV768	10/19/97 7:20:45 a.m.		10/19/97 7:20:45 a.m.	Server_A	
4	AXV567:CBV768	10/19/97 7:20:45 a.m.	10/21/97 6:55:11 p.m.	10/19/97 8:25:55 p.m.	Server_B	
5	C2SD34:681S45	10/19/97 7:59:08 a.m.	10/21/97 4:25:22 p.m.	10/19/97 7:59:08 a.m.	Server_A	Yes
6	C2SD34:681S45	10/19/97 7:59:08 a.m.		10/19/97 8:26:57 p.m.	Server_B	

The document IDs in this example have been shortened to save space.

Document 1 was created in another replica of the Marketing Discussion database on 10/20/97 (by a remote user perhaps) and was modified on 10/20/97, but did not get replicated into the copy on Server_A until 10/21/97. (This is a good example of what happens when you have users with local replicas of a database who do not replicate daily.)

Document 2 was created in the replica of the Marketing Discussion database on Server_B on 10/20/97 (which is why the Created date and Added to file dates are the same), and it was modified on 10/21/97.

Document 3 was created in the Server_A copy of the Marketing Discussion database on 10/19/97 and has not been modified in this copy.

Document 4 is a replica of Document 3 that was placed into the Marketing Discussion database on Server_B during the initial replication (notice that the Document IDs and Created dates are the same). Document 4 was modified on 10/21/97 at 6:55:11 p.m.

Document 5 was created in the Server_A copy of the Marketing Discussion database on 10/19/97 and was deleted from the Server_A database on 10/21/97.

Document 6 is a replica of Document 5 that was placed in the Marketing Discussion replica on Server_B during the initial replication.

Table 23.2 shows the states of the two replica databases after Server_A and Server_B replicate on 10/22/97 at 6:00:00 a.m.

Table 23.2   Replication Example 2

Doc #	Doc ID*	Created	Modified	Added to File	Server	Delete
1	ABC234:364VBC	10/20/97 7:22:40 a.m.	10/20/97 9:31:56 a.m.	10/21/97 6:22:11 a.m.	Server_A	
2	AB1X42:BN456X	10/20/97 12:45:32 p.m.	10/21/97 3:44:11 p.m.	10/20/97 12:45:32 p.m.	Server_B	
3	AXV567:CBV768	10/19/97 7:20:45 a.m.	10/21/97 6:55:11 p.m.	10/22/97 6:00:45 a.m.	Server_A	
4	AXV567:CBV768	10/19/97 7:20:45 a.m.	10/21/97 6:55:11 p.m.	10/19/97 8:25:55 p.m.	Server_B	
5	C2SD34:681S45	10/19/97 7:59:08 a.m.	10/21/97 4:25:22 p.m.	10/19/97 7:59:08 a.m.	Server_A	Yes
6	C2SD34:681S45	10/19/97 7:59:08 a.m.	10/21/97 4:25:22 p.m.	10/22/97 6:05:12 a.m.	Server_B	Yes
7	ABC234:364VBC	10/20/97 7:22:40 a.m.	10/20/97 9:31:56 a.m.	10/22/97 6:05:56 a.m.	Server_B	
8	AB1X42:BN456X	10/20/97 12:45:32 p.m.	10/21/97 3:44:11 p.m.	10/22/97 6:01:32 p.m.	Server_A	

After the scheduled replication on 10/22/97 at 6:00:00 a.m., the replication history of the Marketing Discussion database on Server_A would look something like this (the actual times will vary based on the size of the documents being replicated):

```
Server_A/ABC Company DATA\MDISCUSS.NSF 10/22/97 06:04:23 AM (Receive)
Server_A/ABC Company DATA\MDISCUSS.NSF 10/22/97 06:01:34 PM (Send)
```

After the scheduled replication on 10/22/97 at 6:00:00 a.m., the replication history of the Marketing Discussion database on Server_B would look something like this (the actual times will vary based on the size of the documents being replicated):

```
Server_B/ABC Company DATA\MDISCUSS.NSF 10/22/97 06:00:15 AM (Send)
Server_B/ABC Company DATA\MDISCUSS.NSF 10/22/97 06:05:32 PM (Receive)
```

As you can see in Table 23.2, the databases have been synchronized. The Replicator has created a new instance of Document 1 in Server_B's database (Document 7) because Document 1 was added to Server_A's copy after the first replication with Server_B on 10/19/97.

In the same way, Document 8 in Server_A's copy of the database is a new instance of Document 2, because Document 2 was added to Server_B's copy of the database after the first replication on 10/19/97.

In our example, Document 4 in Server_B's copy is a replica of Document 3 created in Server_B's copy during the initial replication on 10/19/97. On 10/21/97 at 6:55:11 p.m., Document 4 was modified in Server_B's copy. During the replication on 10/22/97, the modifications made to Document 4 were made to Document 3 in Server_A's copy. Notice that in Table 23.2, Document 3 and Document 4 now have the same Created and Modified dates; however, the Added to this file dates reflect the dates when each of these documents was added into its respective database.

Handling Deleted Documents   Document 5 and Document 6 require some special attention because Document 5 has been deleted. Document 6 in Server_B's database is a replica of Document 5 in Server_A's copy. On 10/21/97 at 4:25:22 p.m., Document 5 was deleted from the database on Server_A. If Document 5 was actually physically deleted, the Replicator process would see that Document 6 exists in Server_B's database but not in Server_A's copy after the next replication. It would then create a new replica of Document 6 in Server_A's database.

To solve this problem, Notes handles deletions in a special way. When a document is deleted, a *deletion stub* is created to act as a flag for the Replicator. During the next replication, the Replicator sees the deletion stubs and knows that the documents with matching Document IDs should be deleted and deletion stubs created in their places (this is necessary so that the deletion stubs are populated throughout all replicas of the database).

In our example, when the replication takes place on 10/22/97, the Replicator will see the deletion stub for Document 5 and will delete Document 6 from Server_B's database. Table 23.2 shows that both documents have been deleted.

Changing the Purge Interval   Deletion stubs are relatively small and contain only enough information for the Replicator task to find the corresponding document in each replica of a database. However, because deletion stubs can waste a significant amount of space over time, Notes lets you set a *purge interval* so that deletion stubs can be physically removed from the database after a specified period of time.

The purge interval for a database is one-third the number of days specified in the setting of each database for Remove documents not modified in the last X days (where X is a numeric value that you supply). The default value for this setting is 90 days. If you do not change this value, all deletion stubs will be removed from the specified database every 30 days.

To access this setting, choose File, Database, Properties and then click the Replication Settings button on the Database Property InfoBox that appears, or right-click a database, choose Properties, and click the Replication Settings button on the Database Property InfoBox. Either of these methods launches the Replication Settings dialog box shown in Figure 23.4. Click the Space Savers tab after the Replication Settings InfoBox is displayed.

▶ **See** "Choosing Replication Settings," **p. 886**

Be aware that if the purge interval for a database is more frequent than the replication schedule, documents that you have deleted will reappear in your copy of the database. This happens because the deletion stubs are removed from your copy of the database before they are sent to the server copy of the database. When the server copy next replicates with your copy (whether it's local or another server copy), it will re-create each of the deleted documents.

FIG. 23.4

Use the Replication Settings dialog box to control replication options for each database.

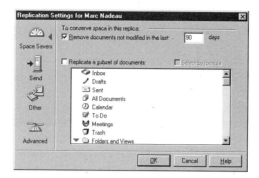

The moral of this story is to ensure that the frequency of replication between replicas of the database is greater than the purge interval for those databases.

 TIP The checkbox for Do not send deletions made in this replica to another replica allows you to delete documents in your database without creating deletion stubs, which means the deletions will not be sent to other replicas. To enable this setting, click the Send icon on the Replication Settings dialog box.

▶ **See** "Limiting What Is Sent to the Server," **p. 889**

Preventing Replication or Save Conflicts At this point, Server_A and Server_B have identical copies of the Marketing Discussion database. Any other replicas of this database that replicate with Server_A or Server_B will also be synchronized.

If you are familiar with relational databases, by now you are most likely thinking, "But what if you and I edit replicas of the same document in different databases between scheduled replications?" When this happens—and it inevitably will—a Replication or Save conflict occurs. Take, for example, a database on Server_A and its replica on Server_B. If you examine Table 23.3 with the knowledge that the two servers last replicated on 10/23/97 at 12:30:01 p.m. and will next replicate on 10/25/97 at 12:30:00 p.m., you can see from the Modified date of the two documents that each was edited in its respective database between scheduled replications.

Table 23.3 Replication Example 3

Doc #	Doc ID*	Created	Modified	Added to File	Server	Delete
1	C34VB1:98D345	10/23/97 7:22:40 a.m.	10/24/97 10:37:46 a.m.	10/23/97 7:22:40 a.m.	Server_A	
2	C34VB1:98D345	10/23/97 7:22:40 a.m.	10/24/97 3:24:12 p.m.	10/23/97 12:30:32 p.m.	Server_B	

The document IDs in this example have been shortened to save space.

By default (and design), the Replicator does not overwrite one user's changes to a replica of a document with the other's changes. Instead, the Replicator chooses a "winner" and makes it the *main*, or *parent*, *document*. The "loser" becomes a *response*, or *child*, *document* of the "winner" and is marked as a Replication or Save conflict. (The document will contain a $Conflict field.) The document that has been edited and saved most frequently becomes the winner. If both documents have been edited and saved the same number of times, the document that was saved most recently becomes the winner.

Lotus realizes that handling this process manually for a large number of databases with many documents and many replica copies would be overwhelming, so they implemented a way, at the form level of each database, to handle these conflicts automatically. Figure 23.5 shows the versioning options available in the Form Properties InfoBox.

FIG. 23.5

The document versioning options for Notes forms allows you to automatically merge conflicts, saving you time and effort.

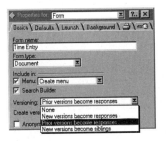

There are four options you can use to help reduce or eliminate Replication or Save conflicts, including Prior versions become responses, New versions become responses, and New versions become siblings. The fourth option, Merge replication conflicts, puts all the conflicts into one document to ease the task of determining what to keep. The Merge replication conflicts option works on a field-by-field level. For example, if a Replication conflict has field A changed in one document and field B changed in the other, the resulting merged document has field A from the first document and field B from the second.

N O T E   Replication or Save conflicts can be resolved manually by editing and saving the child document. This removes the conflict status and elevates the document from a response document to a main (parent) document. You can then decide which document has the most correct information and delete the other documents. In addition, Replication or Save conflicts can be handled programmatically. For more information regarding this topic, consult the Lotus Notes Help database or Lotus Notes documentation.

How the Access Control List (ACL) Affects Replication   Replication is not the all-or-nothing process it may appear to be from the prior example. In fact, the replication process is highly customizable, and the information actually replicated depends on several factors, such as selective replication settings, database ACLs, and Read Access Lists.

First and foremost, replication is subordinate to the database ACL. For instance, if you have two servers in your organization, ABC_1 and ABC_2, and ABC_2 has a replica of a database on

ABC_1, the data that replicates between these two servers is wholly dependent on the access level each server has been granted to the other's copy of the database. Table 23.4 briefly demonstrates the effect of various access levels on the replication process between servers.

Table 23.4 Database Access Levels

ABC_1 Access Level in ABC_2's Database	ABC_2 Access Level in ABC_1's Database	Effect
Manager	Reader	ABC_1 can send ALL changes (data, design, and ACL) to ABC 2. ABC_1 will accept no changes from ABC_2. Generally speaking, a server should have Manager access to all databases that reside on that server; however, certain security needs may merit lower access levels.
Designer	Author	ABC_1 can send data and design changes to ABC_2. ABC_2 can only send new documents created on ABC_2 and modifications to those documents.
Editor	Editor	ABC_1 can only send new documents and modifications to existing documents. (If the Can Delete Documents option is enabled for Editor access, deletions will also be accepted.) ABC_2 will not accept design or ACL changes from ABC_1. Likewise, ABC_2 can send data changes, but cannot alter the design or ACL of the database ABC_1.

N O T E If your changes don't seem to be replicating between replicas of a database, check your Notes Log for messages indicating that the access level is set in the database in question to disallow replication from the other database. The following is an example of a message you might see:

```
Access control is set in DATA\DISCUSS.NSF not to allow
replication from ABC_1\DATA\DISCUSS.NSF
```

This message indicates that server ABC_1 does not have sufficient access rights to replicate with the local database. If this is the case, have your Administrator grant you the required access level in the database's ACL. If you require more detail in your replication log, consider creating a configuration document for the Log_Replication setting. The setting ranges from general information to reporting replication information for each field. ∎

If you have a local replica of a database, you most likely have Manager access to that database.

> **N O T E** ACLs can be enforced locally in Notes 4.6, so it's possible that the database manager would enable this feature and change your local access. If you do not have manager access to a local database, see your Administrator. ■

With Manager access, in addition to creating new documents and editing or deleting existing documents, you can make changes to the design of the database. However, your access level in the server's copy of the database dictates what changes the server will accept from you. If you make changes to the local copy that you are not authorized to make to the server copy, the server will overwrite your changes during the next replication.

▶ **See** "Understanding Database Access," **p. 394**

Limiting Read Access Another security feature of Notes is the capability to add Read Access Lists to forms, views, folders, and documents. When a Read Access List is added to any of these elements, access is limited exclusively to those users, servers, or groups explicitly named in the list.

What this means in terms of replication is that if the name of a server or user is not in the list, that server or user will not have that element replicated to it. For example, if you work on a local replica of a database and create a document that has a Readers field in it, you must specify the names of all users, servers, and groups who can access this document. If you accidentally omit the name of the server where the database is stored, that document would not be replicated to the server and, therefore, would not be accessible to other users. (Typically, if a Readers field is implemented in a form, the database designer writes code to automatically populate the field with the server's name so the document will replicate with the server.)

▶ **See** "Names Fields," **p. 104**

> **N O T E** Read Access Lists and Readers fields can be very powerful security devices; however, they should not be implemented without a thorough understanding of how replication works and the effect these features have on the replication process. Please see the Lotus Notes Help database or Lotus Notes documentation for more information on Readers fields and Read Access Lists. ■

Selective Replication Using the checkbox for Replicate a subset of documents in the Replication Settings dialog box allows you to pull only documents that meet criteria you define. This *selective replication* can greatly reduce the amount of data replicated, thereby reducing the amount of time and disk space required.

Many people think of selective replication as a security feature, allowing you to limit the documents a workstation or server can replicate. However, Lotus clearly states in the Notes manuals that this is not a security feature, because users with only a rudimentary knowledge of Notes can change the selection formula. If you want to limit the documents that certain users can see, consider using Readers fields in the documents and enforcing database ACLs locally.

▶ **See** "Understanding the Data Types," **p. 457**

▶ **See** "Selective Replication," **p. 914**

The Role of Notes Servers

Lotus Notes is a client/server application that relies on networking technology to enable groups of people to collaborate. It consists of two primary components: the Notes server and the Notes workstation. By now, you most likely have worked with the Notes client software extensively and are quite familiar with its functions and features, but becoming familiar with the server is critical if you are responsible for developing Notes applications or administering Notes, or if you want to have a thorough understanding of how Notes does its magic. Because the Notes server provides mail routing, replication, authentication, communication services, and a plethora of other services to users and other servers, it is the glue that holds a Notes installation together. Accessing a Notes server requires very little knowledge on the part of the user (this is by design, as the hard stuff is left to the Notes Administrator). This section explains the role of the Notes server in your Notes installation.

The Notes server is not a file server. A *file server* is a machine that is connected to a network and runs a network operating system (NOS) (for example, Novell NetWare or Microsoft Windows NT) providing access to shared resources such as applications, printers, disk storage, modems, scanners, and other peripherals.

A *Notes server,* on the other hand, is application software running on a machine that is connected to a network. Notes servers are built around the client/server model and provide service for Notes users and other Notes servers. Although it is possible to run a Notes server on the same machine that acts as a file server, Lotus recommends that the Notes server software be run on a separate machine. The Notes server can consume a large amount of resources, and the extra overhead of running on a file server can seriously hamper performance.

The Notes server is essential to any Notes installation, providing the communication mechanism for the workstations. You can think of it as the glue that holds the whole system together. The Notes server provides the following services to Notes clients and other Notes servers:

- Storage and replication of databases
- Directory services
- Mail routing
- Security
- MTA/Gateway interface
- HTTP services/Web Retriever
- Calendaring and scheduling services
- Custom server tasks
- Add-ins

The first half of this chapter explored replication; the following sections will discuss the other services provided by the server.

Directory Services

If you have read Chapter 5, "Using the Notes Address Books," you are already familiar with the directory services role of the Notes server in a Notes installation. All users and servers in a domain share a common Public Address Book.

▶ **See** Chapter 5, "Using the Notes Address Books," **p. 181**

The Public Address Book stores information about all valid Notes users, servers, groups, MTAs, and gateways in the domain, as well as foreign domains, and makes this information available to users, servers, and server processes.

Organizations accessing multiple Public Address Books may use a Master Address Book. The Master Address Book provides naming rules for a domain and can search secondary Public Address Books. The Master Address Book is an important part of Directory Assistance, which is a powerful alternative to cascading address books.

A new service offered with Domino 4.6 is Lightweight Directory Access Protocol (LDAP). A Domino server can be set up as an LDAP server. The Domino LDAP server lets LDAP clients and applications access person and group documents in the Public Address Book. For example, LDAP clients such as Microsoft Internet Explorer or Netscape Communicator can retrieve email addresses and phone numbers from the Public Address Book.

Mail Routing

As you are probably aware from Chapter 4, "Getting Started with Electronic Mail," and Chapter 6, "Advanced Mail," Notes sports a powerful integrated client/server-based store-and-forward mail system built around the cc:Mail interface. The server plays a pivotal role in the mail system for the following reasons:

- The server provides a connection point for Notes clients and other servers.
- The *router* is a server task responsible for mail routing and delivery.
- Each mailbox resides on the user's home server.

In most installations, the router runs constantly on each server, continuously checking for new mail messages in the server's MAIL.BOX database. When the router encounters a new mail message, it examines the recipients' addresses to determine whether this server is the home server of any of the recipients. If it is, a copy of the document is placed in the mailboxes of the recipients on the server.

If the mailbox of any recipient is on a different server or in a different domain, the router task determines the best route for the mail message and transfers it to a MAIL.BOX file on the next server. Once there, the process is repeated until the message has been delivered to all recipients or an error condition is encountered.

N O T E Notes 4.6 has a very powerful mail feature named Shared Mail. Shared mail, when enabled (by default it is not enabled), provides a central object store for mail messages. When multiple recipients are specified for a mail message, only one complete copy is stored on the server, and the recipients receive only the envelope of the mail with a link to the body (this is unknown to the recipient). The benefit of this technology is the amount of space that can be saved on the server's hard disk. For example, if someone mails a 5M WordPro document as an attachment to 10 users in the non-shared model, 50M of disk space would be consumed because a copy of the mail message would be stored in each user's mailbox. Using the shared-mail model, only one 5M copy is stored in the mail object store, and the header (probably no more than 64-100K) is stored in the users' mail files. ▓

Security

From its inception, Lotus Notes was designed as a very secure system that is independent of the platform and operating system. The client/server computing model is, by nature, more secure than file-system based systems, because access to data is tightly controlled by the server. In addition, Notes utilizes RSA encryption technology, which enables user authentication, certification, encryption, and digital signatures to provide substantial security.

N O T E The Rivest, Shamir, and Adleman (RSA) public key encryption scheme is *the* leading public key scheme. In this system, each user has two 512-bit keys: one private key, which only the user holds, and one public key, which is made available to other users. Security is then provided by encrypting messages with the recipient's public key, which can be decrypted only with the recipient's private key. This method is extraordinarily secure because it encrypts data in 64-bit blocks. The potential key combinations that would have to be tested to break just one key number is somewhere in the quadrillions. ▓

Notes servers provide four types of security, as follows:

- ▓ Authentication
- ▓ Access control
- ▓ Digital signatures
- ▓ Encryption

These features will be discussed in the following sections.

Authentication   *Authentication* is a bidirectional verification process that is invoked anytime two servers or a user and a server communicate. A good illustration of authentication is the process of logging in to your Notes server.

N O T E When the first Notes server in an organization is installed, a special "master" ID known as the *Certifier ID* (CERT.ID) is created. When a new ID file is created for use in a Notes installation, it must be certified by the Certifier ID. During the certification process, an electronic "stamp" known as a *certificate* is generated, based on the private key in the Certifier ID, and placed into each new ID file. The certificate verifies that the public key associated with the new ID file is valid.

For a workstation to communicate with a server, it *must* have certificates derived from a common or ancestral Certifier ID. In lay terms, this means that to access a Notes server, your ID file must have been created by the certifier ID for the organization you are trying to access, or one of its descendants, or must have been cross-certified. For more information on certificates and certification, see the online Help database and the Lotus Notes documentation. ▓

The server generates a random number and encrypts it, using the public encryption key stored in the Person document (in the Public Address Book) that corresponds to the user ID in use during the login. The workstation software then uses the matching private encryption key stored in your user ID to decrypt the number and return it to the server. If your workstation returns the correct number (which can happen only if the matching private encryption key is used), you are authenticated as a valid user on this server. If the correct number is not returned, the server does not grant access. The process is then reversed, and your workstation software attempts to authenticate the server.

Access Control *Access control* should be a familiar concept by this point. Each database, document, form, view, and folder can employ access control to grant or deny very specific, well-defined user privileges to individual users, servers, and groups. Server access can also be granted or denied to specific users, servers, and groups through the Access server and Not Access server fields in the Server document. For more information on access control and Access Control Lists, see Chapter 3, "Using Databases."

Electronic Signatures *Electronic signatures* are also based on the RSA encryption scheme. They can be used to guarantee that a message is actually from the sender it claims to be from and that the message has not been altered while being transmitted. More in-depth coverage of this feature was given in Chapter 22, "Security and Encryption."

Encryption *Encryption* is essentially the applying of an encryption key so that unauthorized users will not be able to understand the data if they access it. The data can only be unscrambled with the appropriate *decryption* key. As mentioned earlier in this section, Notes uses the RSA Public Key encryption scheme. Lotus Notes supports three levels of encryption, as follows:

- First, at the network level, data can be encrypted so that if it is intercepted during transfer, it contains no intelligence without the appropriate key.
- At the message level, mail messages can be encrypted so that only recipients with the appropriate key can decrypt them.
- Finally, at the field level, information within a document can be encrypted.

CAUTION

Although encryption is a very powerful security measure, it should be used judiciously and only when absolutely necessary, for two reasons. First, encryption and decryption consume resources and time. The second and more important reason is that all of your encryption keys are stored in your user ID file. If that file becomes corrupted, is accidentally deleted, or otherwise becomes unavailable, you can no longer access any of the information that was encrypted by using that ID.

There are no "back doors" to this system; in fact, not even Lotus can help you if you lose your ID. This is especially critical with field- and message-level encryption. If this is enabled in your system, you should frequently back up your user ID file and keep it protected.

As you can see, Notes provides a security-rich environment that can protect even the most sensitive data from prying eyes, but be aware that many or all of these security features can be circumvented if your user ID or a server ID is compromised. If someone has physical access to your ID file and can crack the password for that ID, the person can assume your identity and see and do anything your ID permits.

To prevent unauthorized access, important ID files such as the Certifier ID and server IDs should be physically secured. Further, all passwords should be difficult to guess. (Your spouse's name or your child's birthday make poor passwords.) In that regard, long passwords are better than short ones, and a mixture of numeric and text characters in a password makes it even harder to crack. Nonetheless, all passwords should be changed frequently.

Server Programs and Add-In Programs

The Notes server software was designed in a highly modular fashion, making it easy for the Notes Administrator to configure a server to perform any or all of the tasks shown in Table 23.5. Many of these tasks are automatically loaded on the server by default settings in the NOTES.INI file. Any server program can be loaded or unloaded at any time without shutting down the Notes server. Also, you can create Program documents in the Public Address Book to launch a server program at a specified time.

To load a server program that is not currently running at the server console, type the following:

```
LOAD <programname> [argument1],[argumentn]
```

where the *<programname>* is the name of the Notes server program to load and *argument* is the command line parameters accepted by this program. Table 23.5 shows the standard Notes server programs.

Table 23.5   Common Server Tasks

Task Name	Program Name to Load	Description
Administration	ADMINP	Performs global name changes and deletions. Useful for maintaining access control lists.
Agent Manager	AMGR	Runs agents on one or more databases.
Billing	BILLING	Collects all generated billing information.
Cataloger	CATALOG	Updates the Database Catalog database.

continues

Table 23.5 Continued

Task Name	Program Name to Load	Description
Database Compactor	COMPACT	Compacts all databases on the server, removing white space and freeing disk space.
Database Fixup	FIXUP	Checks databases for corruption, such as truncated documents. Fixes problems when possible.
Designer	DESIGN	For any database that has a Design Template, synchronizes the design of the database with the template.
Event	EVENT	Starts and performs server event logging.
Indexer	UPDATE	Updates all opened views in a specific database or when other tasks such as the Replicator have changes waiting.
Indexer	UPDALL	Updates all changed views or full text indexes for all databases on the server. This program accepts several command line parameters.
Login	LOGIN	Listens to enabled ports for requests from users of add-in programs.
Object Store	OBJECT	Performs maintenance on databases and mail files that use shared mail.
POP3	POP3	Enables a Domino server to be a POP3 host server. POP3 clients, such as Microsoft Internet Explorer, can retrieve mail from the server.
Chronos	CHRONOS	Runs background macros and any other time-related tasks. This is always loaded by default; there is no program file to load.
Replicator	REPLICA	Replicates databases with other servers.
Router	ROUTER	Routes mail to other servers.
Statistics	STATLOG	Updates database statistics in the Server's log file.

Task Name	Program Name to Load	Description
SMTP/MTA	SMTP	Implements the SMTP/MTA program to enable Simple Message Transfer Protocol messages for SMTP networks such as the Internet.
Web Retriever	WEB	Implements the HTTP protocol to retrieve Web pages and convert them into Notes documents.

For more information about Notes server programs, consult the Help database or the Lotus Notes documentation.

If your server is not running the Designer process and you want to load it, enter the following command at the server console or by using the Remote Console icon in the Notes Administration dialog box (which can be accessed by choosing File, Tools, Server Administration):

```
LOAD DESIGN
```

N O T E Your ability to interact with the Server Console or load any of these tasks might be limited by your access level or a console password. ▓

Notes also lets you load and run *add-in tasks,* which are other programs written specifically to run on a Notes server. Your organization, for example, might have a C programmer write an API program to archive Notes databases at 3:00 a.m. each day. In the next section, you will see that most of the gateways for Notes are actually Notes add-in tasks. Creating custom programs for the Notes server can provide tremendous expansion capabilities.

Gateways

To further expand the capabilities of Lotus Notes and provide easy integration with existing systems, Lotus has developed a wide array of gateways. According to the *LAN Times Encyclopedia of Networking,* a *gateway* is "a computer system or other device that acts as a translator between two systems that do not use the same communication protocols, data formatting structures, languages, and/or architecture."

Some of the gateways currently available for Notes are described in the following sections. As you will see from the large number of gateways, Lotus has made a commitment to connectivity and will continue to provide excellent connectivity with other popular systems.

Incoming/Outgoing Fax Gateway   The Domino Fax Server (DFS) is additional software that allows Notes users to send email messages as faxes and receive faxes as email. When faxes are received, the actual fax (which is graphical as opposed to text) is stored as an attachment in the TIFF format. This software comes with the Lotus Image Viewer (LIV) so the TIFF files can be viewed easily.

Sky-Tel Pager Gateway   The Lotus pager gateway is an OS/2 server add-in task through which Notes mail messages can be sent to Sky-Tel pagers. This gateway requires a free COM port and modem so these messages can be sent immediately.

Microsoft Mail Gateway   Through the Microsoft Mail gateway, which requires a dedicated PC, your Notes mail users can transparently communicate via email with Microsoft mail users.

MHS Gateway   The MHS Gateway software is an OS/2 server add-in task through which Notes mail users can communicate with Novell NetWare messaging services, using Novell's Message Handling Server format.

Lotus Connect for X.25 Gateway   This is an OS/2-based add-in task through which users can connect to an X.25 network.

DEC Message Router   Through this gateway, which runs on VAX/VMS, Notes mail users can communicate with DEC mail users.

Ca-email+ Gateway   Through the Ca-email+ gateway, Notes mail users can communicate with Ca-email+ users. It is a CICS-based application for IBM host machines.

Dedicating Servers by Task

When planning your Notes network, if you envision multiple servers, consider dedicating each server to a specific task to increase performance and greatly simplify the administration of the network. Some suggested dedicated server types to consider are described here.

Mail Server   Mail servers store users' mail databases and route mail. Some of the benefits of a dedicated mail server are as follows:

- When the database server is down, users can still access their mail database, and vice versa.

- Administration is simplified because all the mail databases reside on one server, and network traffic is reduced because the vast majority of messages do not route across the LAN.

- The amount of mail databases you could reasonably expect to store on one server is dependent on the number of concurrent users you expect at any given time and on the server platform you are running.

Database Server   A database server could be used to store only application databases. The following are some of the benefits of setting up a dedicated database server:

- Administration is easier because databases can be grouped by type, replication, or security needs.

- Users can find a database more easily when it's on only a limited number of servers.

- A dedicated server can be "tuned" to achieve optimal performance without considering mail routing, and it's easy to add more database servers as the system expands.

Dialup Server   A dialup server can be set up to provide a single secure point of entry into your network for all remote users. Some benefits of a dedicated dialup server are the following:

- Security is enhanced because remote users connect with only one server that can provide access to other servers.
- LAN traffic can be decreased by putting all of the databases needed by remote users on the dialup server.
- Call tracking and logging is simplified by the single entry point.
- Call costs can be monitored and tuned more easily due to the single entry point.

Passthru Server   A passthru server is set up to allow other Notes servers or users running different LAN protocols to communicate with each other. The passthru server must, of course, run all the protocols needed to connect to each network.

After a passthru server has been configured, it can be used as a stepping stone to get to other servers. Users can go through the passthru server to other servers without needing to know all the routing steps required to make the connection. In addition, dialup users can call the passthru server and then access other servers on the network from the passthru server.

Some benefits of a dedicated passthru server are as follows:

- Dialup users can connect to multiple servers with a single phone call.
- Users on different LANs can communicate with one another through the passthru server.

To set up a passthru server, you must create a Passthru Connection document in the Public Address Book. See Chapter 5, "Using the Notes Address Books," for more information on Passthru Connection documents.

Gateway Servers   A dedicated gateway server can reduce the overhead required to run a gateway as an add-in on a production server. For instance, if you want to run the Domino Fax Server software, it may behoove your company to purchase a separate machine to run it on, as this would reduce the overhead on the Notes server and provide faster performance for the Notes server and the Fax gateway.

Hub Server   A hub server is usually set up as the central server that controls replication and mail routing in a hub-and-spoke Notes network. Hub servers are generally not accessed by end users.

Hot-Swap (Backup) Server   A hot-swap server is fully configured and ready to go in the event that another, mission-critical, server fails. Users can be redirected to the hot-swap server while the other server is down.

Server Clusters   Domino servers can be configured as clusters. A server cluster provides failover protection, workload balancing, cluster replication, and scalability.

Message Transfer Agent (MTA) Server If your organization runs several MTAs, such as the SMTP and the X,400 MTA, or if you will have a large volume of messages passing through an MTA, you should consider setting up an MTA server that does nothing but handle the messaging demands of your installation.

Notes Server Topology Overview

Notes servers can be configured to replicate and route in a variety of ways, depending on factors such as the servers' locations, the number of servers, the frequency with which the servers need to be updated, and the goals of the Administrator (to make administration easier or to reduce costs).

Based on these factors, there are three common replication topologies—hub-and-spoke, binary tree, and peer-to-peer—and it's very important to understand the distinction between the Notes network topology and your actual LAN topology. Notes Network topology determines how servers will replicate and route mail and is not tied to your network topology in any way. For example, your actual network might be comprised of NT servers with a multiple domain model running TCP/IP over Internet in a bus topology, while your Notes servers (running on the NT servers) are configured in a hub-and-spoke scheme. The following sections examine the pros and cons of each of the three Notes topologies.

Hub-and-Spoke Replication

In the hub-and-spoke replication scheme, the hub server initiates all connections, based on scheduled connections (defined in connection documents in the Public Address Book on the server), and controls replication and mail routing with the spokes (see Figure 23.6). As an example, Table 23.6 displays a subset of four connection documents from the Public Address Book on the hub.

Table 23.6 An Example of Hub-and-Spoke Connection Documents

From Computer	To Call Computer	Call at Times	Tasks	Use Port
Hub	Spoke A	11:00 p.m.	Replication, Routing	LAN0
Hub	Spoke B	12:30 a.m.	Replication, Routing	COM1
Hub	Spoke C	2:00 a.m.	Replication, Routing	LAN0
Hub	Spoke D	3:30 a.m.	Replication, Routing	LAN0

This very simple example assumes that all of the servers are in the same domain, that scheduled calling is enabled in each of these connection documents, and that the hub will attempt to call each server only once a day at the specified time.

FIG. 23.6
A graphic representa-
tion of a small hub-
and-spoke network.

A Simple Hub-and-Spoke Replication Scheme

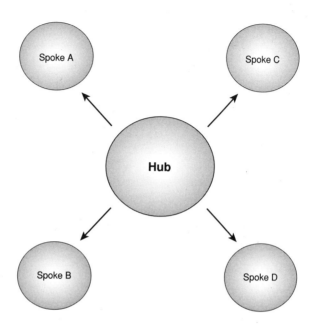

Based on the connection documents in Table 23.6, the hub first calls Spoke A for replication and mail routing. Exactly 90 minutes later, the hub calls Spoke B for replication and mail routing. Every 90 minutes, the hub calls the next spoke. When all the spokes have replicated with the hub, the hub then replicates with other hubs, if any exist.

N O T E   When using the hub-and-spoke replication model, be sure the connection documents have enough time between scheduled calls to enable the hub to finish replication with one spoke before calling the next. Otherwise, some changes may not get transferred correctly. Using the Replication Time Limit setting in the Routing and Replication section of the connection documents ensures a timely replication cycle. ▪

In this model, all of the necessary connection documents are maintained in the Public Address Book on the hub server. The following are some of the advantages of this model:

- ▪ Centralized administration of the Public Address Book is possible.

- ▪ A hub can be used to "bridge" two LANs running different protocols if the hub supports both protocols.

- ▪ Most transactions within the domain are a maximum of two "hops" away, mail routing is peer-to-peer in the same domain, and all mail servers are only one hop away. This helps to drastically reduce the amount of network traffic generated on the LAN.

■ The hub-and-spoke model scales well as the installation grows. In other words, as new servers are added to the network, the hub-and-spoke model makes it easy to integrate these new servers into the network because you need to add only a small number of connection documents.

Binary Tree Replication

In the binary tree method of replication, one server replicates with two servers at a lower level in the tree, and they in turn replicate with two servers at lower levels until all the databases have been replicated. Then the servers at the top level replicate with one another (see Figure 23.7).

FIG. 23.7

A graphic representation of a simple Binary Tree Replication model.

A Simple Binary Tree Replication Scheme

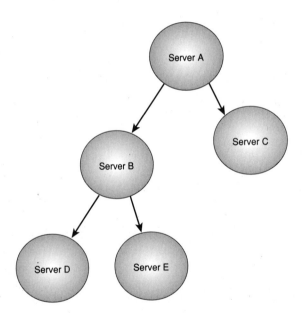

Because it can take a long time for information to move from the top of the tree to the bottom, this method is generally not as efficient as the hub-and-spoke method.

The binary tree method is often used in large international corporations because of the distances between locations and because of political issues.

Peer-to-Peer Replication

The peer-to-peer method of replication dictates that each server in a domain replicate with every other server in the domain (see Figure 23.8).

FIG. 23.8
A simple peer-to-peer replication model.

A Simple Peer-to-Peer Replication Scheme

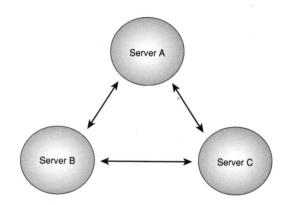

Based on Figure 23.8, the Public Address Book for the domain needs two connection documents for each database, because each database must call all other databases. Peer-to-peer replication is highly inefficient and needs additional administration to handle the greater number of connection documents required. This method should be used only in installations that have very few servers.

Notes Named Networks

Another unique, but important, Notes concept is Notes named networks. A *Notes named network* identifies a group of servers that share a common network protocol and can communicate directly with one another by using that protocol.

In a large LAN environment, it is very common to run a number of network protocols, such as TCP/IP and SPX/IPX or NetBIOS, because certain protocols provide specific advantages over others. For example, NetBIOS is easy to implement and has a very small memory footprint, but it cannot be routed. TCP/IP is more difficult to implement, but it has become a relatively popular LAN protocol because it can be routed and allows easy connections to the Internet.

Because Notes is platform-independent and protocol-independent, you can choose the protocol(s) that best suit the needs of your users. After you have selected your LAN protocols, you simply need to tell your Notes server which protocol(s) it should use—for example, TCP/IP on the NIC and X.PC (the native Notes protocol for serial communications) on COM1. Each individual protocol a server runs dictates that the server be added to a Notes named network for that protocol.

The name you choose for a particular Notes named network is completely up to you; however, using a descriptive name, particularly in a large Notes installation, can make administration easier. The following are some naming suggestions:

- Use a network name that reflects the location of the servers, such as Cincinnati.
- Use a name that indicates the location and network type, such as Lexington TCP/IP.
- Identify the network protocol, such as XPC.

One important reason to group servers in a Notes named network is that users, by default, only see the servers in their Notes named network. This encourages users to access servers that are close to them, as opposed to accessing servers that are more remote and therefore slower and more expensive to access. For example, when a user in the named network Cincinnati TCP/IP chooses File, Open Database, the list of servers contains only those located in Cincinnati and running TCP/IP.

 Although Notes will not display the names of servers outside your Notes named network in operations such as File, Open Database, if you have been granted access to those servers and a physical path exists, you can access them by typing the server's name directly into the servername field.

To view or edit the Notes named network a particular server is in, simply open that server's server document in the Public Address Book and expand the server's Network section. This displays a table indicating the Notes named networks the server belongs to.

Configuring a Notes named network is simple. For example, the server Mars has two ports configured, SPX (running SPX/IPX on one NIC) and TCP (running TCP/IP on a second NIC). Each port is then added to a Notes named network. I arbitrarily chose the names SPX and TCP for the Notes named networks, and as I add new servers running these protocols into the network, I'll add them to these groups. For each port, a network address can be specified to help other servers find this server. The final step is to enable or disable the port by using the Enable/Disable radio buttons.

 You can bind different protocols to the server Network Interface Card (NIC). This allows you to use the server to "bridge" the protocols so users can access servers and databases outside their Notes named network. For example, you can bind TCP/IP and SPX to the NIC card in the server, allowing users running SPX to get to Notes resources on the TCP/IP side.

Understanding Notes named networks is key to successfully implementing Notes. For more in-depth information, please refer to the *Lotus Notes System Administration Guide* or see the Notes Administration Help database.

The Admin Agent

The Admin Agent in Notes 4.6 is a great tool for Notes Administrators. It helps eliminate the tedious and time-consuming task of cleaning up the Public Address Book and database ACLs when a user is deleted, recertified, or renamed.

In Notes 3.x, when a user was deleted, recertified, or renamed, the Administrator had to try to ferret out all the groups containing the user's or server's name, as well as all database ACLs that might be affected by the change. The Admin Agent does the searching for you and automatically takes the following actions according to the Admin Agent's schedule:

- If a user has been deleted, the Admin Agent removes the user from all Public Address Book entries, removes the user from all database ACLs, and offers to delete the user's mail file.

- If a user has been recertified or renamed, the Admin Agent updates all documents related to that user, including group documents, in the Public Address Book and all affected database ACLs so that the user's new information is reflected.

The Notes Administrator Interface

In Notes 3.x, the Administrator had to use several different levels of nonintuitive menus to accomplish administrative tasks. The Notes 4.6 workstation software now has a vastly improved administrative interface that consolidates most administrative functions in one window. To access this interface, choose File, Tools, Server Administration to launch the Lotus Notes Administration window shown in Figure 23.9.

N O T E Remember that your ability to use these features will be determined by your server access level. If you are not named in the Administrator field in the server document, you will not be able to use the Server Administration tool.

When the Administration window is displayed, you will see the Choose a server to administer field (and the corresponding list box below it that displays the servers in your Notes Named Network). You will also see several large buttons that enable you to administer certain key aspects of the server quickly and easily.

N O T E Notice that some of the buttons have small down-arrows displayed on them. When one of these buttons is pressed, you are presented with a menu that displays additional choices. Buttons that do not have a down-arrow launch diretly into another window.

Under the Choose a server to administer field, you will see a list box that should display all the Notes servers in your Public Address Book. If you select any of the servers from the list, the name of the server should be displayed in the Choose a server to administer field. When you have selected a server, you can click any of the eight buttons described in the following sections to begin administrative tasks.

 T I P If you want to access a server that is not displayed in the list and you know the fully distinguished name, you can type the server's name in the Choose a server to administer field and press Enter. Remember, to access that server with the Server Administrator, you must have been named in the server's Administrators field.

FIG. 23.9

The super cool Notes 4.6 System Administrator Interface.

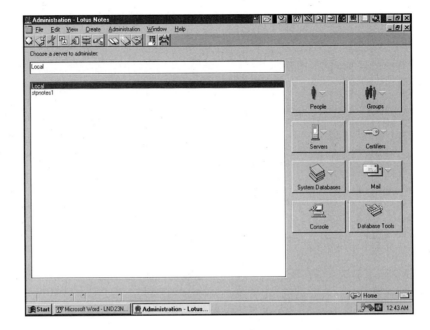

The eight buttons—People, Groups, Servers, Certifiers, System Databases, Mail, Console, and Database Tools—will be covered in detail throughout the remainder of this section.

Changing the List of Users

The People button, when pressed, presents the pop-up menu shown in Figure 23.10.

FIG. 23.10

You can use the People button to easily add or maintain Notes users in your installation.

The first option, People View, launches the People view in the Public Address Book so you can find users quickly and easily.

With the second option, Register Person, the Administrator can register a new Notes user (which creates a new Person document in the Public Address Book and creates a new User ID file).

The last option, Register From File, allows the Administrator to automate the registration process by registering new Notes users from a previously created text file. The text file requires a certain format for this to work correctly. If you intend to use this feature, be sure to read the Notes documentation.

Changing the Groups

The Groups button presents the pop-up menu shown in Figure 23.11.

FIG. 23.11
You can use the Groups button to add or maintain Notes user groups.

The first option, Groups View, launches the Groups view in the Public Address Book.

With the second option, Create Group, the Administrator can create a new Group document in the Public Address Book.

Changing the Server Settings

The Servers button displays the pop-up menu show in Figure 23.12.

FIG. 23.12
Use the Servers button to configure or analyze your servers.

The first option, Servers View, launches the Servers view in the Public Address Book.

The second option, Configure Servers, opens the Public Address Book and launches the Configuration view.

The third option, Directories and Links, launches the directory and link management interface shown in Figure 23.13. This extremely handy feature of Notes 4.6 makes it easy to view, create, modify, and delete directories and directory links. It also shows you the actual directory each link points at and lets you add users to the directory links. In the "old days," the creation and maintenance of directory links had to be done manually with a text editor and, even worse, there was no way to see what links existed or where they pointed without going out to the OS and looking for them.

Through the fourth option, Register Server, the Administrator can register a new Notes server (which creates a Server document in the Public Address Book and a new Server ID).

The fifth option, Log Analysis, displays a dialog box in which the Administrator can configure analysis parameters and run an analysis on the Notes Log. This can be extremely useful when troubleshooting, because it does the searching for you; you no longer have to open the log and manually scan it for specific information. When the analysis is complete, the data is written into the database you specify.

FIG. 23.13

Use the Directories and
Links option to launch
the Manage Directories
and Links dialog box.

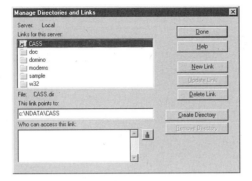

The sixth option, Cluster Analysis, displays a dialog box in which you can perform several
types of analysis on servers within a server cluster. When the analysis is complete, the data is
written into the database you specify.

Controlling Certification

The Certifiers button displays the pop-up menu shown in Figure 23.14.

FIG. 23.14

The Certifiers button can
be used to perform
certification and
registration tasks from
your workstation.

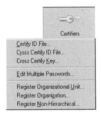

The Certify ID File option enables the Administrator to "stamp" a certificate into an ID file.

The Cross Certify ID File option enables the Administrator to place a cross certificate into an
ID file.

Edit Multiple Passwords allows you to perform maintenance on the User ID files that have
multiple passwords associated with them.

Register Organizational Unit enables the Administrator to certify an organizational unit ID.

Register Organization enables the Administrator to register an organization ID.

Register Non-Hierarchical enables the Administrator to register a Non-Hierarchical ID.

Accessing System Database Information

The System Databases button drops system databases on the chosen server and Configure
statistics reporting for a given server. The system databases include the Public Address
Book, the server's Notes Log, the Database Catalog, the Statistics Reporting Database, the

Administration Requests Database, the Certification Log, the server's Outgoing Mailbox, the Web Server Log, the Web Server Configuration, the Certificate Admin, and the Certificate Authority database.

System Databases are important tools for troubleshooting server administration issues. For example, the Administration Requests Database stores all the Administration processes along with responses to the requests, allowing administrators to track down issues with the Administration Process.

Notes 4.6 offers four new system databases. The Web Server log contains all Web server requests. The Web Server Configuration database enables configuration settings for the Web Server. Administrators can use the Certificate Administration and Authority databases to effectively manage certificates within your organization (see Figure 23.15).

Part

V

Ch

23

N O T E Statistics Reporting is a powerful Notes server administration feature that enables you to track a wide variety of Notes server statistics and thresholds in a special Notes database. If you are responsible for the administration of a Notes installation, look into the features of Statistics Reporting.

FIG. 23.15

The system databases include the Public Address Book, the server's Notes Log, the Database Catalog, the Statistics Reporting Database, the Administration Requests Database, the Certification Log, the server's Outgoing Mailbox, the Web Server Log, the Web Server Configuration, the Certificate Admin, and the Certificate Authority database.

Mail Options

The Mail button displays the pop-up menu shown in Figure 23.16.

The Open Outgoing Mailbox option opens the server's Outgoing Mailbox (MAIL.BOX) and opens the Mail view.

The Send Mail Trace option launches a dialog box in which you can send a Mail Trace to track a mail message's routing path. This is very useful for troubleshooting mail routing problems.

FIG. 23.16

The Mail button can be used to perform key mail-related tasks on the server.

Controlling the Server with the Remote Server Console

The Console button launches the Remote Server Console dialog box shown in Figure 23.17.

FIG. 23.17

The Remote Server Console window can be used to send commands to a server from your workstation.

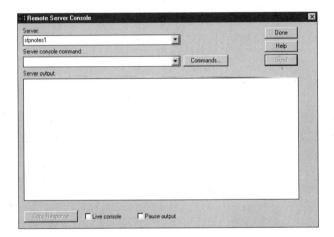

The Remote Sever Console window enables the administrator to choose a server and send commands to it remotely. This very useful tool lets an Administrator troubleshoot or "tweak" a server from a remote location. To use the remote console, you must be named an administrator in the server document on the server you want to administer.

Database Information

The last button, Database Tools, displays the dialog box shown in Figure 23.18.

FIG. 23.18

The database-related tools available from the Databases button.

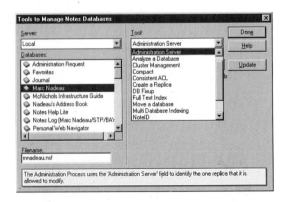

From this dialog box, you can perform a number of administrative tasks. The Server combo box lets you choose the server that hosts the database you are interested in. After you have selected a server, the Database list box presents you with a list of databases on that server. You can then select a database and use the Tools combo box to select an action from the following list to perform on the selected database:

- **Administration Server:** This option lets you set the server that will perform administrative tasks (run the Admin agent), such as updating the ACL when the Address Book changes.

- **Analyze a Database:** This option lets you choose a series of things to scan a database for, such as *user writes*. It also lets you indicate the time frame for the scan and a database into which the output should be written. This is a very powerful feature, because the system can do the searching for you and present you with a summary.

- **Cluster Management:** If you are using server clusters, this option lets you tell the cluster about the status of a database.

- **Compact:** You can select any database and use the Compact option to free up the white space in the database and even discard the view indexes, which also frees up a tremendous amount of space.

- **Consistent ACL:** With this option, you can make a database enforce consistent ACLs across all copies of a database. You must have manager access to the selected database to perform this action.

- **Create a Replica:** This option lets you create a replica copy of the selected database on one or more servers. You must be in the Create Replicas field in the server document of the server where you want to create a replica.

- **DB Fixup:** This option lets you run Fixup on local and multiple databases at the same time. Only reader access on the database is needed to run Fixup.

- **Full Text Index:** This option lets you set the parameters and create a full text index for the selected database.

- **Move a Database:** If you are using server clusters, you can use this option to move a database from one server in the cluster to another.

- **Multi Database Indexing:** This option lets you include the database in an index that spans multiple servers or databases. You must have manager access to implement this option.

- **NoteID:** This option allows you to enter the NoteID of a document and search a database for the specified document. If the document is found, you can then view the document's fields and properties. This search method works on only one database at a time.

- **Quotas:** This option lets you set various parameters that control the size of databases on the server.

- **Replication:** This option acts as a toggle to enable or disable replication for the specified database. You must have manager access to implement this option.

■ **Sign a Database:** This option lets you sign a database, template, or a specific design element (such as an agent), enabling you to add your organization's associated name to the databases or design elements your organization developed. This option is especially important if you purchase shrink-wrap or near shrink-wrap software and need to sign all of the agents so they have execution access to your server(s).

Notes Server Platforms

Lotus Notes is truly a cross-platform application, capable of running most popular operating systems. Notes server software is available for Windows 95, Windows NT, OS/2, various flavors of UNIX, Novell NetWare servers (NLM), and IBM S/390 servers. Lotus gives you the flexibility to choose the platform that is the best fit for your organization, depending on the networks and operating systems in use at your company. Notes was originally developed for an OS/2 server, and the OS/2 server software still provides the most functionality and flexibility, although other server platforms are rapidly catching up. Lotus will also add Native Domino for the AS/400.

Supporting Multiple Licenses

Although a Notes installation can quickly provide a high return on investment, a large Notes installation can be costly. Lotus realized that many Notes users do not need to have access to the full Notes workstation functionality, such as the design tools, and therefore can use a subset of the full client to meet their needs at a reduced cost.

Based on the varying needs for access to Notes functionality, Lotus responded by developing three types of licenses to provide different degrees of access to Notes features and functionality. The three types of licenses are the following:

■ **Lotus Notes Designer for Domino License:** The most costly of the three, this license enables each created user ID full access to all of Notes core services. Most users, unless they will be doing database design, do not need the Notes Designer for Domino client.

■ **Lotus Notes Desktop License:** This is a less costly version of the Full License that has had the database design tools disabled. This license gives users the legal authority to use any Notes database.

■ **Lotus Notes Mail License:** This supports the least number of features and is the least costly of the three types of licenses. In fact, users who have been given the Express License are legally obliged to use only the five databases that ship with this license.

Notes supports a heterogeneous mixture of different license types within a Notes installation. For instance, you might be using a Notes Desktop License while your coworker in the next cubicle is using an Express License.

To find out what type of license you have been issued, choose File, Tools, User ID. You will then be prompted for your password. After you type your password and click Enter, you will see the User ID dialog box (see Figure 23.19).

FIG. 23.19
The License field displays the type of license you have been granted.

Notes and the Internet: An Overview

By now, you've surely felt the shockwave the Internet has sent through the business world. In fact, if you believed the hype surrounding it, you'd most likely not be reading this book, as industry pundits have predicted that the Internet will be the death of Notes. People who have used the Internet, however, know it is just not ready for the mission-critical applications you can build with Notes. In fact, people who truly understand the power of Notes know that Notes and the Internet are complementary—rather than competing—technologies, and Lotus has capitalized on this fact by creating world-class, industry-leading applications that can leverage the Internet to extend the reach of Notes. Lotus has accomplished this through three technologies: the Simple Mail Transport Protocol Message Transfer Agent (STMP MTA), Domino (Hypertext Transport Protocol Services), and the InterNotes Web Publisher.

The Simple Mail Transport Protocol Message Transfer Agent (SMTP MTA)

Internet mail has become incredibly pervasive, in both the business world and the consumer world. In fact, it's estimated that over 30 million people have Internet connectivity, and that number is increasing very rapidly. Lotus saw the need to allow NotesMail users to send Internet mail and provides a powerful native solution in the form of the SMTP MTA.

The SMTP MTA is a powerful, full-featured Message Transfer Agent that not only converts NotesMail messages to SMTP messages and vice versa, but also supports Multi-Part Internet Mail Extensions (MIME), making life easy for users who want to send and receive file attachments.

Implementing the SMTP MTA requires several things. First, you must choose a server on which to run the SMTP MTA tasks and configure your Public Address Book so that mail destined for the Internet is routed to the SMTP MTA server. Second, the server running the SMTP MTA must have a connection to an Internet Service Provider. With these things in place, sending a mail message to an Internet user is as simple as sending mail to a Notes user. For example, if your company configures the SMTP MTA and has a connection to the Internet, you can use Notes to drop a line to a friend by composing a new mail message, entering the email address (for example, **mnadeau@bay.comm**) in the To: field and then just sending the mail message. Notes routes the mail to the SMTP MTA, which converts the mail message into the SMTP format and then routes it to the ISP, which puts the mail "out on the wire."

If you are considering an SMTP solution for your company, the Notes SMTP MTA is an excellent choice.

Domino

Domino (Hypertext Transport Protocol services for Notes) is one of the most exciting things to happen in the Internet world for some time. Domino is a series of Notes server tasks that, when installed, convert Notes databases into HTML dynamically, as requested by a browser.

In a nutshell, this means that you can use a Web browser not only to read information in a Notes database (and see updates to it almost immediately), but also to enter information directly into a Notes database. You can actually create Notes applications that can be accessed over the Web (either over the Internet or an intranet) with a browser or through Notes with a Notes client.

The following scenario demonstrates a typical Domino session based on the following assumptions: your Notes server is running Domino, the server has a connection to the Internet, and the user has a Web browser.

John Doe is a "road warrior" with Windows 95 dialup networking and Netscape Navigator on his notebook. John connects to the ISP from his hotel room and launches Navigator. He enters the URL **http://www.acmecompany.com**, which points to the home page on your Domino server. He clicks the C & S region on the imagemap (which is really a hotspot on a Notes Navigator) and is prompted for a Username and password. After he is authenticated, he is taken to his Mailbox, and his Calendar is displayed. He schedules two new meetings and then checks his mail, accepting an invitation to a meeting next week and sending an email reply with which he includes a doclink to a Notes discussion database—all through his browser!

Not only can Domino convert Notes databases to HTML as a browser makes requests (ensuring the most current data is displayed), but it also supports the HTML 3.0 specs (and you can code HTML directly into the database to tweak it) and supports native Notes ACL-level security over the Internet. If you want to build a dynamic, high-performance, low-maintenance Web site, there is no better solution than Domino.

▶ For more detailed information on Domino, **see** Chapter 26, "Using Domino Server's HTTP Service," **p. 1039**

Working with the Web

Lotus Notes and the Web

This chapter provides an overview of the Internet enhancements of Lotus Notes/Lotus Domino. In case you're unfamiliar with the Internet, this chapter also provides an overview of the Internet and intranets.

Placing the Internet in Context

Over the last few years, the Internet has become an inescapable presence in our world. It has been around, in one form or another, since the late 1960s, growing slowly over most of that time. But in the last few years, it has caught the imagination of the general public, and its growth has become explosive as the number of people using it has doubled and redoubled and redoubled again in a very short period of time. Now you can barely turn on the television or open a magazine without seeing advertisers' Internet addresses plastered across the screen or page.

The original purpose of the Internet was to encourage communication and collaboration among people doing (first) government research and (later) general academic research. For most of its duration, the Internet was a ho-hum, text-only medium. Early on, the tools available for using it were hard to master. These things limited the Internet's audience and appeal.

As time passed, the usefulness of the Internet for long-distance communication and collaboration caught the attention of more and more people. Users of the Internet added new and better tools and protocols to the tool set. Computer technology became widely and cheaply available.

A few years ago, these trends converged to fuel the Internet's present explosive growth. Programmers at CERN (the European Laboratory for Particle Physics) in Switzerland developed a new kind of research tool that involved rich text documents that had links to related documents embedded right in the body of a document. This tool became the World Wide Web. The documents weren't just plain text. They were formatted text, and they could include embedded objects, such as pictures.

Later, programmers at the National Center for Supercomputing Applications (NCSA) created a graphical tool for viewing documents on the World Wide Web. They called this new tool Mosaic, and they distributed it for free to anyone who wanted to use it and further develop it.

Mosaic allowed the user to see not only the text of a Web document on-screen, but also the embedded objects—the pictures, animations, videos clips, and sound bites (actually, you could hear the sound bites). Mosaic turned the World Wide Web into a multimedia version of the Internet. By the time this happened, computers that could use Mosaic—Macintoshes, PCs running Windows, and computers running graphical versions of UNIX—were sitting on millions of desks in universities, offices, and homes all over the world. The computers were the tinder. Mosaic was the flint. Together, they sparked the phenomenon that the Internet is today—a fire that consumes the imagination of marketers, programmers, computer makers, and users all over the world.

Mosaic and the World Wide Web aren't the sole catalysts that transformed the Internet. UseNet newsgroups, Internet Relay Chat, and Internet-based sound and video transmission have all contributed new ways to use the Internet. Along with the Web, these new technologies have turned the Internet into not merely a handy communication medium and research library, but also a marketplace, a playground, and a hotbed of experimentation in new ways to use networked computers.

Furthermore, the growth of networking in general has fed the popularity of the Internet. At its base, the Internet is simply a computer network based on standard network communication protocols. Even if you don't have a use for all the newfangled communication and research tools that have been popping up, you can still connect two computers—say two Notes servers—to the Internet, and they will communicate with each other as if they were both on your office LAN. This allows replication and mail routing between your Notes servers.

To companies in the computer industry, the Internet is a huge opportunity, a huge risk, and a threat to their livelihoods. Someone will make a lot of money selling products that power the Internet, many people will lose a lot of money trying, and many others will wake up one morning to discover that their products no longer have a market because they aren't Internet products.

Part

VI

Ch

24

Thus, we are witness to the browser wars. The programmers who wrote Mosaic later left the NCSA and formed a company, Netscape, where they wrote and released Netscape Navigator, an enhanced version of the Mosaic Web browser. Netscape Navigator (commonly referred to as just "Netscape") quickly gained a dominant market position of maybe 80 percent penetration.

Microsoft woke up one day and realized that the Internet boat was about to sail without them. Microsoft has managed, through its monopoly of the PC operating system market, to become dominant in all the desktop software markets. When they realized they were about to be stranded on the DOS/Windows island as everyone embarked for the new world of the Internet, Microsoft transformed themselves overnight into an Internet products vendor and hopped on board. Microsoft has since made it its goal to knock Netscape off its perch. As a result, over the past two years Netscape and Microsoft have released new versions of their Web browsers—Netscape Navigator and Microsoft Internet Explorer—every three months or so, adding bells and whistles at a furious pace and all but giving the products away.

What Is the Internet?

The Internet is the granddaddy of all internetworks. Its defining characteristic is the TCP/IP protocol suite. People who work with computer networks define them as follows: Two or more computers connected to each other on a single, shared segment of cable (through which they communicate) constitute a local area network (LAN). Two or more LANs connected to each other by an internetworking device such as a bridge or router constitute an internetwork. If two LANs are so physically distant from each other that you couldn't practically wire them to each other directly, but you must use the resources of the telephone company to connect them—and you do so—the resulting internetwork constitutes a wide area network (WAN). Any network that exists primarily so that other networks can connect to it is a backbone network.

The Internet is thousands of networks, all over the world, connected to each other primarily through the telephone networks, which constitute backbone networks.

A protocol is a set of rules. A computer networking protocol defines how computers on a network communicate with each other. A protocol suite is a set of protocols that are related to each other and build on each other. There are many protocol suites, including TCP/IP, IPX/SPX, NetBEUI, SNA, AppleTalk, and others. Most protocol suites were developed by corporate enterprises and are, therefore, proprietary. The evolution of the Internet from the Defense Department experiment included, among other things, the development of the TCP/IP protocol suite; therefore, TCP/IP is not proprietary. In order for any computer to be considered "on the Internet," it must use TCP/IP. If your computer doesn't use TCP/IP, it can still communicate, via a proxy server, with computers on the Internet, but your computer isn't itself on the Internet if it doesn't use TCP/IP.

The TCP/IP suite includes scores of protocols, most of which are acronyms such as TCP and IP, but some of which are more cleverly named, such as Gopher. Here are some of the Internet protocols that are important to your understanding of Notes and its relationship to the Internet:

- Internet Protocol (IP): This is the basic communication protocol that computers use when they transfer information back and forth. All the other Internet protocols rely and build on IP. Some programs use only IP when transferring information to another computer.

  Among other things, IP defines Internet addressing. Every computer on the Internet must have a unique address. IP addresses consist of 32 bits of information that is usually presented in dotted-decimal format—that is, as a series of four decimal numbers separated from each other by periods. Each number may be from 1 to 254. Therefore, an IP address might look like this: 123.123.123.123.

- Serial Line Internet Protocol (SLIP) and Point-to-Point Protocol (PPP): These are the versions of IP that you use if your computer isn't connected to a LAN and you have to connect to the Internet by dial-up telephone. You will use one or the other, not both. PPP is a later, more powerful version of SLIP.

- Transmission Control Protocol (TCP): Adds reliability to IP data transmissions, among other things. Notes uses TCP, not just IP, to transfer data to other Notes computers.

- Domain Name Service (DNS): Since most human beings (not including system administrators) don't want to bother with remembering numeric computer addresses (see the first item in this list), the Internet also lets you give your computer a host name under the Domain Name system.

  Under this system, every computer (or host) belongs to a super domain, which may be one of the three-letter domains such as gov (government), mil (military), edu (educational institution), org (nonprofit organization), or com (commercial enterprise). Or it could be one of the new proposed top-level domains: firm (businesses), store (online businesses), web (for entities emphasizing activities related to the World Wide Web), arts (cultural organizations), rec (recreation/entertainment), info (information services), and nom (personal sites—*nom de plume*). Or it may be a two-letter country code such as us, uk, jp, au, and so on.

Within the super domain, your computer belongs to a private domain, which may in turn have subdomains defined. Thus, a computer named `www.lotus.com` has host name of `www` and is a member of the `lotus` domain, which is in turn part of the `com` superdomain. When sending information to that computer, you can address its `host.domain` name instead of its IP address. Domain name servers that exist in each domain work together to resolve the host name of each computer to its IP address.

- HyperText Transfer Protocol (HTTP): World Wide Web servers and browsers communicate and transfer files to each other using this protocol. It too builds and relies on IP. A Notes server running Domino Web Publisher understands both HTTP and Notes' proprietary method of transferring data to Notes clients and other Notes servers.

- HyperText Markup Language (HTML): This is the set of codes and syntax rules that define the formatting of documents on the World Wide Web. A document written in HTML is called an HTML document. If you look at the document with a Web browser, it appears to be fully formatted. If you look at it with a text editor, you see that it is just plain text with some strange-looking codes tossed in here and there. These codes are enclosed in angle brackets (< and >). HTML also encompasses the embedding of hypertext links into HTML documents. A hypertext link is a pointer to another document. When you click a hypertext link, your Web browser will send an HTTP message to the computer named in the link, requesting the document named in the link.

  HTML continues to go through version changes, like all other aspects of the Web. The current "recommended version" is HTML 3.2; a proposed 4.0 specification is in the works. (For details, check out `http://www.w3.org/TR/WD-html40/`.)

- Uniform Resource Locators (URLs): These are addresses of computers and the files on them. The format of an URL for a computer is

  `protocol://hostname.domainname.superdomain`

  `protocol` is a protocol that the computer named in the URL should use to interpret the accompanying message, and `hostname.domainname.superdomain` is the DNS host name of the target computer.

  The format of an URL for a file is

  `protocol://hostname.domainname.superdomain/dirname/filename`

  `dirname/filename` is the location of the file on the target computer. An example of an URL for a computer would be `http://www.lotus.com`. This indicates that the computer, `www.lotus.com`, should interpret the accompanying message using HTTP. It can do so only if it has Web server or client software running on it.

  In the Notes environment, a Domino server replaces `filename` with a Notes database name and appends a command. A typical Domino-generated URL would use this format:

  `protocol://hostname.domainname.superdomain/dirname/database/command`

  It might look like this:

  `http://www.lotus.com/lotus/usergroups.nsf?OpenDatabase`

  There are lengthy explanations and examples of the Domino `?Commands` in the user documentation.

- File Transfer Protocol (FTP): This is the original Internet protocol that defines how files will be transferred from one computer to another. Nowadays, you can transfer files using either FTP or HTTP.

- Simple Message Transfer Protocol (SMTP): This is the protocol that defines how email messages will be formatted, addressed, and delivered. SMTP doesn't provide for rich text messages, attached files, or hypertext links. As such, SMTP is what some refer to as a first-generation mail system. (File attachment capability defines a second-generation mail system, rich or formatted text defines a third-generation mail system, and hypertext links define a fourth-generation mail system, such as Notes.)

- Multipurpose Internet Multimedia Extensions (MIME): A mail program that complies with MIME can send and receive messages with file attachments and with rich text content. In other words, MIME extends SMTP and other protocols. Your MIME-compliant mail program is effectively a third-generation mail program.

- Post Office Protocol, version 3 (POP3): If your computer doesn't remain connected to the Internet continually, a computer that is constantly connected must hold your incoming mail for you until you do connect and then receive your mail. POP3 defines a way for this whole transaction to take place.

- Network News Transfer Protocol(NNTP): UseNet news servers use this protocol to transfer data back and forth.

- Gopher: This protocol defines how Gopher servers store and organize information.

- Secure Sockets Layer (SSL): Although early Internet protocols took security considerations pretty lightly, with more and more organizations doing commerce over the Web, this has become a major consideration.

  Several security schemes are being employed. One, SSL, proposed and implemented by Netscape, seems to be gaining wide acceptance (including an implementation by Lotus in Domino Server) and has become an Internet standard for implementing secure financial transactions. SSL works much like Notes security. You and the party you want to do business with both receive certificates that identify you from a trusted third party. That way, no impostor can pretend to be the second party that you think you're dealing with. Then you use public key/private key encryption to authenticate each other and protect your data transmissions from eavesdroppers.

Internet Tools

Since the Internet has from its earliest days served as a medium of communication and research, the first available user tools served those purposes. Over time, Internet users have developed more sophisticated tools, but generally they still serve the purposes of enabling electronic communication, research, and collaboration. The earliest Internet tools still in use include the following:

- Terminal emulation: The Telnet protocol lets a person sitting at one computer control and run programs on a remote computer.

■ Email: Electronic messaging, in the form of the Simple Message Transfer Protocol (SMTP), lets people far from each other in time and place carry on long-term conversations.

■ File transfer: File transfer, in the form of the File Transfer Protocol (FTP), allows collaborators in research projects to more easily work together and share the results of their work with each other.

As time has passed, the original communications and research tools have been augmented with newer and better tools. Some (but not all) are listed here.

Here are the communication tools:

■ Internet mailing lists: These are list servers, or computers that maintain mailing lists of people's email addresses. If you're on a mailing list, you can send a message to the list server that maintains it, and the list server will broadcast your message to all the other people on the list. These provide a great way to hold ongoing special-interest discussions among people who can't easily get together face-to-face.

■ UseNet newsgroups: These are Internet-based discussion groups, or bulletin boards. You can post messages on news servers. Others can reply to your messages. Everyone can read and follow the resulting conversations. This is another good way to hold discussions among widely dispersed people.

■ Internet Relay Chat (IRC): These are "live" discussion rooms. You type a short message and press Enter. Your message appears on the screens of everyone in the "chat room." Their messages appear when they press Enter.

■ Internet telephone programs: This is one-to-one, live voice conversation. As with real telephones, it is cheaper for long-distance calls but has much lower voice quality and reliability.

■ CU-SeeMe: This is one-to-one, live voice conversation with video. You can watch each other as you talk to each other.

■ Internet radio and television: Live or recorded, this is voice or video transmission via Internet into your computer.

■ Push technology: This is customized news feeds via the World Wide Web right to your browser. PointCast was a groundbreaker in this category, but now Microsoft has included this technology in the latest 4.x versions of Internet Explorer with its Active Channels.

Here are the research tools:

■ Gopher: Gopher servers let you browse their contents, and the contents of other Gopher servers, in a menu interface. Choose an item on a Gopher menu. It may open to a deeper menu or a document. The menu or document that it opens to could be on the same or a different Gopher server. The universe of Gopher servers interconnected in this way is sometimes called Gopher-space. You might call the menus hypermenus, because they transport you instantly across space to another server entirely.

Part

VI

Ch

24

- World Wide Web: This is mostly what has caught the imagination of the world and fueled the phenomenal growth of the Internet. Documents in Web servers are connected to each other with hyperlinks. In other words, embedded in one Web document are pointers to other Web documents that relate to the first one contextually. You research a topic by activating the hyperlinks and scrolling through page after page until you find the one(s) that have the information you need.

- Search engines: A series of specialized servers on the Web that catalog other Web servers. Familiar search engines include Yahoo (`http://www.yahoo.com`), AltaVista (`http://www.altavista.digital.com`), and HotBot (`http://www.hotbot.com`).

- Finger: You can use Finger to find the names of people in a specific domain so that you can send them email.

There are also several search engines that focus on finding people: Four11 (`http://www.four11.com`) and SwitchBoard (`http://www.switchboard.com`).

The World Wide Web

The World Wide Web is a system of servers and clients. The Web servers store documents, called Web pages, in HTML format and send them to Web clients on request. The more advanced Web servers, such as the Lotus Domino Web Server, may also store pages in database format and convert them to HTML when sending them to requesting Web browsers. The browsers request documents by sending a document's URL to the server. Then the browser formats pages according to the embedded formatting codes and displays them for you. If a browser sends an URL that names only the Web server and not a specific page, the server sends a default page, known as the home page, to the browser. The server sends pages to the browser, or sends a reply if the page is unavailable, using the HTTP protocol.

The most capable Web browsers can do lots more than just request and receive HTML pages from Web servers. They can also retrieve Gopher menus from Gopher servers, directory listings and documents from FTP servers, and articles from news servers. They can send Finger requests. They include a POP3 mail reader. It used to be that you needed different programs to do all these things. Now your Web browser does it all.

Like Notes documents, HTML documents can present virtually any kind of information. They consist of plain text plus embedded formatting codes, or tags, that look something like this: `<HTMLCODE>`. `HTMLCODE` is an actual text string that has a specific meaning to a Web browser. For example, a given code might tell the browser to italicize (`<I>`) the text that follows or to center (`<CENTER>`) the paragraph that follows. It might tell the browser to insert a horizontal rule at this point (`<HR>`). It might tell the browser to retrieve a graphics file from the server and insert it at this location (`<IMG SRC="image.location">`).

That last example is significant. The browser interprets the code to mean that it should retrieve another file. This example specifies a graphics file. But similar codes can specify any kind of file. Among the kinds of files that a browser might retrieve are programs that the browser might execute on the spot. Or, when the file arrives, it might be accompanied by a MIME specification that tells the browser which helper application it should start up that can execute the program properly or otherwise handle the data file correctly. Thus, your browser might start up a program that can play an audio or video file. If your browser can execute Java or ActiveX or programs, you might see an animated graphic right in a Web page displayed on your screen, or a spreadsheet might pop up so that you can calculate, say, a mortgage payment. The possibilities are endless.

Understanding Intranets

The Internet is a public network, available to anyone who wants to connect to it, virtually anywhere in the world. An intranet is a private network that uses Internet protocols.

Many companies have realized how the Internet and the World Wide Web can enhance communication and collaboration in teams of people scattered all over the world. These companies would like to take advantage of the Internet but are afraid of opening their internal computer networks to the lawlessness of the Internet. A popular compromise has been to borrow the technology of the Internet—IP, HTTP, HTML, FTP, and other protocols—and use them internally but without any connection to the Internet per se. The result is an intranet. Notes and its Internet extensions work just as well on the Internet or a corporate intranet.

Understanding Extranets

The latest buzzword is "extranet," which is sort of an intranet site for more than one organization. The automobile companies in Detroit, for example, have set up an extranet called ANX (Automotive Exchange Network), which links the Big Three with the various automotive suppliers. (For more information on ANX, check out `http://www.aiag.org`.)

Domino works well in all three type of Web environments—intranet, Internet, and extranet. The content might differ, but the context is the same.

Lotus' Internet Thrust Toward Total Integration

Like everyone else in the computer industry, Lotus is scrambling to establish its presence and identity on the Internet. For Lotus, the rise of Internet hysteria is an especially great opportunity. In case you haven't noticed, the core purposes of the Internet and Notes are nearly the same. Both the Internet and Notes were originally developed to promote communication and collaboration among groups of people who need to work together but who are rarely (if ever) in the same room at the same time.

Lotus' strategy is to offer Notes/Domino as an Internet applications server—that is, a Web server that incorporates Notes functionality. Lotus' two main thrusts in accomplishing this goal have been to integrate core Internet protocols right into Notes and to develop a series of add-on products that enhance the value of Domino as an Internet applications server. Significant Internet-related enhancements to Notes and add-on Notes products include the following:

▪ Built-in Internet protocols: For years, Notes servers and clients have been able to communicate with others using the TCP/IP protocol suite. Beginning with Release 4.0, Lotus began incorporating extended Internet protocols, including HTML/HTTP, into Notes. Release 4.6 includes HTML/HTTP, FTP, Gopher, MIME, and Finger protocols in the Notes client and HTML/HTTP, SMTP/MIME, NNTP, IMAP4, LDAP, and POP3 in the Domino server.

With release 4.6, the Notes client and server both offer native support for Java as well.

▪ Combined Notes/Web server: Domino Server is both a Web and a Notes server. It stores data both in Notes databases and, optionally, as HTML documents in an HTML data directory. It serves up Notes documents to Notes clients and Web clients, HTML documents, or Notes documents converted to HTML format.

▪ Internet Mail Server: Because the Domino Server complies with the SMTP, MIME, and POP3 protocols, it can serve as a post office for SMTP/MIME mail clients and as an SMTP message transfer agent. Domino Server can also act as a post office for MAPI mail clients. The 4.6 server adds support for IMAP4 and LDAP as well.

▪ Domino Go Web server: The Go server is a standard Web server from Lotus that offers straight HTTP (that is, it doesn't double as a Notes server). The Pro version of the Go Web server comes bundled with Net.Objects and Net.Data.

▪ Server clustering: This is part of Domino Advanced Services, which is an extra-cost add-on to the Domino Server. Server clustering lets configuring multiple Domino servers replicate with each other in real time and appear to the user as a single server. It provides fault tolerance, load balancing, and fail-over.

▪ Server partitioning: This is also part of Domino Advanced Services. You can create multiple server partitions on one computer, which causes the computer to appear to users as multiple Domino servers. This is useful if you want to host multiple Web sites or Domino applications on one computer.

▪ Usage tracking and billing: This is also part of Domino Advanced Services. You can track and compile system usage and use the information to bill users or monitor trends.

▪ Web Navigator: This is a Web browser built right into Notes. If a Notes user has access to the Internet (or an intranet), he or she can use Notes to browse Web sites, Gopher sites, and FTP servers. Retrieved pages are stored in the Web Navigator database.

▶ **See** "Using the Web Navigators," **p. 1003**, for details about this product.

▪ Lotus Weblicator: This brings Notes functionality—including the Notes object store, replication, and agents—to non-Notes Web browsers. In effect, it turns third-party Web browsers, such as Netscape Navigator and Microsoft Internet Explorer, into "Notes Lite." With Weblicator running alongside them, they can retrieve Web pages into a Notes database on the browser computer. You can then use the browser like a Notes client to view the downloaded Web pages off-line. Since they are stored in a Notes database, you can index and search them, you can sort and categorize them in various ways, and you can edit them or fill in CGI forms off-line. Then you can reconnect to Domino servers and replicate back to them any pages you edited. Or you can reconnect to a third-party

Web server any CGI forms you filled in off-line. Weblicator also includes agents that will automate the retrieval of Web pages.

- Web Publisher: This is Lotus' first Notes-to-Web product. With it, you can publish selected Notes databases to a third-party Web server and, under some circumstances, retrieve information from Web users back into a Notes database. See "Working with Web Publisher" on the CD-ROM for details about this product. Regrettably, development of Web Publisher has ceased. The product no longer ships on the CD with the commercial Domino server product, and it's no longer available from the Lotus Web site.

- Notes News: This is a gateway between Notes/Domino servers and UseNet newsgroups. Since news servers are simply a form of bulletin board or discussion forum, they are analogous to Notes discussion databases. Notes News converts selected newsgroups to Notes discussion databases. The articles posted in the newsgroups become Notes documents in the Notes discussion databases. Notes users can then follow newsgroup discussions without ever having to access the news servers directly. If a Notes user contributes to the discussion, Notes News converts the user's contribution to a News article and submits it to the news server. With Domino 4.6, the NNTP protocol has been rolled into the native server rather than being a separate add-on product.

- Notes Network Information Center (NotesNIC): This is a service provided on the Internet by Lotus (actually by its subsidiary Iris Development Corporation, the developer of Notes) to all Notes-using organizations. It is a Notes domain that resides on the Internet. You can set up a Notes server of your own in the NotesNIC domain. Because you are your own server, you control what databases reside on it and all access control lists.

  Being in the NotesNIC domain, the server's Public Address Book includes the servers of all other organizations that have joined the NotesNIC domain—in other words, hundreds of other Notes organizations. You can set up easy mail delivery and database replication between your organizations by going through your respective NotesNIC servers.

- NetApps: To make it as easy as possible for a Notes organization to quickly set up a powerful, Domino-based Web site, Lotus has developed NetApps. These are templates from which you can generate a whole, interactive Web application by filling in a series of forms. You don't have to develop the applications or create the databases yourself. Just fill in the forms, and NetApps does all the programming for you. The purpose of filling in the forms is so you can customize the resulting applications to your own needs, using your own names and vocabulary.

  The templates available with NetApps include the following:

  Notes:Newsstand, available since January 1996, lets you design and publish electronic newsletters, newspapers, and magazines as pages on your Web site. Notes provides the page design and populates the pages with the content you specify.

  Domino.Action is bundled with Domino Server. Use it to bring up a full-service Web site, including home page, corporate information pages, user registration database, discussion/feedback database, and more.

Domino.Merchant is a series of Notes templates that generate a Notes/Web marketing application. It includes a catalog builder, a payment mechanism, SSL security, and a shopping cart metaphor.

Domino.Broadcast for PointCast uses Domino Server and PointCast I-Server software to let you set up a news feed by which you can pipe company news via PointCast to any PointCast subscriber.

Domino.Doc is a separate product that turns a Domino server into a valid document server for either Notes or Web clients.

Domino.Connect integrates Domino databases with a broad range of relational databases.

In essence, what Lotus is trying to accomplish is to make Notes and Domino Server indispensable to anyone who wants to accomplish anything on the Web more elaborate than simple publishing. By marrying Notes technology to Web technology, Lotus gives you the tools to create powerful, interactive Internet applications with ease. Then Lotus makes it even easier by offering application generators that do all the work for you. All you have to do is set up Notes and Domino on a server, connect the server to the Internet, and fill in a series of questionnaires. The application generator then creates all the Notes databases for you. ●

Using the Web Navigators

With the huge rise in popularity of the Internet over the past few years, Lotus realized that it had to incorporate Internet connectivity into Notes. With the release of Notes 4.0 in January 1996, Lotus incorporated a World Wide Web browser called Web Navigator into Notes. It worked through the Notes server, which ran a server task called the Web Retriever that actually went to the Internet to retrieve Web pages. You had to be connected to a Notes server to browse the Web.

In Notes 4.5, Lotus enhanced the Web Navigator so that you could browse through the Notes server as before, or directly from your workstation. You no longer needed to be attached to a Notes server to browse the Web. Realizing that the Notes Web Navigator couldn't keep pace with the rapid evolution of HTML, and reluctant to join Netscape and Microsoft in the browser wars, Lotus allowed you to choose Netscape Navigator or Microsoft's Internet Explorer as an alternative to its own Web Navigator. The major advantage of using Notes' own Web Navigator was that pages pulled from the Internet were stored in a Notes database for offline browsing. Unfortunately, electing to use Navigator or Internet Explorer meant that you had to sacrifice this convenience, because the pages couldn't be stored in the Web Navigator database, thereby negating the main advantage of using Notes to browse the Web. (Lotus's Weblicator product now provides some of the functionality of the Personal Web Navigator to users of Web browsers who don't have access to Notes.)

In Release 4.6, Lotus has gone some of the way toward rectifying this problem by allowing you to integrate Microsoft's Internet Explorer into Notes itself. This capability allows you to view pages pulled from the Internet with the high fidelity of Internet Explorer while also allowing you to access the pages from the Web Navigator database offline, where you can apply the Notes feature set to manage, search, and manipulate the data. ■

Understanding the Web Navigators

Two Web navigators are built into Notes: the server version and the personal version. In the server version, the browser and the database (referred to here as Server Web Navigator) both reside on a Notes server. If you want, however, you can put a replica copy of the database on your workstation. In the personal version, the browser and the database (referred to here as Personal Web Navigator) both reside on the Notes client.

Users can browse the World Wide Web, or the corporate intranet, by either entering a URL into a dialog box or clicking a URL in a Notes document. Whether the server or client does the actual browsing—and whether browsing occurs at all—depends on a setting in the user's current Location document. This allows you to use the server version sometimes, the personal version other times, and, at times, no browser at all.

For example, Jane, an ace account rep, works all morning at her New York City office, preparing for tomorrow's meeting with her client in San Francisco. She flies there during the afternoon and spends the night in a hotel. While in the office, her Office Location document specifies that she use the Server Web Navigator. On the plane, she has no Internet connection, so she can't browse—at least not online. However, if she has a Personal Web Navigator database or a replica copy of the Server Web Navigator database on her laptop, she can browse within the database. Her Island Location document specifies No Retrievals in the Retrieve/open pages field, so if she clicks the URL of a document not in the database, Notes displays an error message. In the hotel, she switches to a Travel Location document, which specifies From Notes Workstation in the Retrieve/open pages field. She dials out to the Internet with her modem and, when she opens a URL, Notes automatically uses the Personal Web Navigator to browse.

Working with the Web Navigators

When you enter a URL in Notes or click one in a Notes or a Web document in Notes, exactly what happens depends on what choices you have made in your current Location document. (These settings are covered in more detail in the section "Setting Up a Location Document for Personal Web Navigator" later in this chapter.)

Figure 25.1 shows your choices for retrieving Web pages if you have chosen Notes as your Internet browser. Your choices are to retrieve/open Web pages directly from the Internet to your workstation (if you have a TCP/IP connection to the Internet); retrieve/open Web pages via a Notes server, called an InterNotes server, that will retrieve the pages on your behalf and pass them on to you; or not to have any retrievals at all.

FIG. 25.1
Selecting the InterNotes server as your preferred method of retrieving Web pages.

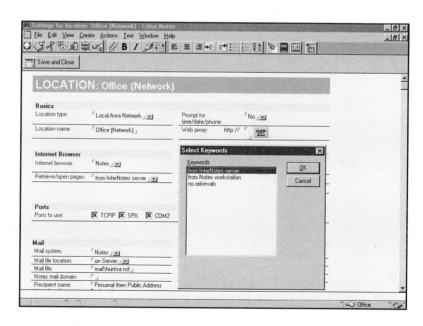

Part
VI

Ch

25

NOTE Don't be confused by the term *InterNotes server*. In this situation, it means a Notes server (that you specify in the InterNotes server field of your Location document) that runs the Web Retriever task. It is a holdover from the days before Domino, when Lotus first built HTML capabilities into Notes. The product was called InterNotes Web Publisher, and it could take Notes databases and create HTML documents from them.

If you choose to use Notes with Internet Explorer as your Internet browser, your choices are restricted to retrieving via the Notes workstation or having no retrievals, as shown in Figure 25.2.

FIG. 25.2

Using Notes with Internet Explorer restricts you to retrieving Web pages from your Notes workstation only.

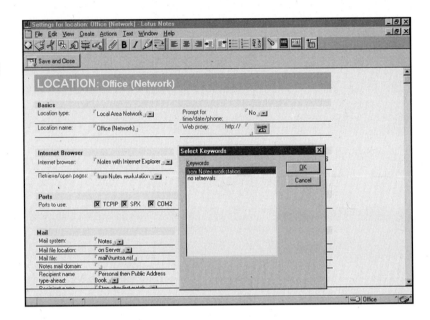

If you choose any other Internet browser (Netscape Navigator, Microsoft Internet Explorer, or Other), Notes merely launches the selected application and passes it a URL.

If you have chosen to browse with the Server Web Navigator, your copy of Notes forwards the URL to your designated Notes server. A server task called Web Retriever forwards the URL to the destination server. If the destination server returns a page, Web Retriever converts it to Notes format. Then the Database Server task stores it in the Server Web Navigator database and forwards a copy to you, and your copy of Notes displays it on your screen (see Figure 25.3).

FIG. 25.3

When you use the Server Web Navigator, your server retrieves pages for you.

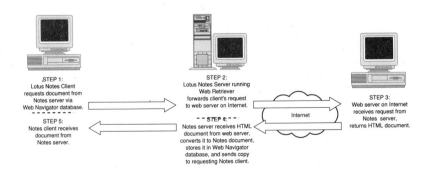

If you have chosen to browse with the Personal Web Navigator, using Notes itself as the Web browser, your own copy of Notes sends the URL to the computer named in it. If the other computer responds by sending a Web page back to you, Notes converts that Web page to Notes format, stores it in the Personal Web Navigator database, and displays it on-screen (see Figure 25.4).

FIG. 25.4

When you use the Personal Web Navigator, your own computer retrieves Web pages directly, without intervention from a Notes server.

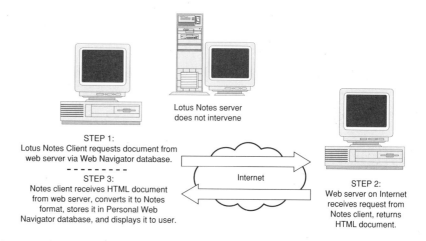

Lotus Notes server does not intervene

STEP 1:
Lotus Notes Client requests document from web server via Web Navigator database.

STEP 3:
Notes client receives HTML document from web server, converts it to Notes format, stores it in Personal Web Navigator database, and displays it to user.

Internet

STEP 2:
Web server on Internet receives request from Notes client, returns HTML document.

Actually, when you enter or click a URL, Notes might not forward the URL to another computer at all. If you ask for a page that either of the Web navigators has retrieved recently, it might simply return to you the copy sitting in its database. This is one of the advantages of using Notes to browse the Web. You can download a whole series of Web pages into your Web Navigator database and read them offline, perhaps while traveling.

Browsing with the Personal Web Navigator using Notes with Internet Explorer as the Internet browser is similar to using the Personal Web Navigator with Notes as the browser. The difference is that when a URL is retrieved, Internet Explorer stores it in its own cache, which is then mirrored in the Personal Web Navigator. If you're working offline, when you open a document from the Personal Web Navigator, the page is actually retrieved from the Internet Explorer cache. In this case, be careful when purging your Internet Explorer cache, or you might find that you receive an error when trying to open a page in your Personal Web Navigator.

Notes works a little differently when you browse the Web than it works when you explore non-Web-related Notes databases. When you open standard Notes documents, each document appears in its own window. However, when you browse with the Web Navigator, your Web pages all appear in the same window. Notes was designed to browse this way because it can't open more than nine subwindows. When you browse the Web, you tend to open so many Web documents so quickly that, if Notes opened a window for each one, you would quickly reach the maximum number of windows and would then have to stop and close a window every time you wanted to jump to a new one.

N O T E The following section explains how to set up Personal Web Navigator. The Server Web Navigator is normally set up by the Notes administrator. If you have to set up Server Web Navigator, you should refer to the documentation and help databases that came with the Notes server. ▨

Setting Up Personal Web Navigator

Before you use Personal Web Navigator, you have to follow these steps to set it up:

1. Meet system requirements for running Notes on your system. See the Notes Workstation Install Guide and the Notes 4.6 Release Notes for information on Notes system requirements.

2. Use a Location document that specifies From Notes Workstation in the Retrieve/open pages field.

3. Open a URL, either by choosing File, Open URL or from a Notes document by clicking an embedded URL, which appears underlined in green. This causes Notes to create the Personal Web Navigator database if it doesn't already exist. This database, which is based on the perweb46.ntf design template, is given the default name of perweb.nsf. It receives and stores all pages retrieved by the Personal Web Navigator.

System Requirements for Personal Web Navigator

The system requirements for Personal Web Navigator, over and above those for the Notes client itself, are the following:

▧ A connection to the Internet or an intranet

▧ TCP/IP running on your workstation

▧ 500M free hard disk space

The last one isn't really a requirement; it's a recommendation by Lotus. Lotus knows that you tend to accumulate Web pages fast when you surf the Web, and your Personal Web Navigator database is likely to get big. There is no specific minimum amount of disk space necessary to run Personal Web Navigator. But remember the axiom that you can never have too much disk space (or RAM or processing power or video resolution or network bandwidth or—well, you get the picture).

If you're connecting to the Internet, there are three possible ways:

▧ A direct connection, via your Local Area Network (LAN) or leased telephone line, to an Internet Service Provider (ISP)

▧ A direct connection, via modem, to an ISP

▧ An indirect connection to an ISP, via a proxy server, to which you will probably connect by LAN

When you're connected to your company's LAN, you probably connect to the Internet across the LAN, either directly to an ISP or indirectly through a proxy server. If you are at home or in a hotel room, you connect directly to an ISP by using your modem.

If you're connecting to your company's intranet, you either connect directly across the LAN or, if you're out of the office, directly by modem or indirectly by proxy server. Because proxy servers protect your LAN from unauthorized access by outsiders, there is no need for you to use a proxy server when you're on the LAN. But going through a proxy server might be the only way to get to your intranet when you're on the outside.

In any event, you must have the TCP/IP protocol stack in your computer's memory in order to use the Personal Web Navigator. The TCP/IP protocol stack is the hallmark of the Internet and intranets. Without it, you aren't on the Internet or intranet.

Setting Up a Location Document for Personal Web Navigator

A variety of settings contained in the Location document affect how you interact with the Web. This section describes them.

▶ **See** "Location Documents," **p. 192**

First you need to edit the Location document that you intend to use with the Personal Web Navigator. Click the Location button in the bottom right of the Notes window, choose the Location you want to change, click the button again, and choose Edit Current. Alternatively, you can access your Personal Address Book, switch to the Advanced/Locations view, and open the desired Location document in edit mode in the normal way.

To browse with Personal Web Navigator, you must be using a Location document that specifies From Notes Workstation in the Retrieve/open pages field, so this is the first change to make. The following fields affect how Notes deals with the Web and the storage of Web pages.

Internet Browser   Choose your Web browser here. You can choose Notes, Notes with Internet Explorer, Netscape Navigator, Microsoft Internet Explorer, or Other.

Retrieve/Open Pages   The choices available to you here depend on your selection in the Internet browser field. You can choose Notes Workstation, from InterNotes server, or no Retrievals.

Web Retriever Configuration Section   To get here, you must expand the Advanced section by clicking the twistie. In this section of the Location document, you control several aspects of the behavior of Personal Web Navigator via the following seven fields:

- Web Navigator database: Holds the filename of the Personal Web Navigator database. If you ever decide to rename or change the location of the database, enter its new path name here.

- Concurrent retrievers: This is the number of retriever processes that can reside in memory concurrently. If you want to browse more intensively than you can with four retrievers, increase this number.

Part
VI

Ch
25

■ Retriever log level: Notes can log retrieval activity to your Notes log. Choose from no logging; Terse, which supplies minimal information; and Verbose, which reports full information to your log.

■ Update cache: The default is Never. The first time the Web Navigator receives a request for a page, it gets it from the designated Web server. It stores the page in the Web Navigator database and displays a copy to you. Thereafter, when you request that page again, the Web Navigator delivers the cached copy of the page instead of retrieving it anew from the Web server. By the default of this field, Web Navigator never checks with the Web server to discover if the page has been updated since it was first retrieved. You can change this to Once per Session or Every Time. If you choose Once per Session, the Web Retriever doesn't check with the Web server if you ask for the same page again in the same browsing session, but it does check with the Web server if you ask for the page again in a future browsing session. If you choose Every Time, then every time you ask for a cached page, before the Web Retriever delivers the cached copy of the page, it queries the originating Web server to see if a new version of the document is on the server.

■ Accept SSL site certificates: The default is No. Change it to Yes to accept Secure Sockets Layer (SSL) certificates from computers with which you do not otherwise share a certificate issued by a third-party Certification Authority (CA). Then, if you do accept a certificate from a computer, you have to take it on faith that the computer you are talking to is really the computer it claims to be, because by accepting a certificate from the computer, you have no way of knowing who issued its public and private keys. However, you still get the other two benefits of SSL security—encryption of data transmissions between the two computers, and assurance that no tampering with any secured message has occurred en route.

■ Accept expired SSL certificates: Just like passports and other trusted forms of identification, SSL certificates have an expiration date. You can choose to accept an expired SSL Certificate.

■ SSL Protocol Version: You can choose only to accept a particular version of SSL for secure transmissions. If the remote system can't utilize that version of SSL, at best you will have an insecure link, and at worst, communication with the remote system might be impossible.

Java Applet Security Section   Use the fields in this section to reduce the risk of a Java applet's compromising the security of the data on your computer or on your LAN as a whole. A Java applet that you receive as part of a Web document is a program and thus can potentially damage your software and data. For example, such a program could make network connections to other hosts and give them access to your system and data. Notes lets you list trusted hosts—computers from which you are reasonably sure you will never receive damaging Java applets—and specify the degree of the Java applets' access to your computer's resources from either trusted or untrusted hosts.

The following fields are found in this section:

- Trusted Hosts: This is where you enter the `host.domain` names (for example, `www.lotus.com`) or IP addresses (for example, `123.123.123.123`) of Web sites that you are reasonably sure will not send you damaging Java applets.

- Network Access for Trusted Hosts: You can select one of the following options for this field:

  Disable Java: Notes doesn't run Java applets.

  No Access Allowed: Notes doesn't permit a Java applet to expose your computer's resources to any other computer.

  Allow Access Only to Originating Host: Notes permits the Java applet to expose your computer's resources only to the computer from which it obtained the Java applet.

  Allow Access to Any Trusted Host: Notes permits the Java applet to expose your computer's resources to any computer in your list of trusted hosts. This setting is the default.

  Allow Access to Any Host: Notes permits the Java applet to expose your computer's resources to any other computer.

- Network Access for Untrusted Hosts: For this field, you can select one of the first three options listed for the Network Access for Trusted Hosts field.

- Trust HTTP proxy: This field is relevant only if you access the Internet through an HTTP proxy server. The default is No, meaning that your computer makes its own determination of whether the host from which a Java applet is received is a trusted host. If you can't run a Java applet, this might be because your computer can't resolve the Web server's host name to its IP address. Changing this field to Yes tells your computer to assume that the HTTP proxy server successfully resolved the host name with the IP address and to go ahead and run the applet according to the Trusted host/Untrusted host settings of the other fields in this section.

You can enable or disable Java applets totally on your workstation by choosing File, Tools, User Preferences and then checking the Enable Java applets option under the Advanced options.

Creating the Personal Web Navigator Database

The last step of setting up the Personal Web Navigator is to create the Personal Web Navigator database. You don't have to do this yourself. All you have to do is retrieve a Web document. You can do this any of several ways: Choose File, Open URL and enter a URL; click the Open URL SmartIcon and enter a URL; or click a URL embedded in any Notes document. An embedded URL looks like a regular URL (for example, **http://www.lotus.com**) and is underlined in green.

TIP If URLs in your Notes documents aren't underlined in green, and Notes doesn't try to retrieve the document when you click the URL, this is probably because you haven't enabled automatic conversion of URLs to Notes hotspots. To enable automatic conversion, follow these steps:

1. Choose File, Tools, User Preferences. The User Preferences dialog box appears.

2. In the Advanced Options field, put a checkmark next to the list beside Make Internet URLs (http://...) into Hotspots.

3. Click OK to accept the change.

When you retrieve that first Web document, Personal Web Navigator creates the Personal Web Navigator database in the Notes data directory on your computer and then tries to retrieve the Web page. If the navigator retrieves the page successfully, it puts the page into the new database.

Setting Internet Options in the Personal Web Navigator Database

Inside the Personal Web Navigator database is an Internet Options document that allows you to configure a variety of options (see Figure 25.5). To access it, choose Actions, Internet Options.

The Internet Options document consists of eight sections, which are covered here.

Startup Options   Here you can specify what happens when you open the Personal Web Navigator database. By default, it opens to a standard Notes three-pane interface in which you see a list of views in the upper-left corner, the documents in the currently selected view in the lower-left corner, and the currently selected document previewed on the right. You can open to a home page if you prefer. To do so, edit the following two fields:

- Put a checkmark in the box labeled Open home page on database open.

- Optionally, enter the URL of the home page to which you want to open in the Home Page field. This defaults to **www.notes.net**, which is a public site run by Iris Associates—developers of Notes.

Search Options   A preferred method of locating information on the Web is to use a search engine to search indexes of documents. The Preferred Search Engine field lets you choose a default search engine from several popular ones. If your own preferred search engine isn't listed, choose Other, and a box will appear where you can type in the URL of the search engine.

Web Ahead Agent Preferences   In the Preload Web pages field, you can choose to retrieve pages one, two, three, or four levels ahead of the current page. If you haven't enabled Web Ahead, the Enable Web Ahead button also appears in this section. If this button doesn't appear, Web Ahead has been enabled. For more information on the Web Ahead feature, see the section "Retrieving Multiple Pages Using Personal Web Navigator's Web Ahead Agent."

Page Minder Agent Preferences   Page Minder is an agent that watches for updates to chosen Web pages and notifies you when it finds them. It runs only when your Notes workstation is running, and it can function only when you are connected to the Internet, but it can keep you up-to-date on important events.

FIG. 25.5

The Internet Options document allows you to control various aspects of the Personal Web Navigator.

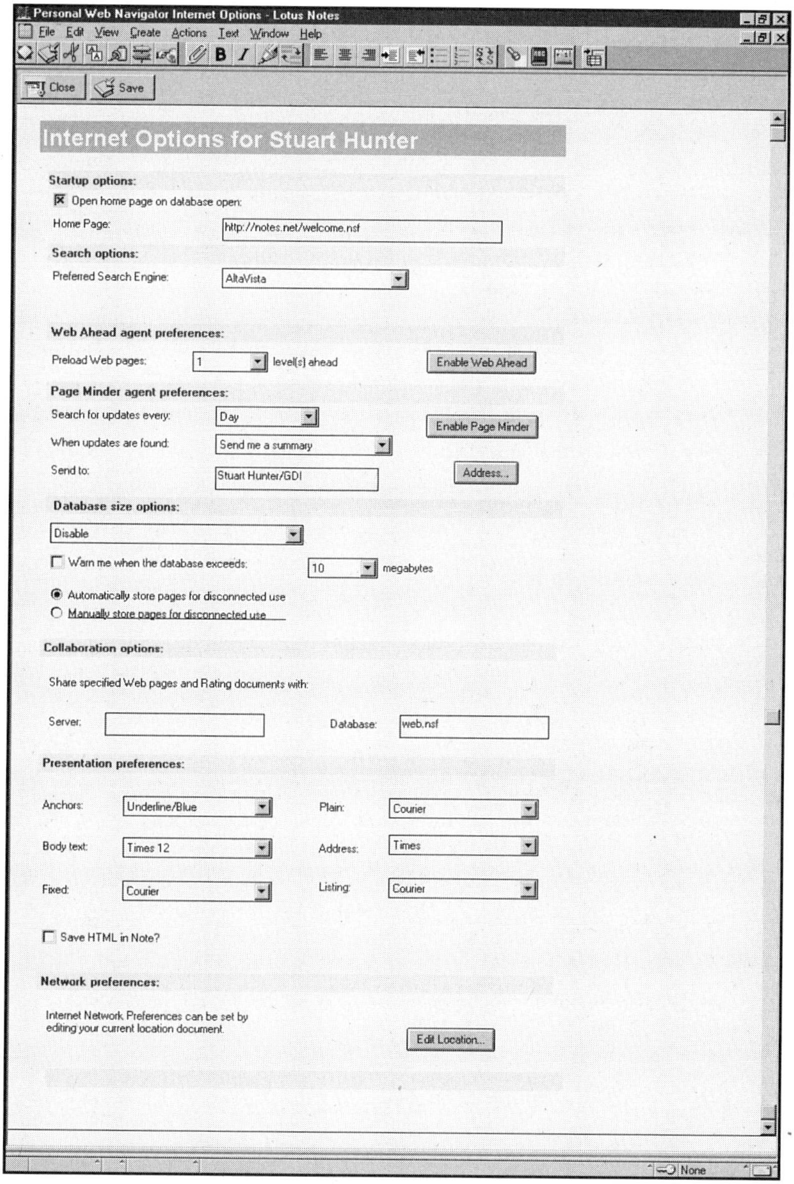

Here are the fields in Page Minder agent preferences:

- Search for updates every: You can choose to search every hour, every four hours, every day, or every week. The default is every day.

- When updates are found: By default, the agent mails you a summary notifying you that the page has changed. You can change this to Send me the actual page to receive the updated page in your mail.

■ Send to: This automatically lists you as the addressee for change notices. You can add or substitute other addressees if you want.

Database Size Options   With all these agents gathering pages from all over the Net in addition to the Web pages you retrieve yourself, you can imagine how quickly your Personal Web Navigator database will eat up disk space. To keep this under control, you can set up automatic purging of old pages in the database. By default, this option is disabled. But you can change it to Reduce full pages to links if not read within or Remove pages from database if not read within and then set a time limit. The time limit default is 30 days. You can change this to 60 or 90 days. Reduce full pages to links means that the pages are purged from the database but their URLs are retained. You will still see the purged pages in the Personal Web Navigator database and, if you click one, Personal Web Navigator retrieves it anew for you. Note that if you're using Notes with Internet Explorer as your Internet browser, your Personal Web Navigator database might not hold all the retrieved files. Your Personal Web Navigator might contain references that are used to identify the retrieved files in the Internet Explorer cache.

You can also have Notes warn you when the Personal Web Navigator database exceeds 5, 10, 25, or 50M in size.

Collaboration Options   One of the drawbacks of using the Personal Web Navigator instead of the Server Web Navigator is that you don't get the benefit of other people's browsing experience. The Server Web Navigator database holds not only your pages but also those of other people browsing through the Server Web Navigator. When other people think a page is particularly useful, beneficial, just plain cool, or, for that matter, really bad, they can rate the page. Server Web Navigator averages the ratings that different people give to a page. Over time, you can really benefit from other people's experiences and opinions.

Although you can't benefit in this way from others' experiences when you use Personal Web Navigator, you can give them the benefit of your experiences by sharing Web pages you have found, as well as your ratings of them. To do so, enter the name of a Notes server in the Server field and a Server Web Navigator database in the Database field.

Then, when you encounter a page that you especially want to bring to others' attention, click the Share button on the Action Bar. A dialog box appears from which you can choose two options (see Figure 25.6):

■ Copy page to shared Web Navigator database: This copies the page to the database specified in the Internet Options document.

■ Create Rating in shared Web Navigator database: When you select this, a rating form appears. Rate the document from 1 to 5, choose a category, write your comments, and click OK. Notes forwards the page to the Server Web Navigator database and creates a Rating document there as well.

FIG. 25.6

Rating and categorizing a Web page to share with colleagues.

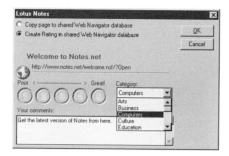

Presentation Preferences   Web documents are made up of plain text and embedded codes. The codes are part of the Internet protocol known as HyperText Markup Language (HTML), and they define the document's formatting. Web browsers interpret the codes and replace them with formatting so that you see a formatted document, not a bunch of inscrutable codes. You can affect how Web Navigator interprets the codes by altering the contents of the following fields:

- Anchors: These are the URL links that appear on HTML pages. They appear, by default, underlined and in blue.
- Body text: Choose a font to display body text within HTML pages.
- Fixed: Choose a font to display text used within code pairs that begin with <CODE>, <KBD>, <SAMPLE>, and <TT>.
- Plain: Choose a font to display text used within code pairs that begin with <PLAINTEXT>, <PRE>, and <EXAMPLE>.
- Address: Choose a font to display text used within the <ADDRESS> code pair.
- Listing: Choose a font to display text used within the <LISTING> code pair.
- Save HTML in Note?: Notes converts HTML documents to Notes format and then saves them in this database. By default, Notes discards the HTML source code. Checking the box in this field causes the server to save the HTML source code in a field called HTMLSource.

Network Preferences   This last section of the Internet Options document includes a button that, when you click it, loads the current Location document so that you can edit it and change your network preferences.

Using Personal Web Navigator

Personal Web Navigator, shown in Figure 25.7, opens to the standard Notes split screen—except that, in this case, the preview pane is open by default and takes up most of the screen, so you see a three-pane screen. Personal Web Navigator has tools to let the Notes user gather information on the Web and keep up with changes in it. It lacks the restrictive features included in the Server Web Navigator, which makes sense.

Part
VI

Ch
25

FIG. 25.7

Unlike Server Web Navigator, Personal Web Navigator opens to the standard Notes three-pane window.

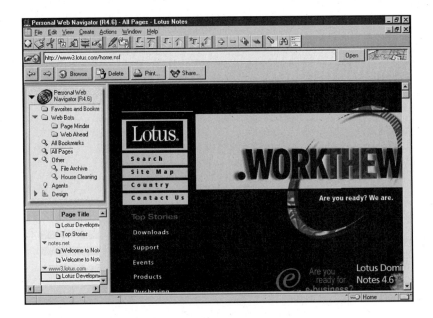

The default list of views and folders includes the following:

■ **Favorites and Bookmarks:** Use this folder to save your favorite Web pages for quick access later. To add a page to this folder, drag and drop the page from the view onto this folder. When you're on the Web, add pages to the Bookmarks folder by clicking the Add Bookmark action button, selecting Favorites and Bookmarks as the folder (although you can choose any folder you want), and choosing Add.

■ · **Web Bots/Page Minder:** When you put a page in this folder, the Page Minder agent (if it is enabled) periodically checks its original site for updates. If it has been updated since you downloaded it, the agent notifies you. See the sections "Page Minder Agent Preferences" and "Using the Page Minder Agent" for more details. When you access this folder, you will see a document called "Using the Page Minder Feature," which provides useful information about setting up and using the agent.

■ **Web Bots/Web Ahead:** When you put a page in this folder, the Web Ahead agent (if it is enabled) retrieves in the background all the pages that it points to. Depending on how you have configured the agent, it might also retrieve all the pages pointed to by those pages, all the pages pointed to by those pages, and all the pages pointed to by those pages—that is, up to four levels of pages. This is a really good way to fill up a hard disk fast. See the section "Web Ahead Agent Preferences" for more details. When you access this folder, you will see a document called "Using the Web Ahead Feature," which provides useful information about setting up and using the agent.

■ **All Bookmarks:** Displays all Web pages that have been bookmarked.

■ **All Pages:** Displays all Web pages stored in the Personal Web Navigator.

- Other/File Archive: Displays all file attachments and their sizes.
- Other/House Cleaning: Displays Web pages sorted by size so that you know which ones to reduce to their URLs.

The Personal Web Navigator Action Bar

The Personal Web Navigator has both View and Form Action Bars. Figure 25.8 shows the Action Bar of the Personal Web Navigator when you're viewing a Web page full-screen. Note that the Share button will appear only if you have set up a valid server and filename in the Collaboration options section of the Internet Options document. If you're using Notes with Internet Explorer as your Internet browser, you might see slightly different buttons. These are described later.

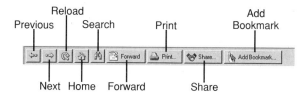

FIG. 25.8
When you view a Web page in the Personal Web Navigator, the Action Bar emulates those in Web browsers.

Part

VI

Ch

25

In the three-pane view, the view Action Bar uses a slightly different button set than the form Action Bar, as shown in Figure 25.9.

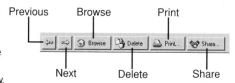

FIG. 25.9
The Action Bar in the three-pane view has different functionality.

The buttons that appear in these two Action Bars are described in Table 25.1.

Table 25.1 Action Buttons

Button	Description
Previous	Goes to the previous page in the History list.
Next	Goes to the next page in the History list.
Reload	Reloads the current Web page from the Internet server.
Home	Goes to the page you defined in the Internet Options document as your Home Web page.

continues

Table 25.1   Continued

Button	Description
Search	Searches for pages on the Web by using the Internet search engine you specified in the Internet Options document.
Forward	Forwards the Web page to someone via email.
Print	Prints the current Web page.
Share	Shares the Web page according to the specifications you made in the Internet Options document. This opens a dialog box in which you can choose to forward the page to someone, copy it to the Server Web Navigator database, or rate it and copy it and your rating to the Server Web Navigator database.
Add Bookmark	Displays the Move to Folder dialog box, where you can choose a folder for the page or create a new folder for it.
Browse	Appears in view only. Goes to the page you defined in the Internet Options document as your Home Web page.
Delete	Appears in view only. Deletes the selected Web page(s) and associated objects. Using the Delete key to delete Web pages doesn't delete the files associated with that page, which will continue to use disk space.

N O T E   If you choose to use Notes with Internet Explorer as your Web browser, the Action Bar that appears when you are viewing a Web page is slightly different. Two extra buttons might appear: A red Stop button will stop the retrieval of the current Web page, and a Keep Page button will appear if you have chosen to store Web pages manually in the Internet Options document. ■

Searching the World Wide Web with the Personal Web Navigator

Up until now, you have worked your way around the Web by typing a URL to go to a specific site. But what if you don't know the URL of a site you want to visit? Or what if you don't know what site would have information of the type you need? For example, suppose you want to search for information about Elvis. You could try typing **www.elvis.com**. Is this a real Web site? Well, type it and find out. Of course, even if you get lucky and correctly guess the name of a site, how do you know what other sites might also have valuable information about Elvis?

A more efficient way to locate information on the Web when you don't know where to look is to use an Internet search engine. You can type in a search term, such as Elvis, and the search engine searches one or more Web indexes for entries that contain the word Elvis. Then it returns a list of links to the sites it found. Most search engines list the sites with the most hits at the top of the list.

Searching for `Elvis` might return an awful lot of hits—perhaps thousands, certainly hundreds, and probably more than you need. So, to narrow your search and find a better match, you can supply additional information to the search engine. For example, Elvis *and* Sands *and* Las Vegas *and* October 1966 is bound to return fewer hits.

Different search engines maintain different lists of Web pages. After working with a few, you'll find one you like best. Or, if you need to do a really exhaustive search, you might run the same search with different search engines. When you select a search engine to use, Web Navigator takes you to the home page of that search engine, where you can type your search criteria. Although you can use any search engine, Notes makes it easy for you to choose CNet, Yahoo!, Lycos, AltaVista, or Excite.

To set a preferred search engine, follow these steps:

1. From the workspace, select the Personal Web Navigator and choose <u>A</u>ctions, <u>I</u>nternet Options.

2. In the Search options section, select the search engine you prefer in the Preferred Search Engine field. If you select CNet, AltaVista, Excite, Lycos, or Yahoo!, save and close this document. If you choose Other, a new field appears, and you must provide a URL, as shown in Figure 25.10. Then save and close this document.

Part

VI

Ch

25

FIG. 25.10

Choose a preferred search engine in the Search Options section of the Internet Options document.

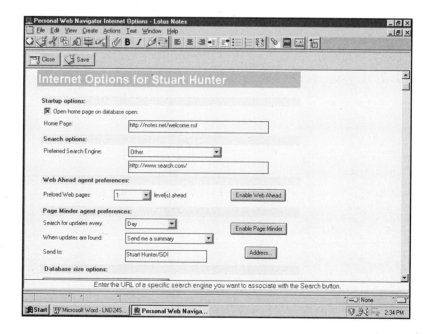

To use the search engine you just selected, follow these steps:

1. Open the Personal Web Navigator to a Web page so that you can see the Action Bar that appears for forms.

2. Click the Search icon on the Action Bar.

3. The Web Navigator retrieves the search engine's Web page. Enter your search criteria.

Some Web pages are themselves indexes of a particular site. If Web Navigator recognizes this, the Search button will display a dialog box to let you search the index rather than opening a page to your selected search engine. Visit **http://www.sec.gov/cgi-bin/srch-edgar** to see an example of an indexed Web page.

After you enter your search criteria, the Web site returns all the documents contained within that match your search criteria, as shown in Figure 25.11.

FIG. 25.11
Results of a search for
`radiator` at Edgar.

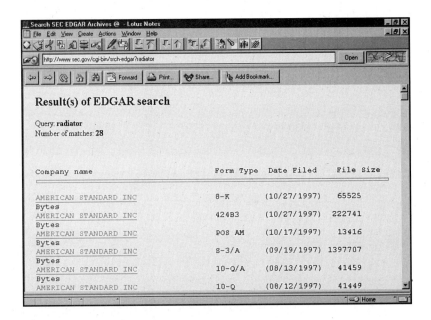

Saving Bookmarks in the Personal Web Navigator

Although you might browse through hundreds or thousands of pages, you will want to return to certain pages repeatedly. You can store these pages in the Favorites and Bookmarks folder. To add an open Web page to this folder, click the Add Bookmark button on the Action Bar. The Move to Folder dialog box appears. Select the Favorites and Bookmarks folder, and click Add.

To add a page to the Favorites and Bookmarks folder from the view pane of the database, drag and drop the page into the Favorites and Bookmarks folder icon.

After you save a page in the Bookmark folder, you might want to save space in your database by reducing the page to a URL. If you choose this option, the only thing that is saved is the URL—not the page itself. When you open a reduced page, the address appears in the Open URL box, and no part of the page is visible. You can see the page by reloading it from the Internet server. To reduce a page to a URL, follow these steps:

1. Open the page from the view pane of the database.
2. Select <u>A</u>ctions, <u>R</u>educe to Bookmark.
3. To view this page again, open the page from the view and select <u>A</u>ctions, <u>R</u>eload.

Recommending or Sharing a Document in the Personal Web Navigator

In the Personal Web Navigator, you can either share or recommend a Web page that interests you.

To recommend a Web page by using the Personal Web Navigator, you first need to supply the name of your Notes server in the Internet Options document, as explained in the section "Setting Internet Options in the Personal Web Navigator Database." Then you can copy the page to the shared Web Navigator database or create a rating for it in the shared Web Navigator Database. Notes automates both of these procedures:

1. Open the Personal Web Navigator.
2. Click a document in the Navigator pane, or open a document.
3. Click the Share button on the Action Bar.
4. A dialog box appears, as shown in Figure 25.12. It offers you two options:
   - Copy page to shared Web Navigator database: This copies the page to the All Documents view of the Server Web Navigator. You must be connected to the Notes server in order to choose this option.
   - Create Rating in shared Web Navigator database: This prompts you to create a rating as you would in the Server Web Navigator database and sends the page with its rating to the Recommended views of the Server Web Navigator.

FIG. 25.12

Sharing a Web page from the Personal Web Navigator.

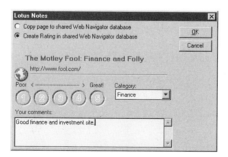

5. Click <u>O</u>K to send the document or the rating and close the dialog box.

Retrieving Multiple, Simultaneous Web Pages

The Personal Web Navigator lets you retrieve up to six pages simultaneously. To allow multiple Web retrievals, follow these steps:

1. Edit your Location document by clicking the location on the status bar and selecting Edit Current.

2. In the Concurrent Retrievers field, select the number of pages you want to be able to retrieve simultaneously. You can choose from two to six.

3. Save your changes and close the document.

After you have edited your Location document, you can retrieve several Web pages at a time. For each Web page you want to open, choose File, Open URL, complete the fields in the Open URL dialog box, and click OK. Or enter successive URLs into the Open URL Search Bar. Personal Web Navigator opens a new window for each Open URL command and retrieves the requested pages into the separate windows simultaneously. To see the pages, use the Window menu to move from page to page, or choose Window, Cascade or Window, Tile to see all your Web pages.

Retrieving Multiple Pages by Using Personal Web Navigator's Web Ahead Agent

Web Ahead is a Notes agent that automatically retrieves into the Personal Web Navigator database all the pages pointed to by URLs on a given page. You can configure Web Ahead to retrieve up to four levels of pages. In other words, you can pull in just the pages pointed to by URLs on the current page, or all those plus all the pages pointed to by the second level of pages, or the third level, or the fourth level.

> **CAUTION**
> You'd better have lots of free disk space if you plan to choose level four.

The idea here is that, instead of manually (and tediously) retrieving all the pages and having to wait around while they arrive, you can start the agent running (or have it run on schedule), go off and do something else, and then come back and browse at your pace (not the Web's) through the copies of the pages waiting in your database.

To use the Web Ahead agent, you must first enable it. To do so, follow these steps:

1. Choose File, Tools, User Preferences to open the User Preferences dialog box.

2. In User Preferences, place a checkmark in the box labeled Enable Scheduled Local Agents. Then click OK to close User Preferences.

3. Open the Internet Options document in the Personal Web Navigator database. Click the Enable Web Ahead button. If asked what server to run it on, choose Local. Click OK. If the Enable Web Ahead button doesn't appear in the Internet Options document, this is because Web Ahead has already been enabled. You can verify this by checking the Agents view of the Web Navigator database. A checkmark should appear in the checkbox next to the Web Ahead listing.

4. Set the number of levels ahead that you want Web Ahead to retrieve.

5. To use the Web Ahead agent, just drag a page into the Web Bots/Web Ahead folder. The agent does the rest automatically. You do, of course, have to have an active connection to the Internet in order for Web Ahead to be able to do its job.

Viewing the Most Current Version of a Web Page

Web pages are updated constantly. When you visit a Web site, you want current information, not last week's news. So there is a chance that a Web page stored in your database could be out-of-date a day later. On the other hand, opening a Web page from the Notes database is a lot faster than opening a Web page on the Web! So, how can you balance between opening pages from the Web and opening pages from the database?

There are three ways you can make sure you are looking at a relatively recent version of a Web page:

- First, you can manually refresh any page when you're looking at it by clicking the Reload button (the circular arrow) on the Action Bar. This causes the Web Retriever running on your workstation to get a new copy of the page from the original source on the Web. It displays the new copy and overwrites the old copy in the Personal Web Navigator database with the new copy.

- Second, you can set the Web Retriever cache options so that, under certain circumstances, the Web Retriever will retrieve a fresh copy of a page when you open it, even though a copy of the page already resides in the Personal Web Navigator database. The drawback of this method is it updates all pages indiscriminately, even pages that are strictly archival and unchanging by nature.

- Third, and best of all, you can activate the Page Minder agent, which will refresh pages that you designate on a scheduled basis. The really nice thing about this method is that the Page Minder will tell you when it has updated a page in the Web Navigator database. You don't have to remember to check for updates.

You set Web Retriever cache options for the Personal Web Navigator by changing the settings of the Update Cache field in the Web Retriever Configuration section (click the Advanced twistie) of the Location document in your Personal Address Book.

Here are the choices in the Update Cache field:

- Never: This is the default setting. Select Never if you don't want your Web pages indiscriminately refreshed when you open them. With Never as your choice, you have to click the Reload button on the Action Bar to refresh your Web pages.

- Once per session: Select this option to refresh your Web page when you open it from the database and not again during your current Notes session.

- Every time: Select this option to refresh a Web page every time you open it from the database, even if the last time you opened it was just a minute earlier during the same Notes session.

Using the Page Minder Agent   To use the Page Minder agent in the Personal Web Navigator, do the following:

1. Enable background agents in User Preferences. Choose <u>F</u>ile, <u>T</u>ools, <u>U</u>ser Preferences. On the Basics page, under Startup Options, put a checkmark next to E<u>n</u>able scheduled local agents. Click OK.

2. Enable the Page Minder agent in the Personal Web Navigator database. You can do this in one of two ways:

   - In the Page Minder agent preferences section of the Internet Options document of the Personal Web Navigator database, click the Enable Page Minder button. (If this button doesn't appear, you have already enabled the agent.)

   - In the Agents view of the Personal Web Navigator database, put a checkmark next to the Page Minder agent listing.

3. Set Page Minder options in the Page Minder agent preferences section of the Internet Options document in the Personal Web Navigator database. You can set the frequency of updates to every hour, every four hours, every day, or every week. You can specify whether you want to receive the updated page or just a notice that the page has been updated in the Web Navigator database. And you can designate the addressees of the new page or notice. See the earlier section "Page Minder Agent Preferences" for more information about the Page Minder option fields in the Internet Options document.

4. Choose which Web pages should be updated by Page Minder. This is the easy part. If you want Page Minder to update a given page for you, just find the page in the Web Navigator database and put a copy of it in the Page Minder folder.

Setting Up Server Web Navigator

Although primarily an administrative function, it is useful to understand in general terms how the Server Web Navigator works and how the configuration affects users.

At its simplest, all the administrator has to do to enable the Server Web Navigator is type `load web` at the server console. This starts the Web Retriever task and automatically creates a file called WEB.NSF (if it doesn't already exist), which is the Server Web Navigator that the users will utilize. Provided that there is a connection to the Internet on that server, users with sufficient security rights to that server will be able to browse the Web through the Server Web Navigator.

This works well when the user is physically accessing the Server Web Navigator and using the tools in that database to retrieve Web pages. There are other ways to request Web pages, such as by selecting <u>F</u>ile, Open UR<u>L</u>, or clicking a highlighted URL in a Notes document. In these situations, the user's workstation needs some way of identifying which Notes server to connect to in order to perform the retrieval.

The user can specify the InterNotes server (the server running the Web Retriever task) by entering its name in the InterNotes server field of the Location document that is currently in use.

In the absence of an entry in that field, the administrator can enter the server name in the InterNotes server field of the server document in the Public Address Book that is the user's home server.

When the user requests a Web page, first the current Location document is checked, and if an InterNotes server is specified, the request is made to that server. If there is no entry, the user's home server document in the Public Address Book will be checked to see if an InterNotes server has been specified. If it has, the Web page will be retrieved from that server. If there is no entry in the Location document, and there is no entry in the home server document in the Public Address Book, the user will receive a warning message, and no page will be retrieved.

Your administrator controls access to the Web in two other places. The server document in the Public Address Book for the server running the Web Retriever task contains a section called Web Retriever Administration. Included in this section are the name of the Server Web Navigator database (normally WEB.NSF), what Internet services are available (HTTP, FTP, Gopher), and which sites are allowed to be accessed. Secondly, the Server Web Navigator database itself includes an Administration document in which such things as the maximum size of the database and purge intervals can be controlled.

Naturally, standard Notes security exists as well. If a user hasn't been granted access to the server running the Web Retriever task, he won't be able to use that server to browse the Web.

Using Server Web Navigator

The Server Web Navigator has been around since Notes 4.0 arrived in January 1996. It was designed with the goals of introducing the World Wide Web to groups of people who might not have experienced it, of extracting synergies from the Web surfing experiences of groups of people so that individual members of the group might benefit from the collective experiences of the whole group, and of letting employers limit the amount and kind of surfing employees do on company time. Server Web Navigator has a Navigator front end that invites the novice user to explore the unknown terrain of the Web by clicking hotspots and discovering where they lead. Server Web Navigator also has tools that allow you to share good and bad Web surfing experiences with other people. Finally, because the Notes server actually does Web browsing for you, you can surf only where and when the server is willing.

The first time you open the Server Web Navigator, you will probably see the Home Navigator, shown in Figure 25.13. It consists of a bunch of hotspots that, when you click them, load a Web page, open another Navigator, or open a dialog box.

FIG. 25.13

The flashy front end of the Server Web Navigator. Click one of the icons and see where it takes you.

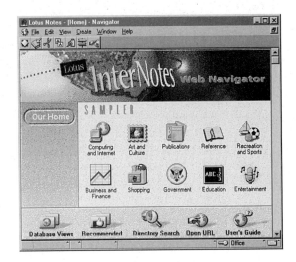

One hotspot, called Our Home, takes you to **www.notes.net**, the public site run by Iris Associates, unless someone has customized the Web Navigator database, in which case it might take you to your own company's home page.

The hotspots in the Sampler section of the Home Navigator all take you to another navigator. The name of the navigator will vary, depending on which hotspot you click. They all look alike, though, showing you hotspots that open three of the more popular Web search engines. Alongside this Navigator, you see a view that displays the documents in the Web Navigator database that fall in the chosen category. Thus, you can browse the database for documents of the chosen type, or you can search the Web for more such documents. Figure 25.14 shows the Entertainment Navigator.

The icons along the bottom of the Home Navigator have the following functions:

- Database Views: Opens the View Navigator, which lists various views of the Web pages already stored in the database.

- Recommended: Opens the Recommended Navigator, where you can see the Rated documents.

- Directory Search: Displays a search form that lets you perform searches with Internet search engines.

- Open URL: Displays a dialog box in which you enter the URL of a Web page in order to open it.

- User's Guide: Opens the online Web Navigator User's Guide database.

When you click Database Views in the Home Navigator, the View Navigator opens. Here, each hotspot opens a particular view of the contents of the Web Navigator database. Table 25.2 describes each button in the View Navigator.

FIG. 25.14

The Entertainment Navigator appears when you click the Entertainment hotspot in the Home Navigator.

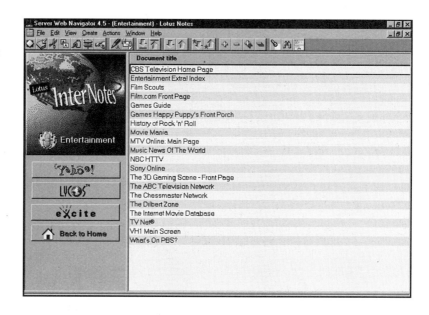

Table 25.2 The View Navigator Buttons

Button	Description
My Bookmarks	Opens pages you saved in your Bookmarks folder. To add a page to the Bookmarks folder, drag and drop the page onto this button. You add pages to the Bookmarks folder from the Web by clicking Bookmarks, selecting My Bookmarks in the Move to Folder dialog box, and clicking Add.
Folders	Opens a standard Folders Navigator.
All Documents	Displays all the Web pages stored in this database.
By Host	Displays all Web pages sorted by their host site.
File Archive	Displays all file attachments and their sizes.
Web Tours	Displays all the saved Web Tours.
Recommended	Opens the Recommended Navigator.
Back to Home	Returns to the Home Navigator.

The Server Web Navigator Action Bar

When you open a document stored in the Server Web Navigator database, an Action Bar appears (see Figure 25.15). It is unlike the Action Bars in other Notes databases (except the Personal Web Navigator database). It emulates the Action Bars that you see in Web browsers such as Mosaic, Netscape Navigator, and Microsoft's Internet Explorer. This Action Bar helps you browse the Web.

FIG. 25.15

The Action Bar of the Server Web Navigator emulates those seen in Web browsers.

The buttons in the Action Bar serve the functions listed in Table 25.3.

Table 25.3   Action Buttons

Button	Description
Home	Goes back to the Home Page Navigator.
Open	Opens the Open URL dialog box.
Previous	Goes to the previous page in the History file.
Next	Goes to the next page in the History file.
History	Opens the History dialog box to save pages to the History or to go to other pages listed in the History.
Reload	Reloads the current Web page from the Internet server.
Recommend	Opens the dialog box to enter your rating of the current Web page.
Forward	Forwards the Web page to someone by email.
Bookmarks	Stores the current Web page in the Bookmarks folder.

The Server Web Navigator Search Bar

The Search Bar is actually a dual-purpose tool. You can use it to enter a URL and retrieve a Web page, or you can search the Web Navigator database for text you enter in the Search Bar. You toggle between the two modes by clicking the icon at the left end of the Search Bar.

In the Web Navigator databases, the Search Bar appears when you're in a view or when a Web document is open; however, when a document is open, you can use the Search Bar only to retrieve Web pages. In other databases, the Search Bar appears only when you are in a view, not when a document is open. The Search Bar appears by default only in databases that have been full-text indexed. If you don't see the Search Bar, select View, Search Bar.

The two versions of the Search Bar are potentially confusing. Make sure the proper icon is showing for the type of search you want to perform. When you want to retrieve a Web page, you might need to click the Search icon to switch to Open URL mode. When you want to search for text within the pages of the database, you might need to click the Open URL icon to switch to search mode (see Figure 25.16).

FIG. 25.16

The Search Bar in full-text search mode. Note which icon appears on the left. Note the button labels on the right and compare them with Figure 25.17.

The buttons on the Open URL Search Bar are described in Table 25.4. The buttons in the Full Text Search Bar are described in Table 25.5.

Table 25.4 The Buttons on the Open URL Search Bar

Button	Description
Open URL	Sets which type of Search Bar you're using.
Text box	Enter the URL you want here.
Open	Opens the specified URL.
Reset	Clears the URL name.
History	If you're connected to the Internet or an intranet when you click this button, Notes displays the History dialog box, from which you can go directly to any page you have visited during the current session. If you aren't connected to the Web, nothing happens when you click this button.

Table 25.5 The Buttons on the Full Text Search Bar

Button	Description
Search	Sets the Search Bar to search for text in the database.
Text	Enter the word or phrase you're looking for.
Index	This button appears only if the database is not indexed. Click it to start the index creation process.
Add Condition	The Create Index button becomes the Add Condition button after you create the index. Use it to display the Search Builder dialog box, where Notes does most of the work of building your search query.
Search	Activates the search.
Reset	Clears the search results from the view pane. The query that produced the search remains in the Search Bar for you to edit.

continues

Part

VI

Ch

25

Table 25.5   Continued

Button	Description
Search Menu	Drops down a menu of search options. The programmers couldn't think of a short description for this button (like, say, "menu"), so, in the spirit of "a word is worth a thousand pictures," they used an inscrutable diagram instead.

Before you search for text, your database must be full-text indexed. If it isn't, the first button in the Search Bar is Create Index. Click it to open the Properties for Database InfoBox and choose the Full Text panel. There you can set options and then begin the index creation process. If you create an index for a Local database, you might have to wait around while Notes creates it. If you haven't enabled local background indexing in User Preferences, you will have to wait. If you have enabled local background indexing, you will still have to wait for Notes to create the index, but you can read your mail or something while waiting, because Notes will create the index in the background. If it is a large database and Notes makes you wait, go get a cup of coffee or something.

Searching the World Wide Web with the Server Web Navigator

To access the search engines in the Server Web Navigator, follow these steps:

1. Open the Server Web Navigator database.

2. Click the Directory Search icon (see Figure 25.17).

FIG. 25.17
The Directory Search icon appears on the Public Web Navigator home page.

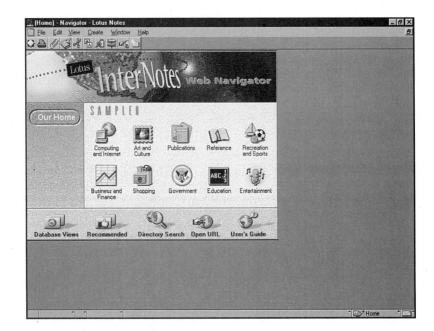

3. Enter the topic to search for in the text box, as shown in Figure 25.18.

FIG. 25.18
Elvis has been entered in the search field.

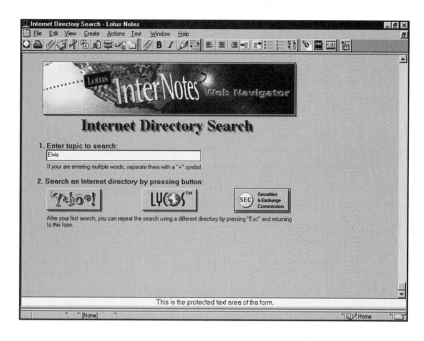

4. Click the search engine you want to use (Yahoo!, Lycos, Excite, or AltaVista).

5. Web Navigator takes you to the site you requested, and the results of your search are displayed on-screen. Figure 25.19 shows the results of searching Yahoo! for Elvis. First, the categories relating to "Elvis" are listed; if you scroll further down, specific sites are shown.

6. You can now scroll through the Elvis list. When you find a page you want to read, click the underlined text.

Using Bookmarks

Perhaps you've had this frustrating experience: You initiate a search and drill deeper and deeper down through layer after layer of information. The address of the page you have reached is

http:\\www.bongo.biz\technotes\dir_423\idea\ohno\iamlost\littlefeat

The phone rings, the system goes down, you get distracted, and you don't make note of the address of this very important document. How do you ever find it again?

You could have saved the page in the Bookmarks folder. The My Bookmarks folder in the Server Web Navigator is a private folder stored on the Notes server; its contents are accessible only by you. If your Notes administrator has elected to periodically purge the Server Web

Navigator database, the contents of the My Bookmarks folder and any subfolders you create under it are not, by default, deleted during the purge (although the Database Manager can override the default).

FIG. 25.19

Yahoo! found 179 references to Elvis.

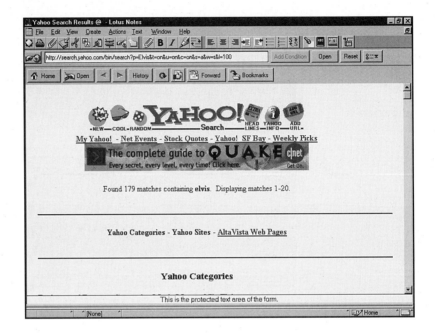

To add an open page to the My Bookmarks folder while using the Server Web Navigator, click the Bookmarks button on the Action Bar. Select the Bookmarks folder and click Add.

To add a page to the My Bookmarks folder from the view pane of the database, drag and drop the page onto the My Bookmarks folder icon in the navigation pane.

Downloading Files with the Server Web Navigator

Some Web pages might have one or more files attached to them. The attached files sometimes appear as embedded icons with filenames beneath them. To retrieve such a file from a Web page, do the following:

1. Click the filename listed in the Web page. This will download the file into a Notes document with the file attached to the bottom of the document (see Figure 25.20).

2. Now you can treat the attachment just like any other in Notes. Double-click the attachment to display the Properties dialog box for the attachment, as shown in Figure 25.21.

3. Click Detach. The Save Attachment dialog box appears, as shown in Figure 25.22.

4. Select a drive, directory, and filename under which to save the file. Click Detach. Notes will save the file. It doesn't actually detach the file itself, just a copy. You can detach another copy later if you want.

FIG. 25.20

The downloaded file is attached to a Notes document.

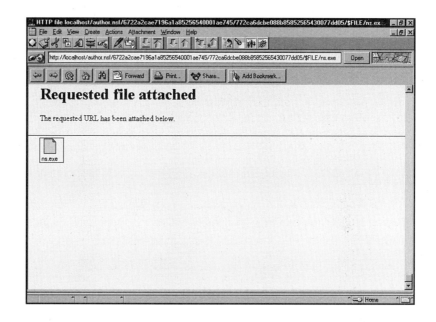

FIG. 25.21

The Properties for Attachment dialog box shows the file's filename, size, and date and time of last modification. You can view, launch, or detach a file.

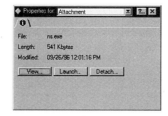

FIG. 25.22

Choose a drive, directory, and filename under which to save your file in the Save Attachment dialog box. Notes will offer to save it under the file's original name.

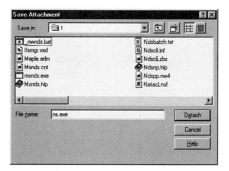

Recommending Web Pages in the Server Web Navigator

The Server Web Navigator lets you make recommendations about useful or interesting Web pages to others within your company who are also Notes users. Because the Server Web Navigator is a shared database, everyone can see each other's recommendations just by looking in the database, so recommending a page is a relatively simple procedure. To recommend a Web page while using the Server Web Navigator, follow these steps:

1. Open the Web page you want to recommend.

2. Click the Recommend button on the Action Bar. You see the dialog box shown in Figure 25.23.

FIG. 25.23

In the Recommend dialog box, you can rate and categorize Web pages.

3. Select a rating from 1 to 5 for this page.

4. Add your comments about this page in the Your comments text field.

5. Select a category for your recommendation.

6. Click <u>O</u>K to save this recommendation.

Viewing Recommended Web Pages

To view the Web pages you and others have recommended in the Server Web Navigator, follow these steps:

1. Open the Server Web Navigator.

2. Click the Recommended button on the Navigator home page.

3. The Recommended Navigator appears on the left of the screen. It lets you view the contents of the recommended Web pages in the following three ways:

- By Category: A list of classifications chosen when Web page ratings were created. A good view for finding pages by topic.

- By Reviewer: Sorted by the person who rated the Web page.

- Top Ten: Shows the top 10 pages with the highest cumulative ratings.

Viewing the Most Current Version of a Web Page

The Server Web Navigator gives you two ways to make sure you're looking at a relatively recent version of a Web page:

■ First, you can manually refresh any page when you're looking at it by clicking the Reload button (the circular blue arrow) on the Action Bar. This causes the Server Web Retriever to get a new copy of the page from the original source on the Web. It displays the new copy and overwrites the old copy in the Server Web Navigator database with the new copy. Also, when you retrieve a page in the Open URL dialog box, you can force Server Web Navigator to ignore any copy of the page that might already be in the Server Web Navigator database and to overwrite that page, if it does exist, with a new copy from the Web. Simply select the Reload from Internet Server option before clicking OK.

■ Second, you can set the Server Web Retriever cache options so that, under certain circumstances, the Web Retriever will retrieve a fresh copy of a page when you open it, even though a copy of the page already resides in the Web Navigator database. The drawback of this method is that it updates all pages indiscriminately, even pages that are strictly archival and unchanging by nature.

You set Web Retriever cache options for the Server Web Navigator by changing the settings of the Update Cache field in the Web Retriever Administration section of the Notes server's Server document in the Public Address Book. (Of course, not just anybody can do this; you have to have adequate access rights to the database and to that document.) Here are the choices in the Update Cache field:

■ Never: This is the default setting. Select it if you don't want your Web pages indiscriminately refreshed when you open them. With Never as your choice, you have to click the Reload button on the Action Bar to refresh your Web pages.

■ Once per session: Select this option to refresh your Web page at the time you open it from the database and not again during your current Notes session. If you're using the Server Web Navigator, Notes will give you a fresh reload even if some other Notes user opened the same page one second before you did.

■ Every time: Select this option to refresh a Web page every time you open it from the database, even if the last time you (or anyone else) opened it was just a minute earlier during the same Notes session.

Forwarding Web Pages to Other Users

You can email a Web page to other Notes users from any view or any open document in the Web Navigator databases. Choose Actions, Forward, click the Actions Forward SmartIcon, or, if a document is open, click the Forward button on the Action Bar. Notes displays the Forward Options dialog box, as shown in Figure 25.24.

Part
VI

Ch

25

FIG. 25.24

You can forward a link or the whole page.

You can choose to forward just the bookmark, which consists of the URL, or the whole Web page. If you choose to forward the whole Web page, Notes opens a mail memo. The Web page appears in the body of the memo, and the subject line is automatically filled in with the title of the Web page. Figure 25.25 shows a Web page ready to be forwarded. Address the memo, add your comments, and click Send.

FIG. 25.25

You can forward a Web page just like any other document. When the recipient opens the forwarded page, the links in it will be live.

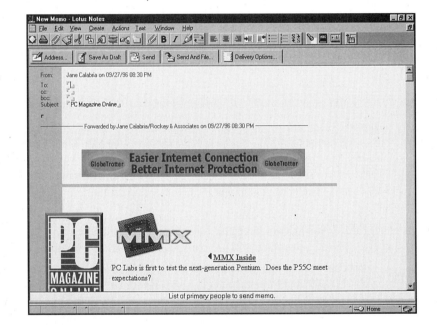

Viewing HTML Code

If you ever do any HTML programming, you might occasionally visit a Web page and say to yourself, "How did they do that?" Really cool colors, formatting, and graphics help attract people to your site.

You can learn how to view the HTML code behind Web pages. So if you see a cool Web page and you want to know more about that page's design, you can view the HTML code on the page and get ideas for your own Web site.

To see the code underlying the HTML documents that Notes retrieves, you must enable the Save HTML in Note option for the Web Navigator database. In Server Web Navigator, you do this in the Administration document, which you open from the Actions menu in the All

Documents view. In Personal Web Navigator, you do this in the Internet Options page, which also can be reached from the Actions menu.

By default, when Notes converts a retrieved HTML page to Notes format, it discards the HTML source code. After you enable the Save HTML in Note option, Notes saves the HTML source code of newly retrieved pages in a hidden field called HTMLSource. You can view the HTML source code only in the Document Properties box of a Web page (see Figure 25.26). It is a little difficult to read in that confined space, however. To ease the pain, copy the HTML source code from the Document Properties dialog box to a text editor or a text field in a Notes document.

FIG. 25.26

HTML code visible in the HTMLSource field.

Viewing HTML Source Code in Notes Documents in a Usable Form

You might think that Lotus would provide a form that displays the HTML source code in a field. But Lotus hasn't yet done so, and you can't create such a form. The HTMLSource field is of data type HTML, which is not a data type you can choose when you create a field in a form. So, even if you create a form that has a field called HTMLSource and you switch to that form when viewing a document, the HTML source code won't appear in that field.

What you can do is select the contents of the HTMLSource field in the Document Properties box, copy the selected text to the clipboard, and paste it into a text editor or a text field in a Notes document.

To view HTML code, follow these steps:

1. Select the Web page in either the Server or Personal Web Navigator.
2. Choose File, Document Properties or click the Properties SmartIcon.
3. Go to the Fields tab.
4. Select the HTMLSource field in the left column to see the HTML code in the right column.
5. Select the HTML code in the right column and copy it to the clipboard.
6. Paste the HTML code into a text editor or a text field in any Notes document. Print a copy if you like. Read it at your leisure.

The Web navigators are a powerful adjunct to the overall functionality of Notes. By allowing you to extend Notes's reach to the far corners of the Internet, the Web navigators truly enhance Notes's role as a repository of all kinds of information. ●

Using Domino Server's HTTP Service

Lotus Notes has always consisted of two components: the *client* and the *server*. In past Notes releases, these components were called the *Notes client* and the *Notes server*. In the summer of 1996, Lotus released a product that turned the Notes server into a combination Notes/Web server. Lotus alternately called this product the *HTTP Service for Lotus Notes* and the *Domino Web Server*. Beginning with the release of Notes 4.5, Lotus folded the Web server add-on so completely into the Notes server that Lotus renamed the Notes server; it is now called the *Lotus Domino server*.

This chapter examines in detail the former add-on from which the Lotus Domino server took its name. To differentiate between the general server functions of the Domino server and the Web-related functions, the Web-server function is called the *HTTP service*.

What Is Domino Server's HTTP Service?

HTTP service is a Lotus Domino server task that adds Web server capabilities to the Domino server. It incorporates several Internet protocols into the Domino server, including HTTP, HTML, URL syntax, CGI, and SSL. (See Chapter 24, "Lotus Notes and the Web," for definitions of these terms.) In effect, Domino is both a Notes server and a Web server. More important, HTTP Service extends to Web users both read and write access to Notes databases. Web users, therefore, can add to and update Notes databases just as though they were using the Notes client. This capability brings 'the power of Notes as a workflow automation tool directly to the Web. In the words of Lotus, this capability makes Notes with Domino not just another Web server, but an Internet application server.

How HTTP Service Works

The HTTP server task adds complete HTTP services to the Domino server. The HTTP side of the server stores HTML files just as any HTTP server does. The Notes side of the server maintains Notes databases. When a Notes client requests services, the "Notes" server provides them. When a Web client requests documents, the HTTP server either provides them itself from its store of HTML files, or it requests the documents from the Notes server; then it converts them from Notes format to HTML and delivers them to the requesting Web client. If a Web client submits a form or a query, the HTTP service converts it to Notes format and submits it to the Notes server, which processes it appropriately (see Figure 26.1).

FIG. 26.1
The Notes database server and the HTTP Web server coexist in the Domino server memory space. One services Notes clients; the other services Web clients.

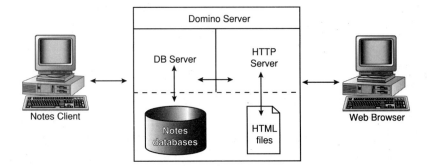

System Requirements

The HTTP service was an add-in to earlier versions of Notes. You had to download it from the Internet (at no charge, of course), and then carefully follow a set of installation instructions to get it running with Notes. Starting with Notes Release 4.5, however, the HTTP service was included with the Domino server as a standard server task, and setup was much easier than before. With Release 4.6, additional web-oriented services have also been included with the core server: POP3 mail server, SMTP MTA, LDAP, NNTP, and so on, along with native ISDN support.

If you put the HTTP service to use on a server, it does increase the load on the processor, RAM, and disk space, although precisely how much depends on how heavily you use the HTTP service. Lotus recommends that a Domino server running the HTTP service have 64M RAM and 1G disk space on the NT platform.

> **N O T E** Running a Domino/HTTP server successfully with only 48M RAM or less is possible. However, with less RAM, the performance is awful. I recommend that you run a production server with an absolute minimum of 64M RAM if you expect a steady stream of users from the Web. You'll find that, in the NT world, 128M RAM gives such a dramatic increase in performance that it's hard not to justify the additional expense for the memory. ▮

Of course, as an HTTP server, your Domino server must run the TCP/IP protocol suite and be accessible to Web users either on the Internet or on your intranet. Notes clients can use any protocol available under Notes to access the server. On the other hand, Web users, by definition, must use TCP/IP.

Configuring Your Site

The server installation process performs most of the setup necessary to implement the HTTP service. To finish configuring it, you must set it to start up when the Domino server starts and edit (or at least review) several sections of the server document.

When you perform a Domino 4.6 server installation, the Install program automatically installs the HTTP files and creates a set of data directories beneath the Notes data directory. They include a "master" directory called Domino and a series of subdirectories off the master, including HTML, intended as the location of any HTML files maintained by Domino; CGI-BIN, the location of CGI scripts to be executed by Domino; and ICONS, the place where Domino stores .GIF versions of Notes icons to be substituted for them when a Notes page is converted to HTML. (See the directory structure in Figure 26.2.) Domino creates an additional subdirectory, CACHE, after you run it for the first time, and another if and when you enable logging.

FIG. 26.2

The Domino server installation process automatically creates the data directories that Domino will use, and it populates the ICONS subdirectory with bitmap files.

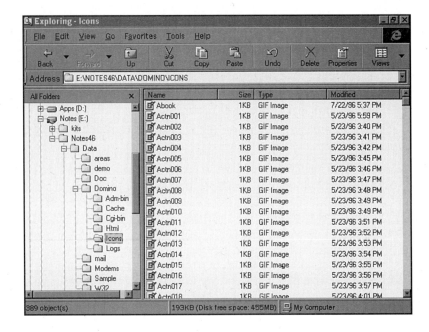

Running the HTTP Service

The server installation and configuration process does not configure the HTTP service to start up when Domino starts. You have to perform that task yourself, by editing the `ServerTasks` variable in the NOTES.INI file. Immediately after server installation, the variable is set as follows:

```
ServerTasks=Replica,Router,Update,Stats,AMgr,Adminp,Sched,CalConn
```

Edit this line by adding `HTTP` to it. When it is edited properly, `ServerTasks` looks like this:

```
ServerTasks=Replica,Router,Update,Stats,AMgr,Adminp,Sched,CalConn,HTTP
```

When you start Domino, this statement causes the HTTP service to start up at that time, along with all the other Domino server tasks listed. Another way to edit this line is by entering the following command at the server console:

```
set configuration
"ServerTasks=Replica,Router,Update,Stats,AMgr,Adminp,Sched,CalConn,HTTP"
```

This statement commands Domino to insert the quoted text into NOTES.INI itself, substituting it for the existing `ServerTasks` variable. By entering this command, you save yourself the trouble of opening, saving, and closing the NOTES.INI file. However, I prefer to edit NOTES.INI directly, because if I mistype a single character of the `set configuration` command, I can impair the functioning of the server. I have less opportunity to make typos if I have to add one word to the end of the statement in a text editor than if I have to retype the whole, long statement in the Notes server console.

You can also start the HTTP server task manually. To do so, enter the following command at the server console:

```
load http
```

Stop the HTTP server task manually by entering the following command at the server console:

```
tell http quit
```

You also have to review and possibly change a multitude of parameters in the server document in the Public Address Book.

Server Document Variables

Two sections of the server document control the actions of the HTTP service: Security and HTTP server. The HTTP server parameters are examined here, and Security parameters will be discussed in the "Domino Security Features" section later in this chapter.

The HTTP server section of the server document has six major parts: Basics, Mapping, Disk and Memory Cache, Logging, Timeouts, and some Operational Information. Initially, you have to make only a few decisions. Later, you can go back and perhaps fine-tune Domino's settings. The fields you must look at up front include those shown in Table 26.1.

> **CAUTION**
>
> The Domino 4.6 server document described in Table 26.1 has changed substantially from the 4.5 version. The 4.6 document contains new sections, new fields, and in general, a different arrangement than the one in 4.5. If the discussion and figures that follow seem to bear little resemblance to the server document you're looking at on your server, you may be looking at a 4.5 version of the address book, even if on a 4.6 server.

Part VI

Ch 26

Table 26.1   Essential HTTP Server Settings

Part	Field	Description
Basics	Host name	The default is blank, which means that the HTTP server gets the host name from the TCP/IP stack in the server's memory. If you have registered an alias with your Domain Name Server, enter the alias here, as shown in Figure 26.3. Otherwise, you can enter the server's IP address so that Web users can access the server by typing the IP address.
Mapping	Home URL	The default is /?Open, which causes the server to send a list of Notes databases as the site home page. If you want to create a real home page, enter its filename here, or clear this field. If you want to designate a home page database, enter its filename here.

FIG. 26.3

The Basics and Mapping portions of the HTTP section of the server document.

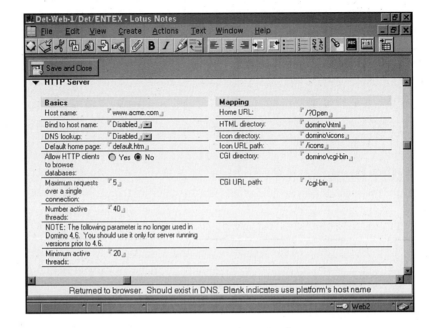

CAUTION

Whenever you make a change in the HTTP server section of the server document, remember to stop and restart the HTTP server task (if it was running). Otherwise, your changes do not take effect.

The rest of the fields are listed as follows, grouped by subsection. Many of them you should never have to change. You may be able to improve the performance of your server by changing some of them.

HTTP Server Basics   HTTP Server Basics is the first subsection of the HTTP server part of the server document. It covers—you guessed it—the basics. Figure 26.3 shows the following:

- Host name: By default, this field is blank, which means that Domino gets the host name from the TCP/IP stack in the server's memory. If you have registered an alias with your Domain Name Server, you can enter the alias here. If the server is not registered with a Domain Name Server, you can enter the server's IP address, which allows users to access the server by typing the IP address in the form `http://192.192.192.11`.

- Bind to Host Name: This field is used for advanced services and partitioned servers. This field allows each IP to answer on its own port 80.

- DNS lookup: This field is disabled by default. If it is enabled, Domino attempts to retrieve the host name of all requesting clients. If the field is disabled, Domino gets only the client's IP address. Because enabling this function requires the server to do more work, it degrades overall server performance. If the server obtains clients' host names, they are recorded in the Domino log files and filter.

- Default home page: This field defaults to default.htm. When a client makes a request that does not specify a page name, Domino serves up this page.

- Allow HTTP Clients to browse databases: This field defaults to yes, which allows clients using browsers to perform the ?open command. If you set it to no, it prevents users from getting a listing of databases.

- Maximum requests over a single connection: This field allows administrators to limit the number of items that can be requested before terminating the connection and thus freeing server resources.

- Maximum active threads and Minimum active threads: These fields default to 40 and 20, respectively. Domino always keeps at least the minimum number of threads open, even when idling. If it reaches the maximum number, it puts any additional requests on hold until threads become free. The more RAM your server has, the higher you should set these values. If your computer seems to spend a lot of time and effort swapping memory to disk, reduce these values. Note that the 4.6 server ignores the Minimum active threads value, although it still exists in the 4.6 PAB for compatibility.

Mapping The fields in the Mapping subsection of the server document specify the physical and mapped locations of Domino's HTML-related data directories. The mapped values are shorthand values that conform to UNIX/URL syntax rules (meaning that they use forward slashes instead of backslashes). Web users enter the mapped locations. The server uses the entries in these fields to translate from the mapped to the actual locations of these directories. As long as you do not change the default setup of the server, you don't need to change most of these values. If you do decide to designate other data directories than the system defaults, you must change the entries in the path fields in this section.

The default data directories, as subdirectories of the Notes data directory, are designated by their relative path names. If you move the data directories out of the Notes data subdirectory tree, enter full versions of the new path names.

The fields in the Mapping subsection are as follow:

- Home URL: This field defaults to /?open, which causes the server to send a list of Notes databases as the site home page (like when a Notes user chooses File, Database, Open). If you want to create a static home page that users see when they enter your host name, put it in the HTML directory, and enter its filename in this field; or you can clear this field for the same effect. If you want to designate a home page database that users will open when they enter your host name, enter its filename here.

- HTML directory: By default, this field is set to domino\html. If the Notes data directory path is c:\notes\data, then this partial path name translates to c:\notes\data\domino\html. If you move the HTML data files to, say, c:\domino\html, then you change this field to c:\domino\html. No corresponding mapped path exists for this directory, because to users seeking static HTML pages from the Domino server, this directory is the root data directory. For example, if a user asks for http://domino.chestnet.com/pagename.htm, the Domino server translates that to c:\notes\data\domino\html\pagename.htm.

■ Icon URL path and Path to icons: The Icon URL path is the name users enter to reach the directory identified in the Path to Icons field. Domino substitutes these graphics files for the actual icons when translating from Notes to HTML file format.

■ CGI URL path and CGI directory: The CGI URL path is the name users enter to reach the actual directory identified in the CGI directory field. CGI scripts are located here.

Disk and Memory Cache Information   When Domino receives a request for a Notes document that includes embedded images or attached files, Domino converts the images to GIF-formatted files and delivers them and the attached files to the requester. It stores copies of both the newly created GIF files and the attachment files in a cache directory. When Domino receives another request for the same document, it can deliver the document faster the second time because it does not have to regenerate the GIFs or detach the attached files again; it retrieves them from the cache instead. This capability increases performance at the expense of disk space.

The fields in this subsection determine how, where, and for how long Domino stores these cached files. You can also set default graphics file settings and HTML output settings here:

■ Cache directory (for GIFs and file attachments): This field indicates the location on disk of the file cache directory. It defaults to domino\cache. Domino creates this directory the first time it runs.

■ Maximum cache size: This field indicates the maximum amount of disk space the files in the cache directory are permitted to occupy. By default, this field is set to 50M. If you have lots of free disk space, consider increasing this number. The benefit is faster delivery of documents to requesters.

■ Delete cache on shutdown: This field is disabled by default. If you enable it, Domino deletes all files from the cache directory whenever you shut down Domino.

■ Garbage collection: Domino uses this process to delete cached files to keep the size of the cache directory within its maximum size (see *Maximum cache size*, described previously). Domino deletes least accessed files first. Disable this option only if you also disable caching. If you disable garbage collection without also disabling caching, the cache can grow beyond its maximum size, eventually taking over all the server's disk space.

■ Garbage collection interval: This field specifies how often the garbage collection process runs; it defaults to every 60 minutes. If the size of the cache exceeds its maximum, garbage collection does not wait until the next scheduled runtime, but runs immediately.

■ Maximum cached commands, designs and users: This field allows administrators to control the size of their cache by limiting the number of pages, graphics, and user sessions.

Conversion/Display   The Conversion/Display section of the server document addresses how Domino deals with graphic images. Specifically, in this section you tell the Domino server how to render graphics that have been pasted into Notes databases.

N O T E This section does not affect images that are referenced by HTML tags. ▪

- Image conversion format: By default, Domino converts images embedded in Notes documents to GIF files. In this field, you can change the format to JPEG if you want.

- Interlaced rendering: This field appears in the server document only if you have selected GIF in the Image conversion format field. Interlaced rendering is enabled by default. When this field enabled, Domino delivers GIFs interlaced; that is, it delivers every eighth line, then every fourth line, then every second line, and then the remaining lines. As a result, the receiver can discern what the image will look like before it is entirely rendered on-screen. Being able to see the image cuts down on the user's frustration factor.

- Progressive rendering: This field appears in the server document only if you have selected JPEG in the Image conversion format field. Progressive rendering is enabled by default. When this field is enabled, the image is rendered at first blurry; then, with each pass, more clearly. Like interlaced GIF rendering, this capability allows the users to tell how the image will look before it is fully rendered.

- JPEG image quality: This field appears in the server document only if you have selected JPEG in the Image conversion format field. JPEG files are compressed in a way that causes them to lose fidelity with the original copy when decompressed. This type of compression is known as *lossy compression*; the other kind, used by GIF among other formats, is *lossless compression*, in which, when decompressed, the image retains 100 percent fidelity with the original. The benefit of using lossy compression is that you can obtain higher compression ratios and thus use less disk space when storing files and less time when transmitting them.

  In this field, you can specify just how tightly JPEGs will compress or, to put it another way, just how much fidelity they will lose when decompressed. A high number in this field means less compression, more fidelity. The default is 75; the range is zero to 100.

- Lines per view page: If a Notes view has more than the number of rows set in this field (the default is 30), then Domino divides the view into multiple view pages for delivery to the requester. Each view page has the number of rows dictated by this field. Every database is affected by this setting.

Part VI

Ch 26

GIF versus JPEG

You have to decide whether to use GIF or JPEG when converting embedded images in Notes documents into graphics files that Web users will be able to see in their browsers. The factors are as follow:

GIF (Graphics Interchange Format) files:

- Are compressed using a lossless compression scheme. This means that the decompressed image is identical to the original.

- Can display a maximum of 256 colors.

- Are better than JPEG for computer-generated art.

continues

continued

JPEG (Joint Photographic Experts Group) files:

- Are compressed using a lossy compression scheme. This means that, when decompressed, the resulting image loses some of the detail that the original image had. The trade-off is higher compression ratios. With JPEG compression, you can also specify ahead of time just how much compression/loss you will get. That is, at compression time you can specify 100 percent fidelity with no compression or progressively less fidelity with correspondingly greater compression. You may wonder why anyone would want to lose fidelity with the original image. Well, it turns out that, with photographic images, the losses aren't particularly noticeable to the human eye. By sacrificing barely noticeable detail, you may be able to reclaim lots of disk space and transmission time. Considering that most video monitors are going to degrade a photographic image anyway, the trade-off may be well worthwhile.

- Can display upwards of 16 million colors.

- Cannot be displayed by some older browsers.

- Are better than GIF for photographic art.

So, which one should you choose? The answer depends on what types of images you are storing in your Notes databases—photographs or computer-generated art. If your Notes databases include predominantly photographs, choose JPEG; if computer-generated art, choose GIF. Sorry, you can't choose database-by-database. You could, however, alter the way you store images in a given database if you want to give viewers the benefits of both image types. For example, if your databases store mostly computer art, but one database stores photographs, you can choose GIF as the default graphics conversion format but then store JPEG copies of embedded photographs as attachments to the documents in which the photographs appear.

Log File Names   Domino optionally maintains Web access and error log files, and you can use either a Notes database or text files as the log.

To use a Notes database for your logs, you simply create a log file from the DOMLOG.NTF template. The Domino server automatically recognizes the database and begins logging into it.

The fields in the Log File Names of the server document are used to allow logging into text files.

You can enable text file logging by entering into the Access log and Error log fields the path names of the directories where access and error logs will be stored. You can enter directory and filenames if you also want to specify the filenames Domino will use when it creates log files. Then you can stop the HTTP server task if it was running and restart it. After restarting, Domino creates the directories you specified, and then it creates the files. The files increase in size quickly. Each day at midnight Domino closes the preceding day's log files and creates new files for the new day. Don't enable logging without good reason; the log files will gradually take over your disk space. If you do enable logging, delete old log files when you no longer need them.

If you enable access logging, Domino creates two log files. If you did not specify a log filename, Domino creates files named agent_log.*mmddyy*, and referer_log.*mmddyy*, where *mmddyy* is the month, day, and year the file was created. Domino records an entry into the current copy of each log whenever it receives a request for a document from a Web user. It enters the identity of the browser program in the agent log and either the IP address or the host name of the requesting computer in the referrer log. It enters host names only if you have enabled DNS lookup. Otherwise, it enters IP addresses. See "HTTP Server Basics," earlier in this chapter, for the details about DNS lookup.

TIP Because Domino appends *mmddyy* to log filenames, reading the files in a text editor becomes a little awkward. If you try to double-click the log file, Windows reports that it does not recognize the extension. If you open your text editor, the log files do not appear in any Open File dialog boxes unless you tell the editor to display all types of files.

A good way to open the file in Notepad under Windows NT 3.5x is to select the log file in File Manager; then you can choose <u>F</u>ile, <u>R</u>un, enter Notepad in front of the name of the file, and click OK.

In Windows 95 or Windows NT 4.x, select the file in Windows Explorer (My Computer, Network Neighborhood), choose <u>F</u>ile, Op<u>e</u>n with, and choose Notepad from the list of files that appears. Better yet, add Notepad to the Send To fly-out menu that appears in Explorer's File menu. Then select the file and choose <u>F</u>ile, Se<u>n</u>d To, Notepad.

To add Notepad to the Send To menu, add a shortcut to it to the Send To folder, which appears either in the Windows folder or in your personal folder under the Profiles folder in the Windows folder. Got that? If not, look it up in Explorer Help by searching for the word *send*.

If you enable error logging, Domino creates three log files: access.*mmddyy*, errors.*mmddyy*, and cgi_error.*mmddyy*. Domino records internal errors in the first two log files and CGI errors in the last. When an internal error occurs, Domino records the identity of the requesting computer and the text of the request in the access log, and it records the Domino-generated error message in the errors log. Figure 26.4 shows the logging subsection of the server document.

The actual field descriptions follow:

- Log Files: The administrator enables text file logging by enabling this field.
- Domlog.nsf: The administrator enables logging into the domlog database by enabling this field.
- Access log format: You can choose to log in a "common" or "extended" format. This choice is determined by the method that you want to employ in analyzing log files.
- Time Format: In this field, you can choose either local time or GMT.
- Directory for log files: Like the directory fields described previously, this field tells the Domino server into what directory to put the logs. Typically, you'll have a log subdirectory off the Domino directory.
- Access log, Agent log, Referer log, and Error log: These fields are no longer necessary in 4.6 (they're superceded by the "Log Files" field) but are still used for servers running earlier versions.

  Each of these fields is used to specify a database and directory for the appropriate log file.

Part
VI

Ch
26

FIG. 26.4

The Logging subsection of the server document.

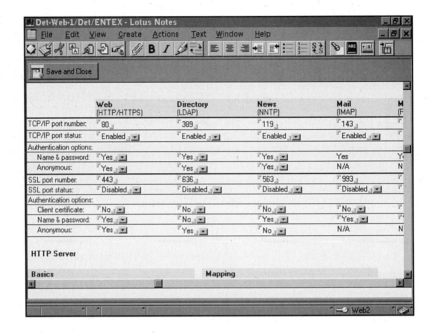

	Web (HTTP/HTTPS)	Directory (LDAP)	News (NNTP)	Mail (IMAP)	M (F
TCP/IP port number:	80	389	119	143	
TCP/IP port status:	Enabled	Enabled	Enabled	Enabled	
Authentication options:					
Name & password:	Yes	Yes	Yes	Yes	Y
Anonymous:	Yes	Yes	Yes	N/A	N
SSL port number:	443	636	563	993	
SSL port status:	Disabled	Disabled	Disabled	Disabled	
Authentication options:					
Client certificate:	No	No	No	No	
Name & password:	Yes	No	Yes	Yes	
Anonymous:	Yes	Yes	No	N/A	N

HTTP Server

Basics   **Mapping**

Exclude from Logging   Use these Exclude from Logging fields to filter entries into the access logs. The several fields here allow you to exclude logging of specific URLs (for example, ignore requests for *.gif, and 'your log files won't be littered with all the requests for images), methods (for example, POST), MIME types (for example, images/avi), agents, return codes (you could ignore certain error messages), or Hosts and Domains. This final option allows you to ignore requests from certain domains or IP addresses; you can choose to exclude from your logs information on what your internal users were doing and only log activities of "real" visitors.

Enter URLs, hosts, or domains that you want to exclude by using "templates" of IP addresses or host/domain names using wildcards. For example, you can enter 192.192.*.* or *.chestnet.com. In this case, accesses to your server are not logged if the accessing host has an IP address that begins with 192.192 or has a host name ending in chestnet.com. Separate entries in this field with spaces. You can use host names in this field only if you have enabled DNS lookup. Otherwise, you can use only IP addresses. See "HTTP Server Basics," earlier in this chapter, for the details about DNS lookup.

Timeouts   All the system timeout variables appear in the Timeouts subsection. They are as follow:

■ Input timeout: When one computer transfers a file to another computer, the computers typically establish a session or connection with each other and maintain that session/connection until the transaction is complete. Some types of servers maintain the connection for a long period of time even though they have no activity with the client.

Web servers, in anticipation of receiving requests from large numbers of strangers, typically drop connections after very short periods of inactivity. Domino is configurable in this regard. This field (which defaults to two minutes) dictates how long the server waits for a request after a client first connects. If no request is forthcoming within the time limit, the server drops the connection.

▪ Output timeout: This field dictates how much time Domino has to fulfill a request before it drops the connection with the requester. The default is 20 minutes, which means, in effect, that Domino is never able to deliver anything that takes longer than that amount of time to download. Its time limit also ensures that a malfunctioning delivery does not hang forever. If Web users will be downloading large files from your server—files that, in the real world of congested Internet pathways, might take more than 20 minutes to transfer to users through 14.4kbps modems—then you might consider increasing the value of this field.

▪ CGI timeout. This field determines the maximum amount of time (defaulting to five minutes) that any CGI script has to get its job done. Among other things, this setting kills a program that gets trapped in a perpetual loop.

▪ Idle thread timeout: This field indicates the same thread referred to in the descriptions of the Maximum and Minimum active threads fields in the section "HTTP Server Basics." As used here, a thread is an independent process that the server maintains to serve requested documents. Multiple threads are available so that the server can service multiple simultaneous requests. Upon startup, Domino creates the number of threads set in the Minimum active threads field. If enough simultaneous page requests come in so that the server needs to activate more threads, it will do so on an as-needed basis. Under no circumstances, however, will Domino open more threads than the number in the Maximum active threads field.

Establishing a new thread takes some time and effort for the computer, so keeping inactive threads alive provides some benefits even though there is no work for them to do. On the other hand, these inactive threads use up memory and processor time, so killing inactive threads also provides some benefits. This field dictates how long after it finishes servicing a request a thread will hang around idle before dying. The default setting of zero minutes means that it never dies. In effect, the number of threads ratchets up, never dropping back down. This setting favors performance over memory conservation.

Internet Ports and Security Configuration

Another important area on the server document is the Internet Ports and Security Configuration section, shown in Figure 26.5, where you can configure all the settings for the various Internet services your Domino server has to offer. The Web settings most relevant to this chapter are covered in the following list, but in this area you also can set configurations for LDAP, POP mail, and so on.

FIG. 26.5

Web services port settings.

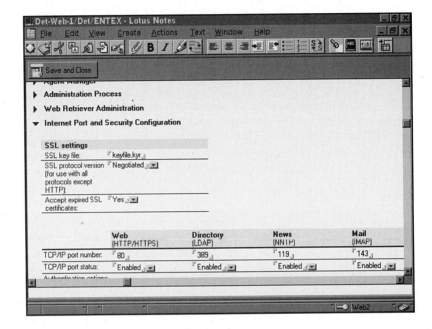

■ TCP/IP port number: The default is 80, which is the standard HTTP port. You need to change this setting only if you are running more than one HTTP server on this computer—that is, if you are running some other HTTP server in addition to Domino. If you do have to change it, you must change it to a port number greater than 1024, and you might prefer to change it to 8008 or 8080, which are commonly used as alternate HTTP port numbers. If you use a port number other than 80, users have to enter it as part of your URL, in the form `http://domino.chestnet.com:8080`.

■ TCP/IP port status: The default for this field is Enabled. You disable this setting only if you want to force users to use the SSL (Secure Sockets Layer) port. If both ports are disabled, the HTTP service does not function properly. See the section "Domino and the SSL Protocol" later in this chapter.

■ Authentication Options: The Name & password field enables HTTP clients to use name and password authentication. The Anonymous field asks whether you want to allow HTTP clients to visit your site without authenticating first.

■ SSL Port Number and Status: The default port is 443, and the default status is enabled, but you can alter these settings.

In addition to the Web options, in this subsection the administrator can configure LDAP, NNTP, IMAP, and POP protocols as well. The defaults are all laid out for you, and, by default, they are all enabled.

Domino Security Features

An amazing thing happens when you start up the HTTP server for the first time. A server that previously would have guarded its databases with all the zeal of a mother bear protecting her cubs suddenly lets almost anyone in the world have entry to them (the databases, not the cubs). Lotus Notes is renowned for its robust security. The typical Domino server requires positive identification of anyone coming to it with a request for data. Even after you identify yourself to it, chances are you will either be turned away or given only the most proscribed access to the data you seek.

All Notes administrators know that the authentication function can be disabled in Lotus Notes. But they also know that disabling has to be done positively, by changing a field in the server document. Now along comes this server task that, by the mere act of loading it, disables the requirement of authentication. If you're new to Notes, you may be thinking right about now, "Okay, so what?" People who have spent some time with traditional Notes servers tend to react to this discovery with shock. The ironic part is that, although loading the HTTP service into memory opens the Domino server's secrets to any Web surfer who wants to come poking around, the Notes server continues to jealously protect that same data whenever a legitimate Notes user comes around. Notes users have to authenticate with the server, whereas mere Web users can have anonymous access.

If this process still doesn't make you light-headed, take a step back and examine Domino's security features from the ground up. To gain access to databases on a standard (non-HTTP) Domino server, a Notes user must first authenticate with the server, then must survive the server's access list, and then get past a layered series of access lists in each database: view access lists, form access lists, document access lists, section access lists, and encrypted fields. One roadblock anywhere along the way, and the user is stopped cold.

In the authentication process, both the user and the server have to prove to each other that they are members of trusted organizations, and they have to prove their identities. This process involves a series of encryptions and decryptions of information using public and private keys. After the server has authenticated the user, the server can still refuse the user access to the server if the user is listed in the Not Access Server field or is not listed in the Access Server field in the Server's server document.

If the user gets past this checkpoint, the server considers any user request to access a database. The server consults the database's Access Control List, where the user may be listed, either individually or as a member of a group, as having Manager access, Designer access, Editor access, Author access, Reader access, Depositor access, or No access. Alternatively, the user may not be listed at all, in which case, the user is granted the Default level of access, which could be any of the listed levels.

▶ **See** "Access Levels," **p. 926**

In Notes 4.6, you can relax the Notes' security by allowing unauthenticated users to access a given server and its databases. An unauthenticated user is one whose identity the server has not ascertained and who, therefore, is essentially anonymous to the server. You permit anonymous access by setting the Allow Anonymous Notes Connections field in the Security section of the server document in the Public Address Book to yes; it defaults to no. You can control the degree of access such users have to given databases by adding Anonymous to each database's Access Control List and specifying the degree of access that Anonymous should have. If you don't add Anonymous to a database Access Control List, anonymous users are granted Default access.

Web Users and Domino Security

When you load the HTTP server task into the server's memory, you permit (by default) unauthenticated Web users to access your server and its databases. As a result, whether you like it or not, Web users now have access to your databases. They have Anonymous access to any database in which Anonymous appears in the database's Access Control List. They have Default access to all other databases.

You can tighten the security of the databases on your Domino server in the following several ways:

- Remove from the Domino server any databases that don't need to be there.
- Altogether deny Web users anonymous access to your server, just the way the server denies access to unauthenticated Notes users, by resetting several fields in the Security section of the server document.
- Set the "Allow HTTP Clients to browse databases" field in the server document to no. See the discussion in the next section, "Limiting Web Access at the Server Level."
- Hide databases from view by resetting fields in each database's Properties InfoBox.
- Review the Access Control List of every database on the server, and ensure either that an entry for Anonymous, with the appropriate degree of access assigned, does appear there or that the degree of access assigned to Default is appropriate for unauthenticated Web users.
- Deny anonymous access to a given database; then require Web users who want access to it to register with you. This technique is known as *basic authentication*. This standard Web authentication technique gives Web users individualized access to your site. That is, after registering with you, they are no longer anonymous. They tell you their names and passwords, and then you let them in—just like Notes users.
- Activate Secure Sockets Layer (SSL) security for Web-based transactions.

Limiting Web Access at the Server Level   The server document contains several fields that apply to Web security. By default, they permit wide-open access to your Notes server. The fields are as follow:

- Allow anonymous HTTP connections: This field defaults to yes. Setting it to no allows only authenticated Web users to access the databases on your site. All Web users, when they request documents from your site, must first enter their names and passwords in a dialog box. The server denies access if the names and passwords submitted do not match those in a Person document in the Public Address Book.

■ Allow HTTP clients to browse databases: This field defaults to yes. By default, anyone who can access your site can retrieve a list of databases there by entering the /?Open command. That is, they can enter something like this: http://domino.chestnet.com/ ?Open. Setting this field to no forces users to authenticate before they can browse in this way.

Limiting Web Access at the Database Level

The fields described in the preceding section limit the types of access that anonymous Web users can gain to your server. You can perform the same tasks on a database level. You can make it difficult for Web users to locate a database on your server by changing two settings in the Database Properties InfoBox. You can control the types of activities Web users can perform in a database by adding a user named Anonymous to the database's Access Control List.

You may not want to altogether disallow browsing with the /?Open command. Instead, you can stop a database from appearing in the list that the /?Open command procures. You do so in the Design panel of that database's Properties InfoBox. Remove the checkmark from the box labeled Show in 'Open Database' Dialog (see Figure 26.6). You can also make sure the checkbox labeled List in Database Catalog is not checked so that users cannot browse in the Database Catalog database for the database you are trying to hide.

However, even if you hide a file so that users cannot discover it by browsing, the users can still open any database whose filename they know by using the following command:

```
http://domino.chestnet.com/dbfilename.nsf/?OpenDatabase
```

FIG. 26.6

Two fields in the Database Properties InfoBox affect users' ability to find databases on the Domino server.

Ultimately, you control user access to databases with the Database Access Control List (ACL). Domino controls anonymous access to databases with two ACL entries: Anonymous and Default. If you add the name Anonymous to a database's ACL, anonymous users have the level of access that you assign to Anonymous. If you don't want anonymous Web users poking around in your Public Address Book, gathering the names and phone numbers of your most valued employees, add Anonymous to the ACL and assign No Access.

If you neglect to add Anonymous to the ACL of a database, don't worry. Anonymous users still get only the level of access assigned to Default. Assign No Access to Default in the ACLs of your most sensitive databases, and only named users can open them.

You can further control user access at the view, form, and document levels. Every view, form, and document in a database has an Access List, located in the object's Properties InfoBox, which defaults to permitting use by everyone with appropriate ACL access. You can limit the membership of any Reader Access List. Notes documents can include Readers or Authors fields. If users with Author ACL access are included in an Authors field, those users can edit the document even though they did not create the document. If users with Reader ACL access are excluded from a Readers field, they cannot read the document. Anonymous users may be included in or excluded from any of these Access Lists or fields. Anonymous users may be members of groups that are, in turn, included in or excluded from any of these Access Lists.

The only sub-database-level access limiters that do not function the same for Web users as for Notes users are signed and encrypted fields. Field signatures and encryption do not function when Web users view a document.

Setting Up Basic Authentication   You can give Web users individualized database access if you create Person documents for those users by entering data in two fields. First, you must enter the user's' names in the User Name field. Second, you must enter passwords into the HTTP Password field. The passwords are encrypted as soon as you save the Person documents.

If you don't feel like personally creating a Person document for every Web user who wants access to your restricted databases, that's okay, because you can set up a Notes registration application that allows Web users to register themselves. Lotus provides a registration application similar to the one used at **www.lotus.com**; it's called Domino Registration Application. Users fill in a form and submit it; then a LotusScript agent creates Person documents for them in the Public Address Book and adds them to a group called Domino Users in the Public Address Book. This application is really great! Lotus uses it to register users at its own Web sites. Download it. Use it as is, customize it, or borrow pieces of it and create your own registration application. Lotus won't mind. Lotus wants you to take the application. So, go for it. Better yet, look for it on the CD-ROM in the back of this book. It is located at **http://notes.net/down.nsf/welcome.**

After Person documents exist for Web users, you can treat the users individually, or groups in which you've placed them, in database ACLs. You can set the access level of Anonymous in a database to No Access, and the access level of the registered users—or more realistically, of a group to which the registered users belong—to Reader or some higher access level. When registered Web users try to access the database, they have to identify themselves by name and password. Notes verifies the information entered against the information in the Public Address Book and then gives appropriate access to the database.

Here's another example: In a database ACL, you can give Reader access to Anonymous and Author access to your registered users (or a group of which they are members). When registered users open the database, Notes goes along and opens it. When the users try to add documents to the database, the server asks the users to identify themselves.

You can also give your registered Notes users Web access to the server by adding a password to the HTTP Password field in their Person documents. Actually, if Default access in the Public

Address Book ACL is set to Author, then your users can perform this task for themselves. Thereafter, your Notes users can access the Notes server using either their Notes clients or their Web browsers.

There's one little catch here, though. Your users have to enter their fully distinguished names when prompted by their Web browsers for names and passwords. The reason for this is that the Notes users' fully distinguished names appear first in the Full Name fields of their Person documents and/or *that's* the way their names appear in the ACL itself. You can remedy this situation by reordering the versions of the users' names in the Full Name fields of their Person documents, so the users' common names (first names, optional middle initials, and last names only) appear first, on a line by themselves. A sample resulting entry in the field looks like this:

```
User name:    Bob Dobbs
              Bob Dobbs/Sales/AcmeCorp
```

Thereafter, your users will be able to enter their common names when prompted by their Web browsers.

Yet another safeguard exists in the ACL of each database that applies to Web users. On the Advanced page of the database ACL, the Maximum Internet browser access field defaults to No Access. You can set it to any ACL access level. It defines the maximum level of access that any non-Notes user will have to that database, no matter what access is shown for the users (or for Anonymous) on the Basics page. For example, if Maximum Internet browser access is set to Author, and a Web user is a member of a group that has Editor access on the Basics page, the Web user still has only Author access. The ACL access level in Maximum Internet browser access prevails over any higher access level granted on the Basics page.

Domino and the SSL Protocol

Domino supports the Secure Sockets Layer (SSL) security protocol for further securing Domino access by Web users. SSL is a public/private key encryption system that supports the following features:

- Encryption of data transferred between the Domino server and Web clients
- Validation that messages between the Domino server and Web clients were not tampered with en route
- Digital signatures

This system, in turn, permits you to establish true user/server authentication between Web users and your Domino Web server, not just the pale imitation that basic Web authentication represents.

The SSL system works like other public/private key systems, such as the security system in Notes. In fact, both Notes and SSL use the RSA (Rivest, Shamir, Adleman) cryptosystem to create their encryption keys. All users and servers possess both private keys and public keys. The users or servers then make the public key available to the world and keep the private key to themselves.

Only the private key can decrypt data that was encrypted with the public key. Only the public key can decrypt data that was encrypted with the private key. If users want to encrypt a message to you, they do so with your public key. Only you have possession of your private key, so only you can decrypt the message. If the author of a message wants to assure you that the message is really from her and not some impostor, she can sign the message with her private key. If you can decrypt the signature with her public key, you can assume it came from her because (presumably) nobody but her has access to her private key.

The weakness of public/private key encryption systems is that someone can send you a public key and tell you it is from anyone in the world—say, for example, Bill Clinton. Then that person can send out all sorts of politically damaging statements, sign them with a private key ostensibly belonging to Bill Clinton, and you might mistakenly say, "I know Bill Clinton said these things because he signed his name to them!"

How do you verify that the public key sent to you really isn't from Bill Clinton at all? You establish positive identification of the person sending you the public key, that's how. Either you have to get the public key in person, satisfying yourself about the identity of the public key's owner, or you have to get someone that you trust to vouch for the person and the public key being offered to you. In SSL parlance, this trusted third party is a Certification Authority (CA). It is the equivalent of the Certifier in Notes.

The CA establishes the identity of the key holders and issues them certificates, signed by the CA, verifying their identity. (Under SSL, the certificates are stored, along with the private and public keys, in a password-protected file called a *keying file*. In Notes, the certificates are stored in *ID files*.) When two people, otherwise total strangers, want to establish a confidential relationship, they can establish each other's identity by presenting to each other the certificates issued to them by the CA. They can trust each other's certificates because they were both signed using the same private key (that belonging to the CA). Both parties know the difficulty they had to undergo to get the certificate; each can assume the other is the person the CA certifies him or her to be.

In the future, anytime these two people want to communicate with each other, they can reestablish each other's identity the same way. The two parties never have to worry that they are talking to an impostor (unless someone stole one of their private keys, of course).

The Notes' implementation of SSL allows great flexibility in establishing a certification scheme. You can self-certify for testing purposes or if you don't need the assurance of certification by a CA. You can become a CA and issue certificates to others. You also can contract with a commercial CA. For example, if you want to set up secure transactions within your own intranet, you can set yourself up as the company CA. Your office issues the certificates to your Domino server and to all the secured users. If you want to set up secure transactions outside your company—say, to conduct sales on the Internet—you can contract with a commercial CA, such as VeriSign (www.verisign.com), to certify you and all users who want to do business with you.

Domino comes with a Notes application, Domino SSL Administration, that automates the establishment of SSL security. It guides you through the process of either self-certifying or submitting a request for a certificate to either your own internal CA or VeriSign. It also guides you through the process of merging the resulting certificate into your keyring file. Finally, if you want to become a CA yourself, this application guides you through that process as well as the process of issuing certificates to others. Describing these processes in detail is beyond the scope of this chapter, but you can obtain more information in two databases that come with the Notes server: the Domino Documentation database, Chapter 5, "Security (SSL)," and the Domino SSL Administration database. You can also download the Notes and the Internet database from notes.net.

Reaching the Domino Site from a Browser

As soon as the HTTP server task is running, you can reach the Domino server from a Web browser. At first, your Domino-based Web site does not look like much to Web users. You can change the default settings in the server document, however, and redesign your databases to take advantage of the features of HTML. You can use a variety of techniques to improve the appearance and usefulness of your Web site.

When you look at a brand new, unrefined Domino Web site through a browser, you first see a list of the databases stored on the Domino Notes server. Each database appears as an HTML hyperlink (see Figure 26.7).

FIG. 26.7

The unadorned Domino Web site displays a list of available databases instead of a home page.

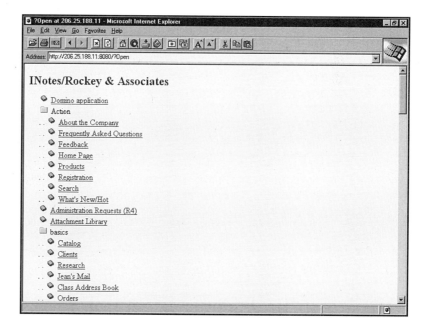

Part
VI

Ch
26

When you click a database hyperlink, by default Domino sends you a list of available views in that database. Each view appears as an HTML hyperlink (see Figure 26.8). If a database is designed to open a graphic navigator when you open it in Notes, that navigator appears instead of the list of views when you open the database in a browser.

FIG. 26.8

When you click one of
the databases, Domino
sends you a list of the
views in the database.

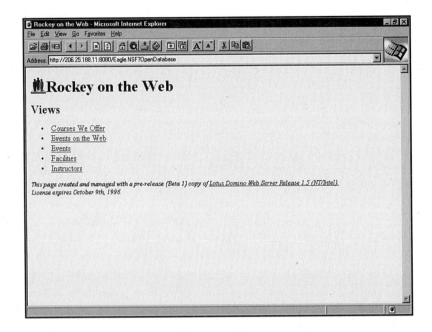

Click a view hyperlink to see the contents of the view—a list of documents, each appearing as
an HTML hyperlink (see Figure 26.9). At the top of the view, you see one or possibly two action
bars. The action bar you see is a row of five navigation graphics that Domino inserts in every
view automatically. The first two graphics take you to the previous and next views, respectively.
The next two graphics either expand or collapse a view category. (Yes, Domino supports collapsible views.) The last takes you to a search screen. If the Notes version of the view has an
action bar associated with it, the action bar items may appear as a row of buttons across the top
of the HTML version of the list of views. Scroll to the bottom of the view, and you see the row
of navigation graphics again, duplicated at the bottom of the view.

Click a document in the view and, you guessed it, the document appears. To see other documents, views, or databases, you can back up to a previous level high enough to display it and
then move down that branch.

In addition to browsing the views, you can perform a full-text search of any database on the site
that has been full-text indexed. When you click the Search icon in the action bar of a view, you
see a Full Text Search screen that looks like the one in Figure 26.10. You might recognize that
the fields in this screen are the same choices that you have when defining a full-text search in
Notes. If the Domino server has been set up for multi-database searching, you may see another
search form, and when you use it to perform a search, Domino will search multiple databases.

FIG. 26.9

Domino adds an action bar to the top and bottom of every view page.

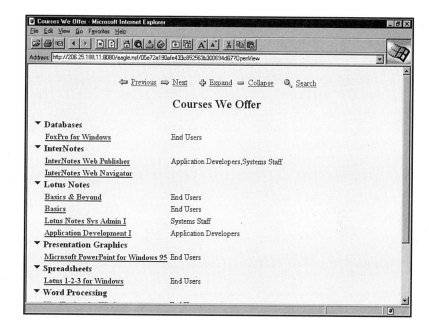

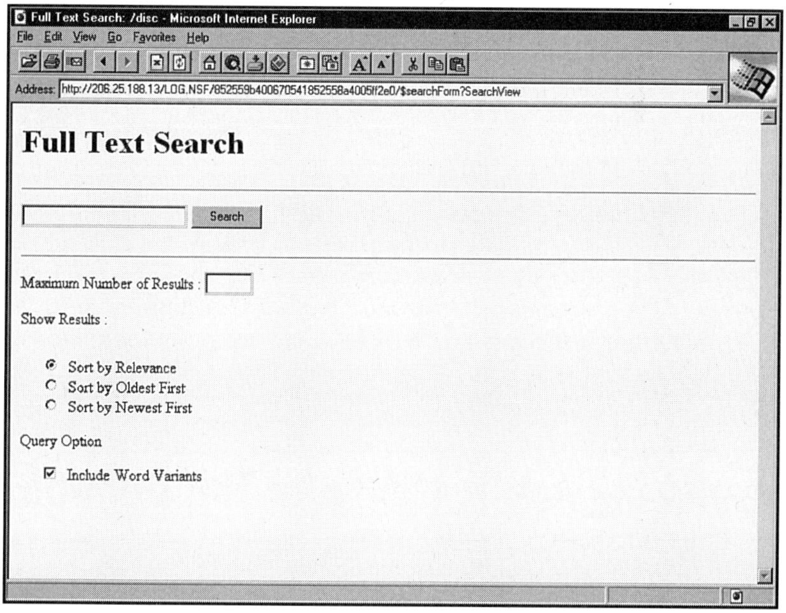

FIG. 26.10

Enter a Boolean (AND, OR, NOT) query in the search window. Notes returns a list of links to documents in the database that meet the terms of your query.

N O T E Unless you consciously make a change to the view, the Domino server automatically puts the search icon in the action bar in every view in a Notes database—whether or not the database is set up for searching!

Your users will see the search window shown in Figure 26.10. They can enter a query but then will receive an error message stating "Database not full text indexed" when they attempt to run the query.

The only two remedies to this potentially embarrassing problem are as follow: Make sure every database is full-text indexed, or modify the way the standard views look by using View Templates (see the section "Embedding Views, View Lists, and Navigators in Forms" later in this chapter). ■

If the Webmaster of a Domino Web site has had an opportunity to modify the parameters of the server document and the databases on the server, then on your first look at the site, you will probably not see a list of databases. Instead, you will see a real home page. The home page may be a file residing in the Domino server's HTML directory, designed by some artist to knock your socks off when you first see it, in hopes that you will come back again and again to the site and tell all your friends and associates about it. Or the home page might be the About This Database document or an opening graphical navigator for one of the databases on the server. Considering what you can do with graphics in Notes, this page might knock your socks off, too.

If the Webmaster has gone to the trouble of creating a home page for you, it undoubtedly will contain links to other documents at the site and perhaps other sites. The links may take you to database home pages, database view pages, document pages, form pages, or HTML files.

If you follow a link to a form page, you see a series of fields into which you can enter data (see Figure 26.11). The form also has at least one Submit button, which, when you click it, returns the filled-in form to the Domino server. Submitting a form to Domino in a Web browser is basically the same process you use in Notes. The form looks different from a typical Notes form. It may not have all the functionality of the same form under Notes, but it does have the same kinds of fields. Most standard Notes @Functions work in it just as in Notes forms. After you click the Submit button, Domino treats the resulting document like a document that any Notes users might have created. That is, it executes any input translation or input validation formulas. It creates a new Notes document based on the form. Any agents that process other documents will act on this one, too.

Developing Applications for the Domino Web Site

The unmodified Domino Web site is a perfectly serviceable but not especially exciting site. It makes the information available but does not exactly send shock waves out over the Internet. What you really want is to modify your Notes databases so that they pack a little punch. Instead of seeing an undifferentiated list of database names and exploring them at random, the Web users can see an attractive and informative home page that focuses their attention on the things you want them to see. Instead of browsing your site more or less aimlessly, the users can see on the home page what is available, what is interesting, and how to get there. Your users don't waste time getting the information they need, and they are less likely to try to get into databases where you don't want them.

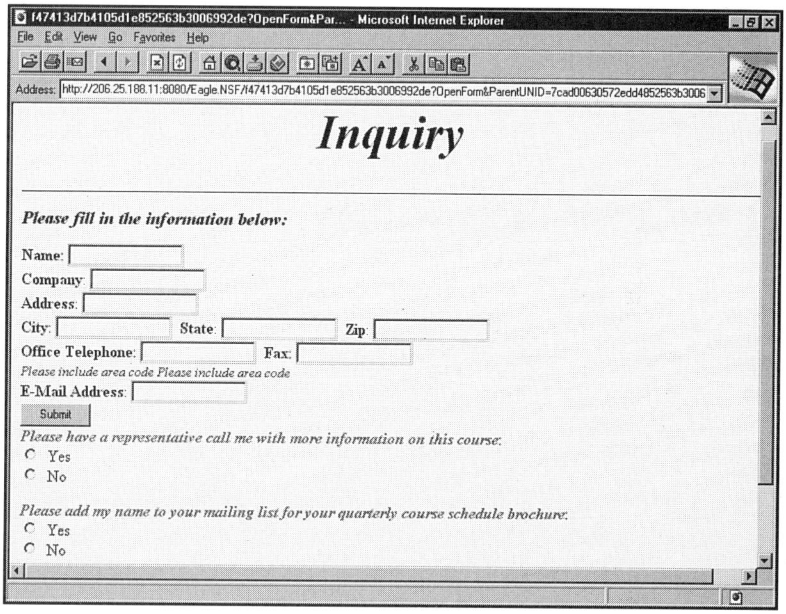

FIG. 26.11
When Web users submit forms, Domino turns them into standard Notes documents and stores them in a database on the Domino server.

More important than making your site inviting is making it interactive. The big advantage that Notes has over the World Wide Web is that Notes was designed from the bottom up to be interactive. The users both create the data and retrieve it. The World Wide Web started out as a one-way information publishing scheme. To get information from the users back into the vanilla Web server, you have to build what amount to kludges by writing scripts in CGI. Because the Web is not inherently a two-way information tool, browsers don't typically provide tools for users to add, edit, or delete documents on Web servers. To provide that functionality, you have to add those capabilities to the views, forms, and documents in your Notes databases.

To make your Domino Web site both more appealing and more interactive, you can do the following:

■ Designate and create a home page document or home page database containing links to all the other pages and databases you want to make available to Web users.

■ Use the numerous Web-oriented templates (such as the new Notes & Web Discussion or Notes & Web Doc Library templates, which were both designed with browser clients in mind). See Appendix A, "Database Templates," for a complete list.

■ Add actions to forms and views to enhance interactivity.

■ Redesign forms to minimize the text formatting limitations of HTML.

- Consider the differences in how Notes and HTML handle graphics.
- Consider enhancing views, forms, and documents with embedded HTML codes.
- Consider enhancing views and forms with special Notes fields designed specifically for Web-enhancing your databases.
- Use Notes graphics navigators as HTML image maps.
- Add CGI variables to input forms to gather information automatically from Web users.
- Use MIME type mappings to inform the Web users' browsers which program to use to open an attached file.

Text-Formatting Considerations

When you're designing any form—whether an About Database form that Web users will view as a home page or a form that will act as a template for documents in a database—you need to be aware of the limitations of HTML text formatting. You shouldn't use the Notes' text-formatting features that do not translate well into HTML.

The Notes' text-formatting features that are supported by HTML include the following:

- Left-aligned, centered, and right-aligned paragraphs
- Table column alignment (but not column widths)
- Extra space characters (preserved only if using a platform's default monospace font—for example, Courier in Windows)
- Font styles (bold, italic, underline, and so on, but not Shadow, Emboss, or Extrude)
- Font colors
- Bulleted and numbered lists
- Named styles

The Notes' text-formatting features that are not supported by HTML include the following:

- Paragraph indentation (whether using tabs or the indentation markers on the ruler)
- Inter-line spacing
- Tab spacing
- Extra space characters (which are removed on translation to HTML except when using a platform's default monospace font—for example, Courier in Windows)
- Fully justified and no-wrap paragraphs (which become left-aligned)
- Font sizes (which are mapped to a limited number of predefined HTML font sizes)

The upshot here is that HTML eliminates white space from paragraphs, no matter how you insert the white space, except for one way—using tables. Inter-line spacing within a paragraph is reduced to single-spacing. Indents disappear, whether they were created using tabs, spaces, or the indent markers on the ruler. With one exception, white space between words disappears, all but one space, whether put there with spaces or tabs.

On the other hand, centered and right-aligned paragraphs are supported. Inter-paragraph spacing is preserved only if inserted with carriage returns; HTML ignores it if you use the Spacing Above/Below fields in the Text Properties InfoBox. Column alignments are preserved in a table. And if you use your computer platform's default monospace font (in Windows, it is Courier, not Courier New), then white space inserted using the Spacebar is preserved.

Domino does support some Notes formatting features by inserting equivalent HTML codes into the text at the time it delivers a form or document to the Web user.

Text Tables   If you want to set up text in columns that translate into HTML columns, you can do so in two ways: by using HTML tables or by using extra spaces with your operating system's default monospace font. Use Notes tables if your Web audience uses graphical browsers that support HTML tables. That includes most of the world. If a large number of the Web users that you cater to (and this number should be a dwindlingly small) use text-based browsers or any browser that does not support HTML tables, you can use manually spaced tables formatted in your computer platform's default monospace font. In Windows, the default is Courier, not Courier New.

When you use Notes tables, the border settings of the top-left cell become the border settings of the whole table in HTML. Plus, you can choose whether to have cell borders.

Font Sizes   Font sizes in Notes map to HTML font sizes, as shown in Table 26.2. The HTML sizes, in turn, map to font sizes on a Web browser according to the browser's configuration. Essentially, there is not a one-to-one correlation between the font sizes Notes uses to display a document and the font sizes a Web browser uses to display the same document.

Table 26.2   Notes Font Sizes versus HTML Font Sizes

Notes Font Point Sizes Less Than or Equal To	Maps to HTML Size
8	1
10	2
12	3
14	4
18	5
24	6
Greater than 24	7

HTML Header styles (the styles typically used by HTML authors to create headlines) are not supported by Domino. Domino does a pretty good job of approximating text sizes, but if you actually want a browser to pick up something as a Header, you need to insert the <H?> HTML tag, where ? represents the size of the header. The largest is 1, and so on.

Graphics Formatting Considerations

You can transfer graphic images from Notes documents to HTML documents in two ways. First, Domino automatically converts embedded graphics of all kinds into files in either GIF or JPEG format (depending on your choice in the HTTP server section of the server document) and sends the resulting graphic file to the Web user along with the HTML document, which has a reference in it to the graphic file.

Second, you can insert passthru HTML code into a form or document. Passthru HTML is a reference to an existing file on your server. When Domino converts the Notes document to HTML and sends it to the users, the reference is passed, unchanged, through to the HTML document. The users receive both the document and the referenced graphics file. A passthru HTML code looks something like this:

```
[<IMG SRC="http://domino.chestnet.com/filename.gif" WIDTH=240 HEIGHT=120>]
```

In the preceding code, `IMG SRC` means image source, `filename` is the name of the file, and the `WIDTH` and `HEIGHT` commands tell the browser the size of the image in pixels. For absolute fidelity to the original image, use the same width and height sizes as the actual image. If you use different sizes, some browsers resize the image accordingly (and, naturally, other browsers ignore the size parameters). If you do resize in any way other than multiplying the original measurements by integers (original measurement ×2 or ×3 or ×4, and so on), the resulting image may look distorted or have moiré patterns.

Domino servers store embedded graphics in two forms: a platform-dependent metafile (Windows Metafile) and a platform-independent bitmap. When you view the document in Notes, you may be looking at either the metafile or the bitmap (depending on the choice made by the person who embedded the file originally). Notes ships the bitmap, not the metafile, to the Web users. Because the metafile and the bitmap may not look exactly alike, the graphic that Notes users and Web users see might be slightly different.

Navigators as Image Maps

An image map is a graphic image, included in an HTML document, that has hotspot links associated with different parts of it. If you click this portion of the image, you are requesting one document; if you click that portion of the image, you are requesting another document. Well-designed image maps are attractive and allow Web users to navigate around easily in your Web site.

Domino converts graphics navigators in Notes databases into image maps in the resulting HTML documents. Domino-created image maps are both *client-side* and *server-side* image maps, meaning that all browsers support them.

To create an image map, you create a graphic navigator, paste the graphic image you want to use into it as a graphic background, and then add hotspots to it that link to other navigators, views, documents, other databases, and so on.

You must, however, consider two caveats. First, any graphics that you paste onto the navigator as anything other than a graphic background disappear from the image map upon translation to HTML. Second, any text that you add in Notes to the navigator also disappears on translation. Therefore, you need to create the entire graphic image, including all graphical and text components, in a graphics program external to Notes. The only thing you do in Notes is paste the image in the navigator as a graphic background, add the hotspots to it, and program the hotspots.

To create a navigator, follow these steps:

1. Create or open in a paint or drawing program the graphic image that will become the image map.

2. Copy the image (or the portion of it that you want) to the clipboard. Most programs allow you to do so by selecting the image (or part of it) and then choosing Edit, Copy. You may also be able to select the image and then press Ctrl+C.

3. Return to Notes. Open the database in which you intend to create the navigator.

4. Create a new navigator by choosing Create, Design, Navigator. A new Navigator design window appears.

5. Choose Design, Navigator Properties. The Navigator Properties InfoBox then appears.

6. Enter a name for the navigator in the Name field of the InfoBox. You can give it an alias as well as a name by naming it in the format Navigator Name|Alias.

7. Paste the clipboard image into the navigator by choosing Create, Graphic Background. Do not paste the image using Edit, Paste; the process doesn't work that way.

8. Assign URL links to different portions of the image. To learn how, see the sections "Creating a Hotspot Rectangle," "Creating a Hotspot Polygon," "Defining Hotspot Properties," and "Assigning an URL to a Hotspot Rectangle or Polygon," later in this chapter.

9. Save and close the navigator.

To define an URL link in a graphical navigator, create a hotspot rectangle or hotspot polygon, and assign the @URLOpen ("URLname") @Function to it (see Figure 26.12).

Creating a Hotspot Rectangle   To create a hotspot rectangle, choose Create, Hotspot Rectangle, or click the red rectangle icon in the toolbar. Your mouse pointer becomes a crosshair. Place the crosshair at one corner of the area to be covered by the rectangle, and then, holding the mouse down button, drag the crosshair to the opposite corner. You see a black rectangle appear as you draw. When you release the mouse button, the black rectangle becomes a red rectangle.

If you are not happy with the resulting rectangle, you can resize it by dragging the corner handles. If no corner handles appear, click anywhere on the rectangle to make them appear.

Creating a Hotspot Polygon   Use the hotspot polygon to define a non-rectangular portion of the graphic image. To create a Hotspot Polygon, choose Create, Hotspot Polygon, or click the red polygon icon in the toolbar. Your mouse pointer becomes a crosshair.

FIG. 26.12

This figure shows a Navigator in Design mode. Note the @URLOpen @Function in the formula pane.

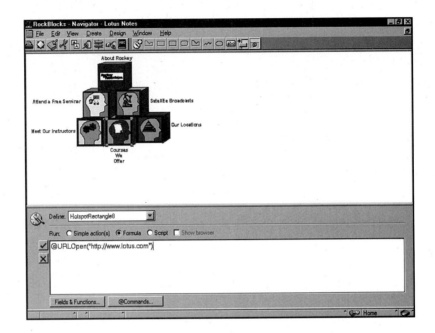

Place the crosshair at one apex of the area to be defined. Click the mouse button to anchor a line at that point. Move the mouse pointer to an adjacent apex. A line connects the first apex to your mouse pointer.

At the second apex, click the mouse again to anchor the other end of the first line, and create an anchor for your next line. Move the mouse pointer to the third apex. Click to create the third line.

Continue until you have reached the last unconnected apex. There you double-click, which creates the second-to-last line and the last line between the last apex and the first apex. The secret to using the Hotspot Polygon tool is to remember to double-click the last apex to close the polygon.

After you finish creating the hotspot polygon, the lines turn red, and corner handles appear when the hotspot polygon is selected. If you want to adjust the shape of the polygon, drag the handles.

Defining Hotspot Properties   After you create a hotspot rectangle or polygon, you can define its properties in the HotspotRectangle/Polygon Properties InfoBox. You can rename it in the Name field, and you can lock or unlock its size and position. You also can define whether the outline of the hotspot appears either when you touch it with the mouse pointer or when you click it. Finally, you can define the weight and color of the outline.

Assigning an URL to a Hotspot Rectangle or Polygon   To assign an URL to a hotspot rectangle or hotspot polygon in a graphic navigator, select the rectangle or polygon while in Design mode. Handles appear at the corners of the object when it is selected. Alternatively, you can select the name of the hotspot from the list in the Define field in the Formula pane of the design window. Then, in the Run field, choose Formula. In the formula pane, enter @URLOpen ("URLname"), where URLname is the URL of the page to which this hotspot should point.

For example, if the hotspot should point to the Lotus Domino Web site, the formula should read @URLOpen("http://domino.lotus.com"). To point to the home page of your own site, the formula could read @URLOpen("/").

Attachments and MIME

If you attach files to Notes documents, they appear in the documents as representative icons. When you double-click the icon in Notes, an Attachment Properties InfoBox appears. On the first tab of the InfoBox, three buttons appear: View, Launch, and Detach. Clicking one of these buttons allows you to view the contents of the file, run the program that created the file, or make a copy of the file on disk.

When Domino sends a Notes document with attachments to Web users, it does two things. First, it copies the attached file to the cache directory. Second, it converts the icon representing the file to a GIF image and turns the GIF into a link hotspot that points to the location on the Domino server of the file. The code behind the link looks something like this:

```
http://www.planetnotes.com/DatabaseName.nsf/ViewUNID/
DocumentUNID/Attachments/CachedFileName/
OriginalAttachmentFileName.ext?OpenElement
```

In the preceding code, DatabaseName is the name of the database in which the HTML document originated. ViewUNID is the Notes' unique identifier (a very long number) of the view in which the document was located. DocumentUNID is the Notes' unique identifier of the original document. CachedFileName is the filename under which Domino stored the cached version of the attached file. OriginalAttachmentFileName.ext is the original filename of the attachment before it was attached to the Notes document. ?OpenElement is the HTTP command to send the attachment to the browser.

If a user clicks the GIF hotspot, the browser retrieves the file and attempts to view it or run it as a program. If the browser cannot figure out how to perform either of these tasks, it presents the viewer with a dialog box offering the options of either saving the file or telling the browser what helper application it should use to launch or view the file. If the user decides to save the file, the browser uses the OriginalAttachmentFileName.ext as the default filename.

The browser figures out how to handle a downloaded file by referring to a file in the Notes data directory, an HTTP configuration file called HTTPD.CNF, placed there by the installation program when the server was installed (or by the Domino installation program if Domino was installed separately from Notes 4.6). HTTPD.CNF is a text file that contains line after line of MIME type mappings as well as lots of other interesting and/or mystifying lines of text.

MIME is an acronym that stands for *Multipurpose Internet Multimedia Extensions*. MIME is an Internet protocol that defines a set of rules for attaching files of all kinds to mail messages and other files (such as HTML files) that computers send to each other across the Net. The early Internet messaging protocols, such as SMTP (Simple Message Transfer Protocol), defined how to format and email messages but did not provide the capability to attach files to messages. In the early days of the Internet, users didn't attach files to messages. They sent the messages by SMTP and transferred the files by a separate process called FTP (File Transfer Protocol). As time passed, developers came up with various ways to attach files to mail messages, but doing so was always a chore until MIME established a standard way of doing it.

A MIME *type mapping* is a line of text that defines a file type and equates its filename extension to a program that can be used to open the file or run the program, if that is what the file is. MIME-compliant programs, such as modern Internet mail programs like Eudora and modern Web browsers, can receive a file attached to or embedded in another file, and then process the attached or embedded file or hand it off to another program to process. A MIME-compliant browser knows how to perform this task by obtaining the file type from the HTTPD.CNF file.

If you get in the habit of attaching a particular type of file to your Notes documents, and you would like Web users to be able to process the files automatically, you can add a type-mapping row to the HTTPD.CNF file to represent your file type. When users download files, Domino sends the information from the type-mapping line to the users along with the files. If the users have the programs needed to process the files, the processing takes place automatically.

The syntax for a MIME type-mapping line is the following:

```
Addtype .extension type/subtype/ encoding [quality[ character-set]] # Comment
```

Addtype is the MIME keyword identifying this as a type-mapping line. .extension is the file extension used to identify the file type. Type/subtype identifies the file type. Examples of types are application, audio, image, and text. Encoding tells how the file is encoded. Types of encoding include binary, 7-bit bytes, and 8-bit bytes. Quality and character set, both optional, identify the file further. The pound sign (#) identifies the text that follows it as a comment.

A sample of type mappings appears in Figure 26.13.

HTML Tags

You don't need to use HTML tags in your databases, but they do offer a handy set of tools for improving the look of your databases when viewed in a Web browser. You can add them in one of the following ways:

- Embed them in any field or on any form by enclosing them in square brackets.
- Use the new 4.6 text property Passthru HTML.
- Place them in a rich text paragraph assigned a style named HTML.
- Place them in a rich text field named HTML.

You can also use HTML tags in formulas, in views, in LotusScript—you name it!

Using Bracketed HTML Codes Because HTML codes are already enclosed in angle brackets, when you embed them in a field by enclosing them in square brackets, they end up being double-bracketed, like [<HTMLcode>] (where HTMLcode is the actual code). When Domino translates the document into HTML, it strips off the square brackets and passes the enclosed code, unchanged, through to the HTML document so that the code appears like this: <HTMLcode>. A good example would be the HTML tag for a horizontal rule. The HTML tag is <hr>, so in your database, you' enter [<hr>].

FIG. 26.13

The HTTPD.CNF file includes line after line of MIME type mappings.

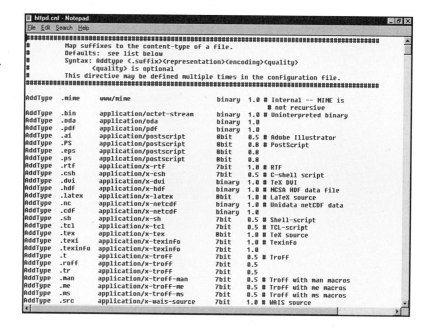

Using Passthru HTML   With Notes 4.6, you can handle HTML in another easy way. Simply choose Text, Passthru HTML, and type your HTML tags. You do not need to enclose the HTML tags in brackets—just in the angle brackets. This method works both in form design and in documents.

Using a Paragraph Style Named HTML   You don't need to use the square brackets using a paragraph style named HTML either. Domino assumes that any text within the paragraph that is enclosed in angle brackets is an HTML code and acts accordingly.

Apply the HTML style to a paragraph by placing the insertion point anywhere in the paragraph and then selecting HTML in either style list (the one in the Text Properties InfoBox or the one in the status bar). You also can assign the style by cycling to it with repeated presses of the Cycle key (F11). Although the goal here is to save yourself the trouble of entering square brackets around every HTML tag in this paragraph, you might just take note that using paragraph styles is also an easy way to apply formatting to any Notes paragraph.

If you don't want Notes users scratching their heads over all the chicken scratchings in an HTML paragraph, use Hide When properties to hide the code from them. With the release of Notes 4.6, your ability to hide HTML from Notes users got even easier. Now you can select a Hide When property to "Hide from Notes 4.6 or later."

To hide the HTML, do the following:

1. Go into the document in Edit mode.
2. Put the insertion point anywhere in the paragraph. You don't need to select the whole paragraph because Hide When properties always affect whole paragraphs, whether you like it or not.
3. Choose Text, Text Properties. The Text Properties InfoBox then appears.
4. Click the window shade tab in the InfoBox. The hide-paragraph properties appear.
5. Check the box "labeled Notes R4.6 or later."
6. Close the InfoBox, and save and close the document.

Using a Text or Rich Text Field Named HTML   Finally, say you have a bunch of existing HTML documents. Maybe they are currently being stored on the third-party Web server that you plan to retire just as soon as you get your Domino Web server running smoothly. You don't want to lose those documents.

Well, you can just move them over to the HTML directory on the Domino server, but then you can't track them with Notes. You still have to manage them manually. What you really should do is import them into one or more Notes databases. That way, Notes can keep track of them for you.

The question is: How can you take these existing HTML documents and store them in Notes documents in such a way that they pass, entire and unchanged, through Domino's translation process to Web users?

The answer is: You can create a form that contains a text or rich text field that you name HTML. If the HTML field is rich text, you should also include at least one other text field so that the document can appear in a view (rich text fields do not appear in view columns). The form can also include other fields, as many (and of whatever data types) as you want. Next, create documents based on the form, and use the HTML field to reference your existing HTML documents. Add a field named HTML to a form, with an HTML file entered as its value, and you pass HTML directly to the browser.

Whenever Domino translates such a document, it not only passes the HTML document through unaltered to the Web users, but—and this is the cool part—it ignores all other fields in the document. It passes only the contents of the HTML field to the Web users.

The other fields are important. They can include all sorts of information about the contents of the HTML field so that you can classify the document. Most important, a year or two after you have forgotten altogether that the document exists, you can go back and draw some clue from the other fields what the document is all about.

There's yet another way to do all this; you can use a new database template to store HTML documents. This template, called Web Pages, is listed in Appendix A, "Database Templates."

Input Forms

Notes was designed from day one, from the ground up, to receive information from Notes users and then give it back to them. Domino's HTTP service was designed from day one, from the ground up, to extend the functionality of Notes to non-Notes users on the Internet. Not only can Domino get information in Notes databases out to the non-Notes world, but non-Notes users can, almost transparently, put information back into Notes and, by natural extension, participate in Notes applications. As Lotus puts it, Domino is the world's first Internet Application Server. It is Notes for the Internet.

Although non-Notes users can participate in Notes applications, keep in mind the following points:

- Notes forms are not as accessible to Web users as they are to Notes users (no "Create" menu exists in a browser).
- Notes forms are not as fully functional on the Web as they are in Notes.

Making Input Forms Accessible to Web Users   The first problem is that, when you, the Web user, want to create, edit, or delete a Notes document from within a browser, you can't just pull down the menu and choose a command. The database designer must make the commands available to you in one of the following three ways:

- As an action on a view or form action bar
- As an action hotspot anywhere in a document or form
- As an HTML link anywhere in a document or form

These commands all appear as clickable buttons, text, or graphics. Users click, and a form appears. The users complete the form, click the Submit button that appears automatically at the bottom of the form, and Domino takes the form, translates it back into Notes format, and stores it in the database.

Actions   Actions are buttons that appear in an action bar at the top of the screen whenever a view or document that has an action bar is present on the screen. When viewed in a Web browser, action bar actions look like cells in a bordered table. The text inside each cell is a link that, when you click it, performs the defined action. In your case, you might want it to do any number of things: create a new document, open an existing document in Edit mode, move a document to a folder, or delete a document.

> **N O T E**   Because of the differences between the Notes client and the browser, you can do several
> things from Notes that you can't do from a browser. ■

To create an action that creates a new document, you can use @Command([Compose]). The steps for creating such an action are as follow:

1. Open in Design mode the view or form in whose action bar the action should appear.
2. Make the action pane appear. Choose View, Action Pane, or drag the action pane border out from the right side of the screen. Alternatively, you can double-click the action pane

border or click the Action Pane SmartIcon (third from the right in a Form window, rightmost in a View window).

The action pane displays a list of all currently defined actions for the current view or form. You can recognize the six Default Actions because each of their names begins with an asterisk.

N O T E You *can't* use one of the six Default Actions. For some reason, the Default Actions don't show up in Domino—whether form actions or view actions.

If you want to create an "Edit Document" action, instead of choosing the existing "Edit Document" Default Action, you need to create your own. It'll work fine. ∎

3. Create another action by choosing <u>C</u>reate, <u>A</u>ction. The word (Untitled) appears in the action pane, and the Action Properties InfoBox for that action appears on the screen.

4. Name the new action in the Title field of the Action Properties InfoBox. The name should be descriptive but short because it will be the text that appears in the action bar in both Notes and the browser.

5. Optionally, choose an icon from the array in the Button Icon field. The icon appears to the left of the actions title in the action bar both in Notes and the browser. Don't skip this step; it's the neatest part of creating an action, and it may be the hardest. (Choosing just the right icon is tough.)

6. Check the box labeled Include Action in Button Bar.

7. Change the action's horizontal position in the action bar (and its vertical position in the Action Menu) by changing the number in the Position field. Number one is the leftmost (topmost) position.

8. If this form is to be used only by Web users, go to the Hide When panel by clicking the window shade icon and, as shown in Figure 26.14, simply click the "Hide from Notes" property on the Hide When tab.

FIG. 26.14

Hide/When properties allow you to "Hide from Notes" or "Hide from Web."

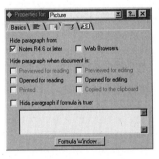

9. Close the Action Properties InfoBox. Make sure the design pane appears in the bottom half of the screen. If it does not, choose <u>V</u>iew, <u>D</u>esign Pane, or drag the design pane border up from the bottom of the screen. Alternatively, you can double-click the design pane border or click the Design Pane SmartIcon (fourth from right in a Form window, second from right in a View window).

10. In the design pane, make sure the Define field says `ActionName(Action)`, where `ActionName` is the title of your action. Make sure the Formula radio button is selected. Then enter the following formula in the formula window:

```
@Command([Compose]; "FormName")
```

11. Save, close, and test the form or view.

If you did everything correctly, your new action should appear in the action bar when the view or form to which you added it is open on the screen. That is, if you did not hide the action from Notes users, it should appear when the form or view is open in Notes and when it is open in a browser. If you hid the form from Notes users, then the action should appear only in a Web browser.

You also might employ the @Function `@UserRoles`, which returns any Roles that the current user fulfills. These Roles appear in the database ACL, mostly. However, if a user is coming in from the Web, `@UserRoles` returns `$$WebClient`.

Again, with the advent of release 4.6, you can now simplify this process by simply checking "Hide from Notes" or "Hide from Web."

The formula in step 10 says to compose a form called `FormName`, where `FormName` is the name of the form the user wants to compose.

To create an action that performs some act upon an existing document, you have to add your action to the action bar of the form with which the document is displayed. You cannot put this kind of action in a view action bar because in a Web browser you cannot tell the action which document in the view it should act upon.

To add an action that opens an existing document in Edit mode, perform the preceding steps, but use this formula in step 10 instead:

```
@Command([EditDocument])
```

You can also hide this action when the document is being edited because the action doesn't do anything in Edit mode when in a Web browser. Interestingly, one of the Default Actions (the ones whose names begin with an asterisk) is Edit Document. You can't use it, however, because the Default Actions do not show up in the action bar when viewed in a Web browser; you have to make your own @Command and duplicate the functionality of the Default Action. (Oh, well. Maybe in the next release...)

To add an action that deletes a document, use the following formula:

```
@Command([EditClear])
```

Notes provides a Simple Action that deletes documents. However, (like Default Actions) Simple Actions do not show up in the action bar when viewed in a Web browser.

By now, maybe you can see the pattern. To add an action that affects an existing document, you have to add it to the form action bar, not to the view action bar. You also have to use an @Command formula even though a Default Action or a Simple Action would do the same thing in Notes that you want your action to do in a Web browser.

Action Hotspots   An *action hotspot* is a block of text—usually surrounded by a box so that it stands out from surrounding text—programmed so that, when you double-click it, some action takes place. It is a Notes equivalent to a text hotspot in an HTML document, and you can program it to open a form in Compose mode, open a document in Edit mode, delete a document, and do all the other things you can do with the action bar as discussed in the preceding section.

To create an action hotspot, you select the block of text that will be clickable. Then you choose Create, Hotspot, Action Hotspot. The HotSpot Button Properties InfoBox appears, but you don't have to do anything in it. Next, in the design pane, choose Formula and enter the following formula, where FormName is the name of the form to be composed:

```
@Command([Compose]; "FormName")
```

In a browser, the hotspot text appears as a standard, different color, underlined HTML link. When you point to it, the mouse pointer changes to a hand. When you click it, a new document, based on the Notes form FormName, opens in Edit mode.

If you want to perform some other action, just substitute the appropriate @Command.

HTML Links   Finally, you can open a form (but not perform any other action) with an HTML link. This link is an HTML code. That is, it is text and it can appear anywhere on a form in Design mode, or you can even add it to a text field in a document. It appears as follows:

```
[<A HREF="/databasename/formname?OpenForm">Click here to create formname</a>]
```

A HREF is the HTML tag that means "add a hypertext reference." databasename and formname are the names of the database and form to be opened, respectively. /databasename/ formname?OpenForm is the command to open the named Notes form in the named Notes database. Click here to create formname is the text that becomes the hotspot. </A> denotes the end of the opening <A> reference (<A> and </A> are paired code).

The resulting link appears and performs as a standard text link in a browser.

Making Input Forms Functional   The second problem with forms in Web browsers is that they behave differently in Web browsers than in Notes. For that reason, you may need to redesign a form so that it is usable in a browser. Or you may decide to create two sets of forms— one for use in Notes, the other for use in Web browsers.

Of course, most of the features of Notes that you apply to forms work the same whether the form appears in a Notes client or a Web browser. For example, Default Value, Input Translation, and Input Validation formulas work the same on both platforms. All types of Computed fields work on both platforms. All data types are available in Web-based forms, with a minor exception. The types of keyword fields that are unique to layout regions are not available in Web-based forms because layout regions themselves do not work at all in Web-based forms.

Field inheritance works slightly different in Web-based forms. Rich text fields cannot inherit from another document. Also, you cannot select a document in a Web-based view, so if you compose a document by clicking a view action, no inheritance takes place. You have to compose a document from within another document for inheritance to work.

Forms on the Web have some features that forms in Notes do not. In particular, you can use HTML tags in Web-based forms to control field input.

For example, you can control the width and maximum number of characters in a text field by entering a tag similar to the following in the Help Description field of a Field Properties InfoBox: [<SIZE=30 MAXLENGTH=50>]. This example sets the width of the field as displayed in a browser at 30 characters and permits entry of up to 50 characters into the field.

You can control how many keywords appear in the browser display of a keyword file by putting a tag similar to the following into the Help Description field of the Field Properties InfoBox: [<SIZE=4>]. This tag causes a scroll bar to appear in the field if more than four keywords are available.

You can control the size and wrap characteristics of a text field with the following tag: [<ROWS=12 COLS=75 WRAP=VIRTUAL>]. This tag causes the text field to display in the browser as a 12-row by 75-column text entry area, and your text wraps within the confines of this space but is transmitted as long, unbroken lines. WRAP=PHYSICAL causes lines to wrap and be transmitted with breaks at wrap points. WRAP=OFF (you guessed it) turns word wrap off so that the typist has to press Enter to force wrapping.

Somewhere along the line, the developers must have realized that using the Help Properties was an unintuitive (if not downright stupid) way to utilize these HTML attributes. So, with Release 4.6, an HTML Attributes event is now associated with virtually every design element in a Notes database. So, instead of entering [<Size = 4>] in the Help Description, you can now enter it in the HTML attributes event for the field. Likewise, savvy HTML coders are aware of elements such as Meta Tags (used to provide keywords for search engines and the like); they can be added in the HTML Attributes for a form.

The Submit Button   Several substantial improvements were made between Release 4.5 and 4.6, and one of the most significant for developers was the ability to use multiple buttons.

Keep in mind that all forms on the Web must have Submit buttons. In Notes, you simply choose File, Save or press Esc, but on the Web, you need a button to do the work.

Domino automatically adds a Submit button to the bottom of any form that a Web user opens. The default Submit button has the word Submit on it. You can move the Submit button or change the words that appear on its face. In 4.5, you could neither alter its behavior nor put more than one Submit button on a form. And you couldn't put any other kind of button on a Web-based form.

In this section, you examine the standard Submit button. Then you will examine the changes in 4.6.

You need to have a Submit button on any form in which you intend Web users to enter information from their browsers.

To move or change the Submit button on a form intended for use by Web users, do the following:

1. Open the form in Design mode.

2. Place the text cursor where you want the Submit button to appear.

3. Choose <u>C</u>reate, <u>H</u>otspot, <u>B</u>utton. A button appears on your form, and the Button Properties InfoBox opens.

4. In the Button Properties InfoBox, enter the desired button text into the button label field. If you leave this field blank, the word Submit will appear when Web users open the form.

5. Save and close the form.

In 4.5, you didn't need to bother programming an action for the button. Domino ignored your programming. The only button it recognized in Web-based forms was the Submit button. In Release 4.6, Domino recognizes multiple buttons, although their functionality is still somewhat limited.

To get multiple buttons working, you first need to select a new property in the Database Properties InfoBox: "Web Access: Use JavaScript when generating pages." This property allows Domino to generate the Notes database complete with multiple buttons. You now can have two buttons on a form: one to simply save this entry, and another to Save and Compose another entry.

> **CAUTION**
>
> If you select the "Use JavaScript" property, Domino then shows *all* buttons you've created, whether or not they're appropriate for Web use. So, be careful.

N O T E   Another consideration in the "'Notes versus Web'" client discussion is *refreshing* a document. Notes users are used to clicking a keyword and having an entire form change, or "refresh." This change occurs as a result of the property "Refresh fields on Keyword Change" in the keyword field being enabled.

HTML doesn't recognize the concept of "refreshing a document." You need to create a script or agent that will save the document and immediately reopen it in Edit mode with the new values in place.

Check the Domino discussion on Notes.Net for lengthy discussions on this and similar topics concerning HTML limitations. ▨

Customizing Responses to User Submissions with the $$Return or $$QuerySaveAgent Fields

When you do submit a form on the Web, a default message, Form processed, appears on the screen. You can customize this response with the $$Return or $$QuerySaveAgent fields. For example, you can cause Domino to respond: Thank you, Rob. One of our representatives will reply to you within one business day.

You do so by adding a computed field to the form that users submit and naming the field $$Return. In the formula pane, you enter a formula defining the response message. The formula that responds with the Thank You message looks something like this:

```
@Return("<H2>Thank you, " + FirstName + ". One of our representatives will reply
to you within one business day.</H2>")
```

The following formula says Thank you, Rob. and displays, on the following line, a hotspot back to the site home page:

```
@Return("<H2>Thank you, " + FirstName + ".</H2><BR><H4><a href=/</a>")
```

You can also use $$Return to run a CGI script or to display a selected HTML page.

The $$QuerySaveAgent field contains a formula that equates to the name of an Agent in the database. $$QuerySaveAgent will then run that Agent as the document is saved. ('A companion $$QueryOpenAgent runs an Agent as the form is opened.)

Typically, $$QuerySaveAgent gives you far more flexibility than $$Return because Agents provide so many more programmatic possibilities than with straight field formulas.

Take your pick, and be sure to check the documentation for examples.

Returning Information with CGI Variables   Finally, you can enter a set of fields that have meaning and function only in Web-based forms. These fields are named after CGI variables. CGI variables are a set of standard variables that CGI programmers can use when writing scripts. CGI variables carry information about the server and client that a CGI script refers to when executing. If fields named for CGI variables appear in an input form, the Web browser automatically enters the values of those variables into the fields. Notes could then use the information when processing a form received from a Web user. See Figure 26.15 for an example of each field name and a corresponding value.

If you add CGI variable fields, they should be text fields. Name them with the CGI variable names whose data you want to collect. Because the users submitting the form will not fill in these fields manually, you should mark them as hidden. To do so, open the Field Properties InfoBox for each such field. Display the Hide When panel by clicking the window shade tab. then mark the fields Hide When Editing.

The CGI variable names that Web Publisher recognizes include those shown in Table 26.3.

Table 26.3   CGI Environment Variables

Variable	Description
Auth_Type	Returns the protocol-specific authentication method used to validate the user, but only if the server supports user authentication and the script is protected
Content_Length	Returns the length of the content, if and as reported by the browser

continues

Table 26.3 Continued

Variable	Description
Content_Type	Returns the content type of the data For queries that have attached information, such as PUT and HTTP POST queries
Gateway_Interface	Returns the server's CGI version number
HTTP_Accept	Returns the MIME types that the client will accept
HTTP_Referer	Returns the URL of the page from which the users opened this form
HTTP_User_Agent	Returns the name and version of the browser used to create this form
HTTPS	Returns On if the server is running the SSL protocol; otherwise, returns Off
Path_Info	Returns the portion of an URL that trails the name of the HTTP server
Path_Translated	Returns the same Path_Info, but in terms of the physical path name not the virtual path name
Query_String	Returns the portion of an URL that trails the question mark
Remote_Addr	Returns the IP address of the browser's host
Remote_Host	Returns the host name of the browser's host
Remote_Ident	Returns the user name of the browser's host
Remote_User	Returns the name by which a Web user is authenticated
Request_Method	Returns the HTTP command the browser used to make the current request
Script_Name	Returns the virtual path name of the script being executed
Server_Name	Returns the server's host name or IP address
Server_Port	Returns the server's HTTP port number
Server_Protocol	Returns the name and version number of the protocol being used by the browser to make this request
Server_Software	Returns the name and version of the HTTP server program
Server_URL	Returns the version of CGI with which the server complies

For more information about CGI variables, see *Special Edition Using CGI*, published by Que.

Links The World Wide Web is made up of hyperlinks. It is a super-document, made up of lots and lots of documents, all of which are connected to each other by hyperlinks. Notes is not merely hyperlinks; it is certainly a whole lot more. Notes supports hyperlinks in the form of document links, view links, and database links, as well as various kinds of hotspots that can link you to navigators, views, forms, and documents. Notes and the Web are a natural fit. Domino automatically converts Notes links into Web hyperlinks. It automatically turns lists into lists of hyperlinks. That is, the list of databases that appears as the default home page is really a list of hyperlinks to the databases. The list of views that appears when you click one of the databases is a list of hyperlinks to the listed views. The views are lists of hyperlinks to the listed documents.

FIG. 26.15

These sample values would appear in the CGI variable fields of a Web input form.

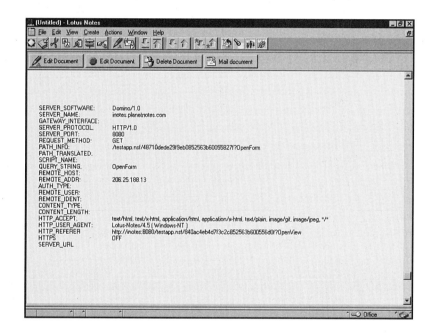

Most links on a Domino server are forged automatically. You have to create only a few of them yourself. If you replace the default home page, you have to add links to your home page by hand. You may also want to add links to other Web sites. You may want to put links in documents that shortcut you back to a view or a home page. Occasionally, you might want to set up a special relationship between two otherwise unlinked documents.

For most of the links you have to create by hand, you can use Notes linking techniques. For some—mostly to pages at other Web sites—you will have to use HTML linking techniques. The linking techniques that Domino recognizes include the following:

- Notes anchor, document, view, and database links
- Link hotspots
- Action hotspots
- Actions on action bars
- Passthru HTML

The question remains: When should you choose one type of link instead of another? As a general rule, you should use links that Notes maintains whenever possible. They include document, view, and database links, and link hotspots. When you use passthru HTML, or an action bar action or action hotspot with @URLOpen, you enter a static URL. Notes cannot automatically update the URL if the address of the resource that it points to changes; you have to change it manually.

Document, View, and Database Links You can link Notes documents to other Notes documents with document links, to Notes views with view links, or to other Notes databases with database links. You create Notes links as follows:

1. Navigate to the document, view, or database icon that you want to link to, and select or open it.

2. With the target selected, choose Edit, Copy as Link, and then Document Link, View Link, or Database Link.

3. Navigate back to the document that will contain the link, and place the insertion point where you want the link to appear.

4. Choose Edit, Paste. A link icon then appears.

New in Release 4.6 is an anchor link, which not only allows you to link to a document, but to a location in the document. For example, if you want to create a link to this chapter and the section immediately following this one, you create the link with the chapter document open and the cursor on the header "Link Hotspots." When you paste that information into the document that will contain the link, the icon will take you directly to this section, not to the top of the document.

Anchor links are common HTML tools. Yet, you should keep in mind that they work just as well within Notes databases and Notes clients.

Link Hotspots Link hotspots act like document, view, and database links but look like boxed text in Notes and underlined text on the Web. You create link hotspots the same way you create standard Notes links, except that in step 4 of the procedure listed in the preceding section, instead of choosing Edit, Paste, you select a block of text and then choose Create, Hotspot, Link Hotspot. The selected text appears to be outlined with a box.

Actions, Action Hotspots, and Passthru HTML Links Instructions for making actions, action hotspots, and passthru HTML links appear in the section "Making Input Forms Accessible to Web Users," earlier in this chapter. To refresh your memory, you use the @OpenURL @Function in actions and action hotspots. A passthru HTML link to another document would look something like this in a Notes document or form:

```
[<A HREF="url.address">clickable text</A>]
```

In the preceding reference, url.address is the actual URL of the page to which this reference points, and clickable text is the text that, in the HTML page as it appears in a Web browser, is highlighted and, when clicked with the mouse, causes the browser to retrieve url.address.

Customizing Database Elements for Viewing on the Web

When you look at a standard Notes database from a Web browser, you see a bare list of views. When you go to a view, you see a bare list of documents. When you open a document, you see a bare document. If you are looking at a navigator, you see nothing else on the screen. If you perform a search, the results come back in a bare screen.

Notes provides a series of tools that allow you to enhance Notes databases so that lists of views, lists of documents, navigators, and search results appear as elements on a page, along with other text and graphics elements. In effect, you can merge views, navigators, and search results with forms.

You can approach this merger of Notes elements in two ways. One approach is to add special fields to forms so that, when users open any documents created with the form, the users see, embedded in the documents where you placed a special field, a list of views, a list of documents (that is, a view), or a navigator. The other approach is to create forms that are templates for views, navigators, or search results, so that when a user opens a view or a navigator or performs a search, the resulting page includes textual and graphic enhancements that normally appear only on forms.

The difference between the two approaches is subtle. The first approach enhances forms (therefore documents) by embedding views, view lists, and navigators in them. The second approach enhances views, navigators, and search results with elements that normally appear only on forms.

Embedding Views, View Lists, and Navigators in Forms   You can embed a list of views, a view, or a navigator in a form by creating fields using the following reserved field names:

- $$ViewList: Returns a list of available views and folders in the database. They appear as they do in the standard Folders navigator.
- $$ViewBody: Returns the contents of a specific view in the database. You can use only one $$ViewBody field per form.
- $$NavigatorBody or $$NavigatorBody_n: Returns a specific navigator in the database. You can use more than one $$NavigatorBody field in a form; if you do use more than one, however, name them $$NavigatorBody_1, $$NavigatorBody_2, and so on.

These fields may be Editable, Computed, Computed for display, or Computed when composed. They should be of data type text. $$ViewBody and $$NavigatorBody field definitions must include string values equal to the name of a view or navigator; or they must include formulas that resolve to the name of a view or navigator. $$ViewList field definitions do not need to include any value.

Create the field where you want the element to appear. You can place these fields in collapsible sections or in tables. These fields have no effect when you're viewing the resulting document from within Notes; they affect only documents viewed from a Web browser.

Creating Custom Views, Navigators, and Search Results Pages   You can create custom views, navigators, or search results pages by creating forms that use the following reserved form names:

- $$ViewTemplate for *viewname*: Where viewname is the alias or name of a view. This form must include a $$ViewBody field for viewname.

- $$ViewTemplateDefault: All views not associated with a specific form using $$ViewTemplate for viewname will be displayed using this form.

- $$NavigatorTemplate for navigatorname: Where navigatorname is the alias or name of a navigator. This form must include a $$NavigatorBody field for navigatorname.

- $$NavigatorTemplateDefault: All navigators not associated with a specific form using $$ViewTemplate for navigatorname will be displayed using this form.

- $$SearchTemplate for viewname: Where viewname is the alias or name of a view. This form must include a $$ViewBody field for viewname; the search results will appear in the $$ViewBody field.

- $$SearchTemplateDefault: All search results from views not associated with a specific search results form using $$SearchTemplate for viewname will be displayed using this form.

- $$SearchSiteTemplate: If you create this form in a site search database, all results of all site searches from this database will display using this form. For more information, see the next section, "Domino Site Searches."

The effect of creating these forms is that, whenever someone opens a view or navigator that is affected by the form, the view or navigator will appear on-screen framed in the form. Whenever someone conducts a search that is affected by one of these forms, the search results will appear framed by the form. So you can include custom text, graphic elements, or anything you want in these forms; the resulting Web pages will look customized, not generic.

Domino Site Searches

When you conduct searches in Lotus Notes, you normally search within individual databases. When you conduct a search on the World Wide Web, you normally search an entire Web site. You can set up Notes to emulate standard Web site searches by having Notes search multiple databases with a single search query.

The Notes' site-search capability is actually more powerful, in a way, than that of a standard Web server because you can configure it so that different subsets of databases get searched in different circumstances. For example, a search conducted from a site home page might involve every site-related database on the server, but a search conducted from within a product information page might only search product-related databases.

To set up site-search capability, you complete the following process:

1. Enable the Include in multi database indexing option for the databases to be included in site searches. Do so in one of two ways. You can select each database, open its Database Properties InfoBox, go to the Design panel, and enable the option. Alternatively, if you

want to enable the option for many databases, you can do so from the Server Administrations screen. There you can open the Tools to Manage Notes Databases dialog box either by choosing Administration, Database Tools or by clicking the Database Tools icon. In the dialog box, you can choose the Web site server in the Server field, choose a database in the Databases field, and choose Multi Database Indexing in the Tool field. After you enable multi-database indexing for all the databases you want, click Done.

2. On the Web site server, create one or more site-search databases by using the Web Site Search (websrch.ntf) design template. Create one site-search database for each multi-database search you want to define.

3. In each site-search database that you create, define the scope of the search by creating a Search Scope Configuration document. This document includes the following fields:

- Scope: Choose Database, Directory, Server, or Domain. For a Web site search, you would normally choose Server. For a partial site search, you might choose Database or Directory.

- Domain: For searches of Domain scope, enter the name of the Notes domain.

- Server: For searches of Server or less scope, enter the name of the Web site server. If you leave this field blank, the search takes place on the server conducting it.

- Filename: For searches of Directory scope, enter the names of one or more directories. For searches of Database scope, enter the names of one or more databases.

- Full Text Index options: Enter No Index, Index Summary Data (not rich text fields), Index Full Document, or Index Full Document and Attachments.

4. Create a full-text index for each site search database that you created in step 2. After the database is indexed, go to the Database By Title view to verify that the databases included in multi-database indexing in step 1 appear in the view.

5. To the forms and documents in your Web site, databases add URLs that bring up the search forms from the site-search databases. The URLs should be in the format

```
http://SiteName/SiteSearchDBName/$SearchForm?SearchSite
```

where SiteName is the Internet domain name or intranet host name of your Web site server, and SiteSearchDBName is the Notes title (not filename) of the site-search database to be queried.

The URL in step 5 retrieves a search form from the database named in the URL. The preceding query returns the Simple search form to the Web users. This form appears in Figure 26.16. The Web users can click a link in the form, which then returns the Advanced search form, pictured in Figure 26.17.

You can also enter a site search manually by using an URL in the form

```
http://SiteName/SearchSiteDBName?SearchSite&Query=SearchString1
+AND+SearchString2…
```

Part
VI

Ch
26

where the plus signs represent the space character and `SearchString1` and `SearchString2` are search strings separated by the logical AND. In other words, this query searches for all documents that include both `SearchString1` and `SearchString2`.

FIG. 26.16

By default, you start a site search by using the Simple search form.

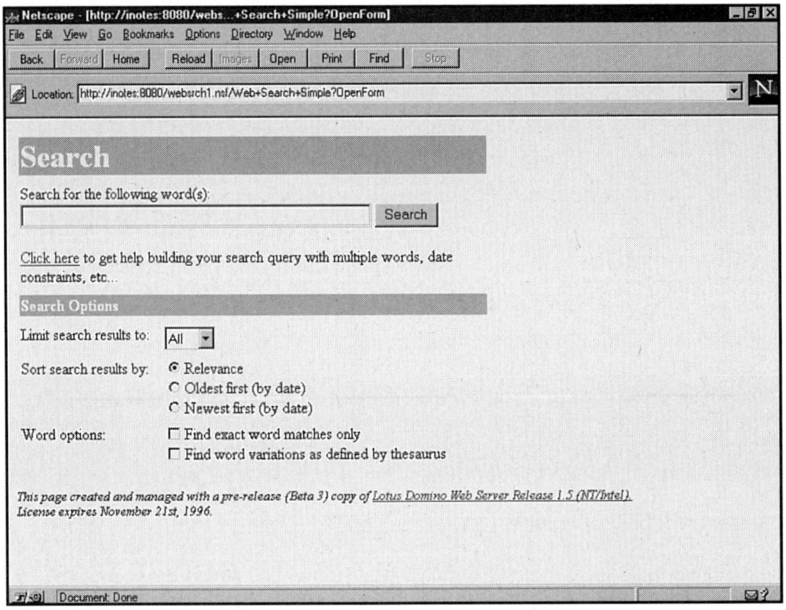

FIG. 26.17

You can then click a link to retrieve the Advanced search form.

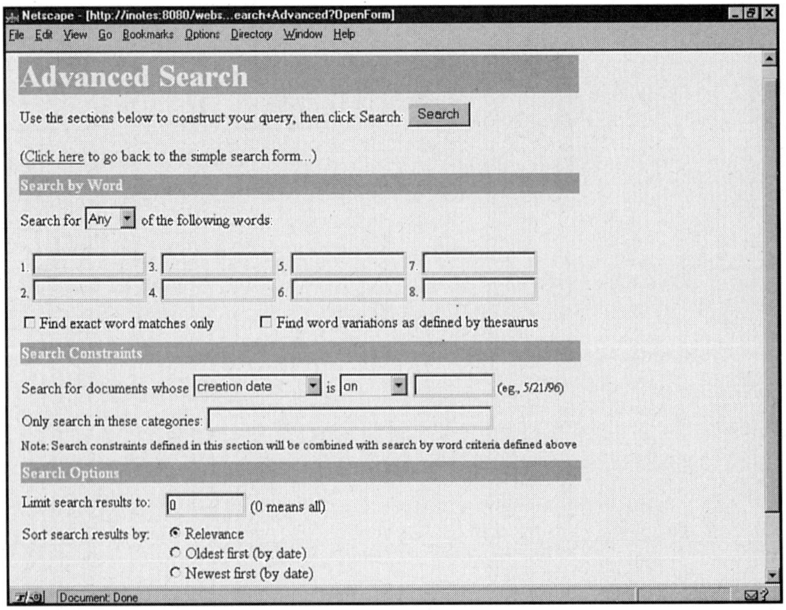

When Web users fill in and submit one of the search forms, or when users enter manual search queries like the one in the previous paragraph, Domino performs a search of the databases defined in the Databases By Title view of the site-search database.

When Domino returns the results of a search, it uses the Results form from the site-search database. This is a bare-bones form: Its title shows the query that produced it; it indicates the number of documents found by the search; and it lists the documents in the order specified in the search (see Figure 26.18).

FIG. 26.18

The Search Results form shows the search query, the number of documents found by the search query, and a list of links to the documents found.

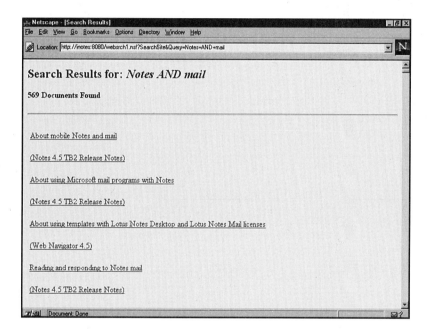

If you prefer, Domino will return the search results on a custom search results form, $$SearchSiteTemplate. See the section "Creating Custom Views, Navigators, and Search Results Pages," earlier in this chapter, for instructions on creating this form. ●

Part
VI

Ch
26

Appendixes

Database Templates

Lotus Notes comes with a selection of application database templates that can be used as the foundation for creating new databases. Database templates are identified by their unique NTF (Notes Template File) file extension. Several of these templates are designed to take advantage of new functionality available in Release 4.6. This appendix briefly describes the database templates included with Release 4.6 that will help you design applications. Database templates used in administration functions aren't covered—with the exception of a few that are often accessed by users and database developers—because they are beyond the scope of this book. If you do need a listing of the administration database templates, you will find a comprehensive list in the Administration Help database, typically located in the DOC subdirectory.

T I P   The Notes Net Web site (http://www.notes.net) has a download section where updated templates are posted. As new updates to Notes 4.6 are released, you might find that some templates are added or discontinued. Check the Lotus Web site for recent updates to templates for Notes. In particular, check out the Best Practices database on the Notes Net Web site for great information on working with templates.

▶ **See** "Using Templates," **p. 381**

Listed after the template description are the template filename and the design template name you use when you create an application in which you want to control updates to the design through the design template. You can read more about designing applications in Chapter 10, "Creating New Databases."

N O T E   The Help documentation in your database lists the availability of several templates from previous versions of Notes. An example is the Discussion R4.5 template. However, these templates aren't installed with Notes 4.6.

The following lists the application templates that are included in Release 4.6 and that you can use when you begin designing applications in Notes. Application templates speed up your development process by providing a starting point for your application design. You can later customize them to further meet your business needs.

- Approval Cycle (R4): Companies can use this database to manage their electronic approval requirements. Based on a flexible design, forms can be created to cater to a variety of approval types, yet designers need to maintain only one set of approval logic. The approval logic, stored in the ApprovalLogic subform, can be modified quickly when a company's approval cycle changes. This template also includes an agent to manage overdue approvals.

  Template filename: APPROVE4.NTF

  Design template name: StdR4Approval

- Database Library: This template is used to create a database that contains a list of public databases to which users can request access. The main difference between the two applications is that entries aren't automatically placed in the Database Library—the database manager must specify that a particular database be listed. This Database Library is ideal for users who want to create a library of the databases they have stored on their particular hardware, or which they manage. Databases are published to a Database Library using File, Database, Publish.

  Template filename: DBLIB4.NTF

  Design template name: StdR4DatabaseLib

- Discussion - Notes & Web (R4.6): Discussion databases are one of the most common Notes application types. A workgroup can use a discussion database as a meeting place to collect and share ideas without having to be physically present. Nearly all workgroups can take advantage of the benefits that discussion databases offer. Financial planners can use them to discuss annual budgets, sales managers can use them to discuss targets, and social committees can use them to plan events. Users can simply follow discussion threads or take a more active role and contribute to discussions. Users can also make anonymous contributions.

Discussion databases have a number of key elements. First, discussion thread hierarchies are easy to maintain through the use of main topic, response, and response-to-response forms. Second, the form layouts are designed to be simple to use, making them ideal for first-time Notes users. Third, views are designed to allow users to quickly navigate contributions by category, author, or favorite documents. Users can even set up interest profiles and be notified via the Newsletter Agent when conditions they specify are met. For example, a user might want to be notified when her name appears in a discussion thread. In addition, there are full archiving capabilities in place to store documents in a separate database when they become obsolete.

This electronic conference room template features the same functionality as the standard Discussion database used in Notes 4.5, with the addition of multiple navigators, alternative view templates, and hotspot actions for Web browser users.

Template filename: DISCSW46.NTF

Design template name: StdR46Disc

- Doc Library - Notes & Web (R4.6): This document storage library database sports the same functionality as the standard Document Library, only it supports linear review workflow processing (rather than linear and parallel workflow processing) and archiving capabilities. It is built to support both Notes users and Web browser users.

Template filename: DOCLBW46.NTF

Design template name: StdR46NetLib

- Document Library (R4): The document library is a database used to capture and store documents. It is an electronic filing cabinet with document review and archiving functions. A document library might contain all the product specifications for an electronic components manufacturer or all drug study information for a pharmaceutical company.

Template filename: DOCLIB4.NTF

Design template name: StdR4DocLib

- Frameset (R4.6): This template gives application developers customizable HTML frame layouts for home pages. You can use this template to create a database of Web pages that are to be published on an intranet or on the Web using the Domino server. Pages in this database are designed to take advantage of frames, an HTML feature that many browsers support.

Template filename: FRAMEW46.NTF

Design template name: StdR46WebFrames

■ Local Free Time Info: This template is used to create a database used by the Calendaring and Scheduling features in Release 4.6. It lets you keep track of users' free time while you're working remote. This is really an administrative-type database template. It is listed here because it's used by end users.

Template filename: BUSYTIME.NTF

Design template name: BusyTime

■ Lotus SmartSuite 96 Library (R4): This Document Library template is designed specifically for Lotus SmartSuite 96 applications. Forms are included for creating 1-2-3 worksheets, freelance presentations, and Word Pro documents. Document review and archiving functions are included. (This template isn't designed for backward compatibility with previous versions of Lotus SmartSuite.)

Template filename: DOCLIBL4.NTF

Design template name: StdR4DocLibLS

■ Mail (R4.6): The Mail template is used to create a database for managing the use, storage, and routing of electronic mail between Notes users. The template contains forms for creating mail, replies, tasks, and Calendaring and Scheduling events. Forms for creating out-of-office profiles and archive criteria assist with mail management.

Template filename: MAIL46.NTF

Design template name: StdR46Mail

■ Mail Web Only (R4.6): This Web Mail template is for use from Web browsers only. The Notes client is only used to modify this template. This Web Mail template isn't intended to function via the Notes client. It will only work properly from a Web browser. The Web Mail template is used to create a database to send and receive electronic mail using a Domino server. The Web Mail template also contains Calendaring and Scheduling features that can be used for personal time management and meeting and appointment scheduling. The Calendar view provides a desktop calendar for ease in viewing scheduled appointments.

Template filename: MAILW46.NTF

Design template name: StdR46WebMail

■ Microsoft Office Library (R4.6): This Document Library template is designed specifically for Microsoft Office applications. Forms are included for creating Excel worksheets, Paintbrush pictures, PowerPoint presentations, and Word documents. Document review and archiving functions are included.

Template filename: DOCLIBM46.NTF

Design template name: StdR46DocLibMS

■ Personal Address Book: The Personal Address Book is the replacement for the full Address Book from prior versions of Notes. Although this database is actually part of the administrative database templates, it is listed here because users might need to access it if their Personal Address Book needs to be upgraded from a prior release. Or perhaps you want to use the template as a starting point for creating other applications similar to the Address Book. This address book is tailored to a user's personal use. Information about a contact's work, home, and email systems is stored in this database. Connection records to other Notes servers are stored in this database, as are location documents that store information about the different locations from which you use Notes.

Template filename: PERNAMES.NTF

Design template name: StdR4PersonalAddressBook

- Personal Journal: This is a database designed to store private documents. Users can elect to encrypt this database to add further security to entries. A personal journal can be used to store documents in draft form, thoughts, ideas, or just about anything you want to record. The journal is created automatically when you install (or upgrade to) Notes 4.6 and is a part of the Favorites portfolio.

    Template filename: JOURNAL4.NTF

    Design template name: StdR4Journal

- Personal Web Navigator: This template is used to create a database that records information about the activity on one or more Notes servers.

    Template filename: PERWEB46.NTF

    Design template name: StdR46PersonalWebNavigator

- Portfolio (R4.6): A portfolio database is a collection of databases. You can use a portfolio to group databases you use frequently or that are related to the work you want to track. For example, you could create a portfolio database for projects and add all project databases you want to track to the portfolio, making it a reference tool. When you open a portfolio database, the left pane contains buttons that correspond to the databases collected in the portfolio. These buttons contain the icon from the databases referenced in the portfolio. The portfolio automatically opens the first database in the list.

    Template filename: PRTFLO46.NTF

    Design template name: StdR46Portfolio

- Search Site: This template is used to create a database for creating and submitting simple or advanced queries that can search for information on a specified site.

    Template filename: SRCHSITE.NTF

    Design template name: StdNotesSearchSite

- Web Pages (R4.6): Use this database to easily create and store Web pages. You can enter data in Notes' rich text format using the Web Page form. You can also add Notes doclinks to pages you create with this form to link your Web pages together. The Domino server automatically translates rich text and doclinks into HTML for the browser. If you want to create pages using HTML, use the Web Page Using HTML form. Note that the Domino server won't translate pages you create with this form; rather, use this database if you have existing HTML pages you want to store.

    Template filename: PAGESW46.NSF

    Design template name: StdR46WebPages

Special Characters

Special characters—usually not found on your keyboard—represent foreign language letters, foreign currency symbols, copyright and trademark characters, and mathematical symbols. By pressing a key combination, you can use special characters in Notes anywhere you can enter text.

Notes uses the keyboard combination Alt+F1 plus special codes to create special characters. For example, to enter the cent symbol (¢), press Alt+F1, then C, then /. Listed in this appendix are the special characters and key combinations for the Windows, OS/2, and UNIX platforms. Macintosh users can look in the Notes Online help under LMBCS (Lotus Multibyte Character Set) for the help document containing characters and codes for the Macintosh.

N O T E   Notes provides several codes for many common characters. You can use whichever seems easiest to type or remember. You can get a full listing of supported LMBCS characters in the "Creating Special Characters" document in the online Help database in Notes. The following list contains some of the more commonly used characters. ▨

Press Alt+F1 Plus...	To Get This Character	Character Description
C,	Ç	C cedilla
u"	ü	u umlaut
e'	é	e acute
a^	â	a circumflex
a"	ä	a umlaut
a`	à	a grave
a*	å	a angstrom
c,	ç	c cedilla
e^	ê	e circumflex
e"	ë	e umlaut
e`	è	e grave
i"	ï	i umlaut
i^	î	i circumflex
i`	ì	i grave
A"	Ä	A umlaut
A*	Å	A angstrom
E'	É	E acute
ae	æ	ae diphthong
AE	Æ	AE diphthong
o^	ô	o circumflex
o"	ö	o umlaut
o`	ò	o grave
u^	û	u circumflex
u`	ù	u grave
y"	ÿ	y umlaut
O"	Ö	O umlaut

U"	Ü	U umlaut
o/	ø	o slash
L= or l= or L- or l-	£	Pound sign
O/	Ø	O slash
xx or XX	×	Multiply
a'	á	a acute
i'	í	i acute
o'	ó	o acute
u'	ú	u acute
n~	ñ	n tilde
N~	Ñ	N tilde
a_ or A_	a	Feminine ordinal indicator
O_ or o_	o	Masculine ordinal indicator
??	¿	Inverted ?
RO or R0 or r0	®	Registered
-]		Start of line
12	½	Half
14	¼	Quarter
!!	¡	Inverted exclamation
<<	«	Left Angle quotes
>>	»	Right Angle quotes
A'	Á	A acute
A^	Â	A circumflex
A`	À	A grave
CO or co or C0 or c0	©	Copyright
c| or c/ or C| or C/	¢	Cent
Y= or y= or Y- or y-	¥	Yen
a~	ã	a tilde
A~	Ã	A tilde
XO or xo or X0 or x0	¤	International Currency

continues

continued

d-	ð	Eth lower
D-	Ð	Eth upper
E^	Ê	E circumflex
E"	Ë	E umlaut
E`	È	E grave
I'	Í	I acute
I^	Î	I circumflex, uppercase
I"	Ï	I umlaut, uppercase
/<space>	¦	Vertical line, broken
I`	Ì	I grave
O'	Ó	O acute, uppercase
ss	ß	German sharp, lowercase
O^	Ô	O circumflex, uppercase
O`	Ò	O grave, uppercase
o~	õ	o tilde, lowercase
O~	Õ	O tilde, uppercase
/u	µ	Greek mu, lowercase
p-	þ	Icelandic Thorn, lowercase
P-	Þ	Icelandic Thorn, uppercase
U'	Ú	U acute, uppercase
U^	Û	U circumflex, uppercase
Ù	Ù	U grave, uppercase
y'	ý	y acute, lowercase
Y'	Ý	Y acute, uppercase
_^		Overline
spacebar then '	´	Acute
-=	–	Hyphen
+-	±	Plus/Minus
34	¾	Three-quarters
!p	¶	Paragraph symbol

so	§	Section symbol
:-	÷	Division
,,	¸	Cedilla
^0	°	Degree
spacebar then "	¨	Umlaut
^.	·	Center dot
^1	¹	1 Superscript
^2	²	2 Superscript
^3	³	3 Superscript

App

B

Using the CD-ROM

N O T E   To view the QUEBOOK.NSF database directly from the CD-ROM without copying the
database to your local drive, you might need to use a copy of Lotus Notes 4.6x. This is due
to the differences in indexing algorithms between Notes 4.6 and previous versions.

If you don't have access to Notes 4.6, and you can't open the database with your current Notes version
directly from the CD, you can copy the QUEBOOK.NSF database to your local hard drive and then, using
your operating system, change the attributes of the file to deselect Read Only. You will now be able to
open the database, because Notes can now create its own index locally. ■

The CD-ROM that accompanies this book contains the book itself in electronic form, with
demo applications, troubleshooting databases, and additional information on Lotus Business
Partners, companion products, and third-party applications. You will find a host of screencams,
applications, technical documents, and more, all stored within a single Notes database on the
CD-ROM. You simply have to open the Notes database on the CD-ROM, read through the
documents to see what is attached, and then detach and/or launch the file attachments. Each
document in the database that contains a file attachment has a brief description of the application and provides instructions on how you might want to work with that file.

In addition to this entire book, the CD-ROM also contains the following:

Program or File	Contributor
ScanMail Evaluation Copy	Trend Micro
TNG Unicenter Resource Information	Computer Associates
Notes Network-Based Training Demo	ReCor Corporation
Remind Project Management Demo	ChangePoint Corporation
Instant I*Net Evaluation Copy, version 1.5A	InfoImage
Lotus Notes Advisor Premier Magazine	Advisor Publications
Lotus Notes Internet Cookbook	Lotus Development Corporation
Sentinel Data Integrator Demo	Mayflower Software
Notes Update Magazine Sample Articles	Xephon
Acrobat Reader	Adobe Systems Incorporated
Modem Survivor's Kit	Lotus Development Corporation
Icon Library	Que Corporation
Recipe Tracker	Que Corporation
Video/CD Tracker	Que Corporation
Administrator's Guidebook	Que Corporation
$alesLink demo	Encompass Software, Inc.
TeamStudio Analyzer	Ives Development
Essential Tools Evaluation Copy	InfoImage
Lotus Notes Designer for Domino Java Programmer's Guide	Lotus Development Corporation

Program or File	Contributor
Involv Intranet Evaluation Copy	ChangePoint Corporation
Internet Explorer 4	Microsoft Corporation

All of this is included, and more!

Working with the Database

All the files on the CD, with the exception of the electronic versions of this book, are located in a single Notes database. Accessing these files is as easy as opening any other Notes database. Follow these steps to access the Special Edition Using Lotus Notes and Domino 4.6 database:

1. Select File, Database, Open. The Open Database dialog box appears.
2. Type D:\QUEBOOK.NSF in the Filename box. (Substitute your CD-ROM drive designation for D:\, if necessary, to access your CD-ROM drive.) You can also use the Browse button to open the CD-ROM and locate the QUEBOOK.NSF file.
3. Click Open.

Notes will open the Special Edition Using Lotus Notes and Domino 4.6 database for you to review its contents. Instructions for using specific files attached to the documents in this database are provided within each document in the "Using This Demo" section. Read through this section to understand how to work with a particular file.

When you exit the database, Notes will leave its icon on your workspace for future use of the database. Double-click the icon for all subsequent accesses to this database. Keep in mind that the CD-ROM needs to be in the CD-ROM drive when you access the database—unless you copied the database to your workspace.

App
C

Using the Electronic Book

This book is available to you as a Notes database that can be easily opened directly from the CD-ROM or copied to your hard drive and then opened. Follow the directions in Chapter 1, "Getting Started with Lotus Notes," to get started accessing this database.

Installing the Internet Explorer

If you don't have a Web browser installed on your machine, you can use Microsoft's Internet Explorer 4.0, included on this CD-ROM.

The Microsoft Internet Explorer can be installed from the self-extracting file in the \EXPLORER directory. Double-click MSIE40M.EXE or use the Control Panel's Add/Remove Programs option and follow the instructions in the install routine. Please be aware that you must have Windows 95 installed on your machine to use this version of Internet Explorer. Other versions of this software can be downloaded from Microsoft's Web site at http://www.microsoft.com/ie.

Index

Symbols

A

J-K

L

Need more information on Lotus Notes 4.6? Check out these other titles from Macmillan Computer Publishing...

10 Minute Guide to Lotus Notes 4.6

If you need training materials that cover the Notes desktop client...

Start from the ground up with the *10 Minute Guide to Lotus Notes 4.6*. This book offers simple, practical help for busy people who need a focused introduction to the Notes 4.6 desktop client. Learn to configure calendaring and scheduling options, use the new Notes 4.6 Favorites database, participate in discussion databases, and search the Web, all using the consumer-tested 10 Minute Guide format. This book is the perfect start to your Notes 4.6 desktop reference collection.

ISBN: 0-7897-1536-8   *$14.99 USA/$21.95 CDN*   *224 pages*

Teach Yourself Lotus Notes 4.6 in 24 Hours

If you want a concentrated look at the features of Notes 4.6, check out *Teach Yourself Lotus Notes 4.6 in 24 Hours*. With this easy-to-use tutorial, you'll learn to customize your workspace, use tables and sections within documents, work with web browsers, work remotely using Notes, and much more. Find all you need to get up-to-speed with Notes 4.6—and do it in only 24 hours!

ISBN: 0-672-31256-5   *$19.99 USA/$28.95 CDN*   *400 pages*

Lotus Notes and Domino Server 4.6 Unleashed

For an in-depth, advanced look at the features of Lotus Notes and Domino 4.6, check out *Lotus Notes and Domino Server 4.6 Unleashed*. With detailed coverage of LotusScript and Notes' Internet capabilities and focusing on the new features of Release 4.6, *Lotus Notes and Domino Server 4.6 Unleashed* will give you a deeper look at the technology that underlies Notes. You'll also find expert advice on how to enhance and optimize the use of Notes and Domino in your organization.

ISBN: 0-672-31142-9   *$59.99 USA/$84.95 CDN*   *1290 pages/1 CD-ROM*

To order one or more of these titles, call 1-800-428-5331 or visit www.mcp.com